Fundamental Accounting Principles

Eighteenth Edition

Accounting I & II

D1199580

John J. Wild
University of Wisconsin at Madison

Kermit D. Larson
University of Texas at Austin

Barbara Chiappetta
Nassau Community College

Columbia Southern University

McGraw Hill **Learning Solutions**

Boston   Burr Ridge, IL   Dubuque, IA   New York   San Francisco   St. Louis
Bangkok   Bogotá   Caracas   Lisbon   London   Madrid
Mexico City   Milan   New Delhi   Seoul   Singapore   Sydney   Taipei   Toronto

The **McGraw·Hill** Companies

Fundamental Accounting Principles, Eighteenth Edition
Accounting I & II
Columbia Southern University

1 2 3 4 5 6 7 8 9 0 DOW DOW 0 9 8 7

ISBN 13: 978-0-07-725801-6
ISBN-10: 0-07-725801-0

Custom Publishing Specialist: Michael Hemmer
Production Editor: Nicole Baumgartner
Printer/Binder: RR Donnelley

Dear Colleagues/Friends,

As we roll out the 18th edition of *Fundamental Accounting Principles*, we wish to thank each of you who adopted the prior edition. As teachers, we appreciate the importance of selecting the best textbook. We are humbled that you have helped make our book the fastest growing accounting principles textbook on the market—with the number of users growing by 45% over the past two editions. Our publisher, McGraw-Hill/Irwin, recognized this remarkable growth by selecting this book for its "Outstanding Revision of the Year" award.

Our goal in this edition is to further that success. In the past couple years, we again listened closely to you, to our own students, and to our colleagues across the country. As a result, this edition addresses the needs of you and your students better than any previous edition. Above all, we enhanced aspects of the book that contribute to its current success: cutting-edge technology, engaging and accurate content, and clear and concise writing.

Instructors and students tell us this edition's technology package caters to different learning styles and helps students better learn accounting. For example, Homework Manager Plus offers new features to enhance student learning and assist instructor grading. iPod Content lets students study on the go, and the new Algorithmic Test Bank provides an infinite number of exam problems. We believe you and your students will find these technology learning tools both easy to use and highly valuable.

We owe a huge debt of gratitude to the hundreds of colleagues like you who took time to discuss with us the needs of today's instructors and students. We feel fortunate to witness our profession's extraordinary devotion to teaching and helping students learn accounting. Your feedback and suggestions are reflected in everything we write. Please accept our heartfelt thanks for your dedication in helping today's students understand and appreciate accounting.

With kindest regards,

John J. Wild   *Kermit D. Larson*   *Barbara Chiappetta*

Fundamental Accounting Principles is #1

For the second consecutive edition, *Fundamental Accounting Principles* rates #1 in both Instructor and Student satisfaction. Both independent research and development reviews confirm that *Fundamental Accounting Principles* is #1 in the following categories...

#1 in Accuracy

#1 in Readability

#1 in Organization

#1 in Topic Coverage

#1 in Problems and Exercises

#1 in Instructor Supplements

#1 in Overall Textbook Satisfaction

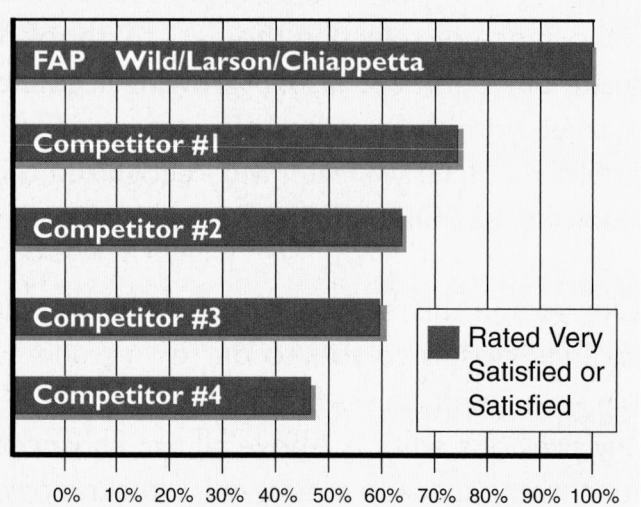

With ratings such as these, it is no surprise that *Fundamental Accounting Principles* is the fastest growing textbook in the accounting principles market.

Take a **look at what instructors are saying** about *Fundamental Accounting Principles*.

Linda Mallory, Central Virginia Community College
"This is an excellent book and one of the best on the market. The topical coverage and the sequence of coverage surpass anything on the market."

Patricia Walczak, Lansing Community College
"Better coverage of the accounting cycle (Chapters 1-4) and the quality of the quick study exercises and exercises at the end of the chapter."

Shirly Kleiner, Johnson County Community College
"Well-written, organized, and covers the main concepts necessary for fundamental accounting courses."

Lynette Yerbury, Salt Lake Community College
"Readable, readable, readable! I love the book. It's easy to read. There are tons of homework problems available."

Larry Swisher, Muskegon Community College
"A good textbook with good homework assignments and supplements backed by an organization that really cares about what instructors want in a textbook."

Janice Stoudemire, Midlands Technical College
"I am impressed with the overall clarity of the managerial chapters. Not only is the readability excellent, but also the authors have an ability to clearly explain both the simple and complex concepts. These chapters are excellent- far better than my current textbook."

Janet Adeyiga, Hampton University
"Demonstration Problems and application to real life cases and problems included in each chapter."

John J. Wild is a professor of accounting and the Robert and Monica Beyer Distinguished Professor at the University of Wisconsin at Madison. He previously held appointments at Michigan State University and the University of Manchester in England. He received his BBA, MS, and PhD from the University of Wisconsin.

Professor Wild teaches accounting courses at both the undergraduate and graduate levels. He has received the Mabel W. Chipman Excellence-in-Teaching Award, the departmental Excellence-in-Teaching Award, and the Teaching Excellence Award from the 2003 and 2005 business graduates at the University of Wisconsin. He also received the Beta Alpha Psi and Roland F. Salmonson Excellence-in-Teaching Award from Michigan State University. Professor Wild is a past KPMG Peat Marwick National Fellow and is a recipient of fellowships from the American Accounting Association and the Ernst and Young Foundation.

Professor Wild is an active member of the American Accounting Association and its sections. He has served on several committees of these organizations, including the Outstanding Accounting Educator Award, Wildman Award, National Program Advisory, Publications, and Research Committees. Professor Wild is author of *Financial Accounting* and *Financial Statement Analysis*, both published by McGraw-Hill/Irwin. His research appears in The Accounting Review, Journal of Accounting Research, Journal of Accounting and Economics, Contemporary Accounting Research, Journal of Accounting, Auditing and Finance, Journal of Accounting and Public Policy, and other journals. He is past associate editor of Contemporary Accounting Research and has served on several editorial boards including The Accounting Review.

Professor Wild, his wife, and four children enjoy travel, music, sports, and community activities.

Kermit D. Larson is the Arthur Andersen & Co. Alumni Professor of Accounting Emeritus at the University of Texas at Austin. He served as chairman of the University of Texas Department of Accounting and was visiting professor at Tulane University. His scholarly articles have been published in a variety of journals, including The Accounting Review, Journal of Accountancy, and Abacus. He is the author of several books, including *Financial Accounting* and *Fundamentals of Financial and Managerial Accounting*, both published by McGraw-Hill/Irwin.

Professor Larson is a member of the American Accounting Association, the Texas Society of CPAs, and the American Institute of CPAs. His positions with the AAA have included vice president, southwest regional vice president, and chairperson of several committees, including the Committee of Concepts and Standards. He was a member of the committee that planned the first AAA doctoral consortium and served as its director.

Professor Larson served as president of the Richard D. Irwin Foundation. He also served on the Accounting Accreditation Committee and on the Accounting Standards Committee of the AACSB. He was a member of the Constitutional Drafting Committee of the Federation of Schools of Accountancy and a member of the Commission on Professional Accounting Education. He has been an expert witness on cases involving mergers, antitrust litigation, consolidation criteria, franchise taxes, and expropriation of assets by foreign governments. Professor Larson served on the Board of Directors and Executive Committee of Tekcon, Inc., and on the National Accountants Advisory Board of Safe-Guard Business Systems. In his leisure time, he enjoys skiing and is an avid sailor and golfer.

Barbara Chiappetta received her BBA in Accountancy and MS in Education from Hofstra University and is a tenured full professor at Nassau Community College. For the past 17 years, she has been an active executive board member of the Teachers of Accounting at Two-Year Colleges (TACTYC), serving 10 years as vice president and as president from 1993 through 1999. As an active member of the American Accounting Association, she has served on the Northeast Regional Steering Committee, chaired the Curriculum Revision Committee of the Two-Year Section, and participated in numerous national committees.

In 1998, Professor Chiappetta was inducted into the American Accounting Association Hall of Fame for the Northeast Region. She received the Nassau Community College dean of instruction's Faculty Distinguished Achievement Award in 1995. Professor Chiappetta was honored with the State University of New York Chancellor's Award for Teaching Excellence in 1997. As a confirmed believer in the benefits of the active learning pedagogy, Professor Chiappetta has authored *Student Learning Tools*, an active learning workbook for a first-year accounting course, published by McGraw-Hill/Irwin.

In her leisure time, Professor Chiappetta enjoys tennis and participates on a U.S.T.A. team. She also enjoys the challenge of bridge. Her husband, Robert, is an entrepreneur in the leisure sport industry. She has two sons—Michael, a lawyer, specializing in intellectual property law in New York, and David, a composer, pursuing a career in music for film in Los Angeles.

Give your students an Edge!

Fundamental Accounting Principles 18e

Help your students ride the wave of Success by giving them the Edge they need to succeed in today's accounting principles course.

Fundamental Accounting Principles (FAP) has helped a generation of students succeed by **giving them an edge** with leading-edge accounting content that engages students, and with state-of-the-art technology.

One of the greatest challenges students confront in a principles course is seeing the relevance of materials. *FAP* tackles this issue head on with **engaging content** and a **motivating style**. Students are motivated when reading materials that are **clear and relevant**. *FAP* stands apart in engaging students. Its chapter-opening vignettes showcase dynamic, successful, entrepreneurial individuals and companies guaranteed to **interest and excite readers**. This edition's featured companies—Best Buy, Circuit City, and Apple—engage students with their annual reports, which are great vehicles for **learning** financial statements. Further, this book's coverage of the accounting cycle fundamentals is widely praised for its **clarity and effectiveness**.

FAP also delivers **cutting-edge technology** to help students succeed. **Homework Manager** provides students with instant grading and feedback for assignments that are completed online. **Homework Manager Plus** integrates an online version of the textbook with our popular Homework Manager system and provides unlimited access to an Online Tutor. A new **Algorithmic Test Bank** in Homework Manager offers infinite variations of numerical test bank questions. *FAP* is also the first book to offer accounting students portable **iPod-ready content**.

We're confident you'll agree that *FAP* **gives your students the edge to succeed**.

Cutting-Edge Content

FAP content continues to set the standard in the principles market. Take a look at Chapter 1 and you'll see how *FAP* leads the market with the best coverage of the accounting cycle. We are the first book to cover equity transactions the way most instruc... ... h it and students learn it–by introducing the separate equity accounts upfront and not w...ing until a chapter or two later. *FAP* also motivates students with engaging chapter openers... students identify with them and can even picture themselves as future entrepreneurs. Also...ach book includes the financial statements of Circuit City, Best Buy, and Apple to further engage students.

Cutting-Edge Technology

FAP offers the most advanced and comprehensive technology on the market in a seamless, easy-to-use platform. As students learn in different ways, *FAP* provides a technology smorgasbord that helps students learn more effectively and efficiently. Homework Manager, eBook options, iPod content, and Topic Tackler are some of the options available. Homework Manager Plus takes learning to another level by integrating an online version of the textbook with all the power of Homework Manager and our online NetTutor service. Technology offerings include the following:

- Homework Manager
- Homework Manager Plus
- iPod content
- Algorithmic Test Bank
- Online Learning Center

- Topic Tackler
- Carol Yacht's General Ledger and Peachtree Complete
- ALEKS for the Accounting Cycle
- ALEKS for Financial Accounting

Cutting-Edge Support

McGraw-Hill/Irwin has mobilized a new force of product specialists committed to training and supporting the technology we offer. Our commitment to instructor service and support is top notch and leads the industry. Our new "McGraw-Hill Cares" program provides you with the fastest answers to your questions or solutions to your training needs. Ask your McGraw-Hill sales rep about our Key Media Support Plan and the McGraw-Hill Cares Program.

Through current and motivating content, cutting-edge technology, and committed service and support programs... *FAP* provides you and your students the edge to succeed in today's principles course.

What Can McGraw-Hill Technology Offer You?

Whether you are just getting started with technology in your course, or you are ready to embrace the latest advances in electronic content delivery and course management, McGraw-Hill/Irwin has the technology you need, and provides training and support that will help you every step of the way.

Our most popular technologies, Homework Manager and Homework Manager Plus, are optional online Homework Management systems that will allow you to assign problems and exercises from the text for your students to work out in an online format. Student results are automatically graded, and the students receive instant feedback on their work. Homework Manager Plus adds an online version of the text and an online tutorial service called NetTutor for direct access while completing homework within Homework Manager.

Students can also use the Online Learning Center associated with this text on their own to enhance their knowledge of accounting. Plus we now offer iPod content for students who want to study on the go with their iPod.

For instructors, we provide all of the crucial instructor supplements on one easy to use Instructor CD-ROM; we can help build a custom class Website for your course using PageOut; we can deliver a fully developed online course for you to conduct through Blackboard, WebCT, or eCollege; and we have a technical support team that will provide training and support for our key technology products.

How Can Students Study on the Go Using Their iPod?

iPod Content

Harness the power of one of the most popular technology tools students use today—the Apple iPod. Our innovative approach allows students to download audio and video presentations right into their iPod and take learning materials with them wherever they go. It makes review and study time as easy as putting in headphones. Visit the *FAP* Online Learning Center (www.mhhe.com/wildFAP18e) to learn more details on available iPod content—and enhance your learning experience today.

How Can My Students Use the Web to Complete Their Homework?

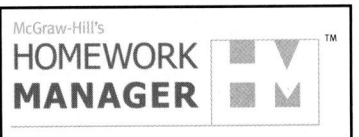

McGraw-Hill's Homework Manager

is a Web-based supplement that duplicates problem structures directly from the end-of-chapter material in your textbook, using algorithms to provide a limitless supply of online self-graded assignments that can be used for student practice, homework, or testing. Each assignment has a unique solution. Say goodbye to cheating in your classroom; say hello to the power and flexibility you've been waiting for in creating assignments. All Quick Studies, Exercises, and Problems are available with Homework Manager.

McGraw-Hill's Homework Manager is also a useful grading tool. All assignments can be delivered over the Web and are graded automatically, with the results stored in your private grade book. Detailed results let you see at a glance how each student does on an assignment or an individual problem—you can even see how many tries it took them to solve it.

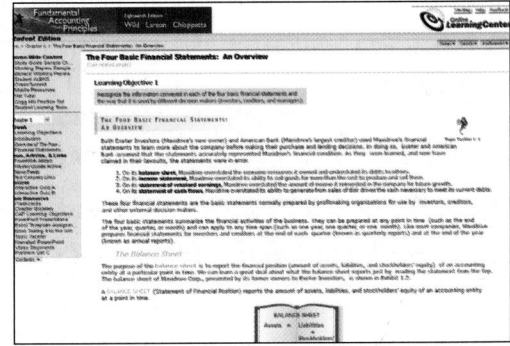

Jim Shelton, Freed-Hardeman University

"Homework Manager is working out really well, and I believe it is significantly contributing to increased performance on exams."

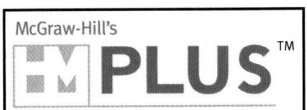

Homework Manager Plus

is an extension of McGraw-Hill's popular Homework Manager System. With Homework Manager Plus you get all of the power of Homework Manager plus an integrated online version of the text, and unlimited access to our NetTutor service. Students simply receive one single access code which provides access to all of the resources available through Homework Manager Plus.

Paula Ratliff, Arkansas State University

"I like the idea that there are online assignments that change algorithmically so that students can practice with them."

When students find themselves needing to reference the textbook in order to complete their homework, now they can simply click on hints and link directly to the most relevant materials associated with the problem or exercise they are working on. If they cannot figure out the problem from referencing the online version of the text, then they can link over to access the NetTutor service. Through NetTutor the student can chat with a live tutor who can provide help and advice towards completing their homework.

How Can Busy Students Get Text-Specific Help at Their Convenience?

NetTutor™

Many students work or have other commitments outside of class, making it difficult for them to get help with their questions during regular school hours. NetTutor is a breakthrough program that connects your students with qualified tutors online so they can get help at their convenience.

Students can communicate with tutors in a variety of ways:

- The Live Tutor Center, where students can view tutor-created spreadsheets, T-accounts, and instant responses to their questions.
- The Q&A Center, which allows students to submit questions anytime and receive answers within 24 hours.
- The Archive Center that lets students browse for answers to previously asked questions. They can also search for questions pertinent to a particular topic.

With Homework Manager Plus, students receive unlimited access to NetTutor for the length of the course. Otherwise, you can package a NetTutor Access Card with your text.

How Can Text-Related Web Resources Enhance My Course?

Online Learning Center (OLC)

We offer an Online Learning Center (OLC) that follows *Fundamental Accounting Principles* chapter by chapter. It doesn't require any building or maintenance on your part. It's ready to go the moment you and your students type in the URL: www.mhhe.com/wildFAP18e.

As students study and learn from *Fundamental Accounting Principles*, they can visit the Student Edition of the OLC Website to work with a multitude of helpful tools:

- Generic Template Working Papers
- Cogg Hill Practice Set
- Chapter Learning Objectives
- Chapter Glossaries
- Key Term Flashcards
- Interactive Chapter Quizzes A & B
- PowerPoint® Presentations
- Narrated PowerPoint® Presentations

- Topic Tackler Plus Tutorial
- Video Segments
- Excel Template Assignments
- Animated Demonstration Problems
- Problem Set C
- More Taking It To The Net Exercises
- *BusinessWeek* articles
- NetTutor

A secured Instructor Edition stores essential course materials to save you prep time before class. Everything you need to run a lively classroom and an efficient course is included. All resources available to students, plus . . .

- Sample Syllabi
- Transition Notes
- Cogg Hill Practice Set Solutions Manual
- General Ledger and Peachtree Solution Files
- Instructor's Manual

- Solutions Manual
- Solutions to Excel Template Assignments
- Solutions to Problem Set C
- Solutions to More Taking It To The Net Exercises

The OLC Website also serves as a doorway to other technology solutions, like course management systems.

Try One of Our New e-Books Options!

For budget-conscious students, every dollar makes a difference. That's why we offer FAP in two convenient, cost-effective digital formats.

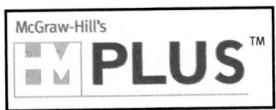

McGraw-Hill's Homework Manager Plus

If you use Homework Manager in your course, your students can purchase McGraw-Hill's Homework Manager Plus for *FAP* 18e. Homework Manager Plus gives students direct access to an online edition of the text while working assignments within Homework Manager. If you get stuck working a problem, simply click the "Hint" link and jump directly to relevant content in the online edition of the text.

Visit the Online Learning Center at www.mhhe.com/wildFAP18e to purchase McGraw-Hill's Homework Manager Plus.

Zinio Digital Edition

A leader in digital media, Zinio offers students using *Fundamental Accounting Principles* 18e the full benefit of its powerful, flexible digital reading system. Using the Zinio reader, you can search your digital textbook, highlight important passages, or jot down electronic notes. Navigating a textbook has never been easier. You can even print pages to study from off line.

To order your Zinio Digital Edition of *Fundamental Accounting Principles* 18e visit www.textbooks.zinio.com.

With either option you choose you'll be blown away by what you can do and how much you'll save.

Roy Carson, Anne Arundel Community College

"I am certain I will make good use of the (Zinio) e-Book, and I suspect students will like it."

McGraw-Hill/Irwin CARES

At McGraw-Hill/Irwin, we understand that getting the most from new technology can be challenging. That's why our services don't stop after you purchase our product. Each professor will receive a customer McGraw-Hill Cares support card that is your complete guide to McGraw-Hill/Irwin technology product support. You can e-mail our Product Specialists 24 hours a day, get product training online, or search our knowledge bank of Frequently Asked Questions on our support Website.

McGraw-Hill/Irwin Customer Care Contact Information

For all Customer Support call **(800) 331-5094**,
Email **hmsupport@mcgraw-hill.com**,
or visit **www.mhhe.com/support**.
One of our Technical Support Analysts will be able to assist you in a timely fashion.

Scott Barhight, Northampton Community College

"McGraw-Hill gives some of the best customer support, including personal support from John Wild the author of the text."

How Can I Make My Classroom Discussions More Interactive?

CPS Classroom Performance System

This is a revolutionary system that brings ultimate interactivity to the classroom. CPS is a wireless response system that gives you immediate feedback from every student in the class. CPS units include easy-to-use software for creating and delivering questions and assessments to your class. With CPS you can ask subjective and objective questions. Then every student simply responds with their individual, wireless response pad, providing instant results. CPS is the perfect tool for engaging students while gathering important assessment data.

eInstruction

> **Janice Stoudemire**, Midlands Technical College
>
> "The supplemental material that this principles accounting text provides is impressive: homework manager, the extensive online learning center, general ledger application software, the topic tackler, net tutor, as well as ALEKS."

How Can McGraw-Hill Help Me Teach My Course Online?

ALEKS®

ALEKS® for the Accounting Cycle and ALEKS® for Financial Accounting

Available from McGraw-Hill over the World Wide Web, ALEKS (Assessment and LEarning in Knowledge Spaces) provides precise assessment and individualized instruction in the fundamental skills your students need to succeed in accounting.

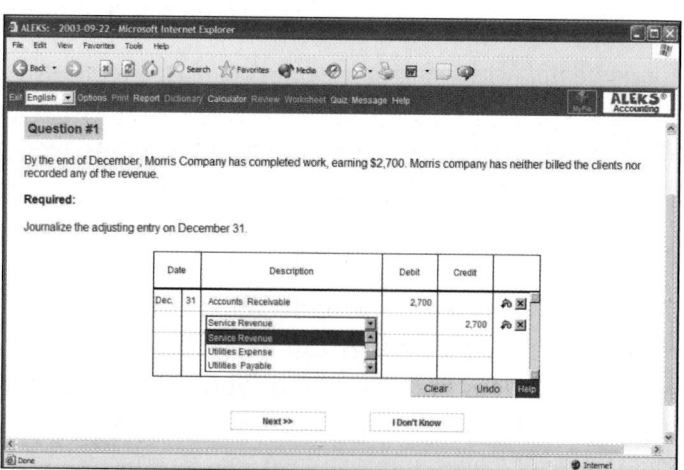

ALEKS motivates your students because ALEKS can tell what a student knows, doesn't know, and is most ready to learn next. ALEKS does this using the ALEKS Assessment and Knowledge Space Theory as an artificial intelligence engine to exactly identify a student's knowledge of accounting. When students focus on precisely what they are ready to learn, they build the confidence and learning momentum that fuel success.

To learn more about adding ALEKS to your principles course, visit www.business.aleks.com.

> **Liz Ott**, Casper College
>
> "I originally adopted the book because of the tools that accompanied it: Homework Manager, ALEKS, CPS."

Online Course Management

No matter what online course management system you use (WebCT, BlackBoard, or eCollege), we have a course content ePack available for *FAP* 18e. Our new ePacks are specifically designed to make it easy for students to navigate and access content online. They are easier than ever to install on the latest version of the course management system available today.

Don't forget that you can count on the highest level of service from McGraw-Hill. Our online course management specialists are ready to assist you with your online course needs. They provide training and will answer any questions you have throughout the life of your adoption. So try our new ePack for *FAP* 18e and make online course content delivery easy and fun.

PageOut: McGraw-Hill's Course Management System

PageOut is the easiest way to create a Website for your accounting course. There is no need for HTML coding, graphic design, or a thick how-to book. Just fill in a series of boxes with simple English and click on one of our professional designs. In no time, your course is online with a Website that contains your syllabus!

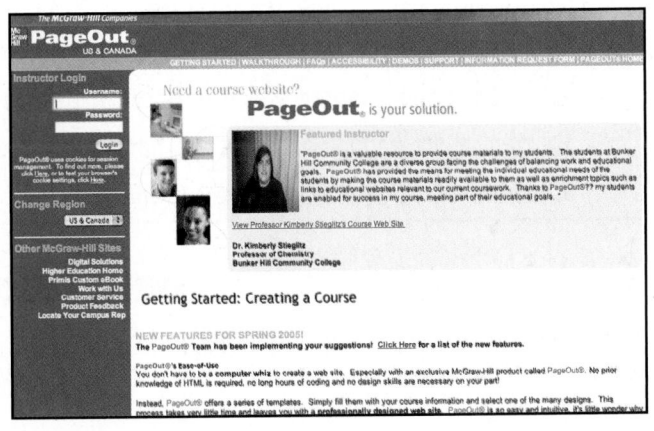

Should you need assistance in preparing your Website, we can help. Our team of product specialists is ready to take your course materials and build a custom Website to your specifications. You simply need to call a McGraw-Hill/Irwin PageOut specialist to start the process. To learn more, please visit www.pageout.net and see "PageOut & Service" below.

Best of all, PageOut is free when you adopt *Fundamental Accounting Principles*!

PageOut Service

Our team of product specialists is happy to help you design your own course Website. Just call 1-800-634-3963, press 0, and ask to speak with a PageOut specialist. You will be asked to send in your course materials and then participate in a brief telephone consultation. Once we have your information, we build your Website for you, from scratch.

What tools bring Accounting to life

Decision Center

Whether we prepare, analyze, or apply accounting information, one skill remains essential: decision-making. To help develop good decision-making habits and to illustrate the relevance of accounting, *Fundamental Accounting Principles* 18e uses a unique pedagogical framework called the Decision Center. This framework is comprised of a variety of approaches and subject areas, giving students insight into every aspect of business decision-making. Answers to Decision Maker and Ethics boxes are at the end of each chapter.

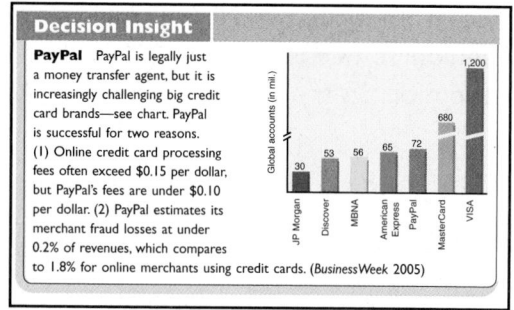

Decision Insight

PayPal PayPal is legally just a money transfer agent, but it is increasingly challenging big credit card brands—see chart. PayPal is successful for two reasons. (1) Online credit card processing fees often exceed $0.15 per dollar, but PayPal's fees are under $0.10 per dollar. (2) PayPal estimates its merchant fraud losses at under 0.2% of revenues, which compares to 1.8% for online merchants using credit cards. (*BusinessWeek* 2005)

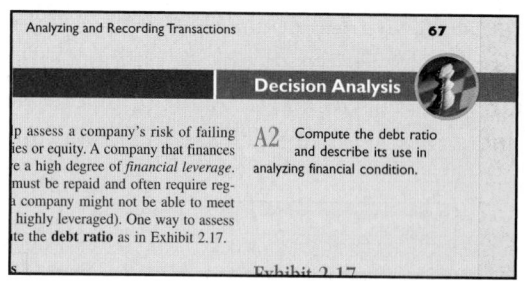

Analyzing and Recording Transactions   67

Decision Analysis

A2 Compute the debt ratio and describe its use in analyzing financial condition.

p assess a company's risk of failing ...ies or equity. A company that finances ...e a high degree of *financial leverage*. ...must be repaid and often require reg— ...a company might not be able to meet ...highly leveraged). One way to assess ...te the **debt ratio** as in Exhibit 2.17.

Exhibit 2.17

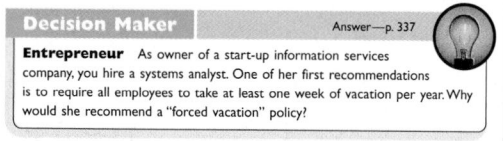

Decision Maker   Answer—p. 337

Entrepreneur As owner of a start-up information services company, you hire a systems analyst. One of her first recommendations is to require all employees to take at least one week of vacation per year. Why would she recommend a "forced vacation" policy?

Decision Ethics   Answer—p. 71

Cashier Your manager requires that you, as cashier, immediately enter each sale. Recently, lunch hour traffic has increased and the assistant manager asks you to avoid delays by taking customers' cash and making change without entering sales. The assistant manager says she will add up cash and enter sales after lunch. She says that, in this way, the register will always match the cash amount when the manager arrives at three o'clock. What do you do?

> "This text has the best introductions of any text that I have reviewed or used. Some texts simply summarize the chapter, which is boring to students. Research indicates that material needs to be written in an 'engaging manner.' That's what these vignettes do—they get the students interested."
>
> **Clarice McCoy,** Brookhaven College

CAP Model

The Conceptual/Analytical/Procedural (CAP) Model allows courses to be specially designed to meet your teaching needs or those of a diverse faculty. This model identifies learning objectives, textual materials, assignments, and test items by C, A, or P, allowing different instructors to teach from the same materials, yet easily customize their courses toward a conceptual, analytical, or procedural approach (or a combination thereof) based on personal preferences.

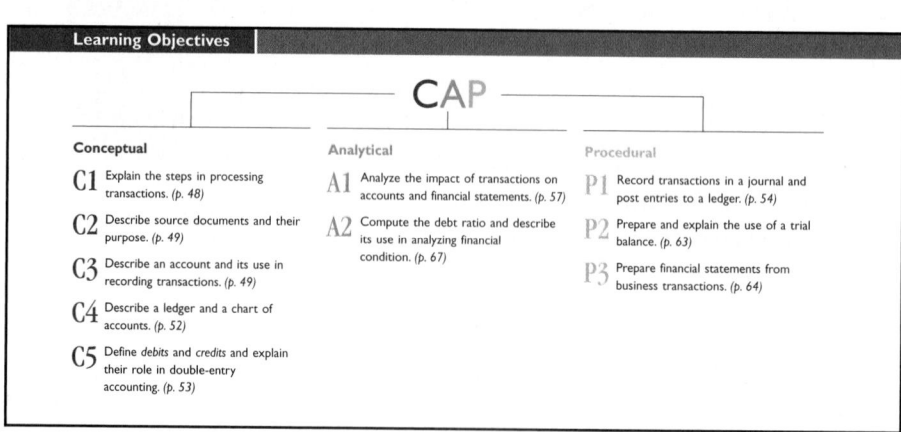

Learning Objectives

CAP

Conceptual

C1 Explain the steps in processing transactions. (p. 48)

C2 Describe source documents and their purpose. (p. 49)

C3 Describe an account and its use in recording transactions. (p. 49)

C4 Describe a ledger and a chart of accounts. (p. 52)

C5 Define *debits* and *credits* and explain their role in double-entry accounting. (p. 53)

Analytical

A1 Analyze the impact of transactions on accounts and financial statements. (p. 57)

A2 Compute the debt ratio and describe its use in analyzing financial condition. (p. 67)

Procedural

P1 Record transactions in a journal and post entries to a ledger. (p. 54)

P2 Prepare and explain the use of a trial balance. (p. 63)

P3 Prepare financial statements from business transactions. (p. 64)

Chapter Preview with Flow Chart

This feature provides a handy textual/visual guide at the start of every chapter. Students can now begin their reading with a clear understanding of what they will learn and when, allowing them to stay more focused and organized along the way.

e explained in earlier chapters. We described how trans-
ons and events are analyzed, journalized, and posted. This
ter describes important adjustments that are often
essary to properly reflect revenues when earned and
enses when incurred. This chapter also describes financial
ement preparation. It explains the closing process that

reporting period an
is shown to be a useful tool for these final steps and in
preparing financial statements. It also explains how accounts
are classified on a balance sheet to increase their usefulness
to decision makers.

Completing the Accounting Cycle

Work Sheet	Closing Process	Accounting Cycle	Classified Balance Sheet
• Benefits of a work sheet • Use of a work sheet	• Temporary and permanent accounts • Closing entries • Post-closing trial balance	• Definition of accounting cycle • Review of accounting cycle	• Classification structure • Classification categories

Quick Check

These short question/answer features reinforce the material immediately preceding them. They allow the reader to pause and reflect on the topics described, then receive immediate feedback before going on to new topics. Answers are provided at the end of each chapter.

Quick Check   Answers—p. 112

1. Describe a company's annual reporting period.
2. Why do companies prepare interim financial statements?
3. What two accounting principles most directly drive the adjusting process?
4. Is cash basis accounting consistent with the matching principle? Why or why not?
5. If your company pays a $4,800 premium on April 1, 2007, for two years' insurance coverage, how much insurance expense is reported in 2008 using cash basis accounting?

"(This book is) visually friendly with many illustrations. Good balance sheet presentation in margin."

Joan Cook, Milwaukee Area Technical College

Marginal Student Annotations

These annotations provide students with additional hints, tips, and examples to help them more fully understand the concepts and retain what they have learned. The annotations also include notes on global implications of accounting and further examples.

luding depreciation) and unearned rev-
ceived *before* a related expense or rev-
use the recognition of an expense (or
or received). The right side of this ex-
hich reflect transactions when cash is
cognized. Adjusting entries are neces-
s, and liabilities are correctly reported.
cts one or more income statement ac-
the Cash account).

Point: Adjusting is a 3-step process:
(1) Determine current account balance,
(2) Determine what current account balance should be, and (3) Record entry to get from step 1 to step 2.

FastForward

FastForward is a case that takes students through the Accounting Cycle, chapters 1-4. The FastForward icon is placed in the margin whenever this case is discussed.

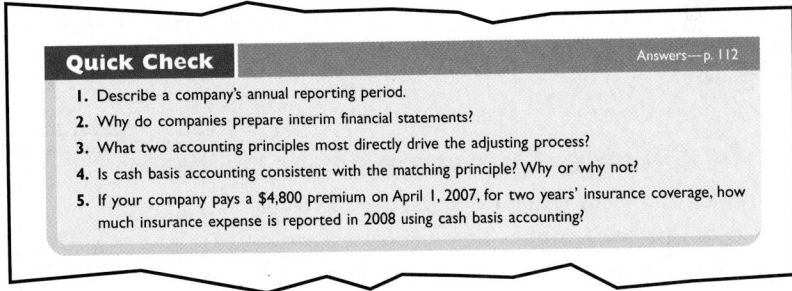

huck Taylor invests $30,000 cash in FastForward.   *FAST Forward*

Assets	=	Liabilities	+	Equity
Cash				**C. Taylor, Capital**
+30,000	=	0	+	30,000

(1)	Cash	101	30,000	
	C. Taylor, Capital	301		30,000

How are chapter concepts

Once a student has finished reading the chapter, how well he or she retains the material can depend greatly on the questions, exercises, and problems that reinforce it. This book leads the way in comprehensive, accurate end-of-chapter assignments.

Demonstration Problems
present both a problem and a complete solution, allowing students to review the entire problem-solving process and achieve success.

Chapter Summaries
provide students with a review organized by learning objectives. Chapter Summaries are a component of the CAP model (see page xiv), which recaps each conceptual, analytical, and procedural objective.

Key Terms
are bolded in the text and repeated at the end of the chapter with page numbers indicating their location. The book also includes a complete Glossary of Key Terms. Key Terms are also available as online flash cards at the book's Website.

Multiple Choice Questions
In response to review and focus group feedback, the author has created Multiple Choice Questions that quickly test chapter knowledge before a student moves on to complete Quick Studies, Exercises, and Problems.

Quick Study
assignments are short exercises that often focus on one learning objective. All are included in Homework Manager. There are usually 8-10 Quick Study assignments per chapter.

Exercises
are one of this book's many strengths and a competitive advantage. There are about 10-15 per chapter and all are included in Homework Manager.

Problem Sets A & B
are proven problems that can be assigned as homework or for in-class projects. Problem Set C is available on the book's Website. All problems are coded according to the CAP model (see page xiv), and all are included in Homework Manager.

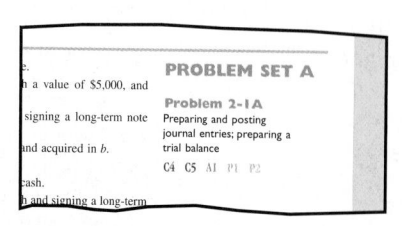

"One of the best features in FAP is the Serial Problem. I find the continuation of a company from a service to a merchandiser, to a manufacturing, and from a sole proprietorship form or business to a corporation, provides the student a real picture of a company's development. It also provides a consistency from one lesson to another."

Barbara Marotta, Northern Virginia Community College, Woodbridge

Beyond the Numbers exercises ask students to use accounting figures and understand their meaning. Students also learn how accounting applies to a variety of business situations. These creative and fun exercises are all new or updated, and are divided into 10 sections:

- Reporting in Action
- Comparative Analysis
- Ethics Challenge
- Communicating in Practice
- Taking It To The Net
- Teamwork in Action
- Hitting the Road
- *BusinessWeek* Activity
- Entrepreneurial Decision
- Global Decision

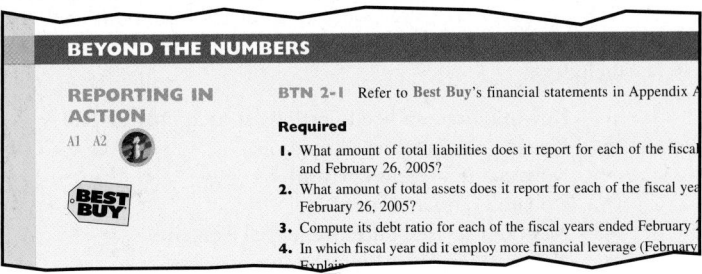

BEYOND THE NUMBERS

REPORTING IN ACTION

A1 A2

BTN 2-1 Refer to Best Buy's financial statements in Appendix A

Required

1. What amount of total liabilities does it report for each of the fiscal and February 26, 2005?
2. What amount of total assets does it report for each of the fiscal ye February 26, 2005?
3. Compute its debt ratio for each of the fiscal years ended February 2
4. In which fiscal year did it employ more financial leverage (February)

Serial Problems use a continuous running case study to illustrate chapter concepts in a familiar context. Serial Problems can be followed continuously from the first chapter or picked up at any later point in the book; enough information is provided to ensure students can get right to work.

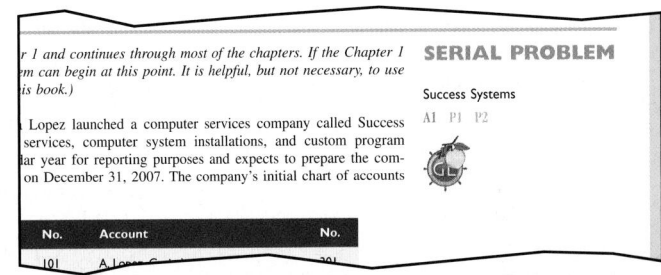

...r 1 and continues through most of the chapters. If the Chapter 1 ...m can begin at this point. It is helpful, but not necessary, to use ...s book.)

SERIAL PROBLEM

Success Systems

A1 P1 P2

...Lopez launched a computer services company called Success ...services, computer system installations, and custom program ...ar year for reporting purposes and expects to prepare the com- ...on December 31, 2007. The company's initial chart of accounts

No.	Account	No.

> "The best feature of this book is the use of real (financial) information in the Beyond the Numbers section. This is something that I do on my own, which can be very time consuming. I also like the Entrepreneurial questions, which are not even addressed in most textbooks."
>
> **Cindy Navaroli,** Chaffey Community College

The End of the Chapter Is Only the Beginning

Our valuable and proven assignments aren't just confined to the book. From problems that require technological solutions to materials found exclusively online, this book's end-of-chapter material is fully integrated with its technology package.

- Quick Studies, Exercises, and Problems available on Homework Manager (see page ix) are marked with an icon.

- Problems supported by the General Ledger Application Software or Peachtree are marked with an icon.

- The Online Learning Center (OLC) includes more Taking It To The Net exercises, Personal Interactive Quizzes, Excel template assignments, and Problem Set C.

mhhe.com/wildFAP18e

- Problems supported with Microsoft Excel template assignments are marked with an icon.

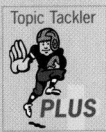

Topic Tackler
PLUS

- Material that receives additional coverage (slide shows, videos, audio, etc.) in Topic Tackler is marked with an icon.

Put Away Your Red Pen

We pride ourselves on the accuracy of this book's assignment materials. Independent research reports that instructors and reviewers point to the accuracy of this book's assignment materials as one of its key competitive advantages.

The authors extend a special thanks to accuracy checkers Barbara Schnathorst, The Write Solution, Inc.; Helen Roybark, Radford University; Beth Woods, CPA, Accuracy Counts; Alice Sineath, Forsyth Technical Community College; Teressa Farough, CPA, and Marilyn Sagrillo, University of Wisconsin - Green Bay.

FAP's revisions are in response to feedback from both instructors and students. Many of these revisions are summarized below. Feedback suggests that *FAP* is the book instructors want to teach from and students want to learn from. Some overall revisions include:

- New multiple choice questions at each chapter-end
- Revised assignments throughout
- New chapter-opening layout
- Updated ratio analyses
- New and revised entrepreneurial elements
- New assignments using chapter openers

- Revised serial problem running through nearly all chapters
- New Circuit City annual report with comparisons to Best Buy, Dixons (UK), and the industry–including new assignments
- New Apple financial statements and assignments

Chapter 1

LoveSac NEW opener with new entrepreneurial assignment

Revised, early introduction to financial statements

Enhanced transaction analysis using expanded accounting equation

New material on frauds such as Tyco and WorldCom

Revised illustration and assignments on ethical decisions

New insight on principles-based accounting

New evidence on small businesses

Enhanced materials on Sarbanes-Oxley

New multiple choice questions

Chapter 2

Cake Love NEW opener with new entrepreneurial assignment

Enhanced introduction to asset accounts

Streamlined introduction to double-entry accounting

New color layout for transaction analysis

New insight on women entrepreneurs

Revised insight on unearned revenues

New insight on manager pay under Sarbanes-Oxley

Chapter 3

Alienware NEW opener with new entrepreneurial assignment

New graphics for prepaid expenses

New graphic for unearned revenues

New insight on gift card sales as unearned revenues

New illustration of accrued revenues

Revised exhibit on accounting adjustments

Enhanced assignments for adjusting entries and ethics

Chapter 4

Betty Rides NEW opener with new entrepreneurial assignment

Streamlined exhibit for closing entries

New assignment on aggressive estimates

Streamlined discussion of work sheet

New visual from closing entries to accounts

Chapter 5

CoCaLo NEW opener with new entrepreneurial assignment

Enhanced illustration on operating cycle

Revised exhibit on merchandisers' closing entries

Streamlined multi-step income statement

Merchandiser work sheet in appendix

Chapter 6

Surf Diva NEW opener with new entrepreneurial assignment

Improved exhibit on cost flow assumptions

Updated exhibit on inventory methods

Enhanced illustration on lower of cost or market

Revised serial problem to add LCM

Chapter 7

Ring Masters NEW opener with new entrepreneurial assignment

Enhanced diagrams on special journals and ledgers

New assignments on identifying the special journal of entry

Updated enterprise resource planning (ERP)

New insights on Internet frauds and controls

Chapter 8

Raising Cane's Chicken Fingers NEW opener with new entrepreneurial assignment

New material on e-commerce, its risks, its controls, and identity theft

New insight on credit card fraud

New illustration on "Hacker" risks

New diagram on controls for over-the-counter cash receipts

Updated data on Internet frauds

New information on check fraud

New data on fees for bank services

Chapter 9

Linditas' NEW opener with new entrepreneurial assignment

New explanation of credit and debit cards

Simplified estimation of uncollectibles

New data on PayPal and credit card growth

Enhanced exhibit on aging of receivables

New data on bad debt percentages

Enhanced exhibit on computing maturity date

Chapter 10

Fairytale Brownies NEW opener with new entrepreneurial assignment

Revised exhibit on plant asset disposals

Updated data on depreciation methods used

Moved plant asset exchanges to appendix

Updated book for new standard on asset exchanges

New assignments on asset disposals, goodwill, and intangibles

Chapter 11

Wildflower Linen NEW opener with new entrepreneurial assignment

New insight on gift card liabilities

Updated IRS tax forms

Updated IRS withholding table

New insight on guaranteed salary liabilities

New insight on extended-warranty contracts

Applied 2006 payroll tax rates throughout

New diagram for contingent liabilities

Chapter 12

Rookie Skateboards **NEW opener** with new entrepreneurial assignment

Enhanced explanation and accounting for limited liability companies

New assignment on limited partnerships

New insight on Broadway partnerships

Chapter 13

Medsite **NEW opener** with new entrepreneurial assignment

Enhanced graphic on equity composition

'Paid-in capital' used in lieu of 'contributed capital'

Moved section on dividends before preferred stock

Streamlined computation of weighted-average shares

Updated and streamlined stock options

New assignments on stock, EPS, and ethics

Moved discontinued and extraordinary items to Chapter 17

Chapter 14

Melton Franchise Systems **NEW opener** with new entrepreneurial assignment

Enhanced exhibit on bond interest computation and entry

Moved debt features to decision analysis section

Streamlined bond-issuing procedures

Moved 'issuing bonds between interest dates' to appendix

Streamlined installment notes

New ratio analysis on debt-to-equity

Chapter 15

TOKYOPOP **NEW opener** with new entrepreneurial assignment

Streamlined and enhanced explanation of investments

New illustration on purchases listed in a foreign currency

New return on assets analysis of Gap

Chapter 16

Ashtae Products **NEW opener** with new entrepreneurial assignment

New diagram on cash effects of changes in current assets and liabilities

Enhanced exhibit on summary adjustments for indirect method

New insight on measuring free cash flow

New assignments on computing operating cash flows, and financing and investing cash flows

Chapter 17

The Motley Fool **REVISED opener** with new entrepreneurial assignment

New horizontal and vertical analysis using Best Buy

Enhanced common-size analysis of Circuit City and Best Buy

New ratio analysis of Best Buy and Circuit City

New debt-to-equity analysis

New appendix on 'sustainable income,' including new requirements for accounting changes

Streamlined intro to comprehensive income

Chapter 18

Garrison Guitars **NEW opener** with new entrepreneurial assignment

New discussion and assignments on manufacturing cycle time and efficiency

Moved unit contribution margin to Chapter 22

New assignments on direct and indirect costs

New assignments on lean manufacturing and operating efficiencies

Enhanced graphics and streamlined discussion of cost flows

Expanded discussion of service businesses and cost controls

Chapter 19

Antelope Valley Medical College **NEW opener** with new entrepreneurial assignment

New insight on target costing

New illustrations and entries for cost flows in a job order system

Enhanced discussion for service businesses

New assignment on Ikea's costing strategy and success

Chapter 20

Duwop **NEW opener** with new entrepreneurial assignment

New discussion on tracking costs in a process operation

New focus on weighted average costing

Moved FIFO costing to appendix

Streamlined process costing illustrations and exhibits

Simplified computation of equivalent units

Streamlined the cost reconciliation and process cost summary

Chapter 21

Jungle Jim's International Market **NEW opener** with new entrepreneurial assignment

Streamlined activity-based costing illustration

Enhanced illustration of performance measurement

New assignment on costing and control of off-site employees

Chapter 22

Chinasprout **NEW opener** with new entrepreneurial assignment

Enhanced illustration and computations for measuring cost behaviors

Expanded explanation and illustration of high-low costing method

New illustration of unit contribution margin

Enhanced illustration of contribution margin income statement

New assignments on cost behavior estimation, and on cost, profits, and product giveaways

Chapter 23

Cloudveil **NEW opener** with new entrepreneurial assignment

Enhanced section on budgeted financial reports

New assignment on benefits of budgeting for startups

Chapter 24

Under Armour **NEW opener** with new entrepreneurial assignment

Enhanced explanation of flexible budgets

Streamlined overhead cost variance analysis

Enhanced budgeting for service businesses

Chapter 25

Progressive Telecom **NEW opener** with new entrepreneurial assignment

Enhanced explanation of depreciation and cash flow

Simplified selected present value calculations

Expanded applications to service businesses

Instructor Supplements

Instructor's Resource CD-ROM

Vol. 1, Chapters 1-12
ISBN13: 9780073266558
ISBN10: 0073266558

FAP 18e, Chapters 1-25
ISBN13: 9780073266374
ISBN10: 007326637X

This is your all-in-one resource. It allows you to create custom presentations from your own materials or from the following text-specific materials provided in the CD's asset library:

- Instructor's Resource Manual
- Solutions Manual
- Test Bank, Computerized Test Bank
- PowerPoint® Presentations *Prepared by Domenico A. Tavella and Tim Samolis, Pittsburgh Technical Institute* Presentations allow for revision of lecture slides, and includes a viewer, allowing screens to be shown with or without the software.
- Excel Template Assignments
- Link to PageOut
- Video Clips

Test Bank

Vol. 1, Chapters 1-12
ISBN13: 9780073266442
ISBN10: 0073266442

Vol. 2, Chapters 13-25
ISBN13: 9780073266398
ISBN10: 0073266396

Revised by Gregory Prescott, Univeristy of South Alabama–Mobile and Gloria Worthy, Southwest Tennessee Community College–Macon Campus.

Instructor's Resource Manual, *FAP* 18e, Chapters 1-25

ISBN13: 9780073266527
ISBN10: 0073266523

Written by Barbara Chiappetta, Nassau Community College, and Patricia Walczak, Lansing Community College.

This manual contains (for each chapter) a Lecture Outline, a chart linking all assignment materials to Learning Objectives, a list of relevant active learning activities, and additional visuals with transparency masters. An electronic version is available on the Website and on the Instructor's Resource CD-ROM.

Algorithmic Test Bank

ISBN13: 9780073266612
ISBN10: 0073266619

Solutions Manual

Vol. 1, Chapters 1-12
ISBN13: 9780073266428
ISBN10: 0073266426

Vol. 2, Chapters 13-25
ISBN13: 9780073266510
ISBN10: 0073266515

Written by John J. Wild and Marilyn Sagrillo.

Solutions Acetates

Vol. 1, Chapters 1-12
ISBN13: 9780073266572
ISBN10: 0073266574

Vol. 2, Chapters 13-25
ISBN13: 9780073266589
ISBN10: 0073266582

Geoffrey Heriot, Greenville Technical College

"The text is well presented and has excellent materials for both students and instructors. It is certainly one of the top texts in an entry level principles of accounting marketplace."

Excel Working Papers CD

Vol. 1, Chapters 1-12
ISBN13: 9780073266411
ISBN10: 0073266418

Vol. 2, Chapters 12-25
ISBN13: 9780073266503
ISBN10: 0073266507

PFA, Chapters 1-17
ISBN13: 9780073266350
ISBN10: 0073266353

Written by John J. Wild.

Working Papers delivered in Excel spreadsheets. Excel Working Papers are available on CD-ROM and can be bundled with the printed Working Papers; see your representative for information.

Working Papers

Vol. 1, Chapters 1-12
ISBN13: 9780073266565
ISBN10: 0073266566

Vol. 2, Chapters 12-25
ISBN13: 9780073266404
ISBN10: 007326640X

PFA, Chapters 1-17
ISBN13: 9780073266367
ISBN10: 0073266361

Written by John J. Wild.

Study Guide

Vol. 1, Chapters 1-12
ISBN13: 9780073266435
ISBN10: 0073266434

Vol. 2, Chapters 12-25
ISBN13: 9780073266381
ISBN10: 0073266388

PFA, Chapters 1-17
ISBN13: 9780073266497
ISBN10: 0073266493

Written by Barbara Chiappetta, Nassau Community College, and Patricia Walczak, Lansing Community College.

Covers each chapter and appendix with reviews of the learning objectives, outlines of the chapters, summaries of chapter materials, and additional problems with solutions.

Carol Yacht's General Ledger & Peachtree Complete 2006 CD-ROM

ISBN 13: 9780073266336
ISBN 10: 0073266337

GL Software developed by Jack E. Terry, ComSource Associates, Inc.

Peachtree templates prepared by Carol Yacht.

The CD-ROM includes fully functioning versions of McGraw-Hill's own General Ledger Application software as well as Peachtree Complete 2006. Problem templates are included that allow you to assign text problems for working in either Yacht's General Ledger or Peachtree Complete 2006.

Zinio eBook

ISBN13: 9780073266473
ISBN10: 0073266477

Topic Tackler Plus DVD

ISBN13: 9780073266534
ISBN10: 0073266531

Prepared by Jeannie Folk, College of DuPage.

See page xvii for complete description.

Contributing Author
The authors and book team wish to thank Marilyn Sagrillo for her excellent contributions.

Marilyn Sagrillo is an associate professor at the University of Wisconsin at Green Bay. She received her BA and MS from Northern Illinois University and her PhD from the University of Wisconsin at Madison. Her scholarly articles are published in *Accounting Enquiries, Journal of Accounting Case Research*, and the *Missouri Society of CPAs Casebook*. She is a member of the American Accounting Association and the Institute of Management Accountants. She previously received the UWGB Founder's Association Faculty Award for Excellence in Teaching. Professor Sagrillo is an active volunteer for the Midwest Renewable Energy Association. She also enjoys reading, traveling, and hiking.

John J. Wild, Kermit D. Larson, Barbara Chiappetta, and McGraw-Hill/Irwin would like to recognize the following instructors for their valuable feedback and involvement in the development of *Fundamental Accounting Principles* 18e. We are thankful for their suggestions, counsel, and encouragement.

Matilda Abavana, Essex County College

Janet Adeyiga, Hampton University

Lelia Austin, Lake City Community College

Mazen Badra, Sanford-Brown College

Thomas Badley, Baker College of Port Huron

Joyce Barden, DeVry University

Scott Barhight, Northampton Community College

Richard Barnhart, Grand Rapids Community College

Mary Barnum, Grand Rapids Community College

Cheryl Baron, Ridgewater College

Dan Bayak, Northampton Community College

Allen Bealle, Delgado Community College

Irene Bembenista, Davenport University

James Benedum, Milwaukee Area Technical College

Joe Berlinski, Prairie State College

Michelle Berube, Florida Metropolitan University

William Black, Raritan Valley CC

Mike Blackett, National American University

Linda Bolduc, Mount Wachusett Community College

Rick Bowden, Oakland CC - Auburn Hills

Deborah Boyce, Mohawk Valley Community College

Nancy Boyd, Middle Tennessee State University

Sarah Brown, University of North Alabama

Mary Burnell, Fairmont State College

Earl Butler, Broward Community College North

Paula Campbell, United Education Institute

Ronald L. Campbell, North Carolina A&T State University

Sharon Campbell, University of North Alabama

Gary Carlson, Kirkwood Community College

Lloyd Carroll, Borough of Manhattan Community College

Roy Carson, Anne Arundel Community College

Al Case, Southern Oregon University

Fatma Cebenoyan, Hunter College

Amy Chataginer, Mississippi Gulf Coast Community College

Sandra Check, Texas School of Business

Bea Chiang, College of New Jersey

Marilyn G. Ciolino, Delgado Community College

Joan Cook, Milwaukee Area Technical College

Ken Couvillion, San Joaquin Delta College

Jim Crowther, Kirkwood Community College

Patricia Davis, Keystone College

Lee Daugherty, Lorain County Community College

Thomas W. DeBerry, North Georgia College and State University

Andrea Deebach, Lake Washington Technical College

Joan H. Demko, Wor-Wic Community College

Linda Dening, Jefferson Community College

Mike Deschamps, Chaffey College

Jack Dodds, Des Moines Area Community College

Patricia Doherty, Old Dominion University

Alex Dontoh, New York University

Ron Douglas, Southwest Minnesota State University

Andy Dressler, Walla Walla College

Michael Farina, Cerritos College

Tim Farmer, University of Missouri-St. Louis

Charles Fazzi, Saint Vincent College

Patricia Feller, Nashville State Community College

Albert Fisher, Community College of Southern Nevada

Carolyn Fitzmorris, Hutchinson Community College

Jim Formosa, Nashville State Technical College

Jayne Fuglister, Cleveland State University

John Gabelman, Columbus State Community College

Dennis Gaffney, Cleveland State University

Dan Galvin, Diablo Valley College

Tesfa G. Gebremedhin, West Virginia University

Harold Gellis, York College

Barbara Gershowitz, Nashville State Community College

Natalie Gillard, Mesalands Community College

Marie Gould, Springfield College

Harry E. Gray, Ivy Tech State College

Ann Gregory, South Plains College

Curtis Gustafson, South Dakota State University

Bill Guthrie, DeVry University - Westminster

Betty Habershon, Prince Georges Community College

Patricia Halliday, Santa Monica College

Fred Hampel, Frontrange Community College

John Hancock, University of California Davis

Mark Handley, Delaware Technical and Community College

Heidi Hansel, Kirkwood Community College

James Hansen, Minnesota State University

Jeannie Harrington, Middle Tennessee State University

William Harvey, Henry Ford Community College

Yvonne Hatami, Boro of Manhattan Community College

Laurie Hays, Western Michigan University

Ken Heaslip, Kean State University

Dianne Henline, Texarkana College

Geoffrey Heriot, Greenville Technical Community College

Bernie Hill, Spokane Community College

Kathy Hill, Leeward Community College

Ted Hopple, Columbus State Community College

Richard Hudanick, Sanford Brown College

Regina C. Ivory, Fort Valley State University

Beverly Jenkins, Phoenix College

Cathy Jeppson, California State University

Bill Johnstone, Montgomery College - Rockville

Jeffery Jones, Community College of Southern Nevada

John Karayan, Occidental College

Naomi Karolinski, Monroe Community College

Sushila Kedia, Grambling University

Howard Keller, Indiana University/Purdue University Indiana

Miriam Keller-Perkins, Berkeley College

Chris Kelly, Community College of Southern Nevada

Chula King, University of West Florida

Debra Kiss, Davenport University

Jay Klein, Florida Metropolitan University

Mary Kline, Blackhawk College

Shirly Kleiner, Johnson County Community College

Christy Kloezeman, Glendale Community College

Susan R. Koch, Austin Peay State University

Jerry Kreuze, Western Michigan University

Tara Laken, Joliet Junior College

Michael Landers, Middlesex County Community College

Sam Lanzafame, Bryant and Stratton

Deborah Leitsch, Goldey-Beacom College

Denise Leggett, Middle Tennessee State University

Natasha Librizzi, Milwaukee Area Technical College

Danny Litt, University of California - Los Angeles

William P. Logan, Middle Georgia College

Dorinda Lynn, Pensacola Junior College

Linda Mallory, Central Virginia Community College

Maria Mari, Miami Dade College

Barbara Marotta, North Virginia Community College, Woodbridge

Mary Maury, St. John's University

Linda McAnally, Sul Ross State University

Larry C. McCabe, Muhlenberg College

Dorothy McCaden, Gibbs College

Cynthia McCall, Des Moines Area Community College

Irene McCarthy, St. John's University

Clarice McCoy, Brookhaven College

Florence McGovern, Bergen Community College

Andrew W. McKee, North Country Community College

Teri Meta, Seminole Community College - Sanford

James E. Miller, Gannon University

Shea Mears, Des Moines Area Community College

Andy Morgret, University of Memphis

David E. Morris, North Georgia College & State University

Audrey Morrison, Pensacola Junior College

Richard Murdock, Ohio State University

Andrea Murowski, Brookdale Community College

Charles Murphy, Bunker Hill Community College

Cindy Navaroli, Chaffey College

Bruce R. Neumann, University of Colorado at Denver

Joe Nicassio, Westmoreland County CC

Dave Nichols, University of Mississippi

Deborah Niemer, Oakland Community College

Jon Nitschke, Montana State University - Great Falls

Eugene O'Donnell, Harcum College

Liz Ott, Casper College

Lydia Parham, Baker College of Flint

Jane Park, California State University

Robert D. Patterson, Penn State Erie

Deborah Pavelka, Roosevelt University

Dennis Pelzek, Waukesha County Technical College

Shirley Powell, Arkansas State University

Greg Prescott, University of Southern Alabama

Lisa Rackley, Rich Mountain Community College

Lavonda Ramey, Schoolcraft College

Nova Randolph, Shawnee Community College

Paula Ratliff, Arkansas State University

Kathie Reeslund, Normandale Community College

Robert Ricketts, Texas Tech University

Paul Rivers, Bunker Hill Community College

Frank Rodjius, Northwestern University

Harold Royer, Miami Dade Community College

Al Ruggiero, Suffolk Community College

John A. Rude, Bloomsburg University

Jerry Scott, Ivy Tech State College

Gary Schader, Kean University

Angela Seidel, Cambria-Rowe Business College

Joe Shambley, Sullivan County Community College

Lynn Shuster, Central Penn College

Lois Slutsky, Broward Community College - South Pembroke Pines

Judy Smith, American InterContinental University

Horace Stearman, Remington College

Stacey Stewart, Colorado Northwestern Community College

Verlindsey Stewart, J.F. Drake State Technical

Bill Stibrany, Allentown Business School

Undine Stinnette, Roosevelt University

Janice Stoudemire, Midlands Technical College

Scott Stroher, Glendale Community College

Pamela Strysick, Broward Community College South

Linda Stuckey, Virginia Western Community College

Ron Summers, Oklahoma City Community College

David R. Swarts, Clinton Community College

Larry Swisher, Muskegon Community College

Domenico A. Tavella, Pittsburgh Technical Institute

Steve Teeter, Utah Valley State University

Katherene Terrell, University of Central Oklahoma

Ronald R. Tidd, Central Washington University

Christine N. Todd, William Woods University

Shafi Ullah, Broward Community College South

Bob Urell, Irvine Valley College

Peter Vander Weyst, Edmonds Community College

Patricia Walczak, Lansing Community College

Kenton Walker, University of Wyoming

Debra A. Warren, Chadron State College

John Weber, DeVry University

Terry Wegner, Casper College

Keith Weidkamp, Sierra College

Christian Widmer, Tidewater Community College

Jack Wiehler, San Joaquin Delta College

Denise N. Wooten, Erie Community College

Patricia Worsham, Riverside Community College-Norco

Gloria Worthy, Southwest Tennessee Community College

Nancy L. Wyant, International College - Fort Myers

Lynette Yerbury, Salt Lake City Community College

Judy Zander, Grossmont College

Charlie Zaruba, Florida Metropolitan University

In addition to the helpful and generous colleagues listed above, we thank the entire McGraw-Hill/Irwin *Fundamental Accounting Principles* 18e team, including Stewart Mattson, Steve Schuetz, Kelly Odom, Lori Koetters, Matthew Baldwin, Michael McCormick, Becky Szura, and Elizabeth Mavetz. We also thank the great marketing and sales support staff, including Krista Bettino, Dan Silverburg, and Liz Farina. Many talented educators and professionals worked hard to create the supplements for this book, and for their efforts we're grateful. Finally, many more people we either did not meet or whose efforts we did not personally witness nevertheless helped to make this book everything that it is, and we thank them all.

John J. Wild   Kermit D. Larson   Barbara Chiappetta

Brief Contents

Contents

Fundamental Accounting Principles

1

Accounting in Business

A Look at This Chapter

Accounting plays a crucial role in the information age. In this chapter, we discuss the importance of accounting to different types of organizations and describe its many users and uses. We explain that ethics are crucial to accounting. We also describe business transactions and how they are reflected in financial statements.

A Look Ahead

Chapter 2 further describes and analyzes business transactions. We explain the analysis and recording of transactions, the ledger and trial balance, and the double-entry system. Chapters 2 and 3 together show (via the accounting cycle) how financial statements reflect business activities.

Learning Objectives

Learning Objectives are classified as conceptual, analytical, or procedural.

CAP

Conceptual

C1 Explain the purpose and importance of accounting in the information age. *(p. 4)*

C2 Identify users and uses of accounting. *(p. 5)*

C3 Identify opportunities in accounting and related fields. *(p. 6)*

C4 Explain why ethics are crucial to accounting. *(p. 8)*

C5 Explain the meaning of generally accepted accounting principles and define and apply several key accounting principles. *(p. 9)*

C6 *Appendix 1B*—Identify and describe the three major activities in organizations. *(p. 24)*

Analytical

A1 Define and interpret the accounting equation and each of its components. *(p. 12)*

A2 Analyze business transactions using the accounting equation. *(p. 13)*

A3 Compute and interpret return on assets. *(p. 20)*

A4 *Appendix 1A*—Explain the relation between return and risk. *(p. 23)*

Procedural

P1 Identify and prepare basic financial statements and explain how they interrelate. *(p. 17)*

> "Ask everyone to give you money... remember, you hold the opportunity for them"
> —Shawn Nelson

I Should Have Thought of That!

*A **Decision Feature** launches each chapter showing the relevance of accounting for a real entrepreneur. An **Entrepreneurial Decision** problem at the end of the assignments returns to this feature with a mini-case.*

SALT LAKE CITY—Trying to get comfortable while watching TV, Shawn Nelson thought "a huge beanbag thing" would be far more relaxing than his old couch. So he made one—a big one! Seven feet across and shaped like a baseball, Shawn's creation was the talk of friends and neighbors. Shortly after making and selling a few "huge beanbag things," Shawn knew it needed a better name. Drawing on the 1960s retro spirit of "love and peace," Shawn named his invention the LoveSac and his company (**LoveSac.com**) was born.

Yet LoveSac's launch was anything but smooth. Shawn began by working out of his mother's basement. He then set up shop at trade shows and even the local drive-in cinema. He got his first big break when **Limited Too** called after seeing his display at a trade show. "I answered the phone," says Shawn, "Twelve thousand Sacs? Sure, no problem." Who was he kidding?

Shawn's credit card debt swelled to over $50,000 as he worked 19-hour days and slept in the aged building in which he manufactured the Sacs. "It nearly broke me emotionally, physically, mentally," Shawn recalls. "We finished the order but ate up all our profits." Without

profits his business, too, would soon be retro. So Shawn approached furniture retailers to ask if they would carry Sacs. "Shawn can still hear the laughter," states LoveSac's Website.

Just when things seemed bleakest, Shawn's cousin suggested he open a retail location. Desperate, Shawn took a three-month lease in a shopping mall. His goal: sell one SuperSac per day. This would cover rent and pay him and his cousin a $5 hourly wage. Shawn then developed a transaction-based accounting system to get a handle on orders and sales. He also selected an organizational form and constructed financial measures and reports.

Incredibly, customers crowded into his store within days of opening. Four weeks later and just before Christmas, customers were lined up outside the door waiting for Sacs to arrive from the factory. By Christmas Eve, Shawn's store was nearly sold out. Today, Shawn has more than 60 stores projected to generate over $30 million in sales. With results like that we'd all croon over Sacs! [Sources: *LoveSac* Website, January 2006; *Entrepreneur*, November 2004; *LA Confidential*, Fall 2004; *Life & Style Weekly*, June 2005.]

Chapter Preview

*A **Preview** opens each chapter with a summary of topics covered.*

Today's world is one of information—its preparation, communication, analysis, and use. Accounting is at the heart of this information age. Knowledge of accounting gives us career opportunities and the insight to take advantage of them. This book introduces concepts, procedures, and analyses that help us make better decisions. In this chapter we describe accounting, the users and uses of accounting information, the forms and activities of organizations, and several accounting principles. We also introduce transaction analysis and financial statements.

Accounting in Business

Importance of Accounting
- Accounting information users
- Opportunities in accounting

Fundamentals of Accounting
- Ethics—key concept
- Generally accepted accounting principles

Transaction Analysis
- Accounting equation
- Transaction analysis— illustrated

Financial Statements
- Income statement
- Statement of owner's equity
- Balance sheet
- Statement of cash flows

Importance of Accounting

C1 Explain the purpose and importance of accounting in the information age.

We live in an information age—a time of communication and immediate access to data, news, facts, and commentary. Information affects how we live, whom we associate with, and the opportunities we have. To fully benefit from the available information, we need knowledge of the information system. An information system consists of the collecting, processing, and reporting of information to decision makers.

Providing information about what businesses own, what they owe, and how they perform is an important aim of accounting. **Accounting** is an information and measurement system that identifies, records, and communicates relevant, reliable, and comparable information about an organization's business activities. *Identifying* business activities requires selecting transactions and events relevant to an organization. Examples are the sale of iPods by **Apple** and the receipt of ticket money by **TicketMaster**. *Recording* business activities requires keeping a chronological log of transactions and events measured in dollars and classified and summarized in a useful format. *Communicating* business activities requires preparing accounting reports such as financial statements. It also requires analyzing and interpreting such reports. (The financial statements and notes of **Best Buy** are shown in Appendix A of this book. This appendix also shows the financial statements of **Circuit City** and **Apple Computer**.) Exhibit 1.1 summarizes accounting activities.

We must guard against a narrow view of accounting. The most common contact with accounting is through credit approvals, checking accounts, tax forms, and payroll. These

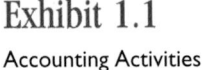

Real company names are printed in bold magenta.

Exhibit 1.1

Accounting Activities

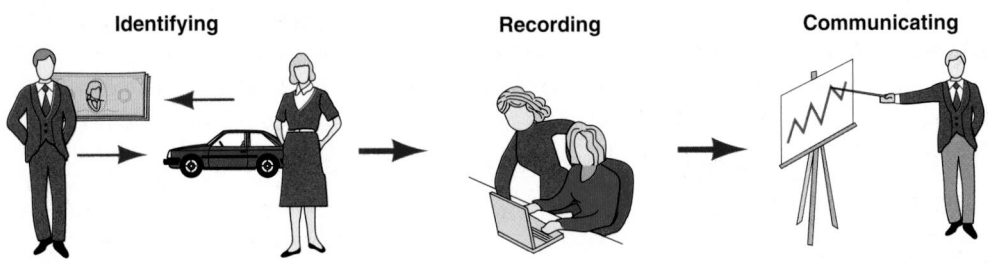

Identifying	Recording	Communicating
Select transactions and events	Input, measure, and classify	Prepare, analyze, and interpret

experiences are limited and tend to focus on the recordkeeping parts of accounting. **Recordkeeping,** or **bookkeeping,** is the recording of transactions and events, either manually or electronically. This is just one part of accounting. Accounting also identifies and communicates information on transactions and events, and it includes the crucial processes of analysis and interpretation.

Technology is a key part of modern business and plays a major role in accounting. Technology reduces the time, effort, and cost of recordkeeping while improving clerical accuracy. Some small organizations continue to perform various accounting tasks manually, but even they are impacted by information technology. As technology has changed the way we store, process, and summarize masses of data, accounting has been freed to expand. Consulting, planning, and other financial services are now closely linked to accounting. These services require sorting through data, interpreting their meaning, identifying key factors, and analyzing their implications.

Margin notes further enhance the textual material.

Point: Technology is only as useful as the accounting data available, and users' decisions are only as good as their understanding of accounting. The best software and recordkeeping cannot make up for lack of accounting knowledge.

Users of Accounting Information

Accounting is often called the *language of business* because all organizations set up an accounting information system to communicate data to help people make better decisions. Exhibit 1.2 shows that the accounting information system serves many kinds of users who can be divided into two groups: external users and internal users.

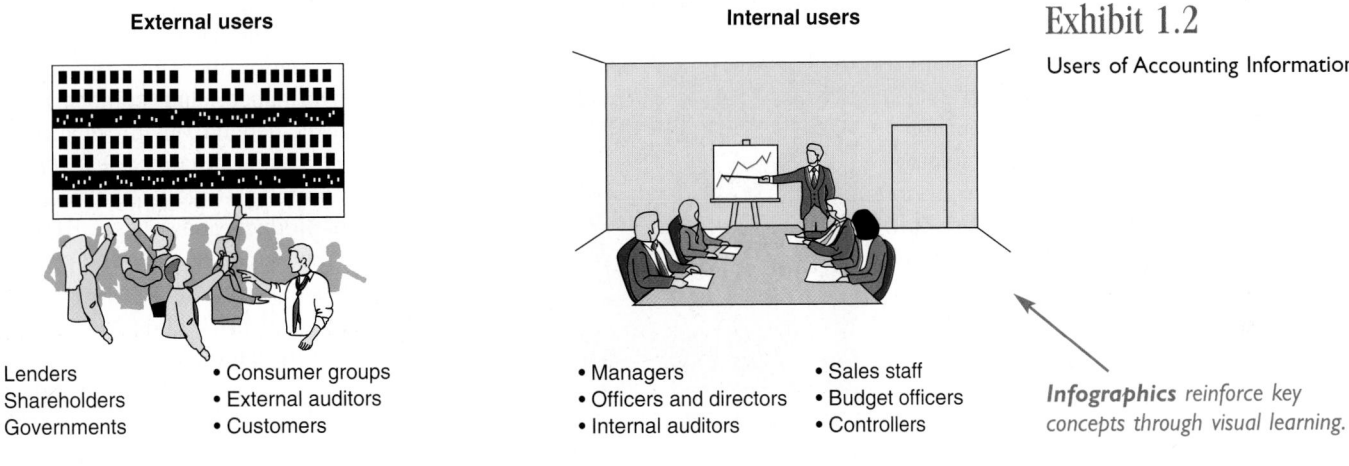

External users

- Lenders
- Shareholders
- Governments
- Consumer groups
- External auditors
- Customers

Internal users

- Managers
- Officers and directors
- Internal auditors
- Sales staff
- Budget officers
- Controllers

Exhibit 1.2

Users of Accounting Information

Infographics reinforce key concepts through visual learning.

External Information Users   **External users** of accounting information are *not* directly involved in running the organization. They include shareholders (investors), lenders, directors, customers, suppliers, regulators, lawyers, brokers, and the press. External users have limited access to an organization's information. Yet their business decisions depend on information that is reliable, relevant, and comparable.

Financial accounting is the area of accounting aimed at serving external users by providing them with financial statements. These statements are known as *general-purpose financial statements*. The term *general-purpose* refers to the broad range of purposes for which external users rely on these statements.

Each external user has special information needs depending on the types of decisions to be made. *Lenders* (creditors) loan money or other resources to an organization. Banks, savings and loans, co-ops, and mortgage and finance companies often are lenders. Lenders look for information to help them assess whether an organization is likely to repay its loans with interest. *Shareholders* (investors) are the owners of a corporation. They use accounting reports in deciding whether to buy, hold, or sell stock. Shareholders typically elect a *board of directors* to oversee their interests in an organization. Since directors are responsible to shareholders, their information needs are similar. *External* (independent) *auditors* examine financial statements to verify that they are prepared according to generally accepted accounting principles. *Employees* and *labor unions* use financial statements to judge the fairness of wages, assess job

C2   Identify users and uses of accounting.

Point: Google has more than 400 mil. shares of stock outstanding.

prospects, and bargain for better wages. *Regulators* often have legal authority over certain activities of organizations. For example, the Internal Revenue Service (IRS) and other tax authorities require organizations to file accounting reports in computing taxes. Other regulators include utility boards that use accounting information to set utility rates and securities regulators that require reports for companies that sell their stock to the public.

Point: Microsoft's high income levels encouraged antitrust actions against it.

Accounting serves the needs of many other external users. *Voters, legislators,* and *government officials* use accounting information to monitor and evaluate government receipts and expenses. *Contributors* to nonprofit organizations use accounting information to evaluate the use and impact of their donations. *Suppliers* use accounting information to judge the soundness of a customer before making sales on credit, and *customers* use financial reports to assess the staying power of potential suppliers.

Internal Information Users   **Internal users** of accounting information are those directly involved in managing and operating an organization. They use the information to help improve the efficiency and effectiveness of an organization. **Managerial accounting** is the area of accounting that serves the decision-making needs of internal users. Internal reports are not subject to the same rules as external reports and instead are designed with the special needs of internal users in mind.

Decision Insight boxes highlight relevant items from practice.

There are several types of internal users, and many are managers of key operating activities. *Research and development managers* need information about projected costs and revenues of any proposed changes in products and services. *Purchasing managers* need to know what, when, and how much to purchase. *Human resource managers* need information about employees' payroll, benefits, performance, and compensation. *Production managers* depend on information to monitor costs and ensure quality. *Distribution managers* need reports for timely, accurate, and efficient delivery of products and services. *Marketing managers* use reports about sales and costs to target consumers, set prices, and monitor consumer needs, tastes, and price concerns. *Service managers* require information on the costs and benefits of looking after products and services. Decisions of these and other internal users depend on accounting reports.

Decision Insight

They Fought the Law   Our economic and social welfare depends on reliable accounting information. A few managers in recent years forgot that and are now paying their dues. They include L. Dennis Kozlowski of **Tyco**, convicted of falsifying accounting records; Bernard Ebbers of **WorldCom**, convicted of an $11 billion accounting scandal, and Andrew Fastow of **Enron**, guilty of hiding debt and inflating income.

Both internal and external users rely on internal controls to monitor and control company activities. *Internal controls* are procedures designed to protect company property and equipment, ensure reliable accounting reports, promote efficiency, and encourage adherence to company policies. Examples are good records, physical controls (locks, passwords, guards), and independent reviews.

Opportunities in Accounting

C3 Identify opportunities in accounting and related fields.

Accounting information affects many aspects of our lives. When we earn money, pay taxes, invest savings, budget earnings, and plan for the future, we are influenced by accounting. Accounting has four broad areas of opportunities: financial, managerial, taxation, and accounting-related. Exhibit 1.3 lists selected opportunities in each area.

The majority of accounting opportunities are in *private accounting,* as shown in Exhibit 1.4. *Public accounting* offers the next largest number of opportunities. Still other opportunities exist in government (and not-for-profit) agencies, including business regulation and investigation of law violations.

Point: The largest accounting firms are Deloitte & Touche, Ernst & Young, PricewaterhouseCoopers, and KPMG.

Accounting specialists are highly regarded. Their professional standing often is denoted by a certificate. Certified public accountants (CPAs) must meet education and experience requirements, pass an examination, and exhibit ethical character. Many accounting specialists hold certificates in addition to or instead of the CPA. Two of the most common are the certificate

Exhibit 1.3

Accounting Opportunities

in management accounting (CMA) and the certified internal auditor (CIA). Employers also look for specialists with designations such as certified bookkeeper (CB), certified payroll professional (CPP), and personal financial specialist (PFS).

Individuals with accounting knowledge are always in demand as they can help with financial analysis, strategic planning, e-commerce, product feasibility analysis, information technology, and financial management. Benefit packages can include flexible work schedules, telecommuting options, career path alternatives, casual work environments, extended vacation time, and child and elder care.

Demand for accounting specialists is boosting salaries. Exhibit 1.5 reports average annual salaries for several accounting positions. Salary variation depends on location, company size, professional designation, experience, and other factors. For example, salaries for chief financial officers (CFO) range from under $75,000 to more than $1 million per year. Likewise, salaries for bookkeepers range from under $30,000 to more than $80,000.

Exhibit 1.4

Accounting Jobs by Area

- Private accounting 60%
- Public accounting 25%
- Government, not-for-profit and education 15%

Point: The Census Bureau reports that for workers 18 and over, higher education yields higher average pay:
Advanced degree $74,602
Bachelor's degree 51,206
High school degree 27,915
No high school degree 18,734

Field	Title (experience)	2006 Salary	2011 Estimate*
Public Accounting	Partner	$181,000	$231,000
	Manager (6–8 years)	89,500	114,000
	Senior (3–5 years)	68,500	87,500
	Junior (0–2 years)	49,000	62,500
Private Accounting	CFO	221,000	282,000
	Controller/Treasurer	140,000	179,000
	Manager (6–8 years)	83,000	106,000
	Senior (3–5 years)	69,000	88,000
	Junior (0–2 years)	47,000	60,000
Recordkeeping	Full-charge bookkeeper	55,000	70,000
	Accounts manager	48,500	62,000
	Payroll manager	52,000	66,000
	Accounting clerk (0–2 years)	35,500	45,000

Exhibit 1.5

Accounting Salaries for Selected Fields

Point: For updated salary information:
www.AICPA.org
Abbott-Langer.com
Kforce.com

* Estimates assume a 5% compounded annual increase over current levels.

Quick Check is a chance to stop and reflect on key points.

Answers—p. 26

Quick Check

1. What is the purpose of accounting?
2. What is the relation between accounting and recordkeeping?
3. Identify some advantages of technology for accounting.
4. Who are the internal and external users of accounting information?
5. Identify at least five types of managers who are internal users of accounting information.
6. What are internal controls and why are they important?

Fundamentals of Accounting

Accounting is guided by principles, standards, concepts, and assumptions. This section describes several of these key fundamentals of accounting.

Ethics—A Key Concept

C4 Explain why ethics are crucial to accounting.

The goal of accounting is to provide useful information for decisions. For information to be useful, it must be trusted. This demands ethics in accounting. **Ethics** are beliefs that distinguish right from wrong. They are accepted standards of good and bad behavior.

Identifying the ethical path is sometimes difficult. The preferred path is a course of action that avoids casting doubt on one's decisions. For example, accounting users are less likely to trust an auditor's report if the auditor's pay depends on the success of the client being audited. To avoid such concerns, ethics rules are often set. For example, auditors are banned from direct investment in their client and cannot accept pay that depends on figures in the client's reports. Exhibit 1.6 gives guidelines for making ethical decisions.

Point: Sarbanes-Oxley Act requires each issuer of securities to disclose whether it has adopted a code of ethics for its senior financial officers and the contents of that code.

Exhibit 1.6

Guidelines for Ethical Decision Making

Identify ethical concerns	Analyze options	Make ethical decision
Use personal ethics to recognize an ethical concern.	Consider all good and bad consequences.	Choose best option after weighing all consequences.

Global: Business ethics differ across countries. This is due to cultural, political, legal, economic, and other important factors.

Point: A survey of executives, educators, and legislators showed that 9 of 10 participants believe organizations are troubled by ethical problems.

Point: The American Institute of Certified Public Accountants' *Code of Professional Conduct* is available at **www.AICPA.org**.

Providers of accounting information often face ethical choices as they prepare financial reports. These choices can affect the price a buyer pays and the wages paid to workers. They can even affect the success of products and services. Misleading information can lead to a wrongful closing of a division that harms workers, customers, and suppliers. There is an old saying worth remembering: *Good ethics are good business.*

Some people extend ethics to *social responsibility,* which refers to a concern for the impact of actions on society. An organization's social responsibility can include donations to hospitals, colleges, community programs, and law enforcement. It also can include programs to reduce pollution, increase product safety, improve worker conditions, and support continuing education. These programs are not limited to large companies. For example, many small businesses offer discounts to students and senior citizens. Still others help sponsor events such as the Special Olympics and summer reading programs.

Graphical displays are often used to illustrate key points.

Generally Accepted Accounting Principles

Financial accounting practice is governed by concepts and rules known as **generally accepted accounting principles (GAAP).** To use and interpret financial statements effectively, we need to understand these principles. GAAP aims to make information in financial statements relevant, reliable, and comparable. *Relevant information* affects the decisions of its users. *Reliable information* is trusted by users. *Comparable information* is helpful in contrasting organizations.

Setting Accounting Principles   Two main groups establish generally accepted accounting principles in the United States. The **Financial Accounting Standards Board (FASB)** is the private group that sets both broad and specific principles. The **Securities and Exchange Commission (SEC)** is the government group that establishes reporting requirements for companies that issue stock to the public.

In today's global economy, there is increased demand by external users for comparability in accounting reports. This often arises when companies wish to raise money from lenders and investors in different countries. To that end, the **International Accounting Standards Board (IASB)** issues *International Financial Reporting Standards* (*IFRS*) that identify preferred accounting practices. The IASB hopes to create more harmony among accounting practices of different countries. If standards are harmonized, one company can potentially use a single set of financial statements in all financial markets. Many countries' standard setters support the IASB, and differences between U.S. GAAP and IASB's practices are fading. Yet, the IASB does not have authority to impose its standards on companies.

Principles of Accounting   Accounting principles are of two types. *General principles* are the basic assumptions, concepts, and guidelines for preparing financial statements. *Specific principles* are detailed rules used in reporting business transactions and events. General principles stem from long-used accounting practices. Specific principles arise more often from the rulings of authoritative groups.

We need to understand both general and specific principles to effectively use accounting information. Several general principles are described in this section and several others are described in later chapters. General principles are portrayed as building blocks of GAAP in Exhibit 1.7. The specific principles are described as we encounter them in the book.

The **objectivity principle** means that accounting information is supported by independent, unbiased evidence. It demands more than a person's opinion. Information is not reliable if it is based only on what a preparer thinks might be true. A preparer can be too optimistic or pessimistic. The objectivity principle is intended to make financial statements useful by ensuring they report reliable and verifiable information.

The **cost principle** means that accounting information is based on actual cost. Cost is measured on a cash or equal-to-cash basis. This means if cash is given for a service, its cost is measured as the amount of cash paid. If something besides cash is exchanged (such as a car traded for a truck), cost is measured as the cash value of what is given up or received. The cost principle emphasizes reliability, and information based on cost is considered objective. To illustrate, suppose a company pays $5,000 for equipment. The cost principle requires

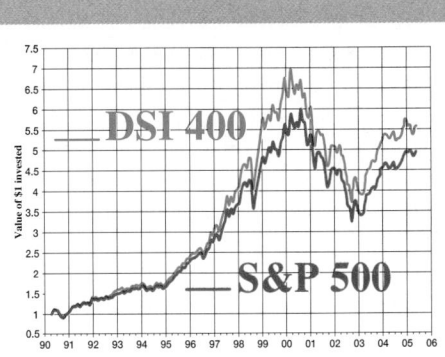
C5 Explain the meaning of generally accepted accounting principles and define and apply several key accounting principles.

Point: State ethics codes require CPAs who audit financial statements to disclose areas where those statements fail to comply with GAAP. If CPAs fail to report noncompliance, they can lose their licenses and be subject to criminal and civil actions and fines.

Point: The cost principle is also called the *historical cost principle.*

Exhibit 1.7

Building Blocks for GAAP

that this purchase be recorded at a cost of $5,000. It makes no difference if the owner thinks this equipment is worth $7,000.

The **going-concern principle** means that accounting information reflects an assumption that the business will continue operating instead of being closed or sold. This implies, for example, that property is reported at cost instead of, say, liquidation values that assume closure.

The **monetary unit principle** means that we can express transactions and events in monetary, or money, units. Money is the common denominator in business. Examples of monetary units are the dollar in the United States, Canada, Australia, and Singapore; the pound sterling in the United Kingdom; and the peso in Mexico, the Philippines, and Chile. The monetary unit a company uses in its accounting reports usually depends on the country where it operates, but many companies today are expressing reports in more than one monetary unit.

Point: For currency conversion: cnnfn.com/markets/currencies

Revenue (sales) is the amount received from selling products and services. The **revenue recognition principle** provides guidance on when a company must recognize revenue. To *recognize* means to record it. If revenue is recognized too early, a company would look more profitable than it is. If revenue is recognized too late, a company would look less profitable than it is. The following three concepts are important to revenue recognition. (1) *Revenue is recognized when earned.* The earnings process is normally complete when services are performed or a seller transfers ownership of products to the buyer. (2) *Proceeds from selling products and services need not be in cash.* A common noncash proceed received by a seller is a customer's promise to pay at a future date, called *credit sales.* (3) *Revenue is measured by the cash received plus the cash value of any other items received.*

Example: When a bookstore sells a textbook on credit is its earnings process complete? *Answer:* The bookstore can record sales for these books minus an amount expected for returns.

The **business entity principle** means that a business is accounted for separately from other business entities, including its owner. The reason for this principle is that separate information about each business is necessary for good decisions. A business entity can take one of three legal forms: *proprietorship, partnership,* or *corporation.*

Point: Abuse of the entity principle was a main culprit in the collapse of **Enron.**

1. A **sole proprietorship,** or simply **proprietorship,** is a business owned by one person. No special legal requirements must be met to start a proprietorship. It is a separate entity for accounting purposes, but it is *not* a separate legal entity from its owner. This means, for example, that a court can order an owner to sell personal belongings to pay a proprietorship's debt. This *unlimited liability* of a proprietorship is a disadvantage. However, an advantage is that a proprietorship's income is not subject to a business income tax but is instead reported and taxed on the owner's personal income tax return. Proprietorship characteristics are summarized in Exhibit 1.8, including those for partnerships and corporations.

2. A **partnership** is a business owned by two or more people, called *partners.* Like a proprietorship, no special legal requirements must be met in starting a partnership. The only requirement is an agreement between partners to run a business together. The agreement can be either oral or written and usually indicates how income and losses are to be shared. A partnership, like a proprietorship, is *not* legally separate from its owners. This means that each partner's share of profits is reported and taxed on that partner's tax return. It also means *unlimited liability* for its partners. However, at least three types of partnerships limit liability. A *limited partnership* (*LP*) includes a general partner(s) with unlimited liability and a limited partner(s) with liability restricted to the amount invested. A *limited liability partnership* (*LLP*) restricts partners'

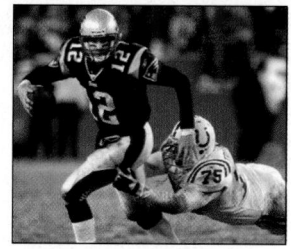

Characteristic	Proprietorship	Partnership	Corporation
Business entity	yes	yes	yes
Legal entity	no	no	yes
Limited liability	no*	no*	yes
Unlimited life	no	no	yes
Business taxed	no	no	yes
One owner allowed	yes	no	yes

Exhibit 1.8

Characteristics of Businesses

* Proprietorships and partnerships that are set up as LLCs provide limited liability.

Lightbulb icon highlights entrepreneurial-related info.

liabilities to their own acts and the acts of individuals under their control. This protects an innocent partner from the negligence of another partner, yet all partners remain responsible for partnership debts. A *limited liability company (LLC)*, offers the limited liability of a corporation and the tax treatment of a partnership (and proprietorship). Most proprietorships and partnerships are now organized as LLCs.

3. A **corporation** is a business legally separate from its owners, meaning it is responsible for its own acts and its own debts. Separate legal status means that a corporation can conduct business with the rights, duties, and responsibilities of a person. A corporation acts through its managers, who are its legal agents. Separate legal status also means that its owners, who are called **shareholders** (or **stockholders**), are not personally liable for corporate acts and debts. This limited liability is its main advantage. A main disadvantage is what's called *double taxation*—meaning that (1) the corporation income is taxed and (2) any distribution of income to its owners through dividends is taxed as part of the owners' personal income, usually at the 15% rate. (*Note:* For lower income taxpayers, the dividend tax is less than 15%, and in some cases zero.) An exception to this is an *S corporation,* a corporation with certain characteristics that give it a tax status that removes its corporate income tax. Owners of S corporations report their share of corporate income with their personal income. Ownership of corporations is divided into units called **shares** or **stock.** When a corporation issues only one class of stock, we call it **common stock** (or *capital stock*).

> **Decision Insight**
>
> **Smaller Is Better** Entrepreneurship is key to modern business and economic success. U.S. small businesses:
>
> - Total about 25 million and employ more than half of the U.S. workforce.
> - Provide 60% to 80% of new jobs annually and pay about 50% of total U.S. payroll.
> - Employ about 40% of high tech workers (such as engineers and scientists).
> - Appeal to 65% of young people who desire to launch their own business.

Decision Ethics boxes are role-playing exercises that stress ethics in accounting and business.

> **Decision Ethics** Answer—p. 25
>
> **Entrepreneur** You and a friend develop a new design for in-line skates that improves speed and performance by 25% to 40%. You plan to form a business to manufacture and market these skates. You and your friend want to minimize taxes, but your prime concern is potential lawsuits from individuals who might be injured on these skates. What form of organization do you set up?

Sarbanes–Oxley

Congress passed the **Sarbanes–Oxley Act,** also called *SOX,* to help curb financial abuses at companies that issue their stock to the public. SOX requires that these public companies apply both accounting oversight and stringent internal controls. The desired results include more transparency, accountability, and truthfulness in reporting transactions.

Compliance with SOX requires extensive documentation and verification of internal controls and increased emphasis on internal control effectiveness. Failure to comply can yield financial penalties, stock market delisting, and criminal prosecution of executives. Management must issue a report stating that internal controls are effective. CEOs and CFOs who knowingly sign off on bogus accounting reports risk millions of dollars in fines and up to 10 years in prison. Auditors also must verify the effectiveness of internal controls.

Point: An **audit** examines whether financial statements are prepared using GAAP. It does *not* attest to the absolute accuracy of the statements.

Point: *BusinessWeek* (2005) reports that external audit costs run about $35,000 for startups, up from $15,000 pre-SOX.

Point: Proprietorships and partnerships are usually managed on a regular basis by their owners. In a corporation, the owners (shareholders) elect a board of directors who appoint managers to run the business.

Quick Check   Answers—p. 26

7. What three-step guidelines can help people make ethical decisions?

8. Why are ethics and social responsibility valuable to organizations?

9. Why are ethics crucial in accounting?

10. Who sets U.S. accounting rules?

11. How are U.S. companies affected by international accounting standards?

12. How are the objectivity and cost principles related?

13. Why is the business entity principle important?

14. Why is the revenue recognition principle important?

15. What are the three basic forms of business organization?

16. Identify the owners of corporations and the terminology for ownership units.

Transaction Analysis and the Accounting Equation

A1 Define and interpret the accounting equation and each of its components.

To understand accounting information, we need to know how an accounting system captures relevant data about transactions, and then classifies, records, and reports data.

Accounting Equation

The accounting system reflects two basic aspects of a company: what it owns and what it owes. **Assets** are resources with future benefits that are owned or controlled by a company. Examples are cash, supplies, equipment, and land. The claims on a company's assets—what it owes—are separated into owner and nonowner claims. **Liabilities** are what a company owes its nonowners (creditors) in future payments, products, or services. **Equity** (also called owner's equity or capital) refers to the claims of its owner(s). Together, liabilities and equity are the source of funds to acquire assets. The relation of assets, liabilities, and equity is reflected in the following **accounting equation:**

$$\text{Assets} = \text{Liabilities} + \text{Equity}$$

Liabilities are usually shown before equity in this equation because creditors' claims must be paid before the claims of owners. (The terms in this equation can be rearranged; for example, Assets − Liabilities = Equity.) The accounting equation applies to all transactions and events, to all companies and forms of organization, and to all points in time. For example, **Best Buy**'s assets equal $10,294, its liabilities equal $5,845, and its equity equals $4,449 ($ in millions). Let's now look at the accounting equation in more detail.

Assets   Assets are resources owned or controlled by a company. These resources are expected to yield future benefits. Examples are Web servers for an online services company, musical instruments for a rock band, and land for a vegetable grower. The term *receivable* is used to refer to an asset that promises a future inflow of resources. A company that provides a service or product on credit is said to have an account receivable from that customer.

Point: The phrase "on credit" implies that the cash payment will occur at a future date.

Liabilities   **Liabilities** are creditors' claims on assets. These claims reflect obligations to provide assets, products or services to others. The term *payable* refers to a liability that promises a future outflow of resources. Examples are wages payable to workers, accounts payable to suppliers, notes payable to banks, and taxes payable to the government.

*Key **terms** are printed in bold and defined again in the end-of-book **glossary.***

Equity   **Equity** is the owner's claim on assets. Equity is equal to assets minus liabilities. This is the reason equity is also called *net assets* or *residual equity*.

Equity for a noncorporate entity—commonly called owner's equity—increases and decreases as follows: owner investments and revenues *increase* equity, whereas owner withdrawals and expenses *decrease* equity. **Owner investments** are assets an owner puts into the company and are included under the generic account **Owner, Capital. Revenues** increase equity and are the assets earned from a company's earnings activities. Examples are consulting services provided, sales of products, facilities rented to others, and commissions from services. **Owner withdrawals** are assets an owner takes from the company for personal use. **Expenses** decrease equity and are the cost of assets or services used to earn revenues. Examples are costs of employee time, use of supplies, and advertising, utilities, and insurance services from others. In sum, equity is the accumulated revenues and owner investments less the accumulated expenses and withdrawals since the company began. This breakdown of equity yields the following **expanded accounting equation.**

Point: Revenues and owner investments increase equity. Expenses and owner withdrawals decrease equity.

Point: Revenues usually result from product sales, services provided, property rentals, and money lending.

$$\text{Assets} = \text{Liabilities} + \overbrace{\underset{\text{Capital}}{\text{Owner,}} - \underset{\text{Withdrawals}}{\text{Owner,}} + \text{Revenues} - \text{Expenses}}^{\text{Equity}}$$

Net income occurs when revenues exceed expenses. Net income increases equity. A **net loss** occurs when expenses exceed revenues, which decreases equity.

Transaction Analysis

Business activities can be described in terms of transactions and events. **External transactions** are exchanges of value between two entities, which yield changes in the accounting equation. **Internal transactions** are exchanges within an entity; they can also affect the accounting equation. An example is a company's use of its supplies, which are reported as expenses when used. **Events** refer to those happenings that affect an entity's accounting equation *and* can be reliably measured. They include business events such as changes in the market value of certain assets and liabilities, and natural events such as floods and fires that destroy assets and create losses. They do not include, for example, the signing of service or product contracts, which by themselves do not impact the accounting equation.

This section uses the accounting equation to analyze 11 selected transactions and events of FastForward, a start-up consulting business, in its first month of operations. Remember that each transaction and event leaves the equation in balance and that assets *always* equal the sum of liabilities and equity.

A2 Analyze business transactions using the accounting equation.

*Topic Tackler **icon** references additional help on the CD.*

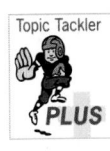

Topic Tackler

PLUS

1-1

Transaction 1: Investment by Owner On December 1, Chuck Taylor forms a consulting business, focused on assessing the performance of athletic footwear and accessories, which he names FastForward. He sets it up as a proprietorship. Taylor owns and manages the business. The marketing plan for the business is to focus primarily on consulting with sports clubs, amateur athletes, and others who place orders for athletic footwear and accessories with manufacturers. Taylor personally invests $30,000 cash in the new company and deposits the cash in a bank account opened under the name of FastForward. After this transaction, the cash (an asset) and the owner's equity each equal $30,000. The source of increase in equity is the owner's investment, which is included in the column titled C. Taylor, Capital. (Owner investments are always included under the title *"Owner name," Capital.*) The effect of this transaction on FastForward is reflected in the accounting equation as follows.

Point: There are 3 basic types of company operations: (1) **Services**—providing services for profit, (2) **Merchandisers**—buying products and reselling them for profit, and (3) **Manufacturers**—creating products and selling them for profit.

	Assets	=	Liabilities	+	Equity
	Cash	=			**C. Taylor, Capital**
(1)	**+$30,000**	=			**+$30,000**

Transaction 2: Purchase Supplies for Cash FastForward uses $2,500 of its cash to buy supplies of brand name athletic footwear for performance testing over the next few months. This transaction is an exchange of cash, an asset, for another kind of asset, supplies. It merely changes the form of assets from cash to supplies. The decrease in cash is exactly equal to the increase in supplies. The supplies of athletic footwear are assets because of the expected future benefits from the test results of their performance. This transaction is reflected in the accounting equation as follows:

	Assets			=	Liabilities	+	Equity
	Cash	**+**	**Supplies**	**=**			**C. Taylor, Capital**
Old Bal.	$30,000			**=**			$30,000
(2)	−2,500	+	$2,500				
New Bal.	$27,500	+	$ 2,500	**=**			$30,000
		$30,000				$30,000	

Transaction 3: Purchase Equipment for Cash FastForward spends $26,000 to acquire equipment for testing athletic footwear. Like transaction 2, transaction 3 is an exchange of one asset, cash, for another asset, equipment. The equipment is an asset because of its expected future benefits from testing athletic footwear. This purchase changes the makeup of assets but does not change the asset total. The accounting equation remains in balance.

	Assets					=	Liabilities	+	Equity
	Cash	**+**	**Supplies**	**+**	**Equipment**	**=**			**C. Taylor, Capital**
Old Bal.	$27,500	+	$2,500			**=**			$30,000
(3)	−26,000			+	$26,000				
New Bal.	$ 1,500	+	$2,500	+	$ 26,000	**=**			$30,000
		$30,000						$30,000	

Transaction 4: Purchase Supplies on Credit Taylor decides he needs more supplies of athletic footwear and accessories. These additional supplies total $7,100, but as we see from the accounting equation in transaction 3, FastForward has only $1,500 in cash. Taylor arranges to purchase them on credit from CalTech Supply Company. Thus, FastForward acquires supplies in exchange for a promise to pay for them later. This purchase increases assets by $7,100 in supplies, and liabilities (called *accounts payable* to CalTech Supply) increase by the same amount. The effects of this purchase follow:

Example: If FastForward pays $500 cash in transaction 4, how does this partial payment affect the liability to CalTech? What would be FastForward's cash balance? *Answers:* The liability to CalTech would be reduced to $6,600 and the cash balance would be reduced to $1,000.

	Assets					=	Liabilities	+	Equity
	Cash	**+**	**Supplies**	**+**	**Equipment**	**=**	**Accounts Payable**	**+**	**C. Taylor, Capital**
Old Bal.	$1,500	+	$2,500	+	$26,000	**=**			$30,000
(4)		+	7,100				+$7,100		
New Bal.	$1,500	+	$9,600	+	$26,000	**=**	$ 7,100	+	$30,000
		$37,100						$37,100	

Transaction 5: Provide Services for Cash FastForward earns revenues by consulting with clients about test results on athletic footwear and accessories. It earns net income only if its revenues are greater than its expenses incurred in earning them. In one of its first jobs, FastForward provides consulting services to an athletic club and immediately collects $4,200 cash. The accounting equation reflects this increase in cash of $4,200 and in equity of $4,200. This increase in equity is identified in the far right column under Revenues because the cash received is earned by providing consulting services.

	Assets					=	Liabilities	+	Equity		
	Cash	+	Supplies	+	Equipment	=	Accounts Payable	+	C. Taylor, Capital	+	Revenues
Old Bal.	$1,500	+	$9,600	+	$26,000	=	$7,100	+	$30,000		
(5)	+4,200									+	$4,200
New Bal.	$5,700	+	$9,600	+	$26,000	=	$7,100	+	$30,000	+	$ 4,200
			$41,300						$41,300		

Transactions 6 and 7: Payment of Expenses in Cash

FastForward pays $1,000 rent to the landlord of the building where its facilities are located. Paying this amount allows FastForward to occupy the space for the month of December. The rental payment is reflected in the following accounting equation as transaction 6. FastForward also pays the biweekly $700 salary of the company's only employee. This is reflected in the accounting equation as transaction 7. Both transactions 6 and 7 are December expenses for FastForward. The costs of both rent and salary are expenses, as opposed to assets, because their benefits are used in December (they have no future benefits after December). These transactions also use up an asset (cash) in carrying out FastForward's operations. The accounting equation shows that both transactions reduce cash and equity. The far right column identifies these decreases as Expenses.

By definition, increases in expenses yield decreases in equity.

	Assets					=	Liabilities	+	Equity				
	Cash	+	Supplies	+	Equipment	=	Accounts Payable	+	C. Taylor, Capital	+	Revenues	−	Expenses
Old Bal.	$5,700	+	$9,600	+	$26,000	=	$7,100	+	$30,000	+	$4,200		
(6)	−1,000											−	$1,000
Bal.	4,700	+	9,600	+	26,000	=	7,100	+	30,000	+	4,200	−	1,000
(7)	− 700											−	700
New Bal.	$4,000	+	$9,600	+	$26,000	=	$7,100	+	$30,000	+	$4,200	−	$ 1,700
			$39,600						$39,600				

Transaction 8: Provide Services and Facilities for Credit

FastForward provides consulting services of $1,600 and rents its test facilities for $300 to an amateur sports club. The rental involves allowing club members to try recommended footwear and accessories at FastForward's testing grounds. The sports club is billed for the $1,900 total. This transaction results in a new asset, called *accounts receivable,* from this client. It also yields an increase in equity from the two revenue components reflected in the Revenues column of the accounting equation:

	Assets								=	Liabilities	+	Equity				
	Cash	+	Accounts Receivable	+	Supplies	+	Equipment	=	Accounts Payable	+	C. Taylor, Capital	+	Revenues	−	Expenses
Old Bal.	$4,000	+		+	$9,600	+	$26,000	=	$7,100	+	$30,000	+	$4,200	−	$1,700
(8)		+	$1,900									+	1,600		
												+	300		
New Bal.	$4,000	+	$ 1,900	+	$9,600	+	$26,000	=	$7,100	+	$30,000	+	$6,100	−	$1,700
				$41,500								$41,500				

Transaction 9: Receipt of Cash from Accounts Receivable

The client in transaction 8 (the amateur sports club) pays $1,900 to FastForward 10 days after it is billed for consulting services. This transaction 9 does not change the total amount of assets and does not affect liabilities or equity. It converts the receivable (an asset) to cash (another asset). It does

Point: Receipt of cash is not always a revenue.

not create new revenue. Revenue was recognized when FastForward rendered the services in transaction 8, not when the cash is now collected. This emphasis on the earnings process instead of cash flows is a goal of the revenue recognition principle and yields useful information to users. The new balances follow:

	Assets						=	Liabilities	+				Equity		
	Cash	+	Accounts Receivable	+	Supplies	+	Equipment	=	Accounts Payable	+	C. Taylor, Capital	+	Revenues	−	Expenses
Old Bal.	$4,000	+	$1,900	+	$9,600	+	$26,000	=	$7,100	+	$30,000	+	$6,100	−	$1,700
(9)	+1,900	−	1,900												
New Bal.	$5,900	+	$ 0	+	$9,600	+	$26,000	=	$7,100	+	$30,000	+	$6,100	−	$1,700

$41,500 $41,500

Transaction 10: Payment of Accounts Payable   FastForward pays CalTech Supply $900 cash as partial payment for its earlier $7,100 purchase of supplies (transaction 4), leaving $6,200 unpaid. The accounting equation shows that this transaction decreases FastForward's cash by $900 and decreases its liability to CalTech Supply by $900. Equity does not change. This event does not create an expense even though cash flows out of FastForward (instead the expense is recorded when FastForward derives the benefits from these supplies).

	Assets						=	Liabilities	+				Equity		
	Cash	+	Accounts Receivable	+	Supplies	+	Equipment	=	Accounts Payable	+	C. Taylor, Capital	+	Revenues	−	Expenses
Old Bal.	$5,900	+	$ 0	+	$9,600	+	$26,000	=	$7,100	+	$30,000	+	$6,100	−	$1,700
(10)	− 900								− 900						
New Bal.	$5,000	+	$ 0	+	$9,600	+	$26,000	=	$6,200	+	$30,000	+	$6,100	−	$1,700

$40,600 $40,600

Transaction 11: Withdrawal of Cash by Owner   The owner of FastForward withdraws $200 cash for personal use. Withdrawals (decreases in equity) are not reported as expenses because they are not part of the company's earnings process. Since withdrawals are not company expenses, they are not used in computing net income.

By definition, increases in withdrawals yield decreases in equity.

	Assets						=	Liabilities	+					Equity		
	Cash	+	Accounts Receivable	+	Supplies	+	Equipment	=	Accounts Payable	+	C. Taylor, Capital	−	C. Taylor, Withdrawals	+	Revenues	−	Expenses
Old Bal.	$5,000	+	$ 0	+	$9,600	+	$26,000	=	$6,200	+	$30,000			+	$6,100	−	$1,700
(11)	− 200											− $200				
New Bal.	$4,800	+	$ 0	+	$9,600	+	$26,000	=	$6,200	+	$30,000	−	$200	+	$6,100	−	$1,700

$40,400 $40,400

Summary of Transactions

Point: Knowing how financial statements are prepared improves our analysis of them. We develop the skills for analysis of financial statements throughout the book. Chapter 17 focuses on financial statement analysis.

We summarize in Exhibit 1.9 the effects of these 11 transactions of FastForward using the accounting equation. Two points should be noted. First, the accounting equation remains in balance after each transaction. Second, transactions can be analyzed by their effects on components of the accounting equation. For example, in transactions 2, 3, and 9, one asset increased while another decreased by equal amounts.

Exhibit 1.9

Summary of Transactions Using the Accounting Equation

	Cash	+	Accounts Receivable	+	Supplies	+	Equipment	=	Accounts Payable	+	C. Taylor, Capital	−	C. Taylor, Withdrawals	+	Revenues	−	Expenses
(1)	$30,000							=			$30,000						
(2)	− 2,500			+	$2,500												
Bal.	27,500			+	2,500			=			30,000						
(3)	−26,000					+	$26,000										
Bal.	1,500			+	2,500	+	26,000	=			30,000						
(4)				+	7,100				+$7,100								
Bal.	1,500			+	9,600	+	26,000	=	7,100	+	30,000						
(5)	+ 4,200													+	$4,200		
Bal.	5,700			+	9,600	+	26,000	=	7,100	+	30,000			+	4,200		
(6)	− 1,000															−	$1,000
Bal.	4,700			+	9,600	+	26,000	=	7,100	+	30,000			+	4,200	−	1,000
(7)	− 700															−	700
Bal.	4,000			+	9,600	+	26,000	=	7,100	+	30,000			+	4,200	−	1,700
(8)		+	$1,900											+	1,600		
														+	300		
Bal.	4,000	+	1,900	+	9,600	+	26,000	=	7,100	+	30,000			+	6,100	−	1,700
(9)	+ 1,900	−	1,900														
Bal.	5,900	+	0	+	9,600	+	26,000	=	7,100	+	30,000			+	6,100	−	1,700
(10)	− 900								− 900								
Bal.	5,000	+	0	+	9,600	+	26,000	=	6,200	+	30,000			+	6,100	−	1,700
(11)	− 200											−	$200				
Bal.	$ 4,800	+	$ 0	+	$ 9,600	+	$ 26,000	=	$ 6,200	+	$ 30,000	−	$ 200	+	$6,100	−	$1,700

Quick Check

Answers—p. 26

17. When is the accounting equation in balance, and what does that mean?

18. How can a transaction not affect any liability and equity accounts?

19. Describe a transaction increasing equity and one decreasing it.

20. Identify a transaction that decreases both assets and liabilities.

Financial Statements

This section shows how financial statements are prepared from the analysis of business transactions. The four financial statements and their purposes are:

P1 Identify and prepare basic financial statements and explain how they interrelate.

1. **Income statement**—describes a company's revenues and expenses along with the resulting net income or loss over a period of time due to earnings activities.
2. **Statement of owner's equity**—explains changes in equity from net income (or loss) and from any owner investments and withdrawals over a period of time.
3. **Balance sheet**—describes a company's financial position (types and amounts of assets, liabilities, and equity) at a point in time.
4. **Statement of cash flows**—identifies cash inflows (receipts) and cash outflows (payments) over a period of time.

We prepare these financial statements using the 11 selected transactions of FastForward. (These statements are technically called *unadjusted*—we explain this in Chapters 2 and 3.)

Topic Tackler
PLUS

1-2

Income Statement

FastForward's income statement for December is shown at the top of Exhibit 1.10. Information about revenues and expenses is conveniently taken from the Equity columns of Exhibit 1.9. Revenues are reported first on the income statement. They include consulting revenues of $5,800 from transactions 5 and 8 and rental revenue of $300 from transaction 8. Expenses are reported after revenues. (For convenience in this chapter, we list larger amounts first, but we can sort expenses in different ways.) Rent and salary expenses are from transactions 6 and 7. Expenses reflect the costs to generate the revenues reported. Net income (or loss) is reported at the bottom of the statement and is the amount earned in December. Owner's investments and withdrawals are *not* part of income.

Statement of Owner's Equity

The statement of owner's equity reports information about how equity changes over the reporting period. This statement shows beginning capital, events that increase it (owner investments and net income), and events that decrease it (withdrawals and net loss). Ending capital is computed in this statement and is carried over and reported on the balance sheet. FastForward's statement of owner's equity is the second report in Exhibit 1.10. The beginning capital balance is measured as of the start of business on December 1. It is zero because FastForward did not exist before then. An existing business reports the beginning balance as of the end of the prior reporting period (such as from November 30). FastForward's statement shows that Taylor's initial investment created $30,000 of equity. It also shows the $4,400 of net income earned during the period. This links the income statement to the statement of owner's equity (see line ①). The statement also reports Taylor's $200 cash withdrawal and FastForward's end-of-period capital balance.

Balance Sheet

FastForward's balance sheet is the third report in Exhibit 1.10. This statement refers to FastForward's financial condition at the close of business on December 31. The left side of the balance sheet lists FastForward's assets: cash, supplies, and equipment. The upper right side of the balance sheet shows that FastForward owes $6,200 to creditors. Any other liabilities (such as a bank loan) would be listed here. The equity (capital) balance is $34,200. Note the link between the ending balance of the statement of owner's equity and the equity balance here—see line ②. (This presentation of the balance sheet is called the *account form:* assets on the left and liabilities and equity on the right. Another presentation is the *report form:* assets on top, followed by liabilities and then equity at the bottom. Either presentation is acceptable.)

Decision Maker

Answer—p. 26

Retailer   You open a wholesale business selling entertainment equipment to retail outlets. You find that most of your customers demand to buy on credit. How can you use the balance sheets of these customers to help you decide which ones to extend credit to?

Statement of Cash Flows

FastForward's statement of cash flows is the final report in Exhibit 1.10. The first section reports cash flows from *operating activities.* It shows the $6,100 cash received from clients and the cash paid for supplies, rent, and employee salaries. Outflows are in parentheses to denote subtraction. Net cash provided by operating activities for December is $1,000. If cash paid exceeded cash received, we would call it "cash used by operating activities." The second section reports *investing activities,* which involve buying and selling assets such as land and equipment that are held for *long-term use* (typically more than one year). The only investing activity is the $26,000 purchase of equipment. The third section shows cash flows from *financing activities,* which include the *long-term* borrowing and repaying of cash from lenders and the owner's cash investments and withdrawals. FastForward reports $30,000 from the owner's

Exhibit 1.10

Financial Statements and
Their Links

FASTFORWARD
Income Statement
For Month Ended December 31, 2007

Revenues

Consulting revenue ($4,200 + $1,600)	$ 5,800	
Rental revenue	300	
Total revenues		$ 6,100

Expenses

Rent expense	1,000	
Salaries expense	700	
Total expenses		1,700
Net income		$ 4,400

Point: A statement's heading identifies the company, the statement title, and the date or time period.

FASTFORWARD
Statement of Owner's Equity
For Month Ended December 31, 2007

C. Taylor, Capital, December 1, 2007		$ 0
Plus: Investments by owner	$30,000	
Net income	4,400	34,400
		34,400
Less: Withdrawals by owner		200
C. Taylor, Capital, December 31, 2007		$34,200

Point: Arrow lines show how the statements are linked. ① Net income is used to compute equity. ② Ending capital is used to prepare the balance sheet. ③ Cash from the balance sheet is used to reconcile the statement of cash flows.

FASTFORWARD
Balance Sheet
December 31, 2007

Assets		Liabilities	
Cash	$ 4,800	Accounts payable	$ 6,200
Supplies	9,600	Total liabilities	6,200
Equipment	26,000		
		Equity	
		C. Taylor, Capital	34,200
Total assets	$40,400	Total liabilities and equity	$ 40,400

Point: The income statement, the statement of owner's equity, and the statement of cash flows are prepared for a *period* of time. The balance sheet is prepared as of a *point* in time.

FASTFORWARD
Statement of Cash Flows
For Month Ended December 31, 2007

Cash flows from operating activities

Cash received from clients ($4,200 + $1,900)	$ 6,100	
Cash paid for supplies ($2,500 + $900)	(3,400)	
Cash paid for rent	(1,000)	
Cash paid to employee	(700)	
Net cash provided by operating activities		$ 1,000

Cash flows from investing activities

Purchase of equipment	(26,000)	
Net cash used by investing activities		(26,000)

Cash flows from financing activities

Investments by owner	30,000	
Withdrawals by owner	(200)	
Net cash provided by financing activities		29,800
Net increase in cash		$ 4,800
Cash balance, December 1, 2007		0
Cash balance, December 31, 2007		$ 4,800

Point: A single ruled line denotes an addition or subtraction. Final totals are double underlined. Negative amounts are often in parentheses.

Point: Investing activities refer to long-term asset investments by the company, *not* to owner investments.

initial investment and the $200 cash withdrawal. The net cash effect of all transactions is a $29,800 cash inflow. The final part of the statement shows FastForward increased its cash balance by $4,800 in December. Since it started with no cash, the ending balance is also $4,800—see line ③.

Quick Check
Answers—p. 26

21. Explain the link between the income statement and the statement of owner's equity.

22. Describe the link between the balance sheet and the statement of owner's equity.

23. Discuss the three major sections of the statement of cash flows.

Decision Analysis (a section at the end of each chapter) introduces and explains ratios helpful in decision making using real company data. Instructors can skip this section and cover all ratios in Chapter 17.

Decision Analysis   Return on Assets

A *Decision Analysis* section at the end of each chapter is devoted to financial statement analysis. We organize financial statement analysis into four areas: (1) liquidity and efficiency, (2) solvency, (3) profitability, and (4) market prospects—Chapter 13 has a ratio listing with definitions and groupings by area. When analyzing ratios, we need benchmarks to identify good, bad, or average levels. Common benchmarks include the company's prior levels and those of its competitors.

A3 Compute and interpret return on assets.

This chapter presents a profitability measure, that of return on assets. Return on assets is useful in evaluating management, analyzing and forecasting profits, and planning activities. **Dell** has its marketing department compute return on assets for *every* order. *Return on assets* (ROA), also called *return on investment* (ROI), is defined in Exhibit 1.11.

Exhibit 1.11

Return on Assets

$$\text{Return on assets} = \frac{\text{Net income}}{\text{Average total assets}}$$

Net income is from the annual income statement, and average total assets is computed by adding the beginning and ending amounts for that same period and dividing by 2. To illustrate, **Best Buy** reports net income of $984 million in 2005. At the beginning of fiscal 2005, its total assets are $8,652 million and at the end of fiscal 2005, they total $10,294 million. Best Buy's return on assets for 2005 is:

$$\text{Return on assets} = \frac{\$984 \text{ mil.}}{(\$8,652 \text{ mil.} + \$10,294 \text{ mil.})/2} = 10.4\%$$

*Each **Decision Analysis** section ends with a role-playing scenario to show the usefulness of ratios.*

Is a 10.4% return on assets good or bad for Best Buy? To help answer this question, we compare (benchmark) Best Buy's return with its prior performance, the returns of competitors (such as **Circuit City**, **RadioShack**, and **CompUSA**), and the returns from alternative investments. Best Buy's return for each of the prior five years is in the second column of Exhibit 1.12, which ranges from 1.3% to 10.4%. These returns show an increase in its productive use of assets in recent years. We also compute Circuit City's returns in the third column of Exhibit 1.12. In four of the five years, Best Buy's return exceeds Circuit City's, and its average return is higher for this period. We also compare Best Buy's return to the normal return for similar merchandisers of electronic products (fourth column). Industry averages are available from services such as **Dun & Bradstreet**'s *Industry Norms and Key Ratios* and **Robert Morris Associates'** *Annual Statement Studies*. When compared to the industry, Best Buy performs well.

Decision Maker
Answer—p. 26

Business Owner   You own a small winter ski resort that earns a 21% return on its assets. An opportunity to purchase a winter ski equipment manufacturer is offered to you. This manufacturer earns a 19% return on its assets. The industry return for this manufacturer is 14%. Do you purchase this manufacturer?

Best Buy Fiscal Year	Return on Assets		
	Best Buy	**Circuit City**	**Industry**
2005	10.4%	1.6%	3.2%
2004	8.6	(2.3)	3.1
2003	1.3	1.9	3.0
2002	9.3	4.6	3.1
2001	10.1	4.1	6.4

Exhibit 1.12

Best Buy, Circuit City, and Industry Returns

*The **Demonstration Problem** is a review of key chapter content. The Planning the Solution offers strategies in solving the problem.*

Demonstration Problem

After several months of planning, Jasmine Worthy started a haircutting business called Expressions. The following events occurred during its first month:

a. On August 1, Worthy invested $3,000 cash and $15,000 of equipment in Expressions.

b. On August 2, Expressions paid $600 cash for furniture for the shop.

c. On August 3, Expressions paid $500 cash to rent space in a strip mall for August.

d. On August 4, it purchased $1,200 of equipment on credit for the shop (using a long-term note payable).

e. On August 5, Expressions opened for business. Cash received from services provided in the first week and a half of business (ended August 15) is $825.

f. On August 15, it provided $100 of haircutting services on account.

g. On August 17, it received a $100 check for services previously rendered on account.

h. On August 17, it paid $125 cash to an assistant for working during the grand opening.

i. Cash received from services provided during the second half of August is $930.

j. On August 31, it paid a $400 installment toward principal on the note payable entered into on August 4.

k. On August 31, Worthy made a $900 cash withdrawal for personal use.

Required

1. Arrange the following asset, liability, and equity titles in a table similar to the one in Exhibit 1.9: Cash; Accounts Receivable; Furniture; Store Equipment; Note Payable; J. Worthy, Capital; J. Worthy, Withdrawals; Revenues; and Expenses. Show the effects of each transaction using the accounting equation.

2. Prepare an income statement for August.

3. Prepare a statement of owner's equity for August.

4. Prepare a balance sheet as of August 31.

5. Prepare a statement of cash flows for August.

6. Determine the return on assets ratio for August.

Planning the Solution

- Set up a table like Exhibit 1.9 with the appropriate columns for accounts.
- Analyze each transaction and show its effects as increases or decreases in the appropriate columns. Be sure the accounting equation remains in balance after each transaction.
- Prepare the income statement, and identify revenues and expenses. List those items on the statement, compute the difference, and label the result as *net income* or *net loss*.
- Use information in the Equity columns to prepare the statement of owner's equity.
- Use information in the last row of the transactions table to prepare the balance sheet.
- Prepare the statement of cash flows; include all events listed in the Cash column of the transactions table. Classify each cash flow as operating, investing, or financing.
- Calculate return on assets by dividing net income by average assets.

Solution to Demonstration Problem

1.

	Cash	+	Accounts Receiv-able	+	Furni-ture	+	Store Equip-ment	=	Note Payable	+	J. Worthy, Capital	−	J. Worthy, Withdrawals	+	Revenues	−	Expenses
Assets								=	**Liabilities** +					**Equity**			
a.	$3,000						$15,000				$18,000						
b.	− 600			+	$600												
Bal.	2,400	+		+	600	+	15,000	=			18,000						
c.	− 500															−	$500
Bal.	1,900	+		+	600	+	15,000	=			18,000						−	500
d.						+	1,200		+$1,200								
Bal.	1,900	+		+	600	+	16,200	=	1,200	+	18,000						−	500
e.	+ 825														+	$ 825	
Bal.	2,725	+		+	600	+	16,200	=	1,200	+	18,000				+	825	−	500
f.		+	$100												+	100	
Bal.	2,725	+	100	+	600	+	16,200	=	1,200	+	18,000				+	925	−	500
g.	+ 100	−	100														
Bal.	2,825	+	0	+	600	+	16,200	=	1,200	+	18,000				+	925	−	500
h.	− 125																−	125
Bal.	2,700	+	0	+	600	+	16,200	=	1,200	+	18,000				+	925	−	625
i.	+ 930														+	930	
Bal.	3,630	+	0	+	600	+	16,200	=	1,200	+	18,000				+	1,855	−	625
j.	− 400								− 400								
Bal.	3,230	+	0	+	600	+	16,200	=	800	+	18,000				+	1,855	−	625
k.	− 900											−	$900				
Bal.	$ 2,330	+	0	+	$600	+	$ 16,200	=	$ 800	+	$ 18,000	−	$900		+	$1,855	−	$625

2.

EXPRESSIONS		
Income Statement		
For Month Ended August 31		
Revenues		
Haircutting services revenue		$1,855
Expenses		
Rent expense	$500	
Wages expense	125	
Total expenses		625
Net Income		$1,230

3.

EXPRESSIONS		
Statement of Owner's Equity		
For Month Ended August 31		
J. Worthy, Capital, August 1*		$ 0
Plus: Investments by owner	$18,000	
Net income	1,230	19,230
		19,230
Less: Withdrawals by owner		900
J. Worthy, Capital, August 31		$18,330

* If Expressions had been an existing business from a prior period, the beginning capital balance would equal the Capital account balance from the end of the prior period.

4.

EXPRESSIONS Balance Sheet August 31			
Assets		**Liabilities**	
Cash	$ 2,330	Note payable	$ 800
Furniture	600	**Equity**	
Store equipment	16,200	J. Worthy, Capital	18,330
Total assets	$19,130	Total liabilities and equity	$19,130

5.

EXPRESSIONS Statement of Cash Flows For Month Ended August 31		
Cash flows from operating activities		
Cash received from customers	$1,855	
Cash paid for rent	(500)	
Cash paid for wages	(125)	
Net cash provided by operating activities		$1,230
Cash flows from investing activities		
Cash paid for furniture		(600)
Cash flows from financing activities		
Cash investments by owner	3,000	
Cash withdrawals by owner	(900)	
Partial repayment of (long-term) note payable	(400)	
Net cash provided by financing activities		1,700
Net increase in cash		$2,330
Cash balance, August I		0
Cash balance, August 31		$2,330

6. Return on assets $= \dfrac{\text{Net income}}{\text{Average assets}} = \dfrac{\$1,230}{(\$18,000^* + \$19,130)/2} = \dfrac{\$1,230}{\$18,565} = \underline{\underline{\textbf{6.63}\%}}$

* Uses the initial \$18,000 investment as the beginning balance for the startup period only.

APPENDIX

Return and Risk Analysis

1A

This appendix explains return and risk analysis and its role in business and accounting.

Net income is often linked to **return.** Return on assets (ROA) is stated in ratio form as income divided by assets invested. For example, banks report return from a savings account in the form of an interest return such as 4%. If we invest in a savings account or in U.S. Treasury bills, we expect a return of around 2% to 7%. We could also invest in a company's stock, or even start our own business. How do we decide among these investment options? The answer depends on our trade-off between return and risk.

A4   Explain the relation between return and risk.

Risk is the uncertainty about the return we will earn. All business investments involve risk, but some investments involve more risk than others. The lower the risk of an investment, the lower is our expected return. The reason that savings accounts pay such a low return is the low risk of not being repaid with interest (the government guarantees most savings accounts from default). If we buy a share of Nike or any other company, we might obtain a large return. However, we have no guarantee of any return; there is even the risk of loss.

Exhibit 1A.1

Average Returns for Bonds with Different Risks

The bar graph in Exhibit 1A.1 shows recent returns for 30-year bonds with different risks. *Bonds* are written promises by organizations to repay amounts loaned with interest. U.S. Treasury bonds provide a low expected return, but they also offer low risk since they are backed by the U.S. government. High-risk corporate bonds offer a much larger potential return but with much higher risk.

The trade-off between return and risk is a normal part of business. Higher risk implies higher, but riskier, expected returns. To help us make better decisions, we use accounting information to assess both return and risk.

APPENDIX

1B Business Activities and the Accounting Equation

C6 Identify and describe the three major activities in organizations.

This appendix explains how the accounting equation is derived from business activities.

There are three major types of business activities: financing, investing, and operating. Each of these requires planning. *Planning* involves defining an organization's ideas, goals, and actions. Most public corporations use the *Management Discussion and Analysis* section in their annual reports to communicate plans. However, planning is not cast in stone. This adds *risk* to both setting plans and analyzing them.

Point: Management must understand accounting data to set financial goals, make financing and investing decisions, and evaluate operating performance.

Point: Investing (assets) and financing (liabilities plus equity) totals are *always* equal.

Financing *Financing activities* provide the means organizations use to pay for resources such as land, buildings, and equipment to carry out plans. Organizations are careful in acquiring and managing financing activities because they can determine success or failure. The two sources of financing are owner and nonowner. *Owner financing* refers to resources contributed by the owner along with any income the owner leaves in the organization. *Nonowner* (or *creditor*) *financing* refers to resources contributed by creditors (lenders). *Financial management* is the task of planning how to obtain these resources and to set the right mix between owner and creditor financing.

Investing *Investing activities* are the acquiring and disposing of resources (assets) that an organization uses to acquire and sell its products or services. Assets are funded by an organization's financing. Organizations differ on the amount and makeup of assets. Some require land and factories to operate. Others need only an office. Determining the amount and type of assets for operations is called *asset management*.

Invested amounts are referred to as *assets*. Financing is made up of creditor and owner financing, which hold claims on assets. Creditors' claims are called *liabilities,* and the owner's claim is called *equity*. This basic equality is called the *accounting equation* and can be written as: Assets = Liabilities + Equity.

Operating *Operating activities* involve using resources to research, develop, purchase, produce, distribute, and market products and services. Sales and revenues are the inflow of assets from selling products and services. Costs and expenses are the outflow of assets to support operating activities. *Strategic management* is the process of determining the right mix of operating activities for the type of organization, its plans, and its market.

Exhibit 1B.1 summarizes business activities. Planning is part of each activity and gives them meaning and focus. Investing (assets) and financing (liabilities and equity) are set opposite each other to stress their balance. Operating activities are below investing and financing activities to show that operating activities are the result of investing and financing.

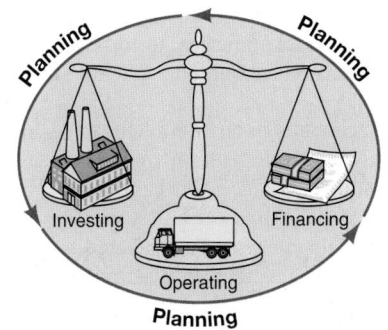

Exhibit 1B.1

Activities in Organizations

— A **Summary** organized by learning objectives concludes each chapter.

Summary

C1 **Explain the purpose and importance of accounting in the information age.** Accounting is an information and measurement system that aims to identify, record, and communicate relevant, reliable, and comparable information about business activities. It helps assess opportunities, products, investments, and social and community responsibilities.

C2 **Identify users and uses of accounting.** Users of accounting are both internal and external. Some users and uses of accounting include (a) managers in controlling, monitoring, and planning; (b) lenders for measuring the risk and return of loans; (c) shareholders for assessing the return and risk of stock; (d) directors for overseeing management; and (e) employees for judging employment opportunities.

C3 **Identify opportunities in accounting and related fields.** Opportunities in accounting include financial, managerial, and tax accounting. They also include accounting-related fields such as lending, consulting, managing, and planning.

C4 **Explain why ethics are crucial to accounting.** The goal of accounting is to provide useful information for decision making. For information to be useful, it must be trusted. This demands ethical behavior in accounting.

C5 **Explain the meaning of generally accepted accounting principles and define and apply several key accounting principles.** Generally accepted accounting principles are a common set of standards applied by accountants. Accounting principles aid in producing relevant, reliable, and comparable information. The business entity principle means that a business is accounted for separately from its owner(s). The objectivity principle means independent, objective evidence supports the information. The cost principle means financial statements are based on actual costs incurred. The monetary unit principle assumes transactions can be reflected in money terms. The going-concern principle means financial statements assume the business will continue. The revenue recognition principle means revenue is recognized when earned.

C6^B **Identify and describe the three major activities in organizations.** Organizations carry out three major activities: financing, investing, and operating. Financing is the means used to pay for resources such as land, buildings, and machines. Investing refers to the buying and selling of resources used in acquiring and selling products and services. Operating activities are those necessary for carrying out the organization's plans.

A1 **Define and interpret the accounting equation and each of its components.** The accounting equation is: Assets = Liabilities + Equity. Assets are resources owned by a company. Liabilities are creditors' claims on assets. Equity is the owner's claim on assets (*the residual*). The expanded accounting equation is: Assets = Liabilities + [Owner Capital − Owner Withdrawals + Revenues − Expenses].

A2 **Analyze business transactions using the accounting equation.** A *transaction* is an exchange of economic consideration between two parties. Examples include exchanges of products, services, money, and rights to collect money. Transactions always have at least two effects on one or more components of the accounting equation. This equation is always in balance.

A3 **Compute and interpret return on assets.** Return on assets is computed as net income divided by average assets. For example, if we have an average balance of $100 in a savings account and it earns $5 interest for the year, the return on assets is $5/$100, or 5%.

A4^A **Explain the relation between return and risk.** *Return* refers to income, and *risk* is the uncertainty about the return we hope to make. All investments involve risk. The lower the risk of an investment, the lower is its expected return. Higher risk implies higher, but riskier, expected return.

P1 **Identify and prepare basic financial statements and explain how they interrelate.** Four financial statements report on an organization's activities: balance sheet, income statement, statement of owner's equity, and statement of cash flows.

Guidance Answers to **Decision Maker** and **Decision Ethics**

Entrepreneur (p. 11) You should probably form the business as a corporation if potential lawsuits are of prime concern. The corporate form of organization protects your personal property from lawsuits directed at the business and places only the corporation's resources at risk. A downside of the corporate form is double taxation: The corporation must pay taxes on its income, and you normally must pay taxes on any money distributed to you from the business (even though the corporation already paid taxes on this money). You should also examine the ethical and socially responsible aspects of starting a business in which you anticipate injuries to others. Formation as an LLC or S corp. should also be explored.

Retailer (p. 18) You can use the accounting equation (Assets = Liabilities + Equity) to help identify risky customers to whom you would likely not want to extend credit. A balance sheet provides amounts for each of these key components. The lower a customer's equity is relative to liabilities, the less likely you would extend credit. A low equity means the business has little value that does not already have creditor claims to it.

Business Owner (p. 20) The 19% return on assets for the manufacturer exceeds the 14% industry return (and many others). This is a positive factor for a potential purchase. Also, the purchase of this manufacturer is an opportunity to spread your risk over two businesses as opposed to one. Still, you should hesitate to purchase a business whose return of 19% is lower than your current resort's return of 21%. You are probably better off directing efforts to increase investment in your resort, assuming you can continue to earn a 21% return.

Guidance Answers to **Quick Checks**

1. Accounting is an information and measurement system that identifies, records, and communicates relevant information to help people make better decisions.

2. Recordkeeping, also called *bookkeeping,* is the recording of financial transactions and events, either manually or electronically. Recordkeeping is essential to data reliability; but accounting is this and much more. Accounting includes identifying, measuring, recording, reporting, and analyzing business events and transactions.

3. Technology offers increased accuracy, speed, efficiency, and convenience in accounting.

4. External users of accounting include lenders, shareholders, directors, customers, suppliers, regulators, lawyers, brokers, and the press. Internal users of accounting include managers, officers, and other internal decision makers involved with strategic and operating decisions.

5. Internal users (managers) include those from research and development, purchasing, human resources, production, distribution, marketing, and servicing.

6. Internal controls are procedures designed to protect assets, ensure reliable accounting reports, promote efficiency, and encourage adherence to company policies. Internal controls are crucial for relevant and reliable information.

7. Ethical guidelines are threefold: (1) identify ethical concerns using personal ethics, (2) analyze options considering all good and bad consequences, and (3) make ethical decisions after weighing all consequences.

8. Ethics and social responsibility yield good behavior, and they often result in higher income and a better working environment.

9. For accounting to provide useful information for decisions, it must be trusted. Trust requires ethics in accounting.

10. Two major participants in setting rules include the SEC and the FASB. (*Note:* Accounting rules reflect society's needs, not those of accountants or any other single constituency).

11. Most U.S. companies are not directly affected by international accounting standards. International standards are put forth as preferred accounting practices. However, stock exchanges and other parties are increasing the pressure to narrow differences in worldwide accounting practices. International accounting standards are playing an important role in that process.

12. The objectivity and cost principles are related in that most users consider information based on cost as objective. Information prepared using both principles is considered highly reliable and often relevant.

13. Users desire information about the performance of a specific entity. If information is mixed between two or more entities, its usefulness decreases.

14. The revenue recognition principle gives preparers guidelines on when to recognize (record) revenue. This is important; for example, if revenue is recognized too early, the statements report revenue sooner than it should and the business looks more profitable than it is. The reverse is also true.

15. The three basic forms of business organization are sole proprietorships, partnerships, and corporations.

16. Owners of corporations are called *shareholders* (or *stockholders*). Corporate ownership is divided into units called *shares* (or *stock*). The most basic of corporate shares is common stock (or capital stock).

17. The accounting equation is: Assets = Liabilities + Equity. This equation is always in balance, both before and after each transaction.

18. A transaction that changes the makeup of assets would not affect liability and equity accounts. FastForward's transactions 2 and 3 are examples. Each exchanges one asset for another.

19. Earning revenue by performing services, as in FastForward's transaction 5, increases equity (and assets). Incurring expenses while servicing clients, such as in transactions 6 and 7, decreases equity (and assets). Other examples include owner investments that increase equity and withdrawals that decrease equity.

20. Paying a liability with an asset reduces both asset and liability totals. One example is FastForward's transaction 10 that reduces a payable by paying cash.

21. An income statement reports a company's revenues and expenses along with the resulting net income or loss. A statement of owner's equity shows changes in equity, including that from net income or loss. Both statements report transactions occurring over a period of time.

22. The balance sheet describes a company's financial position (assets, liabilities, and equity) at a point in time. The equity amount in the balance sheet is obtained from the statement of owner's equity.

23. Cash flows from operating activities report cash receipts and payments from the primary business the company engages in. Cash flows from investing activities involve cash transactions from buying and selling long-term assets. Cash flows from financing activities include long-term cash borrowings and repayments to lenders and the cash investments from and withdrawals by the owner.

A list of key terms with page references concludes each chapter (a complete glossary is at the end of the book and on the book's Website).

Key Terms
mhhe.com/wildFAP18e

Key Terms are available at the book's Website for learning and testing in an online Flashcard Format.

Accounting (p. 4)
Accounting equation (p. 12)
Assets (p. 12)
Audit (p. 11)
Balance sheet (p. 17)
Bookkeeping (p. 5)
Business entity principle (p. 10)
Common stock (p. 11)
Corporation (p. 11)
Cost principle (p. 9)
Equity (p. 12)
Ethics (p. 8)
Events (p. 13)
Expanded accounting equation (p. 13)
Expenses (p. 13)
External transactions (p. 13)
External users (p. 5)
Financial accounting (p. 5)
Financial Accounting Standards Board (FASB) (p. 9)

Generally Accepted Accounting Principles (GAAP) (p. 9)
Going-concern principle (p. 10)
Income (p. 13)
Income statement (p. 17)
Internal transactions (p. 13)
Internal users (p. 6)
International Accounting Standards Board (IASB) (p. 9)
Liabilities (p. 12)
Managerial accounting (p. 6)
Monetary unit principle (p. 10)
Net income (p. 13)
Net loss (p. 13)
Objectivity principle (p. 9)
Owner, Capital (p. 13)
Owner investment (p. 12)
Owner withdrawals (p. 13)
Partnership (p. 10)
Proprietorship (p. 10)

Recordkeeping (p. 5)
Return (p. 23)
Return on assets (p. 20)
Revenue recognition principle (p. 10)
Revenues (p. 13)
Risk (p. 24)
Sarbanes–Oxley Act (p. 11)
Securities and Exchange Commission (SEC) (p. 9)
Shareholders (p. 11)
Shares (p. 11)
Sole proprietorship (p. 10)
Statement of cash flows (p. 17)
Statement of owner's equity (p. 17)
Stock (p. 11)
Stockholders (p. 11)
Withdrawal (p. 13)

Multiple Choice Quiz
Answers on p. 45   mhhe.com/wildFAP18e

Multiple Choice Quizzes A and B are available at the book's Website.

1. A building is offered for sale at $500,000 but is currently assessed at $400,000. The purchaser of the building believes the building is worth $475,000, but ultimately purchases the building for $450,000. The purchaser records the building at:
a. $50,000
b. $400,000
c. $450,000
d. $475,000
e. $500,000

2. On December 30, 2006, KPMG signs a $150,000 contract to provide accounting services to one of its clients in 2007. KPMG has a December 31 year-end. Which accounting principle requires KPMG to record the accounting services revenue from this client in 2007 and not 2006?
a. Business entity principle
b. Revenue recognition principle
c. Monetary unit principle
d. Cost principle
e. Going-concern principle

3. If the assets of a company increase by $100,000 during the year and its liabilities increase by $35,000 during the same year, then the change in equity of the company during the year must have been:
a. An increase of $135,000.
b. A decrease of $135,000.
c. A decrease of $65,000.

d. An increase of $65,000.
e. An increase of $100,000.

4. A company borrows $50,000 cash from Third National Bank. How does this transaction affect the accounting equation for this company?
a. Assets increase by $50,000; liabilities increase by $50,000; no effect on equity.
b. Assets increase by $50,000; no effect on liabilities; equity increases by $50,000.
c. Assets increase by $50,000; liabilities decrease by $50,000; no effect on equity.
d. No effect on assets; liabilities increase by $50,000; equity increases by $50,000.
e. No effect on assets; liabilities increase by $50,000; equity decreases by $50,000.

5. Geek Squad performs services for a customer and bills the customer for $500. How would Geek Squad record this transaction?
a. Accounts receivable increase by $500; revenues increase by $500.
b. Cash increases by $500; revenues increase by $500.
c. Accounts receivable increase by $500; revenues decrease by $500.
d. Accounts receivable increase by $500; accounts payable increase by $500.
e. Accounts payable increase by $500; revenues increase by $500.

Superscript letter ^{A} (^{B}) denotes assignments based on Appendix 1A (1B).

Discussion Questions

1. What is the purpose of accounting in society?

2. Technology is increasingly used to process accounting data. Why then must we study and understand accounting?

3. Identify at least four kinds of external users and describe how they use accounting information.

4. What are at least three questions business owners and managers might be able to answer by looking at accounting information?

5. Identify three actual businesses that offer services and three actual businesses that offer products.

6. Describe the internal role of accounting for organizations.

7. Identify three types of services typically offered by accounting professionals.

8. What type of accounting information might be useful to the marketing managers of a business?

9. Why is accounting described as a service activity?

10. What are some accounting-related professions?

11. How do ethics rules affect auditors' choice of clients?

12. What work do tax accounting professionals perform in addition to preparing tax returns?

13. What does the objectivity principle imply for information reported in financial statements? Why?

14. A business reports its own office stationery on the balance sheet at its $400 cost, although it cannot be sold for more than $10 as scrap paper. Which accounting principle(s) justifies this treatment?

15. Why is the revenue recognition principle needed? What does it demand?

16. Describe the three basic forms of business organization and their key characteristics.

17. Define (a) *assets*, (b) *liabilities*, (c) *equity*, and (d) *net assets*.

18. What events or transactions change equity?

19. Identify the two main categories of accounting principles.

20. What do accountants mean by the term *revenue?*

21. Define *net income* and explain its computation.

22. Identify the four basic financial statements of a business.

23. What information is reported in an income statement?

24. Give two examples of expenses a business might incur.

25. What is the purpose of the statement of owner's equity?

26. What information is reported in a balance sheet?

27. The statement of cash flows reports on what major activities?

28. Define and explain return on assets.

29.^{A}Define return and risk. Discuss the trade-off between them.

30.^{B}Describe the three major business activities in organizations.

31.^{B}Explain why investing (assets) and financing (liabilities and equity) totals are always equal.

32. Refer to the financial statements of **Best Buy** in Appendix A near the end of the book. To what level of significance are dollar amounts rounded? What time period does its income statement cover?

33. Identify the dollar amounts of **Circuit City**'s 2005 assets, liabilities, and equity shown in its statements in Appendix A near the end of the book.

34. Access the SEC EDGAR database (**www.sec.gov**) and retrieve **Apple**'s 2004 10-K (filed 12-03-2004). Identify its auditor. What responsibility does its independent auditor claim regarding Apple's financial statements?

Red numbers denote Discussion Questions that involve decision-making.

Quick Study exercises give readers a brief test of key elements.

Homework Manager repeats assignments on the book's Website, which allows instructors to monitor, promote, and assess student learning. It can be used in practice, homework, or exam mode.

QUICK STUDY

QS 1-1
Identifying accounting terms
C1

(*a*) Identify the meaning of these accounting-related acronyms: GAAP, SEC, FASB and IASB. (*b*) Briefly explain the importance of the knowledge base or organization that is referred to for each of the accounting-related acronyms.

QS 1-2
Identifying accounting users
C2

Identify the following users as either external users (E) or internal users (I).

a. Customers	**d.** Business press	**g.** Shareholders	**j.** FBI and IRS
b. Suppliers	**e.** Managers	**h.** Lenders	**k.** Consumer group
c. Brokers	**f.** District attorney	**i.** Controllers	**l.** Sales staff

---

QS 1-3
Explaining internal control
C1

An important responsibility of many accounting professionals is to design and implement internal control procedures for organizations. Explain the purpose of internal control procedures. Provide two examples of internal controls applied by companies.

Identify at least three main areas of opportunities for accounting professionals. For each area, identify at least three job possibilities linked to accounting.

QS 1-4
Accounting opportunities
C3

Accounting professionals must sometimes choose between two or more acceptable methods of accounting for business transactions and events. Explain why these situations can involve difficult matters of ethical concern.

This icon highlights assignments that enhance decision-making skills. ──────▶

QS 1-5
Identifying ethical concerns
C4

Identify which general accounting principle best describes each of the following practices.

a. In December 2006, Chavez Landscaping received a customer's order and cash prepayment to install sod at a new house that would not be ready for installation until March 2007. Chavez should record the revenue from the customer order in March 2007, not in December 2006.

b. If $51,000 cash is paid to buy land, the land is reported on the buyer's balance sheet at $51,000.

c. Jo Keene owns both Sailing Passions and Dockside Supplies. In preparing financial statements for Dockside Supplies, Keene makes sure that the expense transactions of Sailing Passions are kept separate from Dockside's statements.

QS 1-6
Identifying accounting principles
C5

a. Total assets of Charter Company equal $700,000 and its equity is $420,000. What is the amount of its liabilities?

b. Total assets of Martin Marine equal $500,000 and its liabilities and equity amounts are equal to each other. What is the amount of its liabilities? What is the amount of its equity?

QS 1-7
Applying the accounting equation
A1

Use the accounting equation to compute the missing financial statement amounts (*a*), (*b*), and (*c*).

Company	Assets	=	Liabilities	+	Equity
1	$75,000		$ (a)		$40,000
2	$ (b)		$25,000		$70,000
3	$85,000		$20,000		$ (c)

QS 1-8
Applying the accounting equation
A1

Accounting provides information about an organization's business transactions and events that both affect the accounting equation and can be reliably measured. Identify at least two examples of both (*a*) business transactions and (*b*) business events that meet these requirements.

QS 1-9
Identifying transactions and events
A2

Use **Apple**'s September 25, 2004, financial statements, in Appendix A near the end of the book, to answer the following.

a. Identify the dollar amounts of Apple's 2004 (1) assets, (2) liabilities, and (3) equity.

b. Using Apple's amounts from part *a*, verify that Assets = Liabilities + Equity.

QS 1-10
Identifying and computing assets, liabilities, and equity
A2

Indicate in which financial statement each item would most likely appear: income statement (I), balance sheet (B), statement of owner's equity (E), or statement of cash flows (CF).

a. Assets   **d.** Equipment   **g.** Net decrease (or increase) in cash

b. Cash from operating activities   **e.** Expenses   **h.** Revenues

c. Withdrawals   **f.** Liabilities   **i.** Total liabilities and equity

QS 1-11
Identifying items with financial statements
P1

In a recent year's financial statements, **Home Depot** reported the following results. Compute and interpret its return on assets (assume competitors average a 12% return on assets).

Sales	$73,074 million
Net income	5,001 million
Average total assets	36,672 million

QS 1-12
Computing and interpreting return on assets
A3

EXERCISES

Exercise 1-1

Describing accounting responsibilities

C2   C3

Many accounting professionals work in one of the following three areas.

A. Financial accounting   **B.** Managerial accounting   **C.** Tax accounting

Identify the area of accounting that is most involved in each of the following responsibilities.

_____ **1.** Internal auditing.   _____ **5.** Investigating violations of tax laws.

_____ **2.** External auditing.   _____ **6.** Planning transactions to minimize taxes.

_____ **3.** Cost accounting.   _____ **7.** Preparing external financial statements.

_____ **4.** Budgeting.   _____ **8.** Reviewing reports for SEC compliance.

Exercise 1-2

Identifying accounting users and uses

C2

Much of accounting is directed at servicing the information needs of those users that are external to an organization. Identify at least three external users of accounting information and indicate two questions they might seek to answer through their use of accounting information.

Exercise 1-3

Identifying ethical concerns

C4

Assume the following role and describe a situation in which ethical considerations play an important part in guiding your decisions and actions.

a. You are a student in an introductory accounting course.

b. You are a manager with responsibility for several employees.

c. You are an accounting professional preparing tax returns for clients.

d. You are an accounting professional with audit clients that are competitors in business.

Exercise 1-4

Distinguishing business organizations

C5

The following describe several different business organizations. Determine whether the description refers to a sole proprietorship, partnership, or corporation.

a. Ownership of Zander Company is divided into 1,000 shares of stock.

b. Wallingford is owned by Trent Malone, who is personally liable for the company's debts.

c. Elijah Fong and Ava Logan own Financial Services, a financial services provider. Neither Fong nor Logan has personal responsibility for the debts of Financial Services.

d. Dylan Bailey and Emma Kayley own Speedy Packages, a courier service. Both are personally liable for the debts of the business.

e. IBC Services does not have separate legal existence apart from the one person who owns it.

f. Physio Products does not pay income taxes and has one owner.

g. Aaliyah Services pays its own income taxes and has two owners.

Exercise 1-5

Identifying accounting principles

C5

Match each of the numbered descriptions with the principle it best reflects. Indicate your answer by writing the letter for the appropriate principle in the blank space next to each description.

A. General accounting principle   **E.** Specific accounting principle

B. Cost principle   **F.** Objectivity principle

C. Business entity principle   **G.** Going-concern principle

D. Revenue recognition principle

_____ **1.** Usually created by a pronouncement from an authoritative body.

_____ **2.** Financial statements reflect the assumption that the business continues operating.

_____ **3.** Derived from long-used and generally accepted accounting practices.

_____ **4.** Every business is accounted for separately from its owner or owners.

_____ **5.** Revenue is recorded only when the earnings process is complete.

_____ **6.** Information is based on actual costs incurred in transactions.

_____ **7.** Financial statement data are supported by evidence other than someone's opinion or belief.

Match each of the numbered descriptions with the term or phrase it best reflects. Indicate your answer by writing the letter for the term or phrase in the blank provided.

A. Audit   **C.** Ethics   **E.** SEC   **G.** Net income

B. GAAP   **D.** Tax accounting   **F.** Public accountants   **H.** IASB

_____ **1.** Principles that determine whether an action is right or wrong.

_____ **2.** Accounting professionals who provide services to many clients.

_____ **3.** An accounting area that includes planning future transactions to minimize taxes paid.

_____ **4.** An examination of an organization's accounting system and records that adds credibility to financial statements.

_____ **5.** Amount a business earns after paying all expenses and costs associated with its sales and revenues.

Exercise 1-6
Learning the language of business
C1–C4

Determine the missing amount from each of the separate situations a, b, and c below.

	Assets	=	Liabilities	+	Equity
a.	?	=	$20,000	+	$45,000
b.	$100,000	=	$34,000	+	?
c.	$154,000	=	?	+	$40,000

Exercise 1-7
Using the accounting equation
A1

Provide an example of a transaction that creates the described effects for the separate cases a through g.

a. Decreases an asset and decreases equity.

b. Increases an asset and increases a liability.

c. Decreases a liability and increases a liability.

d. Decreases an asset and decreases a liability.

e. Increases an asset and decreases an asset.

f. Increases a liability and decreases equity.

g. Increases an asset and increases equity.

Exercise 1-8
Identifying effects of transactions on the accounting equation
A1 A2

Zen began a new consulting firm on January 5. The accounting equation showed the following balances after each of the company's first five transactions. Analyze the accounting equation for each transaction and describe each of the five transactions with their amounts.

Exercise 1-9
Analysis using the accounting equation
A1 A2

	Assets									=	Liabilities	+		Equity		
Trans-action	Cash	+	Accounts Receivable	+	Office Supplies	+	Office Furniture	=	Accounts Payable	+	Zen, Capital	+	Revenues			
a.	$40,000	+	$ 0	+	$ 0	+	$ 0	=	$ 0	+	$40,000	+	$ 0			
b.	38,000	+	0	+	3,000	+	0	=	1,000	+	40,000	+	0			
c.	30,000	+	0	+	3,000	+	8,000	=	1,000	+	40,000	+	0			
d.	30,000	+	6,000	+	3,000	+	8,000	=	1,000	+	40,000	+	6,000			
e.	31,000	+	6,000	+	3,000	+	8,000	=	1,000	+	40,000	+	7,000			

Answer the following questions. (*Hint:* Use the accounting equation.)

a. Cadence Office Supplies has assets equal to $123,000 and liabilities equal to $47,000 at year-end. What is the total equity for Cadence at year-end?

b. At the beginning of the year, Addison Company's assets are $300,000 and its equity is $100,000. During the year, assets increase $80,000 and liabilities increase $50,000. What is the equity at the end of the year?

c. At the beginning of the year, Quasar Company's liabilities equal $70,000. During the year, assets increase by $60,000, and at year-end assets equal $190,000. Liabilities decrease $5,000 during the year. What are the beginning and ending amounts of equity?

Exercise 1-10
Using the accounting equation
A1 A2

Check (c) Beg. equity, $60,000

Exercise 1-11

Identifying effects of
transactions using the
accounting equation

A1   A2

Leora Holden began a professional practice on June 1 and plans to prepare financial statements at the
end of each month. During June, Holden (the owner) completed these transactions.

a. Owner invested $60,000 cash along with equipment that had a $15,000 market value.

b. Paid $1,500 cash for rent of office space for the month.

c. Purchased $10,000 of additional equipment on credit (payment due within 30 days).

d. Completed work for a client and immediately collected the $2,500 cash earned.

e. Completed work for a client and sent a bill for $8,000 to be received within 30 days.

f. Purchased additional equipment for $6,000 cash.

g. Paid an assistant $3,000 cash as wages for the month.

h. Collected $5,000 cash on the amount owed by the client described in transaction *e*.

i. Paid $10,000 cash to settle the liability created in transaction *c*.

j. Owner withdrew $1,000 cash for personal use.

Required

Check   Net income, $6,000

Create a table like the one in Exhibit 1.9, using the following headings for columns: Cash; Accounts
Receivable; Equipment; Accounts Payable; Holden, Capital; Holden, Withdrawals; Revenues; and
Expenses. Then use additions and subtractions to show the effects of the transactions on individual items
of the accounting equation. Show new balances after each transaction.

Exercise 1-12

Identifying effects of
transactions on accounting
equation

A1   A2

The following table shows the effects of five transactions (*a* through *e*) on the assets, liabilities, and
equity of Trista's Boutique. Write short descriptions of the probable nature of each transaction.

	Assets				=	Liabilities	+	Equity		
	Cash	+ Accounts Receivable	+ Office Supplies	+ Land	=	Accounts Payable	+ Trista, Capital	+ Revenues
	$ 21,000	+ $ 0	+ $3,000	+ $ 19,000	=	$ 0	+ $43,000	+ $ 0
a.	− 4,000			+ 4,000				
b.			+ 1,000			+1,000		
c.		+ 1,900						+ 1,900
d.	− 1,000					−1,000		
e.	+ 1,900	− 1,900						
	$ 17,900	+ $ 0	+ $4,000	+ $ 23,000	=	$ 0	+ $43,000	+ $1,900

Exercise 1-13

Preparing an income
statement

P1

On October 1, Keisha King organized Real Answers a new consulting firm. On October 31, the company's records show the following items and amounts. Use this information to prepare an October income
statement for the business.

Cash	$11,360	Cash withdrawals by owner	$ 2,000
Accounts receivable	14,000	Consulting fees earned	14,000
Office supplies	3,250	Rent expense	3,550
Land	46,000	Salaries expense	7,000
Office equipment	18,000	Telephone expense	760
Accounts payable	8,500	Miscellaneous expenses	580
Owner investments	84,000		

Check   Net income, $2,110

Exercise 1-14

Preparing a statement of
owner's equity   P1

Use the information in Exercise 1-13 to prepare an October statement of owner's equity for Real
Answers.

Use the information in Exercise 1-13 (if completed, you can also use your solution to Exercise 1-14) to prepare an October 31 balance sheet for Real Answers.

Exercise 1-15
Preparing a balance sheet P1

Use the information in Exercise 1-13 to prepare an October 31 statement of cash flows for Real Answers. Also assume the following:

a. The owner's initial investment consists of $38,000 cash and $46,000 in land.

b. The $18,000 equipment purchase is paid in cash.

c. The accounts payable balance of $8,500 consists of the $3,250 office supplies purchase and $5,250 in employee salaries yet to be paid.

d. The rent, telephone, and miscellaneous expenses are paid in cash.

e. No cash has been collected for the $14,000 consulting services provided.

Exercise 1-16
Preparing a statement of cash flows

P1

Check   Net increase in cash, $11,360

Indicate the section where each of the following would appear on the statement of cash flows.

O. Cash flows from operating activity

I. Cash flows from investing activity

F. Cash flows from financing activity

_____ **1.** Cash paid for advertising   _____ **5.** Cash paid for rent

_____ **2.** Cash paid for wages   _____ **6.** Cash paid on an account payable

_____ **3.** Cash withdrawal by owner   _____ **7.** Cash investment by owner

_____ **4.** Cash purchase of equipment   _____ **8.** Cash received from clients

Exercise 1-17
Identifying sections of the statement of cash flows

P1

Swiss Group reports net income of $40,000 for 2007. At the beginning of 2007, Swiss Group had $200,000 in assets. By the end of 2007, assets had grown to $300,000. What is Swiss Group's 2007 return on assets? How would you assess its performance if competitors average a 10% return on assets?

Exercise 1-18
Analysis of return on assets

A3

Match each transaction or event to one of the following activities of an organization: financing activities (F), investing activities (I), or operating activities (O).

a. _____ An owner contributes resources to the business.

b. _____ An organization sells some of its land.

c. _____ An organization purchases equipment.

d. _____ An organization advertises a new product.

e. _____ The organization borrows money from a bank.

Exercise 1-19[B]
Identifying business activities

C6

> *Problem Set B located at the end of Problem Set A is provided for <u>each</u> problem to reinforce the learning process. Problem Set C (with solutions for instructors) is provided on this book's Website.*

The following financial statement information is from five separate companies.

PROBLEM SET A

Problem 1-1A
Computing missing information using accounting knowledge

A1   A2

	Company A	Company B	Company C	Company D	Company E
December 31, 2006					
Assets	$55,000	$34,000	$24,000	$60,000	$119,000
Liabilities	24,500	21,500	9,000	40,000	?
December 31, 2007					
Assets	58,000	40,000	?	85,000	113,000
Liabilities	?	26,500	29,000	24,000	70,000
During year 2007					
Owner investments	6,000	1,400	9,750	?	6,500
Net income	8,500	?	8,000	14,000	20,000
Owner cash withdrawals	3,500	2,000	5,875	0	11,000

Required

1. Answer the following questions about Company A.

   a. What is the amount of equity on December 31, 2006?

   b. What is the amount of equity on December 31, 2007?

   c. What is the amount of liabilities on December 31, 2007?

2. Answer the following questions about Company B.

   a. What is the amount of equity on December 31, 2006?

   b. What is the amount of equity on December 31, 2007?

   c. What is net income for year 2007?

3. Calculate the amount of assets for Company C on December 31, 2007.

4. Calculate the amount of owner investments for Company D during year 2007.

5. Calculate the amount of liabilities for Company E on December 31, 2006.

Check (1*b*) $41,500

(2*c*) $1,600

(3) $55,875

Problem 1-2A

Identifying effects of transactions on financial statements

A1 A2

Identify how each of the following separate transactions affects financial statements. For the balance sheet, identify how each transaction affects total assets, total liabilities, and total equity. For the income statement, identify how each transaction affects net income. For the statement of cash flows, identify how each transaction affects cash flows from operating activities, cash flows from financing activities, and cash flows from investing activities. For increases, place a "+" in the column or columns. For decreases, place a "−" in the column or columns. If both an increase and a decrease occur, place a "+/−" in the column or columns. The first transaction is completed as an example.

		Balance Sheet			Income Statement	Statement of Cash Flows		
	Transaction	**Total Assets**	**Total Liab.**	**Total Equity**	**Net Income**	**Operating Activities**	**Financing Activities**	**Investing Activities**
1	Owner invests cash in business	+		+			+	
2	Receives cash for services provided							
3	Pays cash for employee wages							
4	Incurs legal costs on credit							
5	Borrows cash by signing long-term note payable							
6	Owner withdraws cash							
7	Buys land by signing note payable							
8	Provides services on credit							
9	Buys office equipment for cash							
10	Collects cash on receivable from (8)							

Problem 1-3A

Preparing an income statement

P1

The following is selected financial information for Elko Energy Company for the year ended December 31, 2007: revenues, $55,000; expenses, $40,000; net income, $15,000.

Required

Prepare the 2007 calendar-year income statement for Elko Energy Company.

Problem 1-4A

Preparing a balance sheet

P1

The following is selected financial information for Amity Company as of December 31, 2007: liabilities, $44,000; equity, $46,000; assets, $90,000.

Required

Prepare the balance sheet for Amity Company as of December 31, 2007.

Following is selected financial information of ABM Co. for the year ended December 31, 2007:

Cash used by investing activities	$(2,000)
Net increase in cash	1,200
Cash used by financing activities	(2,800)
Cash from operating activities	6,000
Cash, December 31, 2006	2,300

Problem 1-5A

Preparing a statement of cash flows

P1

Check Cash balance, Dec. 31, 2007, $3,500

Required

Prepare the 2007 calendar-year statement of cash flows for ABM.

Following is selected financial information for Kasio Co. for the year ended December 31, 2007.

K. Kasio, Capital, Dec. 31, 2007	$14,000	K. Kasio, Withdrawals	$1,000
Net income	8,000	K. Kasio, Capital, Dec. 31, 2006	7,000

Problem 1-6A

Preparing a statement of owner's equity

P1

Required

Prepare the 2007 calendar-year statement of owner's equity for Kasio.

Holden Graham started The Graham Co., a new business that began operations on May 1. Graham Co. completed the following transactions during that first month.

May 1   H. Graham invested $40,000 cash in the business.
     1   Rented a furnished office and paid $2,200 cash for May's rent.
     3   Purchased $1,890 of office equipment on credit.
     5   Paid $750 cash for this month's cleaning services.
     8   Provided consulting services for a client and immediately collected $5,400 cash.
    12   Provided $2,500 of consulting services for a client on credit.
    15   Paid $750 cash for an assistant's salary for the first half of this month.
    20   Received $2,500 cash payment for the services provided on May 12.
    22   Provided $3,200 of consulting services on credit.
    25   Received $3,200 cash payment for the services provided on May 22.
    26   Paid $1,890 cash for the office equipment purchased on May 3.
    27   Purchased $80 of advertising in this month's (May) local paper on credit; cash payment is due June 1.
    28   Paid $750 cash for an assistant's salary for the second half of this month.
    30   Paid $300 cash for this month's telephone bill.
    30   Paid $280 cash for this month's utilities.
    31   Graham withdrew $1,400 cash for personal use.

Problem 1-7A

Analyzing transactions and preparing financial statements

C5   A2   P1

mhhe.com/wildFAP18e

Required

1. Arrange the following asset, liability, and equity titles in a table like Exhibit 1.9: Cash; Accounts Receivable; Office Equipment; Accounts Payable; H. Graham, Capital; H. Graham, Withdrawals; Revenues; and Expenses.

2. Show effects of the transactions on the accounts of the accounting equation by recording increases and decreases in the appropriate columns. Do not determine new account balances after each transaction. Determine the final total for each account and verify that the equation is in balance.

3. Prepare an income statement for May, a statement of owner's equity for May, a May 31 balance sheet, and a statement of cash flows for May.

Check (2) Ending balances: Cash, $42,780; Expenses, $5,110

(3) Net income, $5,990; Total assets, $44,670

Problem 1-8A

Analyzing transactions and
preparing financial statements

C5 A2 P1

mhhe.com/wildFAP18e

Helga Ander started a new business and completed these transactions during December.

Dec. 1   Helga Ander transferred $65,000 cash from a personal savings account to a checking account
          in the name of Ander Electric.
       2   Rented office space and paid $1,000 cash for the December rent.
       3   Purchased $13,000 of electrical equipment by paying $4,800 cash and agreeing to pay the
          $8,200 balance in 30 days.
       5   Purchased office supplies by paying $800 cash.
       6   Completed electrical work and immediately collected $1,200 cash for the work.
       8   Purchased $2,530 of office equipment on credit.
      15   Completed electrical work on credit in the amount of $5,000.
      18   Purchased $350 of office supplies on credit.
      20   Paid $2,530 cash for the office equipment purchased on December 8.
      24   Billed a client $900 for electrical work completed; the balance is due in 30 days.
      28   Received $5,000 cash for the work completed on December 15.
      29   Paid the assistant's salary of $1,400 cash for this month.
      30   Paid $540 cash for this month's utility bill.
      31   Ander withdrew $950 cash for personal use.

Required

1. Arrange the following asset, liability, and equity titles in a table like Exhibit 1.9: Cash; Accounts
   Receivable; Office Supplies; Office Equipment; Electrical Equipment; Accounts Payable; H. Ander,
   Capital; H. Ander, Withdrawals; Revenues; and Expenses.

Check (2) Ending balances: Cash,
$59,180, Accounts Payable, $8,550

2. Use additions and subtractions to show the effects of each transaction on the accounts in the accounting equation. Show new balances after each transaction.

(3) Net income, $4,160;
Total assets, $76,760

3. Use the increases and decreases in the columns of the table from part 2 to prepare an income statement, a statement of owner's equity, and a statement of cash flows for the month. Also prepare a balance sheet as of the end of the month.

Analysis Component

4. Assume that the owner investment transaction on December 1 was $49,000 cash instead of $65,000
   and that Ander Electric obtained the $16,000 difference by borrowing it from a bank. Explain the ef-
   fect of this change on total assets, total liabilities, and total equity.

Problem 1-9A

Analyzing effects of transactions

C5 P1 A1 A2

Isabel Lopez started Biz Consulting, a new business, and completed the following transactions during
its first year of operations.

a. I. Lopez invests $70,000 cash and office equipment valued at $10,000 in the business.

b. Purchased a $150,000 building to use as an office. Biz paid $20,000 in cash and signed a note payable
   promising to pay the $130,000 balance over the next ten years.

c. Purchased office equipment for $15,000 cash.

d. Purchased $1,200 of office supplies and $1,700 of office equipment on credit.

e. Paid a local newspaper $500 cash for printing an announcement of the office's opening.

f. Completed a financial plan for a client and billed that client $2,800 for the service.

g. Designed a financial plan for another client and immediately collected a $4,000 cash fee.

h. Lopez withdrew $3,275 cash for personal use.

i. Received a $1,800 cash payment from the client described in transaction f.

j. Made a $700 cash payment on the equipment purchased in transaction d.

k. Paid $1,800 cash for the office secretary's wages.

Required

1. Create a table like the one in Exhibit 1.9, using the following headings for the columns: Cash; Accounts
   Receivable; Office Supplies; Office Equipment; Building; Accounts Payable; Notes Payable; I. Lopez,
   Capital; I. Lopez, Withdrawals; Revenues; and Expenses.

Check (2) Ending balances: Cash,
$34,525; Expenses, $2,300; Notes
Payable, $130,000

2. Use additions and subtractions to show the effects of these transactions on individual items of the
   accounting equation. Show new balances after each transaction.

(3) Net income, $4,500

3. Once you have completed the table, determine the company's net income.

Coca-Cola and PepsiCo both produce and market beverages that are direct competitors. Key financial figures (in $ millions) for these businesses over the past year follow.

Key Figures ($ millions)	Coca-Cola	PepsiCo
Sales	$21,962	$29,261
Net income	4,847	4,212
Average assets	29,335	26,657

Required

1. Compute return on assets for (*a*) Coca-Cola and (*b*) PepsiCo.

2. Which company is more successful in its total amount of sales to consumers?

3. Which company is more successful in returning net income from its assets invested?

Analysis Component

4. Write a one-paragraph memorandum explaining which company you would invest your money in and why. (Limit your explanation to the information provided.)

Problem 1-10A
Computing and interpreting return on assets

A3

Check (1*a*) 16.5%; (1*b*) 15.8%

Kyzera manufactures, markets, and sells cellular telephones. The average total assets for Kyzera is $250,000. In its most recent year, Kyzera reported net income of $65,000 on revenues of $475,000.

Required

1. What is Kyzera's return on assets?

2. Does return on assets seem satisfactory for Kyzera given that its competitors average a 12% return on assets?

3. What are total expenses for Kyzera in its most recent year?

4. What is the average total amount of liabilities plus equity for Kyzera?

Problem 1-11A
Determining expenses, liabilities, equity, and return on assets

A1   A3

Check (3) $410,000

(4) $250,000

All business decisions involve aspects of risk and return.

Required

Identify both the risk and the return in each of the following activities.

1. Investing $2,000 in a 5% savings account.

2. Placing a $2,500 bet on your favorite sports team.

3. Investing $10,000 in Yahoo! stock.

4. Taking out a $7,500 college loan to earn an accounting degree.

Problem 1-12A[A]
Identifying risk and return

A4

A startup company often engages in the following transactions in its first year of operations. Classify these transactions in one of the three major categories of an organization's business activities.

F. Financing   **I.** Investing   **O.** Operating

_____ **1.** Owner investing land in business.

_____ **2.** Purchasing a building.

_____ **3.** Purchasing land.

_____ **4.** Borrowing cash from a bank.

_____ **5.** Purchasing equipment.

_____ **6.** Selling and distributing products.

_____ **7.** Paying for advertising.

_____ **8.** Paying employee wages.

Problem 1-13A[B]
Describing organizational activities

C6

An organization undertakes various activities in pursuit of business success. Identify an organization's three major business activities, and describe each activity.

Problem 1-14A[B]
Describing organizational activities   C6

PROBLEM SET B

Problem 1-1B
Computing missing information
using accounting knowledge

A1   A2

The following financial statement information is from five separate companies.

	Company V	Company W	Company X	Company Y	Company Z
December 31, 2006					
Assets	$54,000	$ 80,000	$141,500	$92,500	$144,000
Liabilities	25,000	60,000	68,500	51,500	?
December 31, 2007					
Assets	59,000	100,000	186,500	?	170,000
Liabilities	36,000	?	65,800	42,000	42,000
During year 2007					
Owner investments	5,000	20,000	?	48,100	60,000
Net income	?	40,000	18,500	24,000	32,000
Owner cash withdrawals	5,500	2,000	0	20,000	8,000

Check   (1b) $23,000

(2c) $22,000

(4) $135,100

Required

1. Answer the following questions about Company V.
   a. What is the amount of equity on December 31, 2006?
   b. What is the amount of equity on December 31, 2007?
   c. What is the net income or loss for the year 2007?
2. Answer the following questions about Company W.
   a. What is the amount of equity on December 31, 2006?
   b. What is the amount of equity on December 31, 2007?
   c. What is the amount of liabilities on December 31, 2007?
3. Calculate the amount of owner investments for Company X during 2007.
4. Calculate the amount of assets for Company Y on December 31, 2007.
5. Calculate the amount of liabilities for Company Z on December 31, 2006.

Problem 1-2B
Identifying effects of transactions
on financial statements

A1   A2

Identify how each of the following separate transactions affects financial statements. For the balance sheet, identify how each transaction affects total assets, total liabilities, and total equity. For the income statement, identify how each transaction affects net income. For the statement of cash flows, identify how each transaction affects cash flows from operating activities, cash flows from financing activities, and cash flows from investing activities. For increases, place a "+" in the column or columns. For decreases, place a "−" in the column or columns. If both an increase and a decrease occur, place "+/−" in the column or columns. The first transaction is completed as an example.

		Balance Sheet			Income Statement	Statement of Cash Flows		
	Transaction	**Total Assets**	**Total Liab.**	**Total Equity**	**Net Income**	**Operating Activities**	**Financing Activities**	**Investing Activities**
1	Owner invests cash in business	+		+			+	
2	Buys building by signing note payable							
3	Pays cash for salaries incurred							
4	Provides services for cash							
5	Pays cash for rent incurred							
6	Incurs utilities costs on credit							
7	Buys store equipment for cash							
8	Owner withdraws cash							
9	Provides services on credit							
10	Collects cash on receivable from (9)							

Selected financial information for Offshore Co. for the year ended December 31, 2007, follows:

| Revenues . . . . | $68,000 | Expenses . . . . | $40,000 | Net income . . . . | $28,000 |

Problem 1-3B
Preparing an income statement
P1

Required

Prepare the 2007 calendar-year income statement for Offshore Co.

The following is selected financial information for TLC Company as of December 31, 2007.

| Liabilities . . . . | $64,000 | Equity . . . . | $50,000 | Assets . . . . | $114,000 |

Problem 1-4B
Preparing a balance sheet
P1

Required

Prepare the balance sheet for TLC as of December 31, 2007.

Selected financial information of HalfLife Co. for the year ended December 31, 2007, follows:

Cash from investing activities	$1,600
Net increase in cash	400
Cash from financing activities	1,800
Cash used by operating activities	(3,000)
Cash, December 31, 2006	1,300

Problem 1-5B
Preparing a statement of cash flows
P1

Required

Prepare the 2007 calendar-year statement of cash flows for HalfLife Co.

Following is selected financial information of First Act for the year ended December 31, 2007.

| I. Firstact, Capital, Dec. 31, 2007 . . . . | $47,000 | I. Firstact, Withdrawals . . . . | $ 7,000 |
| Net income . . . . | 5,000 | I. Firstact, Capital, Dec. 31, 2006 . . . . | 49,000 |

Problem 1-6B
Preparing a statement of owner's equity
P1

Required

Prepare the 2007 calendar-year statement of owner's equity for First Act.

Holly Nikolas launched a new business, Holly's Maintenance Co., that began operations on June 1. The following transactions were completed by the company during that first month.

Problem 1-7B
Analyzing transactions and preparing financial statements
C5   A2   P1

June	1	H. Nikolas invested $130,000 cash in the business.
	2	Rented a furnished office and paid $6,000 cash for June's rent.
	4	Purchased $2,400 of equipment on credit.
	6	Paid $1,150 cash for the next week's advertising of the opening of the business.
	8	Completed maintenance services for a customer and immediately collected $850 cash.
	14	Completed $7,500 of maintenance services for City Center on credit.
	16	Paid $800 cash for an assistant's salary for the first half of the month.
	20	Received $7,500 cash payment for services completed for City Center on June 14.
	21	Completed $7,900 of maintenance services for Paula's Beauty Shop on credit.
	24	Completed $675 of maintenance services for Build-It Coop on credit.
	25	Received $7,900 cash payment from Paula's Beauty Shop for the work completed on June 21.
	26	Made payment of $2,400 cash for the equipment purchased on June 4.
	28	Paid $800 cash for an assistant's salary for the second half of this month.
	29	Nikolas withdrew $4,000 cash for personal use.
	30	Paid $150 cash for this month's telephone bill.
	30	Paid $890 cash for this month's utilities.

Required

1. Arrange the following asset, liability, and equity titles in a table like Exhibit 1.9: Cash; Accounts Receivable; Equipment; Accounts Payable; H. Nikolas, Capital; H. Nikolas, Withdrawals; Revenues; and Expenses.

2. Show the effects of the transactions on the accounts of the accounting equation by recording increases and decreases in the appropriate columns. Do not determine new account balances after each transaction. Determine the final total for each account and verify that the equation is in balance.

3. Prepare a June income statement, a June statement of owner's equity, a June 30 balance sheet, and a June statement of cash flows.

Problem 1-8B
Analyzing transactions and
preparing financial statements

C5 A2 P1

Truro Excavating Co., owned by Raul Truro, began operations in July and completed the following transactions during that first month.

July 1 R. Truro invested $80,000 cash in the business.
      2 Rented office space and paid $700 cash for the July rent.
      3 Purchased excavating equipment for $5,000 by paying $1,000 cash and agreeing to pay the $4,000 balance in 30 days.
      6 Purchased office supplies for $600 cash.
      8 Completed work for a customer and immediately collected $7,600 cash for the work.
     10 Purchased $2,300 of office equipment on credit.
     15 Completed work for a customer on credit in the amount of $8,200.
     17 Purchased $3,100 of office supplies on credit.
     23 Paid $2,300 cash for the office equipment purchased on July 10.
     25 Billed a customer $5,000 for work completed; the balance is due in 30 days.
     28 Received $8,200 cash for the work completed on July 15.
     30 Paid an assistant's salary of $1,560 cash for this month.
     31 Paid $295 cash for this month's utility bill.
     31 Truro withdrew $1,800 cash for personal use.

Required

1. Arrange the following asset, liability, and equity titles in a table like Exhibit 1.9: Cash; Accounts Receivable; Office Supplies; Office Equipment; Excavating Equipment; Accounts Payable; R. Truro, Capital; R. Truro, Withdrawals; Revenues; and Expenses.

2. Use additions and subtractions to show the effects of each transaction on the accounts in the accounting equation. Show new balances after each transaction.

3. Use the increases and decreases in the columns of the table from part 2 to prepare an income statement, a statement of owner's equity, and a statement of cash flows for the month. Also prepare a balance sheet as of the end of the month.

Analysis Component

4. Assume that the $5,000 purchase of excavating equipment on July 3 was financed from an owner investment of another $5,000 cash in the business (instead of the purchase conditions described in the transaction). Explain the effect of this change on total assets, total liabilities, and total equity.

Problem 1-9B
Analyzing effects of transactions

C5 P1 A1 A2

Nico Mitchell started a new business, Nico's Solutions, that completed the following transactions during its first year of operations.

a. N. Mitchell invests $70,000 cash and office equipment valued at $10,000 in the business.
b. Purchased a $150,000 building to use as an office. The company paid $20,000 in cash and signed a note payable promising to pay the $130,000 balance over the next ten years.
c. Purchased office equipment for $15,000 cash.
d. Purchased $1,200 of office supplies and $1,700 of office equipment on credit.
e. Paid a local newspaper $500 cash for printing an announcement of the office's opening.
f. Completed a financial plan for a client and billed that client $2,800 for the service.
g. Designed a financial plan for another client and immediately collected a $4,000 cash fee.
h. Mitchell withdrew $3,275 cash for personal use.
i. Received $1,800 cash from the client described in transaction f.
j. Made a $700 cash payment on the equipment purchased in transaction d.
k. Paid $1,800 cash for the office secretary's wages.

Required

1. Create a table like the one in Exhibit 1.9, using the following headings for the columns: Cash; Accounts Receivable; Office Supplies; Office Equipment; Building; Accounts Payable; Notes Payable; N. Mitchell, Capital; N. Mitchell, Withdrawals; Revenues; and Expenses.

2. Use additions and subtractions to show the effects of these transactions on individual items of the accounting equation. Show new balances after each transaction.

3. Once you have completed the table, determine the company's net income.

Check (2) Ending balances: Cash, $34,525; Expenses, $2,300; Notes Payable, $130,000

(3) Net income, $4,500

AT&T and Verizon produce and market telecommunications products and are competitors. Key financial figures (in $ millions) for these businesses over the past year follow.

Problem 1-10B
Computing and interpreting return on assets

A3

Key Figures ($ millions)	AT&T	Verizon
Sales	$34,529	$ 67,468
Net income	1,865	3,077
Average assets	40,396	165,963

Required

1. Compute return on assets for (*a*) AT&T and (*b*) Verizon.

2. Which company is more successful in the total amount of sales to consumers?

3. Which company is more successful in returning net income from its assets invested?

Check (1*a*) 4.6%; (1*b*) 1.9%

Analysis Component

4. Write a one-paragraph memorandum explaining which company you would invest your money in and why. (Limit your explanation to the information provided.)

Carbondale Company manufactures, markets, and sells snowmobile equipment. The average total assets for Carbondale Company is $3,000,000. In its most recent year, Carbondale reported net income of $200,000 on revenues of $1,400,000.

Problem 1-11B
Determining expenses, liabilities, equity, and return on assets

A1 A3

Required

1. What is Carbondale Company's return on assets?

2. Does return on assets seem satisfactory for Carbondale given that its competitors average a 9.5% return on assets?

3. What are the total expenses for Carbondale Company in its most recent year?

4. What is the average total amount of liabilities plus equity for Carbondale Company?

Check (3) $1,200,000
(4) $3,000,000

All business decisions involve aspects of risk and return.

Problem 1-12B[A]
Identifying risk and return

A4

Required

Identify both the risk and the return in each of the following activities.

1. Stashing $500 cash under your mattress.

2. Placing a $250 bet on a horse running in the Kentucky Derby.

3. Investing $20,000 in Nike stock.

4. Investing $35,000 in U.S. Savings Bonds.

A startup company often engages in the following activities during its first year of operations. Classify each of the following activities into one of the three major activities of an organization.

Problem 1-13B[B]
Describing organizational activities

C6

F. Financing   **I.** Investing   **O.** Operating

_____ **1.** Providing client services.   _____ **5.** Supervising workers.

_____ **2.** Obtaining a bank loan.   _____ **6.** Owner investing money in business.

_____ **3.** Purchasing machinery.   _____ **7.** Renting office space.

_____ **4.** Research for its products.   _____ **8.** Paying utilities expenses.

Problem 1-14B^B
Describing organizational
activities   C6

Identify in outline format the three major business activities of an organization. For each of these activities, identify at least two specific transactions or events normally undertaken by the business's owners or its managers.

PROBLEM SET C

Problem Set C is available at the book's Website to further reinforce and assess your learning.

The serial problem starts in this chapter and continues throughout most chapters of the book. It is most readily solved if you use the Working Papers that accompany this book.

SERIAL PROBLEM

Success Systems

SP 1   On October 1, 2007, Adriana Lopez launched a computer services company, **Success Systems,** that is organized as a proprietorship and provides consulting services, computer system installations, and custom program development. Lopez adopts the calendar year for reporting purposes and expects to prepare the company's first set of financial statements on December 31, 2007.

Required

Create a table like the one in Exhibit 1.9 using the following headings for columns: Cash; Accounts Receivable; Computer Supplies; Computer System; Office Equipment; Accounts Payable; A. Lopez, Capital; A. Lopez, Withdrawals; Revenues; and Expenses. Then use additions and subtractions to show the effects of the October transactions for Success Systems on the individual items of the accounting equation. Show new balances after each transaction.

Oct.   1   Adriana Lopez invested $75,000 cash, a $25,000 computer system, and $10,000 of office equipment in the business.
       3   Purchased $1,600 of computer supplies on credit from Corvina Office Products.
       6   Billed Easy Leasing $6,200 for services performed in installing a new Web server.
       8   Paid $1,600 cash for the computer supplies purchased from Corvina Office Products on October 3.
      10   Hired Michelle Jones as a part-time assistant for $150 per day, as needed.
      12   Billed Easy Leasing another $1,950 for services performed.
      15   Received $6,200 cash from Easy Leasing toward its account.
      17   Paid $900 cash to repair computer equipment damaged when moving it.
      20   Paid $1,790 cash for an advertisement in the local newspaper.
      22   Received $1,950 cash from Easy Leasing toward its account.
      28   Billed Clark Company $7,300 for services performed.
      31   Paid $1,050 cash for Michelle Jones's wages for seven days of work this month.
      31   Lopez withdrew $4,000 cash for personal use.

Check   Ending balances: Cash, $73,810; Revenues, $15,450; Expenses, $3,740

Beyond the Numbers (BTN) is a special problem section aimed to refine communication, conceptual, analysis, and research skills. It includes many activities helpful in developing an active learning environment.

BEYOND THE NUMBERS

REPORTING IN ACTION

A1 A3 A4

BTN 1-1   Key financial figures for **Best Buy**'s fiscal year ended February 26, 2005, follow.

Key Figure	In Millions
Liabilities + Equity	$10,294
Net income	984
Revenues	27,433

Required

1. What is the total amount of assets invested in Best Buy?
2. What is Best Buy's return on assets? Its assets at February 28, 2004, equal $8,652 (in millions).   **Check**   (2) 10.4%
3. How much are total expenses for Best Buy in fiscal year 2005?
4. Does Best Buy's return on assets seem satisfactory if competitors average a 3.2% return?

Fast Forward

5. Access Best Buy's financial statements (Form 10-K) for fiscal years ending after February 26, 2005, from its Website (BestBuy.com) or from the SEC Website (www.sec.gov) and compute its return on assets for those fiscal years. Compare the February 26, 2005, fiscal year-end return on assets to any subsequent years' returns you are able to compute, and interpret the results.

BTN 1-2   Key comparative figures ($ millions) for both Best Buy and Circuit City follow.

COMPARATIVE ANALYSIS

A1   A3   A4

Key Figure	Best Buy	Circuit City
Liabilities + Equity	$10,294	$3,789
Net income	984	62
Revenues and sales	27,433	10,472

Required

1. What is the total amount of assets invested in (*a*) Best Buy and (*b*) Circuit City?
2. What is the return on assets for (*a*) Best Buy and (*b*) Circuit City? Best Buy's beginning-year assets equal $8,652 (in millions) and Circuit City's beginning-year assets equal $3,731 (in millions).   **Check**   (2b) 1.6%
3. How much are expenses for (*a*) Best Buy and (*b*) Circuit City?
4. Is return on assets satisfactory for (*a*) Best Buy and (*b*) Circuit City? (Assume competitors average a 3.2% return.)
5. What can you conclude about Best Buy and Circuit City from these computations?

BTN 1-3   Craig Thorne works in a public accounting firm and hopes to eventually be a partner. The management of Allnet Company invites Thorne to prepare a bid to audit Allnet's financial statements. In discussing the audit fee, Allnet's management suggests a fee range in which the amount depends on the reported profit of Allnet. The higher its profit, the higher will be the audit fee paid to Thorne's firm.

ETHICS CHALLENGE

C4   C5

Required

1. Identify the parties potentially affected by this audit and the fee plan proposed.
2. What are the ethical factors in this situation? Explain.
3. Would you recommend that Thorne accept this audit fee arrangement? Why or why not?
4. Describe some ethical considerations guiding your recommendation.

BTN 1-4   Refer to this chapter's opening feature about LoveSac. Assume that Shawn Nelson desires to expand his manufacturing facilities to meet customer demand. Shawn and his partners decide they need to meet with his banker to discuss a loan to allow them to expand.

COMMUNICATING IN PRACTICE

A1   C2

Required

1. Prepare a half-page report outlining the information you would request from Shawn if you were the loan officer.
2. Indicate whether the information you request and your loan decision are affected by the form of business organization for the LoveSac store.

The book's Website provides free and easy access to all articles for every BusinessWeek Activity.

TAKING IT TO THE NET

A3

BTN 1-5　Visit the EDGAR database at (www.sec.gov). Access the Form 10-K report of World Wrestling Entertainment (ticker WWE) filed on July 13, 2004, covering its 2004 fiscal year.

Required

1. Item 7 of the 10-K report provides comparative financial highlights of WWE for the years 2000–2004. How would you describe the revenue trend for WWE over this five-year period?

2. Has WWE been profitable (see net income) over this five-year period? Support your answer.

TEAMWORK IN ACTION

C1

BTN 1-6　Teamwork is important in today's business world. Successful teams schedule convenient meetings, maintain regular communications, and cooperate with and support their members. This assignment aims to establish support/learning teams, initiate discussions, and set meeting times.

Required

1. Form teams and open a team discussion to determine a regular time and place for your team to meet between each scheduled class meeting. Notify your instructor via a memorandum or e-mail message as to when and where your team will hold regularly scheduled meetings.

2. Develop a list of telephone numbers and/or e-mail addresses of your teammates.

BusinessWeek ACTIVITY　C1

BTN 1-7　*BusinessWeek* publishes a ranking of the top 1,000 companies based on several performance measures. This issue is called the *BusinessWeek Global 1000*. Obtain the July 25, 2004, publication of this issue—this book's Website maintains free access to this article.

Required

1. What are the top 10 companies on the basis of market value?

2. Are any of the top 10 companies in the same industry? If yes, identify them.

3. How many of the top 10 based on market capitalization are not U.S. companies? List them.

ENTREPRENEURIAL DECISION

A1　A2　

BTN 1-8　Refer to this chapter's opening feature about LoveSac. Assume that Shawn Nelson decides to open a new manufacturing facility to meet customer demand. This new company will be called LoveSac Manufacturing.

Required

1. LoveSac Manufacturing obtains a $500,000 loan and Shawn contributes $250,000 of his own assets in the new company.

    a. What is the new company's total amount of liabilities plus equity?

    b. What is the new company's total amount of assets?

Check　(2) 10.7%

2. If the new company earns $80,000 in net income in the first year of operation, compute its return on asset (assume average assets equal $750,000). Assess its performance if competitors average a 10% return.

HITTING THE ROAD

C2　

BTN 1-9　You are to interview a local business owner. (This can be a friend or relative.) Opening lines of communication with members of the business community can provide personal benefits of business networking. If you do not know the owner, you should call ahead to introduce yourself and explain your position as a student and your assignment requirements. You should request a thirty minute appointment for a face-to-face or phone interview to discuss the form of organization and operations of the business. Be prepared to make a good impression.

Required

1. Identify and describe the main operating activities and the form of organization for this business.

2. Determine and explain why the owner(s) chose this particular form of organization.

3. Identify any special advantages and/or disadvantages the owner(s) experiences in operating with this form of business organization.

BTN 1-10 Dixons (Dixons-Group.com) is the leading European retailer of consumer electronics and competes globally with both **Best Buy** and **Circuit City**. Key financial figures for Dixons follow.

GLOBAL
DECISION

A1 A3 A4

Key Figure*	Pounds in Millions
Average assets	£4,015.9
Net income	243.6
Revenues	6,458.0
Return on assets	6.1%

* Figures prepared in accordance with generally accepted
accounting principles in the United Kingdom.

Required

1. Identify any concerns you have in comparing Dixons' net income and revenue figures to those of Best Buy and Circuit City (in BTN 1-2) for purposes of making business decisions.

2. Identify any concerns you have in comparing Dixons' return on assets ratio to those of Best Buy and Circuit City (computed for BTN 1-2) for purposes of making business decisions.

ANSWERS TO MULTIPLE CHOICE QUIZ

1. c; $450,000 is the actual cost incurred.

2. b; revenue is recorded when earned.

3. d;

Assets	=	Liabilities	+	Equity
+$100,000	=	+35,000	+	?

Change in equity = $100,000 − $35,000 = $65,000

4. a

5. a

2

Analyzing and Recording Transactions

A Look Back

Chapter 1 explained the role of accounting and introduced financial statements. We described different forms of organizations and identified users and uses of accounting. We explained the accounting equation and applied it to transaction analysis.

A Look at This Chapter

This chapter focuses on the accounting process. We describe transactions and source documents as inputs for analysis. We explain the analysis and recording of transactions. The accounting equation, T-account, general ledger, trial balance, and debits and credits are applied tools in the accounting process.

A Look Ahead

Chapter 3 extends our focus on processing information. We explain the importance of adjusting accounts and the procedures in preparing financial statements.

Learning Objectives

CAP

Conceptual

C1 Explain the steps in processing transactions. *(p. 48)*

C2 Describe source documents and their purpose. *(p. 49)*

C3 Describe an account and its use in recording transactions. *(p. 49)*

C4 Describe a ledger and a chart of accounts. *(p. 52)*

C5 Define *debits* and *credits* and explain their role in double-entry accounting. *(p. 53)*

Analytical

A1 Analyze the impact of transactions on accounts and financial statements. *(p. 57)*

A2 Compute the debt ratio and describe its use in analyzing financial condition. *(p. 67)*

Procedural

P1 Record transactions in a journal and post entries to a ledger. *(p. 54)*

P2 Prepare and explain the use of a trial balance. *(p. 63)*

P3 Prepare financial statements from business transactions. *(p. 64)*

"Each individual problem you face is totally surmountable"
—Warren Brown

Making Dough and Loving It

WASHINGTON, DC—Warren Brown started baking cakes to reduce stress, but his friends' appetites demanded more. "Friends were jumping on the bed" saying how much they loved the cakes and insisting that I set up shop, says Warren.

Starting small, Warren baked cakes in his apartment for hours after work each evening. He sold his sweet concoctions mostly to co-workers and friends, and even held a cake open house at the local art gallery. But Warren was determined to grow his business. He took a course in entrepreneurship at his local community college, and there he discovered the importance of financial reporting and accounting.

Launching his fledgling cake business presented Warren with many challenges. He needed to establish inventory accounting, transaction analysis, and accounting entries. "Everything feels like a disaster when it's right in your face," says Warren. "You just have to be calm, look at what you're doing, and fix the problem." Warren fixed the problems and unveiled his shop called Cake Love (**CakeLove.com**), funded with credit cards and a loan. "I opened up this tiny retail, walk-up bakery . . .

[to sell] goodies that are baked from scratch," Warren recalls. Today Cake Love entices the neighborhood with a gentle scent of fresh bakery and a sidewalk view into the kitchen. Warmly painted walls, comfy window seats, and free wireless Internet encourage customers to lounge for hours. "I want it to be relaxed and comfortable," says Warren. "People can bring their work, their kids, their friends, and just relax."

Success led Warren to open a new café across the street. This red-brick, by-the-slice café is where Warren experiments with new treats. "I'm always getting better, improving my skills," he said. Warren continues to grow his company while never losing sight of the financials. He shows a keen appetite for using accounting information to make good business decisions. "But," says Warren, "I love eating what I make more."

"The bigger message of Cake Love is finding your passion and working to reach your goals," says Warren. That's a slice of advice worth more than any amount of dough.

[Sources: *Cake Love Website*, January 2006; *Black Enterprise*, September 2004; *Georgetown Voice*, March 2005; *National Public Radio (NPR) Website*, May 2005; *Inc.com*, April 2005]

Financial statements report on the financial performance and condition of an organization. Knowledge of their preparation, organization, and analysis is important. A main goal of this chapter is to illustrate how transactions are recorded, how they are reflected in financial statements, and how they impact analysis of financial statements. Debits and credits are introduced and identified as a tool in helping analyze and process transactions.

Analyzing and Recording Transactions

Analyzing and Recording Process	**Analyzing and Processing Transactions**	**Trial Balance**
• Source documents • The account and its analysis • Types of accounts	• General ledger • Double-entry accounting • Journalizing and posting • An Illustration	• Trial balance preparation • Search for and correction of errors • Trial balance use

Analyzing and Recording Process

The accounting process identifies business transactions and events, analyzes and records their effects, and summarizes and presents information in reports and financial statements. These reports and statements are used for making investing, lending, and other business decisions. The steps in the accounting process that focus on *analyzing and recording* transactions and events are shown in Exhibit 2.1.

Exhibit 2.1

The Analyzing and Recording Process

Analyze each transaction and event from source documents

Record relevant transactions and events in a journal

Post journal information to ledger accounts

Prepare and analyze the trial balance

C1 Explain the steps in processing transactions.

Business transactions and events are the starting points. Relying on source documents, transactions and events are analyzed using the accounting equation to understand how they affect company performance and financial position. These effects are recorded in accounting records, informally referred to as the *accounting books,* or simply the *books.* Additional steps such as posting and then preparing a trial balance help summarize and classify the effects of transactions and events. Ultimately, the accounting process provides information in useful reports or financial statements to decision makers.

Source Documents

Source documents identify and describe transactions and events entering the accounting process. They are the sources of accounting information and can be in either hard copy or electronic form. Examples are sales tickets, checks, purchase orders, bills from suppliers, employee earnings records, and bank statements. To illustrate, when an item is purchased on credit, the seller usually prepares at least two copies of a sales invoice. One copy is given to the buyer. Another copy, often sent electronically, results in an entry in the seller's information system to record the sale. Sellers use invoices for recording sales and for control; buyers use them for recording purchases and for monitoring purchasing activity. Many cash registers record information for each sale on a tape or electronic file locked inside the register. This record can be used as a source document for recording sales in the accounting records. Source documents, especially if obtained from outside the organization, provide objective and reliable evidence about transactions and events and their amounts.

C2 Describe source documents and their purpose.

Point: To ensure that all sales are rung up on the register, most sellers require customers to have their receipts to exchange or return purchased items.

Decision Ethics
Answer—p. 71

Cashier   Your manager requires that you, as cashier, immediately enter each sale. Recently, lunch hour traffic has increased and the assistant manager asks you to avoid delays by taking customers' cash and making change without entering sales. The assistant manager says she will add up cash and enter sales after lunch. She says that, in this way, the register will always match the cash amount when the manager arrives at three o'clock. What do you do?

The Account and its Analysis

An **account** is a record of increases and decreases in a specific asset, liability, equity, revenue, or expense item. Information from an account is analyzed, summarized, and presented in reports and financial statements. The **general ledger,** or simply **ledger,** is a record containing all accounts used by a company. The ledger is often in electronic form. While most companies' ledgers contain similar accounts, a company often uses one or more unique accounts because of its type of operations. Accounts are arranged into three general categories (based on the accounting equation), as shown in Exhibit 2.2.

C3 Describe an account and its use in recording transactions.

Asset Accounts = Liability Accounts + Equity Accounts

Exhibit 2.2

Accounts Organized by the Accounting Equation

Asset Accounts   Assets are resources owned or controlled by a company and that have expected future benefits. Most accounting systems include (at a minimum) separate accounts for the assets described here.

A *Cash* account reflects a company's cash balance. All increases and decreases in cash are recorded in the Cash account. It includes money and any medium of exchange that a bank accepts for deposit (coins, checks, money orders, and checking account balances).

Accounts receivable are held by a seller and refer to promises of payment from customers to sellers. These transactions are often called *credit sales* or *sales on account* (or *on credit*). Accounts receivable are increased by credit sales and are decreased by customer payments. A company needs a separate record for each customer, but for now, we use the simpler practice of recording all increases and decreases in receivables in a single account called Accounts Receivable.

A *note receivable,* or promissory note, is a written promise of another entity to pay a definite sum of money on a specified future date to the holder of the note. A company holding a promissory note signed by another entity has an asset that is recorded in a Note (or Notes) Receivable account.

Prepaid accounts (also called *prepaid expenses*) are assets that represent prepayments of future expenses (*not* current expenses). When the expenses are later incurred, the amounts in prepaid accounts are transferred to expense accounts. Common examples of prepaid accounts include prepaid insurance, prepaid rent, and prepaid services (such as club memberships). Prepaid accounts expire with the passage of time (such as with rent) or through use (such as

Point: Customers and others who owe a company are called its **debtors.**

Point: A college parking fee is a prepaid account from the student's standpoint. At the beginning of the term, it represents an asset that entitles a student to park on or near campus. The benefits of the parking fee expire as the term progresses. At term-end, prepaid parking (asset) equals zero as it has been entirely recorded as parking expense.

with prepaid meal tickets). When financial statements are prepared, prepaid accounts are adjusted so that (1) all expired and used prepaid accounts are recorded as regular expenses and (2) all unexpired and unused prepaid accounts are recorded as assets (reflecting future use in future periods). To illustrate, when an insurance fee, called a *premium,* is paid in advance, the cost is typically recorded in the asset account Prepaid Insurance. Over time, the expiring portion of the insurance cost is removed from this asset account and reported in expenses on the income statement. Any unexpired portion remains in Prepaid Insurance and is reported on the balance sheet as an asset. (An exception exists for prepaid accounts that will expire or be used before the end of the current accounting period when financial statements are prepared. In this case, the prepayments *can* be recorded immediately as expenses.)

Supplies are assets until they are used. When they are used up, their costs are reported as expenses. The costs of unused supplies are recorded in a Supplies asset account. Supplies are often grouped by purpose—for example office supplies and store supplies. *Office supplies* include stationery, paper, toner, and pens. *Store supplies* include packaging materials, plastic and paper bags, gift boxes and cartons, and cleaning materials. The costs of these unused supplies can be recorded in an Office Supplies or a Store Supplies asset account. When supplies are used, their costs are transferred from the asset accounts to expense accounts.

Equipment is an asset. When equipment is used and gets worn down its cost is gradually reported as an expense (called depreciation). Equipment is often grouped by its purpose—for example, office equipment and store equipment. *Office equipment* includes computers, printers, desks, chairs, shelves, and other office equipment. Costs incurred for these items are recorded in an Office Equipment asset account. The Store Equipment account includes the costs of assets used in a store such as counters, showcases, ladders, hoists, and cash registers.

Buildings such as stores, offices, warehouses, and factories are assets because they provide expected future benefits to those who control or own them. Their costs are recorded in a Buildings asset account. When several buildings are owned, separate accounts are sometimes kept for each of them.

The cost of *land* owned by a business is recorded in a Land account. The cost of buildings located on the land is separately recorded in one or more building accounts.

Decision Insight

Women Entrepreneurs Women-owned small businesses are booming. The Center for Women's Business Research reports that women-owned businesses:

- Total approximately 11 million and employ nearly 20 million workers.
- Generate $2.5 trillion in annual sales and tend to embrace technology.
- Are more likely funded by individual investors (73%) than venture firms (15%).
- Are philanthropic—70% of owners volunteer at least once per month.

Liability Accounts Liabilities are claims (by creditors) against assets, which means they are obligations to transfer assets or provide products or services to other entities. **Creditors** are individuals and organizations that own the right to receive payments from a company. If a company fails to pay its obligations, the law gives creditors a right to force the sale of that company's assets to obtain the money to meet creditors' claims. When assets are sold under these conditions, creditors are paid first, but only up to the amount of their claims. Any remaining money, the residual, goes to the owners of the company. Creditors often use a balance sheet to help decide whether to loan money to a company. A loan is less risky if the borrower's liabilities are small in comparison to assets because there are more resources than claims on resources. The more common liability accounts are described here.

Accounts payable refer to oral or implied promises to pay later, which commonly arise from purchases of merchandise. Payables can also arise from purchases of supplies, equipment, and services. Accounting systems keep separate records about each creditor. We describe these individual records in Chapter 4.

A *note payable* refers to a formal promise, usually denoted by the signing of a promissory note, to pay a future amount. It is recorded in either a Short-Term Note Payable account or a Long-Term Note Payable account, depending on when it must be repaid. We explain details of short- and long-term classification in Chapter 3.

Unearned Revenue refers to a liability that is settled in the future when a company delivers its products or services. When customers pay in advance for products or services (before revenue is earned), the revenue recognition principle requires that the seller consider this payment as unearned revenue. Examples of unearned revenue include magazine subscriptions collected in advance by a publisher, sales of gift certificates by stores, and season ticket sales by sports teams. The seller would record these in liability accounts such as Unearned Subscriptions, Unearned Store Sales, and Unearned Ticket Revenue. When products and services are later delivered, the earned portion of the unearned revenue is transferred to revenue accounts such as Subscription Fees, Store Sales, and Ticket Sales.[1]

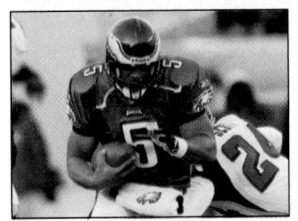

Decision Insight

Revenue Spread The **Philadelphia Eagles** have *Unearned Revenues* of about $50 million in advance ticket sales. When the team plays its home games, it settles this liability to its ticket holders and transfers the amount earned to *Ticket Revenues*.

Point: If a subscription is cancelled the publisher is expected to refund the unused portion to the subscriber.

Accrued liabilities are amounts owed that are not yet paid. Examples are wages payable, taxes payable, and interest payable. These are often recorded in separate liability accounts by the same title. If they are not large in amount, one or more ledger accounts can be added and reported as a single amount on the balance sheet. (Financial statements often have amounts reported that are a summation of several ledger accounts.)

Equity Accounts The owner's claim on a company's assets is called *equity* or *owner's equity*. Equity is the owner's *residual interest* in the assets of a business after deducting liabilities. There are four subcategories of equity: owner's capital, owner's withdrawals, revenues, and expenses. We show this visually in Exhibit 2.3 by expanding the accounting equation.

Point: Equity is also called *net assets*.

Exhibit 2.3

Expanded Accounting Equation

When an owner invests in a company, the invested amount is recorded in an account titled **Owner, Capital** (where the owner's name is inserted in place of "owner"). The account titled *C. Taylor, Capital* is used for FastForward. Any further owner investments are recorded in this account. When an owner withdraws assets for personal use it decreases both company assets and total equity. Withdrawals are not expenses of the business; they are simply the opposite of owner investments. The **Owner, Withdrawals** account is used to record asset distributions to the owner. The account titled *C. Taylor, Withdrawals* is used for FastForward. (Owners of proprietorships cannot receive company salaries because they are not legally separate from their companies; and they cannot enter into company contracts with themselves.)

Point: The Owner's Withdrawals account (also called *Drawing* or *Personal* account) is sometimes referred to as a *contra equity* account because it reduces the normal balance of equity.

Point: The distribution (withdrawal) of assets to the owners of a corporation is called a *dividend*.

Revenues and expenses are the final two categories of equity. Examples of revenue accounts are Sales, Commissions Earned, Professional Fees Earned, Rent Earned, and Interest Revenue. *Revenues increase equity* and result from products and services provided to customers. Examples of expense accounts are Advertising Expense, Store Supplies Expense, Office Salaries Expense, Office Supplies Expense, Rent Expense, Utilities Expense, and Insurance Expense. *Expenses*

---

[1] In practice, account titles vary. As one example, Subscription Fees is sometimes called Subscription Fees Revenue, Subscription Fees Earned, or Earned Subscription Fees. As another example, Rent Earned is sometimes called Rent Revenue, Rental Revenue, or Earned Rent Revenue. We must use good judgment when reading financial statements because titles can differ even within the same industry. For example, product sales are called *revenue* at **Best Buy**, but *net sales and operating revenues* at **Circuit City**. Generally, the term *revenues* or *fees* is more commonly used with service businesses, and *net sales* or *sales* with product businesses.

Decision Insight

Sporting Accounts   The Miami Heat have the following major revenue and expense accounts:

Revenues	Expenses
Basketball ticket sales	Team salaries
TV & radio broadcast fees	Game costs
Advertising revenues	NBA franchise costs
Basketball playoff receipts	Promotional costs

decrease equity and result from assets and services used in a company's operations. The variety of revenues and expenses can be seen by looking at the *chart of accounts* that follows the index at the back of this book. (Different companies sometimes use different account titles than those in this book's chart of accounts. For example, some might use Interest Revenue instead of Interest Earned, or Rental Expense instead of Rent Expense. It is important only that an account title describe the item it represents.)

Analyzing and Processing Transactions

This section explains several tools and processes that comprise an accounting system. These include a ledger, T-accounts, debits and credits, double-entry accounting, journalizing, and posting.

Ledger and Chart of Accounts

C4 Describe a ledger and a chart of accounts.

The collection of all accounts for an information system is called a *ledger* (or *general ledger*). If accounts are in files on a hard drive, the sum of those files is the ledger. If the accounts are pages in a file, that file is the ledger. A company's size and diversity of operations affect the number of accounts needed. A small company can get by with as few as 20 or 30 accounts; a large company can require several thousand. The **chart of accounts** is a list of all accounts a company uses and includes an identification number assigned to each account. A small business might use the following numbering system for its accounts:

101–199	Asset accounts
201–299	Liability accounts
301–399	Equity accounts
401–499	Revenue accounts
501–699	Expense accounts

These numbers provide a three-digit code that is useful in recordkeeping. In this case, the first digit assigned to asset accounts is a 1, the first digit assigned to liability accounts is a 2, and so on. The second and third digits relate to the accounts' subcategories. Exhibit 2.4 shows a partial chart of accounts for FastForward, the focus company of the first few chapters.

Exhibit 2.4

Partial Chart of Accounts for FastForward

Account Number	Account Name	Account Number	Account Name
101	Cash	301	C. Taylor, Capital
106	Accounts receivable	302	C. Taylor, Withdrawals
126	Supplies	403	Consulting revenue
128	Prepaid insurance	406	Rental revenue
167	Equipment	622	Salaries expense
201	Accounts payable	637	Insurance expense
236	Unearned consulting revenue	640	Rent expense
		652	Supplies expense
		690	Utilities expense

Debits and Credits

A **T-account** represents a ledger account and is a tool used to understand the effects of one or more transactions. Its name comes from its shape like the letter *T*. The layout of a T-account (shown in Exhibit 2.5) is (1) the account title on top, (2) a left, or debit side, and (3) a right, or credit, side.

The left side of an account is called the **debit** side, often abbreviated *Dr*. The right side is called the **credit** side, abbreviated *Cr*.[2] To enter amounts on the left side of an account is to *debit* the account. To enter amounts on the

Account Title	
(Left side)	(Right side)
Debit	*Credit*

right side is to *credit* the account. Do not make the error of thinking that the terms *debit* and *credit* mean increase or decrease. Whether a debit or a credit is an increase or decrease depends on the account. For an account where a debit is an increase, the credit is a decrease; for an account where a debit is a decrease, the credit is an increase. The difference between total debits and total credits for an account, including any beginning balance, is the **account balance.** When the sum of debits exceeds the sum of credits, the account has a *debit balance*. It has a *credit balance* when the sum of credits exceeds the sum of debits. When the sum of debits equals the sum of credits, the account has a *zero balance*.

Double-Entry Accounting

Double-entry accounting requires that each transaction affect, and be recorded in, at least two accounts. It also means the *total amount debited must equal the total amount credited* for each transaction. Thus, the sum of the debits for all entries must equal the sum of the credits for all entries, and the sum of debit account balances in the ledger must equal the sum of credit account balances.

The system for recording debits and credits follows from the usual accounting equation—see Exhibit 2.6. Two points are important here. First, like any simple mathematical relation, net increases or decreases on one side have equal net effects on the other side. For example, a net increase in assets must be accompanied by an identical net increase on the liabilities and

Assets		=	Liabilities		+	Equity	
Debit for increases +	Credit for decreases −		Debit for decreases −	Credit for increases +		Debit for decreases −	Credit for increases +

equity side. Recall that some transactions affect only one side of the equation, meaning that two or more accounts on one side are affected, but their net effect on this one side is zero. Second, the left side is the *normal balance* side for assets, and the right side is the *normal balance* side for liabilities and equity. This matches their layout in the accounting equation where assets are on the left side of this equation, and liabilities and equity are on the right.

Recall that equity increases from revenues and owner investments and it decreases from expenses and owner withdrawals. These important equity relations are conveyed by expanding the accounting equation to include debits and credits in double-entry form as shown in Exhibit 2.7.

Increases (credits) to capital and revenues *increase* equity; increases (debits) to withdrawals and expenses *decrease* equity. The normal balance of each account (asset, liability, capital, withdrawals, revenue, or expense) refers to the left or right (debit or credit) side where *increases* are recorded. Understanding these diagrams and rules is required to prepare, analyze, and interpret financial statements.

***

[2] These abbreviations are remnants of 18th-century English recordkeeping practices where the terms *debitor* and *creditor* were used instead of *debit* and *credit*. The abbreviations use the first and last letters of these terms, just as we still do for Saint (St.) and Doctor (Dr.).

C5   Define *debits* and *credits* and explain their role in double-entry accounting.

Exhibit 2.5
The T-Account

Point: Think of *debit* and *credit* as accounting directions for left and right.

"Total debits equal total credits for each entry."

Exhibit 2.6
Debits and Credits in the Accounting Equation

Point: Debits and credits do not mean favorable or unfavorable. A debit to an asset increases it, as does a debit to an expense. A credit to a liability increases it, as does a credit to a revenue.

Exhibit 2.7

Debit and Credit Effects for Component Accounts

The T-account for FastForward's Cash account, reflecting its first 11 transactions (from Exhibit 1.9), is shown in Exhibit 2.8. The total increases in its Cash account are $36,100, the total decreases are $31,300, and the account's debit balance is $4,800.

Exhibit 2.8

Computing the Balance for a T-Account

Cash			
Investment by owner	30,000	Purchase of supplies	2,500
Consulting services revenue earned	4,200	Purchase of equipment	26,000
Collection of account receivable	1,900	Payment of rent	1,000
		Payment of salary	700
		Payment of account payable	900
		Withdrawal by owner	200
Balance	4,800		

Point: The ending balance is on the side with the larger dollar amount.

Quick Check   Answers—p. 72

1. Identify examples of accounting source documents.
2. Explain the importance of source documents.
3. Identify each of the following as either an asset, a liability, or equity: (*a*) Prepaid Rent, (*b*) Unearned Fees, (*c*) Building, (*d*) Wages Payable, and (*e*) Office Supplies.
4. What is an account? What is a ledger?
5. What determines the number and types of accounts a company uses?
6. Does *debit* always mean increase and *credit* always mean decrease?
7. Describe a chart of accounts.

Journalizing and Posting Transactions

P1 Record transactions in a journal and post entries to a ledger.

Processing transactions is a crucial part of accounting. The four usual steps of this process are depicted in Exhibit 2.9. Steps 1 and 2—involving transaction analysis and double-entry accounting—were introduced in prior sections. This section extends that discussion and focuses on steps 3 and 4 of the accounting process. Step 3 is to record each transaction in a journal. A **journal** gives a complete record of each transaction in one place. It also shows debits and credits for each transaction. The process of recording transactions in a journal is called **journalizing.** Step 4 is to transfer (or *post*) entries from the journal to the ledger. The process of transferring journal entry information to the ledger is called **posting.**

Journalizing Transactions   The process of journalizing transactions requires an understanding of a journal. While companies can use various journals, every company uses a **general journal.** It can be used to record any transaction and includes the following information about each transaction: (1) date of transaction, (2) titles of affected accounts, (3) dollar amount

Step 1: Analyze transactions and source documents.

Services Contract
Client Billing
Note Payable
Purchase Ticket
Bank Statement

1	Deposit	30,000
	TOTAL	

Step 2: Apply double-entry accounting.

Cash

Assets = Liability + Equity

Step 3: Record journal entry.

General Journal		
Dec. 1 Cash	30,000	
Taylor, Capital		30,000
Dec. 2 Supplies	2,500	
Cash		2,500

Step 4: Post entry to ledger.

General Journal

Ledger

Exhibit 2.9

Steps in Processing Transactions

of each debit and credit, and (4) explanation of the transaction. Exhibit 2.10 shows how the first two transactions of FastForward are recorded in a general journal. This process is similar for manual and computerized systems. Computerized journals are often designed to look like a manual journal page, and also include error-checking routines that ensure debits equal credits for each entry. Shortcuts allow recordkeepers to select account names and numbers from pull-down menus.

GENERAL JOURNAL

Page 1

Date	Account Titles and Explanation	PR	Debit	Credit
2007 Dec. 1	Cash		30,000	
	C.Taylor, Capital			30,000
	Investment by owner.			
Dec. 2	Supplies		2,500	
	Cash			2,500
	Purchased supplies for cash.			

Exhibit 2.10

Partial General Journal for FastForward

To record entries in a general journal, apply these steps; refer to the entries in Exhibit 2.10 when reviewing these steps. ① Date the transaction: Enter the year at the top of the first column and the month and day on the first line of each journal entry. ② Enter titles of accounts debited and then enter amounts in the Debit column on the same line. Account titles are taken from the chart of accounts and are aligned with the left margin of the Account Titles and Explanation column. ③ Enter titles of accounts credited and then enter amounts in the Credit column on the same line. Account titles are from the chart of accounts and are indented from the left margin of the Account Titles and Explanation column to distinguish them from debited accounts. ④ Enter a brief explanation of the transaction on the line below the entry (it often references a source document). This explanation is indented about half as far as the credited account titles to avoid confusing it with accounts, and it is italicized.

A blank line is left between each journal entry for clarity. When a transaction is first recorded, the **posting reference (PR) column** is left blank (in a manual system). Later, when posting entries to the ledger, the identification numbers of the individual ledger accounts are entered in the PR column.

Balance Column Account T-accounts are simple and direct means to show how the accounting process works. However, actual accounting systems need more structure and therefore use **balance column accounts,** as in Exhibit 2.11.

Exhibit 2.11

Cash Account in Balance Column Format

Cash					Account No. 101
Date	Explanation	PR	Debit	Credit	Balance
2007 Dec. 1		G1	30,000		30,000
Dec. 2		G1		2,500	27,500
Dec. 3		G1		26,000	1,500
Dec. 10		G1	4,200		5,700

The balance column account format is similar to a T-account in having columns for debits and credits. It is different in including transaction date and explanation columns. It also has a column with the balance of the account after each entry is recorded. To illustrate, FastForward's Cash account in Exhibit 2.11 is debited on December 1 for the $30,000 owner investment, yielding a $30,000 debit balance. The account is credited on December 2 for $2,500, yielding a $27,500 debit balance. On December 3, it is credited again, this time for $26,000, and its debit balance is reduced to $1,500. The Cash account is debited for $4,200 on December 10, and its debit balance increases to $5,700; and so on.

The heading of the Balance column does not show whether it is a debit or credit balance. Instead, an account is assumed to have a *normal balance.* Unusual events can sometimes temporarily give an account an abnormal balance. An *abnormal balance* refers to a balance on the side where decreases are recorded. For example, a customer might mistakenly overpay a bill. This gives that customer's account receivable an abnormal (credit) balance. An abnormal balance is often identified by circling it or by entering it in red or some other unusual color. A zero balance for an account is usually shown by writing zeros or a dash in the Balance column to avoid confusion between a zero balance and one omitted in error.

Point: There are no exact rules for writing journal entry explanations. An explanation should be short yet describe why an entry is made.

Point: Computerized systems often provide a code beside a balance such as *dr.* or *cr.* to identify its balance.

Point: A journal is often referred to as the *book of original entry.* The ledger is referred to as the *book of final entry* because financial statements are prepared from it.

Point: Posting is automatic and immediate with accounting software.

Point: Explanations are typically included in ledger accounts only for unusual transactions or events.

Posting Journal Entries Step 4 of processing transactions is to post journal entries to ledger accounts (see Exhibit 2.9). To ensure that the ledger is up-to-date, entries are posted as soon as possible. This might be daily, weekly, or when time permits. All entries must be posted to the ledger before financial statements are prepared to ensure that account balances are up-to-date. When entries are posted to the ledger, the debits in journal entries are transferred into ledger accounts as debits, and credits are transferred into ledger accounts as credits. Exhibit 2.12 shows the four steps to post a journal entry. First, identify the ledger account that is debited in the entry; then, in the ledger, enter the entry date, the journal and page in its PR column, the debit amount, and the new balance of the ledger account. (The letter *G* shows it came from the General Journal.) Second, enter the ledger account number in the PR column of the journal. Steps three and four repeat the first two steps for credit entries and amounts. The posting process creates a link between the ledger and the journal entry. This link is a useful cross-reference for tracing an amount from one record to another.

Analyzing Transactions—An Illustration

A1 Analyze the impact of transactions on accounts and financial statements.

We return to the activities of FastForward to show how double-entry accounting is useful in analyzing and processing transactions. Analysis of each transaction follows the four steps of Exhibit 2.9. First, we review the transaction and any source documents. Second, we analyze the transaction using the accounting equation. Third, we use double-entry accounting to record the transaction in journal entry form. Fourth, the entry is posted (for simplicity, we use T-accounts to

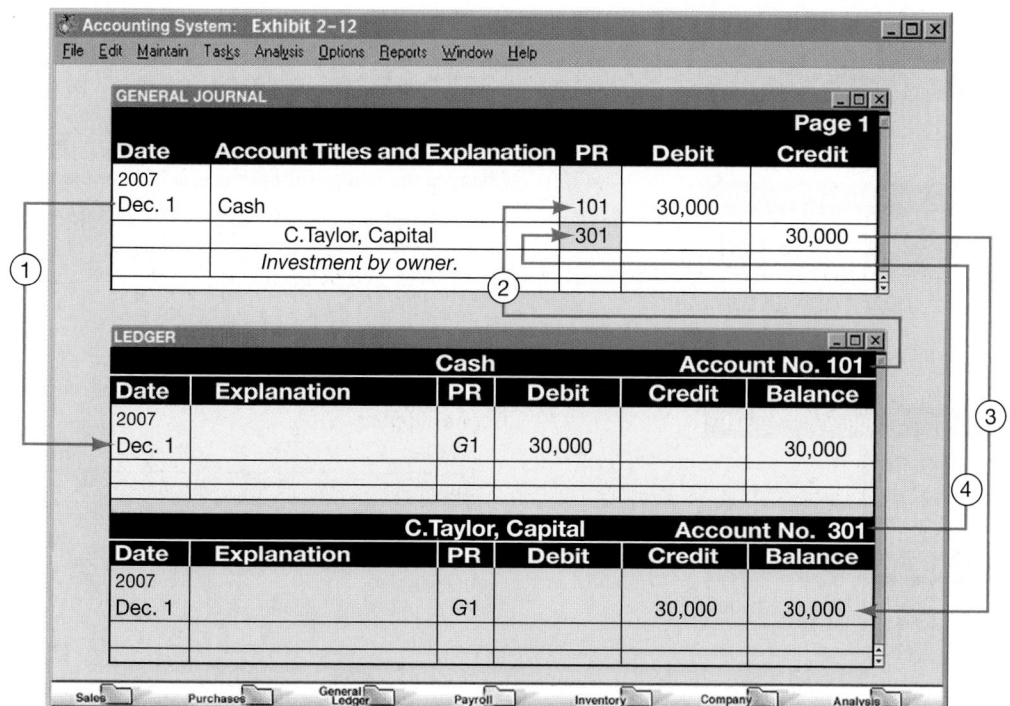

Exhibit 2.12

Posting an Entry to the Ledger

Key:
- ① Identify debit account in Ledger: enter date, journal page, amount, and balance.
- ② Enter the debit account number from the Ledger in the PR column of the journal.
- ③ Identify credit account in Ledger: enter date, journal page, amount, and balance.
- ④ Enter the credit account number from the Ledger in the PR column of the journal.

Point: The fundamental concepts of a manual (pencil-and-paper) system are identical to those of a computerized information system.

represent ledger accounts). We also identify the financial statements affected by each transaction. Study each transaction thoroughly before proceeding to the next. The first 11 transactions are from Chapter 1, and we analyze five additional December transactions of FastForward (numbered 12 through 16) that were omitted earlier.

Topic Tackler
PLUS
2-1

~~FAST~~Forward

1. Investment by Owner

Ledger

Cash		101
(1)	30,000	

C. Taylor, Capital		301
	(1)	30,000

Transaction: Chuck Taylor invests $30,000 cash in FastForward.

Analysis:

Assets	=	Liabilities	+	Equity
Cash				**C. Taylor, Capital**
+30,000	=	0	+	30,000

Double entry:

(1)	Cash	101	30,000	
	C. Taylor, Capital	301		30,000

Statements affected:[3] BLS, SCF, and SE

2. Purchase Supplies for Cash

Ledger

Supplies		126
(2)	2,500	

Cash		101
(1)	30,000	(2) 2,500

Transaction: FastForward pays $2,500 cash for supplies.

Analysis:

Assets		=	Liabilities	+	Equity
Cash	**Supplies**				
−2,500	+2,500	=	0	+	0

Changes the composition of assets but not the total.

Double entry:

(2)	Supplies	126	2,500	
	Cash	101		2,500

Statements affected: BLS and SCF

Point: All transactions are reflected in one or more financial statements. The line "*Statements affected*" identifies the statements impacted for each transaction of FastForward.

---

[3] We use abbreviations for the statements: income statement (IS), balance sheet (BLS), statement of cash flows (SCF), and statement of owner's equity (SE).

3. Purchase Equipment for Cash

Ledger

Equipment	167	
(3)	26,000	

Cash	101	
(1)	30,000	(2)	2,500
		(3)	26,000

Transaction: FastForward pays $26,000 cash for equipment.

Analysis:

Assets		=	Liabilities	+	Equity
Cash	**Equipment**				
−26,000	+26,000	=	0	+	0

Changes the composition of assets but not the total.

Double entry:

(3)	Equipment	167	26,000	
	Cash	101		26,000

Statements affected: BLS and SCF

4. Purchase Supplies on Credit

Ledger

Supplies	126	
(2)	2,500	
(4)	7,100	

Accounts Payable	201	
		(4)	7,100

Transaction: FastForward purchases $7,100 of supplies on credit from a supplier.

Analysis:

Assets	=	Liabilities	+	Equity
Supplies		**Accounts Payable**		
+7,100	=	+7,100	+	0

Double entry:

(4)	Supplies	126	7,100	
	Accounts Payable	201		7,100

Statements affected: BLS

5. Provide Services for Cash

Ledger

Cash	101	
(1)	30,000	(2)	2,500
(5)	4,200	(3)	26,000

Consulting Revenue	403	
		(5)	4,200

Transaction: FastForward provides consulting services and immediately collects $4,200 cash.

Analysis:

Assets	=	Liabilities	+	Equity
Cash				**Consulting Revenue**
+4,200	=	0		+4,200

Double entry:

(5)	Cash	101	4,200	
	Consulting Revenue	403		4,200

Statements affected: BLS, IS, SCF, and SE

6. Payment of Expense in Cash

Ledger

Rent Expense	640	
(6)	1,000	

Cash	101	
(1)	30,000	(2)	2,500
(5)	4,200	(3)	26,000
		(6)	1,000

Transaction: FastForward pays $1,000 cash for December rent.

Analysis:

Assets	=	Liabilities	+	Equity
Cash				**Rent Expense**
−1,000	=	0		−1,000

Double entry:

(6)	Rent Expense	640	1,000	
	Cash	101		1,000

Statements affected: BLS, IS, SCF, and SE

7. Payment of Expense in Cash

Point: *Salary* usually refers to compensation for an employee who receives a fixed amount for a given time period, whereas *wages* usually refers to compensation based on time worked.

Ledger

Salaries Expense	622	
(7)	700	

Cash	101	
(1)	30,000	(2)	2,500
(5)	4,200	(3)	26,000
		(6)	1,000
		(7)	700

Transaction: FastForward pays $700 cash for employee salary.

Analysis:

Assets	=	Liabilities	+	Equity
Cash				**Salaries Expense**
−700	=	0		−700

Double entry:

(7)	Salaries Expense	622	700	
	Cash	101		700

Statements affected: BLS, IS, SCF, and SE

8. Provide Consulting and Rental Services on Credit

Ledger

Accounts Receivable 106	
(8) 1,900	

Consulting Revenue 403	
	(5) 4,200
	(8) 1,600

Rental Revenue 406	
	(8) 300

Transaction: FastForward provides consulting services of $1,600 and rents its test facilities for $300. The customer is billed $1,900 for these services.

Analysis:

Assets	=	Liabilities	+		Equity	
Accounts Receivable				**Consulting Revenue**	**Rental Revenue**	
+1,900	=	0		+1,600	+300	

Double entry:

(8)	Accounts Receivable	106	1,900	
	Consulting Revenue	403		1,600
	Rental Revenue	406		300

Statements affected: BLS, IS, and SE

Point: Transaction 8 is a **compound journal entry,** which affects three or more accounts.

9. Receipt of Cash on Account

Ledger

Cash			101
(1)	30,000	(2)	2,500
(5)	4,200	(3)	26,000
(9)	1,900	(6)	1,000
		(7)	700

Accounts Receivable 106			
(8)	1,900	(9)	1,900

Transaction: FastForward receives $1,900 cash from the client billed in transaction 8.

Analysis:

Assets		=	Liabilities	+	Equity
Cash	**Accounts Receivable**				
+1,900	−1,900	=	0	+	0

Double entry:

(9)	Cash	101	1,900	
	Accounts Receivable	106		1,900

Statements affected: BLS and SCF

Point: The *revenue recognition principle* requires revenue to be recognized when earned, which is when the company provides products and services to a customer. This is not necessarily the same time that the customer pays. A customer can pay before or after products or services are provided.

10. Partial Payment of Accounts Payable

Ledger

Accounts Payable			201
(10)	900	(4)	7,100

Cash			101
(1)	30,000	(2)	2,500
(5)	4,200	(3)	26,000
(9)	1,900	(6)	1,000
		(7)	700
		(10)	900

Transaction: FastForward pays CalTech Supply $900 cash toward the payable of transaction 4.

Analysis:

Assets	=	Liabilities	+	Equity
Cash		**Accounts Payable**		
−900	=	−900	+	0

Double entry:

(10)	Accounts Payable	201	900	
	Cash	101		900

Statements affected: BLS and SCF

11. Withdrawal of Cash by Owner

Ledger

C. Taylor, Withdrawals 302	
(11) 200	

Cash			101
(1)	30,000	(2)	2,500
(5)	4,200	(3)	26,000
(9)	1,900	(6)	1,000
		(7)	700
		(10)	900
		(11)	200

Transaction: Chuck Taylor withdraws $200 cash from FastForward for personal use.

Analysis:

Assets	=	Liabilities	+	Equity
Cash				**C. Taylor, Withdrawals**
−200	=	0		−200

Double entry:

(11)	C. Taylor, Withdrawals	302	200	
	Cash	101		200

Statements affected: BLS, SCF, and SE

12. Receipt of Cash for Future Services

Ledger

Cash			101
(1)	30,000	(2)	2,500
(5)	4,200	(3)	26,000
(9)	1,900	(6)	1,000
(12)	3,000	(7)	700
		(10)	900
		(11)	200

Unearned Consulting Revenue			236
		(12)	3,000

Point: Luca Pacioli, a 15th-century monk, is considered a pioneer in accounting and the first to devise double-entry accounting.

Transaction: FastForward receives $3,000 cash in advance of providing consulting services to a customer.

Analysis:

Assets	=	Liabilities	+	Equity
		Unearned		
Cash		**Consulting Revenue**		
+3,000	=	+3,000	+	0

Accepting $3,000 cash obligates FastForward to perform future services and is a liability. No revenue is earned until services are provided.

Double entry:

(12)	Cash	101	3,000	
	Unearned Consulting Revenue	236		3,000

Statements affected: BLS and SCF

13. Pay Cash for Future Insurance Coverage

Ledger

Prepaid Insurance			128
(13)	2,400		

Cash			101
(1)	30,000	(2)	2,500
(5)	4,200	(3)	26,000
(9)	1,900	(6)	1,000
(12)	3,000	(7)	700
		(10)	900
		(11)	200
		(13)	2,400

Transaction: FastForward pays $2,400 cash (insurance premium) for a 24-month insurance policy. Coverage begins on December 1.

Analysis:

Assets		=	Liabilities	+	Equity
	Prepaid				
Cash	**Insurance**				
−2,400	+2,400	=	0	+	0

Changes the composition of assets from cash to prepaid insurance. Expense is incurred as insurance coverage expires.

Double entry:

(13)	Prepaid Insurance	128	2,400	
	Cash	101		2,400

Statements affected: BLS and SCF

14. Purchase Supplies for Cash

Ledger

Supplies			126
(2)	2,500		
(4)	7,100		
(14)	120		

Cash			101
(1)	30,000	(2)	2,500
(5)	4,200	(3)	26,000
(9)	1,900	(6)	1,000
(12)	3,000	(7)	700
		(10)	900
		(11)	200
		(13)	2,400
		(14)	120

Transaction: FastForward pays $120 cash for supplies.

Analysis:

Assets		=	Liabilities	+	Equity
Cash	**Supplies**				
−120	+120	=	0	+	0

Double entry:

(14)	Supplies	126	120	
	Cash	101		120

Statements affected: BLS and SCF

15. Payment of Expense in Cash

Ledger

Utilities Expense		690
(15)	230	

Cash		101
(1)	30,000	(2)	2,500
(5)	4,200	(3)	26,000
(9)	1,900	(6)	1,000
(12)	3,000	(7)	700
		(10)	900
		(11)	200
		(13)	2,400
		(14)	120
		(15)	230

Transaction: FastForward pays $230 cash for December utilities expense.

Analysis:

Assets	=	Liabilities	+	Equity
Cash				**Utilities Expense**
−230	=	0		−230

Double entry:

(15)	Utilities Expense	690	230	
	Cash	101		230

Statements affected: BLS, IS, SCF, and SE

16. Payment of Expense in Cash

Ledger

Salaries Expense		622
(7)	700	
(16)	700	

Cash		101
(1)	30,000	(2)	2,500
(5)	4,200	(3)	26,000
(9)	1,900	(6)	1,000
(12)	3,000	(7)	700
		(10)	900
		(11)	200
		(13)	2,400
		(14)	120
		(15)	230
		(16)	700

Transaction: FastForward pays $700 cash in employee salary for work performed in the latter part of December.

Analysis:

Assets	=	Liabilities	+	Equity
Cash				**Salaries Expense**
−700	=	0		−700

Double entry:

(16)	Salaries Expense	622	700	
	Cash	101		700

Statements affected: BLS, IS, SCF, and SE

Point: We could merge transactions 15 and 16 into one *compound entry*.

Accounting Equation Analysis

Exhibit 2.13 shows the ledger accounts (in T-account form) of FastForward after all 16 transactions are recorded, posted and the balances computed. The accounts are grouped into three major columns corresponding to the accounting equation: assets, liabilities, and equity. Note several important points. First, as with each transaction, the totals for the three columns must obey the accounting equation. Specifically, assets equal $42,470 ($4,350 + $0 + $9,720 + $2,400 + $26,000); liabilities equal $9,200 ($6,200 + $3,000); and equity equals $33,270 ($30,000 − $200 + $5,800 + $300 − $1,400 − $1,000 − $230). These numbers prove the accounting equation: Assets of $42,470 = Liabilities of $9,200 + Equity of $33,270. Second, the capital, withdrawals, revenue, and expense accounts reflect the transactions that change equity. Third, the revenue and expense account balances will be summarized and reported in the income statement. Fourth, increases and decreases in the cash account make up the elements reported in the statement of cash flows.

	Debit and Credit Rules		
Accounts	Increase (normal bal.)	Decrease
Asset	Debit	Credit
Liability	Credit	Debit
Capital	Credit	Debit
Withdrawals	Debit	Credit
Revenue	Credit	Debit
Expense	Debit	Credit

Point: Technology does not provide the judgment required to analyze most business transactions. Analysis requires the expertise of skilled and ethical professionals.

Exhibit 2.13

Ledger for FastForward (in T-Account Form)

Assets	=	Liabilities	+	Equity

Assets

Cash			101
(1)	30,000	(2)	2,500
(5)	4,200	(3)	26,000
(9)	1,900	(6)	1,000
(12)	3,000	(7)	700
		(10)	900
		(11)	200
		(13)	2,400
		(14)	120
		(15)	230
		(16)	700
Balance	4,350		

Accounts Receivable			106
(8)	1,900	(9)	1,900
Balance	0		

Supplies			126
(2)	2,500		
(4)	7,100		
(14)	120		
Balance	9,720		

Prepaid Insurance		128
(13)	2,400	

Equipment		167
(3)	26,000	

Liabilities

Accounts Payable			201
(10)	900	(4)	7,100
		Balance	6,200

Unearned Consulting Revenue		236
	(12)	3,000

Equity

C. Taylor, Capital		301
	(1)	30,000

C. Taylor, Withdrawals		302
(11)	200	

Consulting Revenue		403
	(5)	4,200
	(8)	1,600
	Balance	5,800

Rental Revenue		406
	(8)	300

Salaries Expense		622
(7)	700	
(16)	700	
Balance	1,400	

Rent Expense		640
(6)	1,000	

Utilities Expense		690
(15)	230	

Accounts in this white area reflect those reported on the income statement.

$42,470	=	$9,200	+	$33,270

Quick Check   Answers—p. 72

8. What types of transactions increase equity? What types decrease equity?

9. Why are accounting systems called *double entry*?

10. For each transaction, double-entry accounting requires which of the following: (*a*) Debits to asset accounts must create credits to liability or equity accounts, (*b*) a debit to a liability account must create a credit to an asset account, or (*c*) total debits must equal total credits.

11. An owner invests $15,000 cash along with equipment having a market value of $23,000 in a company. Prepare the necessary journal entry.

12. Explain what a compound journal entry is.

13. Why are posting reference numbers entered in the journal when entries are posted to ledger accounts?

Trial Balance

Double-entry accounting requires the sum of debit account balances to equal the sum of credit account balances. A trial balance is used to verify this. A **trial balance** is a list of accounts and their balances at a point in time. Account balances are reported in the appropriate debit or credit column of a trial balance. Exhibit 2.14 shows the trial balance for FastForward after its 16 entries have been posted to the ledger. (This is an *unadjusted* trial balance—Chapter 3 explains the necessary adjustments.)

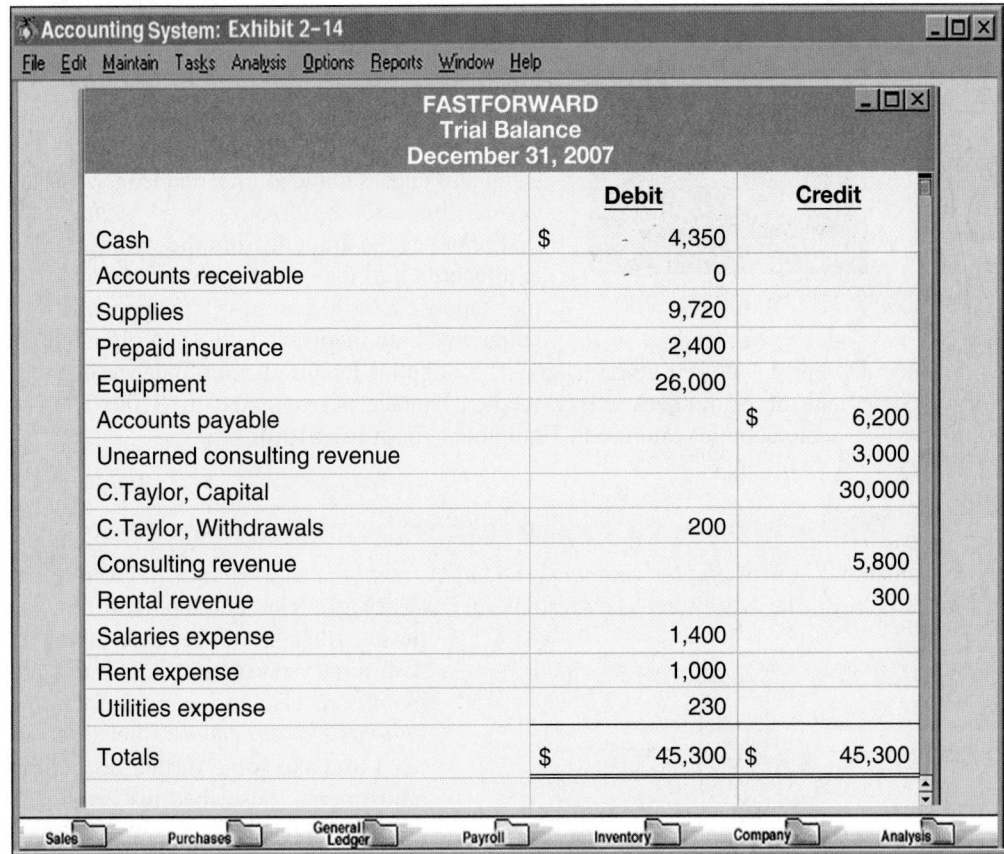

Exhibit 2.14

Trial Balance (unadjusted)

FASTFORWARD
Trial Balance
December 31, 2007

	Debit	Credit
Cash	$ 4,350	
Accounts receivable	0	
Supplies	9,720	
Prepaid insurance	2,400	
Equipment	26,000	
Accounts payable		$ 6,200
Unearned consulting revenue		3,000
C. Taylor, Capital		30,000
C. Taylor, Withdrawals	200	
Consulting revenue		5,800
Rental revenue		300
Salaries expense	1,400	
Rent expense	1,000	
Utilities expense	230	
Totals	$ 45,300	$ 45,300

Preparing a Trial Balance

Preparing a trial balance involves three steps:

P2 Prepare and explain the use of a trial balance.

1. List each account title and its amount (from ledger) in the trial balance. If an account has a zero balance, list it with a zero in its normal balance column (or omit it entirely).
2. Compute the total of debit balances and the total of credit balances.
3. Verify (*prove*) total debit balances equal total credit balances.

Point: The ordering of accounts in a trial balance typically follows their identification number from the chart of accounts.

The total of debit balances equals the total of credit balances for the trial balance in Exhibit 2.14. Equality of these two totals does not guarantee that no errors were made. For example, the column totals still will be equal when a debit or credit of a correct amount is made to a wrong account. Another error that does not cause unequal column totals is when equal debits and credits of an incorrect amount are entered.

Searching for and Correcting Errors   If the trial balance does not balance (when its columns are not equal), the error (or errors) must be found and corrected. An efficient way to search for an error is to check the journalizing, posting, and trial balance preparation in *reverse order*. Step 1 is to verify that the trial balance columns are correctly added. If step 1

Point: A trial balance is *not* a financial statement but a mechanism for checking the equality of debits and credits in the ledger. Financial statements do not have debit and credit columns.

Example: If a credit to Unearned Revenue was incorrectly posted from the journal as a credit to the Revenue ledger account, would the ledger still balance? Would the financial statements be correct? *Answers:* The ledger would balance, but liabilities would be understated, equity would be overstated, and income would be overstated (all because of overstated revenues).

fails to find the error, step 2 is to verify that account balances are accurately entered from the ledger. Step 3 is to see whether a debit (or credit) balance is mistakenly listed in the trial balance as a credit (or debit). A clue to this error is when the difference between total debits and total credits equals twice the amount of the incorrect account balance. If the error is still undiscovered, Step 4 is to recompute each account balance in the ledger. Step 5 is to verify that each journal entry is properly posted. Step 6 is to verify that the original journal entry has equal debits and credits. At this point, the errors should be uncovered.[4]

If an error in a journal entry is discovered before the error is posted, it can be corrected in a manual system by drawing a line through the incorrect information. The correct information is written above it to create a record of change for the auditor. Many computerized systems allow the operator to replace the incorrect information directly.

If an error in a journal entry is not discovered until after it is posted, do not strike through both erroneous entries in the journal and ledger. Instead, correct this error by creating a *correcting entry* that removes the amount from the wrong account and records it to the correct account. As an example, suppose a $100 purchase of supplies is journalized with an incorrect debit to Equipment, and then this incorrect entry is posted to the ledger. The Supplies ledger account balance is understated by $100, and the Equipment ledger account balance is overstated by $100. The correcting entry is: debit Supplies and credit Equipment (both for $100).

Decision Insight

Make CEOs Give Back   In the past few years, CEOs of more than 100 companies received bonuses based on income that later was restated to a lesser amount. Although Sarbanes–Oxley requires repayment of bonuses when restatements result from misconduct, most boards seem loath to enforce it.

Point: The IRS requires companies to keep records that can be audited.

Using a Trial Balance to Prepare Financial Statements

P3   Prepare financial statements from business transactions.

This section shows how to prepare *financial statements* from the trial balance in Exhibit 2.14 and information on the December transactions of FastForward. The statements differ from those in Chapter 1 because of several additional transactions. These statements are also more precisely called *unadjusted statements* because we need to make some further accounting adjustments (described in Chapter 3).

Exhibit 2.15

Links between Financial Statements Across Time

Topic Tackler

PLUS

2-2

How financial statements are linked in time is illustrated in Exhibit 2.15. A balance sheet reports on an organization's financial position at a *point in time*. The income statement, statement of owner's equity, and statement of cash flows report on financial performance over a *period of time*. The three statements in the middle column of Exhibit 2.15 link balance sheets

---

[4] *Transposition* occurs when two digits are switched, or transposed, within a number. If transposition is the only error, it yields a difference between the two trial balance totals that is evenly divisible by 9. For example, assume that a $691 debit in an entry is incorrectly posted to the ledger as $619. Total credits in the trial balance are then larger than total debits by $72 ($691 − $619). The $72 error is *evenly* divisible by 9 (72/9 = 8). The first digit of the quotient (in our example it is 8) equals the difference between the digits of the two transposed numbers (the 9 and the 1). The number of digits in the quotient also tells the location of the transposition, starting from the right. The quotient in our example had only one digit (8), so it tells us the transposition is in the first digit. Consider another example where a transposition error involves posting $961 instead of the correct $691. The difference in these numbers is $270, and its quotient is 30 (270/9). The quotient has two digits, so it tells us to check the second digit from the right for a transposition of two numbers that have a difference of 3.

from the beginning to the end of a reporting period. They explain how financial position changes from one point to another.

Preparers and users (including regulatory agencies) determine the length of the reporting period. A one-year, or annual, reporting period is common, as are semiannual, quarterly, and monthly periods. The one-year reporting period is known as the *accounting,* or *fiscal, year.* Businesses whose accounting year begins on January 1 and ends on December 31 are known as *calendar-year* companies. Many companies choose a fiscal year ending on a date other than December 31. **Best Buy** is a *noncalendar-year* company as reflected in the headings of its February 26 year-end financial statements in Appendix A near the end of the book.

Point: A statement's heading lists the 3 W's: **W**ho—name of organization, **W**hat—name of statement, **W**hen—statement's point in time or period of time.

Income Statement   An income statement reports the revenues earned less the expenses incurred by a business over a period of time. FastForward's income statement for December is shown at the top of Exhibit 2.16. Information about revenues and expenses is conveniently taken from the trial balance in Exhibit 2.14. Net income of $3,470 is reported at the bottom of the statement. Owner investments and dividends are *not* part of income.

Statement of Owner's Equity   The statement of owner's equity reports information about how equity changes over the reporting period. FastForward's statement of owner's equity is the second report in Exhibit 2.16. It shows the $30,000 owner investment, the $3,470 of net income, the $200 withdrawal, and the $33,270 end-of-period (capital) balance. (The beginning balance in the statement of owner's equity is rarely zero; an exception is for the first period of operations. The beginning capital balance in January 2008 is $33,270, which is December's ending balance.)

"It's been a dismal year, let's issue the shareholders report while everyone's hibernating."
© Edward Smith/artizans.com

Balance Sheet   The balance sheet reports the financial position of a company at a point in time, usually at the end of a month, quarter, or year. FastForward's balance sheet is the third report in Exhibit 2.16. This statement refers to financial condition at the close of business on December 31. The left side of the balance sheet lists its assets: cash, supplies, prepaid insurance, and equipment. The upper right side of the balance sheet shows that it owes $6,200 to creditors and $3,000 in services to customers who paid in advance. The equity section shows an ending balance of $33,270. Note the link between the ending balance of the statement of owner's equity and the capital balance here. (Recall that this presentation of the balance sheet is called the *account form:* assets on the left and liabilities and equity on the right. Another presentation is the *report form:* assets on top, followed by liabilities and then equity. Either presentation is acceptable.)

Point: Knowing how financial statements are prepared improves our analysis of them.

Point: An income statement is also called an *earnings statement, a statement of operations,* or a *P&L* (profit and loss) *statement.* A balance sheet is also called a *statement of financial position.*

Decision Maker   Answer—p. 71

Entrepreneur   You open a wholesale business selling entertainment equipment to retail outlets. You find that most of your customers demand to buy on credit. How can you use the balance sheets of these customers to decide which ones to extend credit to?

Presentation Issues   Dollar signs are not used in journals and ledgers. They do appear in financial statements and other reports such as trial balances. The usual practice is to put dollar signs beside only the first and last numbers in a column. **Best Buy**'s financial statements in Appendix A show this. When amounts are entered in a journal, ledger, or trial balance, commas are optional to indicate thousands, millions, and so forth. However, commas are always used in financial statements. Companies also commonly round amounts in reports to the nearest dollar, or even to a higher level. Best Buy is typical of many companies in that it rounds its financial statement amounts to the nearest million. This decision is based on the perceived impact of rounding for users' business decisions.

Point: While revenues increase equity, and expenses decrease equity, the amounts are not reported in detail in the statement of owner's equity. Instead, their effects are reflected through net income.

Exhibit 2.16

Financial Statements and Their Links

FASTFORWARD
Income Statement
For Month Ended December 31, 2007

Revenues		
Consulting revenue ($4,200 + $1,600)	$ 5,800	
Rental revenue	300	
Total revenues		$ 6,100
Expenses		
Rent expense	1,000	
Salaries expense	1,400	
Utilities expense	230	
Total expenses		2,630
Net income		$ 3,470

Point: Arrow lines show how the statements are linked.

FASTFORWARD
Statement of Owner's Equity
For Month Ended December 31, 2007

C. Taylor, Capital, December 1, 2007		$ 0
Plus: Investments by owner	$30,000	
Net income	3,470	33,470
		33,470
Less: Withdrawals by owner		200
C. Taylor, Capital, December 31, 2007		$33,270

FASTFORWARD
Balance Sheet
December 31, 2007

Assets		Liabilities	
Cash	$ 4,350	Accounts payable	$ 6,200
Supplies	9,720	Unearned revenue	3,000
Prepaid insurance . .	2,400	Total liabilities	9,200
Equipment	26,000	**Equity**	
		C. Taylor, Capital	33,270
Total assets	$42,470	Total liabilities and equity .	$ 42,470

Point: To *foot* a column of numbers is to add them.

Example: How would the balance sheet in Exhibit 2.16 change if FastForward pays $2,000 of its payable on December 31 using its Cash account? What would be the new amount of total assets? Would the balance sheet still balance? *Answers:* Cash would be $2,350, accounts payable would be $4,200, total assets (and liabilities plus equity) would be $40,470, and the balance sheet would still balance.

Quick Check

Answers—p. 72

14. Where are dollar signs typically entered in financial statements?
15. If a $4,000 debit to Equipment in a journal entry is incorrectly posted to the ledger as a $4,000 credit, and the ledger account has a resulting debit balance of $20,000, what is the effect of this error on the Trial Balance column totals?
16. Describe the link between the income statement and the statement of owner's equity.
17. Explain the link between the balance sheet and the statement of owner's equity.
18. Define and describe revenues and expenses.
19. Define and describe assets, liabilities, and equity.

Debt Ratio

An important business objective is gathering information to help assess a company's risk of failing to pay its debts. Companies finance their assets with either liabilities or equity. A company that finances a relatively large portion of its assets with liabilities is said to have a high degree of *financial leverage*. Higher financial leverage involves greater risk because liabilities must be repaid and often require regular interest payments (equity financing does not). The risk that a company might not be able to meet such required payments is higher if it has more liabilities (is more highly leveraged). One way to assess the risk associated with a company's use of liabilities is to compute the **debt ratio** as in Exhibit 2.17.

A2 Compute the debt ratio and describe its use in analyzing financial condition.

$$\text{Debt ratio} = \frac{\text{Total liabilities}}{\text{Total assets}}$$

Exhibit 2.17

Debt Ratio

Point: Compare the equity amount to the liability amount to assess the extent of owner versus nonowner financing.

To see how to apply the debt ratio, let's look at **Stride Rite**'s liabilities and assets. Stride Rite makes Keds, Pro-Keds, and other footwear. Exhibit 2.18 computes and reports its debt ratio at the end of each year from 2000 to 2004.

Exhibit 2.18

Computation and Analysis of Debt Ratio

	2004	2003	2002	2001	2000
Total liabilities (in mil.)	$ 74	$ 78	$ 82	$100	$110
Total assets (in mil.)	$321	$345	$335	$362	$359
Debt ratio	0.23	0.23	0.24	0.28	0.31
Industry debt ratio	0.48	0.46	0.45	0.49	0.48

Stride Rite's debt ratio ranges from a low of 0.23 to a high of 0.31. Its ratio is low compared with the industry ratio. Stride Rite reports that it carries no long-term debt, which is unusual. This analysis implies a low risk from its financial leverage. Is this good or bad? To answer that question we need to compare the company's return on the borrowed money to the rate it is paying creditors. If the company's return is higher, it is successfully borrowing money to make more money. A company's success with making money from borrowed money can quickly turn unprofitable if its own return drops below the rate it is paying creditors.

Decision Maker

Answer—p. 71

Investor   You consider buying stock in **Converse**. As part of your analysis, you compute its debt ratio for 2004, 2005, and 2006 as: 0.35, 0.74, and 0.94, respectively. Based on the debt ratio, is Converse a low-risk investment? Has the risk of buying Converse stock changed over this period? (The industry debt ratio averages 0.40.)

Demonstration Problem

(This problem extends the demonstration problem of Chapter 1.) After several months of planning, Jasmine Worthy started a haircutting business called Expressions. The following events occurred during its first month.

a. On August 1, Worthy invested $3,000 cash and $15,000 of equipment in Expressions.

b. On August 2, Expressions paid $600 cash for furniture for the shop.

c. On August 3, Expressions paid $500 cash to rent space in a strip mall for August.

d. On August 4, it purchased $1,200 of equipment on credit for the shop (using a long-term note payable).

e. On August 5, Expressions opened for business. Cash received from services provided in the first week and a half of business (ended August 15) is $825.

f. On August 15, it provided $100 of haircutting services on account.

g. On August 17, it received a $100 check for services previously rendered on account.

h. On August 17, it paid $125 to an assistant for working during the grand opening.

i. Cash received from services provided during the second half of August is $930.

j. On August 31, it paid a $400 installment toward principal on the note payable entered into on August 4.

k. On August 31, Worthy withdrew $900 cash for personal use.

Required

1. Open the following ledger accounts in balance column format (account numbers are in parentheses): Cash (101); Accounts Receivable (102); Furniture (161); Store Equipment (165); Note Payable (240); J. Worthy, Capital (301); J. Worthy, Withdrawals (302); Haircutting Services Revenue (403); Wages Expense (623); and Rent Expense (640). Prepare general journal entries for the transactions.

2. Post the journal entries from (1) to the ledger accounts.

3. Prepare a trial balance as of August 31.

4. Prepare an income statement for August.

5. Prepare a statement of owner's equity for August.

6. Prepare a balance sheet as of August 31.

7. Determine the debt ratio as of August 31.

Extended Analysis

8. In the coming months, Expressions will experience a greater variety of business transactions. Identify which accounts are debited and which are credited for the following transactions. (*Hint:* We must use some accounts not opened in part 1.)

   a. Purchase supplies with cash.

   b. Pay cash for future insurance coverage.

   c. Receive cash for services to be provided in the future.

   d. Purchase supplies on account.

Planning the Solution

- Analyze each transaction and use the debit and credit rules to prepare a journal entry for each.
- Post each debit and each credit from journal entries to their ledger accounts and cross-reference each amount in the posting reference (PR) columns of the journal and ledger.
- Calculate each account balance and list the accounts with their balances on a trial balance.
- Verify that total debits in the trial balance equal total credits.
- To prepare the income statement, identify revenues and expenses. List those items on the statement, compute the difference, and label the result as *net income* or *net loss*.
- Use information in the ledger to prepare the statement of owner's equity.
- Use information in the ledger to prepare the balance sheet.
- Calculate the debt ratio by dividing total liabilities by total assets.
- Analyze the future transactions to identify the accounts affected and apply debit and credit rules.

Solution to Demonstration Problem

1. General journal entries:

GENERAL JOURNAL					_□X
					Page 1
Date	**Account Titles and Explanation**		**PR**	**Debit**	**Credit**
Aug. 1	Cash		101	3,000	
	Store Equipment		165	15,000	
	J. Worthy, Capital		301		18,000
	Owner's investment.				
2	Furniture		161	600	
	Cash		101		600
	Purchased furniture for cash.				
3	Rent Expense		640	500	
	Cash		101		500
	Paid rent for August.				
4	Store Equipment		165	1,200	
	Note Payable		240		1,200
	Purchased additional equipment on credit.				

[continued on next page]

[continued from previous page]

15	Cash	101	825	
	Haircutting Services Revenue	403		825
	Cash receipts from first half of August.			
15	Accounts Receivable	102	100	
	Haircutting Services Revenue	403		100
	To record revenue for services provided on account.			
17	Cash	101	100	
	Accounts Receivable	102		100
	To record cash received as payment on account.			
17	Wages Expense	623	125	
	Cash	101		125
	Paid wages to assistant.			
31	Cash	101	930	
	Haircutting Services Revenue	403		930
	Cash receipts from second half of August.			
31	Note Payable	240	400	
	Cash	101		400
	Paid an installment on the note payable.			
31	J. Worthy, Withdrawals	302	900	
	Cash	101		900
	Cash withdrawal by owner.			

2. Post journal entries from part 1 to the ledger accounts:

General Ledger

Cash   Account No. 101

Date	PR	Debit	Credit	Balance
Aug. 1	G1	3,000		3,000
2	G1		600	2,400
3	G1		500	1,900
15	G1	825		2,725
17	G1	100		2,825
17	G1		125	2,700
31	G1	930		3,630
31	G1		400	3,230
31	G1		900	2,330

Accounts Receivable   Account No. 102

Date	PR	Debit	Credit	Balance
Aug. 15	G1	100		100
17	G1		100	0

Furniture   Account No. 161

Date	PR	Debit	Credit	Balance
Aug. 2	G1	600		600

Store Equipment   Account No. 165

Date	PR	Debit	Credit	Balance
Aug. 1	G1	15,000		15,000
4	G1	1,200		16,200

Note Payable   Account No. 240

Date	PR	Debit	Credit	Balance
Aug. 4	G1		1,200	1,200
31	G1	400		800

J. Worthy, Capital   Account No. 301

Date	PR	Debit	Credit	Balance
Aug. 1	G1		18,000	18,000

J. Worthy, Withdrawals   Account No. 302

Date	PR	Debit	Credit	Balance
Aug. 31	G1	900		900

Haircutting Services Revenue Account No. 403

Date	PR	Debit	Credit	Balance
Aug. 15	G1		825	825
15	G1		100	925
31	G1		930	1,855

Wages Expense   Account No. 623

Date	PR	Debit	Credit	Balance
Aug. 17	G1	125		125

Rent Expense   Account No. 640

Date	PR	Debit	Credit	Balance
Aug. 3	G1	500		500

3. Prepare a trial balance from the ledger:

EXPRESSIONS
Trial Balance
August 31

	Debit	Credit
Cash	$ 2,330	
Accounts receivable	0	
Furniture	600	
Store equipment	16,200	
Note payable		$ 800
J. Worthy, Capital		18,000
J. Worthy, Withdrawals	900	
Haircutting services revenue		1,855
Wages expense	125	
Rent expense	500	
Totals	$20,655	$20,655

4.

EXPRESSIONS
Income Statement
For Month Ended August 31

Revenues		
Haircutting services revenue		$1,855
Operating expenses		
Rent expense	$500	
Wages expense	125	
Total operating expenses		625
Net income		$1,230

5.

EXPRESSIONS
Statement of Owner's Equity
For Month Ended August 31

J. Worthy, Capital, August 1		$ 0
Plus: Investments by owner	$18,000	
Net income	1,230	19,230
		19,230
Less: Withdrawals by owner		900
J. Worthy, Capital, August 31		$18,330

6.

EXPRESSIONS
Balance Sheet
August 31

Assets		Liabilities	
Cash	$ 2,330	Note payable	$ 800
Furniture	600	**Equity**	
Store equipment	16,200	J. Worthy, Capital	18,330
Total assets	$19,130	Total liabilities and equity	$19,130

7. Debt ratio $= \dfrac{\text{Total liabilities}}{\text{Total assets}} = \dfrac{\$800}{\$19,130} = \underline{\underline{\mathbf{4.18\%}}}$

8a. Supplies *debited*
      Cash *credited*

8b. Prepaid Insurance *debited*
      Cash *credited*

8c. Cash *debited*
      Unearned Services Revenue *credited*

8d. Supplies *debited*
      Accounts Payable *credited*

Summary

C1 Explain the steps in processing transactions. The accounting process identifies business transactions and events, analyzes and records their effects, and summarizes and prepares information useful in making decisions. Transactions and events are the starting points in the accounting process. Source documents help in their analysis. The effects of transactions and events are recorded in journals. Posting along with a trial balance helps summarize and classify these effects.

C2 Describe source documents and their purpose. Source documents identify and describe transactions and events. Examples are sales tickets, checks, purchase orders, bills, and bank statements. Source documents provide objective and reliable evidence, making information more useful.

C3 Describe an account and its use in recording transactions. An account is a detailed record of increases and decreases in a specific asset, liability, equity, revenue, or expense. Information from accounts is analyzed, summarized, and presented in reports and financial statements for decision makers.

C4 Describe a ledger and a chart of accounts. The ledger (or general ledger) is a record containing all accounts used by a company and their balances. It is referred to as the *books*. The chart of accounts is a list of all accounts and usually includes an identification number assigned to each account.

C5 Define *debits* and *credits* and explain their role in double-entry accounting. *Debit* refers to left, and *credit* refers to right. Debits increase assets, expenses, and withdrawals while credits decrease them. Credits increase liabilities, owner capital, and revenues; debits decrease them. Double-entry accounting means each transaction affects at least two accounts and has at least one debit and one credit. The system for recording debits and credits follows from the accounting equation. The left side of an account is the normal balance for assets, withdrawals, and expenses, and the right side is the normal balance for liabilities, capital, and revenues.

A1 Analyze the impact of transactions on accounts and financial statements. We analyze transactions using concepts of double-entry accounting. This analysis is performed by determining a transaction's effects on accounts. These effects are recorded in journals and posted to ledgers.

A2 Compute the debt ratio and describe its use in analyzing financial condition. A company's debt ratio is computed as total liabilities divided by total assets. It reveals how much of the assets are financed by creditor (nonowner) financing. The higher this ratio, the more risk a company faces because liabilities must be repaid at specific dates.

P1 Record transactions in a journal and post entries to a ledger. Transactions are recorded in a journal. Each entry in a journal is posted to the accounts in the ledger. This provides information that is used to produce financial statements. Balance column accounts are widely used and include columns for debits, credits, and the account balance.

P2 Prepare and explain the use of a trial balance. A trial balance is a list of accounts from the ledger showing their debit or credit balances in separate columns. The trial balance is a summary of the ledger's contents and is useful in preparing financial statements and in revealing recordkeeping errors.

P3 Prepare financial statements from business transactions. The balance sheet, the statement of owner's equity, the income statement, and the statement of cash flows use data from the trial balance (and other financial statements) for their preparation.

Guidance Answers to **Decision Maker** and **Decision Ethics**

Cashier The advantages to the process proposed by the assistant manager include improved customer service, fewer delays, and less work for you. However, you should have serious concerns about internal control and the potential for fraud. In particular, the assistant manager could steal cash and simply enter fewer sales to match the remaining cash. You should reject her suggestion without the manager's approval. Moreover, you should have an ethical concern about the assistant manager's suggestion to ignore store policy.

Entrepreneur We can use the accounting equation (Assets = Liabilities + Equity) to help us identify risky customers to whom we would likely not want to extend credit. A balance sheet provides amounts for each of these key components. The lower a customer's equity is relative to liabilities, the less likely you would extend credit. A low equity means the business has little value that does not already have creditor claims to it.

Investor The debt ratio suggests the stock of Converse is of higher risk than normal and that this risk is rising. The average industry ratio of 0.40 further supports this conclusion. The 2006 debt ratio for Converse is twice the industry norm. Also, a debt ratio approaching 1.0 indicates little to no equity.

Guidance Answers to **Quick Checks**

1. Examples of source documents are sales tickets, checks, purchase orders, charges to customers, bills from suppliers, employee earnings records, and bank statements.

2. Source documents serve many purposes, including record-keeping and internal control. Source documents, especially if obtained from outside the organization, provide objective and reliable evidence about transactions and their amounts.

3.

Assets	Liabilities	Equity
a,c,e	b,d	—

4. An account is a record in an accounting system that records and stores the increases and decreases in a specific asset, liability, equity, revenue, or expense. The ledger is a collection of all the accounts of a company.

5. A company's size and diversity affect the number of accounts in its accounting system. The types of accounts depend on information the company needs to both effectively operate and report its activities in financial statements.

6. No. Debit and credit both can mean increase or decrease. The particular meaning in a circumstance depends on the *type of account*. For example, a debit increases the balance of asset, withdrawals, and expense accounts, but it decreases the balance of liability, capital, and revenue accounts.

7. A chart of accounts is a list of all of a company's accounts and their identification numbers.

8. Equity is increased by revenues and by owner investments. Equity is decreased by expenses and owner withdrawals.

9. The name *double entry* is used because all transactions affect at least two accounts. There must be at least one debit in one account and at least one credit in another account.

10. Answer is (c).

11.

Cash	15,000	
Equipment	23,000	
Owner, Capital		38,000
Investment by owner of cash and equipment.		

12. A compound journal entry affects three or more accounts.

13. Posting reference numbers are entered in the journal when posting to the ledger as a cross-reference that allows the recordkeeper or auditor to trace debits and credits from one record to another.

14. At a minimum, dollar signs are placed beside the first and last numbers in a column. It is also common to place dollar signs beside any amount that appears after a ruled line to indicate that an addition or subtraction has occurred.

15. The Equipment account balance is incorrectly reported at $20,000—it should be $28,000. The effect of this error understates the trial balance's Debit column total by $8,000. This results in an $8,000 difference between the column totals.

16. An income statement reports a company's revenues and expenses along with the resulting net income or loss. A statement of owner's equity reports changes in equity, including that from net income or loss. Both statements report transactions occurring over a period of time.

17. The balance sheet describes a company's financial position (assets, liabilities, and equity) at a point in time. The capital amount in the balance sheet is obtained from the statement of owner's equity.

18. Revenues are inflows of assets in exchange for products or services provided to customers as part of the main operations of a business. Expenses are outflows or the using up of assets that result from providing products or services to customers.

19. Assets are the resources a business owns or controls that carry expected future benefits. Liabilities are the obligations of a business, representing the claims of others against the assets of a business. Equity reflects the owner's claims on the assets of the business after deducting liabilities.

Key Terms

Key Terms are available at the book's Website for learning and testing in an online Flashcard Format.

Account (p. 49)

Account balance (p. 53)

Balance column account (p. 56)

Chart of accounts (p. 52)

Compound journal entry (p. 59)

Credit (p. 53)

Creditors (p. 50)

Debit (p. 53)

Debt ratio (p. 67)

Double-entry accounting (p. 53)

General journal (p. 54)

Journal (p. 54)

Journalizing (p. 54)

Ledger (p. 49)

Owner, capital (p. 51)

Owner, withdrawals (p. 51)

Posting (p. 54)

Posting reference (PR) column (p. 55)

Source documents (p. 49)

T-account (p. 53)

Trial balance (p. 63)

Unearned revenue (p. 51)

Multiple Choice Quiz   Answers on p. 89   mhhe.com/wildFAP18e

Multiple Choice Quizzes A and B are available at the book's Website.

1. Amalia Company received its utility bill for the current period of $700 and immediately paid it. Its journal entry to record this transaction includes a
   a. Credit to Utility Expense for $700.
   b. Debit to Utility Expense for $700.
   c. Debit to Accounts Payable for $700.
   d. Debit to Cash for $700.
   e. Credit to Capital for $700.

2. On May 1, Mattingly Lawn Service collected $2,500 cash from a customer in advance of five months of lawn service. Mattingly's journal entry to record this transaction includes a
   a. Credit to Unearned Lawn Service Fees for $2,500.
   b. Debit to Lawn Service Fees Earned for $2,500.
   c. Credit to Cash for $2,500.
   d. Debit to Unearned Lawn Service Fees for $2,500.
   e. Credit to Capital for $2,500.

3. Liang Shue contributed $250,000 cash and land worth $500,000 to open his new business, Shue Consulting. Which of the following journal entries does Shue Consulting make to record this transaction?

a. Cash Assets	$750,000	
L. Shue, Capital		$750,000
b. L. Shue, Capital	$750,000	
Assets		$750,000
c. Cash	$250,000	
Land	500,000	
L. Shue, Capital		$750,000
d. L. Shue, Capital	$750,000	
Cash		$250,000
Land		500,000

4. A trial balance prepared at year-end shows total credits exceed total debits by $765. This discrepancy could have been caused by
   a. An error in the general journal where a $765 increase in Accounts Payable was recorded as a $765 decrease in Accounts Payable.
   b. The ledger balance for Accounts Payable of $7,650 being entered in the trial balance as $765.
   c. A general journal error where a $765 increase in Accounts Receivable was recorded as a $765 increase in Cash.
   d. The ledger balance of $850 in Accounts Receivable was entered in the trial balance as $85.
   e. An error in recording a $765 increase in Cash as a credit.

5. A company has total assets of $1,000,000, liabilities of $400,000, and equity of $600,000. What is its debt ratio (rounded to a whole percent)?
   a. 250%
   b. 167%
   c. 67%
   d. 150%
   e. 40%

Discussion Questions

1. Provide the names of two (*a*) asset accounts, (*b*) liability accounts, and (*c*) equity accounts.

2. What is the difference between a note payable and an account payable?

3. Discuss the steps in processing business transactions.

4. What kinds of transactions can be recorded in a general journal?

5. Are debits or credits typically listed first in general journal entries? Are the debits or the credits indented?

6. If assets are valuable resources and asset accounts have debit balances, why do expense accounts also have debit balances?

7. Should a transaction be recorded first in a journal or the ledger? Why?

8. Why does the recordkeeper prepare a trial balance?

9. If an incorrect amount is journalized and posted to the accounts, how should the error be corrected?

10. Identify the four financial statements of a business.

11. What information is reported in an income statement?

12. Why does the user of an income statement need to know the time period that it covers?

13. What information is reported in a balance sheet?

14. Define (*a*) *assets*, (*b*) *liabilities*, (*c*) *equity*, and (*d*) *net assets*.

15. Which financial statement is sometimes called the *statement of financial position?*

16. Review the **Best Buy** balance sheet in Appendix A. Identify three accounts on its balance sheet that carry debit balances and three accounts on its balance sheet that carry credit balances.

17. Review the **Circuit City** balance sheet in Appendix A. Identify an asset with the word *receivable* in its account title and a liability with the word *payable* in its account title.

18. Locate **Apple**'s income statement in Appendix A. What is the title of its revenue account?

Red numbers denote Discussion Questions that involve decision-making.

QUICK STUDY

QS 2-1

Identifying source documents

C2

Identify the items from the following list that are likely to serve as source documents.

a. Sales ticket
b. Income statement
c. Trial balance

d. Telephone bill
e. Invoice from supplier
f. Company revenue account

g. Balance sheet
h. Prepaid insurance
i. Bank statement

QS 2-2

Identifying financial statement items

C3   P3

Identify the financial statement(s) where each of the following items appears. Use I for income statement, E for statement of owner's equity, and B for balance sheet.

a. Cash withdrawal by owner
b. Office equipment
c. Accounts payable

d. Cash
e. Utilities expenses
f. Office supplies

g. Prepaid rent
h. Unearned fees
i. Service fees earned

QS 2-3

Linking debit or credit with normal balance

C5

Indicate whether a debit or credit *decreases* the normal balance of each of the following accounts.

a. Repair Services Revenue
b. Interest Payable
c. Accounts Receivable
d. Salaries Expense

e. Owner Capital
f. Prepaid Insurance
g. Buildings
h. Interest Revenue

i. Owner Withdrawals
j. Unearned Revenue
k. Accounts Payable
l. Office Supplies

QS 2-4

Analyzing debit or credit by account

C5   A1

Identify whether a debit or credit yields the indicated change for each of the following accounts.

a. To increase Land
b. To decrease Cash
c. To increase Utilities Expense
d. To increase Fees Earned
e. To decrease Unearned Revenue

f. To decrease Prepaid Insurance
g. To increase Notes Payable
h. To decrease Accounts Receivable
i. To increase Owner Capital
j. To increase Store Equipment

QS 2-5

Identifying normal balance

C5

Identify the normal balance (debit or credit) for each of the following accounts.

a. Office Supplies
b. Owner Withdrawals
c. Fees Earned

d. Wages Expense
e. Cash
f. Prepaid Insurance

g. Wages Payable
h. Building
i. Owner Capital

QS 2-6

Preparing journal entries

P1

Prepare journal entries for each of the following selected transactions.

a. On January 13, DeShawn Tyler opens a landscaping business called Elegant Lawns by investing $70,000 cash along with equipment having a $30,000 value.

b. On January 21, Elegant Lawns purchases office supplies on credit for $280.

c. On January 29, Elegant Lawns receives $7,800 cash for performing landscaping services.

d. On January 30, Elegant Lawns receives $1,000 cash in advance of providing landscaping services to a customer.

QS 2-7

Identifying a posting error

P2

A trial balance has total debits of $20,000 and total credits of $24,500. Which one of the following errors would create this imbalance? Explain.

a. A $2,250 debit to Rent Expense in a journal entry is incorrectly posted to the ledger as a $2,250 credit, leaving the Rent Expense account with a $3,000 debit balance.

b. A $4,500 debit to Salaries Expense in a journal entry is incorrectly posted to the ledger as a $4,500 credit, leaving the Salaries Expense account with a $750 debit balance.

c. A $2,250 credit to Consulting Fees Earned in a journal entry is incorrectly posted to the ledger as a $2,250 debit, leaving the Consulting Fees Earned account with a $6,300 credit balance.

QS 2-8

Classifying accounts in financial statements

P3

Indicate the financial statement on which each of the following items appears. Use I for income statement, E for statement of owner's equity, and B for balance sheet.

a. Services Revenue
b. Interest Payable
c. Accounts Receivable
d. Salaries Expense

e. Equipment
f. Prepaid Insurance
g. Buildings

h. Interest Revenue
i. Owner Withdrawals
j. Office Supplies

For each of the following (1) identify the type of account as an asset, liability, equity, revenue, or expense, (2) enter *debit* (*Dr.*) or *credit* (*Cr.*) to identify the kind of entry that would increase the account balance, and (3) identify the normal balance of the account.

a. Accounts Payable

b. Postage Expense

c. Prepaid Insurance

d. Land

e. Owner Capital

f. Accounts Receivable

g. Owner Withdrawals

h. Cash

i. Equipment

j. Fees Earned

k. Wages Expense

l. Unearned Revenue

Use the information in each of the following separate cases to calculate the unknown amount.

a. During October, Alameda Company had $102,500 of cash receipts and $103,150 of cash disbursements. The October 31 Cash balance was $18,600. Determine how much cash the company had at the close of business on September 30.

b. On September 30, Valerian Co. had a $102,500 balance in Accounts Receivable. During October, the company collected $102,890 from its credit customers. The October 31 balance in Accounts Receivable was $89,000. Determine the amount of sales on account that occurred in October.

c. Corentine Co. had $152,000 of accounts payable on September 30 and $132,500 on October 31. Total purchases on account during October were $281,000. Determine how much cash was paid on accounts payable during October.

Goro Co. bills a client $62,000 for services provided and agrees to accept the following three items in full payment: (1) $10,000 cash, (2) computer equipment worth $80,000, and (3) assume responsibility for a $28,000 note payable related to the computer equipment. The entry Goro makes to record this transaction includes which one or more of the following?

a. $28,000 increase in a liability account

b. $10,000 increase in the Cash account

c. $10,000 increase in a revenue account

d. $62,000 increase in an asset account

e. $62,000 increase in a revenue account

Prepare general journal entries for the following transactions of a new business called Pose-for-Pics.

Aug. 1	Madison Harris, the owner, invested $6,500 cash and $33,500 of photography equipment in the business.
2	Paid $2,100 cash for an insurance policy covering the next 24 months.
5	Purchased office supplies for $880 cash.
20	Received $3,331 cash in photography fees earned.
31	Paid $675 cash for August utilities.

Use the information in Exercise 2-4 to prepare an August 31 trial balance for Pose-for-Pics. Open these T-accounts: Cash; Office Supplies; Prepaid Insurance; Photography Equipment; M. Harris, Capital; Photography Fees Earned; and Utilities Expense. Post the general journal entries to these T-accounts (which will serve as the ledger), and prepare a trial balance.

Record the transactions below for Amena Company by recording the debit and credit entries directly in the following T-accounts: Cash; Accounts Receivable; Office Supplies; Office Equipment; Accounts Payable; A. Amena, Capital; A. Amena, Withdrawals; Fees Earned; and Rent Expense. Use the letters beside each transaction to identify entries. Determine the ending balance of each T-account.

a. Ahmad Amena, owner, invested $13,325 cash in the business.

b. Purchased office supplies for $475 cash.

c. Purchased $6,235 of office equipment on credit.

d. Received $2,000 cash as fees for services provided to a customer.

e. Paid $6,235 cash to settle the payable for the office equipment purchased in transaction *c*.

f. Billed a customer $3,300 as fees for services provided.

g. Paid $775 cash for the monthly rent.

h. Collected $2,300 cash toward the account receivable created in transaction *f*.

i. Ahmad Amena withdrew $800 cash for personal use.

Exercise 2-7

Preparing a trial balance P2

After recording the transactions of Exercise 2-6 in T-accounts and calculating the balance of each account, prepare a trial balance. Use May 31, 2008, as its report date.

Exercise 2-8

Analyzing and journalizing revenue transactions

A1   P1

Examine the following transactions and identify those that create revenues for Valdez Services, a company owned by Brina Valdez. Prepare general journal entries to record those revenue transactions and explain why the other transactions did not create revenues.

a. Brina Valdez invests $39,350 cash in the business.

b. Provided $2,300 of services on credit.

c. Provided services to a client and immediately received $875 cash.

d. Received $10,200 cash from a client in payment for services to be provided next year.

e. Received $3,500 cash from a client in partial payment of an account receivable.

f. Borrowed $120,000 cash from the bank by signing a promissory note.

Exercise 2-9

Analyzing and journalizing expense transactions

A1   P1

Examine the following transactions and identify those that create expenses for Valdez Services. Prepare general journal entries to record those expense transactions and explain why the other transactions did not create expenses.

a. Paid $12,200 cash for office supplies that were purchased more than 1 year ago.

b. Paid $1,233 cash for the receptionist's salary for the two weeks just completed.

c. Paid $39,200 cash for equipment.

d. Paid $870 cash for this month's utilities.

e. Owner (Valdez) withdrew $4,500 cash for personal use.

Exercise 2-10

Preparing an income statement

C4   P3

On October 1, Diondre Shabazz organized a new consulting firm called OnTech. On October 31, the company's records show the following items and amounts. Use this information to prepare an October income statement for the business.

Cash	$11,360	D. Shabazz, Withdrawals	$ 2,000
Accounts receivable	14,000	Consulting fees earned	14,000
Office supplies	3,250	Rent expense	3,550
Patents	46,000	Salaries expense	7,000
Office equipment	18,000	Telephone expense	760
Accounts payable	8,500	Miscellaneous expenses	580
D. Shabazz, Capital	84,000		

Check Net income, $2,110

Exercise 2-11

Preparing a statement of owner's equity P3

Use the information in Exercise 2-10 to prepare an October statement of owner's equity for OnTech.

Exercise 2-12

Preparing a balance sheet P3

Use the information in Exercise 2-10 (if completed, you can also use your solution to Exercise 2-11) to prepare an October 31 balance sheet for OnTech.

Exercise 2-13

Computing net income

A1   P3

A proprietorship had the following assets and liabilities at the beginning and end of a recent year.

	Assets	Liabilities
Beginning of the year	$ 60,000	$20,000
End of the year	105,000	36,000

Determine the net income earned or net loss incurred by the business during the year for each of the following *separate* cases.

a. Owner made no investments in the business and no withdrawals were made during the year.

b. Owner made no investments in the business but withdrew $1,250 cash per month for personal use.

c. No withdrawals were made during the year but the owner invested an additional $55,000 cash.

d. Owner withdrew $1,250 cash per month for personal use and the owner invested an additional $35,000 cash.

Compute the missing amount in each of the following separate companies *a* through *d*.

Exercise 2-14
Analyzing changes in a company's equity

C5 P3

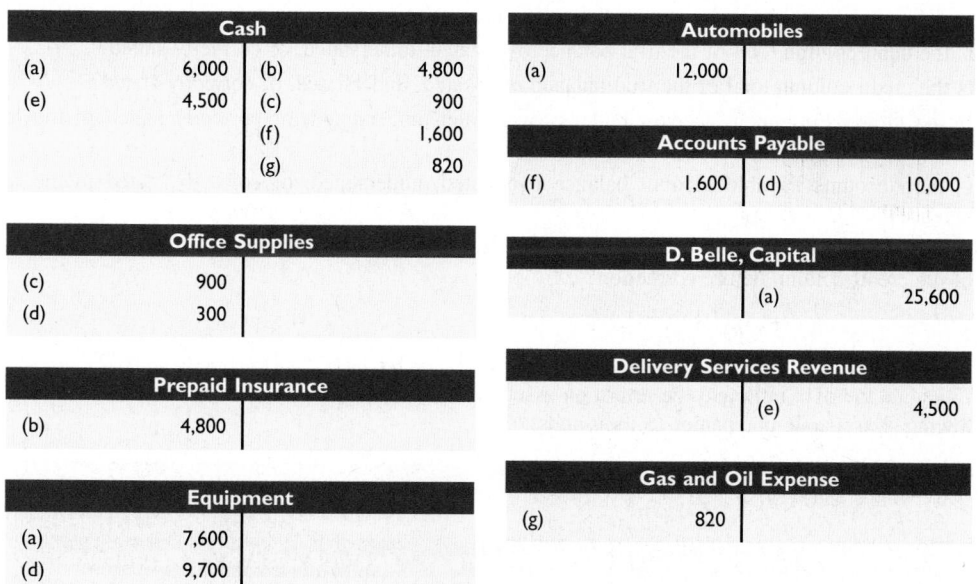

	(a)	(b)	(c)	(d)
Equity, December 31, 2007	$ 0	$ 0	$ 0	$ 0
Owner investments during the year	110,000	?	87,000	210,000
Owner withdrawals during the year	?	(47,000)	(10,000)	(55,000)
Net income (loss) for the year	22,000	90,000	(4,000)	?
Equity, December 31, 2008	104,000	85,000	?	110,000

Assume the following T-accounts reflect Belle Co.'s general ledger and that seven transactions *a* through *g* are posted to them. Provide a short description of each transaction. Include the amounts in your descriptions.

Exercise 2-15
Interpreting and describing transactions from T-accounts

C1 A1

Cash
(a)	6,000	(b)	4,800
(e)	4,500	(c)	900
		(f)	1,600
		(g)	820

Office Supplies
| (c) | 900 |
| (d) | 300 |

Prepaid Insurance
| (b) | 4,800 |

Equipment
| (a) | 7,600 |
| (d) | 9,700 |

Automobiles
| (a) | 12,000 |

Accounts Payable
| (f) | 1,600 | (d) | 10,000 |

D. Belle, Capital
| | | (a) | 25,600 |

Delivery Services Revenue
| | | (e) | 4,500 |

Gas and Oil Expense
| (g) | 820 |

Use information from the T-accounts in Exercise 2-15 to prepare general journal entries for each of the seven transactions *a* through *g*.

Exercise 2-16
Preparing general journal entries A1 P1

Several posting errors are identified in the following table. In column (1), enter the amount of the difference between the two trial balance columns (debit and credit) due to the error. In column (2), identify the trial balance column (debit or credit) with the larger amount if they are not equal. In column (3), identify the account(s) affected by the error. In column (4), indicate the amount by which the account(s) in column (3) is (are) under- or overstated. Item (a) is completed as an example.

Exercise 2-17
Identifying effects of posting errors on the trial balance A1 P2

	Description of Posting Error	(1) Difference between Debit and Credit Columns	(2) Column with the Larger Total	(3) Identify Account(s) Incorrectly Stated	(4) Amount that Account(s) is Over- or Understated
a.	$3,600 debit to Rent Expense is posted as a $1,340 debit.	$2,260	Credit	Rent Expense	Rent Expense understated $2,260
b.	$6,500 credit to Cash is posted twice as two credits to Cash.				
c.	$10,900 debit to the Withdrawals account is debited to Owner's Capital.				
d.	$2,050 debit to Prepaid Insurance is posted as a debit to Insurance Expense.				
e.	$38,000 debit to Machinery is posted as a debit to Accounts Payable.				
f.	$5,850 credit to Services Revenue is posted as a $585 credit.				
g.	$1,390 debit to Store Supplies is not posted.				

Exercise 2-18

Analyzing a trial balance error

A1   P2

You are told the column totals in a trial balance are not equal. After careful analysis, you discover only one error. Specifically, a correctly journalized credit purchase of a computer for $18,950 is posted from the journal to the ledger with a $18,950 debit to Office Equipment and another $18,950 debit to Accounts Payable. The Office Equipment account has a debit balance of $37,100 on the trial balance. Answer each of the following questions and compute the dollar amount of any misstatement.

a. Is the debit column total of the trial balance overstated, understated, or correctly stated?

b. Is the credit column total of the trial balance overstated, understated, or correctly stated?

c. Is the Office Equipment account balance overstated, understated, or correctly stated in the trial balance?

d. Is the Accounts Payable account balance overstated, understated, or correctly stated in the trial balance?

e. If the debit column total of the trial balance is $360,000 before correcting the error, what is the total of the credit column before correction?

Exercise 2-19

Interpreting the debt ratio and return on assets

A2

a. Calculate the debt ratio and the return on assets using the year-end information for each of the following six separate companies ($ thousands).

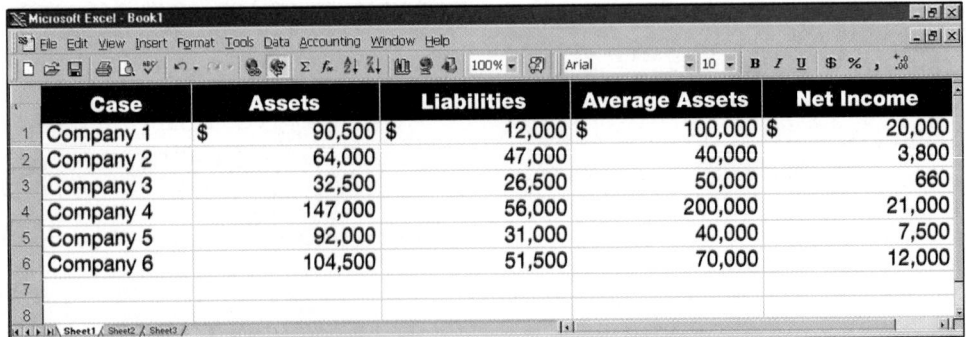

Case	Assets	Liabilities	Average Assets	Net Income
Company 1	$ 90,500	$ 12,000	$ 100,000	$ 20,000
Company 2	64,000	47,000	40,000	3,800
Company 3	32,500	26,500	50,000	660
Company 4	147,000	56,000	200,000	21,000
Company 5	92,000	31,000	40,000	7,500
Company 6	104,500	51,500	70,000	12,000

b. Of the six companies, which business relies most heavily on creditor financing?

c. Of the six companies, which business relies most heavily on equity financing?

d. Which two companies indicate the greatest risk?

e. Which two companies earn the highest return on assets?

f. Which one company would investors likely prefer based on the risk–return relation?

Aracel Engineering completed the following transactions in the month of June.

a. Jenna Aracel, the owner, invested $100,000 cash, office equipment with a value of $5,000, and $60,000 of drafting equipment to launch the business.

b. Purchased land worth $49,000 for an office by paying $6,300 cash and signing a long-term note payable for $42,700.

c. Purchased a portable building with $55,000 cash and moved it onto the land acquired in *b*.

d. Paid $3,000 cash for the premium on an 18-month insurance policy.

e. Completed and delivered a set of plans for a client and collected $6,200 cash.

f. Purchased $20,000 of additional drafting equipment by paying $9,500 cash and signing a long-term note payable for $10,500.

g. Completed $14,000 of engineering services for a client. This amount is to be received in 30 days.

h. Purchased $1,150 of additional office equipment on credit.

i. Completed engineering services for $22,000 on credit.

j. Received a bill for rent of equipment that was used on a recently completed job. The $1,333 rent cost must be paid within 30 days.

k. Collected $7,000 cash in partial payment from the client described in transaction *g*.

l. Paid $1,200 cash for wages to a drafting assistant.

m. Paid $1,150 cash to settle the account payable created in transaction *h*.

n. Paid $925 cash for minor repairs to its drafting equipment.

o. Jenna Aracel withdrew $9,480 cash for personal use.

p. Paid $1,200 cash for wages to a drafting assistant.

q. Paid $2,500 cash for advertisements in the local newspaper during June.

Required

1. Prepare general journal entries to record these transactions (use the account titles listed in part 2).

2. Open the following ledger accounts—their account numbers are in parentheses (use the balance column format): Cash (101); Accounts Receivable (106); Prepaid Insurance (108); Office Equipment (163); Drafting Equipment (164); Building (170); Land (172); Accounts Payable (201); Notes Payable (250); J. Aracel, Capital (301); J. Aracel, Withdrawals (302); Engineering Fees Earned (402); Wages Expense (601); Equipment Rental Expense (602); Advertising Expense (603); and Repairs Expense (604). Post the journal entries from part 1 to the accounts and enter the balance after each posting.

3. Prepare a trial balance as of the end of June.

PROBLEM SET A

Problem 2-1A
Preparing and posting journal entries; preparing a trial balance

C4 C5 A1 P1 P2

Check (2) Ending balances: Cash, $22,945; Accounts Receivable, $29,000; Accounts Payable, $1,333

(3) Trial balance totals, $261,733

Denzel Brooks opens a Web consulting business called Venture Consultants and completes the following transactions in March.

March 1   Brooks invested $150,000 cash along with $22,000 of office equipment in the business.

2   Prepaid $6,000 cash for six months' rent for an office. (*Hint:* Debit Prepaid Rent for $6,000.)

3   Made credit purchases of office equipment for $3,000 and office supplies for $1,200. Payment is due within 10 days.

6   Completed services for a client and immediately received $4,000 cash.

9   Completed a $7,500 project for a client, who must pay within 30 days.

12   Paid $4,200 cash to settle the account payable created on March 3.

19   Paid $5,000 cash for the premium on a 12-month insurance policy.

22   Received $3,500 cash as partial payment for the work completed on March 9.

25   Completed work for another client for $3,820 on credit.

29   Brooks withdrew $5,100 cash for personal use.

30   Purchased $600 of additional office supplies on credit.

31   Paid $500 cash for this month's utility bill.

Problem 2-2A
Preparing and posting journal entries; preparing a trial balance

C4 C5 A1 P1 P2

mhhe.com/wildFAP18e

Required

1. Prepare general journal entries to record these transactions (use the account titles listed in part 2).

2. Open the following ledger accounts—their account numbers are in parentheses (use the balance column format): Cash (101); Accounts Receivable (106); Office Supplies (124); Prepaid Insurance (128); Prepaid Rent (131); Office Equipment (163); Accounts Payable (201); D. Brooks, Capital (301); D. Brooks, Withdrawals (302); Services Revenue (403); and Utilities Expense (690). Post the journal entries from part 1 to the ledger accounts and enter the balance after each posting.

3. Prepare a trial balance as of the end of March.

Problem 2-3A

Preparing and posting journal entries; preparing a trial balance

C4 C5   A1   P1   P2

Kendis Lanelle opened a computer consulting business called Viva Consultants and completed the following transactions in the first month of operations.

April 1   Lanelle invested $80,000 cash along with office equipment valued at $26,000 in the business.
       2   Prepaid $9,000 cash for 12 months' rent for office space. (*Hint:* Debit Prepaid Rent for $9,000.)
       3   Made credit purchases for $8,000 in office equipment and $3,600 in office supplies. Payment is due within 10 days.
       6   Completed services for a client and immediately received $4,000 cash.
       9   Completed a $6,000 project for a client, who must pay within 30 days.
      13   Paid $11,600 cash to settle the account payable created on April 3.
      19   Paid $2,400 cash for the premium on a 12-month insurance policy. (*Hint:* Debit Prepaid Insurance for $2,400.)
      22   Received $4,400 cash as partial payment for the work completed on April 9.
      25   Completed work for another client for $2,890 on credit.
      28   Lanelle withdrew $5,500 cash for personal use.
      29   Purchased $600 of additional office supplies on credit.
      30   Paid $435 cash for this month's utility bill.

Required

1. Prepare general journal entries to record these transactions (use account titles listed in part 2).

2. Open the following ledger accounts—their account numbers are in parentheses (use the balance column format): Cash (101); Accounts Receivable (106); Office Supplies (124); Prepaid Insurance (128); Prepaid Rent (131); Office Equipment (163); Accounts Payable (201); K. Lanelle, Capital (301); K. Lanelle, Withdrawals (302); Services Revenue (403); and Utilities Expense (690). Post journal entries from part 1 to the ledger accounts and enter the balance after each posting.

3. Prepare a trial balance as of April 30.

Problem 2-4A

Computing net income from equity analysis, preparing a balance sheet, and computing the debt ratio

C3   A1   A2   P3

mhhe.com/wildFAP18e

The accounting records of Faviana Adriano Shipping show the following assets and liabilities as of December 31, 2007, and 2008.

	December 31	
	2007	**2008**
Cash	$ 64,300	$ 15,640
Accounts receivable	26,240	19,390
Office supplies	3,160	1,960
Office equipment	44,000	44,000
Trucks	148,000	157,000
Building	0	80,000
Land	0	60,000
Accounts payable	3,500	33,500
Note payable	0	40,000

Late in December 2008, the business purchased a small office building and land for $140,000. It paid $100,000 cash toward the purchase and a $40,000 note payable was signed for the balance. Adriano had to invest $35,000 cash in the business to enable it to pay the $100,000 cash. The owner withdraws $3,000 cash per month for personal use.

Required

1. Prepare balance sheets for the business as of December 31, 2007, and 2008. (*Hint:* You need only report total equity on the balance sheet, and remember that total equity equals the difference between assets and liabilities.)

2. By comparing equity amounts from the balance sheets and using the additional information presented in this problem, prepare a calculation to show how much net income was earned by the business during 2008.

Check   (2) Net income, $23,290

3. Compute the 2008 year-end debt ratio for the business.

(3) Debt ratio, 19.4%

Yi Min started an engineering firm called Min Engineering. He began operations and completed seven transactions in May, which included his initial investment of $18,000 cash. After these transactions, the ledger included the following accounts with normal balances.

Problem 2-5A
Analyzing account balances and reconstructing transactions

C1   C4   A1   P2

Cash	$37,641
Office supplies	890
Prepaid insurance	4,600
Office equipment	12,900
Accounts payable	12,900
Y. Min, Capital	18,000
Y. Min, Withdrawals	3,329
Engineering fees earned	36,000
Rent expense	7,540

Required

1. Prepare a trial balance for this business at the end of May.

Check   (1) Trial balance totals, $66,900

Analysis Components

2. Analyze the accounts and their balances and prepare a list that describes each of the seven most likely transactions and their amounts.

3. Prepare a report of cash received and cash paid showing how the seven transactions in part 2 yield the $37,641 ending Cash balance.

(3) Cash paid, $16,359

Business transactions completed by Hannah Venedict during the month of September are as follows.

a. Venedict invested $60,000 cash along with office equipment valued at $25,000 in her startup business named HV Consulting.

b. Purchased land valued at $40,000 and a building valued at $160,000. The purchase is paid with $30,000 cash and a long-term note payable for $170,000.

c. Purchased $2,000 of office supplies on credit.

d. Venedict invested her personal automobile in the business. The automobile has a value of $16,500 and is to be used exclusively in the business.

e. Purchased $5,600 of additional office equipment on credit.

f. Paid $1,800 cash salary to an assistant.

g. Provided services to a client and collected $8,000 cash.

h. Paid $635 cash for this month's utilities.

i. Paid $2,000 cash to settle the account payable created in transaction *c*.

Problem 2-6A
Recording transactions; posting to ledger; preparing a trial balance

C4   A1   P1   P2

j. Purchased $20,300 of new office equipment by paying $20,300 cash.

k. Completed $6,250 of services for a client, who must pay within 30 days.

l. Paid $1,800 cash salary to an assistant.

m. Received $4,000 cash on the receivable created in transaction *k*.

n. Venedict withdrew $2,800 cash for personal use.

Required

1. Prepare general journal entries to record these transactions (use account titles listed in part 2).

2. Open the following ledger accounts—their account numbers are in parentheses (use the balance column format): Cash (101); Accounts Receivable (106); Office Supplies (108); Office Equipment (163); Automobiles (164); Building (170); Land (172); Accounts Payable (201); Notes Payable (250); H. Venedict, Capital (301); H. Venedict, Withdrawals (302); Fees Earned (402); Salaries Expense (601); and Utilities Expense (602). Post the journal entries from part 1 to the ledger accounts and enter the balance after each posting.

3. Prepare a trial balance as of the end of September.

PROBLEM SET B

Problem 2-1B
Preparing and posting journal entries; preparing a trial balance

C4 C5 A1 P1 P2

At the beginning of April, Bernadette Grechus launched a custom computer solutions company called Softworks. The company had the following transactions during April.

a. Bernadette Grechus invested $65,000 cash, office equipment with a value of $5,750, and $30,000 of computer equipment in the company.

b. Purchased land worth $22,000 for an office by paying $5,000 cash and signing a long-term note payable for $17,000.

c. Purchased a portable building with $34,500 cash and moved it onto the land acquired in *b*.

d. Paid $5,000 cash for the premium on a two-year insurance policy.

e. Provided services to a client and immediately collected $4,600 cash.

f. Purchased $4,500 of additional computer equipment by paying $800 cash and signing a long-term note payable for $3,700.

g. Completed $4,250 of services for a client. This amount is to be received within 30 days.

h. Purchased $950 of additional office equipment on credit.

i. Completed client services for $10,200 on credit.

j. Received a bill for rent of a computer testing device that was used on a recently completed job. The $580 rent cost must be paid within 30 days.

k. Collected $5,100 cash from the client described in transaction *i*.

l. Paid $1,800 cash for wages to an assistant.

m. Paid $950 cash to settle the payable created in transaction *h*.

n. Paid $608 cash for minor repairs to the company's computer equipment.

o. Grechus withdrew $6,230 cash for personal use.

p. Paid $1,800 cash for wages to an assistant.

q. Paid $750 cash for advertisements in the local newspaper during April.

Required

1. Prepare general journal entries to record these transactions (use account titles listed in part 2).

2. Open the following ledger accounts—their account numbers are in parentheses (use the balance column format): Cash (101); Accounts Receivable (106); Prepaid Insurance (108); Office Equipment (163); Computer Equipment (164); Building (170); Land (172); Accounts Payable (201); Notes Payable (250); B. Grechus, Capital (301); B. Grechus, Withdrawals (302); Fees Earned (402); Wages Expense (601); Computer Rental Expense (602); Advertising Expense (603); and Repairs Expense (604). Post the journal entries from part 1 to the accounts and enter the balance after each posting.

3. Prepare a trial balance as of the end of April.

Diella Management Services opens for business and completes these transactions in November.

Nov. 1 Cicely Diella, the owner, invested $30,000 cash along with $15,000 of office equipment in the business.
2 Prepaid $4,500 cash for six months' rent for an office. (*Hint:* Debit Prepaid Rent for $4,500.)
4 Made credit purchases of office equipment for $2,500 and of office supplies for $600. Payment is due within 10 days.
8 Completed work for a client and immediately received $3,400 cash.
12 Completed a $10,200 project for a client, who must pay within 30 days.
13 Paid $3,100 cash to settle the payable created on November 4.
19 Paid $1,800 cash for the premium on a 24-month insurance policy.
22 Received $5,200 cash as partial payment for the work completed on November 12.
24 Completed work for another client for $1,750 on credit.
28 Cicely Diella withdrew $5,300 cash for personal use.
29 Purchased $249 of additional office supplies on credit.
30 Paid $831 cash for this month's utility bill.

Problem 2-2B
Preparing and posting journal entries; preparing a trial balance
C4 C5 A1 P1 P2

Required

1. Prepare general journal entries to record these transactions (use account titles listed in part 2).
2. Open the following ledger accounts—their account numbers are in parentheses (use the balance column format): Cash (101); Accounts Receivable (106); Office Supplies (124); Prepaid Insurance (128); Prepaid Rent (131); Office Equipment (163); Accounts Payable (201); C. Diella, Capital (301); C. Diella, Withdrawals (302); Services Revenue (403); and Utilities Expense (690). Post the journal entries from part 1 to the ledger accounts and enter the balance after each posting.
3. Prepare a trial balance as of the end of November.

Check (2) Ending balances: Cash, $23,069; Accounts Receivable, $6,750; Accounts Payable, $249

(3) Total debits, $60,599

Hussein Management Services opens for business and completes these transactions in September.

Sept. 1 Jamal Hussein, the owner, invests $38,000 cash along with office equipment valued at $15,000 in the business.
2 Prepaid $9,000 cash for 12 months' rent for office space. (*Hint:* Debit Prepaid Rent for $9,000.)
4 Made credit purchases for $8,000 in office equipment and $2,400 in office supplies. Payment is due within 10 days.
8 Completed work for a client and immediately received $3,280 cash.
12 Completed a $15,400 project for a client, who must pay within 30 days.
13 Paid $10,400 cash to settle the payable created on September 4.
19 Paid $1,900 cash for the premium on an 18-month insurance policy. (*Hint:* Debit Prepaid Insurance for $1,900.)
22 Received $7,700 cash as partial payment for the work completed on September 12.
24 Completed work for another client for $2,100 on credit.
28 Jamal Hussein withdrew $5,300 cash for personal use.
29 Purchased $550 of additional office supplies on credit.
30 Paid $860 cash for this month's utility bill.

Problem 2-3B
Preparing and posting journal entries; preparing a trial balance
C4 C5 A1 P1 P2

Required

1. Prepare general journal entries to record these transactions (use account titles listed in part 2).
2. Open the following ledger accounts—their account numbers are in parentheses (use the balance column format): Cash (101); Accounts Receivable (106); Office Supplies (124); Prepaid Insurance (128); Prepaid Rent (131); Office Equipment (163); Accounts Payable (201); J. Hussein, Capital (301); J. Hussein, Withdrawals (302); Service Fees Earned (401); and Utilities Expense (690). Post journal entries from part 1 to the ledger accounts and enter the balance after each posting.
3. Prepare a trial balance as of the end of September.

Check (2) Ending balances: Cash, $21,520; Accounts Receivable, $9,800; Accounts Payable, $550

(3) Total debits, $74,330

Problem 2-4B

Computing net income from equity analysis, preparing a balance sheet, and computing the debt ratio

C3   A1   A2   P3

The accounting records of Tama Co. show the following assets and liabilities as of December 31, 2007, and 2008.

	December 31	
	2007	**2008**
Cash	$20,000	$ 5,000
Accounts receivable	35,000	25,000
Office supplies	8,000	13,500
Office equipment	40,000	40,000
Machinery	28,500	28,500
Building	0	250,000
Land	0	50,000
Accounts payable	4,000	12,000
Note payable	0	250,000

Late in December 2008, the business purchased a small office building and land for $300,000. It paid $50,000 cash toward the purchase and a $250,000 note payable was signed for the balance. Tama, the owner, had to invest an additional $15,000 cash to enable it to pay the $50,000 cash. The owner withdraws $250 cash per month for personal use.

Required

1. Prepare balance sheets for the business as of December 31, 2007, and 2008. (*Hint:* You need only report total equity on the balance sheet, and remember that total equity equals the difference between assets and liabilities.)

Check   (2) Net income, $10,500

2. By comparing equity amounts from the balance sheets and using the additional information presented in the problem, prepare a calculation to show how much net income was earned by the business during 2008.

(3) Debt ratio, 63.6%

3. Calculate the December 31, 2008, debt ratio for the business.

Problem 2-5B

Analyzing account balances and reconstructing transactions

C1   C4   A1   P2

Roshaun Gould started a Web consulting firm called Gould Solutions. He began operations and completed seven transactions in April that resulted in the following accounts, which all have normal balances.

Cash	$19,982
Office supplies	760
Prepaid rent	1,800
Office equipment	12,250
Accounts payable	12,250
R. Gould, Capital	15,000
R. Gould, Withdrawals	5,200
Consulting fees earned	20,400
Operating expenses	7,658

Required

Check   (1) Trial balance total, $47,650

1. Prepare a trial balance for this business at the end of April.

Analysis Component

2. Analyze the accounts and their balances and prepare a list that describes each of the seven most likely transactions and their amounts.

(3) Cash paid, $15,418

3. Prepare a report of cash received and cash paid showing how the seven transactions in part 2 yield the $19,982 ending Cash balance.

Nuncio Consulting completed the following transactions during June.

a. Armand Nuncio, the owner, invested $35,000 cash along with office equipment valued at $11,000 in the new business.

b. Purchased land valued at $7,500 and a building valued at $40,000. The purchase is paid with $15,000 cash and a long-term note payable for $32,500.

c. Purchased $500 of office supplies on credit.

d. Nuncio invested his personal automobile in the business. The automobile has a value of $8,000 and is to be used exclusively in the business.

e. Purchased $1,200 of additional office equipment on credit.

f. Paid $1,000 cash salary to an assistant.

g. Provided services to a client and collected $3,200 cash.

h. Paid $540 cash for this month's utilities.

i. Paid $500 cash to settle the payable created in transaction *c*.

j. Purchased $3,400 of new office equipment by paying $3,400 cash.

k. Completed $4,200 of services for a client, who must pay within 30 days.

l. Paid $1,000 cash salary to an assistant.

m. Received $2,200 cash on the receivable created in transaction *k*.

n. Armand Nuncio withdrew $1,100 cash for personal use.

Problem 2-6B
Recording transactions; posting to ledger; preparing a trial balance

C4   A1   P1   P2

Required

1. Prepare general journal entries to record these transactions (use account titles listed in part 2).

2. Open the following ledger accounts—their account numbers are in parentheses (use the balance column format): Cash (101); Accounts Receivable (106); Office Supplies (108); Office Equipment (163); Automobiles (164); Building (170); Land (172); Accounts Payable (201); Notes Payable (250); A. Nuncio, Capital (301); A. Nuncio, Withdrawals (302); Fees Earned (402); Salaries Expense (601); and Utilities Expense (602). Post the journal entries from part 1 to the ledger accounts and enter the balance after each posting.

3. Prepare a trial balance as of the end of June.

Check   (2) Ending balances: Cash, $17,860; Office Equipment, $15,600

(3) Trial balance totals, $95,100

 Problem Set C is available at the book's Website to further reinforce and assess your learning.

PROBLEM SET C

(This serial problem started in Chapter 1 and continues through most of the chapters. If the Chapter 1 segment was not completed, the problem can begin at this point. It is helpful, but not necessary, to use the Working Papers that accompany this book.)

SERIAL PROBLEM

Success Systems

A1   P1   P2

SP 2   On October 1, 2007, Adriana Lopez launched a computer services company called Success Systems, which provides consulting services, computer system installations, and custom program development. Lopez adopts the calendar year for reporting purposes and expects to prepare the company's first set of financial statements on December 31, 2007. The company's initial chart of accounts follows.

Account	No.	Account	No.
Cash	101	A. Lopez, Capital	301
Accounts Receivable	106	A. Lopez, Withdrawals	302
Computer Supplies	126	Computer Services Revenue	403
Prepaid Insurance	128	Wages Expense	623
Prepaid Rent	131	Advertising Expense	655
Office Equipment	163	Mileage Expense	676
Computer Equipment	167	Miscellaneous Expenses	677
Accounts Payable	201	Repairs Expense—Computer	684

Required

1. Prepare journal entries to record each of the following transactions for Success Systems.

Oct. 1 Lopez invested $75,000 cash, a $25,000 computer system, and $10,000 of office equipment in the business.

2 Paid $3,500 cash for four months' rent. (*Hint:* Debit Prepaid Rent for $3,500.)

3 Purchased $1,600 of computer supplies on credit from Corvina Office Products.

5 Paid $2,400 cash for one year's premium on a property and liability insurance policy. (*Hint:* Debit Prepaid Insurance for $2,400.)

6 Billed Easy Leasing $6,200 for services performed in installing a new Web server.

8 Paid $1,600 cash for the computer supplies purchased from Corvina Office Products on October 3.

10 Hired Michelle Jones as a part-time assistant for $150 per day, as needed.

12 Billed Easy Leasing another $1,950 for services performed.

15 Received $6,200 cash from Easy Leasing on its account.

17 Paid $900 cash to repair computer equipment that was damaged when moving it.

20 Paid $1,790 cash for an advertisement in the local newspaper.

22 Received $1,950 cash from Easy Leasing on its account.

28 Billed Clark Company $7,300 for services performed.

31 Paid $1,050 cash for Michelle Jones's wages for seven days' work.

31 Lopez withdrew $4,000 cash for personal use.

Nov. 1 Reimbursed Lopez in cash for business automobile mileage allowance (Lopez logged 1,200 miles at $0.32 per mile).

2 Received $3,600 cash from Edge Corporation for computer services performed.

5 Purchased computer supplies for $1,750 cash from Corvina Office Products.

8 Billed Gomez Co. $6,500 for services performed.

13 Received notification from Alex's Engineering Co. that Success Systems' bid of $7,000 for an upcoming project is accepted.

18 Received $5,000 cash from Clark Company as partial payment of the October 28 bill.

22 Donated $300 cash to the United Way in the company's name.

24 Completed work for Alex's Engineering Co. and sent it a bill for $7,000.

25 Sent another bill to Clark Company for the past-due amount of $2,300.

28 Reimbursed Lopez in cash for business automobile mileage (1,500 miles at $0.32 per mile).

30 Paid $2,100 cash for Michelle Jones's wages for 14 days' work.

30 Lopez withdrew $2,500 cash for personal use.

Check (2) Cash, Nov. 30 bal., $68,996

(3) Trial bal. totals, $142,550

2. Open ledger accounts (in balance column format) and post the journal entries from part 1 to them.

3. Prepare a trial balance as of the end of November.

REPORTING IN ACTION

A1 A2

BTN 2-1 Refer to Best Buy's financial statements in Appendix A for the following questions.

Required

1. What amount of total liabilities does it report for each of the fiscal years ended February 28, 2004, and February 26, 2005?

2. What amount of total assets does it report for each of the fiscal years ended February 28, 2004, and February 26, 2005?

3. Compute its debt ratio for each of the fiscal years ended February 28, 2004, and February 26, 2005.

4. In which fiscal year did it employ more financial leverage (February 28, 2004, or February 26, 2005)? Explain.

Fast Forward

5. Access its financial statements (10-K report) for a fiscal year ending after February 26, 2005, from its Website (BestBuy.com) or the SEC's EDGAR database (www.sec.gov). Recompute its debt ratio for any subsequent year's data and compare it with the February 26, 2005, debt ratio.

BTN 2-2 Key comparative figures ($ thousands) for both **Best Buy** and **Circuit City** follow.

| Key Figures | Best Buy | | Circuit City | |
	Current Year	Prior Year	Current Year	Prior Year
Total liabilities	$ 5,845,000	$5,230,000	$1,701,948	$1,506,565
Total assets	10,294,000	8,652,000	3,789,382	3,730,526

1. What is the debt ratio for Best Buy in the current year and for the prior year?

2. What is the debt ratio for Circuit City in the current year and for the prior year?

3. Which of the two companies has a higher degree of financial leverage? What does this imply?

BTN 2-3 Review the *Decision Ethics* case from the first part of this chapter involving the cashier. The guidance answer suggests that you should not comply with the assistant manager's request.

Required

Propose and evaluate two other courses of action that you might consider, and explain why.

BTN 2-4 Lila Corentine is an aspiring entrepreneur and your friend. She is having difficulty understanding the purposes of financial statements and how they fit together across time.

Required

Write a one-page memorandum to Corentine explaining the purposes of the four financial statements and how they are linked across time.

BTN 2-5 Access EDGAR online (www.SEC.gov) and locate the 2004 fiscal year 10-K report of **Amazon.com** (ticker AMZN) filed on March 11, 2005. Review its financial statements reported for fiscal years ended 2002, 2003, and 2004 to answer the following questions:

Required

1. What are the amounts of its net income or net loss reported for each of these three years?

2. Does Amazon's operations provide cash or use cash for each of these three years?

3. If Amazon has a 2002 net loss, how is it possible that its cash balance at December 31, 2002, shows an increase relative to its balance at January 1, 2002?

BTN 2-6 The expanded accounting equation consists of assets, liabilities, capital, withdrawals, revenues, and expenses. It can be used to reveal insights into changes in a company's financial position.

Required

1. Form *learning teams* of six (or more) members. Each team member must select one of the six components and each team must have at least one expert on each component: (*a*) assets, (*b*) liabilities, (*c*) capital, (*d*) withdrawals, (*e*) revenues, and (*f*) expenses.

2. Form *expert teams* of individuals who selected the same component in part 1. Expert teams are to draft a report that each expert will present to his or her learning team addressing the following:

    a. Identify for its component the (i) increase and decrease side of the account and (ii) normal balance side of the account.

    b. Describe a transaction, with amounts, that increases its component.

c. Using the transaction and amounts in (*b*), verify the equality of the accounting equation and then explain any effects on the income statement and statement of cash flows.

d. Describe a transaction, with amounts, that decreases its component.

e. Using the transaction and amounts in (*d*), verify the equality of the accounting equation and then explain any effects on the income statement and statement of cash flows.

3. Each expert should return to his/her learning team. In rotation, each member presents his/her expert team's report to the learning team. Team discussion is encouraged.

BusinessWeek
ACTIVITY

A2

BTN 2-7 Read the article "After Sarbanes–Oxley, XBRL?" in the February 8, 2005, issue of *BusinessWeek*. (Access the book's Website for a free link.)

Required

1. Briefly explain why investors and analysts would want companies to report their financial information to the SEC with XBRL tags.

2. Why would companies be reluctant to include XBRL tags on the financial information they file with the SEC?

3. Is there an advantage to companies in using XBRL for internal reporting? Explain.

ENTREPRENEURIAL
DECISION

A1   A2   P3

BTN 2-8 Angel Martin is a young entrepreneur who operates Martin Music Services, offering singing lessons and instruction on musical instruments. Martin wishes to expand but needs a $30,000 loan. The bank requests Martin to prepare a balance sheet and key financial ratios. Martin has not kept formal records but is able to provide the following accounts and their amounts as of December 31, 2008:

Cash	$ 3,600	Accounts Receivable . . .	$ 9,600	Prepaid Insurance	$ 1,500
Prepaid Rent	9,400	Store Supplies	6,600	Equipment	50,000
Accounts Payable	2,200	Unearned Lesson Fees . .	15,600	Total Equity*	62,900
Annual net income	40,000				

* The total equity amount reflects all owner investments, withdrawals, revenues, and expenses as of December 31, 2008.

Required

1. Prepare a balance sheet as of December 31, 2008, for Martin Music Services. (You need only report the total equity amount on the balance sheet.)

2. Compute Martin's debt ratio and its return on assets (the latter ratio is defined in Chapter 1). Assume average assets equal its ending balance.

3. Do you think the prospects of a $30,000 bank loan are good? Why or why not?

A1   A2   P3

BTN 2-9 Assume Warren Brown of **Cake Love** plans on expanding his café to accommodate more customers. He is considering financing his expansion in one of two ways: (1) contributing more of his own funds to the business or (2) borrowing the funds from a bank.

Required

Identify the issues that Brown should consider when trying to decide on the method for financing his expansion.

HITTING THE
ROAD

C1

BTN 2-10 Obtain a recent copy of the most prominent newspaper distributed in your area. Research the classified section and prepare a report answering the following questions (attach relevant classified clippings to your report). Alternatively, you may want to search the Web for the required information. One suitable Website is **America's Job Bank** (**www.AJB.org**). For documentation, you should print copies of Websites accessed.

1. Identify the number of listings for accounting positions and the various accounting job titles.

2. Identify the number of listings for other job titles, with examples, that require or prefer accounting knowledge/experience but are not specifically accounting positions.

3. Specify the salary range for the accounting and accounting-related positions if provided.

4. Indicate the job that appeals to you, the reason for its appeal, and its requirements.

BTN 2-11   Dixons (Dixons–Group.com) competes with several companies, including Best Buy and Circuit City. Key financial ratios for the current fiscal year follow.

Key Figure	Dixons	Best Buy	Circuit City
Return on assets	7.3%	9.6%	1.6%
Debt ratio	62.1%	56.8%	44.9%

Required

1. Which company is most profitable according to its return on assets?
2. Which company is most risky according to the debt ratio?
3. Which company deserves increased investment based on a joint analysis of return on assets and the debt ratio? Explain.

ANSWERS TO MULTIPLE CHOICE QUIZ

1. b; debit Utility Expense for $700, and credit Cash for $700.
2. a; debit Cash for $2,500, and credit Unearned Lawn Service Fees for $2,500.
3. c; debit Cash for $250,000, debit Land for $500,000, and credit L. Shue, Capital for $750,000.

4. d
5. e; Debt ratio = $400,000/$1,000,000 = 40%

3

Adjusting Accounts and Preparing Financial Statements

A Look Back

Chapter 2 explained the analysis and recording of transactions. We showed how to apply and interpret company accounts, T-accounts, double-entry accounting, ledgers, postings, and trial balances.

A Look at This Chapter

This chapter explains the timing of reports and the need to adjust accounts. Adjusting accounts is important for recognizing revenues and expenses in the proper period. We describe the adjusted trial balance and how it is used to prepare financial statements.

A Look Ahead

Chapter 4 highlights the completion of the accounting cycle. We explain the important final steps in the accounting process. These include closing procedures, the post-closing trial balance, and reversing entries.

Learning Objectives

CAP

Conceptual

C1 Explain the importance of periodic reporting and the time period principle. (p. 92)

C2 Explain accrual accounting and how it improves financial statements. (p. 93)

C3 Identify the types of adjustments and their purpose. (p. 94)

Analytical

A1 Explain how accounting adjustments link to financial statements. (p. 102)

A2 Compute profit margin and describe its use in analyzing company performance. (p. 105)

Procedural

P1 Prepare and explain adjusting entries. (p. 95)

P2 Explain and prepare an adjusted trial balance. (p. 103)

P3 Prepare financial statements from an adjusted trial balance. (p. 103)

P4 *Appendix 3A*—Explain the alternatives in accounting for prepaids. (p. 109)

"I'm never content with what we've accomplished"
—Nelson Gonzalez (on right; Alex Aguila on left)

Alienware Aims for the Outer Limits

MIAMI—Alex Aguila and Nelson Gonzalez are demanding gamers. Frustrated by the limited power of available PCs, they started **Alienware (alienware.com)** to build computers optimized for game playing. "Everyone told us, 'This is insane,' " recalls Aguila. "We got laughed out of every bank in Miami."

Undaunted, Aguila and Gonzalez scraped together the little cash they had. "Alienware started with $10,000 and a prayer," says Aguila. Building their initial PCs in a garage, the young duo quickly developed a system to account for everything, including cash, inventory, payables, equipment, and sales. They also adopted the unearned revenue model of early PC-makers: First customers pay, and then you build. Thanks to a relentless focus on a neglected niche of hardcore gamers, and positive reviews in gaming magazines, Alienware's sales are soaring.

The unearned revenue model is a blessing for Aguila and Gonzalez. It means no bad debts on customer receivables because cash is received in advance. The model also means little inventory to support because parts are ordered as needed for production. Although the no-inventory model works well for Alienware, Aguila readily admits, "It takes a strong management team to [run the model] effectively."

Aguila and Gonzalez continue to fine-tune their accounting system. They remain focused on measures of sales, income, assets, and growth. That type of attention allows the company to enjoy profitability and measured growth. But, says Gonzalez, "I have a strong suspicion that there are not too many hardcore gamers in our accounting department!"

Today, Aguila and Gonzalez say Alienware is the largest minority-owned U.S. computer maker. But they expect Alienware to continue to push the outer limits. "For me, running this company is like playing a computer game," says Gonzalez. "It feels great when you win but the next day you're back looking for a higher score, a faster time, more points, better magic."

[Sources: *Alienware Website*, January 2006; *Entrepreneur*, March 2005 and November 2003; *Wired*, August 2004; *Ownt.com Website*, February 2003; *Newsweek*, 2005]

Financial statements reflect revenues when earned and expenses when incurred. This is known as *accrual accounting*. Accrual accounting requires several steps. We described many of these steps in Chapter 2. We showed how companies use accounting systems to collect information about *external* transactions and events. We also explained how journals, ledgers, and other tools are useful in preparing financial statements. This chapter describes the accounting process for producing useful information involving *internal* transactions and events. An important part of this process is adjusting the account balances so that financial statements at the end of a reporting period reflect the effects of all transactions. We then explain the important steps in preparing financial statements.

Adjusting Accounts and Preparing Financial Statements

Timing and Reporting	Adjusting Accounts	Preparing Financial Statements
• Accounting period • Accrual versus cash • Recognition of revenues and expenses	• Prepaid expenses • Unearned revenues • Accrued expenses • Accrued revenues • Adjusted trial balance	• Income statement • Statement of owner's equity • Balance sheet

Timing and Reporting

Regular, or periodic, reporting is an important part of the accounting process. This section describes the impact on the accounting process of the point in time or the period of time that a report refers to.

The Accounting Period

C1 Explain the importance of periodic reporting and the time period principle.

"Best Buy announces earnings per share of . . ."

The value of information is often linked to its timeliness. Useful information must reach decision makers frequently and promptly. To provide timely information, accounting systems prepare reports at regular intervals. This results in an accounting process impacted by the time period (or periodicity) principle. The **time period principle** assumes that an organization's activities can be divided into specific time periods such as a month, a three-month quarter, a six-month interval, or a year. Exhibit 3.1 shows various **accounting,**

Exhibit 3.1

Accounting Periods

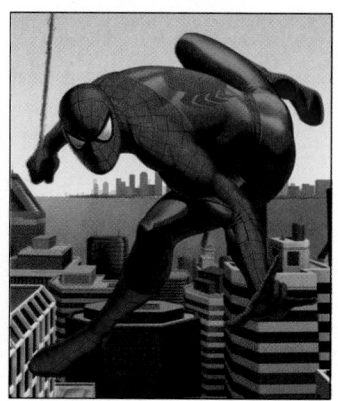

or *reporting,* **periods.** Most organizations use a year as their primary accounting period. Reports covering a one-year period are known as **annual financial statements.** Many organizations also prepare **interim financial statements** covering one, three, or six months of activity.

The annual reporting period is not always a calendar year ending on December 31. An organization can adopt a **fiscal year** consisting of any 12 consecutive months. It is also acceptable to adopt an annual reporting period of 52 weeks. For example, Gap's fiscal year consistently ends the final week of January or the first week of February each year.

Companies with little seasonal variation in sales often choose the calendar year as their fiscal year. For example, the financial statements of Marvel Enterprises (the company that controls characters such as Spider-Man, X-Men, and Shang-Chi) reflect a fiscal year that ends on December 31. Companies experiencing seasonal variations in sales often choose a **natural business year** end, which is when sales activities are at their lowest level for the year. The natural business year for retailers such as Wal-Mart, Target, and Staples usually ends around January 31, after the holiday season.

Accrual Basis versus Cash Basis

After external transactions and events are recorded, several accounts still need adjustments before their balances appear in financial statements. This need arises because internal transactions and events remain unrecorded. **Accrual basis accounting** uses the adjusting process to recognize revenues when earned and expenses when incurred (matched with revenues).

Cash basis accounting recognizes revenues when cash is received and records expenses when cash is paid. This means that cash basis net income for a period is the difference between cash receipts and cash payments. Cash basis accounting is not consistent with generally accepted accounting principles.

It is commonly held that accrual accounting better reflects business performance than information about cash receipts and payments. Accrual accounting also increases the *comparability* of financial statements from one period to another. Yet cash basis accounting is useful for several business decisions—which is the reason companies must report a statement of cash flows.

To see the difference between these two accounting systems, let's consider FastForward's Prepaid Insurance account. FastForward paid $2,400 for 24 months of insurance coverage beginning on December 1, 2007. Accrual accounting requires that $100 of insurance expense be reported on December's income statement. Another $1,200 of expense is reported in year 2008, and the remaining $1,100 is reported as expense in the first 11 months of 2009. Exhibit 3.2 illustrates this allocation of insurance cost across these three years. The accrual basis balance sheet reports any unexpired premium as a Prepaid Insurance asset.

C2 Explain accrual accounting and how it improves financial statements.

Topic Tackler
PLUS
3-1

Point: IBM's revenues from services to customers are recorded when services are performed. Its revenues from product sales are recorded when products are shipped.

Exhibit 3.2

Accrual Basis Accounting for Allocating Prepaid Insurance to Expense

Transaction: Purchase 24 months' insurance beginning December 2007	Insurance Expense 2007				Insurance Expense 2008				Insurance Expense 2009			
	Jan $0	Feb $0	Mar $0	Apr $0	Jan $100	Feb $100	Mar $100	Apr $100	Jan $100	Feb $100	Mar $100	Apr $100
	May $0	June $0	July $0	Aug $0	May $100	June $100	July $100	Aug $100	May $100	June $100	July $100	Aug $100
	Sept $0	Oct $0	Nov $0	Dec $100	Sept $100	Oct $100	Nov $100	Dec $100	Sept $100	Oct $100	Nov $100	Dec $0

A cash basis income statement for December 2007 reports insurance expense of $2,400, as shown in Exhibit 3.3. The cash basis income statements for years 2008 and 2009 report no insurance expense. The cash basis balance sheet never reports an insurance asset because it is immediately expensed. Cash basis income for 2007–2009 fails to match the cost of insurance with the insurance benefits received for those years and months.

Point: Recording revenue early overstates current-period revenue and income; recording it late understates current-period revenue and income.

Recognizing Revenues and Expenses

We use the time period principle to divide a company's activities into specific time periods, but not all activities are complete when financial statements are prepared. Thus, adjustments often are required to get correct account balances.

Exhibit 3.3

Cash Basis Accounting for Allocating Prepaid Insurance to Expense

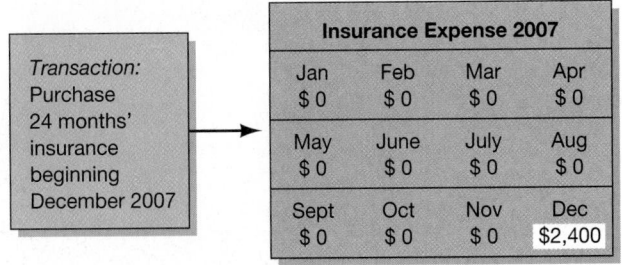

Transaction: Purchase 24 months' insurance beginning December 2007	Insurance Expense 2007			
	Jan $0	Feb $0	Mar $0	Apr $0
	May $0	June $0	July $0	Aug $0
	Sept $0	Oct $0	Nov $0	Dec $2,400

Insurance Expense 2008			
Jan $0	Feb $0	Mar $0	Apr $0
May $0	June $0	July $0	Aug $0
Sept $0	Oct $0	Nov $0	Dec $0

Insurance Expense 2009			
Jan $0	Feb $0	Mar $0	Apr $0
May $0	June $0	July $0	Aug $0
Sept $0	Oct $0	Nov $0	Dec $0

Point: Recording expense early overstates current-period expense and understates current-period income; recording it late understates current-period expense and overstates current-period income.

We rely on two principles in the adjusting process: revenue recognition and matching. Chapter 1 explained that the *revenue recognition principle* requires that revenue be recorded when earned, not before and not after. Most companies earn revenue when they provide services and products to customers. A major goal of the adjusting process is to have revenue recognized (reported) in the time period when it is earned.

The **matching principle** aims to record expenses in the same accounting period as the revenues that are earned as a result of these expenses. This matching of expenses with the revenue benefits is a major part of the adjusting process.

Matching expenses with revenues often requires us to predict certain events. When we use financial statements, we must understand that they require estimates and therefore include measures that are not precise. **Walt Disney**'s annual report explains that its production costs from movies, such as *Pirates of the Caribbean,* are matched to revenues based on a ratio of current revenues from the movie divided by its predicted total revenues.

Quick Check
Answers—p. 112

1. Describe a company's annual reporting period.
2. Why do companies prepare interim financial statements?
3. What two accounting principles most directly drive the adjusting process?
4. Is cash basis accounting consistent with the matching principle? Why or why not?
5. If your company pays a $4,800 premium on April 1, 2007, for two years' insurance coverage, how much insurance expense is reported in 2008 using cash basis accounting?

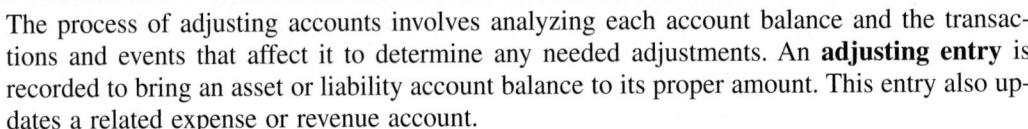

Adjusting Accounts

C3 Identify the types of adjustments and their purpose.

The process of adjusting accounts involves analyzing each account balance and the transactions and events that affect it to determine any needed adjustments. An **adjusting entry** is recorded to bring an asset or liability account balance to its proper amount. This entry also updates a related expense or revenue account.

Framework for Adjustments

Adjustments are necessary for transactions and events that extend over more than one period. It is helpful to group adjustments by the timing of cash receipt or cash payment in relation to the recognition of the related revenues or expenses. Exhibit 3.4 identifies the four types of adjustments.

Topic Tackler

PLUS

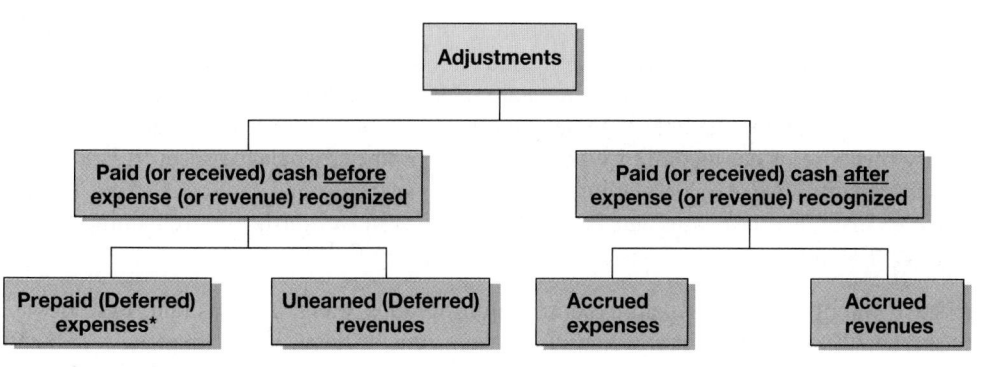

Exhibit 3.4

Types of Adjustments

The left side of this exhibit shows prepaid expenses (including depreciation) and unearned revenues, which reflect transactions when cash is paid or received *before* a related expense or revenue is recognized. They are also called *deferrals* because the recognition of an expense (or revenue) is *deferred* until after the related cash is paid (or received). The right side of this exhibit shows accrued expenses and accrued revenues, which reflect transactions when cash is paid or received *after* a related expense or revenue is recognized. Adjusting entries are necessary for each of these so that revenues, expenses, assets, and liabilities are correctly reported. It is helpful to remember that each adjusting entry affects one or more income statement accounts *and* one or more balance sheet accounts (but not the Cash account).

Point: Adjusting is a 3-step process: (1) Determine current account balance, (2) Determine what current account balance should be, and (3) Record entry to get from step 1 to step 2.

Prepaid (Deferred) Expenses

Prepaid expenses refer to items *paid for* in advance of receiving their benefits. Prepaid expenses are assets. When these assets are used, their costs become expenses. Adjusting entries for prepaids increase expenses and decrease assets as shown in the T-accounts of Exhibit 3.5. Such adjustments reflect transactions and events that use up prepaid expenses (including passage of time). To illustrate the accounting for prepaid expenses, this section focuses on prepaid insurance, supplies, and depreciation.

P1 Prepare and explain adjusting entries.

Exhibit 3.5

Adjusting for Prepaid Expenses

Prepaid Insurance   We illustrate prepaid insurance using FastForward's payment of $2,400 for 24 months of insurance benefits beginning on December 1, 2007. With the passage of time, the benefits of the insurance gradually expire and a portion of the Prepaid Insurance asset becomes expense. For instance, one month's insurance coverage expires by December 31, 2007. This expense is $100, or 1/24 of $2,400. The adjusting entry to record this expense and reduce the asset, along with T-account postings, follows.

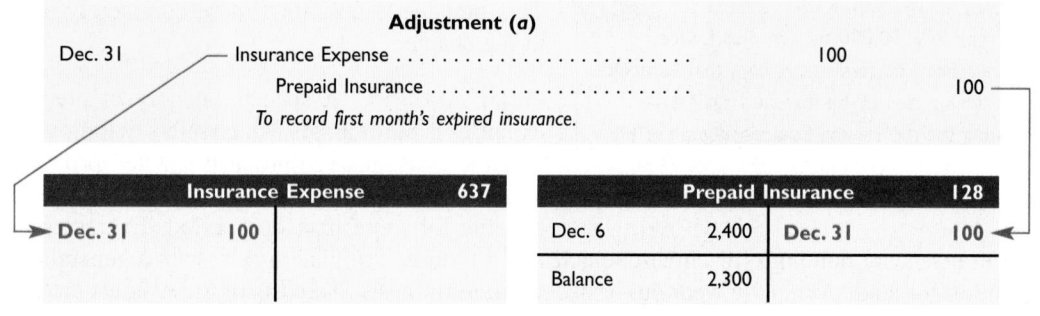

Assets = Liabilities + Equity
−100   −100

Point: Many companies record adjusting entries only at the end of each year because of the time and cost necessary.

Point: Source documents provide information for most daily transactions, and in many businesses the recordkeepers record them. Adjustments require more knowledge and are usually handled by senior accounting professionals.

After adjusting and posting, the $100 balance in Insurance Expense and the $2,300 balance in Prepaid Insurance are ready for reporting in financial statements. *Not* making the adjustment on or before December 31 would (1) understate expenses by $100 and overstate net income by $100 for the December income statement and (2) overstate both prepaid insurance (assets) and equity (because of net income) by $100 in the December 31 balance sheet. It is also evident from Exhibit 3.2 that 2008's adjustments must transfer a total of $1,200 from Prepaid Insurance to Insurance Expense, and 2009's adjustments must transfer the remaining $1,100 to Insurance Expense.

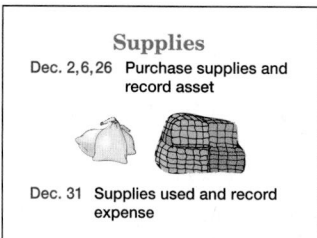

Supplies Supplies

Dec. 2, 6, 26 Purchase supplies and record asset

Dec. 31 Supplies used and record expense

Supplies Supplies are a prepaid expense requiring adjustment. To illustrate, FastForward purchased $9,720 of supplies in December and used some of them. When financial statements are prepared at December 31, the cost of supplies used during December must be recognized. When FastForward computes (takes a physical count of) its remaining unused supplies at December 31, it finds $8,670 of supplies remaining of the $9,720 total supplies. The $1,050 difference between these two amounts is December's supplies expense. The adjusting entry to record this expense and reduce the Supplies asset account, along with T-account postings, follows:

Assets = Liabilities + Equity
−1,050   −1,050

Adjustment (b)

Dec. 31	Supplies Expense	1,050	
	Supplies		1,050
	To record supplies used.		

Supplies Expense		652
Dec. 31	**1,050**	

Supplies			126
Dec. 2	2,500	**Dec. 31**	**1,050**
6	7,100		
26	120		
Balance	8,670		

The balance of the Supplies account is $8,670 after posting—equaling the cost of the remaining supplies. *Not* making the adjustment on or before December 31 would (1) understate expenses by $1,050 and overstate net income by $1,050 for the December income statement and (2) overstate both supplies and equity (because of net income) by $1,050 in the December 31 balance sheet.

Point: An alternative method to record prepaids is to initially debit expense for the total amount. Appendix 3A discusses this alternative. The adjusted financial statement information is identical under either method.

Other Prepaid Expenses Other prepaid expenses, such as Prepaid Rent, are accounted for exactly as Insurance and Supplies are. We should also note that some prepaid expenses are both paid for and fully used up within a single accounting period. One example is when a company pays monthly rent on the first day of each month. This payment creates a prepaid expense on the first day of each month that fully expires by the end of the month. In these special cases, we can record the cash paid with a debit to an expense account instead of an asset account. This practice is described more completely later in the chapter.

Decision Maker   Answer—p. 111

Investor A small publishing company signs a well-known athlete to write a book. The company pays the athlete $500,000 to sign plus future book royalties. A note to the company's financial statements says that "prepaid expenses include $500,000 in author signing fees to be matched against future expected sales." Is this accounting for the signing bonus acceptable? How does it affect your analysis?

Depreciation A special category of prepaid expenses is **plant assets,** which refers to long-term tangible assets used to produce and sell products and services. Plant assets are expected to provide benefits for more than one period. Examples of plant assets are buildings, machines, vehicles, and fixtures. All plant assets, with a general exception for land, eventually wear out or decline in usefulness. The costs of these assets are deferred but are gradually reported as expenses in the income statement over the assets' useful lives (benefit periods). **Depreciation** is the process of allocating the costs of these assets over their expected useful lives. Depreciation expense is recorded with an adjusting entry similar to that for other prepaid expenses.

To illustrate, recall that FastForward purchased equipment for $26,000 in early December to use in earning revenue. This equipment's cost must be depreciated. The equipment is expected to have a useful life (benefit period) of four years and to be worth about $8,000 at the end of four years. This means the *net* cost of this equipment over its useful life is $18,000 ($26,000 − $8,000). We can use any of several methods to allocate this $18,000 net cost to expense. FastForward uses a method called **straight-line depreciation,** which allocates equal amounts of an asset's net cost to depreciation during its useful life. Dividing the $18,000 net cost by the 48 months in the asset's useful life gives a monthly cost of $375 ($18,000/48). The adjusting entry to record monthly depreciation expense, along with T-account postings, follows:

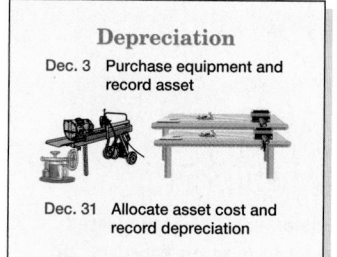

Depreciation

Dec. 3 Purchase equipment and record asset

Dec. 31 Allocate asset cost and record depreciation

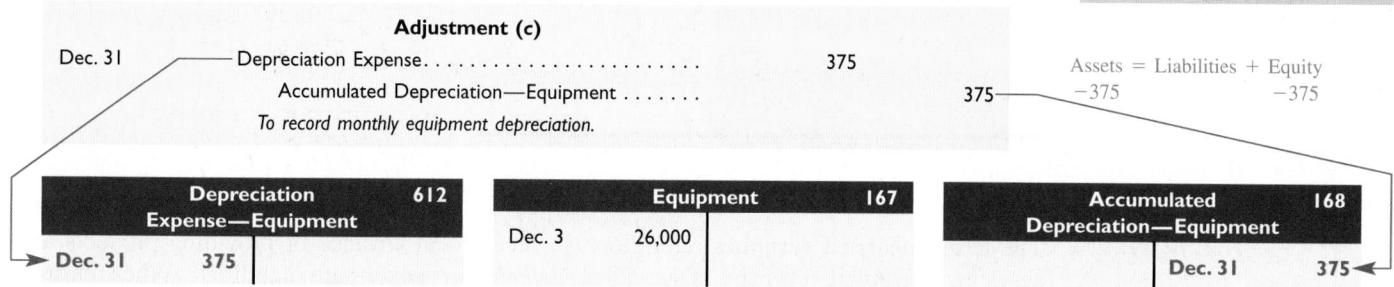

Adjustment (c)

Dec. 31   Depreciation Expense........................   375

Accumulated Depreciation—Equipment.......   375

To record monthly equipment depreciation.

Assets = Liabilities + Equity
−375   −375

Depreciation Expense—Equipment	612
Dec. 31 375	

Equipment	167
Dec. 3 26,000	

Accumulated Depreciation—Equipment	168
Dec. 31 375	

After posting the adjustment, the Equipment account ($26,000) less its Accumulated Depreciation ($375) account equals the $25,625 net cost of the 47 remaining months in the benefit period. The $375 balance in the Depreciation Expense account is reported in the December income statement. *Not* making the adjustment at December 31 would (1) understate expenses by $375 and overstate net income by $375 for the December income statement and (2) overstate both assets and equity (because of income) by $375 in the December 31 balance sheet.

Accumulated depreciation is kept in a separate contra account. A **contra account** is an account linked with another account, it has an opposite normal balance, and it is reported as a subtraction from that other account's balance. For instance, FastForward's contra account of Accumulated Depreciation—Equipment is subtracted from the Equipment account in the balance sheet (see Exhibit 3.7).

A contra account allows balance sheet readers to know both the full costs of assets and the total amount of depreciation. By knowing both these amounts, decision makers can better assess a company's capacity and its need to replace assets. For example, FastForward's balance sheet shows both the $26,000 original cost of equipment and the $375 balance in the accumulated depreciation contra account. This information reveals that the equipment is close to new. If FastForward reports equipment only at its net amount of $25,625, users cannot assess the equipment's age or its need for replacement. The title of the contra account, *Accumulated Depreciation,* indicates that this account includes total depreciation expense for all prior periods for which the asset was used. To illustrate, the Equipment and the Accumulated Depreciation accounts appear as in Exhibit 3.6 on February 28, 2008, after three months of adjusting entries.

Decision Maker   Answer—p. 112

Entrepreneur You are preparing an offer to purchase a family-run restaurant. The depreciation schedule for the restaurant's building and equipment shows costs of $175,000 and accumulated depreciation of $155,000. This leaves a net for building and equipment of $20,000. Is this information useful in helping you decide on a purchase offer?

The $1,125 balance in the accumulated depreciation account is subtracted from its related $26,000 asset cost. The difference ($24,875) between these two balances is the cost of the asset that has not yet been depreciated. This difference is called the **book value,** or

Exhibit 3.6

Accounts after Three Months of Depreciation Adjustments

Equipment		167
Dec. 3	26,000	

Accumulated Depreciation—Equipment		168
	Dec. 31	375
	Jan. 31	375
	Feb. 28	375
	Balance	1,125

net amount, which equals the asset's costs less its accumulated depreciation. These account balances are reported in the assets section of the February 28 balance sheet in Exhibit 3.7.

Exhibit 3.7

Equipment and Accumulated Depreciation on February 28 Balance Sheet

Assets		
Cash		$ ___
⋮		
Equipment	$26,000	
Less accumulated depreciation	1,125	24,875
Total Assets		$ ___

> Commonly titled *Equipment, net*

Unearned (Deferred) Revenues

The term **unearned revenues** refers to cash received in advance of providing products and services. Unearned revenues, also called *deferred revenues,* are liabilities. When cash is accepted, an obligation to provide products or services is accepted. As products or services are provided, the unearned revenues become *earned* revenues. Adjusting entries for unearned revenues involve increasing revenues and decreasing unearned revenues, as shown in Exhibit 3.8.

Exhibit 3.8

Adjusting for Unearned Revenues

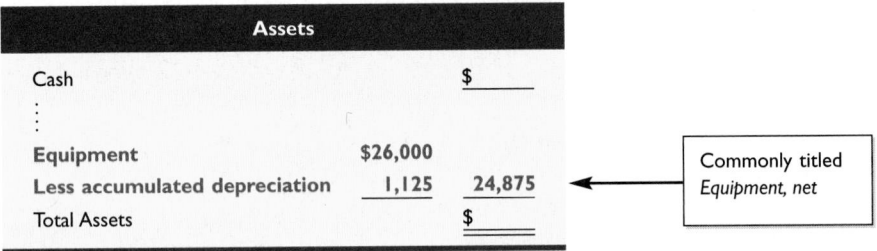

Point: To *defer* is to postpone. We postpone reporting amounts received as revenues until they are earned.

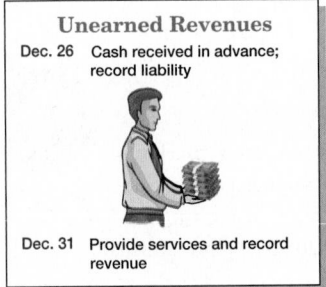

Unearned Revenues

Dec. 26   Cash received in advance; record liability

Dec. 31   Provide services and record revenue

An example of unearned revenues is from **The New York Times Company**, which reports unexpired (unearned) subscriptions of nearly $80 million: "Proceeds from . . . subscriptions are deferred at the time of sale and are recognized in earnings on a pro rata basis over the terms of the subscriptions." Unearned revenues are nearly 10% of the current liabilities for the Times. Another example comes from the **Boston Celtics**. When the Celtics receive cash from advance ticket sales and broadcast fees, they record it in an unearned revenue account called *Deferred Game Revenues.* The Celtics recognize this unearned revenue with adjusting entries on a game-by-game basis. Since the NBA regular season begins in October and ends in April, revenue recognition is mainly limited to this period. For a recent season, the Celtics' quarterly revenues were $0 million for July–September; $34 million for October–December; $48 million for January–March; and $17 million for April–June.

FastForward has unearned revenues. It agreed on December 26 to provide consulting services to a client for a fixed fee of $3,000 for 60 days. On that same day, this client paid the 60-day fee in advance, covering the period December 27 to February 24. The entry to record the cash received in advance is

Assets = Liabilities + Equity
+3,000   +3,000

Dec. 26	Cash	3,000	
	Unearned Consulting Revenue		3,000
	Received advance payment for services over the next 60 days.		

This advance payment increases cash and creates an obligation to do consulting work over the next 60 days. As time passes, FastForward will earn this payment through consulting. By December 31, it has provided five days' service and earned 5/60 of the $3,000 unearned revenue. This amounts to $250 ($3,000 × 5/60). The *revenue recognition principle* implies that $250 of unearned revenue must be reported as revenue on the December income statement. The adjusting entry to reduce the liability account and recognize earned revenue, along with T-account postings, follows.

Adjustment (d)

Dec. 31	Unearned Consulting Revenue.	250
	Consulting Revenue	250
	To record earned revenue that was received in advance ($3,000 × 5/60).	

Assets = Liabilities + Equity
          −250   +250

Unearned Consulting Revenue			236
Dec. 31	250	Dec. 26	3,000
		Balance	2,750

Consulting Revenue			403
		Dec. 5	4,200
		12	1,600
		31	250
		Balance	6,050

The adjusting entry transfers $250 from unearned revenue (a liability account) to a revenue account. *Not* making the adjustment (1) understates revenue and net income by $250 in the December income statement and (2) overstates unearned revenue and understates equity by $250 on the December 31 balance sheet.

Accounting for unearned revenues is crucial to many companies. For example, the **National Retail Federation** reports that gift card sales, which are unearned revenues for sellers, are approaching $20 billion annually. Gift cards are now the top-selling holiday gift.

Accrued Expenses

Accrued expenses refer to costs that are incurred in a period but are both unpaid and unrecorded. Accrued expenses must be reported on the income statement of the period when incurred. Adjusting entries for recording accrued expenses involves increasing expenses and increasing liabilities as shown in Exhibit 3.9. This adjustment recognizes expenses incurred in a period but not yet paid. Common examples of accrued expenses are salaries, interest, rent, and taxes. We use salaries and interest to show how to adjust accounts for accrued expenses.

Exhibit 3.9

Adjusting for Accrued Expenses

Point: Accrued expenses are also called *accrued liabilities.*

Accrued Salaries Expense   FastForward's employee earns $70 per day, or $350 for a five-day workweek beginning on Monday and ending on Friday. This employee is paid every two weeks on Friday. On December 12 and 26, the wages are paid, recorded in the journal, and posted to the ledger. The calendar in Exhibit 3.10 shows three working days after the December 26 payday (29, 30, and 31). This means the employee has earned three days' salary by the close of business on Wednesday, December 31, yet this salary cost is not paid or recorded.

Point: Instead assume: (1) the last payday for the year is Dec. 19, (2) the next payday is Jan. 2, and (3) Dec. 25 is a paid holiday. Record the Dec. 31 adjusting entry. *Answer:* We must accrue pay for 8 working days (8 × $70):
Salaries Expense . . . 560
  Salaries Payable 560

Exhibit 3.10

Salary Accrual and Paydays

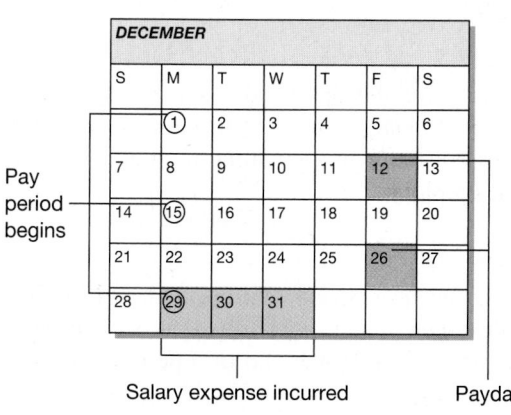

The financial statements would be incomplete if FastForward fails to report the added expense and liability to the employee for unpaid salary from December 29–31. The adjusting entry to account for accrued salaries, along with T-account postings, follows.

Assets = Liabilities + Equity
+210   −210

Adjustment (e)

Dec. 31	Salaries Expense.............................	210	
	Salaries Payable..........................		210
	To record three days' accrued salary (3 × $70).		

Salaries Expense		**622**
Dec. 12	700	
26	700	
31	210	
Balance	1,610	

Salaries Payable		**209**
	Dec. 31	210

Salaries expense of $1,610 is reported on the December income statement and $210 of salaries payable (liability) is reported in the balance sheet. *Not* making the adjustment (1) understates salaries expense and overstates net income by $210 in the December income statement and (2) understates salaries payable (liabilities) and overstates equity by $210 on the December 31 balance sheet.

Accrued Interest Expense Companies commonly have accrued interest expense on notes payable and other long-term liabilities at the end of a period. Interest expense is incurred with the passage of time. Unless interest is paid on the last day of an accounting period, we need to adjust for interest expense incurred but not yet paid. This means we must accrue interest cost from the most recent payment date up to the end of the period. The formula for computing accrued interest is:

Principal amount owed × Annual interest rate × Fraction of year since last payment date.

To illustrate, if a company has a $6,000 loan from a bank at 6% annual interest, then 30 days' accrued interest expense is $30—computed as $6,000 × 0.06 × 30/360. The adjusting entry would be to debit Interest Expense for $30 and credit Interest Payable for $30.

Future Payment of Accrued Expenses Adjusting entries for accrued expenses foretell cash transactions in future periods. Specifically, accrued expenses at the end of one accounting period result in *cash payment* in a *future* period(s). To illustrate, recall that FastForward recorded accrued salaries of $210. On January 9, the first payday of the next period, the following entry settles the accrued liability (salaries payable) and records salaries expense for seven days of work in January.

Assets = Liabilities + Equity
−700   −210   −490

Jan. 9	Salaries Payable (3 days at $70 per day)...........	210	
	Salaries Expense (7 days at $70 per day)	490	
	Cash		700
	Paid two weeks' salary including three days accrued in December.		

The $210 debit reflects the payment of the liability for the three days' salary accrued on December 31. The $490 debit records the salary for January's first seven working days (including the New Year's Day holiday) as an expense of the new accounting period. The $700 credit records the total amount of cash paid to the employee.

Accrued Revenues

The term **accrued revenues** refers to revenues earned in a period that are both unrecorded and not yet received in cash (or other assets). An example is a technician who bills customers only when the job is done. If one-third of a job is complete by the end of a period, then the technician must record one-third of the expected billing as revenue in that period—even though there is no billing or collection. The adjusting entries for accrued revenues increase assets and increase revenues as shown in Exhibit 3.11. Accrued revenues commonly arise from services, products, interest, and rent. We use service fees and interest to show how to adjust for accrued revenues.

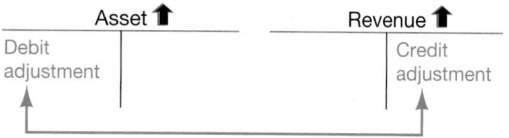

Exhibit 3.11

Adjusting for Accrued Revenues

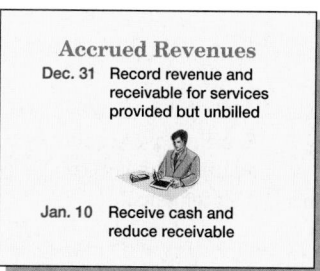

Accrued Revenues

Dec. 31 Record revenue and receivable for services provided but unbilled

Jan. 10 Receive cash and reduce receivable

Accrued Services Revenue Accrued revenues are not recorded until adjusting entries are made at the end of the accounting period. These accrued revenues are earned but unrecorded because either the buyer has not yet paid for them or the seller has not yet billed the buyer. FastForward provides an example. In the second week of December, it agreed to provide 30 days of consulting services to a local sports club for a fixed fee of $2,700. The terms of the initial agreement call for FastForward to provide services from December 12, 2007, through January 10, 2008, or 30 days of service. The club agrees to pay FastForward $2,700 on January 10, 2008, when the service period is complete. At December 31, 2007, 20 days of services have already been provided. Since the contracted services are not yet entirely provided, FastForward has neither billed the club nor recorded the services already provided. Still, FastForward has earned two-thirds of the 30-day fee, or $1,800 ($2,700 × 20/30). The *revenue recognition principle* implies that it must report the $1,800 on the December income statement. The balance sheet also must report that the club owes FastForward $1,800. The year-end adjusting entry to account for accrued services revenue is

	Adjustment (f)		
Dec. 31	Accounts Receivable.	1,800	
	Consulting Revenue.		1,800
	To record 20 days' accrued revenue.		

Assets = Liabilities + Equity
+1,800   +1,800

Accounts Receivable			**106**
Dec. 12	1,900	Dec. 22	1,900
31	1,800		
Balance	1,800		

Consulting Revenue		**403**
	Dec. 5	4,200
	12	1,600
	31	250
	31	1,800
	Balance	7,850

Accounts receivable are reported on the balance sheet at $1,800, and the $7,850 of consulting revenue is reported on the income statement. *Not* making the adjustment would understate (1) both consulting revenue and net income by $1,800 in the December income statement and (2) both accounts receivable (assets) and equity by $1,800 on the December 31 balance sheet.

Example: What is the adjusting entry if the 30-day consulting period began on December 22? *Answer:* One-third of the fee is earned:
Accounts Receivable . . . 900
    Consulting Revenue . . . 900

Accrued Interest Revenue In addition to the accrued interest expense we described earlier, interest can yield an accrued revenue when a debtor owes money (or other assets) to a company. If a company is holding notes or accounts receivable that produce interest revenue, we must adjust the accounts to record any earned and yet uncollected interest revenue. The adjusting entry is similar to the one for accruing services revenue. Specifically, we debit Interest Receivable (asset) and credit Interest Revenue.

Decision Maker

Answer—p. 112

Loan Officer The owner of an electronics store applies for a business loan. The store's financial statements reveal large increases in current-year revenues and income. Analysis shows that these increases are due to a promotion that let consumers buy now and pay nothing until January 1 of next year. The store recorded these sales as accrued revenue. Does your analysis raise any concerns?

Future Receipt of Accrued Revenues Accrued revenues at the end of one accounting period result in *cash receipts* in a *future* period(s). To illustrate, recall that FastForward made an adjusting entry for $1,800 to record 20 days' accrued revenue earned from its consulting contract. When FastForward receives $2,700 cash on January 10 for the entire contract amount, it makes the following entry to remove the accrued asset (accounts receivable) and recognize the revenue earned in January. The $2,700 debit reflects the cash received. The $1,800 credit reflects the removal of the receivable, and the $900 credit records the revenue earned in January.

Assets = Liabilities + Equity
+2,700   +900
−1,800

Jan. 10	Cash	2,700	
	Accounts Receivable (20 days at $90 per day)		1,800
	Consulting Revenue (10 days at $90 per day)		900
	Received cash for the accrued asset and recorded *earned consulting revenue for January.*		

Links to Financial Statements

A1 Explain how accounting adjustments link to financial statements.

The process of adjusting accounts is intended to bring an asset or liability account balance to its correct amount. It also updates a related expense or revenue account. These adjustments are necessary for transactions and events that extend over more than one period. (Adjusting entries are posted like any other entry.)

Exhibit 3.12 summarizes the four types of transactions requiring adjustment. Understanding this exhibit is important to understanding the adjusting process and its importance to financial statements. Remember that each adjusting entry affects one or more income statement accounts *and* one or more balance sheet accounts (but not cash).

Exhibit 3.12

Summary of Adjustments and Financial Statement Links

	BEFORE Adjusting		
Category	**Balance Sheet**	**Income Statement**	**Adjusting Entry**
Prepaid expenses†	Asset overstated	Expense understated	**Dr. Expense**
	Equity overstated		**Cr. Asset***
Unearned revenues†	Liability overstated	Revenue understated	**Dr. Liability**
	Equity understated		**Cr. Revenue**
Accrued expenses	Liability understated	Expense understated	**Dr. Expense**
	Equity overstated		**Cr. Liability**
Accrued revenues	Asset understated	Revenue understated	**Dr. Asset**
	Equity understated		**Cr. Revenue**

* For depreciation, the credit is to Accumulated Depreciation (contra asset).

† Exhibit assumes that Prepaid Expenses are initially recorded as assets and that Unearned Revenues are initially recorded as liabilities.

Information about some adjustments is not always available until several days or even weeks after the period-end. This means that some adjusting and closing entries are recorded later than, but dated as of, the last day of the period. One example is a company that receives a utility bill on January 10 for costs incurred for the month of December. When it receives the bill, the company records the expense and the payable as of December 31. Other examples include long-distance phone usage and costs of many Web billings. The December income statement reflects these additional expenses incurred, and the December 31 balance sheet includes these payables, although the amounts were not actually known on December 31.

Decision Ethics   Answer—p. 112

Financial Officer   At year-end, the president instructs you, the financial officer, not to record accrued expenses until next year because they will not be paid until then. The president also directs you to record in current-year sales a recent purchase order from a customer that requires merchandise to be delivered two weeks after the year-end. Your company would report a net income instead of a net loss if you carry out these instructions. What do you do?

Quick Check   Answers—p. 112

6. If an adjusting entry for accrued revenues of $200 at year-end is omitted, what is this error's effect on the year-end income statement and balance sheet?

7. What is a contra account? Explain its purpose.

8. What is an accrued expense? Give an example.

9. Describe how an unearned revenue arises. Give an example.

Adjusted Trial Balance

An **unadjusted trial balance** is a list of accounts and balances prepared *before* adjustments are recorded. An **adjusted trial balance** is a list of accounts and balances prepared *after* adjusting entries have been recorded and posted to the ledger.

Exhibit 3.13 shows both the unadjusted and the adjusted trial balances for FastForward at December 31, 2007. The order of accounts in the trial balance is usually set up to match the order in the chart of accounts. Several new accounts arise from the adjusting entries. Each adjustment (see middle columns) is identified by a letter in parentheses that links it to an adjusting entry explained earlier. Each amount in the Adjusted Trial Balance columns is computed by taking that account's amount from the Unadjusted Trial Balance columns and adding or subtracting any adjustment(s). To illustrate, Supplies has a $9,720 Dr. balance in the unadjusted columns. Subtracting the $1,050 Cr. amount shown in the adjustments columns yields an adjusted $8,670 Dr. balance for Supplies. An account can have more than one adjustment, such as for Consulting Revenue. Also, some accounts might not require adjustment for this period, such as Accounts Payable.

P2 Explain and prepare an adjusted trial balance.

Exhibit 3.13

Unadjusted and Adjusted Trial Balances

FASTFORWARD
Trial Balances
December 31, 2007

Acct. No.	Account Title	Unadjusted Trial Balance Dr.	Unadjusted Trial Balance Cr.	Adjustments Dr.	Adjustments Cr.	Adjusted Trial Balance Dr.	Adjusted Trial Balance Cr.
101	Cash	$ 4,350				$ 4,350	
106	Accounts receivable	0		(f) $1,800		1,800	
126	Supplies	9,720			(b) $1,050	8,670	
128	Prepaid insurance	2,400			(a) 100	2,300	
167	Equipment	26,000				26,000	
168	Accumulated depreciation—Equip.		$ 0		(c) 375		$ 375
201	Accounts payable		6,200				6,200
209	Salaries payable		0		(e) 210		210
236	Unearned consulting revenue		3,000	(d) 250			2,750
301	C. Taylor, Capital		30,000				30,000
302	C. Taylor, Withdrawals	200				200	
403	Consulting revenue		5,800		(d) 250		7,850
					(f) 1,800		
406	Rental revenue		300				300
612	Depreciation expense—Equip.	0		(c) 375		375	
622	Salaries expense	1,400		(e) 210		1,610	
637	Insurance expense	0		(a) 100		100	
640	Rent expense	1,000				1,000	
652	Supplies expense	0		(b) 1,050		1,050	
690	Utilities expense	230				230	
	Totals	$45,300	$45,300	$3,785	$3,785	$47,685	$47,685

Preparing Financial Statements

We can prepare financial statements directly from information in the *adjusted* trial balance. An adjusted trial balance (see the right-most columns in Exhibit 3.13) includes all accounts and balances appearing in financial statements, and is easier to work from than the entire ledger when preparing financial statements.

Exhibit 3.14 shows how revenue and expense balances are transferred from the adjusted trial balance to the income statement (red lines). The net income and the withdrawals amount are then used to prepare the statement of owner's equity (black lines). Asset and liability balances

P3 Prepare financial statements from an adjusted trial balance.

Exhibit 3.14

Preparing Financial Statements (Adjusted Trial Balance from Exhibit 3.13)

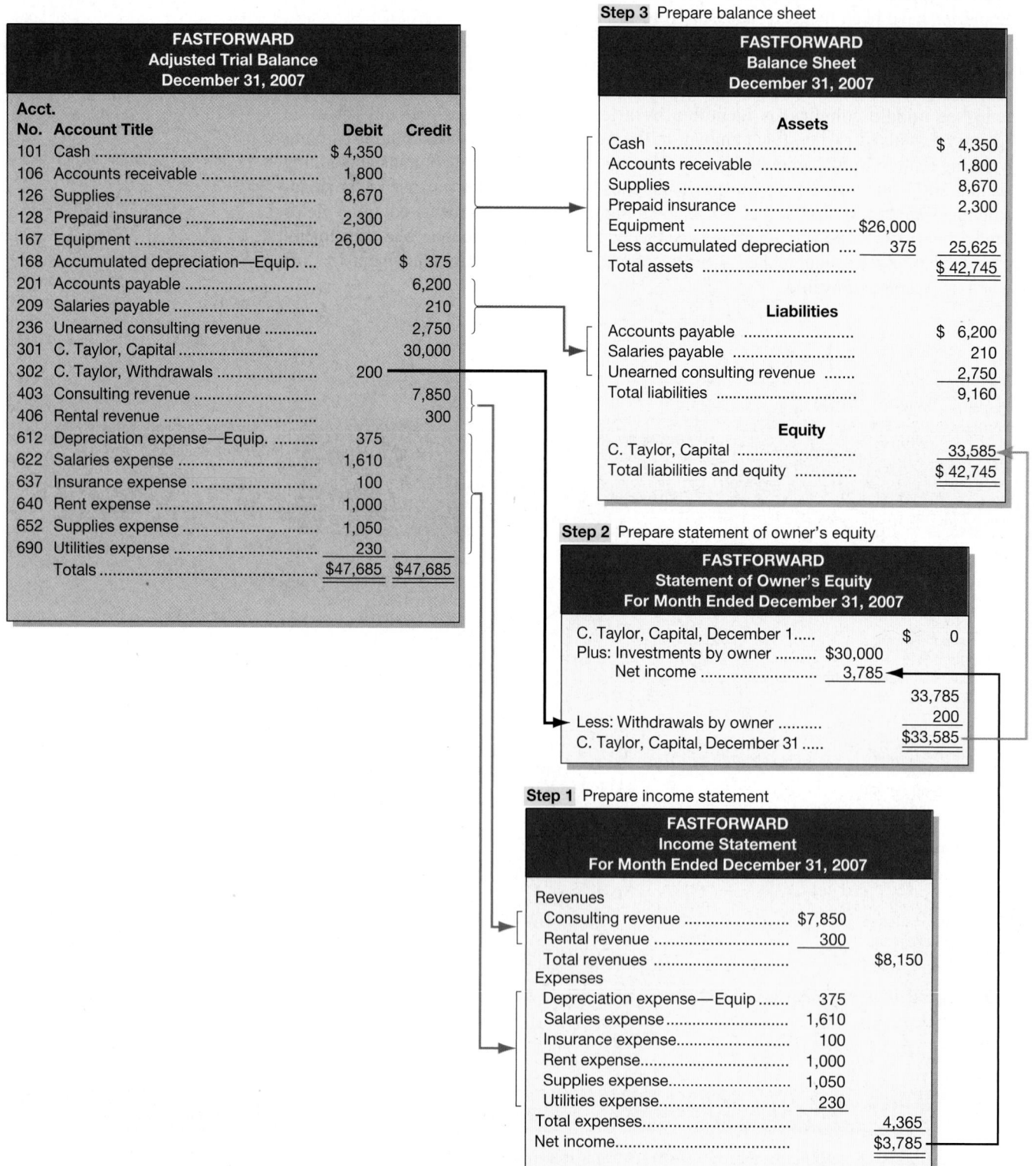

FASTFORWARD
Adjusted Trial Balance
December 31, 2007

Acct. No.	Account Title	Debit	Credit
101	Cash	$ 4,350	
106	Accounts receivable	1,800	
126	Supplies	8,670	
128	Prepaid insurance	2,300	
167	Equipment	26,000	
168	Accumulated depreciation—Equip.		$ 375
201	Accounts payable		6,200
209	Salaries payable		210
236	Unearned consulting revenue		2,750
301	C. Taylor, Capital		30,000
302	C. Taylor, Withdrawals	200	
403	Consulting revenue		7,850
406	Rental revenue		300
612	Depreciation expense—Equip.	375	
622	Salaries expense	1,610	
637	Insurance expense	100	
640	Rent expense	1,000	
652	Supplies expense	1,050	
690	Utilities expense	230	
	Totals	$47,685	$47,685

Step 3 Prepare balance sheet

FASTFORWARD
Balance Sheet
December 31, 2007

Assets

Cash		$ 4,350
Accounts receivable		1,800
Supplies		8,670
Prepaid insurance		2,300
Equipment	$26,000	
Less accumulated depreciation	375	25,625
Total assets		$ 42,745

Liabilities

Accounts payable	$ 6,200
Salaries payable	210
Unearned consulting revenue	2,750
Total liabilities	9,160

Equity

C. Taylor, Capital	33,585
Total liabilities and equity	$ 42,745

Step 2 Prepare statement of owner's equity

FASTFORWARD
Statement of Owner's Equity
For Month Ended December 31, 2007

C. Taylor, Capital, December 1		$ 0
Plus: Investments by owner	$30,000	
Net income	3,785	
		33,785
Less: Withdrawals by owner		200
C. Taylor, Capital, December 31		$33,585

Step 1 Prepare income statement

FASTFORWARD
Income Statement
For Month Ended December 31, 2007

Revenues		
Consulting revenue	$7,850	
Rental revenue	300	
Total revenues		$8,150
Expenses		
Depreciation expense—Equip	375	
Salaries expense	1,610	
Insurance expense	100	
Rent expense	1,000	
Supplies expense	1,050	
Utilities expense	230	
Total expenses		4,365
Net income		$3,785

on the adjusted trial balance are then transferred to the balance sheet (blue lines). The ending capital is determined on the statement of owner's equity and transferred to the balance sheet (green lines).

We usually prepare financial statements in the following order: income statement, statement of owner's equity, and balance sheet. This order makes sense since the balance sheet uses information from the statement of owner's equity, which in turn uses information from the income statement. The statement of cash flows is usually the final statement prepared.

Point: Sarbanes-Oxley Act requires that financial statements filed with the SEC be certified by the CEO and CFO, including a declaration that the statements fairly present the issuer's operations and financial condition. Violators can receive a $5,000,000 fine and/or up to 20 years imprisonment.

Quick Check

Answers—p. 112

10. Music-Mart records $1,000 of accrued salaries on December 31. Five days later, on January 5 (the next payday), salaries of $7,000 are paid. What is the January 5 entry?

11. Jordan Air has the following information in its unadjusted and adjusted trial balances.

	Unadjusted		Adjusted	
	Debit	Credit	Debit	Credit
Prepaid insurance	$6,200		$5,900	
Salaries payable		$ 0		$1,400

What are the adjusting entries that Jordan Air likely recorded?

12. What accounts are taken from the adjusted trial balance to prepare an income statement?

13. In preparing financial statements from an adjusted trial balance, what statement is usually prepared second?

Profit Margin

Decision Analysis

A useful measure of a company's operating results is the ratio of its net income to net sales. This ratio is called **profit margin,** or *return on sales,* and is computed as in Exhibit 3.15.

A2 Compute profit margin and describe its use in analyzing company performance.

$$\text{Profit margin} = \frac{\text{Net income}}{\text{Net sales}}$$

Exhibit 3.15

Profit Margin

This ratio is interpreted as reflecting the percent of profit in each dollar of sales. To illustrate how we compute and use profit margin, let's look at the results of **Limited Brands, Inc.,** in Exhibit 3.16 for the period 2002–2005.

	2005	2004	2003	2002
Net income (in mil.)	$ 705	$ 717	$ 502	$ 519
Net sales (in mil.)	$9,408	$8,934	$8,445	$8,423
Profit margin	7.5%	8.0%	5.9%	6.2%
Industry profit margin	1.4%	1.5%	1.7%	1.5%

Exhibit 3.16

Limited Brands' Profit Margin

The Limited's average profit margin is 6.9% during this period. This favorably compares to the average industry profit margin of 1.5%. Moreover, Limited's most recent two years' profit margins are markedly better than earlier years.

Thus, while 2003 was less successful in generating profits on its sales, Limited's performance has improved in 2004–2005. Future success, of course, depends on Limited maintaining and preferably increasing its profit margin.

Demonstration Problem 1

The following information relates to Fanning's Electronics on December 31, 2008. The company, which uses the calendar year as its annual reporting period, initially records prepaid and unearned items in balance sheet accounts (assets and liabilities, respectively).

a. The company's weekly payroll is $8,750, paid each Friday for a five-day workweek. Assume December 31, 2008, falls on a Monday, but the employees will not be paid their wages until Friday, January 4, 2009.

b. Eighteen months earlier, on July 1, 2007, the company purchased equipment that cost $20,000. Its useful life is predicted to be five years, at which time the equipment is expected to be worthless (zero salvage value).

c. On October 1, 2008, the company agreed to work on a new housing development. The company is paid $120,000 on October 1 in advance of future installation of similar alarm systems in 24 new homes. That amount was credited to the Unearned Services Revenue account. Between October 1 and December 31, work on 20 homes was completed.

d. On September 1, 2008, the company purchased a 12-month insurance policy for $1,800. The transaction was recorded with an $1,800 debit to Prepaid Insurance.

e. On December 29, 2008, the company completed a $7,000 service that has not been billed and not recorded as of December 31, 2008.

Required

1. Prepare any necessary adjusting entries on December 31, 2008, in relation to transactions and events *a* through *e*.

2. Prepare T-accounts for the accounts affected by adjusting entries, and post the adjusting entries. Determine the adjusted balances for the Unearned Revenue and the Prepaid Insurance accounts.

3. Complete the following table and determine the amounts and effects of your adjusting entries on the year 2008 income statement and the December 31, 2008, balance sheet. Use up (down) arrows to indicate an increase (decrease) in the Effect columns.

Entry	Amount in the Entry	Effect on Net Income	Effect on Total Assets	Effect on Total Liabilities	Effect on Total Equity

Planning the Solution

- Analyze each situation to determine which accounts need to be updated with an adjustment.
- Calculate the amount of each adjustment and prepare the necessary journal entries.
- Show the amount of each adjustment in the designated accounts, determine the adjusted balance, and identify the balance sheet classification of the account.
- Determine each entry's effect on net income for the year and on total assets, total liabilities, and total equity at the end of the year.

Solution to Demonstration Problem 1

1. Adjusting journal entries.

(a) Dec. 31	Wages Expense	1,750	
	Wages Payable		1,750
	To accrue wages for the last day of the year		
	($8,750 × 1/5).		
(b) Dec. 31	Depreciation Expense—Equipment	4,000	
	Accumulated Depreciation—Equipment		4,000
	To record depreciation expense for the year		
	($20,000/5 years = $4,000 per year).		
(c) Dec. 31	Unearned Services Revenue	100,000	
	Services Revenue		100,000
	To recognize services revenue earned		
	($120,000 × 20/24).		

[continued on next page]

[continued from previous page]

(d) Dec. 31	Insurance Expense		600	
	Prepaid Insurance			600
	To adjust for expired portion of insurance			
	($1,800 × 4/12).			
(e) Dec. 31	Accounts Receivable.		7,000	
	Services Revenue			7,000
	To record services revenue earned.			

2. T-accounts for adjusting journal entries *a* through *e*.

Wages Expense			
(a)	1,750		

Wages Payable			
		(a)	1,750

Depreciation Expense—Equipment			
(b)	4,000		

Accumulated Depreciation—Equipment			
		(b)	4,000

Unearned Revenue			
		Unadj. Bal.	120,000
(c)	100,000		
		Adj. Bal.	20,000

Services Revenue			
		(c)	100,000
		(e)	7,000
		Adj. Bal.	107,000

Insurance Expense			
(d)	600		

Prepaid Insurance			
Unadj. Bal.	1,800		
		(d)	600

Accounts Receivable			
(e)	7,000		

Adj. Bal.	1,200		

3. Financial statement effects of adjusting journal entries.

Entry	Amount in the Entry	Effect on Net Income	Effect on Total Assets	Effect on Total Liabilities	Effect on Total Equity
a	$ 1,750	$ 1,750 ↓	No effect	$ 1,750 ↑	$ 1,750 ↓
b	4,000	4,000 ↓	$4,000 ↓	No effect	4,000 ↓
c	100,000	100,000 ↑	No effect	$100,000 ↓	100,000 ↑
d	600	600 ↓	$ 600 ↓	No effect	600 ↓
e	7,000	7,000 ↑	$7,000 ↑	No effect	7,000 ↑

Demonstration Problem 2

Use the following adjusted trial balance to answer questions 1–3.

CHOI COMPANY Adjusted Trial Balance December 31		
	Debit	**Credit**
Cash	$ 3,050	
Accounts receivable	400	
Prepaid insurance	830	
Supplies	80	
Equipment	217,200	

[continued on next page]

[continued from previous page]

Accumulated depreciation—Equipment		$ 29,100
Wages payable		880
Interest payable		3,600
Unearned rent		460
Long-term notes payable		150,000
M. Choi, Capital		40,340
M. Choi, Withdrawals	21,000	
Rent earned		57,500
Wages expense	25,000	
Utilities expense	1,900	
Insurance expense	3,200	
Supplies expense	250	
Depreciation expense—Equipment	5,970	
Interest expense	3,000	
Totals	$281,880	$281,880

1. Prepare the annual income statement from the adjusted trial balance of Choi Company.

Answer:

CHOI COMPANY Income Statement For Year Ended December 31		
Revenues		
Rent earned		$57,500
Expenses		
Wages expense	$25,000	
Utilities expense	1,900	
Insurance expense	3,200	
Supplies expense	250	
Depreciation expense—Equipment	5,970	
Interest expense	3,000	
Total expenses		39,320
Net income		$18,180

2. Prepare a statement of owner's equity from the adjusted trial balance of Choi Company. Choi's capital account balance of $40,340 consists of a $30,340 balance from the prior year-end, plus a $10,000 owner investment during the current year.

Answer:

CHOI COMPANY Statement of Owner's Equity For Year Ended December 31		
M. Choi, Capital, December 31 prior year-end		$30,340
Plus: Owner investments	$10,000	
Net income	18,180	28,180
....		58,520
Less: Withdrawals by owner		21,000
M. Choi, Capital, December 31 current year-end		$37,520

3. Prepare a balance sheet from the adjusted trial balance of Choi Company.

Answer:

CHOI COMPANY Balance Sheet December 31		
Assets		
Cash		$ 3,050
Accounts receivable		400
Prepaid insurance		830
Supplies		80
Equipment	$217,200	
Less accumulated depreciation	29,100	188,100
Total assets		$192,460
Liabilities		
Wages payable		$ 880
Interest payable		3,600
Unearned rent		460
Long-term notes payable		150,000
Total liabilities		154,940
Equity		
M. Choi, Capital		37,520
Total liabilities and equity		$192,460

Alternative Accounting for Prepayments

This appendix explains an alternative in accounting for prepaid expenses and unearned revenues.

Recording the Prepayment of Expenses in Expense Accounts

An alternative method is to record *all* prepaid expenses with debits to expense accounts. If any prepaids remain unused or unexpired at the end of an accounting period, then adjusting entries must transfer the cost of the unused portions from expense accounts to prepaid expense (asset) accounts. This alternative method is acceptable. The financial statements are identical under either method, but the adjusting entries are different. To illustrate the differences between these two methods, let's look at FastForward's cash payment of December 6 for 24 months of insurance coverage beginning on December 1. FastForward recorded that payment with a debit to an asset account, but it could have recorded a debit to an expense account. These alternatives are shown in Exhibit 3A.1.

P4 Explain the alternatives in accounting for prepaids.

		Payment Recorded as Asset	Payment Recorded as Expense
Dec. 6	Prepaid Insurance	2,400	
	Cash	2,400	
Dec. 6	Insurance Expense		2,400
	Cash		2,400

Exhibit 3A.1

Alternative Initial Entries for Prepaid Expenses

At the end of its accounting period on December 31, insurance protection for one month has expired. This means $100 ($2,400/24) of insurance coverage expired and is an expense for December. The adjusting entry depends on how the original payment was recorded. This is shown in Exhibit 3A.2.

Exhibit 3A.2

Adjusting Entry for Prepaid Expenses for the Two Alternatives

		Payment Recorded as Asset	Payment Recorded as Expense
Dec. 31	Insurance Expense	100	
	Prepaid Insurance	100	
Dec. 31	Prepaid Insurance		2,300
	Insurance Expense		2,300

When these entries are posted to the accounts in the ledger, we can see that these two methods give identical results. The December 31 adjusted account balances in Exhibit 3A.3 show Prepaid Insurance of $2,300 and Insurance Expense of $100 for both methods.

Exhibit 3A.3

Account Balances under Two Alternatives for Recording Prepaid Expenses

Payment Recorded as Asset			
Prepaid Insurance			**128**
Dec. 6	2,400	Dec. 31	100
Balance	2,300		

Insurance Expense			**637**
Dec. 31	100		

Payment Recorded as Expense			
Prepaid Insurance			**128**
Dec. 31	2,300		

Insurance Expense			**637**
Dec. 6	2,400	Dec. 31	2,300
Balance	100		

Recording the Prepayment of Revenues in Revenue Accounts

As with prepaid expenses, an alternative method is to record *all* unearned revenues with credits to revenue accounts. If any revenues are unearned at the end of an accounting period, then adjusting entries must transfer the unearned portions from revenue accounts to unearned revenue (liability) accounts. This alternative method is acceptable. The adjusting entries are different for these two alternatives, but the financial statements are identical. To illustrate the accounting differences between these two methods, let's look at FastForward's December 26 receipt of $3,000 for consulting services covering the period December 27 to February 24. FastForward recorded this transaction with a credit to a liability account. The alternative is to record it with a credit to a revenue account, as shown in Exhibit 3A.4.

Exhibit 3A.4

Alternative Initial Entries for Unearned Revenues

		Receipt Recorded as Liability	Receipt Recorded as Revenue
Dec. 26	Cash	3,000	
	Unearned Consulting Revenue	3,000	
Dec. 26	Cash		3,000
	Consulting Revenue		3,000

By the end of its accounting period on December 31, FastForward has earned $250 of this revenue. This means $250 of the liability has been satisfied. Depending on how the initial receipt is recorded, the adjusting entry is as shown in Exhibit 3A.5.

Exhibit 3A.5

Adjusting Entry for Unearned Revenues for the Two Alternatives

		Receipt Recorded as Liability	Receipt Recorded as Revenue
Dec. 31	Unearned Consulting Revenue	250	
	Consulting Revenue	250	
Dec. 31	Consulting Revenue		2,750
	Unearned Consulting Revenue		2,750

After adjusting entries are posted, the two alternatives give identical results. The December 31 adjusted account balances in Exhibit 3A.6 show unearned consulting revenue of $2,750 and consulting revenue of $250 for both methods.

Receipt Recorded as Liability			
Unearned Consulting Revenue			236
Dec. 31	250	Dec. 26	3,000
		Balance	2,750

Consulting Revenue			403
		Dec. 31	250

Receipt Recorded as Revenue			
Unearned Consulting Revenue			236
		Dec. 31	2,750

Consulting Revenue			403
Dec. 31	2,750	Dec. 26	3,000
		Balance	250

Exhibit 3A.6

Account Balances under Two Alternatives for Recording Unearned Revenues

Summary

C1 Explain the importance of periodic reporting and the time period principle. The value of information is often linked to its timeliness. To provide timely information, accounting systems prepare periodic reports at regular intervals. The time period principle assumes that an organization's activities can be divided into specific time periods for periodic reporting.

C2 Explain accrual accounting and how it improves financial statements. Accrual accounting recognizes revenue when earned and expenses when incurred—not necessarily when cash inflows and outflows occur. This information is valuable in assessing a company's financial position and performance.

C3 Identify the types of adjustments and their purpose. Adjustments can be grouped according to the timing of cash receipts and cash payments relative to when they are recognized as revenues or expenses as follows: prepaid expenses, unearned revenues, accrued expenses, and accrued revenues. Adjusting entries are necessary so that revenues, expenses, assets, and liabilities are correctly reported.

A1 Explain how accounting adjustments link to financial statements. Accounting adjustments bring an asset or liability account balance to its correct amount. They also update related expense or revenue accounts. Every adjusting entry affects one or more income statement accounts *and* one or more balance sheet accounts. An adjusting entry never affects cash.

A2 Compute profit margin and describe its use in analyzing company performance. *Profit margin* is defined as the reporting period's net income divided by its net sales. Profit margin reflects on a company's earnings activities by showing how much income is in each dollar of sales.

P1 Prepare and explain adjusting entries. *Prepaid expenses* refer to items paid for in advance of receiving their benefits.

Prepaid expenses are assets. Adjusting entries for prepaids involve increasing (debiting) expenses and decreasing (crediting) assets. *Unearned* (or *prepaid*) *revenues* refer to cash received in advance of providing products and services. Unearned revenues are liabilities. Adjusting entries for unearned revenues involves increasing (crediting) revenues and decreasing (debiting) unearned revenues. *Accrued expenses* refer to costs incurred in a period that are both unpaid and unrecorded. Adjusting entries for recording accrued expenses involve increasing (debiting) expenses and increasing (crediting) liabilities. *Accrued revenues* refer to revenues earned in a period that are both unrecorded and not yet received in cash. Adjusting entries for recording accrued revenues involve increasing (debiting) assets and increasing (crediting) revenues.

P2 Explain and prepare an adjusted trial balance. An adjusted trial balance is a list of accounts and balances prepared after recording and posting adjusting entries. Financial statements are often prepared from the adjusted trial balance.

P3 Prepare financial statements from an adjusted trial balance. Revenue and expense balances are reported on the income statement. Asset, liability, and equity balances are reported on the balance sheet. We usually prepare statements in the following order: income statement, statement of owner's equity, balance sheet, and statement of cash flows.

P4^A Explain the alternatives in accounting for prepaids. Charging all prepaid expenses to expense accounts when they are purchased is acceptable. When this is done, adjusting entries must transfer any unexpired amounts from expense accounts to asset accounts. Crediting all unearned revenues to revenue accounts when cash is received is also acceptable. In this case, the adjusting entries must transfer any unearned amounts from revenue accounts to unearned revenue accounts.

Guidance Answers to **Decision Maker** and **Decision Ethics**

Investor   Prepaid expenses are items paid for in advance of receiving their benefits. They are assets and are expensed as they are used up. The publishing company's treatment of the signing bonus is acceptable provided future book sales can at least match the $500,000 expense. As an investor, you are concerned about the risk of future book sales. The riskier the likelihood of future book sales is, the more likely your analysis is to treat the $500,000, or a portion of it, as an expense, not a prepaid expense (asset).

Entrepreneur Depreciation is a process of cost allocation, not asset valuation. Knowing the depreciation schedule is not especially useful in your estimation of what the building and equipment are currently worth. Your own assessment of the age, quality, and usefulness of the building and equipment is more important.

Loan Officer Your concern in lending to this store arises from analysis of current-year sales. While increased revenues and income are fine, your concern is with collectibility of these promotional sales. If the owner sold products to customers with poor records of paying

bills, then collectibility of these sales is low. Your analysis must assess this possibility and recognize any expected losses.

Financial Officer Omitting accrued expenses and recognizing revenue early can mislead financial statement users. One action is to request a second meeting with the president so you can explain that accruing expenses when incurred and recognizing revenue when earned are required practices. If the president persists, you might discuss the situation with legal counsel and any auditors involved. Your ethical action might cost you this job, but the potential pitfalls for falsification of statements, reputation and personal integrity loss, and other costs are too great.

Guidance Answers to **Quick Checks**

1. An annual reporting (or accounting) period covers one year and refers to the preparation of annual financial statements. The annual reporting period is not always a calendar year that ends on December 31. An organization can adopt a fiscal year consisting of any consecutive 12 months or 52 weeks.

2. Interim financial statements (covering less than one year) are prepared to provide timely information to decision makers.

3. The revenue recognition principle and the matching principle lead most directly to the adjusting process.

4. No. Cash basis accounting is not consistent with the matching principle because it reports revenue when received, not necessarily when earned, and expenses when paid, not necessarily in the period when the expenses were incurred as a result of the revenues earned.

5. No expense is reported in 2008. Under cash basis accounting, the entire $4,800 is reported as an expense in April 2007 when the premium is paid.

6. If the accrued revenues adjustment of $200 is not made, then both revenues and net income are understated by $200 on the current year's income statement, and both assets and equity are understated by $200 on the balance sheet.

7. A contra account is an account that is subtracted from the balance of a related account. Use of a contra account provides more information than simply reporting a net amount.

8. An accrued expense is a cost incurred in a period that is both unpaid and unrecorded prior to adjusting entries. One example is salaries earned but not yet paid at period-end.

9. An unearned revenue arises when a firm receives cash (or other assets) from a customer before providing the services or products to the customer. A magazine subscription paid in advance is one example; season ticket sales is another.

10.

Salaries Payable	1,000	
Salaries Expense	6,000	
Cash		7,000
Paid salary including accrual from December.		

11. The probable adjusting entries of Jordan Air are:

Insurance Expense	300	
Prepaid Insurance		300
To record insurance expired.		
Salaries Expense	1,400	
Salaries Payable		1,400
To record accrued salaries.		

12. Revenue accounts and expense accounts.

13. Statement of owner's equity.

Key Terms

mhhe.com/wildFAP18e

Key Terms are available at the book's Website for learning and testing in an online Flashcard Format.

Accounting period (pp. 92–93)
Accrual basis accounting (p. 93)
Accrued expenses (p. 99)
Accrued revenues (p. 100)
Adjusted trial balance (p. 103)
Adjusting entry (p. 94)
Annual financial statements (p. 93)
Book value (p. 97)

Cash basis accounting (p. 93)
Contra account (p. 97)
Depreciation (p. 97)
Fiscal year (p. 93)
Interim financial statements (p. 93)
Matching principle (p. 94)
Natural business year (p. 93)
Plant assets (p. 96)

Prepaid expenses (p. 95)
Profit margin (p. 105)
Straight-line depreciation method (p. 97)
Time period principle (p. 92)
Unadjusted trial balance (p. 103)
Unearned revenues (p. 98)

Multiple Choice Quiz   Answers on p. 132   mhhe.com/wildFAP18e

Multiple Choice Quizzes A and B are available at the book's Website.

1. A company forgot to record accrued and unpaid employee wages of $350,000 at period-end. This oversight would
   a. Understate net income by $350,000.
   b. Overstate net income by $350,000.
   c. Have no effect on net income.
   d. Overstate assets by $350,000.
   e. Understate assets by $350,000.

2. Prior to recording adjusting entries, the Office Supplies account has a $450 debit balance. A physical count of supplies shows $125 of unused supplies still available. The required adjusting entry is:
   a. Debit Office Supplies $125; Credit Office Supplies Expense $125.
   b. Debit Office Supplies $325; Credit Office Supplies Expense $325.
   c. Debit Office Supplies Expense $325; Credit Office Supplies $325.
   d. Debit Office Supplies Expense $325; Credit Office Supplies $125.
   e. Debit Office Supplies Expense $125; Credit Office Supplies $125.

3. On May 1, 2008, a two-year insurance policy was purchased for $24,000 with coverage to begin immediately. What is the amount of insurance expense that appears on the company's income statement for the year ended December 31, 2008?

   a. $4,000
   b. $8,000
   c. $12,000
   d. $20,000
   e. $24,000

4. On November 1, 2008, Stockton Co. receives $3,600 cash from Hans Co. for consulting services to be provided evenly over the period November 1, 2008, to April 30, 2009—at which time Stockton credited $3,600 to Unearned Consulting Fees. The adjusting entry on December 31, 2008 (Stockton's year-end) would include a
   a. Debit to Unearned Consulting Fees for $1,200.
   b. Debit to Unearned Consulting Fees for $2,400.
   c. Credit to Consulting Fees Earned for $2,400.
   d. Debit to Consulting Fees Earned for $1,200.
   e. Credit to Cash for $3,600.

5. If a company had $15,000 in net income for the year, and its sales were $300,000 for the same year, what is its profit margin?
   a. 20%
   b. 2,000%
   c. $285,000
   d. $315,000
   e. 5%

Superscript letter ^{A} denotes assignments based on Appendix 3A.

Discussion Questions

1. What is the difference between the cash basis and the accrual basis of accounting?
2. Why is the accrual basis of accounting generally preferred over the cash basis?
3. What type of business is most likely to select a fiscal year that corresponds to its natural business year instead of the calendar year?
4. What is a prepaid expense and where is it reported in the financial statements?
5. What type of assets require adjusting entries to record depreciation?
6. What contra account is used when recording and reporting the effects of depreciation? Why is it used?
7. What is unearned revenue and where is it reported in financial statements?
8. What is an accrued revenue? Give an example.

9.^{A}If a company initially records prepaid expenses with debits to expense accounts, what type of account is debited in the adjusting entries for those prepaid expenses?
10. Review the balance sheet of **Best Buy** in Appendix A. Identify the asset accounts that require adjustment before annual financial statements can be prepared. What would be the effect on the income statement if these asset accounts were not adjusted?
11. Review the balance sheet of **Circuit City** in Appendix A. In addition to Prepayments, identify two accounts (either assets or liabilities) requiring adjusting entries.
12. Refer to **Apple**'s balance sheet in Appendix A. If it made an adjustment for unpaid wages at year-end, where would the accrued wages expense be reported on its balance sheet?

Red numbers denote Discussion Questions that involve decision-making.

QUICK STUDY

QS 3-1

Identifying accounting adjustments

C3

Classify the following adjusting entries as involving prepaid expenses (PE), unearned revenues (UR), accrued expenses (AE), or accrued revenues (AR).

a. _____ To record revenue earned that was previously received as cash in advance.

b. _____ To record wages expense incurred but not yet paid (nor recorded).

c. _____ To record revenue earned but not yet billed (nor recorded).

d. _____ To record expiration of prepaid insurance.

e. _____ To record annual depreciation expense.

QS 3-2

Recording and analyzing adjusting entries

A1

Adjusting entries affect at least one balance sheet account and at least one income statement account. For the following entries, identify the account to be debited and the account to be credited. Indicate which of the accounts is the income statement account and which is the balance sheet account.

a. Entry to record revenue earned that was previously received as cash in advance.

b. Entry to record wage expenses incurred but not yet paid (nor recorded).

c. Entry to record revenue earned but not yet billed (nor recorded).

d. Entry to record expiration of prepaid insurance.

e. Entry to record annual depreciation expense.

QS 3-3

Adjusting prepaid expenses

P1

a. On July 1, 2008, Lamis Company paid $1,200 for six months of insurance coverage. No adjustments have been made to the Prepaid Insurance account, and it is now December 31, 2008. Prepare the journal entry to reflect expiration of the insurance as of December 31, 2008.

b. Shandi Company has a Supplies account balance of $500 on January 1, 2008. During 2008, it purchased $2,000 of supplies. As of December 31, 2008, a supplies inventory shows $800 of supplies available. Prepare the adjusting journal entry to correctly report the balance of the Supplies account and the Supplies Expense account as of December 31, 2008.

QS 3-4

Adjusting for depreciation

P1

a. Chika Company purchases $20,000 of equipment on January 1, 2008. The equipment is expected to last five years and be worth $2,000 at the end of that time. Prepare the entry to record one year's depreciation expense of $3,600 for the equipment as of December 31, 2008.

b. Madra Company purchases $10,000 of land on January 1, 2008. The land is expected to last indefinitely. What depreciation adjustment, if any, should be made with respect to the Land account as of December 31, 2008?

QS 3-5

Accruing salaries

A1 P1

Lakia Rowa employs one college student every summer in her coffee shop. The student works the five weekdays and is paid on the following Monday. (For example, a student who works Monday through Friday, June 1 through June 5, is paid for that work on Monday, June 8.) Rowa adjusts her books monthly, if needed, to show salaries earned but unpaid at month-end. The student works the last week of July—Friday is August 1. If the student earns $100 per day, what adjusting entry must Rowa make on July 31 to correctly record accrued salaries expense for July?

QS 3-6

Adjusting for unearned revenues

A1 P1

a. Tao receives $10,000 cash in advance for 4 months of legal services on October 1, 2008, and records it by debiting Cash and crediting Unearned Revenue both for $10,000. It is now December 31, 2008, and Tao has provided legal services as planned. What adjusting entry should Tao make to account for the work performed from October 1 through December 31, 2008?

b. A. Caden started a new publication called *Contest News*. Her subscribers pay $24 to receive 12 issues. With every new subscriber, Caden debits Cash and credits Unearned Subscription Revenue for the amounts received. Caden has 100 new subscribers as of July 1, 2008. She sends *Contest News* to each of these subscribers every month from July through December. Assuming no changes in subscribers, prepare the journal entry that Caden must make as of December 31, 2008, to adjust the Subscription Revenue account and the Unearned Subscription Revenue account.

During the year, Sereno Co. recorded prepayments of expenses in asset accounts, and cash receipts of unearned revenues in liability accounts. At the end of its annual accounting period, the company must make three adjusting entries: (1) accrue salaries expense, (2) adjust the Unearned Services Revenue account to recognize earned revenue, and (3) record services revenue earned for which cash will be received the following period. For each of these adjusting entries (1), (2), and (3), indicate the account from *a* through *i* to be debited and the account to be credited.

QS 3-7
Preparing adjusting entries
C3 P1

a. Prepaid Salaries   **d.** Unearned Services Revenue   **g.** Accounts Receivable
b. Cash   **e.** Salaries Expense   **h.** Accounts Payable
c. Salaries Payable   **f.** Services Revenue   **i.** Equipment

---

The following information is taken from Brooke Company's unadjusted and adjusted trial balances.

QS 3-8
Interpreting adjusting entries
C2 P2

	Unadjusted		Adjusted	
	Debit	Credit	Debit	Credit
Prepaid insurance	$4,100		$3,700	
Interest payable		$ 0		$800

Given this information, which of the following is likely included among its adjusting entries?

a. A $400 debit to Insurance Expense and an $800 debit to Interest Payable.
b. A $400 debit to Insurance Expense and an $800 debit to Interest Expense.
c. A $400 credit to Prepaid Insurance and an $800 debit to Interest Payable.

In its first year of operations, Ronna Co. earned $45,000 in revenues and received $37,000 cash from these customers. The company incurred expenses of $25,500 but had not paid $5,250 of them at year-end. Ronna also prepaid $6,750 cash for expenses that would be incurred the next year. Calculate the first year's net income under both the cash basis and the accrual basis of accounting.

QS 3-9
Computing accrual and cash income
C1 C2

In making adjusting entries at the end of its accounting period, Chao Consulting failed to record $1,600 of insurance coverage that had expired. This $1,600 cost had been initially debited to the Prepaid Insurance account. The company also failed to record accrued salaries expense of $1,000. As a result of these two oversights, the financial statements for the reporting period will [choose one] (1) understate assets by $1,600; (2) understate expenses by $2,600; (3) understate net income by $1,000; or (4) overstate liabilities by $1,000.

QS 3-10
Determining effects of adjusting entries
C3 A1

Sidone Company reported net income of $48,152 and net sales of $425,000 for the current year. Calculate Sidone's profit margin and interpret the result. Assume that Sidone's competitors achieve an average profit margin of 15%.

QS 3-11
Analyzing profit margin
A2

Calvin Consulting initially records prepaid and unearned items in income statement accounts. Given Calvin Consulting's accounting practices, which of the following applies to the preparation of adjusting entries at the end of its first accounting period?

QS 3-12ᴬ
Preparing adjusting entries
C3 P4

a. Earned but unbilled (and unrecorded) consulting fees are recorded with a debit to Unearned Consulting Fees and a credit to Consulting Fees Earned.
b. Unpaid salaries are recorded with a debit to Prepaid Salaries and a credit to Salaries Expense.
c. The cost of unused office supplies is recorded with a debit to Supplies Expense and a credit to Office Supplies.
d. Unearned fees (on which cash was received in advance earlier in the period) are recorded with a debit to Consulting Fees Earned and a credit to Unearned Consulting Fees.

EXERCISES

Exercise 3-1

Classifying adjusting entries

C3

In the blank space beside each adjusting entry, enter the letter of the explanation A through F that most closely describes the entry.

A. To record this period's depreciation expense.

B. To record accrued salaries expense.

C. To record this period's use of a prepaid expense.

D. To record accrued interest revenue.

E. To record accrued interest expense.

F. To record the earning of previously unearned income.

_____ 1.	Interest Expense	2,208
	Interest Payable	2,208
_____ 2.	Insurance Expense	3,180
	Prepaid Insurance	3,180
_____ 3.	Unearned Professional Fees	19,250
	Professional Fees Earned	19,250
_____ 4.	Interest Receivable	3,300
	Interest Revenue	3,300
_____ 5.	Depreciation Expense	38,217
	Accumulated Depreciation	38,217
_____ 6.	Salaries Expense	13,280
	Salaries Payable	13,280

Exercise 3-2

Preparing adjusting entries

P1

Check (c) Dr. Office Supplies Expense, $3,882; (e) Dr. Insurance Expense, $5,800

Prepare adjusting journal entries for the year ended (date of) December 31, 2008, for each of these separate situations. Assume that prepaid expenses are initially recorded in asset accounts. Also assume that fees collected in advance of work are initially recorded as liabilities.

a. Depreciation on the company's equipment for 2008 is computed to be $18,000.

b. The Prepaid Insurance account had a $6,000 debit balance at December 31, 2008, before adjusting for the costs of any expired coverage. An analysis of the company's insurance policies showed that $1,100 of unexpired insurance coverage remains.

c. The Office Supplies account had a $700 debit balance on December 31, 2007; and $3,480 of office supplies was purchased during the year. The December 31, 2008, physical count showed $298 of supplies available.

d. Two-thirds of the work related to $15,000 of cash received in advance was performed this period.

e. The Prepaid Insurance account had a $6,800 debit balance at December 31, 2008, before adjusting for the costs of any expired coverage. An analysis of insurance policies showed that $5,800 of coverage had expired.

f. Wage expenses of $3,200 have been incurred but are not paid as of December 31, 2008.

Exercise 3-3

Preparing adjusting entries

P1

Check (e) Dr. Insurance Expense, $2,800; (f) Cr. Interest Revenue, $1,000

For each of the following separate cases, prepare adjusting entries required of financial statements for the year ended (date of) December 31, 2008. (Assume that prepaid expenses are initially recorded in asset accounts and that fees collected in advance of work are initially recorded as liabilities.)

a. One-third of the work related to $15,000 cash received in advance is performed this period.

b. Wages of $8,000 are earned by workers but not paid as of December 31, 2008.

c. Depreciation on the company's equipment for 2008 is $18,531.

d. The Office Supplies account had a $240 debit balance on December 31, 2007. During 2008, $5,239 of office supplies is purchased. A physical count of supplies at December 31, 2008, shows $487 of supplies available.

e. The Prepaid Insurance account had a $4,000 balance on December 31, 2007. An analysis of insurance policies shows that $1,200 of unexpired insurance benefits remain at December 31, 2008.

f. The company has earned (but not recorded) $1,000 of interest from investments in CDs for the year ended December 31, 2008. The interest revenue will be received on January 10, 2009.

g. The company has a bank loan and has incurred (but not recorded) interest expense of $2,500 for the year ended December 31, 2008. The company must pay the interest on January 2, 2009.

Lopez Management has five part-time employees, each of whom earns $250 per day. They are normally paid on Fridays for work completed Monday through Friday of the same week. They were paid in full on Friday, December 28, 2008. The next week, the five employees worked only four days because New Year's Day was an unpaid holiday. Show (a) the adjusting entry that would be recorded on Monday, December 31, 2008, and (b) the journal entry that would be made to record payment of the employees' wages on Friday, January 4, 2009.

Exercise 3-4
Adjusting and paying accrued wages

C1 P1

Determine the missing amounts in each of these four separate situations a through d.

	a	b	c	d
Supplies available—prior year-end	$ 400	$1,200	$1,260	?
Supplies purchased during the current year	2,800	6,500	?	$3,000
Supplies available—current year-end	650	?	1,350	700
Supplies expense for the current year	?	1,200	8,400	4,588

Exercise 3-5
Determining cost flows through accounts

C1 A1 P1

The following three separate situations require adjusting journal entries to prepare financial statements as of April 30. For each situation, present both the April 30 adjusting entry and the subsequent entry during May to record the payment of the accrued expenses.

a. On April 1, the company retained an attorney at a flat monthly fee of $3,500. This amount is payable on the 12th of the following month.

b. An $800,000 note payable requires $8,000 of interest to be paid at the 20th day of each month. The interest was last paid on April 20 and the next payment is due on May 20. As of April 30, $2,667 of interest expense has accrued.

c. Total weekly salaries expense for all employees is $10,000. This amount is paid at the end of the day on Friday of each five-day workweek. April 30 falls on Tuesday of this year, which means that the employees had worked two days since the last payday. The next payday is May 3.

Exercise 3-6
Adjusting and paying accrued expenses

A1 P1

Check (b) May 20 Dr. Interest Expense, $5,333

On March 1, 2006, a company paid an $18,000 premium on a 36-month insurance policy for coverage beginning on that date. Refer to that policy and fill in the blanks in the following table.

Balance Sheet Insurance Asset Using		Insurance Expense Using		
	Accrual Basis	Cash Basis		Accrual Basis	Cash Basis
Dec. 31, 2006	$_____	$_____	2006	$_____	$_____
Dec. 31, 2007	_____	_____	2007	_____	_____
Dec. 31, 2008	_____	_____	2008	_____	_____
Dec. 31, 2009	_____	_____	2009	_____	_____
			Total	$_____	$_____

Exercise 3-7
Determining assets and expenses for accrual and cash accounting

C2

Check 2008 insurance expense: Accrual, $6,000; Cash, $0. Dec. 31, 2008, asset: Accrual, $1,000; Cash, $0.

Following are two income statements for Alexis Co. for the year ended December 31. The left column is prepared before any adjusting entries are recorded, and the right column includes the effects of adjusting entries. The company records cash receipts and payments related to unearned and prepaid items in balance sheet accounts. Analyze the statements and prepare the eight adjusting entries that likely were recorded. (Note: 30% of the $7,000 adjustment for Fees Earned has been earned but not billed, and the other 70% has been earned by performing services that were paid for in advance.)

Exercise 3-8
Analyzing and preparing adjusting entries

A1 P1 P3

ALEXIS CO. Income Statements For Year Ended December 31	Unadjusted	Adjusted
Revenues		
Fees earned	$18,000	$25,000
Commissions earned	36,500	36,500
Total revenues	$54,500	61,500
Expenses		
Depreciation expense—Computers	0	1,600
Depreciation expense—Office furniture	0	1,850
Salaries expense	13,500	15,750
Insurance expense	0	1,400
Rent expense	3,800	3,800
Office supplies expense	0	580
Advertising expense	2,500	2,500
Utilities expense	1,245	1,335
Total expenses	21,045	28,815
Net income	$33,455	$32,685

Exercise 3-9
Computing and interpreting profit margin

A2

Use the following information to compute profit margin for each separate company *a* through *e*.

		Net Income	Net Sales			Net Income	Net Sales
a.		$ 4,390	$ 44,830	**d.**		$65,234	$1,458,999
b.		97,644	398,954	**e.**		80,158	435,925
c.		111,385	257,082				

Which of the five companies is the most profitable according to the profit margin ratio? Interpret that company's profit margin ratio.

Exercise 3-10^A
Adjusting for prepaids recorded as expenses and unearned revenues recorded as revenues

P4

Ricardo Construction began operations on December 1. In setting up its accounting procedures, the company decided to debit expense accounts when it prepays its expenses and to credit revenue accounts when customers pay for services in advance. Prepare journal entries for items *a* through *d* and the adjusting entries as of its December 31 period-end for items *e* through *g*.

a. Supplies are purchased on December 1 for $2,000 cash.

b. The company prepaid its insurance premiums for $1,540 cash on December 2.

c. On December 15, the company receives an advance payment of $13,000 cash from a customer for remodeling work.

d. On December 28, the company receives $3,700 cash from another customer for remodeling work to be performed in January.

e. A physical count on December 31 indicates that Ricardo has $1,840 of supplies available.

Check   (f) Cr. Insurance Expense, $1,200; (g) Dr. Remodeling Fees Earned, $11,130

f. An analysis of the insurance policies in effect on December 31 shows that $340 of insurance coverage had expired.

g. As of December 31, only one remodeling project has been worked on and completed. The $5,570 fee for this project had been received in advance.

Exercise 3-11^A
Recording and reporting revenues received in advance

P4

Costanza Company experienced the following events and transactions during July.

July   1   Received $3,000 cash in advance of performing work for Vivian Solana.
      6   Received $7,500 cash in advance of performing work for Iris Haru.
    12   Completed the job for Solana.
    18   Received $8,500 cash in advance of performing work for Amina Jordan.
    27   Completed the job for Haru.
    31   None of the work for Jordan has been performed.

a. Prepare journal entries (including any adjusting entries as of the end of the month) to record these events using the procedure of initially crediting the Unearned Fees account when payment is received from a customer in advance of performing services.

b. Prepare journal entries (including any adjusting entries as of the end of the month) to record these events using the procedure of initially crediting the Fees Earned account when payment is received from a customer in advance of performing services.

c. Under each method, determine the amount of earned fees reported on the income statement for July and the amount of unearned fees reported on the balance sheet as of July 31.

Check (c) Fees Earned, $10,500

For each of the following entries, enter the letter of the explanation that most closely describes it in the space beside each entry. (You can use letters more than once.)

PROBLEM SET A

Problem 3-1A
Identifying adjusting entries with explanations

C3   P1

A. To record receipt of unearned revenue.
B. To record this period's earning of prior unearned revenue.
C. To record payment of an accrued expense.
D. To record receipt of an accrued revenue.
E. To record an accrued expense.

F. To record an accrued revenue.
G. To record this period's use of a prepaid expense.
H. To record payment of a prepaid expense.
I. To record this period's depreciation expense.

_____ 1.	Interest Expense	1,000	
	Interest Payable		1,000
_____ 2.	Depreciation Expense	4,000	
	Accumulated Depreciation		4,000
_____ 3.	Unearned Professional Fees	3,000	
	Professional Fees Earned		3,000
_____ 4.	Insurance Expense	4,200	
	Prepaid Insurance		4,200
_____ 5.	Salaries Payable	1,400	
	Cash		1,400
_____ 6.	Prepaid Rent	4,500	
	Cash		4,500
_____ 7.	Salaries Expense	6,000	
	Salaries Payable		6,000
_____ 8.	Interest Receivable	5,000	
	Interest Revenue		5,000
_____ 9.	Cash	9,000	
	Accounts Receivable (from consulting)		9,000
_____ 10.	Cash	7,500	
	Unearned Professional Fees		7,500
_____ 11.	Cash	2,000	
	Interest Receivable		2,000
_____ 12.	Rent Expense	2,000	
	Prepaid Rent		2,000

Arnez Co. follows the practice of recording prepaid expenses and unearned revenues in balance sheet accounts. Arnez's annual accounting period ends on December 31, 2008. The following information concerns the adjusting entries to be recorded as of that date.

Problem 3-2A
Preparing adjusting and subsequent journal entries

C1 A1 P1

a. The Office Supplies account started the year with a $4,000 balance. During 2008, the company purchased supplies for $13,400, which was added to the Office Supplies account. The inventory of supplies available at December 31, 2008, totaled $2,554.

b. An analysis of the company's insurance policies provided the following facts.

Policy	Date of Purchase	Months of Coverage	Cost
A	April 1, 2007	24	$14,400
B	April 1, 2008	36	12,960
C	August 1, 2008	12	2,400

The total premium for each policy was paid in full (for all months) at the purchase date, and the Prepaid Insurance account was debited for the full cost. (Year-end adjusting entries for Prepaid Insurance were properly recorded in all prior years.)

c. The company has 15 employees, who earn a total of $1,960 in salaries each working day. They are paid each Monday for their work in the five-day workweek ending on the previous Friday. Assume that December 31, 2008, is a Tuesday, and all 15 employees worked the first two days of that week. Because New Year's Day is a paid holiday, they will be paid salaries for five full days on Monday, January 6, 2009.

d. The company purchased a building on January 1, 2008. It cost $960,000 and is expected to have a $45,000 salvage value at the end of its predicted 30-year life. Annual depreciation is $30,500.

e. Since the company is not large enough to occupy the entire building it owns, it rented space to a tenant at $3,000 per month, starting on November 1, 2008. The rent was paid on time on November 1, and the amount received was credited to the Rent Earned account. However, the tenant has not paid the December rent. The company has worked out an agreement with the tenant, who has promised to pay both December and January rent in full on January 15. The tenant has agreed not to fall behind again.

f. On November 1, the company rented space to another tenant for $2,800 per month. The tenant paid five months' rent in advance on that date. The payment was recorded with a credit to the Unearned Rent account.

Check (1b) Dr. Insurance Expense, $11,440 (1d) Dr. Depreciation Expense, $30,500

Required

1. Use the information to prepare adjusting entries as of December 31, 2008.

2. Prepare journal entries to record the first subsequent cash transaction in 2009 for parts *c* and *e*.

Problem 3-3A

Preparing adjusting entries, adjusted trial balance, and financial statements

A1 P1 P2 P3

mhhe.com/wildFAP18e

Wells Technical Institute (WTI), a school owned by Tristana Wells, provides training to individuals who pay tuition directly to the school. WTI also offers training to groups in off-site locations. Its unadjusted trial balance as of December 31, 2008, follows. WTI initially records prepaid expenses and unearned revenues in balance sheet accounts. Descriptions of items *a* through *h* that require adjusting entries on December 31, 2008, follow.

Additional Information Items

a. An analysis of the school's insurance policies shows that $2,400 of coverage has expired.

b. An inventory count shows that teaching supplies costing $2,800 are available at year-end 2008.

c. Annual depreciation on the equipment is $13,200.

d. Annual depreciation on the professional library is $7,200.

e. On November 1, the school agreed to do a special six-month course (starting immediately) for a client. The contract calls for a monthly fee of $2,500, and the client paid the first five months' fees in advance. When the cash was received, the Unearned Training Fees account was credited. The fee for the sixth month will be recorded when it is collected in 2009.

f. On October 15, the school agreed to teach a four-month class (beginning immediately) for an individual for $3,000 tuition per month payable at the end of the class. The services are being provided as agreed, and no payment has yet been received.

g. The school's two employees are paid weekly. As of the end of the year, two days' wages have accrued at the rate of $100 per day for each employee.

h. The balance in the Prepaid Rent account represents rent for December.

```
┌─────────────────────────────────────────────────────────────────────────────────────┐
│ ☒ Microsoft Excel - Book1                                              _ ┌ 8 ┐ x     │
│ ⁑ File Edit View Insert Format Tools Data Accounting Window Help          _ ┌ 8 ┐ x  │
│ D 📄 🖫 🖨 🔍 ᢟ │ ᳌ ⋅ ⋄ ⋅ │ 🍷 🐝 │ Σ ƒₓ ⅍ ⅏ 🛗 🥤 📇 100% ▾ 🔊 │ Arial   ▾ 10 ▾ │ B I U │ $ % , 🖗 🤝 │
```

	WELLS TECHNICAL INSTITUTE Unadjusted Trial Balance December 31, 2008		
1		**Debit**	**Credit**
2			
3	Cash	$ 34,000	
4	Accounts receivable	0	
5	Teaching supplies	8,000	
6	Prepaid insurance	12,000	
7	Prepaid rent	3,000	
8	Professional library	35,000	
9	Accumulated depreciation—Professional library		$ 10,000
10	Equipment	80,000	
11	Accumulated depreciation—Equipment		15,000
12	Accounts payable		26,000
13	Salaries payable		0
14	Unearned training fees		12,500
15	T. Wells, Capital		90,000
16	T. Wells, Withdrawals	50,000	
17	Tuition fees earned		123,900
18	Training fees earned		40,000
19	Depreciation expense—Professional library	0	
20	Depreciation expense—Equipment	0	
21	Salaries expense	50,000	
22	Insurance expense	0	
23	Rent expense	33,000	
24	Teaching supplies expense	0	
25	Advertising expense	6,000	
26	Utilities expense	6,400	
27	Totals	$ 317,400	$ 317,400
28			

`│◄ ◄ ►│\ Sheet1 ⟨ Sheet2 ⟨ Sheet3 /`

Required

1. Prepare T-accounts (representing the ledger) with balances from the unadjusted trial balance.
2. Prepare the necessary adjusting journal entries for items *a* through *h* and post them to the T-accounts. Assume that adjusting entries are made only at year-end.
3. Update balances in the T-accounts for the adjusting entries and prepare an adjusted trial balance.
4. Prepare Wells Technical Institute's income statement and statement of owner's equity for the year 2008 and prepare its balance sheet as of December 31, 2008.

Check   (2e) Cr. Training Fees Earned, $5,000; (2f) Cr. Tuition Fees Earned, $7,500; (3) Adj. Trial balance totals, $345,700; (4) Net income, $49,600; Ending T. Wells, Capital $89,600

A six-column table for JKL Company follows. The first two columns contain the unadjusted trial balance for the company as of July 31, 2008. The last two columns contain the adjusted trial balance as of the same date.

Problem 3-4A
Interpreting unadjusted and adjusted trial balances, and preparing financial statements

C3   A1   P1   P2   P3

e**X**cel
mhhe.com/wildFAP18e

Required

Analysis Component

1. Analyze the differences between the unadjusted and adjusted trial balances to determine the eight adjustments that likely were made. Show the results of your analysis by inserting these adjustment amounts in the table's two middle columns. Label each adjustment with a letter *a* through *h* and provide a short description of it at the bottom of the table.

Preparation Component

2. Use the information in the adjusted trial balance to prepare the company's (*a*) income statement and its statement of owner's equity for the year ended July 31, 2008 (*note:* J. Logan, Capital at July 31, 2007, was $40,000, and the current-year withdrawals were $5,000), and (*b*) the balance sheet as of July 31, 2008.

Check   (2) Net income, $4,960; J. Logan, Capital (7/31/2008), $39,960; Total assets, $124,960

	Unadjusted Trial Balance		Adjustments		Adjusted Trial Balance	
Cash	$ 34,000				$ 34,000	
Accounts receivable	14,000				22,000	
Office supplies	16,000				2,000	
Prepaid insurance	8,540				2,960	
Office equipment	84,000				84,000	
Accum. depreciation— Office equip.		$ 14,000				$ 20,000
Accounts payable		9,100				10,000
Interest payable		0				1,000
Salaries payable		0				7,000
Unearned consulting fees		18,000				15,000
Long-term notes payable		52,000				52,000
J. Logan, Capital		40,000				40,000
J. Logan, Withdrawals	5,000				5,000	
Consulting fees earned		123,240				134,240
Depreciation expense— Office equip.	0				6,000	
Salaries expense	67,000				74,000	
Interest expense	1,200				2,200	
Insurance expense	0				5,580	
Rent expense	14,500				14,500	
Office supplies expense	0				14,000	
Advertising expense	12,100				13,000	
Totals	$256,340	$256,340			$279,240	$279,240

Problem 3-5A

Preparing financial statements from the adjusted trial balance and calculating profit margin

P3 A1 A2

The adjusted trial balance for Chiara Company as of December 31, 2008, follows.

	Debit	Credit
Cash	$ 30,000	
Accounts receivable	52,000	
Interest receivable	18,000	
Notes receivable (due in 90 days)	168,000	
Office supplies	16,000	
Automobiles	168,000	
Accumulated depreciation—Automobiles		$ 50,000
Equipment	138,000	
Accumulated depreciation—Equipment		18,000
Land	78,000	
Accounts payable		96,000
Interest payable		20,000
Salaries payable		19,000
Unearned fees		30,000
Long-term notes payable		138,000
R. Chiara, Capital		255,800
R. Chiara, Withdrawals	46,000	
Fees earned		484,000
Interest earned		24,000

[continued on next page]

[continued from previous page]

Depreciation expense—Automobiles	26,000	
Depreciation expense—Equipment	18,000	
Salaries expense	188,000	
Wages expense	40,000	
Interest expense	32,000	
Office supplies expense	34,000	
Advertising expense	58,000	
Repairs expense—Automobiles	24,800	
Totals	$1,134,800	$1,134,800

Required

1. Use the information in the adjusted trial balance to prepare (a) the income statement for the year ended December 31, 2008; (b) the statement of owner's equity for the year ended December 31, 2008; and (c) the balance sheet as of December 31, 2008.

2. Calculate the profit margin for year 2008.

Check (1) Total assets, $600,000

Gomez Co. had the following transactions in the last two months of its year ended December 31.

Nov. 1 Paid $1,800 cash for future newspaper advertising.
   1 Paid $2,460 cash for 12 months of insurance through October 31 of the next year.
   30 Received $3,600 cash for future services to be provided to a customer.
Dec. 1 Paid $3,000 cash for a consultant's services to be received over the next three months.
   15 Received $7,950 cash for future services to be provided to a customer.
   31 Of the advertising paid for on November 1, $1,200 worth is not yet used.
   31 A portion of the insurance paid for on November 1 has expired. No adjustment was made in November to Prepaid Insurance.
   31 Services worth $1,500 are not yet provided to the customer who paid on November 30.
   31 One-third of the consulting services paid for on December 1 have been received.
   31 The company has performed $3,300 of services that the customer paid for on December 15.

Problem 3-6A^A
Recording prepaid expenses and unearned revenues

P1 P4

Required

1. Prepare entries for these transactions under the method that records prepaid expenses as assets and records unearned revenues as liabilities. Also prepare adjusting entries at the end of the year.

2. Prepare entries for these transactions under the method that records prepaid expenses as expenses and records unearned revenues as revenues. Also prepare adjusting entries at the end of the year.

Analysis Component

3. Explain why the alternative sets of entries in requirements 1 and 2 do not result in different financial statement amounts.

For each of the following entries, enter the letter of the explanation that most closely describes it in the space beside each entry. (You can use letters more than once.)

A. To record payment of a prepaid expense.
B. To record this period's use of a prepaid expense.
C. To record this period's depreciation expense.
D. To record receipt of unearned revenue.
E. To record this period's earning of prior unearned revenue.
F. To record an accrued expense.
G. To record payment of an accrued expense.
H. To record an accrued revenue.
I. To record receipt of accrued revenue.

PROBLEM SET B

Problem 3-1B
Identifying adjusting entries with explanations

C3 P1

_____	1.	Interest Receivable	3,500	
		Interest Revenue		3,500
_____	2.	Salaries Payable	9,000	
		Cash		9,000
_____	3.	Depreciation Expense	8,000	
		Accumulated Depreciation		8,000
_____	4.	Cash	9,000	
		Unearned Professional Fees		9,000
_____	5.	Insurance Expense	4,000	
		Prepaid Insurance		4,000
_____	6.	Interest Expense	5,000	
		Interest Payable		5,000
_____	7.	Cash	1,500	
		Accounts Receivable (from services)		1,500
_____	8.	Salaries Expense	7,000	
		Salaries Payable		7,000
_____	9.	Cash	1,000	
		Interest Receivable		1,000
_____	10.	Prepaid Rent	3,000	
		Cash		3,000
_____	11.	Rent Expense	7,500	
		Prepaid Rent		7,500
_____	12.	Unearned Professional Fees	6,000	
		Professional Fees Earned		6,000

Problem 3-2B

Preparing adjusting and subsequent journal entries

C1 A1 P1

Natsu Co. follows the practice of recording prepaid expenses and unearned revenues in balance sheet accounts. Natsu's annual accounting period ends on October 31, 2008. The following information concerns the adjusting entries that need to be recorded as of that date.

a. The Office Supplies account started the fiscal year with a $600 balance. During the fiscal year, the company purchased supplies for $4,570, which was added to the Office Supplies account. The supplies available at October 31, 2008, totaled $800.

b. An analysis of the company's insurance policies provided the following facts.

Policy	Date of Purchase	Months of Coverage	Cost
A	April 1, 2007	24	$6,000
B	April 1, 2008	36	7,200
C	August 1, 2008	12	1,320

The total premium for each policy was paid in full (for all months) at the purchase date, and the Prepaid Insurance account was debited for the full cost. (Year-end adjusting entries for Prepaid Insurance were properly recorded in all prior fiscal years.)

c. The company has four employees, who earn a total of $1,000 for each workday. They are paid each Monday for their work in the five-day workweek ending on the previous Friday. Assume that October 31, 2008, is a Monday, and all five employees worked the first day of that week. They will be paid salaries for five full days on Monday, November 7, 2008.

d. The company purchased a building on November 1, 2007, that cost $175,000 and is expected to have a $40,000 salvage value at the end of its predicted 25-year life. Annual depreciation is $5,400.

e. Since the company does not occupy the entire building it owns, it rented space to a tenant at $1,000 per month, starting on September 1, 2008. The rent was paid on time on September 1, and the amount received was credited to the Rent Earned account. However, the October rent has not been paid. The company has worked out an agreement with the tenant, who has promised to pay both October and November rent in full on November 15. The tenant has agreed not to fall behind again.

f. On September 1, the company rented space to another tenant for $725 per month. The tenant paid five months' rent in advance on that date. The payment was recorded with a credit to the Unearned Rent account.

Required

1. Use the information to prepare adjusting entries as of October 31, 2008.

2. Prepare journal entries to record the first subsequent cash transaction in November 2008 for parts *c* and *e*.

Check   (1*b*) Dr. Insurance Expense, $4,730; (1*d*) Dr. Depreciation Expense, $5,400.

Following is the unadjusted trial balance for Augustus Institute as of December 31, 2008, which initially records prepaid expenses and unearned revenues in balance sheet accounts. The Institute provides one-on-one training to individuals who pay tuition directly to the business and offers extension training to groups in off-site locations. Shown after the trial balance are items *a* through *h* that require adjusting entries as of December 31, 2008.

Problem 3-3B
Preparing adjusting entries, adjusted trial balance, and financial statements

A1   P1   P2   P3

	Debit	Credit
AUGUSTUS INSTITUTE		
Unadjusted Trial Balance		
December 31, 2008		
Cash	$ 60,000	
Accounts receivable	0	
Teaching supplies	70,000	
Prepaid insurance	19,000	
Prepaid rent	3,800	
Professional library	12,000	
Accumulated depreciation—Professional library		$ 2,500
Equipment	40,000	
Accumulated depreciation—Equipment		20,000
Accounts payable		11,200
Salaries payable		0
Unearned training fees		28,600
C. Augustus, Capital		71,500
C. Augustus, Withdrawals	20,000	
Tuition fees earned		129,200
Training fees earned		68,000
Depreciation expense—Professional library	0	
Depreciation expense—Equipment	0	
Salaries expense	44,200	
Insurance expense	0	
Rent expense	29,600	
Teaching supplies expense	0	
Advertising expense	19,000	
Utilities expense	13,400	
Totals	$ 331,000	$ 331,000

Additional Information Items

a. An analysis of the Institute's insurance policies shows that $9,500 of coverage has expired.

b. An inventory count shows that teaching supplies costing $20,000 are available at year-end 2008.

c. Annual depreciation on the equipment is $5,000.

d. Annual depreciation on the professional library is $2,400.

e. On November 1, the Institute agreed to do a special five-month course (starting immediately) for a client. The contract calls for a $14,300 monthly fee, and the client paid the first two months' fees in advance. When the cash was received, the Unearned Training Fees account was credited. The last three months' fees will be recorded when collected in 2009.

f. On October 15, the Institute agreed to teach a four-month class (beginning immediately) to an individual for $2,300 tuition per month payable at the end of the class. The class started on October 15, but no payment has yet been received.

g. The Institute's only employee is paid weekly. As of the end of the year, three days' wages have accrued at the rate of $150 per day.

h. The balance in the Prepaid Rent account represents rent for December.

Required

1. Prepare T-accounts (representing the ledger) with balances from the unadjusted trial balance.

2. Prepare the necessary adjusting journal entries for items *a* through *h*, and post them to the T-accounts. Assume that adjusting entries are made only at year-end.

3. Update balances in the T-accounts for the adjusting entries and prepare an adjusted trial balance.

4. Prepare Augustus Institute's income statement and statement of owner's equity for the year 2008, and prepare its balance sheet as of December 31, 2008.

Problem 3-4B
Interpreting unadjusted and adjusted trial balances, and preparing financial statements

C3 A1 P1 P2 P3

A six-column table for Yan Consulting Company follows. The first two columns contain the unadjusted trial balance for the company as of December 31, 2008, and the last two columns contain the adjusted trial balance as of the same date.

	Unadjusted Trial Balance		Adjustments		Adjusted Trial Balance	
Cash	$ 45,000				$ 45,000	
Accounts receivable	60,000				66,660	
Office supplies	40,000				17,000	
Prepaid insurance	8,200				3,600	
Office equipment	120,000				120,000	
Accumulated depreciation— Office equip.		$ 20,000				$ 30,000
Accounts payable		26,000				32,000
Interest payable		0				2,150
Salaries payable		0				16,000
Unearned consulting fees		40,000				27,800
Long-term notes payable		75,000				75,000
Z. Yan, Capital		80,200				80,200
Z. Yan, Withdrawals	20,000				20,000	
Consulting fees earned		234,600				253,460
Depreciation expense— Office equip.	0				10,000	
Salaries expense	112,000				128,000	
Interest expense	8,600				10,750	
Insurance expense	0				4,600	
Rent expense	20,000				20,000	
Office supplies expense	0				23,000	
Advertising expense	42,000				48,000	
Totals	$475,800	$475,800			$516,610	$516,610

Required

Analysis Component

1. Analyze the differences between the unadjusted and adjusted trial balances to determine the eight adjustments that likely were made. Show the results of your analysis by inserting these adjustment amounts in the table's two middle columns. Label each adjustment with a letter *a* through *h* and provide a short description of it at the bottom of the table.

Preparation Component

2. Use the information in the adjusted trial balance to prepare this company's (*a*) income statement and its statement of owner's equity for the year ended December 31, 2008 (*note:* Z. Yan, Capital at December 31, 2007, was $80,200, and the current-year withdrawals were $20,000), and (*b*) the balance sheet as of December 31, 2008.

The adjusted trial balance for Speedy Courier as of December 31, 2008, follows.

Problem 3-5B
Preparing financial statements from the adjusted trial balance and calculating profit margin

P3 A1 A2

	Debit	Credit
Cash	$ 58,000	
Accounts receivable	120,000	
Interest receivable	7,000	
Notes receivable (due in 90 days)	210,000	
Office supplies	22,000	
Trucks	134,000	
Accumulated depreciation—Trucks		$ 58,000
Equipment	270,000	
Accumulated depreciation—Equipment		200,000
Land............................	100,000	
Accounts payable		134,000
Interest payable		20,000
Salaries payable		28,000
Unearned delivery fees		120,000
Long-term notes payable		200,000
L. Horace, Capital		125,000
L. Horace, Withdrawals	50,000	
Delivery fees earned		611,800
Interest earned		34,000
Depreciation expense—Trucks	29,000	
Depreciation expense—Equipment	48,000	
Salaries expense	74,000	
Wages expense	300,000	
Interest expense	15,000	
Office supplies expense	31,000	
Advertising expense	27,200	
Repairs expense—Trucks	35,600	
Totals	$1,530,800	$1,530,800

Required

1. Use the information in the adjusted trial balance to prepare (*a*) the income statement for the year ended December 31, 2008, (*b*) the statement of owner's equity for the year ended December 31, 2008, and (*c*) the balance sheet as of December 31, 2008.

2. Calculate the profit margin for year 2008.

Check   (1) Total assets, $663,000

Tremor Co. had the following transactions in the last two months of its fiscal year ended May 31.

Problem 3-6B[A]
Recording prepaid expenses and unearned revenues

P1 P4

Apr. 1   Paid $2,450 cash to an accounting firm for future consulting services.
      1   Paid $3,600 cash for 12 months of insurance through March 31 of the next year.
     30   Received $8,500 cash for future services to be provided to a customer.
May 1   Paid $4,450 cash for future newspaper advertising.
     23   Received $10,450 cash for future services to be provided to a customer.
     31   Of the consulting services paid for on April 1, $2,000 worth has been received.
     31   A portion of the insurance paid for on April 1 has expired. No adjustment was made in April to Prepaid Insurance.
     31   Services worth $4,600 are not yet provided to the customer who paid on April 30.
     31   Of the advertising paid for on May 1, $2,050 worth is not yet used.
     31   The company has performed $5,500 of services that the customer paid for on May 23.

Required

1. Prepare entries for these transactions under the method that records prepaid expenses and unearned revenues in balance sheet accounts. Also prepare adjusting entries at the end of the year.

2. Prepare entries for these transactions under the method that records prepaid expenses and unearned revenues in income statement accounts. Also prepare adjusting entries at the end of the year.

Analysis Component

3. Explain why the alternative sets of entries in parts 1 and 2 do not result in different financial statement amounts.

PROBLEM SET C   **Problem Set C is available at the book's Website to further reinforce and assess your learning.**

SERIAL PROBLEM   *This serial problem began in Chapter 1 and continues through most of the book. If previous chapter segments were not completed, the serial problem can still begin at this point. It is helpful, but not necessary, that you use the Working Papers that accompany the book.*

Success Systems

SP 3   After the success of the company's first two months, Adriana Lopez continues to operate Success Systems. (Transactions for the first two months are described in the serial problem of Chapter 2.) The November 30, 2007, unadjusted trial balance of Success Systems (reflecting its transactions for October and November of 2007) follows.

No.	Account Title	Debit	Credit
101	Cash	$ 68,996	
106	Accounts receivable	15,800	
126	Computer supplies	3,350	
128	Prepaid insurance	2,400	
131	Prepaid rent	3,500	
163	Office equipment	10,000	
164	Accumulated depreciation—Office equipment		$ 0
167	Computer equipment	25,000	
168	Accumulated depreciation—Computer equipment		0
201	Accounts payable		0
210	Wages payable		0
236	Unearned computer services revenue		0
301	A. Lopez, Capital		110,000
302	A. Lopez, Withdrawals	6,500	
403	Computer services revenue		32,550
612	Depreciation expense—Office equipment	0	
613	Depreciation expense—Computer equipment	0	
623	Wages expense	3,150	
637	Insurance expense	0	
640	Rent expense	0	
652	Computer supplies expense	0	
655	Advertising expense	1,790	
676	Mileage expense	864	
677	Miscellaneous expenses	300	
684	Repairs expense—Computer	900	
	Totals	$142,550	$142,550

Success Systems had the following transactions and events in December 2007.

Dec. 2 Paid $1,200 cash to Hilldale Mall for Success Systems' share of mall advertising costs.
3 Paid $500 cash for minor repairs to the company's computer.
4 Received $7,000 cash from Alex's Engineering Co. for the receivable from November.
10 Paid cash to Michelle Jones for six days of work at the rate of $150 per day.
14 Notified by Alex's Engineering Co. that Success's bid of $9,000 on a proposed project has been accepted. Alex's paid a $2,500 cash advance to Success Systems.
15 Purchased $2,100 of computer supplies on credit from Cain Office Products.
16 Sent a reminder to Gomez Co. to pay the fee for services recorded on November 8.
20 Completed a project for Chang Corporation and received $3,620 cash.
22–26 Took the week off for the holidays.
28 Received $3,000 cash from Gomez Co. on its receivable.
29 Reimbursed Lopez's business automobile mileage (800 miles at $0.32 per mile).
31 Lopez withdrew $2,000 cash for personal use.

The following additional facts are collected for use in making adjusting entries prior to preparing financial statements for the company's first three months:

a. The December 31 inventory count of computer supplies shows $775 still available.

b. Three months have expired since the 12-month insurance premium was paid in advance.

c. As of December 31, Michelle Jones has not been paid for four days of work at $150 per day.

d. The company's computer is expected to have a five-year life with no salvage value.

e. The office equipment is expected to have a four-year life with no salvage value.

f. Three of the four months' prepaid rent has expired.

Required

1. Prepare journal entries to record each of the December transactions and events for Success Systems. Post those entries to the accounts in the ledger.

2. Prepare adjusting entries to reflect *a* through *f*. Post those entries to the accounts in the ledger.

3. Prepare an adjusted trial balance as of December 31, 2007.

4. Prepare an income statement for the three months ended December 31, 2007.

5. Prepare a statement of owner's equity for the three months ended December 31, 2007.

6. Prepare a balance sheet as of December 31, 2007.

Check (3) Adjusted trial balance totals, $153,245

(6) Total assets, $122,635

BEYOND THE NUMBERS

BTN 3-1 Refer to Best Buy's financial statements in Appendix A to answer the following.

1. Identify and write down the revenue recognition principle as explained in the chapter.

2. Research Best Buy's footnotes to discover how it applies the revenue recognition principle. Report what you discover.

3. What is Best Buy's profit margin for fiscal years ended February 26, 2005, and February 28, 2004.

Fast Forward

4. Access Best Buy's financial statements (10-K) for fiscal years ending after February 26, 2005, at its Website (BestBuy.com) or the SEC's EDGAR database (www.sec.gov). Compare the February 26, 2005, fiscal year profit margin to any subsequent year's profit margin that you are able to calculate.

REPORTING IN ACTION

C1 C2 A1 A2

BTN 3-2 Key figures for the recent two years of both Best Buy and Circuit City follow.

COMPARATIVE ANALYSIS

A2

Key Figures ($ thousands)	Best Buy		Circuit City	
	Current Year	Prior Year	Current Year	Prior Year
Net income	$ 984,000	$ 705,000	$ 61,658	$ (89,269)
Net sales	27,433,000	24,548,000	10,472,364	9,857,057

Required

1. Compute profit margins for (*a*) Best Buy and (*b*) Circuit City for the two years of data shown.
2. Which company is more successful on the basis of profit margin? Explain.

ETHICS CHALLENGE

C1 C2 A1

BTN 3-3   Jerome Boland works for Sea Biscuit Co. He and Farah Smith, his manager, are preparing adjusting entries for annual financial statements. Boland computes depreciation and records it as

Depreciation Expense—Equipment 123,000	
Accumulated Depreciation—Equipment	123,000

Smith agrees with his computation but says the credit entry should be directly to the Equipment account. She argues that while accumulated depreciation is technically correct, "it is less hassle not to use a contra account and just credit the Equipment account directly. And besides, the balance sheet shows the same amount for total assets under either method."

Required

1. How should depreciation be recorded? Do you support Boland or Smith?
2. Evaluate the strengths and weaknesses of Smith's reasons for preferring her method.
3. Indicate whether the situation Boland faces is an ethical problem. Explain.

COMMUNICATING IN PRACTICE

C1 A2

BTN 3-4   The class should be divided into teams. Teams are to select an industry (such as automobile manufacturing, airlines, defense contractors), and each team member is to select a different company in that industry. Each team member is to acquire the annual report of the company selected. Annual reports can be downloaded from company Websites or from the SEC's EDGAR database at (WWW.SEC.GOV).

Required

1. Use the annual report to compute the return on assets, debt ratio, and profit margin.
2. Communicate with team members via a meeting, e-mail, or telephone to discuss the meaning of the ratios, how different companies compare to each other, and the industry norm. The team must prepare a single memo reporting the ratios for each company and identifying the conclusions or consensus of opinion reached during the team's discussion. The memo is to be copied and distributed to the instructor and all classmates.

TAKING IT TO THE NET

C1 A2

BTN 3-5   Access the Gap's Website (gap.com) to answer the following requirements.

Required

1. What are Gap's main brands?
2. Access Gap's annual report either at the company's Website or at (WWW.SEC.GOV). What is Gap's fiscal year-end?
3. What is Gap's net sales for the period ended January 29, 2005?
4. What is Gap's net income for the period ended January 29, 2005?
5. Compute Gap's profit margin for the year ended January 29, 2005.
6. Do you believe Gap's decision to use a year-end of late January or early February relates to its natural business year? Explain.

TEAMWORK IN ACTION

C3 A1 P1

BTN 3-6   Four types of adjustments are described in the chapter: (1) prepaid expenses, (2) unearned revenues, (3) accrued expenses, and (4) accrued revenues.

Required

1. Form *learning teams* of four (or more) members. Each team member must select one of the four adjustments as an area of expertise (each team must have at least one expert in each area).

2. Form *expert teams* from the individuals who have selected the same area of expertise. Expert teams are to discuss and write a report that each expert will present to his or her learning team addressing the following:

   a. Description of the adjustment and why it's necessary.

   b. Example of a transaction or event, with dates and amounts, that requires adjustment.

   c. Adjusting entry(ies) for the example in requirement *b*.

   d. Status of the affected account(s) before and after the adjustment in requirement *c*.

   e. Effects on financial statements of not making the adjustment.

3. Each expert should return to his or her learning team. In rotation, each member should present his or her expert team's report to the learning team. Team discussion is encouraged.

BTN 3-7   Read the article "Fuzzy Numbers" in the October 4, 2004, issue of *BusinessWeek*. Also read the followup letters in the "Reader's Report" in the October 25, 2004, issue of *BusinessWeek* for additional insights into the issue of estimates in financial reporting.

BusinessWeek
ACTIVITY

C2

Required

1. Why are estimates required under accrual accounting?
2. What are some potential problems with using estimates?
3. What are some ways that companies inflate or deflate earnings and cash flows?
4. What does the article suggest as solutions?

BTN 3-8   Review the opening feature of this chapter dealing with Alex Aguila and Nelson Gonzalez of **Alienware**.

**ENTREPRENEURIAL
DECISION**

A2

Required

1. Assume that Alienware sells a $3,000 computer to a customer, collecting the $3,000 cash in advance. Prepare the journal entry for the (*a*) collection of the cash and (*b*) subsequent delivery of the computer to the customer.

2. How can keeping no inventories help to improve Alienware's profit margin?

3. Aguila and Gonzalez understand that many companies carry inventories, and they are thinking of increasing their inventories. They desire your advice on the pros and cons of carrying inventory. Provide at least one reason for and one reason against carrying inventories.

BTN 3-9   Visit the Website of a major company that interests you. Use the Investor Relations link at the Website to obtain the toll-free telephone number of the Investor Relations Department. Call the company, ask to speak to Investor Relations, and request a copy of the company's most recent annual report. You should receive the requested report within one to two weeks. Once you have received your report, use it throughout the term to see that the principles you are learning in class are being applied in practice.

**HITTING THE
ROAD**

C1

BTN 3-10   **Dixons** is the United Kingdom's largest retailer of consumer electronics. Access its financial statements for the year ended May 1, 2004, at the company's Website (www.dixons-group.com).

**GLOBAL
DECISION**

A2 C1 C2

Required

1. Locate the notes to its financial statements, and read note *1.3 Turnover*. What does Dixons title its sales revenue account? When is sales revenue recognized by Dixons?

2. What is Dixons' profit margin for the year ended May 1, 2004?

3. Compute Dixons' current ratio for both the current year and the prior year. (Dixons' balance sheet is in a slightly different format than the examples in the text: current assets follow fixed assets, and current liabilities follow current assets.)

ANSWERS TO MULTIPLE CHOICE QUIZ

1. b; the forgotten adjusting entry is: *dr.* Wages Expense, *cr.* Wages Payable.

2. c; Supplies used = $450 − $125 = $325

3. b; Insurance expense = $24,000 × (8/24) = $8,000; adjusting entry is: *dr.* Insurance Expense for $8,000, *cr.* Prepaid Insurance for $8,000.

4. a; Consulting fees earned = $3,600 × (2/6) = $1,200; adjusting entry is: *dr.* Unearned Consulting Fee for $1,200, *cr.* Consulting Fees Earned for $1,200.

5. e; Profit margin = $15,000/$300,000 = 5%

4

Completing the Accounting Cycle

A Look Back

Chapter 3 explained the timing of reports. We described why adjusting accounts is important for recognizing revenues and expenses in the proper period. We prepared an adjusted trial balance and used it to prepare financial statements.

A Look at This Chapter

This chapter emphasizes the final steps in the accounting process and reviews the entire accounting cycle. We explain the closing process, including accounting procedures and the use of a post-closing trial balance. We show how a work sheet aids in preparing financial statements.

A Look Ahead

Chapter 5 looks at accounting for merchandising activities. We describe the sale and purchase of merchandise and their implications for preparing and analyzing financial statements.

Learning Objectives

CAP

Conceptual

C1 Explain why temporary accounts are closed each period. *(p. 140)*

C2 Identify steps in the accounting cycle. *(p. 144)*

C3 Explain and prepare a classified balance sheet. *(p. 145)*

Analytical

A1 Compute the current ratio and describe what it reveals about a company's financial condition. *(p. 147)*

Procedural

P1 Prepare a work sheet and explain its usefulness. *(p. 136)*

P2 Describe and prepare closing entries. *(p. 141)*

P3 Explain and prepare a post-closing trial balance. *(p. 142)*

P4 *Appendix 4A*—Prepare reversing entries and explain their purpose. *(p. 153)*

"We really focus on our products . . . we put our all into them"
—Janet Freeman

Taming the Mountain . . . In Style

PORTLAND—Success did not come easy for Janet Freeman. "I grew up thinking that getting hurt . . . and being cold, wet, and hungry was normal," she says. That background explains Janet's determination and work ethic: Traits that serve her well as owner and founder of **Betty Rides** (**BettyRides.com**), a snowboard apparel and accessories company.

Her sister's demand that snowboarding clothing show off her figure started Janet along her entrepreneurial path. "She kept bugging me until I did it," says Janet of her initial foray into snowboard fashion. She quickly realized that females were an underserved segment in the snowboarding apparel market.

But for Betty Rides to be successful, it needed to control costs. "I didn't run up huge bills on advertising," says Janet. "When other people were staying in fancy hotels . . . I was staying in cheap places." She controlled materials costs while closely monitoring both revenues and customer needs. She used the accounting system and closing entries to help identify and match costs with revenues for specific time periods. Janet relied on classified balance sheets so she'd know when to pay bills. And she worked with a bookkeeper that, says Janet, "helped us simplify our chart of accounts and clarify the payroll entries."

Janet continues to make good business decisions. "We really focus on our product," says Janet. "We don't skimp on our pieces . . . we put our all into them." She adds that women "want fit, function, value, and to look beautiful as well."

The downside of owning a business is that it cuts into Janet's time to snowboard. But, Janet says, she and the team now "do product testing while we ride," and that it still "makes me feel like a teenager." Janet also loves the entrepreneurial ride, noting, "Everyday I wake up and say— 'I'm the luckiest person on earth.'"

[Sources: *Betty Rides Website,* January 2006; *Transworld Business,* February 2005; *Transworld Snowboarding,* March 2003; *In Balance Services Website,* July 2005.]

Many of the important steps leading to financial statements were explained in earlier chapters. We described how transactions and events are analyzed, journalized, and posted. This chapter describes important adjustments that are often necessary to properly reflect revenues when earned and expenses when incurred. This chapter also describes financial statement preparation. It explains the closing process that readies revenue, expense, and withdrawal accounts for the next reporting period and updates the capital account. A work sheet is shown to be a useful tool for these final steps and in preparing financial statements. It also explains how accounts are classified on a balance sheet to increase their usefulness to decision makers.

Completing the Accounting Cycle			
Work Sheet	**Closing Process**	**Accounting Cycle**	**Classified Balance Sheet**
• Benefits of a work sheet • Use of a work sheet	• Temporary and permanent accounts • Closing entries • Post-closing trial balance	• Definition of accounting cycle • Review of accounting cycle	• Classification structure • Classification categories

Work Sheet as a Tool

Information preparers use various analyses and internal documents when organizing information for internal and external decision makers. Internal documents are often called **working papers.** One widely used working paper is the **work sheet,** which is a useful tool for preparers in working with accounting information. It is usually not available to external decision makers.

Benefits of a Work Sheet

P1 Prepare a work sheet and explain its usefulness.

A work sheet is *not* a required report, yet using a manual or electronic work sheet has several potential benefits. Specifically, a work sheet:

■ Aids the preparation of financial statements.

■ Reduces the possibility of errors when working with many accounts and adjustments.

■ Links accounts and adjustments to their impacts in financial statements.

■ Assists in planning and organizing an audit of financial statements—as it can be used to reflect any adjustments necessary.

■ Helps in preparing interim (monthly and quarterly) financial statements when the journalizing and posting of adjusting entries are postponed until the year-end.

■ Shows the effects of proposed or "what if" transactions.

Point: Since a work sheet is *not* a required report or an accounting record, its format is flexible and can be modified by its user to fit his/her preferences.

Use of a Work Sheet

When a work sheet is used to prepare financial statements, it is constructed at the end of a period before the adjusting process. The complete work sheet includes a list of the accounts, their balances and adjustments, and their sorting into financial statement columns. It provides two columns each for the unadjusted trial balance, the adjustments, the adjusted trial balance, the income statement, and the balance sheet (including the statement of owner's equity). To describe and interpret the work sheet, we use the information from FastForward. Preparing the work sheet has five important steps. Each step, 1 through 5, is color-coded and explained with reference to Exhibits 4.1 and 4.2.

① Step 1. Enter Unadjusted Trial Balance

Refer to Exhibit 4.1. The first step in preparing a work sheet is to list the title of every account and its account number that is expected to appear on its financial statements. This includes all accounts in the ledger plus any new ones from adjusting entries. Most adjusting entries—including expenses from salaries, supplies, depreciation, and insurance—are predictable and recurring. The unadjusted balance for each account is then entered in the appropriate Debit or Credit column of the unadjusted trial balance columns. The totals of these two columns must be equal. Exhibit 4.1 shows FastForward's work sheet after completing this first step. Sometimes blank lines are left on the work sheet based on past experience to indicate where lines will be needed for adjustments to certain accounts. Exhibit 4.1 shows Consulting Revenue as one example. An alternative is to squeeze adjustments on one line or to combine the effects of two or more adjustments in one amount. In the unusual case when an account is not predicted, we can add a new line for such an account following the *Totals* line.

② Step 2. Enter Adjustments

Refer to Exhibit 4.1a (turn over first transparency). The second step in preparing a work sheet is to enter adjustments in the Adjustments columns. The adjustments shown are the same ones shown in Exhibit 3.13. An identifying letter links the debit and credit of each adjusting entry. This is called *keying* the adjustments. After preparing a work sheet, adjusting entries must still be entered in the journal and posted to the ledger. The Adjustments columns provide the information for those entries.

Point: A recordkeeper often can complete the procedural task of journalizing and posting adjusting entries by using a work sheet and the guidance that *keying* provides.

③ Step 3. Prepare Adjusted Trial Balance

Refer to Exhibit 4.1b (turn over second transparency). The adjusted trial balance is prepared by combining the adjustments with the unadjusted balances for each account. As an example, the Prepaid Insurance account has a $2,400 debit balance in the Unadjusted Trial Balance columns. This $2,400 debit is combined with the $100 credit in the Adjustments columns to give Prepaid Insurance a $2,300 debit in the Adjusted Trial Balance columns. The totals of the Adjusted Trial Balance columns confirm the equality of debits and credits.

Point: To avoid omitting the transfer of an account balance, start with the first line (cash) and continue in account order.

④ Step 4. Sort Adjusted Trial Balance Amounts to Financial Statements

Refer to Exhibit 4.1c (turn over third transparency). This step involves sorting account balances from the adjusted trial balance to their proper financial statement columns. Expenses go to the Income Statement Debit column and revenues to the Income Statement Credit column. Assets and withdrawals go to the Balance Sheet & Statement of Owner's Equity Debit column. Liabilities and owner's capital go to the Balance Sheet & Statement of Owner's Equity Credit column.

⑤ Step 5. Total Statement Columns, Compute Income or Loss, and Balance Columns

Refer to Exhibit 4.1d (turn over fourth transparency). Each financial statement column (from Step 4) is totaled. The difference between the totals of the Income Statement columns is net income or net loss. This occurs because revenues are entered in the Credit column and expenses in the Debit column. If the Credit total exceeds the Debit total, there is net income. If the Debit total exceeds the Credit total, there is a net loss. For FastForward, the Credit total exceeds the Debit total, giving a $3,785 net income.

The net income from the Income Statement columns is then entered in the Balance Sheet & Statement of Owner's Equity Credit column. Adding net income to the last Credit column implies that it is to be added to owner's capital. If a loss occurs, it is added to the Debit column. This implies that it is to be subtracted from owner's capital. The ending balance of owner's

[continued on p. 140]

Exhibit 4.1

Work Sheet with Unadjusted Trial Balance

File Edit View Insert Format Tools Data Window Help

FastForward
Work Sheet
For Month Ended December 31, 2007

No.	Account	Unadjusted Trial Balance Dr.	Cr.	Adjustments Dr.	Cr.	Adjusted Trial Balance Dr.	Cr.	Income Statement Dr.	Cr.	Balance Sheet & Statement of Owner's Equity Dr.	Cr.
101	Cash	4,350									
106	Accounts receivable	0									
126	Supplies	9,720									
128	Prepaid insurance	2,400									
167	Equipment	26,000									
168	Accumulated depreciation—Equip.		0								
201	Accounts payable		6,200								
209	Salaries payable		0								
236	Unearned consulting revenue		3,000								
301	C. Taylor, Capital		30,000								
302	C. Taylor, Withdrawals	200									
403	Consulting revenue		5,800								
406	Rental revenue		300								
612	Depreciation expense—Equip.	0									
622	Salaries expense	1,400									
637	Insurance expense	0									
640	Rent expense	1,000									
652	Supplies expense	0									
690	Utilities expense	230									
	Totals	45,300	45,300								

Sheet1 Sheet2 Sheet3

List all accounts from the ledger and those expected to arise from adjusting entries.

Enter all amounts available from ledger accounts. Column totals must be equal.

A work sheet collects and summarizes information used to prepare adjusting entries, financial statements, and closing entries.

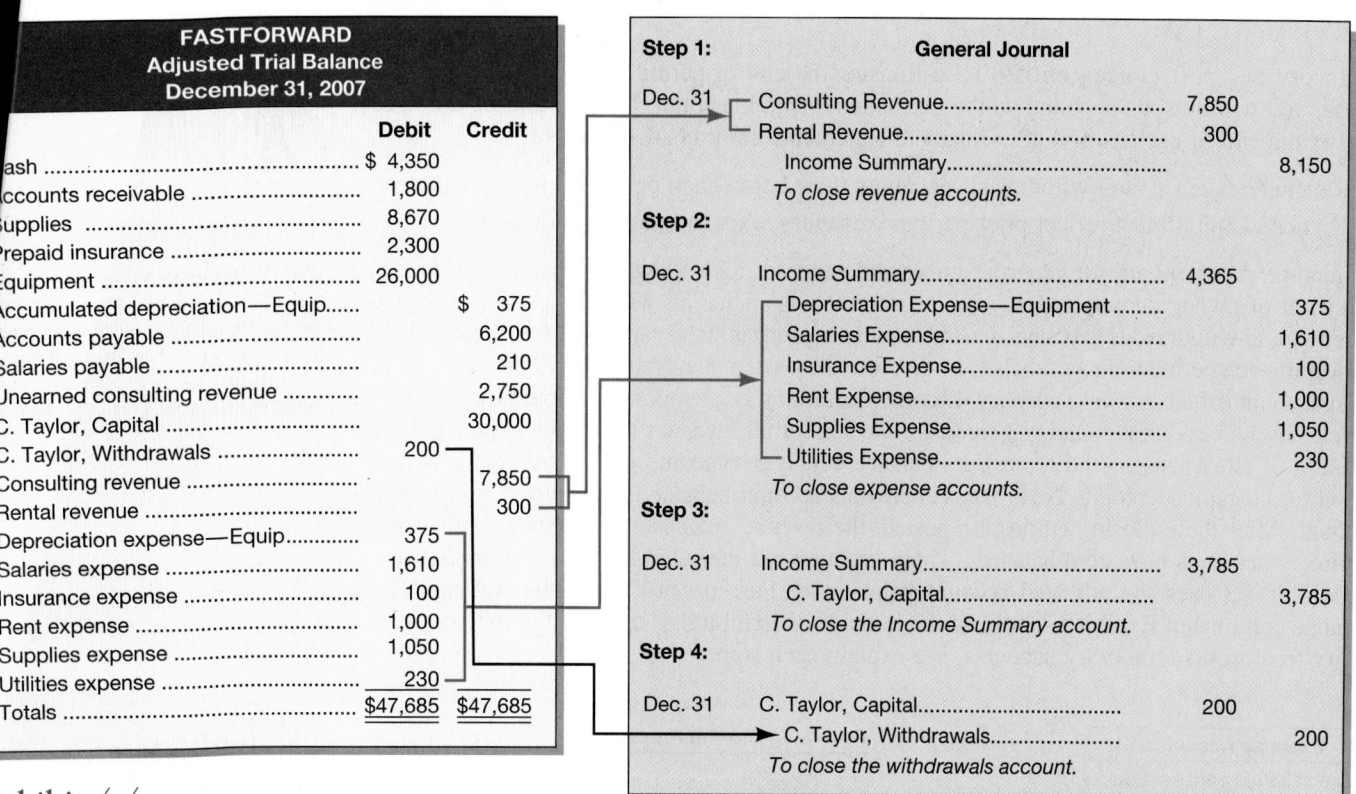

FASTFORWARD
Adjusted Trial Balance
December 31, 2007

	Debit	Credit
Cash	$ 4,350	
Accounts receivable	1,800	
Supplies	8,670	
Prepaid insurance	2,300	
Equipment	26,000	
Accumulated depreciation—Equip.		$ 375
Accounts payable		6,200
Salaries payable		210
Unearned consulting revenue		2,750
C. Taylor, Capital		30,000
C. Taylor, Withdrawals	200	
Consulting revenue		7,850
Rental revenue		300
Depreciation expense—Equip.	375	
Salaries expense	1,610	
Insurance expense	100	
Rent expense	1,000	
Supplies expense	1,050	
Utilities expense	230	
Totals	$47,685	$47,685

Step 1:

General Journal

Dec. 31	Consulting Revenue	7,850	
	Rental Revenue	300	
	Income Summary		8,150
	To close revenue accounts.		

Step 2:

Dec. 31	Income Summary	4,365	
	Depreciation Expense—Equipment		375
	Salaries Expense		1,610
	Insurance Expense		100
	Rent Expense		1,000
	Supplies Expense		1,050
	Utilities Expense		230
	To close expense accounts.		

Step 3:

Dec. 31	Income Summary	3,785	
	C. Taylor, Capital		3,785
	To close the Income Summary account.		

Step 4:

Dec. 31	C. Taylor, Capital	200	
	C. Taylor, Withdrawals		200
	To close the withdrawals account.		

Exhibit 4.4

Preparing Closing Entries

Point: The Income Summary is used only for closing entries.

period. This second closing entry for FastForward is step 2 in Exhibit 4.4. Exhibit 4.3 shows that posting this entry gives each expense account a zero balance.

Step 3: Close Income Summary to Owner's Capital After steps 1 and 2, the balance of Income Summary is equal to December's net income of $3,785. The third closing entry transfers the balance of the Income Summary account to the capital account. This entry closes the Income Summary account and is step 3 in Exhibit 4.4. The Income Summary account has a zero balance after posting this entry. It continues to have a zero balance until the closing process again occurs at the end of the next period. (If a net loss occurred because expenses exceeded revenues, the third entry is reversed: debit Owner Capital and credit Income Summary.)

Step 4: Close Withdrawals Account to Owner's Capital The fourth closing entry transfers any debit balance in the withdrawals account to the owner's capital account—see step 4 in Exhibit 4.4. This entry gives the withdrawals account a zero balance, and the account is now ready to accumulate next period's withdrawals. This entry also reduces the capital account balance to the $33,585 amount reported on the balance sheet.

We could also have selected the accounts and amounts needing to be closed by identifying individual revenue, expense, and withdrawals accounts in the ledger. This is illustrated in Exhibit 4.4 where we prepare closing entries using the adjusted trial balance.[1] (Information for closing entries is also in the financial statement columns of a work sheet.)

Post-Closing Trial Balance

P3 Explain and prepare a post-closing trial balance.

Exhibit 4.5 shows the entire ledger of FastForward as of December 31 after adjusting and closing entries are posted. (The transaction and adjusting entries are in Chapters 2 and 3.) The temporary accounts (revenues, expenses, and withdrawals) have ending balances equal to zero.

---

[1] The closing process has focused on proprietorships. It is identical for partnerships with the exception that each owner has separate capital and withdrawals accounts (for steps 3 and 4). The closing process for a corporation is similar with the exception that it uses a Retained Earnings account instead of a Capital account, and a Dividend account instead of a Withdrawals account.

Exhibit 4.2

Financial Statements Prepared from the Work Sheet

FASTFORWARD
Income Statement
For Month Ended December 31, 2007

Revenues		
Consulting revenue	$ 7,850	
Rental revenue	300	
Total revenues		$ 8,150
Expenses		
Depreciation expense—Equipment	375	
Salaries expense	1,610	
Insurance expense	100	
Rent expense	1,000	
Supplies expense	1,050	
Utilities expense	230	
Total expenses		4,365
Net income		$ 3,785

FASTFORWARD
Statement of Owner's Equity
For Month Ended December 31, 2007

C. Taylor, Capital, December 1		$ 0
Add: Investment by owner	$30,000	
Net income	3,785	33,785
		33,785
Less: Withdrawals by owner		200
C. Taylor, Capital, December 31		$33,585

FASTFORWARD
Balance Sheet
December 31, 2007

Assets		
Cash		$ 4,350
Accounts receivable		1,800
Supplies		8,670
Prepaid insurance		2,300
Equipment	$26,000	
Accumulated depreciation—Equipment	(375)	25,625
Total assets		$42,745

Liabilities		
Accounts payable		$ 6,200
Salaries payable		210
Unearned consulting revenue		2,750
Total liabilities		9,160

Equity		
C. Taylor, Capital		33,585
Total liabilities and equity		$42,745

Decision Maker

Answer—p. 153

Entrepreneur You make a printout of the electronic work sheet used to prepare financial statements. There is no depreciation adjustment, yet you own a large amount of equipment. Does the absence of depreciation adjustment concern you?

capital does not appear in the last two columns as a single amount, but it is computed in the statement of owner's equity using these account balances. When net income or net loss is added to the proper Balance Sheet & Statement of Owner's Equity column, the totals of the last two columns must balance. If they do not, one or more errors have been made. The error can either be mathematical or involve sorting one or more amounts to incorrect columns.

Work Sheet Applications and Analysis

A work sheet does not substitute for financial statements. It is a tool we can use at the end of an accounting period to help organize data and prepare financial statements. FastForward's financial statements are shown in Exhibit 4.2. Its income statement amounts are taken from the Income Statement columns of the work sheet. Similarly, amounts for its balance sheet and its statement of owner's equity are taken from the Balance Sheet & Statement of Owner's Equity columns of the work sheet.

A work sheet is also useful to journalize adjusting entries as the information is in the Adjustments columns. It is important to remember that a work sheet is not a journal. This means that even when a work sheet is prepared, it is necessary to both journalize adjustments and post them to the ledger.

Work sheets are also useful in analyzing the effects of proposed, or what-if, transactions. This is done by entering financial statement amounts in the Unadjusted (what-if) columns. Proposed transactions are then entered in the Adjustments columns. We then compute "adjusted" amounts from these proposed transactions. The extended amounts in the financial statement columns show the effects of these proposed transactions. These financial statement columns yield **pro forma financial statements** because they show the statements *as if* the proposed transactions occurred.

Quick Check

Answers—p. 154

1. Where do we get the amounts to enter in the Unadjusted Trial Balance columns of a work sheet?
2. What are the advantages of using a work sheet to help prepare adjusting entries?
3. What are the overall benefits of a work sheet?

Closing Process

C1 Explain why temporary accounts are closed each period.

The **closing process** is an important step at the end of an accounting period *after* financial statements have been completed. It prepares accounts for recording the transactions and the events of the *next* period. In the closing process we must (1) identify accounts for closing, (2) record and post the closing entries, and (3) prepare a post-closing trial balance. The purpose of the closing process is twofold. First, it resets revenue, expense, and withdrawals account balances to zero at the end of each period. This is done so that these accounts can properly measure income and withdrawals for the next period. Second, it helps in summarizing a period's revenues and expenses. This section explains the closing process.

Temporary and Permanent Accounts

Temporary Accounts

| Revenues |
| Expenses |
| Owner Withdrawals |
| Income Summary |

Permanent Accounts

| Assets |
| Liabilities |
| Owner Capital |

Temporary (or *nominal*) **accounts** accumulate data related to one accounting period. They include all income statement accounts, the withdrawals account, and the Income Summary account. They are temporary because the accounts are opened at the beginning of a period, used to record transactions and events for that period, and then closed at the end of the period. *The closing process applies only to temporary accounts.* **Permanent** (or *real*) **accounts** report on activities related to one or more future accounting periods. They carry their ending balances into the next period and generally consist of all balance sheet accounts. These asset, liability, and equity accounts are not closed.

Recording Closing Entries

To record and post **closing entries** is to transfer the end-of-period balances in revenue, expense, and withdrawals accounts to the permanent capital account. Closing entries are necessary at the end of each period after financial statements are prepared because

- Revenue, expense, and withdrawals accounts must begin each period with zero balances.
- Owner's capital must reflect prior periods' revenues, expenses, and withdrawals.

An income statement aims to report revenues and expenses for a *specific accounting period*. The statement of owner's equity reports similar information, including withdrawals. Since revenue, expense, and withdrawals accounts accumulate information separately for each period, they must start each period with zero balances. To close these accounts, we transfer their balances first to an account called *Income Summary*. **Income Summary** is a temporary account (only used for the closing process) that contains a credit for the sum of all revenues (and gains) and a debit for the sum of all expenses (and losses). Its balance equals net income or net loss and it is transferred to the capital account. Next, the withdrawals account balance is transferred to the capital account. After these closing entries are posted, the revenue, expense, withdrawals, and Income Summary accounts have zero balances. These accounts are then said to be *closed* or *cleared*.

Exhibit 4.3 uses the adjusted account balances of FastForward (from the Adjusted Trial Balance columns of Exhibit 4.1 or from the left side of Exhibit 4.4) to show the four steps necessary to close its temporary accounts. We explain each step.

Point: To understand the process, focus on its outcome: the capital account balance, ending balance, and getting accounts to show zero balances for purposes of accumulating data for period.

Exhibit 4.3

Four-Step Closing Process

Expense Accounts	
Depreciation Expense—Equip.	
Balance 375	375
Salaries Expense	
Balance 1,610	1,610
Insurance Expense	
Balance 100	100
Rent Expense	
Balance 1,000	1,000
Supplies Expense	
Balance 1,050	1,050
Utilities Expense	
Balance 230	230

Four-Step Closing Process

① Close revenue accounts
② Close expense accounts
③ Close income summary account
④ Close withdrawals account

Income Summary	
4,365	8,150
3,785	Balance 3,785

Revenue Accounts	
Consulting Revenue	
7,850	Balance 7,850
Rental Revenue	
300	Balance 300

C. Taylor, Capital	
	Balance 30,000
200	3,785
	Balance 33,585

C. Taylor, Withdrawals	
Balance 200	200

Point: C. Taylor, Capital is the only *permanent account* in Exhibit 4.3.

Step 1: Close Credit Balances in Revenue Accounts to Income Summary The first closing entry transfers credit balances in revenue (and gain) accounts to the Income Summary account. We bring accounts with credit balances to zero by debiting them. For FastForward, this journal entry is step 1 in Exhibit 4.4. This entry closes revenue accounts and leaves them with zero balances. The accounts are now ready to record revenues when they occur in the next period. The $8,150 credit entry to Income Summary equals total revenues for the period.

P2 Describe and prepare closing entries.

Step 2: Close Debit Balances in Expense Accounts to Income Summary The second closing entry transfers debit balances in expense (and loss) accounts to the Income Summary account. We bring expense accounts' debit balances to zero by crediting them. With a balance of zero, these accounts are ready to accumulate a record of expenses for the next

Point: It is possible to close revenue and expense accounts directly to owner's capital. Computerized accounting systems do this.

Exhibit 4.5

General Ledger after the Closing Process for FastForward

Asset Accounts

Cash   Acct. No. 101

Date	Explan.	PR	Debit	Credit	Balance
2007					
Dec. 1		G1	30,000		30,000
2		G1		2,500	27,500
3		G1		26,000	1,500
5		G1	4,200		5,700
6		G1		2,400	3,300
12		G1		1,000	2,300
12		G1		700	1,600
22		G1	1,900		3,500
24		G1		900	2,600
24		G1		200	2,400
26		G1	3,000		5,400
26		G1		120	5,280
26		G1		230	5,050
26		G1		700	**4,350**

Accounts Receivable   Acct. No. 106

Date	Explan.	PR	Debit	Credit	Balance
2007					
Dec. 12		G1	1,900		1,900
22		G1		1,900	0
31	Adj.	G1	1,800		**1,800**

Supplies   Acct. No. 126

Date	Explan.	PR	Debit	Credit	Balance
2007					
Dec. 2		G1	2,500		2,500
6		G1	7,100		9,600
26		G1	120		9,720
31	Adj.	G1		1,050	**8,670**

Prepaid Insurance   Acct. No. 128

Date	Explan.	PR	Debit	Credit	Balance
2007					
Dec. 6		G1	2,400		2,400
31	Adj.	G1		100	**2,300**

Equipment   Acct. No. 167

Date	Explan.	PR	Debit	Credit	Balance
2007					
Dec. 3		G1	26,000		**26,000**

Accumulated Depreciation—Equipment   Acct. No. 168

Date	Explan.	PR	Debit	Credit	Balance
2007					
Dec. 31	Adj.	G1		375	**375**

Liability and Equity Accounts

Accounts Payable   Acct. No. 201

Date	Explan.	PR	Debit	Credit	Balance
2007					
Dec. 6		G1		7,100	7,100
24		G1	900		**6,200**

Salaries Payable   Acct. No. 209

Date	Explan.	PR	Debit	Credit	Balance
2007					
Dec. 31	Adj	G1		210	**210**

Unearned Consulting Revenue   Acct. No. 236

Date	Explan.	PR	Debit	Credit	Balance
2007					
Dec. 26		G1		3,000	3,000
31	Adj.	G1	250		**2,750**

C. Taylor, Capital   Acct. No. 301

Date	Explan.	PR	Debit	Credit	Balance
2007					
Dec. 1		G1		30,000	30,000
31	Closing	G1		3,785	33,785
31	Closing	G1	200		33,585

C. Taylor, Withdrawals   Acct. No. 302

Date	Explan.	PR	Debit	Credit	Balance
2007					
Dec. 24		G1	200		200
31	Closing	G1		200	0

Revenue and Expense Accounts (including Income Summary)

Consulting Revenue   Acct. No. 403

Date	Explan.	PR	Debit	Credit	Balance
2007					
Dec. 5		G1		4,200	4,200
12		G1		1,600	5,800
31	Adj.	G1		250	6,050
31	Adj.	G1		1,800	7,850
31	Closing	G1	7,850		0

Rental Revenue   Acct. No. 406

Date	Explan.	PR	Debit	Credit	Balance
2007					
Dec. 12		G1		300	300
31	Closing	G1	300		0

Depreciation Expense—Equipment   Acct. No. 612

Date	Explan.	PR	Debit	Credit	Balance
2007					
Dec. 31	Adj.	G1	375		375
31	Closing	G1		375	0

Salaries Expense   Acct. No. 622

Date	Explan.	PR	Debit	Credit	Balance
2007					
Dec. 12		G1	700		700
26		G1	700		1,400
31	Adj.	G1	210		1,610
31	Closing	G1		1,610	0

Insurance Expense   Acct. No. 637

Date	Explan.	PR	Debit	Credit	Balance
2007					
Dec. 31	Adj.	G1	100		100
31	Closing	G1		100	0

Rent Expense   Acct. No. 640

Date	Explan.	PR	Debit	Credit	Balance
2007					
Dec. 12		G1	1,000		1,000
31	Closing	G1		1,000	0

Supplies Expense   Acct. No. 652

Date	Explan.	PR	Debit	Credit	Balance
2007					
Dec. 31	Adj.	G1	1,050		1,050
31	Closing	G1		1,050	0

Utilities Expense   Acct. No. 690

Date	Explan.	PR	Debit	Credit	Balance
2007					
Dec. 26		G1	230		230
31	Closing	G1		230	0

Income Summary   Acct. No. 901

Date	Explan.	PR	Debit	Credit	Balance
2007					
Dec. 31	Closing	G1		8,150	8,150
31	Closing	G1	4,365		3,785
31	Closing	G1	3,785		0

A **post-closing trial balance** is a list of permanent accounts and their balances from the ledger after all closing entries have been journalized and posted. It lists the balances for all accounts not closed. These accounts comprise a company's assets, liabilities, and equity, which are identical to those in the balance sheet. The aim of a post-closing trial balance is to verify that (1) total debits equal total credits for permanent accounts and (2) all temporary accounts have zero balances. FastForward's post-closing trial balance is shown in Exhibit 4.6. The post-closing trial balance usually is the last step in the accounting process.

Exhibit 4.6

Post-Closing Trial Balance

FASTFORWARD Post-Closing Trial Balance December 31, 2007	Debit	Credit
Cash	$ 4,350	
Accounts receivable	1,800	
Supplies	8,670	
Prepaid insurance	2,300	
Equipment	26,000	
Accumulated depreciation—Equipment		$ 375
Accounts payable		6,200
Salaries payable		210
Unearned consulting revenue		2,750
C. Taylor, Capital		33,585
Totals	$43,120	$43,120

Accounting Cycle

C2 Identify steps in the accounting cycle.

The term **accounting cycle** refers to the steps in preparing financial statements. It is called a *cycle* because the steps are repeated each reporting period. Exhibit 4.7 shows the 10 steps in the cycle, beginning with analyzing transactions and ending with a post-closing trial balance

Exhibit 4.7

Steps in the Accounting Cycle*

Explanations

1. Analyze transactions	Analyze transactions to prepare for journalizing.
2. Journalize	Record accounts, including debits and credits, in a journal.
3. Post	Transfer debits and credits from the journal to the ledger.
4. Prepare unadjusted trial balance	Summarize unadjusted ledger accounts and amounts.
5. Adjust	Record adjustments to bring account balances up to date; journalize and post adjusting entries.
6. Prepare adjusted trial balance	Summarize adjusted ledger accounts and amounts.
7. Prepare statements	Use adjusted trial balance to prepare financial statements.
8. Close	Journalize and post entries to close temporary accounts.
9. Prepare post-closing trial balance	Test clerical accuracy of the closing procedures.
10. Reverse (optional)	Reverse certain adjustments in the next period—optional step; see Appendix 4A.

*Steps 4, 6, and 9 can be done on a work sheet. A work sheet is useful in *planning* adjustments, but adjustments (step 5) must always be journalized and posted. Steps 3, 4, 6, and 9 are automatic with a computerized system.

Exhibit 4.2

Financial Statements Prepared
from the Work Sheet

FASTFORWARD
Income Statement
For Month Ended December 31, 2007

Revenues		
Consulting revenue	$ 7,850	
Rental revenue	300	
Total revenues		$ 8,150
Expenses		
Depreciation expense—Equipment	375	
Salaries expense	1,610	
Insurance expense	100	
Rent expense	1,000	
Supplies expense	1,050	
Utilities expense	230	
Total expenses		4,365
Net income		$ 3,785

FASTFORWARD
Statement of Owner's Equity
For Month Ended December 31, 2007

C. Taylor, Capital, December 1		$ 0
Add: Investment by owner	$30,000	
Net income	3,785	33,785
		33,785
Less: Withdrawals by owner		200
C. Taylor, Capital, December 31		$33,585

FASTFORWARD
Balance Sheet
December 31, 2007

Assets		
Cash		$ 4,350
Accounts receivable		1,800
Supplies		8,670
Prepaid insurance		2,300
Equipment	$26,000	
Accumulated depreciation—Equipment	(375)	25,625
Total assets		$42,745
Liabilities		
Accounts payable		$ 6,200
Salaries payable		210
Unearned consulting revenue		2,750
Total liabilities		9,160
Equity		
C. Taylor, Capital		33,585
Total liabilities and equity		$42,745

capital does not appear in the last two columns as a single amount, but it is computed in the statement of owner's equity using these account balances. When net income or net loss is added to the proper Balance Sheet & Statement of Owner's Equity column, the totals of the last two columns must balance. If they do not, one or more errors have been made. The error can either be mathematical or involve sorting one or more amounts to incorrect columns.

Work Sheet Applications and Analysis

A work sheet does not substitute for financial statements. It is a tool we can use at the end of an accounting period to help organize data and prepare financial statements. FastForward's financial statements are shown in Exhibit 4.2. Its income statement amounts are taken from the Income Statement columns of the work sheet. Similarly, amounts for its balance sheet and its statement of owner's equity are taken from the Balance Sheet & Statement of Owner's Equity columns of the work sheet.

A work sheet is also useful to journalize adjusting entries as the information is in the Adjustments columns. It is important to remember that a work sheet is not a journal. This means that even when a work sheet is prepared, it is necessary to both journalize adjustments and post them to the ledger.

Work sheets are also useful in analyzing the effects of proposed, or what-if, transactions. This is done by entering financial statement amounts in the Unadjusted (what-if) columns. Proposed transactions are then entered in the Adjustments columns. We then compute "adjusted" amounts from these proposed transactions. The extended amounts in the financial statement columns show the effects of these proposed transactions. These financial statement columns yield **pro forma financial statements** because they show the statements *as if* the proposed transactions occurred.

Quick Check   Answers—p. 154

1. Where do we get the amounts to enter in the Unadjusted Trial Balance columns of a work sheet?
2. What are the advantages of using a work sheet to help prepare adjusting entries?
3. What are the overall benefits of a work sheet?

Closing Process

C1 Explain why temporary accounts are closed each period.

The **closing process** is an important step at the end of an accounting period *after* financial statements have been completed. It prepares accounts for recording the transactions and the events of the *next* period. In the closing process we must (1) identify accounts for closing, (2) record and post the closing entries, and (3) prepare a post-closing trial balance. The purpose of the closing process is twofold. First, it resets revenue, expense, and withdrawals account balances to zero at the end of each period. This is done so that these accounts can properly measure income and withdrawals for the next period. Second, it helps in summarizing a period's revenues and expenses. This section explains the closing process.

Temporary Accounts

| Revenues |
| Expenses |
| Owner Withdrawals |
| Income Summary |

Permanent Accounts

| Assets |
| Liabilities |
| Owner Capital |

Temporary and Permanent Accounts

Temporary (or *nominal*) **accounts** accumulate data related to one accounting period. They include all income statement accounts, the withdrawals account, and the Income Summary account. They are temporary because the accounts are opened at the beginning of a period, used to record transactions and events for that period, and then closed at the end of the period. *The closing process applies only to temporary accounts.* **Permanent** (or *real*) **accounts** report on activities related to one or more future accounting periods. They carry their ending balances into the next period and generally consist of all balance sheet accounts. These asset, liability, and equity accounts are not closed.

Recording Closing Entries

To record and post **closing entries** is to transfer the end-of-period balances in revenue, expense, and withdrawals accounts to the permanent capital account. Closing entries are necessary at the end of each period after financial statements are prepared because

Topic Tackler
PLUS
4-1

- Revenue, expense, and withdrawals accounts must begin each period with zero balances.
- Owner's capital must reflect prior periods' revenues, expenses, and withdrawals.

An income statement aims to report revenues and expenses for a *specific accounting period*. The statement of owner's equity reports similar information, including withdrawals. Since revenue, expense, and withdrawals accounts must accumulate information separately for each period, they must start each period with zero balances. To close these accounts, we transfer their balances first to an account called *Income Summary*. **Income Summary** is a temporary account (only used for the closing process) that contains a credit for the sum of all revenues (and gains) and a debit for the sum of all expenses (and losses). Its balance equals net income or net loss and it is transferred to the capital account. Next, the withdrawals account balance is transferred to the capital account. After these closing entries are posted, the revenue, expense, withdrawals, and Income Summary accounts have zero balances. These accounts are then said to be *closed* or *cleared*.

Exhibit 4.3 uses the adjusted account balances of FastForward (from the Adjusted Trial Balance columns of Exhibit 4.1 or from the left side of Exhibit 4.4) to show the four steps necessary to close its temporary accounts. We explain each step.

Point: To understand the closing process, focus on its *outcomes—updating* the capital account balance to its proper ending balance, and getting *temporary accounts* to show *zero balances* for purposes of accumulating data for the next period.

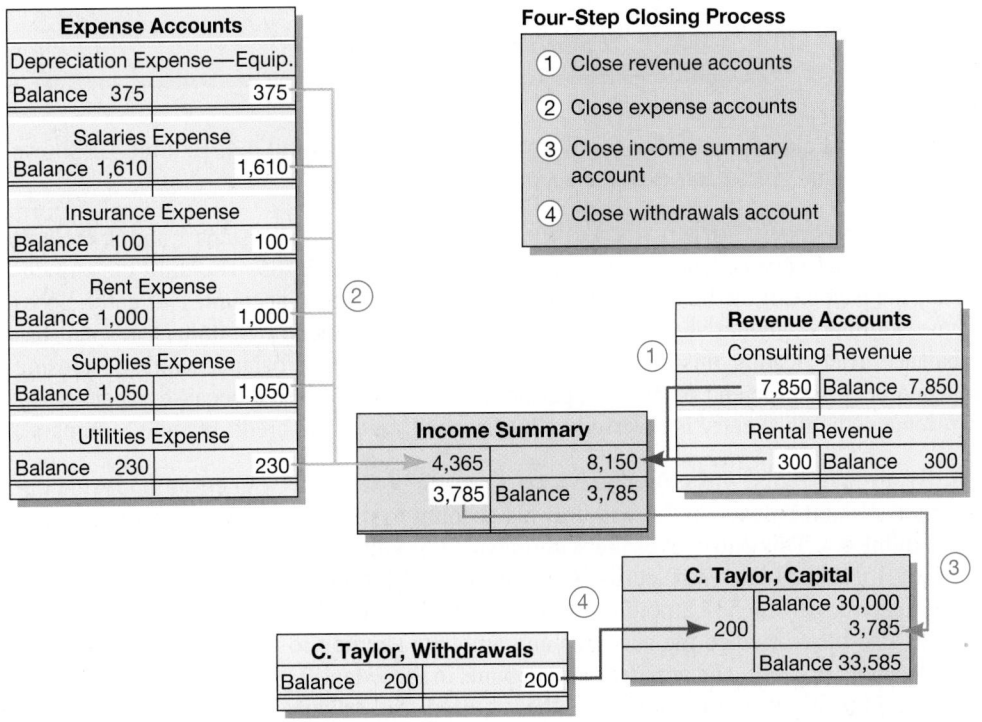

Exhibit 4.3

Four-Step Closing Process

Point: C. Taylor, Capital is the only *permanent account* in Exhibit 4.3.

Step 1: Close Credit Balances in Revenue Accounts to Income Summary

The first closing entry transfers credit balances in revenue (and gain) accounts to the Income Summary account. We bring accounts with credit balances to zero by debiting them. For FastForward, this journal entry is step 1 in Exhibit 4.4. This entry closes revenue accounts and leaves them with zero balances. The accounts are now ready to record revenues when they occur in the next period. The $8,150 credit entry to Income Summary equals total revenues for the period.

Step 2: Close Debit Balances in Expense Accounts to Income Summary

The second closing entry transfers debit balances in expense (and loss) accounts to the Income Summary account. We bring expense accounts' debit balances to zero by crediting them. With a balance of zero, these accounts are ready to accumulate a record of expenses for the next

P2   Describe and prepare closing entries.

Point: It is possible to close revenue and expense accounts directly to owner's capital. Computerized accounting systems do this.

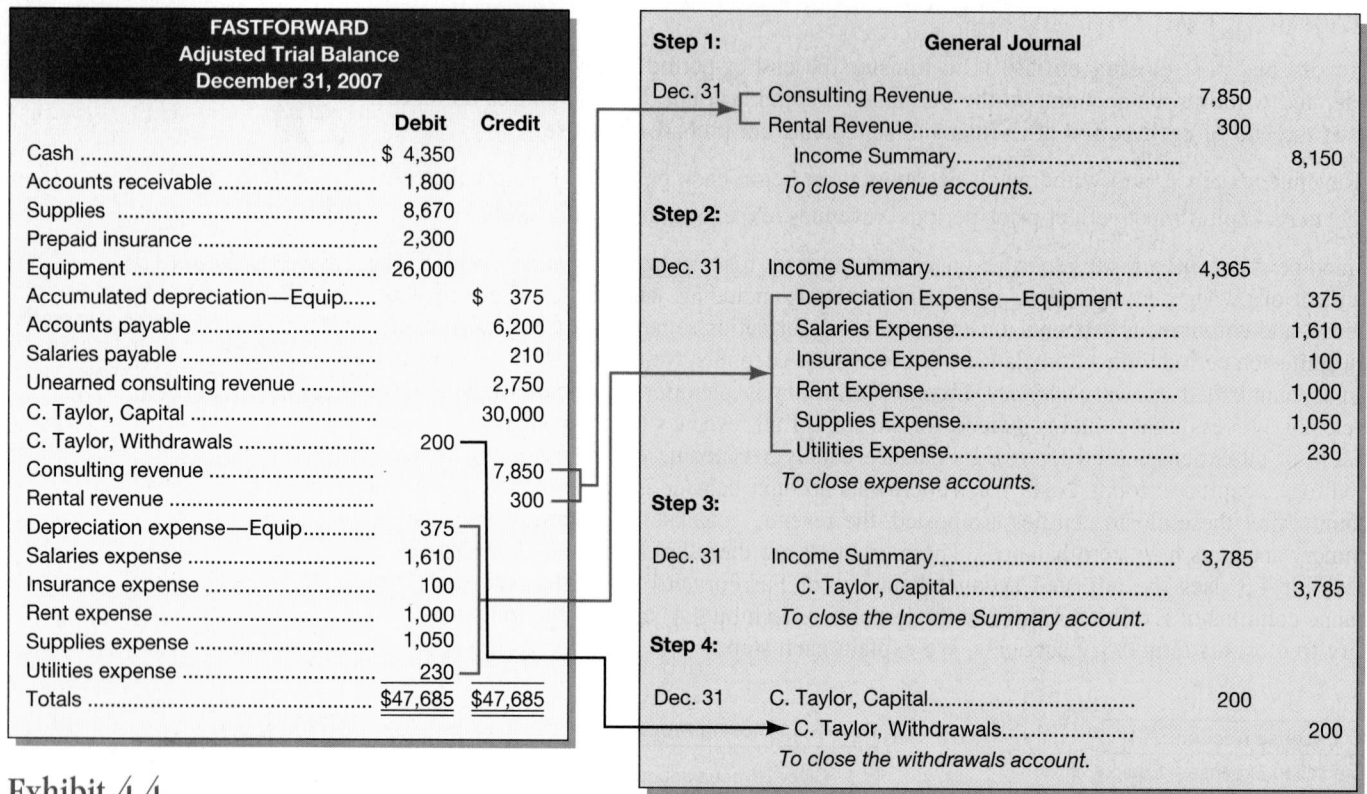

Exhibit 4.4

Preparing Closing Entries

period. This second closing entry for FastForward is step 2 in Exhibit 4.4. Exhibit 4.3 shows that posting this entry gives each expense account a zero balance.

Point: The Income Summary is used only for closing entries.

Step 3: Close Income Summary to Owner's Capital   After steps 1 and 2, the balance of Income Summary is equal to December's net income of $3,785. The third closing entry transfers the balance of the Income Summary account to the capital account. This entry closes the Income Summary account and is step 3 in Exhibit 4.4. The Income Summary account has a zero balance after posting this entry. It continues to have a zero balance until the closing process again occurs at the end of the next period. (If a net loss occurred because expenses exceeded revenues, the third entry is reversed: debit Owner Capital and credit Income Summary.)

Step 4: Close Withdrawals Account to Owner's Capital   The fourth closing entry transfers any debit balance in the withdrawals account to the owner's capital account—see step 4 in Exhibit 4.4. This entry gives the withdrawals account a zero balance, and the account is now ready to accumulate next period's withdrawals. This entry also reduces the capital account balance to the $33,585 amount reported on the balance sheet.

We could also have selected the accounts and amounts needing to be closed by identifying individual revenue, expense, and withdrawals accounts in the ledger. This is illustrated in Exhibit 4.4 where we prepare closing entries using the adjusted trial balance.[1] (Information for closing entries is also in the financial statement columns of a work sheet.)

Post-Closing Trial Balance

P3   Explain and prepare a post-closing trial balance.

Exhibit 4.5 shows the entire ledger of FastForward as of December 31 after adjusting and closing entries are posted. (The transaction and adjusting entries are in Chapters 2 and 3.) The temporary accounts (revenues, expenses, and withdrawals) have ending balances equal to zero.

---

[1] The closing process has focused on proprietorships. It is identical for partnerships with the exception that each owner has separate capital and withdrawals accounts (for steps 3 and 4). The closing process for a corporation is similar with the exception that it uses a Retained Earnings account instead of a Capital account, and a Dividend account instead of a Withdrawals account.

Exhibit 4.5

General Ledger after the Closing Process for FastForward

Asset Accounts

Cash — Acct. No. 101

Date	Explan.	PR	Debit	Credit	Balance
2007					
Dec. 1		G1	30,000		30,000
2		G1		2,500	27,500
3		G1		26,000	1,500
5		G1	4,200		5,700
6		G1		2,400	3,300
12		G1		1,000	2,300
12		G1		700	1,600
22		G1	1,900		3,500
24		G1		900	2,600
24		G1		200	2,400
26		G1	3,000		5,400
26		G1		120	5,280
26		G1		230	5,050
26		G1		700	4,350

Accounts Receivable — Acct. No. 106

Date	Explan.	PR	Debit	Credit	Balance
2007					
Dec. 12		G1	1,900		1,900
22		G1		1,900	0
31	Adj.	G1	1,800		1,800

Supplies — Acct. No. 126

Date	Explan.	PR	Debit	Credit	Balance
2007					
Dec. 2		G1	2,500		2,500
6		G1	7,100		9,600
26		G1	120		9,720
31	Adj.	G1		1,050	8,670

Prepaid Insurance — Acct. No. 128

Date	Explan.	PR	Debit	Credit	Balance
2007					
Dec. 6		G1	2,400		2,400
31	Adj.	G1		100	2,300

Equipment — Acct. No. 167

Date	Explan.	PR	Debit	Credit	Balance
2007					
Dec. 3		G1	26,000		26,000

Accumulated Depreciation— Equipment — Acct. No. 168

Date	Explan.	PR	Debit	Credit	Balance
2007					
Dec. 31	Adj.	G1		375	375

Liability and Equity Accounts

Accounts Payable — Acct. No. 201

Date	Explan.	PR	Debit	Credit	Balance
2007					
Dec. 6		G1		7,100	7,100
24		G1	900		6,200

Salaries Payable — Acct. No. 209

Date	Explan.	PR	Debit	Credit	Balance
2007					
Dec. 31	Adj	G1		210	210

Unearned Consulting Revenue — Acct. No. 236

Date	Explan.	PR	Debit	Credit	Balance
2007					
Dec. 26		G1		3,000	3,000
31	Adj.	G1	250		2,750

C. Taylor, Capital — Acct. No. 301

Date	Explan.	PR	Debit	Credit	Balance
2007					
Dec. 1		G1		30,000	30,000
31	Closing	G1		3,785	33,785
31	Closing	G1	200		33,585

C. Taylor, Withdrawals — Acct. No. 302

Date	Explan.	PR	Debit	Credit	Balance
2007					
Dec. 24		G1	200		200
31	Closing	G1		200	0

Revenue and Expense Accounts (including Income Summary)

Consulting Revenue — Acct. No. 403

Date	Explan.	PR	Debit	Credit	Balance
2007					
Dec. 5		G1		4,200	4,200
12		G1		1,600	5,800
31	Adj.	G1		250	6,050
31	Adj.	G1		1,800	7,850
31	Closing	G1	7,850		0

Rental Revenue — Acct. No. 406

Date	Explan.	PR	Debit	Credit	Balance
2007					
Dec. 12		G1		300	300
31	Closing	G1	300		0

Depreciation Expense— Equipment — Acct. No. 612

Date	Explan.	PR	Debit	Credit	Balance
2007					
Dec. 31	Adj.	G1	375		375
31	Closing	G1		375	0

Salaries Expense — Acct. No. 622

Date	Explan.	PR	Debit	Credit	Balance
2007					
Dec. 12		G1	700		700
26		G1	700		1,400
31	Adj.	G1	210		1,610
31	Closing	G1		1,610	0

Insurance Expense — Acct. No. 637

Date	Explan.	PR	Debit	Credit	Balance
2007					
Dec. 31	Adj.	G1	100		100
31	Closing	G1		100	0

Rent Expense — Acct. No. 640

Date	Explan.	PR	Debit	Credit	Balance
2007					
Dec. 12		G1	1,000		1,000
31	Closing	G1		1,000	0

Supplies Expense — Acct. No. 652

Date	Explan.	PR	Debit	Credit	Balance
2007					
Dec. 31	Adj.	G1	1,050		1,050
31	Closing	G1		1,050	0

Utilities Expense — Acct. No. 690

Date	Explan.	PR	Debit	Credit	Balance
2007					
Dec. 26		G1	230		230
31	Closing	G1		230	0

Income Summary — Acct. No. 901

Date	Explan.	PR	Debit	Credit	Balance
2007					
Dec. 31	Closing	G1		8,150	8,150
31	Closing	G1	4,365		3,785
31	Closing	G1	3,785		0

A **post-closing trial balance** is a list of permanent accounts and their balances from the ledger after all closing entries have been journalized and posted. It lists the balances for all accounts not closed. These accounts comprise a company's assets, liabilities, and equity, which are identical to those in the balance sheet. The aim of a post-closing trial balance is to verify that (1) total debits equal total credits for permanent accounts and (2) all temporary accounts have zero balances. FastForward's post-closing trial balance is shown in Exhibit 4.6. The post-closing trial balance usually is the last step in the accounting process.

Exhibit 4.6

Post-Closing Trial Balance

FASTFORWARD Post-Closing Trial Balance December 31, 2007		
	Debit	**Credit**
Cash	$ 4,350	
Accounts receivable	1,800	
Supplies	8,670	
Prepaid insurance	2,300	
Equipment	26,000	
Accumulated depreciation—Equipment		$ 375
Accounts payable		6,200
Salaries payable		210
Unearned consulting revenue		2,750
C. Taylor, Capital		33,585
Totals	$43,120	$43,120

Accounting Cycle

C2   Identify steps in the accounting cycle.

The term **accounting cycle** refers to the steps in preparing financial statements. It is called a *cycle* because the steps are repeated each reporting period. Exhibit 4.7 shows the 10 steps in the cycle, beginning with analyzing transactions and ending with a post-closing trial balance

Exhibit 4.7

Steps in the Accounting Cycle*

Explanations

1. Analyze transactions	Analyze transactions to prepare for journalizing.
2. Journalize	Record accounts, including debits and credits, in a journal.
3. Post	Transfer debits and credits from the journal to the ledger.
4. Prepare unadjusted trial balance	Summarize unadjusted ledger accounts and amounts.
5. Adjust	Record adjustments to bring account balances up to date; journalize and post adjusting entries.
6. Prepare adjusted trial balance	Summarize adjusted ledger accounts and amounts.
7. Prepare statements	Use adjusted trial balance to prepare financial statements.
8. Close	Journalize and post entries to close temporary accounts.
9. Prepare post-closing trial balance	Test clerical accuracy of the closing procedures.
10. Reverse (optional)	Reverse certain adjustments in the next period—optional step; see Appendix 4A.

*Steps 4, 6, and 9 can be done on a work sheet. A work sheet is useful in *planning* adjustments, but adjustments (step 5) must always be journalized and posted. Steps 3, 4, 6, and 9 are automatic with a computerized system.

or reversing entries. Steps 1 through 3 usually occur regularly as a company enters into transactions. Steps 4 through 9 are done at the end of a period. Reversing entries in step 10 are optional and are explained in Appendix 4A.

Quick Check
Answers—p. 154

4. What are the major steps in preparing closing entries?

5. Why are revenue and expense accounts called *temporary*? Can you identify and list any other temporary accounts?

6. What accounts are listed on the post-closing trial balance?

Classified Balance Sheet

Our discussion to this point has been limited to unclassified financial statements. This section describes a classified balance sheet. Chapter 5 describes a classified income statement. An **unclassified balance sheet** is one whose items are broadly grouped into assets, liabilities, and equity. One example is FastForward's balance sheet in Exhibit 4.2. A **classified balance sheet** organizes assets and liabilities into important subgroups that provide more information to decision makers.

C3 Explain and prepare a classified balance sheet.

Classification Structure

A classified balance sheet has no required layout, but it usually contains the categories in Exhibit 4.8. One of the more important classifications is the separation between current and noncurrent items for both assets and liabilities. Current items are those expected to come due (either collected or owed) within one year or the company's operating cycle, whichever is longer. The **operating cycle** is the time span from when *cash is used* to acquire goods and services until *cash is received* from the sale of goods and services. "Operating" refers to company operations and "cycle" refers to the circular flow of cash used for company inputs and then cash received from its outputs. The length of a company's operating cycle depends on its activities. For a service company, the operating cycle is the time span between (1) paying employees who perform the services and (2) receiving cash from customers. For a merchandiser selling products, the operating cycle is the time span between (1) paying suppliers for merchandise and (2) receiving cash from customers.

Topic Tackler
PLUS
4-2

Assets	Liabilities and Equity
Current assets	Current liabilities
Noncurrent assets	Noncurrent liabilities
Long-term investments	Equity
Plant assets	
Intangible assets	

Exhibit 4.8

Typical Categories in a Classified Balance Sheet

Point: Current is also called *short-term*, and noncurrent is also called *long-term*.

Most operating cycles are less than one year. This means most companies use a one-year period in deciding which assets and liabilities are current. A few companies have an operating cycle longer than one year. For instance, producers of certain beverages (wine) and products (ginseng) that require aging for several years have operating cycles longer than one year. A balance sheet lists current assets before noncurrent assets and current liabilities before noncurrent liabilities. This consistency in presentation allows users to quickly identify current assets that are most easily converted to cash and current liabilities that are shortly coming due. Items in current assets and current liabilities are listed in the order of how quickly they will be converted to, or paid in, cash.

Classification Categories

This section describes the most common categories in a classified balance sheet. The balance sheet for Snowboarding Components in Exhibit 4.9 shows these typical categories. Its assets

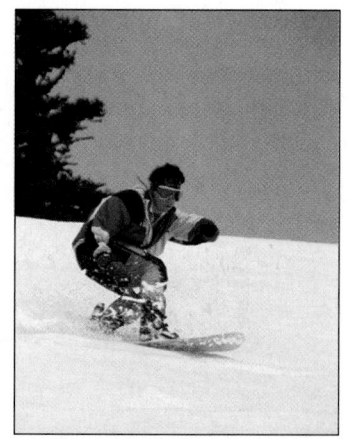

Exhibit 4.9

Example of a Classified
Balance Sheet

SNOWBOARDING COMPONENTS
Balance Sheet
January 31, 2008

Assets

Current assets

Cash	$ 6,500	
Short-term investments	2,100	
Accounts receivable, net	4,400	
Merchandise inventory	27,500	
Prepaid expenses	2,400	
Total current assets		$ 42,900
Long-term investments		
Notes receivable	1,500	
Investments in stocks and bonds	18,000	
Land held for future expansion	48,000	
Total long-term investments		67,500
Plant assets		
Store equipment .... $ 33,200		
Less accumulated depreciation 8,000	25,200	
Buildings 170,000		
Less accumulated depreciation 45,000	125,000	
Land	73,200	
Total plant assets		223,400
Intangible assets		10,000
Total assets		$343,800

Liabilities

Current liabilities

Accounts payable	$15,300	
Wages payable	3,200	
Notes payable	3,000	
Current portion of long-term liabilities	7,500	
Total current liabilities		$ 29,000
Long-term liabilities (net of current portion)		150,000
Total liabilities		179,000

Equity

T. Hawk, Capital		164,800
Total liabilities and equity		$343,800

are classified as either current or noncurrent. Its noncurrent assets include three main categories: long-term investments, plant assets, and intangible assets. Its liabilities are classified as either current or long term. Not all companies use the same categories of assets and liabilities for their balance sheets. **K2 Inc.**'s balance sheet lists only three asset classes: current assets; property, plant and equipment; and other assets.

Point: Short-term investments maturing within three months are combined with cash on both the balance sheet and cash flow statement. This combination is called *cash and cash equivalents*.

Current Assets   **Current assets** are cash and other resources that are expected to be sold, collected, or used within one year or the company's operating cycle, whichever is longer. Examples are cash, short-term investments, accounts receivable, short-term notes receivable, goods for sale (called *merchandise* or *inventory*), and prepaid expenses. The individual prepaid expenses of a company are usually small in amount compared to many other assets and are often combined and shown as a single item. The prepaid expenses in Exhibit 4.9 likely include items such as prepaid insurance, prepaid rent, office supplies, and store supplies. Prepaid expenses are usually listed last because they will not be converted to cash (instead, they are used).

Long-Term Investments A second major balance sheet classification is **long-term** (or *noncurrent*) **investments.** Notes receivable and investments in stocks and bonds are long-term assets when they are expected to be held for more than the longer of one year or the operating cycle. Land held for future expansion is a long-term investment because it is *not* used in operations.

Global: In the U.K. and many countries influenced by U.K. reporting, noncurrent assets are listed first and current assets are listed second.

Plant Assets Plant assets are tangible assets that are both *long lived* and *used to produce* or *sell products and services.* Examples are equipment, machinery, buildings, and land that are used to produce or sell products and services. The order listing for plant assets is usually from most liquid to least liquid such as equipment and machinery to buildings and land.

Point: Plant assets are also called *fixed assets; property, plant and equipment;* or *long-lived assets.*

Intangible Assets **Intangible assets** are long-term resources that benefit business operations. They usually lack physical form and have uncertain benefits. Examples are patents, trademarks, copyrights, franchises, and goodwill. Their value comes from the privileges or rights granted to or held by the owner. **Huffy Corporation** reports intangible assets of $45 million, which is more than 15 percent of its total assets. Its intangibles include trademarks, patents, and licensing agreements.

Current Liabilities **Current liabilities** are obligations due to be paid or settled within one year or the operating cycle, whichever is longer. They are usually settled by paying out current assets such as cash. Current liabilities often include accounts payable, notes payable, wages payable, taxes payable, interest payable, and unearned revenues. Also, any portion of a long-term liability due to be paid within one year or the operating cycle, whichever is longer, is a current liability. Unearned revenues are current liabilities when they will be settled by delivering products or services within one year or the operating cycle, whichever is longer. Current liabilities are reported in the order of those to be settled first.

Point: Many financial ratios are distorted if accounts are not classified correctly. We must be especially careful when analyzing accounts whose balances are separated into short and long term.

Long-Term Liabilities **Long-term liabilities** are obligations *not* due within one year or the operating cycle, whichever is longer. Notes payable, mortgages payable, bonds payable, and lease obligations are common long-term liabilities. If a company has both short- and long-term items in each of these categories, they are commonly separated into two accounts in the ledger.

Point: Many companies report two or more subgroups for long-term liabilities. See the balance sheets in Appendix A for examples.

Equity Equity is the owner's claim on assets. For a proprietorship, this claim is reported in the equity section with an owner's capital account. (For a partnership, the equity section reports a capital account for each partner. For a corporation, the equity section is divided into two main subsections, common stock and retained earnings.)

Quick Check

Answers—p. 154

7. Classify the following assets as (1) current assets, (2) plant assets, or (3) intangible assets:
   (*a*) land used in operations, (*b*) office supplies, (*c*) receivables from customers due in 10 months, (*d*) insurance protection for the next nine months, (*e*) trucks used to provide services to customers, (*f*) trademarks.
8. Cite two examples of assets classified as investments on the balance sheet.
9. Explain the operating cycle for a service company.

Current Ratio   Decision Analysis

An important use of financial statements is to help assess a company's ability to pay its debts in the near future. Such analysis affects decisions by suppliers when allowing a company to buy on credit. It also affects decisions by creditors when lending money to a company, including loan terms such as interest rate, due date, and collateral requirements. It can also affect a manager's decisions about using cash to

A1 Compute the current ratio and describe what it reveals about a company's financial condition.

pay debts when they come due. The **current ratio** is one measure of a company's ability to pay its short-term obligations. It is defined in Exhibit 4.10 as current assets divided by current liabilities:

Exhibit 4.10

Current Ratio

$$\text{Current ratio} = \frac{\text{Current assets}}{\text{Current liabilities}}$$

Using financial information from **Limited Brands, Inc.**, we compute its current ratio for the recent four-year period. The results are in Exhibit 4.11.

Exhibit 4.11

Limited Brands' Current Ratio

	2005	2004	2003	2002
Current assets (in mil.)	$2,684	$4,433	$3,606	$2,784
Current liabilities (in mil.)	$1,451	$1,388	$1,259	$1,454
Current ratio	1.8	3.2	2.9	1.9
Industry current ratio	2.5	2.7	3.0	2.9

Decision Maker

Answer—p. 153

Analyst You are analyzing the financial condition of a fitness club to assess its ability to meet upcoming loan payments. You compute its current ratio as 1.2. You also find that a major portion of accounts receivable is due from one client who has not made any payments in the past 12 months. Removing this receivable from current assets drops the current ratio to 0.7. What do you conclude?

Limited Brands' current ratio averaged 2.5 for 2002–2005. The current ratio for each of these years suggests that the company's short-term obligations can be covered with its short-term assets. However, if its ratio were to approach 1.0, Limited would expect to face challenges in covering liabilities. If the ratio were *less* than 1.0, current liabilities would exceed current assets, and the company's ability to pay short-term obligations could be in doubt.

Demonstration Problem

The partial work sheet of Midtown Repair Company at December 31, 2008, follows.

	Adjusted Trial Balance		Income Statement		Balance Sheet and Statement of Owner's Equity	
	Debit	**Credit**	**Debit**	**Credit**	**Debit**	**Credit**
Cash	95,600					
Notes receivable (current)	50,000					
Prepaid insurance	16,000					
Prepaid rent	4,000					
Equipment	170,000					
Accumulated depreciation—Equipment		57,000				
Accounts payable		52,000				
Long-term notes payable		63,000				
C. Trout, Capital		178,500				
C. Trout, Withdrawals	30,000					
Repair services revenue		180,800				
Interest revenue		7,500				
Depreciation expense—Equipment	28,500					
Wages expense	85,000					
Rent expense	48,000					
Insurance expense	6,000					
Interest expense	5,700					
Totals	538,800	538,800				

Required

1. Complete the work sheet by extending the adjusted trial balance totals to the appropriate financial statement columns.
2. Prepare closing entries for Midtown Repair Company.
3. Set up the Income Summary and the C. Trout, Capital account in the general ledger (in balance column format) and post the closing entries to these accounts.
4. Determine the balance of the C. Trout, Capital account to be reported on the December 31, 2008, balance sheet.
5. Prepare an income statement, statement of owner's equity, and classified balance sheet (in report form) as of December 31, 2008.

Planning the Solution

- Extend the adjusted trial balance account balances to the appropriate financial statement columns.
- Prepare entries to close the revenue accounts to Income Summary, to close the expense accounts to Income Summary, to close Income Summary to the capital account, and to close the withdrawals account to the capital account.
- Post the first and second closing entries to the Income Summary account. Examine the balance of income summary and verify that it agrees with the net income shown on the work sheet.
- Post the third and fourth closing entries to the capital account.
- Use the work sheet's two right-most columns and your answer in part 4 to prepare the classified balance sheet.

Solution to Demonstration Problem

1. Completing the work sheet.

	Adjusted Trial Balance		Income Statement		Balance Sheet and Statement of Owner's Equity	
	Debit	Credit	Debit	Credit	Debit	Credit
Cash	95,600				95,600	
Notes receivable (current)	50,000				50,000	
Prepaid insurance	16,000				16,000	
Prepaid rent	4,000				4,000	
Equipment	170,000				170,000	
Accumulated depreciation—Equipment ...		57,000				57,000
Accounts payable		52,000				52,000
Long-term notes payable		63,000				63,000
C. Trout, Capital		178,500				178,500
C. Trout, Withdrawals	30,000				30,000	
Repair services revenue		180,800		180,800		
Interest revenue		7,500		7,500		
Depreciation expense—Equipment	28,500		28,500			
Wages expense	85,000		85,000			
Rent expense	48,000		48,000			
Insurance expense	6,000		6,000			
Interest expense	5,700		5,700			
Totals	538,800	538,800	173,200	188,300	365,600	350,500
Net Income			15,100			15,100
Totals			188,300	188,300	365,600	365,600

2. Closing entries.

Dec. 31	Repair Services Revenue......................	180,800	
	Interest Revenue	7,500	
	Income Summary		188,300
	To close revenue accounts.		

[continued on next page]

[continued from previous page]

Dec. 31	Income Summary	173,200	
	Depreciation Expense—Equipment.		28,500
	Wages Expense.		85,000
	Rent Expense		48,000
	Insurance Expense.		6,000
	Interest Expense		5,700
	To close expense accounts.		
Dec. 31	Income Summary	15,100	
	C. Trout, Capital		15,100
	To close the Income Summary account.		
Dec. 31	C. Trout, Capital	30,000	
	C. Trout, Withdrawals		30,000
	To close the withdrawals account.		

3. Set up the Income Summary and the capital ledger accounts and post the closing entries.

	Income Summary					Account No. 901
Date	**Explanation**	**PR**	**Debit**	**Credit**	**Balance**	
2008						
Jan. 1	Beginning balance				0	
Dec. 31	Close revenue accounts			188,300	188,300	
31	Close expense accounts		173,200		15,100	
31	Close income summary		15,100		0	

	C. Trout, Capital					Account No. 301
Date	**Explanation**	**PR**	**Debit**	**Credit**	**Balance**	
2008						
Jan. 1	Beginning balance				178,500	
Dec. 31	Close Income Summary			15,100	193,600	
31	Close C. Trout, Withdrawals		30,000		163,600	

4. The final capital balance of $163,600 (from part 3) will be reported on the December 31, 2008, balance sheet. The final capital balance reflects the increase due to the net income earned during the year and the decrease for the owner's withdrawals during the year.

5.

MIDTOWN REPAIR COMPANY		
Income Statement		
For Year Ended December 31, 2008		
Revenues		
Repair services revenue	$180,800	
Interest revenue	7,500	
Total revenues		$188,300
Expenses		
Depreciation expense—Equipment	28,500	
Wages expense	85,000	
Rent expense	48,000	
Insurance expense	6,000	
Interest expense	5,700	
Total expenses		173,200
Net income		$ 15,100

MIDTOWN REPAIR COMPANY
Statement of Owner's Equity
For Year Ended December 31, 2008

C. Trout, Capital, December 31, 2007		$178,500
Add: Investment by owner	$ 0	
Net income	15,100	15,100
		193,600
Less: Withdrawals by owner		30,000
C. Trout, Capital, December 31, 2008		$163,600

MIDTOWN REPAIR COMPANY
Balance Sheet
December 31, 2008

Assets

Current assets		
Cash		$ 95,600
Notes receivable		50,000
Prepaid insurance		16,000
Prepaid rent		4,000
Total current assets		165,600
Plant assets		
Equipment	$170,000	
Less: Accumulated depreciation—Equipment	(57,000)	
Total plant assets		113,000
Total assets		$278,600

Liabilities

Current liabilities		
Accounts payable		$ 52,000
Long-term liabilities		
Long-term notes payable		63,000
Total liabilities		115,000

Equity

C. Trout, Capital		163,600
Total liabilities and equity		$278,600

Reversing Entries

4A

Reversing entries are optional. They are recorded in response to accrued assets and accrued liabilities that were created by adjusting entries at the end of a reporting period. The purpose of reversing entries is to simplify a company's recordkeeping. Exhibit 4A.1 shows an example of FastForward's reversing entries. The top of the exhibit shows the adjusting entry FastForward recorded on December 31 for its employee's earned but unpaid salary. The entry recorded three days' salary of $210, which increased December's total salary expense to $1,610. The entry also recognized a liability of $210. The expense is reported on December's income statement. The expense account is then closed. The ledger on January 1,

Point: As a general rule, adjusting entries that create new asset or liability accounts are likely candidates for reversing.

Exhibit 4A.1

Reversing Entries for an
Accrued Expense

Accrue salaries expense on December 31, 2007

Salaries Expense 210
    Salaries Payable 210

Salaries Expense

Date	Expl.	Debit	Credit	Balance
2007				
Dec. 12	(7)	700		700
26	(16)	700		1,400
31	(e)	210		1,610

Salaries Payable

Date	Expl.	Debit	Credit	Balance
2007				
Dec. 31	(e)		210	210

 — OR —

No reversing entry recorded on January 1, 2008

NO ENTRY

Salaries Expense

Date	Expl.	Debit	Credit	Balance
2008				

Salaries Payable

Date	Expl.	Debit	Credit	Balance
2007				
Dec. 31	(e)		210	210
2008				

Reversing entry recorded on January 1, 2008

Salaries Payable 210
    Salaries Expense 210

Salaries Expense*

Date	Expl.	Debit	Credit	Balance
2008				
Jan. 1			210	⟨210⟩

Salaries Payable

Date	Expl.	Debit	Credit	Balance
2007				
Dec. 31	(e)		210	210
2008				
Jan. 1		210		0

Pay the accrued and current salaries on January 9, the first payday in 2008

Salaries Expense 490
Salaries Payable 210
    Cash 700

Salaries Expense

Date	Expl.	Debit	Credit	Balance
2008				
Jan. 9		490		490

Salaries Payable

Date	Expl.	Debit	Credit	Balance
2007				
Dec. 31	(e)		210	210
2008				
Jan. 9		210		0

Salaries Expense 700
    Cash 700

Salaries Expense*

Date	Expl.	Debit	Credit	Balance
2008				
Jan. 1			210	⟨210⟩
Jan. 9		700		490

Salaries Payable

Date	Expl.	Debit	Credit	Balance
2007				
Dec. 31	(e)		210	210
2008				
Jan. 1		210		0

*Under both approaches, the expense and liability accounts have
identical balances after the cash payment on January 9.*

Salaries Expense $490
Salaries Payable .... $ 0

*Circled numbers in the Balance column indicate abnormal balances.

2005, shows a $210 liability and a zero balance in the Salaries Expense account. At this point, the choice is made between using or not using reversing entries.

Accounting *without* Reversing Entries

The path down the left side of Exhibit 4A.1 is described in the chapter. To summarize here, when the next payday occurs on January 9, we record payment with a compound entry that debits both the expense and liability accounts and credits Cash. Posting that entry creates a $490 balance in the expense account and reduces the liability account balance to zero because the debt has been settled. The disadvantage of this approach is the slightly more complex entry required on January 9. Paying the accrued liability means that this entry differs from the routine entries made on all other paydays. To construct the proper entry on January 9, we must recall the effect of the December 31 adjusting entry. Reversing entries overcome this disadvantage.

Accounting *with* Reversing Entries

The right side of Exhibit 4A.1 shows how a reversing entry on January 1 overcomes the disadvantage of the January 9 entry when not using reversing entries. A reversing entry is the exact opposite of an adjusting entry. For FastForward, the Salaries Payable liability account is debited for $210, meaning that this account now has a zero balance after the entry is posted. The Salaries Payable account temporarily understates the liability, but this is not a problem since financial statements are not prepared before the liability is settled on January 9. The credit to the Salaries Expense account is unusual because it gives the account an *abnormal credit balance*. We highlight an abnormal balance by circling it. Because of the reversing entry, the January 9 entry to record payment is straightforward. This entry debits the Salaries Expense account and credits Cash for the full $700 paid. It is the same as all other entries made to record 10 days' salary for the employee. Notice that after the payment entry is posted, the Salaries Expense account has a $490 balance that reflects seven days' salary of $70 per day (see the lower right side of Exhibit 4A.1). The zero balance in the Salaries Payable account is now correct. The lower section of Exhibit 4A.1 shows that the expense and liability accounts have exactly the same balances whether reversing entries are used or not. This means that both approaches yield identical results.

P4 Prepare reversing entries and explain their purpose.

Summary

C1 Explain why temporary accounts are closed each period. Temporary accounts are closed at the end of each accounting period for two main reasons. First, the closing process updates the capital account to include the effects of all transactions and events recorded for the period. Second, it prepares revenue, expense, and withdrawals accounts for the next reporting period by giving them zero balances.

C2 Identify steps in the accounting cycle. The accounting cycle consists of 10 steps: (1) analyze transactions, (2) journalize, (3) post, (4) prepare an unadjusted trial balance, (5) adjust accounts, (6) prepare an adjusted trial balance, (7) prepare statements, (8) close, (9) prepare a post-closing trial balance, and (10) prepare (optional) reversing entries.

C3 Explain and prepare a classified balance sheet. Classified balance sheets report assets and liabilities in two categories: current and noncurrent. Noncurrent assets often include long-term investments, plant assets, and intangible assets. Owner's equity for proprietorships (and partnerships) report the capital account balance. A corporation separates equity into common stock and retained earnings.

A1 Compute the current ratio and describe what it reveals about a company's financial condition. A company's current ratio is defined as current assets divided by current liabilities. We use it to evaluate a company's ability to pay its current liabilities out of current assets.

P1 Prepare a work sheet and explain its usefulness. A work sheet can be a useful tool in preparing and analyzing financial statements. It is helpful at the end of a period in preparing adjusting entries, an adjusted trial balance, and financial statements. A work sheet usually contains five pairs of columns: Unadjusted Trial Balance, Adjustments, Adjusted Trial Balance, Income Statement, and Balance Sheet & Statement of Owner's Equity.

P2 Describe and prepare closing entries. Closing entries involve four steps: (1) close credit balances in revenue (and gain) accounts to Income Summary, (2) close debit balances in expense (and loss) accounts to Income Summary, (3) close Income Summary to the capital account, and (4) close withdrawals account to owner's capital.

P3 Explain and prepare a post-closing trial balance. A post-closing trial balance is a list of permanent accounts and their balances after all closing entries have been journalized and posted. Its purpose is to verify that (1) total debits equal total credits for permanent accounts and (2) all temporary accounts have zero balances.

P4^A Prepare reversing entries and explain their purpose. Reversing entries are an optional step. They are applied to accrued expenses and revenues. The purpose of reversing entries is to simplify subsequent journal entries. Financial statements are unaffected by the choice to use or not use reversing entries.

Guidance Answers to **Decision Maker** and **Decision Ethics**

Entrepreneur Yes, you are concerned about the absence of a depreciation adjustment. Equipment does depreciate, and financial statements must recognize this occurrence. Its absence suggests an error or a misrepresentation.

Analyst A current ratio of 1.2 suggests that current assets are sufficient to cover current liabilities, but it implies a minimal buffer in case of errors in measuring current assets or current liabilities. Removing the past due receivable reduces the current ratio to 0.7. Your assessment is that the club will have some difficulty meeting its loan payments.

Guidance Answers to **Quick Checks**

1. Amounts in the Unadjusted Trial Balance columns are taken from current account balances in the ledger. The balances for new accounts expected to arise from adjusted entries can be left blank or set at zero.

2. A work sheet offers the advantage of listing on one page all necessary information to make adjusting entries.

3. A work sheet can help in (a) accounting efficiency and avoiding errors, (b) linking transactions and events to their effects in financial statements, (c) showing adjustments for audit purposes, (d) preparing interim financial statements, and (e) showing effects from proposed, or what-if, transactions.

4. The major steps in preparing closing entries are to close (1) credit balances in revenue accounts to Income Summary, (2) debit balances in expense accounts to Income Summary, (3) Income Summary to owner's capital, and (4) any withdrawals account to owner's capital.

5. Revenue (and gain) and expense (and loss) accounts are called *temporary* because they are opened and closed each period. The Income Summary and owner's withdrawals accounts are also temporary.

6. Permanent accounts make up the post-closing trial balance, which consist of asset, liability, and equity accounts.

7. Current assets: (*b*), (*c*), (*d*). Plant assets: (*a*), (*e*). Item (*f*) is an intangible asset.

8. Investment in common stock, investment in bonds, and land held for future expansion.

9. For a service company, the operating cycle is the usual time between (1) paying employees who do the services and (2) receiving cash from customers for services provided.

Key Terms

Key Terms are available at the book's Website for learning and testing in an online Flashcard Format.

Accounting cycle (p. 144)
Classified balance sheet (p. 145)
Closing entries (p. 141)
Closing process (p. 140)
Current assets (p. 146)
Current liabilities (p. 147)
Current ratio (p. 148)

Income Summary (p. 141)
Intangible assets (p. 147)
Long-term investments (p. 147)
Long-term liabilities (p. 147)
Operating cycle (p. 145)
Permanent accounts (p. 140)
Post-closing trial balance (p. 144)

Pro forma financial statements (p. 140)
Reversing entries (p. 151)
Temporary accounts (p. 140)
Unclassified balance sheet (p. 145)
Working papers (p. 136)
Work sheet (p. 136)

Multiple Choice Quiz   Answers on p. 175   mhhe.com/wildFAP18e

Multiple Choice Quizzes A and B are available at the book's Website.

1. G. Venda, owner of Venda Services, withdrew $25,000 from the business during the current year. The entry to close the withdrawals account at the end of the year is:

a.	G. Venda, Withdrawals	25,000
	G. Venda, Capital	25,000
b.	Income Summary	25,000
	G. Venda, Capital	25,000
c.	G. Venda, Withdrawals	25,000
	Cash	25,000
d.	G. Venda, Capital	25,000
	Salary Expense	25,000
e.	G. Venda, Capital	25,000
	G. Venda, Withdrawals	25,000

2. The following information is available for the R. Kandamil Company before closing the accounts. After all of the closing entries are made, what will be the balance in the R. Kandamil, Capital account?

Total revenues	$300,000
Total expenses	195,000
R. Kandamil, Capital	100,000
R. Kandamil, Withdrawals	45,000

a. $360,000
b. $250,000
c. $160,000
d. $150,000
e. $60,000

3. Based on the following information from Repicor Company's balance sheet, what is Repicor Company's current ratio?

Current assets	$ 75,000
Investments	30,000
Plant assets	300,000
Current liabilities	50,000
Long-term liabilities	60,000
D. Repicor, Capital	295,000

  a. 2.10
  b. 1.50
  c. 1.00
  d. 0.95
  e. 0.67

4. Which of the following errors would cause the balance sheet and statement of owner's equity columns of a work sheet to be out of balance?

  a. Entering a revenue amount in the balance sheet and statement of owner's equity debit column.
  b. Entering a liability amount in the balance sheet and statement of owner's equity credit column.
  c. Entering an expense account in the balance sheet and statement of owner's equity debit column.
  d. Entering an asset account in the income statement debit column.
  e. Entering a liability amount in the income statement credit column.

5. The temporary account used only in the closing process to hold the amounts of revenues and expenses before the net difference is added or subtracted from the owner's capital account is called the
  a. Closing account.
  b. Nominal account.
  c. Income Summary account.
  d. Balance Column account.
  e. Contra account.

Superscript letter ^A denotes assignments based on Appendix 4A.

Discussion Questions

1. What accounts are affected by closing entries? What accounts are not affected?

2. What two purposes are accomplished by recording closing entries?

3. What are the steps in recording closing entries?

4. What is the purpose of the Income Summary account?

5. Explain whether an error has occurred if a post-closing trial balance includes a Depreciation Expense account.

6. What tasks are aided by a work sheet?

7. Why are the debit and credit entries in the Adjustments columns of the work sheet identified with letters?

8. What is a company's operating cycle?

9. What classes of assets and liabilities are shown on a typical classified balance sheet?

10. How is unearned revenue classified on the balance sheet?

11. What are the characteristics of plant assets?

12.^A How do reversing entries simplify recordkeeping?

13.^A If a company recorded accrued salaries expense of $500 at the end of its fiscal year, what reversing entry could be made? When would it be made?

14. Refer to the balance sheet for **Best Buy** in Appendix A. What five noncurrent asset categories are used on its classified balance sheet?

15. Refer to **Circuit City**'s balance sheet in Appendix A. Identify the accounts listed as current liabilities.

16. Refer to **Apple**'s financial statements in Appendix A. What journal entry was likely recorded as of September 25, 2004, to close its Income Summary account?

 Red numbers denote Discussion Questions that involve decision-making.

Gloriosa Company began the current period with a $28,000 credit balance in the M. Gloriosa, Capital account. At the end of the period, the company's adjusted account balances include the following temporary accounts with normal balances.

Service fees earned	$45,000	Interest revenue	$6,000
Salaries expense	29,000	M. Gloriosa, Withdrawals	7,200
Depreciation expense	9,000	Utilities expense	3,000

QUICK STUDY

QS 4-1
Determining effects of closing entries

C1 P2

After closing the revenue and expense accounts, what will be the balance of the Income Summary account? After all closing entries are journalized and posted, what will be the balance of the M. Gloriosa, Capital account?

QS 4-2

Identifying the accounting cycle

C2

List the following steps of the accounting cycle in their proper order.

a. Posting the journal entries.

b. Journalizing and posting adjusting entries.

c. Preparing the adjusted trial balance.

d. Journalizing and posting closing entries.

e. Analyzing transactions and events.

f. Preparing the financial statements.

g. Preparing the unadjusted trial balance.

h. Journalizing transactions and events.

i. Preparing the post-closing trial balance.

QS 4-3

Classifying balance sheet items

C3

The following are common categories on a classified balance sheet.

A. Current assets

B. Long-term investments

C. Plant assets

D. Intangible assets

E. Current liabilities

F. Long-term liabilities

For each of the following items, select the letter that identifies the balance sheet category where the item typically would appear.

_____ **1.** Land not currently used in operations

_____ **2.** Notes payable (due in three years)

_____ **3.** Accounts receivable

_____ **4.** Trademarks

_____ **5.** Accounts payable

_____ **6.** Store equipment

_____ **7.** Wages payable

_____ **8.** Cash

QS 4-4

Identifying current accounts and computing the current ratio

C3 A1

Compute Chavez Company's current ratio using the following information.

Accounts receivable	$18,000	Long-term notes payable	$21,000
Accounts payable	11,000	Office supplies	2,800
Buildings	45,000	Prepaid insurance	3,500
Cash	7,000	Unearned services revenue	3,000

QS 4-5

Interpreting a work sheet

P1

The following information is taken from the work sheet for Warton Company as of December 31, 2008. Using this information, determine the amount for B. Warton, Capital, that should be reported on its December 31, 2008, balance sheet.

	Income Statement		Balance Sheet and Statement of Owner's Equity	
	Dr.	**Cr.**	**Dr.**	**Cr.**
B. Warton, Capital				72,000
B. Warton, Withdrawals			39,000	
Totals	122,000	181,000		

QS 4-6

Applying a work sheet

P1

In preparing a work sheet, indicate the financial statement Debit column to which a normal balance in the following accounts should be extended. Use I for the Income Statement Debit column and B for the Balance Sheet and Statement of Owner's Equity Debit column.

_____ **a.** Equipment

_____ **b.** Owner, Withdrawals

_____ **c.** Prepaid rent

_____ **d.** Depreciation expense—Equipment

_____ **e.** Accounts receivable

_____ **f.** Insurance expense

List the following steps in preparing a work sheet in their proper order by writing numbers 1–5 in the blank spaces provided.

a. _____ Total the statement columns, compute net income (loss), and complete work sheet.

b. _____ Extend adjusted balances to appropriate financial statement columns.

c. _____ Prepare an unadjusted trial balance on the work sheet.

d. _____ Prepare an adjusted trial balance on the work sheet.

e. _____ Enter adjustments data on the work sheet.

QS 4-7
Ordering work sheet steps

P1

The ledger of Claudell Company includes the following unadjusted normal balances: Prepaid Rent $1,000, Services Revenue $55,600, and Wages Expense $25,000. Adjusting entries are required for **(a)** prepaid rent expense used, $200; **(b)** accrued services revenue $900; and **(c)** accrued wages expense $700. Enter these unadjusted balances and the necessary adjustments on a work sheet and complete the work sheet for these accounts. *Note:* You must include the following accounts: Accounts Receivable, Wages Payable, and Rent Expense.

QS 4-8
Preparing a partial work sheet

P1

The ledger of Mai Company includes the following accounts with normal balances: D. Mai, Capital $9,000; D. Mai, Withdrawals $800; Services Revenue $13,000; Wages Expense $8,400; and Rent Expense $1,600. Prepare the necessary closing entries from the available information at December 31.

QS 4-9
Prepare closing entries from the ledger   P2

Identify the accounts listed in QS 4-9 that would be included in a post-closing trial balance.

QS 4-10
Identify post-closing accounts   P3

On December 31, 2007, Yates Co. prepared an adjusting entry for $12,000 of earned but unrecorded management fees. On January 16, 2008, Yates received $26,700 cash in management fees, which included the accrued fees earned in 2007. Assuming the company uses reversing entries, prepare the January 1, 2008, reversing entry and the January 16, 2008, cash receipt entry.

QS 4-11[A]
Reversing entries

P4

Use the March 31 fiscal year-end information from the following ledger accounts (assume that all accounts have normal balances) to prepare closing journal entries and then post those entries to the appropriate ledger accounts.

EXERCISES

Exercise 4-1
Preparing and posting closing entries

P2

General Ledger					

M. Muncel, Capital Acct. No. 301

Date	PR	Debit	Credit	Balance
Mar. 31	G2			40,000

M. Muncel, Withdrawals Acct. No. 302

Date	PR	Debit	Credit	Balance
Mar. 31	G2			22,000

Services Revenue Acct. No. 401

Date	PR	Debit	Credit	Balance
Mar. 31	G2			76,000

Depreciation Expense Acct. No. 603

Date	PR	Debit	Credit	Balance
Mar. 31	G2			15,000

Salaries Expense Acct. No. 622

Date	PR	Debit	Credit	Balance
Mar. 31	G2			20,000

Insurance Expense Acct. No. 637

Date	PR	Debit	Credit	Balance
Mar. 31	G2			4,400

Rent Expense Acct. No. 640

Date	PR	Debit	Credit	Balance
Mar. 31	G2			8,400

Income Summary Acct. No. 901

Date	PR	Debit	Credit	Balance

Check M. Muncel, Capital (ending balance), $46,200

Exercise 4-2
Preparing closing entries and a
post-closing trial balance

P2   P3

The adjusted trial balance for Salonika Marketing Co. follows. Complete the four right-most columns of the table by first entering information for the four closing entries (keyed *1* through *4*) and second by completing the post-closing trial balance.

No.	Account Title	Adjusted Trial Balance Dr.	Adjusted Trial Balance Cr.	Closing Entry Information Dr.	Closing Entry Information Cr.	Post-Closing Trial Balance Dr.	Post-Closing Trial Balance Cr.
101	Cash	$ 9,200					
106	Accounts receivable	25,000					
153	Equipment	42,000					
154	Accumulated depreciation—Equipment		$ 17,500				
193	Franchise	31,000					
201	Accounts payable		15,000				
209	Salaries payable		4,200				
233	Unearned fees		3,600				
301	E. Salonika, Capital		68,500				
302	E. Salonika, Withdrawals	15,400					
401	Marketing fees earned		80,000				
611	Depreciation expense—Equipment	12,000					
622	Salaries expense	32,500					
640	Rent expense	13,000					
677	Miscellaneous expenses	8,700					
901	Income summary						
	Totals	$188,800	$188,800				

Exercise 4-3
Preparing closing entries and a
post-closing trial balance

C1   P2   P3

The following adjusted trial balance contains the accounts and balances of Cruz Company as of December 31, 2008, the end of its fiscal year. (1) Prepare the December 31, 2008, closing entries for Cruz Company. (2) Prepare the December 31, 2008, post-closing trial balance for Cruz Company.

No.	Account Title	Debit	Credit
101	Cash	$19,000	
126	Supplies	13,000	
128	Prepaid insurance	3,000	
167	Equipment	24,000	
168	Accumulated depreciation—Equipment		$ 7,500
301	T. Cruz, Capital		47,600
302	T. Cruz, Withdrawals	7,000	
404	Services revenue		44,000
612	Depreciation expense—Equipment	3,000	
622	Salaries expense	22,000	
637	Insurance expense	2,500	
640	Rent expense	3,400	
652	Supplies expense	2,200	
	Totals	$99,100	$99,100

Check   (2) T. Cruz, Capital (ending),
$51,500; Total debits, $59,000

Use the following adjusted trial balance of Wilson Trucking Company to prepare the (1) income statement, and (2) statement of owner's equity, for the year ended December 31, 2008. The K. Wilson, Capital account balance is $175,000 at December 31, 2007.

Exercise 4-4
Preparing the financial statements
C2

Account Title	Debit	Credit
Cash	$ 8,000	
Accounts receivable	17,500	
Office supplies	3,000	
Trucks	172,000	
Accumulated depreciation—Trucks		$ 36,000
Land	85,000	
Accounts payable		12,000
Interest payable		4,000
Long-term notes payable		53,000
K. Wilson, Capital		175,000
K. Wilson, Withdrawals	20,000	
Trucking fees earned		130,000
Depreciation expense—Trucks	23,500	
Salaries expense	61,000	
Office supplies expense	8,000	
Repairs expense—Trucks	12,000	
Totals	$410,000	$410,000

Use the information in the adjusted trial balance reported in Exercise 4-4 to prepare Wilson Trucking Company's classified balance sheet.

Exercise 4-5
Preparing a classified balance sheet C3

Check Total assets, $249,500;
K. Wilson, Capital, $180,500

Use the information in the adjusted trial balance reported in Exercise 4-4 to compute the current ratio as of the balance sheet date. Interpret the current ratio for the Wilson Trucking Company. (Assume that the industry average for the current ratio is 1.5.)

Exercise 4-6
Computing the current ratio

A1

Calculate the current ratio in each of the following separate cases. Identify the company case with the strongest liquidity position. (These cases represent competing companies in the same industry.)

Exercise 4-7
Computing and analyzing the current ratio

A1

	Current Assets	Current Liabilities
Case 1	$ 79,000	$ 32,000
Case 2	105,000	76,000
Case 3	45,000	49,000
Case 4	85,500	81,600
Case 5	61,000	100,000

Use the following information from the Adjustments columns of a 10-column work sheet to prepare the necessary adjusting journal entries (a) through (e).

Exercise 4-8
Preparing adjusting entries from a work sheet

P1

		Adjustments	
No.	Account Title	Debit	Credit
109	Interest receivable	(d) $ 880	
124	Office supplies		(b) $1,750
128	Prepaid insurance		(a) 900

[continued on next page]

[continued from previous page]

164	Accumulated depreciation—Office equipment		(c)	2,200
209	Salaries payable		(e)	560
409	Interest revenue		(d)	880
612	Depreciation expense—Office equipment	(c) 2,200		
620	Office salaries expense	(e) 560		
636	Insurance expense—Office equipment	(a) 332		
637	Insurance expense—Store equipment	(a) 568		
650	Office supplies expense	(b) 1,750		
	Totals	$6,290	$6,290	

Exercise 4-9

Extending adjusted account balances on a work sheet

P1

These 16 accounts are from the Adjusted Trial Balance columns of a company's 10-column work sheet. In the blank space beside each account, write the letter of the appropriate financial statement column (A, B, C, or D) to which a normal account balance is extended.

A. Debit column for the Income Statement columns.

B. Credit column for the Income Statement columns.

C. Debit column for the Balance Sheet and Statement of Owner's Equity columns.

D. Credit column for the Balance Sheet and Statement of Owner's Equity columns.

_____ **1.** Interest Revenue
_____ **2.** Machinery
_____ **3.** Owner, Withdrawals
_____ **4.** Depreciation Expense
_____ **5.** Accounts Payable
_____ **6.** Service Fees Revenue
_____ **7.** Owner, Capital
_____ **8.** Interest Expense

_____ **9.** Accounts Receivable
_____ **10.** Accumulated Depreciation
_____ **11.** Office Supplies
_____ **12.** Insurance Expense
_____ **13.** Interest Receivable
_____ **14.** Cash
_____ **15.** Rent Expense
_____ **16.** Wages Payable

Exercise 4-10

Extending accounts in a work sheet

P1

The Adjusted Trial Balance columns of a 10-column work sheet for Planta Company follow. Complete the work sheet by extending the account balances into the appropriate financial statement columns and by entering the amount of net income for the reporting period.

No.	Account Title	Debit	Credit
101	Cash	$ 7,000	
106	Accounts receivable	27,200	
153	Trucks	42,000	
154	Accumulated depreciation—Trucks		$ 17,500
183	Land	32,000	
201	Accounts payable		15,000
209	Salaries payable		4,200
233	Unearned fees		3,600
301	F. Planta, Capital		65,500
302	F. Planta, Withdrawals	15,400	
401	Plumbing fees earned		84,000
611	Depreciation expense—Trucks	6,500	
622	Salaries expense	38,000	
640	Rent expense	13,000	
677	Miscellaneous expenses	8,700	
	Totals	$189,800	$189,800

Check   Net income, $17,800

These partially completed Income Statement columns from a 10-column work sheet are for Brown's Bike Rental Company. (1) Use the information to determine the amount that should be entered on the net income line of the work sheet. (2) Prepare the company's closing entries. The owner, H. Brown, did not make any withdrawals this period.

Exercise 4-11
Completing the income statement columns and preparing closing entries

P1   P2

Account Title	Debit	Credit
Rent earned		120,000
Salaries expense	46,300	
Insurance expense	7,400	
Office supplies expense	16,000	
Bike repair expense	4,200	
Depreciation expense—Bikes	20,500	
Totals		
Net income		
Totals		

Check   Net income, $25,600

The following unadjusted trial balance contains the accounts and balances of Dylan Delivery Company as of December 31, 2008, its first year of operations.

(1) Use the following information about the company's adjustments to complete a 10-column work sheet for Dylan.

a. Unrecorded depreciation on the trucks at the end of the year is $40,000.

b. The total amount of accrued interest expense at year-end is $6,000.

c. The cost of unused office supplies still available at the year-end is $2,000.

(2) Prepare the year-end closing entries for Dylan, and determine the capital amount to be reported on its year-end balance sheet.

Exercise 4-12
Preparing a work sheet and recording closing entries

P1   P2

Microsoft Excel - Book1
File Edit View Insert Format Tools Data Accounting Window Help

Account Title	Debit	Credit
1		
2 Cash	$ 16,000	
3 Accounts receivable	34,000	
4 Office supplies	5,000	
5 Trucks	350,000	
6 Accumulated depreciation—Trucks		$ 80,000
7 Land	160,000	
8 Accounts payable		24,000
9 Interest payable		5,000
10 Long-term notes payable		100,000
11 S. Dylan, Capital		307,000
12 S. Dylan, Withdrawals	34,000	
13 Delivery fees earned		263,000
14 Depreciation expense—Truck	40,000	
15 Salaries expense	110,000	
16 Office supplies expense	15,000	
17 Interest expense	5,000	
18 Repairs expense—trucks	10,000	
19 Totals	$779,000	$779,000
20		

Check   Adj. trial balance totals, $820,000; Net income, $39,000

The following two events occurred for Trey Co. on October 31, 2008, the end of its fiscal year.

a. Trey rents a building from its owner for $2,800 per month. By a prearrangement, the company delayed paying October's rent until November 5. On this date, the company paid the rent for both October and November.

Exercise 4-13ᴬ
Preparing reversing entries

P4

b. Trey rents space in a building it owns to a tenant for $850 per month. By prearrangement, the tenant delayed paying the October rent until November 8. On this date, the tenant paid the rent for both October and November.

Required

1. Prepare adjusting entries that Trey must record for these events as of October 31.

2. Assuming Trey does *not* use reversing entries, prepare journal entries to record Trey's payment of rent on November 5 and the collection of rent on November 8 from Trey's tenant.

3. Assuming that Trey uses reversing entries, prepare reversing entries on November 1 and the journal entries to record Trey's payment of rent on November 5 and the collection of rent on November 8 from Trey's tenant.

Exercise 4-14ᴬ

Preparing reversing entries

P4

Hawk Company records prepaid assets and unearned revenues in balance sheet accounts. The following information was used to prepare adjusting entries for Hawk Company as of August 31, the end of the company's fiscal year.

a. The company has earned $6,000 in unrecorded service fees.

b. The expired portion of prepaid insurance is $3,700.

c. The company has earned $2,900 of its Unearned Service Fees account balance.

d. Depreciation expense for office equipment is $3,300.

e. Employees have earned but have not been paid salaries of $3,400.

Prepare any necessary reversing entries for the accounting adjustments *a* through *e* assuming that Hawk uses reversing entries in its accounting system.

PROBLEM SET A

Problem 4-1A

Determining balance sheet classifications

C3

In the blank space beside each numbered balance sheet item, enter the letter of its balance sheet classification. If the item should not appear on the balance sheet, enter a *Z* in the blank.

A. Current assets
B. Long-term investments
C. Plant assets
D. Intangible assets
E. Current liabilities
F. Long-term liabilities
G. Equity

_____ **1.** Long-term investment in stock
_____ **2.** Depreciation expense—Building
_____ **3.** Prepaid rent
_____ **4.** Interest receivable
_____ **5.** Taxes payable
_____ **6.** Automobiles
_____ **7.** Notes payable (due in 3 years)
_____ **8.** Accounts payable
_____ **9.** Prepaid insurance
_____ **10.** Owner, Capital
_____ **11.** Unearned services revenue

_____ **12.** Accumulated depreciation— Trucks
_____ **13.** Cash
_____ **14.** Buildings
_____ **15.** Store supplies
_____ **16.** Office equipment
_____ **17.** Land (used in operations)
_____ **18.** Repairs expense
_____ **19.** Office supplies
_____ **20.** Current portion of long-term note payable

Problem 4-2A

Applying the accounting cycle

C1 C2 P2 P3

eXcel

mhhe.com/wildFAP18e

On April 1, 2008, Jiro Nozomi created a new travel agency, Adventure Travel. The following transactions occurred during the company's first month.

April 1 Nozomi invested $30,000 cash and computer equipment worth $20,000 in the business.
     2 Rented furnished office space by paying $1,800 cash for the first month's (April) rent.
     3 Purchased $1,000 of office supplies for cash.
    10 Paid $2,400 cash for the premium on a 12-month insurance policy. Coverage begins on April 11.
    14 Paid $1,600 cash for two weeks' salaries earned by employees.
    24 Collected $8,000 cash on commissions from airlines on tickets obtained for customers.
    28 Paid another $1,600 cash for two weeks' salaries earned by employees.
    29 Paid $350 cash for minor repairs to the company's computer.
    30 Paid $750 cash for this month's telephone bill.
    30 Nozomi withdrew $1,500 cash for personal use.

The company's chart of accounts follows:

101	Cash		405	Commissions Earned
106	Accounts Receivable		612	Depreciation Expense—Computer Equip.
124	Office Supplies		622	Salaries Expense
128	Prepaid Insurance		637	Insurance Expense
167	Computer Equipment		640	Rent Expense
168	Accumulated Depreciation—Computer Equip.		650	Office Supplies Expense
209	Salaries Payable		684	Repairs Expense
301	J. Nozomi, Capital		688	Telephone Expense
302	J. Nozomi, Withdrawals		901	Income Summary

Required

1. Use the balance column format to set up each ledger account listed in its chart of accounts.
2. Prepare journal entries to record the transactions for April and post them to the ledger accounts. The company records prepaid and unearned items in balance sheet accounts.
3. Prepare an unadjusted trial balance as of April 30.
4. Use the following information to journalize and post adjusting entries for the month:
   a. Two-thirds of one month's insurance coverage has expired.
   b. At the end of the month, $600 of office supplies are still available.
   c. This month's depreciation on the computer equipment is $500.
   d. Employees earned $420 of unpaid and unrecorded salaries as of month-end.
   e. The company earned $1,750 of commissions that are not yet billed at month-end.
5. Prepare the income statement and the statement of owner's equity for the month of April and the balance sheet at April 30, 2008.
6. Prepare journal entries to close the temporary accounts and post these entries to the ledger.
7. Prepare a post-closing trial balance.

Check (3) Unadj. trial balance totals, $58,000

(4a) Dr. Insurance Expense, $133

(5) Net income, $2,197; J. Nozomi, Capital (4/30/2008), $50,697; Total assets, $51,117

(7) P-C trial balance totals, $51,617

The adjusted trial balance of Karise Repairs on December 31, 2008, follows.

Problem 4-3A

Preparing trial balances, closing entries, and financial statements

C3   P2   P3

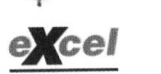
mhhe.com/wildFAP18e

	KARISE REPAIRS Adjusted Trial Balance December 31, 2008		
No.	**Account Title**	**Debit**	**Credit**
101	Cash	$ 14,000	
124	Office supplies	1,300	
128	Prepaid insurance	2,050	
167	Equipment	50,000	
168	Accumulated depreciation—Equipment		$ 5,000
201	Accounts payable		14,000
210	Wages payable		600
301	C. Karise, Capital		33,000
302	C. Karise, Withdrawals	16,000	
401	Repair fees earned		90,950
612	Depreciation expense—Equipment	5,000	
623	Wages expense	37,500	
637	Insurance expense	800	
640	Rent expense	10,600	
650	Office supplies expense	3,600	
690	Utilities expense	2,700	
	Totals	$143,550	$143,550

Required

1. Prepare an income statement and a statement of owner's equity for the year 2008, and a classified balance sheet at December 31, 2008. There are no owner investments in 2008.

2. Enter the adjusted trial balance in the first two columns of a six-column table. Use columns three and four for closing entry information and the last two columns for a post-closing trial balance. Insert an Income Summary account as the last item in the trial balance.

3. Enter closing entry information in the six-column table and prepare journal entries for them.

Analysis Component

4. Assume for this part only that:

   a. None of the $800 insurance expense had expired during the year. Instead, assume it is a prepayment of the next period's insurance protection.

   b. There are no earned and unpaid wages at the end of the year. (*Hint:* Reverse the $600 wages payable accrual.)

   Describe the financial statement changes that would result from these two assumptions.

Problem 4-4A

Preparing closing entries, financial statements, and ratios

C3   A1   P2

The adjusted trial balance for Tybalt Construction as of December 31, 2008, follows.

No.	Account Title	Debit	Credit
	TYBALT CONSTRUCTION		
	Adjusted Trial Balance		
	December 31, 2008		
101	Cash	$ 5,000	
104	Short-term investments	23,000	
126	Supplies	8,100	
128	Prepaid insurance	7,000	
167	Equipment	40,000	
168	Accumulated depreciation—Equipment		$ 20,000
173	Building	150,000	
174	Accumulated depreciation—Building		50,000
183	Land	55,000	
201	Accounts payable		16,500
203	Interest payable		2,500
208	Rent payable		3,500
210	Wages payable		2,500
213	Property taxes payable		900
233	Unearned professional fees		7,500
251	Long-term notes payable		67,000
301	O. Tybalt, Capital		126,400
302	O. Tybalt, Withdrawals	13,000	
401	Professional fees earned		97,000
406	Rent earned		14,000
407	Dividends earned		2,000
409	Interest earned		2,100
606	Depreciation expense—Building	11,000	
612	Depreciation expense—Equipment	6,000	
623	Wages expense	32,000	
633	Interest expense	5,100	
637	Insurance expense	10,000	
640	Rent expense	13,400	
652	Supplies expense	7,400	
682	Postage expense	4,200	
683	Property taxes expense	5,000	
684	Repairs expense	8,900	
688	Telephone expense	3,200	
690	Utilities expense	4,600	
	Totals	$411,900	$411,900

O. Tybalt invested $5,000 cash in the business during year 2008 (the December 31, 2007, credit balance of the O. Tybalt, Capital account was $121,400). Tybalt Construction is required to make a $7,000 payment on its long-term notes payable during 2009.

Required

1. Prepare the income statement and the statement of owner's equity for the calendar-year 2008, and the classified balance sheet at December 31, 2008.

2. Prepare the necessary closing entries at December 31, 2008.

3. Use the information in the financial statements to compute these ratios: (*a*) return on assets (total assets at December 31, 2007, was $200,000), (*b*) debt ratio, (*c*) profit margin ratio (use total revenues as the denominator), and (*d*) current ratio.

Check (1) Total assets (12/31/2008), $218,100; Net income, $4,300

The following unadjusted trial balance is for Ace Construction Co. as of the end of its 2008 fiscal year. The June 30, 2007, credit balance of the owner's capital account was $53,660, and the owner invested $35,000 cash in the company during the 2008 fiscal year.

Problem 4-5A
Preparing a work sheet, adjusting and closing entries, and financial statements

C3   P1   P2

No.	Account Title	Debit	Credit
	ACE CONSTRUCTION CO.		
	Unadjusted Trial Balance		
	June 30, 2008		
101	Cash	$ 18,500	
126	Supplies	9,900	
128	Prepaid insurance	7,200	
167	Equipment	132,000	
168	Accumulated depreciation—Equipment		$ 26,250
201	Accounts payable		6,800
203	Interest payable		0
208	Rent payable		0
210	Wages payable		0
213	Property taxes payable		0
251	Long-term notes payable		25,000
301	V. Ace, Capital		88,660
302	V. Ace, Withdrawals	33,000	
401	Construction fees earned		132,100
612	Depreciation expense—Equipment	0	
623	Wages expense	46,860	
633	Interest expense	2,750	
637	Insurance expense	0	
640	Rent expense	12,000	
652	Supplies expense	0	
683	Property taxes expense	7,800	
684	Repairs expense	2,910	
690	Utilities expense	5,890	
	Totals	$ 278,810	$ 278,810

Required

1. Prepare a 10-column work sheet for fiscal year 2008, starting with the unadjusted trial balance and including adjustments based on these additional facts.

a. The supplies available at the end of fiscal year 2008 had a cost of $3,300.

b. The cost of expired insurance for the fiscal year is $3,800.

c. Annual depreciation on equipment is $8,400.

d. The June utilities expense of $650 is not included in the unadjusted trial balance because the bill arrived after the trial balance was prepared. The $650 amount owed needs to be recorded.

e. The company's employees have earned $1,800 of accrued wages at fiscal year-end.

f. The rent expense incurred and not yet paid or recorded at fiscal year-end is $500.

g. Additional property taxes of $1,000 have been assessed for this fiscal year but have not been paid or recorded in the accounts.

h. The long-term note payable bears interest at 12% per year. The unadjusted Interest Expense account equals the amount paid for the first 11 months of the 2008 fiscal year. The $250 accrued interest for June has not yet been paid or recorded. (Note that the company is required to make a $5,000 payment toward the note payable during the 2009 fiscal year.)

2. Use the work sheet to enter the adjusting and closing entries; then journalize them.

Check (3) Total assets, $122,550;
Current liabilities, $16,000; Net income,
$30,890

3. Prepare the income statement and the statement of owner's equity for the year ended June 30 and the classified balance sheet at June 30, 2008.

Analysis Component

4. Analyze the following separate errors and describe how each would affect the 10-column work sheet. Explain whether the error is likely to be discovered in completing the work sheet and, if not, the effect of the error on the financial statements.

   a. Assume that the adjustment for supplies used consisted of a credit to Supplies for $3,300 and a debit for $3,300 to Supplies Expense.

   b. When the adjusted trial balance in the work sheet is completed, assume that the $18,500 Cash balance is incorrectly entered in the Credit column.

Problem 4-6A[A]

Preparing adjusting, reversing, and next period entries

P4

The following six-column table for Hawkeye Ranges includes the unadjusted trial balance as of December 31, 2008.

	HAWKEYE RANGES December 31, 2008					
	Unadjusted Trial Balance		**Adjustments**		**Adjusted Trial Balance**	
Account Title	Dr.	Cr.	Dr.	Cr.	Dr.	Cr.
Cash	$ 14,000					
Accounts receivable	0					
Supplies	6,500					
Equipment	135,000					
Accumulated depreciation— Equipment		$ 30,000				
Interest payable		0				
Salaries payable		0				
Unearned member fees		15,000				
Notes payable		75,000				
P. Hawkeye, Capital		50,250				
P. Hawkeye, Withdrawals	21,125					
Member fees earned		42,000				
Depreciation expense— Equipment	0					
Salaries expense	30,000					
Interest expense	5,625					
Supplies expense	0					
Totals	$212,250	$212,250				

Required

1. Complete the six-column table by entering adjustments that reflect the following information.

   a. As of December 31, 2008, employees had earned $1,200 of unpaid and unrecorded salaries. The next payday is January 4, at which time $1,500 of salaries will be paid.

   b. The cost of supplies still available at December 31, 2008, is $3,000.

   c. The notes payable requires an interest payment to be made every three months. The amount of unrecorded accrued interest at December 31, 2008, is $1,875. The next interest payment, at an amount of $2,250, is due on January 15, 2009.

   d. Analysis of the unearned member fees account shows $5,800 remaining unearned at December 31, 2008.

   e. In addition to the member fees included in the revenue account balance, the company has earned another $9,300 in unrecorded fees that will be collected on January 31, 2009. The company is also expected to collect $10,000 on that same day for new fees earned in January 2009.

   f. Depreciation expense for the year is $15,000.

2. Prepare journal entries for the adjustments entered in the six-column table for part 1.

3. Prepare journal entries to reverse the effects of the adjusting entries that involve accruals.

4. Prepare journal entries to record the cash payments and cash collections described for January.

Check (1) Adjusted trial balance totals, $239,625

In the blank space beside each numbered balance sheet item, enter the letter of its balance sheet classification. If the item should not appear on the balance sheet, enter a *Z* in the blank.

A. Current assets
B. Long-term investments
C. Plant assets
D. Intangible assets

E. Current liabilities
F. Long-term liabilities
G. Equity

PROBLEM SET B

Problem 4-1B
Determining balance sheet classifications

C3

_____ **1.** Commissions earned
_____ **2.** Interest receivable
_____ **3.** Long-term investment in stock
_____ **4.** Prepaid insurance
_____ **5.** Machinery
_____ **6.** Notes payable (due in 15 years)
_____ **7.** Copyrights
_____ **8.** Current portion of long-term note payable
_____ **9.** Accumulated depreciation—Trucks
_____ **10.** Office equipment

_____ **11.** Rent receivable
_____ **12.** Salaries payable
_____ **13.** Income taxes payable
_____ **14.** Owner, Capital
_____ **15.** Office supplies
_____ **16.** Interest payable
_____ **17.** Rent revenue
_____ **18.** Notes receivable (due in 120 days)
_____ **19.** Land (used in operations)
_____ **20.** Depreciation expense—Trucks

On July 1, 2008, Lula Plume created a new self-storage business, Safe Storage Co. The following transactions occurred during the company's first month.

Problem 4-2B
Applying the accounting cycle

C1 C2 P2 P3

July 1   Plume invested $30,000 cash and buildings worth $150,000 in the business.
     2   Rented equipment by paying $2,000 cash for the first month's (July) rent.
     5   Purchased $2,400 of office supplies for cash.
   10   Paid $7,200 cash for the premium on a 12-month insurance policy. Coverage begins on July 11.
   14   Paid an employee $1,000 cash for two weeks' salary earned.
   24   Collected $9,800 cash for storage fees from customers.
   28   Paid another $1,000 cash for two weeks' salary earned by an employee.
   29   Paid $950 cash for minor repairs to a leaking roof.
   30   Paid $400 cash for this month's telephone bill.
   31   Plume withdrew $2,000 cash for personal use.

The company's chart of accounts follows:

101	Cash	401	Storage Fees Earned
106	Accounts Receivable	606	Depreciation Expense—Buildings
124	Office Supplies	622	Salaries Expense
128	Prepaid Insurance	637	Insurance Expense
173	Buildings	640	Rent Expense
174	Accumulated Depreciation—Buildings	650	Office Supplies Expense
209	Salaries Payable	684	Repairs Expense
301	L. Plume, Capital	688	Telephone Expense
302	L. Plume, Withdrawals	901	Income Summary

Required

1. Use the balance column format to set up each ledger account listed in its chart of accounts.

2. Prepare journal entries to record the transactions for July and post them to the ledger accounts. Record prepaid and unearned items in balance sheet accounts.

3. Prepare an unadjusted trial balance as of July 31.

4. Use the following information to journalize and post adjusting entries for the month:

   a. Two-thirds of one month's insurance coverage has expired.

   b. At the end of the month, $1,525 of office supplies are still available.

   c. This month's depreciation on the buildings is $1,500.

   d. An employee earned $100 of unpaid and unrecorded salary as of month-end.

   e. The company earned $1,150 of storage fees that are not yet billed at month-end.

5. Prepare the income statement and the statement of owner's equity for the month of July and the balance sheet at July 31, 2008.

6. Prepare journal entries to close the temporary accounts and post these entries to the ledger.

7. Prepare a post-closing trial balance.

Problem 4-3B

Preparing trial balances, closing entries, and financial statements

C3 P2 P3

Santo Company's adjusted trial balance on December 31, 2008, follows.

No.	Account Title	Debit	Credit
	SANTO COMPANY		
	Adjusted Trial Balance		
	December 31, 2008		
101	Cash	$ 14,450	
125	Store supplies	5,140	
128	Prepaid insurance	1,200	
167	Equipment	31,000	
168	Accumulated depreciation—Equipment		$ 8,000
201	Accounts payable		1,500
210	Wages payable		2,700
301	P. Holt, Capital		35,650
302	P. Holt, Withdrawals	15,000	
401	Repair fees earned		54,700
612	Depreciation expense—Equipment	2,000	
623	Wages expense	26,400	
637	Insurance expense	600	
640	Rent expense	3,600	
651	Store supplies expense	1,200	
690	Utilities expense	1,960	
	Totals	$102,550	$102,550

Required

1. Prepare an income statement and a statement of owner's equity for the year 2008, and a classified balance sheet at December 31, 2008. There are no owner investments in 2008.

2. Enter the adjusted trial balance in the first two columns of a six-column table. Use the middle two columns for closing entry information and the last two columns for a post-closing trial balance. Insert an Income Summary account (No. 901) as the last item in the trial balance.

3. Enter closing entry information in the six-column table and prepare journal entries for them.

Analysis Component

4. Assume for this part only that:

   a. None of the $600 insurance expense had expired during the year. Instead, assume it is a prepayment of the next period's insurance protection.

   b. There are no earned and unpaid wages at the end of the year. (*Hint:* Reverse the $2,700 wages payable accrual.)

Describe the financial statement changes that would result from these two assumptions.

The adjusted trial balance for Anara Co. as of December 31, 2008, follows.

No.	ANARA CO. Adjusted Trial Balance December 31, 2008 Account Title	Debit	Credit
101	Cash	$ 7,400	
104	Short-term investments	11,200	
126	Supplies	4,600	
128	Prepaid insurance	1,000	
167	Equipment	24,000	
168	Accumulated depreciation—Equipment		$ 4,000
173	Building	100,000	
174	Accumulated depreciation—Building		10,000
183	Land	30,500	
201	Accounts payable		3,500
203	Interest payable		1,750
208	Rent payable		400
210	Wages payable		1,280
213	Property taxes payable		3,330
233	Unearned professional fees		750
251	Long-term notes payable		40,000
301	P. Anara, Capital		92,800
302	P. Anara, Withdrawals	8,000	
401	Professional fees earned		59,600
406	Rent earned		4,500
407	Dividends earned		1,000
409	Interest earned		1,320
606	Depreciation expense—Building	2,000	
612	Depreciation expense—Equipment	1,000	
623	Wages expense	18,500	
633	Interest expense	1,550	
637	Insurance expense	1,525	
640	Rent expense	3,600	
652	Supplies expense	1,000	
682	Postage expense	410	
683	Property taxes expense	4,825	
684	Repairs expense	679	
688	Telephone expense	521	
690	Utilities expense	1,920	
	Totals	$224,230	$224,230

P. Anara invested $40,000 cash in the business during year 2008 (the December 31, 2007, credit balance of the P. Anara, Capital account was $52,800). Anara Company is required to make an $8,400 payment on its long-term notes payable during 2009.

Required

1. Prepare the income statement and the statement of owner's equity for the calendar year 2008 and the classified balance sheet at December 31, 2008.

2. Prepare the necessary closing entries at December 31, 2008.

3. Use the information in the financial statements to calculate these ratios: (*a*) return on assets (total assets at December 31, 2007, was $160,000), (*b*) debt ratio, (*c*) profit margin ratio (use total revenues as the denominator), and (*d*) current ratio.

Problem 4-5B

Preparing a work sheet, adjusting and closing entries, and financial statements

C3 P1 P2

The following unadjusted trial balance is for Power Demolition Company as of the end of its April 30, 2008, fiscal year. The April 30, 2007, credit balance of the owner's capital account was $46,900, and the owner invested $40,000 cash in the company during the 2008 fiscal year.

	File Edit View Insert Format Tools Data Window Help		
	POWER DEMOLITION COMPANY **Unadjusted Trial Balance** **April 30, 2008**		
No.	**Account Title**	**Debit**	**Credit**
101	Cash	$ 7,000	
126	Supplies	16,000	
128	Prepaid insurance	12,600	
167	Equipment	200,000	
168	Accumulated depreciation—Equipment		$ 14,000
201	Accounts payable		6,800
203	Interest payable		0
208	Rent payable		0
210	Wages payable		0
213	Property taxes payable		0
251	Long-term notes payable		30,000
301	J. Bonair, Capital		86,900
302	J. Bonair, Withdrawals	12,000	
401	Demolition fees earned		187,000
612	Depreciation expense—Equipment	0	
623	Wages expense	41,400	
633	Interest expense	3,300	
637	Insurance expense	0	
640	Rent expense	13,200	
652	Supplies expense	0	
683	Property taxes expense	9,700	
684	Repairs expense	4,700	
690	Utilities expense	4,800	
	Totals	$ 324,700	$ 324,700

Required

1. Prepare a 10-column work sheet for fiscal year 2008, starting with the unadjusted trial balance and including adjustments based on these additional facts.

   a. The supplies available at the end of fiscal year 2008 had a cost of $7,900.

   b. The cost of expired insurance for the fiscal year is $10,600.

   c. Annual depreciation on equipment is $7,000.

   d. The April utilities expense of $800 is not included in the unadjusted trial balance because the bill arrived after the trial balance was prepared. The $800 amount owed needs to be recorded.

   e. The company's employees have earned $2,000 of accrued wages at fiscal year-end.

   f. The rent expense incurred and not yet paid or recorded at fiscal year-end is $3,000.

   g. Additional property taxes of $550 have been assessed for this fiscal year but have not been paid or recorded in the accounts.

   h. The long-term note payable bears interest at 12% per year. The unadjusted Interest Expense account equals the amount paid for the first 11 months of the 2008 fiscal year. The $300 accrued interest for April has not yet been paid or recorded. (Note that the company is required to make a $10,000 payment toward the note payable during the 2009 fiscal year.)

2. Enter the adjusting and closing entry information in the work sheet; then journalize them.

3. Prepare the income statement and the statement of owner's equity for the year ended April 30, and the classified balance sheet at April 30, 2008.

Check (3) Total assets, $195,900; current liabilities, $23,450; Net income, $77,550

Analysis Component

4. Analyze the following separate errors and describe how each would affect the 10-column work sheet. Explain whether the error is likely to be discovered in completing the work sheet and, if not, the effect of the error on the financial statements.

a. Assume the adjustment for expiration of the insurance coverage consisted of a credit to Prepaid Insurance for $2,000 and a debit for $2,000 to Insurance Expense.

b. When the adjusted trial balance in the work sheet is completed, assume that the $4,700 Repairs Expense account balance is extended to the Debit column of the balance sheet columns.

The following six-column table for Solutions Co. includes the unadjusted trial balance as of December 31, 2008.

Problem 4-6B[A]

Preparing adjusting, reversing, and next period entries

P4

SOLUTIONS CO.
December 31, 2008

Account Title	Unadjusted Trial Balance		Adjustments		Adjusted Trial Balance	
	Dr.	Cr.	Dr.	Cr.	Dr.	Cr.
Cash	$ 10,000					
Accounts receivable	0					
Supplies	7,600					
Machinery	50,000					
Accumulated depreciation—Machinery		$ 20,000				
Interest payable		0				
Salaries payable		0				
Unearned rental fees		7,200				
Notes payable		30,000				
G. Clay, Capital		14,200				
G. Clay, Withdrawals	9,500					
Rental fees earned		32,450				
Depreciation expense—Machinery	0					
Salaries expense	24,500					
Interest expense	2,250					
Supplies expense	0					
Totals	$103,850	$103,850				

Required

1. Complete the six-column table by entering adjustments that reflect the following information:

    a. As of December 31, 2008, employees had earned $400 of unpaid and unrecorded wages. The next payday is January 4, at which time $1,200 in wages will be paid.

    b. The cost of supplies still available at December 31, 2008, is $3,450.

    c. The notes payable requires an interest payment to be made every three months. The amount of unrecorded accrued interest at December 31, 2008, is $800. The next interest payment, at an amount of $900, is due on January 15, 2009.

    d. Analysis of the unearned rental fees shows that $3,200 remains unearned at December 31, 2008.

    e. In addition to the machinery rental fees included in the revenue account balance, the company has earned another $2,450 in unrecorded fees that will be collected on January 31, 2009. The company is also expected to collect $5,400 on that same day for new fees earned in January 2009.

    f. Depreciation expense for the year is $3,800.

Check (1) Adjusted trial balance totals, $111,300

2. Prepare journal entries for the adjustments entered in the six-column table for part 1.

3. Prepare journal entries to reverse the effects of the adjusting entries that involve accruals.

4. Prepare journal entries to record the cash payments and cash collections described for January.

PROBLEM SET C

Problem Set C is available at the book's Website to further reinforce and assess your learning.

SERIAL PROBLEM

Success Systems   P2   P3

(This serial problem began in Chapter 1 and continues through most of the book. If previous chapter segments were not completed, the serial problem can begin at this point. It is helpful, but not necessary, that you use the Working Papers that accompany the book.)

SP 4   The December 31, 2007, adjusted trial balance of Success Systems (reflecting its transactions from October through December of 2007) follows.

No.	Account Title	Debit	Credit
101	Cash	$ 80,260	
106	Accounts receivable	5,800	
126	Computer supplies	775	
128	Prepaid insurance	1,800	
131	Prepaid rent	875	
163	Office equipment	10,000	
164	Accumulated depreciation—Office equipment		$ 625
167	Computer equipment	25,000	
168	Accumulated depreciation—Computer equipment		1,250
201	Accounts payable		2,100
210	Wages payable		600
236	Unearned computer services revenue		2,500
301	A. Lopez, Capital		110,000
302	A. Lopez, Withdrawals	8,500	
403	Computer services revenue		36,170
612	Depreciation expense—Office equipment	625	
613	Depreciation expense—Computer equipment	1,250	
623	Wages expense	4,650	
637	Insurance expense	600	
640	Rent expense	2,625	
652	Computer supplies expense	4,675	
655	Advertising expense	2,990	
676	Mileage expense	1,120	
677	Miscellaneous expenses	300	
684	Repairs expense—Computer	1,400	
901	Income summary		0
	Totals	$153,245	$153,245

Required

Check Post-closing trial balance totals, $124,510

1. Record and post the necessary closing entries for Success Systems.
2. Prepare a post-closing trial balance as of December 31, 2007.

BEYOND THE NUMBERS

REPORTING IN ACTION

C1   P2

BTN 4-1   Refer to Best Buy's financial statements in Appendix A to answer the following.

Required

1. For the fiscal year ended February 26, 2005, what amount is credited to Income Summary to summarize its revenues earned?
2. For the fiscal year ended February 26, 2005, what amount is debited to Income Summary to summarize its expenses incurred?

3. For the fiscal year ended February 26, 2005, what is the balance of its Income Summary account before it is closed?

4. In its statement of cash flows for the year ended February 26, 2005, what amount of cash is paid in dividends to common stockholders?

Fast Forward

5. Access Best Buy's annual report for fiscal years ending after February 26, 2005, at its Website (BestBuy.com) or the SEC's EDGAR database (www.sec.gov). How has the amount of net income closed to Income Summary changed in the fiscal years ending after February 26, 2005? How has the amount of cash paid as dividends changed in the fiscal years ending after February 26, 2005?

BTN 4-2   Key figures for the recent two years of both **Best Buy** and **Circuit City** follow.

Key Figures ($ thousands)	Best Buy		Circuit City	
	Current Year	Prior Year	Current Year	Prior Year
Current assets	$6,903,000	$5,724,000	$2,685,715	$2,919,061
Current liabilities	4,959,000	4,501,000	1,263,846	1,138,198

COMPARATIVE ANALYSIS

A1

Required

1. Compute the current ratio for both years and both companies.

2. Which company has the better ability to pay short-term obligations according to the current ratio?

3. Analyze and comment on each company's current ratios for the past two years.

4. How do Best Buy's and Circuit City's current ratios compare to their industry average ratio of 1.6?

BTN 4-3   On January 20, 2008, Tamira Nelson, the accountant for Picton Enterprises, is feeling pressure to complete the annual financial statements. The company president has said he needs up-to-date financial statements to share with the bank on January 21 at a dinner meeting that has been called to discuss Picton's obtaining loan financing for a special building project. Tamira knows that she will not be able to gather all the needed information in the next 24 hours to prepare the entire set of adjusting entries that must be posted before the financial statements accurately portray the company's performance and financial position for the fiscal period ended December 31, 2007. Tamira ultimately decides to estimate several expense accruals at the last minute. When deciding on estimates for the expenses, she uses low estimates because she does not want to make the financial statements look worse than they are. Tamira finishes the financial statements before the deadline and gives them to the president without mentioning that several account balances are estimates that she provided.

ETHICS CHALLENGE

C2

Required

1. Identify several courses of action that Tamira could have taken instead of the one she took.

2. If you were in Tamira's situation, what would you have done? Briefly justify your response.

BTN 4-4   Assume that one of your classmates states that a company's books should be ongoing and therefore not closed until that business is terminated. Write a one-half page memo to this classmate explaining the concept of the closing process by drawing analogies between (1) a scoreboard for an athletic event and the revenue and expense accounts of a business or (2) a sports team's record book and the capital account. (*Hint:* Think about what would happen if the scoreboard is not cleared before the start of a new game.)

COMMUNICATING IN PRACTICE

C1 P2

TAKING IT TO THE NET

A1

BTN 4-5   Access Motley Fool's discussion of the current ratio at www.Fool.com/School/BalanceSheet/BalanceSheet05.htm. (Note that if the page changed, search the site for the *current ratio*.)

Required

1. What level for the current ratio is generally regarded as sufficient to meet near-term operating needs?
2. Once you have calculated the current ratio for a company, what should you compare it against?
3. What are the implications for a company that has a current ratio that is too high?

TEAMWORK IN ACTION

P1 P2 P3

BTN 4-6   The unadjusted trial balance and information for the accounting adjustments of Noseworthy Investigators follow. Each team member involved in this project is to assume one of the four responsibilities listed. After completing each of these responsibilities, the team should work together to prove the accounting equation utilizing information from teammates (1 and 4). If your equation does not balance, you are to work as a team to resolve the error. The team's goal is to complete the task as quickly and accurately as possible.

Unadjusted Trial Balance		
Account Title	**Debit**	**Credit**
Cash	$16,000	
Supplies	12,000	
Prepaid insurance	3,000	
Equipment	25,000	
Accumulated depreciation—Equipment		$ 7,000
Accounts payable		3,000
D. Noseworthy, Capital		34,000
D. Noseworthy, Withdrawals	6,000	
Investigation fees earned		33,000
Rent expense	15,000	
Totals	$77,000	$77,000

Additional Year-End Information

a. Insurance that expired in the current period amounts to $2,200.
b. Equipment depreciation for the period is $4,000.
c. Unused supplies total $5,000 at period-end.
d. Services in the amount of $800 have been provided but have not been billed or collected.

Responsibilities for Individual Team Members

1. Determine the accounts and adjusted balances to be extended to the balance sheet columns of the work sheet for Noseworthy. Also determine total assets and total liabilities.
2. Determine the adjusted revenue account balance and prepare the entry to close this account.
3. Determine the adjusted account balances for expenses and prepare the entry to close these accounts.
4. Prepare T-accounts for both D. Noseworthy, Capital (reflecting the unadjusted trial balance amount) and Income Summary. Prepare the third and fourth closing entries. Ask teammates assigned to parts 2 and 3 for the postings for Income Summary. Obtain amounts to complete the third closing entry and post both the third and fourth closing entries. Provide the team with the ending capital account balance.
5. The entire team should prove the accounting equation using post-closing balances.

BusinessWeek **ACTIVITY**

A1 C3

BTN 4-7   Read the editorial "The New Earnings Game" in the October 4, 2004, issue of *BusinessWeek*. (Access the book's Website for a free link.)

Required

1. According to this editorial, how are accounting estimates used in a company's financial reports?
2. What does the author see as the problem when companies prepare their accounting estimates?

3. What is the author's opinion of companies that make the most aggressive estimates and report the most exaggerated earnings?

BTN 4-8 Review this chapter's opening feature involving Janet Freeman and her business Betty Rides.

1. Explain how a classified balance sheet can help Janet Freeman know what bills are due when, and whether she has the resources to pay those bills.

2. Why is it important for Janet to match costs and revenues in a specific time period? How do closing entries help her in this regard?

3. What objectives are met when Janet applies closing procedures each fiscal year-end?

BTN 4-9 Select a company that you can visit in person or interview on the telephone. Call ahead to the company to arrange a time when you can interview an employee (preferably an accountant) who helps prepare the annual financial statements. Inquire about the following aspects of its *accounting cycle:*

1. Does the company prepare interim financial statements? What time period(s) is used for interim statements?

2. Does the company use the cash or accrual basis of accounting?

3. Does the company use a work sheet in preparing financial statements? Why or why not?

4. Does the company use a spreadsheet program? If so, which software program is used?

5. How long does it take after the end of its reporting period to complete annual statements?

BTN 4-10 Dixons is the United Kingdom's largest retailer of consumer electronics. Access its financial statements for the year ended May 1, 2004, at the company's Website (www.dixons-group.com). The following selected information is available from Dixons' financial statements.

(£ millions)	Current Year	Prior Year
Current assets	£2,303.9	£2,220.4
Current liabilities	1,565.8	1,679.0

Required

1. Compute Dixons' current ratio for both the current year and the prior year. (Dixons' balance sheet is in a slightly different format than the examples in the text. Current assets follow fixed assets, and current liabilities follow current assets.)

2. Comment on any change from the prior year to the current year for the current ratio.

ANSWERS TO MULTIPLE CHOICE QUIZ

1. e

2. c

3. b

4. a

5. c

5

Accounting for Merchandising Operations

A Look Back

Chapters 3 and 4 focused on the final steps of the accounting process. We explained the importance of proper revenue and expense recognition and described the adjusting and closing processes. We also prepared financial statements.

A Look at This Chapter

This chapter emphasizes merchandising activities. We explain how reporting merchandising activities differs from reporting service activities. We also analyze and record merchandise purchases and sales transactions and explain the adjustments and closing process for merchandisers.

A Look Ahead

Chapter 6 extends our analysis of merchandising activities and focuses on the valuation of inventory. Topics include the items in inventory, costs assigned, costing methods used, and inventory estimation techniques.

Learning Objectives

CAP

Conceptual

C1 Describe merchandising activities and identify income components for a merchandising company. *(p. 178)*

C2 Identify and explain the inventory asset of a merchandising company. *(p. 179)*

C3 Describe both perpetual and periodic inventory systems. *(p. 179)*

C4 Analyze and interpret cost flows and operating activities of a merchandising company. *(p. 187)*

Analytical

A1 Compute the acid-test ratio and explain its use to assess liquidity. *(p. 193)*

A2 Compute the gross margin ratio and explain its use to assess profitability. *(p. 193)*

Procedural

P1 Analyze and record transactions for merchandise purchases using a perpetual system. *(p. 180)*

P2 Analyze and record transactions for merchandise sales using a perpetual system. *(p. 185)*

P3 Prepare adjustments and close accounts for a merchandising company. *(p. 188)*

P4 Define and prepare multiple-step and single-step income statements. *(p. 191)*

P5 *Appendix 5A—*Record and compare merchandising transactions using both periodic and perpetual inventory systems. *(p. 198)*

"We're selling a feeling to the consumer"
—Renee Pepys Lowe

CoCaLo Creates Sweet Dreams

COSTA MESA, CA—"I always had my mother to lean on," admits Renee Pepys Lowe. But when her mother decided to sell her small business in which Renee worked, Renee lost her job. "That was a big change," recalls Renee. "I did a lot of soul-searching."

Renee rebounded by starting an infant bedding and nursery accessories company, CoCaLo (**CoCaLo.com**)—named after her daughters, Courtenay and Catherine Lowe. Renee envisioned a company with fashionable, high-quality products at affordable prices. Fortunately, she says her designers have "a remarkable talent for seeing what fabrics, colors, and textures can look like in combination."

After only five years, CoCaLo now projects over $15 million in annual sales. But the early days were not easy. "You really have to take a lot of risks," says Renee. "It's all about allowing everyone to have a bedding collection with style, without having to spend a thousand dollars to get it." Adds Renee, "The scariest part for me is that I'm responsible for . . . finances, loans [and all aspects of accounting]."

To succeed, Renee needed to make smart business decisions. She set up an accounting system to capture and communicate costs and sales information. Effectively tracking merchandising activities is needed to set prices and create policies for discounts and allowances, returns on sales and purchases. A perpetual inventory system enabled CoCaLo to stock the right type and amount of merchandise and to avoid the costs of out-of-stock and excess inventory.

Mastering accounting for merchandising is a means to an end for Renee. "I love this business," she says. "There's something about giving new parents the tools to create a room they can feel proud of." Judging by CoCaLo's sales, there are plenty of proud parents out there.

[Sources: *CoCaLo Website,* January 2006, *Entrepreneur,* November 2003, *Kids Today,* July 2004]

Merchandising activities are a major part of modern business. Consumers expect a wealth of products, discount prices, inventory on demand, and high quality. This chapter introduces the business and accounting practices used by companies engaged in merchandising activities. We show how financial statements reflect these merchandising activities and explain the new financial statement items created by merchandising activities. We also analyze and record merchandise purchases and sales, and explain the adjustments and the closing process for merchandising companies.

Merchandising Activities

C1 Describe merchandising activities and identify income components for a merchandising company.

Point: Fleming, SuperValu, and SYSCO are wholesalers. Gap, Oakley, and Wal-Mart are retailers.

Previous chapters emphasized the accounting and reporting activities of service companies. A merchandising company's activities differ from those of a service company. **Merchandise** consists of products, also called *goods,* that a company acquires to resell to customers. A **merchandiser** earns net income by buying and selling merchandise. Merchandisers are often identified as either wholesalers or retailers. A **wholesaler** is an *intermediary* that buys products from manufacturers or other wholesalers and sells them to retailers or other wholesalers. A **retailer** is an intermediary that buys products from manufacturers or wholesalers and sells them to consumers. Many retailers sell both products and services.

Reporting Income for a Merchandiser

Net income to a merchandiser equals revenues from selling merchandise minus both the cost of merchandise sold to customers and the cost of other expenses for the period (see Exhibit 5.1). The usual accounting term for revenues from selling merchandise is *sales,* and the term used

Exhibit 5.1

Computing Income for a Merchandising Company versus a Service Company

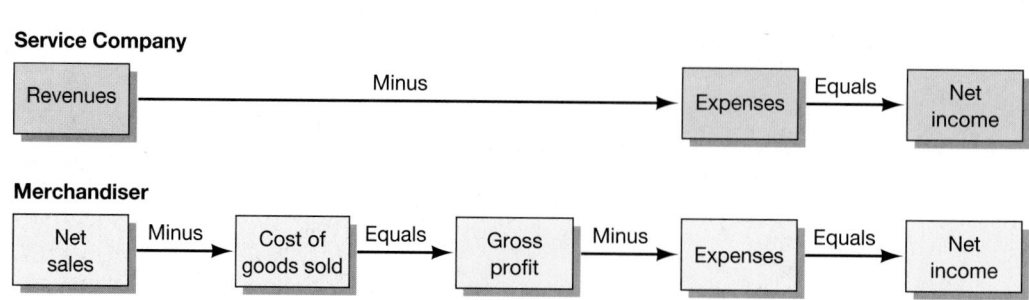

for the expense of buying and preparing the merchandise is **cost of goods sold.** (Many service companies use the term *sales* instead of revenues; and cost of goods sold is also called *cost of sales.*)

The income statement for Z-Mart in Exhibit 5.2 illustrates these key components of a merchandiser's net income. The first two lines show that products are acquired at a cost of $230,400 and sold for $314,700. The third line shows an $84,300 **gross profit,** also called **gross margin,** which equals net sales less cost of goods sold. Other expenses of $71,400 are reported, which leaves $12,900 in net income.

Z-MART Income Statement For Year Ended December 31, 2008	
Net sales	$314,700
Cost of goods sold	230,400
Gross profit	84,300
Expenses	71,400
Net income	$ 12,900

Exhibit 5.2

Merchandiser's Income Statement

Point: Analysis of gross profit is important to effective business decisions, and is described later in the chapter.

Reporting Inventory for a Merchandiser

A merchandiser's balance sheet includes a current asset called *merchandise inventory,* an item not on a service company's balance sheet. **Merchandise inventory,** or simply *inventory,* refers to products that a company owns and intends to sell. The cost of this asset includes the cost incurred to buy the goods, ship them to the store, and make them ready for sale.

C2 Identify and explain the inventory asset of a merchandising company.

Operating Cycle for a Merchandiser

A merchandising company's operating cycle begins by purchasing merchandise and ends by collecting cash from selling the merchandise. The length of an operating cycle differs across the types of businesses. Department stores often have operating cycles of two to five months. Operating cycles for grocery merchants usually range from two to eight weeks.

Exhibit 5.3 illustrates an operating cycle for a merchandiser with credit sales. The cycle moves from (*a*) cash purchases of merchandise to (*b*) inventory for sale to (*c*) credit sales to (*d*) accounts receivable to (*e*) cash. Companies try to keep their operating cycles short because assets tied up in inventory and receivables are not productive.

Exhibit 5.3

Merchandiser's Operating Cycle

Point: Cash sales shorten operating cycles.

Inventory Systems

Cost of goods sold is the cost of merchandise sold to customers during a period. It is often the largest single expense on a merchandiser's income statement. **Inventory** refers to products a company owns and expects to sell in its normal operations. Exhibit 5.4 shows that a company's merchandise available for sale consists of what it begins with (beginning inventory) and what it purchases (net cost of purchases). The merchandise available is either sold (cost of goods sold) or kept for future sales (ending inventory).

Exhibit 5.4

Merchandiser's Cost Flow for a Single Time Period

Two alternative inventory accounting systems can be used to collect information about cost of goods sold and cost of inventory: *perpetual system* or *periodic system*. The **perpetual**

C3 Describe both perpetual and periodic inventory systems.

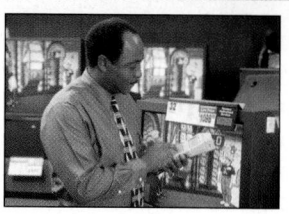

inventory system continually updates accounting records for merchandising transactions—specifically, for those records of inventory available for sale and inventory sold. The **periodic inventory system** updates the accounting records for merchandise transactions only at the *end of a period*. Technological advances and competitive pressures have dramatically increased the use of the perpetual system.

Quick Check   Answers—p. 204

1. Describe a merchandiser's cost of goods sold.
2. What is gross profit for a merchandising company?
3. Explain why use of the perpetual inventory system has dramatically increased.

The following sections on purchasing, selling, and adjusting merchandise use the perpetual system. Appendix 5A uses the periodic system (with the perpetual results on the side). An instructor can choose to cover either one or both inventory systems.

Accounting for Merchandise Purchases

The cost of merchandise purchased for resale is recorded in the Merchandise Inventory asset account. To illustrate, Z-Mart records a $1,200 cash purchase of merchandise on November 2 as follows:

Assets = Liabilities + Equity
+1,200
−1,200

Nov. 2	Merchandise Inventory	1,200	
	Cash		1,200
	Purchased merchandise for cash.		

P1   Analyze and record transactions for merchandise purchases using a perpetual system.

The invoice for this merchandise is shown in Exhibit 5.5. The buyer usually receives the original invoice, and the seller keeps a copy. This *source document* serves as the purchase invoice of Z-Mart (buyer) and the sales invoice for Trex (seller). The amount recorded for merchandise inventory includes its purchase cost, shipping fees, taxes, and any other costs necessary to make it ready for sale. This section explains how we compute the recorded cost of merchandise purchases.

Topic Tackler
PLUS

5-1

Trade Discounts

When a manufacturer or wholesaler prepares a catalog of items it has for sale, it usually gives each item a **list price,** also called a *catalog price.* However, an item's intended *selling price* equals list price minus a given percent called a **trade discount.** The amount of trade discount usually depends on whether a buyer is a wholesaler, retailer, or final consumer. A wholesaler buying in large quantities is often granted a larger discount than a retailer buying in smaller quantities. A buyer records the net amount of list price minus trade discount. For example, in the November 2 purchase of merchandise by Z-Mart, the merchandise was listed in the seller's catalog at $2,000 and Z-Mart received a 40% trade discount. This meant that Z-Mart's purchase price was $1,200, computed as $2,000 − (40% × $2,000).

Point: The Merchandise Inventory account reflects the cost of goods available for resale.

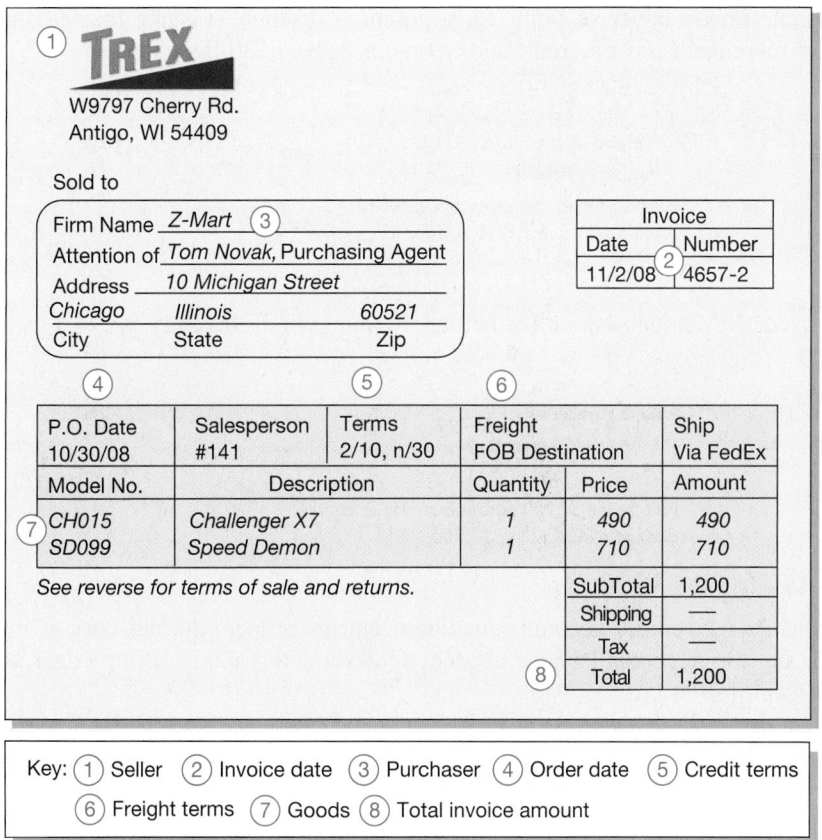

Exhibit 5.5

Invoice

Key: ① Seller ② Invoice date ③ Purchaser ④ Order date ⑤ Credit terms
     ⑥ Freight terms ⑦ Goods ⑧ Total invoice amount

Purchase Discounts

The purchase of goods on credit requires a clear statement of expected future payments and dates to avoid misunderstandings. **Credit terms** for a purchase include the amounts and timing of payments from a buyer to a seller. Credit terms usually reflect an industry's practices. To illustrate, when sellers require payment within 10 days after the end of the month of the invoice date, the invoice will show credit terms as "n/10 EOM," which stands for net 10 days after end of month (**EOM**). When sellers require payment within 30 days after the invoice date, the invoice shows credit terms of "n/30," which stands for *net 30 days*.

Exhibit 5.6 portrays credit terms. The amount of time allowed before full payment is due is called the **credit period.** Sellers can grant a **cash discount** to encourage buyers to pay earlier. A buyer views a cash discount as a **purchase discount.** A seller views a cash discount as a **sales discount.** Any cash discounts are described in the credit terms on the invoice. For example, credit terms of "2/10, n/60" mean that full payment is due within a 60-day credit period, but the buyer can deduct 2% of the invoice amount if payment is made within 10 days of the invoice date. This reduced payment applies only for the **discount period.**

Point: Since both the buyer and seller know the invoice date, this date is used in determining the discount and credit periods.

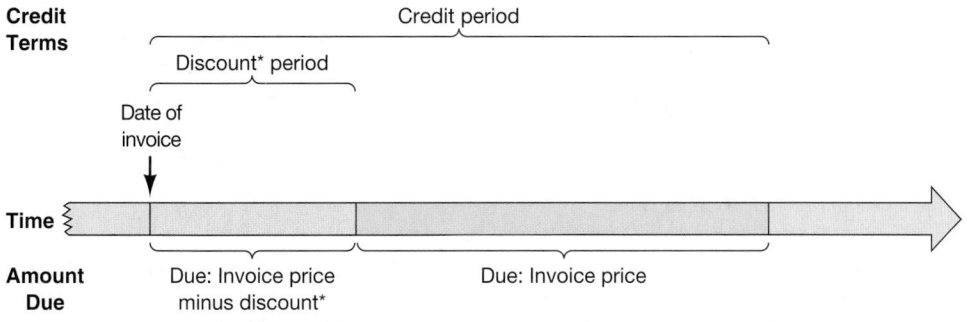

Exhibit 5.6

Credit Terms

*Discount refers to a purchase discount for a buyer and a sales discount for a seller.

Point: Appendix 5A repeats journal entries *a* through *f* using a periodic inventory system.

To illustrate how a buyer accounts for a purchase discount, assume that Z-Mart's $1,200 purchase of merchandise is on credit with terms of 2/10, n/30. Its entry is

Assets = Liabilities + Equity
+1,200   +1,200

(a) Nov. 2	Merchandise Inventory	1,200	
	Accounts Payable		1,200
	Purchased merchandise on credit, invoice		
	dated Nov. 2, terms 2/10, n/30.		

If Z-Mart pays the amount due on (or before) November 12, the entry is

Assets = Liabilities + Equity
−24   −1,200
−1,176

(b) Nov. 12	Accounts Payable	1,200	
	Merchandise Inventory		24
	Cash		1,176
	Paid for the $1,200 purchase of Nov. 2 less the		
	discount of $24 (2% × $1,200).		

Point: These entries illustrate what is called the *gross method* of accounting for purchases with discount terms.

The Merchandise Inventory account after these entries reflects the net cost of merchandise purchased, and the Accounts Payable account shows a zero balance. Both ledger accounts, in T-account form, follow:

Merchandise Inventory			
Nov. 2	1,200	Nov. 12	24
Balance	1,176		

Accounts Payable			
Nov. 12	1,200	Nov. 2	1,200
		Balance	0

Decision Maker

Answer—p. 203

Entrepreneur You purchase a batch of products on terms of 3/10, n/90, but your company has limited cash and you must borrow funds at an 11% annual rate if you are to pay within the discount period. Do you take advantage of the purchase discount?

A buyer's failure to pay within a discount period can be expensive. To illustrate, if Z-Mart does not pay within the 10-day 2% discount period, it can delay payment by 20 more days. This delay costs Z-Mart $24, computed as 2% × $1,200. Most buyers take advantage of a purchase discount because of the usually high interest rate implied from not taking it.[1] Also, good cash management means that no invoice is paid until the last day of the discount or credit period.

Purchase Returns and Allowances

Purchase returns refer to merchandise a buyer acquires but then returns to the seller. A *purchase allowance* is a reduction in the cost of defective or unacceptable merchandise that a buyer acquires. Buyers often keep defective but still marketable merchandise if the seller grants an acceptable allowance.

Point: The sender (maker) of a *debit memorandum* will debit the account of the memo's receiver. The memo's receiver will credit the account of the sender.

When a buyer returns or takes an allowance on merchandise, the buyer issues a **debit memorandum** to inform the seller of a debit made to the seller's account in the buyer's records. To illustrate, on November 15 Z-Mart (buyer) issues a $300 debit memorandum for an allowance

---

[1] The *implied annual interest rate* formula is:

$$(365 \text{ days} \div [\text{Credit period} - \text{Discount period}]) \times \text{Cash discount rate}.$$

For terms of 2/10, n/30, missing the 2% discount for an additional 20 days is equal to an annual interest rate of 36.5%, computed as (365 days/[30 days − 10 days]) × 2% discount rate. *Favorable purchase discounts* are those with implied annual interest rates that exceed the purchaser's annual rate for borrowing money.

from Trex for defective merchandise. Z-Mart's November 15 entry to update its Merchandise Inventory account to reflect the purchase allowance is

(c) Nov. 15	Accounts Payable	300		Assets = Liabilities + Equity
	Merchandise Inventory		300	−300 −300
	Allowance for defective merchandise.			

If this had been a return, then the total *recorded cost* (all costs less any discounts) of the defective merchandise would be entered. The buyer's cost of returned and defective merchandise is usually offset against the buyer's current account payable balance to the seller. When cash is refunded, the Cash account is debited instead of Accounts Payable.

When goods are returned, a buyer can take a purchase discount on only the remaining balance of the invoice. For example, suppose Z-Mart purchases $1,000 of merchandise offered with a 2% cash discount. Two days later, Z-Mart returns $100 of goods before paying the invoice. When Z-Mart later pays within the discount period, it takes the 2% discount only on the $900 remaining balance. The discount is $18 (2% × $900) and the cash payment is $882 ($900 − $18).

Example: Z-Mart pays $980 cash for $1,000 of merchandise purchased within its 2% discount period. Later, Z-Mart returns $100 of the original $1,000 merchandise. The return entry is
Cash 98
  Merchandise Inventory . . . 98

Transportation Costs and Ownership Transfer

The buyer and seller must agree on who is responsible for paying any freight costs and who bears the risk of loss during transit for merchandising transactions. This is essentially the same as asking at what point ownership transfers from the seller to the buyer. The point of transfer is called the **FOB** (*free on board*) point, which determines who pays transportation costs (and often other incidental costs of transit such as insurance).

Exhibit 5.7 identifies two alternative points of transfer. (1) *FOB shipping point,* also called *FOB factory,* means the buyer accepts ownership when the goods depart the seller's place of business. The buyer is then responsible for paying shipping costs and bearing the risk of damage or loss when goods are in transit. The goods are part of the buyer's inventory when they are in transit since ownership has transferred to the buyer. **Cannondale**, a major bike manufacturer, uses FOB shipping point. (2) *FOB destination* means ownership of goods transfers to the buyer when the goods arrive at the buyer's place of business. The seller is responsible for paying shipping charges and bears the risk of damage or loss in transit. The seller does not

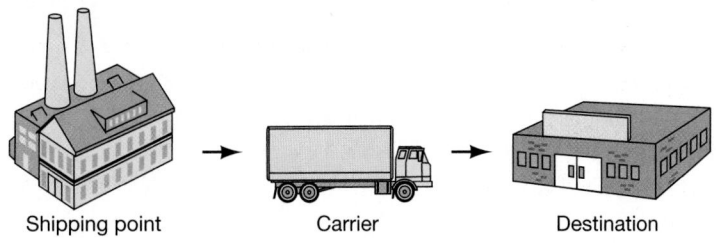

	Shipping point	Carrier	Destination

Exhibit 5.7

Ownership Transfer and Transportation Costs

	Ownership Transfers when Goods Passed to	Transportation Costs Paid by
FOB shipping point	Carrier	Buyer
FOB destination	Buyer	Seller

Point: The party not responsible for shipping costs sometimes pays the carrier. In these cases, the party paying these costs either bills the party responsible or, more commonly, adjusts its account payable or account receivable with the other party. For example, a buyer paying a carrier when terms are FOB destination can decrease its account payable to the seller by the amount of shipping cost.

record revenue from this sale until the goods arrive at the destination because this transaction is not complete before that point.

Z-Mart's $1,200 purchase on November 2 is on terms of FOB destination. This means Z-Mart is not responsible for paying transportation costs. When a buyer is responsible for paying transportation costs, the payment is made to a carrier or directly to the seller depending on the agreement. The cost principle requires that any necessary transportation costs of a buyer (often called *transportation-in* or *freight-in*) be included as part of the cost of purchased merchandise. To illustrate, Z-Mart's entry to record a $75 freight charge from an independent carrier for merchandise purchased FOB shipping point is

Assets = Liabilities + Equity
+75
−75

(d) Nov. 24	Merchandise Inventory	75	
	Cash		75
	Paid freight costs on purchased merchandise.		

A seller records the costs of shipping goods to customers in a Delivery Expense account when the seller is responsible for these costs. Delivery Expense, also called *transportation-out* or *freight-out,* is reported as a selling expense in the seller's income statement.

In summary, purchases are recorded as debits to Merchandise Inventory. Any later purchase discounts, returns, and allowances are credited (decreases) to Merchandise Inventory. Transportation-in is debited (added) to Merchandise Inventory. Z-Mart's itemized costs of merchandise purchases for year 2008 are in Exhibit 5.8.

Exhibit 5.8

Itemized Costs of Merchandise Purchases

Z-MART **Itemized Costs of Merchandise Purchases** **For Year Ended December 31, 2008**	
Invoice cost of merchandise purchases	$235,800
Less: Purchase discounts received	(4,200)
Purchase returns and allowances	(1,500)
Add: Costs of transportation-in	2,300
Total cost of merchandise purchases	**$232,400**

Point: Some companies have separate accounts for purchase discounts, returns and allowances, and transportation-in. These accounts are then transferred to Merchandise Inventory at period-end. This is a *hybrid system* of perpetual and periodic. That is, Merchandise Inventory is updated on a perpetual basis but only for purchases and cost of goods sold.

The accounting system described here does not provide separate records (accounts) for total purchases, total purchase discounts, total purchase returns and allowances, and total transportation-in. Yet nearly all companies collect this information in supplementary records because managers need this information to evaluate and control each of these cost elements. **Supplementary records,** also called *supplemental records,* refer to information outside the usual general ledger accounts.

Quick Check

Answers—p. 204

4. How long are the credit and discount periods when credit terms are 2/10, n/60?
5. Identify which items are subtracted from the *list* amount and not recorded when computing purchase price: (a) freight-in; (b) trade discount; (c) purchase discount; (d) purchase return.
6. What does FOB mean? What does FOB *destination* mean?

Accounting for Merchandise Sales

Merchandising companies also must account for sales, sales discounts, sales returns and allowances, and cost of goods sold. A merchandising company such as Z-Mart reflects these items in its gross profit computation, as shown in Exhibit 5.9. This section explains how this information is derived from transactions.

Exhibit 5.9

Gross Profit Computation

Z-MART Computation of Gross Profit For Year Ended December 31, 2008		
Sales		$321,000
Less: Sales discounts	$4,300	
Sales returns and allowances	2,000	6,300
Net sales		314,700
Cost of goods sold		230,400
Gross profit		**$ 84,300**

Sales of Merchandise

Each sales transaction for a seller of merchandise involves two parts. One part is the revenue received in the form of an asset from a customer. The second part is the recognition of the cost of merchandise sold to a customer. Accounting for a sales transaction under the perpetual system requires recording information about both parts. This means that each sales transaction for merchandisers, whether for cash or on credit, requires two entries: one for revenue and one for cost. To illustrate, Z-Mart sold $2,400 of merchandise on credit on November 3. The revenue part of this transaction is recorded as

P2 Analyze and record transactions for merchandise sales using a perpetual system.

Point: Growth of superstores such as **Price Club** and **Costco** is fed by the efficient use of perpetual inventory.

(e) Nov. 3	Accounts Receivable.	2,400	
	Sales.		2,400
	Sold merchandise on credit.		

Assets = Liabilities + Equity
+2,400   +2,400

This entry reflects an increase in Z-Mart's assets in the form of an accounts receivable. It also shows the increase in revenue (Sales). If the sale is for cash, the debit is to Cash instead of Accounts Receivable.

    The cost part of each sales transaction ensures that the Merchandise Inventory account under a perpetual inventory system reflects the updated cost of the merchandise available for sale. For example, the cost of the merchandise Z-Mart sold on November 3 is $1,600, and the entry to record the cost part of this sales transaction is

Topic Tackler

PLUS

5-2

(e) Nov. 3	Cost of Goods Sold.	1,600	
	Merchandise Inventory.		1,600
	To record the cost of Nov. 3 sale.		

Assets = Liabilities + Equity
−1,600   −1,600

Point: The Cost of Goods Sold account is only used in a perpetual system.

Sales Discounts

Sales discounts on credit sales can benefit a seller by decreasing the delay in receiving cash and reducing future collection efforts.

    At the time of a credit sale, a seller does not know whether a customer will pay within the discount period and take advantage of a purchases discount. This means the seller usually does not record a sales discount until a customer actually pays within the discount period. To illustrate, Z-Mart completes a credit sale for $1,000 on November 12 with terms of 2/10, n/60. The entry to record the revenue part of this sale is

Decision Insight

Suppliers and Demands Merchandising companies often bombard suppliers with demands. These include discounts for bar coding and technology support systems, and fines for shipping errors. Merchandisers' goals are to reduce inventories, shorten lead times, and eliminate errors.

Nov. 12	Accounts Receivable.	1,000	
	Sales.		1,000
	Sold merchandise under terms of 2/10, n/60.		

Assets = Liabilities + Equity
+1,000   +1,000

This entry records the receivable and the revenue as if the customer will pay the full amount. The customer has two options, however. One option is to wait 60 days until January 11 and pay the full $1,000. In this case, Z-Mart records that payment as

Assets = Liabilities + Equity
+1,000
−1,000

Jan. 11	Cash	1,000	
	Accounts Receivable		1,000
	Received payment for Nov. 12 sale.		

The customer's second option is to pay $980 within a 10-day period ending November 22. If the customer pays on (or before) November 22, Z-Mart records the payment as

Assets = Liabilities + Equity
+980   −20
−1,000

Nov. 22	Cash	980	
	Sales Discounts	20	
	Accounts Receivable		1,000
	Received payment for Nov. 12 sale less discount.		

Sales Discounts is a contra revenue account, meaning the Sales Discounts account is deducted from the Sales account when computing a company's net sales (see Exhibit 5.9). Management monitors Sales Discounts to assess the effectiveness and cost of its discount policy.

Sales Returns and Allowances

Sales returns refer to merchandise that customers return to the seller after a sale. Many companies allow customers to return merchandise for a full refund. *Sales allowances* refer to reductions in the selling price of merchandise sold to customers. This can occur with damaged or defective merchandise that a customer is willing to purchase with a decrease in selling price. Sales returns and allowances usually involve dissatisfied customers and the possibility of lost future sales, and managers need information about returns and allowances to monitor these problems.

To illustrate, recall Z-Mart's sale of merchandise on November 3 for $2,400 that had cost $1,600. Assume that the customer returns part of the merchandise on November 6, and the returned items sell for $800 and cost $600. The revenue part of this transaction must reflect the decrease in sales from the customer's return of merchandise as follows:

Decision Insight

Return to Sender Book merchandisers such as **Barnes & Noble** and **Borders Books** can return unsold books to publishers at purchase price. Publishers say returns of new hardcover books run between 35% and 50%.

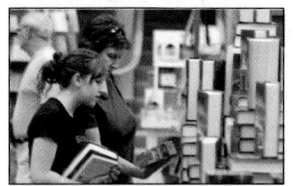

Assets = Liabilities + Equity
−800   −800

(f) Nov. 6	Sales Returns and Allowances	800	
	Accounts Receivable		800
	Customer returns merchandise of Nov. 3 sale.		

If the merchandise returned to Z-Mart is not defective and can be resold to another customer, Z-Mart returns these goods to its inventory. The entry to restore the cost of such goods to the Merchandise Inventory account is

Assets = Liabilities + Equity
+600   +600

Nov. 6	Merchandise Inventory	600	
	Cost of Goods Sold		600
	Returned goods added to inventory.[2]		

----

[2] This entry changes if the goods returned are defective—that is, the returned inventory is recorded at its estimated value, not its cost. To illustrate, if the goods (costing $600) returned to Z-Mart are defective and estimated to be worth $150, the following entry is made: Dr. Merchandise Inventory for $150, Dr. Loss from Defective Merchandise for $450, and Cr. Cost of Goods Sold for $600.

To illustrate sales allowances, assume that $800 of the merchandise Z-Mart sold on November 3 is defective but the buyer decides to keep it because Z-Mart offers a $100 price reduction. Z-Mart records the allowance and decreases expected assets as follows:

Nov. 6	Sales Returns and Allowances	100	
	Accounts Receivable		100
	To record sales allowance on Nov. 3 sale.		

Assets = Liabilities + Equity
−100   −100

The seller usually prepares a credit memorandum to confirm a buyer's return or allowance. A seller's **credit memorandum** informs a buyer of the seller's credit to the buyer's Account Receivable (on the seller's books).

Point: The sender (maker) of a credit memorandum will *credit* the account of the receiver. The receiver of a credit memorandum will *debit* the account of the sender.

Quick Check
Answers—p. 204

7. Why are sales discounts and sales returns and allowances recorded in contra revenue accounts instead of directly in the Sales account?

8. Under what conditions are two entries necessary to record a sales return?

9. When merchandise is sold on credit and the seller notifies the buyer of a price allowance, does the seller create and send a credit memorandum or a debit memorandum?

Completing the Accounting Cycle

Exhibit 5.10 shows the flow of merchandising costs during a period and where these costs are reported at period-end. This chapter already discussed how a merchandiser's purchases and sales transactions during a period are analyzed, recorded, and reported. Specifically, beginning inventory plus the net cost of purchases is the merchandise available for sale. As inventory is sold, its cost is recorded in cost of goods sold on the income statement; what remains is ending inventory on the balance sheet. Note that a period's ending inventory is the next period's beginning inventory.

Each of the steps in the accounting cycle described in Chapter 4 for a service company applies to a merchandiser. This section extends that discussion to three

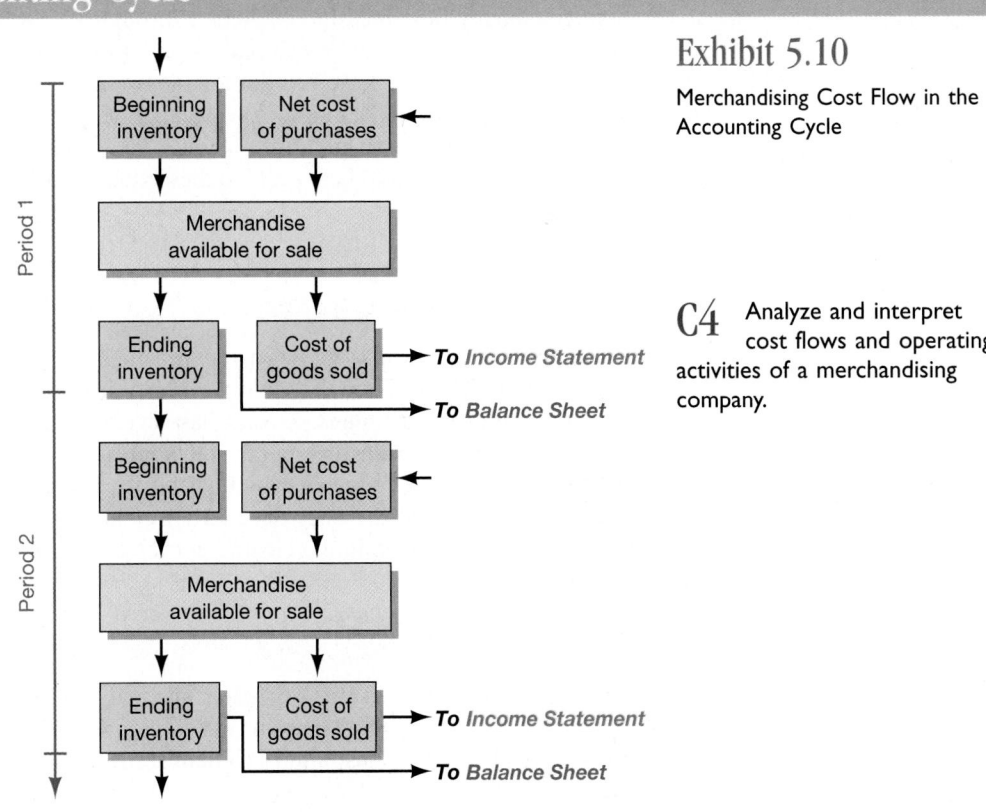

Exhibit 5.10

Merchandising Cost Flow in the Accounting Cycle

C4 Analyze and interpret cost flows and operating activities of a merchandising company.

remaining steps of the accounting cycle for a merchandiser—adjustments, statement preparation, and closing.

Adjusting Entries for Merchandisers

Adjusting entries are generally the same for merchandising companies and service companies, including those for prepaid expenses (including depreciation), accrued expenses, unearned revenues, and accrued revenues. However, a merchandiser using a perpetual inventory system is usually required to make another adjustment to update the Merchandise Inventory account to reflect any loss of merchandise, including theft and deterioration. **Shrinkage** is the term used to refer to the loss of inventory and it is computed by comparing a physical count of inventory with recorded amounts. A physical count is usually performed at least once annually.

Point: About two-thirds of shoplifting losses are thefts by employees.

To illustrate, Z-Mart's Merchandise Inventory account at the end of year 2008 has a balance of $21,250, but a physical count reveals that only $21,000 of inventory exists. The adjusting entry to record this $250 shrinkage is

Assets = Liabilities + Equity
−250   −250

Dec. 31	Cost of Goods Sold	250	
	Merchandise Inventory		250
	To adjust for $250 shrinkage revealed by a physical count of inventory.		

Preparing Financial Statements

The financial statements of a merchandiser, and their preparation, are similar to those for a service company described in Chapters 2 through 4. The income statement mainly differs by the inclusion of *cost of goods sold* and *gross profit*. Also, net sales is affected by discounts, returns, and allowances, and some additional expenses are possible such as delivery expense and loss from defective merchandise. The balance sheet mainly differs by the inclusion of *merchandise inventory* as part of current assets. The statement of owner's equity is unchanged. A work sheet can be used to help prepare these statements, and one is illustrated in Appendix 5B for Z-Mart.

Point: Staples's costs of shipping merchandise to its stores is included in the costs of its inventories as required by the cost principle.

Closing Entries for Merchandisers

Closing entries are similar for service companies and merchandising companies using a perpetual system. The difference is that we must close some new temporary accounts that arise from merchandising activities. Z-Mart has several temporary accounts unique to merchandisers: Sales (of goods), Sales Discounts, Sales Returns and Allowances, and Cost of Goods Sold. Their existence in the ledger means that the first two closing entries for a merchandiser are slightly different from the ones described in Chapter 4 for a service company. These differences are set in boldface in the closing entries of Exhibit 5.11.

Point: The Inventory account is not affected by the closing process under a perpetual system.

Summary of Merchandising Entries

Exhibit 5.12 summarizes the key adjusting and closing entries of a merchandiser (using a perpetual inventory system) that are different from those of a service company described in prior chapters (the Demonstration Problem 2 illustrates these merchandising entries).

Step 1: Close Credit Balances in Temporary Accounts to Income Summary.

Z-Mart has one temporary account with a credit balance; it is closed with this entry:

Dec. 31	**Sales**	321,000	
	Income Summary		321,000
	To close credit balances in temporary accounts.		

Step 2: Close Debit Balances in Temporary Accounts to Income Summary.

The second entry closes temporary accounts having debit balances such as Cost of Goods Sold, Sales Discounts, and Sales Returns and Allowances and is shown here:

Dec. 31	Income Summary	308,100	
	Sales Discounts		4,300
	Sales Returns and Allowances		2,000
	Cost of Goods Sold		230,400
	Depreciation Expense—Store Equipment		3,000
	Depreciation Expense—Office Equipment.		700
	Office Salaries Expense		25,300
	Sales Salaries Expense		18,500
	Insurance Expense.		600
	Rent Expense—Office Space		900
	Rent Expense—Selling Space		8,100
	Office Supplies Expense.		1,800
	Store Supplies Expense		1,200
	Advertising Expense		11,300
	To close debit balances in temporary accounts.		

Step 3: Close Income Summary to Owner's Capital.

The third closing entry is exactly the same for a merchandising company and a service company. It updates the owner's capital account for the net income or loss and is shown below. The $12,900 amount in the entry is net income reported on the income statement in Exhibit 5.2.

Dec. 31	Income Summary	12,900	
	K. Marty, Capital		12,900
	To close the Income Summary account.		

Step 4: Close Withdrawals Account to Owner's Capital.

The fourth closing entry is exactly the same for a merchandising company and a service company. It closes the withdrawals account and adjusts the owner's capital account balance to the amount shown on the balance sheet. This entry follows. After the entries in this exhibit are posted, all temporary accounts are set to zero and are ready to record events for the next period. Further, the capital account now reflects all current and prior period transactions.

Dec. 31	K. Marty, Capital	4,000	
	K. Marty, Withdrawals		4,000
	To close the withdrawals account.		

Exhibit 5.11

Closing Entries for a Merchandiser

Exhibit 5.12

Summary of Merchandising Entries

	Merchandising Transactions	Merchandising Entries	Dr.	Cr.
Purchases	Purchasing merchandise for resale.	Merchandise Inventory . . . . Cash or Accounts Payable	#	#
	Paying freight costs on purchases; FOB shipping point.	Merchandise Inventory . . . . Cash	#	#

	Paying within discount period.	Accounts Payable . . . .
		    Merchandise Inventory . . . .
		    Cash . . . .
			#	#
				#

	Recording purchase returns or allowances.	Cash or Accounts Payable . . . . Merchandise Inventory	#	#
Sales	Selling merchandise.	Cash or Accounts Receivable . . . . Sales	#	#
		Cost of Goods Sold . . . . Merchandise Inventory	#	#
	Receiving payment within discount period.	Cash . . . . Sales Discounts . . . . Accounts Receivable	# #	#
	Granting sales returns or allowances.	Sales Returns and Allowances . . . . Cash or Accounts Receivable	#	#
		Merchandise Inventory . . . . Cost of Goods Sold	#	#
	Paying freight costs on sales; FOB destination.	Delivery Expense . . . . Cash	#	#

	Merchandising Events	Adjusting and Closing Entries		
Adjusting	Adjusting due to shrinkage (occurs when recorded amount larger than physical inventory).	Cost of Goods Sold . . . . Merchandise Inventory	#	#
Closing	Closing temporary accounts with credit balances.	Sales . . . . Income Summary	#	#

	Closing temporary accounts with debit balances.	Income Summary . . . .
		    Sales Returns and Allowances . . . . . .
		    Sales Discounts . . . .
		    Cost of Goods Sold . . . .
		    Delivery Expense . . . .
		    "Other Expenses" . . . .
			#	#
				#
				#
				#
				#

Quick Check

Answers—p. 204

10. When a merchandiser uses a perpetual inventory system, why is it sometimes necessary to adjust the Merchandise Inventory balance with an adjusting entry?

11. What temporary accounts do you expect to find in a merchandising business but not in a service business?

12. Describe the closing entries normally made by a merchandising company.

Financial Statement Formats

Generally accepted accounting principles do not require companies to use any one presentation format for financial statements so we see many different formats in practice. This section describes two common income statement formats: multiple-step and single-step. The classified balance sheet of a merchandiser is also explained.

Multiple-Step Income Statement

A **multiple-step income statement** format shows detailed computations of net sales and other costs and expenses, and reports subtotals for various classes of items. Exhibit 5.13 shows a multiple-step income statement for Z-Mart. The statement has three main parts: (1) *gross profit,* determined by net sales less cost of goods sold, (2) *income from operations,* determined by gross profit less operating expenses, and (3) *net income,* determined by income from operations adjusted for nonoperating items.

P4   Define and prepare multiple-step and single-step income statements.

Exhibit 5.13

Multiple-Step Income Statement

Z-MART
Income Statement
For Year Ended December 31, 2008

Sales		$321,000
Less: Sales discounts	$ 4,300	
Sales returns and allowances	2,000	6,300
Net sales		314,700
Cost of goods sold		230,400
Gross profit		84,300
Operating Expenses		
Selling expenses		
Depreciation expense—Store equipment	3,000	
Sales salaries expense	18,500	
Rent expense—Selling space	8,100	
Store supplies expense	1,200	
Advertising expense	11,300	
Total selling expenses	42,100	
General and administrative expenses		
Depreciation expense—Office equipment	700	
Office salaries expense	25,300	
Insurance expense	600	
Rent expense—Office space	900	
Office supplies expense	1,800	
Total general and administrative expenses	29,300	
Total operating expenses		71,400
Income from operations		12,900
Other revenues and gains (expenses and losses)		
Interest revenue	1,000	
Gain on sale of building	2,500	
Interest expense	(1,500)	
Total other revenue and gains (expenses and losses)		2,000
Net income		$ 14,900

Gross profit computation

Income from operations computation

Nonoperating activities computation

   Operating expenses are classified into two sections. **Selling expenses** include the expenses of promoting sales by displaying and advertising merchandise, making sales, and delivering goods to customers. **General and administrative expenses** support a company's overall operations and include expenses related to accounting, human resource management, and financial management. Expenses are allocated between sections when they contribute to more than one. Z-Mart allocates rent expense of $9,000 from its store building between two sections: $8,100 to selling expense and $900 to general and administrative expense.

   Nonoperating activities consist of other expenses, revenues, losses, and gains that are unrelated to a company's operations. They are reported in two sections. (1) *Other revenues and gains,* which often include interest revenue, dividend revenue, rent revenue, and gains from asset disposals. (2) *Other expenses and losses,* which often include interest expense, losses from

Point: Z-Mart did not have any nonoperating activities, however, Exhibit 5.13 includes some for illustrative purposes.

asset disposals, and casualty losses. When a company has no reportable nonoperating activities, its income from operations is simply labeled net income.

Single-Step Income Statement

A **single-step income statement** is another widely used format, and is shown in Exhibit 5.14 for Z-Mart. It lists cost of goods sold as another expense and shows only one subtotal for total expenses. Expenses are grouped into very few, if any, categories. Many companies use formats that combine features of both the single- and multiple-step statements. Provided that income statement items are shown sensibly, management can choose the format. (In later chapters, we describe some items, such as extraordinary gains and losses, that must be reported in certain locations on the income statement.) Similar presentation options are available for the statement of owner's equity and statement of cash flows.

Point: Many companies report interest expense and interest revenue in separate categories after operating income and before subtracting income tax expense. As one example, see **Best Buy's** income statement in Appendix A.

Exhibit 5.14

Single-Step Income Statement

Z-MART Income Statement For Year Ended December 31, 2008		
Revenues		
Net sales		$314,700
Interest revenue		1,000
Gain on sale of building		2,500
Total revenues		318,200
Expenses		
Cost of goods sold	$230,400	
Selling expenses	42,100	
General and administrative expenses	29,300	
Interest expense	1,500	
Total expenses		303,300
Net income		$ 14,900

Decision Insight

Head Start   Incubators offer start-ups a space plus services such as management advice, office support, and financial, legal, and technical help. Studies show that nearly 90% of entrepreneurs that "hatch" from incubators (usually after two to three years) are still in business six years later—which is more than double the usual success rate.

Classified Balance Sheet

The merchandiser's classified balance sheet reports merchandise inventory as a current asset, usually after accounts receivable according to an asset's nearness to liquidity. Inventory is usually less liquid than accounts receivable because inventory must first be sold before cash can be received; but it is more liquid than supplies and prepaid expenses. Exhibit 5.15 shows the current asset section of Z-Mart's classified balance sheet (other sections are as shown in Chapter 4).

Exhibit 5.15

Classified Balance Sheet (partial) of a Merchandiser

Z-MART Balance Sheet (partial) December 31, 2008	
Assets	
Current assets	
Cash	$ 8,200
Accounts receivable	11,200
Merchandise inventory	21,000
Office supplies	550
Store supplies	250
Prepaid insurance	300
Total current assets	$ 41,500

Acid-Test and Gross Margin Ratios	Decision Analysis

Acid-Test Ratio

For many merchandisers, inventory makes up a large portion of current assets. Inventory must be sold and any resulting accounts receivable must be collected before cash is available. Chapter 4 explained that the current ratio, defined as current assets divided by current liabilities, is useful in assessing a company's ability to pay current liabilities. Since it is sometimes unreasonable to assume that inventories are a source of payment for current liabilities, we look to other measures.

A1 Compute the acid-test ratio and explain its use to assess liquidity.

One measure of a merchandiser's ability to pay its current liabilities (referred to as its *liquidity*) is the acid-test ratio. It differs from the current ratio by excluding less liquid current assets such as inventory and prepaid expenses that take longer to be converted to cash. The **acid-test ratio,** also called *quick ratio,* is defined as *quick assets* (cash, short-term investments, and current receivables) divided by current liabilities—see Exhibit 5.16.

$$\text{Acid-test ratio} = \frac{\text{Cash and equivalents} + \text{Short-term investments} + \text{Current receivables}}{\text{Current liabilities}}$$

Exhibit 5.16

Acid-Test (Quick) Ratio

Exhibit 5.17 shows both the acid-test and current ratios of retailer **JCPenney** for fiscal years 2002 through 2005. JCPenney's acid-test ratio reveals a general increase from 2002–2005 that exceeds the average for the retailing industry. Further, JCPenney's current ratio (never less than 1.7) suggests that its short-term obligations can be confidently covered with short-term assets.

($ millions)	2005	2004	2003	2002
Total quick assets	$5,091	$3,227	$2,698	$3,538
Total current assets	$8,427	$6,590	$5,758	$8,677
Total current liabilities	$3,447	$3,754	$2,563	$4,499
Acid-test ratio	1.48	0.86	1.05	0.79
Current ratio	2.44	1.76	2.25	1.93
Industry acid-test ratio	0.6	0.5	0.6	0.5
Industry current ratio	2.7	2.7	2.5	2.6

Exhibit 5.17

JCPenney's Acid-Test and Current Ratios

An acid-test ratio less than 1.0 means that current liabilities exceed quick assets. A rule of thumb is that the acid-test ratio should have a value near, or higher than, 1.0 to conclude that a company is unlikely to face near-term liquidity problems. A value much less than 1.0 raises liquidity concerns unless a company can generate enough cash from inventory sales or if much of its liabilities are not due until late in the next period. Similarly, a value slightly larger than 1.0 can hide a liquidity problem if payables are due shortly and receivables are not collected until late in the next period. Analysis of JCPenney reveals a slight concern with its liquidity in 2002 and 2004, especially when benchmarked against the industry. However, in other years, JCPenney's acid-test ratios exceed the norm and are at reasonable levels (and its inventory is fairly liquid).

Point: Successful use of a just-in-time inventory system can narrow the gap between the acid-test ratio and the current ratio.

Decision Maker Answer—p. 203

Supplier A retailer requests to purchase supplies on credit from your company. You have no prior experience with this retailer. The retailer's current ratio is 2.1, its acid-test ratio is 0.5, and inventory makes up most of its current assets. Do you extend credit?

Gross Margin Ratio

The cost of goods sold makes up much of a merchandiser's expenses. Without sufficient gross profit, a merchandiser will likely fail. Users often compute the gross margin ratio to help understand this relation. It differs from the profit margin ratio in that it excludes all costs except cost of goods sold. The **gross margin ratio** is defined as *gross margin* (net sales minus cost of goods sold) divided by net sales—see Exhibit 5.18.

A2 Compute the gross margin ratio and explain its use to assess profitability.

$$\text{Gross margin ratio} = \frac{\text{Net sales} - \text{Cost of goods sold}}{\text{Net sales}}$$

Exhibit 5.18

Gross Margin Ratio

Financial Officer   Your company has a 36% gross margin ratio and a 17% net profit margin ratio. Industry averages are 44% for gross margin and 16% for net profit margin. Do these comparative results concern you?

Exhibit 5.19 shows the gross margin ratio of **JCPenney** for fiscal years 2002–2005. For JCPenney, each $1 of sales in 2005 yielded about 39¢ in gross margin to cover all other expenses and still produce a profit. This 39¢ margin is up from 34¢ in 2002. This increase is an important (and positive) development. Success for merchandisers such as JCPenney depends on adequate gross margin.

Point: The power of a ratio is often its ability to identify areas for more detailed analysis.

Overall, both the acid-test ratio and the gross margin ratio suggest that the financial condition and performance of JCPenney has markedly improved over the past four years.

Exhibit 5.19

JCPenney's Gross Margin Ratio

($ millions)	2005	2004	2003	2002
Gross margin	$ 7,139	$ 6,620	$ 6,334	$ 6,082
Net sales	$18,424	$17,786	$17,633	$18,092
Gross margin ratio	38.7%	37.2%	35.9%	33.6%

Demonstration Problem 1

Use the following adjusted trial balance and additional information to complete the requirements:

KC ANTIQUES
Adjusted Trial Balance
December 31, 2008

	Debit	Credit
Cash	$ 20,000	
Merchandise inventory	60,000	
Store supplies	1,500	
Equipment	45,600	
Accumulated depreciation—Equipment		$ 16,600
Accounts payable		9,000
Salaries payable		2,000
K. Carter, Capital		79,000
K. Carter, Withdrawals	10,000	
Sales		343,250
Sales discounts	5,000	
Sales returns and allowances	6,000	
Cost of goods sold	159,900	
Depreciation expense—Store equipment	4,100	
Depreciation expense—Office equipment	1,600	
Sales salaries expense	30,000	
Office salaries expense	34,000	
Insurance expense	11,000	
Rent expense (70% is store, 30% is office)	24,000	
Store supplies expense	5,750	
Advertising expense	31,400	
Totals	$449,850	$449,850

KC Antiques' *supplementary records* for 2008 reveal the following itemized costs for merchandising activities:

Invoice cost of merchandise purchases	$150,000
Purchase discounts received	2,500
Purchase returns and allowances	2,700
Cost of transportation-in	5,000

Required

1. Use the supplementary records to compute the total cost of merchandise purchases for 2008.
2. Prepare a 2008 multiple-step income statement. (Inventory at December 31, 2007, is $70,100.)
3. Prepare a single-step income statement for 2008.
4. Prepare closing entries for KC Antiques at December 31, 2008.
5. Compute the acid-test ratio and the gross margin ratio. Explain the meaning of each ratio and interpret them for KC Antiques.

Planning the Solution

- Compute the total cost of merchandise purchases for 2008.
- To prepare the multiple-step statement, first compute net sales. Then, to compute cost of goods sold, add the net cost of merchandise purchases for the year to beginning inventory and subtract the cost of ending inventory. Subtract cost of goods sold from net sales to get gross profit. Then classify expenses as selling expenses or general and administrative expenses.
- To prepare the single-step income statement, begin with net sales. Then list and subtract the expenses.
- The first closing entry debits all temporary accounts with credit balances and opens the Income Summary account. The second closing entry credits all temporary accounts with debit balances. The third entry closes the Income Summary account to the capital account, and the fourth entry closes the withdrawals account to the capital account.
- Identify the quick assets on the adjusted trial balance. Compute the acid-test ratio by dividing quick assets by current liabilities. Compute the gross margin ratio by dividing gross profit by net sales.

Solution to Demonstration Problem 1

1.

Invoice cost of merchandise purchases	$150,000
Less: Purchases discounts received	2,500
Purchase returns and allowances	2,700
Add: Cost of transportation-in	5,000
Total cost of merchandise purchases	$149,800

2. Multiple-step income statement

KC ANTIQUES
Income Statement
For Year Ended December 31, 2008

Sales		$343,250
Less: Sales discounts	$ 5,000	
Sales returns and allowances	6,000	11,000
Net sales		332,250
Cost of goods sold*		159,900
Gross profit		172,350
Expenses		
Selling expenses		
Depreciation expense—Store equipment	4,100	
Sales salaries expense	30,000	
Rent expense—Selling space	16,800	
Store supplies expense	5,750	
Advertising expense	31,400	
Total selling expenses	88,050	

[continued on next page]

[continued from previous page]

General and administrative expenses			
Depreciation expense—Office equipment	1,600		
Office salaries expense	34,000		
Insurance expense	11,000		
Rent expense—Office space	7,200		
Total general and administrative expenses	53,800		
Total operating expenses		141,850	
Net income		$ 30,500	

* Cost of goods sold can also be directly computed (applying concepts from Exhibit 5.4):

Merchandise inventory, December 31, 2007	$ 70,100
Total cost of merchandise purchases (from part 1)	149,800
Goods available for sale	219,900
Merchandise inventory, December 31, 2008	60,000
Cost of goods sold	$159,900

3. Single-step income statement

KC ANTIQUES
Income Statement
For Year Ended December 31, 2008

Net sales		$332,250
Expenses		
Cost of goods sold	$159,900	
Selling expenses	88,050	
General and administrative expenses	53,800	
Total expenses		301,750
Net income		$ 30,500

4.

Dec. 31	Sales	343,250	
	Income Summary		343,250
	To close credit balances in temporary accounts.		
Dec. 31	Income Summary	312,750	
	Sales Discounts		5,000
	Sales Returns and Allowances		6,000
	Cost of Goods Sold		159,900
	Depreciation Expense—Store Equipment		4,100
	Depreciation Expense—Office Equipment		1,600
	Sales Salaries Expense		30,000
	Office Salaries Expense		34,000
	Insurance Expense		11,000
	Rent Expense		24,000
	Store Supplies Expense		5,750
	Advertising Expense		31,400
	To close debit balances in temporary accounts.		
Dec. 31	Income Summary	30,500	
	K. Carter, Capital		30,500
	To close the Income Summary account.		
Dec. 31	K. Carter, Capital	10,000	
	K. Carter, Withdrawals		10,000
	To close the withdrawals account.		

5. Acid-test ratio = (Cash and equivalents + Short-term investments + Current receivables)/
        Current liabilities
    = Cash/(Accounts payable + Salaries payable)
    = $20,000/($9,000 + $2,000) = $20,000/$11,000 = 1.82

Gross margin ratio = Gross profit/Net sales = $172,350/$332,250 = 0.52 (or 52%)

KC Antiques has a healthy acid-test ratio of 1.82. This means it has more than $1.80 in liquid assets to satisfy each $1.00 in current liabilities. The gross margin of 0.52 shows that KC Antiques spends 48¢ ($1.00 − $0.52) of every dollar of net sales on the costs of acquiring the merchandise it sells. This leaves 52¢ of every dollar of net sales to cover other expenses incurred in the business and to provide a profit.

Demonstration Problem 2

Prepare journal entries to record the following merchandising transactions for both the seller (BMX) and buyer (Sanuk).

May 4   BMX sold $1,500 of merchandise on account to Sanuk, terms FOB shipping point, n/45, invoice dated May 4. The cost of the merchandise was $900.

May 6   Sanuk paid transportation charges of $30 on the May 4 purchase from BMX.

May 8   BMX sold $1,000 of merchandise on account to Sanuk, terms FOB destination, n/30, invoice dated May 8. The cost of the merchandise was $700.

May 10   BMX paid transportation costs of $50 for delivery of merchandise sold to Sanuk on May 8.

May 16   BMX issued Sanuk a $200 credit memorandum for merchandise returned. The merchandise was purchased by Sanuk on account on May 8. The cost of the merchandise returned was $140.

May 18   BMX received payment from Sanuk for purchase of May 8.

May 21   BMX sold $2,400 of merchandise on account to Sanuk, terms FOB shipping point, 2/10, n/EOM. BMX prepaid transportation costs of $100, which were added to the invoice. The cost of the merchandise was $1,440.

May 31   BMX received payment from Sanuk for purchase of May 21, less discount (2% × $2,400).

Solution to Demonstration Problem 2

BMX (Seller)

May 4	Accounts Receivable—Sanuk	1,500	
	Sales		1,500
	Cost of Goods Sold	900	
	Merchandise Inventory		900
6	No entry.		
8	Accounts Receivable—Sanuk	1,000	
	Sales		1,000
	Cost of Goods Sold	700	
	Merchandise Inventory		700
10	Delivery Expense	50	
	Cash		50
16	Sales Returns & Allowances	200	
	Accounts Receivable—Sanuk		200
	Merchandise Inventory	140	
	Cost of Goods Sold		140
18	Cash	800	
	Accounts Receivable—Sanuk		800
21	Accounts Receivable—Sanuk	2,400	
	Sales		2,400
	Accounts Receivable—Sanuk	100	
	Cash		100
	Cost of Goods Sold	1,440	
	Merchandise Inventory		1,440
31	Cash	2,452	
	Sales Discounts	48	
	Accounts Receivable—Sanuk		2,500

Sanuk (Buyer)

	Merchandise Inventory	1,500	
	Accounts Payable—BMX		1,500
	Merchandise Inventory	30	
	Cash		30
	Merchandise Inventory	1,000	
	Accounts Payable—BMX		1,000
	No entry.		
	Accounts Payable—BMX	200	
	Merchandise Inventory		200
	Accounts Payable—BMX	800	
	Cash		800
	Merchandise Inventory	2,500	
	Accounts Payable—BMX		2,500
	Accounts Payable—BMX	2,500	
	Merchandise Inventory		48
	Cash		2,452

5A Periodic (and Perpetual) Inventory System

A **periodic inventory system** requires updating the inventory account only at the *end of a period* to reflect the quantity and cost of both the goods available and the goods sold. Thus, during the period, the Merchandise Inventory balance remains unchanged. It reflects the beginning inventory balance until it is updated at the end of the period. During the period the cost of merchandise is recorded in a temporary *Purchases* account. When a company sells merchandise, it records revenue but not the cost of the goods sold. At the end of the period when a company prepares financial statements, it takes a *physical count of inventory* by counting the quantities and costs of merchandise available. The cost of goods sold is then computed by subtracting the ending inventory amount from the cost of merchandise available for sale.

Recording Merchandise Transactions

P5 Record and compare merchandising transactions using both periodic and perpetual inventory systems.

Under a periodic system, purchases, purchase returns and allowances, purchase discounts, and transportation-in transactions are recorded in separate temporary accounts. At period-end, each of these temporary accounts is closed and the Merchandise Inventory account is updated. To illustrate, journal entries under the periodic inventory system are shown for the most common transactions (codes *a* through *f* link these transactions to those in the chapter, and we drop explanations for simplicity). For comparison, perpetual system journal entries are shown to the right of each periodic entry.

Purchases   The periodic system uses a temporary *Purchases* account that accumulates the cost of all purchase transactions during each period. Z-Mart's November 2 entry to record the purchase of merchandise for $1,200 on credit with terms of 2/10, n/30 is

(a)

Periodic			Perpetual		
Purchases	1,200		Merchandise Inventory	1,200	
Accounts Payable		1,200	Accounts Payable		1,200

Purchase Discounts   The periodic system uses a temporary *Purchase Discounts* account that accumulates discounts taken on purchase transactions during the period. If payment in (*a*) is delayed until after the discount period expires, the entry is to debit Accounts Payable and credit Cash for $1,200 each. However, if Z-Mart pays the supplier for the previous purchase in (*a*) within the discount period, the required payment is $1,176 ($1,200 × 98%) and is recorded as

(b)

Periodic			Perpetual		
Accounts Payable	1,200		Accounts Payable	1,200	
Purchase Discounts		24	Merchandise Inventory		24
Cash		1,176	Cash		1,176

Purchase Returns and Allowances   Z-Mart returned merchandise purchased on November 2 because of defects. In the periodic system, the temporary *Purchase Returns and Allowances* account accumulates the cost of all returns and allowances during a period. The recorded cost (including discounts) of the defective merchandise is $300, and Z-Mart records the November 15 return with this entry:

(c)

Periodic			Perpetual		
Accounts Payable	300		Accounts Payable	300	
Purchase Returns and Allowances		300	Merchandise Inventory		300

Transportation-In   Z-Mart paid a $75 freight charge to transport merchandise to its store. In the periodic system, this cost is charged to a temporary *Transportation-In* account.

(d)

Periodic			Perpetual		
Transportation-In	75		Merchandise Inventory	75	
Cash		75	Cash		75

Sales   Under the periodic system, the cost of goods sold is *not* recorded at the time of each sale. (We later show how to compute total cost of goods sold at the end of a period.) Z-Mart's November 3 entry to record sales of $2,400 in merchandise on credit (when its cost is $1,600) is:

(e)

Periodic			Perpetual		
Accounts Receivable	2,400		Accounts Receivable	2,400	
Sales		2,400	Sales		2,400
			Cost of Goods Sold	1,600	
			Merchandise Inventory		1,600

Sales Returns   A customer returned part of the merchandise from the transaction in (*e*), where the returned items sell for $800 and cost $600. (*Recall:* The periodic system records only the revenue effect, not the cost effect, for sales transactions.) Z-Mart restores the merchandise to inventory and records the November 6 return as

(f)

Periodic			Perpetual		
Sales Returns and			Sales Returns and		
Allowances	800		Allowances	800	
Accounts Receivable ...		800	Accounts Receivable		800
			Merchandise Inventory	600	
			Cost of Goods Sold		600

Adjusting and Closing Entries

The periodic and perpetual inventory systems have slight differences in adjusting and closing entries. The period-end Merchandise Inventory balance (unadjusted) is $19,000 under the periodic system and $21,250 under the perpetual system. Since the periodic system does not update the Merchandise Inventory balance during the period, the $19,000 amount is the beginning inventory. However, the $21,250 balance under the perpetual system is the recorded ending inventory before adjusting for any inventory shrinkage.

A physical count of inventory taken at the end of the period reveals $21,000 of merchandise available. The adjusting and closing entries for the two systems are shown in Exhibit 5A.1. The periodic

Exhibit 5A.1

Comparison of Adjusting and Closing Entries—Periodic and Perpetual

PERIODIC		
Adjusting Entry—Shrinkage		
None		

PERPETUAL		
Adjusting Entry—Shrinkage		
Cost of Goods Sold	250	
Merchandise Inventory		250

PERIODIC — Closing Entries		
(1) Sales	321,000	
Merchandise Inventory	21,000	
Purchase Discounts	4,200	
Purchase Returns and Allowances	1,500	
Income Summary		347,700
(2) Income Summary	334,800	
Sales Discounts		4,300
Sales Returns and Allowances		2,000
Merchandise Inventory		19,000
Purchases		235,800
Transportation-In		2,300
Depreciation Expense—Store eq.		3,000
Depreciation Expense—Office eq. ...		700

PERPETUAL — Closing Entries		
(1) Sales	321,000	
Income Summary		321,000
(2) Income Summary	308,100	
Sales Discounts		4,300
Sales Returns and Allowances		2,000
Cost of Goods Sold		230,400
Depreciation Expense—Store eq.		3,000
Depreciation Expense—Office eq. ...		700

[continued on next page]

[continued from previous page]

Office Salaries Expense		25,300
Sales Salaries Expense		18,500
Insurance Expense		600
Rent Expense—Office space		900
Rent Expense—Selling space		8,100
Office Supplies Expense		1,800
Store Supplies Expense		1,200
Advertising Expense		11,300
(3) Income Summary	12,900	
K. Marty, Capital		12,900
(4) K. Marty, Capital	4,000	
K. Marty, Withdrawals		4,000

Office Salaries Expense		25,300
Sales Salaries Expense		18,500
Insurance Expense		600
Rent Expense—Office space		900
Rent Expense—Selling space		8,100
Office Supplies Expense		1,800
Store Supplies Expense		1,200
Advertising Expense		11,300
(3) Income Summary	12,900	
K. Marty, Capital		12,900
(4) K. Marty, Capital	4,000	
K. Marty, Withdrawals		4,000

system records the ending inventory of $21,000 in the Merchandise Inventory account (which includes shrinkage) in the first closing entry and removes the $19,000 beginning inventory balance from the account in the second closing entry.[3]

By updating Merchandise Inventory and closing Purchases, Purchase Discounts, Purchase Returns and Allowances, and Transportation-In, the periodic system transfers the cost of goods sold amount to Income Summary. Review the periodic side of Exhibit 5A.1 and notice that the boldface items affect Income Summary as follows.

Credit to Income Summary in the first closing entry includes amounts from:	
Merchandise inventory (ending)	$ 21,000
Purchase discounts	4,200
Purchase returns and allowances	1,500
Debit to Income Summary in the second closing entry includes amounts from:	
Merchandise inventory (beginning)	(19,000)
Purchases	(235,800)
Transportation-in	(2,300)
Net effect on Income Summary	**$(230,400)**

This $230,400 effect on Income Summary is the cost of goods sold amount. The periodic system transfers cost of goods sold to the Income Summary account but without using a Cost of Goods Sold account. Also, the periodic system does not separately measure shrinkage. Instead, it computes cost of goods available for sale, subtracts the cost of ending inventory, and defines the difference as cost of goods sold, which includes shrinkage.

Preparing Financial Statements

The financial statements of a merchandiser using the periodic system are similar to those for a service company described in prior chapters. The income statement mainly differs by the inclusion of *cost of goods sold* and *gross profit*—of course, net sales is affected by discounts, returns, and allowances. The cost of goods sold section under the periodic system follows

Calculation of Cost of Goods Sold For Year Ended December 31, 2008		
Beginning inventory	$ 19,000	
Cost of goods purchased	232,400	
Cost of goods available for sale	251,400	
Less ending inventory	21,000	
Cost of goods sold	$230,400	

---

[3] This approach is called the *closing entry method*. An alternative approach, referred to as the *adjusting entry method*, would not make any entries to Merchandise Inventory in the closing entries of Exhibit 5A.1, but instead would make two adjusting entries. Using Z-Mart data, the two adjusting entries would be: (1) Dr. Income Summary and Cr. Merchandise Inventory for $19,000 each, and (2) Dr. Merchandise Inventory and Cr. Income Summary for $21,000 each. The first entry removes the beginning balance of Merchandise Inventory, and the second entry records the actual ending balance.

The balance sheet mainly differs by the inclusion of *merchandise inventory* in current assets—see Exhibit 5.15. The statement of owner's equity is unchanged. Finally, a work sheet can be used to help prepare these statements. The only differences under the periodic system from the work sheet illustrated in Appendix 5B using the perpetual system are highlighted as follows in blue boldface font.

	No.	Account	Unadjusted Trial Balance Dr.	Cr.	Adjustments Dr.	Cr.	Adjusted Trial Balance Dr.	Cr.	Income Statement Dr.	Cr.	Balance Sheet Dr.	Cr.
3	101	Cash	8,200				8,200				8,200	
4	106	Accounts receivable	11,200				11,200				11,200	
5	119	Merchandise Inventory	19,000				19,000		19,000	21,000	21,000	
6	124	Office supplies	2,350			(c) 1,800	550				550	
7	125	Store supplies	1,450			(b) 1,200	250				250	
8	128	Prepaid insurance	900			(a) 600	300				300	
9	163	Office equipment	4,200				4,200				4,200	
10	164	Accum. depr.—Office equip.		700		(e) 700		1,400				1,400
11	165	Store equipment	30,000				30,000				30,000	
12	166	Accum. depr.—Store equip.		3,000		(d) 3,000		6,000				6,000
13	201	Accounts payable		16,000				16,000				16,000
14	209	Salaries payable				(f) 800		800				800
15	301	K. Marty, Capital		42,600				42,600				42,600
16	302	K. Marty, Withdrawals	4,000				4,000				4,000	
17	413	Sales		321,000				321,000		321,000		
18	414	Sales returns and allowances	2,000				2,000		2,000			
19	415	Sales discounts	4,300				4,300		4,300			
20a	505	Purchases	235,800				235,800		235,800			
20b	506	Purchases returns & allowance		1,500				1,500		1,500		
20c	507	Purchases discounts		4,200				4,200		4,200		
20d	508	Transportation-in	2,300				2,300		2,300			
21	612	Depr. expense—Store equip.			(d) 3,000		3,000		3,000			
22	613	Depr. expense—Office equip.			(e) 700		700		700			
23	620	Office salaries expense	25,000		(f) 300		25,300		25,300			
24	621	Sales salaries expense	18,000		(f) 500		18,500		18,500			
25	637	Insurance expense			(a) 600		600		600			
26	641	Rent expense—Office space	900				900		900			
27	642	Rent expense—Selling space	8,100				8,100		8,100			
28	650	Office supplies expense			(c) 1,800		1,800		1,800			
29	651	Store supplies expense			(b) 1,200		1,200		1,200			
30	655	Advertising expense	11,300				11,300		11,300			
31		Totals	389,000	389,000	8,100	8,100	393,500	393,500	334,800	347,700	79,700	66,800
32		Net income							12,900			12,900
33		Totals							347,700	347,700	79,700	79,700

Quick Check
Answer—p. 204

13. What account is used in a perpetual inventory system but not in a periodic system?

14. Which of the following accounts are temporary accounts under a periodic system?
(*a*) Merchandise Inventory; (*b*) Purchases; (*c*) Transportation-In.

15. How is cost of goods sold computed under a periodic inventory system?

16. Do reported amounts of ending inventory and net income differ if the adjusting entry method of recording the change in inventory is used instead of the closing entry method?

APPENDIX

5B

Work Sheet—Perpetual System

Exhibit 5B.1 shows the work sheet for preparing financial statements of a merchandiser. It differs slightly from the work sheet layout in Chapter 4—the differences are in red boldface. Also, the adjustments in the work sheet reflect the following: (*a*) Expiration of $600 of prepaid insurance. (*b*) Use of $1,200 of store supplies. (*c*) Use of $1,800 of office supplies. (*d*) Depreciation of $3,000 for store equipment. (*e*) Depreciation of $700 for office equipment. (*f*) Accrual of $300 of unpaid office salaries and $500 of unpaid store salaries. (*g*) Inventory shrinkage of $250. Once the adjusted amounts are extended into the financial statement columns, the information is used to develop financial statements.

Exhibit 5B.1

Work Sheet for Merchandiser (using a perpetual system)

No.	Account	Unadjusted Trial Balance Dr.	Cr.	Adjustments Dr.	Cr.	Adjusted Trial Balance Dr.	Cr.	Income Statement Dr.	Cr.	Balance Sheet Dr.	Cr.
101	Cash	8,200				8,200				8,200	
106	Accounts receivable	11,200				11,200				11,200	
119	Merchandise Inventory	21,250			(g) 250	21,000				21,000	
124	Office supplies	2,350			(c) 1,800	550				550	
125	Store supplies	1,450			(b) 1,200	250				250	
128	Prepaid insurance	900			(a) 600	300				300	
163	Office equipment	4,200				4,200				4,200	
164	Accum. depr.—Office equip.		700		(e) 700		1,400				1,400
165	Store equipment	30,000				30,000				30,000	
166	Accum. depr.—Store equip.		3,000		(d) 3,000		6,000				6,000
201	Accounts payable		16,000				16,000				16,000
209	Salaries payable				(f) 800		800				800
301	K. Marty, Capital		42,600				42,600				42,600
302	K. Marty, Withdrawals	4,000				4,000				4,000	
413	Sales		321,000				321,000		321,000		
414	Sales returns and allowances	2,000				2,000		2,000			
415	Sales discounts	4,300				4,300		4,300			
502	Cost of goods sold	230,150		(g) 250		230,400		230,400			
612	Depr. expense—Store equip.			(d) 3,000		3,000		3,000			
613	Depr. expense—Office equip.			(e) 700		700		700			
620	Office salaries expense	25,000		(f) 300		25,300		25,300			
621	Sales salaries expense	18,000		(f) 500		18,500		18,500			
637	Insurance expense			(a) 600		600		600			
641	Rent expense—Office space	900				900		900			
642	Rent expense—Selling space	8,100				8,100		8,100			
650	Office supplies expense			(c) 1,800		1,800		1,800			
651	Store supplies expense			(b) 1,200		1,200		1,200			
655	Advertising expense	11,300				11,300		11,300			
	Totals	383,300	383,300	8,350	8,350	387,800	387,800	308,100	321,000	79,700	66,800
	Net income							12,900			12,900
	Totals							321,000	321,000	79,700	79,700

Summary

C1 Describe merchandising activities and identify income components for a merchandising company. Merchandisers buy products and resell them. Examples of merchandisers include Wal-Mart, Home Depot, The Limited, and Barnes & Noble. A merchandiser's costs on the income statement include an amount for cost of goods sold. Gross profit, or gross margin, equals sales minus cost of goods sold.

C2 Identify and explain the inventory asset of a merchandising company. The current asset section of a merchandising company's balance sheet includes *merchandise inventory,* which refers to the products a merchandiser sells and are available for sale at the balance sheet date.

C3 Describe both perpetual and periodic inventory systems. A perpetual inventory system continuously tracks the cost of goods available for sale and the cost of goods sold. A periodic system accumulates the cost of goods purchased during the period and does not compute the amount of inventory or the cost of goods sold until the end of a period.

C4 Analyze and interpret cost flows and operating activities of a merchandising company. Cost of merchandise purchases flows into Merchandise Inventory and from there to Cost of Goods Sold on the income statement. Any remaining inventory is reported as a current asset on the balance sheet.

A1 Compute the acid-test ratio and explain its use to assess liquidity. The acid-test ratio is computed as quick assets (cash, short-term investments, and current receivables) divided by current liabilities. It indicates a company's ability to pay its current liabilities with its existing quick assets. An acid-test ratio equal to or greater than 1.0 is often adequate.

A2 Compute the gross margin ratio and explain its use to assess profitability. The gross margin ratio is computed as gross margin (net sales minus cost of goods sold) divided by net sales. It indicates a company's profitability before considering other expenses.

P1 Analyze and record transactions for merchandise purchases using a perpetual system. For a perpetual inventory system, purchases of inventory (net of trade discounts) are added to the Merchandise Inventory account. Purchase discounts and purchase returns and allowances are subtracted from Merchandise Inventory, and transportation-in costs are added to Merchandise Inventory.

P2 Analyze and record transactions for merchandise sales using a perpetual system. A merchandiser records sales at list price less any trade discounts. The cost of items sold is transferred from Merchandise Inventory to Cost of Goods Sold. Refunds or credits given to customers for unsatisfactory merchandise are recorded in Sales Returns and Allowances, a contra account to Sales. If merchandise is returned and restored to inventory, the cost of this merchandise is removed from Cost of Goods Sold and transferred back to Merchandise Inventory. When cash discounts from the sales price are offered and customers pay within the discount period, the seller records Sales Discounts, a contra account to Sales.

P3 Prepare adjustments and close accounts for a merchandising company. With a perpetual system, it is often necessary to make an adjustment for inventory shrinkage. This is computed by comparing a physical count of inventory with the Merchandise Inventory balance. Shrinkage is normally charged to Cost of Goods Sold. Temporary accounts closed to Income Summary for a merchandiser include Sales, Sales Discounts, Sales Returns and Allowances, and Cost of Goods Sold.

P4 Define and prepare multiple-step and single-step income statements. Multiple-step income statements include greater detail for sales and expenses than do single-step income statements. They also show details of net sales and report expenses in categories reflecting different activities.

P5^A Record and compare merchandising transactions using both periodic and perpetual inventory systems. Transactions involving the sale and purchase of merchandise are recorded and analyzed under both the periodic and perpetual inventory systems. Adjusting and closing entries for both inventory systems are illustrated and explained.

Guidance Answers to **Decision Maker** and **Decision Ethics**

Entrepreneur For terms of 3/10, n/90, missing the 3% discount for an additional 80 days equals an implied annual interest rate of 13.69%, computed as (365 days ÷ 80 days) × 3%. Since you can borrow funds at 11% (assuming no other processing costs), it is better to borrow and pay within the discount period. You save 2.69% (13.69% − 11%) in interest costs by paying early.

Credit Manager Your decision is whether to comply with prior policy or to create a new policy and not abuse discounts offered by suppliers. Your first step should be to meet with your superior to find out if the late payment policy is the actual policy and, if so, its rationale. If it is the policy to pay late, you must apply your own sense of ethics. One point of view is that the late payment policy is unethical. A deliberate plan to make late payments means the company lies

when it pretends to make payment within the discount period. Another view is that the late payment policy is acceptable. In some markets, attempts to take discounts through late payments are accepted as a continued phase of "price negotiation." Also, your company's suppliers can respond by billing your company for the discounts not accepted because of late payments. However, this is a dubious viewpoint, especially since the prior manager proposes that you dishonestly explain late payments as computer or mail problems and since some suppliers have complained.

Supplier A current ratio of 2.1 suggests sufficient current assets to cover current liabilities. An acid-test ratio of 0.5 suggests, however, that quick assets can cover only about one-half of current liabilities. This implies that the retailer depends on money from sales of inventory to pay current liabilities. If sales of inventory decline or profit margins decrease, the likelihood that this retailer will default on its payments increases. Your decision is probably not to extend credit. If you do extend credit, you are likely to closely monitor the retailer's financial condition. (It is better to hold unsold inventory than uncollectible receivables.)

Financial Officer   Your company's net profit margin is about equal to the industry average and suggests typical industry perform-

ance. However, gross margin reveals that your company is paying far more in cost of goods sold or receiving far less in sales price than competitors. Your attention must be directed to finding the problem with cost of goods sold, sales, or both. One positive note is that your company's expenses make up 19% of sales (36% − 17%). This favorably compares with competitors' expenses that make up 28% of sales (44% − 16%).

Guidance Answers to **Quick Checks**

1. Cost of goods sold is the cost of merchandise purchased from a supplier that is sold to customers during a specific period.

2. Gross profit (or gross margin) is the difference between net sales and cost of goods sold.

3. Widespread use of computing and related technology has dramatically increased the use of the perpetual inventory system.

4. Under credit terms of 2/10, n/60, the credit period is 60 days and the discount period is 10 days.

5. (b) trade discount.

6. *FOB* means "free on board." It is used in identifying the point when ownership transfers from seller to buyer. *FOB destination* means that the seller transfers ownership of goods to the buyer when they arrive at the buyer's place of business. It also means that the seller is responsible for paying shipping charges and bears the risk of damage or loss during shipment.

7. Recording sales discounts and sales returns and allowances separately from sales gives useful information to managers for internal monitoring and decision making.

8. When a customer returns merchandise *and* the seller restores the merchandise to inventory, two entries are necessary. One entry

records the decrease in revenue and credits the customer's account. The second entry debits inventory and reduces cost of goods sold.

9. Credit memorandum—seller credits accounts receivable from buyer.

10. Merchandise Inventory may need adjusting to reflect shrinkage.

11. Sales (of goods), Sales Discounts, Sales Returns and Allowances, and Cost of Goods Sold (and maybe Delivery Expense).

12. Four closing entries: (1) close credit balances in temporary accounts to Income Summary, (2) close debit balances in temporary accounts to Income Summary, (3) close Income Summary to owner's capital, and (4) close withdrawals account to owner's capital.

13. Cost of Goods Sold.

14. (b) Purchases and (c) Transportation-In.

15. Under a periodic inventory system, the cost of goods sold is determined at the end of an accounting period by adding the net cost of goods purchased to the beginning inventory and subtracting the ending inventory.

16. Both methods report the same ending inventory and income.

Key Terms   mhhe.com/wildFAP18e

Key Terms are available at the book's Website for learning and testing in an online Flashcard Format.

Acid-test ratio (p. 193)	**Gross margin** (p. 179)	**Purchase discount** (p. 181)
Cash discount (p. 181)	**Gross margin ratio** (p. 193)	**Retailer** (p. 178)
Cost of goods sold (p. 179)	**Gross profit** (p. 179)	**Sales discount** (p. 181)
Credit memorandum (p. 187)	**Inventory** (p. 179)	**Selling expenses** (p. 191)
Credit period (p. 181)	**List price** (p. 180)	**Shrinkage** (p. 188)
Credit terms (p. 181)	**Merchandise** (p. 178)	**Single-step income statement** (p. 192)
Debit memorandum (p. 182)	**Merchandise inventory** (p. 179)	**Supplementary records** (p. 184)
Discount period (p. 181)	**Merchandiser** (p. 178)	**Trade discount** (p. 180)
EOM (p. 181)	**Multiple-step income statement** (p. 191)	**Wholesaler** (p. 178)
FOB (p. 183)	**Periodic inventory system** (p. 180)	
General and administrative expenses (p. 191)	**Perpetual inventory system** (p. 179)	

Multiple Choice Quizzes A and B are available at the book's Website.

1. A company has $550,000 in net sales and $193,000 in gross profit. This means its cost of goods sold equals
   a. $743,000
   b. $550,000
   c. $357,000
   d. $193,000
   e. $(193,000)

2. A company purchased $4,500 of merchandise on May 1 with terms of 2/10, n/30. On May 6, it returned $250 of that merchandise. On May 8, it paid the balance owed for merchandise, taking any discount it is entitled to. The cash paid on May 8 is
   a. $4,500
   b. $4,250
   c. $4,160
   d. $4,165
   e. $4,410

3. A company has cash sales of $75,000, credit sales of $320,000, sales returns and allowances of $13,700, and sales discounts of $6,000. Its net sales equal
   a. $395,000
   b. $375,300

   c. $300,300
   d. $339,700
   e. $414,700

4. A company's quick assets are $37,500, its current assets are $80,000, and its current liabilities are $50,000. Its acid-test ratio equals
   a. 1.600
   b. 0.750
   c. 0.625
   d. 1.333
   e. 0.469

5. A company's net sales are $675,000, its costs of goods sold are $459,000, and its net income is $74,250. Its gross margin ratio equals
   a. 32%
   b. 68%
   c. 47%
   d. 11%
   e. 34%

Superscript letter ^{A} (^{B}) denotes assignments based on Appendix 5A (5B).

Discussion Questions

1. In comparing the accounts of a merchandising company with those of a service company, what additional accounts would the merchandising company likely use, assuming it employs a perpetual inventory system?

2. What items appear in financial statements of merchandising companies but not in the statements of service companies?

3. Explain how a business can earn a positive gross profit on its sales and still have a net loss.

4. Why do companies offer a cash discount?

5. How does a company that uses a perpetual inventory system determine the amount of inventory shrinkage?

6. Distinguish between cash discounts and trade discounts. Is the amount of a trade discount on purchased merchandise recorded in the accounts?

7. What is the difference between a sales discount and a purchase discount?

8. Why would a company's manager be concerned about the quantity of its purchase returns if its suppliers allow unlimited returns?

9. Does the sender (maker) of a debit memorandum record a debit or a credit in the recipient's account? What entry (debit or credit) does the recipient record?

10. What is the difference between the single-step and multiple-step income statement formats?

11. Refer to the balance sheet and income statement for **Best Buy** in Appendix A. What does the company title its inventory account? Does the company present a detailed calculation of its cost of goods sold?

12. Refer to the income statement for **Circuit City** in Appendix A. What does Circuit City title its cost of goods sold account?

13. Refer to the income statement of **Apple** in Appendix A. Does its income statement report a gross profit figure? If yes, what is the amount?

14. Buyers negotiate purchase contracts with suppliers. What type of shipping terms should a buyer attempt to negotiate to minimize freight-in costs?

Red numbers denote Discussion Questions that involve decision-making.

QUICK STUDY

QS 5-1
Recording purchases—
perpetual system   P1

Prepare journal entries to record each of the following purchases transactions of a merchandising company. Show supporting calculations and assume a perpetual inventory system.

Mar. 5   Purchased 600 units of product with a list price of $10 per unit. The purchaser is granted a trade discount of 20%; terms of the sale are 2/10, n/60; invoice is dated March 5.
Mar. 7   Returned 25 defective units from the March 5 purchase and received full credit.
Mar. 15   Paid the amount due from the March 5 purchase, less the return on March 7.

QS 5-2
Recording sales—
perpetual system

P2

Prepare journal entries to record each of the following sales transactions of a merchandising company. Show supporting calculations and assume a perpetual inventory system.

Apr. 1   Sold merchandise for $3,000, granting the customer terms of 2/10, EOM; invoice dated April 1. The cost of the merchandise is $1,800.
Apr. 4   The customer in the April 1 sale returned merchandise and received credit for $600. The merchandise, which had cost $360, is returned to inventory.
Apr. 11   Received payment for the amount due from the April 1 sale less the return on April 4.

QS 5-3
Computing and analyzing
gross margin

C1   A2

Compute net sales, gross profit, and the gross margin ratio for each separate case *a* through *d*. Interpret the gross margin ratio for case *a*.

	a	b	c	d
Sales	$150,000	$550,000	$38,700	$255,700
Sales discounts	5,200	17,500	600	4,200
Sales returns and allowances	20,000	6,000	5,300	900
Cost of goods sold	79,600	329,700	24,300	126,900

QS 5-4
Accounting for shrinkage—
perpetual system

P3

Nix'It Company's ledger on July 31, its fiscal year-end, includes the following selected accounts that have normal balances (Nix'It uses the perpetual inventory system):

Merchandise inventory	$ 37,800	Cost of goods sold	$105,000
U. Nix, Capital	122,300	Depreciation expense	10,300
Sales	160,200	Salaries expense	32,500
Sales discounts	4,700	Miscellaneous expenses	5,000
Sales returns and allowances	6,500		

A physical count of its July 31 year-end inventory discloses that the cost of the merchandise inventory still available is $35,900. Prepare the entry to record any inventory shrinkage.

QS 5-5
Closing entries   P3

Refer to QS 5-4 and prepare journal entries to close the balances in temporary revenue and expense accounts. Remember to consider the entry for shrinkage that is made to solve QS 5-4.

QS 5-6
Computing and interpreting
acid-test ratio

A1

Use the following information on current assets and current liabilities to compute and interpret the acid-test ratio. Explain what the acid-test ratio of a company measures.

Cash	$1,500	Prepaid expenses	$ 700
Accounts receivable	2,800	Accounts payable	5,750
Inventory	6,000	Other current liabilities	850

QS 5-7
Contrasting liquidity ratios   A1

Identify similarities and differences between the acid-test ratio and the current ratio. Compare and describe how the two ratios reflect a company's ability to meet its current obligations.

QS 5-8[A]
Contrasting periodic and
perpetual systems

C3

Identify whether each description best applies to a periodic or a perpetual inventory system.

a. Provides more timely information to managers.
b. Requires an adjusting entry to record inventory shrinkage.
c. Updates the inventory account only at period-end.
d. Markedly increased in frequency and popularity in business within the past decade.
e. Records cost of goods sold each time a sales transaction occurs.

Refer to QS 5-1 and prepare journal entries to record each of the merchandising transactions assuming that the periodic inventory system is used.

QS 5-9[A]
Recording purchases—
periodic system   P5

Refer to QS 5-2 and prepare journal entries to record each of the merchandising transactions assuming that the periodic inventory system is used.

QS 5-10[A]
Recording purchases—
periodic system   P5

Prepare journal entries to record the following transactions for a retail store. Assume a perpetual inventory system.

EXERCISES

Exercise 5-1
Recording entries for
merchandise purchases

P1

Apr. 2   Purchased merchandise from Lyon Company under the following terms: $4,600 price, invoice dated April 2, credit terms of 2/15, n/60, and FOB shipping point.
      3   Paid $300 for shipping charges on the April 2 purchase.
      4   Returned to Lyon Company unacceptable merchandise that had an invoice price of $600.
     17   Sent a check to Lyon Company for the April 2 purchase, net of the discount and the returned merchandise.
     18   Purchased merchandise from Frist Corp. under the following terms: $8,500 price, invoice dated April 18, credit terms of 2/10, n/30, and FOB destination.
     21   After negotiations, received from Frist a $1,100 allowance on the April 18 purchase.
     28   Sent check to Frist paying for the April 18 purchase, net of the discount and allowance.

Check   April 28, Cr. Cash $7,252

Santa Fe Company purchased merchandise for resale from Mesa Company with an invoice price of $24,000 and credit terms of 3/10, n/60. The merchandise had cost Mesa $16,000. Santa Fe paid within the discount period. Assume that both buyer and seller use a perpetual inventory system.

1. Prepare entries that the buyer should record for the purchase and the cash payment.

2. Prepare entries that the seller should record for the sale and the cash collection.

3. Assume that the buyer borrowed enough cash to pay the balance on the last day of the discount period at an annual interest rate of 8% and paid it back on the last day of the credit period. Compute how much the buyer saved by following this strategy. (Assume a 365-day year and round dollar amounts to the nearest cent.)

Exercise 5-2
Analyzing and recording
merchandise transactions—
both buyer and seller

P1 P2

Check   (3) $465 savings

Insert the letter for each term in the blank space beside the definition that it most closely matches.

A. Cash discount   **E.** FOB shipping point   **H.** Purchase discount
B. Credit period   **F.** Gross profit   **I.** Sales discount
C. Discount period   **G.** Merchandise inventory   **J.** Trade discount
D. FOB destination

_____ **1.** Reduction below list or catalog price that is negotiated in setting the price of goods.
_____ **2.** Reduction in a receivable or payable if it is paid within the discount period.
_____ **3.** Time period that can pass before a customer's payment is due.
_____ **4.** Difference between net sales and the cost of goods sold.
_____ **5.** Ownership of goods is transferred when the seller delivers goods to the carrier.
_____ **6.** Ownership of goods is transferred when delivered to the buyer's place of business.
_____ **7.** Goods a company owns and expects to sell to its customers.
_____ **8.** Purchaser's description of a cash discount received from a supplier of goods.
_____ **9.** Seller's description of a cash discount granted to buyers in return for early payment.
____ **10.** Time period in which a cash discount is available.

Exercise 5-3
Applying merchandising terms

C1

Allied Parts was organized on May 1, 2008, and made its first purchase of merchandise on May 3. The purchase was for 2,000 units at a price of $10 per unit. On May 5, Allied Parts sold 1,500 of the units for $14 per unit to Baker Co. Terms of the sale were 2/10, n/60. Prepare entries for Allied Parts

Exercise 5-4
Recording sales returns and
allowances   P2

to record the May 5 sale and each of the following separate transactions *a* through *c* using a perpetual inventory system.

a. On May 7, Baker returns 200 units because they did not fit the customer's needs. Allied Parts restores the units to its inventory.

b. On May 8, Baker discovers that 300 units are damaged but are still of some use and, therefore, keeps the units. Allied Parts sends Baker a credit memorandum for $600 to compensate for the damage.

Check (c) Dr. Sales Returns and Allowances $680

c. On May 15, Baker discovers that 100 units are the wrong color. Baker keeps 60 of these units because Allied sends a $120 credit memorandum to compensate. However, Baker returns the remaining 40 units to Allied. Allied restores the 40 returned units to its inventory.

Exercise 5-5
Recording purchase returns and allowances   P1

Refer to Exercise 5-4 and prepare the appropriate journal entries for Baker Co. to record the May 5 purchase and each of the three separate transactions *a* through *c*. Baker is a retailer that uses a perpetual inventory system and purchases these units for resale.

Exercise 5-6
Analyzing and recording merchandise transactions— both buyer and seller

P1   P2

On May 11, Sydney Co. accepts delivery of $40,000 of merchandise it purchases for resale from Troy Corporation. With the merchandise is an invoice dated May 11, with terms of 3/10, n/90, FOB shipping point. The goods cost Troy $30,000. When the goods are delivered, Sydney pays $345 to Express Shipping for delivery charges on the merchandise. On May 12, Sydney returns $1,400 of goods to Troy, who receives them one day later and restores them to inventory. The returned goods had cost Troy $800. On May 20, Sydney mails a check to Troy Corporation for the amount owed. Troy receives it the following day. (Both Sydney and Troy use a perpetual inventory system)

Check (1) May 20, Cr. Cash $37,442

1. Prepare journal entries that Sydney Co. records for these transactions.

2. Prepare journal entries that Troy Corporation records for these transactions.

Exercise 5-7
Sales returns and allowances

C1   P2

Business decision makers desire information on sales returns and allowances. (1) Explain why a company's manager wants the accounting system to record customers' returns of unsatisfactory goods in the Sales Returns and Allowances account instead of the Sales account. (2) Explain whether this information would be useful for external decision makers.

Exercise 5-8
Computing revenues, expenses, and income

C1   C4

Using your accounting knowledge, fill in the blanks in the following separate income statements *a* through *e*. Identify any negative amount by putting it in parentheses.

	a	b	c	d	e
Sales	$62,000	$43,500	$46,000	$?	$25,600
Cost of goods sold					
Merchandise inventory (beginning)	8,000	17,050	7,500	8,000	4,560
Total cost of merchandise purchases	38,000	?	?	32,000	6,600
Merchandise inventory (ending)	?	(3,000)	(9,000)	(6,600)	?
Cost of goods sold	34,050	16,000	?	?	7,000
Gross profit	?	?	3,750	45,600	?
Expenses	10,000	10,650	12,150	3,600	6,000
Net income (loss)	$?	$16,850	$ (8,400)	$42,000	$?

Exercise 5-9
Recording effects of merchandising activities

C4

The following supplementary records summarize Tosca Company's merchandising activities for year 2008. Set up T-accounts for Merchandise Inventory and Cost of Goods Sold. Then record the summarized activities in those T-accounts and compute account balances.

Cost of merchandise sold to customers in sales transactions	$196,000
Merchandise inventory, December 31, 2007	25,000
Invoice cost of merchandise purchases	192,500
Shrinkage determined on December 31, 2008	800
Cost of transportation-in	2,900
Cost of merchandise returned by customers and restored to inventory	2,100
Purchase discounts received	1,700
Purchase returns and allowances	4,000

Check Merchandise Inventory (12/31/2008), $20,000

The following list includes selected permanent accounts and all of the temporary accounts from the December 31, 2008, unadjusted trial balance of Emiko Co., a business owned by Kumi Emiko. Use these account balances along with the additional information to journalize (*a*) adjusting entries and (*b*) closing entries. Emiko Co. uses a perpetual inventory system.

Exercise 5-10

Preparing adjusting and closing entries for a merchandiser

P3

	Debit	Credit
Merchandise inventory	$ 30,000	
Prepaid selling expenses	5,600	
K. Emiko, Withdrawals	33,000	
Sales		$529,000
Sales returns and allowances	17,500	
Sales discounts	5,000	
Cost of goods sold	212,000	
Sales salaries expense	48,000	
Utilities expense	15,000	
Selling expenses	36,000	
Administrative expenses	105,000	

Additional Information

Accrued sales salaries amount to $1,700. Prepaid selling expenses of $3,000 have expired. A physical count of year-end merchandise inventory shows $28,450 of goods still available.

Check Entry to close Income Summary: Cr. K. Emiko, Capital $84,250

A retail company recently completed a physical count of ending merchandise inventory to use in preparing adjusting entries. In determining the cost of the counted inventory, company employees failed to consider that $3,000 of incoming goods had been shipped by a supplier on December 31 under an FOB shipping point agreement. These goods had been recorded in Merchandise Inventory as a purchase, but they were not included in the physical count because they were in transit. Explain how this overlooked fact affects the company's financial statements and the following ratios: return on assets, debt ratio, current ratio, profit margin ratio, and acid-test ratio.

Exercise 5-11

Interpreting a physical count error as inventory shrinkage

A1 A2 P3

Compute the current ratio and acid-test ratio for each of the following separate cases. Which company case is in the best position to meet short-term obligations? Explain.

Exercise 5-12

Computing and analyzing acid-test and current ratios

A1

	Case X	Case Y	Case Z
Cash	$ 900	$ 810	$1,000
Short-term investments	0	0	600
Current receivables	0	1,090	700
Inventory	3,000	1,100	4,100
Prepaid expenses	1,300	500	900
Total current assets	$5,200	$3,500	$7,300
Current liabilities	$2,200	$1,200	$3,750

Journalize the following merchandising transactions for Chilton Systems assuming it uses (*a*) a periodic inventory system and (*b*) a perpetual inventory system.

Exercise 5-13[A]

Preparing journal entries for both the periodic and perpetual systems

P1 P2 P5

1. On November 1, Chilton Systems purchases merchandise for $1,500 on credit with terms of 2/5, n/30, FOB shipping point; invoice dated November 1.

2. On November 5, Chilton Systems pays cash for the November 1 purchase.

3. On November 7, Chilton Systems discovers and returns $200 of defective merchandise purchased on November 1 for a cash refund.

4. On November 10, Chilton Systems pays $90 cash for transportation costs with the November 1 purchase.

5. On November 13, Chilton Systems sells merchandise for $1,600 on credit. The cost of the merchandise is $800.

6. On November 16, the customer returns merchandise from the November 13 transaction. The returned items sell for $300 and cost $150.

Exercise 5-14^A
Recording purchases—
periodic system   P5

Refer to Exercise 5-1 and prepare journal entries to record each of the merchandising transactions assuming that the periodic inventory system is used.

Exercise 5-15^A
Recording purchases and
sales—periodic system   P5

Refer to Exercise 5-2 and prepare journal entries to record each of the merchandising transactions assuming that the periodic inventory system is used by both the buyer and the seller. (Skip the part 3 requirement.)

Exercise 5-16^A
Buyer and seller transactions—
periodic system   P5

Refer to Exercise 5-6 and prepare journal entries to record each of the merchandising transactions assuming that the periodic inventory system is used by both the buyer and the seller.

PROBLEM SET A

Problem 5-1A
Preparing journal entries for
merchandising activities—
perpetual system

P1   P2

Check   July 12, Dr. Cash $882
July 16, Cr. Cash $5,940

July 24, Cr. Cash $1,960
July 30, Dr. Cash $980

Prepare journal entries to record the following merchandising transactions of Blink Company, which applies the perpetual inventory system. (*Hint:* It will help to identify each receivable and payable; for example, record the purchase on July 1 in Accounts Payable—Boden.)

July 1   Purchased merchandise from Boden Company for $6,000 under credit terms of 1/15, n/30, FOB shipping point, invoice dated July 1.
  2   Sold merchandise to Creek Co. for $900 under credit terms of 2/10, n/60, FOB shipping point, invoice dated July 2. The merchandise had cost $500.
  3   Paid $125 cash for freight charges on the purchase of July 1.
  8   Sold merchandise that had cost $1,300 for $1,700 cash.
  9   Purchased merchandise from Leight Co. for $2,200 under credit terms of 2/15, n/60, FOB destination, invoice dated July 9.
  11   Received a $200 credit memorandum from Leight Co. for the return of part of the merchandise purchased on July 9.
  12   Received the balance due from Creek Co. for the invoice dated July 2, net of the discount.
  16   Paid the balance due to Boden Company within the discount period.
  19   Sold merchandise that cost $800 to Art Co. for $1,200 under credit terms of 2/15, n/60, FOB shipping point, invoice dated July 19.
  21   Issued a $200 credit memorandum to Art Co. for an allowance on goods sold on July 19.
  24   Paid Leight Co. the balance due after deducting the discount.
  30   Received the balance due from Art Co. for the invoice dated July 19, net of discount.
  31   Sold merchandise that cost $4,800 to Creek Co. for $7,000 under credit terms of 2/10, n/60, FOB shipping point, invoice dated July 31.

Problem 5-2A
Preparing journal entries for
merchandising activities—
perpetual system

P1   P2

Check   Aug. 9, Dr. Delivery
Expense, $125

Prepare journal entries to record the following merchandising transactions of Sheng Company, which applies the perpetual inventory system. (*Hint:* It will help to identify each receivable and payable; for example, record the purchase on August 1 in Accounts Payable—Arotek.)

Aug. 1   Purchased merchandise from Arotek Company for $7,500 under credit terms of 1/10, n/30, FOB destination, invoice dated August 1.
  4   At Arotek's request, Sheng paid $200 cash for freight charges on the August 1 purchase, reducing the amount owed to Arotek.
  5   Sold merchandise to Laird Corp. for $5,200 under credit terms of 2/10, n/60, FOB destination, invoice dated August 5. The merchandise had cost $4,000.
  8   Purchased merchandise from Waters Corporation for $5,400 under credit terms of 1/10, n/45, FOB shipping point, invoice dated August 8. The invoice showed that at Sheng's request, Waters paid the $140 shipping charges and added that amount to the bill. (*Recall:* Discounts are not applied to freight and shipping charges.)
  9   Paid $125 cash for shipping charges related to the August 5 sale to Laird Corp.
  10   Laird returned merchandise from the August 5 sale that had cost Sheng $400 and been sold for $600. The merchandise was restored to inventory.

12   After negotiations with Waters Corporation concerning problems with the merchandise purchased on August 8, Sheng received a credit memorandum from Waters granting a price reduction of $700.

15   Received balance due from Laird Corp. for the August 5 sale less the return on August 10.

18   Paid the amount due Waters Corporation for the August 8 purchase less the price reduction granted.

19   Sold merchandise to Tux Co. for $4,800 under credit terms of 1/10, n/30, FOB shipping point, invoice dated August 19. The merchandise had cost $2,400.

22   Tux requested a price reduction on the August 19 sale because the merchandise did not meet specifications. Sheng sent Tux a $500 credit memorandum to resolve the issue.

29   Received Tux's cash payment for the amount due from the August 19 sale.

30   Paid Arotek Company the amount due from the August 1 purchase.

Aug. 18, Cr. Cash $4,793

Aug. 29, Dr. Cash $4,257

The following unadjusted trial balance is prepared at fiscal year-end for Nelson Company.

Problem 5-3A

Preparing adjusting entries and income statements; and computing gross margin, acid-test, and current ratios

A1 A2 P3 P4

e**X**cel

mhhe.com/wildFAP18e

File Edit View Insert Format Tools Data Accounting Window Help		
NELSON COMPANY **Unadjusted Trial Balance** **January 31, 2008**		
	Debit	**Credit**
2 Cash	$ 1,000	
3 Merchandise inventory	12,500	
4 Store supplies	5,800	
5 Prepaid insurance	2,400	
6 Store equipment	42,900	
7 Accumulated depreciation—Store equipment		$ 15,250
8 Accounts payable		10,000
9 J. Nelson, Capital		32,000
10 J. Nelson, Withdrawals	2,200	
11 Sales		111,950
12 Sales discounts	2,000	
13 Sales returns and allowances	2,200	
14 Cost of good sold	38,400	
15 Depreciation expense—Store equipment	0	
16 Salaries expense	35,000	
17 Insurance expense	0	
18 Rent expense	15,000	
19 Store supplies expense	0	
20 Advertising expense	9,800	
21 Totals	$169,200	$169,200

Sheet1 Sheet2 Sheet3

Rent expense and salaries expense are equally divided between selling activities and the general and administrative activities. Nelson Company uses a perpetual inventory system.

Required

1. Prepare adjusting journal entries to reflect each of the following:

   a. Store supplies still available at fiscal year-end amount to $1,750.

   b. Expired insurance, an administrative expense, for the fiscal year is $1,400.

   c. Depreciation expense on store equipment, a selling expense, is $1,525 for the fiscal year.

   d. To estimate shrinkage, a physical count of ending merchandise inventory is taken. It shows $10,900 of inventory is still available at fiscal year-end.

2. Prepare a multiple-step income statement for fiscal year 2008.

3. Prepare a single-step income statement for fiscal year 2008.

4. Compute the current ratio, acid-test ratio, and gross margin ratio as of January 31, 2008.

Check (2) Gross profit, $67,750;
(3) Total expenses, $106,775; Net income, $975

Problem 5-4A
Computing merchandising
amounts and formatting
income statements

C4   P4

Valley Company's adjusted trial balance on August 31, 2008, its fiscal year-end, follows.

	Debit	Credit
Merchandise inventory	$ 41,000	
Other (noninventory) assets	130,400	
Total liabilities		$ 25,000
K. Valley, Capital		104,550
K. Valley, Withdrawals	8,000	
Sales		225,600
Sales discounts	2,250	
Sales returns and allowances	12,000	
Cost of goods sold	74,500	
Sales salaries expense	32,000	
Rent expense—Selling space	8,000	
Store supplies expense	1,500	
Advertising expense	13,000	
Office salaries expense	28,500	
Rent expense—Office space	3,600	
Office supplies expense	400	
Totals	$355,150	$355,150

On August 31, 2007, merchandise inventory was $25,400. Supplementary records of merchandising activities for the year ended August 31, 2008, reveal the following itemized costs:

Invoice cost of merchandise purchases	$92,000
Purchase discounts received	2,000
Purchase returns and allowances	4,500
Costs of transportation-in	4,600

Required

1. Compute the company's net sales for the year.

Check (2) $90,100;

2. Compute the company's total cost of merchandise purchased for the year.

(3) Gross profit, $136,850;
   Net income, $49,850;

3. Prepare a multiple-step income statement that includes separate categories for selling expenses and for general and administrative expenses.

(4) Total expenses, $161,500

4. Prepare a single-step income statement that includes these expense categories: cost of goods sold, selling expenses, and general and administrative expenses.

Problem 5-5A
Preparing closing entries and
interpreting information about
discounts and returns

C4   P3

Check (1) $49,850 Dr. to close
   Income Summary
   (3) Current-year rate, 5.3%

Use the data for Valley Company in Problem 5-4A to complete the following requirements.

Required

1. Prepare closing entries as of August 31, 2008 (the perpetual inventory system is used).

Analysis Component

2. The company makes all purchases on credit, and its suppliers uniformly offer a 3% sales discount. Does it appear that the company's cash management system is accomplishing the goal of taking all available discounts? Explain.

3. In prior years, the company experienced a 4% returns and allowance rate on its sales, which means approximately 4% of its gross sales were eventually returned outright or caused the company to grant allowances to customers. How do this year's results compare to prior years' results?

Refer to the data and information in Problem 5-3A.

Required

Prepare and complete the entire 10-column work sheet for Nelson Company. Follow the structure of Exhibit 5B.1 in Appendix 5B.

Problem 5-6A[B]
Preparing a work sheet for
a merchandiser
P3

Prepare journal entries to record the following merchandising transactions of Yarvelle Company, which applies the perpetual inventory system. (*Hint:* It will help to identify each receivable and payable; for example, record the purchase on May 2 in Accounts Payable—Havel.)

May	2	Purchased merchandise from Havel Co. for $10,000 under credit terms of 1/15, n/30, FOB shipping point, invoice dated May 2.
	4	Sold merchandise to Heather Co. for $11,000 under credit terms of 2/10, n/60, FOB shipping point, invoice dated May 4. The merchandise had cost $5,600.
	5	Paid $250 cash for freight charges on the purchase of May 2.
	9	Sold merchandise that had cost $2,000 for $2,500 cash.
	10	Purchased merchandise from Duke Co. for $3,650 under credit terms of 2/15, n/60, FOB destination, invoice dated May 10.
	12	Received a $400 credit memorandum from Duke Co. for the return of part of the merchandise purchased on May 10.
	14	Received the balance due from Heather Co. for the invoice dated May 4, net of the discount.
	17	Paid the balance due to Havel Co. within the discount period.
	20	Sold merchandise that cost $1,450 to Tameron Co. for $2,800 under credit terms of 2/15, n/60, FOB shipping point, invoice dated May 20.
	22	Issued a $400 credit memorandum to Tameron Co. for an allowance on goods sold from May 20.
	25	Paid Duke Co. the balance due after deducting the discount.
	30	Received the balance due from Tameron Co. for the invoice dated May 20, net of discount and allowance.
	31	Sold merchandise that cost $3,600 to Heather Co. for $7,200 under credit terms of 2/10, n/60, FOB shipping point, invoice dated May 31.

PROBLEM SET B

Problem 5-1B
Preparing journal entries for
merchandising activities—
perpetual system

P1   P2

Check   May 14, Dr. Cash $10,780
May 17, Cr. Cash $9,900

May 30, Dr. Cash $2,352

Prepare journal entries to record the following merchandising transactions of Mason Company, which applies the perpetual inventory system. (*Hint:* It will help to identify each receivable and payable; for example, record the purchase on July 3 in Accounts Payable—OLB.)

July	3	Purchased merchandise from OLB Corp. for $15,000 under credit terms of 1/10, n/30, FOB destination, invoice dated July 3.
	4	At OLB's request, Mason paid $150 cash for freight charges on the July 3 purchase, reducing the amount owed to OLB.
	7	Sold merchandise to Brill Co. for $11,500 under credit terms of 2/10, n/60, FOB destination, invoice dated July 7. The merchandise had cost $7,750.
	10	Purchased merchandise from Rupert Corporation for $14,200 under credit terms of 1/10, n/45, FOB shipping point, invoice dated July 10. The invoice showed that at Mason's request, Rupert paid the $500 shipping charges and added that amount to the bill. (*Recall:* Discounts are not applied to freight and shipping charges.)
	11	Paid $300 cash for shipping charges related to the July 7 sale to Brill Co.
	12	Brill returned merchandise from the July 7 sale that had cost Mason $1,450 and been sold for $1,850. The merchandise was restored to inventory.
	14	After negotiations with Rupert Corporation concerning problems with the merchandise purchased on July 10, Mason received a credit memorandum from Rupert granting a price reduction of $2,000.
	17	Received balance due from Brill Co. for the July 7 sale less the return on July 12.
	20	Paid the amount due Rupert Corporation for the July 10 purchase less the price reduction granted.
	21	Sold merchandise to Brown for $11,000 under credit terms of 1/10, n/30, FOB shipping point, invoice dated July 21. The merchandise had cost $7,000.
	24	Brown requested a price reduction on the July 21 sale because the merchandise did not meet specifications. Mason sent Brown a credit memorandum for $1,300 to resolve the issue.
	30	Received Brown's cash payment for the amount due from the July 21 sale.
	31	Paid OLB Corp. the amount due from the July 3 purchase.

Problem 5-2B
Preparing journal entries for
merchandising activities—
perpetual system

P1   P2

Check   July 17, Dr. Cash $9,457
July 20, Cr. Cash $12,578

July 30, Dr. Cash $9,603

Problem 5-3B

Preparing adjusting entries and income statements; and computing gross margin, acid-test, and current ratios

A1 A2 P3 P4

The following unadjusted trial balance is prepared at fiscal year-end for Foster Products Company.

	File Edit View Insert Format Tools Data Accounting Window Help		
	FOSTER PRODUCTS COMPANY Unadjusted Trial Balance October 31, 2008		
		Debit	**Credit**
2	Cash	$ 7,400	
3	Merchandise inventory	24,000	
4	Store supplies	9,700	
5	Prepaid insurance	6,600	
6	Store equipment	81,800	
7	Accumulated depreciation—Store equipment		$ 32,000
8	Accounts payable		18,000
9	D. Foster, Capital		43,000
10	D. Foster, Withdrawals	2,000	
11	Sales		227,100
12	Sales discounts	1,000	
13	Sales returns and allowances	5,000	
14	Cost of good sold	75,800	
15	Depreciation expense—Store equipment	0	
16	Salaries expense	63,000	
17	Insurance expense	0	
18	Rent expense	26,000	
19	Store supplies expense	0	
20	Advertising expense	17,800	
21	Totals	$320,100	$320,100

Rent expense and salaries expense are equally divided between selling activities and the general and administrative activities. Foster Products Company uses a perpetual inventory system.

Required

1. Prepare adjusting journal entries to reflect each of the following.

   a. Store supplies still available at fiscal year-end amount to $3,700.

   b. Expired insurance, an administrative expense, for the fiscal year is $2,800.

   c. Depreciation expense on store equipment, a selling expense, is $3,000 for the fiscal year.

   d. To estimate shrinkage, a physical count of ending merchandise inventory is taken. It shows $21,300 of inventory is still available at fiscal year-end.

Check (2) Gross profit, $142,600; (3) Total expenses, $197,100; Net income, $24,000

2. Prepare a multiple-step income statement for fiscal year 2008.

3. Prepare a single-step income statement for fiscal year 2008.

4. Compute the current ratio, acid-test ratio, and gross margin ratio as of October 31, 2008.

Problem 5-4B

Computing merchandising amounts and formatting income statements

C1 C4 P4

Barkley Company's adjusted trial balance on March 31, 2008, its fiscal year-end, follows.

	Debit	Credit
Merchandise inventory	$ 56,500	
Other (noninventory) assets	202,600	
Total liabilities		$ 42,500
C. Barkley, Capital		164,425
C. Barkley, Withdrawals	3,000	

[continued on next page]

[continued from previous page]

Sales		332,650
Sales discounts	5,875	
Sales returns and allowances	20,000	
Cost of goods sold	115,600	
Sales salaries expense	44,500	
Rent expense—Selling space	16,000	
Store supplies expense	3,850	
Advertising expense	26,000	
Office salaries expense	40,750	
Rent expense—Office space	3,800	
Office supplies expense	1,100	
Totals	$539,575	$539,575

On March 31, 2007, merchandise inventory was $37,500. Supplementary records of merchandising activities for the year ended March 31, 2008, reveal the following itemized costs.

Invoice cost of merchandise purchases	$138,500
Purchase discounts received	2,950
Purchase returns and allowances	6,700
Costs of transportation-in	5,750

Required

1. Calculate the company's net sales for the year.
2. Calculate the company's total cost of merchandise purchased for the year.
3. Prepare a multiple-step income statement that includes separate categories for selling expenses and for general and administrative expenses.
4. Prepare a single-step income statement that includes these expense categories: cost of goods sold, selling expenses, and general and administrative expenses.

Check   (2) $134,600;

(3) Gross profit, $191,175; Net income, $55,175;

(4) Total expenses, $251,600

Use the data for Barkley Company in Problem 5-4B to complete the following requirements:

Required

1. Prepare closing entries as of March 31, 2008 (the perpetual inventory system is used).

Analysis Component

2. The company makes all purchases on credit, and its suppliers uniformly offer a 3% sales discount. Does it appear that the company's cash management system is accomplishing the goal of taking all available discounts? Explain.

3. In prior years, the company experienced a 5% returns and allowance rate on its sales, which means approximately 5% of its gross sales were eventually returned outright or caused the company to grant allowances to customers. How do this year's results compare to prior years' results?

Problem 5-5B
Preparing closing entries and interpreting information about discounts and returns

C4 P3

Check   (1) $55,175 Dr. to close Income Summary

(3) Current-year rate, 6.0%

Refer to the data and information in Problem 5-3B.

Required

Prepare and complete the entire 10-column work sheet for Foster Products Company. Follow the structure of Exhibit 5B.1 in Appendix 5B.

Problem 5-6B[B]
Preparing a work sheet for a merchandiser

P3

PROBLEM SET C

Problem Set C is available at the book's Website to further reinforce and assess your learning.

SERIAL PROBLEM

Success Systems

(This serial problem began in Chapter 1 and continues through most of the book. If previous chapter segments were not completed, the serial problem can begin at this point. It is helpful, but not necessary, that you use the Working Papers that accompany the book.)

SP 5   Adriana Lopez created Success Systems on October 1, 2007. The company has been successful, and its list of customers has grown. To accommodate the growth, the accounting system is modified to set up separate accounts for each customer. The following chart of accounts includes the account number used for each account and any balance as of December 31, 2007. Lopez decided to add a fourth digit with a decimal point to the 106 account number that had been used for the single Accounts Receivable account. This modification allows the company to continue using the existing chart of accounts.

No.	Account Title	Dr.	Cr.
101	Cash	$80,260	
106.1	Alex's Engineering Co.	0	
106.2	Wildcat Services	0	
106.3	Easy Leasing	0	
106.4	Clark Co.	2,300	
106.5	Chang Corp.	0	
106.6	Gomez Co.	3,500	
106.7	Delta Co.	0	
106.8	KC, Inc.	0	
106.9	Dream, Inc.	0	
119	Merchandise inventory	0	
126	Computer supplies	775	
128	Prepaid insurance	1,800	
131	Prepaid rent	875	
163	Office equipment	10,000	
164	Accumulated depreciation—Office equipment		625
167	Computer equipment	25,000	
168	Accumulated depreciation—Computer equipment		1,250
201	Accounts payable		2,100

No.	Account Title	Dr.	Cr.
210	Wages payable		600
236	Unearned computer services revenue		2,500
301	A. Lopez, Capital		117,435
302	A. Lopez, Withdrawals	0	
403	Computer services revenue		0
413	Sales		0
414	Sales returns and allowances	0	
415	Sales discounts	0	
502	Cost of goods sold	0	
612	Depreciation expense—Office equipment	0	
613	Depreciation expense—Computer equipment	0	
623	Wages expense	0	
637	Insurance expense	0	
640	Rent expense	0	
652	Computer supplies expense	0	
655	Advertising expense	0	
676	Mileage expense	0	
677	Miscellaneous expenses	0	
684	Repairs expense—Computer	0	

In response to requests from customers, Lopez will begin selling computer software. The company will extend credit terms of 1/10, n/30, FOB shipping point, to all customers who purchase this merchandise. However, no cash discount is available on consulting fees. Additional accounts (Nos. 119, 413, 414, 415, and 502) are added to its general ledger to accommodate the company's new merchandising activities. Also, Success Systems does not use reversing entries and, therefore, all revenue and expense accounts have zero balances as of January 1, 2008. Its transactions for January through March follow:

Jan. 4   Paid cash to Michelle Jones for five days' work at the rate of $150 per day. Four of the five days relate to wages payable that were accrued in the prior year.

5   Adriana Lopez invested an additional $10,000 cash in the business.

7   Purchased $5,700 of merchandise from Kansas Corp. with terms of 1/10, n/30, FOB shipping point, invoice dated January 7.

9   Received $3,500 cash from Gomez Co. as full payment on its account.

11 Completed a five-day project for Alex's Engineering Co. and billed it $6,500, which is the to-
tal price of $9,000 less the advance payment of $2,500.

Check Jan. 11, Dr. Unearned Computer Services Revenue $2,500

13 Sold merchandise with a retail value of $6,000 and a cost of $4,080 to Chang Corp., invoice
dated January 13.

15 Paid $400 cash for freight charges on the merchandise purchased on January 7.

16 Received $5,600 cash from Delta Co. for computer services provided.

17 Paid Kansas Corp. for the invoice dated January 7, net of the discount.

20 Chang Corp. returned $500 of defective merchandise from its invoice dated January 13. The
returned merchandise, which had a $340 cost, is discarded. (The policy of Success Systems is
to leave the cost of defective products in cost of goods sold.)

Check Jan. 20, No entry to Cost of Goods Sold

22 Received the balance due from Chang Corp., net of both the discount and the credit for the
returned merchandise.

24 Returned defective merchandise to Kansas Corp. and accepted a credit against future purchases.
The defective merchandise invoice cost, net of the discount, was $496.

26 Purchased $9,500 of merchandise from Kansas Corp. with terms of 1/10, n/30, FOB destination,
invoice dated January 26.

26 Sold merchandise with a $3,196 cost for $4,700 on credit to KC, Inc., invoice dated January 26.

29 Received a $496 credit memorandum from Kansas Corp. concerning the merchandise returned
on January 24.

31 Paid cash to Michelle Jones for 10 days' work at $150 per day.

Feb. 1 Paid $2,625 cash to Summit Mall for another three months' rent in advance.

3 Paid Kansas Corp. for the balance due, net of the cash discount, less the $496 amount in the
credit memorandum.

5 Paid $800 cash to the local newspaper for an advertising insert in today's paper.

11 Received the balance due from Alex's Engineering Co. for fees billed on January 11.

15 Adriana Lopez withdrew $5,200 cash for personal use.

23 Sold merchandise with a $2,584 cost for $3,800 on credit to Delta Co., invoice dated
February 23.

26 Paid cash to Michelle Jones for eight days' work at $150 per day.

27 Reimbursed Adriana Lopez for business automobile mileage (1,000 miles at $0.32 per mile).

Mar. 8 Purchased $3,250 of computer supplies from Cain Office Products on credit, invoice dated
March 8.

9 Received the balance due from Delta Co. for merchandise sold on February 23.

11 Paid $1,200 cash for minor repairs to the company's computer.

16 Received $6,250 cash from Dream, Inc., for computing services provided.

19 Paid the full amount due to Cain Office Products, including amounts created on December 15
(of $2,100) and March 8.

24 Billed Easy Leasing for $11,000 of computing services provided.

25 Sold merchandise with a $2,652 cost for $3,900 on credit to Wildcat Services, invoice dated
March 25.

30 Sold merchandise with a $1,700 cost for $2,500 on credit to Clark Company, invoice dated
March 30.

31 Reimbursed Adriana Lopez for business automobile mileage (600 miles at $0.32 per mile).

The following additional facts are available for preparing adjustments on March 31 prior to financial
statement preparation:

a. The March 31 amount of computer supplies still available totals $1,950.

b. Three more months have expired since the company purchased its annual insurance policy at a $2,400
cost for 12 months of coverage.

c. Michelle Jones has not been paid for seven days of work at the rate of $150 per day.

d. Three months have passed since any prepaid rent has been transferred to expense. The monthly rent
expense is $875.

e. Depreciation on the computer equipment for January 1 through March 31 is $1,250.

f. Depreciation on the office equipment for January 1 through March 31 is $625.

g. The March 31 amount of merchandise inventory still available totals $680.

Required

1. Prepare journal entries to record each of the January through March transactions.

2. Post the journal entries in part 1 to the accounts in the company's general ledger. (*Note:* Begin with
the ledger's post-closing adjusted balances as of December 31, 2007.)

Check (2) Ending balances: Cash, $87,266; Sales, $20,900;

(3) Unadj. totals, $182,060;
Adj. totals, $184,985;

(4) Net income, $24,336;

(5) A. Lopez, Capital
(3/31/08), $146,571;

(6) Total assets, $147,621

3. Prepare a partial work sheet consisting of the first six columns (similar to the one shown in Exhibit 5B.1) that includes the unadjusted trial balance, the March 31 adjustments (*a*) through (*g*), and the adjusted trial balance. Do not prepare closing entries and do not journalize the adjustments or post them to the ledger.

4. Prepare an income statement (from the adjusted trial balance in part 3) for the three months ended March 31, 2008. Use a single-step format. List all expenses without differentiating between selling expenses and general and administrative expenses.

5. Prepare a statement of owner's equity (from the adjusted trial balance in part 3) for the three months ended March 31, 2008.

6. Prepare a classified balance sheet (from the adjusted trial balance) as of March 31, 2008.

BEYOND THE NUMBERS

REPORTING IN ACTION

C4 A1

BTN 5-1   Refer to Best Buy's financial statements in Appendix A to answer the following.

Required

1. Assume that the amounts reported for inventories and cost of sales reflect items purchased in a form ready for resale. Compute the net cost of goods purchased for the fiscal year ended February 26, 2005.

2. Compute the current ratio and acid-test ratio as of February 26, 2005, and February 28, 2004. Interpret and comment on the ratio results. How does Best Buy compare to the industry average of 1.6 for the current ratio and 0.7 for the acid-test ratio?

Fast Forward

3. Access Best Buy's financial statements (form 10-K) for fiscal years ending after February 26, 2005, from its Website (BestBuy.com) or the SEC's EDGAR database (www.sec.gov). Recompute and interpret the current ratio and acid-test ratio for these current fiscal years.

COMPARATIVE ANALYSIS

A2

BTN 5-2   Key comparative figures ($ millions) for both Best Buy and Circuit City follow.

Key Figures	Best Buy		Circuit City	
	Current Year	Prior Year	Current Year	Prior Year
Revenues (net sales)	$27,433	$24,548	$10,472	$9,857
Cost of sales	20,938	18,677	7,904	7,573

Required

1. Compute the dollar amount of gross margin and the gross margin ratio for the two years shown for both companies.

2. Which company earns more in gross margin for each dollar of net sales? How do they compare to the industry average of 29%?

3. Did the gross margin ratio improve or decline for these companies?

ETHICS CHALLENGE

C1 P2

BTN 5-3   Amy Martin is a student who plans to attend approximately four professional events a year at her college. Each event necessitates a financial outlay of $100–$200 for a new suit and accessories. After incurring a major hit to her savings for the first event, Amy developed a different approach. She buys the suit on credit the week before the event, wears it to the event, and returns it the next week to the store for a full refund on her charge card.

Required

1. Comment on the ethics exhibited by Amy and possible consequences of her actions.

2. How does the merchandising company account for the suits that Amy returns?

BTN 5-4   You are the financial officer for Music Plus, a retailer that sells goods for home entertainment needs. The business owner, Vic Velakturi, recently reviewed the annual financial statements you prepared and sent you an e-mail stating that he thinks you overstated net income. He explains that although he has invested a great deal in security, he is sure shoplifting and other forms of inventory shrinkage have occurred, but he does not see any deduction for shrinkage on the income statement. The store uses a perpetual inventory system.

COMMUNICATING IN PRACTICE

C3 C4 P3

Required

Prepare a brief memorandum that responds to the owner's concerns.

BTN 5-5   Access the SEC's EDGAR database (www.SEC.gov) and obtain the April 29, 2005, filing of its fiscal 2005 10-K report (for year ended January 29, 2005) for J. Crew Group, Inc.

TAKING IT TO THE NET

A2 C1

Required

Prepare a table that reports the gross margin ratios for J. Crew using the revenues and cost of goods sold data from J. Crew's income statement for each of its most recent four years. Analyze and comment on the trend in its gross margin ratio.

BTN 5-6   Official Brands' general ledger and supplementary records at the end of its current period reveal the following.

TEAMWORK IN ACTION

C1 C4

Sales	$600,000	Merchandise inventory (beginning of period)	$ 98,000
Sales returns	20,000	Invoice cost of merchandise purchases	360,000
Sales discounts	13,000	Purchase discounts received	9,000
Cost of transportation-in	22,000	Purchase returns and allowances	11,000
Operating expenses	50,000	Merchandise inventory (end of period)	84,000

Required

1. *Each* member of the team is to assume responsibility for computing *one* of the following items. You are not to duplicate your teammates' work. Get any necessary amounts to compute your item from the appropriate teammate. Each member is to explain his or her computation to the team in preparation for reporting to the class.

   a. Net sales   **d.** Gross profit

   b. Total cost of merchandise purchases   **e.** Net income

   c. Cost of goods sold

2. Check your net income with the instructor. If correct, proceed to step 3.

3. Assume that a physical inventory count finds that actual ending inventory is $76,000. Discuss how this affects previously computed amounts in step 1.

Point: In teams of four, assign the same student *a* and *e*. Rotate teams for reporting on a different computation and the analysis in step 3.

BTN 5-7   Read the article, "Gift Cards: No Gift to Investors" in the March 14, 2005, of *BusinessWeek*. (This book's Website provides a free link.)

BusinessWeek ACTIVITY

C1 C4

1. What is the difference between gift cards and the loyalty programs that retailers offer?

2. Assume that we purchase a $50 gift card from Best Buy as a gift for a family member. Prepare the journal entries that Best Buy would make (*a*) to record that gift card purchase and (*b*) to record a purchase of merchandise with that gift card.

3. The article talks about Best Buy's "Reward Zone" incentive plan, where shoppers earn $5 on every $125 in purchases. The article explains that Best Buy initially deducted the Reward Zone dollars from revenue. Assume that Best Buy has $125,000 in revenues and allows $5,000 in "Reward Zone" dollars. Prepare the journal entries that Best Buy would make to record these two transactions.

4. Is the method described in part 3 consistent across all retailers who offer such incentive programs? Describe the other methods that are used by retailers to keep track of these programs.

5. What method does the FASB recommend to keep track of these programs?

6. What effect do the different methods have on the financial statements of the different retailers? Why is this important to investors and other readers of financial statements?

ENTREPRENEURIAL DECISION

C1 C4 P4

BTN 5-8 Refer to the opening feature about CoCaLo. Assume that Renee Pepys Lowe estimates current annual sales at approximately $10 million and reports the following income statement.

CoCaLo Income Statement For Year Ended January 31, 2007	
Net sales	$10,000,000
Cost of sales	6,100,000
Expenses (other than cost of sales)	2,000,000
Net income	$ 1,900,000

CoCaLo sells to various retailers, ranging from small shops to large chains such as Target. Assume that Renee Pepys Lowe currently offers credit terms of 1/15, n/60, and ships FOB destination. To improve her cash flow, Lowe is considering changing her credit terms to 3/10, n/30. In addition, she proposes to change her shipping terms to FOB shipping point. She expects that the increase in discount rate will increase her net sales by 9%, but her gross margin ratio (and ratio of cost of sales divided by net sales) is expected to remain unchanged. She also expects that her delivery expenses will be zero under this proposal; thus, her expenses other than cost of sales are expected to increase only 6%.

Required

1. Prepare a forecasted income statement for the year ended January 31, 2008, based on the proposal.

2. Based on the forecasted income statement alone (from part 1), do you recommend CoCaLo implement the new sales policies? Explain.

3. What else should Lowe consider before she decides whether or not to implement the new policies? Explain.

HITTING THE ROAD

C1

Point: This activity complements the Ethics Challenge assignment.

BTN 5-9 Arrange an interview (in person or by phone) with the manager of a retail shop in a mall or in the downtown area of your community. Explain to the manager that you are a student studying merchandising activities and the accounting for sales returns and sales allowances. Ask the manager what the store policy is regarding returns. Also find out if sales allowances are ever negotiated with customers. Inquire whether management perceives that customers are abusing return policies and what actions management takes to counter potential abuses. Be prepared to discuss your findings in class.

GLOBAL DECISION

A2 P4

BTN 5-10 Dixons (Dixons-Group.com), Best Buy, and Circuit City are all competitors in the global marketplace. Key comparative figures for each company follow.

	Net Sales	Cost of Sales
Dixons*	£ 6,458	£ 5,821
Best Buy†	$27,433	$20,938
Circuit City†	$10,472	$ 7,904

* £ millions for Dixons.

† $ millions for Best Buy and Circuit City.

Required

1. Rank the three companies (highest to lowest) based on the gross margin ratio.
2. Which of the companies uses a multiple-step income statement format? (Access their annual reports.)
3. Which company's income statement would likely be most easily interpreted by potential investors? Provide a brief justification for your choice.

ANSWERS TO MULTIPLE CHOICE QUIZ

1. c; Gross profit = $550,000 − $193,000 = $357,000

2. d; ($4,500 − $250) × (100% − 2%) = $4,165

3. b; Net sales = $75,000 + $320,000 − $13,700 − $6,000 = $375,300

4. b; Acid-test ratio = $37,500/$50,000 = 0.750

5. a; Gross margin ratio = ($675,000 − $459,000)/$675,000 = 32%

6

Inventories and Cost of Sales

A Look Back

Chapter 5 focused on merchandising activities and how they are reported. We analyzed and recorded purchases and sales and explained accounting adjustments and closing for merchandisers.

A Look at This Chapter

This chapter emphasizes accounting for inventory. We describe methods for assigning costs to inventory and we explain the items and costs making up merchandise inventory. We also discuss methods of estimating and measuring inventory.

A Look Ahead

Chapter 7 emphasizes accounting information systems. We describe system principles, the system components, use of special journals and subsidiary ledgers, and technology-based systems.

Learning Objectives

CAP

Conceptual

C1 Identify the items making up merchandise inventory. (p. 224)

C2 Identify the costs of merchandise inventory. (p. 225)

Analytical

A1 Analyze the effects of inventory methods for both financial and tax reporting. (p. 231)

A2 Analyze the effects of inventory errors on current and future financial statements. (p. 234)

A3 Assess inventory management using both inventory turnover and days' sales in inventory. (p. 236)

Procedural

P1 Compute inventory in a perpetual system using the methods of specific identification, FIFO, LIFO, and weighted average. (p. 226)

P2 Compute the lower of cost or market amount of inventory. (p. 233)

P3 Appendix 6A—Compute inventory in a periodic system using the methods of specific identification, FIFO, LIFO, and weighted average. (p. 241)

P4 Appendix 6B—Apply both the retail inventory and gross profit methods to estimate inventory. (p. 245)

Decision Feature

Surf Divas Carry an Aloha Attitude

LA JOLLA, CA—Surfing is the lives of twin sisters, Izzy and Coco Tihanyi. "Our dad [a Hungarian immigrant] had us paddling on his long board at age three," recalls Izzy. Years later, "our mom would pick us up after school and take us straight to the beach," adds Coco. "She'd pack a picnic, and we'd do our homework stretched out on towels." It was only natural that this dynamic duo would launch Surf Diva (**SurfDiva.com**) to provide surfing lessons, training, gear, and apparel.

Yet the entrepreneurial waters were rough at times. Izzy and Coco struggled with inventory and sales, and had to deal with discounts, returns, and allowances. One challenge is maintaining appropriate inventories while controlling costs. This hurdle will continue as Surf Diva tries to double sales in the next year through additional marketing. "We're really focused on building the brand," says Izzy. "Every dime we spend on marketing apparel is focused on women. We're a real surf company with real roots."

But business success requires more than good products, admits Izzy. "Being a Surf Diva is an attitude—enjoying life, giving yourself challenges, having dreams, and following those dreams." Although the divas continue to measure, monitor, and manage inventories and costs, for them it is a natural existence. "This is our lives—we live it, breathe it, surf it."

"Surfing is spirituality on a stick," Izzy explains. "When you leave your problems on land and marvel at the sunset from the water, everything becomes liquid gold." Coco chimes in, "Surfing takes care of you both emotionally and physically." Adds Izzy, "Don't let the boys have all the fun."

[Sources: *Surf Diva Website,* January 2006; *USA Today,* March 2005; *Transworld Business,* February 2005; *Harcourt Website,* July 2005; *iVillage,* December 2004; *San Diego Union-Tribune,* February 2005]

Merchandisers' activities include the purchasing and reselling of merchandise. We explained accounting for merchandisers in Chapter 5, including that for purchases and sales. In this chapter, we extend the study and analysis of inventory by explaining the methods used to assign costs to merchandise inventory *and* to cost of goods sold. Retailers, wholesalers, and other merchandising companies that purchase products for resale use the principles and methods described here. Understanding inventory accounting helps in the analysis and interpretation of financial statements, and in helping people run their own businesses.

Inventory Basics

This section identifies the items and costs making up merchandise inventory. It also describes the importance of internal controls in taking a physical count of inventory.

Determining Inventory Items

C1 Identify the items making up merchandise inventory.

Merchandise inventory includes all goods that a company owns and holds for sale. This rule holds regardless of where the goods are located when inventory is counted. Certain inventory items require special attention, including goods in transit, goods on consignment, and goods that are damaged or obsolete.

Goods in Transit Does a purchaser's inventory include goods in transit from a supplier? The answer is that if ownership has passed to the purchaser, the goods are included in the purchaser's inventory. We determine this by reviewing the shipping terms: *FOB destination* or *FOB shipping point.* If the purchaser is responsible for paying freight, ownership passes when goods are loaded on the transport vehicle. If the seller is responsible for paying freight, ownership passes when goods arrive at their destination.

Goods on Consignment Goods on consignment are goods shipped by the owner, called the **consignor,** to another party, the **consignee.** A consignee sells goods for the owner. The consignor continues to own the consigned goods and reports them in its inventory. **Upper Deck,** for instance, pays sports celebrities such as Tiger Woods to sign memorabilia, which are offered to shopping networks on consignment. Upper Deck, the consignor, must report these items in its inventory until sold.

Goods Damaged or Obsolete Damaged and obsolete (and deteriorated) goods are not counted in inventory if they cannot be sold. If these goods can be sold at a reduced price, they are included in inventory at a conservative estimate of their **net realizable value.** Net realizable value is sales price minus the cost of making the sale. The period when damage or obsolescence (or deterioration) occurs is the period when the loss in value is reported.

Determining Inventory Costs

Merchandise inventory includes costs of expenditures necessary, directly or indirectly, to bring an item to a salable condition and location. This means that the cost of an inventory item includes its invoice cost minus any discount, and plus any added or incidental costs necessary to put it in a place and condition for sale. Added or incidental costs can include import duties, freight, storage, insurance, and costs incurred in an aging process (for example, aging wine or cheese).

C2 Identify the costs of merchandise inventory.

Accounting principles prescribe that incidental costs be assigned to inventory. Also, the *matching principle* states that inventory costs should be recorded against revenue in the period when inventory is sold. However, some companies use the *materiality principle* (*cost-to-benefit constraint*) to avoid assigning incidental costs of acquiring merchandise to inventory. These companies argue either that incidental costs are immaterial or that the effort in assigning these costs to inventory outweighs the benefit.

Internal Controls and Taking a Physical Count

The Inventory account under a perpetual system is updated for each purchase and sale, but events can cause the account balance to be different from the actual inventory available. Such events include theft, loss, damage, and errors. Thus, nearly all companies take a *physical count of inventory* at least once each year—informally called *taking an inventory*. This often occurs at the end of a fiscal year or when inventory amounts are low. This physical count is used to adjust the Inventory account balance to the actual inventory available.

A business must apply internal controls when taking a physical count of inventory that would usually include the following:

- *Prenumbered inventory tickets* are prepared and distributed to *counters*—each ticket must be accounted for.
- Counters of inventory are assigned that do not include those responsible for inventory.
- Counters confirm the validity of inventory, including its existence, amount, and quality.
- A second count should be performed by a different counter.
- A manager confirms that all inventories are ticketed once, and only once.

Point: The Inventory account is a controlling account for the inventory subsidiary ledger. This *subsidiary ledger* contains a separate record (units and costs) for each separate product, and it can be in electronic or paper form. Subsidiary records assist managers in planning and monitoring inventory.

Inventory Costing Under a Perpetual System

Accounting for inventory affects both the balance sheet and the income statement. A major goal in accounting for inventory is to properly match costs with sales. We use the *matching principle* to decide how much of the cost of the goods available for sale is deducted from sales and how much is carried forward as inventory and matched against future sales.

Management decisions in accounting for inventory involve the following

- Costing method (specific identification, FIFO, LIFO, or weighted average).
- Inventory system (perpetual or periodic).
- Items included in inventory and their costs.
- Use of market values or other estimates.

Decisions on these points affect the reported amounts for inventory, cost of goods sold, gross profit, income, current assets, and other accounts.

One of the most important issues in accounting for inventory is determining the per unit costs assigned to inventory items. When all units are purchased at the same unit cost, this process is simple. When identical items are purchased at different costs, however, a question arises as to which amounts to record in cost of goods sold and which amounts remain in inventory.

Four methods are commonly used to assign costs to inventory and to cost of goods sold: (1) specific identification; (2) first-in, first-out; (3) last-in, first-out; and (4) weighted average.

Exhibit 6.1

Frequency in Use of Inventory Methods

LIFO 30%   FIFO 46%

Weighted Average 20%   Other* 4%

*Includes specific identification.

Exhibit 6.1 shows the frequency in the use of these methods.

Each method assumes a particular pattern for how costs flow through inventory. Each of these four methods is acceptable whether or not the actual physical flow of goods follows the cost flow assumption. Physical flow of goods depends on the type of product and the way it is stored. (Perishable goods such as fresh fruit demand that a business attempt to sell them in a first-in, first-out physical flow. Other products such as crude oil and minerals such as coal, gold, decorative stone can be sold in a last-in, first-out physical flow.) **Physical flow and cost flow need not be the same.**

Inventory Cost Flow Assumptions

P1 Compute inventory in a perpetual system using the methods of specific identification, FIFO, LIFO, and weighted average.

This section introduces inventory cost flow assumptions. Assume that three identical units are purchased separately at the following three dates and costs: May 1 at $45, May 3 at $65, and May 6 at $70. One unit is then sold on May 7 for $100. Exhibit 6.2 gives a visual layout of the flow of costs to either the gross profit section of the income statement or the inventory reported on the balance sheet for FIFO, LIFO, and weighted average.

(1) *FIFO assumes costs flow in the order incurred.* The unit purchased on May 1 for $45 is the earliest cost incurred—it is sent to cost of goods sold on the income statement. The remaining two units ($65 and $70) are reported in inventory on the balance sheet.

Point: It is helpful to recall the cost flow from Exhibit 5.4.

Beginning inventory + Net cost of purchases

= Merchandise available for sale

Ending inventory + Cost of goods sold

(2) *LIFO assumes costs flow in the reverse order incurred.* The unit purchased on May 6 for $70 is the most recent cost incurred—it is sent to cost of goods sold on the income statement. The remaining two units ($45 and $65) are reported in inventory on the balance sheet.

(3) *Weighted average assumes costs flow at an average of the costs available.* The units available at the May 7 sale average $60 in cost, computed as ($45 + $65 + $70)/3. One unit's $60 average cost is sent to cost of goods sold on the income statement. The remaining two units' average costs are reported in inventory at $120 on the balance sheet.

Cost flow assumptions can markedly impact gross profit and inventory numbers. Exhibit 6.2 shows that gross profit as a percent of net sales ranges from 30% to 55% due to nothing else but the cost flow assumption.

Exhibit 6.2

Cost Flow Assumptions

The following sections on inventory costing methods use the perpetual system. Appendix 6A uses the periodic system. An instructor can choose to cover either one or both inventory systems.

Inventory Costing Illustration

This section provides a comprehensive illustration of inventory costing methods. We use information from Trekking, a sporting goods store. Among its many products, Trekking carries one type of mountain bike whose sales are directed at resorts that provide inexpensive mountain bikes for complimentary guest use. Its customers usually purchase in amounts of 10 or more bikes. We use Trekking's data from August 2008. Its mountain bike (unit) inventory at the beginning of August and its purchases and sales during August are shown in Exhibit 6.3. It ends August with 12 bikes remaining in inventory.

Point: Inventories are a large portion of current assets for most wholesalers, retailers, and manufacturers. Accounting for inventories is key to determining cost of goods sold and gross profit.

Exhibit 6.3

Purchases and Sales of Goods

Date	Activity	Units Acquired at Cost	Units Sold at Retail	Unit Inventory
Aug. 1	Beginning inventory	10 units @ $ 91 = $ 910		10 units
Aug. 3	Purchases	15 units @ $106 = $ 1,590		25 units
Aug. 14	Sales		20 units @ $130	5 units
Aug. 17	Purchases	20 units @ $115 = $ 2,300		25 units
Aug. 28	Purchases	10 units @ $119 = $ 1,190		35 units
Aug. 31	Sales		23 units @ $150	12 units
	Totals	55 units $5,990	43 units	

Trekking uses the perpetual inventory system, which means that its merchandise inventory account is continually updated to reflect purchases and sales. **(Appendix 6A describes the assignment of costs to inventory using a periodic system.)** Regardless of what inventory method or system is used, cost of goods available for sale must be allocated between cost of goods sold and ending inventory.

Point: The perpetual inventory system is now the most dominant system for U.S. businesses.

Point: Cost of goods sold plus ending inventory equals cost of goods available for sale.

Specific Identification

When each item in inventory can be identified with a specific purchase and invoice, we can use **specific identification** (also called *specific invoice inventory pricing*) to assign costs. We

Point: Three key variables determine the dollar value of ending inventory: (1) inventory quantity, (2) costs of inventory, and (3) cost flow assumption.

also need sales records that identify exactly which items were sold and when. Trekking's internal documents reveal that 7 of the 12 unsold units in ending inventory were from the August 28 purchase and 5 were from the August 17 purchase. We use this information and the specific identification method to assign costs to the 12 units in ending inventory and to the 43 units sold as shown in Exhibit 6.4. Carefully study this exhibit and the boxed explanations to see the flow of costs both in and out of inventory. Each unit, whether sold or remaining in inventory, has its own specific cost attached to it.

Exhibit 6.4

Specific Identification
Computations

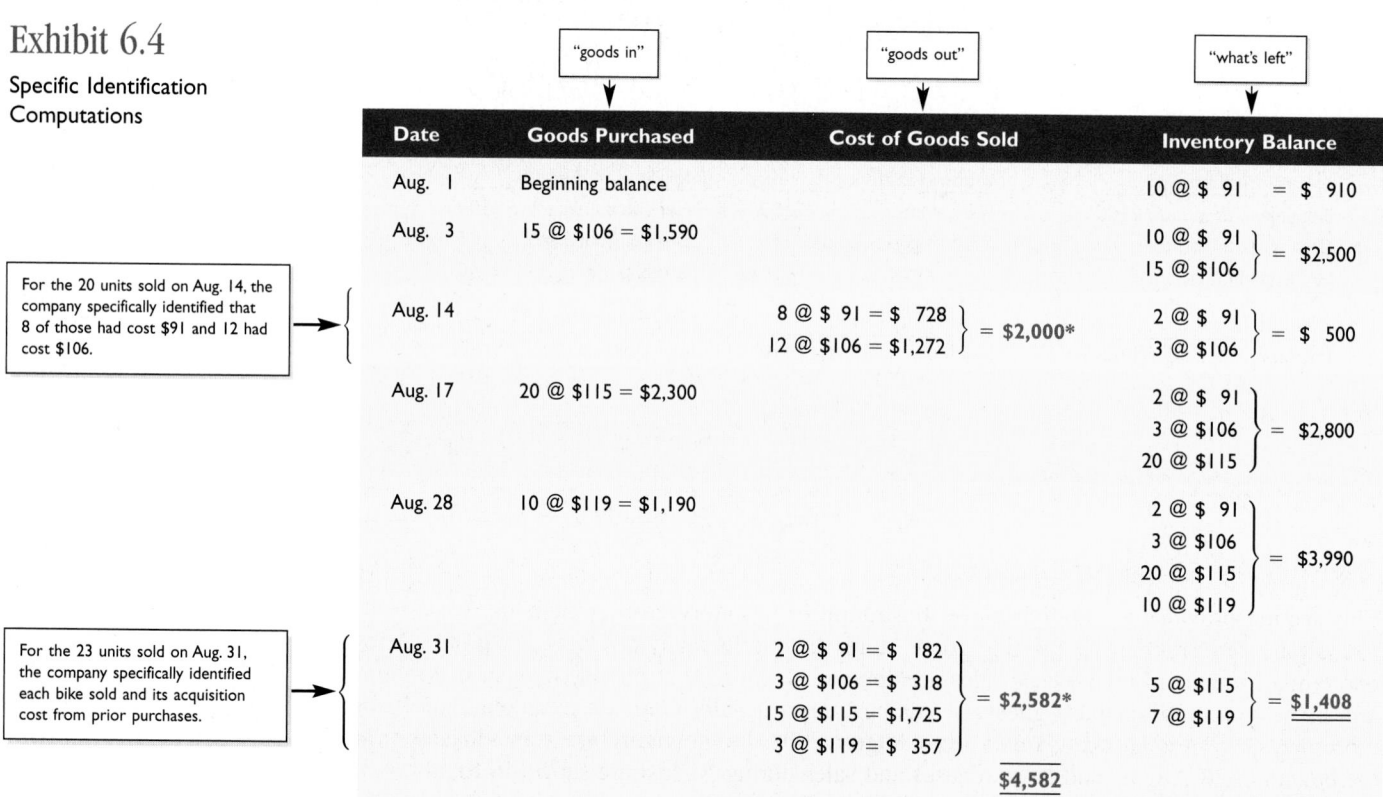

* Identification of items sold (and their costs) is obtained from internal documents that track each unit from its purchase to its sale.

When using specific identification, Trekking's cost of goods sold reported on the income statement totals **$4,582**, the sum of $2,000 and $2,582 from the third column of Exhibit 6.4. Trekking's ending inventory reported on the balance sheet is **$1,408**, which is the final inventory balance from the fourth column of Exhibit 6.4.

The purchases and sales entries for Exhibit 6.4 follow (the colored boldface numbers are those determined by the cost flow assumption).

Point: Specific identification is usually only practical for companies with expensive, custom-made inventory.

	Purchases		
Aug. 3	Merchandise Inventory	1,590	
	Accounts Payable		1,590
17	Merchandise Inventory	2,300	
	Accounts Payable		2,300
28	Merchandise Inventory	1,190	
	Accounts Payable		1,190

	Sales		
Aug. 14	Accounts Receivable	2,600	
	Sales		2,600
14	Cost of Goods Sold	**2,000**	
	Merchandise Inventory		**2,000**
31	Accounts Receivable	3,450	
	Sales		3,450
31	Cost of Goods Sold	**2,582**	
	Merchandise Inventory		**2,582**

First-In, First-Out

The **first-in, first-out (FIFO)** method of assigning costs to both inventory and cost of goods sold assumes that inventory items are sold in the order acquired. When sales occur, the costs of the earliest units acquired are charged to cost of goods sold. This leaves the costs from the most recent purchases in ending inventory. Use of FIFO for computing the cost of inventory and cost of goods sold is shown in Exhibit 6.5.

Point: The "Goods Purchased" column is identical for all methods. Data are taken from Exhibit 6.3.

Date	Goods Purchased	Cost of Goods Sold	Inventory Balance
Aug. 1	Beginning balance		10 @ $ 91 = $ 910
Aug. 3	15 @ $106 = $1,590		10 @ $ 91 15 @ $106 } = $2,500
Aug. 14		10 @ $ 91 = $ 910 10 @ $106 = $1,060 } = $1,970	5 @ $106 = $ 530
Aug. 17	20 @ $115 = $2,300		5 @ $106 20 @ $115 } = $2,830
Aug. 28	10 @ $119 = $1,190		5 @ $106 20 @ $115 10 @ $119 } = $4,020
Aug. 31		5 @ $106 = $ 530 18 @ $115 = $2,070 } = $2,600 **$4,570**	2 @ $115 10 @ $119 } = $1,420

Exhibit 6.5

FIFO Computations—
Perpetual System

> For the 20 units sold on Aug. 14, the first 10 sold are assigned the earliest cost of $91 (from beg. bal.). The next 10 sold are assigned the next earliest cost of $106.

> For the 23 units sold on Aug. 31, the first 5 sold are assigned the earliest available cost of $106 (from Aug. 3 purchase). The next 18 sold are assigned the next earliest cost of $115 (from Aug. 17 purchase).

Trekking's FIFO cost of goods sold reported on its income statement (reflecting the 43 units sold) is **$4,570** ($1,970 + $2,600), and its ending inventory reported on the balance sheet (reflecting the 12 units unsold) is **$1,420**.

The purchases and sales entries for Exhibit 6.5 follow (the colored boldface numbers are those affected by the cost flow assumption).

Point: Under FIFO, a unit sold is assigned the earliest (oldest) cost from inventory. This leaves the most recent costs in ending inventory.

Purchases		
Aug. 3 Merchandise Inventory	1,590	
Accounts Payable		1,590
17 Merchandise Inventory	2,300	
Accounts Payable		2,300
28 Merchandise Inventory	1,190	
Accounts Payable		1,190

Sales		
Aug. 14 Accounts Receivable	2,600	
Sales		2,600
14 Cost of Goods Sold	1,970	
Merchandise Inventory		1,970
31 Accounts Receivable	3,450	
Sales		3,450
31 Cost of Goods Sold	2,600	
Merchandise Inventory		2,600

Last-In, First-Out

The **last-in, first-out (LIFO)** method of assigning costs assumes that the most recent purchases are sold first. These more recent costs are charged to the goods sold, and the costs of the earliest purchases are assigned to inventory. As with other methods, LIFO is acceptable even when the physical flow of goods does not follow a last-in, first-out pattern. One appeal of LIFO is that by assigning costs from the most recent purchases to cost of goods sold, LIFO comes closest to matching current costs of goods sold with revenues (compared to FIFO or weighted average). Exhibit 6.6 shows how LIFO assigns the costs of mountain bikes to the 12 units in ending inventory and to the 43 units sold.

Topic Tackler

PLUS

6-1

Point: Under LIFO, a unit sold is assigned the most recent (latest) cost from inventory. This leaves the oldest costs in inventory.

Exhibit 6.6

LIFO Computations—
Perpetual System

Date	Goods Purchased	Cost of Goods Sold	Inventory Balance
Aug. 1	Beginning balance		10 @ $ 91 = $ 910
Aug. 3	15 @ $106 = $1,590		10 @ $ 91 ⎫ = $ 2,500 15 @ $106 ⎭
Aug. 14		15 @ $106 = $1,590 ⎫ = $2,045 5 @ $ 91 = $ 455 ⎭	5 @ $ 91 = $ 455
Aug. 17	20 @ $115 = $2,300		5 @ $ 91 ⎫ = $ 2,755 20 @ $115 ⎭
Aug. 28	10 @ $119 = $1,190		5 @ $ 91 ⎫ 20 @ $115 ⎬ = $ 3,945 10 @ $119 ⎭
Aug. 31		10 @ $119 = $1,190 ⎫ = $2,685 13 @ $115 = $1,495 ⎭	5 @ $ 91 ⎫ = $1,260 7 @ $115 ⎭
		$4,730	

For the 20 units sold on Aug. 14, the first 15 sold are assigned the most recent cost of $106. The next 5 sold are assigned the next most recent cost of $91.

For the 23 units sold on Aug. 31, the first 10 sold are assigned the most recent cost of $119. The next 13 sold are assigned the next most recent cost of $115.

Trekking's LIFO cost of goods sold reported on the income statement is **$4,730** ($2,045 + $2,685), and its ending inventory reported on the balance sheet is **$1,260**.

The purchases and sales entries for Exhibit 6.6 follow (the colored boldface numbers are those affected by the cost flow assumption).

	Purchases		
Aug. 3	Merchandise Inventory	1,590	
	Accounts Payable		1,590
17	Merchandise Inventory	2,300	
	Accounts Payable		2,300
28	Merchandise Inventory	1,190	
	Accounts Payable		1,190

	Sales		
Aug. 14	Accounts Receivable.	2,600	
	Sales		2,600
14	Cost of Goods Sold	**2,045**	
	Merchandise Inventory. . . .		**2,045**
31	Accounts Receivable.	3,450	
	Sales		3,450
31	Cost of Goods Sold	**2,685**	
	Merchandise Inventory. . . .		**2,685**

Weighted Average

The **weighted average** (also called **average cost**) method of assigning cost requires that we use the weighted average cost per unit of inventory at the time of each sale. Weighted average cost per unit at the time of each sale equals the cost of goods available for sale divided by the units available. The results using weighted average for Trekking are shown in Exhibit 6.7.

Point: Under weighted average, a unit sold is assigned the average cost of all items currently available for sale at the date of each sale.

Trekking's cost of goods sold reported on the income statement (reflecting the 43 units sold) is **$4,622** ($2,000 + $2,622), and its ending inventory reported on the balance sheet (reflecting the 12 units unsold) is **$1,368**.

The purchases and sales entries for Exhibit 6.7 follow (the colored boldface numbers are those affected by the cost flow assumption).

	Purchases		
Aug. 3	Merchandise Inventory	1,590	
	Accounts Payable		1,590
17	Merchandise Inventory	2,300	
	Accounts Payable		2,300
28	Merchandise Inventory	1,190	
	Accounts Payable		1,190

	Sales		
Aug. 14	Accounts Receivable.	2,600	
	Sales		2,600
14	Cost of Goods Sold	**2,000**	
	Merchandise Inventory. . . .		**2,000**
31	Accounts Receivable.	3,450	
	Sales		3,450
31	Cost of Goods Sold	**2,622**	
	Merchandise Inventory. . . .		**2,622**

Date	Goods Purchased	Cost of Goods Sold	Inventory Balance
Aug. 1	Beginning balance		10 @ $ 91 = $ 910
Aug. 3	15 @ $106 = $1,590		10 @ $ 91 15 @ $106 } = $2,500 (or $100 per unit)[a]
Aug. 14		20 @ $100 = $2,000	5 @ $100 = $ 500 (or $100 per unit)[b]
Aug. 17	20 @ $115 = $2,300		5 @ $100 20 @ $115 } = $2,800 (or $112 per unit)[c]
Aug. 28	10 @ $119 = $1,190		5 @ $100 20 @ $115 10 @ $119 } = $3,990 (or $114 per unit)[d]
Aug. 31		23 @ $114 = $2,622	12 @ $114 = $1,368 (or $114 per unit)[e]
		$4,622	

Exhibit 6.7

Weighted Average Computations—Perpetual System

> For the 20 units sold on Aug. 14, the cost assigned is the $100 *average cost* per unit from the inventory balance column at the time of sale.

> For the 23 units sold on Aug. 31, the cost assigned is the $114 *average cost* per unit from the inventory balance column at the time of sale.

[a] $100 per unit = ($2,500 inventory balance ÷ 25 units in inventory).

[b] $100 per unit = ($500 inventory balance ÷ 5 units in inventory).

[c] $112 per unit = ($2,800 inventory balance ÷ 25 units in inventory).

[d] $114 per unit = ($3,990 inventory balance ÷ 35 units in inventory).

[e] $114 per unit = ($1,368 inventory balance ÷ 12 units in inventory).

Advances in technology have greatly reduced the cost of a perpetual inventory system. Many companies are now asking whether they can afford *not* to have a perpetual inventory system because timely access to inventory information is a competitive advantage and it can help reduce the level of inventory, which reduces costs.

Decision Insight

Social Profits A survey found 76% of consumers would switch from their current product to one with a "good cause" if price and quality are equal. Another survey found 35% would actually pay more. Many entrepreneurs combine their business with their social passions for a win-win scenario.

Financial Statement Effects of Costing Methods

When purchase prices do not change, each inventory costing method assigns the same cost amounts to inventory and to cost of goods sold. When purchase prices are different, however, the methods nearly always assign different cost amounts. We show these differences in Exhibit 6.8 using Trekking's data.

A1 Analyze the effects of inventory methods for both financial and tax reporting.

TREKKING COMPANY For Month Ended August 31	Specific Identification	FIFO	LIFO	Weighted Average
Income Statement				
Sales	$6,050	$6,050	$6,050	$6,050
Cost of goods sold	4,582	4,570	4,730	4,622
Gross profit	1,468	1,480	1,320	1,428
Expenses	450	450	450	450
Income before taxes	1,018	1,030	870	978
Income tax expense (30%)	305	309	261	293
Net income	$ 713	$ 721	$ 609	$ 685
Balance Sheet				
Inventory	$1,408	$1,420	$1,260	$1,368

Exhibit 6.8

Financial Statement Effects of Inventory Costing Methods

When purchase costs *regularly rise,* as in Trekking's case, the following occurs:

Point: FIFO is preferred when costs are rising and managers have incentives to report higher income for reasons such as bonus plans, job security, and reputation.

■ FIFO assigns the lowest amount to cost of goods sold—yielding the highest gross profit and net income.

■ LIFO assigns the highest amount to cost of goods sold—yielding the lowest gross profit and net income, which also yields a temporary tax advantage by postponing payment of some income tax.

■ Weighted average yields results between FIFO and LIFO.

■ Specific identification always yields results that depend on which units are sold.

Point: LIFO inventory is often less than the inventory's replacement cost because LIFO inventory is valued using the oldest inventory purchase costs.

When costs *regularly decline,* the reverse occurs for FIFO and LIFO.

All four inventory costing methods are acceptable. However, a company must disclose the inventory method it uses in its financial statements or notes. Each method offers certain advantages as follows:

■ FIFO assigns an amount to inventory on the balance sheet that approximates its current cost; it also mimics the actual flow of goods for most businesses.

■ LIFO assigns an amount to cost of goods sold on the income statement that approximates its current cost; it also better matches current costs with revenues in computing gross profit.

■ Weighted average tends to smooth out erratic changes in costs.

■ Specific identification exactly matches the costs of items with the revenues they generate.

Decision Maker   Answer—p. 247

Financial Planner   One of your clients asks if the inventory account of a company using FIFO needs any "adjustments" for analysis purposes in light of recent inflation. What is your advice? Does your advice depend on changes in the costs of these inventories?

Tax Effects of Costing Methods   Trekking's segment income statement in Exhibit 6.8 includes income tax expense (at a rate of 30%) because it was formed as a corporation. Since inventory costs affect net income, they have potential tax effects. Trekking gains a temporary tax advantage by using LIFO. Many companies use LIFO for this reason.

Companies can and often do use different costing methods for financial reporting and tax reporting. *The only exception is when LIFO is used for tax reporting; in this case, the IRS requires that it also be used in financial statements*—called the LIFO conformity rule.

Consistency in Using Costing Methods

The **consistency principle** prescribes that a company use the same accounting methods period after period so that financial statements are comparable across periods—the only exception is when a change from one method to another will improve its financial reporting. The *full-disclosure principle* prescribes that the notes to the statements report this type of change, its justification, and its effect on income.

Decision Ethics   Answer—p. 247

Inventory Manager   Your compensation as inventory manager includes a bonus plan based on gross profit. Your superior asks your opinion on changing the inventory costing method from FIFO to LIFO. Since costs are expected to continue to rise, your superior predicts that LIFO would match higher current costs against sales, thereby lowering taxable income (and gross profit). What do you recommend?

The consistency principle does *not* require a company to use one method exclusively. For example, it can use different methods to value different categories of inventory.

4. Describe one advantage for each of the inventory costing methods: specific identification, FIFO, LIFO, and weighted average.

5. When costs are rising, which method reports higher net income—LIFO or FIFO?

6. When costs are rising, what effect does LIFO have on a balance sheet compared to FIFO?

7. A company takes a physical count of inventory at the end of 2008 and finds that ending inventory is understated by $10,000. Would this error cause cost of goods sold to be overstated or understated in 2008? In year 2009? If so, by how much?

Valuing Inventory at LCM and the Effects of Inventory Errors

This section examines the role of market costs in determining inventory on the balance sheet and also the financial statement effects of inventory errors.

Lower of Cost or Market

We explained how to assign costs to ending inventory and cost of goods sold using one of four costing methods (FIFO, LIFO, weighted average, or specific identification). However, *accounting principles require that inventory be reported at the market value (cost) of replacing inventory when market value is lower than cost.* Merchandise inventory is then said to be reported on the balance sheet at the **lower of cost or market (LCM).**

P2 Compute the lower of cost or market amount of inventory.

Computing the Lower of Cost or Market   *Market* in the term *LCM* is defined as the current replacement cost of purchasing the same inventory items in the usual manner. A decline in replacement cost reflects a loss of value in inventory. When the recorded cost of inventory is higher than the replacement cost, a loss is recognized. When the recorded cost is lower, no adjustment is made.

LCM is applied in one of three ways: (1) to each individual item separately, (2) to major categories of items, or (3) to the entire inventory. The less similar the items that make up inventory, the more likely companies are to apply LCM to individual items. To illustrate, we apply LCM to the ending inventory of a motorsports retailer in Exhibit 6.9.

Point: Advances in technology encourage the individual-item approach for LCM.

Inventory Items	Units	Per Unit Cost	Per Unit Market	Total Cost	Total Market	LCM Applied to Items	LCM Applied to Categories	LCM Applied to Whole
Cycles								
Roadster	20	$8,000	$7,000	$160,000	$140,000	$ 140,000		
Sprint	10	5,000	6,000	50,000	60,000	50,000		
Category subtotal				210,000	200,000		$ 200,000	
Off-Road								
Trax-4	8	5,000	6,500	40,000	52,000	40,000		
Blazer	5	9,000	7,000	45,000	35,000	35,000		
Category subtotal				85,000	87,000		85,000	
Totals				$295,000	$287,000	$265,000	$285,000	$287,000

Exhibit 6.9

Lower of Cost or Market Computations

Items: $140,000 is the lower of $160,000 or $140,000

Categories: $200,000 is the lower of $210,000 or $200,000

Whole: $287,000 is the lower of $295,000 or $287,000

Reported inventory depends on which of the 3 different LCM methods are applied

When LCM is applied to the *entire* inventory, the market amount is $287,000. Since this market amount is $8,000 lower than the $295,000 recorded cost, the $287,000 amount is reported for inventory on the balance sheet. When LCM is applied to the major *categories* of inventory, the market is $285,000. When LCM is applied to individual *items* of inventory, the market is $265,000. Since market amounts for these cases is less than the $295,000 recorded cost, the market amount is reported for inventory. Any one of these three applications of LCM is acceptable. The retailer **Best Buy** applies LCM and reports that its "merchandise inventories are recorded at the lower of average cost or market."

Recording the Lower of Cost or Market Inventory must be adjusted downward when market is less than cost. To illustrate, if LCM is applied to the individual items of inventory in Exhibit 6.9, the Merchandise Inventory account must be adjusted from the $295,000 recorded cost down to the $265,000 market amount as follows.

Cost of Goods Sold.	30,000	
Merchandise Inventory.		30,000
To adjust inventory cost to market.		

Accounting rules require that inventory be adjusted to market when market is less than cost, but inventory usually cannot be written up to market when market exceeds cost. If recording inventory down to market is acceptable, why are companies not allowed to record inventory up to market? One view is that a gain from a market increase should not be realized until a sales transaction verifies the gain. However, this problem also applies when market is less than cost. A second and primary reason is the **conservatism principle,** which prescribes the use of the less optimistic amount when more than one estimate of the amount to be received or paid exists and these estimates are about equally likely.

Financial Statement Effects of Inventory Errors

A2 Analyze the effects of inventory errors on current and future financial statements.

Companies must take care in both taking a physical count of inventory and in assigning a cost to it. An inventory error causes misstatements in cost of goods sold, gross profit, net income, current assets, and equity. It also causes misstatements in the next period's statements because ending inventory of one period is the beginning inventory of the next. As we consider the financial statement effects in this section, it is helpful if you recall the following accounting relation:

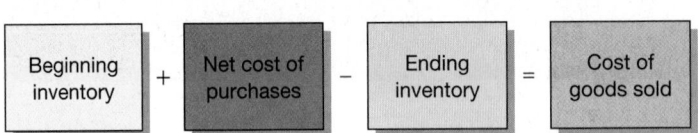

Income Statement Effects Exhibit 6.10 shows the effects of inventory errors on key amounts in the current period's income statement. Inventory errors yield opposite effects in cost of goods sold and net income. Inventory errors also carry over to the next period, yielding reverse effects.

6-2

Exhibit 6.10

Effects of Inventory Errors on the Current Period's Income Statement

Inventory Error	Cost of Goods Sold	Net Income
Understate ending inventory	Overstated	Understated
Understate beginning inventory	Understated	Overstated
Overstate ending inventory*	Understated	Overstated
Overstate beginning inventory*	Overstated	Understated

* These errors are less likely under a perpetual system because they imply more inventory than is recorded (or less shrinkage than expected). Thus, management will normally follow up and discover and correct these errors before they impact any accounts.

To illustrate, consider an inventory error for a company with $100,000 in sales for each of the years 2006, 2007, and 2008. If this company maintains a steady $20,000 inventory level during this period and makes $60,000 in purchases in each of these years, its cost of goods sold is $60,000 and its gross profit is $40,000 each year. What if this company errs in computing its 2006 ending inventory and reports $16,000 instead of the correct amount of $20,000? The effects of this error are shown in Exhibit 6.11. The $4,000 understatement of the year 2006 ending inventory causes a $4,000 overstatement in year 2006 cost of goods sold and a $4,000 understatement in both gross profit and net income for year 2006. Since year 2006 ending inventory becomes year 2007 beginning inventory, this error causes an understatement in 2007 cost of goods sold and a $4,000 overstatement in both gross profit and net income for year 2007. Notice that an inventory error in period 1 (2006) does not affect the period 3, year 2008. An inventory error is said to be *self-correcting* because it always yields an offsetting error in the next period. This, however, does not make inventory errors less serious. Managers, lenders, owners, and other users make important decisions from analysis of changes in net income and cost of goods sold.

Point: A former internal auditor at **Coca-Cola** alleges that just before midnight at the 2002 period-end, fully loaded Coke trucks were ordered to drive about 2 feet away from the loading dock so that Coke could record millions of dollars in extra sales.

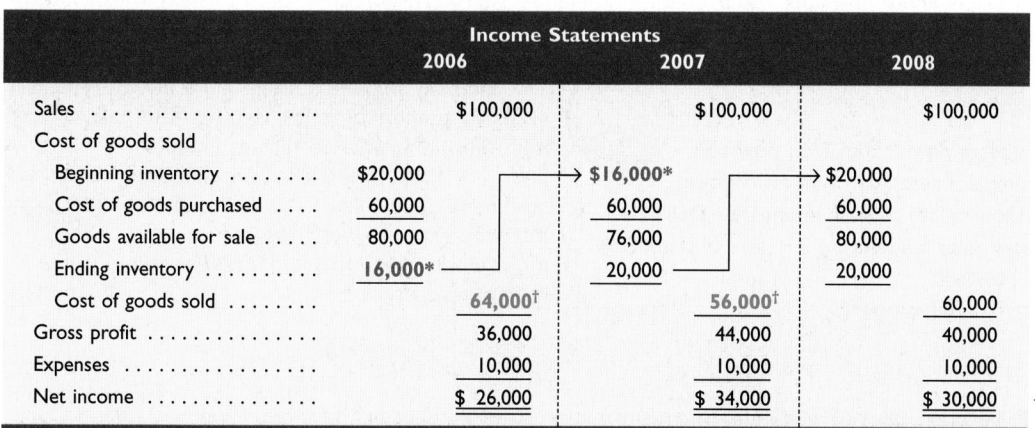

Income Statements			
	2006	**2007**	**2008**
Sales	$100,000	$100,000	$100,000
Cost of goods sold			
Beginning inventory	$20,000	→ $16,000*	→ $20,000
Cost of goods purchased	60,000	60,000	60,000
Goods available for sale	80,000	76,000	80,000
Ending inventory	16,000*	20,000	20,000
Cost of goods sold	64,000†	56,000†	60,000
Gross profit	36,000	44,000	40,000
Expenses	10,000	10,000	10,000
Net income	$ 26,000	$ 34,000	$ 30,000

Correct income is $30,000 for each year

* Correct amount is $20,000.   † Correct amount is $60,000.

Exhibit 6.11

Effects of Inventory Errors on Three Periods' Income Statements

Balance Sheet Effects   Balance sheet effects of an inventory error can be seen by considering the components of the accounting equation: Assets = Liabilities + Equity. For example, understating ending inventory understates both current and total assets. An understatement in ending inventory also yields an understatement in equity because of the understatement in net income. Exhibit 6.12 shows the effects of inventory errors on the current period's balance sheet amounts. Errors in *beginning* inventory do not yield misstatements in the end-of-period balance sheet, but they do affect that current period's income statement.

Example: If year 2006 ending inventory in Exhibit 6.11 is overstated by $3,000 (not understated by $4,000), what is the effect on cost of goods sold, gross profit, assets, and equity? *Answer:* Cost of goods sold is understated by $3,000 in 2006 and overstated by $3,000 in 2007. Gross profit and net income are overstated in 2006 and understated in 2007. Assets and equity are overstated in 2006.

Inventory Error	Assets	Equity
Understate ending inventory	Understated	Understated
Overstate ending inventory	Overstated	Overstated

Exhibit 6.12

Effects of Inventory Errors on Current Period's Balance Sheet

Quick Check   Answer—p. 248

8. Use LCM applied separately to the following individual items to compute ending inventory.

Product	Units	Unit Recorded Cost	Unit Market Cost
A	20	$ 6	$ 5
B	40	9	8
C	10	12	15

Inventory Turnover

A3 Assess inventory management using both inventory turnover and days' sales in inventory.

Earlier chapters described two important ratios useful in evaluating a company's short-term liquidity: current ratio and acid-test ratio. A merchandiser's ability to pay its short-term obligations also depends on how quickly it sells its merchandise inventory. **Inventory turnover,** also called *merchandise inventory turnover,* is one ratio used to assess this and is defined in Exhibit 6.13.

Exhibit 6.13

Inventory Turnover

$$\text{Inventory turnover} = \frac{\text{Cost of goods sold}}{\text{Average inventory}}$$

Point: We must take care when comparing turnover ratios across companies that use different costing methods (such as FIFO and LIFO).

This ratio reveals how many *times* a company turns over (sells) its inventory during a period. If a company's inventory greatly varies within a year, average inventory amounts can be computed from interim periods such as quarters or months.

Users apply inventory turnover to help analyze short-term liquidity and to assess whether management is doing a good job controlling the amount of inventory available. A low ratio compared to that of competitors suggests inefficient use of assets. The company may be holding more inventory than it needs to support its sales volume. Similarly, a very high ratio compared to that of competitors suggests inventory might be too low. This can cause lost sales if customers must back-order merchandise. Inventory turnover has no simple rule except to say *a high ratio is preferable provided inventory is adequate to meet demand.*

Decision Insight

Dell-ocity From its roots in a college dorm room, Dell now sells over 50 million dollars' worth of computers each day from its Website. The speed of Web technology has allowed Dell to slash inventories. Dell's inventory turnover is 102 and its days' sales in inventory is 4 days. Michael Dell asserts, "Speed is everything in this business."

Days' Sales in Inventory

Point: Inventory turnover is higher and days' sales in inventory is lower for industries such as foods and other perishable products. The reverse holds for nonperishable product industries.

To better interpret inventory turnover, many users measure the adequacy of inventory to meet sales demand. **Days' sales in inventory,** also called *days' stock on hand,* is a ratio that reveals how much inventory is available in terms of the number of days' sales. It can be interpreted as the number of days one can sell from inventory if no new items are purchased. This ratio is often viewed as a measure of the buffer against out-of-stock inventory and is useful in evaluating liquidity of inventory. It is defined in Exhibit 6.14.

Exhibit 6.14

Days' Sales in Inventory

$$\text{Days' sales in inventory} = \frac{\text{Ending inventory}}{\text{Cost of goods sold}} \times 365$$

Point: Days' sales in inventory for many Ford models has risen: Freestyle, 122 days; Montego, 109 days; Five Hundred, 118 days. The industry average is 73 days. (*BusinessWeek* 2005)

Days' sales in inventory focuses on ending inventory and it estimates how many days it will take to convert inventory at the end of a period into accounts receivable or cash. Notice that days' sales in inventory focuses on *ending* inventory whereas inventory turnover focuses on *average* inventory.

Analysis of Inventory Management

Inventory management is a major emphasis for merchandisers. They must both plan and control inventory purchases and sales. Toys "R" Us is one of those merchandisers. Its inventory in fiscal year 2005 was $1,884 million. This inventory constituted 43% of its current assets and 19% of its total assets. We apply the analysis tools in this section to Toys "R" Us, as shown in Exhibit 6.15.

Exhibit 6.15

Inventory Turnover and Days' Sales in Inventory for Toys "R" Us

($ millions)	2005	2004	2003	2002	2001
Cost of goods sold	$7,506	$7,646	$7,799	$7,604	$7,815
Ending inventory	$1,884	$2,094	$2,190	$2,041	$2,307
Inventory turnover	3.8 times	3.6 times	3.7 times	3.5 times	3.6 times
Industry inventory turnover	2.6 times	2.6 times	2.6 times	2.5 times	2.8 times
Days' sales in inventory	92 days	100 days	102 days	98 days	108 days
Industry days' sales in inventory	139 days	141 days	139 days	146 days	130 days

Its 2005 inventory turnover of 3.8 times means that Toys "R" Us turns over its inventory 3.8 times per year, or once every 96 days (365 days ÷ 3.8). We prefer inventory turnover to be high provided inventory is not out of stock and the company is not losing customers. The 2005 days' sales in inventory of 92 days reveals that it is carrying 92 days of sales in inventory. This inventory buffer seems more than adequate. Toys "R" Us would benefit from further management efforts to increase inventory turnover and reduce inventory levels.

Decision Maker   Answer—p. 247

Entrepreneur   Analysis of your retail store yields an inventory turnover of 5.0 and a days' sales in inventory of 73 days. The industry norm for inventory turnover is 4.4 and for days' sales in inventory is 74 days. What is your assessment of inventory management?

DILBERT reprinted by permission of United Feature Syndicate, Inc.

Demonstration Problem

Craig Company uses a perpetual inventory system for its one product. Its beginning inventory, purchases, and sales during calendar year 2008 follow.

Date	Activity	Units Acquired at Cost	Units Sold at Retail	Unit Inventory
Jan. 1	Beg. Inventory ..	400 units @ $14 = $ 5,600		400 units
Jan. 15	Sale		200 units @ $30	200 units
March 10	Purchase	200 units @ $15 = $ 3,000		400 units
April 1	Sale		200 units @ $30	200 units
May 9	Purchase	300 units @ $16 = $ 4,800		500 units
Sept. 22	Purchase	250 units @ $20 = $ 5,000		750 units
Nov. 1	Sale		300 units @ $35	450 units
Nov. 28	Purchase	100 units @ $21 = $ 2,100		550 units
	Totals	1,250 units $20,500	700 units	

Additional tracking data for specific identification: (1) January 15 sale—200 units @ $14, (2) April 1 sale—200 units @ $15, and (3) November 1 sale—200 units @ $14 and 100 units @ $20.

Required

1. Calculate the cost of goods available for sale.

2. Apply the four different methods of inventory costing (FIFO, LIFO, weighted average, and specific identification) to calculate ending inventory and cost of goods sold under each method.

3. In preparing financial statements for year 2008, the financial officer was instructed to use FIFO but failed to do so and instead computed cost of goods sold according to LIFO. Determine the impact on year 2008's income from the error. Also determine the effect of this error on year 2009's income. Assume no income taxes.

4. Management wants a report that shows how changing from FIFO to another method would change net income. Prepare a table showing (1) the cost of goods sold amount under each of the four methods, (2) the amount by which each cost of goods sold total is different from the FIFO cost of goods sold, and (3) the effect on net income if another method is used instead of FIFO.

Planning the Solution

- Compute cost of goods available for sale by multiplying the units of beginning inventory and each purchase by their unit costs to determine the total cost of goods available for sale.
- Prepare a perpetual FIFO table starting with beginning inventory and showing how inventory changes after each purchase and after each sale (see Exhibit 6.5).
- Prepare a perpetual LIFO table starting with beginning inventory and showing how inventory changes after each purchase and after each sale (see Exhibit 6.6).
- Make a table of purchases and sales recalculating the average cost of inventory prior to each sale to arrive at the weighted average cost of ending inventory. Total the average costs associated with each sale to determine cost of goods sold (see Exhibit 6.7).
- Prepare a table showing the computation of cost of goods sold and ending inventory using the specific identification method (see Exhibit 6.4).
- Compare the year-end 2008 inventory amounts under FIFO and LIFO to determine the misstatement of year 2008 income that results from using LIFO. The errors for year 2008 and 2009 are equal in amount but opposite in effect.
- Create a table showing cost of goods sold under each method and how net income would differ from FIFO net income if an alternate method is adopted.

Solution to Demonstration Problem

1. Cost of goods available for sale (this amount is the same for all methods).

Date		Units	Unit Cost	Cost
Jan. 1	Beg. Inventory	400	$14	$ 5,600
March 10	Purchase	200	15	3,000
May 9	Purchase	300	16	4,800
Sept. 22	Purchase	250	20	5,000
Nov. 28	Purchase	100	21	2,100
	Total goods available for sale	1,250		$20,500

2a. FIFO perpetual method.

Date	Goods Purchased	Cost of Goods Sold	Inventory Balance
Jan. 1	Beginning balance		400 @ $14 = $ 5,600
Jan. 15		200 @ $14 = $2,800	200 @ $14 = $ 2,800
Mar. 10	200 @ $15 = $3,000		200 @ $14 } 200 @ $15 } = $ 5,800
April 1		200 @ $14 = $2,800	200 @ $15 = $ 3,000
May 9	300 @ $16 = $4,800		200 @ $15 } 300 @ $16 } = $ 7,800
Sept. 22	250 @ $20 = $5,000		200 @ $15 } 300 @ $16 } = $12,800 250 @ $20 }
Nov. 1		200 @ $15 = $3,000 100 @ $16 = $1,600	200 @ $16 } 250 @ $20 } = $ 8,200
Nov. 28	100 @ $21 = $2,100		200 @ $16 } 250 @ $20 } = $10,300 100 @ $21 }
	Total cost of goods sold	$10,200	

Note to students: **In a classroom situation,** once we compute cost of goods available for sale, we can compute the amount for either cost of goods sold or ending inventory—it is a matter of preference. **In practice,** the costs of items sold are identified as sales are made and immediately transferred from the inventory account to the cost of goods sold account. The previous solution showing the line-by-line approach illustrates actual application in practice. The following alternate solutions illustrate that, once the concepts are understood, other solution approaches are available—although this is only shown for FIFO, it could be shown for all methods.

Alternate Methods to Compute FIFO Perpetual Numbers

[FIFO Alternate No. 1: Computing cost of goods sold first]

Cost of goods available for sale (from part 1)			$ 20,500
Cost of goods sold			
Jan. 15 Sold (200 @ $14)	$2,800		
April 1 Sold (200 @ $14)	2,800		
Nov. 1 Sold (200 @ $15 and 100 @ $16)	4,600	10,200	
Ending inventory		**$10,300**	

[FIFO Alternate No. 2: Computing ending inventory first]

Cost of goods available for sale (from part 1)			$ 20,500
Ending inventory*			
Nov. 28 Purchase (100 @ $21)	$2,100		
Sept. 22 Purchase (250 @ $20)	5,000		
May 9 Purchase (200 @ $16)	3,200		
Ending inventory		10,300	
Cost of goods sold		**$10,200**	

* Since FIFO assumes that the earlier costs are the first to flow out, we determine ending inventory by assigning the most recent costs to the remaining items.

2b. LIFO perpetual method.

Date	Goods Purchased	Cost of Goods Sold	Inventory Balance
Jan. 1	Beginning balance		400 @ $14 = $ 5,600
Jan. 15		200 @ $14 = $2,800	200 @ $14 = $ 2,800
Mar. 10	200 @ $15 = $3,000		200 @ $14 200 @ $15 } = $ 5,800
April 1		200 @ $15 = $3,000	200 @ $14 = $ 2,800
May 9	300 @ $16 = $4,800		200 @ $14 300 @ $16 } = $ 7,600
Sept. 22	250 @ $20 = $5,000		200 @ $14 300 @ $16 250 @ $20 } = $12,600
Nov. 1		250 @ $20 = $5,000 50 @ $16 = $ 800	200 @ $14 250 @ $16 } = $ 6,800
Nov. 28	100 @ $21 = $2,100		200 @ $14 250 @ $16 100 @ $21 } = $ 8,900
Total cost of goods sold		**$11,600**	

2c. Weighted average perpetual method.

Date	Goods Purchased	Cost of Goods Sold	Inventory Balance
Jan. 1	Beginning balance		400 @ $14 = $ 5,600
Jan. 15		200 @ $14 = $2,800	200 @ $14 = $ 2,800
Mar. 10	200 @ $15 = $3,000		200 @ $14 ⎱ = $ 5,800 200 @ $15 ⎰ (avg. cost is $14.5)
April 1		200 @ $14.5 = $2,900	200 @ $14.5 = $ 2,900
May 9	300 @ $16 = $4,800		200 @ $14.5 ⎱ = $ 7,700 300 @ $16 ⎰ (avg. cost is $15.4)
Sept. 22	250 @ $20 = $5,000		200 @ $14.5 ⎱ 300 @ $16 ⎬ = $ 12,700 250 @ $20 ⎰ (avg. cost is $16.93)
Nov. 1		300 @ $16.93 = $5,079	450 @ $16.93 = $ 7,618.5
Nov. 28	100 @ $21 = $2,100		450 @ $16.93 ⎱ = **$9,718.5** 100 @ $21 ⎰
Total cost of goods sold*		**$10,779**	

* The cost of goods sold ($10,779) plus ending inventory ($9,718.5) is $2.5 less than the cost of goods available for sale ($20,500) due to rounding.

2d. Specific identification method.

Date	Goods Purchased	Cost of Goods Sold	Inventory Balance
Jan. 1	Beginning balance		400 @ $14 = $ 5,600
Jan. 15		200 @ $14 = $2,800	200 @ $14 = $ 2,800
Mar. 10	200 @ $15 = $3,000		200 @ $14 ⎱ = $ 5,800 200 @ $15 ⎰
April 1		200 @ $15 = $3,000	200 @ $14 = $ 2,800
May 9	300 @ $16 = $4,800		200 @ $14 ⎱ = $ 7,600 300 @ $16 ⎰
Sept. 22	250 @ $20 = $5,000		200 @ $14 ⎱ 300 @ $16 ⎬ = $12,600 250 @ $20 ⎰
Nov. 1		200 @ $14 = $2,800 100 @ $20 = $2,000	300 @ $16 ⎱ = $ 7,800 150 @ $20 ⎰
Nov. 28	100 @ $21 = $2,100		300 @ $16 ⎱ 150 @ $20 ⎬ = $ 9,900 100 @ $21 ⎰
Total cost of goods sold		**$10,600**	

3. Mistakenly using LIFO when FIFO should have been used overstates cost of goods sold in year 2008 by $1,400, which is the difference between the FIFO and LIFO amounts of ending inventory. It understates income in 2008 by $1,400. In year 2009, income is overstated by $1,400 because of the understatement in beginning inventory.

4. Analysis of the effects of alternative inventory methods.

	Cost of Goods Sold	Difference from FIFO Cost of Goods Sold	Effect on Net Income if Adopted Instead of FIFO
FIFO	$10,200	—	—
LIFO	11,600	+$1,400	$1,400 lower
Weighted average	10,779	+ 579	579 lower
Specific identification	10,600	+ 400	400 lower

Inventory Costing under a Periodic System

6A

The basic aim of the periodic system and the perpetual system is the same: to assign costs to inventory and cost of goods sold. The same four methods are used to assign costs under both systems: specific identification; first-in, first-out; last-in, first-out; and weighted average. We use information from Trekking to show how to assign costs using these four methods with a periodic system. Data for sales and purchases are reported in the chapter (see Exhibit 6.3). Recall that we explained the accounting under a periodic system in Appendix 5A.

P3 Compute inventory in a periodic system using the methods of specific identification, FIFO, LIFO, and weighted average.

Specific Identification

We use the information in Exhibit 6.3 and the specific identification method to assign costs to the 12 units in ending inventory and to the 43 units sold as shown in Exhibit 6A.1. Carefully study Exhibit 6A.1 to

Exhibit 6A.1

Specific Identification Computations

Date	Goods Purchased	Cost of Goods Sold	Inventory Balance
Aug. 1	Beginning balance		10 @ $ 91 = $ 910
Aug. 3	15 @ $106 = $1,590		10 @ $ 91 15 @ $106 } = $2,500
Aug. 14		8 @ $ 91 = $ 728 12 @ $106 = $1,272 } = $2,000*	2 @ $ 91 3 @ $106 } = $ 500
Aug. 17	20 @ $115 = $2,300		2 @ $ 91 3 @ $106 20 @ $115 } = $2,800
Aug. 28	10 @ $119 = $1,190		2 @ $ 91 3 @ $106 20 @ $115 10 @ $119 } = $3,990
Aug. 31		2 @ $ 91 = $ 182 3 @ $106 = $ 318 15 @ $115 = $1,725 3 @ $119 = $ 357 } = $2,582* $4,582	5 @ $115 7 @ $119 } = $1,408

For the 20 units sold on Aug. 14, the company specifically identified that 8 of those had cost $91 and 12 had cost $106.

For the 23 units sold on Aug. 31, the company specifically identified each bike sold and its acquisition cost from prior purchases.

"goods in"   "goods out"   "what's left"

* Identification of items sold (and their costs) is obtained from internal documents that track each unit from its purchase to its sale.

see the flow of costs both in and out of inventory. Notice that each unit, whether sold or remaining in inventory, has its own specific cost attached to it.

Point: The assignment of costs to the goods sold and to inventory using specific identification is the same for both the perpetual and periodic systems.

When using specific identification, Trekking's cost of goods sold reported on the income statement totals **$4,582**, the sum of $2,000 and $2,582 from the third column of Exhibit 6A.1. Trekking's ending inventory reported on the balance sheet is **$1,408**, which is the final inventory balance from the fourth column of Exhibit 6A.1. The purchases and sales entries for Exhibit 6A.1 follow (the colored boldface numbers are those affected by the cost flow assumption).

Purchases		
Aug. 3 Purchases	1,590	
Accounts Payable		1,590
17 Purchases	2,300	
Accounts Payable		2,300
28 Purchases	1,190	
Accounts Payable		1,190

Sales		
Aug. 14 Accounts Receivable	2,600	
Sales		2,600
31 Accounts Receivable	3,450	
Sales		3,450
Adjusting Entry		
31 Merchandise Inventory	1,408	
Income Summary		498
Merchandise Inventory . . .		910

First-In, First-Out

The first-in, first-out (FIFO) method of assigning cost to both inventory and cost of goods sold using the periodic system is shown in Exhibit 6A.2.

Exhibit 6A.2

FIFO Computations— Periodic System

Exhibit 6.3 shows that the 12 units in ending inventory consist of 10 units from the latest purchase on Aug. 28 and 2 units from the next latest purchase on Aug. 17.

Total cost of 55 units available for sale (from Exhibit 6.3)		$5,990
Less ending inventory priced using FIFO		
10 units from August 28 purchase at $119 each	$1,190	
2 units from August 17 purchase at $115 each	230	
Ending inventory		1,420
Cost of goods sold		$4,570

Point: The assignment of costs to the goods sold and to inventory using FIFO is the same for both the perpetual and periodic systems.

Trekking's ending inventory reported on the balance sheet is **$1,420**, and its cost of goods sold reported on the income statement is **$4,570**. These amounts are the same as those computed using the perpetual system. This always occurs because the most recent purchases are in ending inventory under both systems. The purchases and sales entries for Exhibit 6A.2 follow (the colored boldface numbers are those affected by the cost flow assumption).

Purchases		
Aug. 3 Purchases	1,590	
Accounts Payable		1,590
17 Purchases	2,300	
Accounts Payable		2,300
28 Purchases	1,190	
Accounts Payable		1,190

Sales		
Aug. 14 Accounts Receivable	2,600	
Sales		2,600
31 Accounts Receivable	3,450	
Sales		3,450
Adjusting Entry		
31 Merchandise Inventory	1,420	
Income Summary		510
Merchandise Inventory		910

Last-In, First-Out

The last-in, first-out (LIFO) method of assigning costs to the 12 remaining units in inventory (and to the 43 units in cost of goods sold) using the periodic system is shown in Exhibit 6A.3.

Total cost of 55 units available for sale (from Exhibit 6.3)		$5,990
Less ending inventory priced using LIFO		
10 units in beginning inventory at $91 each	$910	
2 units from August 3 purchase at $106 each	212	
Ending inventory		1,122
Cost of goods sold		$4,868

Exhibit 6A.3

LIFO Computations—
Periodic System

> Exhibit 6.3 shows that the 12 units in ending inventory consist of 10 units from the earliest purchase (beg. inv.) and 2 units from the next earliest purchase on Aug. 3.

Trekking's ending inventory reported on the balance sheet is $1,122, and its cost of goods sold reported on the income statement is $4,868. When LIFO is used with the periodic system, cost of goods sold is assigned costs from the most recent purchases for the period. With a perpetual system, cost of goods sold is assigned costs from the most recent purchases at the point of *each sale*. The purchases and sales entries for Exhibit 6A.3 follow (the colored boldface numbers are those affected by the cost flow assumption).

Purchases		
Aug. 3 Purchases	1,590	
Accounts Payable		1,590
17 Purchases	2,300	
Accounts Payable		2,300
28 Purchases	1,190	
Accounts Payable		1,190

Sales		
Aug. 14 Accounts Receivable	2,600	
Sales		2,600
31 Accounts Receivable	3,450	
Sales		3,450
Adjusting Entry		
31 Merchandise Inventory	1,122	
Income Summary		212
Merchandise Inventory		910

Weighted Average

The weighted average method of assigning cost involves three important steps. The first two steps are shown in Exhibit 6A.4. First, multiply the per unit cost for beginning inventory and each particular purchase by the corresponding number of units (from Exhibit 6.3). Second, add these amounts and divide by the total number of units available for sale to find the weighted average cost per unit.

Step 1:	10 units @ $ 91 = $ 910
	15 units @ $106 = 1,590
	20 units @ $115 = 2,300
	10 units @ $119 = 1,190
	55 $5,990
Step 2:	$5,990/55 units = $108.91 weighted average cost per unit

Exhibit 6A.4

Weighted Average Cost per Unit

Example: In Exhibit 6A.4, if 5 more units had been purchased at $120 each, what would be the weighted average cost per unit?
Answer: $109.83 ($6,590/60)

The third step is to use the weighted average cost per unit to assign costs to inventory and to the units sold as shown in Exhibit 6A.5.

Step 3:	Total cost of 55 units available for sale (from Exhibit 6.3)	$ 5,990
	Less **ending inventory** priced on a weighted average cost basis: 12 units at $108.91 each (from Exhibit 6A.4)	1,307
	Cost of goods sold	$4,683

Exhibit 6A.5

Weighted Average Computations—Periodic

Trekking's ending inventory reported on the balance sheet is $1,307, and its cost of goods sold reported on the income statement is $4,683 when using the weighted average (periodic) method. The purchases

Point: Weighted average usually yields different results for the perpetual and the periodic systems because under a perpetual system it recomputes the per unit cost prior to each sale, whereas under a periodic system, the per unit cost is computed only at the end of a period.

and sales entries for Exhibit 6A.5 follow (the colored boldface numbers are those affected by the cost flow assumption).

Purchases		
Aug. 3 Purchases	1,590	
Accounts Payable		1,590
17 Purchases	2,300	
Accounts Payable		2,300
28 Purchases	1,190	
Accounts Payable		1,190

Sales		
Aug. 14 Accounts Receivable	2,600	
Sales		2,600
31 Accounts Receivable	3,450	
Sales		3,450

Adjusting Entry		
31 Merchandise Inventory.........	1,307	
Income Summary		397
Merchandise Inventory		910

Financial Statement Effects

Point: LIFO inventory is often less than the inventory's replacement cost because LIFO inventory is valued using the oldest inventory purchase costs.

When purchase prices do not change, each inventory costing method assigns the same cost amounts to inventory and to cost of goods sold. When purchase prices are different, however, the methods nearly always assign different cost amounts. We show these differences in Exhibit 6A.6 using Trekking's data.

Exhibit 6A.6

Financial Statement Effects of Inventory Costing Methods

TREKKING COMPANY For Month Ended August 31				
	Specific Identification	FIFO	LIFO	Weighted Average
Income Statement				
Sales	$ 6,050	$ 6,050	$ 6,050	$ 6,050
Cost of goods sold	4,582	4,570	4,868	4,683
Gross profit	1,468	1,480	1,182	1,367
Expenses	450	450	450	450
Income before taxes	1,018	1,030	732	917
Income tax expense (30%)	305	309	220	275
Net income	$ 713	$ 721	$ 512	$ 642
Balance Sheet				
Inventory	$1,408	$1,420	$1,122	$1,307

When purchase costs *regularly rise,* as in Trekking's case, observe the following:

■ FIFO assigns the lowest amount to cost of goods sold—yielding the highest gross profit and net income.

■ LIFO assigns the highest amount to cost of goods sold—yielding the lowest gross profit and net income, which also yields a temporary tax advantage by postponing payment of some income tax.

■ Weighted average yields results between FIFO and LIFO.

■ Specific identification always yields results that depend on which units are sold.

When costs *regularly decline,* the reverse occurs for FIFO and LIFO.

All four inventory costing methods are acceptable in practice. A company must disclose the inventory method it uses. Each method offers certain advantages as follows:

■ FIFO assigns an amount to inventory on the balance sheet that approximates its current cost; it also mimics the actual flow of goods for most businesses.

■ LIFO assigns an amount to cost of goods sold on the income statement that approximates its current cost; it also better matches current costs with revenues in computing gross profit.

■ Weighted average tends to smooth out erratic changes in costs.

■ Specific identification exactly matches the costs of items with the revenues they generate.

Quick Check   Answers—p. 248

9. A company reports the following beginning inventory and purchases, and it ends the period with 30 units in inventory.

Beginning Inventory	100 units at $10 cost per unit
Purchase 1	40 units at $12 cost per unit
Purchase 2	20 units at $14 cost per unit

a. Compute ending inventory using the FIFO periodic system.
b. Compute cost of goods sold using the LIFO periodic system.

APPENDIX

Inventory Estimation Methods

6B

Inventory sometimes requires estimation for two reasons. First, companies often require **interim statements** (financial statements prepared for periods of less than one year), but they only annually take a physical count of inventory. Second, companies may require an inventory estimate if some casualty such as fire or flood makes taking a physical count impossible. Estimates are usually only required for companies that use the periodic system. Companies using a perpetual system would presumably have updated inventory data.

This appendix describes two methods to estimate inventory.

P4 Apply both the retail inventory and gross profit methods to estimate inventory.

Retail Inventory Method

To avoid the time-consuming and expensive process of taking a physical inventory each month or quarter, some companies use the **retail inventory method** to estimate cost of goods sold and ending inventory. Some companies even use the retail inventory method to prepare the annual statements. **Home Depot**, for instance, says in its annual report: "Inventories are stated at the lower of cost (first-in, first-out) or market, as determined by the retail inventory method." A company may also estimate inventory for audit purposes or when inventory is damaged or destroyed.

The retail inventory method uses a three-step process to estimate ending inventory. We need to know the amount of inventory a company had at the beginning of the period in both *cost* and *retail* amounts. We already explained how to compute the cost of inventory. The *retail amount of inventory* refers to its dollar amount measured using selling prices of inventory items. We also need to know the net amount of goods purchased (minus returns, allowances, and discounts) in the period, both at cost and at retail. The amount of net sales at retail is also needed. The process is shown in Exhibit 6B.1.

The reasoning behind the retail inventory method is that if we can get a good estimate of the cost-to-retail ratio, we can multiply ending inventory at retail by this ratio to estimate ending inventory at cost. We show in Exhibit 6B.2 how these steps are applied to estimate ending inventory for a typical company. First, we find that $100,000 of goods (at retail selling prices) was available for sale. We see that $70,000 of these goods were sold, leaving $30,000 (retail value) of merchandise in ending inventory. Second, the cost of these goods is 60%

Point: When a retailer takes a physical inventory, it can restate the retail value of inventory to a cost basis by applying the cost-to-retail ratio. It can also estimate the amount of shrinkage by comparing the inventory computed with the amount from a physical inventory.

Exhibit 6B.1

Retail Inventory Method of Inventory Estimation

Exhibit 6B.2

Estimated Inventory Using the Retail Inventory Method

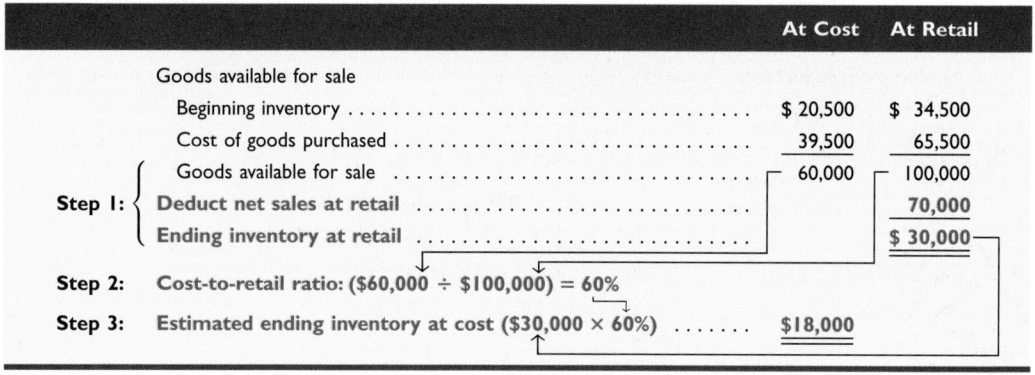

		At Cost	At Retail
Goods available for sale			
Beginning inventory		$ 20,500	$ 34,500
Cost of goods purchased		39,500	65,500
Step 1: Goods available for sale		60,000	100,000
Deduct net sales at retail			70,000
Ending inventory at retail			$ 30,000
Step 2: Cost-to-retail ratio: ($60,000 ÷ $100,000) = 60%			
Step 3: Estimated ending inventory at cost ($30,000 × 60%)		$18,000	

Example: What is the cost of ending inventory in Exhibit 6B.2 if the cost of beginning inventory is $22,500 and its retail value is $34,500? *Answer:* $30,000 × 62% = $18,600

of the $100,000 retail value. Third, since cost for these goods is 60% of retail, the estimated cost of ending inventory is $18,000.

Gross Profit Method

The **gross profit method** estimates the cost of ending inventory by applying the gross profit ratio to net sales (at retail). This type of estimate often is needed when inventory is destroyed, lost, or stolen. These cases require an inventory estimate so that a company can file a claim with its insurer. Users also apply this method to see whether inventory amounts from a physical count are reasonable. This method uses the historical relation between cost of goods sold and net sales to estimate the proportion of cost of goods sold making up current sales. This cost of goods sold estimate is then subtracted from cost of goods available for sale to estimate the ending inventory at cost. These two steps are shown in Exhibit 6B.3.

Exhibit 6B.3

Gross Profit Method of Inventory Estimation

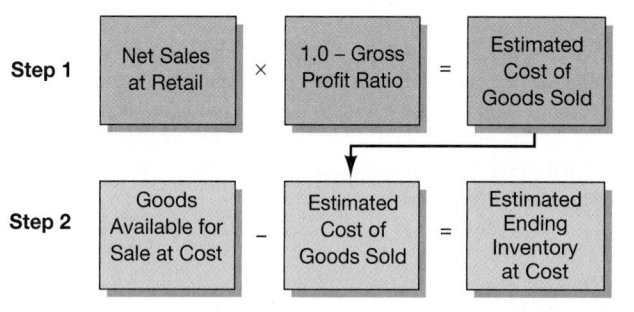

Point: A fire or other catastrophe can result in an insurance claim for lost inventory or income. Backup and off-site storage of data help ensure coverage for such losses.

Point: Reliability of the gross profit method depends on a good estimate of the gross profit ratio.

To illustrate, assume that a company's inventory is destroyed by fire in March 2008. When the fire occurs, the company's accounts show the following balances for January through March: sales, $31,500; sales returns, $1,500; inventory (January 1, 2008), $12,000; and cost of goods purchased, $20,500. If this company's gross profit ratio is 30%, then 30% of each net sales dollar is gross profit and 70% is cost of goods sold. We show in Exhibit 6B.4 how this 70% is used to estimate lost inventory of $11,500. To understand this exhibit, think of subtracting cost of goods sold from the goods available for sale to get ending inventory.

Exhibit 6B.4

Estimated Inventory Using the Gross Profit Method

Goods available for sale	
Inventory, January 1, 2008	$12,000
Cost of goods purchased	20,500
Goods available for sale (at cost)	32,500
Net sales at retail ($31,500 − $1,500)	$30,000
Step 1: Estimated cost of goods sold ($30,000 × 70%)	(21,000) ← × 0.70
Step 2: Estimated March inventory at cost	$11,500

Quick Check
Answers—p. 248

10. Using the retail method and the following data, estimate the cost of ending inventory.

	Cost	Retail
Beginning inventory	$324,000	$530,000
Cost of goods purchased	195,000	335,000
Net sales		320,000

Summary

C1 **Identify the items making up merchandise inventory.**
Merchandise inventory refers to goods owned by a company and held for resale. Three special cases merit our attention. Goods in transit are reported in inventory of the company that holds ownership rights. Goods on consignment are reported in the consignor's inventory. Goods damaged or obsolete are reported in inventory at their net realizable value.

C2 **Identify the costs of merchandise inventory.** Costs of merchandise inventory include expenditures necessary to bring an item to a salable condition and location. This includes its invoice cost minus any discount plus any added or incidental costs necessary to put it in a place and condition for sale.

A1 **Analyze the effects of inventory methods for both financial and tax reporting.** When purchase costs are rising or falling, the inventory costing methods are likely to assign different costs to inventory. Specific identification exactly matches costs and revenues. Weighted average smooths out cost changes. FIFO assigns an amount to inventory closely approximating current replacement cost. LIFO assigns the most recent costs incurred to cost of goods sold and likely better matches current costs with revenues.

A2 **Analyze the effects of inventory errors on current and future financial statements.** An error in the amount of ending inventory affects assets (inventory), net income (cost of goods sold), and equity for that period. Since ending inventory is next period's beginning inventory, an error in ending inventory affects next period's cost of goods sold and net income. Inventory errors in one period are offset in the next period.

A3 **Assess inventory management using both inventory turnover and days' sales in inventory.** We prefer a high inventory turnover, provided that goods are not out of stock and customers are not turned away. We use days' sales in inventory to assess the likelihood of goods being out of stock. We prefer a small number of days' sales in inventory if we can serve customer needs and provide a buffer for uncertainties.

P1 **Compute inventory in a perpetual system using the methods of specific identification, FIFO, LIFO, and weighted average.** Costs are assigned to the cost of goods sold account *each time* a sale occurs in a perpetual system. Specific identification assigns a cost to each item sold by referring to its actual cost (for example, its net invoice cost). Weighted average assigns a cost to items sold by dividing the current balance in the inventory account by the total items available for sale to determine cost per unit. We then multiply the number of units sold by this cost per unit to get the cost of each sale. FIFO assigns cost to items sold assuming that the earliest units purchased are the first units sold. LIFO assigns cost to items sold assuming that the most recent units purchased are the first units sold.

P2 **Compute the lower of cost or market amount of inventory.** Inventory is reported at market cost when market is *lower* than recorded cost, called the *lower of cost or market (LCM) inventory*. Market is typically measured as replacement cost. Lower of cost or market can be applied separately to each item, to major categories of items, or to the entire inventory.

P3[A] **Compute inventory in a periodic system using the methods of specific identification, FIFO, LIFO, and weighted average.** Periodic inventory systems allocate the cost of goods available for sale between cost of goods sold and ending inventory *at the end of a period*. Specific identification and FIFO give identical results whether the periodic or perpetual system is used. LIFO assigns costs to cost of goods sold assuming the last units purchased for the period are the first units sold. The weighted average cost per unit is computed by dividing the total cost of beginning inventory and net purchases for the period by the total number of units available. Then, it multiplies cost per unit by the number of units sold to give cost of goods sold.

P4[B] **Apply both the retail inventory and gross profit methods to estimate inventory.** The retail inventory method involves three steps: (1) goods available at retail minus net sales at retail equals ending inventory at retail, (2) goods available at cost divided by goods available at retail equals the cost-to-retail ratio, and (3) ending inventory at retail multiplied by the cost-to-retail ratio equals estimated ending inventory at cost. The gross profit method involves two steps: (1) net sales at retail multiplied by 1 minus the gross profit ratio equals estimated cost of goods sold, and (2) goods available at cost minus estimated cost of goods sold equals estimated ending inventory at cost.

Guidance Answers to **Decision Maker** and **Decision Ethics**

Financial Planner The FIFO method implies that the oldest costs are the first ones assigned to cost of goods sold. This leaves the most recent costs in ending inventory. You report this to your client and note that in most cases, the ending inventory of a company using FIFO is reported at or near its replacement cost. This means that your client need not in most cases adjust the reported value of inventory. Your answer changes only if there are major increases in replacement cost compared to the cost of recent purchases reported in inventory. When major increases in costs occur, your client might wish to adjust inventory (for internal reports) for the difference between the reported cost of inventory and its replacement cost. (*Note:* Decreases in costs of purchases are recognized under the lower of cost or market adjustment.)

Inventory Manager It seems your company can save (or at least postpone) taxes by switching to LIFO, but the switch is likely to reduce bonus money that you think you have earned and deserve. Since the U.S. tax code requires companies that use LIFO for tax reporting also to use it for financial reporting, your options are further constrained. Your best decision is to tell your superior about the tax savings with LIFO. You also should discuss your bonus plan and how this is likely to hurt you unfairly. You might propose to compute inventory under the LIFO method for reporting purposes but use the FIFO method for your bonus calculations. Another solution is to revise the bonus plan to reflect the company's use of the LIFO method.

Entrepreneur Your inventory turnover is markedly higher than the norm, whereas days' sales in inventory approximates the norm. Since your turnover is already 14% better than average, you are probably best served by directing attention to days' sales in inventory. You should see whether you can reduce the level of inventory while maintaining service to customers. Given your higher turnover, you should be able to hold less inventory.

Guidance Answers to **Quick Checks**

1. The matching principle.
2. Target reports these goods in its inventory.
3. Total cost assigned to the painting is $12,180, computed as $11,400 + $130 + $150 + $100 + $400.
4. Specific identification exactly matches costs and revenues. Weighted average tends to smooth out cost changes. FIFO assigns an amount to inventory that closely approximates current replacement cost. LIFO assigns the most recent costs incurred to cost of goods sold and likely better matches current costs with revenues.
5. FIFO—it gives a lower cost of goods sold, a higher gross profit, and a higher net income when costs are rising.
6. When costs are rising, LIFO gives a lower inventory figure on the balance sheet as compared to FIFO. FIFO's inventory amount approximates current replacement costs.
7. Cost of goods sold would be overstated by $10,000 in 2008 and understated by $10,000 in year 2009.

8. The reported LCM inventory amount (using items) is $540, computed as $[(20 \times \$5) + (40 \times \$8) + (10 \times \$12)]$.
9.[A]a. FIFO periodic inventory = $(20 \times \$14) + (10 \times \$12)$
$= \$400$
 b. LIFO periodic cost of goods sold
$= (20 \times \$14) + (40 \times \$12) + (70 \times \$10)$
$= \$1,460$
10.[B]Estimated ending inventory (at cost) is $327,000. It is computed as follows:

Step 1: $(\$530,000 + \$335,000) - \$320,000 = \$545,000$

Step 2: $\dfrac{\$324,000 + \$195,000}{\$530,000 + \$335,000} = 60\%$

Step 3: $\$545,000 \times 60\% = \underline{\$327,000}$

Key Terms   mhhe.com/wildFAP18e

Key Terms are available at the book's Website for learning and testing in an online Flashcard Format.

Average cost (p. 230)
Conservatism principle (p. 234)
Consignee (p. 224)
Consignor (p. 224)
Consistency principle (p. 232)
Days' sales in inventory (p. 236)

First-in, first-out (FIFO) (p. 229)
Gross profit method (p. 246)
Interim statements (p. 245)
Inventory turnover (p. 236)
Last-in, first-out (LIFO) (p. 229)
Lower of cost or market (LCM) (p. 233)

Net realizable value (p. 224)
Retail inventory method (p. 245)
Specific identification (p. 227)
Weighted average (p. 230)

Multiple Choice Quiz   Answers on p. 262–263   mhhe.com/wildFAP18e

Multiple Choice Quizzes A and B are available at the book's Website.

Use the following information from Marvel Company for the month of July to answer questions 1 through 4.

July 1	Beginning inventory	75 units @ $25 each
July 3	Purchase	348 units @ $27 each
July 8	Sale	300 units
July 15	Purchase	257 units @ $28 each
July 23	Sale	275 units

1. Assume that Marvel uses a perpetual FIFO inventory system. What is the dollar value of its ending inventory?
   a. $2,940   d. $2,852
   b. $2,685   e. $2,705
   c. $2,625
2. Assume that Marvel uses a perpetual LIFO inventory system. What is the dollar value of its ending inventory?
   a. $2,940   d. $2,852
   b. $2,685   e. $2,705
   c. $2,625

3. Assume that Marvel uses a perpetual specific identification inventory system. Its ending inventory consists of 20 units from beginning inventory, 40 units from the July 3 purchase, and 45 units from the July 15 purchase. What is the dollar value of its ending inventory?
   a. $2,940   d. $2,852
   b. $2,685   e. $2,840
   c. $2,625
4.[A] Assume that Marvel uses a *periodic* FIFO inventory system. What is the dollar value of its ending inventory?
   a. $2,940   d. $2,852
   b. $2,685   e. $2,705
   c. $2,625
5. A company has cost of goods sold of $85,000 and ending inventory of $18,000. Its days' sales in inventory equals:
   a. 49.32 days   d. 77.29 days
   b. 0.21 days   e. 1,723.61 days
   c. 4.72 days

Superscript letter ^{A} $(^B)$ denotes assignments based on Appendix 6A (6B).

Discussion Questions

1. Describe how costs flow from inventory to cost of goods sold for the following methods: (*a*) FIFO and (*b*) LIFO.

2. Where is the amount of merchandise inventory disclosed in the financial statements?

3. Why are incidental costs sometimes ignored in inventory costing? Under what principle is this permitted?

4. If costs are declining, will the LIFO or FIFO method of inventory valuation yield the lower cost of goods sold? Why?

5. What does the full-disclosure principle prescribe if a company changes from one acceptable accounting method to another?

6. Can a company change its inventory method each accounting period? Explain.

7. Does the accounting principle of consistency preclude any changes from one accounting method to another?

8. If inventory errors are said to correct themselves, why are accounting users concerned when such errors are made?

9. Explain the following statement: "Inventory errors correct themselves."

10. What is the meaning of *market* as it is used in determining the lower of cost or market for inventory?

11. What guidance does the principle of conservatism offer?

12. What factors contribute to (or cause) inventory shrinkage?

13.^{A}What accounts are used in a periodic inventory system but not in a perpetual inventory system?

14.^{B}When preparing interim financial statements, what two methods can companies utilize to estimate cost of goods sold and ending inventory?

15. Refer to Best Buy's financial statements in Appendix A. On February 26, 2005, what percent of current assets are represented by inventory?

16. Refer to Circuit City's financial statements in Appendix A. Compute its cost of goods available for sale for the year ended February 28, 2005.

17. What percent of Apple's current assets are inventory as of September 25, 2004, and as of September 25, 2003?

 Red numbers denote Discussion Questions that involve decision-making.

A company reports the following beginning inventory and purchases for the month of January. On January 26, 355 units were sold. What is the cost of the 160 units that remain in ending inventory at January 31, assuming costs are assigned based on a perpetual inventory system and use of (*a*) FIFO, (*b*) LIFO, and (*c*) weighted average? (Round unit costs to the nearest cent.)

QUICK STUDY

QS 6-1
Inventory costing methods
P1

	Units	Unit Cost
Beginning inventory on January 1	320	$3.00
Purchase on January 9	85	3.20
Purchase on January 25	110	3.30

Check (c) $496

Wattan Company reports beginning inventory of 10 units at $60 each. Every week for four weeks it purchases an additional 10 units at respective costs of $61, $62, $65, and $70 per unit for weeks 1 through 4. Calculate the cost of goods available for sale and the units available for sale for this four-week period.

QS 6-2
Computing goods available for sale
P1

Trey Monson starts a merchandising business on December 1 and enters into three inventory purchases:

December 7	10 units @ $ 7 cost
December 14	20 units @ $ 8 cost
December 21	15 units @ $10 cost

Monson sells 15 units for $20 each on December 15. Eight of the sold units are from the December 7 purchase and seven are from the December 14 purchase. Monson uses a perpetual inventory system. Determine the costs assigned to the December 31 ending inventory based on (*a*) FIFO, (*b*) LIFO, (*c*) weighted average, and (*d*) specific identification.

QS 6-3
Assigning costs to inventory—perpetual systems
P1

Check (c) $265

QS 6-4
Contrasting inventory costing methods
A1

Identify the inventory costing method best described by each of the following separate statements. Assume a period of increasing costs.

1. Yields a balance sheet inventory amount often markedly less than its replacement cost.
2. Matches recent costs against net sales.
3. Results in a balance sheet inventory amount approximating replacement cost.
4. Provides a tax advantage (deferral) to a corporation when costs are rising.
5. The preferred method when each unit of product has unique features that markedly affect cost.

QS 6-5
Inventory ownership
C1

1. At year-end, Liu Co. had shipped $750 of merchandise FOB destination to Kwon Co. Which company should include the $750 of merchandise in transit as part of its year-end inventory?
2. Jabar Company has shipped $600 of goods to Chi Co., and Chi Co. has arranged to sell the goods for Jabar. Identify the consignor and the consignee. Which company should include any unsold goods as part of its inventory?

QS 6-6
Inventory ownership
C1

Homestead Crafts, a distributor of handmade gifts, operates out of owner Emma Flynn's house. At the end of the current period, Emma reports she has 1,300 units (products) in her basement, 20 of which were damaged by water and cannot be sold. She also has another 350 units in her van, ready to deliver per a customer order, terms FOB destination, and another 80 units out on consignment to a friend who owns a retail store. How many units should Emma include in her company's period-end inventory?

QS 6-7
Inventory costs
C2

A car dealer acquires a used car for $14,000, terms FOB shipping point. Additional costs in obtaining and offering the car for sale include $250 for transportation-in, $900 for import duties, $300 for insurance during shipment, $150 for advertising, and $1,250 for sales staff salaries. For computing inventory, what cost is assigned to the used car?

QS 6-8
Inventory costs
C2

Majors & Son, antique dealers, purchased the contents of an estate for $38,500. Terms of the purchase were FOB shipping point, and the cost of transporting the goods to Majors & Son's warehouse was $2,100. Majors & Son insured the shipment at a cost of $250. Prior to putting the goods up for sale, they cleaned and refurbished them at a cost of $800. Determine the cost of the inventory acquired from the estate.

QS 6-9
Applying LCM to inventories
P2

Amulet Trading Co. has the following products in its ending inventory. Compute lower of cost or market for inventory (a) as a whole and (b) applied separately to each product.

Product	Quantity	Cost per Unit	Market per Unit
Mountain bikes	11	$600	$550
Skateboards	13	350	425
Gliders	26	800	700

QS 6-10
Inventory errors
A2

In taking a physical inventory at the end of year 2008, Peña Company erroneously forgot to count certain units. Explain how this error affects the following: (a) 2008 cost of goods sold, (b) 2008 gross profit, (c) 2008 net income, (d) 2009 net income, (e) the combined two-year income, and (f) income for years after 2009.

QS 6-11
Analyzing inventory A3

Endor Company begins the year with $150,000 of goods in inventory. At year-end, the amount in inventory has increased to $180,000. Cost of goods sold for the year is $1,200,000. Compute Endor's inventory turnover and days' sales in inventory. Assume that there are 365 days in the year.

QS 6-12ᴬ
Costing methods—periodic system P3

Refer to QS 6-1 and assume the periodic inventory system is used. Determine the costs assigned to the ending inventory when costs are assigned based on (a) FIFO, (b) LIFO, and (c) weighted average. (Round unit costs to the nearest cent.)

QS 6-13ᴬ
Costing methods—periodic system P3

Refer to QS 6-3 and assume the periodic inventory system is used. Determine the costs assigned to the December 31 ending inventory when costs are assigned based on (a) FIFO, (b) LIFO, (c) weighted average, and (d) specific identification.

Kauai Store's inventory is destroyed by a fire on September 5, 2008. The following data for year 2008 are available from the accounting records. Estimate the cost of the inventory destroyed.

QS 6-14[B]
Estimating inventories—gross profit method

P4

Jan. 1 inventory	$190,000
Jan. 1 through Sept. 5 purchases (net)	$352,000
Jan. 1 through Sept. 5 sales (net)	$685,000
Year 2008 estimated gross profit rate	44%

EXERCISES

Laker Company reported the following January purchases and sales data for its only product.

Exercise 6-1
Inventory costing methods—perpetual

P1

Date	Activities	Units Acquired at Cost	Units Sold at Retail
Jan. 1	Beginning inventory	140 units @ $6.00 = $ 840	
Jan. 10	Sales		100 units @ $15
Jan. 20	Purchase	300 units @ $5.60 = 1,680	
Jan. 25	Sales		250 units @ $15
Jan. 30	Purchase	100 units @ $5.00 = 500	
	Totals	540 units $3,020	350 units

Laker uses a perpetual inventory system. Ending inventory consists of 190 units, 100 from the January 30 purchase, 70 from the January 20 purchase, and 20 from beginning inventory. Determine the cost assigned to ending inventory and to cost of goods sold using (*a*) specific identification, (*b*) weighted average, (*c*) FIFO, and (*d*) LIFO.

Check   Ending inventory: LIFO, $1,020; WA, $1,008

Use the data in Exercise 6-1 to prepare comparative income statements for the month of January for Laker Company similar to those shown in Exhibit 6.8 for the four inventory methods. Assume expenses are $1,250, and that the applicable income tax rate is 30%.

Exercise 6-2
Income effects of inventory methods

A1

1. Which method yields the highest net income?

2. Does net income using weighted average fall between that using FIFO and LIFO?

3. If costs were rising instead of falling, which method would yield the highest net income?

Hemming Co. reported the following current-year purchases and sales data for its only product.

Exercise 6-3
Inventory costing methods (perpetual)—FIFO and LIFO

P1

Date	Activities	Units Acquired at Cost	Units Sold at Retail
Jan. 1	Beginning inventory	200 units @ $10 = $ 2,000	
Jan. 10	Sales		150 units @ $40
Mar. 14	Purchase	350 units @ $15 = 5,250	
Mar. 15	Sales		300 units @ $40
July 30	Purchase	450 units @ $20 = 9,000	
Oct. 5	Sales		430 units @ $40
Oct. 26	Purchase	100 units @ $25 = 2,500	
	Totals	1,100 units $18,750	880 units

Hemming uses a perpetual inventory system. Determine the costs assigned to ending inventory and to cost of goods sold using (*a*) FIFO and (*b*) LIFO. Compute the gross margin for each method.

Check   Ending inventory: LIFO, $4,150

Refer to the data in Exercise 6-3. Assume that ending inventory is made up of 45 units from the March 14 purchase, 75 units from the July 30 purchase, and all the units of the October 26 purchase. Using the specific identification method, calculate (*a*) the cost of goods sold and (*b*) the gross profit.

Exercise 6-4
Specific identification   P1

Martinez Company's ending inventory includes the following items. Compute the lower of cost or market for ending inventory (*a*) as a whole and (*b*) applied separately to each product.

Exercise 6-5
Lower of cost or market   P2

Product	Units	Per Unit Cost	Per Unit Market
Helmets	24	$50	$54
Bats	17	78	72
Shoes	38	95	91
Uniforms	42	36	36

Check (b) $7,394

Exercise 6-6

Analysis of inventory errors

A2

Check 2007 reported gross profit, $330,000

Vibrant Company had $850,000 of sales in each of three consecutive years 2007–2009, and it purchased merchandise costing $500,000 in each of those years. It also maintained a $250,000 physical inventory from the beginning to the end of that three-year period. In accounting for inventory, it made an error at the end of year 2007 that caused its year-end 2007 inventory to appear on its statements as $230,000 rather than the correct $250,000.

1. Determine the correct amount of the company's gross profit in each of the years 2007–2009.

2. Prepare comparative income statements as in Exhibit 6.11 to show the effect of this error on the company's cost of goods sold and gross profit for each of the years 2007–2009.

Exercise 6-7

Inventory turnover and days' sales in inventory

A3

Use the following information for Palmer Co. to compute inventory turnover for 2008 and 2007, and its days' sales in inventory at December 31, 2008 and 2007. (Round answers to the tenth place.) Comment on Palmer's efficiency in using its assets to increase sales from 2007 to 2008.

	2008	2007	2006
Cost of goods sold	$643,825	$426,650	$391,300
Ending inventory	97,400	87,750	92,500

Exercise 6-8

Comparing LIFO numbers to FIFO numbers; ratio analysis

A1 A3

Cruz Company uses LIFO for inventory costing and reports the following financial data. It also recomputed inventory and cost of goods sold using FIFO for comparison purposes.

	2008	2007
LIFO inventory	$160	$110
LIFO cost of goods sold	740	680
FIFO inventory	240	145
FIFO cost of goods sold	660	645
Current assets (using LIFO)	220	180
Current liabilities	200	170

Check (1) FIFO: Current ratio, 1.5; Inventory turnover, 3.4 times

1. Compute its current ratio, inventory turnover, and days' sales in inventory for 2008 using (a) LIFO numbers and (b) FIFO numbers. (Round answers to the tenth place.)

2. Comment on and interpret the results of part 1.

Exercise 6-9[A]

Inventory costing— periodic system P3

Refer to Exercise 6-1 and assume the periodic inventory system is used. Determine the costs assigned to ending inventory and to cost of goods sold using (a) specific identification, (b) weighted average, (c) FIFO, and (d) LIFO. (Round unit costs to the tenth of a cent.)

Exercise 6-10[A]

Inventory costing— periodic system P3

Refer to Exercise 6-3 and assume the periodic inventory system is used. Determine the costs assigned to ending inventory and to cost of goods sold using (a) FIFO, and (b) LIFO. Compute the gross margin for each method.

Exercise 6-11[A]

Alternative cost flow assumptions—periodic

P3

Martinez Co. reported the following current-year data for its only product. The company uses a periodic inventory system, and its ending inventory consists of 150 units—50 from each of the last three purchases. Determine the cost assigned to ending inventory and to cost of goods sold using (a) specific identification, (b) weighted average, (c) FIFO, and (d) LIFO. (Round unit costs to the cent.) Which method yields the highest net income?

Jan.	1	Beginning inventory	100 units @ $2.00 = $ 200
Mar.	7	Purchase	220 units @ $2.25 = 495
July	28	Purchase	540 units @ $2.50 = 1,350
Oct.	3	Purchase	480 units @ $2.80 = 1,344
Dec.	19	Purchase	160 units @ $2.90 = 464
		Totals	1,500 units $3,853

Check   Inventory; LIFO, $312.50; FIFO, $435

Flora's Gifts reported the following current-year data for its only product. The company uses a periodic inventory system, and its ending inventory consists of 150 units—50 from each of the last three purchases. Determine the cost assigned to ending inventory and to cost of goods sold using (a) specific identification, (b) weighted average, (c) FIFO, and (d) LIFO. (Round unit costs to the cent.) Which method yields the lowest net income?

Exercise 6-12^A
Alternative cost flow assumptions—periodic

P3

Jan.	1	Beginning inventory	140 units @ $3.00 = $ 420
Mar.	7	Purchase	300 units @ $2.80 = 840
July	28	Purchase	400 units @ $2.50 = 1,000
Oct.	3	Purchase	550 units @ $2.30 = 1,265
Dec.	19	Purchase	125 units @ $2.00 = 250
		Totals	1,515 units $3,775

Check   Inventory: LIFO, $448; FIFO, $307.50

In 2008, Dakota Company had net sales (at retail) of $260,000. The following additional information is available from its records at the end of 2008. Use the retail inventory method to estimate Dakota's 2008 ending inventory at cost.

Exercise 6-13^B
Estimating ending inventory—retail method

P4

	At Cost	At Retail
Beginning inventory	$ 63,800	$128,400
Cost of goods purchased	115,060	196,800

Check   End. Inventory, $35,860

On January 1, JKR Store had $225,000 of inventory at cost. In the first quarter of the year, it purchased $795,000 of merchandise, returned $11,550, and paid freight charges of $18,800 on purchased merchandise, terms FOB shipping point. The store's gross profit averages 30%. The store had $1,000,000 of net sales (at retail) in the first quarter of the year. Use the gross profit method to estimate its cost of inventory at the end of the first quarter.

Exercise 6-14^B
Estimating ending inventory—gross profit method

P4

Montoure Company uses a perpetual inventory system. It entered into the following calendar-year 2008 purchases and sales transactions.

PROBLEM SET A

Problem 6-1A
Alternative cost flows—perpetual

P1

Date		Activities	Units Acquired at Cost	Units Sold at Retail
Jan.	1	Beginning inventory	600 units @ $45/unit	
Feb.	10	Purchase	350 units @ $42/unit	
Mar.	13	Purchase	200 units @ $29/unit	
Mar.	15	Sales		600 units @ $75/unit
Aug.	21	Purchase	150 units @ $50/unit	
Sept.	5	Purchase	545 units @ $46/unit	
Sept.	10	Sales		650 units @ $75/unit
		Totals	1,845 units	1,250 units

Required

1. Compute cost of goods available for sale and the number of units available for sale.

2. Compute the number of units in ending inventory.

3. Compute the cost assigned to ending inventory using (a) FIFO, (b) LIFO, (c) specific identification— units sold consist of 500 units from beginning inventory, 300 from the February 10 purchase, 200 from the March 13 purchase, 50 from the August 21 purchase, and 200 from the September 5 purchase, and (d) weighted average—round per unit costs to tenth of a cent and inventory balances to the dollar.

4. Compute gross profit earned by the company for each of the four costing methods in part 3.

Check   (3) Ending inventory: FIFO, $27,570; LIFO, $27,000; WA, $26,422;

(4) LIFO gross profit, $40,680

Analysis Component

5. If the company's manager earns a bonus based on a percent of gross profit, which method of inventory costing will the manager likely prefer?

Problem 6-2A
Analysis of inventory errors

A2

mhhe.com/wildFAP18e

Navajo Company's financial statements report the following. Navajo recently discovered that in making physical counts of inventory, it had made the following errors: Inventory on December 31, 2007, is understated by $56,000, and inventory on December 31, 2008, is overstated by $20,000.

		For Year Ended December 31		
Key Figures		**2007**	**2008**	**2009**
(a)	Cost of goods sold	$ 615,000	$ 957,000	$ 780,000
(b)	Net income	230,000	285,000	241,000
(c)	Total current assets	1,255,000	1,365,000	1,200,000
(d)	Total equity	1,387,000	1,530,000	1,242,000

Required

1. For each key financial statement figure—(a), (b), (c), and (d) above—prepare a table similar to the following to show the adjustments necessary to correct the reported amounts.

Figure: _____	**2007**	**2008**	**2009**
Reported amount			
Adjustments for: 12/31/2007 error			
12/31/2008 error			
Corrected amount			

Check (1) Corrected net income: 2007, $286,000; 2008, $209,000; 2009, $261,000

Analysis Component

2. What is the error in total net income for the combined three-year period resulting from the inventory errors? Explain.

3. Explain why the understatement of inventory by $56,000 at the end of 2007 results in an understatement of equity by the same amount in that year.

Problem 6-3A
Lower of cost or market

P2

A physical inventory of Liverpool Unlimited taken at December 31 reveals the following.

File Edit View Insert Format Tools Data Accounting Window Help

			Per Unit	
	Item	**Units**	**Cost**	**Market**
3	Audio equipment			
4	Receivers	345	$ 90	$ 98
5	CD players	260	111	100
6	MP3 players	326	86	95
7	Speakers	204	52	41
8	Video equipment			
9	Handheld LCDs	480	150	125
10	VCRs	291	93	84
11	Camcorders	212	310	322
12	Car audio equipment			
13	Satellite radios	185	70	84
14	CD/MP3 radios	170	97	105

Sheet1 / Sheet2 / Sheet3 /

Required

Calculate the lower of cost or market for the inventory (a) as a whole, (b) by major category, and (c) applied separately to each item.

Check (b) $280,702; (c) $273,054

Seminole Company began year 2008 with 25,000 units of product in its January 1 inventory costing $15 each. It made successive purchases of its product in year 2008 as follows. The company uses a periodic inventory system. On December 31, 2008, a physical count reveals that 40,000 units of its product remain in inventory.

Problem 6-4A[A]

Alternative cost flows—periodic

P3

Mar. 7	30,000 units @ $18 each
May 25	32,000 units @ $22 each
Aug. 1	22,000 units @ $24 each
Nov. 10	35,000 units @ $27 each

Required

1. Compute the number and total cost of the units available for sale in year 2008.

2. Compute the amounts assigned to the 2008 ending inventory and the cost of goods sold using (*a*) FIFO, (*b*) LIFO, and (*c*) weighted average.

Check (2) Cost of goods sold: FIFO, $2,027,000; LIFO, $2,447,000; WA, $2,233,111

QP Corp. sold 6,500 units of its product at $50 per unit in year 2008 and incurred operating expenses of $5 per unit in selling the units. It began the year with 700 units in inventory and made successive purchases of its product as follows.

Problem 6-5A[A]

Income comparisons and cost flows—periodic

A1 P3

Jan. 1	Beginning inventory	700 units @ $18 per unit
Feb. 20	Purchase	1,600 units @ $19 per unit
May 16	Purchase	800 units @ $20 per unit
Oct. 3	Purchase	500 units @ $21 per unit
Dec. 11	Purchase	3,500 units @ $22 per unit
	Total	7,100 units

Required

1. Prepare comparative income statements similar to Exhibit 6.8 for the three inventory costing methods of FIFO, LIFO, and weighted average. Include a detailed cost of goods sold section as part of each statement. The company uses a periodic inventory system, and its income tax rate is 30%.

2. How would the financial results from using the three alternative inventory costing methods change if QP had been experiencing declining costs in its purchases of inventory?

3. What advantages and disadvantages are offered by using (*a*) LIFO and (*b*) FIFO? Assume the continuing trend of increasing costs.

Check (1) Net income: LIFO, $109,760; FIFO, $111,440; WA, $110,866

The records of Alaska Company provide the following information for the year ended December 31:

Problem 6-6A[B]

Retail inventory method

P4

mhhe.com/wildFAP18e

	At Cost	At Retail
January 1 beginning inventory	$ 469,010	$ 928,950
Cost of goods purchased	3,376,050	6,381,050
Sales		5,595,800
Sales returns		42,800

Required

1. Use the retail inventory method to estimate the company's year-end inventory at cost.

2. A year-end physical inventory at retail prices yields a total inventory of $1,686,900. Prepare a calculation showing the company's loss from shrinkage at cost and at retail.

Check (1) Inventory, $924,182 cost; (2) Inventory shortage at cost, $36,873

Wayward Company wants to prepare interim financial statements for the first quarter. The company wishes to avoid making a physical count of inventory. Wayward's gross profit rate averages 34%. The following information for the first quarter is available from its records.

Problem 6-7A[B]

Gross profit method

P4

January 1 beginning inventory	$ 302,580
Cost of goods purchased	941,040
Sales	1,211,160
Sales returns	8,398

Required

Use the gross profit method to estimate the company's first-quarter ending inventory.

PROBLEM SET B

Problem 6-1B
Alternative cost flows—perpetual

P1

Aloha Company uses a perpetual inventory system. It entered into the following calendar-year 2008 purchases and sales transactions.

Date	Activities	Units Acquired at Cost	Units Sold at Retail
Jan. 1	Beginning inventory	700 units @ $55/unit	
Jan. 10	Purchase	550 units @ $56/unit	
Feb. 13	Purchase	220 units @ $57/unit	
Feb. 15	Sales		900 units @ $90/unit
July 21	Purchase	270 units @ $58/unit	
Aug. 5	Purchase	445 units @ $59/unit	
Aug. 10	Sales		750 units @ $90/unit
	Total	2,185 units	1,650 units

Required

1. Compute cost of goods available for sale and the number of units available for sale.

2. Compute the number of units in ending inventory.

3. Compute the cost assigned to ending inventory using (*a*) FIFO, (*b*) LIFO, (*c*) specific identification—units sold consist of 700 units from beginning inventory, 500 units from the January 10 purchase, 220 units from the February 13 purchase, 200 units from the July 21 purchase, and 30 units from the August 5 purchase, and (*d*) weighted average—round per unit costs to tenth of a cent and inventory balances to the dollar.

4. Compute gross profit earned by the company for each of the four costing methods in part 3.

Analysis Component

5. If the company's manager earns a bonus based on a percent of gross profit, which method of inventory costing will the manager likely prefer?

Problem 6-2B
Analysis of inventory errors

A2

Hallam Company's financial statements report the following. Hallam recently discovered that in making physical counts of inventory, it had made the following errors: Inventory on December 31, 2007, is overstated by $18,000, and inventory on December 31, 2008, is understated by $26,000.

		For Year Ended December 31		
Key Figures		**2007**	**2008**	**2009**
(*a*)	Cost of goods sold	$207,200	$213,800	$197,030
(*b*)	Net income	175,800	212,270	184,910
(*c*)	Total current assets	276,000	277,500	272,950
(*d*)	Total equity	314,000	315,000	346,000

Required

1. For each key financial statement figure—(*a*), (*b*), (*c*), and (*d*) above—prepare a table similar to the following to show the adjustments necessary to correct the reported amounts.

Figure: _____	2007	2008	2009
Reported amount	_____	_____	_____
Adjustments for: 12/31/2007 error	_____	_____	_____
12/31/2008 error	_____	_____	_____
Corrected amount	_____	_____	_____

Analysis Component

2. What is the error in total net income for the combined three-year period resulting from the inventory errors? Explain.

3. Explain why the overstatement of inventory by $18,000 at the end of 2007 results in an overstatement of equity by the same amount in that year.

A physical inventory of Office Necessities taken at December 31 reveals the following.

Problem 6-3B
Lower of cost or market
P2

Item	Units	Cost	Market
		Per Unit	
Office furniture			
Desks	536	$261	$305
Credenzas	395	227	256
Chairs	687	49	43
Bookshelves	421	93	82
Filing cabinets			
Two-drawer	114	81	70
Four-drawer	298	135	122
Lateral	75	104	118
Office equipment			
Fax machines	370	168	200
Copiers	475	317	288
Telephones	302	125	117

Required

Compute the lower of cost or market for the inventory (*a*) as a whole, (*b*) by major category, and (*c*) applied separately to each item.

Check (b) $601,697; (c) $580,054

Seneca Co. began year 2008 with 6,500 units of product in its January 1 inventory costing $35 each. It made successive purchases of its product in year 2008 as follows. The company uses a periodic inventory system. On December 31, 2008, a physical count reveals that 18,500 units of its product remain in inventory.

Problem 6-4B[A]
Alternative cost flows—periodic
P3

Jan. 4	....	11,500 units @ $33 each
May 18	....	13,400 units @ $32 each
July 9	....	11,000 units @ $29 each
Nov. 21	....	16,500 units @ $26 each

Required

1. Compute the number and total cost of the units available for sale in year 2008.

2. Compute the amounts assigned to the 2008 ending inventory and the cost of goods sold using (*a*) FIFO, (*b*) LIFO, and (*c*) weighted average.

Check (2) Cost of goods sold: FIFO, $1,296,800; LIFO, $1,160,800; WA, $1,223,523

Shepard Company sold 2,000 units of its product at $108 per unit in year 2008 and incurred operating expenses of $14 per unit in selling the units. It began the year with 840 units in inventory and made successive purchases of its product as follows.

Problem 6-5B[A]
Income comparisons and cost flows—periodic
A1 P3

Jan. 1	Beginning inventory	840 units @ $58 per unit
April 2	Purchase	600 units @ $59 per unit
June 14	Purchase	500 units @ $61 per unit
Aug. 29	Purchase	700 units @ $64 per unit
Nov. 18	Purchase	900 units @ $65 per unit
	Total	3,540 units

Required

1. Prepare comparative income statements similar to Exhibit 6.8 for the three inventory costing methods of FIFO, LIFO, and weighted average. Include a detailed cost of goods sold section as part of each statement. The company uses a periodic inventory system, and its income tax rate is 30%.

2. How would the financial results from using the three alternative inventory costing methods change if Shepard had been experiencing decreasing prices in its purchases of inventory?

3. What advantages and disadvantages are offered by using (*a*) LIFO and (*b*) FIFO? Assume the continuing trend of increasing costs.

Problem 6-6B[B]
Retail inventory method

P4

The records of Macklin Co. provide the following information for the year ended December 31.

	At Cost	At Retail
January 1 beginning inventory	$ 90,022	$115,610
Cost of goods purchased	502,250	761,830
Sales		782,300
Sales returns		3,460

Required

1. Use the retail inventory method to estimate the company's year-end inventory.

2. A year-end physical inventory at retail prices yields a total inventory of $80,450. Prepare a calculation showing the company's loss from shrinkage at cost and at retail.

Problem 6-7B[B]
Gross profit method

P4

Otingo Equipment Co. wants to prepare interim financial statements for the first quarter. The company wishes to avoid making a physical count of inventory. Otingo's gross profit rate averages 35%. The following information for the first quarter is available from its records.

January 1 beginning inventory	$ 802,880
Cost of goods purchased	2,209,630
Sales	3,760,250
Sales returns	79,300

Required

Use the gross profit method to estimate the company's first quarter ending inventory.

PROBLEM SET C

Problem Set C is available at the book's Website to further reinforce and assess your learning.

SERIAL PROBLEM

(This serial problem began in Chapter 1 and continues through most of the book. If previous chapter segments were not completed, the serial problem can begin at this point.)

Success Systems

SP 6
Part A

Adriana Lopez of Success Systems is evaluating her inventory to determine whether it must be adjusted based on lower of cost or market rules. Lopez has three different types of software in her inventory and the following information is available for each.

		Per Unit	
Inventory Items	Units	Cost	Market
Office productivity	3	$ 75	$73
Desktop publishing	2	100	98
Accounting	3	85	90

Required

1. Compute the lower of cost or market for ending inventory assuming Lopez applies the lower of cost or market rule to inventory as a whole. Must Lopez adjust the reported inventory value? Explain.

2. Assume that Lopez had instead applied the lower of cost or market rule to each product in inventory. Under this assumption, must Lopez adjust the reported inventory value? Explain.

Part B

Selected accounts and balances for the three months ended March 31, 2008, for Success Systems follows.

January 1 beginning inventory	$ 0
Cost of goods sold	14,272
March 31 ending inventory	680

Required

1. Compute inventory turnover and days' sales in inventory for the three months ended March 31, 2008.

2. Assess its performance if competitors average 10 times for inventory turnover and 29 days for days' sales in inventory.

BEYOND THE NUMBERS

BTN 6-1   Refer to **Best Buy**'s financial statements in Appendix A to answer the following.

REPORTING IN ACTION

C2   A3

Required

1. What amount of inventories did Best Buy hold as a current asset on February 26, 2005? On February 28, 2004?

2. Inventories represent what percent of total assets on February 26, 2005? On February 28, 2004?

3. Comment on the relative size of Best Buy's inventories compared to its other types of assets.

4. What accounting method did Best Buy use to compute inventory amounts on its balance sheet?

5. Compute inventory turnover for fiscal year ended February 26, 2005, and days' sales in inventory as of February 26, 2005.

Fast Forward

6. Access Best Buy's financial statements for fiscal years ended after February 26, 2005, from its Website (BestBuy.com) or the SEC's EDGAR database (www.sec.gov). Answer questions 1 through 5 using the current Best Buy information and compare results to those prior years.

BTN 6-2   Key comparative figures ($ millions) for both **Best Buy** and **Circuit City** follow.

COMPARATIVE ANALYSIS

A3

	Best Buy			Circuit City		
Key Figures	**Current Year**	**One Year Prior**	**Two Years Prior**	**Current Year**	**One Year Prior**	**Two Years Prior**
Inventory	$ 2,851	$ 2,607	$ 2,077	$1,460	$1,517	$1,410
Cost of sales	20,938	18,677	15,998	7,904	7,573	7,648

Required

1. Compute inventory turnover for both companies for the most recent two years shown.

2. Compute days' sales in inventory for both companies for the three years shown.

3. Comment on and interpret your findings from parts 1 and 2. Assume an industry average for inventory turnover of 5.5.

ETHICS CHALLENGE

A1

BTN 6-3   Golf Challenge Corp. is a retail sports store carrying golf apparel and equipment. The store is at the end of its second year of operation and is struggling. A major problem is that its cost of inventory has continually increased in the past two years. In the first year of operations, the store assigned inventory costs using LIFO. A loan agreement the store has with its bank, its prime source of financing, requires the store to maintain a certain profit margin and current ratio. The store's owner is currently looking over Golf Challenge's preliminary financial statements for its second year. The numbers are not favorable. The only way the store can meet the required financial ratios agreed on with the bank is to change from LIFO to FIFO. The store originally decided on LIFO because of its tax advantages. The owner recalculates ending inventory using FIFO and submits those numbers and statements to the loan officer at the bank for the required bank review. The owner thankfully reflects on the available latitude in choosing the inventory costing method.

Required

1. How does Golf Challenge's use of FIFO improve its net profit margin and current ratio?
2. Is the action by Golf Challenge's owner ethical? Explain.

COMMUNICATING IN PRACTICE

A1

BTN 6-4   You are a financial adviser with a client in the wholesale produce business that just completed its first year of operations. Due to weather conditions, the cost of acquiring produce to resell has escalated during the later part of this period. Your client, Javonte Gish, mentions that because her business sells perishable goods, she has striven to maintain a FIFO flow of goods. Although sales are good, the increasing cost of inventory has put the business in a tight cash position. Gish has expressed concern regarding the ability of the business to meet income tax obligations.

Required

Prepare a memorandum that identifies, explains, and justifies the inventory method you recommend your client, Ms. Gish, adopt.

TAKING IT TO THE NET

A3

BTN 6-5   Access the 2004 annual 10-K report for **Oakley, Inc.** (Ticker OO), filed on March 16, 2005, from the EDGAR filings at www.sec.gov.

Required

1. What product does Oakley sell that is especially popular with college students?
2. What inventory method does Oakley use? (*Hint:* See the notes to its financial statements.)
3. Compute Oakley's gross margin and gross margin ratio for the 2004 calendar year. Comment on your computations—assume an industry average of 35% for the gross margin ratio.
4. Compute Oakley's inventory turnover and days' sales in inventory for the year ended December 31, 2004. Comment on your computations—assume an industry average of 3.9 for inventory turnover.

TEAMWORK IN ACTION

A1 P1

Point: Step 1 allows four choices or areas for expertise. Larger teams will have some duplication of choice, but the specific identification method should not be duplicated.

BTN 6-6   Each team member has the responsibility to become an expert on an inventory method. This expertise will be used to facilitate teammates' understanding of the concepts relevant to that method.

1. Each learning team member should select an area for expertise by choosing one of the following inventory methods: specific identification, LIFO, FIFO, or weighted average.
2. Form expert teams made up of students who have selected the same area of expertise. The instructor will identify where each expert team will meet.
3. Using the following data, each expert team must collaborate to develop a presentation that illustrates the relevant concepts and procedures for its inventory method. Each team member must write the presentation in a format that can be shown to the learning team.

Data

Wiseman Company uses a perpetual inventory system. It had the following beginning inventory and current year purchases of its product.

Jan.	1	Beginning inventory	50 units @ $100 =	$ 5,000
Jan.	14	Purchase	150 units @ $120 =	18,000
Apr.	30	Purchase	200 units @ $150 =	30,000
Sept.	26	Purchase	300 units @ $200 =	60,000

Wiseman Company transacted sales on the following dates at a $350 per unit sales price.

Jan.	10	30 units	(specific cost: 30 @ $100)
Feb.	15	100 units	(specific cost: 100 @ $120)
Oct.	5	350 units	(specific cost: 100 @ $150 and 250 @ $200)

Concepts and Procedures to Illustrate in Expert Presentation

a. Identify and compute the costs to assign to the units sold. (Round unit costs to the tenth of a cent.)

b. Identify and compute the costs to assign to the units in ending inventory.

c. How likely is it that this inventory costing method will reflect the actual physical flow of goods? How relevant is that factor in determining whether this is an acceptable method to use?

d. What is the impact of this method versus others in determining net income and income taxes?

e. How closely does the ending inventory amount reflect replacement cost?

4. Re-form learning teams. In rotation, each expert is to present to the team the presentation developed in part 3. Experts are to encourage and respond to questions.

BusinessWeek ACTIVITY

A3

BTN 6-7   Read the article "A Surprise in Office Depot's In-Box?" in the October 25, 2004, issue of *BusinessWeek*. A friend has also read the article and is puzzled by the paragraph that deals with **Office Depot**'s inventory management. Your friend comments: "I thought having inventory was a good thing. You can't sell products to customers unless you have merchandise. Why is Office Depot's increasing inventory turnover a good thing? Don't they run the risk of running out of merchandise to sell and disappointing customers?"

Required

Prepare written responses to your friend's questions.

ENTREPRENEURIAL DECISION

A3

BTN 6-8   Review the chapter's opening feature highlighting Izzy and Coco Tihanyi and their company, **Surf Diva**. Assume that Surf Diva consistently maintains an inventory level of $300,000, meaning that its average and ending inventory levels are the same. Also assume its annual cost of sales is $1,200,000. To cut costs, Izzy and Coco propose to slash inventory to a constant level of $150,000 with no impact on cost of sales. They plan to work with suppliers to get quicker deliveries and to order smaller quantities more often.

Required

1. Compute the company's inventory turnover and its days' sales in inventory under (*a*) current conditions and (*b*) proposed conditions.

2. Evaluate and comment on the merits of Izzy and Coco's proposal given your analysis in part 1. Identify any concerns you might have about the proposal.

HITTING THE ROAD

C1 C2

BTN 6-9   Visit four retail stores with another classmate. In each store, identify whether the store uses a bar-coding system to help manage its inventory. Try to find at least one store that does not use bar-coding. If a store does not use bar-coding, ask the store's manager or clerk whether he or she knows which type of inventory method the store employs. Create a table that shows columns for the name of store visited, type of merchandise sold, use or nonuse of bar-coding, and the inventory method used if bar-coding is not employed. You might also inquire as to what the store's inventory turnover is and how often physical inventory is taken.

GLOBAL DECISION

A3

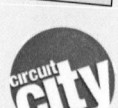

BTN 6-10   Key figures (£ millions) for Dixons (Dixons-Group.com) follow.

Key Figures	Current Year	One Year Prior	Two Years Prior
Inventory*	777.1	699.9	615.7
Cost of sales	5,777.0	5,108.6	4,303.1

* Titled "stock" in Dixons' reports and excludes properties held for development or resale.

Required

1. Use these data and those from BTN 6-2 to compute (a) inventory turnover and (b) days' sales in inventory for the most recent two years shown for Dixons, Best Buy, and Circuit City.
2. Comment on and interpret your findings from part 1.

ANSWERS TO MULTIPLE CHOICE QUIZ

1. a; FIFO perpetual

Date	Goods Purchased	Cost of Goods Sold	Inventory Balance
July 1			75 units @ $25 = $ 1,875
July 3	348 units @ $27 = $9,396		75 units @ $25 } 348 units @ $27 } = $ 11,271
July 8		75 units @ $25 } 225 units @ $27 } = $ 7,950	123 units @ $27 = $ 3,321
July 15	257 units @ $28 = $7,196		123 units @ $27 } 257 units @ $28 } = $ 10,517
July 23		123 units @ $27 } 152 units @ $28 } = $ 7,577	105 units @ $28 = $ 2,940
		$15,527	

2. b; LIFO perpetual

Date	Goods Purchased	Cost of Goods Sold	Inventory Balance
July 1			75 units @ $25 = $ 1,875
July 3	348 units @ $27 = $9,396		75 units @ $25 } 348 units @ $27 } = $ 11,271
July 8		300 units @ $27 = $ 8,100	75 units @ $25 } 48 units @ $27 } = $ 3,171
July 15	257 units @ $28 = $7,196		75 units @ $25 } 48 units @ $27 } 257 units @ $28 } = $ 10,367
July 23		257 units @ $28 } 18 units @ $27 } = $ 7,682	75 units @ $25 } 30 units @ $27 } = $ 2,685
		$15,782	

3. e; Specific identification perpetual—Ending inventory computation.

20 units @ $25	$ 500	
40 units @ $27	1,080	
45 units @ $28	1,260	
105 units	$2,840	

4. a; FIFO periodic—Ending inventory computation.

105 units @ $28 each = $2,940; The FIFO periodic inventory computation is identical to the FIFO perpetual inventory computation (see question 1).

5. d; Days' sales in inventory = (Ending inventory/Cost of goods sold × 365)

= ($18,000/$85,000) × 365 = 77.29 days

7

Accounting Information Systems

A Look Back

Chapters 5 and 6 focused on merchandising activities and accounting for inventory. We explained inventory systems, accounting for inventory transactions, and methods for assigning costs to inventory.

A Look at This Chapter

This chapter emphasizes accounting information systems. We describe fundamental system principles, the system's components, use of special journals and subsidiary ledgers, and technology-based systems.

A Look Ahead

Chapter 8 focuses on internal controls and accounting for cash and cash equivalents. We explain good internal control procedures and their importance.

Learning Objectives

CAP

Conceptual

C1 Identify fundamental principles of accounting information systems. (p. 266)

C2 Identify components of accounting information systems. (p. 267)

C3 Explain the goals and uses of special journals. (p. 269)

C4 Describe the use of controlling accounts and subsidiary ledgers. (p. 270)

C5 Explain how technology-based information systems impact accounting. (p. 280)

Analytical

A1 Compute segment return on assets and use it to evaluate segment performance. (p. 282)

Procedural

P1 Journalize and post transactions using special journals. (p. 271)

P2 Prepare and prove the accuracy of subsidiary ledgers. (p. 273)

P3 *Appendix 7A*—Journalize and post transactions using special journals in a periodic inventory system. (p. 286)

Decision Feature

Master of the Rings

MASSILLON, OH—Tony Lee dreamed of attending college and one day owning a business. But he set his dream aside to join the Army and serve in the Gulf War fresh out of high school. Soon after Tony returned home, he and his girlfriend had a baby girl and Tony needed a job. He found work as a janitor at Eaton Corporation, a manufacturer of steel rings.

While cleaning restrooms and sweeping floors, Tony hoped a machine job would come his way at Eaton. After one year, Tony got a chance to run a machine making steel rings. But Tony's determination drove him to learn how to operate every machine in the factory. Afterward, he set his sights on handling customer complaints, buying raw materials, and preparing and interpreting accounting reports.

Tony still dreamed of attending college but could not afford it. So he instead spent many nights studying accounting at the local library. He learned how accounting tracks business activities. He learned about internal controls, special journals, accounting ledgers, and systems technology. And he read biographies of Warren Buffet and Jack Welch.

When Eaton announced its closing in 2003, Tony wasted no time. Using his knowledge of factory operations and accounting, he prepared a buyout proposal. He projected accounting results and identified changes necessary for the company to survive. Tony then wrote a detailed business plan, analyzed competitors, and arranged for potential financing. Tony even sold his beloved motorcycle and took a second mortgage on his family's home to resuscitate the company. Within two months, Tony and six other investors owned the ring manufacturer—renamed **Ring Masters (Ring-Masters.net).** Says one investor, "Tony knew the product, knew the customer, and had a tremendous amount of loyalty from the employees."

Today, Ring Masters produces over 200,000 steel rings every day. Sales are up nearly 20% to around $3 million annually, and Tony hopes to double that within five years. Tony Lee is truly "Master of the Rings."

[Sources: *Ring Masters Website,* January 2006, *Stark Development Board Website,* July 2005, *The Plain Dealer,* July 2005, *Inc.,* April 2005]

With increases in the number and complexity of business activities, the demands placed on accounting information systems increase. Accounting information systems must meet this challenge in an efficient and effective manner. In this chapter, we learn about fundamental principles guiding information systems, and we study components making up these systems. We also explain procedures that use special journals and subsidiary ledgers to make accounting information systems more efficient. An understanding of the details of accounting reports makes us better decision makers when using financial information, and it improves our ability to analyze and interpret financial statements.

Accounting Information Systems

System Principles	System Components	Special Journals	System Technology
• Control • Relevance • Compatibility • Flexibility • Cost-Benefit	• Source documents • Input devices • Processors • Storage • Output devices	• Subsidiary ledgers • Sales journal • Cash receipts journal • Purchases journal • Cash disbursements journal	• Computers • Data processing • Networks • Enterprise resource planning (ERP)

Fundamental System Principles

C1 Identify fundamental principles of accounting information systems.

Accounting information systems collect and process data from transactions and events, organize them in useful reports, and communicate results to decision makers. With the increasing complexity of business and the growing need for information, accounting information systems are more important than ever. All decision makers need to have a basic knowledge of how accounting information systems work. This knowledge gives decision makers a competitive edge as they gain a better understanding of information constraints, measurement limitations, and potential applications. It allows them to make more informed decisions and to better balance the risks and returns of different strategies. This section explains five basic principles of accounting information systems, shown in Exhibit 7.1.

Exhibit 7.1

System Principles

Control
Cost-Benefit Principle
System Principles
Relevance
Flexibility
Compatibility

Control Principle

Managers need to control and monitor business activities. The **control principle** prescribes that an accounting information system have internal controls. **Internal controls** are methods and procedures allowing managers to control and monitor business activities. They include policies to direct operations toward common goals, procedures to ensure reliable financial reports, safeguards to protect company assets, and methods to achieve compliance with laws and regulations.

Point: A hacker stole 300,000 credit card numbers from online music retailer CDUniverse due to internal control failure.

Relevance Principle

Decision makers need relevant information to make informed decisions. The **relevance principle** prescribes that an accounting information system report useful, understandable, timely, and pertinent information for effective decision making. The system must be designed to capture data that make a difference in decisions. To ensure this, we must consider all decision makers when identifying relevant information for disclosure.

Compatibility Principle

Accounting information systems must be consistent with the aims of a company. The **compatibility principle** prescribes that an accounting information system conform with a company's activities, personnel, and structure. It also must adapt to a company's unique characteristics. The system must not be intrusive but must work in harmony with and be driven by company goals. Most start-up entrepreneurs require only a simple information system. Harley-Davidson, on the other hand, demands both a merchandising and a manufacturing information system able to assemble data from its global operations.

> **Decision Insight**
>
> **Digital Is Forever** E-communications have helped bring down many employees, including the CEO of Boeing. To comply with Sarbanes-Oxley, more and more companies now archive and monitor e-mails, instant messages, blog postings, and Net-based phone calls. Using natural-language software, companies sift through digital communications in milliseconds, checking for trade secrets, bad language, porn, and pirated files.

Flexibility Principle

Accounting information systems must be able to adjust to changes. The **flexibility principle** prescribes that an accounting information system be able to adapt to changes in the company, business environment, and needs of decisions makers. Technological advances, competitive pressures, consumer tastes, regulations, and company activities constantly evolve. A system must be designed to adapt to these changes.

Cost-Benefit Principle

The **cost-benefit principle** prescribes that the benefits from an activity in an accounting information system outweigh the costs of that activity. The costs and benefits of an activity such as producing a specific report will impact the decisions of both external and internal users. Decisions regarding other systems principles (control, relevance, compatibility, and flexibility) are also affected by the cost-benefit principle.

Point: Law requires that *all* employers destroy credit-check and other employee records *before* tossing them. A cross-cut shredder is the tool of choice.

Components of Accounting Systems

Accounting information systems consist of people, records, methods, and equipment. The systems are designed to capture information about a company's transactions and to provide output including financial, managerial, and tax reports. All accounting information systems have these same goals, and thus share some basic components. These components apply whether or not a system is heavily computerized, yet the components of computerized systems usually provide more accuracy, speed, efficiency, and convenience than those of manual systems.

The five basic **components of accounting systems** are source documents, input devices, information processors, information storage, and output devices. Exhibit 7.2 shows these components as a series of steps, yet we know that much two-way communication occurs between many of these components. We briefly describe each of these key components in this section.

C2   Identify components of accounting information systems.

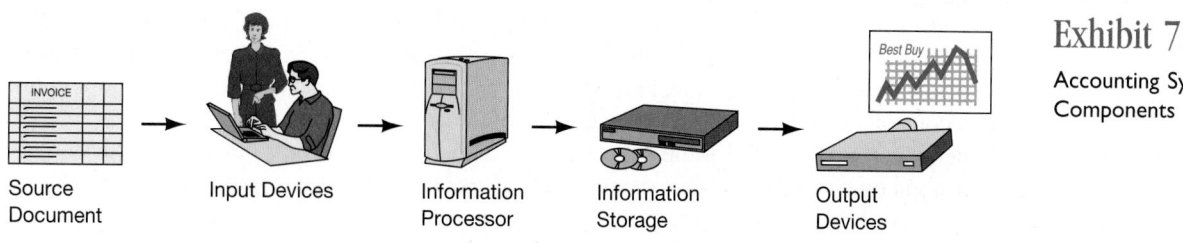

Source Document   Input Devices   Information Processor   Information Storage   Output Devices

Exhibit 7.2

Accounting System Components

Source Documents

We introduced source documents in Chapters 1 and 2 and explained their importance for both business transactions and information collection. Source documents provide the basic information processed by an accounting system. Examples of source documents include bank statements and checks, invoices from suppliers, billings to customers, cash register files, and employee earnings records. Source documents can be paper, although they increasingly are taking the form of electronic files and Web communications. A growing number of companies are sending documents directly from their systems to their customers' and suppliers' systems. The Web is playing a major role in this transformation from paper-based to *paperless* systems.

Accurate source documents are crucial to accounting information systems. Input of faulty or incomplete information seriously impairs the reliability and relevance of the information system. We commonly refer to this as "garbage in, garbage out." Information systems are set up with attention on control procedures to limit the possibility of entering faulty data in the system.

Input Devices

Point: Understanding a manual accounting system is useful in understanding an electronic system.

Input devices capture information from source documents and enable its transfer to the system's information processing component. These devices often involve converting data on source documents from written or electronic form to a form usable for the system. Journal entries, both electronic and paper based, are a type of input device. Keyboards, scanners, and modems are some of the most common input devices in practice today. For example, bar code readers capture code numbers and transfer them to the organization's computer for processing. Moreover, a scanner can capture writing samples and other input directly from source documents.

Controls are used to ensure that only authorized individuals input data to the system. Controls increase the system's reliability and allow information to be traced back to its source.

Information Processors

Point: *BusinessWeek* (2005) reports that 75% of all e-mail traffic in the past year was spam.

Information processors are systems that interpret, transform, and summarize information for use in analysis and reporting. An important part of an information processor in accounting systems is professional judgment. Accounting principles are never so structured that they limit the need for professional judgment. Other parts of an information processor include journals, ledgers, working papers, and posting procedures. Each assists in transforming raw data to useful information.

Increasingly, computer technology (both computing hardware and software) is assisting manual information processors. This assistance is freeing accounting professionals to take on increased analysis, interpretive, and managerial roles. Web-based application service providers (ASPs) offer another type of information processor.

Information Storage

Point: A financial accounting database can be designed to support a wide range of internal reports for management.

Information storage is the accounting system component that keeps data in a form accessible to information processors. After being input and processed, data are stored for use in future analyses and reports. The database must be accessible to preparers of periodic financial reports. Auditors rely on this database when they audit both financial statements and a company's controls. Companies also maintain files of source documents.

Older systems consisted almost exclusively of paper documents, but most modern systems depend on electronic storage devices. Advances in information storage enable accounting systems to increasingly store more detailed data. This means managers have more data to access and work with in planning and controlling business activities. Note that information storage can be online, meaning that data can be accessed whenever, and from wherever, it is needed. Offline storage means access often requires assistance and authorization. Information storage is increasingly augmented by Web sources such as SEC databases, benchmarking services, and financial and product markets.

Output Devices

Output devices are the means to take information out of an accounting system and make it available to users. Common output devices are printers, monitors, LCD projectors, and Web communications. Output devices provide users a variety of items including graphics, analysis reports, bills to customers, checks to suppliers, employee paychecks, financial statements, and internal reports. When requests for output occur, an information processor takes the needed data from a database and prepares the necessary report, which is then sent to an output device.

A special type of output is an electronic funds transfer (EFT). One example is the transfer of payroll from the company's bank account to its employees' bank accounts. This requires an interface to allow a company's accounting system to send payroll data directly to the bank's accounting system. This interface can involve a company recording its payroll data on CD and forwarding it to the bank. The bank then uses this output to transfer wages earned to employees' accounts.

Quick Check Answers—pp. 291–292

1. Identify the five primary components of an accounting information system.
2. What is the aim of information processors in an accounting system?
3. How are data in the information storage component of an accounting system used?

Special Journals in Accounting

This section describes the underlying records of accounting information systems. Designed correctly, these records support efficiency in processing transactions and events. They are part of all systems in various forms and are increasingly electronic. Even in technologically advanced systems, a basic understanding of the records we describe in this section aids in using, interpreting, and applying accounting information. It also improves our knowledge of computer-based systems. Remember that all accounting systems have common purposes and internal workings whether or not they depend on technology.

This section focuses on special journals and subsidiary ledgers that are an important part of accounting systems. We describe how special journals are used to capture transactions, and we explain how subsidiary ledgers are set up to capture details of accounts. This section uses a *perpetual* inventory system, and the special journals are set up using this system. Appendix 7A describes the change in special journals required for a *periodic* system. We also include a note at the bottom of each of the special journals explaining the change required if a company uses a periodic system.

C3 Explain the goals and uses of special journals.

Basics of Special Journals

A **general journal** is an all-purpose journal in which we can record any transaction. Use of a general journal for all transactions is usually more costly for a business *and* is a less effective control procedure. Moreover, for less technologically advanced systems, use of a general journal requires that each debit and each credit entered be individually posted to its respective ledger account. To enhance internal control and reduce costs, transactions are organized into common groups. A **special journal** is used to record and post transactions of similar type. Most transactions of a merchandiser, for instance, can be categorized into the journals shown in Exhibit 7.3. This section assumes the use of these four special journals along with the general journal. The general journal continues to be used for transactions not covered by special journals and for adjusting, closing, and correcting entries. We show in the following discussion that special journals are *efficient tools in helping journalize and post transactions.* This is done, for instance, by accumulating debits and credits of similar transactions, which allows posting of amounts as column *totals* rather than as individual amounts. The advantage of this system increases as the number of transactions increases. Special journals allow an *efficient division of labor,* which is also an effective control procedure.

Exhibit 7.3

Using Special Journals with a General Journal

   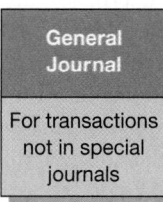

It is important to note that special journals and subsidiary ledgers *are designed in a manner that is best suited for each business.* The most likely candidates for special journal status are recurring transactions—for many businesses those are sales, cash receipts, purchases, and cash disbursements. However, good systems design for a business could involve collapsing sales and cash receipts in one journal, or purchases and cash disbursement in another. It could also involve adding more special journals or additional subsidiary ledgers for other recurring transactions. This design decision extends to journal and ledger format. That is, the selection on number of columns, column headings, and so forth is based on what is best suited for each business. Thus, read the following sections as one example of a common systems design, but not the only design.

Subsidiary Ledgers

To understand special journals, it is necessary to understand the workings of a **subsidiary ledger,** which is a list of individual accounts with a common characteristic. A subsidiary ledger contains detailed information on specific accounts in the general ledger. Information systems often include several subsidiary ledgers. Two of the most important are:

■ *Accounts receivable ledger*—stores transaction data of individual customers.
■ *Accounts payable ledger*—stores transaction data of individual suppliers.

Individual accounts in subsidiary ledgers are often arranged alphabetically, which is the approach taken here. We describe accounts receivable and accounts payable ledgers in this section. Our discussion of special journals uses these ledgers.

Accounts Receivable Ledger　When we recorded credit sales in prior chapters, we debited (increased) Accounts Receivable. When a company has more than one credit customer, the accounts receivable records must show how much *each* customer purchased, paid, and has yet to pay. This information is collected by keeping a separate account receivable for each credit customer. A separate account for each customer *could* be kept in the general ledger with the other financial statement accounts, but this is uncommon. Instead, the general ledger usually has a single Accounts Receivable account, and a *subsidiary ledger* is set up to keep a separate account for each customer. This subsidiary ledger is called the **accounts receivable ledger** (also called *accounts receivable subsidiary ledger* or *customers ledger*), and it can exist in electronic or paper form.

Exhibit 7.4 shows the relation between the Accounts Receivable account and its individual accounts in the subsidiary ledger. After all items are posted, the balance in the Accounts Receivable account must equal the sum of all balances of its customers' accounts. The Accounts Receivable account is said to control the accounts receivable ledger and is called a **controlling account.** Since the accounts receivable ledger is a supplementary record controlled by an account in the general ledger, it is called a *subsidiary* ledger.

Point: When a general ledger account has a subsidiary ledger, any transaction that impacts one of them also impacts the other—some refer to this as *general and subsidiaries ledgers kept in tandem.*

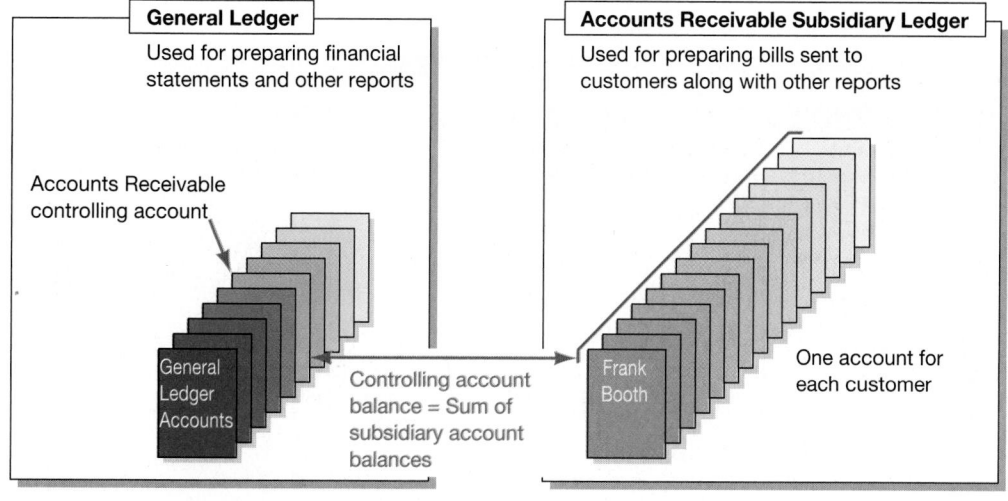

Exhibit 7.4

Accounts Receivable Controlling Account and Its Subsidiary Ledger

Accounts Payable Ledger   There are other controlling accounts and subsidiary ledgers. We know, for example, that many companies buy on credit from several suppliers. This means that companies must keep a separate account for each supplier by keeping an Accounts Payable controlling account in the general ledger and a separate account for each supplier (creditor) in an **accounts payable ledger** (also called *accounts payable subsidiary ledger* or *creditors ledger*).

Other Subsidiary Ledgers   Subsidiary ledgers are common for several other accounts. A company with many classes of equipment, for example, might keep only one Equipment account in its general ledger, but its Equipment account would control a subsidiary ledger in which each class of equipment is recorded in a separate account. Similar treatment is common for investments, inventory, and any accounts needing separate detailed records. Brunswick reports sales information by product line in its annual report. Yet its accounting system keeps much more detailed sales records. Brunswick, for instance, sells hundreds of different products and must be able to analyze the sales performance of each. This detail can be captured by many different general ledger sales accounts but is instead captured by using supplementary records that function like subsidiary ledgers. Overall, subsidiary ledgers are applied in many different ways to ensure that the accounting system captures sufficient details to support analyses that decision makers need.

Point: Subsidiary ledgers: (1) remove excessive details from general ledger, (2) provide up-to-date info on customer or other specific account balances, (3) aid in error identification for individual accounts, and (4) help with division of labor (recordkeeping tasks).

Sales Journal

A typical **sales journal** is used to record sales of inventory *on credit*. Sales of inventory for cash are not recorded in a sales journal but in a cash receipts journal. Sales of noninventory assets on credit are recorded in the general journal.

P1   Journalize and post transactions using special journals.

Topic Tackler

PLUS

7-2

Point: Each transaction in the sales journal includes a debit to accounts receivable and a credit to sales.

Journalizing Credit sale transactions are recorded with information about each sale entered separately in a sales journal. This information is often taken from a copy of the sales ticket or invoice prepared at the time of sale. The top portion of Exhibit 7.5 shows a typical sales journal from a merchandiser. It has columns for recording the date, customer's name, invoice number, posting reference, and the retail and cost amounts of each credit sale. The sales journal in this exhibit is called a **columnar journal,** which is any journal with more than one column.

Each transaction recorded in the sales journal yields an entry in the "Accounts Receivable Dr., Sales Cr." column. We usually need only one column for these two accounts. (An exception is when managers need more information about taxes, returns, and other sales details.) Each transaction in the sales journal also yields an entry in the "Cost of Goods Sold Dr., Inventory Cr." column. This entry reflects the perpetual inventory system of tracking costs with each sale. To illustrate, on February 2, this company sold merchandise on account to Jason

Exhibit 7.5

Sales Journal with Posting*

File Edit Maintain Tasks Analysis Options Reports Window Help

Sales Journal — Page 3

Date	Account Debited	Invoice Number	PR	Accounts Receivable Dr. Sales Cr.	Cost of Goods Sold Dr. Inventory Cr.
Feb. 2	Jason Henry	307	✓	450	315
7	Albert Co.	308	✓	500	355
13	Kam Moore	309	✓	350	260
15	Paul Roth	310	✓	200	150
22	Jason Henry	311	✓	225	155
25	Frank Booth	312	✓	175	95
28	Albert Co.	313	✓	250	170
28	Totals			2,150	1,500
				(106/413)	(502/119)

Totals are posted at the end of the period to General Ledger accounts.

Individual line item amounts in the Accounts Receivable Dr. and Sales Cr. column are posted immediately to the subsidiary ledger.

Customer accounts are in a subsidiary ledger and the financial statement accounts are in the General Ledger.

Accounts Receivable Ledger

Albert Co.

Date	PR	Debit	Credit	Balance
Feb. 7	S3	500		500
28	S3	250		750

Frank Booth

Date	PR	Debit	Credit	Balance
Feb. 25	S3	175		175

Jason Henry

Date	PR	Debit	Credit	Balance
Feb. 2	S3	450		450
22	S3	225		675

Kam Moore

Date	PR	Debit	Credit	Balance
Feb. 13	S3	350		350

Paul Roth

Date	PR	Debit	Credit	Balance
Feb. 15	S3	200		200

General Ledger

Accounts Receivable No. 106

Date	PR	Debit	Credit	Balance
Feb. 28	S3	2,150		2,150

Inventory No. 119

Date	PR	Debit	Credit	Balance
Feb. 1	bal.			15,700
28	S3		1,500	14,200

Sales No. 413

Date	PR	Debit	Credit	Balance
Feb. 28	S3		2,150	2,150

Cost of Goods Sold No. 502

Date	PR	Debit	Credit	Balance
Feb. 28	S3	1,500		1,500

Sales   Purchases   General Ledger   Payroll   Inventory   Company   Analysis

*The Sales Journal in a *periodic* system would exclude the column on the far right titled "Cost of Goods Sold Dr., Inventory Cr." (see Exhibit 7A.1).

Henry for $450. The invoice number is 307, and the cost of this merchandise is $315. This information is captured on one line in the sales journal. No further explanations or entries are necessary, saving time and effort. Moreover, this sales journal is consistent with most inventory systems that use bar codes to record both sales and costs with each sale transaction. Note that the Posting Reference (PR) column is not used when entering transactions but instead is used when posting.

Point: Continuously updated customer accounts provide timely information for customer inquiries on those accounts. Keeping creditor accounts updated provides timely information on current amounts owed.

Posting A sales journal is posted as reflected in the arrow lines of Exhibit 7.5. Two types of posting can be identified: (1) posting to the subsidiary ledger(s) and (2) posting to the general ledger.

Posting to subsidiary ledger. Individual transactions in the sales journal are posted regularly (typically concurrently) to customer accounts in the accounts receivable ledger. These postings keep customer accounts up-to-date, which is important for the person granting credit to customers. When sales recorded in the sales journal are individually posted to customer accounts in the accounts receivable ledger, check marks are entered in the sales journal's PR column. Check marks are used rather than account numbers because customer accounts usually are arranged alphabetically in the accounts receivable ledger. Note that posting debits to Accounts Receivable twice—once to Accounts Receivable and once to the customer's subsidiary account—does not violate the accounting equation of debits equal credits. The equality of debits and credits is always maintained in the general ledger.

Point: PR column is only checked *after* the amount(s) is posted.

Posting to general ledger. The sales journal's account columns are totaled at the end of each period (the month of February in this case). For the "sales" column, the $2,150 total is debited to Accounts Receivable and credited to Sales in the general ledger (see Exhibit 7.5). For the "cost" column, the $1,500 total is debited to Cost of Goods Sold and credited to Inventory in the general ledger. When totals are posted to accounts in the general ledger, the account numbers are entered below the column total in the sales journal for tracking. For example, we enter (106/413) below the total in the sales column after this amount is posted to account number 106 (Accounts Receivable) and account number 413 (Sales).

Point: Postings are automatic in a computerized system.

A company identifies in the PR column of its subsidiary ledgers the journal and page number from which an amount is taken. We identify a journal by using an initial. Items posted from the sales journal carry the initial **S** before their journal page numbers in a PR column. Likewise, items from the cash receipts journal carry the initial **R**; items from the cash disbursements journal carry the initial **D**; items from the purchases journal carry the initial **P**; and items from the general journal carry the initial **G**.

Proving the Ledgers Account balances in the general ledger and subsidiary ledgers are periodically proved (or reviewed) for accuracy after posting. To do this we first prepare a trial balance of the general ledger to confirm that debits equal credits. Second, we test a subsidiary ledger by preparing a *schedule* of individual accounts and amounts. A **schedule of accounts receivable** lists each customer and the balance owed. If this total equals the balance of the Accounts Receivable controlling account, the accounts in the accounts receivable ledger are assumed correct. Exhibit 7.6 shows a schedule of accounts receivable drawn from the accounts receivable ledger of Exhibit 7.5.

P2 Prepare and prove the accuracy of subsidiary ledgers.

Exhibit 7.6

Schedule of Accounts Receivable

Schedule of Accounts Receivable February 28	
Albert Co.	$ 750
Frank Booth	175
Jason Henry	675
Kam Moore	350
Paul Roth	200
Total accounts receivable	$2,150

Additional Issues We consider three additional issues with the sales journal: (1) recording sales taxes, (2) recording sales returns and allowances, and (3) using actual sales invoices as a journal.

Point: In accounting, the word *schedule* generally means a list.

Sales taxes. Governmental agencies such as cities and states often require sellers to collect sales taxes from customers and to periodically send these taxes to the appropriate agency. When using a columnar sales journal, we can keep a record of taxes collected by adding a Sales Taxes Payable column as follows.

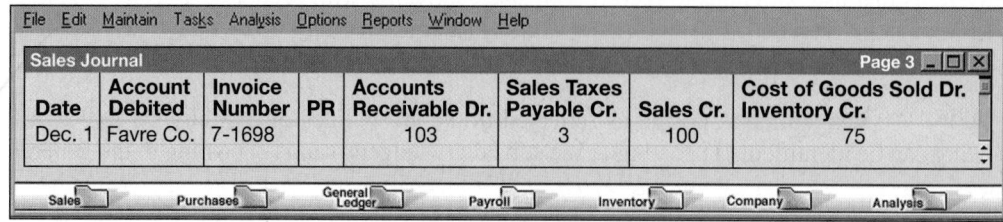

Individual amounts in the Accounts Receivable column would continue to be posted immediately to customer accounts in the accounts receivable ledger. Individual amounts in the Sales Taxes Payable and Sales columns are not posted. Column totals would continue to be posted as usual. (A company that collects sales taxes on its cash sales can also use a Sales Taxes Payable column in its cash receipts journal.)

Sales returns and allowances.   A company with only a few sales returns and allowances can record them in a general journal with an entry such as the following:

Assets = Liabilities + Equity			
−175	−175		

May 17	Sales Returns and Allowances	414	175	
	Accounts Receivable—Ray Ball.	106/✓		175
	Customer returned merchandise.			

The debit in this entry is posted to the Sales Returns and Allowances account (no. 414). The credit is posted to both the Accounts Receivable controlling account (no. 106) and to the customer's account. When we enter the account number and the check mark, 106/✓, in the PR column on the credit line, this means both the Accounts Receivable controlling account in the general ledger and the Ray Ball account in the accounts receivable ledger are credited for $175. [*Note:* If the returned goods can be resold to another customer, the company would debit (increase) the Inventory account and credit (decrease) the Cost of Goods Sold account. If the returned goods are defective (worthless), the company could simply leave their costs in the Cost of Goods Sold account (see Chapter 5).] A company with a large number of sales returns and allowances can save time by recording them in a separate sales returns and allowances journal.

Sales invoices as a sales journal.   To save costs, some small companies avoid using a sales journal for credit sales and instead post each sales invoice amount directly to the customer's account in the accounts receivable ledger. They then put copies of invoices in a file. At the end of the period, they total all invoices for that period and make a general journal entry to debit Accounts Receivable and credit Sales for the total amount. The file of invoice copies acts as a sales journal. This is called *direct posting of sales invoices*.

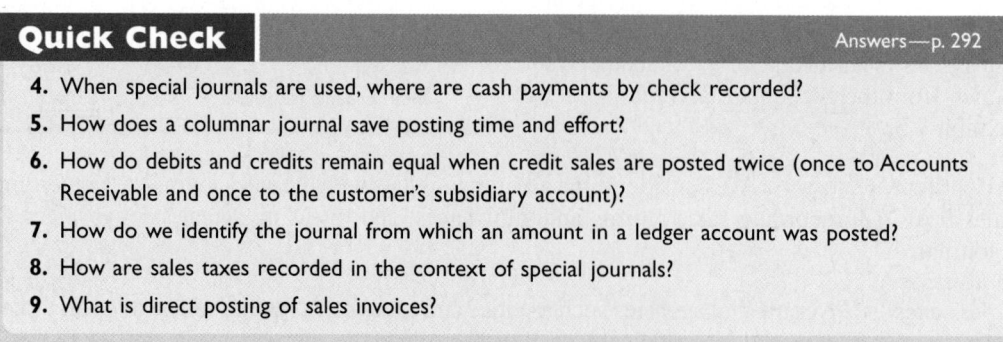

Quick Check   Answers—p. 292

4. When special journals are used, where are cash payments by check recorded?

5. How does a columnar journal save posting time and effort?

6. How do debits and credits remain equal when credit sales are posted twice (once to Accounts Receivable and once to the customer's subsidiary account)?

7. How do we identify the journal from which an amount in a ledger account was posted?

8. How are sales taxes recorded in the context of special journals?

9. What is direct posting of sales invoices?

Cash Receipts Journal

A **cash receipts journal** is typically used to record all receipts of cash. Exhibit 7.7 shows one common form of the cash receipts journal.

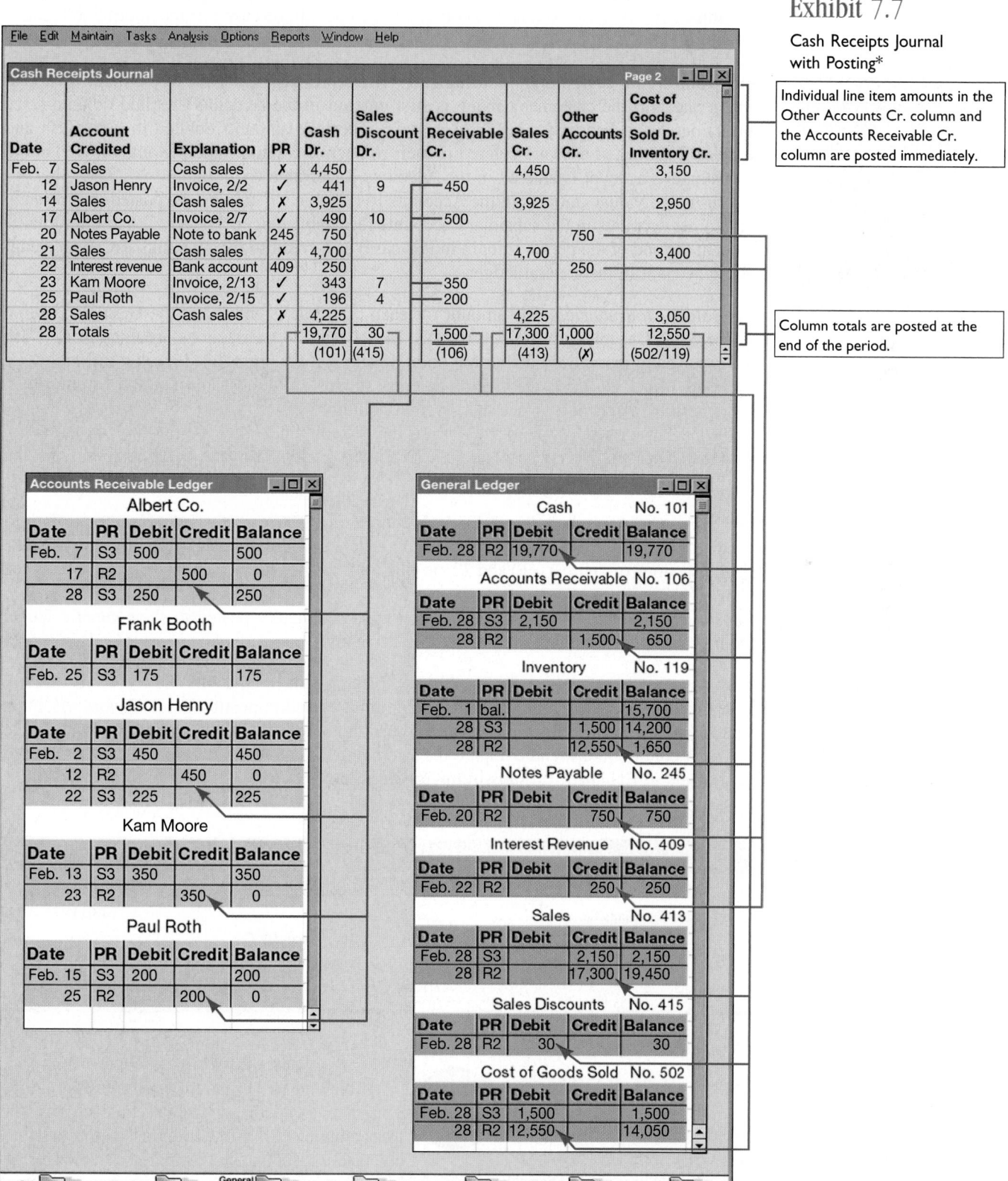

Exhibit 7.7

Cash Receipts Journal with Posting*

Individual line item amounts in the Other Accounts Cr. column and the Accounts Receivable Cr. column are posted immediately.

Column totals are posted at the end of the period.

*The Cash Receipts Journal in a *periodic* system would exclude the column on the far right titled "Cost of Goods Dr., Inventory Cr." (see Exhibit 7A.2).

Point: Each transaction in the cash receipts journal involves a debit to Cash. Credit accounts will vary.

Journalizing and Posting

Cash receipts can be separated into one of three types: (1) cash from credit customers in payment of their accounts, (2) cash from cash sales, and (3) cash from other sources. The cash receipts journal in Exhibit 7.7 has a separate credit column for each of these three sources. We describe how to journalize transactions from each of these three sources. (An Explanation column is included in the cash receipts journal to identify the source.)

Cash from credit customers.   *Journalizing.* To record cash received in payment of a customer's account, the customer's name is first entered in the Account Credited column—see transactions dated February 12, 17, 23, and 25. Then the amounts debited to both Cash and the Sales Discount (if any) are entered in their respective columns, and the amount credited to the customer's account is entered in the Accounts Receivable Cr. column.

Posting. Individual amounts in the Accounts Receivable Cr. column are posted immediately to customer accounts in the subsidiary accounts receivable ledger. The $1,500 column total is posted at the end of the period (month in this case) as a credit to the Accounts Receivable controlling account in the general ledger.

Point: Some software packages put cash sales in the sales journal.

Cash sales.   *Journalizing.* The amount for each cash sale is entered in the Cash Dr. column and the Sales Cr. column. The February 7, 14, 21, and 28 transactions are examples. (Cash sales are usually journalized daily or at point of sale, but are journalized weekly in Exhibit 7.7 for brevity.) Each cash sale also yields an entry to Cost of Goods Sold Dr. and Inventory Cr. for the cost of merchandise—see the far right column.

Posting. For cash sales, we place an *x* in the PR column to indicate that its amount is not individually posted. We do post the $17,300 Sales Cr. total and the $12,550 total from the "cost" column.

Example: Record in the cash receipts journal a $700 cash sale of land when the land carries a $700 original cost. *Answer:* Debit the Cash column for $700, and credit the Other Accounts column for $700 (the account credited is Land).

Cash from other sources.   *Journalizing.* Examples of cash from other sources are money borrowed from a bank, cash interest received on account, and cash sale of noninventory assets. The transactions of February 20 and 22 are illustrative. The Other Accounts Cr. column is used for these transactions.

Posting. Amounts from these transactions are immediately posted to their general ledger accounts and the PR column identifies those accounts.

Footing, Crossfooting, and Posting

To be sure that total debits and credits in a columnar journal are equal, we often crossfoot column totals before posting them. To *foot* a column of numbers is to add it. To *crossfoot* in this case is to add the Debit column totals, then add the Credit column totals, and compare the two sums for equality. Footing and crossfooting of the numbers in Exhibit 7.7 results in the report in Exhibit 7.8.

Point: Subsidiary ledgers and their controlling accounts are *in balance* only after all posting is complete.

Exhibit 7.8

Footing and Crossfooting Journal Totals

Debit Columns		Credit Columns	
Cash Dr.	$19,770	Accounts Receivable Cr.	$ 1,500
Sales Discounts Dr.	30	Sales Cr.	17,300
Cost of Goods Sold Dr.	12,550	Other Accounts Cr.	1,000
		Inventory Cr.	12,550
Total	$32,350	Total	$32,350

Decision Maker   Answer—p. 291

Entrepreneur   You want to know how promptly customers are paying their bills. This information can help you plan your cash payments and decide whether to extend credit. Where do you find this information?

At the end of the period, after crossfooting the journal to confirm that debits equal credits, the total amounts from the columns of the cash receipts journal are posted to their general ledger accounts. The Other Accounts Cr. column total is not posted because the individual amounts are directly posted to their general ledger accounts. We place an *x* below the Other Accounts Cr. column to indicate that this column total is not posted. The account numbers for the column totals that are posted are entered in parentheses below each column. (*Note:* Posting items immediately from the Other Accounts Cr. column with a delayed posting of their offsetting items in the Cash column total causes the general ledger to be out of balance during the period. Posting the Cash Dr. column total at the end of the period corrects this imbalance in the general ledger before the trial balance and financial statements are prepared.)

Purchases Journal

A **purchases journal** is typically used to record all credit purchases, including those for inventory. Purchases for cash are recorded in the Cash Disbursements Journal.

Journalizing   Entries in the purchases journal in Exhibit 7.9 reflect purchase invoices or other source documents. We use the invoice date and terms to compute the date when payment

Point: The number of special journals and the design of each are based on a company's specific needs.

Exhibit 7.9
Purchases Journal with Posting*

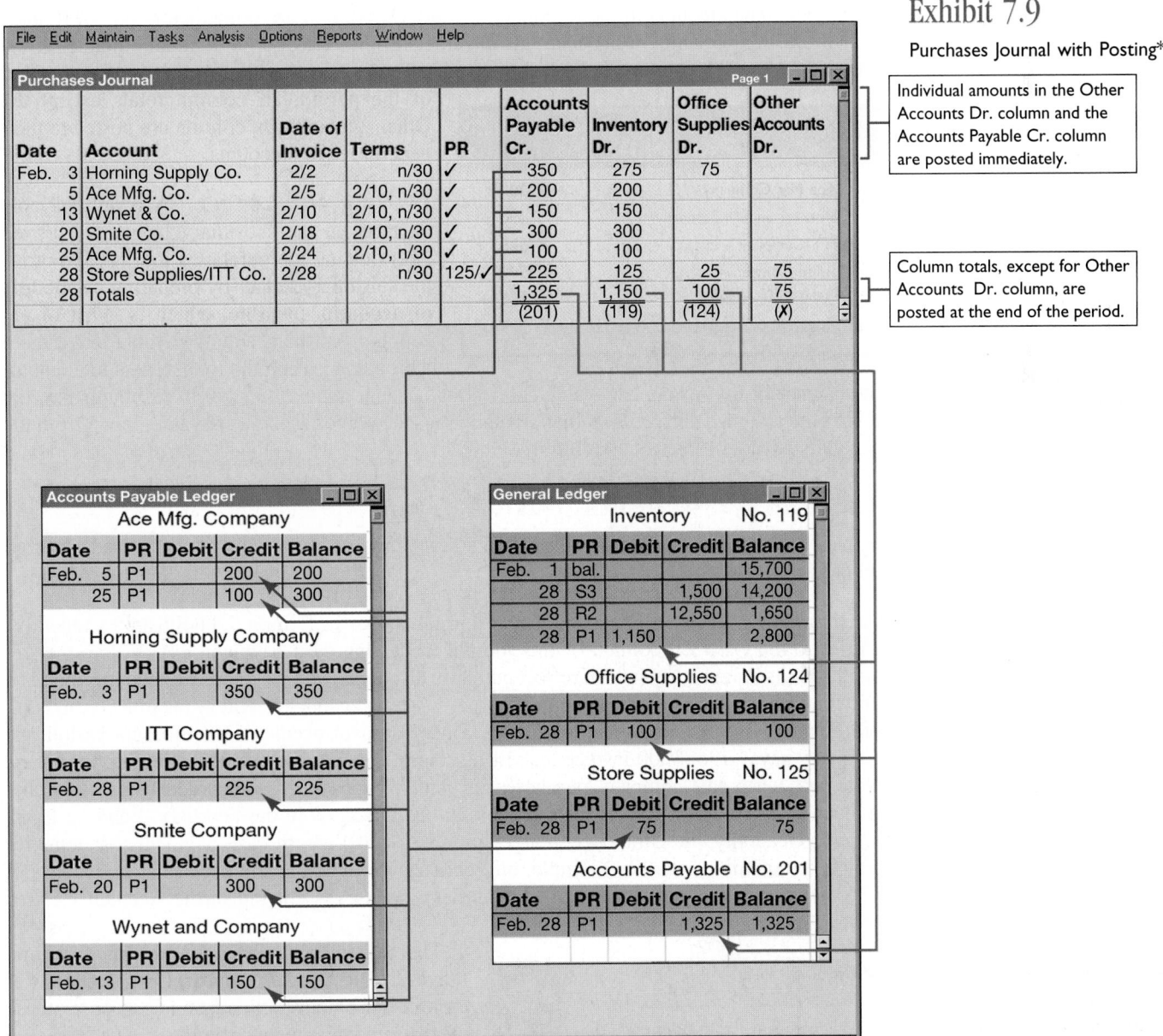

Individual amounts in the Other Accounts Dr. column and the Accounts Payable Cr. column are posted immediately.

Column totals, except for Other Accounts Dr. column, are posted at the end of the period.

*The Purchases Journal in a *periodic* system replaces "Inventory Dr." with "Purchases Dr." (see Exhibit 7A.3).

for each purchase is due. The Accounts Payable Cr. column is used to record the amounts owed to each creditor. Inventory purchases are recorded in the Inventory Dr. column.

To illustrate, inventory costing $200 is purchased from Ace Manufacturing on February 5. The creditor's name (Ace) is entered in the Account column, the invoice date is entered in the Date of Invoice column, the purchase terms are entered in the Terms column, and the $200 amount is entered in the Accounts Payable Cr. and the Inventory Dr. columns. When a purchase involves an amount recorded in the Other Accounts Dr. column, we use the Account column to identify the general ledger account debited. For example, the February 28 transaction involves purchases of inventory, office supplies, and store supplies from ITT. The journal has no column for store supplies, so the Other Accounts Dr. column is used. In this case, Store Supplies is entered in the Account column along with the creditor's name (ITT). This purchases journal also includes a separate column for credit purchases of office supplies. A separate column such as this is useful when several transactions involve debits to the same account. Each company uses its own judgment in deciding on the number of separate columns necessary.

Point: Each transaction in the purchases journal involves a credit to Accounts Payable. Debit accounts will vary.

Point: The Other Accounts Dr. column allows the purchases journal to be used for any purchase transaction on credit.

Posting   The amounts in the Accounts Payable Cr. column are immediately posted to individual creditor accounts in the accounts payable subsidiary ledger. Individual amounts in the Other Accounts Dr. column are immediately posted to their general ledger accounts. At the end of the period, all column totals except the Other Accounts Dr. column are posted to their general ledger accounts.

Exhibit 7.10

Schedule of Accounts Payable

Schedule of Accounts Payable February 28	
Ace Mfg. Company	$ 300
Horning Supply Company	350
ITT Company	225
Smite Company	300
Wynet & Company	150
Total accounts payable	$1,325

Point: The balance in the Accounts Payable controlling account must equal the sum of the individual account balances in the accounts payable subsidiary ledger after posting.

Proving the Ledger   Accounts payable balances in the subsidiary ledger are proved after posting the purchases journal. We prove the subsidiary ledger by preparing a **schedule of accounts payable,** which is a list of accounts from the accounts payable ledger with their balances and the total. If this total equals the balance of the Accounts Payable controlling account, the accounts in the accounts payable ledger are assumed correct. Exhibit 7.10 shows a schedule of accounts payable drawn from the accounts payable ledger of Exhibit 7.9.

Cash Disbursements Journal

A **cash disbursements journal,** also called a *cash payments journal,* is typically used to record all cash payments.

Journalizing   The cash disbursements journal shown in Exhibit 7.11 illustrates repetitive entries to the Cash Cr. column of this journal (reflecting cash payments). Also note the frequent credits to Inventory (which reflect purchase discounts) and the debits to Accounts Payable. For example, on February 15, the company pays Ace on account (credit terms of 2/10, n/30—see February 5 transaction in Exhibit 7.9). Since payment occurs in the discount period, the company pays $196 ($200 invoice less $4 discount). The $4 discount is credited to Inventory. Note that when this company purchases inventory for cash, it is recorded using the Other Accounts Dr. column and the Cash Cr. column as illustrated in the February 3 and 12 transactions. Generally, the Other Accounts column is used to record cash payments on items for which no column exists. For example, on February 15, the company pays salaries expense of $250. The title of the account debited (Salaries Expense) is entered in the Account Debited column.

Point: Each transaction in the cash disbursements journal involves a credit to Cash. Debit accounts will vary.

The cash disbursements journal has a column titled Ck. No. (check number). For control over cash disbursements, all payments except for those of small amounts are made by check. Checks should be prenumbered and each check's number entered in the journal in numerical order in the column

Decision Maker   Answer—p. 291

Controller   You wish to analyze your company's cash payments to suppliers and its purchases discounts. Where do you find this information?

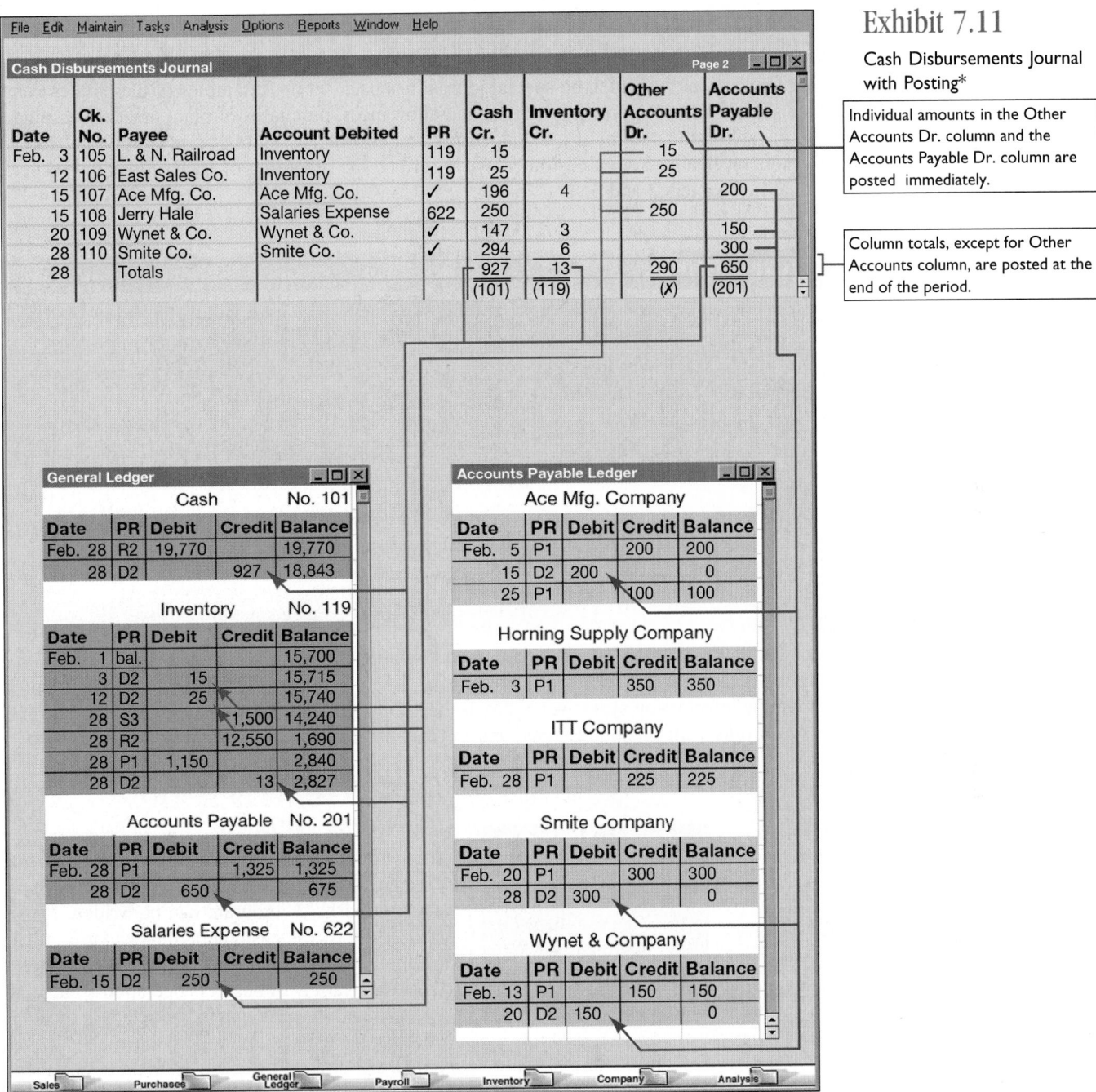

Exhibit 7.11

Cash Disbursements Journal with Posting*

Individual amounts in the Other Accounts Dr. column and the Accounts Payable Dr. column are posted immediately.

Column totals, except for Other Accounts column, are posted at the end of the period.

*The Cash Disbursements Journal in a *periodic* system replaces "Inventory Cr." with "Purchases Discounts Cr." (see Exhibit 7A.4).

headed Ck. No. This makes it possible to scan the numbers in the column for omitted checks. When a cash disbursements journal has a column for check numbers, it is sometimes called a **check register.**

Posting Individual amounts in the Other Accounts Dr. column of a cash disbursements journal are immediately posted to their general ledger accounts. Individual amounts in the Accounts Payable Dr. column are also immediately posted to creditors' accounts in the subsidiary Accounts Payable ledger. At the end of the period, we crossfoot column totals and post the Accounts Payable Dr. column total to the Accounts Payable controlling account. Also, the Inventory Cr. column total is posted to the Inventory account, and the Cash Cr. column total is posted to the Cash account.

General Journal Transactions

When special journals are used, we still need a general journal for adjusting, closing, and any other transactions for which no special journal has been set up. Examples of these other transactions might include purchases returns and allowances, purchases of plant assets by issuing a note payable, sales returns if a sales returns and allowances journal is not used, and receipt of a note receivable from a customer. We described the recording of transactions in a general journal in Chapters 2 and 3.

Quick Check
Answers—p. 292

10. What are the normal recording and posting procedures when using special journals and controlling accounts with subsidiary ledgers?

11. What is the process for posting to a subsidiary ledger and its controlling account?

12. How do we prove the accuracy of account balances in the general ledger and subsidiary ledgers after posting?

13. Why does a company need a general journal when using special journals for sales, purchases, cash receipts, and cash disbursements?

Technology-Based Accounting Systems

C5 Explain how technology-based information systems impact accounting.

Accounting information systems are supported with technology, which can range from simple calculators to advanced computerized systems. Since technology is increasingly important in accounting information systems, we discuss the impact of computer technology, how data processing works with accounting data, and the role of computer networks.

Decision Insight

Middleware is software allowing different computer programs in a company or across companies to work together. It allows transfer of purchase orders, invoices, and other electronic documents between accounting systems. For example, suppliers can monitor inventory levels of their buyers for production and shipping purposes.

Computer Technology in Accounting

Computer technology provides accuracy, speed, efficiency, and convenience in performing accounting tasks. A program can be written, for instance, to process customers' merchandise orders. Multipurpose off-the-shelf software applications exist for a variety of business operations. These include familiar accounting programs such as Peachtree® and QuickBooks®. Off-the-shelf programs are designed to be user friendly and menu driven, and many operate more efficiently as *integrated* systems. In an integrated system, actions taken in one part of the system automatically affect related parts. When a credit sale is recorded in an integrated system, for instance, several parts of the system are automatically updated, such as posting.

Decision Insight

A new generation of accounting support is available. With the touch of a key, users can create real-time inventory reports showing all payments, charges, and credit limits at any point in the accounting cycle. Many services also include "alert signals" notifying the company when, for example, a large order exceeds a customer's credit limit or when purchases need to be made or when a bank balance is running low. These alerts occur via e-mail, fax, PDA, or phone.

Computer technology can dramatically reduce the time and effort devoted to recordkeeping. Less effort spent on recordkeeping means more time for accounting professionals to concentrate on analysis and managerial decision making. These advances have created a greater demand for accounting professionals who understand financial reports and can draw insights and information from mountains of processed data. Accounting professionals have expertise in determining relevant and reliable information for decision making. They also can assess the effects of transactions and events on a company and its financial statements.

Data Processing in Accounting

Accounting systems differ with regard to how input is entered and processed. **Online processing** enters and processes data as soon as source documents are available. This means that databases are immediately updated. **Batch processing** accumulates source documents for a period of time and then processes them all at once such as daily, weekly, or monthly. The advantage of online processing is timeliness. This often requires additional costs related to both software and hardware requirements. Companies such as Intuit (**Intuit.com**) are making online processing of accounting data a reality for many businesses. The advantage of batch processing is that it requires only periodic updating of databases. Records used to send bills to customers, for instance, might require updating only once a month. The disadvantage of batch processing is the lack of updated databases for management to use when making business decisions.

Point: Companies that have reported missing or stolen employee data such as names and Social Security numbers include Time Warner, Polo Ralph Lauren, Lexis/Nexis, ChoicePoint, and DSW Shoes.

Computer Networks in Accounting

Networking, or linking computers with each other, can create information advantages (and cost efficiencies). **Computer networks** are links among computers giving different users and different computers access to common databases, programs, and hardware. Many college computer labs, for instance, are networked. A small computer network is called a *local area network (LAN);* it links machines with *hard-wire* hookups. Large computer networks extending over long distances often rely on *modem* or *wireless* communication.

Demand for information sometimes requires advanced networks such as the systems Federal Express and UPS use to track packages and bill customers and the system Wal-Mart uses to monitor inventory levels in its stores. These networks include many computers and satellite communications to gather information and to provide ready access to its databases from all locations.

Enterprise Resource Planning Software

Enterprise resource planning (ERP) software includes the programs that manage a company's vital operations. They extend from order taking to manufacturing to accounting. When working properly, these integrated programs can speed decision making, identify costs for reduction, and give managers control over operations with the click of a mouse. For many managers, ERP software allows them to scrutinize business, identify where inventories are piling up, and see what plants are most efficient. The software is designed to link every part of a company's operations. This software allowed Monsanto to slash production planning from six weeks to three, trim its inventories, and increase its bargaining power with suppliers. Monsanto estimates that this software saves the company $200 million per year.

ERP has several suppliers. SAP leads the market, with Oracle, which gobbled up PeopleSoft and J. D. Edwards, a distant second (*AMR Research*). SAP software is used by more than half of the world's 500 largest companies. It links ordering, inventory, production, purchasing, planning, tracking, and human resources. A transaction or event triggers an immediate chain reaction of events throughout the enterprise. It is making companies more efficient and profitable.

Total ERP Market: About $25 Billion

- Other 23%
- SAP 40%
- Sage Group 7%
- Microsoft's Business Solutions 5%
- SSA Global 4%
- Oracle-PeopleSoft 21%

Point: *BusinessWeek* (2005) reports
that the number of Internet fraud
complaints has soared as follows:

2002   48,252
2004   207,449

ERP is pushing into cyberspace and customer relationship management (CRM). Now companies can share data with customers and suppliers. Applesauce maker **Mott's** is using SAP so that distributors can check the status of orders and place them over the Net, and the **Coca-Cola Company** uses it to ship soda on time. ERP is also increasingly used by small business. For example, **NetSuite**'s accounting services to small and medium businesses are powered by Oracle's system.

Quick Check

Answers—p. 292

14. Identify an advantage of an integrated computer-based accounting system.
15. What advantages do computer systems offer over manual systems?
16. Identify an advantage of computer networks.
17. Describe ERP software and its potential advantages to businesses.

Decision Analysis   Segment Return on Assets

Good accounting information systems collect financial data for a company's various segments. A *segment* refers to a part of a company that is separately identified by its products or services, or by the geographic market it serves. **Harley-Davidson** reports that it operates in two business segments: (1) motorcycles and related and (2) financial services. Users of financial statements are especially interested in segment information to better understand a company's activities because segments often vary on profitability, risk, and growth.

Companies must report segment information, including their sales, operating income, identifiable assets, capital expenditures, and depreciation. However, managers are reluctant to release information that can harm competitive position. Exhibit 7.12 shows survey results on the number of companies with different (reported) segments.

One measure of success for business segments is the **segment return on assets** ratio defined as follows.

Exhibit 7.12

Companies Reporting Operations
by These Segments*

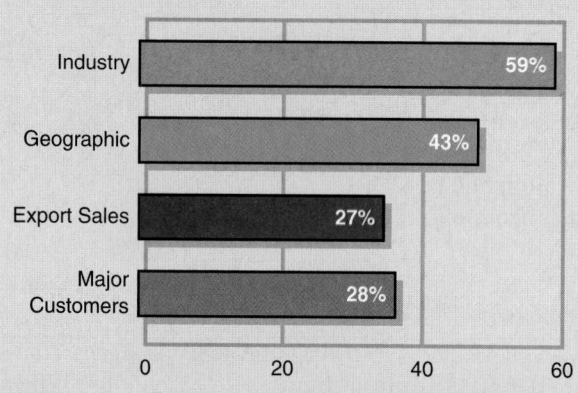

*Total exceeds 100% because companies can
report more than one type of segment.

A1 Compute segment return on assets and use it to evaluate segment performance.

$$\text{Segment return on assets} = \frac{\text{Segment operating income}}{\text{Segment average assets}}$$

Exhibit 7.13

Harley-Davidson's Segment
Return on Assets ($ millions)

This ratio reflects on the profitability of a segment. Exhibit 7.13 shows the segments' operating income, average assets, and return on assets for Harley-Davidson from 2002 through 2004.

Segment*	2004			2003			2002
	Operating Income	Average Assets	Return on Assets	Operating Income	Average Assets	Return on Assets	Return on Assets
Motorcycles & related . . .	$1,190	$1,712	70%	$997	$1,660	60%	54%
Financial services	189	2,022	9%	168	1,672	10%	8%

* A segment's operating income is usually measured as income before taxes, and assets is usually measured as identifiable assets.

The trend in Harley's segment return on assets is increasing for its motorcycle segment, but not for its financial services segment. Also, its motorcycle segment is much more profitable (70%) than its financial services (9%) segment. Harley should consider further investment in its motorcycle segment if such returns can be sustained. Analysis can also be extended to geographical segments and any other segments that companies report.

Decision Maker

Answer—p. 291

Banker A bicycle merchandiser requests a loan from you to expand operations. Its net income is $220,000, reflecting a 10% increase over the prior year. You ask about segment results. The owner reports that $160,000 of net income is from Cuban operations, reflecting a 60% increase over the prior year. The remaining $60,000 of net income is from U.S. operations, reflecting a 40% decrease. Does this segment information impact your loan decision?

Demonstration Problem—Perpetual System

Pepper Company completed the following selected transactions and events during March of this year. (Terms of all credit sales for the company are 2/10, n/30.)

Mar. 4 Sold merchandise on credit to Jennifer Nelson, Invoice No. 954, for $16,800 (cost is $12,200).

6 Purchased $1,220 of office supplies on credit from Mack Company. Invoice dated March 3, terms n/30.

6 Sold merchandise on credit to Dennie Hoskins, Invoice No. 955, for $10,200 (cost is $8,100).

11 Purchased $52,600 of merchandise, invoice dated March 6, terms 2/10, n/30, from Defore Industries.

12 Borrowed $26,000 cash by giving Commerce Bank a long-term promissory note payable.

14 Received cash payment from Jennifer Nelson for the March 4 sale less the discount (Invoice No. 954).

16 Received a $200 credit memorandum from Defore Industries for unsatisfactory merchandise Pepper purchased on March 11 and later returned.

16 Received cash payment from Dennie Hoskins for the March 6 sale less the discount (Invoice No. 955).

18 Purchased $22,850 of store equipment on credit from Schmidt Supply, invoice dated March 15, terms n/30.

20 Sold merchandise on credit to Marjorie Allen, Invoice No. 956, for $5,600 (cost is $3,800).

21 Sent Defore Industries Check No. 516 in payment of its March 6 dated invoice less the return and the discount.

22 Purchased $41,625 of merchandise, invoice dated March 18, terms 2/10, n/30, from Welch Company.

26 Issued a $600 credit memorandum to Marjorie Allen for defective merchandise Pepper sold on March 20 and Allen later returned.

31 Issued Check No. 517, payable to Payroll, in payment of $15,900 sales salaries for the month. Cashed the check and paid the employees.

31 Cash sales for the month are $134,680 (cost is $67,340). (Cash sales are recorded daily but are recorded only once here to reduce repetitive entries.)

Required

1. Open the following selected general ledger accounts: Cash (101), Accounts Receivable (106) Inventory (119), Office Supplies (124), Store Equipment (165), Accounts Payable (201), Long-Term Notes Payable (251), Sales (413), Sales Returns and Allowances (414), Sales Discounts (415), Cost of Goods Sold (502), and Sales Salaries Expense (621). Open the following accounts receivable ledger accounts: Marjorie Allen, Dennie Hoskins, and Jennifer Nelson. Open the following accounts payable ledger accounts: Defore Industries, Mack Company, Schmidt Supply, and Welch Company.

2. Enter the transactions using a sales journal, a purchases journal, a cash receipts journal, a cash disbursements journal, and a general journal similar to the ones illustrated in the chapter. Regularly post to the individual customer and creditor accounts. Also, post any amounts that should be posted as individual amounts to general ledger accounts. Foot and crossfoot the journals and make the month-end postings. *Pepper Co. uses the perpetual inventory system.*

3. Prepare a trial balance for the selected general ledger accounts in part 1 and prove the accuracy of subsidiary ledgers by preparing schedules of accounts receivable and accounts payable.

Planning the Solution

- Set up the required general ledger, the subsidiary ledger accounts, and the five required journals as illustrated in the chapter.

- Read and analyze each transaction and decide in which special journal (or general journal) the transaction is recorded.
- Record each transaction in the proper journal (and post the appropriate individual amounts).
- Once you have recorded all transactions, total the journal columns. Post from each journal to the appropriate ledger accounts.
- Prepare a trial balance to prove the equality of the debit and credit balances in your general ledger.
- Prepare schedules of accounts receivable and accounts payable. Compare the totals of these schedules to the Accounts Receivable and Accounts Payable controlling account balances, making sure that they agree.

Solution to Demonstration Problem — Perpetual System

Sales Journal   Page 2 _ □ ×

Date	Account Debited	Invoice Number	PR	Accounts Receivable Dr. Sales Cr.	Cost of Goods Sold Dr. Inventory Cr.
Mar. 4	Jennifer Nelson	954	✓	16,800	12,200
6	Dennie Hoskins	955	✓	10,200	8,100
20	Marjorie Allen	956	✓	5,600	3,800
31	Totals			32,600	24,100
				(106/413)	(502/119)

Cash Receipts Journal   Page 3 _ □ ×

Date	Account Credited	Explanation	PR	Cash Dr.	Sales Discount Dr.	Accounts Receivable Cr.	Sales Cr.	Other Accounts Cr.	Cost of Goods Sold Dr. Inventory Cr.
Mar. 12	L.T. Notes Payable	Note to bank	251	26,000				26,000	
14	Jennifer Nelson	Invoice 954, 3/4	✓	16,464	336	16,800			
16	Dennie Hoskins	Invoice 955, 3/6	✓	9,996	204	10,200			
31	Sales	Cash sales	x	134,680			134,680		67,340
31	Totals			187,140	540	27,000	134,680	26,000	67,340
				(101)	(415)	(106)	(413)	(x)	(502/119)

Purchases Journal   Page 3 _ □ ×

Date	Account	Date of Invoice	Terms	PR	Accounts Payable Cr.	Inventory Dr.	Office Supplies Dr.	Other Accounts Dr.
Mar. 6	Office Supplies/Mack Co	3/3	n/30	✓	1,220		1,220	
11	Defore Industries	3/6	2/10, n/30	✓	52,600	52,600		
18	Store Equipment/Schmidt Supp	3/15	n/30	165/✓	22,850			22,850
22	Welch Company	3/18	2/10, n/30	✓	41,625	41,625		
31	Totals				118,295	94,225	1,220	22,850
					(201)	(119)	(124)	(x)

Cash Disbursements Journal   Page 3 _ □ ×

Date	Ck. No.	Payee	Account Debited	PR	Cash Cr.	Inventory Cr.	Other Accounts Dr.	Accounts Payable Dr.
Mar. 21	516	Defore Industries	Defore Industries	✓	51,352	1,048		52,400
31	517	Payroll	Sales Salaries Expense	621	15,900		15,900	
31		Totals			67,252	1,048	15,900	52,400
					(101)	(119)	(x)	(201)

General Journal			Page 2
Mar. 16	Accounts Payable—Defore Industries	201/✓	200	
	Inventory	119		200
	To record credit memorandum received.			
26	Sales Returns and Allowances	414	600	
	Accounts Receivable—Marjorie Allen	106/✓		600
	To record credit memorandum issued.			

Accounts Receivable Ledger

Marjorie Allen

Date	PR	Debit	Credit	Balance
Mar. 20	S2	5,600		5,600
26	G2		600	5,000

Dennie Hoskins

Date	PR	Debit	Credit	Balance
Mar. 6	S2	10,200		10,200
16	R3		10,200	0

Jennifer Nelson

Date	PR	Debit	Credit	Balance
Mar. 4	S2	16,800		16,800
14	R3		16,800	0

Accounts Payable Ledger

Defore Industries

Date	PR	Debit	Credit	Balance
Mar. 11	P3		52,600	52,600
16	G2	200		52,400
21	D3	52,400		0

Mack Company

Date	PR	Debit	Credit	Balance
Mar. 6	P3		1,220	1,220

Schmidt Supply

Date	PR	Debit	Credit	Balance
Mar. 18	P3		22,850	22,850

Welch Company

Date	PR	Debit	Credit	Balance
Mar. 22	P3		41,625	41,625

General Ledger (Partial Listing)

Cash   Acct. No. 101

Date	PR	Debit	Credit	Balance
Mar. 31	R3	187,140		187,140
31	D3		67,252	119,888

Accounts Receivable   Acct. No. 106

Date	PR	Debit	Credit	Balance
Mar. 26	G2		600	(600)
31	S2	32,600		32,000
31	R3		27,000	5,000

Inventory   Acct. No. 119

Date	PR	Debit	Credit	Balance
Mar. 16	G2		200	(200)
21	D3		1,048	(1,248)
31	P3	94,225		92,977
31	S2		24,100	68,877
31	R3		67,340	1,537

Office Supplies   Acct. No. 124

Date	PR	Debit	Credit	Balance
Mar. 31	P3	1,220		1,220

Store Equipment   Acct. No. 165

Date	PR	Debit	Credit	Balance
Mar. 18	P3	22,850		22,850

Accounts Payable   Acct. No. 201

Date	PR	Debit	Credit	Balance
Mar. 16	G2	200		(200)
31	P3		118,295	118,095
31	D3	52,400		65,695

Long-Term Notes Payable   Acct. No. 251

Date	PR	Debit	Credit	Balance
Mar. 12	R3		26,000	26,000

Sales   Acct. No. 413

Date	PR	Debit	Credit	Balance
Mar. 31	S2		32,600	32,600
31	R3		134,680	167,280

Sales Returns and Allowances   Acct. No. 414

Date	PR	Debit	Credit	Balance
Mar. 26	G2	600		600

Sales Discounts   Acct. No. 415

Date	PR	Debit	Credit	Balance
Mar. 31	R3	540		540

Cost of Goods Sold   Acct. No. 502

Date	PR	Debit	Credit	Balance
Mar. 31	R3	67,340		67,340
31	S2	24,100		91,440

Sales Salaries Expense   Acct. No. 621

Date	PR	Debit	Credit	Balance
Mar. 31	D3	15,900		15,900

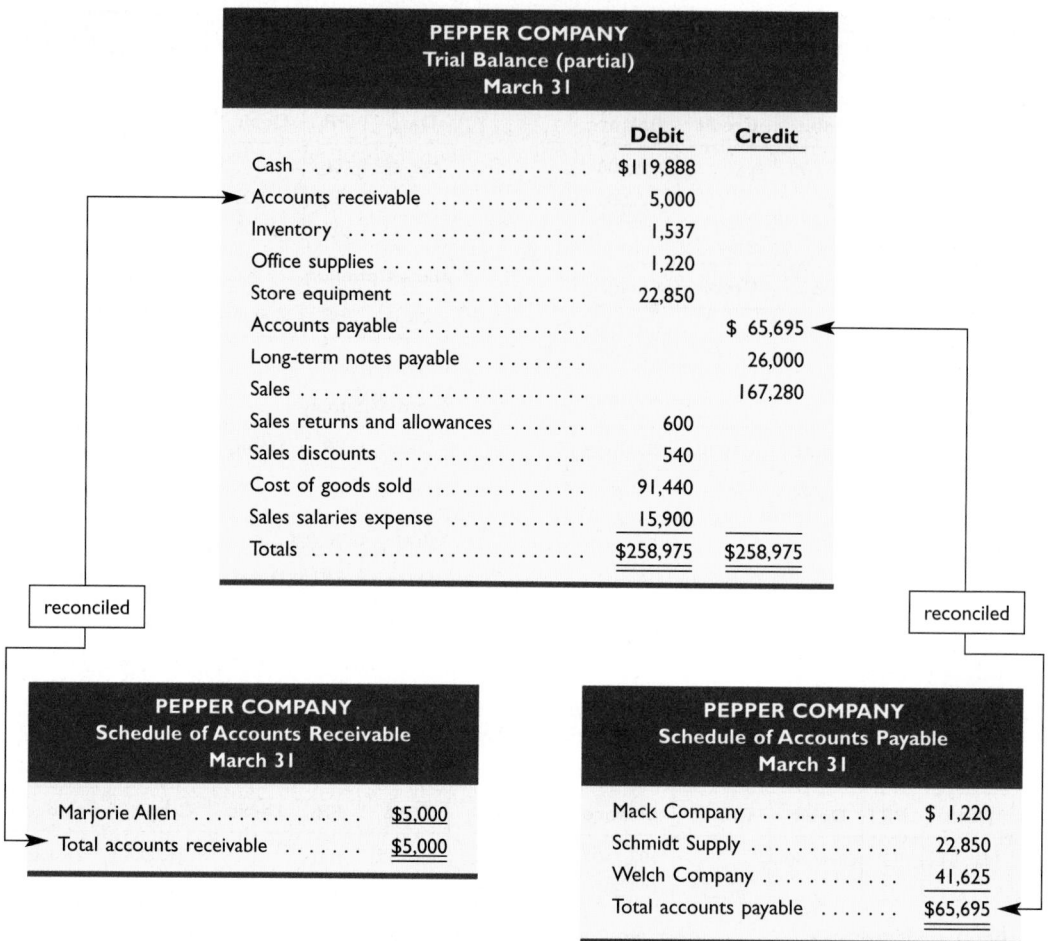

APPENDIX

7A

Special Journals under a Periodic System

P3 Journalize and post transactions using special journals in a periodic inventory system.

This appendix describes special journals under a periodic inventory system. Each journal is slightly impacted. The sales journal and the cash receipts journal both require one less column (namely that of Cost of Goods Sold Dr., Inventory Cr.). The Purchases Journal replaces the Inventory Dr. column with a Purchases Dr. column in a periodic system. The cash disbursements journal replaces the Inventory Cr. column with a Purchases Discounts Cr. column in a periodic system. These changes are illustrated.

Sales Journal

The sales journal using the periodic inventory system is shown in Exhibit 7A.1. The difference in the sales journal between the perpetual and periodic system is the exclusion of the column to record cost of goods sold and inventory amounts for each sale. The periodic system does *not* record the increase in cost of goods sold and the decrease in inventory at the time of each sale.

Sales Journal — Page 3

Date	Account Debited	Invoice Number	PR	Accounts Receivable Dr. Sales Cr.
Feb. 2	Jason Henry	307	✓	450
7	Albert Co.	308	✓	500
13	Kam Moore	309	✓	350
15	Paul Roth	310	✓	200
22	Jason Henry	311	✓	225
25	Frank Booth	312	✓	175
28	Albert Co.	313	✓	250
28	Total			2,150
				(106/413)

Exhibit 7A.1

Sales Journal—Periodic System

Cash Receipts Journal

The cash receipts journal using the periodic system is shown in Exhibit 7A.2. Note the absence of the column on the far right side to record debits to Cost of Goods Sold and credits to Inventory for the cost of merchandise sold (seen under the perpetual system). Consistent with the cash receipts journal shown in Exhibit 7.7, we show only the weekly (summary) cash sale entries.

Exhibit 7A.2

Cash Receipts Journal— Periodic System

Cash Receipts Journal — Page 2

Date	Account Credited	Explanation	PR	Cash Dr.	Sales Discount Dr.	Accounts Receivable Cr.	Sales Cr.	Other Accounts Cr.
Feb. 7	Sales	Cash sales	x	4,450			4,450	
12	Jason Henry	Invoice 307, 2/2	✓	441	9	450		
14	Sales	Cash sales	x	3,925			3,925	
17	Albert Co.	Invoice 308, 2/7	✓	490	10	500		
20	Notes Payable	Note to bank	245	750				750
21	Sales	Cash sales	x	4,700			4,700	
22	Interest revenue	Bank account	409	250				250
23	Kam Moore	Invoice 309, 2/13	✓	343	7	350		
25	Paul Roth	Invoice 310, 2/15	✓	196	4	200		
28	Sales	Cash sales	x	4,225			4,225	
28	Totals			19,770	30	1,500	17,300	1,000
				(101)	(415)	(106)	(413)	(x)

Purchases Journal

The purchases journal using the periodic system is shown in Exhibit 7A.3. This journal under a perpetual system included an Inventory column where the periodic system now has a Purchases column.

Exhibit 7A.3

Purchases Journal— Periodic System

Purchases Journal — Page 1

Date	Account	Date of Invoice	Terms	PR	Accounts Payable Cr.	Purchases Dr.	Office Supplies Dr.	Other Accounts Dr.
Feb. 3	Horning Supply Co.	2/2	n/30	✓	350	275	75	
5	Ace Mfg. Co.	2/5	2/10, n/30	✓	200	200		
13	Wynet and Co.	2/10	2/10, n/30	✓	150	150		
20	Smite Co.	2/18	2/10, n/30	✓	300	300		
25	Ace Mfg. Co.	2/24	2/10, n/30	✓	100	100		
28	Store Supplies/ITT Co.	2/28	n/30	125/✓	225	125	25	75
28	Totals				1,325	1,150	100	75
					(201)	(505)	(124)	(x)

Cash Disbursements Journal

The cash disbursements journal using a periodic system is shown in Exhibit 7A.4. This journal under the perpetual system included an Inventory column where the periodic system now has the Purchases Discounts column.

Exhibit 7A.4

Cash Disbursements Journal—Periodic System

Cash Disbursements Journal — Page 2 _□×

Date	Ck. No.	Payee	Account Debited	PR	Cash Cr.	Purchases Discounts Cr.	Other Accounts Dr.	Accounts Payable Dr.
Feb. 3	105	L. and N. Railroad	Purchases	505	15		15	
12	106	East Sales Co.	Purchases	505	25		25	
15	107	Ace Mfg. Co.	Ace Mfg. Co.	✓	196	4		200
15	108	Jerry Hale	Salaries Expense	622	250		250	
20	109	Wynet and Co.	Wynet and Co.	✓	147	3		150
28	110	Smite Co.	Smite Co.	✓	294	6		300
28			Totals		927	13	290	650
					(101)	(507)	(x)	(201)

Demonstration Problem—Periodic System

Refer to Pepper Company's selected transactions described under the Demonstration Problem—Perpetual System to fulfill the following requirements.

Required

1. Open the following selected general ledger accounts: Cash (101), Accounts Receivable (106), Office Supplies (124), Store Equipment (165), Accounts Payable (201), Long-Term Notes Payable (251), Sales (413), Sales Returns and Allowances (414), Sales Discounts (415), Purchases (505), Purchases Returns and Allowances (506), Purchases Discounts (507), and Sales Salaries Expense (621). Open the following accounts receivable ledger accounts: Marjorie Allen, Dennie Hoskins, and Jennifer Nelson. Open the following accounts payable ledger accounts: Defore Industries, Mack Company, Schmidt Supply, and Welch Company.

2. Enter the transactions using a sales journal, a purchases journal, a cash receipts journal, a cash disbursements journal, and a general journal similar to the ones illustrated in Appendix 7A. Regularly post to the individual customer and creditor accounts. Also, post any amounts that should be posted as individual amounts to general ledger accounts. Foot and crossfoot the journals and make the month-end postings. *Pepper Co. uses the periodic inventory system in this problem.*

3. Prepare a trial balance for the selected general ledger accounts in part 1 and prove the accuracy of subsidiary ledgers by preparing schedules of accounts receivable and accounts payable.

Solution to Demonstration Problem — Periodic System

Sales Journal — Page 2 _□×

Date	Account Debited	Invoice Number	PR	Accounts Receivable Dr. Sales Cr.
Mar. 4	Jennifer Nelson	954	✓	16,800
6	Dennie Hoskins	955	✓	10,200
20	Marjorie Allen	956	✓	5,600
31	Totals			32,600
				(106/413)

Cash Receipts Journal — Page 3 _□×

Date	Account Credited	Explanation	PR	Cash Dr.	Sales Discount Dr.	Accounts Receivable Cr.	Sales Cr.	Other Accounts Cr.
Mar. 12	L.T. Notes Payable	Note to bank	251	26,000				26,000
14	Jennifer Nelson	Invoice 954, 3/4	✓	16,464	336	16,800		
16	Dennie Hoskins	Invoice 955, 3/6	✓	9,996	204	10,200		
31	Sales	Cash sales	x	134,680			134,680	
31	Totals			187,140	540	27,000	134,680	26,000
				(101)	(415)	(106)	(413)	(x)

Purchases Journal   Page 3 ▫□✕

Date	Account	Date of Invoice	Terms	PR	Accounts Payable Cr.	Purchases Dr.	Office Supplies Dr.	Other Accounts Dr.
Mar. 6	Office Supplies/Mack Co	3/3	n/30	✓	1,220		1,220	
11	Defore Industries	3/6	2/10, n/30	✓	52,600	52,600		
18	Store Equipment/Schmidt Supp	3/15	n/30	165/✓	22,850			22,850
22	Welch Company	3/18	2/10, n/30	✓	41,625	41,625		
31	Totals				118,295	94,225	1,220	22,850
					(201)	(505)	(124)	(x)

Cash Disbursements Journal   Page 3 ▫□✕

Date	Ck. No.	Payee	Account Debited	PR	Cash Cr.	Purch. Discount Cr.	Other Accounts Dr.	Accounts Payable Dr.
Feb. 21	516	Defore Industries	Defore Industries	✓	51,352	1,048		52,400
31	517	Payroll	Sales Salaries Expense	621	15,900		15,900	
31		Totals			67,252	1,048	15,900	52,400
					(101)	(507)	(x)	(201)

General Journal			Page 2
Mar. 16	Accounts Payable—Defore Industries	201/✓	200	
	Purchases Returns and Allowances	506		200
	To record credit memorandum received.			
26	Sales Returns and Allowances	414	600	
	Accounts Receivable—Marjorie Allen	106/✓		600
	To record credit memorandum issued.			

Accounts Receivable Ledger

Marjorie Allen

Date	PR	Debit	Credit	Balance
Mar. 20	S2	5,600		5,600
26	G2		600	5,000

Dennie Hoskins

Date	PR	Debit	Credit	Balance
Mar. 6	S2	10,200		10,200
16	R3		10,200	0

Jennifer Nelson

Date	PR	Debit	Credit	Balance
Mar. 4	S2	16,800		16,800
14	R3		16,800	0

Accounts Payable Ledger

Defore Industries

Date	PR	Debit	Credit	Balance
Mar. 11	P3		52,600	52,600
16	G2	200		52,400
21	D3	52,400		0

Mack Company

Date	PR	Debit	Credit	Balance
Mar. 6	P3		1,220	1,220

Schmidt Supply

Date	PR	Debit	Credit	Balance
Mar. 18	P3		22,850	22,850

Welch Company

Date	PR	Debit	Credit	Balance
Mar. 22	P3		41,625	41,625

General Ledger (Partial Listing)

Cash   Acct. No. 101

Date	PR	Debit	Credit	Balance
Mar. 31	R3	187,140		187,140
31	D3		67,252	119,888

Accounts Receivable   Acct. No. 106

Date	PR	Debit	Credit	Balance
Mar. 26	G2		600	(600)
31	S2	32,600		32,000
31	R3		27,000	5,000

Office Supplies   Acct. No. 124

Date	PR	Debit	Credit	Balance
Mar. 31	P3	1,220		1,220

Store Equipment   Acct. No. 165

Date	PR	Debit	Credit	Balance
Mar. 18	P3	22,850		22,850

Accounts Payable   Acct. No. 201

Date	PR	Debit	Credit	Balance
Mar. 16	G2	200		(200)
31	P3		118,295	118,095
31	D3	52,400		65,695

Long-Term Notes Payable   Acct. No. 251

Date	PR	Debit	Credit	Balance
Mar. 12	R3		26,000	26,000

Sales   Acct. No. 413

Date	PR	Debit	Credit	Balance
Mar. 31	S2		32,600	32,600
31	R3		134,680	167,280

Sales Returns and Allowances   Acct. No. 414

Date	PR	Debit	Credit	Balance
Mar. 26	G2	600		600

Sales Discounts   Acct. No. 415

Date	PR	Debit	Credit	Balance
Mar. 31	R3	540		540

Purchases   Acct. No. 505

Date	PR	Debit	Credit	Balance
Mar. 31	P3	94,225		94,225

Purchases Returns and Allowances   Acct. No. 506

Date	PR	Debit	Credit	Balance
Mar. 16	G2		200	200

Purchases Discounts   Acct. No. 507

Date	PR	Debit	Credit	Balance
Mar. 31	D3		1,048	1,048

Sales Salaries Expense   Acct. No. 621

Date	PR	Debit	Credit	Balance
Mar. 31	D3	15,900		15,900

PEPPER COMPANY
Trial Balance (partial)
March 31

	Debit	Credit
Cash	$119,888	
Accounts receivable	5,000	
Office supplies	1,220	
Store equipment	22,850	
Accounts payable		$ 65,695
Long-term notes payable		26,000
Sales		167,280
Sales returns and allowances	600	
Sales discounts	540	
Purchases	94,225	
Purchases returns and allowances		200
Purchases discounts		1,048
Sales salaries expense	15,900	
Totals	$260,223	$260,223

PEPPER COMPANY
Schedule of Accounts Receivable
March 31

Marjorie Allen	$5,000
Total accounts receivable	$5,000

PEPPER COMPANY
Schedule of Accounts Payable
March 31

Mack Company	$ 1,220
Schmidt Supply	22,850
Welch Company	41,625
Total accounts payable	$65,695

Summary

C1 **Identify fundamental principles of accounting information systems.** Accounting information systems are governed by five fundamental principles: control, relevance, compatibility, flexibility, and cost-benefit.

C2 **Identify components of accounting information systems.** The five basic components of an accounting information system are source documents, input devices, information processors, information storage, and output devices.

C3 **Explain the goals and uses of special journals.** Special journals are used for recording transactions of similar type, each meant to cover one kind of transaction. Four of the most common special journals are the sales journal, cash receipts journal, purchases journal, and cash disbursements journal. Special journals are efficient and cost-effective tools in the journalizing and posting processes.

C4 **Describe the use of controlling accounts and subsidiary ledgers.** A general ledger keeps controlling accounts such as Accounts Receivable and Accounts Payable, but details on individual accounts making up the controlling account are kept in subsidiary ledgers (such as an accounts receivable ledger). The balance in a controlling account must equal the sum of its subsidiary account balances after posting is complete.

C5 **Explain how technology-based information systems impact accounting.** Technology-based information systems aim to increase the accuracy, speed, efficiency, and convenience of accounting procedures.

A1 **Compute segment return on assets and use it to evaluate segment performance.** A business segment is a part of a company that is separately identified by its products or services or by the geographic market it serves. Analysis of a company's segments is aided by the segment return on assets (segment operating income divided by segment average assets).

P1 **Journalize and post transactions using special journals.** Each special journal is devoted to similar kinds of transactions. Transactions are journalized on one line of a special journal, with columns devoted to specific accounts, dates, names, posting references, explanations, and other necessary information. Posting is threefold: (1) individual amounts in the Other Accounts column are posted to their general ledger accounts on a regular (daily) basis, (2) individual amounts in a column whose total is *not* posted to a controlling account at the end of a period (month) are posted regularly (daily) to their general ledger accounts, and (3) total amounts for all columns except the Other Accounts column are posted at the end of a period (month) to their column's account title in the general ledger.

P2 **Prepare and prove the accuracy of subsidiary ledgers.** Account balances in the general ledger and its subsidiary ledgers are tested for accuracy after posting is complete. This procedure is twofold: (1) prepare a trial balance of the general ledger to confirm that debits equal credits and (2) prepare a schedule to confirm that the controlling account's balance equals the subsidiary ledger's balance.

P3^A **Journalize and post transactions using special journals in a periodic inventory system.** Transactions are journalized and posted using special journals in a periodic system. The methods are similar to those in a perpetual system; the primary difference is that both cost of goods sold and inventory are not adjusted at the time of each sale. This usually results in the deletion (or renaming) of one or more columns devoted to these accounts in each special journal.

Guidance Answers to **Decision Maker** and **Decision Ethics**

Accountant The main issue is whether commissions have an actual or perceived impact on the integrity and objectivity of your advice. You probably should not accept a commission arrangement (the AICPA Code of Ethics prohibits it when you perform the audit or a review). In any event, you should tell the client of your commission arrangement. Also, you need to seriously examine the merits of agreeing to a commission arrangement when you are in a position to exploit it.

Entrepreneur The accounts receivable ledger has much of the information you need. It lists detailed information for each customer's account, including the amounts, dates for transactions, and dates of payments. It can be reorganized into an "aging schedule" to show how long customers wait before paying their bills.

Controller Much of the information you need is in the accounts payable ledger. It contains information for each supplier, the amounts due, and when payments are made. This subsidiary ledger along with information on credit terms should enable you to conduct your analyses.

Banker This merchandiser's segment information is likely to greatly impact your loan decision. The risks associated with the company's two sources of net income are quite different. While net income is up by 10%, U.S. operations are performing poorly and Cuban operations are subject to many uncertainties. These uncertainties depend on political events, legal issues, business relationships, Cuban economic conditions, and a host of other risks. Overall, net income results suggested a low-risk loan opportunity, but the segment information reveals a high-risk situation.

Guidance Answers to **Quick Checks**

1. The five components are source documents, input devices, information processors, information storage, and output devices.

2. Information processors interpret, transform, and summarize the recorded accounting information so that it can be used in analysis, interpretation, and decision making.

3. Data saved in information storage are used to prepare periodic financial reports and special-purpose internal reports as well as source documentation for auditors.

4. All cash payments by check are recorded in the cash disbursements journal.

5. Columnar journals allow us to accumulate repetitive debits and credits and post them as column totals rather than as individual amounts from each entry.

6. The equality of debits and credits is kept within the general ledger. The subsidiary ledger keeps the customer's individual account and is used only for supplementary information.

7. An initial and the page number of the journal from which the amount was posted are entered in the PR column next to the amount.

8. A separate column for Sales Taxes Payable can be included in both the cash receipts journal and the sales journal.

9. This refers to a procedure of using copies of sales invoices as a sales journal. Each invoice amount is posted directly to the customer's account. All invoices are totaled at period-end for posting to the general ledger accounts.

10. The normal recording and posting procedures are threefold. First, transactions are entered in a special journal if applicable. Second, individual amounts are posted to any subsidiary ledger accounts. Third, column totals are posted to general ledger accounts if not already individually posted.

11. Controlling accounts are debited periodically for an amount or amounts equal to the sum of their respective debits in the subsidiary ledgers (equals journal column totals), and they are credited periodically for an amount or amounts equal to the sum of their respective credits in the subsidiary ledgers (from journal column totals).

12. Tests for accuracy of account balances in the general ledger and subsidiary ledgers are twofold. First, we prepare a trial balance of the general ledger to confirm that debits equal credits. Second, we prove the subsidiary ledgers by preparing schedules of accounts receivable and accounts payable.

13. The general journal is still needed for adjusting, closing, and correcting entries and for special transactions such as sales returns, purchases returns, and certain asset purchases.

14. Integrated systems can save time and minimize errors. This is so because actions taken in one part of the system automatically affect and update related parts.

15. Computer systems offer increased accuracy, speed, efficiency, and convenience.

16. Computer networks can create advantages by linking computers, and giving different users and different computers access to common databases, programs, and hardware.

17. ERP software involves integrated programs, from order taking to manufacturing to accounting. It can speed decision-making, help identify costs for reduction, and aid managers in controlling operations.

Key Terms

mhhe.com/wildFAP18e

Key Terms are available at the book's Website for learning and testing in an online Flashcard Format.

Accounting information systems (p. 266)
Accounts payable ledger (p. 271)
Accounts receivable ledger (p. 271)
Batch processing (p. 281)
Cash disbursements journal (p. 278)
Cash receipts journal (p. 275)
Check register (p. 279)
Columnar journal (p. 272)
Compatibility principle (p. 267)
Components of accounting systems (p. 267)

Computer networks (p. 281)
Controlling account (p. 271)
Control principle (p. 266)
Cost-benefit principle (p. 267)
Enterprise resource planning (ERP) software (p. 281)
Flexibility principle (p. 267)
General journal (p. 270)
Information processors (p. 268)
Information storage (p. 268)
Input devices (p. 268)

Internal controls (p. 266)
Online processing (p. 281)
Output devices (p. 269)
Purchases journal (p. 277)
Relevance principle (p. 266)
Sales journal (p. 271)
Schedule of accounts payable (p. 278)
Schedule of accounts receivable (p. 273)
Segment return on assets (p. 282)
Special journal (p. 270)
Subsidiary ledger (p. 270)

Multiple Choice Quiz

Answers on p. 309   mhhe.com/wildFAP18e

Multiple Choice Quizzes A and B are available at the book's Website.

1. The sales journal is used to record
 a. Credit sales
 b. Cash sales
 c. Cash receipts
 d. Cash purchases
 e. Credit purchases

2. The purchases journal is used to record
 a. Credit sales
 b. Cash sales
 c. Cash receipts
 d. Cash purchases
 e. Credit purchases

3. The ledger that contains the financial statement accounts of a company is the
   a. General journal
   b. Column balance journal
   c. Special ledger
   d. General ledger
   e. Special journal
4. A subsidiary ledger that contains a separate account for each supplier (creditor) to the company is the
   a. Controlling account
   b. Accounts payable ledger
   c. Accounts receivable ledger
   d. General ledger
   e. Special journal
5. Enterprise resource planning software
   a. Refers to programs that help manage company operations.
   b. Is another name for spreadsheet programs.
   c. Uses batch processing of business information.
   d. Is substantially declining in use.
   e. Is another name for database programs.

Superscript ^{A} denotes assignments based on Appendix 7A.

Discussion Questions

1. What are the five fundamental principles of accounting information systems?
2. What are five basic components of an accounting system?
3. What are source documents? Give two examples.
4. What is the purpose of an input device? Give examples of input devices for computer systems.
5. What is the difference between data that are stored off-line and data that are stored online?
6. What purpose is served by the output devices of an accounting system?
7. When special journals are used, they are usually used to record each of four different types of transactions. What are these four types of transactions?
8. What notations are entered into the Posting Reference column of a ledger account?
9. When a general journal entry is used to record sales returns, the credit of the entry must be posted twice. Does this cause the trial balance to be out of balance? Explain.

10. Describe the procedures involving the use of copies of a company's sales invoices as a sales journal.
11. Credits to customer accounts and credits to Other Accounts are individually posted from a cash receipts journal such as the one in Exhibit 7.7. Why not put both types of credits in the same column and save journal space?
12. Why should sales to and receipts of cash from credit customers be recorded and posted immediately?
13. Locate the note that discusses **Best Buy**'s operations by segments in Appendix A. In what two segments does it predominantly operate?
14. Does the income statement of **Circuit City** in Appendix A indicate the net income earned by its business segments? If so, list them.
15. Does the balance sheet of **Apple** in Appendix A indicate the identifiable assets owned by its business segments? If so, list them.

 Red numbers denote Discussion Questions that involve decision-making.

Place the letter of each system principle in the blank next to its best description.

A. Control principle
B. Relevance principle
C. Compatibility principle
D. Flexibility principle
E. Cost-benefit principle

1. _____ The principle prescribes the accounting information system to help monitor activities.
2. _____ The principle prescribes the accounting information system to adapt to the unique characteristics of the company.
3. _____ The principle prescribes the accounting information system to change in response to technological advances and competitive pressures.
4. _____ The principle that affects all other accounting information system principles.
5. _____ The principle prescribes the accounting information system to provide timely information for effective decision making.

QUICK STUDY

QS 7-1
Accounting information
system principles

C1

QS 7-2
Accounting information system
C2

Fill in the blanks to complete the following descriptions.

1. With _____ processing, source documents are accumulated for a period and then processed all at the same time, such as once a day, week, or month.

2. A computer _____ allows different computer users to share access to data and programs.

3. A _____ is an input device that captures writing and other input directly from source documents.

4. _____ _____ _____ software comprises programs that help manage a company's vital operations, from manufacturing to accounting.

QS 7-3
Accounting information
system components
C2

Identify the most likely role in an accounting system played by each of the numbered items 1 through 12 by assigning a letter from the list A through E on the left.

A. Source documents
B. Input devices
C. Information processors
D. Information storage
E. Output devices

_____ **1.** Computer keyboard
_____ **2.** Computer printer
_____ **3.** Computer monitor
_____ **4.** MP3 player
_____ **5.** Bank statement
_____ **6.** Computer software
_____ **7.** Bar code reader
_____ **8.** Digital camera
_____ **9.** Invoice from a supplier
_____ **10.** Zip drive
_____ **11.** Computer scanner
_____ **12.** Filing cabinet

QS 7-4
Identifying the special journal
of entry
C3

Wilcox Electronics uses a sales journal, a purchases journal, a cash receipts journal, a cash disbursements journal, and a general journal as illustrated in this chapter. Wilcox recently completed the following transactions *a* through *h*. Identify the journal in which each transaction should be recorded.

a. Sold merchandise on credit.
b. Purchased shop supplies on credit.
c. Paid an employee's salary in cash.
d. Borrowed cash from the bank.

e. Sold merchandise for cash.
f. Purchased merchandise on credit.
g. Purchased inventory for cash.
h. Paid cash to a creditor.

QS 7-5
Entries in the general journal
C3

Biloxi Gifts uses a sales journal, a purchases journal, a cash receipts journal, a cash disbursements journal, and a general journal as illustrated in this chapter. Journalize its November transactions that should be recorded in the general journal. For those not recorded in the general journal, identify the special journal where each should be recorded.

Nov. 2 Purchased $2,600 of merchandise on credit from the Midland Co., terms 2/10, n/30.
      12 The owner, T. Biloxi, contributed an automobile worth $17,000 to the business.
      16 Sold $1,200 of merchandise (cost is $800) on credit to K. Myer, terms n/30.
      19 K. Myer returned $175 of (worthless) merchandise originally purchased on November 16 (assume the cost of this merchandise is left in cost of goods sold).

QS 7-6
Analyzing segment reports
A1

Apple Computer reports the following income (and average assets in parentheses) for each of its geographic segments—$ millions: Americas, $465 ($529); Europe, $280 ($256); and Japan, $115 ($122). Apple also reports the following sales (only) by product segments: iPod, $1,306; Power Macintosh, $1,419; PowerBook, $1,589; iBook, $961; iMac, $954; Other, $2,050. Compute Apple's return on assets for each of its geographic segments, and assess the relative performance of these segments. Compute the percentage of total sales for each of its top three product sellers.

Finer Company uses a sales journal, a purchases journal, a cash receipts journal, a cash disbursement journal, and a general journal. The following transactions occur in the month of March.

EXERCISES

Mar. 2   Sold merchandise costing $300 to B. Facer for $450 cash, invoice no. 5703.
       5   Purchased $2,400 of merchandise on credit from Marchant Corp.
       7   Sold merchandise costing $800 to J. Dryer for $1,250, terms 2/10, n/30, invoice no. 5704.
       8   Borrowed $9,000 cash by signing a note payable to the bank.
      12   Sold merchandise costing $200 to R. Lamb for $340, terms n/30, invoice no. 5705.
      16   Received $1,225 cash from J. Dryer to pay for the purchase of March 7.
      19   Sold used store equipment for $900 cash to Golf, Inc.
      25   Sold merchandise costing $500 to T. Taylor for $750, terms n/30, invoice no. 5706.

Exercise 7-1
Sales journal—perpetual

P1

Prepare headings for a sales journal like the one in Exhibit 7.5. Journalize the March transactions that should be recorded in this sales journal.

Refer to Exercise 7-1 and for each of the March transactions identify the journal in which it would be recorded. Assume the company uses a sales journal, purchases journal, cash receipts journal, cash disbursements journal, and general journal as illustrated in this chapter.

Exercise 7-2
Identifying journal of entry

C3

Prepare headings for a sales journal like the one in Exhibit 7A.1. Journalize the March transactions shown in Exercise 7-1 that should be recorded in the sales journal assuming that the periodic inventory system is used.

Exercise 7-3[A]
Sales journal—periodic

P3

Ali Co. uses a sales journal, a purchases journal, a cash receipts journal, a cash disbursements journal, and a general journal. The following transactions occur in the month of November.

Exercise 7-4
Cash receipts journal—perpetual

P1

Nov. 3   Purchased $3,200 of merchandise on credit from Hart Co., terms n/20.
       7   Sold merchandise costing $840 on credit to J. Than for $1,000, subject to a $20 sales discount if paid by the end of the month.
       9   Borrowed $3,750 cash by signing a note payable to the bank.
      13   J. Ali, the owner, contributed $5,000 cash to the company.
      18   Sold merchandise costing $250 to B. Cox for $330 cash.
      22   Paid Hart Co. $3,200 cash for the merchandise purchased on November 3.
      27   Received $980 cash from J. Than in payment of the November 7 purchase.
      30   Paid salaries of $1,650 in cash.

Prepare headings for a cash receipts journal like the one in Exhibit 7.7. Journalize the November transactions that should be recorded in the cash receipts journal.

Refer to Exercise 7-4 and for each of the November transactions identify the journal in which it would be recorded. Assume the company uses a sales journal, purchases journal, cash receipts journal, cash disbursements journal, and general journal as illustrated in this chapter.

Exercise 7-5
Identifying journal of entry

C3

Prepare headings for a cash receipts journal like the one in Exhibit 7A.2. Journalize the November transactions shown in Exercise 7-4 that should be recorded in the cash receipts journal assuming that the periodic inventory system is used.

Exercise 7-6[A]
Cash receipts journal—periodic

P3

Exercise 7-7

Purchases journal—perpetual

P1

Alivan Company uses a sales journal, a purchases journal, a cash receipts journal, a cash disbursements journal, and a general journal. The following transactions occur in the month of June.

June 1   Purchased $9,100 of merchandise on credit from Lucas, Inc., terms n/30.
       8   Sold merchandise costing $800 on credit to R. Panke for $1,400 subject to a $25 sales discount if paid by the end of the month.
     14   Purchased $340 of store supplies from Park Company on credit, terms n/30.
     17   Purchased $380 of office supplies on credit from Ray Company, terms n/30.
     24   Sold merchandise costing $400 to L. Barnett for $630 cash.
     28   Purchased store supplies from Pringle's for $90 cash.
     29   Paid Lucas, Inc., $9,100 cash for the merchandise purchased on June 1.

Prepare headings for a purchases journal like the one in Exhibit 7.9. Journalize the June transactions that should be recorded in the purchases journal.

Exercise 7-8

Identifying journal of entry

C3

Refer to Exercise 7-7 and for each of the June transactions identify the journal in which it would be recorded. Assume the company uses a sales journal, purchases journal, cash receipts journal, cash disbursements journal, and general journal as illustrated in this chapter.

Exercise 7-9^A

Purchases journal—periodic

P3

Prepare headings for a purchases journal like the one in Exhibit 7A.3. Journalize the June transactions from Exercise 7-7 that should be recorded in the purchases journal assuming the periodic inventory system is used.

Exercise 7-10

Cash disbursements journal—perpetual

P1

Marx Supply uses a sales journal, a purchases journal, a cash receipts journal, a cash disbursements journal, and a general journal. The following transactions occur in the month of April.

Apr. 3   Purchased merchandise for $2,950 on credit from Seth, Inc., terms 2/10, n/30.
      9   Issued check no. 210 to Kitt Corp. to buy store supplies for $650.
    12   Sold merchandise costing $500 on credit to C. Myers for $770, terms n/30.
    17   Issued check no. 211 for $1,400 to pay off a note payable to City Bank.
    20   Purchased merchandise for $4,500 on credit from Lite, terms 2/10, n/30.
    28   Issued check no. 212 to Lite to pay the amount due for the purchase of April 20, less the discount.
    29   Paid salary of $1,800 to B. Dock by issuing check no. 213.
    30   Issued check no. 214 to Seth, Inc., to pay the amount due for the purchase of April 3.

Prepare headings for a cash disbursements journal like the one in Exhibit 7.11. Journalize the April transactions that should be recorded in the cash disbursements journal.

Exercise 7-11

Identifying journal of entry

C3

Refer to Exercise 7-10 and for each of the April transactions identify the journal in which it would be recorded. Assume the company uses a sales journal, purchases journal, cash receipts journal, cash disbursements journal, and general journal as illustrated in this chapter.

Exercise 7-12^A

Cash disbursements journal—periodic P3

Prepare headings for a cash disbursements journal like the one in Exhibit 7A.4. Journalize the April transactions from Exercise 7-10 that should be recorded in the cash disbursements journal assuming that the periodic inventory system is used.

Exercise 7-13

Special journal transactions and error discovery

P1

Houst Pharmacy uses the following journals: sales journal, purchases journal, cash receipts journal, cash disbursements journal, and general journal. On June 5, Houst purchased merchandise priced at $14,000, subject to credit terms of 2/10, n/30. On June 14, the pharmacy paid the net amount due for the merchandise. In journalizing the payment, the pharmacy debited Accounts Payable for $14,000 but failed to record the cash discount on the purchases. Cash was properly credited for the actual $13,720 paid. (*a*) In what journals would the June 5 and the June 14 transactions be recorded? (*b*) What procedure is likely to discover the error in journalizing the June 14 transaction?

At the end of May, the sales journal of Mountain View appears as follows.

Exercise 7-14

Posting to subsidiary ledger accounts; preparing a schedule of accounts receivable

P1 P2

Sales Journal					▢◻✕
Date	Account Debited	Invoice Number	PR	Accounts Receivable Dr. Sales Cr.	Cost of Goods Sold Dr. Inventory Cr.
May 6	Aaron Reckers	190		3,880	3,120
10	Sara Reed	191		2,940	2,325
17	Anna Page	192		1,850	1,480
25	Sara Reed	193		1,340	1,075
31	Totals			10,010	8,000

Mountain View also recorded the return of defective merchandise with the following entry.

May 20	Sales Returns and Allowances	350	
	Accounts Receivable—Anna Page		350
	Customer returned (worthless) merchandise.		

Required

1. Open an accounts receivable subsidiary ledger that has a T-account for each customer listed in the sales journal. Post to the customer accounts the entries in the sales journal and any portion of the general journal entry that affects a customer's account.

2. Open a general ledger that has T-accounts for Accounts Receivable, Inventory, Sales, Sales Returns and Allowances, and Cost of Goods Sold. Post the sales journal and any portion of the general journal entry that affects these accounts.

3. Prepare a schedule of accounts receivable and prove that its total equals the balance in the Accounts Receivable controlling account.

Check (3) Accounts Receivable, $9,660

Keeler Company posts its sales invoices directly and then binds them into a Sales Journal. Keeler had the following credit sales to these customers during June.

Exercise 7-15

Accounts receivable ledger; posting from sales journal

P1 P2

June 2	Joe Mack	$ 4,600
8	Eric Horner	7,100
10	Tess Cox	14,400
14	Hong Jiang	21,500
20	Tess Cox	12,200
29	Joe Mack	8,300
	Total credit sales	$68,100

Required

1. Open an accounts receivable subsidiary ledger having a T-account for each customer. Post the invoices to the subsidiary ledger.

2. Open an Accounts Receivable controlling T-account and a Sales T-account to reflect general ledger accounts. Post the end-of-month total from the sales journal to these accounts.

3. Prepare a schedule of accounts receivable and prove that its total equals the Accounts Receivable controlling account balance.

A company that records credit purchases in a purchases journal and records purchases returns in a general journal made the following errors. Indicate when each error should be discovered.

Exercise 7-16

Purchases journal and error identification

P1

1. Made an addition error in determining the balance of a creditor's subsidiary account.

2. Made an addition error in totaling the Office Supplies column of the purchases journal.

3. Posted a purchases return to the Accounts Payable account and to the creditor's subsidiary account but did not post the purchases return to the Inventory account.

4. Posted a purchases return to the Inventory account and to the Accounts Payable account but did not post to the creditor's subsidiary account.

5. Correctly recorded a $4,000 purchase in the purchases journal but posted it to the creditor's subsidiary account as a $400 purchase.

Exercise 7-17
Computing and analyzing segment
return on assets

A1

Refer to Exhibit 7.13 and complete the segment return on assets table for Teton Company. Analyze your findings and identify the segment with the highest, and that with the lowest, segment return on assets.

Segment	Segment Operating Income (in $ mil.)		Segment Assets (in $ mil.)		Segment Return on Assets
	2007	2006	2007	2006	2007
Specialty					
Skiing Group	$ 72	$ 68	$ 591	$ 450	
Skating Group	19	16	63	52	
Specialty Footwear	32	29	165	146	
Other Specialty	21	14	47	34	
Subtotal	144	127	866	682	
General Merchandise					
South America	42	46	315	284	
United States	17	18	62	45	
Europe	15	13	24	22	
Subtotal	74	77	401	351	
Total	$218	$204	$1,267	$1,033	

Check   Europe segment return, 65.2%

PROBLEM SET A

Problem 7-1A
Special journals, subsidiary
ledgers, and schedule of accounts
receivable—perpetual

C4   P1   P2

Wiset Company completes these transactions during April of the current year (the terms of all its credit sales are 2/10, n/30).

Apr. 2   Purchased $14,300 of merchandise on credit from Noth Company, invoice dated April 2, terms 2/10, n/60.

3   Sold merchandise on credit to Page Alistair, Invoice No. 760, for $4,000 (cost is $3,000).

3   Purchased $1,480 of office supplies on credit from Custer, Inc. Invoice dated April 2, terms n/10 EOM.

4   Issued Check No. 587 to *World View* for advertising expense, $899.

5   Sold merchandise on credit to Paula Kohr, Invoice No. 761, for $8,000 (cost is $6,500).

6   Received an $80 credit memorandum from Custer, Inc., for the return of some of the office supplies received on April 3.

9   Purchased $12,125 of store equipment on credit from Hal's Supply, invoice dated April 9, terms n/10 EOM.

11   Sold merchandise on credit to Nic Nelson, Invoice No. 762, for $10,500 (cost is $7,000).

12   Issued Check No. 588 to Noth Company in payment of its April 2 invoice, less the discount.

13   Received payment from Page Alistair for the April 3 sale, less the discount.

13   Sold $5,100 of merchandise on credit to Page Alistair (cost is $3,600), Invoice No. 763.

14   Received payment from Paula Kohr for the April 5 sale, less the discount.

16   Issued Check No. 589, payable to Payroll, in payment of sales salaries expense for the first half of the month, $10,750. Cashed the check and paid employees.

16   Cash sales for the first half of the month are $52,840 (cost is $35,880). (Cash sales are recorded daily from cash register data but are recorded only twice in this problem to reduce repetitive entries.)

17   Purchased $13,750 of merchandise on credit from Grant Company, invoice dated April 17, terms 2/10, n/30.

18   Borrowed $60,000 cash from First State Bank by signing a long-term note payable.

20   Received payment from Nic Nelson for the April 11 sale, less the discount.

20   Purchased $830 of store supplies on credit from Hal's Supply, invoice dated April 19, terms n/10 EOM.

23   Received a $750 credit memorandum from Grant Company for the return of defective merchandise received on April 17.

23   Received payment from Page Alistair for the April 13 sale, less the discount.

25   Purchased $11,375 of merchandise on credit from Noth Company, invoice dated April 24, terms 2/10, n/60.

26   Issued Check No. 590 to Grant Company in payment of its April 17 invoice, less the return and the discount.

27   Sold $3,170 of merchandise on credit to Paula Kohr, Invoice No. 764 (cost is $2,520).

27   Sold $6,700 of merchandise on credit to Nic Nelson, Invoice No. 765 (cost is $4,305).

30   Issued Check No. 591, payable to Payroll, in payment of the sales salaries expense for the last half of the month, $10,750.

30   Cash sales for the last half of the month are $73,975 (cost is $58,900).

Required

1. Prepare a sales journal like that in Exhibit 7.5 and a cash receipts journal like that in Exhibit 7.7. Number both journal pages as page 3. Then review the transactions of Wiset Company and enter those that should be journalized in the sales journal and those that should be journalized in the cash receipts journal. Ignore any transactions that should be journalized in a purchases journal, a cash disbursements journal, or a general journal.

2. Open the following general ledger accounts: Cash, Accounts Receivable, Inventory, Long-Term Notes Payable, Cost of Goods Sold, Sales, and Sales Discounts. Enter the March 31 balances for Cash ($85,000), Inventory ($125,000), and Long-Term Notes Payable ($210,000). Also open accounts receivable subsidiary ledger accounts for Paula Kohr, Page Alistair, and Nic Nelson.

3. Verify that amounts that should be posted as individual amounts from the journals have been posted. (Such items are immediately posted.) Foot and crossfoot the journals and make the month-end postings.

4. Prepare a trial balance of the general ledger and prove the accuracy of the subsidiary ledger by preparing a schedule of accounts receivable.

Check   Trial balance totals, $434,285

Analysis Component

5. Assume that the total for the schedule of Accounts Receivable does not equal the balance of the controlling account in the general ledger. Describe steps you would take to discover the error(s).

Assume that Wiset Co. in Problem 7-1A uses the periodic inventory system.

Required

1. Prepare headings for a sales journal like the one in Exhibit 7A.1. Prepare headings for a cash receipts journal like the one in Exhibit 7A.2. Journalize the April transactions shown in Problem 7-1A that should be recorded in the sales journal and the cash receipts journal assuming the *periodic* inventory system is used.

2. Open the general ledger accounts with balances as shown in Problem 7-1A (do not open a Cost of Goods Sold ledger account). Under the periodic system, an Inventory account exists but is inactive until its balance is updated to the correct inventory balance at year-end. In this problem, the Inventory account remains inactive but must be included to correctly complete the trial balance.

3. Complete parts 3, 4, and 5 of Problem 7-1A using the results of parts 1 and 2 of this problem.

Problem 7-2A^A
Special journals, subsidiary ledgers, and schedule of accounts receivable—periodic

C4   P2   P3

Check   Trial balance totals, $434,285

The April transactions of Wiset Company are described in Problem 7-1A.

Required

1. Prepare a general journal, a purchases journal like that in Exhibit 7.9, and a cash disbursements journal like that in Exhibit 7.11. Number all journal pages as page 3. Review the April transactions of Wiset Company and enter those transactions that should be journalized in the general journal, the purchases journal, or the cash disbursements journal. Ignore any transactions that should be journalized in a sales journal or cash receipts journal.

2. Open the following general ledger accounts: Cash, Inventory, Office Supplies, Store Supplies, Store Equipment, Accounts Payable, Long-Term Notes Payable, Sales Salaries Expense, and Advertising Expense. Enter the March 31 balances of Cash ($85,000), Inventory ($125,000), and Long-Term Notes Payable ($210,000). Also open accounts payable subsidiary ledger accounts for Hal's Supply, Noth Company, Grant Company, and Custer, Inc.

3. Verify that amounts that should be posted as individual amounts from the journals have been posted. (Such items are immediately posted.) Foot and crossfoot the journals and make the month-end postings.

4. Prepare a trial balance of the general ledger and a schedule of accounts payable.

Problem 7-3A
Special journals, subsidiary ledgers, and schedule of accounts payable—perpetual

C4   P1   P2

Check   Trial balance totals, $235,730

Problem 7-4A^A
Special journals, subsidiary ledgers, and schedule of accounts payable—periodic

C4   P2   P3

Check   Trial balance totals, $237,026

Refer to Problem 7-1A and assume that Wiset Co. uses the periodic inventory system.

Required

1. Prepare a general journal, a purchases journal like that in Exhibit 7A.3, and a cash disbursements journal like that in Exhibit 7A.4. Number all journal pages as page 3. Review the April transactions of Wiset Company (Problem 7-1A) and enter those transactions that should be journalized in the general journal, the purchases journal, or the cash disbursements journal. Ignore any transaction that should be journalized in a sales journal or cash receipts journal.

2. Open the following general ledger accounts: Cash, Inventory, Office Supplies, Store Supplies, Store Equipment, Accounts Payable, Long-Term Notes Payable, Purchases, Purchases Returns and Allowances, Purchases Discounts, Sales Salaries Expense, and Advertising Expense. Enter the March 31 balances of Cash ($85,000), Inventory ($125,000), and Long-Term Notes Payable ($210,000). Also open accounts payable subsidiary ledger accounts for Hal's Supply, Noth Company, Grant Company, and Custer, Inc.

3. Complete parts 3 and 4 of Problem 7-3A using the results of parts 1 and 2 of this problem.

Problem 7-5A
Special journals, subsidiary ledgers, trial balance—perpetual

C4   P1   P2

mhhe.com/wildFAP18e

Church Company completes these transactions and events during March of the current year (terms for all its credit sales are 2/10, n/30).

Mar. 1   Purchased $43,600 of merchandise from Van Industries, invoice dated March 1, terms 2/15, n/30.

     2   Sold merchandise on credit to Min Cho, Invoice No. 854, for $16,800 (cost is $8,400).

     3   Purchased $1,230 of office supplies on credit from Gabel Company, invoice dated March 3, terms n/10 EOM.

     3   Sold merchandise on credit to Linda Witt, Invoice No. 855, for $10,200 (cost is $5,800).

     6   Borrowed $82,000 cash from Federal Bank by signing a long-term note payable.

     9   Purchased $21,850 of office equipment on credit from Spell Supply, invoice dated March 9, terms n/10 EOM.

     10   Sold merchandise on credit to Jovita Albany, Invoice No. 856, for $5,600 (cost is $2,900).

     12   Received payment from Min Cho for the March 2 sale less the discount.

     13   Sent Van Industries Check No. 416 in payment of the March 1 invoice less the discount.

     13   Received payment from Linda Witt for the March 3 sale less the discount.

     14   Purchased $32,625 of merchandise from the CD Company, invoice dated March 13, terms 2/10, n/30.

     15   Issued Check No. 417, payable to Payroll, in payment of sales salaries expense for the first half of the month, $18,300. Cashed the check and paid the employees.

     15   Cash sales for the first half of the month are $34,680 (cost is $20,210). (Cash sales are recorded daily, but are recorded only twice here to reduce repetitive entries.)

     16   Purchased $1,770 of store supplies on credit from Gabel Company, invoice dated March 16, terms n/10 EOM.

     17   Received a $2,425 credit memorandum from CD Company for the return of unsatisfactory merchandise purchased on March 14.

     19   Received a $630 credit memorandum from Spell Supply for office equipment received on March 9 and returned for credit.

     20   Received payment from Jovita Albany for the sale of March 10 less the discount.

     23   Issued Check No. 418 to CD Company in payment of the invoice of March 13 less the return and the discount.

     27   Sold merchandise on credit to Jovita Albany, Invoice No. 857, for $14,910 (cost is $7,220).

     28   Sold merchandise on credit to Linda Witt, Invoice No. 858, for $4,315 (cost is $3,280).

     31   Issued Check No. 419, payable to Payroll, in payment of sales salaries expense for the last half of the month, $18,300. Cashed the check and paid the employees.

     31   Cash sales for the last half of the month are $30,180 (cost is $16,820).

     31   Verify that amounts impacting customer and creditor accounts were posted and that any amounts that should have been posted as individual amounts to the general ledger accounts were posted. Foot and crossfoot the journals and make the month-end postings.

Required

1. Open the following general ledger accounts: Cash; Accounts Receivable; Inventory (March 1 beg. bal. is $10,000); Office Supplies; Store Supplies; Office Equipment; Accounts Payable; Long-Term

Notes Payable; Z. Church, Capital (March 1 beg. bal. is $10,000); Sales; Sales Discounts; Cost of Goods Sold; and Sales Salaries Expense. Open the following accounts receivable subsidiary ledger accounts: Jovita Albany, Min Cho, and Linda Witt. Open the following accounts payable subsidiary ledger accounts: Gabel Company, Van Industries, Spell Supply, and CD Company.

2. Enter these transactions in a sales journal like Exhibit 7.5, a purchases journal like Exhibit 7.9, a cash receipts journal like Exhibit 7.7, a cash disbursements journal like Exhibit 7.11, or a general journal. Number all journal pages as page 2.

3. Prepare a trial balance of the general ledger and prove the accuracy of the subsidiary ledgers by preparing schedules of both accounts receivable and accounts payable.

Check Trial balance totals, $232,905

Assume that Church Company in Problem 7-5A uses the periodic inventory system.

Problem 7-6A^A
Special journals, subsidiary ledgers, trial balance—periodic

C4 P2 P3

mhhe.com/wildFAP18e

Required

1. Open the following general ledger accounts: Cash; Accounts Receivable; Inventory (March 1 beg. bal. is $10,000); Office Supplies; Store Supplies; Office Equipment; Accounts Payable; Long-Term Notes Payable; Z. Church, Capital (March 1 beg. bal. is $10,000); Sales; Sales Discounts; Purchases; Purchases Returns and Allowances; Purchases Discounts; and Sales Salaries Expense. Open the following accounts receivable subsidiary ledger accounts: Jovita Albany, Min Cho, and Linda Witt. Open the following Accounts Payable subsidiary ledger accounts: Gabel Company, Van Industries, Spell Supply, and CD Company.

2. Enter the transactions from Problem 7-5A in a sales journal like that in Exhibit 7A.1, a purchases journal like that in Exhibit 7A.3, a cash receipts journal like that in Exhibit 7A.2, a cash disbursements journal like that in Exhibit 7A.4, or a general journal. Number journal pages as page 2.

3. Prepare a trial balance of the general ledger and prove the accuracy of the subsidiary ledgers by preparing schedules of both accounts receivable and accounts payable.

Check Trial balance totals, $236,806

Acorn Industries completes these transactions during July of the current year (the terms of all its credit sales are 2/10, n/30).

PROBLEM SET B

Problem 7-1B
Special journals, subsidiary ledgers, schedule of accounts receivable—perpetual

C4 P1 P2

July 1 Purchased $6,500 of merchandise on credit from Teton Company, invoice dated June 30, terms 2/10, n/30.
3 Issued Check No. 300 to *The Weekly* for advertising expense, $625.
5 Sold merchandise on credit to Kim Nettle, Invoice No. 918, for $19,200 (cost is $10,500).
6 Sold merchandise on credit to Ruth Blake, Invoice No. 919, for $7,500 (cost is $4,300).
7 Purchased $1,250 of store supplies on credit from Plaine, Inc., invoice dated July 7, terms n/10 EOM.
8 Received a $250 credit memorandum from Plaine, Inc., for the return of store supplies received on July 7.
9 Purchased $38,220 of store equipment on credit from Charm's Supply, invoice dated July 8, terms n/10 EOM.
10 Issued Check No. 301 to Teton Company in payment of its June 30 invoice, less the discount.
13 Sold merchandise on credit to Ashton Moore, Invoice No. 920, for $8,550 (cost is $5,230).
14 Sold merchandise on credit to Kim Nettle, Invoice No. 921, for $5,100 (cost is $3,800).
15 Received payment from Kim Nettle for the July 5 sale, less the discount.
15 Issued Check No. 302, payable to Payroll, in payment of sales salaries expense for the first half of the month, $31,850. Cashed the check and paid employees.
15 Cash sales for the first half of the month are $118,350 (cost is $76,330). (Cash sales are recorded daily using data from the cash registers but are recorded only twice in this problem to reduce repetitive entries.)
16 Received payment from Ruth Blake for the July 6 sale, less the discount.
17 Purchased $7,200 of merchandise on credit from Drake Company, invoice dated July 17, terms 2/10, n/30.
20 Purchased $650 of office supplies on credit from Charm's Supply, invoice dated July 19, terms n/10 EOM.
21 Borrowed $15,000 cash from College Bank by signing a long-term note payable.
23 Received payment from Ashton Moore for the July 13 sale, less the discount.
24 Received payment from Kim Nettle for the July 14 sale, less the discount.

24   Received a $2,400 credit memorandum from Drake Company for the return of defective merchandise received on July 17.

26   Purchased $9,770 of merchandise on credit from Teton Company, invoice dated July 26, terms 2/10, n/30.

27   Issued Check No. 303 to Drake Company in payment of its July 17 invoice, less the return and the discount.

29   Sold merchandise on credit to Ruth Blake, Invoice No. 922, for $17,500 (cost is $10,850).

30   Sold merchandise on credit to Ashton Moore, Invoice No. 923, for $16,820 (cost is $9,840).

31   Issued Check No. 304, payable to Payroll, in payment of the sales salaries expense for the last half of the month, $31,850.

31   Cash sales for the last half of the month are $80,244 (cost is $53,855).

Required

1. Prepare a sales journal like that in Exhibit 7.5 and a cash receipts journal like that in Exhibit 7.7. Number both journals as page 3. Then review the transactions of Acorn Industries and enter those transactions that should be journalized in the sales journal and those that should be journalized in the cash receipts journal. Ignore any transactions that should be journalized in a purchases journal, a cash disbursements journal, or a general journal.

2. Open the following general ledger accounts: Cash, Accounts Receivable, Inventory, Long-Term Notes Payable, Cost of Goods Sold, Sales, and Sales Discounts. Enter the June 30 balances for Cash ($100,000), Inventory ($200,000), and Long-Term Notes Payable ($300,000). Also open accounts receivable subsidiary ledger accounts for Kim Nettle, Ashton Moore, and Ruth Blake.

3. Verify that amounts that should be posted as individual amounts from the journals have been posted. (Such items are immediately posted.) Foot and crossfoot the journals and make the month-end postings.

Check   Trial balance totals, $588,264   4. Prepare a trial balance of the general ledger and prove the accuracy of the subsidiary ledger by preparing a schedule of accounts receivable.

Analysis Component

5. Assume that the total for the schedule of Accounts Receivable does not equal the balance of the controlling account in the general ledger. Describe steps you would take to discover the error(s).

Problem 7-2B[A]
Special journals, subsidiary ledgers, and schedule of accounts receivable—periodic

C4 P2 P3

Assume that Acorn Industries in Problem 7-1B uses the periodic inventory system.

Required

1. Prepare headings for a sales journal like the one in Exhibit 7A.1. Prepare headings for a cash receipts journal like the one in Exhibit 7A.2. Journalize the July transactions shown in Problem 7-1B that should be recorded in the sales journal and the cash receipts journal assuming the periodic inventory system is used.

2. Open the general ledger accounts with balances as shown in Problem 7-1B (do not open a Cost of Goods Sold ledger account). Under the periodic system, an Inventory account exists but is inactive until its balance is updated to the correct inventory balance at year-end. In this problem, the Inventory account remains inactive but must be included to correctly complete the trial balance.

Check   Trial balance totals, $588,264   3. Complete parts 3, 4, and 5 of Problem 7-1B using the results of parts 1 and 2 of this problem.

Problem 7-3B
Special journals, subsidiary ledgers, and schedule of accounts payable—perpetual

C4 P1 P2

The July transactions of Acorn Industries are described in Problem 7-1B.

Required

1. Prepare a general journal, a purchases journal like that in Exhibit 7.9, and a cash disbursements journal like that in Exhibit 7.11. Number all journal pages as page 3. Review the July transactions of Acorn Industries and enter those transactions that should be journalized in the general journal, the purchases journal, or the cash disbursements journal. Ignore any transactions that should be journalized in a sales journal or cash receipts journal.

2. Open the following general ledger accounts: Cash, Inventory, Office Supplies, Store Supplies, Store Equipment, Accounts Payable, Long-Term Notes Payable, Sales Salaries Expense, and Advertising Expense. Enter the June 30 balances of Cash ($100,000), Inventory ($200,000), and Long-Term Notes Payable ($300,000). Also open accounts payable subsidiary ledger accounts for Charm's Supply, Teton Company, Drake Company, and Plaine, Inc.

3. Verify that amounts that should be posted as individual amounts from the journals have been posted. (Such items are immediately posted.) Foot and crossfoot the journals and make the month-end postings.

4. Prepare a trial balance of the general ledger and a schedule of accounts payable.

Check Trial balance totals, $349,640

Refer to Problem 7-1B and assume that Acorn uses the periodic inventory system.

Problem 7-4B[A]

Special journals, subsidiary ledgers, and schedule of accounts payable—periodic

C4 P2 P3

Required

1. Prepare a general journal, a purchases journal like that in Exhibit 7A.3, and a cash disbursements journal like that in Exhibit 7A.4. Number all journal pages as page 3. Review the July transactions of Acorn Company (Problem 7-1B) and enter those transactions that should be journalized in the general journal, the purchases journal, or the cash disbursements journal. Ignore any transaction that should be journalized in a sales journal or cash receipts journal.

2. Open the following general ledger accounts: Cash, Inventory, Office Supplies, Store Supplies, Store Equipment, Accounts Payable, Long-Term Notes Payable, Purchases, Purchases Returns and Allowances, Purchases Discounts, Sales Salaries Expense, and Advertising Expense. Enter the June 30 balances of Cash ($100,000), Inventory ($200,000), and Long-Term Notes Payable ($300,000). Also open accounts payable subsidiary ledger accounts for Teton Company, Plaine, Inc., Charm's Supply, and Drake Company.

3. Complete parts 3 and 4 of Problem 7-3B using the results of parts 1 and 2 of this problem.

Check Trial balance totals, $352,266

Grassley Company completes these transactions during November of the current year (terms for all its credit sales are 2/10, n/30).

Problem 7-5B

Special journals, subsidiary ledgers, trial balance—perpetual

C4 P1 P2

Nov. 1 Purchased $5,058 of office equipment on credit from Brun Supply, invoice dated November 1, terms n/10 EOM.

2 Borrowed $88,500 cash from Wisconsin Bank by signing a long-term note payable.

4 Purchased $33,500 of merchandise from BLR Industries, invoice dated November 3, terms 2/10, n/30.

5 Purchased $1,040 of store supplies on credit from Grebe Company, invoice dated November 5, terms n/10 EOM.

8 Sold merchandise on credit to Cyd Rounder, Invoice No. 439, for $6,550 (cost is $3,910).

10 Sold merchandise on credit to Carlos Mantel, Invoice No. 440, for $13,500 (cost is $8,500).

11 Purchased $2,557 of merchandise from Lo Company, invoice dated November 10, terms 2/10, n/30.

12 Sent BLR Industries Check No. 633 in payment of its November 3 invoice less the discount.

15 Issued Check No. 634, payable to Payroll, in payment of sales salaries expense for the first half of the month, $6,585. Cashed the check and paid the employees.

15 Cash sales for the first half of the month are $18,170 (cost is $9,000). (Cash sales are recorded daily but are recorded only twice in this problem to reduce repetitive entries.)

15 Sold merchandise on credit to Tori Tripp, Invoice No. 441, for $5,250 (cost is $2,450).

16 Purchased $459 of office supplies on credit from Grebe Company, invoice dated November 16, terms n/10 EOM.

17 Received a $557 credit memorandum from Lo Company for the return of unsatisfactory merchandise purchased on November 11.

18 Received payment from Cyd Rounder for the November 8 sale less the discount.

19 Received payment from Carlos Mantel for the November 10 sale less the discount.

19 Issued Check No. 635 to Lo Company in payment of its invoice of November 10 less the return and the discount.

22 Sold merchandise on credit to Carlos Mantel, Invoice No. 442, for $3,695 (cost is $2,060).

24 Sold merchandise on credit to Tori Tripp, Invoice No. 443, for $4,280 (cost is $2,130).

25 Received payment from Tori Tripp for the sale of November 15 less the discount.

26 Received a $922 credit memorandum from Brun Supply for the return of office equipment purchased on November 1.

30 Issued Check No. 636, payable to Payroll, in payment of sales salaries expense for the last half of the month, $6,585. Cashed the check and paid the employees.

30 Cash sales for the last half of the month are $16,703 (cost is $10,200).

30 Verify that amounts impacting customer and creditor accounts were posted and that any amounts that should have been posted as individual amounts to the general ledger accounts were posted. Foot and crossfoot the journals and make the month-end postings.

Required

1. Open the following general ledger accounts: Cash; Accounts Receivable; Inventory (November 1 beg. bal. is $40,000); Office Supplies; Store Supplies; Office Equipment; Accounts Payable; Long-Term Notes Payable; C. Grassley, Capital (Nov. 1 beg. bal. is $40,000); Sales; Sales Discounts; Cost of Goods Sold; and Sales Salaries Expense. Open the following accounts receivable subsidiary ledger accounts: Carlos Mantel, Tori Tripp, and Cyd Rounder. Open the following accounts payable subsidiary ledger accounts: Grebe Company, BLR Industries, Brun Supply, and Lo Company.

2. Enter these transactions in a sales journal like that in Exhibit 7.5, a purchases journal like that in Exhibit 7.9, a cash receipts journal like that in Exhibit 7.7, a cash disbursements journal like that in Exhibit 7.11, or a general journal. Number all journal pages as page 2.

Check   Trial balance totals, $202,283

3. Prepare a trial balance of the general ledger and prove the accuracy of the subsidiary ledgers by preparing schedules of both accounts receivable and accounts payable.

Problem 7-6B[A]
Special journals, subsidiary
ledgers, trial balance—periodic

C4 P2 P3

Assume that Grassley Company in Problem 7-5B uses the periodic inventory system.

Required

1. Open the following general ledger accounts: Cash; Accounts Receivable; Inventory (November 1 beg. bal. is $40,000); Office Supplies; Store Supplies; Office Equipment; Accounts Payable; Long-Term Notes Payable; C. Grassley, Capital (Nov. 1 beg. bal. is $40,000); Sales; Sales Discounts; Purchases; Purchases Returns and Allowances; Purchases Discounts; and Sales Salaries Expense. Open the following accounts receivable subsidiary ledger accounts: Carlos Mantel, Tori Tripp, and Cyd Rounder. Open the following accounts payable subsidiary ledger accounts: Grebe Company, BLR Industries, Brun Supply, and Lo Company.

2. Enter the transactions from Problem 7-5B in a sales journal like that in Exhibit 7A.1, a purchases journal like that in Exhibit 7A.3, a cash receipts journal like that in Exhibit 7A.2, a cash disbursements journal like that in Exhibit 7A.4, or a general journal. Number journal pages as page 2.

Check   Trial balance totals, $203,550

3. Prepare a trial balance of the general ledger and prove the accuracy of the subsidiary ledgers by preparing schedules of both accounts receivable and accounts payable.

PROBLEM SET C

 Problem Set C is available at the book's Website to further reinforce and assess your learning.

SERIAL PROBLEM

Success Systems

(This serial problem began in Chapter 1 and continues through most of the book. If previous chapter segments were not completed, the serial problem can begin at this point. It is helpful, but not necessary, that you use the Working Papers that accompany the book.)

SP 7   Assume that A. Lopez expands Success Systems' accounting system to include special journals.

Required

1. Locate the transactions related to January through March 2008 for Success Systems in Chapter 5.

2. Enter the Success Systems transactions for January through March in a sales journal like that in Exhibit 7.5 (insert "n/a" in the Invoice column), a cash receipts journal like that in Exhibit 7.7, a purchases journal like that in Exhibit 7.9 (use Computer Supplies heading instead of Office Supplies), and a cash disbursements journal like that in Exhibit 7.11 (insert "n/a" in the Check Number column), or a general journal. Number journal pages as page 2. If the transaction does not specify the name of the payee, state "not specified" in the Payee column of the cash disbursements journal.

3. The transactions on the following dates should be journalized in the general journal: January 5, 11, 20, 24, and 29 (no entry required) and March 24. Do not record and post the adjusting entries for the end of March.

(If the Working Papers that accompany this book are not available, omit this comprehensive problem.) Assume it is Monday, May 1, the first business day of the month, and you have just been hired as the accountant for Paloma Company, which operates with monthly accounting periods. All of the company's accounting work is completed through the end of April and its ledgers show April 30 balances. During your first month on the job, the company experiences the following transactions and events (terms for all its credit sales are 2/10, n/30 unless stated differently):

May 1 Issued Check No. 3410 to J&K Management Co. in payment of the May rent, $3,710. (Use two lines to record the transaction. Charge 80% of the rent to Rent Expense—Selling Space and the balance to Rent Expense—Office Space.)

2 Sold merchandise on credit to Bowman Company, Invoice No. 8785, for $6,100 (cost is $4,100).

2 Issued a $175 credit memorandum to Net, Inc., for defective (worthless) merchandise sold on April 28 and returned for credit. The total selling price (gross) was $4,725.

3 Received a $798 credit memorandum from Parker Products for the return of merchandise purchased on April 29.

4 Purchased the following on credit from Gates Supply Co.: merchandise, $37,072; store supplies, $574; and office supplies, $83. Invoice dated May 4, terms n/10 EOM.

5 Received payment from Net, Inc., for the balance from the April 28 sale less the May 2 return and the discount.

8 Issued Check No. 3411 to Parker Products to pay for the $7,098 of merchandise purchased on April 29 less the May 3 return and a 2% discount.

9 Sold store supplies to the merchant next door at their cost of $350 cash.

10 Purchased $4,074 of office equipment on credit from Gates Supply Co., invoice dated May 10, terms n/10 EOM.

11 Received payment from Bowman Company for the May 2 sale less the discount.

11 Purchased $8,800 of merchandise from Gatsby, Inc., invoice dated May 10, terms 2/10, n/30.

12 Received an $854 credit memorandum from Gates Supply Co. for the return of defective office equipment received on May 10.

15 Issued Check No. 3412, payable to Payroll, in payment of sales salaries, $5,320, and office salaries, $3,150. Cashed the check and paid the employees.

15 Cash sales for the first half of the month are $59,220 (cost is $38,200). (Cash sales are recorded daily but are recorded only twice here to reduce repetitive entries.)

15 Post to the customer and creditor accounts. Also post individual items that are not included in column totals at the end of the month to the general ledger accounts. (Such items are posted daily but are posted only twice each month because they are few in number.)

16 Sold merchandise on credit to Bowman Company, Invoice No. 8786, for $3,990 (cost is $1,890).

17 Purchased $13,650 of merchandise from Joey Corp., invoice dated May 14, terms 2/10, n/60.

19 Issued Check No. 3413 to Gatsby, Inc., in payment of its May 10 invoice less the discount.

22 Sold merchandise to Karim Services, Invoice No. 8787, for $6,850 (cost is $4,990), terms 2/10, n/60.

23 Issued Check No. 3414 to Joey Corp. in payment of its May 14 invoice less the discount.

24 Purchased the following on credit from Gates Supply Co.: merchandise, $8,120; store supplies, $630; and office supplies, $280. Invoice dated May 24, terms n/10 EOM.

25 Purchased $3,080 of merchandise from Parker Products, invoice dated May 23, terms 2/10, n/30.

26 Sold merchandise on credit to Dexter Corp., Invoice No. 8788, for $14,210 (cost is $8,230).

26 Issued Check No. 3415 to Trinity Power in payment of the May electric bill, $1,283.

29 The owner of Paloma Company, Paloma Chavez, used Check No. 3416 to withdraw $7,000 cash from the business for personal use.

30 Received payment from Karim Services for the May 22 sale less the discount.

30 Issued Check No. 3417, payable to Payroll, in payment of sales salaries, $5,320, and office salaries, $3,150. Cashed the check and paid the employees.

31 Cash sales for the last half of the month are $70,052 (cost is $45,500).

31 Post to the customer and creditor accounts. Also post individual items that are not included in column totals at the end of the month to the general ledger accounts. Foot and crossfoot the journals and make the month-end postings.

Required

1. Enter these transactions in a sales journal, a purchases journal, a cash receipts journal, a cash disbursements journal, or a general journal as illustrated in this chapter (number all journal pages as page 2). Post when instructed to do so. Assume a perpetual inventory system.

2. Prepare a trial balance in the Trial Balance columns of the work sheet form provided with the working papers. Complete the work sheet using the following information for accounting adjustments.

    a. Expired insurance, $553.

    b. Ending store supplies inventory, $2,232.

    c. Ending office supplies inventory, $504.

    d. Depreciation of store equipment, $567.

    e. Depreciation of office equipment, $329.

    Prepare and post adjusting and closing entries.

3. Prepare a May 2008 multiple-step income statement, a May 2008 statement of owner's equity, and a May 31, 2008, classified balance sheet.

4. Prepare a post-closing trial balance. Also prove the accuracy of subsidiary ledgers by preparing schedules of both accounts receivable and accounts payable.

BEYOND THE NUMBERS

REPORTING IN ACTION

A1

BTN 7-1 Refer to Best Buy's financial statements in Appendix A to answer the following.

1. Identify the note that reports on Best Buy's business segments.

2. Describe the focus and activities of each of Best Buy's business segments.

Fast Forward

3. Access Best Buy's annual report for fiscal years ending after February 26, 2005, from its Website (BestBuy.com) or the SEC's EDGAR database (www.SEC.gov). Has Best Buy changed its reporting policy regarding segment information? Explain.

COMPARATIVE ANALYSIS

A1

BTN 7-2 Key figures for Best Buy and Circuit City follow ($ millions).

Best Buy Segment	Current Year Segment Income	Current Year Segment Assets	One Year Prior Segment Income	One Year Prior Segment Assets	Two Years Prior Segment Income	Two Years Prior Segment Assets
Domestic	$1,393	$8,372	$1,267	$7,547	$1,002	$6,282
International	49	1,922	37	1,105	8	858

Circuit City Segment	Current Year Segment Income	Current Year Segment Assets	One Year Prior Segment Income	One Year Prior Segment Assets	Two Years Prior Segment Income	Two Years Prior Segment Assets
Domestic	$58	$3,355	$(34)	$3,129	$(33)	$3,122
International	32	435	—	—	—	—

Required

1. Compute the segment return on assets for each of the segments of Best Buy and Circuit City for each of the two most recent years shown. (You can only calculate the return on the international segment assets for the most recent year for Circuit City.)

2. Interpret and comment on your results of part 1.

BTN 7-3   Erica Gray, CPA, is a sole practitioner. She has been practicing as an auditor for 10 years. Recently a long-standing audit client asked Gray to design and implement an integrated computer-based accounting information system. The fees associated with this additional engagement with the client are very attractive. However, Gray wonders if she can remain objective on subsequent audits in her evaluation of the client's accounting system and its records if she was responsible for its design and implementation. Gray knows that professional auditing standards require her to remain independent in fact and appearance from her auditing clients.

Required

1. What do you believe auditing standards are mainly concerned with when they require independence in fact? In appearance?

2. Why is it important that auditors remain independent of their clients?

3. Do you think Gray can accept this engagement and remain independent? Justify your response.

BTN 7-4   Your friend, Wendy Geiger, owns a small retail store that sells candies and nuts. Geiger acquires her goods from a few select vendors. She generally makes purchase orders by phone and on credit. Sales are primarily for cash. Geiger keeps her own manual accounting system using a general journal and a general ledger. At the end of each business day, she records one summary entry for cash sales. Geiger recently began offering items in creative gift packages. This has increased sales substantially, and she is now receiving orders from corporate and other clients who order large quantities and prefer to buy on credit. As a result of increased credit transactions in both purchases and sales, keeping the accounting records has become extremely time consuming. Geiger wants to continue to maintain her own manual system and calls you for advice. Write a memo to her advising how she might modify her current manual accounting system to accommodate the expanded business activities. Geiger is accustomed to checking her ledger by using a trial balance. Your memo should explain the advantages of what you propose and of any other verification techniques you recommend.

BTN 7-5   Access the March 8, 2005, filing of the fiscal 2005 10-K report for Dell Computer (ticker DELL) at www.sec.gov. Read the footnote that details Dell's segment information and answer the following.

1. Dell's operations are divided among which three geographic segments?

2. In fiscal year 2005, which geographic area had the largest dollar amount of operating income? Which had the largest amount of identifiable assets?

3. Compute the return on assets for each segment for fiscal year 2005. Use operating income and average total assets by segment for your calculation. Which segment has the highest return on assets?

4. For what product groups does Dell provide segment data? What percent of Dell's net revenue is earned by each product group?

BTN 7-6   Each member of the team is to assume responsibility for one of the following tasks:

a. Journalizing in the purchases journal.

b. Journalizing in the cash disbursements journal.

c. Maintaining and verifying the Accounts Payable ledger.

d. Journalizing in the sales journal and the general journal.

e. Journalizing in the cash receipts journal.

f. Maintaining and verifying the Accounts Receivable ledger.

The team should abide by the following procedures in carrying out responsibilities.

Required

1. After tasks *a–f* are assigned, each team member is to quickly read the list of transactions in Problem 7-5A, identifying with initials the journal in which each transaction is to be recorded. Upon completion, the team leader is to read transaction dates, and the appropriate team member is to vocalize responsibility. Any disagreement between teammates must be resolved.

2. Journalize and continually update subsidiary ledgers. Journal recorders should alert teammates assigned to subsidiary ledgers when an entry must be posted to their subsidiary.

3. Team members responsible for tasks *a*, *b*, *d*, and *e* are to summarize and prove journals; members responsible for tasks *c* and *f* are to prepare both payables and receivables schedules.

4. The team leader is to take charge of the general ledger, rotating team members to obtain amounts to be posted. The person responsible for a journal must complete posting references in that journal. Other team members should verify the accuracy of account balance computations. To avoid any abnormal account balances, post in the following order: P, S, G, R, D. (*Note:* Posting any necessary individual general ledger amounts is also done at this time.)

5. The team leader is to read out general ledger account balances while another team member fills in the trial balance form. Concurrently, one member should keep a running balance of debit account balance totals and another credit account balance totals. Verify the final total of the trial balance and the schedules. If necessary, the team must resolve any errors. Turn in the trial balance and schedules to the instructor.

BusinessWeek ACTIVITY

C1 C2

BTN 7-7   Read the article "A Big Lift from the Little Guys" in the August 8, 2005, issue of *BusinessWeek*. (This book's Website provides a free link.)

Required

1. What is the expected growth of IT spending for software in 2006?

2. Why are enterprise-software vendors beginning to focus their attention on the small- and medium-sized business (SMB) market?

3. What is the author's assessment of SAP's success in the SMB market? Explain.

ENTREPRENEURIAL DECISION

P1

BTN 7-8   Refer to the chapter's opening feature about Tony Lee and his **Ring Masters** company.

Required

1. Identify the special journals that Ring Masters would be likely to use in its operations. Also identify any subsidiary ledgers that Ring Masters would likely use.

2. Tony Lee hopes to double his sales from the current $3 million annually within five years. Assume that Lee's sales growth is as follows.

Year	One Year Hence	Two Years Hence	Three Years Hence	Four Years Hence	Five Years Hence
Growth in Sales	0%	20%	15%	25%	20%

Compute Lee's projected sales for each year (round to nearest dollar). If this pattern of sales growth holds, will Lee achieve his goal of doubling sales in five years?

GLOBAL DECISION

A1

Dixons

BTN 7-9   Access and refer to the April 2005 annual report for **Dixons** at <u>Dixons-Group.com</u>.

Required

1. Skim the notes to the financial statements until you find information relating to Dixons' geographic segments. Identify those segments.

2. What financial figures does it disclose for each geographic segment?

3. Does Dixons have a dominant segment? Explain.

ANSWERS TO MULTIPLE CHOICE QUIZ

1. a

2. e

3. d

4. b

5. a

8

Cash and Internal Controls

A Look Back

Chapter 7 focused on accounting information systems. We explained the principles and components of information systems, the use of special journals and subsidiary ledgers, and technology-based systems.

A Look at This Chapter

This chapter extends our study of accounting to internal control and the analysis of cash. We describe procedures that are good for internal control. We also explain the control of and the accounting for cash, including control features of banking activities.

A Look Ahead

Chapter 9 focuses on receivables. We explain how to account and report on receivables and their related accounts. This includes estimating uncollectible receivables and computing interest earned.

Learning Objectives

CAP

Conceptual

C1 Define internal control and identify its purpose and principles. *(p. 312)*

C2 Define cash and cash equivalents and explain how to report them. *(p. 317)*

C3 Identify control features of banking activities. *(p. 323)*

Analytical

A1 Compute the days' sales uncollected ratio and use it to assess liquidity. *(p. 329)*

Procedural

P1 Apply internal control to cash receipts and disbursements. *(p. 317)*

P2 Explain and record petty cash fund transactions. *(p. 320)*

P3 Prepare a bank reconciliation. *(p. 326)*

P4 *Appendix 8A*—Describe the voucher system to control cash disbursements. *(p. 332)*

P5 *Appendix 8B*—Apply the net method to control purchase discounts. *(p. 335)*

"I'm living my dream every day . . . you have to love it to be successful"
—Todd Graves

Going Fishing for Chicken Fingers

BATON ROUGE, LA—To launch his business, Todd Graves needed to go fishing. "After writing my business plan, buying a cheap suit, and borrowing a briefcase," says Todd, "I went to see every bank in town to fund my first chicken finger restaurant." Not a single bank would lend him the money.

Desperate, Todd left for Alaska to work as a salmon fisherman. The pay was great but the job dangerous. "Boats would often ram each other to get better sets for their nets." Having saved enough money to get started, Todd returned to Louisiana and launched **Raising Cane's Chicken Fingers (RaisingCanes.com).** Today, his restaurants generate millions in annual sales and continue to grow.

Although chicken fingers are key to Raising Cane's success, Todd's management of internal controls and cash is equally impressive. Several controls keep restaurant activities in check and safeguard assets. These include cash register procedures, inventory controls, and employee management. Todd even safeguards the sauce recipe!

Tight controls boost productivity and cut expenses, but these controls are applied thoughtfully. "We make it a priority to respect, recognize, and reward our crew," says Todd. "It's something we call Cane's Love." The restaurants also apply good cash management, including controls over cash receipts, disbursements, petty cash, and bank reconciliations.

Internal controls are crucial for Todd since on busy days his nearly 30 restaurants attract thousands of customers and their cash. "We have a vision: To be known all over the world," says Todd. "I'm fortunate. I don't have a job; I have a passion. Your passion and culture are what set you apart." So, what is the end game for Raising Cane's? "I don't have an end game," says Todd. "Ray Kroc didn't have an end game. Dave Thomas didn't have an end game." Now that is a winning game plan.

[Sources: *Raising Cane's Chicken Fingers Website;* January 2006; *Entrepreneur,* October 2004 and November 2003; *Business Report,* November 2004; *LSU Reveille,* February 2004]

We all are aware of reports and experiences involving theft and fraud. These occurrences affect us in several ways: We lock doors, chain bikes, review sales receipts, and acquire alarm systems. A company also takes actions to safeguard, control, and manage what it owns. Experience tells us that small companies are most vulnerable, usually due to weak internal controls. It is management's responsibility to set up policies and procedures to safeguard a company's assets, especially cash. To do so, management *and* employees must understand and apply principles of internal control. This chapter describes these principles and how to apply them. It focuses special attention on cash because it is easily transferable and is often at high risk of loss.

Internal Control

This section describes internal control and its fundamental principles. We also discuss the impact of technology on internal control and the limitations of control procedures.

Purpose of Internal Control

C1 Define internal control and identify its purpose and principles.

Managers (or owners) of small businesses often control the entire operation. These managers usually purchase all assets, hire and manage employees, negotiate all contracts, and sign all checks. They know from personal contact and observation whether the business is actually receiving the assets and services paid for. Most companies, however, cannot maintain this close personal supervision. They must delegate responsibilities and rely on formal procedures rather than personal contact in controlling business activities.

Point: With company growth comes increased reporting and controls to safeguard assets and manage operations.

Managers use an internal control system to monitor and control business activities. An **internal control system** consists of the policies and procedures managers use to

- Protect assets.
- Ensure reliable accounting.
- Promote efficient operations.
- Urge adherence to company policies.

A properly designed internal control system is a key part of systems design, analysis, and performance. Managers place a high priority on internal control systems because they can prevent avoidable losses, help managers plan operations, and monitor company and employee performance. Internal controls do not provide guarantees, but they lower the company's risk of loss.

Principles of Internal Control

8-1

Internal control policies and procedures vary from company to company according to such factors as the nature of the business and its size. Certain fundamental internal control principles apply to all companies. The **principles of internal control** are to

1. Establish responsibilities.
2. Maintain adequate records.
3. Insure assets and bond key employees.
4. Separate recordkeeping from custody of assets.
5. Divide responsibility for related transactions.
6. Apply technological controls.
7. Perform regular and independent reviews.

This section explains these seven principles and describes how internal control procedures minimize the risk of fraud and theft. These procedures also increase the reliability and accuracy of accounting records.

Establish Responsibilities   Proper internal control means that responsibility for a task is clearly established and assigned to one person. When a problem occurs in a company where responsibility is not identified, determining who is at fault is difficult. For instance, if two sales-clerks share the same cash register and there is a cash shortage, neither clerk can be held accountable. To prevent this problem, one clerk might be given responsibility for handling all cash sales. Alternately, a company can use a register with separate cash drawers for each clerk. Most of us have waited at a retail counter during a shift change while employees swap cash drawers.

Maintain Adequate Records   Good recordkeeping is part of an internal control system. It helps protect assets and ensures that employees use prescribed procedures. Reliable records are also a source of information that managers use to monitor company activities. When detailed records of equipment are kept, for instance, items are unlikely to be lost or stolen without detection. Similarly, transactions are less likely to be entered in wrong accounts if a chart of accounts is set up and carefully used. Many preprinted forms and internal documents are also designed for use in a good internal control system. When sales slips are properly designed, for instance, sales personnel can record needed information efficiently with less chance of errors or delays to customers. When sales slips are prenumbered and controlled, each one issued is the responsibility of one salesperson, preventing the salesperson from pocketing cash by making a sale and destroying the sales slip. Computerized point-of-sale systems achieve the same control results.

Insure Assets and Bond Key Employees   Good internal control means that assets are adequately insured against casualty and that employees handling large amounts of cash and easily transferable assets are bonded. An employee is *bonded* when a company purchases an insurance policy, or a bond, against losses from theft by that employee. Bonding reduces the risk of loss. It also discourages theft because bonded employees know an independent bonding company will be involved when theft is uncovered and is unlikely to be sympathetic with an employee involved in theft.

Separate Recordkeeping from Custody of Assets   A person who controls or has access to an asset must not keep that asset's accounting records. This principle reduces the risk of theft or waste of an asset because the person with control over it knows that another person keeps its records. Also, a recordkeeper who does not have access to the asset has no reason to falsify records. This means that to steal an asset and hide the theft from the records, two or more people must *collude*— or agree in secret to commit the fraud.

Point: Sarbanes-Oxley Act requires that each annual report contain an *internal control report*, which must: (1) state managers' responsibility for establishing and maintaining adequate internal controls for financial reporting; and (2) assess the effectiveness of those controls.

Point: Many companies have a mandatory vacation policy for employees who handle cash. When another employee must cover for the one on vacation, it is more difficult to hide cash frauds.

Point: The Association of Certified Fraud Examiners (**cfenet.com**) estimates that employee fraud costs small companies more than $100,000 per incident.

Decision Insight

Tag Control   A novel technique exists for marking physical assets. It involves embedding a less than one-inch-square tag of fibers that creates a unique optical signature recordable by scanners. Manufacturers hope to embed tags in everything from compact discs and credit cards to designer clothes.

Divide Responsibility for Related Transactions Good internal control divides responsibility for a transaction or a series of related transactions between two or more individuals or departments. This is to ensure that the work of one individual acts as a check on the other. This principle, often called *separation of duties,* is not a call for duplication of work. Each employee or department should perform unduplicated effort. Examples of transactions with divided responsibility are placing purchase orders, receiving merchandise, and paying vendors. These tasks should not be given to one individual or department. Assigning responsibility for two or more of these tasks to one party increases mistakes and perhaps fraud. Having an independent person, for example, check incoming goods for quality and quantity encourages more care and attention to detail than having the person who placed the order do the checking. Added protection can result from identifying a third person to approve payment of the invoice. A company can even designate a fourth person with authority to write checks as another protective measure.

Apply Technological Controls Cash registers, check protectors, time clocks, and personal identification scanners are examples of devices that can improve internal control. Technology often improves the effectiveness of controls. A cash register with a locked-in tape or electronic file makes a record of each cash sale. A check protector perforates the amount of a check into its face and makes it difficult to alter the amount. A time clock registers the exact time an employee both arrives at and departs from the job. Mechanical change and currency counters quickly and accurately count amounts, and personal scanners limit access to only authorized individuals. Each of these and other technological controls are an effective part of many internal control systems.

Decision Insight

About Face Face-recognition software snaps a digital picture of the face and converts key facial features—say, the distance between the eyes—into a series of numerical values. These can be stored on an ID or ATM card as a simple bar code to prohibit unauthorized access.

Perform Regular and Independent Reviews Changes in personnel, stress of time pressures, and technological advances present opportunities for shortcuts and lapses. To counter these factors, regular reviews of internal control systems are needed to ensure that procedures are followed. These reviews are preferably done by internal auditors not directly involved in the activities. Their impartial perspective encourages an evaluation of the efficiency as well as the effectiveness of the internal control system. Many companies also pay for audits by independent, external auditors. These external auditors test the company's financial records to give an opinion as to whether its financial statements are presented fairly. Before external auditors decide on how much testing is needed, they evaluate the effectiveness of the internal control system. This evaluation is often helpful to a client.

Decision Maker

Answer—p. 337

Entrepreneur As owner of a start-up information services company, you hire a systems analyst. One of her first recommendations is to require all employees to take at least one week of vacation per year. Why would she recommend a "forced vacation" policy?

Technology and Internal Control

The fundamental principles of internal control are relevant no matter what the technological state of the accounting system, from purely manual to fully automated systems. Technology impacts an internal control system in several important ways. Perhaps the most obvious is that technology allows us quicker access to databases and information. Used effectively, technology greatly improves managers' abilities to monitor and control business activities. This section describes some technological impacts we must be alert to.

Reduced Processing Errors Technologically advanced systems reduce the number of errors in processing information. Provided the software and data entry are correct, the risk of mechanical and mathematical errors is nearly eliminated. However, we must remember that erroneous software or data entry does exist. Also, less human involvement in data processing can cause data entry errors to go undiscovered. Moreover, errors in software can produce consistent but erroneous processing of transactions. Continually checking and monitoring all types of systems are important.

More Extensive Testing of Records A company's review and audit of electronic records can include more extensive testing when information is easily and rapidly accessed. When accounting records are kept manually, auditors and others likely select only small samples of data to test. When data are accessible with computer technology, however, auditors can quickly analyze large samples or even the entire database.

Limited Evidence of Processing Many data processing steps are increasingly done by computer. Accordingly, fewer hard-copy items of documentary evidence are available for review. Yet technologically advanced systems can provide new evidence. They can, for instance, record who made the entries, the date and time, the source of the entry, and so on. Technology can also be designed to require the use of passwords or other identification before access to the system is granted. This means that internal control depends more on the design and operation of the information system and less on the analysis of its resulting documents.

Point: External decision makers look to several sources when assessing a company's internal controls. Sources include the auditor's report, management report on controls (if available), management discussion and analysis, and financial press.

Crucial Separation of Duties Technological advances in accounting information systems often yield some job eliminations or consolidations. While those who remain have the special skills necessary to operate advanced programs and equipment, a company with a reduced workforce risks losing its crucial separation of duties. The company must establish ways to control and monitor employees to minimize risk of error and fraud. For instance, the person who designs and programs the information system must not be the one who operates it. The company must also separate control over programs and files from the activities related to cash receipts and disbursements. For instance, a computer operator should not control check-writing activities. Achieving acceptable separation of duties can be especially difficult and costly in small companies with few employees.

> **Decision Insight**
>
> **Happiest Fraud Victim** Certified Fraud Examiners Website reports the following: Andrew Cameron stole Jacqueline Boanson's credit card. Cameron headed to the racetrack and promptly charged two bets for $150 on the credit card—winning $400. Unfortunately for Cameron the racetrack refused to pay him cash as its policy is to credit winnings from bets made on a credit card to that same card. Cameron was later nabbed; and the racetrack let Ms. Boanson keep the winnings.

Increased E-Commerce Technology has encouraged the growth of e-commerce. Amazon.com and eBay are examples of companies that have successfully exploited e-commerce. Most companies have some e-commerce transactions. All such transactions involve at least three risks. (1) *Credit card number theft* is a risk of using, transmitting, and storing such data online. This increases the cost of e-commerce. (2) *Computer viruses* are malicious programs that attach themselves to innocent files for purposes of infecting and harming other files and programs. (3) *Impersonation* online can result in charges of sales to bogus accounts, purchases of inappropriate materials, and the unknowing giving up of confidential information to hackers. Companies use both firewalls and encryption to combat some of these risks—firewalls are points of entry to a system that require passwords to continue, and encryption is a mathematical process to rearrange contents that cannot be read without the process code. Nearly 5% of Americans already report being victims of identity theft, and roughly 10 million say their privacy has been compromised.

"Worst case of identity theft I've ever seen!"

Copyright 2004 by Randy Glasbergen. www.glasbergen.com

Limitations of Internal Control

All internal control policies and procedures have limitations which usually arise from either (1) the human element, or (2) the cost-benefit principle.

Internal control policies and procedures are applied by people. This human element creates several potential limitations that we can categorize as either (1) human error or (2) human fraud. *Human error* can occur from negligence, fatigue, misjudgment, or confusion. *Human fraud* involves intent by people to defeat internal controls, such as *management override,* for personal gain. Fraud also includes collusion to thwart the separation of duties. The human element highlights the importance of establishing an *internal control environment* to convey management's commitment to internal control policies and procedures.

Point: Cybercrime.gov pursues computer and intellectual property crimes, including that of e-commerce.

The second major limitation on internal control is the *cost-benefit principle,* which dictates that the costs of internal controls must not exceed their benefits. Analysis of costs and benefits must consider all factors, including the impact on morale. Most companies, for instance, have a legal right to read employees' e-mails, yet companies seldom exercise that right unless they are confronted with evidence of potential harm to the company. The same holds for drug testing, phone tapping, and hidden cameras. The bottom line is that managers must establish internal control policies and procedures with a net benefit to the company.

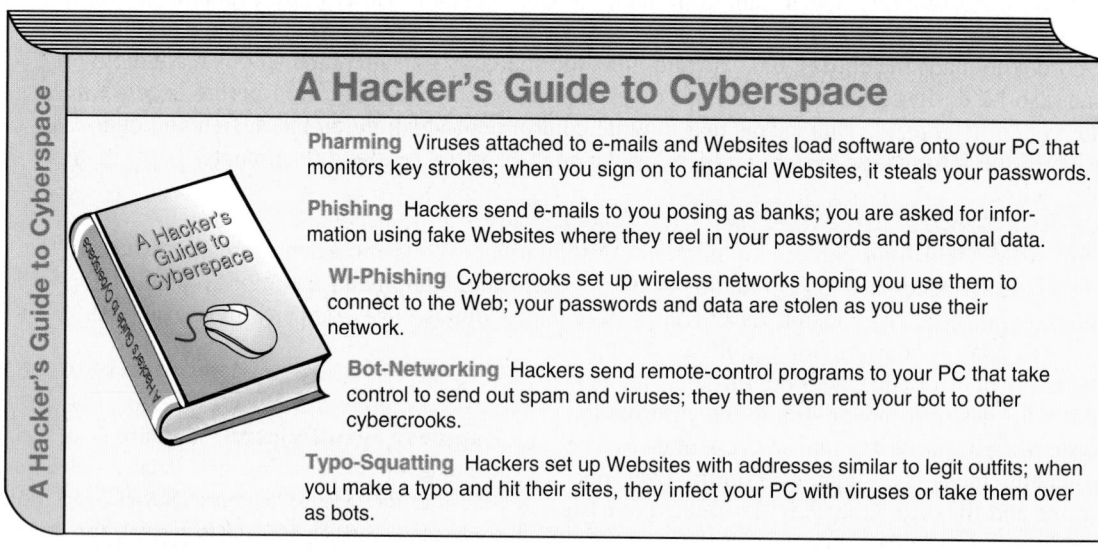

A Hacker's Guide to Cyberspace

Pharming Viruses attached to e-mails and Websites load software onto your PC that monitors key strokes; when you sign on to financial Websites, it steals your passwords.

Phishing Hackers send e-mails to you posing as banks; you are asked for information using fake Websites where they reel in your passwords and personal data.

WI-Phishing Cybercrooks set up wireless networks hoping you use them to connect to the Web; your passwords and data are stolen as you use their network.

Bot-Networking Hackers send remote-control programs to your PC that take control to send out spam and viruses; they then even rent your bot to other cybercrooks.

Typo-Squatting Hackers set up Websites with addresses similar to legit outfits; when you make a typo and hit their sites, they infect your PC with viruses or take them over as bots.

Quick Check

Answers—p. 337

1. Principles of internal control suggest that (choose one): (*a*) Responsibility for a series of related transactions (such as placing orders, receiving and paying for merchandise) should be assigned to one employee; (*b*) Responsibility for individual tasks should be shared by more than one employee so that one serves as a check on the other; or (*c*) Employees who handle considerable cash and easily transferable assets should be bonded.

2. What are some impacts of computing technology on internal control?

Control of Cash

Cash is a necessary asset of every company. Most companies also own *cash equivalents* (defined below), which are assets similar to cash. Cash and cash equivalents are the most liquid of all assets and are easily hidden and moved. An effective system of internal controls protects these assets and it should meet three basic guidelines:

1. Handling cash is separate from recordkeeping of cash.
2. Cash receipts are promptly deposited in a bank.
3. Cash disbursements are made by check.

The first guideline applies separation of duties to minimize errors and fraud. When duties are separated, two or more people must collude to steal cash and conceal this action in the accounting records. The second guideline uses immediate (say, daily) deposits of all cash receipts to produce a timely independent record of the cash received. It also reduces the likelihood of cash theft (or loss) and the risk that an employee could personally use the money before depositing it. The third guideline uses payments by check to develop an independent bank record of cash disbursements. This guideline also reduces the risk of cash theft (or loss).

Decision Insight

Days' Cash Expense Coverage The ratio of *cash (and cash equivalents) to average daily cash expenses* indicates the number of days a company can operate without additional cash inflows. It reflects on company liquidity.

This section begins with definitions of cash and cash equivalents. Discussion then focuses on controls and accounting for both cash receipts and disbursements. The exact procedures used to achieve control over cash vary across companies. They depend on factors such as company size, number of employees, volume of cash transactions, and sources of cash.

Cash, Cash Equivalents, and Liquidity

Good accounting systems help in managing the amount of cash and controlling who has access to it. Cash is the usual means of payment when paying for assets, services, or liabilities. **Liquidity** refers to a company's ability to pay for its near-term obligations. Cash and similar assets are called **liquid assets** because they can be readily used to settle such obligations. A company needs liquid assets to effectively operate.

Cash includes currency and coins along with the amounts on deposit in bank accounts, checking accounts (called *demand deposits*), and many savings accounts (called *time deposits*). Cash also includes items that are acceptable for deposit in these accounts such as customer checks, cashier checks, certified checks, and money orders. **Cash equivalents** are short-term, highly liquid investment assets meeting two criteria: (1) readily convertible to a known cash amount and (2) sufficiently close to their due date so that their market value is not sensitive to interest rate changes. Only investments purchased within three months of their due date usually satisfy these criteria. Examples of cash equivalents are short-term investments in assets such as U.S. Treasury bills and money market funds. To increase their return, many companies invest idle cash in cash equivalents. Most companies combine cash equivalents with cash as a single item on the balance sheet.

C2 Define cash and cash equivalents and explain how to report them.

Point: The most liquid assets are usually reported first on a balance sheet; the least liquid assets are reported last.

Point: Google reports cash and cash equivalents of $186 million in its balance sheet. This amount makes up over 20% of its total assets.

Control of Cash Receipts

Internal control of cash receipts ensures that cash received is properly recorded and deposited. Cash receipts can arise from transactions such as cash sales, collections of customer accounts, receipts of interest earned, bank loans, sales of assets, and owner investments. This section explains internal control over two important types of cash receipts: over-the-counter and by mail.

P1 Apply internal control to cash receipts and disbursements.

Over-the-Counter Cash Receipts For purposes of internal control, over-the-counter cash receipts from sales should be recorded on a cash register at the time of each sale. To help ensure that correct amounts are entered, each register should be located so customers can read the amounts entered. Clerks also should be required to enter each sale before wrapping merchandise and to give the customer a receipt for each sale. The design of each cash register should provide a permanent, locked-in record of each transaction. In many systems, the register is directly linked with computing and accounting services. Less advanced registers simply print a record of each transaction on a paper tape or electronic file locked inside the register.

Decision Insight

Cash Budget Projected cash receipts and cash disbursements are often summarized in a *cash budget*. Provided that sufficient cash exists for effective operations, companies wish to minimize the cash they hold because of its low return versus other investment opportunities.

Proper internal control prescribes that custody over cash should be separate from its record-keeping. For over-the-counter cash receipts, this separation begins with the cash sale. The clerk who has access to cash in the register should not have access to its locked-in record. At the end of the clerk's work period, the clerk should count the cash in the register, record the amount, and turn over the cash and a record of its amount to the company cashier. The cashier, like the clerk, has access to the cash but should not have access to accounting records (or the register tape or file). A third employee, often a supervisor, compares the record of total register transactions (or the register tape or file) with the cash receipts reported by the cashier. This record is the basis for a journal entry recording over-the-counter cash receipts. The third employee has access to the records for

Decision Insight

Perpetual Accounting Wal-Mart uses a network of information links with its point-of-sale cash registers to coordinate sales, purchases, and distribution. Its supercenters, for instance, ring up to 15,000 separate sales on heavy days. By using cash register information, the company can fix pricing mistakes quickly and capitalize on sales trends.

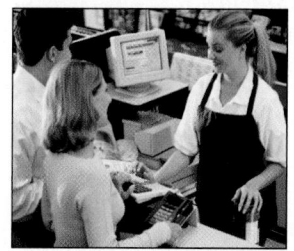

cash but not to the actual cash. The clerk and the cashier have access to cash but not to the accounting records. None of them can make a mistake or divert cash without the difference being revealed—see the following diagram.

Clerk rings up cash sales on register; clerk prepares cash count sheet (and keeps copy) and sends to company cashier along with the cash

Supervisor reads register data, prepares register sheet (and keeps copy), and sends both to company cashier

Cashier prepares cash records, deposit slip, and journal entry

Point: Retailers often require cashiers to restrictively endorse checks immediately on receipt by stamping them "For deposit only."

Cash over and short. Sometimes errors in making change are discovered from differences between the cash in a cash register and the record of the amount of cash receipts. Although a clerk is careful, one or more customers can be given too much or too little change. This means that at the end of a work period, the cash in a cash register might not equal the record of cash receipts. This difference is reported in the **Cash Over and Short** account, also called *Cash Short and Over,* which is an income statement account recording the income effects of cash overages and cash shortages. To illustrate, if a cash register's record shows $550 but the count of cash in the register is $555, the entry to record cash sales and its overage is

Assets = Liabilities + Equity
+555   + 5
              +550

Cash	555	
Cash Over and Short		5
Sales		550
To record cash sales and a cash overage.		

On the other hand, if a cash register's record shows $625 but the count of cash in the register is $621, the entry to record cash sales and its shortage is:

Assets = Liabilities + Equity
+621   − 4
              +625

Cash	621	
Cash Over and Short.	4	
Sales.		625
To record cash sales and a cash shortage.		

Since customers are more likely to dispute being shortchanged than being given too much change, the Cash Over and Short account usually has a debit balance at the end of an accounting period. A debit balance reflects an expense. It can be shown on the income statement as part of general and administrative expenses. (Since the amount is usually small, it is often combined with other small expenses and reported as part of *miscellaneous expenses;* or as part of *miscellaneous revenues* if it has a credit balance.)

Point: Collusion implies that two or more individuals are knowledgeable or involved with the activities of the other(s).

Cash Receipts by Mail Control of cash receipts that arrive through the mail starts with the person who opens the mail. Preferably, two people are assigned the task of, and are present for, opening the mail. In this case, theft of cash receipts by mail requires collusion between these two employees. Specifically, the person(s) opening the mail enters a list (in triplicate) of money received. This list should contain a record of each sender's name, the amount, and an explanation of why the money is sent. The first copy is sent with the money to the cashier. A second copy is sent to the recordkeeper in the accounting area. A third copy is kept by the clerks who opened the mail. The cashier deposits the money in a bank, and the recordkeeper records the amounts received in the accounting records.

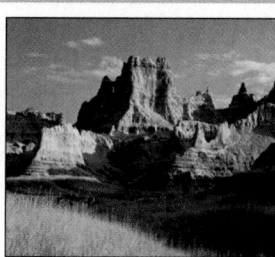

This process reflects good internal control. That is, when the bank balance is reconciled by another person (explained later in the chapter), errors or acts of fraud by the mail clerks, the cashier, or the recordkeeper are revealed. They are revealed because the bank's record of cash deposited must agree with the records from each of the three. Moreover, if the mail clerks do not report all receipts correctly, customers will question their account balances. If the cashier does not deposit all receipts, the bank balance does not agree with the recordkeeper's cash balance. The recordkeeper and the person who reconciles the bank balance do not have access to cash and therefore have no opportunity to divert cash to themselves. This system makes errors and fraud highly unlikely. The exception is employee collusion.

Point: A complete set of financial statements includes a statement of cash flows, which provides useful information about a company's sources and uses of cash and cash equivalents.

Control of Cash Disbursements

Control of cash disbursements is especially important as most large thefts occur from payment of fictitious invoices. One key to controlling cash disbursements is to require all expenditures to be made by check. The only exception is small payments made from petty cash. Another key is to deny access to the accounting records to anyone other than the owner who has the authority to sign checks. A small business owner often signs checks and knows from personal contact that the items being paid for are actually received. This arrangement is impossible in large businesses. Instead, internal control procedures must be substituted for personal contact. Such procedures are designed to assure the check signer that the obligations recorded are properly incurred and should be paid. This section describes these and other internal control procedures, including the voucher system and petty cash system. The management of cash disbursements for purchases is described in Appendix 8B.

Voucher System of Control   A **voucher system** is a set of procedures and approvals designed to control cash disbursements and the acceptance of obligations. The voucher system of control establishes procedures for

- Verifying, approving, and recording obligations for eventual cash disbursement.
- Issuing checks for payment of verified, approved, and recorded obligations.

A reliable voucher system follows standard procedures for every transaction. This applies even when multiple purchases are made from the same supplier.

A voucher system's control over cash disbursements begins when a company incurs an obligation that will result in payment of cash. A key factor in this system is that only approved departments and individuals are authorized to incur such obligations. The system often limits the type of obligations that a department or individual can incur. In a large retail store, for instance, only a purchasing department should be authorized to incur obligations for merchandise inventory. Another key factor is that procedures for purchasing, receiving, and paying for merchandise are divided among several departments (or individuals). These departments include the one requesting the purchase, the purchasing department, the receiving department,

Point: MCI, formerly **WorldCom,** paid a whopping $500 million in SEC fines for accounting fraud. Among the charges were that it inflated earnings by as much as $10 billion. Its CEO, Bernard Ebbers, was sentenced to 25 years.

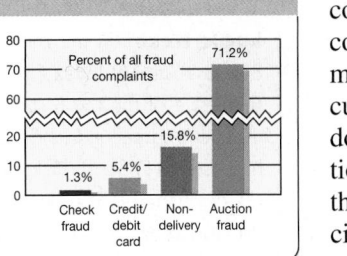
and the accounting department. To coordinate and control responsibilities of these departments, a company uses several different business documents. Exhibit 8.1 shows how documents are accumulated in a **voucher,** which is an internal document (or file) used to accumulate information to control cash disbursements and to ensure that a transaction is properly recorded. This specific example begins with a *purchase requisition* and concludes with a *check* drawn against cash. Appendix 8A describes each document entering and leaving a voucher system. It also describes the internal control objective served by each document.

Exhibit 8.1

Document Flow in a Voucher System

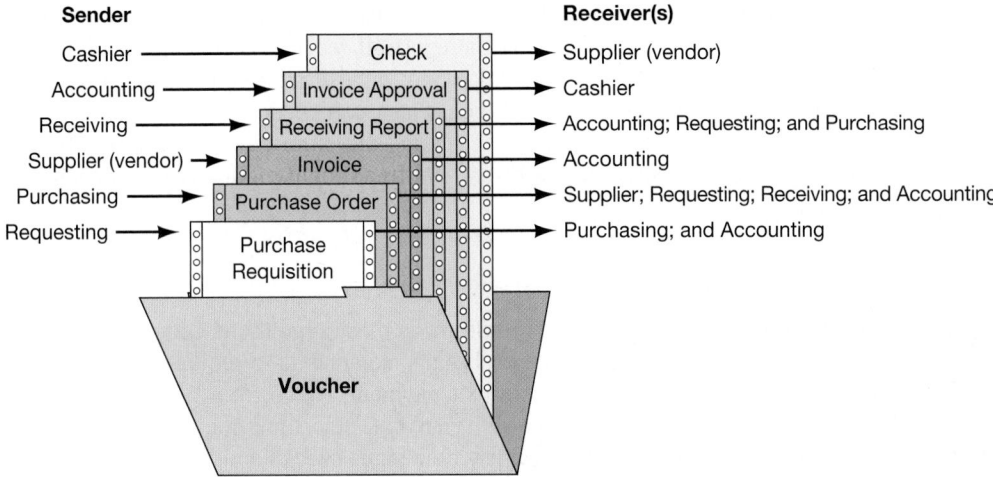

A voucher system should be applied not only to purchases of inventory but to all expenditures. To illustrate, when a company receives a monthly telephone bill, it should review and verify the charges, prepare a voucher (file), and insert the bill. This transaction is then recorded with a journal entry. If the amount is currently due, a check is issued. If not, the voucher is filed for payment on its due date. If no voucher is prepared, verifying the invoice and its amount after several days or weeks can be difficult. Also, without records, a dishonest employee could collude with a dishonest supplier to get more than one payment for an obligation, payment for excessive amounts, or payment for goods and services not received. An effective voucher system helps prevent such frauds.

Point: A *voucher* is an internal document (or file).

Quick Check   Answers—p. 337

3. Why must a company hold liquid assets?

4. Why does a company hold cash equivalent assets in addition to cash?

5. Identify at least two assets that are classified as cash equivalents.

6. Good internal control procedures for cash include which of the following? (*a*) All cash disbursements, other than those for very small amounts, are made by check; (*b*) One employee counts cash received from sales and promptly deposits cash receipts; or (*c*) Cash receipts by mail are opened by one employee who is then responsible for recording and depositing them.

7. Should all companies require a voucher system? At what point in a company's growth would you recommend a voucher system?

P2 Explain and record petty cash fund transactions.

Petty Cash System of Control A basic principle for controlling cash disbursements is that all payments must be made by check. An exception to this rule is made for *petty cash disbursements,* which are the small payments required for items such as postage, courier fees, minor repairs, and low-cost supplies. To avoid the time and cost of writing checks for small amounts, a company sets up a petty cash fund to make small payments. (**Petty cash** activities are part of an *imprest system,* which designates advance money to establish the fund, to withdraw from the fund, and to reimburse the fund.)

Operating a petty cash fund. Establishing a petty cash fund requires estimating the total amount of small payments likely to be made during a short period such as a week or month. A check is then drawn by the company cashier for an amount slightly in excess of this estimate. This check is recorded with a debit to the Petty Cash account (an asset) and a credit to Cash. The check is cashed, and the currency is given to an employee designated as the *petty cashier* or *petty cash custodian*. The petty cashier is responsible for keeping this cash safe, making payments from the fund, and keeping records of it in a secure place referred to as the *petty cashbox.*

For example, when each cash disbursement is made, the person receiving payment should sign a prenumbered *petty cash receipt,* also called *petty cash ticket*—see Exhibit 8.2. The petty cash receipt is then placed in the petty cashbox with the remaining money. Under this system, the sum of all receipts plus the remaining cash equals the total fund amount. A $100 petty cash fund, for instance, contains any combination of cash and petty cash receipts that totals $100 (examples are $80 cash plus $20 in receipts, or $10 cash plus $90 in receipts). Each disbursement reduces cash and increases the amount of receipts in the petty cashbox.

Point: A petty cash fund is used only for business expenses.

Petty Cash Receipt No. 9 Z-Mart	
For ___Freight charges___	Date ___11/5/08___
Charge to ___Merchandise Inventory___	Amount ___$6.75___
Approved by ___Jim Gills___	Received by ___Dick Fitch___

Exhibit 8.2

Petty Cash Receipt

The petty cash fund should be reimbursed when it is nearing zero and at the end of an accounting period when financial statements are prepared. For this purpose, the petty cashier sorts the paid receipts by the type of expense or account and then totals the receipts. The petty cashier presents all paid receipts to the company cashier, who stamps all receipts *paid* so they cannot be reused, files them for recordkeeping, and gives the petty cashier a check for their sum. When this check is cashed and the money placed in the cashbox, the total money in the cashbox is restored to its original amount. The fund is now ready for a new cycle of petty cash payments.

Point: Petty cash receipts with either no signature or a forged signature usually indicate misuse of petty cash. Companies respond with surprise petty cash counts for verification.

Illustrating a petty cash fund. To illustrate, assume Z-Mart establishes a petty cash fund on November 1 and designates one of its office employees as the petty cashier. A $75 check is drawn, cashed, and the proceeds given to the petty cashier. The entry to record the setup of this petty cash fund is

Nov. I	Petty Cash.	75	
	Cash		75
	To establish a petty cash fund.		

Assets = Liabilities + Equity
+75
−75

After the petty cash fund is established, the *Petty Cash account is not debited or credited again unless the amount of the fund is changed.* (A fund should be increased if it requires reimbursement too frequently. On the other hand, if the fund is too large, some of its money should be redeposited in the Cash account.)

Next, assume that Z-Mart's petty cashier makes several November payments from petty cash. Each person who received payment is required to sign a receipt. On November 27, after making a $26.50 cash payment for tile cleaning, only $3.70 cash remains in the fund. The petty cashier then summarizes and totals the petty cash receipts as shown in Exhibit 8.3.

Point: Reducing or eliminating a petty cash fund would require a credit to Petty Cash.

Point: Although *individual* petty cash disbursements are not evidenced by a check, the initial petty cash fund is evidenced by a check, and later petty cash expenditures are evidenced by a check to replenish them *in total.*

Exhibit 8.3

Petty Cash Payments Report

ZMART		
Petty Cash Payments Report		
Miscellaneous Expenses		
Nov. 2 Washing windows	$20.00	
Nov. 27 Tile cleaning	26.50	$ 46.50
Merchandise Inventory (transportation-in)		
Nov. 5 Transport of merchandise purchased	6.75	
Nov. 20 Transport of merchandise purchased	8.30	15.05
Delivery Expense		
Nov. 18 Customer's package delivered		5.00
Office Supplies Expense		
Nov. 15 Purchase of office supplies immediately used		4.75
Total		$71.30

Point: This report can also include receipt number and names of those who approved and received cash payment (see Demo Problem 2).

The petty cash payments report and all receipts are given to the company cashier in exchange for a $71.30 check to reimburse the fund. The petty cashier cashes the check and puts the $71.30 cash in the petty cashbox. The company records this reimbursement as follows.

Assets	=	Liabilities	+	Equity
−71.30				−46.50
				−15.05
				− 5.00
				− 4.75

Nov. 27	Miscellaneous Expenses	46.50	
	Merchandise Inventory	15.05	
	Delivery Expense	5.00	
	Office Supplies Expense	4.75	
	Cash		71.30
	To reimburse petty cash.		

A petty cash fund is usually reimbursed at the end of an accounting period so that expenses are recorded in the proper period, even if the fund is not low on money. If the fund is not reimbursed at the end of a period, the financial statements would show both an overstated cash asset and understated expenses (or assets) that were paid out of petty cash. Some companies do not reimburse the petty cash fund at the end of each period under the principle that this amount is immaterial to users of financial statements.

Point: To avoid errors in recording petty cash reimbursement, follow these steps: (1) prepare payments report, (2) compute cash needed by subtracting cash remaining from total fund amount, (3) record entry, and (4) check "Dr. = Cr." in entry. Any difference is Cash Over and Short.

Event	Petty Cash	Cash	Expenses
Set up fund	Dr.	Cr.	—
Reimburse fund .	—	Cr.	Dr.
Increase fund ...	Dr.	Cr.	—
Decrease fund ..	Cr.	Dr.	—

Increasing or decreasing a petty cash fund. A decision to increase or decrease a petty cash fund is often made when reimbursing it. To illustrate, assume Z-Mart decides to *increase* its petty cash fund from $75 to $100 on November 27 when it reimburses the fund. The entries required are to (1) reimburse the fund as usual (see the preceding November 27 entry), and (2) increase the fund amount as follows.

Nov. 27	Petty Cash.................................	25	
	Cash		25
	To increase the petty cash fund amount.		

Alternatively, if Z-Mart *decreases* the petty cash fund from $75 to $55 on November 27, the entry is to (1) credit Petty Cash for $20 (decreasing the fund from $75 to $55) and (2) debit Cash for $20 (reflecting the $20 transfer from Petty Cash to Cash).

Cash over and short. Sometimes a petty cashier fails to get a receipt for payment or overpays for the amount due. When this occurs and the fund is later reimbursed, the petty cash payments report plus the cash remaining will not total to the fund balance. This mistake causes the fund to be *short*. This shortage is recorded as an expense in the reimbursing entry with a debit to the Cash Over and Short account. (An overage in the petty cash fund is recorded with a credit to Cash Over and Short in the reimbursing entry.) To illustrate, prepare the entry to reimburse a $200 petty cash fund when its payments report shows $178 in miscellaneous expenses and $15 cash remains.

Miscellaneous Expenses....................................	178 ◄	
Cash Over and Short....................................	7 ◄	
Cash...		185
To reimburse petty cash.		

Quick Check

Answers—p. 337

8. Why are some cash payments made from a petty cash fund, and not by check?

9. Why should a petty cash fund be reimbursed at the end of an accounting period?

10. Identify at least two results of reimbursing a petty cash fund.

Banking Activities as Controls

Banks (and other financial institutions) provide many services, including helping companies control cash. Banks safeguard cash, provide detailed and independent records of cash transactions, and are a source of cash financing. This section describes these services and the documents provided by banking activities that increase managers' control over cash.

Basic Bank Services

This section explains basic bank services—such as the bank account, the bank deposit, and checking—that contribute to the control of cash.

C3 Identify control features of banking activities.

Bank Account, Deposit, and Check   A *bank account* is a record set up by a bank for a customer. It permits a customer to deposit money for safekeeping and helps control withdrawals. To limit access to a bank account, all persons authorized to write checks on the account must sign a **signature card,** which bank employees use to verify signatures on checks. Many companies have more than one bank account to serve different needs and to handle special transactions such as payroll.

Each bank deposit is supported by a **deposit ticket,** which lists items such as currency, coins, and checks deposited along with their corresponding dollar amounts. The bank gives the customer a copy of the deposit ticket or a deposit receipt as proof of the deposit. Exhibit 8.4 shows one type of deposit ticket.

To withdraw money from an account, the depositor can use a **check,** which is a document signed by the depositor instructing the bank to pay a specified amount of money to a designated recipient. A check involves three parties: a *maker* who signs the check, a *payee* who is the recipient, and a *bank* (or *payer*) on which the check is drawn. The bank provides a depositor the checks that are serially numbered and imprinted with the name and address of both the depositor and bank. Both checks and deposit tickets are imprinted with identification codes in magnetic ink for computer

Decision Insight

Web-bank   Many companies balance checkbooks and pay bills online. Customers value the convenience of banking services anytime, anywhere. Services include the ability to stop payment on a check, move money between accounts, get up-to-date balances, and identify cleared checks and deposits.

Exhibit 8.4

Deposit Ticket

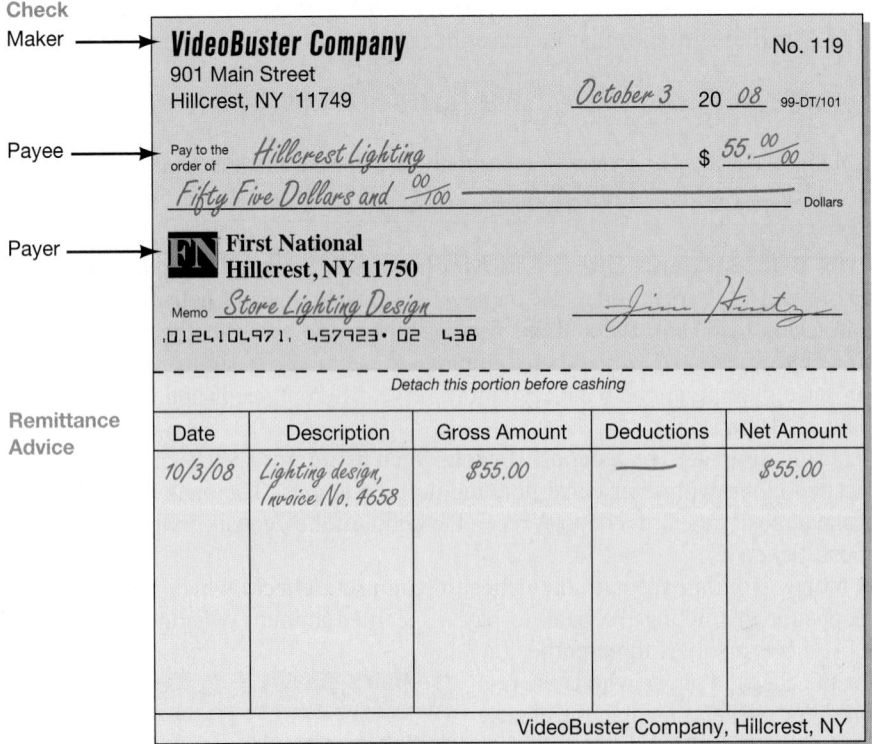

processing. Exhibit 8.5 shows one type of check. It is accompanied with an optional *remittance advice* explaining the payment. When a remittance advice is unavailable, the *memo* line is often used for a brief explanation.

Exhibit 8.5

Check with Remittance Advice

Electronic Funds Transfer   **Electronic funds transfer (EFT)** is the electronic communication transfer of cash from one party to another. No paper documents are necessary. Banks simply transfer cash from one account to another with a journal entry. Companies are increasingly using EFT because of its convenience and low cost. For instance, it can cost up to 50 cents to process a check through the banking system, whereas EFT cost is near zero. We now commonly see items such as payroll, rent, utilities, insurance, and interest payments being handled by EFT. The bank statement lists cash withdrawals by EFT with the checks and other deductions. Cash receipts by EFT are listed with deposits and other additions. A bank statement is sometimes a depositor's only notice of an EFT.

Bank Statement

Usually once a month, the bank sends each depositor a **bank statement** showing the activity in the account. Different banks use different formats for their bank statements, but all of them include the following items of information:

1. Beginning-of-period balance of the depositor's account.
2. Checks and other debits decreasing the account during the period.
3. Deposits and other credits increasing the account during the period.
4. End-of-period balance of the depositor's account.

This information reflects the bank's records. Exhibit 8.6 shows one type of bank statement. Identify each of these four items in that statement. Part Ⓐ of Exhibit 8.6 summarizes changes in the account. Part Ⓑ lists paid checks along with other debits. Part Ⓒ lists deposits and credits to the account, and part Ⓓ shows the daily account balances.

Point: Good internal control is to deposit all cash receipts daily and make all payments for goods and services by check. This controls access to cash and creates an independent record of all cash activities.

Exhibit 8.6

Bank Statement

Member FDIC — First National, Hillcrest, NY 11750 — Bank Statement

VideoBuster Company
901 Main Street
Hillcrest, NY 11749

October 31, 2008 — Statement Date

494 504 2 — Account Number

Previous Balance	Total Checks and Debits	Total Deposits and Credits	Current Balance
1,609.58	723.00	1,163.42	2,050.00

Ⓑ Checks and Debits

Date	No.	Amount
10/03	119	55.00
10/09	120	200.00
10/10	121	120.00
10/12		23.00 DM
10/14	122	70.00
10/16	123	25.00
10/23	125	15.00
10/25		20.00 NSF
		10.00 DM
10/26	127	50.00
10/29	128	135.00

Ⓒ Deposits and Credits

Date	Amount
10/02	240.00
10/09	180.00
10/15	100.00
10/16	150.00
10/23	485.00 CM
10/31	8.42 IN

Ⓓ Daily Balance

Date	Amount
10/01	1,609.58
10/02	1,849.58
10/03	1,794.58
10/09	1,774.58
10/10	1,654.58
10/12	1,631.58
10/14	1,561.58
10/15	1,661.58
10/16	1,786.58
10/23	2,256.58
10/25	2,226.58
10/26	2,176.58
10/29	2,041.58
10/31	2,050.00

Symbols: **CM**–Credit Memo **EC**–Error Correction **NSF**–Non-Sufficient Funds **SC**–Service Charge
DM–Debit Memo **IN**–Interest Earned **OD**–Overdraft

< Reconcile the account immediately. >

In reading a bank statement note that a depositor's account is a liability on the bank's records. This is so because the money belongs to the depositor, not the bank. When a depositor increases the account balance, the bank records it with a *credit* to that liability account. This means that debit memos from the bank produce *credits* on the depositor's books, and credit memos from the bank produce *debits* on the depositor's books.

Enclosed with a bank statement is a list of the depositor's canceled checks (or the actual canceled checks) along with any debit or credit memoranda affecting the account. **Canceled checks** are checks the bank has paid and deducted from the customer's account during the period. Other deductions that can appear on a bank statement include (1) service charges and fees assessed by the bank, (2) checks deposited that are uncollectible, (3) corrections of previous errors, (4) withdrawals through automated teller machines (ATMs), and (5) periodic payments arranged in advance by a depositor. (Most company checking accounts do not allow ATM withdrawals because of the company's desire to make all disbursements by check.) Except for service charges, the bank notifies the depositor of each deduction with a debit memorandum when the bank reduces the balance. A copy of each debit memorandum is usually sent with the statement.

Transactions that increase the depositor's account include amounts the bank collects on behalf of the depositor and the corrections of previous errors. Credit memoranda notify the depositor of all increases when they are recorded. A copy of each credit memorandum is often sent with the bank statement. Banks that pay interest on checking accounts often compute the amount of interest earned on the average cash balance and would credit it to the depositor's account each period. In Exhibit 8.6, the bank credits $8.42 of interest to the account.

Bank Reconciliation

When a company deposits all cash receipts and makes all cash payments (except petty cash) by check, it can use the bank statement for proving the accuracy of its cash records. This is done using a **bank reconciliation,** which is a report explaining any differences between the checking account balance according to the depositor's records and the balance reported on the bank statement.

Purpose of Bank Reconciliation   The balance of a checking account reported on the bank statement rarely equals the balance in the depositor's accounting records. This is usually due to information that one party has that the other does not. We must therefore prove the accuracy of both the depositor's records and those of the bank. This means we must *reconcile* the two balances and explain or account for any differences in them. Among the factors causing the bank statement balance to differ from the depositor's book balance are these:

- **Outstanding checks. Outstanding checks** are checks written (or drawn) by the depositor, deducted on the depositor's records, and sent to the payees but not yet received by the bank for payment at the bank statement date.

- **Deposits in transit** (also called **outstanding deposits**). **Deposits in transit** are deposits made and recorded by the depositor but not yet recorded on the bank statement. For example, companies can make deposits (in the night depository) at the end of a business day after the bank is closed. If such a deposit occurred on a bank statement date, it would not appear on this period's statement. The bank would record such a deposit on the next business day, and it would appear on the next period's bank statement. Deposits mailed to the bank near the end of a period also can be in transit and unrecorded when the statement is prepared.

- **Deductions for uncollectible items and for services.** A company sometimes deposits another party's check that is uncollectible (usually meaning the balance in such an account is not large enough to cover the check). This check is called a *non-sufficient funds (NSF)* check. The bank would have initially credited the depositor's account for the amount of the check. When the bank learns the check is uncollectible, it debits (reduces) the depositor's account for the amount of that check. The bank may also charge the depositor a fee for processing an uncollectible check and notify the depositor of the deduction by sending a debit memorandum. The depositor should record each deduction when a debit memorandum is received, but an entry is sometimes not made until the bank reconciliation is prepared. Other possible bank charges to a depositor's account that are first reported on a bank statement include printing new checks and service fees.

- **Additions for collections and for interest.** Banks sometimes act as collection agents for their depositors by collecting notes and other items. Banks can also receive electronic funds

---

transfers to the depositor's account. When a bank collects an item, it is added to the depositor's account, less any service fee. The bank also sends a credit memorandum to notify the depositor of the transaction. When the memorandum is received, the depositor should record it; yet it sometimes remains unrecorded until the bank reconciliation is prepared. The bank statement also includes a credit for any interest earned.

■ **Errors.** Both banks and depositors can make errors. Bank errors might not be discovered until the depositor prepares the bank reconciliation. Also, depositor errors are sometimes discovered when the bank balance is reconciled. Error testing includes: (a) comparing deposits on the bank statement with deposits in the accounting records and (b) comparing canceled checks on the bank statement with checks recorded in the accounting records.

Point: Small businesses with few employees often allow recordkeepers to both write checks and keep the general ledger. If this is done, it is essential that the owner do the bank reconciliation.

Point: The person preparing the bank reconciliation should not be responsible for processing cash receipts, managing checks, or maintaining cash records.

Illustration of a Bank Reconciliation We follow nine steps in preparing the bank reconciliation. It is helpful to refer to the bank reconciliation in Exhibit 8.7 when studying steps ① through ⑨.

Exhibit 8.7

Bank Reconciliation

	VIDEOBUSTER Bank Reconciliation October 31, 2008						
①	Bank statement balance		$ 2,050.00	⑤	Book balance		$ 1,404.58
②	Add			⑥	Add		
	Deposit of Oct. 31 in transit		145.00		Collect $500 note less $15 fee	$485.00	
			2,195.00		Interest earned	8.42	493.42
③	Deduct						1,898.00
	Outstanding checks			⑦	Deduct		
	No. 124	$150.00			Check printing charge	23.00	
	No. 126	200.00	350.00		NSF check plus service fee	30.00	53.00
④	**Adjusted bank balance**		**$1,845.00**	⑧	**Adjusted book balance**		**$1,845.00**

⑨ Balances are equal (reconciled)

① Identify the bank statement balance of the cash account (*balance per bank*). VideoBuster's bank balance is $2,050.

② Identify and list any unrecorded deposits and any bank errors understating the bank balance. Add them to the bank balance. VideoBuster's $145 deposit placed in the bank's night depository on October 31 is not recorded on its bank statement.

③ Identify and list any outstanding checks and any bank errors overstating the bank balance. Deduct them from the bank balance. VideoBuster's comparison of canceled checks with its books shows two checks outstanding: No. 124 for $150 and No. 126 for $200.

④ Compute the *adjusted bank balance,* also called the *corrected* or *reconciled balance.*

⑤ Identify the company's book balance of the cash account (*balance per book*). VideoBuster's book balance is $1,404.58.

⑥ Identify and list any unrecorded credit memoranda from the bank, any interest earned, and errors understating the book balance. Add them to the book balance. Enclosed with VideoBuster's bank statement is a credit memorandum showing the bank collected a note receivable for the company on October 23. The note's proceeds of $500 (minus a $15 collection fee) are credited to the company's account. VideoBuster's bank statement also shows a credit of $8.42 for interest earned on the average cash balance. There was no prior notification of this item, and it is not yet recorded.

⑦ Identify and list any unrecorded debit memoranda from the bank, any service charges, and errors overstating the book balance. Deduct them from the book balance. Debits on VideoBuster's bank statement that are not yet recorded include (a) a $23 charge for check printing and (b) an NSF check for $20 plus a related $10 processing fee. (The NSF check is dated October 16 and was included in the book balance.)

Point: Outstanding checks are identified by comparing canceled checks on the bank statement with checks recorded. This includes identifying any outstanding checks listed on the *previous* period's bank reconciliation that are not included in the canceled checks on this period's bank statement.

8 Compute the *adjusted book balance,* also called *corrected* or *reconciled balance.*

9 Verify that the two adjusted balances from steps 4 and 8 are equal. If so, they are reconciled. If not, check for accuracy and missing data to achieve reconciliation.

Point: Adjusting entries could be combined into one compound entry.

Decision Insight

Not-So-Free Banking   Fees for bank services are rising—see chart. Bounce protection alone yields $8 billion in annual bank income, or nearly 30% of all bank fees. Regulators are taking notice. Indiana regulators warned that if fees exceeded a 72% annual rate, they would consider it a felony. (*BusinessWeek* 2005)

Adjusting Entries from a Bank Reconciliation   A bank reconciliation often identifies unrecorded items that need recording by the company. In VideoBuster's reconciliation, the adjusted balance of $1,845 is the correct balance as of October 31. But the company's accounting records show a $1,404.58 balance. We must prepare journal entries to adjust the book balance to the correct balance. *It is important to remember that only the items reconciling the book balance require adjustment.* A review of Exhibit 8.7 indicates that four entries are required for VideoBuster.

Collection of note.   The first entry is to record the proceeds of its note receivable collected by the bank less the expense of having the bank perform that service.

Assets = Liabilities + Equity
+485   −15
−500

Oct. 31	Cash......................................	485	
	Collection Expense.........................	15	
	Notes Receivable		500
	To record the collection fee and proceeds for a note collected by the bank.		

Interest earned.   The second entry records interest credited to its account by the bank.

Assets = Liabilities + Equity
+8.42   +8.42

Oct. 31	Cash......................................	8.42	
	Interest Revenue.......................		8.42
	To record interest earned on the cash balance in the checking account.		

Check printing.   The third entry records expenses for the check printing charge.

Assets = Liabilities + Equity
−23   −23

Oct. 31	Miscellaneous Expenses	23	
	Cash		23
	Check printing charge.		

NSF check.   The fourth entry records the NSF check that is returned as uncollectible. The $20 check was originally received from T. Woods in payment of his account and then deposited. The bank charged $10 for handling the NSF check and deducted $30 total from VideoBuster's account. This means the entry must reverse the effects of the original entry made when the check was received and must record (add) the $10 bank fee.

Point: The company will try to collect the entire NSF amount of $30.

Assets = Liabilities + Equity
+30
−30

Oct. 31	Accounts Receivable—T. Woods................	30	
	Cash		30
	To charge Woods' account for $20 NSF check and $10 bank fee.		

Point: The Demo Problem 1 shows an adjusting entry for an error correction.

After these four entries are recorded, the book balance of cash is adjusted to the correct amount of $1,845 (computed as $1,404.58 + $485 + $8.42 − $23 − $30). The Cash T-account to the side shows the same computation.

Cash			
Beg. bal.	1,404.58		
⑥	493.42	⑦	23.00
			30.00
Adj. bal.	1,845.00		

Quick Check

Answers—pp. 337–338

11. What is a bank statement?

12. What is the meaning of the phrase *to reconcile a bank balance?*

13. Why do we reconcile the bank statement balance of cash and the depositor's book balance of cash?

14. List at least two items affecting the bank balance side of a bank reconciliation and indicate whether the items are added or subtracted.

15. List at least three items affecting the book balance side of a bank reconciliation and indicate whether the items are added or subtracted.

Days' Sales Uncollected

Decision Analysis

Many companies attract customers by selling to them on credit. This means that cash receipts from customers are delayed until accounts receivable are collected. Users of accounting information often want to know how quickly a company can convert its accounts receivable into cash. This is important for evaluating a company's liquidity. One measure of the receivables' nearness to cash is the **days' sales uncollected,** also called *days' sales in receivables.* This measure is computed by dividing the current balance of receivables by net credit sales over the year just completed and then multiplying by 365 (number of days in a year). Since net credit sales usually are not reported to external users, the net sales (or revenues) figure is commonly used in the computation as in Exhibit 8.8.

A1 Compute the days' sales uncollected ratio and use it to assess liquidity.

$$\text{Days' sales uncollected} = \frac{\text{Accounts receivable}}{\text{Net sales}} \times 365$$

Exhibit 8.8

Days' Sales Uncollected

We use days' sales uncollected to estimate how much time is likely to pass before the current amount of accounts receivable is received in cash. For evaluation purposes, we need to compare this estimate to that for other companies in the same industry. We also make comparisons between current and prior periods.

To illustrate, we select data from the annual reports of two toy manufacturers, **Hasbro** and **Mattel**. Their days' sales uncollected figures are shown in Exhibit 8.9.

Exhibit 8.9

Analysis using Days' Sales Uncollected

Company	Figure ($ millions)	2004	2003	2002	2001
Hasbro	Accounts receivable	$579	$608	$555	$572
	Net sales	$2,998	$3,139	$2,816	$2,856
	Days' sales uncollected	70 days	71 days	72 days	73 days
Mattel	Accounts receivable	$759	$544	$491	$666
	Net sales	$5,103	$4,960	$4,885	$4,688
	Days' sales uncollected	54 days	40 days	37 days	52 days

Days' sales uncollected for Hasbro in 2004 is computed as ($579/$2,998) × 365 days = 70 days. This means that it will take about 70 days to collect cash from ending accounts receivable. This number reflects one or more of the following factors: a company's ability to collect receivables, customer financial health, customer payment strategies, and discount terms. To further assess days' sales uncollected for Hasbro, we compare it to three prior years and to those of Mattel. We see that Hasbro's days' sales uncollected has changed little over the past four years. In comparison, Mattel improved on days' sales uncollected for 2002 (37) and 2003 (40), but then worsened for 2004 (54). Yet, for all years, Mattel is superior to Hasbro on this measure. The less time that money is tied up in receivables often translates into increased profitability.

Decision Maker

Answer—p. 337

Sales Representative The sales staff is told to take action to help reduce days' sales uncollected. What can you, a salesperson, do to reduce days' sales uncollected?

Demonstration Problem 1

Prepare a bank reconciliation for Jamboree Enterprises for the month ended November 30, 2008. The following information is available to reconcile Jamboree Enterprises' book balance of cash with its bank statement balance as of November 30, 2008:

a. After all posting is complete on November 30, the company's book balance of Cash has a $16,380 debit balance, but its bank statement shows a $38,520 balance.

b. Checks No. 2024 for $4,810 and No. 2026 for $5,000 are outstanding.

c. In comparing the canceled checks on the bank statement with the entries in the accounting records, it is found that Check No. 2025 in payment of rent is correctly drawn for $1,000 but is erroneously entered in the accounting records as $880.

d. The November 30 deposit of $17,150 was placed in the night depository after banking hours on that date, and this amount does not appear on the bank statement.

e. In reviewing the bank statement, a check written by Jumbo Enterprises in the amount of $160 was erroneously drawn against Jamboree's account.

f. A credit memorandum enclosed with the bank statement indicates that the bank collected a $30,000 note and $900 of related interest on Jamboree's behalf. This transaction was not recorded by Jamboree prior to receiving the statement.

g. A debit memorandum for $1,100 lists a $1,100 NSF check received from a customer, Marilyn Welch. Jamboree had not recorded the return of this check before receiving the statement.

h. Bank service charges for November total $40. These charges were not recorded by Jamboree before receiving the statement.

Planning the Solution

• Set up a bank reconciliation with a bank side and a book side (as in Exhibit 8.7). Leave room to both add and deduct items. Each column will result in a reconciled, equal balance.

• Examine each item *a* through *h* to determine whether it affects the book or the bank balance and whether it should be added or deducted from the bank or book balance.

• After all items are analyzed, complete the reconciliation and arrive at a reconciled balance between the bank side and the book side.

• For each reconciling item on the book side, prepare an adjusting entry. Additions to the book side require an adjusting entry that debits Cash. Deductions on the book side require an adjusting entry that credits Cash.

Solution to Demonstration Problem 1

JAMBOREE ENTERPRISES
Bank Reconciliation
November 30, 2008

Bank statement balance		$ 38,520	Book balance			$ 16,380
Add			Add			
Deposit of Nov. 30	$17,150		Collection of note	$30,000		
Bank error (Jumbo)	160	17,310	Interest earned	900	30,900	
		55,830				47,280
Deduct			Deduct			
Outstanding checks			NSF check (M. Welch) . . .	1,100		
No. 2024	4,810		Recording error (# 2025) .	120		
No. 2026	5,000	9,810	Service charge	40	1,260	
Adjusted bank balance . . .		**$46,020**	**Adjusted book balance** . .			**$46,020**

Required Adjusting Entries for Jamboree

Nov. 30	Cash		30,900	
	Notes Receivable		30,000
	Interest Earned		900
	To record collection of note with interest.		

[continued on next page]

[continued from previous page]

Nov. 30	Accounts Receivable—M. Welch	1,100	
	Cash		1,100
	To reinstate account due from an NSF check.		
Nov. 30	Rent Expense	120	
	Cash		120
	To correct recording error on check no. 2025.		
Nov. 30	Bank Service Charges.	40	
	Cash		40
	To record bank service charges.		

Demonstration Problem 2

Bacardi Company established a $150 petty cash fund with Dean Martin as the petty cashier. When the fund balance reached $19 cash, Martin prepared a petty cash payment report, which follows.

Petty Cash Payments Report				
Receipt No.	**Account Charged**		**Approved by**	**Received by**
12	Delivery Expense	$ 29	Martin	A. Smirnoff
13	Merchandise Inventory	18	Martin	J. Daniels
15	(Omitted)	32	Martin	C. Carlsberg
16	Miscellaneous Expense	41	(Omitted)	J. Walker
	Total	$120		

Required

1. Identify four internal control weaknesses from the payment report.
2. Prepare general journal entries to record:
   a. Establishment of the petty cash fund.
   b. Reimbursement of the fund. (Assume for this part only that petty cash receipt no. 15 was issued for miscellaneous expenses.)
3. What is the Petty Cash account balance immediately before reimbursement? Immediately after reimbursement?

Solution to Demonstration Problem 2

1. Four internal control weaknesses are
   a. Petty cash ticket no. 14 is missing. Its omission raises questions about the petty cashier's management of the fund.
   b. The $19 cash balance means that $131 has been withdrawn ($150 − $19 = $131). However, the total amount of the petty cash receipts is only $120 ($29 + $18 + $32 + $41). The fund is $11 short of cash ($131 − $120 = $11). Was petty cash receipt no. 14 issued for $11? Management should investigate.
   c. The petty cashier (Martin) did not sign petty cash receipt no. 16. This omission could have been an oversight on his part or he might not have authorized the payment. Management should investigate.
   d. Petty cash receipt no. 15 does not indicate which account to charge. This omission could have been an oversight on the petty cashier's part. Management could check with C. Carlsberg and the petty cashier (Martin) about the transaction. Without further information, debit Miscellaneous Expense.
2. Petty cash general journal entries.
   a. Entry to establish the petty cash fund.   b. Entry to reimburse the fund.

Petty Cash	150	
Cash		150

Delivery Expense	29	
Merchandise Inventory	18	
Miscellaneous Expense ($41 + $32)	73	
Cash Over and Short	11	
Cash		131

3. The Petty Cash account balance *always* equals its fund balance, in this case $150. This account balance does not change unless the fund is increased or decreased.

APPENDIX

8A Documents in a Voucher System

P4   Describe the voucher system to control cash disbursements.

This appendix describes the important business documents of a voucher system of control.

Purchase Requisition   Department managers are usually not allowed to place orders directly with suppliers for control purposes. Instead, a department manager must inform the purchasing department of its needs by preparing and signing a **purchase requisition,** which lists the merchandise needed and requests that it be purchased—see Exhibit 8A.1. Two copies of the purchase requisition are sent to the purchasing department, which then sends one copy to the accounting department. When the accounting department receives a purchase requisition, it creates and maintains a voucher for this transaction. The requesting department keeps the third copy.

Exhibit 8A.1

Purchase Requisition

Purchase Requisition	No. 917
Z-Mart	

From ___ Sporting Goods Department ___   **Date** _____ October 28, 2008 _____

To _____ Purchasing Department _____   **Preferred Vendor** ___ Trex _____

Request purchase of the following item(s):

Model No.	Description	Quantity
CH 015	Challenger X7	1
SD 099	SpeedDemon	1

Reason for Request _____ Replenish inventory _____

Approval for Request _____ _J.Z._ _____

For Purchasing Department use only: Order Date __10/30/08__   P.O. No. _____P98_____

Point: It is important to note that a voucher system is designed to uniquely meet the needs of a specific business. Thus, you should read this appendix as one example of a common voucher system design, but *not* the only design.

Purchase Order   A **purchase order** is a document the purchasing department uses to place an order with a **vendor** (seller or supplier). A purchase order authorizes a vendor to ship ordered merchandise at the stated price and terms—see Exhibit 8A.2. When the purchasing department receives a purchase requisition, it prepares at least five copies of a purchase order. The copies are distributed as follows: *copy 1* to the vendor as a purchase request and as authority to ship merchandise; *copy 2,* along with a copy of the purchase requisition, to the accounting department, where it is entered in the voucher and used in approving payment of the invoice; *copy 3* to the requesting department to inform its manager that action is being taken; *copy 4* to the receiving department without order quantity so it can compare with goods received and provide independent count of goods received; and *copy 5* retained on file by the purchasing department.

Invoice   An **invoice** is an itemized statement of goods prepared by the vendor listing the customer's name, items sold, sales prices, and terms of sale. An invoice is also a bill sent to the buyer from the supplier. From the vendor's point of view, it is a *sales invoice.* The buyer, or **vendee,** treats it as a *purchase invoice.* When receiving a purchase order, the vendor ships the ordered merchandise to the buyer and includes or mails a copy of the invoice covering the shipment to the buyer. The invoice is sent to the buyer's accounting department where it is placed in the voucher. (Refer back to Exhibit 5.5, which shows Z-Mart's purchase invoice.)

Receiving Report Many companies maintain a separate department to receive all merchandise and purchased assets. When each shipment arrives, this receiving department counts the goods and checks them for damage and agreement with the purchase order. It then prepares four or more copies of a **receiving report,** which is used within the company to notify the appropriate persons that ordered goods have been received and to describe the quantities and condition of the goods. One copy is sent to accounting and placed in the voucher. Copies are also sent to the requesting department and the purchasing department to notify them that the goods have arrived. The receiving department retains a copy in its files.

Invoice Approval When a receiving report arrives, the accounting department should have copies of the following documents in the voucher: purchase requisition, purchase order, and invoice. With the information in these documents, the accounting department can record the purchase and approve its payment. In approving an invoice for payment, it checks and compares information across all documents. To facilitate this checking and to ensure that no step is omitted, it often uses an **invoice approval,** also called *check authorization*—see Exhibit 8A.3. An invoice approval is a checklist of steps necessary for approving an invoice for recording and payment. It is a separate document either filed in the voucher or preprinted (or stamped) on the voucher.

As each step in the checklist is approved, the person initials the invoice approval and records the current date. Final approval implies the following steps have occurred:

1. **Requisition check:** Items on invoice are requested per purchase requisition.
2. **Purchase order check:** Items on invoice are ordered per purchase order.
3. **Receiving report check:** Items on invoice are received, per receiving report.
4. **Invoice check: Price:** Invoice prices are as agreed with the vendor.
   Calculations: Invoice has no mathematical errors.
   Terms: Terms are as agreed with the vendor.

Point: Recording a purchase is initiated by an invoice approval, not an invoice. An invoice approval verifies that the amount is consistent with that requested, ordered, and received. This controls and verifies purchases and related liabilities.

Voucher Once an invoice has been checked and approved, the voucher is complete. A complete voucher is a record summarizing a transaction. Once the voucher certifies a transaction, it authorizes recording an obligation. A voucher also contains approval for paying the obligation on an appropriate date. The physical form of a voucher varies across companies. Many are designed so that the invoice and other related source documents are placed inside the voucher, which can be a folder.

Completion of a voucher usually requires a person to enter certain information on both the inside and outside of the voucher. Typical information required on the inside of a voucher is shown in Exhibit 8A.4, and that for the outside is shown in Exhibit 8A.5. This information is taken from the invoice and the supporting documents filed in the voucher. A complete voucher is sent to an authorized individual (often called an *auditor*). This person performs a final review, approves the accounts and amounts for debiting (called the *accounting distribution*), and authorizes recording of the voucher.

Exhibit 8A.4

Inside of a Voucher

Z-Mart
Chicago, Illinois

Voucher No. 4657

Date Oct. 28, 2008
Pay to Trex
City Antigo   State Wisconsin

For the following: (attach all invoices and supporting documents)

Date of Invoice	Terms	Invoice Number and Other Details	Terms
Nov. 2, 2008	2/15, n/30	Invoice No. 4657	1,200
		Less discount	24
		Net amount payable	1,176

Payment approved

N. O. Neal

Auditor

After a voucher is approved and recorded (in a journal called a **voucher register**), it is filed by its due date. A check is then sent on the payment date from the cashier, the voucher is marked "paid", and the voucher is sent to the accounting department and recorded (in a journal called the **check register**). The person issuing checks relies on the approved voucher and its signed supporting documents as proof that an obligation has been incurred and must be paid. The purchase requisition and purchase order confirm the purchase was authorized. The receiving report shows that items have been received, and the invoice approval form verifies that the invoice has been checked for errors. There is little chance for error and even less chance for fraud without collusion unless all the documents and signatures are forged.

Exhibit 8A.5

Outside of a Voucher

Voucher No. 4657

Accounting Distribution

Account Debited	Amount
Merch. Inventory	1,200
Store Supplies	
Office Supplies	
Sales Salaries	
Other	
Total Vouch. Pay. Cr.	1,200

Due Date   November 12, 2008
Pay to   Trex
City   Antigo
State   Wisconsin

Summary of charges:
Total charges   1,200
Discount   24
Net payment   1,176

Record of payment:
Paid
Check No.

Control of Purchase Discounts

8B

This appendix explains how a company can better control its cash *disbursements* to take advantage of favorable purchases discounts. Chapter 5 described the entries to record the receipt and payment of an invoice for a merchandise purchase with and without discount terms. Those entries were prepared under what is called the **gross method** of recording purchases, which initially records the invoice at its *gross* amount ignoring any cash discount.

The **net method** is another means of recording purchases, which initially records the invoice at its *net* amount of any cash discount. The net method gives management an advantage in controlling and monitoring cash payments involving purchase discounts.

P5 Apply the net method to control purchase discounts.

To explain, when invoices are recorded at *gross* amounts, the amount of any discounts taken is deducted from the balance of the Merchandise Inventory account when cash payment is made. This means that the amount of any discounts lost is not reported in any account or on the income statement. Lost discounts recorded in this way are unlikely to come to the attention of management. When purchases are recorded at *net* amounts, a **Discounts Lost** expense account is recorded and brought to management's attention. Management can then seek to identify the reason for discounts lost such as oversight, carelessness, or unfavorable terms. (Chapter 5 explains how managers assess whether a discount is favorable or not.)

Perpetual Inventory System   To illustrate, assume that a company purchases merchandise on November 2 at a $1,200 invoice price with terms of 2/10, n/30. Its November 2 entries under the gross and net methods are

Gross Method		Net Method	
Merchandise Inventory	1,200	Merchandise Inventory	1,176
Accounts Payable	1,200	Accounts Payable	1,176

If the invoice is paid on November 12 within the discount period, it records the following

Gross Method		Net Method	
Accounts Payable	1,200	Accounts Payable	1,176
Merchandise Inventory	24	Cash	1,176
Cash	1,176		

If the invoice is *not* paid within the discount period, it records the following November 12 entry (which is the date corresponding to the end of the discount period)

Gross Method	Net Method	
No entry	Discounts Lost	24
	Accounts Payable	24

Then, when the invoice is later paid on December 2, outside the discount period, it records the following

Gross Method		Net Method	
Accounts Payable	1,200	Accounts Payable	1,200
Cash	1,200	Cash	1,200

(The discount lost can be recorded when the cash payment is made with a single entry. However, in this case, when financial statements are prepared after a discount is lost and before the cash payment is made, an adjusting entry is required to recognize any unrecorded discount lost in the period when incurred.)

Periodic Inventory System   The preceding entries assume a perpetual inventory system. If a company is using a *periodic system,* its November 2 entries under the gross and net methods are

Gross Method—Periodic		
Purchases	1,200	
Accounts Payable		1,200

Net Method—Periodic		
Purchases	1,176	
Accounts Payable		1,176

If the invoice is paid on November 12 within the discount period, it records the following

Gross Method—Periodic		
Accounts Payable	1,200	
Purchases Discounts		24
Cash		1,176

Net Method—Periodic		
Accounts Payable	1,176	
Cash		1,176

If the invoice is *not* paid within the discount period, it records the following November 12 entry

Gross Method—Periodic		
No entry		

Net Method—Periodic		
Discounts Lost	24	
Accounts Payable		24

Then, when the invoice is later paid on December 2, outside the discount period, it records the following

Gross Method—Periodic		
Accounts Payable	1,200	
Cash		1,200

Net Method—Periodic		
Accounts Payable	1,200	
Cash		1,200

Summary

C1   Define internal control and identify its purpose and principles. An internal control system consists of the policies and procedures managers use to protect assets, ensure reliable accounting, promote efficient operations, and urge adherence to company policies. It can prevent avoidable losses and help managers both plan operations and monitor company and human performance. Principles of good internal control include establishing responsibilities, maintaining adequate records, insuring assets and bonding employees, separating recordkeeping from custody of assets, dividing responsibilities for related transactions, applying technological controls, and performing regular independent reviews.

C2   Define cash and cash equivalents and explain how to report them. Cash includes currency, coins, and amounts on (or acceptable for) deposit in checking and savings accounts. Cash equivalents are short-term, highly liquid investment assets readily convertible to a known cash amount and sufficiently close to their maturity date so that market value is not sensitive to interest rate changes. Cash and cash equivalents are liquid assets because they are readily converted into other assets or can be used to pay for goods, services, or liabilities.

C3   Identify control features of banking activities. Banks offer several services that promote the control and safeguarding of cash. A bank account is a record set up by a bank permitting a customer to deposit money for safekeeping and to draw checks on it. A bank deposit is money contributed to the account with a deposit ticket as proof. A check is a document signed by the depositor instructing the bank to pay a specified amount of money to a designated recipient.

A1   Compute the days' sales uncollected ratio and use it to assess liquidity. Many companies attract customers by selling to them on credit. This means that cash receipts from customers are delayed until accounts receivable are collected. Users want to know how quickly a company can convert its accounts receivable into cash. The days' sales uncollected ratio, one measure reflecting company liquidity, is computed by dividing the ending balance of receivables by annual net sales, and then multiplying by 365.

P1   Apply internal control to cash receipts and disbursements. Internal control of cash receipts ensures that all cash received is properly recorded and deposited. Attention focuses on two important types of cash receipts: over-the-counter and by mail. Good internal control for over-the-counter cash receipts includes use of a cash register, customer review, use of receipts, a permanent transaction record, and separation of the custody of cash from its recordkeeping. Good internal control for cash receipts by mail includes at least two people assigned to open mail and a listing of each sender's name, amount, and explanation.

P2   **Explain and record petty cash fund transactions.** Petty cash disbursements are payments of small amounts for items such as postage, courier fees, minor repairs, and supplies. A company usually sets up one or more petty cash funds. A petty fund cashier is responsible for safekeeping the cash, making payments from this fund, and keeping receipts and records. A Petty Cash account is debited only when the fund is established or increased in amount. When the fund is replenished, petty cash disbursements are recorded with debits to expense (or asset) accounts and a credit to cash.

P3   **Prepare a bank reconciliation.** A bank reconciliation proves the accuracy of the depositor's and the bank's records. The bank statement balance is adjusted for items such as outstanding checks and unrecorded deposits made on or before the bank statement date but not reflected on the statement. The book balance is adjusted for items such as service charges, bank collections for the depositor, and interest earned on the account.

P4A   **Describe the voucher system to control cash disbursements.** A voucher system is a set of procedures and approvals designed to control cash disbursements and acceptance of obligations. The voucher system of control relies on several important documents, including the voucher and its supporting files. A key factor in this system is that only approved departments and individuals are authorized to incur certain obligations.

P5B   **Apply the net method to control purchase discounts.** The net method aids management in monitoring and controlling purchase discounts. When invoices are recorded at gross amounts, the amount of discounts taken is deducted from the balance of the Inventory account. This means that the amount of any discounts lost is not reported in any account and is unlikely to come to the attention of management. When purchases are recorded at net amounts, a Discounts Lost account is brought to management's attention as an operating expense. Management can then seek to identify the reason for discounts lost, such as oversight, carelessness, or unfavorable terms.

Guidance Answers to **Decision Maker** and **Decision Ethics**

Entrepreneur   A forced vacation policy is part of a good system of internal controls. When employees are forced to take vacations, their ability to hide any fraudulent behavior decreases because others must perform the vacationers' duties. A replacement employee potentially can uncover fraudulent behavior or falsified records. A forced vacation policy is especially important for employees in sensitive positions of handling money or in control of easily transferable assets.

Internal Auditor   Since you were asked to postpone your count, along with the fact the fund consists of 14 new $20 bills, you have legitimate concerns about whether money is being used for personal use. It is possible the most recent reimbursement of the fund was for $280 (14 × $20) or more. In that case, this reimbursement can leave the fund with sequentially numbered $20 bills. But if the most recent reimbursement was for less than $280, the presence of 14 sequentially

numbered $20 bills suggests that the new bills were obtained from a bank as replacement for bills that had been removed. Neither situation shows that the cashier is stealing money, but the second case indicates that the cashier "borrowed" the cash and later replaced it after the auditor showed up. In writing your report, you must not conclude that the cashier is unethical unless other evidence supports it. You should consider additional surprise counts of this petty cashier over the next few weeks.

Sales Representative   A salesperson can take several steps to reduce days' sales uncollected. These include (1) decreasing the ratio of sales on account to total sales by encouraging more cash sales, (2) identifying customers most delayed in their payments and encouraging earlier payments or cash sales, and (3) applying stricter credit policies to eliminate credit sales to customers that never pay.

Guidance Answers to **Quick Checks**

1. (*c*)

2. Technology reduces processing errors. It also allows more extensive testing of records, limits the amount of hard evidence, and highlights the importance of separation of duties.

3. A company holds liquid assets so that it can purchase other assets, buy services, and pay obligations.

4. It owns cash equivalents because they yield a return greater than what cash earns (and are readily exchanged for cash).

5. Examples of cash equivalents are 90-day U.S. Treasury bills, money market funds, and commercial paper (notes).

6. (*a*)

7. A voucher system is used when an owner/manager can no longer control purchasing procedures through personal supervision and direct participation.

8. If all cash payments are made by check, numerous checks for small amounts must be written. Since this practice is expensive and time-consuming, a petty cash fund is often established for making small (immaterial) cash payments.

9. If the petty cash fund is not reimbursed at the end of an accounting period, the transactions involving petty cash are not yet recorded and the petty cash asset is overstated.

10. First, petty cash transactions are recorded when the petty cash fund is reimbursed. Second, reimbursement provides cash to allow the fund to continue being used. Third, reimbursement identifies any cash shortage or overage in the fund.

11. A bank statement is a report prepared by the bank describing the activities in a depositor's account.

12. To reconcile a bank balance means to explain the difference between the cash balance in the depositor's accounting records and the cash balance on the bank statement.

13. The purpose of the bank reconciliation is to determine whether the bank or the depositor has made any errors and whether the bank has entered any transactions affecting the account that the depositor has not recorded.

14. Unrecorded deposits—added
Outstanding checks—subtracted

15. Interest earned—added   Debit memos—subtracted
Credit memos—added   NSF checks—subtracted
                            Bank service charges—subtracted

Key Terms   mhhe.com/wildFAP18e

Key Terms are available at the book's Website for learning and testing in an online Flashcard Format.

Bank reconciliation (p. 326)	**Discounts lost** (p. 335)	**Principles of internal control** (p. 313)
Bank statement (p. 325)	**Electronic funds transfer (EFT)** (p. 324)	**Purchase order** (p. 332)
Canceled checks (p. 326)	**Gross method** (p. 335)	**Purchase requisition** (p. 332)
Cash (p. 317)	**Internal control system** (p. 312)	**Receiving report** (p. 333)
Cash equivalents (p. 317)	**Invoice** (p. 332)	**Signature card** (p. 323)
Cash Over and Short (p. 318)	**Invoice approval** (p. 333)	**Vendee** (p. 332)
Check (p. 323)	**Liquid assets** (p. 317)	**Vendor** (p. 332)
Check register (p. 334)	**Liquidity** (p. 317)	**Voucher** (p. 320)
Days' sales uncollected (p. 329)	**Net method** (p. 335)	**Voucher register** (p. 334)
Deposits in transit (p. 326)	**Outstanding checks** (p. 326)	**Voucher system** (p. 319)
Deposit ticket (p. 323)	**Petty cash** (p. 321)	

Multiple Choice Quiz   Answers on p. 351   mhhe.com/wildFAP18e

Multiple Choice Quizzes A and B are available at the book's Website.

1. A company needs to replenish its $500 petty cash fund. Its petty cash box has $75 cash and petty cash receipts of $420. The journal entry to replenish the fund includes
  a. A debit to Cash for $75.
  b. A credit to Cash for $75.
  c. A credit to Petty Cash for $420.
  d. A credit to Cash Over and Short for $5.
  e. A debit to Cash Over and Short for $5.

2. The following information is available for Hapley Company:
  • The November 30 bank statement shows a $1,895 balance.
  • The general ledger shows a $1,742 balance at November 30.
  • A $795 deposit placed in the bank's night depository on November 30 does not appear on the November 30 bank statement.
  • Outstanding checks amount to $638 at November 30.
  • A customer's $335 note was collected by the bank in November. A collection fee of $15 was deducted by the bank and the difference deposited in Hapley's account.
  • A bank service charge of $10 is deducted by the bank and appears on the November 30 bank statement.

  How will the customer's note appear on Hapley's November 30 bank reconciliation?
  a. $320 appears as an addition to the book balance of cash.
  b. $320 appears as a deduction from the book balance of cash.
  c. $320 appears as an addition to the bank balance of cash.
  d. $320 appears as a deduction from the bank balance of cash.
  e. $335 appears as an addition to the bank balance of cash.

3. Using the information from question 2, what is the reconciled balance on Hapley's November 30 bank reconciliation?
  a. $2,052
  b. $1,895
  c. $1,742
  d. $2,201
  e. $1,184

4. A company had net sales of $84,000 and accounts receivable of $6,720. Its days' sales uncollected is
  a. 3.2 days
  b. 18.4 days
  c. 230.0 days
  d. 29.2 days
  e. 12.5 days

5. B A company records its purchases using the net method. On August 1, it purchases merchandise on account for $6,000 with terms of 2/10, n/30. The August 1 journal entry to record this transaction includes a
  a. Debit to Merchandise Inventory for $6,000.
  b. Debit to Merchandise Inventory for $5,880.
  c. Debit to Merchandise Inventory for $120.
  d. Debit to Accounts Payable for $5,880.
  e. Credit to Accounts Payable for $6,000.

Superscript letter ^A *(*^B*) denotes assignments based on Appendix 8A (8B).*

Discussion Questions

1. List the seven broad principles of internal control.

2. Internal control procedures are important in every business, but at what stage in the development of a business do they become especially critical?

3. Why should responsibility for related transactions be divided among different departments or individuals?

4. Why should the person who keeps the records of an asset not be the person responsible for its custody?

5. When a store purchases merchandise, why are individual departments not allowed to directly deal with suppliers?

6. What are the limitations of internal controls?

7. Which of the following assets is most liquid? Which is least liquid? Inventory, building, accounts receivable, or cash.

8. What is a petty cash receipt? Who should sign it?

9. Why should cash receipts be deposited on the day of receipt?

10. Best Buy's statement of cash flows in Appendix A describes changes in cash and cash equivalents for the year ended February 26, 2005. What amount is provided (used) by investing activities? What amount is provided (used) by financing activities?

11. Refer to Circuit City's balance sheet in Appendix A. How does its cash compare with its other current assets (both in amount and percent) as of February 28, 2005. Compare and assess the cash amount at February 28, 2005, with its amount at February 29, 2004.

12. Apple's balance sheet in Appendix A reports that cash and equivalents decreased during the fiscal year ended September 25, 2004. Identify at least three major causes of this change in cash and equivalents.

 Red numbers denote Discussion Questions that involve decision-making.

An internal control system consists of all policies and procedures used to protect assets, ensure reliable accounting, promote efficient operations, and urge adherence to company policies.

1. What is the main objective of internal control procedures? How is that objective achieved?
2. Why should recordkeeping for assets be separated from custody over those assets?
3. Why should the responsibility for a transaction be divided between two or more individuals or departments?

QUICK STUDY

QS 8-1
Internal control objectives

C1

Good accounting systems help with the management and control of cash and cash equivalents.

1. Define and contrast the terms *liquid asset* and *cash equivalent.*
2. Why would companies invest their idle cash in cash equivalents?

QS 8-2
Cash, liquidity, and return

C1   C2

Good accounting systems help in managing cash and controlling who has access to it.

1. What items are included in the category of cash?
2. What items are included in the category of cash equivalents?
3. What does the term *liquidity* refer to?

QS 8-3
Cash and equivalents

C2

A good system of internal control for cash provides adequate procedures for protecting both cash receipts and cash disbursements.

1. What are three basic guidelines that help achieve this protection?
2. Identify two control systems or procedures for cash disbursements.

QS 8-4
Internal control for cash

P1

---

1. The petty cash fund of the Brooks Agency is established at $85. At the end of the current period, the fund contained $14.80 and had the following receipts: film rentals, $21.30, refreshments for meetings, $30.85 (both expenditures to be classified as Entertainment Expense); postage, $8.95; and printing, $9.10. Prepare journal entries to record (*a*) establishment of the fund and (*b*) reimbursement of the fund at the end of the current period.

2. Identify the two events that cause a Petty Cash account to be credited in a journal entry.

QS 8-5
Petty cash accounting

P2

QS 8-6
Bank reconciliation

P3

1. For each of the following items, indicate whether its amount (i) affects the bank or book side of a bank reconciliation and (ii) represents an addition or a subtraction in a bank reconciliation.

a. Interest on cash balance   **d.** Outstanding checks   **g.** Unrecorded deposits

b. Bank service charges   **e.** Credit memos

c. Debit memos   **f.** NSF checks

2. Which of the items in part 1 require an adjusting journal entry?

QS 8-7
Days' sales uncollected

A1

The following annual account balances are taken from Armour Sports at December 31.

	2008	2007
Accounts receivable	$ 85,692	$ 80,485
Net sales	2,691,855	2,396,858

What is the change in the number of days' sales uncollected between years 2007 and 2008? According to this analysis, is the company's collection of receivables improving? Explain your answer.

QS 8-8^A
Documents in a voucher system

P4

Management uses a voucher system to help control and monitor cash disbursements. Identify at least four key documents that are part of a voucher system of control.

QS 8-9^B
Purchase discounts

P5

An important part of cash management is knowing when, and if, to take purchase discounts. (*a*) Which accounting method uses a Discounts Lost account? (*b*) What is the advantage of this method for management?

EXERCISES

Exercise 8-1
Analyzing internal control

C1

Franco Company is a rapidly growing start-up business. Its recordkeeper, who was hired one year ago, left town after the company's manager discovered that a large sum of money had disappeared over the past six months. An audit disclosed that the recordkeeper had written and signed several checks made payable to her fiancé and then recorded the checks as salaries expense. The fiancé, who cashed the checks but never worked for the company, left town with the recordkeeper. As a result, the company incurred an uninsured loss of $184,000. Evaluate Franco's internal control system and indicate which principles of internal control appear to have been ignored.

Exercise 8-2
Control of cash receipts by mail

P1

Some of Crown Company's cash receipts from customers are received by the company with the regular mail. Crown's recordkeeper opens these letters and deposits the cash received each day. (*a*) Identify any internal control problem(s) in this arrangement. (*b*) What changes do you recommend?

Exercise 8-3
Internal control
recommendations

C1

What internal control procedures would you recommend in each of the following situations?

1. A concession company has one employee who sells sunscreen, T-shirts, and sunglasses at the beach. Each day, the employee is given enough sunscreen, shirts and sunglasses to last through the day and enough cash to make change. The money is kept in a box at the stand.

2. An antique store has one employee who is given cash and sent to garage sales each weekend. The employee pays cash for this merchandise that the antique store resells.

Exercise 8-4
Petty cash fund accounting

P2

Check (2) Cr. Cash $162

Palmona Co. establishes a $200 petty cash fund on January 1. On January 8, the fund shows $38 in cash along with receipts for the following expenditures: postage, $74; transportation-in, $29; delivery expenses, $16; and miscellaneous expenses, $43. Palmona uses the perpetual system in accounting for merchandise inventory. Prepare journal entries to (1) establish the fund on January 1, (2) reimburse it on January 8, and (3) both reimburse the fund and increase it to $450 on January 8, assuming no entry in part 2. (*Hint*: Make two separate entries for part 3.)

Waupaca Company establishes a $350 petty cash fund on September 9. On September 30, the fund shows $104 in cash along with receipts for the following expenditures: transportation-in, $40; postage expenses, $123; and miscellaneous expenses, $80. The petty cashier could not account for a $3 shortage in the fund. Waupaca uses the perpetual system in accounting for merchandise inventory. Prepare (1) the September 9 entry to establish the fund, (2) the September 30 entry to reimburse the fund, and (3) an October 1 entry to increase the fund to $400.

Exercise 8-5
Petty cash fund with a shortage

P2

Check   (2) Cr. Cash $246 and (3) Cr. Cash $50

Prepare a table with the following headings for a monthly bank reconciliation dated September 30.

Exercise 8-6
Bank reconciliation and adjusting entries

P3

| Bank Balance | | Book Balance | | | Not Shown on the Reconciliation |
Add	Deduct	Add	Deduct	Adjust	

For each item 1 through 12, place an *x* in the appropriate column to indicate whether the item should be added to or deducted from the book or bank balance, or whether it should not appear on the reconciliation. If the book balance is to be adjusted, place a *Dr.* or *Cr.* in the Adjust column to indicate whether the Cash balance should be debited or credited. At the left side of your table, number the items to correspond to the following list.

1. NSF check from customer returned on September 25 but not yet recorded by this company.

2. Interest earned on the September cash balance in the bank.

3. Deposit made on September 5 and processed by the bank on September 6.

4. Checks written by another depositor but charged against this company's account.

5. Bank service charge for September.

6. Checks outstanding on August 31 that cleared the bank in September.

7. Check written against the company's account and cleared by the bank; erroneously not recorded by the company's recordkeeper.

8. Principal and interest on a note receivable to this company is collected by the bank but not yet recorded by the company.

9. Checks written and mailed to payees on October 2.

10. Checks written by the company and mailed to payees on September 30.

11. Night deposit made on September 30 after the bank closed.

12. Special bank charge for collection of note in part 8 on this company's behalf.

The voucher system of control is designed to control cash disbursements and the acceptance of obligations.

1. The voucher system of control establishes procedures for what two processes?

2. What types of expenditures should be overseen by a voucher system of control?

3. When is the voucher initially prepared? Explain.

Exercise 8-7
Voucher system

P1

Del Gato Clinic deposits all cash receipts on the day when they are received and it makes all cash payments by check. At the close of business on June 30, 2008, its Cash account shows an $11,589 debit balance. Del Gato Clinic's June 30 bank statement shows $10,555 on deposit in the bank. Prepare a bank reconciliation for Del Gato Clinic using the following information:

a. Outstanding checks as of June 30 total $1,829.

b. The June 30 bank statement included a $16 debit memorandum for bank services.

c. Check No. 919, listed with the canceled checks, was correctly drawn for $467 in payment of a utility bill on June 15. Del Gato Clinic mistakenly recorded it with a debit to Utilities Expense and a credit to Cash in the amount of $476.

d. The June 30 cash receipts of $2,856 were placed in the bank's night depository after banking hours and were not recorded on the June 30 bank statement.

Exercise 8-8
Bank reconciliation

P3

Check   Reconciled bal., $11,582

Exercise 8-9
Adjusting entries from
bank reconciliation   P3

Prepare the adjusting journal entries that Del Gato Clinic must record as a result of preparing the bank reconciliation in Exercise 8-8.

Exercise 8-10
Liquid assets and
accounts receivable

A1

Deacon Co. reported annual net sales for 2007 and 2008 of $665,000 and $747,000, respectively. Its year-end balances of accounts receivable follow: December 31, 2007, $61,000; and December 31, 2008, $93,000. (*a*) Calculate its days' sales uncollected at the end of each year. (*b*) Evaluate and comment on any changes in the amount of liquid assets tied up in receivables.

Exercise 8-11[A]
Documents in a voucher system

P4

Match each document in a voucher system in column one with its description in column two.

Document	**Description**
1. Purchase requisition	**A.** An itemized statement of goods prepared by the vendor listing the customer's name, items sold, sales prices, and terms of sale.
2. Purchase order	**B.** An internal file used to store documents and information to control cash disbursements and to ensure that a transaction is properly authorized and recorded.
3. Invoice	
4. Receiving report	**C.** A document used to place an order with a vendor that authorizes the vendor to ship ordered merchandise at the stated price and terms.
5. Invoice approval	
6. Voucher	**D.** A checklist of steps necessary for the approval of an invoice for recording and payment; also known as a check authorization.
	E. A document used by department managers to inform the purchasing department to place an order with a vendor.
	F. A document used to notify the appropriate persons that ordered goods have arrived, including a description of the quantities and condition of goods.

Exercise 8-12[B]
Record invoices at
gross or net amounts

P5

Piere Imports uses the perpetual system in accounting for merchandise inventory and had the following transactions during the month of October. Prepare entries to record these transactions assuming that Piere Imports records invoices (*a*) at gross amounts and (*b*) at net amounts.

Oct. 2   Purchased merchandise at a $3,000 price, invoice dated October 2, terms 2/10, n/30.
    10   Received a $500 credit memorandum (at full invoice price) for the return of merchandise that it purchased on October 2.
    17   Purchased merchandise at a $5,400 price, invoice dated October 16, terms 2/10, n/30.
    26   Paid for the merchandise purchased on October 17, less the discount.
    31   Paid for the merchandise purchased on October 2. Payment was delayed because the invoice was mistakenly filed for payment today. This error caused the discount to be lost.

PROBLEM SET A

Problem 8-1A
Analyzing internal control

C1

For each of these five separate cases, identify the principle(s) of internal control that is violated. Recommend what the business should do to ensure adherence to principles of internal control.

1. Chi Han records all incoming customer cash receipts for his employer and posts the customer payments to their respective accounts.

2. At Tico Company, Julia and Justine alternate lunch hours. Julia is the petty cash custodian, but if someone needs petty cash when she is at lunch, Justine fills in as custodian.

3. Nori Nozumi posts all patient charges and payments at the Hopeville Medical Clinic. Each night Nori backs up the computerized accounting system to a tape and stores the tape in a locked file at her desk.

4. Benedict Shales prides himself on hiring quality workers who require little supervision. As office manager, Benedict gives his employees full discretion over their tasks and for years has seen no reason to perform independent reviews of their work.

5. Cala Farah's manager has told her to reduce costs. Cala decides to raise the deductible on the plant's property insurance from $5,000 to $10,000. This cuts the property insurance premium in half. In a related move, she decides that bonding the plant's employees is a waste of money since the company has not experienced any losses due to employee theft. Cala saves the entire amount of the bonding insurance premium by dropping the bonding insurance.

Nakashima Gallery had the following petty cash transactions in February of the current year.

Feb. 2   Wrote a $400 check, cashed it, and gave the proceeds and the petty cashbox to Chloe Addison, the petty cashier.

     5   Purchased bond paper for the copier for $14.15 that is immediately used.

     9   Paid $32.50 COD shipping charges on merchandise purchased for resale, terms FOB shipping point. Nakashima uses the perpetual system to account for merchandise inventory.

    12   Paid $7.95 postage to express mail a contract to a client.

    14   Reimbursed Adina Sharon, the manager, $68 for business mileage on her car.

    20   Purchased stationery for $67.77 that is immediately used.

    23   Paid a courier $20 to deliver merchandise sold to a customer, terms FOB destination.

    25   Paid $13.10 COD shipping charges on merchandise purchased for resale, terms FOB shipping point.

    27   Paid $54 for postage expenses.

    28   The fund had $120.42 remaining in the petty cash box. Sorted the petty cash receipts by accounts affected and exchanged them for a check to reimburse the fund for expenditures.

    28   The petty cash fund amount is increased by $100 to a total of $500.

Required

1. Prepare the journal entry to establish the petty cash fund.

2. Prepare a petty cash payments report for February with these categories: delivery expense, mileage expense, postage expense, merchandise inventory (for transportation-in), and office supplies expense. Sort the payments into the appropriate categories and total the expenditures in each category.

3. Prepare the journal entries for part 2 to both (*a*) reimburse and (*b*) increase the fund amount.

Problem 8-2A
Establish, reimburse, and increase petty cash

P2

Check (3a) Cr. Cash $279.58

Kiona Co. set up a petty cash fund for payments of small amounts. The following transactions involving the petty cash fund occurred in May (the last month of the company's fiscal year).

May 1   Prepared a company check for $300 to establish the petty cash fund.

    15   Prepared a company check to replenish the fund for the following expenditures made since May 1.

       a.   Paid $88 for janitorial services.

       b.   Paid $53.68 for miscellaneous expenses.

       c.   Paid postage expenses of $53.50.

       d.   Paid $47.15 to *The County Gazette* (the local newspaper) for an advertisement.

       e.   Counted $62.15 remaining in the petty cash box.

    16   Prepared a company check for $200 to increase the fund to $500.

    31   The petty cashier reports that $288.20 cash remains in the fund. A company check is drawn to replenish the fund for the following expenditures made since May 15.

       f.   Paid postage expenses of $147.36.

       g.   Reimbursed the office manager for business mileage, $23.50.

       h.   Paid $34.75 to deliver merchandise to a customer, terms FOB destination.

    31   The company decides that the May 16 increase in the fund was too large. It reduces the fund by $100, leaving a total of $400.

Required

1. Prepare journal entries to establish the fund on May 1, to replenish it on May 15 and on May 31, and to reflect any increase or decrease in the fund balance on May 16 and May 31.

Analysis Component

2. Explain how the company's financial statements are affected if the petty cash fund is not replenished and no entry is made on May 31.

Problem 8-3A
Establish, reimburse, and adjust petty cash

P2

Check (1) Cr. to Cash: May 15, $237.85; May 16, $200

The following information is available to reconcile Branch Company's book balance of cash with its bank statement cash balance as of July 31, 2008.

a. After all posting is complete on July 31, the company's Cash account has a $27,497 debit balance, but its July bank statement shows a $27,233 cash balance.

b. Check No. 3031 for $1,482 and Check No. 3040 for $558 were outstanding on the June 30 bank reconciliation. Check No. 3040 is listed with the July canceled checks, but Check No. 3031 is not. Also, Check No. 3065 for $382 and Check No. 3069 for $2,281, both written in July, are not among the canceled checks on the July 31 statement.

Problem 8-4A
Prepare a bank reconciliation and record adjustments

P3
eXcel
mhhe.com/wildFAP18e

c. In comparing the canceled checks on the bank statement with the entries in the accounting records, it is found that Check No. 3056 for July rent was correctly written and drawn for $1,270 but was erroneously entered in the accounting records as $1,250.

d. A credit memorandum enclosed with the July bank statement indicates the bank collected $8,000 cash on a noninterest-bearing note for Branch, deducted a $45 collection fee, and credited the remainder to its account. Branch had not recorded this event before receiving the statement.

e. A debit memorandum for $805 lists a $795 NSF check plus a $10 NSF charge. The check had been received from a customer, Evan Shaw. Branch has not yet recorded this check as NSF.

f. Enclosed with the July statement is a $25 debit memorandum for bank services. It has not yet been recorded because no previous notification had been received.

g. Branch's July 31 daily cash receipts of $11,514 were placed in the bank's night depository on that date, but do not appear on the July 31 bank statement.

Required

Check (1) Reconciled balance, $34,602; (2) Cr. Note Receivable $8,000

1. Prepare the bank reconciliation for this company as of July 31, 2008.

2. Prepare the journal entries necessary to bring the company's book balance of cash into conformity with the reconciled cash balance as of July 31, 2008.

Analysis Component

3. Assume that the July 31, 2008, bank reconciliation for this company is prepared and some items are treated incorrectly. For each of the following errors, explain the effect of the error on (i) the adjusted bank statement cash balance and (ii) the adjusted cash account book balance.

    a. The company's unadjusted cash account balance of $27,497 is listed on the reconciliation as $27,947.

    b. The bank's collection of the $8,000 note less the $45 collection fee is added to the bank statement cash balance on the reconciliation.

Problem 8-5A

Prepare a bank reconciliation and record adjustments

P3

mhhe.com/wildFAP18e

Chavez Company most recently reconciled its bank statement and book balances of cash on August 31 and it reported two checks outstanding, No. 5888 for $1,028.05 and No. 5893 for $494.25. The following information is available for its September 30, 2008, reconciliation.

From the September 30 Bank Statement

Previous Balance	Total Checks and Debits	Total Deposits and Credits	Current Balance
16,800.45	9,620.05	11,272.85	18,453.25

Checks and Debits			Deposits and Credits		Daily Balance	
Date	No.	Amount	Date	Amount	Date	Amount
09/03	5888	1,028.05	09/05	1,103.75	08/31	16,800.45
09/04	5902	719.90	09/12	2,226.90	09/03	15,772.40
09/07	5901	1,824.25	09/21	4,093.00	09/04	15,052.50
09/17		600.25 NSF	09/25	2,351.70	09/05	16,156.25
09/20	5905	937.00	09/30	12.50 IN	09/07	14,332.00
09/22	5903	399.10	09/30	1,485.00 CM	09/12	16,558.90
09/22	5904	2,090.00			09/17	15,958.65
09/28	5907	213.85			09/20	15,021.65
09/29	5909	1,807.65			09/21	19,114.65
					09/22	16,625.55
					09/25	18,977.25
					09/28	18,763.40
					09/29	16,955.75
					09/30	18,453.25

From Chavez Company's Accounting Records

Cash Receipts Deposited		
Date		**Cash Debit**
Sept. 5		1,103.75
12		2,226.90
21		4,093.00
25		2,351.70
30		1,682.75
		11,458.10

Cash Disbursements		
Check No.		**Cash Credit**
5901		1,824.25
5902		719.90
5903		399.10
5904		2,060.00
5905		937.00
5906		982.30
5907		213.85
5908		388.00
5909		1,807.65
		9,332.05

Cash					Acct. No. 101	
Date		**Explanation**	**PR**	**Debit**	**Credit**	**Balance**
Aug. 31		Balance				15,278.15
Sept. 30		Total receipts	R12	11,458.10		26,736.25
30		Total disbursements	D23		9,332.05	17,404.20

Additional Information

Check No. 5904 is correctly drawn for $2,090 to pay for computer equipment; however, the recordkeeper misread the amount and entered it in the accounting records with a debit to Computer Equipment and a credit to Cash of $2,060. The NSF check shown in the statement was originally received from a customer, S. Nilson, in payment of her account. Its return has not yet been recorded by the company. The credit memorandum is from the collection of a $1,500 note for Chavez Company by the bank. The bank deducted a $15 collection fee. The collection and fee are not yet recorded.

Required

1. Prepare the September 30, 2008, bank reconciliation for this company.

2. Prepare the journal entries to adjust the book balance of cash to the reconciled balance.

Check   (1) Reconciled balance, $18,271.45 (2) Cr. Note Receivable $1,500

Analysis Component

3. The bank statement reveals that some of the prenumbered checks in the sequence are missing. Describe three situations that could explain this.

For each of these five separate cases, identify the principle(s) of internal control that is violated. Recommend what the business should do to ensure adherence to principles of internal control.

1. Latisha Tally is the company's computer specialist and oversees its computerized payroll system. Her boss recently asked her to put password protection on all office computers. Latisha has put a password in place that allows only the boss access to the file where pay rates are changed and personnel are added or deleted from the payroll.

2. Marker Theater has a computerized order-taking system for its tickets. The system is active all week and backed up every Friday night.

3. Sutton Company has two employees handling acquisitions of inventory. One employee places purchase orders and pays vendors. The second employee receives the merchandise.

4. The owner of Super Pharmacy uses a check protector to perforate checks, making it difficult for anyone to alter the amount of the check. The check protector is on the owner's desk in an office that contains company checks and is normally unlocked.

PROBLEM SET B

Problem 8-1B
Analyzing internal control

C1

5. Lavina Company is a small business that has separated the duties of cash receipts and cash disbursements. The employee responsible for cash disbursements reconciles the bank account monthly.

Problem 8-2B

Establish, reimburse, and increase petty cash

P2

Blues Music Center had the following petty cash transactions in March of the current year.

March 5 Wrote a $250 check, cashed it, and gave the proceeds and the petty cashbox to Jen Rouse, the petty cashier.
6 Paid $12.50 COD shipping charges on merchandise purchased for resale, terms FOB shipping point. Blues uses the perpetual system to account for merchandise inventory.
11 Paid $10.75 delivery charges on merchandise sold to a customer, terms FOB destination.
12 Purchased file folders for $14.13 that are immediately used.
14 Reimbursed Bob Geldof, the manager, $11.65 for office supplies purchased and used.
18 Purchased printer paper for $20.54 that is immediately used.
27 Paid $45.10 COD shipping charges on merchandise purchased for resale, terms FOB shipping point.
28 Paid postage expenses of $18.
30 Reimbursed Geldof $56.80 for business car mileage.
31 Cash of $61.53 remained in the fund. Sorted the petty cash receipts by accounts affected and exchanged them for a check to reimburse the fund for expenditures.
31 The petty cash fund amount is increased by $50 to a total of $300.

Required

1. Prepare the journal entry to establish the petty cash fund.

Check (2) Total expenses $189.47

2. Prepare a petty cash payments report for March with these categories: delivery expense, mileage expense, postage expense, merchandise inventory (for transportation-in), and office supplies expense. Sort the payments into the appropriate categories and total the expenses in each category.

(3a) Cr. Cash $188.47

3. Prepare the journal entries for part 2 to both (a) reimburse and (b) increase the fund amount.

Problem 8-3B

Establishing, reimbursing, and adjusting petty cash

P2

Moya Co. establishes a petty cash fund for payments of small amounts. The following transactions involving the petty cash fund occurred in January (the last month of the company's fiscal year).

Jan. 3 A company check for $150 is written and made payable to the petty cashier to establish the petty cash fund.
14 A company check is written to replenish the fund for the following expenditures made since January 3.
  a. Purchased office supplies for $14.29 that are immediately used up.
  b. Paid $19.60 COD shipping charges on merchandise purchased for resale, terms FOB shipping point. Moya uses the perpetual system to account for inventory.
  c. Paid $38.57 to All-Tech for minor repairs to a computer.
  d. Paid $12.82 for items classified as miscellaneous expenses.
  e. Counted $62.28 remaining in the petty cash box.
15 Prepared a company check for $50 to increase the fund to $200.
31 The petty cashier reports that $17.35 remains in the fund. A company check is written to replenish the fund for the following expenditures made since January 14.
  f. Paid $50 to *The Smart Shopper* for an advertisement in January's newsletter.
  g. Paid $48.19 for postage expenses.
  h. Paid $78 to Smooth Delivery for delivery of merchandise, terms FOB destination.
31 The company decides that the January 15 increase in the fund was too little. It increases the fund by another $50, leaving a total of $250.

Required

Check (1) Cr. to Cash: Jan. 14, $87.72; Jan. 15, $50

1. Prepare journal entries to establish the fund on January 3, to replenish it on January 14 and January 31, and to reflect any increase or decrease in the fund balance on January 15 and 31.

Analysis Component

2. Explain how the company's financial statements are affected if the petty cash fund is not replenished and no entry is made on January 31.

The following information is available to reconcile Severino Co.'s book balance of cash with its bank statement cash balance as of December 31, 2008.

a. After posting is complete, the December 31 cash balance according to the accounting records is $32,878.30, and the bank statement cash balance for that date is $46,822.40.

b. Check No. 1273 for $4,589.30 and Check No. 1282 for $400.00, both written and entered in the accounting records in December, are not among the canceled checks. Two checks, No. 1231 for $2,289.00 and No. 1242 for $410.40, were outstanding on the most recent November 30 reconciliation. Check No. 1231 is listed with the December canceled checks, but Check No. 1242 is not.

c. When the December checks are compared with entries in the accounting records, it is found that Check No. 1267 had been correctly drawn for $3,456 to pay for office supplies but was erroneously entered in the accounting records as $3,465.

d. Two debit memoranda are enclosed with the statement and are unrecorded at the time of the reconciliation. One debit memorandum is for $762.50 and dealt with an NSF check for $745 received from a customer, Titus Industries, in payment of its account. The bank assessed a $17.50 fee for processing it. The second debit memorandum is a $99.00 charge for check printing. Severino did not record these transactions before receiving the statement.

e. A credit memorandum indicates that the bank collected $19,000 cash on a note receivable for the company, deducted a $20 collection fee, and credited the balance to the company's Cash account. Severino did not record this transaction before receiving the statement.

f. Severino's December 31 daily cash receipts of $9,583.10 were placed in the bank's night depository on that date, but do not appear on the December 31 bank statement.

Required

1. Prepare the bank reconciliation for this company as of December 31, 2008.

2. Prepare the journal entries necessary to bring the company's book balance of cash into conformity with the reconciled cash balance as of December 31, 2008.

Analysis Component

3. Explain the nature of the communications conveyed by a bank when the bank sends the depositor (*a*) a debit memorandum and (*b*) a credit memorandum.

Problem 8-4B
Prepare a bank reconciliation and record adjustments

P3

Check   (1) Reconciled balance, $51,005.80; (2) Cr. Note Receivable $19,000

Shamara Systems Co. most recently reconciled its bank balance on April 30 and reported two checks outstanding at that time, No. 1771 for $781.00 and No. 1780 for $1,425.90. The following information is available for its May 31, 2008, reconciliation.

Problem 8-5B
Prepare a bank reconciliation and record adjustments

P3

From the May 31 Bank Statement

Previous Balance	Total Checks and Debits	Total Deposits and Credits	Current Balance
18,290.70	13,094.80	16,566.80	21,762.70

Checks and Debits			Deposits and Credits		Daily Balance	
Date	No.	Amount	Date	Amount	Date	Amount
05/01	1771	781.00	05/04	2,438.00	04/30	18,290.70
05/02	1783	382.50	05/14	2,898.00	05/01	17,509.70
05/04	1782	1,285.50	05/22	1,801.80	05/02	17,127.20
05/11	1784	1,449.60	05/25	7,350.00 CM	05/04	18,279.70
05/18		431.80 NSF	05/26	2,079.00	05/11	16,830.10
05/25	1787	8,032.50			05/14	19,728.10
05/26	1785	63.90			05/18	19,296.30
05/29	1788	654.00			05/22	21,098.10
05/31		14.00 SC			05/25	20,415.60
					05/26	22,430.70
					05/29	21,776.70
					05/31	21,762.70

From Shamara Systems' Accounting Records

Cash Receipts Deposited				Cash Disbursements		
Date		**Cash Debit**		**Check No.**		**Cash Credit**
May	4	2,438.00		1782		1,285.50
	14	2,898.00		1783		382.50
	22	1,801.80		1784		1,449.60
	26	2,079.00		1785		63.90
	31	2,727.30		1786		353.10
		11,944.10		1787		8,032.50
				1788		644.00
				1789		639.50
						12,850.60

Cash						Acct. No. 101
Date		**Explanation**	**PR**	**Debit**	**Credit**	**Balance**
Apr.	30	Balance				16,083.80
May	31	Total receipts	R7	11,944.10		28,027.90
	31	Total disbursements	D8		12,850.60	15,177.30

Additional Information

Check No. 1788 is correctly drawn for $654 to pay for May utilities; however, the recordkeeper misread the amount and entered it in the accounting records with a debit to Utilities Expense and a credit to Cash for $644. The bank paid and deducted the correct amount. The NSF check shown in the statement was originally received from a customer, W. Sox, in payment of her account. The company has not yet recorded its return. The credit memorandum is from a $7,400 note that the bank collected for the company. The bank deducted a $50 collection fee and deposited the remainder in the company's account. The collection and fee have not yet been recorded.

Required

1. Prepare the May 31, 2008, bank reconciliation for Shamara Systems.

2. Prepare the journal entries to adjust the book balance of cash to the reconciled balance.

Analysis Component

3. The bank statement reveals that some of the prenumbered checks in the sequence are missing. Describe three possible situations to explain this.

PROBLEM SET C

Problem Set C is available at the book's Website to further reinforce and assess your learning.

SERIAL PROBLEM

Success Systems

P3

(This serial problem began in Chapter 1 and continues through most of the book. If previous chapter segments were not completed, the serial problem can begin at this point. It is helpful, but not necessary, that you use the Working Papers that accompany the book.)

SP 8 Adriana Lopez receives the March bank statement for Success Systems on April 11, 2008. The March 31 bank statement shows an ending cash balance of $86,896. A comparison of the bank statement with the general ledger Cash account, No. 101, reveals the following.

a. Lopez notices that the bank erroneously cleared a $470 check against her account that she did not issue. The check documentation included with the bank statement shows that this check was actually issued by a company named Sierra Systems.

b. On March 25, the bank issued a $50 debit memorandum for the safety deposit box that Success Systems agreed to rent from the bank beginning March 25.

c. On March 26, the bank issued a $75 debit memorandum for printed checks that Success Systems ordered from the bank.

d. On March 31, the bank issued a credit memorandum for $33 interest earned on Success Systems's checking account for the month of March.

e. Lopez notices that the check she issued for $192 on March 31, 2008, has not yet cleared the bank.

f. Lopez verifies that all deposits made in March do appear on the March bank statement.

g. The general ledger Cash account, No. 101, shows an ending cash balance per books as $87,266 (prior to any reconciliation).

Required

1. Prepare a bank reconciliation for Success Systems for the month ended March 31, 2008.

2. Prepare any necessary adjusting entries. Use Miscellaneous Expenses, No. 677, for any bank charges. Use Interest Revenue, No. 404, for any interest earned on the checking account for the month of March.

BEYOND THE NUMBERS

BTN 8-1   Refer to **Best Buy**'s financial statements in Appendix A to answer the following.

1. For both fiscal year-ends February 26, 2005, and February 28, 2004, identify the total amount of cash and cash equivalents. Determine the percent this amount represents of total current assets, total current liabilities, total shareholders' equity, and total assets for both years. Comment on any trends.

2. For fiscal years ended February 26, 2005, and February 28, 2004, use the information in the statement of cash flows to determine the percent change between the beginning and ending year amounts of cash and cash equivalents.

3. Compute the days' sales uncollected as of February 26, 2005, and February 28, 2004. Has the collection of receivables improved? Are accounts receivable an important asset for Best Buy? Explain.

Fast Forward

4. Access Best Buy's financial statements for fiscal years ending after February 26, 2005, from its Website (BestBuy.com) or the SEC's EDGAR database (www.sec.gov). Recompute its days' sales uncollected for fiscal years ending after February 26, 2005. Compare this to the days' sales uncollected for 2005 and 2004.

REPORTING IN ACTION

C2 A1

BTN 8-2   Key comparative figures ($ millions) for both **Best Buy** and **Circuit City** follow.

	Best Buy		Circuit City	
Key Figures	**Current Year**	**Prior Year**	**Current Year**	**Prior Year**
Accounts receivable	$ 375	$ 343	$ 173	$ 171
Net sales	27,433	24,548	10,472	9,857

COMPARATIVE ANALYSIS

A1

Required

Compute days' sales uncollected for both companies for each of the two years shown. Comment on any trends for both companies. Which company has the larger percent change in days' sales uncollected?

BTN 8-3   Harriet Knox, Ralph Patton, and Marcia Diamond work for a family physician, Dr. Gwen Conrad, who is in private practice. Dr. Conrad is knowledgeable about office management practices and has segregated the cash receipt duties as follows. Knox opens the mail and prepares a triplicate list of money received. She sends one copy of the list to Patton, the cashier, who deposits the receipts daily in the bank. Diamond, the recordkeeper, receives a copy of the list and posts payments to patients' accounts. About once a month the office clerks have an expensive lunch they pay for as follows. First, Patton endorses a patient's check in Dr. Conrad's name and cashes it at the bank. Knox then destroys the

ETHICS CHALLENGE

C1

remittance advice accompanying the check. Finally, Diamond posts payment to the customer's account as a miscellaneous credit. The three justify their actions by their relatively low pay and knowledge that Dr. Conrad will likely never miss the money.

Required

1. Who is the best person in Dr. Conrad's office to reconcile the bank statement?
2. Would a bank reconciliation uncover this office fraud?
3. What are some procedures to detect this type of fraud?
4. Suggest additional internal controls that Dr. Conrad could implement.

COMMUNICATING IN PRACTICE

P5

BTN 8-4[B]   Assume you are a business consultant. The owner of a company sends you an e-mail expressing concern that the company is not taking advantage of its discounts offered by vendors. The company currently uses the gross method of recording purchases. The owner is considering a review of all invoices and payments from the previous period. Due to the volume of purchases, however, the owner recognizes this is time-consuming and costly. The owner seeks your advice about monitoring purchase discounts in the future. Provide a response in memorandum form.

TAKING IT TO THE NET

C1 P1

BTN 8-5   Visit the Association of Certified Fraud Examiners Website at **cfenet.com**. Research the fraud facts (see press room—fraud statistics) presented at this site and fill in the blanks in the following statements.

1. It is estimated that ____% of 2003 revenues were lost as a result of occupational fraud and abuse. Applied to the U.S. gross domestic product, this translates to losses of approximately $____ billion.
2. Small businesses are the most vulnerable to occupational fraud and abuse. The average scheme in a small business causes $____ in losses. The average scheme in the largest companies costs $____.
3. The most common method for detecting occupational fraud is through tips from ____, customers, vendors, and anonymous sources. The second most common method of discovery is ____.
4. The typical occupational fraud perpetrator is a first-time offender. Only ____% of occupational fraudsters in this study were known to have prior convictions for fraud-related offenses.
5. All occupational frauds fall into one of three categories: ____, corruption, or ____statements.
6. Over ____% of occupational frauds involve asset misappropriations. Cash is the targeted asset ____% of the time.
7. Corruption schemes account for ____% of all occupational frauds, and they cause over $____ in losses, on average.
8. Fraudulent statements are the most costly form of occupational fraud with median losses of $____ million per scheme.
9. Frauds committed by employees cause median losses of $____, while frauds committed by owners cause median losses of $____.
10. Losses caused by perpetrators older than 60 are ____times higher than losses caused by employees 25 and younger.

TEAMWORK IN ACTION

C1

BTN 8-6   Organize the class into teams. Each team must prepare a list of 10 internal controls a consumer could observe in a typical retail department store. When called upon, the team's spokesperson must be prepared to share controls identified by the team that have not been shared by another team's spokesperson.

***BusinessWeek* ACTIVITY**

C1 P1

BTN 8-7   Read the article "No Accounting for Being Disorganized" in the March 10, 2004, issue of *BusinessWeek*. (The book's Website provides a free link.)

Required

1. Why does Steven Cohen, the author of the article, urge small business owners to be accounting literate?
2. How does Cohen suggest that small business owners "get savvy"?
3. What does Cohen recommend an owner do to stop theft and fraud?
4. What suggestions does Cohen offer for small business owners?

BTN 8-8 Review the opening feature of this chapter that highlights Todd Graves and his company Raising Cane's Chicken Fingers.

ENTREPRENEURIAL DECISION

C1 P1

Required

1. List the seven principles of internal control and explain how Graves could implement each of them in his restaurants.

2. Do you believe that Graves will need to add additional controls as his business expands? Explain.

BTN 8-9 Visit an area of your college that serves the student community with either products or services. Some examples are food services, libraries, and book stores. Identify and describe between four and eight internal controls being implemented.

HITTING THE ROAD

C1

BTN 8-10 The following information is from Dixons' (Dixons-Group.com) financial statements.

GLOBAL DECISION

C2

Dixons

(£ millions)	Current Year	Prior Year
Cash	293.3	152.0
Accounts receivable*	427.2	1,018.8
Current assets	2,303.9	1,090.2
Total assets	3,873.8	4,158.0
Current liabilities	1,565.8	1,679.0
Shareholders' equity	1,467.7	1,376.5
Net sales[†]	6,458.0	5,719.8

*Titled: Debtors—falling due within one year.   [†]Titled: Turnover.

Required

1. For each year, compute the percentage that cash represents of total assets, current liabilities, and shareholders' equity. Comment on any trends in these percentages.

2. Determine the percentage change between the current and prior year cash balances.

3. Compute the days' sales uncollected at the end of both the current year and the prior year. Has the collection of receivables improved? Explain.

ANSWERS TO MULTIPLE CHOICE QUIZ

1. e; The entry follows.

Debits to expenses (or assets)	420	
Cash Over and Short	5	
Cash		425

2. a; recognizes cash collection of note by bank.

3. a; the bank reconciliation follows.

4. d; ($6,720/$84,000) × 365 = 29.2 days

5. b; The entry follows.

Merchandise Inventory*	5,880	
Accounts Payable		5,880

*$6,000 × 98%

Bank Reconciliation November 30			
Balance per bank statement	$1,895	Balance per books	$1,742
Add: Deposit in transit	795	Add: Note collected less fee	320
Deduct: Outstanding checks	(638)	Deduct: Service charge	(10)
Reconciled balance	$2,052	Reconciled balance	$2,052

9

Accounting for Receivables

A Look Back

Chapter 8 focused on internal control and reporting for cash. We described internal control procedures and the accounting for and management of cash.

A Look at This Chapter

This chapter emphasizes receivables. We explain that they are liquid assets and describe how companies account for and report them. We also discuss the importance of estimating uncollectibles.

A Look Ahead

Chapter 10 focuses on plant assets, natural resources, and intangible assets. We explain how to account for, report, and analyze these long-term assets.

Learning Objectives

CAP

Conceptual

C1 Describe accounts receivable and how they occur and are recorded. *(p. 354)*

C2 Describe a note receivable and the computation of its maturity date and interest. *(p. 364)*

C3 Explain how receivables can be converted to cash before maturity. *(p. 367)*

Analytical

A1 Compute accounts receivable turnover and use it to help assess financial condition. *(p. 368)*

Procedural

P1 Apply the direct write-off and allowance methods to account for accounts receivable. *(p. 358)*

P2 Estimate uncollectibles using methods based on sales and accounts receivable. *(p. 361)*

P3 Record the receipt of a note receivable. *(p. 365)*

P4 Record the honoring and dishonoring of a note and adjustments for interest. *(p. 366)*

Decision Feature

Heating up the Salsa Business

DENVER, CO—Nothing was ever handed to Linda Torres-Winters. "Growing up as a migrant farm worker, I picked tomatoes as a child," recalls Linda. "We lived in one big room, side by side—seven children." Little did she know that one day she would use the know-how gained from picking and working with tomatoes to launch Linditas' (LinditasSalsa.com), a maker of instant salsa mixes. Linda now markets her products in nearly 1,000 stores in more than 10 states.

Linda drew on her experiences and challenges to achieve success. "I always wanted to do something for my family and be somebody," she says proudly. Linda points out that it all came together when she decided "to create an authentic salsa based upon my Hispanic culture and heritage."

"I can remember my mother making the best salsas," Linda says. With that inspiration and her own determination, she created the instant salsa mix. The mix contains dehydrated spices and vegetables—the consumer need only add tomatoes for homemade salsa, any time, anywhere.

Linda creates high-quality salsas, but keeps prices competitive. She pays special attention to buyers and maintains control over receivables. Decisions involving sales on credit and policies for extending credit can make or break a startup. This is an added burden, but Linda points out, "You get back what you put in."

Linda puts in time getting to know her customers, including who pays and when. She uses this information to plan purchases, cash payments, and so forth. Adds Linda, we know our customers—inside and out—including their payment patterns. In this way, says Linda, she can estimate uncollectibles and minimize bad debts.

With a passion for people, Linda never loses sight of the personal touch in business. Yet she also understands the importance of the financial touch. As always, Linda balances these needs with customer relationships. "Like anything else," says Linda. "You have to work it." And work it she has.

[Sources: *Linditas' Website,* January 2006; *SBA Website,* July 2005; *Hispanic Trends,* October 2002; *Denver Business Journal,* January 1999]

This chapter focuses on accounts receivable and short-term notes receivable. We describe each of these assets, their uses, and how they are accounted for and reported in financial statements. This knowledge helps us use accounting information to make better business decisions. It can also help in predicting future company performance and financial condition as well as in managing one's own business.

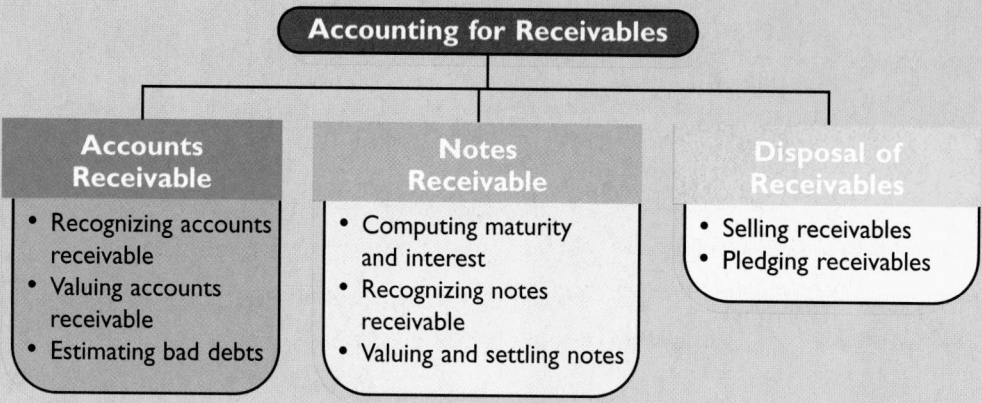

Accounts Receivable

A *receivable* is an amount due from another party. The two most common receivables are accounts receivable and notes receivable. Other receivables include interest receivable, rent receivable, tax refund receivable, and receivables from employees. **Accounts receivable** are amounts due from customers for credit sales. This section begins by describing how accounts receivable occur. It includes receivables that occur when customers use credit cards issued by third parties and when a company gives credit directly to customers. When a company does extend credit directly to customers, it (1) maintains a separate account receivable for each customer and (2) accounts for bad debts from credit sales.

Recognizing Accounts Receivable

C1 Describe accounts receivable and how they occur and are recorded.

Accounts receivable occur from credit sales to customers. The amount of credit sales has increased in recent years, reflecting several factors including an efficient financial system. Retailers such as **Limited Brands** and **Best Buy** hold millions of dollars in accounts receivable. Similar amounts are held by wholesalers such as **SUPERVALU** and **SYSCO**. Exhibit 9.1 shows recent dollar amounts of accounts receivable and their percent of total assets for four well-known companies.

Exhibit 9.1

Accounts Receivable for Selected Companies

Sales on Credit Credit sales are recorded by increasing (debiting) Accounts Receivable. A company must also maintain a separate account for each customer that tracks how much that customer purchases, has already paid, and still owes. This information provides the basis for sending bills to customers and for other business analyses. To maintain this information, companies that extend credit directly to their customers keep a separate account receivable for each one of them. The general ledger continues to have a single Accounts Receivable account along with the other financial statement accounts, but a supplementary record is created to maintain a separate account for each customer. This supplementary record is called the *accounts receivable ledger*.

Exhibit 9.2 shows the relation between the Accounts Receivable account in the general ledger and its individual customer accounts in the accounts receivable ledger for TechCom, a small electronics wholesaler. This exhibit reports a $3,000 ending balance of TechCom's accounts receivable for June 30. TechCom's transactions are mainly in cash, but it has two major credit customers: CompStore and RDA Electronics. Its *schedule of accounts receivable* shows that the $3,000 balance of the Accounts Receivable account in the general ledger equals the total of its two customers' balances in the accounts receivable ledger.

Point: Receivables, cash, cash equivalents, and short-term investments make up the most liquid assets of a company.

Exhibit 9.2

General Ledger and the Accounts Receivable Ledger (before July 1 transactions)

To see how accounts receivable from credit sales are recognized in the accounting records, we look at two transactions on July 1 between TechCom and its credit customers—see Exhibit 9.3. The first is a credit sale of $950 to CompStore. A credit sale is posted with both a debit to the Accounts Receivable account in the general ledger and a debit to the customer account in the accounts receivable ledger. The second transaction is a collection of $720 from RDA Electronics from a prior credit sale. Cash receipts from a credit customer are posted with a credit to the Accounts Receivable account in the general ledger and flows through to credit the customer account in the accounts receivable ledger. (Posting debits or credits to Accounts Receivable in two separate ledgers does not violate the requirement that debits equal credits. The equality of debits and credits is maintained in the general ledger. The accounts receivable ledger is a *supplementary* record providing information on each customer.)

Exhibit 9.3

Accounts Receivable Transactions

Assets = Liabilities + Equity
+950   +950
Assets = Liabilities + Equity
+720
−720

July 1	Accounts Receivable—CompStore	950	
	Sales.		950
	To record credit sales*		
July 1	Cash	720	
	Accounts Receivable—RDA Electronics		720
	To record collection of credit sales.		

* We omit the entry to Dr. Cost of Sales and Cr. Merchandise Inventory to focus on sales and receivables.

Exhibit 9.4 shows the general ledger and the accounts receivable ledger after recording the two July 1 transactions. The general ledger shows the effects of the sale, the collection, and the resulting balance of $3,230. These events are also reflected in the individual customer accounts: RDA Electronics has an ending balance of $280, and CompStore's ending balance is $2,950. The $3,230 sum of the individual accounts equals the debit balance of the Accounts Receivable account in the general ledger.

Like TechCom, many large retailers such as **Sears** and **JCPenney** sell on credit. Many also maintain their own credit cards to grant credit to approved customers and to earn interest on

Point: Software helps merchants build Web storefronts quickly and easily. Merchants simply enter product details such as names and prices, and out comes a respectable-looking Website complete with order forms. They also offer security with credit card orders and can track sales and site visits.

Exhibit 9.4

General Ledger and
the Accounts Receivable Ledger
(after July 1 transactions)

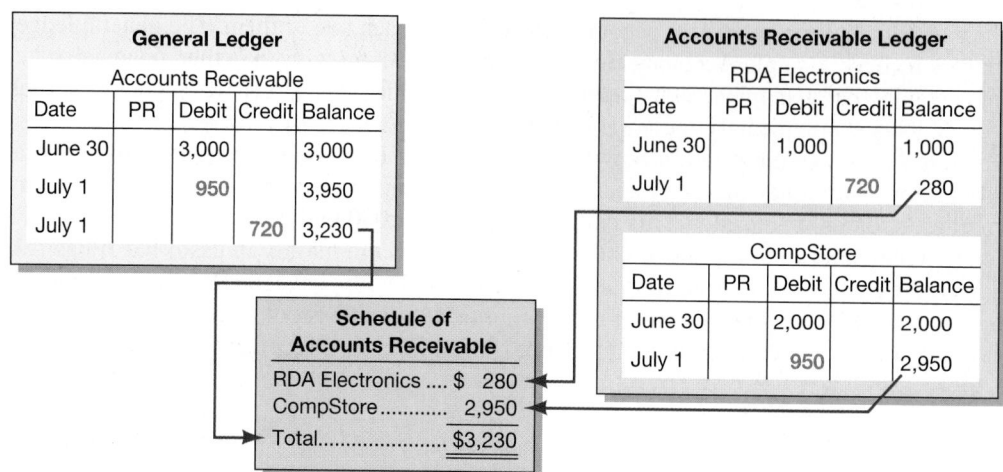

General Ledger

Accounts Receivable

Date	PR	Debit	Credit	Balance
June 30		3,000		3,000
July 1		950		3,950
July 1			720	3,230

Accounts Receivable Ledger

RDA Electronics

Date	PR	Debit	Credit	Balance
June 30		1,000		1,000
July 1			720	280

CompStore

Date	PR	Debit	Credit	Balance
June 30		2,000		2,000
July 1		950		2,950

**Schedule of
Accounts Receivable**

RDA Electronics	$ 280
CompStore	2,950
Total	$3,230

any balance not paid within a specified period of time. This allows them to avoid the fee charged by credit card companies. The entries in this case are the same as those for TechCom except for the possibility of added interest revenue. If a customer owes interest on a bill, we debit Interest Receivable and credit Interest Revenue for that amount.

Credit Card Sales   Many companies allow their customers to pay for products and services using third-party credit cards such as **Visa**, **MasterCard**, or **American Express**, and debit cards (also called ATM or bank cards). This practice gives customers the ability to make purchases without cash or checks. Once credit is established with a credit card company or bank, the customer does not have to open an account with each store. Customers using these cards can make single monthly payments instead of several payments to different creditors and can defer their payments.

Sellers allow customers to use third-party credit cards and debit cards instead of granting credit directly for several reasons. First, the seller does not have to evaluate each customer's credit standing or make decisions about who gets credit and how much. Second, the seller avoids the risk of extending credit to customers who cannot or do not pay. This risk is transferred to the card company. Third, the seller typically receives cash from the card company sooner than had it granted credit directly to customers. Fourth, a variety of credit options for customers offers a potential increase in sales volume. **Sears** historically offered credit only to customers using a Sears card but later changed its policy to permit customers to charge purchases to third-party credit card companies in a desire to increase sales. It reported: "SearsCharge increased its share of Sears retail sales even as the company expanded the payment options available to its customers with the acceptance . . . of [Visa,] MasterCard, and American Express in addition to the [Sears] Card."

Point: Visa USA transacted more than $1 trillion in 2005 from its credit, debit, and prepaid cards.

There are guidelines in how companies account for credit card and debit card sales. Some credit cards, but mostly debit cards, credit a seller's Cash account immediately upon deposit. In this case the seller deposits a copy of each card sales receipt in its bank account just as it deposits a customer's check. Some other cards require the seller to remit a copy (often electronically) of each receipt to the card company. Until payment is received, the seller has an account receivable from the card company. In both cases, the seller pays a fee for services provided by the card company, often ranging from 1% to 5% of card sales. This charge is deducted from the credit to the seller's account or the cash payment to the seller.

The procedures used in accounting for credit card sales depend on whether cash is received immediately on deposit or cash receipt is delayed until the credit card company makes the payment. To illustrate, if TechCom has $100 of credit card sales with a 4% fee, and its $96 cash is received immediately on deposit, the entry is

Point: Web merchants pay twice as much in credit card association fees as other retailers because they suffer 10 times as much fraud.

July 15	Cash	96	
	Credit Card Expense	4	
	Sales		100
	*To record credit card sales less a 4% credit card expense.**		

Assets = Liabilities + Equity
+96   +100
             −4

* We omit the entry to Dr. Cost of Sales and Cr. Merchandise Inventory to focus on credit card expense.

However, if instead TechCom must remit electronically the credit card sales receipts to the credit card company and wait for the $96 cash payment, the entry on the date of sale is

July 15	**Accounts Receivable—Credit Card Co.**	96	
	Credit Card Expense	4	
	Sales		100
	*To record credit card sales less 4% credit card expense.**		

Assets = Liabilities + Equity
+96   +100
             −4

* We omit the entry to Dr. Cost of Sales and Cr. Merchandise Inventory to focus on credit card expense.

When cash is later received from the credit card company, usually through electronic funds transfer, the entry is

July 20	Cash	96	
	Accounts Receivable—Credit Card Co.		96
	To record cash receipt.		

Assets = Liabilities + Equity
+96
−96

Some firms report credit card expense in the income statement as a type of discount deducted from sales to get net sales. Other companies classify it as a selling expense or even as an administrative expense. Arguments can be made for each alternative.

Point: Third-party credit card costs can be large. JCPenney recently reported third-party credit card costs exceeding $10 million.

Installment Sales and Receivables Many companies allow their credit customers to make periodic payments over several months. For example, **Harley-Davidson** holds more than $900 million in installment receivables. The seller refers to such assets as *installment accounts receivable,* which are amounts owed by customers from credit sales for which payment is required in periodic amounts over an extended time period. Source documents for installment accounts receivable include sales slips or invoices describing the sales transactions. The customer is usually charged interest. Although installment accounts receivable may have credit periods of more than one year, they are classified as current assets if the seller regularly offers customers such terms.

Quick Check   Answers—p. 372

1. In recording credit card sales, when do you debit Accounts Receivable and when do you debit Cash?

2. A company accumulates sales receipts and remits them to the credit card company for payment. When are the credit card expenses recorded? When are these expenses incurred?

Valuing Accounts Receivable

When a company directly grants credit to its customers, it expects that some customers will not pay what they promised. The accounts of these customers are *uncollectible accounts,*

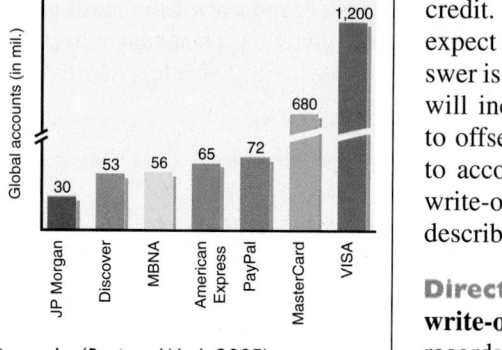
commonly called **bad debts.** The total amount of uncollectible accounts is an expense of selling on credit. Why do companies sell on credit if they expect some accounts to be uncollectible? The answer is that companies believe that granting credit will increase total sales and net income enough to offset bad debts. Companies use two methods to account for uncollectible accounts: (1) direct write-off method and (2) allowance method. We describe both.

Direct Write-Off Method The **direct write-off method** of accounting for bad debts records the loss from an uncollectible account receivable when it is determined to be uncollectible. No attempt is made to predict bad debts

P1 Apply the direct write-off and allowance methods to account for accounts receivable.

expense. To illustrate, if TechCom determines on January 23 that it cannot collect $520 owed to it by its customer J. Kent, it recognizes the loss using the direct write-off method as follows:

Assets = Liabilities + Equity
−520   −520

Jan. 23	Bad Debts Expense	520	
	Accounts Receivable—J. Kent		520
	To write off an uncollectible account.		

The debit in this entry charges the uncollectible amount directly to the current period's Bad Debts Expense account. The credit removes its balance from the Accounts Receivable account in the general ledger (and its subsidiary ledger).

Sometimes an account written off is later collected. This can be due to factors such as continual collection efforts or a customer's good fortune. If the account of J. Kent that was written off directly to Bad Debts Expense is later collected in full, the following two entries record this recovery.

Point: Managers realize that some portion of credit sales will be uncollectible, but which credit sales are uncollectible is unknown.

Assets = Liabilities + Equity
+520   +520

Assets = Liabilities + Equity
+520
−520

Mar. 11	Accounts Receivable—J. Kent.	520	
	Bad Debts Expense.		520
	To reinstate account previously written off.		
Mar. 11	Cash.	520	
	Accounts Receivable—J. Kent		520
	To record full payment of account.		

Point: If a customer fails to pay within the credit period, most companies send out repeated billings and make other efforts to collect.

Companies must weigh at least two accounting principles when considering the use of the direct write-off method: the (1) matching principle and (2) materiality principle.

Matching principle applied to bad debts. The **matching principle** requires expenses to be reported in the same accounting period as the sales they helped produce. This means that if extending credit to customers helped produce sales, the bad debts expense linked to those sales is matched and reported in the same period. The direct write-off method usually does not best match sales and expenses because bad debts expense is not recorded until an account becomes uncollectible, which often occurs in a period after that of the credit sale. To match bad debts expense with the sales it produces therefore requires a company to estimate future uncollectibles.

Point: Pier 1 Imports reports $7 million of bad debts expense matched against $461 million of credit sales in a recent fiscal year.

Materiality principle applied to bad debts. The **materiality principle** states that an amount can be ignored if its effect on the financial statements is unimportant to users' business decisions. The materiality principle permits the use of the direct write-off method when bad debts expenses are very small in relation to a company's other financial statement items such as sales and net income.

Allowance Method The **allowance method** of accounting for bad debts matches the *estimated* loss from uncollectible accounts receivable against the sales they helped produce. We must use estimated losses because when sales occur, management does not know which customers will not pay their bills. This means that at the end of each period, the allowance method requires an estimate of the total bad debts expected to result from that period's sales. This method has two advantages over the direct write-off method: (1) it records estimated bad debts expense in the period when the related sales are recorded and (2) it reports accounts receivable on the balance sheet at the estimated amount of cash to be collected.

Recording bad debts expense. The allowance method estimates bad debts expense at the end of each accounting period and records it with an adjusting entry. TechCom, for instance, had credit sales of $300,000 during its first year of operations. At the end of the first year, $20,000 of credit sales remained uncollected. Based on the experience of similar businesses, TechCom estimated that $1,500 of its accounts receivable would be uncollectible. This estimated expense is recorded with the following adjusting entry.

9-1

Point: Under the direct write-off method, expense is recorded each time an account is written off. Under the allowance method, expense is recorded with an adjusting entry equal to the total estimated uncollectibles for that period's sales.

Dec. 31	Bad Debts Expense	1,500	
	Allowance for Doubtful Accounts.		1,500
	To record estimated bad debts.		

$$\text{Assets} = \text{Liabilities} + \text{Equity}$$
$$-1,500 \qquad\qquad -1,500$$

The estimated Bad Debts Expense of $1,500 is reported on the income statement (as either a selling expense or an administrative expense) and offsets the $300,000 credit sales it helped produce. The **Allowance for Doubtful Accounts** is a contra asset account. A contra account is used instead of reducing accounts receivable directly because at the time of the adjusting entry, the company does not know which customers will not pay. After the bad debts adjusting entry is posted, TechCom's account balances (in T-account form) for Accounts Receivable and its Allowance for Doubtful Accounts are as shown in Exhibit 9.5.

Point: Credit approval is usually not assigned to the selling dept. because its goal is to increase sales, and it may approve customers at the cost of increased bad debts. Instead, approval is assigned to a separate credit-granting or administrative dept.

Accounts Receivable			**Allowance for Doubtful Accounts**		
Dec. 31	20,000			Dec. 31	1,500

Exhibit 9.5

General Ledger Balances after Bad Debts Adjusting Entry

The Allowance for Doubtful Accounts credit balance of $1,500 has the effect of reducing accounts receivable to its estimated realizable value. **Realizable value** refers to the expected proceeds from converting an asset into cash. Although credit customers owe $20,000 to TechCom, only $18,500 is expected to be realized in cash collections from these customers. In the balance sheet, the Allowance for Doubtful Accounts is subtracted from Accounts Receivable and is often reported as shown in Exhibit 9.6.

Point: Bad Debts Expense is also called *Uncollectible Accounts Expense.* The Allowance for Doubtful Accounts is also called *Allowance for Uncollectible Accounts.*

Current assets		
Accounts receivable	$20,000	
Less allowance for doubtful accounts	1,500	$18,500

Exhibit 9.6

Balance Sheet Presentation of the Allowance for Doubtful Accounts

Sometimes the Allowance for Doubtful Accounts is not reported separately. This alternative presentation is shown in Exhibit 9.7 (also see Appendix A).

Current assets	
Accounts receivable (net of $1,500 doubtful accounts)	$18,500

Exhibit 9.7

Alternative Presentation of the Allowance for Doubtful Accounts

Writing off a bad debt.   When specific accounts are identified as uncollectible, they are written off against the Allowance for Doubtful Accounts. To illustrate, TechCom decides that J. Kent's $520 account is uncollectible and makes the following entry to write it off.

Assets = Liabilities + Equity
+520
−520

Jan. 23	Allowance for Doubtful Accounts	520	
	Accounts Receivable—J. Kent		520
	To write off an uncollectible account.		

Posting this write-off entry to the Accounts Receivable account removes the amount of the bad debt from the general ledger (it is also posted to the accounts receivable subsidiary ledger). The general ledger accounts now appear as in Exhibit 9.8 (assuming no other transactions affecting these accounts).

Exhibit 9.8

General Ledger Balances after Write-Off

Accounts Receivable				Allowance for Doubtful Accounts			
Dec. 31	20,000						
		Jan. 23	520	Jan. 23	520	Dec. 31	1,500

The write-off does not affect the realizable value of accounts receivable as shown in Exhibit 9.9. Neither total assets nor net income is affected by the write-off of a specific account. Instead, both assets and net income are affected in the period when bad debts expense is predicted and recorded with an adjusting entry.

Exhibit 9.9

Realizable Value before and after Write-Off of a Bad Debt

	Before Write-Off	After Write-Off
Accounts receivable	$ 20,000	$ 19,480
Less allowance for doubtful accounts	1,500	980
Estimated realizable accounts receivable	**$18,500**	**$18,500**

Recovering a bad debt.   When a customer fails to pay and the account is written off as uncollectible, his or her credit standing is jeopardized. To help restore credit standing, a customer sometimes volunteers to pay all or part of the amount owed. A company makes two entries when collecting an account previously written off by the allowance method. The first is to reverse the write-off and reinstate the customer's account. The second entry records the collection of the reinstated account. To illustrate, if on March 11 Kent pays in full his account previously written off, the entries are

Assets = Liabilities + Equity
+520
−520

Assets = Liabilities + Equity
+520
−520

Mar. 11	Accounts Receivable—J. Kent	520	
	Allowance for Doubtful Accounts		520
	To reinstate account previously written off.		
Mar. 11	Cash	520	
	Accounts Receivable—J. Kent		520
	To record full payment of account.		

In this illustration, Kent paid the entire amount previously written off, but sometimes a customer pays only a portion of the amount owed. A question then arises as to whether the entire balance of the account or just the amount paid is returned to accounts receivable. This is a matter of judgment. If we believe this customer will later pay in full, we return the entire amount owed to accounts receivable, but if we expect no further collection, we return only the amount paid.

Estimating Bad Debts Expense

Companies with direct credit sales must attempt to estimate bad debts expense to both manage their receivables and set credit policies. The allowance method also requires an estimate of bad debts expense to prepare an adjusting entry at the end of each accounting period. There are two common methods. One is based on the income statement relation between bad debts expense and sales. The second is based on the balance sheet relation between accounts receivable and the allowance for doubtful accounts.

Percent of Sales Method   The *percent of sales method* uses income statement relations to estimate bad debts. It is based on the idea that a given percent of a company's credit sales for the period are uncollectible. To illustrate, assume that Musicland has credit sales of $400,000 in year 2008. Based on past experience, Musicland estimates 0.6% of credit sales to be uncollectible. This implies that Musicland expects $2,400 of bad debts expense from its sales (computed as $400,000 \times 0.006 = \$2,400$). The adjusting entry to record this estimated expense is

Dec. 31	Bad Debts Expense	2,400	
	Allowance for Doubtful Accounts.		2,400
	To record estimated bad debts.		

P2 Estimate uncollectibles using methods based on sales and accounts receivable.

Point: The focus is on *credit* sales because cash sales do not produce bad debts. If cash sales are a small or stable percent of credit sales, total sales can be used.

Assets = Liabilities + Equity
−2,400   −2,400

Point: When using the *percent of sales method* for estimating uncollectibles, the estimate of bad debts is the number used in the adjusting entry.

The allowance account ending balance on the balance sheet for this method would rarely equal the bad debts expense on the income statement. This is so because unless a company is in its first period of operations, its allowance account has a zero balance only if the prior amounts written off as uncollectible *exactly* equal the prior estimated bad debts expenses. (When computing bad debts expense as a percent of sales, managers monitor and adjust the percent so it is not too high or too low.)

Accounts Receivable Methods   The *accounts receivable methods* use balance sheet relations to estimate bad debts—mainly the relation between accounts receivable and the allowance amount. The goal of the bad debts adjusting entry for these methods is to make the Allowance for Doubtful Accounts balance equal to the portion of accounts receivable that is estimated to be uncollectible. The estimated balance for the allowance account is obtained in one of two ways: (1) computing the percent uncollectible from the total accounts receivable or (2) aging accounts receivable.

Percent of accounts receivable method.   The *percent of accounts receivable method* assumes that a given percent of a company's receivables is uncollectible. This percent is based on past experience and is impacted by current conditions such as economic trends and customer difficulties. The total dollar amount of all receivables is multiplied by this percent to get the estimated dollar amount of uncollectible accounts—reported in the balance sheet as the Allowance for Doubtful Accounts.

To illustrate, assume that Musicland has $50,000 of accounts receivable on December 31, 2008. Experience suggests 5% of its receivables are uncollectible. This means that after the adjusting entry is posted, we want the Allowance for Doubtful Accounts to show a $2,500 credit balance (5% of $50,000). (*Note:* Its beginning balance is $2,200, which is 5% of the $44,000 accounts receivable on December 31, 2007—see Exhibit 9.10.) Also during 2008, accounts of customers are written off on February 6, July 10, and November 20. Thus, the account has a

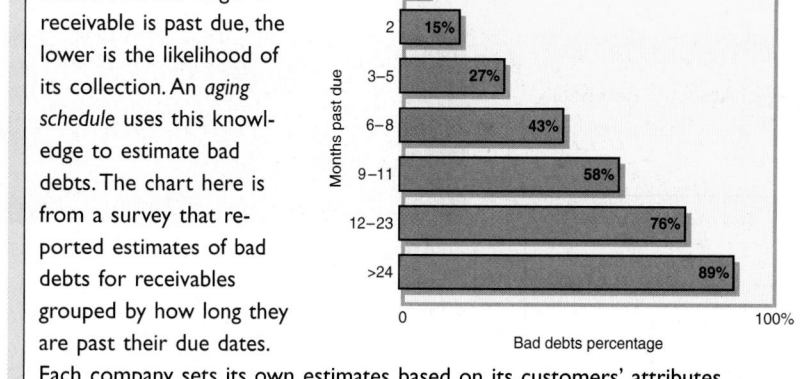

Decision Insight

Aging Pains Experience shows that the longer a receivable is past due, the lower is the likelihood of its collection. An *aging schedule* uses this knowledge to estimate bad debts. The chart here is from a survey that reported estimates of bad debts for receivables grouped by how long they are past their due dates. Each company sets its own estimates based on its customers' attributes.

Months past due — Bad debts percentage:
1: 6%
2: 15%
3–5: 27%
6–8: 43%
9–11: 58%
12–23: 76%
>24: 89%

Point: When using an accounts receivable method for estimating uncollectibles, the allowance account balance is adjusted to equal the estimate of uncollectibles.

$200 credit balance prior to the December 31, 2008, adjustment. The adjusting entry to give the allowance account the estimated $2,500 balance is

Assets = Liabilities + Equity
−2,300   −2,300

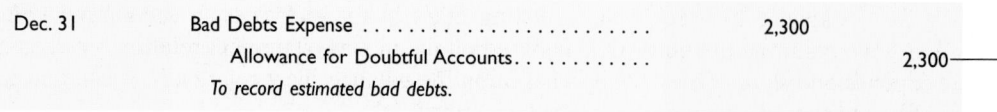

Dec. 31	Bad Debts Expense	2,300	
	Allowance for Doubtful Accounts.		2,300
	To record estimated bad debts.		

Exhibit 9.10 shows the effects of these transactions and adjustments on the allowance amount.

Exhibit 9.10

Allowance for Doubtful Accounts after Bad Debts Adjusting Entry

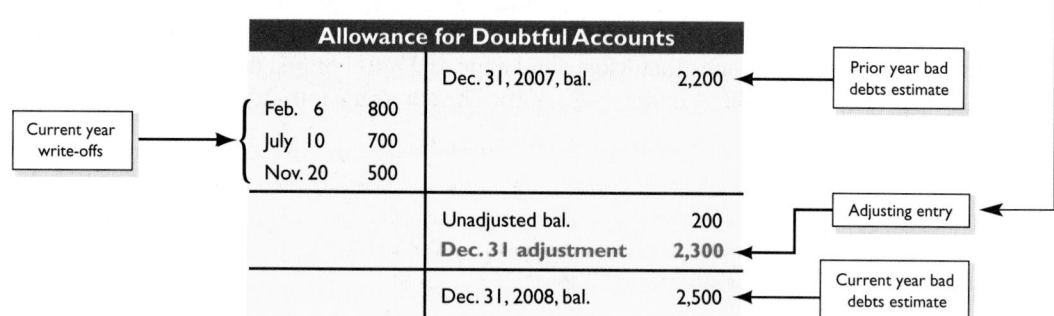

Aging of accounts receivable method.   The **aging of accounts receivable** method uses both past and current receivables information to estimate the allowance amount. Specifically, each receivable is classified by how long it is past its due date. Then estimates of uncollectible amounts are made assuming that the longer an amount is past due, the more likely it is to be uncollectible. Classifications are often based on 30-day periods. After the amounts are classified (or aged), experience is used to estimate the percent of each uncollectible class. These percents are applied to the amounts in each class and then totaled to get the estimated balance of the Allowance for Doubtful Accounts. This computation is performed by setting up a schedule such as Exhibit 9.11.

Exhibit 9.11

Aging of Accounts Receivable

Each receivable is grouped by how long it is past its due date

Each age group is multiplied by its estimated bad debts percent

Estimated bad debts for each group are totaled

MUSICLAND
Schedule of Accounts Receivable by Age
December 31, 2008

Customer	Totals	Not Yet Due	1 to 30 Days Past Due	31 to 60 Days Past Due	61 to 90 Days Past Due	Over 90 Days Past Due
Carlie Abbott	$ 450	$ 450				
Jamie Allen	710			$ 710		
Chavez Andres	500	300	$ 200			
Belicia Company	740				$ 100	$ 640
Zamora Services	1,000	810	190			
Total receivables	$ 50,000	$37,000	$6,500	$3,700	$1,900	$ 900
Percent uncollectible		× 2%	× 5%	× 10%	× 25%	× 40%
Estimated uncollectible	$ 2,270	$ 740	$ 325	$ 370	$ 475	$ 360

Exhibit 9.11 lists each customer's individual balances assigned to one of five classes based on its days past due. The amounts in each class are totaled and multiplied by the estimated percent of uncollectible accounts for each class. The percents used are regularly reviewed to reflect changes in the company and economy.

Point: Using both current and past data, spreadsheet software is useful for estimating bad debts under different assumptions.

To explain, Musicland has $3,700 in accounts receivable that are 31 to 60 days past due. Its management estimates 10% of the amounts in this age class are uncollectible, or a total of $370 (computed as $3,700 × 10%).

Unadjusted balance	$ 200 credit
Estimated balance	2,270 credit
Required adjustment	$2,070 credit

Exhibit 9.12

Computation of the Required Adjustment for an Accounts Receivable Method

Similar analysis is done for each of the other four classes. The final total of $2,270 ($740 + $325 + 370 + $475 + $360) shown in the first column is the estimated balance for the Allowance for Doubtful Accounts. Exhibit 9.12 shows that since the allowance account has an unadjusted credit balance of $200, the required adjustment to the Allowance for Doubtful Accounts is $2,070. This yields the following end-of-period adjusting entry.

Dec. 31	Bad Debts Expense	2,070	
	Allowance for Doubtful Accounts.		2,070
	To record estimated bad debts.		

Assets = Liabilities + Equity
−2,070   −2,070

Alternatively, if the allowance account had an unadjusted *debit* balance of $500 (instead of the $200 credit balance), its required adjustment would be computed as follows.

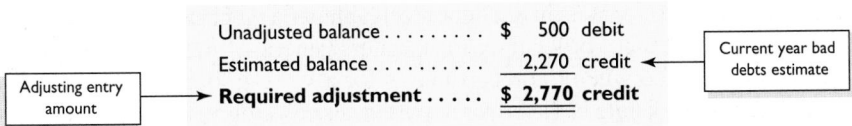

Unadjusted balance	$ 500 debit
Estimated balance	2,270 credit
Required adjustment	**$ 2,770 credit**

The entry to record the end-of-period adjustment for this alternative case is

Dec. 31	Bad Debts Expense	2,770	
	Allowance for Doubtful Accounts.		2,770
	To record estimated bad debts.		

Assets = Liabilities + Equity
−2,770   −2,770

The aging of accounts receivable method is a more detailed examination of specific accounts and is usually the most reliable of the estimation methods.

Exhibit 9.13 summarizes the principles guiding all three estimation methods and their focus of analysis. Percent of sales, with its income statement focus, does a good job at matching bad debts expense with sales. The accounts receivable methods, with their balance sheet focus, do a better job at reporting accounts receivable at realizable value.

Decision Maker   Answer—p. 372

Labor Union Chief One week prior to labor contract negotiations, financial statements are released showing no income growth. A 10% growth was predicted. Your analysis finds that the company increased its allowance for uncollectibles from 1.5% to 4.5% of receivables. Without this change, income would show a 9% growth. Does this analysis impact negotiations?

Exhibit 9.13

Methods to Estimate Bad Debts

Answers—p. 372

Quick Check

3. Why must bad debts expense be estimated if such an estimate is possible?

4. What term describes the balance sheet valuation of Accounts Receivable less the Allowance for Doubtful Accounts?

5. Why is estimated bad debts expense credited to a contra account (Allowance for Doubtful Accounts) rather than to the Accounts Receivable account?

6. SnoBoard Company's year-end balance in its Allowance for Doubtful Accounts is a credit of $440. By aging accounts receivable, it estimates that $6,142 is uncollectible. Prepare SnoBoard's year-end adjusting entry for bad debts.

7. Record entries for these transactions assuming the allowance method is used:

   Jan.   10   The $300 account of customer Cool Jam is determined uncollectible.

   April 12   Cool Jam unexpectedly pays in full the account deemed uncollectible on Jan. 10.

Notes Receivable

C2   Describe a note receivable and the computation of its maturity date and interest.

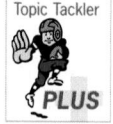

Topic Tackler PLUS

9-2

A **promissory note** is a written promise to pay a specified amount of money, usually with interest, either on demand or at a definite future date. Promissory notes are used in many transactions, including paying for products and services, and lending and borrowing money. Sellers sometimes ask for a note to replace an account receivable when a customer requests additional time to pay a past-due account. For legal reasons, sellers generally prefer to receive notes when the credit period is long and when the receivable is for a large amount. If a lawsuit is needed to collect from a customer, a note is the buyer's written acknowledgment of the debt, its amount, and its terms.

Exhibit 9.14 shows a simple promissory note dated July 10, 2008. For this note, Julia Browne promises to pay TechCom or to its order (according to TechCom's instructions) a specified amount of money ($1,000), called the **principal of a note,** at a definite future date (October 8, 2008). As the one who signed the note and promised to pay it at maturity, Browne is the **maker of the note.** As the person to whom the note is payable, TechCom is the **payee of the note.** To Browne, the note is a liability called a *note payable*. To TechCom, the same note is an asset called a *note receivable*. This note bears interest at 12%, as written on the note. **Interest** is the charge for using (not paying) the money until a later date. To a borrower, interest is an expense. To a lender, it is revenue.

Exhibit 9.14

Promissory Note

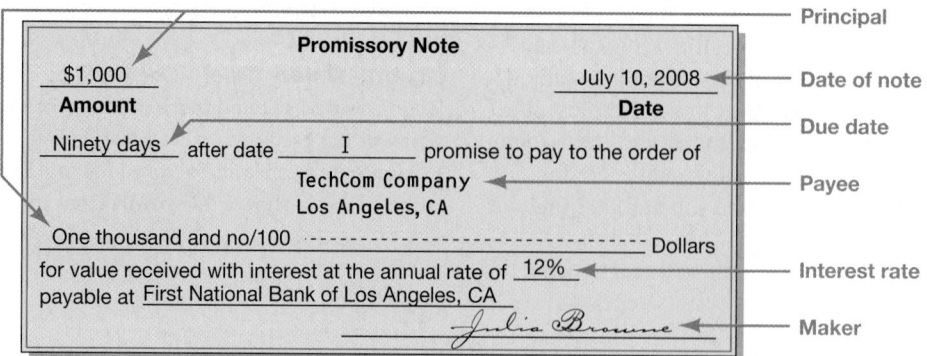

Computing Maturity and Interest

This section describes key computations for notes including the determination of maturity date, period covered, and interest computation.

Maturity Date and Period   The **maturity date of a note** is the day the note (principal and interest) must be repaid. The *period* of a note is the time from the note's (contract) date to its maturity date. Many notes mature in less than a full year, and the period they cover is often expressed in days. When the time of a note is expressed in days, its maturity date is the specified number of days after the note's date. As an example, a five-day note dated June 15 matures and is due on June 20. A 90-day note dated July 10 matures on October 8. This October 8 due date is computed as shown in Exhibit 9.15. The period of a note is sometimes expressed in months or years. When months are used, the note matures and is payable in the month of its maturity on the *same day of the month* as its original date. A nine-month note dated July 10, for instance, is payable on April 10. The same analysis applies when years are used.

Days in July	31
Minus the date of the note	10
Days remaining in July	21 ◄———— July 11–31
Add days in August	31 ◄———— Aug. 1–31
Add days in September	30 ◄———— Sept. 1–30
Days to equal 90 days, or **maturity date of October 8**	8 ◄———— Oct. 1–8
Period of the note in days	90

Exhibit 9.15

Maturity Date Computation

Interest Computation *Interest* is the cost of borrowing money for the borrower or, alternatively, the profit from lending money for the lender. Unless otherwise stated, the rate of interest on a note is the rate charged for the use of the principal for one year. The formula for computing interest on a note is shown in Exhibit 9.16.

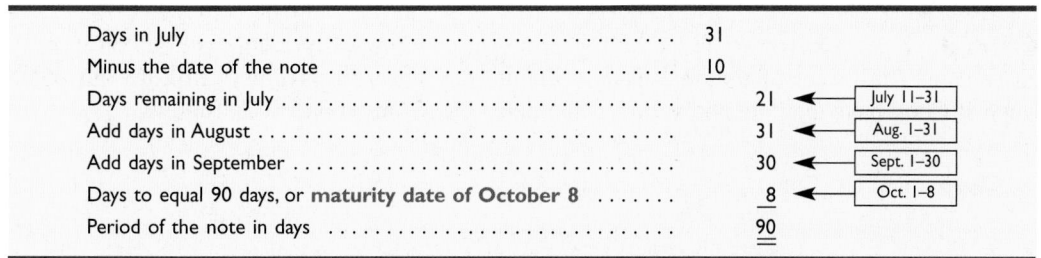

$$\begin{matrix} \textbf{Principal} \\ \textbf{of the note} \end{matrix} \times \begin{matrix} \textbf{Annual} \\ \textbf{interest rate} \end{matrix} \times \begin{matrix} \textbf{Time expressed} \\ \textbf{in years} \end{matrix} = \textbf{Interest}$$

Exhibit 9.16

Computation of Interest Formula

To simplify interest computations, a year is commonly treated as having 360 days (called the *banker's rule* in the business world). **We treat a year as having 360 days for interest computations in the examples and assignments.** Using the promissory note in Exhibit 9.14 where we have a 90-day, 12%, $1,000 note, the total interest is computed as follows.

$$\$1,000 \times 12\% \times \frac{90}{360} = \$1,000 \times 0.12 \times 0.25 = \$30$$

Recognizing Notes Receivable

Notes receivable are usually recorded in a single Notes Receivable account to simplify record-keeping. The original notes are kept on file, including information on the maker, rate of interest, and due date. (When a company holds a large number of notes, it sometimes sets up a controlling account and a subsidiary ledger for notes. This is similar to the handling of accounts receivable.) To illustrate the recording for the receipt of a note, we use the $1,000, 90-day, 12% promissory note in Exhibit 9.14. TechCom received this note at the time of a product sale to Julia Browne. This transaction is recorded as follows.

P3 Record the receipt of a note receivable.

July 10*	Notes Receivable.	1,000	
	Sales.		1,000
	Sold goods in exchange for a 90-day, 12% note.		

Assets = Liabilities + Equity
+1,000   +1,000

* We omit the entry to Dr. Cost of Sales and Cr. Merchandise Inventory to focus on sales and receivables.

When a seller accepts a note from an overdue customer as a way to grant a time extension on a past-due account receivable, it will often collect part of the past-due balance in cash. This partial payment forces a concession from the customer, reduces the customer's debt (and the seller's risk), and produces a note for a smaller amount. To illustrate, assume that TechCom agreed to accept $232 in cash along with a $600, 60-day, 15% note from Jo Cook to settle

Point: Notes receivable often are a major part of a company's assets. Likewise, notes payable often are a large part of a company's liabilities.

her $832 past-due account. TechCom made the following entry to record receipt of this cash and note.

Assets = Liabilities + Equity					
+232	Oct. 5	Cash.	232	
+600		Notes Receivable.	600	
−832		Accounts Receivable—J. Cook.		832
		Received cash and note to settle account.		

Valuing and Settling Notes

P4 Record the honoring and dishonoring of a note and adjustments for interest.

Recording an Honored Note The principal and interest of a note are due on its maturity date. The maker of the note usually *honors* the note and pays it in full. To illustrate, when J. Cook pays the note above on its due date, TechCom records it as follows.

Assets = Liabilities + Equity					
+615 +15	Dec. 4	Cash.	615	
−600		Notes Receivable		600
		Interest Revenue.		15
		Collect note with interest of $600 × 15% × 60/360.		

Interest Revenue, also called *Interest Earned,* is reported on the income statement.

Recording a Dishonored Note When a note's maker is unable or refuses to pay at maturity, the note is *dishonored.* The act of dishonoring a note does not relieve the maker of the obligation to pay. The payee should use every legitimate means to collect. How do companies report this event? The balance of the Notes Receivable account should include only those notes that have not matured. Thus, when a note is dishonored, we remove the amount of this note from the Notes Receivable account and charge it back to an account receivable from its maker. To illustrate, TechCom holds an $800, 12%, 60-day note of Greg Hart. At maturity, Hart dishonors the note. TechCom records this dishonoring of the note as follows.

Point: When posting a dishonored note to a customer's account, an explanation is included so as not to misinterpret the debit as a sale on account.

Assets = Liabilities + Equity					
+816 +16	Oct. 14	Accounts Receivable—G. Hart	816	
−800		Interest Revenue.		16
		Notes Receivable		800
		To charge account of G. Hart for a dishonored note and interest of $800 × 12% × 60/360.		

Point: Reporting the details of notes is consistent with the **full disclosure principle,** which requires financial statements (including footnotes) to report all relevant information.

Charging a dishonored note back to the account of its maker serves two purposes. First, it removes the amount of the note from the Notes Receivable account and records the dishonored note in the maker's account. Second, and more important, if the maker of the dishonored note applies for credit in the future, his or her account will reveal all past dealings, including the dishonored note. Restoring the account also reminds the company to continue collection efforts from Hart for both principal and interest. The entry records the full amount, including interest, to ensure that it is included in collection efforts.

Recording End-of-Period Interest Adjustment When notes receivable are outstanding at the end of a period, any accrued interest earned is computed and recorded. To illustrate, on December 16, TechCom accepts a $3,000, 60-day, 12% note from a customer in granting an extension on a past-due account. When TechCom's accounting period ends on December 31, $15 of interest has accrued on this note ($3,000 × 12% × 15/360). The following adjusting entry records this revenue.

Assets = Liabilities + Equity					
+15 +15	Dec. 31	Interest Receivable.	15	
		Interest Revenue.		15
		To record accrued interest earned.		

Interest Revenue appears on the income statement, and Interest Receivable appears on the balance sheet as a current asset. When the December 16 note is collected on February 14, TechCom's entry to record the cash receipt is

Feb. 14	Cash	3,060	
	Interest Revenue		45
	Interest Receivable		15
	Notes Receivable		3,000
	Received payment of note and its interest.		

Assets = Liabilities + Equity
+3,060   +45
−15
−3,000

Total interest earned on the 60-day note is $60. The $15 credit to Interest Receivable on February 14 reflects the collection of the interest accrued from the December 31 adjusting entry. The $45 interest earned reflects TechCom's revenue from holding the note from January 1 to February 14 of the current period.

Quick Check

Answers—p. 372

8. Irwin purchases $7,000 of merchandise from Stamford on December 16, 2007. Stamford accepts Irwin's $7,000, 90-day, 12% note as payment. Stamford's accounting period ends on December 31, and it does not make reversing entries. Prepare entries for Stamford on December 16, 2007, and December 31, 2007.

9. Using the information in Quick Check 8, prepare Stamford's March 16, 2008, entry if Irwin dishonors the note.

Disposing of Receivables

Companies can convert receivables to cash before they are due. Reasons for this include the need for cash or the desire not to be involved in collection activities. Converting receivables is usually done either by (1) selling them or (2) using them as security for a loan. A recent survey shows that about 20% of companies obtain cash from either selling receivables or pledging them as security. In some industries such as textiles, apparel and furniture, this is common practice.

Selling Receivables

A company can sell all or a portion of its receivables to a finance company or bank. The buyer, called a *factor,* charges the seller a *factoring fee* and then the buyer takes ownership of the receivables and receives cash when they come due. By incurring a factoring fee, the seller receives cash earlier and can pass the risk of bad debts to the factor. The seller can also choose to avoid costs of billing and accounting for the receivables. To illustrate, if TechCom sells $20,000 of its accounts receivable and is charged a 4% factoring fee, it records this sale as follows.

C3 Explain how receivables can be converted to cash before maturity.

Global: Firms in export sales increasingly sell their receivables to factors.

Aug. 15	Cash	19,200	
	Factoring Fee Expense	800	
	Accounts Receivable		20,000
	Sold accounts receivable for cash, less 4% fee.		

Assets = Liabilities + Equity
+19,200   −800
−20,000

The accounting for sales of notes receivable is similar to that for accounts receivable. The detailed entries are covered in advanced courses.

Pledging Receivables

A company can raise cash by borrowing money and *pledging* its receivables as security for the loan. Pledging receivables does not transfer the risk of bad debts to the lender because the

Point: When accounts receivable are sold, each subsidiary ledger account is credited along with the controlling account for the total.

borrower retains ownership of the receivables. If the borrower defaults on the loan, the lender has a right to be paid from the cash receipts of the receivable when collected. To illustrate, when TechCom borrows $35,000 and pledges its receivables as security, it records this transaction as follows.

Assets = Liabilities + Equity
+35,000   +35,000

Aug. 20	Cash	35,000	
	Notes Payable		35,000
	Borrowed money with a note secured by pledging receivables.		

Since pledged receivables are committed as security for a specific loan, the borrower's financial statements disclose the pledging of them. TechCom, for instance, includes the following note with its statements: *Accounts receivable of $40,000 are pledged as security for a $35,000 note payable.*

Decision Analysis   Accounts Receivable Turnover

A1 Compute accounts receivable turnover and use it to help assess financial condition.

For a company selling on credit, we want to assess both the quality and liquidity of its accounts receivable. *Quality* of receivables refers to the likelihood of collection without loss. Experience shows that the longer receivables are outstanding beyond their due date, the lower the likelihood of collection. *Liquidity* of receivables refers to the speed of collection. **Accounts receivable turnover** is a measure of both the quality and liquidity of accounts receivable. It indicates how often, on average, receivables are received and collected during the period. The formula for this ratio is shown in Exhibit 9.17.

Exhibit 9.17

Accounts Receivable Turnover

$$\text{Accounts receivable turnover} = \frac{\text{Net sales}}{\text{Average accounts receivable}}$$

We prefer to use net *credit* sales in the numerator because cash sales do not create receivables. However, since financial statements rarely report net credit sales, our analysis uses net sales. The denominator is the *average* accounts receivable balance, computed as (Beginning balance + Ending balance) ÷ 2. TechCom has an accounts receivable turnover of 5.1. This indicates its average accounts receivable balance is converted into cash 5.1 times during the period. Exhibit 9.18 shows graphically this turnover activity for TechCom.

Exhibit 9.18

Rate of Accounts Receivable Turnover for TechCom

5.1 times per year

| 1 | 2 | 3 | 4 | 5 |

Jan.   Feb.   March   Apr.   May   June   July   Aug.   Sept.   Oct.   Nov.   Dec.

Accounts receivable turnover also reflects how well management is doing in granting credit to customers in a desire to increase sales. A high turnover in comparison with competitors suggests that management should consider using more liberal credit terms to increase sales. A low turnover suggests management should consider stricter credit terms and more aggressive collection efforts to avoid having its resources tied up in accounts receivable.

Point: Credit risk ratio is computed by dividing the Allowance for Doubtful Accounts by Accounts Receivable. The higher this ratio, the higher is credit risk.

To illustrate, we take data from two competitors: **Dell Inc.** and **Apple Computer.** Exhibit 9.19 shows accounts receivable turnover for both companies.

Exhibit 9.19

Analysis Using Accounts Receivable Turnover

Company	Figure ($ millions)	2004	2003	2002
Dell	Net sales	$49,205	$41,444	$35,404
	Average accounts receivable	$ 4,025	$ 3,111	$ 2,428
	Accounts receivable turnover	12.2	13.3	14.6
Apple	Net sales	$ 8,279	$ 6,207	$ 5,742
	Average accounts receivable	$ 770	$ 666	$ 516
	Accounts receivable turnover	10.8	9.3	11.1

Dell's 2004 turnover is computed ($ millions) as $49,205/$4,025 = 12.2. This means that Dell's average accounts receivable balance was converted into cash 12.2 times in 2004. However, its turnover worsened in 2004 (versus its prior two years), but it is superior to that of Apple. Is Dell's turnover too high? Since sales are markedly growing over this time period, Dell's turnover does not appear to be too high. Instead, both Dell and Apple seem to be doing well in managing receivables—with a cautionary note to monitor Dell's recent decline in its receivables turnover. Turnover for competitors is generally in the range of 7 to 11 for this same period.[1]

Decision Maker   Answer—p. 372

Family Physician Your practice is barely profitable, so you hire a health care analyst. The analyst highlights several points including the following: "*Accounts receivable turnover is too low. Tighter credit policies are recommended along with discontinuing service to those most delayed in payments.*" How do you interpret these recommendations? What actions do you take?

Demonstration Problem

Clayco Company completes the following selected transactions during year 2008.

July 14   Writes off a $750 account receivable arising from a sale to Briggs Company that dates to 10 months ago. (Clayco Company uses the allowance method.)

30   Clayco Company receives a $1,000, 90-day, 10% note in exchange for merchandise sold to Sumrell Company (the merchandise cost $600).

Aug. 15   Receives $2,000 cash plus a $10,000 note from JT Co. in exchange for merchandise that sells for $12,000 (its cost is $8,000). The note is dated August 15, bears 12% interest, and matures in 120 days.

Nov. 1   Completed a $200 credit card sale with a 4% fee (the cost of sales is $150). The cash is received immediately from the credit card company.

3   Sumrell Company refuses to pay the note that was due to Clayco Company on October 28. Prepare the journal entry to charge the dishonored note plus accrued interest to Sumrell Company's accounts receivable.

5   Completed a $500 credit card sale with a 5% fee (the cost of sales is $300). The payment from the credit card company is received on Nov. 9.

15   Received the full amount of $750 from Briggs Company that was previously written off on July 14. Record the bad debts recovery.

Dec. 13   Received payment of principal plus interest from JT for the August 15 note.

Required

1. Prepare journal entries to record these transactions on Clayco Company's books.

2. Prepare an adjusting journal entry as of December 31, 2008, assuming the following:

  a. Bad debts expense is estimated to be $20,400 by aging accounts receivable. The unadjusted balance of the Allowance for Doubtful Accounts is $1,000 debit.

  b. Alternatively, assume that bad debts expense is estimated using the percent of sales method. The Allowance for Doubtful Accounts had a $1,000 debit balance before adjustment, and the company estimates bad debts to be 1% of its credit sales of $2,000,000.

Planning the Solution

- Examine each transaction to determine the accounts affected, and then record the entries.
- For the year-end adjustment, record the bad debts expense for the two approaches.

---

[1] As an estimate of *average days' sales uncollected,* we compute how many days (*on average*) it takes to collect receivables as follows: 365 days ÷ accounts receivable turnover. An increase in this *average collection period* can signal a decline in customers' financial condition.

Solution to Demonstration Problem

1.

July 14	Allowance for Doubtful Accounts	750	
	Accounts Receivable—Briggs Co.		750
	Wrote off an uncollectible account.		
July 30	Notes Receivable—Sumrell Co.	1,000	
	Sales.		1,000
	Sold merchandise for a 90-day, 10% note.		
July 30	Cost of Goods Sold.	600	
	Merchandise Inventory.		600
	To record the cost of July 30 sale.		
Aug. 15	Cash	2,000	
	Notes Receivable—JT Co.	10,000	
	Sales.		12,000
	Sold merchandise to customer for $2,000 cash and $10,000 note.		
Aug. 15	Cost of Goods Sold	8,000	
	Merchandise Inventory.		8,000
	To record the cost of Aug. 15 sale.		
Nov. 1	Cash	192	
	Credit Card Expense	8	
	Sales.		200
	To record credit card sale less a 4% credit card expense.		
Nov. 1	Cost of Goods Sold	150	
	Merchandise Inventory.		150
	To record the cost of Nov. 1 sale.		
Nov. 3	Accounts Receivable—Sumrell Co.	1,025	
	Interest Revenue.		25
	Notes Receivable—Sumrell Co.		1,000
	To charge account of Sumrell Company for a $1,000 dishonored note and interest of $1,000 × 10% × 90/360.		
Nov. 5	Accounts Receivable—Credit Card Co.	475	
	Credit Card Expense	25	
	Sales.		500
	To record credit card sale less a 5% credit card expense.		
Nov. 5	Cost of Goods Sold.	300	
	Merchandise Inventory.		300
	To record the cost of Nov. 5 sale.		
Nov. 9	Cash	475	
	Accounts Receivable—Credit Card Co.		475
	To record cash receipt from Nov. 5 sale.		
Nov. 15	Accounts Receivable—Briggs Co.	750	
	Allowance for Doubtful Accounts.		750
	To reinstate the account of Briggs Company previously written off.		
Nov. 15	Cash	750	
	Accounts Receivable—Briggs Co.		750
	Cash received in full payment of account.		
Dec. 13	Cash	10,400	
	Interest Revenue.		400
	Note Receivable—JT Co.		10,000
	Collect note with interest of $10,000 × 12% × 120/360.		

2a. Aging of accounts receivable method.

Dec. 31	Bad Debts Expense	21,400	
	Allowance for Doubtful Accounts.		21,400
	To adjust allowance account from a $1,000		
	debit balance to a $20,400 credit balance.		

2b. Percent of sales method.*

Dec. 31	Bad Debts Expense	20,000	
	Allowance for Doubtful Accounts.		20,000
	To provide for bad debts as 1% × $2,000,000		
	in credit sales.		

---

* For the income statement approach, which requires estimating bad debts as a percent of sales or credit sales, the Allowance account balance is *not* considered when making the adjusting entry.

Summary

C1 **Describe accounts receivable and how they occur and are recorded.** Accounts receivable are amounts due from customers for credit sales. A subsidiary ledger lists amounts owed by each customer. Credit sales arise from at least two sources: (1) sales on credit and (2) credit card sales. *Sales on credit* refers to a company's granting credit directly to customers. Credit card sales involve customers' use of third-party credit cards.

C2 **Describe a note receivable and the computation of its maturity date and interest.** A note receivable is a written promise to pay a specified amount of money at a definite future date. The maturity date is the day the note (principal and interest) must be repaid. Interest rates are normally stated in annual terms. The amount of interest on the note is computed by expressing time as a fraction of one year and multiplying the note's principal by this fraction and the annual interest rate.

C3 **Explain how receivables can be converted to cash before maturity.** Receivables can be converted to cash before maturity in three ways. First, a company can sell accounts receivable to a factor, who charges a factoring fee. Second, a company can borrow money by signing a note payable that is secured by pledging the accounts receivable. Third, notes receivable can be discounted at (sold to) a financial institution.

A1 **Compute accounts receivable turnover and use it to help assess financial condition.** Accounts receivable turnover is a measure of both the quality and liquidity of accounts receivable. The accounts receivable turnover measure indicates how often, on average, receivables are received and collected during the period. Accounts receivable turnover is computed as net sales divided by average accounts receivable.

P1 **Apply the direct write-off and allowance methods to account for accounts receivable.** The direct write-off method charges Bad Debts Expense when accounts are written off as uncollectible. This method is acceptable only when the amount of bad debts expense is immaterial. Under the allowance method, bad debts expense is recorded with an adjustment at the end of each accounting period that debits the Bad Debts Expense account and credits the Allowance for Doubtful Accounts. The uncollectible accounts are later written off with a debit to the Allowance for Doubtful Accounts.

P2 **Estimate uncollectibles using methods based on sales and accounts receivable.** Uncollectibles are estimated by focusing on either (1) the income statement relation between bad debts expense and credit sales or (2) the balance sheet relation between accounts receivable and the allowance for doubtful accounts. The first approach emphasizes the matching principle using the income statement. The second approach emphasizes realizable value of accounts receivable using the balance sheet.

P3 **Record the receipt of a note receivable.** A note received is recorded at its principal amount by debiting the Notes Receivable account. The credit amount is to the asset, product, or service provided in return for the note.

P4 **Record the honoring and dishonoring of a note and adjustments for interest.** When a note is honored, the payee debits the money received and credits both Notes Receivable and Interest Revenue. Dishonored notes are credited to Notes Receivable and debited to Accounts Receivable (to the account of the maker in an attempt to collect), and Interest Revenue is recorded for interest earned for the time the note is held.

Guidance Answers to **Decision Maker** and **Decision Ethics**

Entrepreneur Analysis of credit card sales should weigh the benefits against the costs. The primary benefit is the potential to increase sales by attracting customers who prefer the convenience of

credit cards. The primary cost is the fee charged by the credit card company for providing this service. Analysis should therefore estimate the expected increase in dollar sales from allowing credit card sales and then subtract (1) the normal costs and expenses and (2) the credit card fees associated with this expected increase in dollar sales. If your analysis shows an increase in profit from allowing credit card sales, your store should probably accept them.

Labor Union Chief   Yes, this information is likely to impact your negotiations. The obvious question is why the company markedly increased this allowance. The large increase in this allowance means a substantial increase in bad debts expense *and* a decrease in earnings. This change (coming immediately prior to labor contract discussions) also raises concerns since it reduces the union's bargaining power for increased compensation. You want to ask management for supporting documentation justifying this increase. You also want data for two or three prior years and

similar data from competitors. These data should give you some sense of whether the change in the allowance for uncollectibles is justified.

Family Physician   The recommendations are twofold. First, the analyst suggests more stringent screening of patients' credit standing. Second, the analyst suggests dropping patients who are most overdue in payments. You are likely bothered by both suggestions. They are probably financially wise recommendations, but you are troubled by eliminating services to those less able to pay. One alternative is to follow the recommendations while implementing a care program directed at patients less able to pay for services. This allows you to continue services to patients less able to pay and lets you discontinue services to patients able but unwilling to pay.

Guidance Answers to **Quick Checks**

1. If cash is immediately received when credit card sales receipts are deposited, the company debits Cash at the time of sale. If the company does not receive payment until after it submits receipts to the credit card company, it debits Accounts Receivable at the time of sale. (Cash is later debited when payment is received from the credit card company.)

2. Credit card expenses are usually *recorded* and *incurred* at the time of their related sales, not when cash is received from the credit card company.

3. If possible, bad debts expense must be matched with the sales that gave rise to the accounts receivable. This requires that companies estimate future bad debts at the end of each period before they learn which accounts are uncollectible.

4. Realizable value (also called *net realizable value*).

5. The estimated amount of bad debts expense cannot be credited to the Accounts Receivable account because the specific customer accounts that will prove uncollectible cannot yet be identified and removed from the accounts receivable subsidiary ledger. Moreover, if only the Accounts Receivable account is credited, its balance would not equal the sum of its subsidiary account balances.

6.

Dec. 31	Bad Debts Expense	5,702	
	Allowance for Doubtful Accounts		5,702

7.

Jan. 10	Allowance for Doubtful Accounts	300	
	Accounts Receivable—Cool Jam		300
Apr. 12	Accounts Receivable—Cool Jam	300	
	Allowance for Doubtful Accounts		300
Apr. 12	Cash	300	
	Accounts Receivable—Cool Jam		300

8.

Dec. 16	Note Receivable—Irwin	7,000	
	Sales		7,000
Dec. 31	Interest Receivable	35	
	Interest Revenue		35
	($7,000 × 12% × 15/360)		

9.

Mar. 16	Accounts Receivable—Irwin	7,210	
	Interest Revenue		175
	Interest Receivable		35
	Notes Receivable—Irwin		7,000

Key Terms   mhhe.com/wildFAP18e

Key Terms are available at the book's Website for learning and testing in an online Flashcard Format.

Accounts receivable (p. 354)
Accounts receivable turnover (p. 368)
Aging of accounts receivable (p. 362)
Allowance for Doubtful Accounts (p. 359)
Allowance method (p. 359)
Bad debts (p. 358)

Direct write-off method (p. 358)
Interest (p. 364)
Maker of the note (p. 364)
Matching principle (p. 358)
Materiality principle (p. 358)
Maturity date of a note (p. 364)

Payee of the note (p. 364)
Principal of a note (p. 364)
Promissory note (or note) (p. 364)
Realizable value (p. 359)

Multiple Choice Quiz   Answers on p. 383   mhhe.com/wildFAP18e

Multiple Choice Quizzes A and B are available at the book's Website.

1. A company's Accounts Receivable balance at its December 31 year-end is $125,650, and its Allowance for Doubtful Accounts has a credit balance of $328 before year-end adjustment. Its net sales are $572,300. It estimates that 4% of outstanding accounts receivable are uncollectible. What amount of Bad Debts Expense is recorded at December 31?
   a. $5,354
   b. $328
   c. $5,026
   d. $4,698
   e. $34,338

2. A company's Accounts Receivable balance at its December 31 year-end is $489,300, and its Allowance for Doubtful Accounts has a debit balance of $554 before year-end adjustment. Its net sales are $1,300,000. It estimates that 6% of outstanding accounts receivable are uncollectible. What amount of Bad Debts Expense is recorded at December 31?
   a. $29,912
   b. $28,804
   c. $78,000
   d. $29,358
   e. $554

3. Total interest accrued on a $7,500, 5%, 90-day note is
   a. $93.75
   b. $375.00
   c. $1,125.00
   d. $31.25
   e. $125.00

4. A company receives a $9,000, 8%, 60-day note. The maturity value of the note is
   a. $120
   b. $9,000
   c. $9,120
   d. $720
   e. $9,720

5. A company has net sales of $489,600 and average accounts receivable of $40,800. What is its accounts receivable turnover?
   a. 0.08
   b. 30.41
   c. 1,341.00
   d. 12.00
   e. 111.78

Discussion Questions

1. How do sellers benefit from allowing their customers to use credit cards?

2. Why does the direct write-off method of accounting for bad debts usually fail to match revenues and expenses?

3. Explain the accounting principle of materiality.

4. Explain why writing off a bad debt against the Allowance for Doubtful Accounts does not reduce the estimated realizable value of a company's accounts receivable.

5. Why does the Bad Debts Expense account usually not have the same adjusted balance as the Allowance for Doubtful Accounts?

6. Why might a business prefer a note receivable to an account receivable?

7. Refer to the financial statements of **Best Buy** in Appendix A. In its presentation of accounts receivable, Best Buy does not mention uncollectible accounts, nor does it list its receivables as "net." Why do you believe that Best Buy does not include information about uncollectible accounts?

8. Refer to the balance sheet of **Circuit City** in Appendix A. Does it use the direct write-off method or allowance method to account for doubtful accounts? What is the realizable value of its accounts receivable as of February 28, 2005?

9. Refer to the financial statements of **Apple** in Appendix A. What are Apple's gross accounts receivable at September 25, 2004? What percentage of its accounts receivable does Apple believe to be uncollectible at September 25, 2004?

Red numbers denote Discussion Questions that involve decision-making.

Prepare journal entries for the following credit card sales transactions (the company uses the perpetual inventory system).

1. Sold $20,000 of merchandise, that cost $15,000, on MasterCard credit cards. The net cash receipts from sales are immediately deposited in the seller's bank account. MasterCard charges a 5% fee.

2. Sold $5,000 of merchandise, that cost $3,000, on an assortment of credit cards. Net cash receipts are received 5 days later, and a 4% fee is charged.

QUICK STUDY

QS 9-1
Credit card sales
C1

QS 9-2
Allowance method for bad debts
P1

Gomez Corp. uses the allowance method to account for uncollectibles. On October 31, it wrote off an $800 account of a customer, C. Green. On December 9, it receives a $300 payment from Green.

1. Prepare the journal entry or entries for October 31.

2. Prepare the journal entry or entries for December 9; assume no additional money is expected from Green.

QS 9-3
Percent of accounts receivable method
P1

Warner Company's year-end unadjusted trial balance shows accounts receivable of $99,000, allowance for doubtful accounts of $600 (credit), and sales of $280,000. Uncollectibles are estimated to be 1.5% of accounts receivable.

1. Prepare the December 31 year-end adjusting entry for uncollectibles.

2. What amount would have been used in the year-end adjusting entry if the allowance account had a year-end unadjusted debit balance of $300?

QS 9-4
Percent of sales method   P2

Assume the same facts as in QS 9-3, except that Warner estimates uncollectibles as 0.5% of sales. Prepare the December 31 year-end adjusting entry for uncollectibles.

QS 9-5
Note receivable
P3 P4

On August 2, 2005, Jun Co. receives a $6,000, 90-day, 12% note from customer Ryan Albany as payment on his $6,000 account. Prepare Jun's journal entries for August 2 and for the note's maturity date assuming the note is honored by Albany.

QS 9-6
Note receivable
C2 P4

Dominika Company's December 31 year-end unadjusted trial balance shows a $10,000 balance in Notes Receivable. This balance is from one 6% note dated December 1, with a period of 45 days. Prepare journal entries for December 31 and for the note's maturity date assuming it is honored.

QS 9-7
Accounts receivable turnover
A1

The following data are taken from the comparative balance sheets of Rodriguez Company. Compute and interpret its accounts receivable turnover for year 2008 (competitors average a turnover of 7.5).

	2008	2007
Accounts receivable	$153,400	$138,500
Net sales	854,200	910,600

EXERCISES

Exercise 9-1
Accounting for credit card sales
C1

Levine Company uses the perpetual inventory system and allows customers to use two credit cards in charging purchases. With the Omni Bank Card, Levine receives an immediate credit to its account when it deposits sales receipts. Omni assesses a 4% service charge for credit card sales. The second credit card that Levine accepts is the Continental Card. Levine sends its accumulated receipts to Continental on a weekly basis and is paid by Continental about a week later. Continental assesses a 2.5% charge on sales for using its card. Prepare journal entries to record the following selected credit card transactions of Levine Company:

Apr. 8   Sold merchandise for $8,400 (that had cost $6,000) and accepted the customer's Omni Bank Card. The Omni receipts are immediately deposited in Levine's bank account.

12   Sold merchandise for $5,600 (that had cost $3,500) and accepted the customer's Continental Card. Transferred $5,600 of credit card receipts to Continental, requesting payment.

20   Received Continental's check for the April 12 billing, less the service charge.

Exercise 9-2
Accounts receivable subsidiary ledger; schedule of accounts receivable
C1

Morales Company recorded the following selected transactions during November 2008.

Nov. 5	Accounts Receivable—Ski Shop	4,615	
	Sales.....................................		4,615
10	Accounts Receivable—Welcome Enterprises	1,350	
	Sales.....................................		1,350
13	Accounts Receivable—Zia Natara...............	832	
	Sales.....................................		832
21	Sales Returns and Allowances	209	
	Accounts Receivable—Zia Natara		209
30	Accounts Receivable—Ski Shop	2,713	
	Sales.....................................		2,713

1. Open a general ledger having T-accounts for Accounts Receivable, Sales, and Sales Returns and Allowances. Also open an accounts receivable subsidiary ledger having a T-account for each customer. Post these entries to both the general ledger and the accounts receivable ledger.

2. Prepare a schedule of accounts receivable (see Exhibit 9.4) and compare its total with the balance of the Accounts Receivable controlling account as of November 30.

Check Accounts Receivable ending balance, $9,301

At year-end (December 31), Chan Company estimates its bad debts as 0.5% of its annual credit sales of $975,000. Chan records its Bad Debts Expense for that estimate. On the following February 1, Chan decides that the $580 account of P. Park is uncollectible and writes it off as a bad debt. On June 5, Park unexpectedly pays the amount previously written off. Prepare the journal entries of Chan to record these transactions and events of December 31, February 1, and June 5.

Exercise 9-3
Percent of sales method; write-off

P1 P2

At each calendar year-end, Booyah Supply Co. uses the percent of accounts receivable method to estimate bad debts. On December 31, 2008, it has outstanding accounts receivable of $55,000, and it estimates that 2% will be uncollectible. Prepare the adjusting entry to record bad debts expense for year 2008 under the assumption that the Allowance for Doubtful Accounts has (*a*) a $415 credit balance before the adjustment and (*b*) a $291 debit balance before the adjustment.

Exercise 9-4
Percent of accounts receivable method

P1 P2

On June 30, Petrov Co. has $128,700 of accounts receivable. Prepare journal entries to record the following selected July transactions. Also prepare any footnotes to the July 31 financial statements that result from these transactions. (The company uses the perpetual inventory system.)

July 4   Sold $7,245 of merchandise (that had cost $5,000) to customers on credit.
      9   Sold $20,000 of accounts receivable to Main Bank. Main charges a 4% factoring fee.
     17   Received $5,859 cash from customers in payment on their accounts.
     27   Borrowed $10,000 cash from Main Bank, pledging $12,500 of accounts receivable as security for the loan.

Exercise 9-5
Selling and pledging accounts receivable

C3

Prepare journal entries to record these selected transactions for Vitalo Company.

Nov. 1   Accepted a $6,000, 180-day, 8% note dated November 1 from Kelly White in granting a time extension on her past-due account receivable.
Dec. 31   Adjusted the year-end accounts for the accrued interest earned on the White note.
Apr. 30   White honors her note when presented for payment.

Exercise 9-6
Honoring a note

P4

Prepare journal entries to record the following selected transactions of Ridge Company.

Mar. 21   Accepted a $9,500, 180-day, 8% note dated March 21 from Taurean Jackson in granting a time extension on his past-due account receivable.
Sept. 17 Jackson dishonors his note when it is presented for payment.
Dec. 31   After exhausting all legal means of collection, Ridge Company writes off Jackson account against the Allowance for Doubtful Accounts.

Exercise 9-7
Dishonoring a note

P4

Prepare journal entries for the following selected transactions of Dulcinea Company.

2007

Dec. 13   Accepted a $9,500, 60-day, 8% note dated December 13 in granting Miranda Lee a time extension on her past-due account receivable.
     31   Prepared an adjusting entry to record the accrued interest on the Lee note.

2008

Feb. 11   Received Lee's payment for principal and interest on the note dated December 13.
Mar. 3   Accepted a $5,000, 10%, 90-day note dated March 3 in granting a time extension on the past-due account receivable of Tomas Company.
     17   Accepted a $2,000, 30-day, 9% note dated March 17 in granting Hiroshi Cheng a time extension on his past-due account receivable.
Apr. 16   Cheng dishonors his note when presented for payment.
May   1   Wrote off the Cheng account against the Allowance for Doubtful Accounts.
June 1   Received the Tomas payment for principal and interest on the note dated March 3.

Exercise 9-8
Notes receivable transactions and entries

C2 P3 P4

Check Dec. 31, Cr. Interest Revenue $38

Feb. 11, Dr. Cash $9,627

June 1, Dr. Cash $5,125

Exercise 9-9

Accounts receivable turnover

A1

The following information is from the annual financial statements of Raheem Company. Compute its accounts receivable turnover for 2007 and 2008. Compare the two years results and give a possible explanation for any change (competitors average a turnover of 7).

	2008	2007	2006
Net sales	$405,000	$336,000	$388,000
Accounts receivable (year-end)	44,800	41,400	34,800

PROBLEM SET A

Problem 9-1A

Sales on account and
credit card sales

C1

Check June 17, Dr. Cash $10,003

Mayfair Co. allows select customers to make purchases on credit. Its other customers can use either of two credit cards: Zisa or Access. Zisa deducts a 3% service charge for sales on its credit card and credits the bank account of Mayfair immediately when credit card receipts are deposited. Mayfair deposits the Zisa credit card receipts each business day. When customers use Access credit cards, Mayfair accumulates the receipts for several days before submitting them to Access for payment. Access deducts a 2% service charge and usually pays within one week of being billed. Mayfair completes the following transactions in June. (The terms of all credit sales are 2/15, n/30, and all sales are recorded at the gross price.)

June 4   Sold $650 of merchandise (that had cost $400) on credit to Natara Morris.
      5   Sold $6,900 of merchandise (that had cost $4,200) to customers who used their Zisa cards.
      6   Sold $5,872 of merchandise (that had cost $3,800) to customers who used their Access cards.
      8   Sold $4,335 of merchandise (that had cost $2,900) to customers who used their Access cards.
    10   Submitted Access card receipts accumulated since June 6 to the credit card company for payment.
    13   Wrote off the account of Abigail McKee against the Allowance for Doubtful Accounts. The $429 balance in McKee's account stemmed from a credit sale in October of last year.
    17   Received the amount due from Access.
    18   Received Morris's check in full payment for the purchase of June 4.

Required

Prepare journal entries to record the preceding transactions and events. (The company uses the perpetual inventory system. Round amounts to the nearest dollar.)

Problem 9-2A

Accounts receivable transactions
and bad debts adjustments

C1 P1 P2

Check (d) Dr. Bad Debts Expense
$28,169

(h) Dr. Bad Debts Expense
$32,198

Liang Company began operations on January 1, 2007. During its first two years, the company completed a number of transactions involving sales on credit, accounts receivable collections, and bad debts. These transactions are summarized as follows.

2007

a. Sold $1,345,400 of merchandise (that had cost $975,000) on credit, terms n/30.

b. Wrote off $18,300 of uncollectible accounts receivable.

c. Received $669,200 cash in payment of accounts receivable.

d. In adjusting the accounts on December 31, the company estimated that 1.5% of accounts receivable will be uncollectible.

2008

e. Sold $1,525,600 of merchandise (that had cost $1,250,000) on credit, terms n/30.

f. Wrote off $27,800 of uncollectible accounts receivable.

g. Received $1,204,600 cash in payment of accounts receivable.

h. In adjusting the accounts on December 31, the company estimated that 1.5% of accounts receivable will be uncollectible.

Required

Prepare journal entries to record Liang's 2007 and 2008 summarized transactions and its year-end adjustments to record bad debts expense. (The company uses the perpetual inventory system. Round amounts to the nearest dollar.)

At December 31, 2008, Aaliyah Company reports the following results for its calendar-year.

| Cash sales . . . . | $1,905,000 |
| Credit sales . . . . | 5,682,000 |

Problem 9-3A
Estimating and reporting bad debts

P1 P2

In addition, its unadjusted trial balance includes the following items.

| Accounts receivable . . . . | $1,270,100 debit |
| Allowance for doubtful accounts . . . . | 16,580 debit |

Required

1. Prepare the adjusting entry for Aaliyah Co. to recognize bad debts under each of the following independent assumptions:

   a. Bad debts are estimated to be 1.5% of credit sales.

   b. Bad debts are estimated to be 1% of total sales.

   c. An aging analysis estimates that 5% of year-end accounts receivable are uncollectible.

2. Show how Accounts Receivable and the Allowance for Doubtful Accounts appear on its December 31, 2008, balance sheet given the facts in part 1a.

3. Show how Accounts Receivable and the Allowance for Doubtful Accounts appear on its December 31, 2008, balance sheet given the facts in part 1c.

Check Bad Debts Expense:
(1a) $85,230, (1c) $80,085

Jarden Company has credit sales of $3.6 million for year 2008. On December 31, 2008, the company's Allowance for Doubtful Accounts has an unadjusted credit balance of $14,500. Jarden prepares a schedule of its December 31, 2008, accounts receivable by age. On the basis of past experience, it estimates the percent of receivables in each age category that will become uncollectible. This information is summarized here.

Problem 9-4A
Aging accounts receivable and accounting for bad debts

P1 P2

File Edit View Insert Format Tools Data Accounting Window Help

	December 31, 2008 Accounts Receivable	Age of Accounts Receivable	Expected Percent Uncollectible
1 2			
3	$830,000	Not yet due	1.25%
4	254,000	1 to 30 days past due	2.00
5	86,000	31 to 60 days past due	6.50
6	38,000	61 to 90 days past due	32.75
7	12,000	Over 90 days past due	68.00
8			

Sheet1 / Sheet2 / Sheet3 /

Required

1. Estimate the required balance of the Allowance for Doubtful Accounts at December 31, 2008, using the aging of accounts receivable method.

2. Prepare the adjusting entry to record bad debts expense at December 31, 2008.

Check (2) Dr. Bad Debts Expense
$27,150

Analysis Component

3. On June 30, 2009, Jarden Company concludes that a customer's $4,750 receivable (created in 2008) is uncollectible and that the account should be written off. What effect will this action have on Jarden's 2009 net income? Explain.

The following selected transactions are from Ohlmeyer Company.

Problem 9-5A
Analyzing and journalizing notes receivable transactions

C2 C3 P3 P4

2007

Dec. 16   Accepted a $10,800, 60-day, 8% note dated this day in granting Danny Todd a time extension on his past-due account receivable.

    31   Made an adjusting entry to record the accrued interest on the Todd note.

2008

Feb. 14   Received Todd's payment of principal and interest on the note dated December 16.

Mar. 2   Accepted a $6,120, 8%, 90-day note dated this day in granting a time extension on the past-due account receivable from Midnight Co.

17   Accepted a $2,400, 30-day, 7% note dated this day in granting Ava Privet a time extension on her past-due account receivable.

Apr. 16   Privet dishonored her note when presented for payment.

June 2   Midnight Co. refuses to pay the note that was due to Ohlmeyer Co. on May 31. Prepare the journal entry to charge the dishonored note plus accrued interest to Midnight Co.'s accounts receivable.

July 17   Received payment from Midnight Co. for the maturity value of its dishonored note plus interest for 46 days beyond maturity at 8%.

Aug. 7   Accepted a $7,450, 90-day, 10% note dated this day in granting a time extension on the past-due account receivable of Mulan Co.

Sept. 3   Accepted a $2,120, 60-day, 10% note dated this day in granting Noah Carson a time extension on his past-due account receivable.

Nov. 2   Received payment of principal plus interest from Carson for the September 3 note.

Nov. 5   Received payment of principal plus interest from Mulan for the August 7 note.

Dec. 1   Wrote off the Ava Privet account against Allowance for Doubtful Accounts.

Required

1. Prepare journal entries to record these transactions and events. (Round amounts to the nearest dollar.)

Analysis Component

2. What reporting is necessary when a business pledges receivables as security for a loan and the loan is still outstanding at the end of the period? Explain the reason for this requirement and the accounting principle being satisfied.

PROBLEM SET B

Problem 9-1B
Sales on account and credit card sales

C1

Archer Co. allows select customers to make purchases on credit. Its other customers can use either of two credit cards: Commerce Bank or Aztec. Commerce Bank deducts a 3% service charge for sales on its credit card and immediately credits the bank account of Archer when credit card receipts are deposited. Archer deposits the Commerce Bank credit card receipts each business day. When customers use the Aztec card, Archer accumulates the receipts for several days and then submits them to Aztec for payment. Aztec deducts a 2% service charge and usually pays within one week of being billed. Archer completed the following transactions in August (terms of all credit sales are 2/10, n/30; and all sales are recorded at the gross price).

Aug. 4   Sold $3,700 of merchandise (that had cost $2,000) on credit to MacKenzie Carpenter.

10   Sold $5,200 of merchandise (that had cost $2,800) to customers who used their Commerce Bank credit cards.

11   Sold $1,250 of merchandise (that had cost $900) to customers who used their Aztec cards.

14   Received Carpenter's check in full payment for the purchase of August 4.

15   Sold $3,240 of merchandise (that had cost $1,800) to customers who used their Aztec cards.

18   Submitted Aztec card receipts accumulated since August 11 to the credit card company for payment.

22   Wrote off the account of Craw Co. against the Allowance for Doubtful Accounts. The $498 balance in Craw's account stemmed from a credit sale in November of last year.

25   Received the amount due from Aztec.

Required

Prepare journal entries to record the preceding transactions and events. (The company uses the perpetual inventory system. Round amounts to the nearest dollar.)

Problem 9-2B
Accounts receivable transactions and bad debts adjustments

C1 P1 P2

Sherman Co. began operations on January 1, 2007, and completed several transactions during 2007 and 2008 that involved sales on credit, accounts receivable collections, and bad debts. These transactions are summarized as follows.

2007

a. Sold $685,320 of merchandise (that had cost $500,000) on credit, terms n/30.

b. Received $482,300 cash in payment of accounts receivable.

c. Wrote off $9,350 of uncollectible accounts receivable.

d. In adjusting the accounts on December 31, the company estimated that 1% of accounts receivable will be uncollectible.

Check (*d*) Dr. Bad Debts Expense $11,287

2008

e. Sold $870,200 of merchandise (that had cost $650,000) on credit, terms n/30.

f. Received $990,800 cash in payment of accounts receivable.

g. Wrote off $11,090 of uncollectible accounts receivable.

h. In adjusting the accounts on December 31, the company estimated that 1% of accounts receivable will be uncollectible.

(*h*) Dr. Bad Debts Expense $9,773

Required

Prepare journal entries to record Sherman's 2007 and 2008 summarized transactions and its year-end adjusting entry to record bad debts expense. (The company uses the perpetual inventory system. Round amounts to the nearest dollar.)

At December 31, 2008, Ingleton Company reports the following results for the year.

Cash sales	$1,025,000
Credit sales	1,342,000

In addition, its unadjusted trial balance includes the following items.

Accounts receivable	$575,000 debit
Allowance for doubtful accounts	7,500 credit

Problem 9-3B
Estimating and reporting bad debts

P1 P2

Required

1. Prepare the adjusting entry for Ingleton Co. to recognize bad debts under each of the following independent assumptions:

   a. Bad debts are estimated to be 2.5% of credit sales.

   b. Bad debts are estimated to be 1.5% of total sales.

   c. An aging analysis estimates that 6% of year-end accounts receivable are uncollectible.

2. Show how Accounts Receivable and the Allowance for Doubtful Accounts appear on its December 31, 2008, balance sheet given the facts in part 1*a*.

3. Show how Accounts Receivable and the Allowance for Doubtful Accounts appear on its December 31, 2008, balance sheet given the facts in part 1*c*.

Check Bad debts expense:
(1*b*) $35,505, (1*c*) $27,000

Hovak Company has credit sales of $4.5 million for year 2008. At December 31, 2008, the company's Allowance for Doubtful Accounts has an unadjusted debit balance of $3,400. Hovak prepares a schedule of its December 31, 2008, accounts receivable by age. On the basis of past experience, it estimates the percent of receivables in each age category that will become uncollectible. This information is summarized here:

Problem 9-4B
Aging accounts receivable and accounting for bad debts

P1 P2

File Edit View Insert Format Tools Data Accounting Window Help		
December 31, 2008 Accounts Receivable	**Age of Accounts Receivable**	**Expected Percent Uncollectible**
$396,400	Not yet due	2.0%
277,800	1 to 30 days past due	4.0
48,000	31 to 60 days past due	8.5
6,600	61 to 90 days past due	39.0
2,800	Over 90 days past due	82.0

Required

1. Compute the required balance of the Allowance for Doubtful Accounts at December 31, 2008, using the aging of accounts receivable method.

2. Prepare the adjusting entry to record bad debts expense at December 31, 2008.

Analysis Component

3. On July 31, 2009, Hovak concludes that a customer's $3,455 receivable (created in 2008) is uncollectible and that the account should be written off. What effect will this action have on Hovak's 2009 net income? Explain.

Problem 9-5B
Analyzing and journalizing notes receivable transactions

C2 C3 P3 P4

The following selected transactions are from Springer Company.

2007

Nov. 1   Accepted a $4,800, 90-day, 8% note dated this day in granting Steve Julian a time extension on his past-due account receivable.

Dec. 31   Made an adjusting entry to record the accrued interest on the Julian note.

2008

Jan. 30   Received Julian's payment for principal and interest on the note dated November 1.

Feb. 28   Accepted a $12,600, 8%, 30-day note dated this day in granting a time extension on the past-due account receivable from King Co.

Mar. 1   Accepted a $6,200, 60-day, 12% note dated this day in granting Myron Shelley a time extension on his past-due account receivable.

    30   The King Co. dishonored its note when presented for payment.

April 30   Received payment of principal plus interest from M. Shelley for the March 1 note.

June 15   Accepted a $2,000, 60-day, 8% note dated this day in granting a time extension on the past-due account receivable of Ryder Solon.

    21   Accepted a $9,500, 90-day, 9% note dated this day in granting Joe Felton a time extension on his past-due account receivable.

Aug. 14   Received payment of principal plus interest from R. Solon for the note of June 15.

Sep. 19   Received payment of principal plus interest from J. Felton for the June 21 note.

Nov. 30   Wrote off King Co.'s account against Allowance for Doubtful Accounts.

Required

1. Prepare journal entries to record these transactions and events. (Round amounts to the nearest dollar.)

Analysis Component

2. What reporting is necessary when a business pledges receivables as security for a loan and the loan is still outstanding at the end of the period? Explain the reason for this requirement and the accounting principle being satisfied.

PROBLEM SET C

Problem Set C is available at the book's Website to further reinforce and assess your learning.

SERIAL PROBLEM

Success Systems

(This serial problem began in Chapter 1 and continues through most of the book. If previous chapter segments were not completed, the serial problem can begin at this point. It is helpful, but not necessary, that you use the Working Papers that accompany the book.)

SP 9   Adriana Lopez, owner of Success Systems, realizes that she needs to begin accounting for bad debts expense. Assume that Success Systems has total revenues of $52,195 during the first three months of 2008, and that the Accounts Receivable balance on March 31, 2008, is $24,400.

Required

1. Prepare the adjusting entry needed for Success Systems to recognize bad debts expense on March 31, 2008, under each of the following independent assumptions (assume a zero unadjusted balance in the Allowance for Doubtful Accounts at March 31).

  a. Bad debts are estimated to be 1% of total revenues.

  b. Bad debts are estimated to be 2% of accounts receivable.

2. Assume that Success Systems's Accounts Receivable balance at June 30, 2008, is $26,500 and that one account of $100 has been written off against the Allowance for Doubtful Accounts since March 31, 2008. If Lopez uses the method prescribed in Part 1*b*, what adjusting journal entry must be made to recognize bad debts expense on June 30, 2008?

3. Should Lopez consider adopting the direct write-off method of accounting for bad debts expense rather than one of the allowance methods considered in part 1? Explain.

BEYOND THE NUMBERS

BTN 9-1   Refer to **Best Buy**'s financial statements in Appendix A to answer the following.

1. What is the amount of Best Buy's accounts receivable as of February 26, 2005?

2. Compute Best Buy's accounts receivable turnover as of February 26, 2005.

3. How long does it take, *on average,* for Best Buy to collect receivables? Why is this period so short? Do you believe that customers actually pay the amounts due within this short period? Explain.

4. Best Buy's most liquid assets include (*a*) cash and cash equivalents, (*b*) short-term investments, and (*c*) receivables. Compute the percentage that these liquid assets makeup of current liabilities as of February 26, 2005. Do the same computations for February 28, 2004. Comment on the company's ability to satisfy its current liabilities at the 2005 fiscal year-end compared to the 2004 fiscal year.

5. What criteria did Best Buy use to classify items as cash equivalents?

REPORTING IN ACTION

A1

Fast Forward

6. Access Best Buy's financial statements for fiscal years after February 26, 2005, at its Website (www.BestBuy.com) or the SEC's EDGAR database (www.sec.gov). Recompute parts 2 and 4 and comment on any changes since February 26, 2005.

BTN 9-2   Key comparative figures ($ millions) for both **Best Buy** and **Circuit City** follow.

COMPARATIVE ANALYSIS

A1 P2

Figures	Best Buy			Circuit City		
	Current Year	One-Year Prior	Two-Years Prior	Current Year	One-Year Prior	Two-Years Prior
Accounts receivable, net ...	$ 375	$ 343	$ 312	$ 173	$ 171	$ 140
Net sales	27,433	24,548	20,943	10,472	9,857	10,055

Required

1. Compute the accounts receivable turnover for both Best Buy and Circuit City for each of the two most recent years using the data shown.

2. Using results from part 1, compute how many days it takes each company, *on average,* to collect receivables. Why are these periods so short? Do you believe that receivables are actually collected this quickly? Explain.

3. Which company is more efficient in collecting its accounts receivable? Explain.

Hint: Average collection period equals 365 divided by the accounts receivable turnover.

BTN 9-3   Anton Blair is the manager of a medium-size company. A few years ago, Blair persuaded the owner to base a part of his compensation on the net income the company earns each year. Each December he estimates year-end financial figures in anticipation of the bonus he will receive. If the bonus is not as high as he would like, he offers several recommendations to the accountant for year-end adjustments. One of his favorite recommendations is for the controller to reduce the estimate of doubtful accounts.

ETHICS CHALLENGE

P1 P2

Required

1. What effect does lowering the estimate for doubtful accounts have on the income statement and balance sheet?

2. Do you believe Blair's recommendation to adjust the allowance for doubtful accounts is within his right as manager, or do you believe this action is an ethics violation? Justify your response.

3. What type of internal control(s) might be useful for this company in overseeing the manager's recommendations for accounting changes?

COMMUNICATING IN PRACTICE

P1 P2

BTN 9-4   As the accountant for Pure-Air Distributing, you attend a sales managers' meeting devoted to a discussion of credit policies. At the meeting, you report that bad debts expense is estimated to be $59,000 and accounts receivable at year-end amount to $1,750,000 less a $43,000 allowance for doubtful accounts. Sid Omar, a sales manager, expresses confusion over why bad debts expense and the allowance for doubtful accounts are different amounts. Write a one-page memorandum to him explaining why a difference in bad debts expense and the allowance for doubtful accounts is not unusual. The company estimates bad debts expense as 2% of sales.

TAKING IT TO THE NET

C1

BTN 9-5   Access eBay's, February 28, 2005, filing of its 10-K report for the year ended December 31, 2004, at www.sec.gov.

Required

1. What is the amount of eBay's net accounts receivable at December 31, 2004, and at December 31, 2003?

2. Note 7 to its financial statements lists eBay's gross accounts receivable, allowance for doubtful accounts, allowance for authorized credits, and net accounts receivable. For the two years ended December 31, 2004 and 2003, compute its allowance for doubtful accounts as a percent of gross accounts receivable.

3. Do you believe that these percentages are reasonable based on what you know about eBay? Explain.

TEAMWORK IN ACTION

P2

BTN 9-6   Each member of a team is to participate in estimating uncollectibles using the aging schedule and percents shown in Problem 9-4A. The division of labor is up to the team. Your goal is to accurately complete this task as soon as possible. After estimating uncollectibles, check your estimate with the instructor. If the estimate is correct, the team then should prepare the adjusting entry and the presentation of accounts receivable (net) for the December 31, 2008, balance sheet.

BusinessWeek ACTIVITY

C1 P1

BTN 9-7   Read the article "How to Beat the Deadbeats" in the February 24, 2005, issue of *BusinessWeek*. (The book's Website provides a free link.)

Required

1. What does Carol Frischer say is the reason that small businesses have problems collecting on their receivables?

2. What does Frischer recommend businesses do to collect their receivables?

ENTREPRENEURIAL DECISION

C1

BTN 9-8   Linda Torres-Winters of Linditas' is introduced in the chapter's opening feature. Torres-Winters currently sells her salsa through stores in 10 states. Assume she is considering two proposals.
Plan A. Torres-Winters would begin selling her product online directly to customers through her Website. Online customers would use their credit cards. Linditas' currently has the capability of selling through its Website with no additional investment in hardware or software. Credit sales are expected to increase by $250,000 per year. Costs associated with this plan are: cost of these sales will be $135,500, credit card fees will be 4.75% of sales, and additional recordkeeping and shipping costs will be 6% of sales. These online sales will reduce the sales to stores by $35,000 because some customers will now purchase items online directly from Linditas'. Sales to stores have a 25% gross margin percentage.
Plan B. Torres-Winters would expand her market to more stores. She would make additional credit sales of $500,000 to those stores. Costs associated with those sales are: cost of sales will be $375,000, additional recordkeeping and shipping will be 4% of sales, and uncollectible accounts will be 6.2% of sales.

Required

1. Compute the additional annual net income or loss expected under (a) Plan A and (b) Plan B.

2. Should Torres-Winters pursue either plan? Discuss both the financial and nonfinancial factors relevant to this decision.

 Check   (1b) Net income, $74,000

BTN 9-9   Many commercials include comments similar to the following: "Bring your **VISA**" or "We do not accept **American Express**." Conduct your own research by contacting at least five companies via interviews, phone calls, or the Internet to determine the reason(s) companies discriminate in their use of credit cards. (The instructor may assign this as a team activity.)

HITTING THE ROAD

C1

BTN 9-10   Dixons (<u>Dixons-Group.com</u>) is a retailer of consumer electronics and competes globally with companies such as **Best Buy** and **Circuit City**. Review the May 1, 2004, balance sheet of Dixons to answer the following.

GLOBAL DECISION

C1 P1

Required

1. Does "Accounts Receivable" appear on Dixons' balance sheet? Does its absence imply that Dixons does not have any accounts receivable? What do you believe Dixons titles its receivables? (*Hint:* Dixons titles its accounts payable "Creditors—falling due within one year.") Does this title make sense based on what you know about accounting transactions? Explain.

2. Which presentation of receivables do you prefer—Dixons' or the Best Buy and Circuit City presentations in Appendix A? Explain.

ANSWERS TO MULTIPLE CHOICE QUIZ

1. d; Desired balance in Allowance for Doubtful Accounts = $ 5,026 cr.
($125,650 × 0.04)
Current balance in Allowance for Doubtful Accounts =   (328) cr.
Bad Debts Expense to be recorded   = $ 4,698

2. a; Desired balance in Allowance for Doubtful Accounts = $29,358 cr.
($489,300 × 0.06)
Current balance in Allowance for Doubtful Accounts =   554 dr.
Bad Debts Expense to be recorded   = $29,912

3. a; $7,500 × 0.05 × 90/360 = $93.75

4. c; Principle amount $9,000
Interest accrued . . . .   120 ($9,000 × 0.08 × 60/360)
Maturity value $9,120

5. d; $489,600/$40,800 = 12

10

Plant Assets, Natural Resources, and Intangibles

A Look Back

Chapters 8 and 9 focused on short-term assets: cash, cash equivalents, and receivables. We explained why they are known as liquid assets and described how companies account and report for them.

A Look at This Chapter

This chapter introduces us to long-term assets. We explain how to account for a long-term asset's cost, the allocation of an asset's cost to periods benefiting from it, the recording of additional costs after an asset is purchased, and the disposal of an asset.

A Look Ahead

Chapter 11 focuses on current liabilities. We explain how they are computed, recorded, and reported in financial statements. We also explain the accounting for company payroll and contingencies.

Learning Objectives

CAP

Conceptual

C1 Describe plant assets and issues in accounting for them. (p. 386)

C2 Explain depreciation and the factors affecting its computation. (p. 389)

C3 Explain depreciation for partial years and changes in estimates. (p. 394)

Analytical

A1 Compare and analyze alternative depreciation methods. (p. 393)

A2 Compute total asset turnover and apply it to analyze a company's use of assets. (p. 404)

Procedural

P1 Apply the cost principle to compute the cost of plant assets. (p. 387)

P2 Compute and record depreciation using the straight-line, units-of-production, and declining-balance methods. (p. 390)

P3 Distinguish between revenue and capital expenditures, and account for them. (p. 396)

P4 Account for asset disposal through discarding or selling an asset. (p. 398)

P5 Account for natural resource assets and their depletion. (p. 400)

P6 Account for intangible assets. (p. 401)

P7 Appendix 10A—Account for asset exchanges. (p. 407)

"We always look at what our competition is doing"
—Eileen Spitalny
(David Kravetz on right)

Recipe for a Real-Life Fairy Tale

CHANDLER, AZ—Once upon a time in a land of great sunshine, an inspired man and woman conjured up an enchanting brownie and everyone lived happily ever after. This real-life story features Eileen Spitalny and David Kravetz, founders of Fairytale Brownies (**FairytaleBrownies.com**).

Lifelong friends Eileen and David found themselves one evening in a friend's moonlit catering kitchen. There they concocted a most amazing brownie based on an ancient family recipe belonging to David's mother. The two made a promise to start a business together, and the brownie made history.

Fairytale Brownies' 40 employees now churn out 25,000 brownies each day, generating nearly $8 million in annual sales. A major challenge for Eileen and David is maintaining the right kind and amount of plant assets to meet demand and be profitable. Key to Fairytale's success is monitoring and controlling such plant asset costs, which range from ovens, packaging equipment, baking accessories, and delivery vans to building facilities and land costs.

Eileen and David feel that packaging equipment is especially crucial. "We believe that our packaging is 50 percent of the sale," says David. This view led Fairytale Brownies to recently upgrade its packaging by investing in new wrapping equipment and film and printing technology. "We know the brownies are great but the packaging really gives the product [its] premium look," notes David. And packaging helps drive sales, most of which are mail order and about 30 percent of those are online.

Eileen and David believe in communicating their accounting reports and plant asset decisions to all employees. "It's an open book," says David. "We share all the numbers and keep our doors open to our employees." Employees come to realize that sales must cover plant asset costs and provide a return adequate to pay expenses and wages and still meet income goals. It also helps to have the greatest brownies in all of Fairyland. [Sources: *Fairytale Brownies Website,* January 2006; *Business Journal,* February 2005; *bizAZ,* September 2004; *Arizona Business Gazette,* October 2004; *Entrepreneur,* November 2001]

This chapter focuses on long-term assets used to operate a company. These assets can be grouped into plant assets, natural resource assets, and intangible assets. Plant assets are a major investment for most companies. They make up a large part of assets on most balance sheets, and they yield depreciation, often one of the largest expenses on income statements. The acquisition or building of a plant asset is often referred to as a *capital expenditure*. Capital expenditures are important events because they impact both the short- and long-term success of a company. Natural resource assets and intangible assets have similar impacts. This chapter describes the purchase and use of these assets. We also explain what distinguishes these assets from other types of assets, how to determine their cost, how to allocate their costs to periods benefiting from their use, and how to dispose of them.

Plant Assets, Natural Resources, and Intangibles

Plant Assets
- Cost determination
- Depreciation
- Additional expenditures
- Disposals

Natural Resources
- Cost determination
- Depletion
- Plant assets used in extracting resources

Intangible Assets
- Cost determination
- Amortization
- Types of intangibles

Section 1—Plant Assets

Plant assets are tangible assets used in a company's operations that have a useful life of more than one accounting period. Plant assets are also called *plant and equipment; property, plant, and equipment;* or *fixed assets.* For many companies, plant assets make up the single largest class of assets they own. Exhibit 10.1 shows plant assets as a percent of total assets for several companies. Not only do they make up a large percent of these companies' assets but also their dollar values are large. **McDonald's** plant assets, for instance, are reported at more than $20 billion, and **Wal-Mart** reports plant assets of more than $65 billion.

Exhibit 10.1

Plant Assets of Selected Companies

eBay | 9% | $710 mil.
Wal-Mart | $65,408 mil. | 54%
Anheuser-Busch | $8,847 mil. | 55%
McDonald's | $20,703 mil. | 74%

0   20   40   60   80
As a percent of total assets

C1 Describe plant assets and issues in accounting for them.

Plant assets are set apart from other assets by two important features. First, *plant assets are used in operations.* This makes them different from, for instance, inventory that is held for sale and not used in operations. The distinctive feature here is use, not type of asset. A company that purchases a computer to resell it, reports it on the balance sheet as inventory. If the same company purchases this computer to use in operations, however, it is a plant asset. Another example is land held for future expansion, which is reported as a long-term investment. However, if this land holds a factory used in operations, the land is part of plant assets. Another example is equipment held for use in the event of a breakdown or for peak periods of production, which is reported in plant assets. If this same equipment is removed from use and held for sale, however, it is not reported in plant assets.

The second important feature is that *plant assets have useful lives extending over more than one accounting period.* This makes plant assets different from current assets such as supplies that are normally consumed in a short time period after they are placed in use.

Point: Google's plant assets of $379 million make up 11% of its total assets.

The accounting for plant assets reflects these two features. Since plant assets are used in operations, we try to match their costs against the revenues they generate. Also, since their useful lives extend over more than one period, our matching of costs and revenues must extend over several periods. Specifically, we value plant assets (balance sheet effect) and then allocate their costs to periods benefiting from their use (income statement effect).

Exhibit 10.2 shows four main issues in accounting for plant assets: (1) computing the costs of plant assets, (2) allocating the costs of plant assets (less any salvage amounts) against revenues for the periods they benefit, (3) accounting for expenditures such as repairs and improvements to plant assets, and (4) recording the disposal of plant assets. The following sections discuss these issues.

Point: It can help to view plant assets as prepaid expenses that benefit several future accounting periods.

Topic Tackler

PLUS

10-1

Exhibit 10.2

Issues in Accounting for Plant Assets

Decline in asset value over its useful life

Acquisition	**Use**	**Disposal**
1. Compute cost	2. Allocate cost to periods benefited	4. Record disposal
	3. Account for subsequent expenditures	

Cost Determination

Plant assets are recorded at cost when acquired. This is consistent with the *cost principle.* **Cost** includes all normal and reasonable expenditures necessary to get the asset in place and ready for its intended use. The cost of a factory machine, for instance, includes its invoice cost less any cash discount for early payment, plus any necessary freight, unpacking, assembling, installing, and testing costs. Examples are the costs of building a base or foundation for a machine, providing electrical hook-ups, and testing the asset before using it in operations.

To be recorded as part of the cost of a plant asset, an expenditure must be normal, reasonable, and necessary in preparing it for its intended use. If an asset is damaged during unpacking, the repairs are not added to its cost. Instead, they are charged to an expense account. Nor is a paid traffic fine for moving heavy machinery on city streets without a proper permit part of the machinery's cost; but payment for a proper permit is included in the cost of machinery. Charges are sometimes incurred to modify or customize a new plant asset. These charges are added to the asset's cost. We explain in this section how to determine the cost of plant assets for each of its four major classes.

Land

When land is purchased for a building site, its cost includes the total amount paid for the land, including any real estate commissions, title insurance fees, legal fees, and any accrued property taxes paid by the purchaser. Payments for surveying, clearing, grading, and draining also are in-

P1 Apply the cost principle to compute the cost of plant assets.

cluded in the cost of land. Other costs include government assessments, whether incurred at the time of purchase or later, for items such as public roadways, sewers, and sidewalks. These assessments are included because they permanently add to the land's value. Land purchased as a building site sometimes includes structures that must be removed. In such cases, the total purchase price is charged to the Land account as is the cost of removing the structures, less any amounts recovered through sale of salvaged materials. To illustrate, assume that **Starbucks**

Exhibit 10.3

Computing Cost of Land

Cash price of land	$ 167,000
Net cost of garage removal	13,000
Closing costs	10,000
Cost of land	$190,000

paid $167,000 cash to acquire land for a retail store. This land had an old service garage that was removed at a net cost of $13,000 ($15,000 in costs less $2,000 proceeds from salvaged materials). Additional closing costs total $10,000, consisting of brokerage fees ($8,000), legal fees ($1,500), and title costs ($500). The cost of this land to Starbucks is $190,000 and is computed as shown in Exhibit 10.3.

Land Improvements

Land has an unlimited life and is not usually used up over time. **Land improvements** such as parking lot surfaces, driveways, fences, shrubs, and lighting systems, however, have limited useful lives and are used up. While the costs of these improvements increase the usefulness of the land, they are charged to a separate Land Improvement account so that their costs can be allocated to the periods they benefit.

Buildings

A Building account is charged for the costs of purchasing or constructing a building that is used in operations. When purchased, a building's costs usually include its purchase price, brokerage

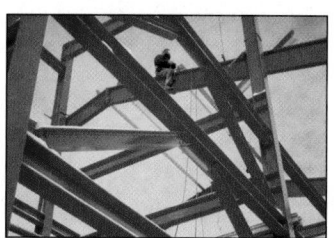

fees, taxes, title fees, and attorney fees. Its costs also include all expenditures to ready it for its intended use, including any necessary repairs or renovations such as wiring, lighting, flooring, and wall coverings. When a company constructs a building or any plant asset for its own use, its costs include materials and labor plus a reasonable amount of indirect overhead cost. Overhead includes the costs of items such as heat, lighting, power, and depreciation on machinery used to construct the asset. Costs of construction also include design fees, building permits, and insurance during construction. However, costs such as insurance to cover the asset *after* it is placed in use are operating expenses.

Machinery and Equipment

The costs of machinery and equipment consist of all costs normal and necessary to purchase them and prepare them for their intended use. These include the purchase price, taxes, transportation charges, insurance while in transit, and the installing, assembling, and testing of the machinery and equipment.

Lump-Sum Purchase

Example: If appraised values in Exhibit 10.4 are land, $24,000; land improvements, $12,000; and building, $84,000, what cost is assigned to the building? *Answer:*

(1) $24,000 + $12,000 + $84,000 = $120,000 (total appraisal)

(2) $84,000/$120,000 = 70% (building's percent of total)

(3) 70% × $90,000 = $63,000 (building's apportioned cost)

Plant assets sometimes are purchased as a group in a single transaction for a lump-sum price. This transaction is called a *lump-sum purchase,* or *group, bulk,* or *basket purchase.* When this occurs, we allocate the cost of the purchase among the different types of assets acquired based on their *relative market values,* which can be estimated by appraisal or by using the tax-assessed valuations of the assets. To illustrate, assume Oakley paid $90,000 cash to acquire a group of items consisting of land appraised at $30,000, land improvements appraised at $10,000, and a building appraised at $60,000. The $90,000 cost is allocated on the basis of these appraised values as shown in Exhibit 10.4.

Exhibit 10.4

Computing Costs in a Lump-Sum Purchase

	Appraised Value	Percent of Total	Apportioned Cost
Land	$ 30,000	30% ($30,000/$100,000)	$27,000 ($90,000 × 30%)
Land improvements	10,000	10 ($10,000/$100,000)	9,000 ($90,000 × 10%)
Building	60,000	60 ($60,000/$100,000)	54,000 ($90,000 × 60%)
Totals	$100,000	100%	$ 90,000

Quick Check

Answers—p. 410

1. Identify the asset class for each of the following: (*a*) supplies, (*b*) office equipment, (*c*) inventory, (*d*) land for future expansion, and (*e*) trucks used in operations.

2. Identify the account charged for each of the following: (*a*) purchase price of a vacant lot to be used in operations and (*b*) cost of paving that same vacant lot.

3. Compute the amount recorded as the cost of a new machine given the following payments related to its purchase: gross purchase price, $700,000; sales tax, $49,000; purchase discount taken, $21,000; freight cost—terms FOB shipping point, $3,500; normal assembly costs, $3,000; cost of necessary machine platform, $2,500; cost of parts used in maintaining machine, $4,200.

Depreciation

Depreciation is the process of allocating the cost of a plant asset to expense in the accounting periods benefiting from its use. Depreciation does not measure the decline in the asset's market value each period, nor does it measure the asset's physical deterioration. Since depreciation reflects the cost of using a plant asset, depreciation charges are only recorded when the asset is actually in service. This section describes the factors we must consider in computing depreciation, the depreciation methods used, revisions in depreciation, and depreciation for partial periods.

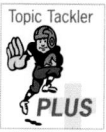

10-2

Factors in Computing Depreciation

Factors that determine depreciation are (1) cost, (2) salvage value, and (3) useful life.

C2 Explain depreciation and the factors affecting its computation.

Cost   The **cost** of a plant asset consists of all necessary and reasonable expenditures to acquire it and to prepare it for its intended use.

Salvage Value   The total amount of depreciation to be charged off over an asset's benefit period equals the asset's cost minus its salvage value. **Salvage value,** also called *residual value* or *scrap value,* is an estimate of the asset's value at the end of its benefit period. This is the amount the owner expects to receive from disposing the asset at the end of its benefit period. If the asset is expected to be traded in on a new asset, its salvage value is the expected trade-in value.

Point: If we expect additional costs in preparing a plant asset for disposal, the salvage value equals the expected amount from disposal less any disposal costs.

Useful Life   The **useful life** of a plant asset is the length of time it is productively used in a company's operations. Useful life, also called *service life,* might not be as long as the asset's total productive life. For example, the productive life of a computer can be eight years or more. Some companies, however, trade in old computers for new ones every two years. In this case, these computers have a two-year useful life, meaning the cost of these computers (less their expected trade-in values) is charged to depreciation expense over a two-year period.

Point: Useful life and salvage value are estimates. Estimates require judgment based on consideration of all available information.

Several variables often make the useful life of a plant asset difficult to predict. A major variable is the wear and tear from use in operations. Two other variables, inadequacy and obsolescence, also demand consideration. **Inadequacy** refers to the insufficient capacity of a company's plant assets to meet its growing productive demands. **Obsolescence** refers to a plant asset that is no longer useful in producing goods or services with a competitive advantage because of new inventions and improvements. Both inadequacy and obsolescence are difficult to predict because of demand changes, new inventions, and

Decision Insight

Life Line   Life expectancy of plant assets is often in the eye of the beholder. For instance, **Hershey Foods** and **Tootsie Roll** are competitors, yet their equipment's life expectancies are different. Hershey depreciates equipment over 3 to 15 years, but Tootsie Roll depreciates them over 5 to 20 years. Such differences markedly impact financial statements.

Global: While U.S. accounting must consider inadequacy and obsolescence in estimating useful life, the accounting in many other countries does not.

improvements. A company usually disposes of an inadequate or obsolete asset before it wears out.

A company is often able to better predict a new asset's useful life when it has past experience with a similar asset. When it has no such experience, a company relies on the experience of others or on engineering studies and judgment. In note 1 of its annual report, **Hershey Foods**, a snacks manufacturer, reports the following useful lives:

Buildings	25–40 years
Machinery and Equipment	3–15 years

Depreciation Methods

Depreciation methods are used to allocate a plant asset's cost over the accounting periods in its useful life. The most frequently used method of depreciation is the straight-line method. Another common depreciation method is the units-of-production method. We explain both of these methods in this section. This section also describes accelerated depreciation methods, with a focus on the declining-balance method.

The computations in this section use information about a machine that inspects athletic shoes before packaging. Manufacturers such as **Converse**, **Reebok**, **Adidas**, and **Fila** use this machine. Data for this machine are in Exhibit 10.5.

Exhibit 10.5

Data for Athletic Shoe-Inspecting Machine

Cost	$10,000
Salvage value	1,000
Depreciable cost	$ 9,000
Useful life	
Accounting periods	5 years
Units inspected	36,000 shoes

P2 Compute and record depreciation using the straight-line, units-of-production, and declining-balance methods.

Straight-Line Method **Straight-line depreciation** charges the same amount of expense to each period of the asset's useful life. A two-step process is used. We first compute the *depreciable cost* of the asset; this amount is also called the *cost to be depreciated*. It is computed by subtracting the asset's salvage value from its total cost. Second, depreciable cost is divided by the number of accounting periods in the asset's useful life. The formula for straight-line depreciation, along with its computation for the inspection machine described above, is shown in Exhibit 10.6.

Exhibit 10.6

Straight-Line Depreciation Formula and Example

$$\frac{\text{Cost} - \text{Salvage value}}{\text{Useful life in periods}} = \frac{\$10,000 - \$1,000}{5 \text{ years}} = \$1,800 \text{ per year}$$

If this machine is purchased on December 31, 2006, and used throughout its predicted useful life of five years, the straight-line method allocates an equal amount of depreciation to each of the years 2007 through 2011. We make the following adjusting entry at the end of each of the five years to record straight-line depreciation of this machine:

Assets = Liabilities + Equity
−1,800   −1,800

Dec. 31	Depreciation Expense	1,800	
	Accumulated Depreciation—Machinery		1,800
	To record annual depreciation.		

Example: If salvage value of the machine is estimated to be $2,500, what is the annual depreciation expense? *Answer:* ($10,000 − $2,500)/5 years = $1,500

The $1,800 Depreciation Expense is reported on the income statement among operating expenses. The $1,800 Accumulated Depreciation is a contra asset account to the Machinery account in the balance sheet. The graph on the left in Exhibit 10.7 shows the $1,800 per year expenses reported in each of the five years. The graph on the right shows the amounts reported on each of the six December 31 balance sheets while the company owns the asset.

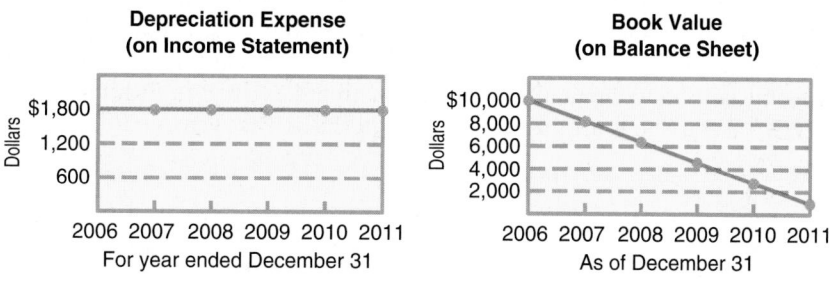

Exhibit 10.7

Financial Statement Effects of Straight-Line Depreciation

The net balance sheet amount is the asset's **book value** and is computed as the asset's total cost less its accumulated depreciation. For example, at the end of year 2 (December 31, 2008), its book value is $6,400 and is reported in the balance sheet as follows:

Machinery	$10,000	
Less accumulated depreciation	3,600	$6,400

The book value of this machine declines by $1,800 each year due to depreciation. From the graphs in Exhibit 10.7 we can see why this method is called straight line.

We also can compute the *straight-line depreciation rate,* defined as 100% divided by the number of periods in the asset's useful life. For the inspection machine, this rate is 20% (100% ÷ 5 years). We use this rate, along with other information, to compute the machine's *straight-line depreciation schedule* shown in Exhibit 10.8. Note three points in Exhibit 10.8. First, depreciation expense is the same each period. Second, accumulated depreciation is the sum of current and prior periods' depreciation expense. Third, book value declines each period until it equals salvage value at the end of the machine's useful life.

Point: Depreciation requires estimates for salvage value and useful life. Decision ethics are relevant when managers might be tempted to choose estimates to achieve desired results on financial statements.

	Depreciation for the Period			End of Period	
Annual Period	Depreciable Cost*	Depreciation Rate	Depreciation Expense	Accumulated Depreciation	Book Value†
2006	—	—	—	—	$10,000
2007	$9,000	20%	$1,800	$1,800	8,200
2008	9,000	20	1,800	3,600	6,400
2009	9,000	20	1,800	5,400	4,600
2010	9,000	20	1,800	7,200	2,800
2011	9,000	20	1,800	9,000	1,000

Exhibit 10.8

Straight-Line Depreciation Schedule

* $10,000 − $1,000.   † Book value is total cost minus accumulated depreciation.

Units-of-Production Method   The straight-line method charges an equal share of an asset's cost to each period. If plant assets are used up in about equal amounts each accounting period, this method produces a reasonable matching of expenses with revenues. However, the use of some plant assets varies greatly from one period to the next. A builder, for instance, might use a piece of construction equipment for a month and then not use it again for several months. When equipment use varies from period to period, the units-of-production depreciation method can better match expenses with revenues. **Units-of-production depreciation** charges a varying amount to expense for each period of an asset's useful life depending on its usage.

A two-step process is used to compute units-of-production depreciation. We first compute *depreciation per unit* by subtracting the asset's salvage value from its total cost and then dividing by the total number of units expected to be produced during its useful life. Units of production can be expressed in product or other units such as hours used or miles driven. The second step is to compute depreciation expense for the period by multiplying the units produced in the period by the depreciation per unit. The formula for units-of-production depreciation, along with its computation for the machine described in Exhibit 10.5, is shown in Exhibit 10.9. (7,000 shoes are inspected and sold in its first year.)

Exhibit 10.9

Units-of-Production Depreciation Formula and Example

Step 1

$$\text{Depreciation per unit} = \frac{\text{Cost} - \text{Salvage value}}{\text{Total units of production}} = \frac{\$10,000 - \$1,000}{36,000 \text{ shoes}} = \$0.25 \text{ per shoe}$$

Step 2

$$\text{Depreciation expense} = \text{Depreciation per unit} \times \text{Units produced in period}$$
$$\$0.25 \text{ per shoe} \times 7,000 \text{ shoes} = \$1,750$$

Using data on the number of shoes inspected by the machine, we can compute the *units-of-production depreciation schedule* shown in Exhibit 10.10. For example, depreciation for the first year is $1,750 (7,000 shoes at $0.25 per shoe). Depreciation for the second year is $2,000 (8,000 shoes at $0.25 per shoe). Other years are similarly computed. Exhibit 10.10 shows that (1) depreciation expense depends on unit output, (2) accumulated depreciation is the sum of current and prior periods' depreciation expense, and (3) book value declines each period until it equals salvage value at the end of the asset's useful life. **Boise Cascade** is one of many companies using the units-of-production depreciation method. It reports that most of its "paper and wood products manufacturing facilities determine depreciation by a units-of-production method."

Example: Refer to Exhibit 10.10. If the number of shoes inspected in 2011 is 5,500, what is depreciation expense for that year?
Answer: $1,250 (never depreciate below salvage value)

Exhibit 10.10

Units-of-Production Depreciation Schedule

| Annual Period | Depreciation for the Period | | | End of Period | |
	Number of Units	Depreciation per Unit	Depreciation Expense	Accumulated Depreciation	Book Value
2006	—	—	—	—	$10,000
2007	7,000	$0.25	$1,750	$1,750	8,250
2008	8,000	0.25	2,000	3,750	6,250
2009	9,000	0.25	2,250	6,000	4,000
2010	7,000	0.25	1,750	7,750	2,250
2011	5,000	0.25	1,250	9,000	1,000

Declining-Balance Method An **accelerated depreciation method** yields larger depreciation expenses in the early years of an asset's life and less depreciation in later years. Of several accelerated methods, the most common is the **declining-balance method** of depreciation, which uses a depreciation rate that is a multiple of the straight-line rate and applies it to the asset's beginning-of-period book value. The amount of depreciation declines each period because book value declines each period.

A common depreciation rate for the declining-balance method is double the straight-line rate. This is called the *double-declining-balance* (*DDB*) method. This method is applied in three steps: (1) compute the asset's straight-line depreciation rate, (2) double the straight-line rate, and (3) compute depreciation expense by multiplying this rate by the asset's beginning-of-period book value. To illustrate, let's return to the machine in Exhibit 10.5 and apply the

Point: In the DDB method, *double* refers to the rate and *declining balance* refers to book value. The rate is applied to beginning book value each period.

double-declining-balance method to compute depreciation expense. Exhibit 10.11 shows the first-year depreciation computation for the machine. The three-step process is to (1) divide 100% by five years to determine the straight-line rate of 20% per year, (2) double this 20% rate to get the declining-balance rate of 40% per year, and (3) compute depreciation expense as 40% multiplied by the beginning-of-period book value.

Exhibit 10.11

Double-Declining-Balance Depreciation Formula

Step 1

Straight-line rate = 100% ÷ Useful life = 100% ÷ 5 years = 20%

Step 2

Double-declining-balance rate = 2 × Straight-line rate = 2 × 20% = 40%

Step 3

Depreciation expense = Double-declining-balance rate × Beginning-period book value

40% × \$10,000 = \$4,000 (for 2007)

The *double-declining-balance depreciation schedule* is shown in Exhibit 10.12. The schedule follows the formula except for year 2011, when depreciation expense is \$296. This \$296 is not equal to 40% × \$1,296, or \$518.40. If we had used the \$518.40 for depreciation expense in 2011, ending book value would equal \$777.60, which is less than the \$1,000 salvage value. Instead, the \$296 is computed by subtracting the \$1,000 salvage value from the \$1,296 book value at the beginning of the fifth year (the year when DDB depreciation cuts into salvage value).

Example: What is DDB depreciation expense in year 2010 if the salvage value is \$2,000? *Answer:* \$2,160 − \$2,000 = \$160

Exhibit 10.12

Double-Declining-Balance Depreciation Schedule

Annual Period	Depreciation for the Period			End of Period	
	Beginning of Period Book Value	Depreciation Rate	Depreciation Expense	Accumulated Depreciation	Book Value
2006	—	—	—	—	\$10,000
2007	\$10,000	40%	\$4,000	\$4,000	6,000
2008	6,000	40	2,400	6,400	3,600
2009	3,600	40	1,440	7,840	2,160
2010	2,160	40	864	8,704	1,296
2011	1,296	40	296*	9,000	**1,000**

* Year 2011 depreciation is \$1,296 − \$1,000 = \$296 (never depreciate book value below salvage value).

Comparing Depreciation Methods Exhibit 10.13 shows depreciation expense for each year of the machine's useful life under each of the three depreciation methods. While the amount of depreciation expense per period differs for different methods, total depreciation expense is the same over the machine's useful life.

A1 Compare and analyze alternative depreciation methods.

Exhibit 10.13

Depreciation Expense for the Different Methods

Period	Straight-Line	Units-of-Production	Double-Declining-Balance
2007	\$1,800	\$1,750	\$4,000
2008	1,800	2,000	2,400
2009	1,800	2,250	1,440
2010	1,800	1,750	864
2011	1,800	1,250	296
Totals	**\$9,000**	**\$9,000**	**\$9,000**

Each method starts with a total cost of \$10,000 and ends with a salvage value of \$1,000. The difference is the pattern in depreciation expense over the useful life. The book value of the

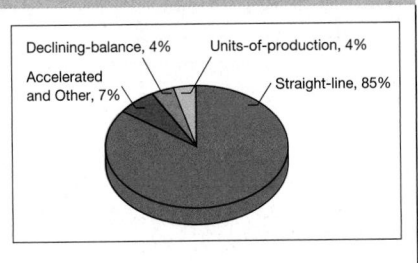

asset when using straight-line is always greater than the book value from using double-declining-balance, except at the beginning and end of the asset's useful life, when it is the same. Also, the straight-line method yields a steady pattern of depreciation expense while the units-of-production depreciation depends on the number of units produced. Each of these methods is acceptable because it allocates cost in a systematic and rational manner.

Depreciation for Tax Reporting   The records a company keeps for financial accounting purposes are usually separate from the records it keeps for tax accounting purposes. This is so because financial accounting aims to report useful information on financial performance and position, whereas tax accounting reflects government objectives in raising revenues. Differences between these two accounting systems are normal and expected. Depreciation is a common example of how the records differ. For example, many companies use accelerated depreciation in computing taxable income. Reporting higher depreciation expense in the early years of an asset's life reduces the company's taxable income in those years and increases it in later years, when the depreciation expense is lower. The company's goal here is to *postpone* its tax payments. This means the company can use these resources now to earn additional income before payment is due.

Point: Understanding depreciation for financial accounting will help in learning MACRS for tax accounting. Rules for MACRS are available from www.IRS.gov.

Global: A few countries require the depreciation method chosen for financial reporting to match the method chosen for tax reporting.

The U.S. federal income tax law has rules for depreciating assets. These rules include the **Modified Accelerated Cost Recovery System (MACRS),** which allows straight-line depreciation for some assets, but it requires accelerated depreciation for most kinds of assets. MACRS separates depreciable assets into different classes and defines the depreciable life and rate for each class. MACRS is not acceptable for financial reporting because it often allocates costs over an arbitrary period that is less than the asset's useful life. Details of MACRS are covered in tax accounting courses.

Partial-Year Depreciation

C3 Explain depreciation for partial years and changes in estimates.

Plant assets are purchased and disposed of at various times. When an asset is purchased (or disposed of) at a time other than the beginning or end of an accounting period, depreciation is recorded for part of a year. This is done so that the year of purchase or the year of disposal is charged with its share of the asset's depreciation.

To illustrate, assume that the machine in Exhibit 10.5 is purchased and placed in service on October 8, 2006, and the annual accounting period ends on December 31. Since this machine is purchased and used for nearly three months in 2006, the calendar-year income statement should report depreciation expense on the machine for that part of the year. Normally, depreciation assumes that the asset is purchased on the first day of the month nearest the actual date of purchase. In this case, since the purchase occurred on October 8, we assume an October 1 purchase date. This means that three months' depreciation is recorded in 2006. Using straight-line depreciation, we compute three months' depreciation of $450 as follows.

$$\frac{\$10,000 - \$1,000}{5 \text{ years}} \times \frac{3}{12} = \$450$$

Example: If the machine's salvage value is zero and purchase occurs on Oct. 8, 2006, how much depreciation is recorded at Dec. 31, 2006?
Answer: $10,000/5 × 3/12 = $500

A similar computation is necessary when an asset disposal occurs during a period. To illustrate, assume that the machine is sold on June 24, 2011. Depreciation is recorded for the period January 1 through June 24 when it is disposed of. This partial year's depreciation, computed to the nearest whole month, is

$$\frac{\$10,000 - \$1,000}{5 \text{ years}} \times \frac{6}{12} = \$900$$

Change in Estimates for Depreciation

Depreciation is based on estimates of salvage value and useful life. During the useful life of an asset, new information may indicate that these estimates are inaccurate. If our estimate of an asset's useful life and/or salvage value changes, what should we do? The answer is to use the new estimate to compute depreciation for current and future periods. This means that we revise the depreciation expense computation by spreading the cost yet to be depreciated over the remaining useful life. This approach is used for all depreciation methods.

Point: Remaining depreciable cost equals book value less revised salvage value at the point of revision.

Let's return to the machine described in Exhibit 10.8 using straight-line depreciation. At the beginning of this asset's third year, its book value is $6,400, computed as $10,000 minus $3,600. Assume that at the beginning of its third year, the estimated number of years remaining in its useful life changes from three to four years *and* its estimate of salvage value changes from $1,000 to $400. Straight-line depreciation for each of the four remaining years is computed as shown in Exhibit 10.14.

Point: Income is overstated (and depreciation understated) when useful life is too high; a useful life that is too low yields opposite results.

$$\frac{\textbf{Book value} - \textbf{Revised salvage value}}{\textbf{Revised remaining useful life}} = \frac{\$6,400 - \$400}{4 \text{ years}} = \$1,500 \text{ per year}$$

Exhibit 10.14

Computing Revised Straight-Line Depreciation

Thus, $1,500 of depreciation expense is recorded for the machine at the end of the third through sixth years—each year of its remaining useful life. Since this asset was depreciated at $1,800 per year for the first two years, it is tempting to conclude that depreciation expense was over-stated in the first two years. However, these expenses reflected the best information available at that time. We do not go back and restate prior years' financial statements for this type of new information. Instead, we adjust the current and future periods' statements to reflect this new information. Revising an estimate of the useful life or salvage value of a plant asset is re-ferred to as a **change in an accounting estimate** and is reflected in current and future financial statements, not in prior statements.

Example: If at the beginning of its second year the machine's remaining useful life changes from four to three years and salvage value from $1,000 to $400, how much straight-line depreciation is recorded in remaining years? *Answer:* Revised depreciation = ($8,200 − $400)/3 = $2,600.

Reporting Depreciation

Both the cost and accumulated depreciation of plant assets are reported on the balance sheet or in its notes. **Yahoo!**, for instance, reports the following.

Land and buildings	$242,244
Computers and equipment	560,907
Furniture, fixtures, and leasehold improvements	116,554
Property and equipment, gross	919,705
Less accumulated depreciation	388,009
Property and equipment, net	$531,696

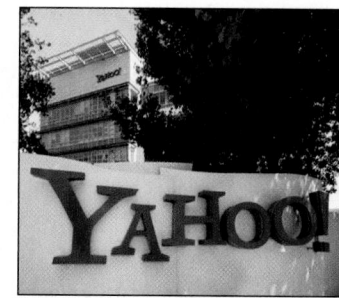

Many companies also show plant assets on one line with the net amount of cost less accumu-lated depreciation. When this is done, the amount of accumulated depreciation is disclosed in a note. **Circuit City** reports only the net amount of its property and equipment in its balance sheet in Appendix A. To satisfy the full-disclosure principle, Circuit City describes its depre-ciation methods in its Note 2 and the amounts comprising plant assets in its Note 8—not shown in Appendix A.

Point: A company usually keeps records for each asset showing its cost and depreciation to date. The combined records for individual assets are a type of *plant asset subsidiary ledger.*

Reporting both the cost and accumulated depreciation of plant assets helps users compare the assets of different companies. For example, a company holding assets costing $50,000 and accumulated depreciation of $40,000 is likely in a situation different from a company with new

Answer—p. 409

Controller You are the controller for a struggling company. Its operations require regular investments in equipment, and depreciation is its largest expense. Its competitors frequently replace equipment—often depreciated over three years. The company president instructs you to revise useful lives of equipment from three to six years and to use a six-year life on all new equipment. What actions do you take?

assets costing $10,000. While the net undepreciated cost of $10,000 is the same in both cases, the first company may have more productive capacity available but likely is facing the need to replace older assets. These insights are not provided if the two balance sheets report only the $10,000 book values.

Users must remember that plant assets are reported on a balance sheet at their undepreciated costs (book value), not at market values. This emphasis on costs rather than market values is based on the *going-concern principle* described in Chapter 1. This principle states that, unless there is evidence to the contrary, we assume that a company continues in business. This implies that plant assets are held and used long enough to recover their cost through the sale of products and services. Since plant assets are not for sale, their market values are not reported.

Accumulated Depreciation is a contra asset account with a normal credit balance. It does *not* reflect funds accumulated to buy new assets when the assets currently owned are replaced. If a company has funds available to buy assets, the funds are shown on the balance sheet among liquid assets such as Cash or Investments.

Point: Depreciation is higher and income lower in the short run when using accelerated versus straight-line methods.

Quick Check   Answers—p. 410

4. On January 1, 2008, a company pays $77,000 to purchase office furniture with a zero salvage value. The furniture's useful life is somewhere between 7 and 10 years. What is the year 2008 straight-line depreciation on the furniture using (*a*) a 7-year useful life and (*b*) a 10-year useful life?

5. What does the term *depreciation* mean in accounting?

6. A company purchases a machine for $96,000 on January 1, 2008. Its useful life is five years or 100,000 units of product, and its salvage value is $8,000. During 2008, 10,000 units of product are produced. Compute the book value of this machine on December 31, 2008, assuming (*a*) straight-line depreciation and (*b*) units-of-production depreciation.

7. In early January 2008, a company acquires equipment for $3,800. The company estimates this equipment to have a useful life of three years and a salvage value of $200. Early in 2010, the company changes its estimates to a total four-year useful life and zero salvage value. Using the straight-line method, what is depreciation for the year ended 2010?

Additional Expenditures

P3 Distinguish between revenue and capital expenditures, and account for them.

Point: When an amount is said to be *capitalized* to an account, the amount is added to the account's normal balance.

After a company acquires a plant asset and puts it into service, it often makes additional expenditures for that asset's operation, maintenance, repair, and improvement. In recording these expenditures, it must decide whether to capitalize or expense them (to capitalize an expenditure is to debit the asset account). The issue is whether more useful information is provided by reporting these expenditures as current period expenses or by adding them to the plant asset's cost and depreciating them over its remaining useful life.

Revenue expenditures, also called *income statement expenditures,* are additional costs of plant assets that do not materially increase the asset's life or productive capabilities. They are recorded as expenses and deducted from revenues in the current period's income statement. Examples of revenue expenditures are cleaning, repainting, adjustments, and lubricants. **Capital expenditures,** also called *balance sheet expenditures,* are additional costs of plant assets that provide benefits extending beyond the current period. They are debited to asset accounts and reported on the balance sheet. Capital expenditures increase or improve the type or amount of service an asset provides. Examples are roofing replacement, plant expansion, and major overhauls of machinery and equipment.

Financial Statement Effect			
Cost Category	**Accounting**	**Expense Timing**	**Current Income**
Revenue expenditure	Income stmt. account debited	Expensed currently	Lower
Capital expenditure	Balance sheet account debited	Expensed in future	Higher

Financial statements are affected for several years by the accounting choice of recording costs as either revenue expenditures or capital expenditures. Managers must be careful in classifying them. This classification decision is based on whether these expenditures are identified as either ordinary repairs or as betterments and extraordinary repairs.

Ordinary Repairs

Ordinary repairs are expenditures to keep an asset in normal, good operating condition. They are necessary if an asset is to perform to expectations over its useful life. Ordinary repairs do not extend an asset's useful life beyond its original estimate or increase its productivity beyond original expectations. Examples are normal costs of cleaning, lubricating, adjusting, and replacing small parts of a machine. Ordinary repairs are treated as *revenue expenditures*. This means their costs are reported as expenses on the current period income statement. Following this rule, **Brunswick** reports that "maintenance and repair costs are expensed as incurred."

Point: Many companies apply the *materiality principle* to treat *low-cost plant assets* (say, less than $500) as revenue expenditures.

Betterments and Extraordinary Repairs

Accounting for betterments and extraordinary repairs is similar. **Betterments,** also called *improvements,* are expenditures that make a plant asset more efficient or productive. A betterment often involves adding a component to an asset or replacing one of its old components with a better one, and does not always increase an asset's useful life. An example is replacing manual controls on a machine with automatic controls. One special type of betterment is an *addition,* such as adding a new wing or dock to a warehouse. Since a betterment benefits future periods, it is debited to the asset account as a capital expenditure. The new book value (less salvage value) is then depreciated over the asset's remaining useful life. To illustrate, suppose a company pays $8,000 for a machine with an eight-year useful life and no salvage value. After three years and $3,000 of depreciation, it adds an automated control system to the machine at a cost of $1,800. This results in reduced labor costs in future periods. The cost of the betterment is added to the Machinery account with this entry.

Example: Assume a company owns a Web server. Identify each item as a revenue or capital expenditure: (1) purchase price, (2) necessary wiring, (3) platform for operation, (4) circuits to increase capacity, (5) cleaning after each three months of use, (6) repair of a faulty connection, and (7) replaced a worn cooling fan. *Answer:* Capital expenditures: 1, 2, 3, 4; Revenue expenditures: 5, 6, 7.

Jan. 2	Machinery	1,800	
	Cash		1,800
	To record installation of automated system.		

Assets = Liabilities + Equity
+1,800
−1,800

After the betterment, the remaining cost to be depreciated is $6,800, computed as $8,000 − $3,000 + $1,800. Depreciation expense for the remaining five years is $1,360 per year, computed as $6,800/5 years.

Point: Both extraordinary repairs and betterments demand revised depreciation schedules.

Extraordinary repairs are expenditures extending the asset's useful life beyond its original estimate. Extraordinary repairs are *capital expenditures* because they benefit future periods. Their costs are debited to the asset account. For example, **America West Airlines** reports: "cost of major scheduled airframe, engine and certain component overhauls are capitalized (and expensed) . . . over the periods benefited."

Decision Maker   Answer—p. 409

Entrepreneur   Your startup Internet services company needs cash, and you are preparing financial statements to apply for a short-term loan. A friend suggests that you treat as many expenses as possible as capital expenditures. What are the impacts on financial statements of this suggestion? What do you think is the aim of this suggestion?

Disposals of Plant Assets

Plant assets are disposed of for several reasons. Some are discarded because they wear out or become obsolete. Others are sold because of changing business plans. Regardless of the reason, disposals of plant assets occur in one of three basic ways: discarding, sale, or exchange. The general steps in accounting for a disposal of plant assets is described in Exhibit 10.15.

Exhibit 10.15

Accounting for Disposals of Plant Assets

1. Record depreciation up to the date of disposal—this also updates Accumulated Depreciation.
2. Record the removal of the disposed asset's account balances—including its Accumulated Depreciation.
3. Record any cash (and/or other assets) received or paid in the disposal.
4. Record any gain or loss—computed by comparing the disposed asset's book value with the market value of any assets received.*

* An exception to step 4 is the case of an exchange that lacks *commercial substance*—See Appendix 10A.

Discarding Plant Assets

P4 Account for asset disposal through discarding or selling an asset.

A plant asset is *discarded* when it is no longer useful to the company and it has no market value. To illustrate, assume that a machine costing $9,000 with accumulated depreciation of $9,000 is discarded. When accumulated depreciation equals the asset's cost, it is said to be *fully depreciated* (zero book value). The entry to record the discarding of this asset is

Assets = Liabilities + Equity
+9,000
−9,000

June 5	Accumulated Depreciation—Machinery............	9,000	
	Machinery.............................		9,000
	To discard fully depreciated machinery.		

This entry reflects all four steps of Exhibit 10.15. Step 1 is unnecessary since the machine is fully depreciated. Step 2 is reflected in the debit to Accumulated Depreciation and credit to Machinery. Since no other asset is involved, step 3 is irrelevant. Finally, since book value is zero and no other asset is involved, no gain or loss is recorded in step 4.

How do we account for discarding an asset that is not fully depreciated or one whose depreciation is not up-to-date? To answer this, consider equipment costing $8,000 with accumulated depreciation of $6,000 on December 31 of the prior fiscal year-end. This equipment is being depreciated using the straight-line method over eight years with zero salvage. On July 1 of the current year it is discarded. Step 1 is to bring depreciation up-to-date.

Point: Recording depreciation expense up-to-date gives an up-to-date book value for determining gain or loss.

Assets = Liabilities + Equity
−500   −500

July 1	Depreciation Expense.......................	500	
	Accumulated Depreciation—Equipment		500
	To record 6 months' depreciation ($1,000 × 6/12).		

Steps 2 through 4 of Exhibit 10.15 are reflected in the second (and final) entry.

Assets = Liabilities + Equity
+6,500   −1,500
−8,000

July 1	Accumulated Depreciation—Equipment...........	6,500	
	Loss on Disposal of Equipment................	1,500	
	Equipment		8,000
	To discard equipment with a $1,500 book value.		

Point: Gain or loss is determined by comparing "value given" (book value) to "value received."

The loss is computed by comparing the equipment's $1,500 book value ($8,000 − $6,000 − $500) with the zero net cash proceeds. This loss is reported in the Other Expenses and Losses section of the income statement. Discarding an asset can sometimes require a cash payment that would increase the loss. The income statement reports any loss from discarding an asset, and the balance sheet reflects the changes in the asset and accumulated depreciation accounts.

Selling Plant Assets

Companies often sell plant assets when they restructure or downsize operations. To illustrate the accounting for selling plant assets, we consider BTO's March 31 sale of equipment that cost $16,000 and has accumulated depreciation of $12,000 at December 31 of the prior calendar year-end. Annual depreciation on this equipment is $4,000 computed using straight-line depreciation. Step 1 of this sale is to record depreciation expense and update accumulated depreciation to March 31 of the current year.

March 31	Depreciation Expense..........................	1,000	
	Accumulated Depreciation—Equipment		1,000
	To record 3 months' depreciation ($4,000 × 3/12).		

Assets = Liabilities + Equity
−1,000   −1,000

Steps 2 through 4 of Exhibit 10.15 can be reflected in one final entry that depends on the amount received from the asset's sale. We consider three different possibilities.

Sale at Book Value   If BTO receives $3,000, an amount equal to the equipment's book value as of March 31, no gain or loss occurs on disposal. The entry is

March 31	Cash.....................................	3,000	
	Accumulated Depreciation—Equipment..........	13,000	
	Equipment		16,000
	To record sale of equipment for no gain or loss.		

Assets = Liabilities + Equity
+3,000
+13,000
−16,000

Sale above Book Value   If BTO receives $7,000, an amount that is $4,000 above the equipment's book value as of March 31, a gain on disposal occurs. The entry is

March 31	Cash.....................................	7,000	
	Accumulated Depreciation—Equipment..........	13,000	
	Gain on Disposal of Equipment		4,000
	Equipment		16,000
	To record sale of equipment for a $4,000 gain.		

Assets = Liabilities + Equity
+7,000   +4,000
+13,000
−16,000

Sale below Book Value   If BTO receives $2,500, an amount that is $500 below the equipment's book value as of March 31, a loss on disposal occurs. The entry is

March 31	Cash.....................................	2,500	
	Loss on Disposal of Equipment................	500	
	Accumulated Depreciation—Equipment..........	13,000	
	Equipment		16,000
	To record sale of equipment for a $500 loss.		

Assets = Liabilities + Equity
+2,500   −500
+13,000
−16,000

Quick Check
Answers—p. 410

8. Early in the fifth year of a machine's six-year useful life, it is overhauled, and its useful life is extended to nine years. This machine originally cost $108,000 and the overhaul cost is $12,000. Prepare the entry to record the overhaul cost.

9. Explain the difference between revenue expenditures and capital expenditures and how both are recorded.

10. What is a betterment? How is a betterment recorded?

11. A company acquires equipment on January 10, 2008, at a cost of $42,000. Straight-line depreciation is used with a five-year life and $7,000 salvage value. On June 27, 2009, the company sells this equipment for $32,000. Prepare the entry(ies) for June 27, 2009.

Section 2—Natural Resources

Natural resources are assets that are physically consumed when used. Examples are standing timber, mineral deposits, and oil and gas fields. Since they are consumed when used, they are often called *wasting assets*. These assets represent soon-to-be inventories of raw materials that will be converted into one or more products by cutting, mining, or pumping. Until that conversion takes place, they are noncurrent assets and are shown in a balance sheet using titles such as timberlands, mineral deposits, or oil reserves. Natural resources are reported under either plant assets or its own separate category. **Alcoa**, for instance, reports its natural resources under the balance sheet title *Properties, plants and equipment*. In a note to its financial statements, Alcoa reports a separate amount for *Land and land rights, including mines*. **Weyerhaeuser**, on the other hand, reports its timber holdings in a separate balance sheet category titled *Timber and timberlands*.

Cost Determination and Depletion

P5 Account for natural resource assets and their depletion.

Natural resources are recorded at cost, which includes all expenditures necessary to acquire the resource and prepare it for its intended use. **Depletion** is the process of allocating the cost of a natural resource to the period when it is consumed. Natural resources are reported on the balance sheet at cost less *accumulated depletion*. The depletion expense per period is usually based on units extracted from cutting, mining, or pumping. This is similar to units-of-production depreciation. **Exxon Mobil** uses this approach to amortize the costs of discovering and operating its oil wells.

To illustrate depletion of natural resources, let's consider a mineral deposit with an estimated 250,000 tons of available ore. It is purchased for $500,000, and we expect zero salvage value. The depletion charge per ton of ore mined is $2, computed as $500,000 ÷ 250,000 tons. If 85,000 tons are mined and sold in the first year, the depletion charge for that year is $170,000. These computations are detailed in Exhibit 10.16.

Exhibit 10.16

Depletion Formula and Example

Step 1

$$\text{Depletion per unit} = \frac{\text{Cost} - \text{Salvage value}}{\text{Total units of capacity}} = \frac{\$500,000 - \$0}{250,000 \text{ tons}} = \$2 \text{ per ton}$$

Step 2

$$\text{Depletion expense} = \text{Depletion per unit} \times \text{Units extracted and sold in period}$$
$$= \$2 \times 85,000 = \$170,000$$

Depletion expense for the first year is recorded as follows.

Assets	= Liabilities +	Equity
−170,000		−170,000

Dec. 31	Depletion Expense—Mineral Deposit	170,000	
	Accumulated Depletion—Mineral Deposit		170,000
	To record depletion of the mineral deposit.		

The period-end balance sheet reports the mineral deposit as shown in Exhibit 10.17.

Exhibit 10.17

Balance Sheet Presentation of Natural Resources

Mineral deposit	$500,000	
Less accumulated depletion	**170,000**	$330,000

Since all 85,000 tons of the mined ore are sold during the year, the entire $170,000 of depletion is reported on the income statement. If some of the ore remains unsold at year-end, however, the depletion related to the unsold ore is carried forward on the balance sheet and reported as Ore Inventory, a current asset.

Plant Assets Used in Extracting Resources

The conversion of natural resources by mining, cutting, or pumping usually requires machinery, equipment, and buildings. When the usefulness of these plant assets is directly related to the depletion of a natural resource, their costs are depreciated using the units-of-production method in proportion to the depletion of the natural resource. For example, if a machine is permanently installed in a mine and 10% of the ore is mined and sold in the period, then 10% of the machine's cost (less any salvage value) is allocated to depreciation expense. The same procedure is used when a machine is abandoned once resources have been extracted. If, however, a machine will be moved to and used at another site when extraction is complete, the machine is depreciated over its own useful life.

Section 3—Intangible Assets

Intangible assets are nonphysical assets (used in operations) that confer on their owners long-term rights, privileges, or competitive advantages. Examples are patents, copyrights, licenses, leaseholds, franchises, goodwill, and trademarks. Lack of physical substance does not necessarily make an asset intangible. Notes and accounts receivable, for instance, lack physical substance, but they are not intangibles. This section identifies the more common types of intangible assets and explains the accounting for them.

P6   Account for intangible assets.

Cost Determination and Amortization

An intangible asset is recorded at cost when purchased. Its cost is systematically allocated to expense over its estimated useful life through the process of **amortization.** If an intangible asset has an **indefinite useful life**—meaning that no legal, regulatory, contractual, competitive, economic, or other factors limit its useful life—it should not be amortized. (If an intangible with an indefinite useful life is later judged to have a limited useful life, it is amortized over that limited useful life.) Amortization of intangible assets is similar to depreciation of plant assets and the depletion of natural resources in that it is a process of cost allocation. However, only the straight-line method is used for amortizing intangibles *unless* the company can show that another method is preferred. The effects of amortization are recorded in a contra account (Accumulated Amortization). The gross acquisition cost of intangible assets is disclosed in the balance sheet along with their accumulated amortization (these disclosures are new per *SFAS 142*). The eventual disposal of an intangible asset involves removing its book value, recording any other asset(s) received or given up, and recognizing any gain or loss for the difference.

Point: Goodwill is not amortized; instead, it is annually tested for impairment.

Point: The cost to acquire a Website address is an intangible asset.

Many intangibles have limited useful lives due to laws, contracts, or other asset characteristics. Examples are patents, copyrights, and leaseholds. Other intangibles such as goodwill, trademarks, and trade names have useful lives that cannot be easily determined. The cost of intangible assets is amortized over the periods expected to benefit by their use, but in no case can this period be longer than the asset's legal existence. The values of some intangible assets such as goodwill continue indefinitely into the future and are not amortized. (An intangible asset that is not amortized is tested annually for **impairment**—if necessary, an impairment loss is recorded. Details for this test are in advanced courses.)

Intangible assets are often shown in a separate section of the balance sheet immediately after plant assets. **Callaway Golf,** for instance, follows this approach in reporting nearly $150 million of intangible assets in its balance sheet. Companies usually disclose their amortization periods for intangibles. The remainder of our discussion focuses on accounting for specific types of intangible assets.

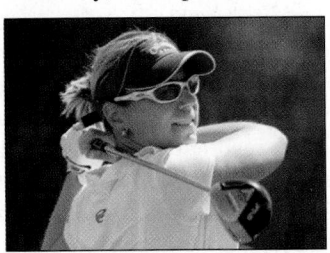

Types of Intangibles

Patents   The federal government grants patents to encourage the invention of new technology, mechanical devices, and production processes. A **patent** is an exclusive right granted to its owner to manufacture and sell a patented item or to use a process for 20 years. When patent rights are purchased, the cost to acquire the rights is debited to an account called Patents. If the owner engages in lawsuits to successfully defend a patent, the cost of lawsuits is debited to the Patents account. However, the costs of research and development leading to a new patent are expensed when incurred.

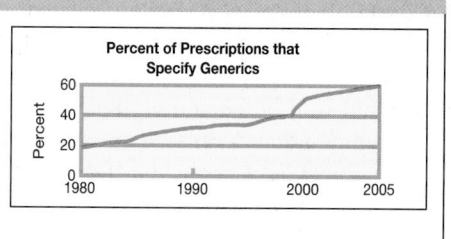

A patent's cost is amortized over its estimated useful life (not to exceed 20 years). If we purchase a patent costing $25,000 with a useful life of 10 years, we make the following adjusting entry at the end of each of the 10 years to amortize one-tenth of its cost:

Assets	=	Liabilities	+	Equity
−2,500				−2,500

Dec. 31	Amortization Expense—Patents	2,500	
	Accumulated Amortization—Patents		2,500
	To amortize patent costs over its useful life.		

The $2,500 debit to Amortization Expense appears on the income statement as a cost of the product or service provided under protection of the patent. The Accumulated Amortization—Patents account is a contra asset account to Patents.

Copyrights   A **copyright** gives its owner the exclusive right to publish and sell a musical, literary, or artistic work during the life of the creator plus 70 years, although the useful life of most copyrights is much shorter. The costs of a copyright are amortized over its useful life. The only identifiable cost of many copyrights is the fee paid to the Copyright Office of the federal government or international agency granting the copyright. If this fee is immaterial, it is charged directly to an expense account, but if the identifiable costs of a copyright are material, they are capitalized (recorded in an asset account) and periodically amortized by debiting an account called Amortization Expense—Copyrights.

Leaseholds   Property is rented under a contract called a **lease.** The property's owner, called the **lessor,** grants the lease. The one who secures the right to possess and use the property is called the **lessee.** A **leasehold** refers to the rights the lessor grants to the lessee under the terms of the lease. A leasehold is an intangible asset for the lessee.

Point: A leasehold account implies existence of future benefits that the lessee controls because of a prepayment. It also meets the definition of an asset.

Certain leases require no advance payment from the lessee but require monthly rent payments. In this case, we do not set up a Leasehold account. Instead, the monthly payments are debited to a Rent Expense account. If a long-term lease requires the lessee to pay the final period's rent in advance when the lease is signed, the lessee records this advance payment with a debit to the Leasehold account. Since the advance payment is not used until the final period, the Leasehold account balance remains intact until that final period when its balance is transferred to Rent Expense. (Some long-term leases give the lessee essentially the same rights as a purchaser. This results in a tangible asset and a liability reported by the lessee. Chapter 14 describes these so-called *capital leases.*)

A long-term lease can increase in value when current rental rates for similar property rise while the required payments under the lease remain constant. This increase in value of a lease is not reported on the lessee's balance sheet. However, if the property is subleased and the new tenant makes a cash payment to the original lessee for the rights under the old lease, the new tenant debits this payment to a Leasehold account, which is amortized to Rent Expense over the remaining life of the lease.

Leasehold Improvements   A lessee sometimes pays for alterations or improvements to the leased property such as partitions, painting, and storefronts. These alterations and improvements are called **leasehold improvements,** and the lessee debits these costs to a Leasehold Improvements account. Since leasehold improvements become part of the property and revert to the lessor at the end of the lease, the lessee amortizes these costs over the life of the lease or the life of the improvements, whichever is shorter. The amortization entry debits Amortization Expense—Leasehold Improvements and credits Accumulated Amortization—Leasehold Improvements.

Franchises and Licenses   **Franchises** and **licenses** are rights that a company or government grants an entity to deliver a product or service under specified conditions. Many organizations grant franchise and license rights—**McDonald's**, **Pizza Hut**, and **Major League Baseball** are just a few examples. The costs of franchises and licenses are debited to a Franchises and Licenses asset account and are amortized over the lives of the agreements.

Trademarks and Trade Names   Companies often adopt unique symbols or select unique names and brands in marketing their products. A **trademark** or **trade (brand) name** is a symbol, name, phrase, or jingle identified with a company, product, or service. Examples are Nike swoosh, Marlboro Man, Big Mac, Coca-Cola, and Corvette. Ownership and exclusive right to use a trademark or trade name is often established by showing that one company used it before another. Ownership is best established by registering a trademark or trade name with the government's Patent Office. The cost of developing, maintaining, or enhancing the value of a trademark or trade name (such as advertising) is charged to expense when incurred. If a trademark or trade name is purchased, however, its cost is debited to an asset account and then amortized over its expected useful life.

Point: McDonald's "golden arches" is one of the world's most valuable trademarks, yet this asset is not shown on McDonald's balance sheet.

Goodwill   **Goodwill** has a specific meaning in accounting. Goodwill is the amount by which a company's value exceeds the value of its individual assets and liabilities. This usually implies that the company as a whole has certain valuable attributes not measured among its individual assets and liabilities. These can include superior management, skilled workforce, good supplier or customer relations, quality products or services, good location, or other competitive advantages.

Point: IBM's balance sheet reports more than $8 billion of goodwill.

To keep accounting information from being too subjective, goodwill is not recorded unless an entire company or business segment is purchased. Purchased goodwill is measured by taking the purchase price of the company and subtracting the market value of its individual net assets (excluding goodwill). For instance, **Yahoo!** paid nearly $3.0 billion to acquire **GeoCities**; about $2.8 of the $3.0 billion was for goodwill and other intangibles.

Point: Accounting for goodwill is different for financial accounting and tax accounting. The IRS requires the amortization of goodwill over 15 years.

Goodwill is measured as the excess of the cost of an acquired entity over the value of the acquired net assets. Goodwill is recorded as an asset, and it is *not* amortized. Instead, goodwill is annually tested for impairment. If the book value of goodwill does not exceed its fair (market) value, goodwill is not impaired. However, if the book value of goodwill does exceed its fair value, an impairment loss is recorded equal to that excess. (Details of this test are in advanced courses.)

Quick Check

Answers—p. 410

12. Give an example of a natural resource and of an intangible asset.

13. A company pays $650,000 for an ore deposit. The deposit is estimated to have 325,000 tons of ore that will be mined over the next 10 years. During the first year, it mined, processed, and sold 91,000 tons. What is that year's depletion expense?

14. On January 6, 2008, a company pays $120,000 for a patent with a remaining 17-year legal life to produce a toy expected to be marketable for three years. Prepare entries to record its acquisition and the December 31, 2008, amortization entry.

Decision Analysis

Total Asset Turnover

A2 Compute total asset turnover and apply it to analyze a company's use of assets.

A company's assets are important in determining its ability to generate sales and earn income. Managers devote much attention to deciding what assets a company acquires, how much it invests in assets, and how to use assets most efficiently and effectively. One important measure of a company's ability to use its assets is **total asset turnover,** defined in Exhibit 10.18.

Exhibit 10.18

Total Asset Turnover

$$\text{Total asset turnover} = \frac{\text{Net sales}}{\text{Average total assets}}$$

[handwritten: 35494 / 14500]

The numerator reflects the net amounts earned from the sale of products and services. The denominator reflects the average total resources devoted to operating the company and generating sales.

To illustrate, let's look at total asset turnover in Exhibit 10.19 for two competing companies: Coors and Anheuser-Busch.

Exhibit 10.19

Analysis Using Total Asset Turnover

Company	Figure ($ millions)	2004	2003	2002
Coors	Net sales	$ 4,306	$ 4,000	$ 3,776
	Average total assets	$ 4,551	$ 4,392	$ 3,019
	Total asset turnover	0.95	0.91	1.25
Anheuser-Busch	Net sales	$14,934	$14,147	$13,566
	Average total assets	$15,431	$14,405	$14,032
	Total asset turnover	0.97	0.98	0.97

Point: An estimate of **plant asset useful life** equals the plant asset cost divided by depreciation expense.

Point: The **plant asset age** is estimated by dividing accumulated depreciation by depreciation expense. Older plant assets can signal needed asset replacements; it may also signal less efficient assets.

To show how we use total asset turnover, let's look at Coors. We express Coors's use of assets in generating net sales by saying "it turned its assets over 0.95 times during 2004." This means that each $1.00 of assets produced $0.95 of net sales. Is a total asset turnover of 0.95 good or bad? It is safe to say that all companies desire a high total asset turnover. Like many ratio analyses, however, a company's total asset turnover must be interpreted in comparison with that of prior years and of its competitors. Interpreting the total asset turnover also requires an understanding of the company's operations. Some operations are capital intensive, meaning that a relatively large amount is invested in assets to generate sales. This suggests a relatively lower total asset turnover. Other companies' operations are labor intensive, meaning that they generate sales more by the efforts of people than the use of assets. In that case, we expect a higher total asset turnover. Companies with low total asset turnover require higher profit margins (examples are hotels and real estate); companies with high total asset turnover can succeed with lower profit margins; examples are food stores and toy merchandisers. Coors's turnover recently declined, but it is similar to that for Anheuser-Busch. Total asset turnover for Coors's competitors, available in industry publications such as Dun & Bradstreet, is generally in the range of 1.0 to 1.1 over this same period. Overall, Coors appears to be competitive and performing similarly to its competitors on total asset turnover.

Decision Maker

Answer—p. 410

Environmentalist A paper manufacturer claims it cannot afford more environmental controls. It points to its low total asset turnover of 1.9 and argues that it cannot compete with companies whose total asset turnover is much higher. Examples cited are food stores (5.5) and auto dealers (3.8). How do you respond?

Demonstration Problem

On July 14, 2007, Tulsa Company pays $600,000 to acquire a fully equipped factory. The purchase involves the following assets.

Asset	Appraised Value	Salvage Value	Useful Life	Depreciation Method
Land	$160,000			Not depreciated
Land improvements	80,000	$ 0	10 years	Straight-line
Building	320,000	100,000	10 years	Double-declining-balance
Machinery	240,000	20,000	10,000 units	Units-of-production*
Total	$800,000			

* The machinery is used to produce 700 units in 2007 and 1,800 units in 2008.

Required

1. Allocate the total $600,000 purchase cost among the separate assets.
2. Compute the 2007 (six months) and 2008 depreciation expense for each asset and compute total depreciation expense for both years.
3.^AOn the first day of 2009, Tulsa exchanged machinery that was acquired on July 14, 2007, and $5,000 cash for machinery with a $210,000 market value. Journalize the exchange of these assets assuming the exchange lacked commercial substance.
4. On the last day of calendar year 2009, Tulsa discarded machinery that had been on its books for five years. The machinery's original cost was $12,000 (estimated life of five years) and its salvage value was $2,000. No depreciation had been recorded for the fifth year when the disposal occurred. Journalize the fifth year of depreciation (straight-line method) and the asset's disposal.
5. At the beginning of year 2009, Tulsa purchased a patent for $100,000 cash. The company estimated the patent's useful life to be 10 years. Journalize the patent acquisition and its amortization for the year 2009.
6. Late in the year 2009, Tulsa acquired an ore deposit for $600,000 cash. It added roads and built mine shafts for an additional cost of $80,000. Salvage value of the mine is estimated to be $20,000. The company estimated 330,000 tons of available ore. In year 2009, Tulsa mined and sold 10,000 tons of ore. Journalize the mine's acquisition and its first year's depletion.

Planning the Solution

- Complete a three-column table showing the following amounts for each asset: appraised value, percent of total value, and apportioned cost.
- Using allocated costs, compute depreciation for 2007 (only one-half year) and 2008 (full year) for each asset. Summarize those computations in a table showing total depreciation for each year.
- Remember that gains and losses on asset exchanges that lack commercial substance are not recognized. Make a journal entry to add the acquired machinery to the books and to remove the old machinery, along with its accumulated depreciation, and to record the cash given in the exchange.
- Remember that depreciation must be recorded up-to-date before discarding an asset. Calculate and record depreciation expense for the fifth year using the straight-line method. Since salvage value is not received at the end of a discarded asset's life, the amount of any salvage value becomes a loss on disposal. Record the loss on the disposal as well as the removal of the discarded asset and its related accumulated depreciation.
- Record the patent (an intangible asset) at its purchase price. Use straight-line amortization over its useful life to calculate amortization expense.
- Record the ore deposit (a natural resource asset) at its cost, including any added costs to ready the mine for use. Calculate depletion per ton using the depletion formula. Multiply the depletion per ton by the amount of tons mined and sold to calculate depletion expense for the year.

Solution to Demonstration Problem

1. Allocation of the total cost of $600,000 among the separate assets.

Asset	Appraised Value	Percent of Total Value	Apportioned Cost
Land	$160,000	20%	$120,000 ($600,000 × 20%)
Land improvements	80,000	10	60,000 ($600,000 × 10%)
Building	320,000	40	240,000 ($600,000 × 40%)
Machinery	240,000	30	180,000 ($600,000 × 30%)
Total	$800,000	100%	$ 600,000

2. Depreciation for each asset. (*Note:* Land is not depreciated.)

Land Improvements	
Cost	$ 60,000
Salvage value	0
Depreciable cost	$ 60,000
Useful life	10 years
Annual depreciation expense ($60,000/10 years)	$ 6,000
2007 depreciation ($6,000 × 6/12)	$ 3,000
2008 depreciation	$ 6,000

[continued on next page]

[continued from previous page]

Building

    Straight-line rate = 100%/10 years = 10%

    Double-declining-balance rate = 10% × 2 = 20%

2007 depreciation ($240,000 × 20% × 6/12) . . . .   **$ 24,000**

2008 depreciation [($240,000 − $24,000) × 20%] . . . .   **$ 43,200**

Machinery

Cost	$ 180,000
Salvage value	20,000
Depreciable cost	$ 160,000
Total expected units of production	10,000 units
Depreciation per unit ($160,000/10,000 units)	$ 16
2007 depreciation ($16 × 700 units)	$ 11,200
2008 depreciation ($16 × 1,800 units)	$ 28,800

Total depreciation expense:

	2007	2008
Land improvements	$ 3,000	$ 6,000
Building	24,000	43,200
Machinery	11,200	28,800
Total	$38,200	$78,000

3. Record the asset exchange: The book value on the exchange date is $180,000 (cost) − $40,000 (accumulated depreciation). The book value of the machinery given up in the exchange ($140,000) plus the $5,000 cash paid is less than the $210,000 value of the machine acquired. The entry to record this exchange of assets that lacks commercial substance does not recognize the $65,000 "gain":

Machinery (new)	145,000*	
Accumulated Depreciation—Machinery (old)	40,000	
Machinery (old)		180,000
Cash		5,000
To record asset exchange that lacks commercial substance.		

* Market value of the acquired asset of $210,000 minus $65,000 "gain".

4. Record the depreciation up to date on the discarded asset.

Depreciation Expense—Machinery	2,000	
Accumulated Depreciation—Machinery		2,000
To record depreciation on date of disposal: ($12,000 − $2,000)/5		

Record the removal of the discarded asset and its loss on disposal.

Accumulated Depreciation—Machinery	10,000	
Loss on Disposal of Machinery	2,000	
Machinery		12,000
To record the discarding of machinery with a $2,000 book value.		

5.

Patent	100,000	
Cash		100,000
To record patent acquisition.		

Amortization Expense—Patent	10,000	
Accumulated Amortization—Patent		10,000
To record amortization expense: $100,000/10 years = $10,000.		

6.

Ore Deposit	680,000	
Cash		680,000
To record ore deposit acquisition and its related costs.		

Depletion Expense—Ore Deposit	20,000	
Accumulated Depletion—Ore Deposit		20,000
To record depletion expense: ($680,000 − $20,000)/330,000 tons =		
$2 per ton. 10,000 tons mined and sold × $2 = $20,000 depletion.		

Exchanging Plant Assets

P7^A Account for asset exchanges.

Many plant assets such as machinery, automobiles, and office equipment are disposed of by exchanging them for newer assets. In a typical exchange of plant assets, a *trade-in allowance* is received on the old asset and the balance is paid in cash. Accounting for the exchange of assets depends on whether the transaction has *commercial substance* (per *SFAS 153*). If an asset exchange has commercial substance, a gain or loss is recorded based on the difference between the book value of the asset(s) given up and the market value of the asset(s) received. If an asset exchange lacks commercial substance, no gain or loss is recorded, and the asset(s) received is recorded based on the book value of the asset(s) given up. An exchange has commercial substance if the company's future cash flows change as a result of the transaction. This section describes the accounting for the exchange of assets.

Exchange with Commercial Substance: A Loss Let's assume that a company exchanges both old equipment and $33,000 in cash for new equipment; assume this transaction has commercial substance. The old equipment originally cost $36,000 and has accumulated depreciation of $20,000 at the time of exchange. The new equipment has a market value of $42,000. These details are reflected in the middle (Loss) columns of Exhibit 10A.1.

Point: Trade-in allowance minus book value equals the gain (or loss if negative) on exchange.

Asset Exchange Has Commercial Substance	Loss		Gain	
Market value of asset received		$42,000		$52,000
Book value of assets given up:				
Equipment ($36,000 − $20,000)	$16,000		$16,000	
Cash	33,000	49,000	33,000	49,000
Gain (loss) on exchange		$(7,000)		$ 3,000

Exhibit 10A.1

Computing Gain or Loss on Asset Exchange with Commercial Substance

The entry to record this asset exchange is

Assets = Liabilities + Equity
+42,000   −7,000
+20,000
−36,000
−33,000

Jan. 3	Equipment (**new**)........................	42,000	
	Loss on Exchange of Assets	7,000	
	Accumulated Depreciation—Equipment (**old**)	20,000	
	Equipment (**old**).........................		36,000
	Cash		33,000
	To record exchange (with commercial substance) of		
	old equipment and cash for new equipment.		

Point: Parenthetical journal entry notes to "new" and "old" equipment are for illustration only. Both the debit and credit are to the same Equipment account in the general ledger.

The book value of the assets given up consists of the $33,000 cash and the $16,000 ($36,000 − $20,000) book value of the old equipment. The total $49,000 book value of assets given up is compared to the $42,000 market value of the new equipment received. This yields a loss of $7,000 ($42,000 − $49,000).

Exchange with Commercial Substance: A Gain Let's assume the same facts as in the preceding asset exchange *except* that the new equipment received has a market value of $52,000 instead of $42,000. The entry to record this asset exchange is

Assets = Liabilities + Equity
+52,000   +3,000
+20,000
−36,000
−33,000

Jan. 3	Equipment (**new**)........................	52,000	
	Accumulated Depreciation—Equipment (**old**)	20,000	
	Equipment (**old**).........................		36,000
	Cash		33,000
	Gain on Exchange of Assets.................		3,000
	To record exchange (with commercial substance)		
	of old equipment and cash for new equipment.		

Exchanges without Commercial Substance Let's assume the same facts as in the preceding asset exchange involving new equipment received with a market value of $52,000, but let's instead assume the transaction *lacks commercial substance*. The entry to record this asset exchange is

Assets = Liabilities + Equity
+49,000
+20,000
−36,000
−33,000

Jan. 3	Equipment (**new**)........................	49,000	
	Accumulated Depreciation—Equipment (**old**)	20,000	
	Equipment (**old**).........................		36,000
	Cash		33,000
	To record exchange (without commercial substance)		
	of old equipment and cash for new equipment.		

Point: No gain or loss is recognized for asset exchanges without commercial substance.

The $3,000 gain recorded when the transaction has commercial substance is *not* recognized in this entry because of the rule prohibiting recording a gain or loss on asset exchanges without commercial substance. The $49,000 recorded for the new equipment equals its cash price ($52,000) less the unrecognized gain ($3,000) on the exchange. The $49,000 cost recorded is called the *cost basis* of the new machine. This cost basis is the amount we use to compute depreciation and its book value. The cost basis of the new asset also can be computed by summing the book values of the assets given up as shown in Exhibit 10A.2. The same analysis and approach is taken for a loss on an asset exchange without commercial substance.

Exhibit 10A.2

Cost Basis of New Asset when Gain Not Recorded on Asset Exchange without Commercial Substance

Cost of old equipment	$ 36,000
Less accumulated depreciation	20,000
Book value of old equipment	16,000
Cash paid in the exchange	33,000
Cost recorded for new	
equipment	**$49,000**

Quick Check   Answer—p. 410

15. A company trades an old Web server for a new one. The cost of the old server is $30,000, and its accumulated depreciation at the time of the trade is $23,400. The new server has a cash price of $45,000. Prepare entries to record the trade under two different assumptions where the company receives a trade-in allowance of (*a*) $3,000 and the exchange has commercial substance, and (*b*) $7,000 and the exchange lacks commercial substance.

Summary

C1   Describe plant assets and issues in accounting for them. Plant assets are tangible assets used in the operations of a company and have a useful life of more than one accounting period. Plant assets are set apart from other tangible assets by two important features: use in operations and useful lives longer than one period. The four main accounting issues with plant assets are (1) computing their costs, (2) allocating their costs to the periods they benefit, (3) accounting for subsequent expenditures, and (4) recording their disposal.

C2   Explain depreciation and the factors affecting its computation. *Depreciation* is the process of allocating to expense the cost of a plant asset over the accounting periods that benefit from its use. Depreciation does not measure the decline in a plant asset's market value or its physical deterioration. Three factors determine depreciation: cost, salvage value, and useful life. Salvage value is an estimate of the asset's value at the end of its benefit period. Useful (service) life is the length of time an asset is productively used.

C3   Explain depreciation for partial years and changes in estimates. Partial-year depreciation is often required because assets are bought and sold throughout the year. Depreciation is revised when changes in estimates such as salvage value and useful life occur. If the useful life of a plant asset changes, for instance, the remaining cost to be depreciated is spread over the remaining (revised) useful life of the asset.

A1   Compare and analyze alternative depreciation methods. The amount of depreciation expense per period is usually different for different methods, yet total depreciation expense over an asset's life is the same for all methods. Each method starts with the same total cost and ends with the same salvage value. The difference is in the pattern of depreciation expense over the asset's life. Common methods are straight-line, double-declining-balance, and units-of-production.

A2   Compute total asset turnover and apply it to analyze a company's use of assets. Total asset turnover measures a company's ability to use its assets to generate sales. It is defined as net sales divided by average total assets. While all companies desire a high total asset turnover, it must be interpreted in comparison with that for prior years and its competitors.

P1   Apply the cost principle to compute the cost of plant assets. Plant assets are recorded at cost when purchased. Cost includes all normal and reasonable expenditures necessary to get the asset in place and ready for its intended use. The cost of a lump-sum purchase is allocated among its individual assets.

P2   Compute and record depreciation using the straight-line, units-of-production, and declining-balance methods. The straight-line method divides cost less salvage value by the asset's useful life to determine depreciation expense per period. The units-of-production method divides cost less salvage value by the estimated number of units the asset will produce over its life to determine depreciation per unit. The declining-balance method multiplies the asset's beginning-of-period book value by a factor that is often double the straight-line rate.

P3   Distinguish between revenue and capital expenditures, and account for them. Revenue expenditures expire in the current period and are debited to expense accounts and matched with current revenues. Ordinary repairs are an example of revenue expenditures. Capital expenditures benefit future periods and are debited to asset accounts. Examples of capital expenditures are extraordinary repairs and betterments.

P4   Account for asset disposal through discarding or selling an asset. When a plant asset is discarded or sold, its cost and accumulated depreciation are removed from the accounts. Any cash proceeds from discarding or selling an asset are recorded and compared to the asset's book value to determine gain or loss.

P5   Account for natural resource assets and their depletion. The cost of a natural resource is recorded in a noncurrent asset account. Depletion of a natural resource is recorded by allocating its cost to depletion expense using the units-of-production method. Depletion is credited to an Accumulated Depletion account.

P6   Account for intangible assets. An intangible asset is recorded at the cost incurred to purchase it. The cost of an intangible asset with a definite useful life is allocated to expense using the straight-line method, and is called *amortization.* Goodwill and intangible assets with an indefinite useful life are not amortized—they are annually tested for impairment. Intangible assets include patents, copyrights, leaseholds, goodwill, and trademarks.

P7^A Account for asset exchanges. For an asset exchange with commercial substance, a gain or loss is recorded based on the difference between the book value of the asset given up and the market value of the asset received. For an asset exchange without commercial substance, no gain or loss is recorded, and the asset received is recorded based on book value of the asset given up.

Guidance Answers to **Decision Maker** and **Decision Ethics**

Controller   The president's instructions may reflect an honest and reasonable prediction of the future. Since the company is struggling financially, the president may have concluded that the normal pattern of replacing assets every three years cannot continue. Perhaps the strategy is to avoid costs of frequent replacements and stretch use of equipment a few years longer until financial conditions improve. However, if you believe the president's decision is unprincipled, you might confront the president with your opinion that it is unethical to change the estimate to increase income. Another possibility is to wait and see whether the auditor will prohibit this change in estimate. In either case, you should insist that the statements be based on reasonable estimates.

Entrepreneur   Treating an expense as a capital expenditure means that reported expenses will be lower and income higher in the short run. This is so because a capital expenditure is not expensed immediately but is spread over the asset's useful life. Treating an expense as a capital expenditure also means that asset and equity totals are reported at larger amounts in the short run. This continues until the asset is fully depreciated. Your friend is probably trying to help, but the suggestion is misguided. Only an expenditure benefiting future periods is a capital expenditure.

Environmentalist The paper manufacturer's comparison of its total asset turnover with food stores and auto dealers is misdirected. These other industries' turnovers are higher because their profit margins are lower (about 2%). Profit margins for the paper industry are usually 3% to 3.5%. You need to collect data from competitors in the paper industry to show that a 1.9 total asset turnover is about the norm for this industry. You might also want to collect data on this company's revenues and expenses, along with compensation data for its high-ranking officers and employees.

Guidance Answers to **Quick Checks**

1. a. Supplies—current assets
   b. Office equipment—plant assets
   c. Inventory—current assets
   d. Land for future expansion—long-term investments
   e. Trucks used in operations—plant assets

2. a. Land   **b.** Land Improvements

3. $700,000 + $49,000 − $21,000 + $3,500 + $3,000 + $2,500 = $737,000

4. a. Straight-line with 7-year life: ($77,000/7) = $11,000
   b. Straight-line with 10-year life: ($77,000/10) = $7,700

5. Depreciation is a process of allocating the cost of plant assets to the accounting periods that benefit from the assets' use.

6. a. Book value using straight-line depreciation:
   $96,000 − [($96,000 − $8,000)/5] = $78,400
   b. Book value using units of production:
   $96,000 − [($96,000 − $8,000) × (10,000/100,000)] = $87,200

7. ($3,800 − $200)/3 = $1,200 (original depreciation per year)
   $1,200 × 2 = $2,400 (accumulated depreciation)
   ($3,800 − $2,400)/2 = $700 (revised depreciation)

8.

Machinery	12,000	
Cash		12,000

9. A revenue expenditure benefits only the current period and should be charged to expense in the current period. A capital expenditure yields benefits that extend beyond the end of the current period and should be charged to an asset.

10. A betterment involves modifying an existing plant asset to make it more efficient, usually by replacing part of the asset with an improved or superior part. The cost of a betterment is debited to the asset account.

11.

Depreciation Expense	3,500	
Accumulated Depreciation		3,500
Cash	32,000	
Accumulated Depreciation	10,500	
Gain on Sale of Equipment		500
Equipment		42,000

12. Examples of natural resources are timberlands, mineral deposits, and oil reserves. Examples of intangible assets are patents, copyrights, leaseholds, leasehold improvements, goodwill, trademarks, and licenses.

13. ($650,000/325,000 tons) × 91,000 tons = $182,000

14.

Jan. 6	Patents	120,000	
	Cash		120,000
Dec. 31	Amortization Expense	40,000*	
	Accumulated		
	Amortization—Patents		40,000

* $120,000/3 years = $40,000.

15.

(a)	Equipment (new)	45,000	
	Loss on Exchange of Assets	3,600	
	Accumulated Depreciation—Equipment (old)	23,400	
	Equipment (old)		30,000
	Cash ($45,000 − $3,000)		42,000
(b)	Equipment (new)*	44,600	
	Accumulated Depreciation—Equipment (old)	23,400	
	Equipment (old)		30,000
	Cash ($45,000 − $7,000)		38,000

* Includes $400 unrecognized gain.

Key Terms

mhhe.com/wildFAP18e

Key Terms are available at the book's Website for learning and testing in an online Flashcard Format.

Accelerated depreciation method (p. 392)
Amortization (p. 401)
Betterments (p. 397)
Book value (p. 391)
Capital expenditures (p. 396)
Change in an accounting estimate (p. 395)
Copyright (p. 402)
Cost (p. 389)

Declining-balance method (p. 392)
Depletion (p. 400)
Depreciation (p. 389)
Extraordinary repairs (p. 397)
Franchises (p. 403)
Goodwill (p. 403)
Impairment (p. 401)
Inadequacy (p. 389)

Indefinite useful life (p. 401)
Intangible assets (p. 401)
Land improvements (p. 388)
Lease (p. 402)
Leasehold (p. 402)
Leasehold improvements (p. 403)
Lessee (p. 402)
Lessor (p. 402)

Licenses (p. 403)

Modified Accelerated Cost Recovery System (MACRS) (p. 394)

Natural resources (p. 400)

Obsolescence (p. 389)

Ordinary repairs (p. 397)

Patent (p. 402)

Plant assets (p. 386)

Revenue expenditures (p. 396)

Salvage value (p. 389)

Straight-line depreciation (p. 390)

Total asset turnover (p. 404)

Trademark or trade (brand) name (p. 403)

Units-of-production depreciation (p. 391)

Useful life (p. 389)

Multiple Choice Quiz   Answers on p. 425   mhhe.com/wildFAP18e

Multiple Choice Quizzes A and B are available at the book's Website.

1. A company paid $326,000 for property that included land, land improvements, and a building. The land was appraised at $175,000, the land improvements were appraised at $70,000, and the building was appraised at $105,000. What is the allocation of property costs to the three assets purchased?
   a. Land, $150,000; Land Improvements, $60,000; Building, $90,000
   b. Land, $163,000; Land Improvements, $65,200; Building, $97,800
   c. Land, $150,000; Land Improvements, $61,600; Building, $92,400
   d. Land, $159,000; Land Improvements, $65,200; Building, $95,400
   e. Land, $175,000; Land Improvements, $70,000; Building, $105,000

2. A company purchased a truck for $35,000 on January 1, 2007. The truck is estimated to have a useful life of four years and an estimated salvage value of $1,000. Assuming that the company uses straight-line depreciation, what is depreciation expense on the truck for the year ended December 31, 2008?
   a. $8,750
   b. $17,500
   c. $8,500
   d. $17,000
   e. $25,500

3. A company purchased machinery for $10,800,000 on January 1, 2007. The machinery has a useful life of 10 years

and an estimated salvage value of $800,000. What is depreciation expense on the machinery for the year ended December 31, 2008, assuming that the double-declining-balance method is used?
   a. $2,160,000
   b. $3,888,000
   c. $1,728,000
   d. $2,000,000
   e. $1,600,000

4. A company sold a machine that originally cost $250,000 for $120,000 when accumulated depreciation on the machine was $100,000. The gain or loss recorded on the sale of this machine is
   a. $0 gain or loss.
   b. $120,000 gain.
   c. $30,000 loss.
   d. $30,000 gain.
   e. $150,000 loss.

5. A company had average total assets of $500,000, gross sales of $575,000, and net sales of $550,000. The company's total asset turnover is
   a. 1.15
   b. 1.10
   c. 0.91
   d. 0.87
   e. 1.05

Superscript letter ᴬ *denotes assignments based on Appendix 10A.*

Discussion Questions

1. What characteristics of a plant asset make it different from other assets?

2. What is the general rule for costs inclusion for plant assets?

3. What is different between land and land improvements?

4. Why is the cost of a lump sum purchase allocated to the individual assets acquired?

5. Does the balance in the Accumulated Depreciation— Machinery account represent funds to replace the machinery when it wears out? If not, what does it represent?

6. Why is the Modified Accelerated Cost Recovery System not generally accepted for financial accounting purposes?

7. What accounting principle justifies charging low-cost plant asset purchases immediately to an expense account?

8. What is the difference between ordinary repairs and extraordinary repairs? How should each be recorded?

9. Identify events that might lead to disposal of a plant asset.

10. What is the process of allocating the cost of natural resources to expense as they are used?

11. Is the declining-balance method an acceptable way to compute depletion of natural resources? Explain.

12. What are the characteristics of an intangible asset?

13. What general procedures are applied in accounting for the acquisition and potential cost allocation of intangible assets?

14. When do we know that a company has goodwill? When can goodwill appear in a company's balance sheet?

15. Assume that a company buys another business and pays for its goodwill. If the company plans to incur costs each year to maintain the value of the goodwill, must it also amortize this goodwill?

16. How is total asset turnover computed? Why would a financial statement user be interested in total asset turnover?

17. Refer to **Best Buy**'s balance sheet in Appendix A. What plant and equipment assets does Best Buy list on its balance sheet? What is the book value of its total plant and equipment assets at February 26, 2005?

18. Refer to **Circuit City**'s balance sheet in Appendix A. What does it title its plant assets? What is the book value of its plant assets at February 28, 2005?

19. Refer to the September 25, 2004, balance sheet of **Apple** in Appendix A. What long-term assets discussed in this chapter are reported by the company?

 Red numbers denote Discussion Questions that involve decision-making.

QUICK STUDY

QS 10-1
Cost of plant assets

P1

Kegler Bowling installs automatic scorekeeping equipment with an invoice cost of $190,000. The electrical work required for the installation costs $20,000. Additional costs are $4,000 for delivery and $13,700 for sales tax. During the installation, a component of the equipment is carelessly left on a lane and hit by the automatic lane-cleaning machine. The cost of repairing the component is $1,850. What is the total recorded cost of the automatic scorekeeping equipment?

QS 10-2
Defining assets

C1

Identify the main difference between (1) plant assets and current assets, (2) plant assets and inventory, and (3) plant assets and long-term investments.

QS 10-3
Depreciation methods

P2

On January 2, 2008, the Cerritos Band acquires sound equipment for concert performances at a cost of $65,800. The band estimates it will use this equipment for four years, during which time it anticipates performing about 200 concerts. It estimates that after four years it can sell the equipment for $2,000. During year 2008, the band performs 45 concerts. Compute the year 2008 depreciation using the (1) straight-line method and (2) units-of-production method.

QS 10-4
Computing revised depreciation

C3

Refer to the facts in QS 10-3. Assume that Cerritos Band chose straight-line depreciation but realizes early in the second year that due to concert bookings beyond expectations, this equipment will last only a total of three years. The salvage value remains unchanged. Compute the revised depreciation for both the second and third years.

QS 10-5
Double-declining-balance method

P2

A fleet of refrigerated delivery trucks is acquired on January 5, 2008, at a cost of $830,000 with an estimated useful life of eight years and an estimated salvage value of $75,000. Compute the depreciation expense for the first three years using the double-declining-balance method.

QS 10-6
Revenue and capital expenditures

P3

1. Classify the following as either a revenue or a capital expenditure.
  a. Paid $40,000 cash to replace a compressor on a refrigeration system that extends its useful life by four years.
  b. Paid $200 cash per truck for the cost of their annual tune-ups.
  c. Paid $175 for the monthly cost of replacement filters on an air-conditioning system.
  d. Completed an addition to an office building for $225,000 cash.

2. Prepare the journal entries to record transactions *a* and *d* of part 1.

Hortez Co. owns equipment that cost $76,800, with accumulated depreciation of $40,800. Hortez sells the equipment for cash. Record the sale of the equipment assuming Hortez sells the equipment for (1) $47,000 cash, (2) $36,000 cash, and (3) $31,000 cash.

QS 10-7
Disposal of assets
P4

Corentine Company acquires an ore mine at a cost of $1,400,000. It incurs additional costs of $400,000 to access the mine, which is estimated to hold 1,000,000 tons of ore. The estimated value of the land after the ore is removed is $200,000.

1. Prepare the entry(ies) to record the cost of the ore mine.

2. Prepare the year-end adjusting entry if 180,000 tons of ore are mined and sold the first year.

QS 10-8
Natural resources and depletion
P5

Which of the following assets are reported on the balance sheet as intangible assets? Which are reported as natural resources? (a) Oil well, (b) Trademark, (c) Leasehold, (d) Gold mine, (e) Building, (f) Copyright, (g) Franchise, (h) Timberland.

QS 10-9
Classify assets
P5   P6

On January 4 of this year, Bibiana Boutique incurs a $105,000 cost to modernize its store. Improvements include new floors, ceilings, wiring, and wall coverings. These improvements are estimated to yield benefits for 10 years. Bibiana leases its store and has eight years remaining on the lease. Prepare the entry to record (1) the cost of modernization and (2) amortization at the end of this current year.

QS 10-10
Intangible assets and amortization
P6

Aneko Company reports the following ($ millions): net sales of $14,880 for 2008 and $13,990 for 2007; end-of-year total assets of $15,869 for 2008 and $17,819 for 2007. Compute its total asset turnover for 2008, and assess its level if competitors average a total asset turnover of 2.0 times.

QS 10-11
Computing total asset turnover
A2

Caleb Co. owns a machine that costs $42,400 with accumulated depreciation of $18,400. Caleb exchanges the machine for a newer model that has a market value of $52,000. Record the exchange assuming Caleb also paid cash of (1) $30,000 and the exchange has commercial substance, and (2) $22,000 and the exchange lacks commercial substance.

QS 10-12ᴬ
Asset exchange
P7

Rizio Co. purchases a machine for $12,500, terms 2/10, n/60, FOB shipping point. The seller prepaid the $360 freight charges, adding the amount to the invoice and bringing its total to $12,860. The machine requires special steel mounting and power connections costing $895. Another $475 is paid to assemble the machine and get it into operation. In moving the machine to its steel mounting, $180 in damages occurred. Also, $40 of materials is used in adjusting the machine to produce a satisfactory product. The adjustments are normal for this machine and are not the result of the damages. Compute the cost recorded for this machine. (Rizio pays for this machine within the cash discount period.)

EXERCISES

Exercise 10-1
Cost of plant assets
P1

Cala Manufacturing purchases a large lot on which an old building is located as part of its plans to build a new plant. The negotiated purchase price is $280,000 for the lot plus $110,000 for the old building. The company pays $33,500 to tear down the old building and $47,000 to fill and level the lot. It also pays a total of $1,540,000 in construction costs—this amount consists of $1,452,200 for the new building and $87,800 for lighting and paving a parking area next to the building. Prepare a single journal entry to record these costs incurred by Cala, all of which are paid in cash.

Exercise 10-2
Recording costs of assets
C1   P1

Exercise 10-3

Lump-sum purchase
of plant assets   C1

Liltua Company pays $375,280 for real estate plus $20,100 in closing costs. The real estate consists of land appraised at $157,040; land improvements appraised at $58,890; and a building appraised at $176,670. Allocate the total cost among the three purchased assets and prepare the journal entry to record the purchase.

Exercise 10-4

Depreciation methods

P2

In early January 2007, NewTech purchases computer equipment for $154,000 to use in operating activities for the next four years. It estimates the equipment's salvage value at $25,000. Prepare tables showing depreciation and book value for each of the four years assuming (1) straight-line and (2) double-declining-balance depreciation.

Exercise 10-5

Depreciation methods

P2

Check (3) $6,960

Ramirez Company installs a computerized manufacturing machine in its factory at the beginning of the year at a cost of $43,500. The machine's useful life is estimated at 10 years, or 385,000 units of product, with a $5,000 salvage value. During its second year, the machine produces 32,500 units of product. Determine the machine's second-year depreciation under the (1) straight-line, (2) units-of-production, and (3) double-declining-balance methods.

Exercise 10-6

Depreciation methods;
partial year depreciation   C3

On April 1, 2007, Cyclone Backhoe Co. purchases a trencher for $280,000. The machine is expected to last five years and have a salvage value of $40,000. Compute depreciation expense for year 2008 using the (1) straight-line and (2) double-declining-balance methods.

Exercise 10-7

Revising depreciation

C3

Check (2) $3,710

Apex Fitness Club uses straight-line depreciation for a machine costing $23,860, with an estimated four-year life and a $2,400 salvage value. At the beginning of the third year, Apex determines that the machine has three more years of remaining useful life, after which it will have an estimated $2,000 salvage value. Compute (1) the machine's book value at the end of its second year and (2) the amount of depreciation for each of the final three years given the revised estimates.

Exercise 10-8

Income effects of
depreciation methods

A1

Check (2) Year 3 NI, $54,170

Tory Enterprises pays $238,400 for equipment that will last five years and have a $43,600 salvage value. By using the machine in its operations for five years, the company expects to earn $88,500 annually, after deducting all expenses except depreciation. Prepare a table showing income before depreciation, depreciation expense, and net (pretax) income for each year and for the total five-year period, assuming (1) straight-line depreciation and (2) double-declining-balance depreciation.

Exercise 10-9

Extraordinary repairs;
plant asset age

P3

Check (3) $211,350

Veradis Company owns a building that appears on its prior year-end balance sheet at its original $572,000 cost less $429,000 accumulated depreciation. The building is depreciated on a straight-line basis assuming a 20-year life and no salvage value. During the first week in January of the current calendar year, major structural repairs are completed on the building at a $68,350 cost. The repairs extend its useful life for 7 years beyond the 20 years originally estimated.

1. Determine the building's age (plant asset age) as of the prior year-end balance sheet date.
2. Prepare the entry to record the cost of the structural repairs that are paid in cash.
3. Determine the book value of the building immediately after the repairs are recorded.
4. Prepare the entry to record the current calendar year's depreciation.

Oki Company pays $264,000 for equipment expected to last four years and have a $29,000 salvage value. Prepare journal entries to record the following costs related to the equipment.

1. During the second year of the equipment's life, $22,000 cash is paid for a new component expected to increase the equipment's productivity by 10% a year.

2. During the third year, $6,250 cash is paid for normal repairs necessary to keep the equipment in good working order.

3. During the fourth year, $14,870 is paid for repairs expected to increase the useful life of the equipment from four to five years.

Exercise 10-10
Ordinary repairs, extraordinary repairs and betterments
P3

Diaz Company owns a milling machine that cost $250,000 and has accumulated depreciation of $182,000. Prepare the entry to record the disposal of the milling machine on January 3 under each of the following independent situations.

1. The machine needed extensive repairs, and it was not worth repairing. Diaz disposed of the machine, receiving nothing in return.

2. Diaz sold the machine for $35,000 cash.

3. Diaz sold the machine for $68,000 cash.

4. Diaz sold the machine for $80,000 cash.

Exercise 10-11
Disposal of assets
P4

Rayya Co. purchases and installs a machine on January 1, 2007, at a total cost of $105,000. Straight-line depreciation is taken each year for four years assuming a seven-year life and no salvage value. The machine is disposed of on July 1, 2011, during its fifth year of service. Prepare entries to record the partial year's depreciation on July 1, 2011, and to record the disposal under the following separate assumptions: (1) the machine is sold for $45,500 cash and (2) Rayya receives an insurance settlement of $25,000 resulting from the total destruction of the machine in a fire.

Exercise 10-12
Partial year depreciation; disposal of plant asset
P4

On April 2, 2008, Montana Mining Co. pays $3,721,000 for an ore deposit containing 1,525,000 tons. The company installs machinery in the mine costing $213,500, with an estimated seven-year life and no salvage value. The machinery will be abandoned when the ore is completely mined. Montana began mining on May 1, 2008, and mined and sold 166,200 tons of ore during the remaining eight months of 2008. Prepare the December 31, 2008, entries to record both the ore deposit depletion and the mining machinery depreciation. Mining machinery depreciation should be in proportion to the mine's depletion.

Exercise 10-13
Depletion of natural resources
P2 P5

Milano Gallery purchases the copyright on an oil painting for $418,000 on January 1, 2008. The copyright legally protects its owner for 19 more years. However, the company plans to market and sell prints of the original for only 10 years. Prepare entries to record the purchase of the copyright on January 1, 2008, and its annual amortization on December 31, 2008.

Exercise 10-14
Amortization of intangible assets
P6

On January 1, 2008, Robinson Company purchased Franklin Company at a price of $2,500,000. The fair market value of the net assets purchased equals $1,800,000.

1. What is the amount of goodwill that Robinson records at the purchase date?

2. Explain how Robinson would determine the amount of goodwill amortization for the year ended December 31, 2008?

3. Robinson Company believes that its employees provide superior customer services, and through their efforts, Robinson Company believes it has created $900,000 of goodwill. How would Robinson Company record this goodwill?

Exercise 10-15
Goodwill
P6

Exercise 10-16

Cash flows related to assets

C1

Refer to the statement of cash flows for **Circuit City** in Appendix A for the fiscal year ended September 25, 2004, to answer the following:

1. What amount of cash is used to purchase property and equipment?

2. How much depreciation and amortization are recorded?

3. What total amount of net cash is used in investing activities?

Exercise 10-17

Evaluating efficient use of assets

A2

Lok Co. reports net sales of $5,865,000 for 2007 and $8,689,000 for 2008. End-of-year balances for total assets are: 2006, $1,686,000; 2007, $1,800,000; and 2008, $1,982,000. (*a*) Compute Lok's total asset turnover for 2007 and 2008. (*b*) Comment on Lok's efficiency in using its assets if its competitors average a total asset turnover of 3.0.

Exercise 10-18[A]

Exchanging assets

P7

Check (2) $14,500

Gilly Construction trades in an old tractor for a new tractor, receiving a $29,000 trade-in allowance and paying the remaining $83,000 in cash. The old tractor had cost $96,000, and straight-line accumulated depreciation of $52,500 had been recorded to date under the assumption that it would last eight years and have a $12,000 salvage value. Answer the following questions assuming the exchange has commercial substance.

1. What is the book value of the old tractor at the time of exchange?

2. What is the loss on this asset exchange?

3. What amount should be recorded (debited) in the asset account for the new tractor?

Exercise 10-19[A]

Recording plant asset disposals

P4 P7

Check (2) Dr. Machinery, $54,575

On January 2, 2008, Bering Co. disposes of a machine costing $44,000 with accumulated depreciation of $24,625. Prepare the entries to record the disposal under each of the following separate assumptions.

1. Machine is sold for $18,250 cash.

2. Machine is traded in on a newer machine having a $60,200 cash price. A $25,000 trade-in allowance is received, and the balance is paid in cash. Assume the asset exchange lacks commercial substance.

3. Machine is traded in on a newer machine having a $60,200 cash price. A $15,000 trade-in allowance is received, and the balance is paid in cash. Assume the asset exchange has commercial substance.

PROBLEM SET A

Problem 10-1A

Plant asset costs;
depreciation methods

C1 C2 A1 P1 P2

mhhe.com/wildFAP18e

Check (2) $30,000

         (3) $10,800

Timberly Construction negotiates a lump-sum purchase of several assets from a company that is going out of business. The purchase is completed on January 1, 2008, at a total cash price of $900,000 for a building, land, land improvements, and four vehicles. The estimated market values of the assets are building, $508,800; land, $297,600; land improvements, $28,800; and four vehicles, $124,800. The company's fiscal year ends on December 31.

Required

1. Prepare a table to allocate the lump-sum purchase price to the separate assets purchased. Prepare the journal entry to record the purchase.

2. Compute the depreciation expense for year 2008 on the building using the straight-line method, assuming a 15-year life and a $27,000 salvage value.

3. Compute the depreciation expense for year 2008 on the land improvements assuming a five-year life and double-declining-balance depreciation.

Analysis Component

4. Defend or refute this statement: Accelerated depreciation results in payment of less taxes over the asset's life.

Problem 10-2A

Asset cost allocation;
straight-line depreciation

C1 C2 P1 P2

mhhe.com/wildFAP18e

In January 2008, Mitzu Co. pays $2,600,000 for a tract of land with two buildings on it. It plans to demolish Building 1 and build a new store in its place. Building 2 will be a company office; it is appraised at $644,000, with a useful life of 20 years and a $60,000 salvage value. A lighted parking lot near Building 1 has improvements (Land Improvements 1) valued at $420,000 that are expected to last another 12 years with no salvage value. Without the buildings and improvements, the tract of land is valued at $1,736,000. Mitzu also incurs the following additional costs:

Cost to demolish Building 1	$ 328,400
Cost of additional land grading	175,400
Cost to construct new building (Building 3), having a useful life of 25 years and a $392,000 salvage value	2,202,000
Cost of new land improvements (Land Improvements 2) near Building 2 having a 20-year useful life and no salvage value	164,000

Required

1. Prepare a table with the following column headings: Land, Building 2, Building 3, Land Improvements 1, and Land Improvements 2. Allocate the costs incurred by Mitzu to the appropriate columns and total each column.

2. Prepare a single journal entry to record all the incurred costs assuming they are paid in cash on January 1, 2008.

3. Using the straight-line method, prepare the December 31 adjusting entries to record depreciation for the 12 months of 2008 when these assets were in use.

Check (1) Land costs, $2,115,800; Building 2 costs, $598,000

(3) Depr.—Land Improv. 1 and 2, $32,500 and $8,200

Champion Contractors completed the following transactions and events involving the purchase and operation of equipment in its business.

2007

Jan. 1 Paid $287,600 cash plus $11,500 in sales tax and $1,500 in transportation (FOB shipping point) for a new loader. The loader is estimated to have a four-year life and a $20,600 salvage value. Loader costs are recorded in the Equipment account.

Jan. 3 Paid $4,800 to enclose the cab and install air conditioning in the loader to enable operations under harsher conditions. This increased the estimated salvage value of the loader by another $1,400.

Dec. 31 Recorded annual straight-line depreciation on the loader.

2008

Jan. 1 Paid $5,400 to overhaul the loader's engine, which increased the loader's estimated useful life by two years.

Feb. 17 Paid $820 to repair the loader after the operator backs it into a tree.

Dec. 31 Recorded annual straight-line depreciation on the loader.

Required

Prepare journal entries to record these transactions and events.

Problem 10-3A
Computing and revising depreciation; revenue and capital expenditures

C3 P1 P3

Check Dec. 31, 2007, Dr. Depr. Expense—Equip., $70,850

Check Dec. 31, 2008, Dr. Depr. Expense—Equip., $43,590

Yoshi Company completed the following transactions and events involving its delivery trucks.

2007

Jan. 1 Paid $20,515 cash plus $1,485 in sales tax for a new delivery truck estimated to have a five-year life and a $2,000 salvage value. Delivery truck costs are recorded in the Trucks account.

Dec. 31 Recorded annual straight-line depreciation on the truck.

2008

Dec. 31 Due to new information obtained earlier in the year, the truck's estimated useful life was changed from five to four years, and the estimated salvage value was increased to $2,400. Recorded annual straight-line depreciation on the truck.

2009

Dec. 31 Recorded annual straight-line depreciation on the truck.

Dec. 31 Sold the truck for $5,300 cash.

Required

Prepare journal entries to record these transactions and events.

Problem 10-4A
Computing and revising depreciation; selling plant assets

C3 P2 P4

Check Dec. 31, 2008, Dr. Depr. Expense—Trucks, $5,200

Dec. 31, 2009, Dr. Loss on Disposal of Trucks, $2,300

Problem 10-5A
Depreciation methods

A1 P2

A machine costing $257,500 with a four-year life and an estimated $20,000 salvage value is installed in Luther Company's factory on January 1. The factory manager estimates the machine will produce 475,000 units of product during its life. It actually produces the following units: year 1, 220,000; year 2, 124,600; year 3, 121,800; and year 4, 15,200. The total number of units produced by the end of year 4 exceeds the original estimate—this difference was not predicted. (The machine must not be depreciated below its estimated salvage value.)

Required

Prepare a table with the following column headings and compute depreciation for each year (and total depreciation of all years combined) for the machine under each depreciation method.

Check Year 4: Units-of-Production Depreciation, $4,300; DDB Depreciation, $12,187

Year	Straight-Line	Units-of-Production	Double-Declining-Balance

Problem 10-6A
Disposal of plant assets

P1 P2 P4

Onslow Co. purchases a used machine for $178,000 cash on January 2 and readies it for use the next day at a $2,840 cost. On January 3, it is installed on a required operating platform costing $1,160, and it is further readied for operations. The company predicts the machine will be used for six years and have a $14,000 salvage value. Depreciation is to be charged on a straight-line basis. On December 31, at the end of its fifth year in operations, it is disposed of.

Required

1. Prepare journal entries to record the machine's purchase and the costs to ready and install it. Cash is paid for all costs incurred.

Check (2b) Depr. Exp., $28,000

2. Prepare journal entries to record depreciation of the machine at December 31 of (a) its first year in operations and (b) the year of its disposal.

3. Prepare journal entries to record the machine's disposal under each of the following separate assumptions: (a) it is sold for $15,000 cash; (b) it is sold for $50,000 cash; and (c) it is destroyed in a fire and the insurance company pays $30,000 cash to settle the loss claim.

(3c) Dr. Loss from Fire, $12,000

Problem 10-7A
Natural resources

P5

On July 23 of the current year, Dakota Mining Co. pays $4,715,000 for land estimated to contain 5,125,000 tons of recoverable ore. It installs machinery costing $410,000 that has a 10-year life and no salvage value and is capable of mining the ore deposit in eight years. The machinery is paid for on July 25, seven days before mining operations begin. The company removes and sells 480,000 tons of ore during its first five months of operations. Depreciation of the machinery is in proportion to the mine's depletion as the machinery will be abandoned after the ore is mined.

Required

Check (c) Depletion, $441,600
(d) Depreciation, $38,400

Prepare entries to record (a) the purchase of the land, (b) the cost and installation of machinery, (c) the first five months' depletion assuming the land has a net salvage value of zero after the ore is mined, and (d) the first five months' depreciation on machinery.

Analysis Component

Describe both the similarities and differences in amortization, depletion, and depreciation.

Problem 10-8A
Intangible assets

P6

On July 1, 2003, Falk Company signed a contract to lease space in a building for 15 years. The lease contract calls for annual (prepaid) rental payments of $80,000 on each July 1 throughout the life of the lease and for the lessee to pay for all additions and improvements to the leased property. On June 25, 2008, Falk decides to sublease the space to Ryan & Associates for the remaining 10 years of the lease—Ryan pays $200,000 to Falk for the right to sublease and it agrees to assume the obligation to pay the $80,000 annual rent to the building owner beginning July 1, 2008. After taking possession of the leased space, Ryan pays for improving the office portion of the leased space at a $130,000 cost. The improvements are paid for on July 5, 2008, and are estimated to have a useful life equal to the 16 years remaining in the life of the building.

Required

1. Prepare entries for Ryan to record (*a*) its payment to Falk for the right to sublease the building space, (*b*) its payment of the 2008 annual rent to the building owner, and (*c*) its payment for the office improvements.

2. Prepare Ryan's year-end adjusting entries required at December 31, 2008, to (*a*) amortize the $200,000 cost of the sublease, (*b*) amortize the office improvements, and (*c*) record rent expense.

Nagy Company negotiates a lump-sum purchase of several assets from a contractor who is relocating. The purchase is completed on January 1, 2008, at a total cash price of $1,800,000 for a building, land, land improvements, and five trucks. The estimated market values of the assets are building, $890,000; land, $427,200; land improvements, $249,200; and five trucks, $213,600. The company's fiscal year ends on December 31.

PROBLEM SET B

Problem 10-1B
Plant asset costs; depreciation methods

C1 C2 A1 P1 P2

Required

1. Prepare a table to allocate the lump-sum purchase price to the separate assets purchased. Prepare the journal entry to record the purchase.

2. Compute the depreciation expense for year 2008 on the building using the straight-line method, assuming a 12-year life and a $120,000 salvage value.

3. Compute the depreciation expense for year 2008 on the land improvements assuming a 10-year life and double-declining-balance depreciation.

Analysis Component

4. Defend or refute this statement: Accelerated depreciation results in payment of more taxes over the asset's life.

In January 2008, ProTech pays $1,550,000 for a tract of land with two buildings. It plans to demolish Building A and build a new shop in its place. Building B will be a company office; it is appraised at $482,800, with a useful life of 15 years and a $99,500 salvage value. A lighted parking lot near Building B has improvements (Land Improvements B) valued at $142,000 that are expected to last another five years with no salvage value. Without the buildings and improvements, the tract of land is valued at $795,200. ProTech also incurs the following additional costs.

Problem 10-2B
Asset cost allocation; straight-line depreciation

C1 C2 P1 P2

Cost to demolish Building A	$ 122,000
Cost of additional land grading	174,500
Cost to construct new building (Building C), having a useful life of 20 years and a $258,000 salvage value	1,458,000
Cost of new land improvements (Land Improvements C) near building C, having a 10-year useful life and no salvage value	103,500

Required

1. Prepare a table with the following column headings: Land, Building B, Building C, Land Improvements B, and Land Improvements C. Allocate the costs incurred by ProTech to the appropriate columns and total each column.

2. Prepare a single journal entry to record all incurred costs assuming they are paid in cash on January 1, 2008.

3. Using the straight-line method, prepare the December 31 adjusting entries to record depreciation for the 12 months of 2008 when these assets were in use.

Mercury Delivery Service completed the following transactions and events involving the purchase and operation of equipment for its business.

Problem 10-3B
Computing and revising depreciation; revenue and capital expenditures

C3 P1 P3

2007

Jan. 1 Paid $25,860 cash plus $1,810 in sales tax for a new delivery van that was estimated to have a five-year life and a $3,670 salvage value. Van costs are recorded in the Equipment account.

Jan. 3 Paid $1,850 to install sorting racks in the van for more accurate and quicker delivery of packages. This increases the estimated salvage value of the van by another $230.

Dec. 31 Recorded annual straight-line depreciation on the van.

2008

Jan.   1   Paid $2,080 to overhaul the van's engine, which increased the van's estimated useful life by
            two years.
May 10   Paid $800 to repair the van after the driver backed it into a loading dock.
Dec. 31   Record annual straight-line depreciation on the van. (Round to the nearest dollar.)

Check   Dec. 31, 2008, Dr. Depr.
Expense—Equip., $3,763

Required

Prepare journal entries to record these transactions and events.

Problem 10-4B
Computing and revising
depreciation; selling plant assets

C3   P2   P4

York Instruments completed the following transactions and events involving its machinery.

2007

Jan.   1   Paid $107,800 cash plus $6,470 in sales tax for a new machine. The machine is estimated to
            have a six-year life and a $9,720 salvage value.
Dec. 31   Recorded annual straight-line depreciation on the machinery.

2008

Check   Dec. 31, 2008, Dr. Depr.
Expense—Machinery, $27,500

Dec. 31   Due to new information obtained earlier in the year, the machine's estimated useful life was
            changed from six to four years, and the estimated salvage value was increased to $14,345.
            Recorded annual straight-line depreciation on the machinery.

2009

Dec. 31, 2009, Dr. Loss on
Disposal of Machine, $16,605

Dec. 31   Recorded annual straight-line depreciation on the machinery.
Dec. 31   Sold the machine for $25,240 cash.

Required

Prepare journal entries to record these transactions and events.

Problem 10-5B
Depreciation methods

A1   P2

On January 2, Manning Co. purchases and installs a new machine costing $324,000 with a five-year life
and an estimated $30,000 salvage value. Management estimates the machine will produce 1,470,000 units
of product during its life. Actual production of units is as follows: year 1, 355,600; year 2, 320,400; year 3,
317,000; year 4, 343,600; and year 5, 138,500. The total number of units produced by the end of year 5
exceeds the original estimate—this difference was not predicted. (The machine must not be depreciated
below its estimated salvage value.)

Required

Prepare a table with the following column headings and compute depreciation for each year (and total
depreciation of all years combined) for the machine under each depreciation method.

Check   DDB depreciation, Year 3,
$46,656; U-of-P depreciation, Year 4,
$68,720

Year	Straight-Line	Units-of-Production	Double-Declining-Balance

---

Problem 10-6B
Disposal of plant assets

P1   P2   P4

On January 1, Walker purchases a used machine for $150,000 and readies it for use the next day at a
cost of $3,510. On January 4, it is mounted on a required operating platform costing $4,600, and it is
further readied for operations. Management estimates the machine will be used for seven years and have
an $18,110 salvage value. Depreciation is to be charged on a straight-line basis. On December 31, at the
end of its sixth year of use, the machine is disposed of.

Required

Check   (2b) Depr. Exp., $20,000

1. Prepare journal entries to record the machine's purchase and the costs to ready and install it. Cash
     is paid for all costs incurred.

2. Prepare journal entries to record depreciation of the machine at December 31 of (*a*) its first year in
     operations and, (*b*) the year of its disposal.

(3c) Dr. Loss from Fire,
$13,110

3. Prepare journal entries to record the machine's disposal under each of the following separate as-
     sumptions: (*a*) it is sold for $28,000 cash; (*b*) it is sold for $52,000 cash; and (*c*) it is destroyed in a
     fire and the insurance company pays $25,000 cash to settle the loss claim.

On February 19 of the current year, Quartzite Co. pays $5,400,000 for land estimated to contain 4 million tons of recoverable ore. It installs machinery costing $400,000 that has a 16-year life and no salvage value and is capable of mining the ore deposit in 12 years. The machinery is paid for on March 21, eleven days before mining operations begin. The company removes and sells 254,000 tons of ore during its first nine months of operations. Depreciation of the machinery is in proportion to the mine's depletion as the machinery will be abandoned after the ore is mined.

Problem 10-7B
Natural resources
P5

Required

Prepare entries to record (*a*) the purchase of the land, (*b*) the cost and installation of machinery, (*c*) the first nine months' depletion assuming the land has a net salvage value of zero after the ore is mined, and (*d*) the first nine months' depreciation on machinery.

Check (*c*) Depletion, $342,900;
(*d*) Depreciation, $25,400

Analysis Component

Describe both the similarities and differences in amortization, depletion, and depreciation.

On January 1, 2001, Mason Co. entered into a 12-year lease on a building. The lease contract requires (1) annual (prepaid) rental payments of $36,000 each January 1 throughout the life of the lease and (2) for the lessee to pay for all additions and improvements to the leased property. On January 1, 2008, Mason decides to sublease the space to Stewart Co. for the remaining five years of the lease—Stewart pays $40,000 to Mason for the right to sublease and agrees to assume the obligation to pay the $36,000 annual rent to the building owner beginning January 1, 2008. After taking possession of the leased space, Stewart pays for improving the office portion of the leased space at a $20,000 cost. The improvements are paid for on January 3, 2008, and are estimated to have a useful life equal to the 13 years remaining in the life of the building.

Problem 10-8B
Intangible assets
P6

Required

1. Prepare entries for Stewart to record (*a*) its payment to Mason for the right to sublease the building space, (*b*) its payment of the 2008 annual rent to the building owner, and (*c*) its payment for the office improvements.
2. Prepare Stewart's year-end adjusting entries required on December 31, 2008, to (*a*) amortize the $40,000 cost of the sublease, (*b*) amortize the office improvements, and (*c*) record rent expense.

Check Dr. Rent Expense: (2*a*) $8,000,
(2*c*) $36,000

 Problem Set C is available at the book's Website to further reinforce and assess your learning.

PROBLEM SET C

(This serial problem began in Chapter 1 and continues through most of the book. If previous chapter segments were not completed, the serial problem can begin at this point. It is helpful, but not necessary, for you to use the Working Papers that accompany the book.)

SERIAL PROBLEM

Success Systems

SP 10 Selected ledger account balances for Success Systems follow.

	For Three Months Ended December 31, 2007	For Three Months Ended March 31, 2008
Office equipment	$ 10,000	$ 10,000
Accumulated depreciation— . . . . Office equipment	625	1,250
Computer equipment	25,000	25,000
Accumulated depreciation— . . . . Computer equipment	1,250	2,500
Total revenue	36,170	51,195
Total assets	122,635	147,621

Required

1. Assume that Success Systems does not acquire additional office equipment or computer equipment in 2008. Compute the amounts for the year ended December 31, 2008, for Depreciation Expense—Office Equipment and for Depreciation Expense—Computer Equipment (assume use of the straight-line method).

2. Given the assumptions in part 1, what is the book value of both the Office Equipment account and the Computer Equipment account as of December 31, 2008?

3. Compute the 3-month total asset turnover for Success Systems as of March 31, 2008. Use total revenue for the numerator and average the December 31, 2007, total assets and the March 31, 2008, total assets for the denominator. Interpret its total asset turnover if competitors average 2.5 for annual periods.

BEYOND THE NUMBERS

REPORTING IN ACTION

A1   A2

BTN 10-1   Refer to the financial statements of **Best Buy** in Appendix A to answer the following.

1. What percent of the original cost of Best Buy's property and equipment remains to be depreciated as of February 26, 2005, and at February 28, 2004? Assume these assets have no salvage value.

2. Over what length(s) of time is Best Buy amortizing its intangible assets?

3. What is the change in total property and equipment (before accumulated depreciation) for the year ended February 26, 2005? What is the amount of cash provided (used) by investing activities for property and equipment for the year ended February 26, 2005? What is one possible explanation for the difference between these two amounts?

4. Compute its total asset turnover for the year ended February 26, 2005, and the year ended February 28, 2004. Assume total assets at March 1, 2003 are $7,694 ($ millions).

Fast Forward

5. Access Best Buy's financial statements for fiscal years ending after February 26, 2005, at its Website (**BestBuy.com**) or the SEC's EDGAR database (**www.SEC.gov**). Recompute Best Buy's total asset turnover for the additional years' data you collect. Comment on any differences relative to the turnover computed in part 4.

COMPARATIVE ANALYSIS

A2

BTN 10-2   Key comparative figures ($ millions) for **Best Buy** and **Circuit City** follow.

Key Figures	Best Buy			Circuit City		
	Current Year	One Year Prior	Two Years Prior	Current Year	One Year Prior	Two Years Prior
Total assets	$10,294	$ 8,652	$ 7,694	$ 3,789	$3,731	$ 3,945
Net sales	27,433	24,548	20,943	10,472	9,857	10,055

Required

1. Compute total asset turnover for the most recent two years for both Best Buy and Circuit City using the data shown.

2. Which company is more efficient in generating net sales given the total assets it employs? Assume an industry average of 2.4.

ETHICS CHALLENGE

C1   C2

BTN 10-3   Flo Choi owns a small business and manages its accounting. Her company just finished a year in which a large amount of borrowed funds was invested in a new building addition as well as in equipment and fixture additions. Choi's banker requires her to submit semiannual financial statements so he can monitor the financial health of her business. He has warned her that if profit margins erode, he might raise the interest rate on the borrowed funds to reflect the increased loan risk from the bank's point of view. Choi knows profit margin is likely to decline this year. As she prepares year-end adjusting

entries, she decides to apply the following depreciation rule: All asset additions are considered to be in use on the first day of the following month. (The previous rule assumed assets are in use on the first day of the month nearest to the purchase date.)

Required

1. Identify decisions that managers like Choi must make in applying depreciation methods.

2. Is Choi's rule an ethical violation, or is it a legitimate decision in computing depreciation?

3. How will Choi's new depreciation rule affect the profit margin of her business?

BTN 10-4 Teams are to select an industry, and each team member is to select a different company in that industry. Each team member is to acquire the financial statements (form 10-K) of the company selected—see the company's Website or the SEC's EDGAR database (www.sec.gov). Use the financial statements to compute total asset turnover. Communicate with teammates via a meeting, e-mail, or telephone to discuss the meaning of this ratio, how different companies compare to each other, and the industry norm. The team must prepare a one-page report that describes the ratios for each company and identifies the conclusions reached during the team's discussion.

COMMUNICATING IN PRACTICE

A2

BTN 10-5 Access the **Yahoo!** (ticker: YHOO) 10-K report for the year ended December 31, 2004, filed on March 11, 2005, at www.sec.gov.

TAKING IT TO THE NET

C1 P6

Required

1. What amount of goodwill is reported on Yahoo!'s balance sheet? What percentage of total assets does its goodwill represent? Is goodwill a major asset for Yahoo! Explain.

2. Locate Note 4 to its financial statements. Identify the change in goodwill from January 1, 2003, to December 31, 2004. Comment on the change in goodwill over this period.

3. Locate Note 5 to its financial statements. What other intangible assets does Yahoo! report at December 31, 2004? What proportion of total assets do the other intangibles represent?

4. What does Yahoo! indicate is the life of "Trademark, trade name, and domain name" according to its Note 5? Comment on the difference between the estimated economic life and the legal life of Yahoo!'s trademark.

BTN 10-6 Each team member is to become an expert on one depreciation method to facilitate teammates' understanding of that method. Follow these procedures:

a. Each team member is to select an area for expertise from one of the following depreciation methods: straight-line, units-of-production, or double-declining-balance.

b. Expert teams are to be formed from those who have selected the same area of expertise. The instructor will identify the location where each expert team meets.

c. Using the following data, expert teams are to collaborate and develop a presentation answering the requirements. Expert team members must write the presentation in a format they can show to their learning teams.

Data and Requirements On January 8, 2007, Whitewater Riders purchases a van to transport rafters back to the point of departure at the conclusion of the rafting adventures they operate. The cost of the van is $44,000. It has an estimated salvage value of $2,000 and is expected to be used for four years and driven 60,000 miles. The van is driven 12,000 miles in 2007, 18,000 miles in 2008, 21,000 in 2009, and 10,000 in 2010.

1. Compute annual depreciation expense for each year of the van's estimated useful life.

2. Explain when and how annual depreciation is recorded.

3. Explain the impact on income of this depreciation method versus others over the van's life.

4. Identify the van's book value for each year of its life and illustrate the reporting of this amount for any one year.

d. Re-form original learning teams. In rotation, experts are to present to their teams the results from part *c*. Experts are to encourage and respond to questions.

TEAMWORK IN ACTION

C2 A1 P2

Point: This activity can follow an overview of each method. Step 1 allows for three areas of expertise. Larger teams will have some duplication of areas, but the straight-line choice should not be duplicated. Expert teams can use the book and consult with the instructor.

**BusinessWeek
ACTIVITY**

C1 P6

BTN 10-7   Read the article "Global Brands" from the August 1, 2005, issue of *BusinessWeek*. (The book's Website provides a free link.)

Required

1. How does *BusinessWeek* determine the value of a brand?

2. What five brands have increased in value the most from 2004 to 2005?

3. If you reviewed the financial statements of the companies that own the five brands identified in part 2, would you expect to see those asset values reported on their balance sheets? Explain. (You might look at **Apple**'s balance sheet in Appendix A to see if you can find the value of its intangible assets. Does it match up with the brand value as determined by *BusinessWeek?*)

**ENTREPRENEURIAL
DECISION**

A2

BTN 10-8   Review the chapter's opening feature involving **Fairytale Brownies**. The company currently has net sales of $8,000,000. Assume that it is planning an expansion that will increase net sales by $4,000,000. To accomplish this expansion, Fairytale Brownies must increase its average total assets from $2,500,000 to $3,000,000.

Required

1. Compute the company's total asset turnover under (*a*) current conditions and (*b*) proposed conditions.

2. Evaluate and comment on the merits of the proposal given your analysis in part 1. Identify any concerns you would express about the proposal.

**HITTING THE
ROAD**

C1 P5 P6

BTN 10-9   Team up with one or more classmates for this activity. Identify companies in your community or area that must account for at least one of the following assets: natural resource; patent; lease; leasehold improvement; copyright; trademark; or goodwill. You might find a company having more than one type of asset. Once you identify a company with a specific asset, describe the accounting this company uses to allocate the cost of that asset to the periods benefited from its use.

GLOBAL DECISION

A2

BTN 10-10   **Dixons**, **Best Buy**, and **Circuit City** are all competitors in the global marketplace. Key comparative figures (in millions) for these companies' recent annual accounting periods follow.

Key Figures	Dixons (£ millions)			Best Buy		Circuit City	
	Current Year	Prior Year	Two Years Prior	Current Year	Prior Year	Current Year	Prior Year
Total assets	£3,980.5	£3,873.8	£4,158.0	$10,294	$ 8,652	$ 3,789	$ 3,731
Net sales	6,982.7	6,491.7	5,758.4	27,433	24,548	10,472	9,857
Total asset turnover	?	?	—	2.90	3.00	2.79	2.57

Required

1. Compute total asset turnover for the most recent two years for Dixons using the data shown.

2. Which company of the three is most efficient in generating net sales given the total assets it employs?

ANSWERS TO MULTIPLE CHOICE QUIZ

1. b;

	Appraisal Value	%	Total Cost	Allocated
Land	$175,000	50%	$326,000	$163,000
Land improvements	70,000	20	326,000	65,200
Building	105,000	30	326,000	97,800
Totals	$350,000			$326,000

2. c; ($35,000 − $1,000)/4 years = $8,500 per year.

3. c; 2007: $10,800,000 × (2 × 10%) = $2,160,000
      2008: ($10,800,000 − $2,160,000) × (2 × 10%) = $1,728,000

4. c;

Cost of machine	$250,000
Accumulated depreciation	100,000
Book value	150,000
Cash received	120,000
Loss on sale	$ 30,000

5. b; $550,000/$500,000 = 1.10

11

Current Liabilities and Payroll Accounting

A Look Back

Chapter 10 focused on long-term assets including plant assets, natural resources, and intangibles. We showed how to account for and analyze those assets.

A Look at This Chapter

This chapter emphasizes current liabilities. We explain how to identify, compute, record, and report current liabilities in financial statements. We also analyze and interpret these liabilities, including those related to employee costs.

A Look Ahead

Chapter 12 explains the partnership form of organization. It also describes the accounting concepts and procedures for partnership transactions.

Learning Objectives

CAP

Conceptual

C1 Describe current and long-term liabilities and their characteristics. *(p. 428)*

C2 Identify and describe known current liabilities. *(p. 430)*

C3 Explain how to account for contingent liabilities. *(p. 439)*

Analytical

A1 Compute the times interest earned ratio and use it to analyze liabilities. *(p. 441)*

Procedural

P1 Prepare entries to account for short-term notes payable. *(p. 431)*

P2 Compute and record *employee* payroll deductions and liabilities. *(p. 433)*

P3 Compute and record *employer* payroll expenses and liabilities. *(p. 435)*

P4 Account for estimated liabilities, including warranties and bonuses. *(p. 437)*

P5 *Appendix 11A*—Identify and describe the details of payroll reports, records, and procedures. *(p. 444)*

"You must follow through on your promises and do the best work you can"
—Youngsong Martin

Dressing Up for Business Success

FOUNTAIN VALLEY, CA—Youngsong Martin found the plain, dreary look of most social and business events extremely disappointing. She recalls, "I was too familiar with the institutional look of those metal-rimmed chairs in banquet halls and ballrooms, drab folding chairs at many outdoor events, and the rather ordinary tablecloths and napkins." Martin reacted by launching Wildflower Linen (**WildflowerLinens.com**) to provide custom table linens, chair covers, and sashes to dress up banquets, meetings, weddings, and special events of all sorts.

"I derive more pleasure than I had imagined," explains Martin. "It has been a dream come true to 'dress' entire events." Martin also enjoys the service side and getting "to know customers on a more personal level."

But the business side is where Martin needed the most help. "You don't really realize what's involved with running a business until you actually do it," says Martin. "I definitely needed help with the management and financial aspects." Martin needed to attend to many facets of business, including the important task of managing liabilities for payroll, supplies, employee benefits, vacations, training, and taxes. Her effective management of liabilities, especially payroll and employee benefits, was crucial to getting Wildflower where it is today. Martin stresses that if you want to succeed in business, then monitoring and controlling liabilities is a must.

"It's one thing to think you know where your money's going," stresses Martin. "But it's quite another to actually write expenses down and see how they affect your operations." This includes measuring and analyzing current liabilities. Martin says she must "analyze expenses and determine if they are necessary to help keep my business growing. It's almost like I'm getting an MBA." With nearly 15 employees and growing revenue, Martin has dressed up her business with more than just linens.

[Sources: *Wildflower Linen Website,* January 2006; *SCORE.org Website,* July 2005; *Special Events Business Advisors Website,* July 2005]

Previous chapters introduced liabilities such as accounts payable, notes payable, wages payable, and unearned revenues. This chapter further explains these liabilities and additional ones such as warranties, taxes, payroll, vacation pay, and bonuses. It also describes contingent liabilities and introduces some basic long-term liabilities. The focus is on how to define, classify, measure, report, and analyze these liabilities so that this information is useful to business decision makers.

Current Liabilities and Payroll Accounting

Liability Characteristics	Known Liabilities	Estimated Liabilities	Contingent Liabilities
• Definition • Classification • Uncertainty	• Accounts payable • Sales taxes payable • Unearned revenues • Short-term notes • Payroll liabilities	• Health and pension benefits • Vacation benefits • Bonus plans • Warranty liabilities	• Accounting for contingencies • Reasonably possible contingencies

Characteristics of Liabilities

This section discusses important characteristics of liabilities and how liabilities are classified and reported.

Defining Liabilities

C1 Describe current and long-term liabilities and their characteristics.

A *liability* is a probable future payment of assets or services that a company is presently obligated to make as a result of past transactions or events. This definition includes three crucial factors:

■ A past transaction or event.
■ A present obligation.
■ A future payment of assets or services.

Exhibit 11.1

Characteristics of a Liability

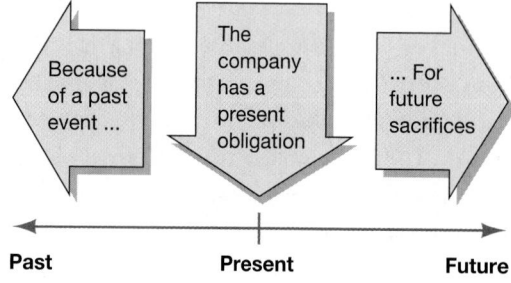

Because of a past event ...

The company has a present obligation

... For future sacrifices

Past   Present   Future

These three important elements are portrayed visually in Exhibit 11.1. Liabilities do not include all expected future payments. For example, most companies expect to pay wages to their employees in upcoming months and years, but these future payments are not liabilities because no past event such as employee work resulted in a present obligation. Instead, such liabilities arise when employees perform their work and earn the wages.

Classifying Liabilities

Information about liabilities is more useful when the balance sheet identifies them as either current or long term. Decision makers need to know when obligations are due so they can plan for them and take appropriate action.

Current Liabilities **Current liabilities,** also called *short-term liabilities,* are obligations due within one year or the company's operating cycle, whichever is longer. They are expected to be paid using current assets or by creating other current liabilities. Common examples of current liabilities are accounts payable, short-term notes payable, wages payable, warranty liabilities, lease liabilities, taxes payable, and unearned revenues.

Current liabilities differ across companies because they depend on the type of company operations. **Univision Communications**, for instance, reported the following current liabilities related to its Spanish-language media operations ($000s):

Point: Improper classification of liabilities can distort key ratios used in financial statement analysis and decision making.

Music copyright and artist royalties	$38,920
Program rights obligations	18,323
English programming	4,718

Harley-Davidson reports a much different set of current liabilities. It discloses current liabilities made up of items such as warranty, recall, and dealer incentive liabilities.

Long-Term Liabilities A company's obligations not expected to be paid within the longer of one year or the company's operating cycle are reported as **long-term liabilities.** They can include long-term notes payable, warranty liabilities, lease liabilities, and bonds payable. They are sometimes reported on the balance sheet in a single long-term liabilities total or in multiple categories. **Domino's Pizza**, for instance, reports long-term liabilities of $982 million. They are reported after current liabilities. A single liability also can be divided between the current and noncurrent sections if a company expects to make payments toward it in both the short and long term. Domino's reports ($ millions) long-term debt, $941; and current portion of long-term debt, $19. The second item is reported in current liabilities. We sometimes see liabilities that do not have a fixed due date but instead are payable on the creditor's demand. These are reported as current liabilities because of the possibility of payment in the near term. Exhibit 11.2 shows amounts of current liabilities and as a percent of total liabilities for selected companies.

Point: The current ratio will be overstated if a company fails to classify any portion of long-term debt due next period as a current liability.

Six Flags	$295 mil. 10%
AMF Bowling	$104 mil. 27%
K2 Inc	$349 mil. 45%
Apple Computer	$2,680 mil. 90%

As a percent of total liabilities

Exhibit 11.2

Current Liabilities of Selected Companies

Uncertainty in Liabilities

Accounting for liabilities involves addressing three important questions: Whom to pay? When to pay? How much to pay? Answers to these questions are often decided when a liability is incurred. For example, if a company has a $100 account payable to a specific individual, payable on March 15, the answers are clear. The company knows whom to pay, when to pay, and how much to pay. However, the answers to one or more of these questions are uncertain for some liabilities.

Uncertainty in Whom to Pay Liabilities can involve uncertainty in whom to pay. For instance, a company can create a liability with a known amount when issuing a note that is payable to its holder. In this case, a specific amount is payable to the note's holder at a specified date, but the company does not know who the holder is until that date. Despite this uncertainty, the company reports this liability on its balance sheet.

Point: An *accrued expense* is an unpaid expense that is also a liability. This is the reason accrued expenses are also called *accrued liabilities.*

Uncertainty in When to Pay   A company can have an obligation of a known amount to a known creditor but not know when it must be paid. For example, a legal services firm can accept fees in advance from a client who plans to use the firm's services in the future. This means that the firm has a liability that it settles by providing services at an unknown future date. Although this uncertainty exists, the legal firm's balance sheet must report this liability. These types of obligations are reported as current liabilities because they are likely to be settled in the short term.

Uncertainty in How Much to Pay   A company can be aware of an obligation but not know how much will be required to settle it. For example, a company using electrical power is billed only after the meter has been read. This cost is incurred and the liability created before a bill is received. A liability to the power company is reported as an estimated amount if the balance sheet is prepared before a bill arrives.

Quick Check   Answers—p. 452

1. What is a liability? Identify its crucial characteristics.
2. Is every expected future payment a liability?
3. If a liability is payable in 15 months, is it classified as current or long term?

Known (Determinable) Liabilities

Most liabilities arise from situations with little uncertainty. They are set by agreements, contracts, or laws and are measurable. These liabilities are **known liabilities,** also called *definitely determinable liabilities.* Known liabilities include accounts payable, notes payable, payroll, sales taxes, unearned revenues, and leases. We describe how to account for these known liabilities in this section.

Accounts Payable

C2   Identify and describe known current liabilities.

Accounts payable, or trade accounts payable, are amounts owed to suppliers for products or services purchased on credit. Accounting for accounts payable is primarily explained and illustrated in our discussion of merchandising activities in Chapters 5 and 6.

Sales Taxes Payable

Nearly all states and many cities levy taxes on retail sales. Sales taxes are stated as a percent of selling prices. The seller collects sales taxes from customers when sales occur and remits these collections (often monthly) to the proper government agency. Since sellers currently owe these collections to the government, this amount is a current liability. **Home Depot**, for instance, reports sales taxes payable of $412 million in its recent annual report. To illustrate, if Home Depot sells materials on August 31 for $6,000 cash that are subject to a 5% sales tax, the revenue portion of this transaction is recorded as follows:

Assets = Liabilities + Equity	Aug. 31	Cash......................................	6,300	
+6,300 +300 +6,000		Sales....................................		6,000
		Sales Taxes Payable ($6,000 × 0.05).........		300
		To record cash sales and 5% sales tax.		

Sales Taxes Payable is debited and Cash credited when it remits these collections to the government. Sales Taxes Payable is not an expense. It arises because laws require sellers to collect this cash from customers for the government.[1]

Unearned Revenues

Unearned revenues (also called *deferred revenues, collections in advance,* and *prepayments*) are amounts received in advance from customers for future products or services. Advance ticket sales for sporting events or music concerts are examples. The **Atlanta Falcons,** for instance, report "deferred game revenues" from advance ticket sales in its balance sheet. To illustrate, assume the Falcons sell $5 million of season tickets for 8 home games; its entry is

Point: To *defer* a revenue means to postpone recognition of a revenue collected in advance until it is earned. Sport teams must defer recognition of ticket sales until games are played.

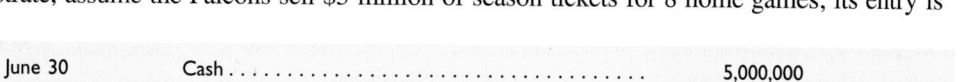

June 30	Cash.	5,000,000	
	Unearned Season Ticket Revenue.		5,000,000
	To record sale of season tickets.		

Assets = Liabilities + Equity
+5,000,000 +5,000,000

When a home game is played, the Falcons record revenue for that portion earned.

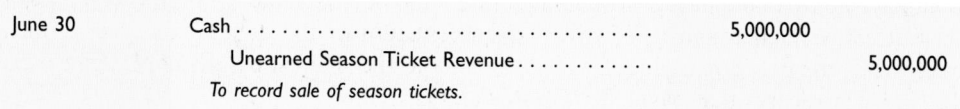

Oct. 31	Unearned Season Ticket Revenue	625,000	
	Season Ticket Revenue		625,000
	To record season ticket revenues earned.		

Assets = Liabilities + Equity
              −625,000   +625,000

Unearned Season Ticket Revenue is an unearned revenue account and is reported as a current liability. Unearned revenues also arise with airline ticket sales, magazine subscriptions, construction projects, hotel reservations, and custom orders.

Short-Term Notes Payable

A **short-term note payable** is a written promise to pay a specified amount on a definite future date within one year or the company's operating cycle, whichever is longer. These promissory notes are negotiable (as are checks), meaning they can be transferred from party to party by endorsement.

Decision Insight

Reward Programs   Gift card sales now exceed $100 billion annually, and reward (also called loyalty) programs are growing. There are no exact rules for how retailers account for rewards. When **Best Buy** launched its "Reward Zone," shoppers earned $5 on each $125 spent and had 90 days to spend it. Retailers make assumptions about how many reward program dollars will be spent and how to report it. Best Buy sets up a liability and reduces revenue by the same amount. **Talbots** does not reduce revenue but instead increases selling expense. **Men's Wearhouse** records rewards in cost of goods sold, whereas **Neiman Marcus** subtracts them from revenue. The FASB is reviewing reward programs.

The written documentation provided by notes is helpful in resolving disputes and for pursuing legal actions involving these liabilities. Most notes payable bear interest to compensate for use of the money until payment is made. Short-term notes payable can arise from many transactions. A company that purchases merchandise on credit can sometimes extend the credit period by signing a note to replace an account payable. Such notes also can arise when money is borrowed from a bank. We describe both of these cases.

P1 Prepare entries to account for short-term notes payable.

Point: Required characteristics for negotiability of a note: (1) unconditional promise, (2) in writing, (3) specific amount, and (4) definite due date.

Note Given to Extend Credit Period   A company can replace an account payable with a note payable. A common example is a creditor that requires the substitution of an interest-bearing note for an overdue account payable that does not bear interest. A less common situation

---

[1] Sales taxes can be computed from total sales receipts when sales taxes are not separately identified on the register. To illustrate, assume a 5% sales tax and $420 in total sales receipts (which includes sales taxes). Sales are computed as follows:

$$\text{Sales} = \text{Total sales receipts}/(1 + \text{Sales tax percentage}) = \$420/1.05 = \$400$$

Thus, the sales tax amount equals total sales receipts minus sales, or $420 − $400 = $20.

occurs when a debtor's weak financial condition motivates the creditor to accept a note, sometimes for a lesser amount, and to close the account to ensure that this customer makes no additional credit purchases.

To illustrate, let's assume that on August 23, Irwin asks to extend its past-due $600 account payable to McGraw. After some negotiations, McGraw agrees to accept $100 cash and a 60-day, 12%, $500 note payable to replace the account payable. Irwin records the transaction with this entry:

Assets = Liabilities + Equity
−100   −600
          +500

Aug. 23	Accounts Payable—McGraw.................	600	
	Cash		100
	Notes Payable—McGraw..................		500
	Gave $100 cash and a 60-day, 12% note for payment on account.		

Point: Accounts payable are detailed in a subsidiary ledger, but notes payable are sometimes not. A file with copies of notes often serves as a subsidiary ledger.

Signing the note does not resolve Irwin's debt. Instead, the form of debt is changed from an account payable to a note payable. McGraw prefers the note payable over the account payable because it earns interest and it is written documentation of the debt's existence, term, and amount. When the note comes due, Irwin pays the note and interest by giving McGraw a check for $510. Irwin records that payment with this entry:

Assets = Liabilities + Equity
−510   −500   −10

Oct. 22	Notes Payable—McGraw....................	500	
	Interest Expense	10	
	Cash		510
	Paid note with interest ($500 × 12% × 60/360).		

Point: Companies commonly compute interest using a 360-day year. This is known as the *banker's rule*.

Interest expense is computed by multiplying the principal of the note ($500) by the annual interest rate (12%) for the fraction of the year the note is outstanding (60 days/360 days).

Note Given to Borrow from Bank   A bank nearly always requires a borrower to sign a promissory note when making a loan. When the note matures, the borrower repays the note with an amount larger than the amount borrowed. The difference between the amount borrowed and the amount repaid is *interest*. This section considers a type of note whose signer promises to pay *principal* (the amount borrowed) plus interest. In this case, the *face value* of the note equals principal. Face value is the value shown on the face (front) of the note. To illustrate, assume that a company needs $2,000 for a project and borrows this money from a bank at 12% annual interest. The loan is made on September 30, 2007, and is due in 60 days. Specifically, the borrowing company signs a note with a face value equal to the amount borrowed. The note includes a statement similar to this: *"I promise to pay $2,000 plus interest at 12% within 60 days after September 30."* This simple note is shown in Exhibit 11.3.

Point: When money is borrowed from a bank, the loan is reported as an asset (receivable) on the bank's balance sheet.

Exhibit 11.3

Note with Face Value Equal to Amount Borrowed

Promissory Note	
$2,000	Sept. 30, 2007
Face Value	**Date**
Sixty days after date, _____I_____ promise to pay to the order of	
National Bank	
Boston, MA	
Two thousand and no/100 ----------------------------- **Dollars**	
plus interest at the annual rate of _12%_ .	
Janet Lee	

The borrower records its receipt of cash and the new liability with this entry:

Assets = Liabilities + Equity
+2,000   +2,000

Sept. 30	Cash..	2,000	
	Notes Payable..........................		2,000
	Borrowed $2,000 cash with a 60-day, 12%, $2,000 note.		

When principal and interest are paid, the borrower records payment with this entry:

Nov. 29	Notes Payable	2,000	
	Interest Expense	40	
	Cash		2,040
	Paid note with interest ($2,000 × 12% × 60/360).		

Assets = Liabilities + Equity
−2,040   −2,000   −40

End-of-period interest adjustment. When the end of an accounting period occurs between the signing of a note payable and its maturity date, the *matching principle* requires us to record the accrued but unpaid interest on the note. To illustrate, let's return to the note in Exhibit 11.3, but assume that the company borrows $2,000 cash on December 16, 2007, instead of September 30. This 60-day note matures on February 14, 2008, and the company's fiscal year ends on December 31. Thus, we need to record interest expense for the final 15 days in December.

Specifically, we know that 15 days of the 60-day loan period for the $2,000, 12% note have elapsed by December 31. This means that one-fourth (15 days/60 days) of the $40 total interest is an expense of year 2007. The borrower records this expense with the following adjusting entry:

2007			
Dec. 31	Interest Expense	10	
	Interest Payable		10
	To record accrued interest on note ($2,000 × 12% × 15/360).		

Assets = Liabilities + Equity
+10   −10

Example: If this note is dated December 1 instead of December 16, how much expense is recorded on December 31? *Answer:*
$2,000 × 12% × 30/360 = $20

When this note matures on February 14, the borrower must recognize 45 days of interest expense for year 2008 and remove the balances of the two liability accounts:

2008			
Feb. 14	Interest Expense*	30	
	Interest Payable	10	
	Notes Payable	2,000	
	Cash		2,040
	*Paid note with interest. *($2,000 × 12% × 45/360)*		

Assets = Liabilities + Equity
−2,040   −10   −30
             −2,000

Payroll Liabilities

An employer incurs several expenses and liabilities from having employees. These expenses and liabilities are often large and arise from salaries and wages earned, from employee benefits, and from payroll taxes levied on the employer. **Anheuser-Busch**, for instance, reports payroll-related current liabilities of more than $291 million from "accrued salaries, wages and benefits." We discuss payroll liabilities and related accounts in this section. The appendix to this chapter describes details about payroll reports, records, and procedures.

P2 Compute and record *employee* payroll deductions and liabilities.

Point: Internal control is important for payroll accounting. Managers must monitor (1) employee hiring, (2) timekeeping, (3) payroll listings, and (4) payroll payments. Poor controls led the U.S. Army to pay nearly $10 million to deserters, fictitious soldiers, and other unauthorized entities.

***Employee* Payroll Deductions**   **Gross pay** is the total compensation an employee earns including wages, salaries, commissions, bonuses, and any compensation earned before deductions such as taxes. (*Wages* usually refer to payments to employees at an hourly rate. *Salaries* usually refer to payments to employees at a monthly or yearly rate.) **Net pay,** also called

Decision Insight

A company's delay or failure to pay withholding taxes to the government has severe consequences. For example, a 100% penalty can be levied, with interest, on the unpaid balance. The government can even close a company, take its assets, and pursue legal actions against those involved.

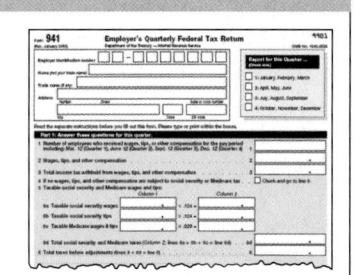

take-home pay, is gross pay less all deductions. **Payroll deductions,** commonly called *withholdings,* are amounts withheld from an employee's gross pay, either required or voluntary. Required deductions result from laws and include income taxes and Social Security taxes. Voluntary deductions, at an employee's option, include pension and health contributions, union dues, and charitable giving. Exhibit 11.4 shows the typical payroll deductions of an employee. The employer withholds payroll deductions from employees' pay and is obligated to transmit this money to the designated organization. The employer records payroll deductions as current liabilities until these amounts are transmitted. This section discusses the major payroll deductions.

Exhibit 11.4

Payroll Deductions

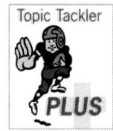

Topic Tackler
PLUS
11-1

Employee FICA taxes.   The federal Social Security system provides retirement, disability, survivorship, and medical benefits to qualified workers. Laws *require* employers to withhold **Federal Insurance Contributions Act (FICA) taxes** from employees' pay to cover costs of the system. Employers usually separate FICA taxes into two groups: (1) retirement, disability, and survivorship and (2) medical. For the first group, the Social Security system provides monthly cash payments to qualified retired workers for the rest of their lives. These payments are often called *Social Security benefits.* Taxes related to this group are often called *Social Security taxes.* For the second group, the system provides monthly payments to deceased workers' surviving families and to disabled workers who qualify for assistance. These payments are commonly called *Medicare benefits;* like those in the first group, they are paid with *Medicare taxes* (part of FICA taxes).

Law requires employers to withhold FICA taxes from each employee's salary or wages on each payday. The taxes for Social Security and Medicare are computed separately. For example, for the year 2006, the amount withheld from each employee's pay for Social Security tax was 6.2% of the first $94,200 the employee earns in the calendar year, or a maximum of $5,840. The Medicare tax was 1.45% of *all* amounts the employee earns; there is no maximum limit to Medicare tax.

Employers must pay withheld taxes to the Internal Revenue Service (IRS) on specific filing dates during the year. Employers who fail to send the withheld taxes to the IRS on time can be assessed substantial penalties. Until all the taxes are sent to the IRS, they are included in employers' current liabilities. For any changes in rates or with the maximum earnings level, check the IRS Website at **www.IRS.gov** or the SSA Website at **www.SSA.gov**.

Point: The sources of U.S. tax receipts are roughly as follows:

10%	Corporate income tax
50	Personal income tax
35	FICA and FUTA taxes
5	Other taxes

Employee income tax. Most employers are required to withhold federal income tax from each employee's paycheck. The amount withheld is computed using tables published by the IRS. The amount depends on the employee's annual earnings rate and the number of *withholding allowances* the employee claims. Allowances reduce the amount of taxes one owes the government. The more allowances one claims, the less tax the employer will withhold. Employees can claim allowances for themselves and their dependents. They also can claim additional allowances if they expect major declines in their taxable income for medical expenses. (An employee who claims more allowances than appropriate is subject to a fine.) Most states and many local governments require employers to withhold income taxes from employees' pay and to remit them promptly to the proper government agency. Until they are paid, withholdings are reported as a current liability on the employer's balance sheet.

Point: Part-time employees may claim "exempt from withholding" if they did not have any income tax liability in the prior year and do not expect any in the current year.

Point: IRS withholding tables are based on projecting weekly (or other period) pay into an annual figure.

Employee voluntary deductions. Beyond Social Security, Medicare, and income taxes, employers often withhold other amounts from employees' earnings. These withholdings arise from employee requests, contracts, unions, or other agreements. They can include amounts for charitable giving, medical insurance premiums, pension contributions, and union dues. Until they are paid, such withholdings are reported as part of employers' current liabilities.

Recording employee payroll deductions. Employers must accrue payroll expenses and liabilities at the end of each pay period. To illustrate, assume that an employee earns a salary of $2,000 per month. At the end of January, the employer's entry to accrue payroll expenses and liabilities for this employee is

Jan. 31	Salaries Expense............................	2,000	
	FICA—Social Security Taxes Payable (6.2%).....		124
	FICA—Medicare Taxes Payable (1.45%)........		29
	Employee Federal Income Taxes Payable*......		213
	Employee Medical Insurance Payable*.........		85
	Employee Union Dues Payable*.............		25
	Accrued Payroll Payable...................		1,524
	To record accrued payroll for January.		

Assets = Liabilities + Equity
+124 −2,000
+29
+213
+85
+25
+1,524

* Amounts taken from employer's accounting records.

Salaries Expense (debit) shows that the employee earns a gross salary of $2,000. The first five payables (credits) show the liabilities the employer owes on behalf of this employee to cover FICA taxes, income taxes, medical insurance, and union dues. The Accrued Payroll Payable account (credit) records the $1,524 net pay the employee receives from the $2,000 gross pay earned. When the employee is paid, another entry (or a series of entries) is required to record the check written and distributed (or funds transferred). The entry to record cash payment to this employee is to debit Accrued Payroll Payable and credit Cash for $1,524.

Employer Payroll Taxes Employers must pay payroll taxes in addition to those required of employees. Employer taxes include FICA and unemployment taxes.

Decision Insight

Baseball Liabilities Baseball's current liabilities include guaranteed player salaries. The Yankees have $148 million in 2006 guaranteed payroll, while the Pittsburgh Pirates have $6 million. Alex Rodriguez and Derek Jeter are each guaranteed over $20 million.

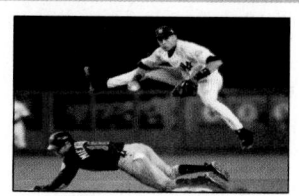

Employer FICA tax. Employers must pay FICA taxes *equal in amount to* the FICA taxes withheld from their employees. An employer's tax is credited to the same FICA Taxes Payable accounts used to record the Social Security and Medicare taxes withheld from employees. (A self-employed person must pay both the employee and employer FICA taxes.)

P3 Compute and record *employer* payroll expenses and liabilities.

Federal and state unemployment taxes. The federal government participates with states in a joint federal and state unemployment insurance program. Each state administers its program. These programs provide unemployment benefits to qualified workers. The federal government approves state programs and pays a portion of their administrative expenses.

Federal Unemployment Taxes (FUTA). Employers are subject to a federal unemployment tax on wages and salaries paid to their employees. For the year 2006, employers were required to pay FUTA taxes of as much as 6.2% of the first $7,000 earned by each employee. This federal tax can be reduced by a credit of up to 5.4% for taxes paid to a state program. As a result, the net federal unemployment tax is often only 0.8%.

State Unemployment Taxes (SUTA). All states support their unemployment insurance programs by placing a payroll tax on employers. (A few states require employees to make a contribution. In the book's assignments, we assume that this tax is only on the employer.) In most states, the base rate for SUTA taxes is 5.4% of the first $7,000 paid each employee. This base rate is adjusted according to an employer's merit rating. The state assigns a **merit rating** that reflects a company's stability or instability in employing workers. A good rating reflects stability in employment and means an employer can pay less than the 5.4% base rate. A low rating reflects high turnover or seasonal hirings and layoffs. To illustrate, an employer with 50 employees each of whom earns $7,000 or more per year saves $15,400 annually if it has a merit rating of 1.0% versus 5.4%. This is computed by comparing taxes of $18,900 at the 5.4% rate to only $3,500 at the 1.0% rate.

Decision Ethics

Answer—p. 452

Web Designer You take a summer job working for a family friend who runs a small IT service. On your first payday, the owner slaps you on the back, gives you full payment in cash, winks, and adds: "No need to pay those high taxes, eh." What action, if any, do you take?

Recording employer payroll taxes. Employer payroll taxes are an added expense beyond the wages and salaries earned by employees. These taxes are often recorded in an entry separate from the one recording payroll expenses and deductions. To illustrate, assume that the $2,000 recorded salaries expense from the previous example is earned by an employee whose earnings have not yet reached $5,000 for the year. This means the entire salaries expense for this period is subject to tax because year-to-date pay is under $7,000. Also assume that the federal unemployment tax rate is 0.8% and the state unemployment tax rate is 5.4%. Consequently, the FICA portion of the employer's tax is $153, computed by multiplying both the 6.2% and 1.45% by the $2,000 gross pay. Moreover, state unemployment (SUTA) taxes are $108 (5.4% of the $2,000 gross pay), and federal unemployment (FUTA) taxes are $16 (0.8% of $2,000). The entry to record the employer's payroll tax expense and related liabilities is

Example: If the employer's merit rating in this example reduces its SUTA rate to 2.9%, what is its SUTA liability?
Answer: SUTA payable = $2,000 × 2.9% = $58

Assets = Liabilities + Equity
  +124 −277
  +29
  +108
  +16

Jan. 31	Payroll Taxes Expense............................	277	
	FICA—Social Security Taxes Payable (6.2%)		124
	FICA—Medicare Taxes Payable (1.45%)		29
	State Unemployment Taxes Payable		108
	Federal Unemployment Taxes Payable.........		16
	To record employer payroll taxes.		

Multi-Period Known Liabilities

Many known liabilities extend over multiple periods. These often include unearned revenues and notes payable. For example, if **Sports Illustrated** sells a four-year magazine subscription, it records amounts received for this subscription in an Unearned Subscription Revenues account. Amounts in this account are liabilities, but are they current or long term? They are *both*. The portion of the Unearned Subscription Revenues account that will be fulfilled in the next year is reported as a current liability. The remaining portion is reported as a long-term liability.

The same analysis applies to notes payable. For example, a borrower reports a three-year note payable as a long-term liability in the first two years it is outstanding. In the third year, the borrower reclassifies this note as a current liability since it is due within one year or the operating cycle, whichever is longer. The **current portion of long-term debt** refers to that part of long-term debt due within one year or the operating cycle, whichever is longer. Long-term debt is reported under long-term liabilities, but the *current portion due* is reported under current liabilities. To illustrate, assume that a $7,500 debt is paid in installments of $1,500 per year for five years. The $1,500 due within the year is reported as a current liability. No journal entry is necessary for this reclassification. Instead, we simply classify the amounts for debt as either current or long term when the balance sheet is prepared.

Point: Alternatively, some accounting systems do make an entry to transfer the current amount due out of Long-Term Debt and into the Current Portion of Long-Term Debt.

Some known liabilities are rarely reported in long-term liabilities. These include accounts payable, sales taxes, and wages and salaries.

Quick Check

Answers—p. 452

4. Why does a creditor prefer a note payable to a past-due account payable?

5. A company pays its one employee $3,000 per month. This company's FUTA rate is 0.8% on the first $7,000 earned; its SUTA rate is 4.0% on the first $7,000; its Social Security tax rate is 6.2% of the first $94,200; and its Medicare tax rate is 1.45% of all amounts earned. The entry to record this company's March payroll includes what amount for total payroll taxes expense?

6. Identify whether the employer or employee or both incurs each of the following: (a) FICA taxes, (b) FUTA taxes, (c) SUTA taxes, and (d) withheld income taxes.

Estimated Liabilities

An **estimated liability** is a known obligation that is of an uncertain amount but that can be reasonably estimated. Common examples are employee benefits such as pensions, health care and vacation pay, and warranties offered by a seller. We discuss each of these in this section. Other examples of estimated liabilities include property taxes and certain contracts to provide future services.

P4   Account for estimated liabilities, including warranties and bonuses.

Health and Pension Benefits

Many companies provide **employee benefits** beyond salaries and wages. An employer often pays all or part of medical, dental, life, and disability insurance. Many employers also contribute to *pension plans,* which are agreements by employers to provide benefits (payments) to employees after retirement. Many companies also provide medical care and insurance benefits to their retirees. When payroll taxes and charges for employee benefits are totaled, payroll cost often exceeds employees' gross earnings by 25% or more.

Decision Insight

Postgame Spoils Baseball was the first pro sport to set up a pension, originally up to $100 per month depending on years played. Many former players now take home six-figure pensions. Cal Ripken Jr.'s pension when he reaches 62 is estimated at $160,000 per year (he played 21 seasons). The requirement is only 43 games for a full pension and just one game for full medical benefits.

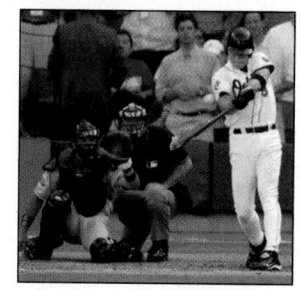

To illustrate, assume that an employer agrees to (1) pay an amount for medical insurance equal to $8,000 and (2) contribute an additional 10% of the employees' $120,000 gross salary to a retirement program. The entry to record these accrued benefits is

Jan. 31	Employee Benefits Expense....................	20,000	
	Employee Medical Insurance Payable..........		8,000
	Employee Retirement Program Payable........		12,000
	To record costs of employee benefits.		

Assets = Liabilities + Equity
+8,000   −20,000
+12,000

Vacation Benefits

Many employers offer paid vacation benefits, also called *paid absences*. To illustrate, assume that salaried employees earn 2 weeks' vacation per year. This benefit increases employers' payroll expenses because employees are paid for 52 weeks but work for only 50 weeks. Total annual salary is the same, but the cost per week worked is greater than the amount paid per week. For example, if an employee is paid $20,800 for 52 weeks but works only 50 weeks, the total weekly expense to the employer is $416 ($20,800/50 weeks) instead of the $400 cash paid weekly to the employee ($20,800/52 weeks). The $16 difference between these two amounts is recorded weekly as follows:

Assets = Liabilities + Equity
       +16   −16

Vacation Benefits Expense.....................	16	
Vacation Benefits Payable.................		16
To record vacation benefits accrued.		

Vacation Benefits Expense is an operating expense, and Vacation Benefits Payable is a current liability. When the employee takes a vacation, the employer reduces (debits) the Vacation Benefits Payable and credits Cash (no additional expense is recorded).

Bonus Plans

Global: Bonuses are considered part of salary expense in most countries. In Japan, bonuses to members of the board of directors and to external auditors are directly charged against equity rather than treated as an expense.

Many companies offer bonuses to employees, and many of the bonuses depend on net income. To illustrate, assume that an employer offers a bonus to its employees equal to 5% of the company's annual net income (to be equally shared by all). The company's expected annual net income is $210,000. The year-end adjusting entry to record this benefit is

Assets = Liabilities + Equity
       +10,000   −10,000

Dec. 31	Employee Bonus Expense*	10,000	
	Bonus Payable.........................		10,000
	To record expected bonus costs.		

* Bonus Expense (B) equals 5% of the quantity $210,000 minus the bonus—computed as:

$$B = 0.05 (\$210,000 - B)$$
$$B = \$10,500 - 0.05B$$
$$1.05B = \$10,500$$
$$\mathbf{B = \$10,500/1.05 = \$10,000}$$

When the bonus is paid, Bonus Payable is debited and Cash is credited for $10,000.

Warranty Liabilities

Point: Kodak recently reported $62 million on its balance sheet for warranty obligations.

A **warranty** is a seller's obligation to replace or correct a product (or service) that fails to perform as expected within a specified period. Most new cars, for instance, are sold with a warranty covering parts for a specified period of time. **Ford Motor Company** reported more than $16 billion in "dealer and customer allowances and claims" in its annual report. To comply with the *full disclosure* and *matching principles,* the seller reports the expected warranty expense in the period when revenue from the sale of the product or service is reported. The seller reports this warranty obligation as a liability, although the existence, amount, payee, and date of future sacrifices are uncertain. This is because such warranty costs are probable and the amount can be estimated using, for instance, past experience with warranties.

To illustrate, a dealer sells a used car for $16,000 on December 1, 2007, with a maximum one-year or 12,000-mile warranty covering parts. This dealer's experience shows that warranty expense averages about 4% of a car's selling price, or $640 in this case ($16,000 × 4%). The dealer records the estimated expense and liability related to this sale with this entry:

Assets = Liabilities + Equity
       +640   −640

2007			
Dec. 1	Warranty Expense	640	
	Estimated Warranty Liability................		640
	To record estimated warranty expense.		

This entry alternatively could be made as part of end-of-period adjustments. Either way, the estimated warranty expense is reported on the 2007 income statement and the warranty liability on the 2007 balance sheet. To further extend this example, suppose the customer returns the car for warranty repairs on January 9, 2008. The dealer performs this work by replacing parts costing $200. The entry to record partial settlement of the estimated warranty liability is

Point: Recognition of expected warranty liabilities is necessary to comply with the matching and full disclosure principles.

2008			
Jan. 9	Estimated Warranty Liability	200	
	Auto Parts Inventory.		200
	To record costs of warranty repairs.		

Assets = Liabilities + Equity
−200   −200

This entry reduces the balance of the estimated warranty liability. Warranty expense was previously recorded in 2007, the year the car was sold with the warranty. Finally, what happens if total warranty expenses are more or less than the estimated 4%, or $640? The answer is that management should monitor actual warranty expenses to see whether the 4% rate is accurate. If experience reveals a large difference from the estimate, the rate for current and future sales should be changed. Differences are expected, but they should be small.

Multi-Period Estimated Liabilities

Estimated liabilities can be both current and long term. For example, pension liabilities to employees are long term to workers who will not retire within the next period. For employees who are retired or will retire within the next period, a portion of pension liabilities is current. Other examples include employee health benefits and warranties. Specifically, many warranties are for 30 or 60 days in length. Estimated costs under these warranties are properly reported in current liabilities. Many other automobile warranties are for three years or 36,000 miles. A portion of these warranties is reported as long term.

Quick Check   Answers—p. 452

7. Estimated liabilities involve an obligation to pay which of these? (*a*) An uncertain but reasonably estimated amount owed on a known obligation or (*b*) A known amount to a specific entity on an uncertain due date.

8. A car is sold for $15,000 on June 1, 2007, with a one-year warranty on parts. Warranty expense is estimated at 1.5% of selling price at each calendar year-end. On March 1, 2008, the car is returned for warranty repairs costing $135. The amount recorded as warranty expense on March 1 is (*a*) $0; (*b*) $60; (*c*) $75; (*d*) $135; (*e*) $225.

Contingent Liabilities

A **contingent liability** is a potential obligation that depends on a future event arising from a past transaction or event. An example is a pending lawsuit. Here, a past transaction or event leads to a lawsuit whose result depends on the outcome of the suit. Future payment of a contingent liability depends on whether an uncertain future event occurs.

C3 Explain how to account for contingent liabilities.

Accounting for Contingent Liabilities

Accounting for contingent liabilities depends on the likelihood that a future event will occur and the ability to estimate the future amount owed if this event occurs. Three different possibilities are identified in the following chart: record liability, disclose in notes, or no disclosure.

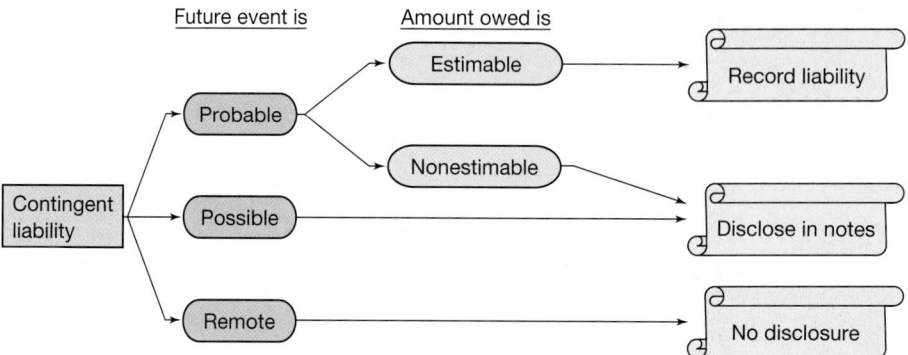

The conditions that determine each of these three possibilities follow:

(1) The future event is *probable* (likely) and the amount owed can be *reasonably estimated*. We then record this amount as a liability. Examples are the estimated liabilities described earlier such as warranties, vacation pay, and income taxes.

(2) The future event is *reasonably possible* (could occur). Then, we disclose information about this contingent liability in notes to the financial statements.

(3) The future event is *remote* (unlikely). We do not record or disclose information on remote contingent liabilities.

Point: A contingency is an *if*. Namely, if a future event occurs, then financial consequences are likely for the entity.

Reasonably Possible Contingent Liabilities

This section identifies and discusses contingent liabilities that commonly fall in the second category—when the future event is reasonably possible. Disclosing information about contingencies in this category is motivated by the *full-disclosure principle,* which requires information relevant to decision makers be reported and not ignored.

Point: A sale of a note receivable is often a contingent liability. It becomes a liability if the original signer of the note fails to pay it at maturity.

Potential Legal Claims   Many companies are sued or at risk of being sued. The accounting issue is whether the defendant should recognize a liability on its balance sheet or disclose a contingent liability in its notes while a lawsuit is outstanding and not yet settled. The answer is that a potential claim is recorded in the accounts *only* if payment for damages is probable and the amount can be reasonably estimated. If the potential claim cannot be reasonably estimated or is less than probable but reasonably possible, it is disclosed. **Ford Motor Company**, for example, includes the following note in its annual report: "Various legal actions, governmental investigations and proceedings and claims are pending . . . arising out of alleged defects in our products."

Debt Guarantees   Sometimes a company guarantees the payment of debt owed by a supplier, customer, or another company. The guarantor usually discloses the guarantee in its financial statement notes as a contingent liability. If it is probable that the debtor will default, the guarantor needs to record and report the guarantee in its financial statements as a liability. The **Boston Celtics** report a unique guarantee when it comes to coaches and players: "Certain of the contracts provide for guaranteed payments which must be paid even if the employee [player] is injured or terminated."

Other Contingencies Other examples of contingencies include environmental damages, possible tax assessments, insurance losses, and government investigations. **Sunoco**, for instance, reports that "federal, state and local laws . . . result in liabilities and loss contingencies. Sunoco accrues . . . cleanup costs [that] are probable and reasonably estimable. Management believes it is reasonably possible (i.e., less than probable but greater than remote) that additional . . . losses will be incurred." Many of Sunoco's contingencies are revealed only in notes.

Uncertainties All organizations face uncertainties from future events such as natural disasters and the development of new competing products or services. These uncertainties are not contingent liabilities because they are future events *not* arising from past transactions. Accordingly, they are not disclosed.

Point: Auditors and managers often have different views about whether a contingency is recorded, disclosed, or omitted.

Topic Tackler
PLUS

11-2

Quick Check

Answers—p. 452

9. A future payment is reported as a liability on the balance sheet if payment is contingent on a future event that (*a*) is reasonably possible but the payment cannot be reasonably estimated; (*b*) is probable and the payment can be reasonably estimated; or (*c*) is not probable but the payment is known.

10. Under what circumstances is a future payment reported in the notes to the financial statements as a contingent liability?

Times Interest Earned Ratio

Decision Analysis

A company incurs interest expense on many of its current and long-term liabilities. Examples extend from its short-term notes and the current portion of long-term liabilities to its long-term notes and bonds. Interest expense is often viewed as a *fixed expense* because the amount of these liabilities is likely to remain in one form or another for a substantial period of time. This means that the amount of interest is unlikely to vary due to changes in sales or other operating activities. While fixed expenses can be advantageous when a company is growing, they create risk. This risk stems from the possibility that a company might be unable to pay fixed expenses if sales decline. To illustrate, consider Diego Co.'s results for 2007 and two possible outcomes for year 2008 in Exhibit 11.5.

A1 Compute the times interest earned ratio and use it to analyze liabilities.

($ thousands)	2007	2008 Projections	
		Sales Increase	Sales Decrease
Sales	$600	$900	$300
Expenses (75% of sales)	450	675	225
Income before interest	150	225	75
Interest expense (fixed)	60	60	60
Net income	$ 90	$165	$ 15

Exhibit 11.5

Actual and Projected Results

Expenses excluding interest are at, and expected to remain at, 75% of sales. Expenses such as these that change with sales volume are called *variable expenses*. However, interest expense is at, and expected to remain at, $60,000 per year due to its fixed nature.

The middle numerical column of Exhibit 11.5 shows that Diego's income nearly doubles to $165,000 if sales increase by 50% to $900,000. In contrast, the far right column shows that income falls sharply if sales decline by 50%. These results reveal that the amount of fixed interest expense affects a company's risk of its ability to pay interest, which is numerically reflected in the **times interest earned** ratio in Exhibit 11.6.

$$\text{Times interest earned} = \frac{\text{Income before interest expense and income taxes}}{\text{Interest expense}}$$

Exhibit 11.6

Times Interest Earned

For 2007, Diego's times interest earned is computed as $150,000/$60,000, or 2.5 times. This ratio suggests that Diego faces low to moderate risk because its sales must decline sharply before it would be unable to cover its interest expenses. (Diego is an LLC and does not pay income taxes.)

Experience shows that when times interest earned falls below 1.5 to 2.0 and remains at that level or lower for several periods, the default rate on liabilities increases sharply. This reflects increased risk for companies and their creditors. We also must interpret the times interest earned ratio in light of information about the variability of a company's income before interest. If income is stable from year to year or if it is growing, the company can afford to take on added risk by borrowing. If its income greatly varies from year to year, fixed interest expense can increase the risk that it will not earn enough income to pay interest.

Decision Maker   Answer—p. 452

Entrepreneur   You wish to invest in a franchise for either one of two national chains. Each franchise has an expected annual net income *after* interest and taxes of $100,000. Net income for the first franchise includes a regular fixed interest charge of $200,000. The fixed interest charge for the second franchise is $40,000. Which franchise is riskier to you if sales forecasts are not met? Does your decision change if the first franchise has more variability in its income stream?

Demonstration Problem

The following transactions and events took place at Kern Company during its recent calendar-year reporting period (Kern does not use reversing entries):

a. In September 2007, Kern sold $140,000 of merchandise covered by a 180-day warranty. Prior experience shows that costs of the warranty equal 5% of sales. Compute September's warranty expense and prepare the adjusting journal entry for the warranty liability as recorded at September 30. Also prepare the journal entry on October 8 to record a $300 cash expenditure to provide warranty service on an item sold in September.

b. On October 12, 2007, Kern arranged with a supplier to replace Kern's overdue $10,000 account payable by paying $2,500 cash and signing a note for the remainder. The note matures in 90 days and has a 12% interest rate. Prepare the entries recorded on October 12, December 31, and January 10, 2008, related to this transaction.

c. In late December, Kern learns it is facing a product liability suit filed by an unhappy customer. Kern's lawyer advises that although it will probably suffer a loss from the lawsuit, it is not possible to estimate the amount of damages at this time.

d. Sally Kline works for Kern. For the pay period ended November 30, her gross earnings are $3,000. Kline has $800 deducted for federal income taxes and $200 for state income taxes from each paycheck. Additionally, a $35 premium for her health care insurance and a $10 donation for the United Way are deducted. Kline pays FICA Social Security taxes at a rate of 6.2% and FICA Medicare taxes at a rate of 1.45%. She has not earned enough this year to be exempt from any FICA taxes. Journalize the accrual of salaries expense of Kline's wages by Kern.

e. On November 1, Kern borrows $5,000 cash from a bank in return for a 60-day, 12%, $5,000 note. Record the note's issuance on November 1 and its repayment with interest on December 31.

f.[B] Kern has estimated and recorded its quarterly income tax payments. In reviewing its year-end tax adjustments, it identifies an additional $5,000 of income tax expense that should be recorded. A portion of this additional expense, $1,000, is deferrable to future years. Record this year-end income taxes expense adjusting entry.

g. For this calendar-year, Kern's net income is $1,000,000, its interest expense is $275,000, and its income taxes expense is $225,000. Calculate Kern's times interest earned ratio.

Planning the Solution

- For *a,* compute the warranty expense for September and record it with an estimated liability. Record the October expenditure as a decrease in the liability.
- For *b,* eliminate the liability for the account payable and create the liability for the note payable. Compute interest expense for the 80 days that the note is outstanding in 2007 and record it as an additional liability. Record the payment of the note, being sure to include the interest for the 10 days in 2008.

- For *c*, decide whether the company's contingent liability needs to be disclosed or accrued (recorded) according to the two necessary criteria: probable loss and reasonably estimable.
- For *d*, set up payable accounts for all items in Kline's paycheck that require deductions. After deducting all necessary items, credit the remaining amount to Accrued Payroll Payable.
- For *e*, record the issuance of the note. Calculate 60 days' interest due using the 360-day convention in the interest formula.
- For *f*, determine how much of the income taxes expense is payable in the current year and how much needs to be deferred.
- For *g*, apply and compute times interest earned.

Solution to Demonstration Problem

a. Warranty expense = 5% × $140,000 = $7,000

Sept. 30	Warranty Expense	7,000	
	Estimated Warranty Liability		7,000
	To record warranty expense for the month.		
Oct. 8	Estimated Warranty Liability	300	
	Cash		300
	To record the cost of the warranty service.		

b. Interest expense for 2007 = 12% × $7,500 × 80/360 = $200

Interest expense for 2008 = 12% × $7,500 × 10/360 = $25

Oct. 12	Accounts Payable	10,000	
	Notes Payable		7,500
	Cash		2,500
	Paid $2,500 cash and gave a 90-day, 12% note to extend the due date on the account.		
Dec. 31	Interest Expense	200	
	Interest Payable		200
	To accrue interest on note payable.		
Jan. 10	Interest Expense	25	
	Interest Payable	200	
	Notes Payable	7,500	
	Cash		7,725
	Paid note with interest, including the accrued interest payable.		

c. Disclose the pending lawsuit in the financial statement notes. Although the loss is probable, no liability can be accrued since the loss cannot be reasonably estimated.

d.

Nov. 30	Salaries Expense	3,000.00	
	FICA—Social Security Taxes Payable (6.2%)		186.00
	FICA—Medicare Taxes Payable (1.45%)		43.50
	Employee Federal Income Taxes Payable		800.00
	Employee State Income Taxes Payable		200.00
	Employee Medical Insurance Payable		35.00
	Employee United Way Payable		10.00
	Accrued Payroll Payable		1,725.50
	To record Kline's accrued payroll.		

e.

Nov. 1	Cash	5,000	
	Notes Payable		5,000
	Borrowed cash with a 60-day, 12% note.		

When the note and interest are paid 60 days later, Kern Company records this entry:

Dec. 31	Notes Payable	5,000	
	Interest Expense	100	
	Cash		5,100
	Paid note with interest ($5,000 × 12% × 60/360).		

f.

Dec. 31	Income Taxes Expense	5,000	
	Income Taxes Payable.		4,000
	Deferred Income Tax Liability.		1,000
	To record added income taxes expense and the deferred tax liability.		

g. Times interest earned $= \dfrac{\$1,000,000 + \$275,000 + \$225,000}{\$275,000} = \underline{\underline{5.45 \text{ times}}}$

APPENDIX

11A Payroll Reports, Records, and Procedures

Understanding payroll procedures and keeping adequate payroll reports and records are essential to a company's success. This appendix focuses on payroll accounting and its reports, records, and procedures.

Payroll Reports

Most employees and employers are required to pay local, state, and federal payroll taxes. Payroll expenses involve liabilities to individual employees, to federal and state governments, and to other organizations such as insurance companies. Beyond paying these liabilities, employers are required to prepare and submit reports explaining how they computed these payments.

P5 Identify and describe the details of payroll reports, records, and procedures.

Reporting FICA Taxes and Income Taxes   The Federal Insurance Contributions Act (FICA) requires each employer to file an Internal Revenue Service (IRS) **Form 941,** the *Employer's Quarterly Federal Tax Return,* within one month after the end of each calendar quarter. A sample Form 941 is shown in Exhibit 11A.1 for Phoenix Sales & Service, a landscape design company. Accounting information and software are helpful in tracking payroll transactions and reporting the accumulated information on Form 941. Specifically, the employer reports total wages subject to income tax withholding on line 2 of Form 941. (For simplicity, this appendix uses *wages* to refer to both wages and salaries.) The income tax withheld is reported on line 3. The combined amount of employee and employer FICA (Social Security) taxes for Phoenix Sales & Service is reported on line 5a (taxable Social Security wages, $36,599 × 12.4% = $4,538.28). The 12.4% is the sum of the Social Security tax withheld, computed as 6.2% tax withheld from the employee wages for the quarter plus the 6.2% tax levied on the employer. The combined amount of employee Medicare wages is reported on line 5c. The 2.9% is the sum of 1.45% withheld from employee wages for the quarter plus 1.45% tax levied on the employer. Total FICA taxes are reported on line 5d and are added to the total income taxes withheld of $3,056.47 to yield a total of $8,656.12. For this year, assume that income up to $94,200 is subject to Social Security tax. There is no income limit on amounts subject to Medicare tax. Congress sets annual limits on the amount owed for Social Security tax.

Form **941**

Employer's Quarterly Federal Tax Return
Department of the Treasury — Internal Revenue Service

Employer identification number: 8 6 – 3 2 1 4 5 8 7

Name *(not your trade name)*: Phoenix Sales & Service

Trade name *(if any)*:

Address:
1214 Mill Road
Number / Street / Suite or room number
Phoenix / AZ / 85621
City / State / ZIP code

Report for this Quarter ...
(Check one.)

- [ ] 1: January, February, March
- [ ] 2: April, May, June
- [ ] 3: July, August, September
- [X] 4: October, November, December

Part 1: Answer these questions for this quarter.

1 Number of employees who received wages, tips, or other compensation for the pay period including: *Mar. 12* (Quarter 1), *June 12* (Quarter 2), *Sept. 12* (Quarter 3), *Dec. 12* (Quarter 4) **1** `1`

2 Wages, tips, and other compensation **2** `36,599.00`

3 Total income tax withheld from wages, tips, and other compensation **3** `3,056.47`

4 If no wages, tips, and other compensation are subject to social security or Medicare tax . [ ] Check and go to line 6.

5 Taxable social security and Medicare wages and tips:

	Column 1		Column 2
5a Taxable social security wages	36,599.00	× .124 =	4,538.28
5b Taxable social security tips	.	× .124 =	.
5c Taxable Medicare wages & tips	36,599.00	× .029 =	1,061.37

5d Total social security and Medicare taxes (*Column 2,* lines 5a + 5b + 5c = line 5d) . **5d** `5,599.65`

6 Total taxes before adjustments (lines 3 + 5d = line 6) **6** `8,656.12`

7 Tax adjustments (If your answer is a negative number, write it in brackets.):

7a Current quarter's fractions of cents `.`

7b Current quarter's sick pay `.`

7c Current quarter's adjustments for tips and group-term life insurance `.`

7d Current year's income tax withholding (Attach Form 941c) `.`

7e Prior quarters' social security and Medicare taxes (Attach Form 941c) `.`

7f Special additions to federal income tax (reserved use) `.`

7g Special additions to social security and Medicare (reserved use) `.`

7h Total adjustments (Combine all amounts: lines 7a through 7g.) **7h** `0.00`

8 Total taxes after adjustments (Combine lines 6 and 7h.) **8** `8,656.12`

9 Advance earned income credit (EIC) payments made to employees **9** `.`

10 Total taxes after adjustment for advance EIC (lines 8 – 9 = line 10) **10** `8,656.12`

11 Total deposits for this quarter, including overpayment applied from a prior quarter **11** `8,656.12`

12 Balance due (lines 10 – 11 = line 12) Make checks payable to the *United States Treasury* . **12** `0.00`

13 Overpayment (If line 11 is more than line 10, write the difference here.) `0.00` Check one [ ] Apply to next return. [ ] Send a refund.

Part 2: Tell us about your deposit schedule for this quarter.

If you are unsure about whether you are a monthly schedule depositor or a semiweekly schedule depositor, see *Pub. 15 (Circular E)*, section 11.

14 A Z Write the state abbreviation for the state where you made your deposits OR write "MU" if you made your deposits in *multiple* states.

15 Check one: [ ] Line 10 is less than $2,500. Go to Part 3.

[X] You were a monthly schedule depositor for the entire quarter. Fill out your tax liability for each month. Then go to Part 3.

Tax liability:	Month 1	3,079.11
	Month 2	2,049.77
	Month 3	3,527.24
	Total	8,656.12	Total must equal line 10.

[ ] You were a semiweekly schedule depositor for any part of this quarter. Fill out *Schedule B (Form 941): Report of Tax Liability for Semiweekly Schedule Depositors*, and attach it to this form.

Part 3: Tell us about your business. If a question does NOT apply to your business, leave it blank.

16 If your business has closed and you do not have to file returns in the future [ ] Check here, and

enter the final date you paid wages / /

17 If you are a seasonal employer and you do not have to file a return for every quarter of the year [ ] Check here.

Part 4: May we contact your third-party designee?

Do you want to allow an employee, a paid tax preparer, or another person to discuss this return with the IRS? See the instructions for details.

[ ] Yes. Designee's name

Phone (   )   –   Personal Identification Number (PIN) [ ][ ][ ][ ][ ]

[X] No.

Part 5: Sign here

Under penalties of perjury, I declare that I have examined this return, including accompanying schedules and statements, and to the best of my knowledge and belief, it is true, correct, and complete.

✕ Sign your name here

Print name and title

Date / / Phone (   )   –

Although the IRS may not be at the end of the rainbow, this cartoon reinforces the importance of taxation in all business activities and management decisions.

Federal depository banks are authorized to accept deposits of amounts payable to the federal government. Deposit requirements depend on the amount of tax owed. For example, when the sum of FICA taxes plus the employee income taxes is less than $2,500 for a quarter, the taxes can be paid when Form 941 is filed. Companies with large payrolls are often required to pay monthly or even semiweekly.

Reporting FUTA Taxes and SUTA Taxes   An employer's federal unemployment taxes (FUTA) are reported on an annual basis by filing an *Annual Federal Unemployment Tax Return,* IRS **Form 940.** It must be mailed on or before January 31 following the end of each tax year. Ten more days are allowed if all required tax deposits are filed on a timely basis and the full amount of tax is paid on or before January 31. FUTA payments are made quarterly to a federal depository bank if the total amount due exceeds $500. If $500 or less is due, the taxes are remitted annually. Requirements for paying and reporting state unemployment taxes (SUTA) vary depending on the laws of each state. Most states require quarterly payments and reports.

Reporting Wages and Salaries   Employers are required to give each employee an annual report of his or her wages subject to FICA and federal income taxes along with the amounts of these taxes withheld. This report is called a *Wage and Tax Statement,* or **Form W-2.** It must be given to employees before January 31 following the year covered by the report. Exhibit 11A.2 shows Form W-2 for one of the employees at Phoenix Sales & Service. Copies of the W-2 Form must be sent to the Social Security Administration, where the amount of the employee's wages subject to FICA taxes and FICA taxes withheld are posted to each employee's Social Security account. These posted amounts become the basis for determining an employee's retirement and survivors' benefits. The Social Security Administration also transmits to the IRS the amount of each employee's wages subject to federal income taxes and the amount of taxes withheld.

Payroll Records

Employers must keep payroll records in addition to reporting and paying taxes. These records usually include a payroll register and an individual earnings report for each employee.

Payroll Register   A **payroll register** usually shows the pay period dates, hours worked, gross pay, deductions, and net pay of each employee for each pay period. Exhibit 11A.3 shows a payroll register for Phoenix Sales & Service. It is organized into nine columns:

Col. 1   Employee identification (ID); Employee name; Social Security number (SS No.); Reference (check number); and Date (date check issued)
Col. 2   Pay Type (regular and overtime)
Col. 3   Pay Hours (number of hours worked as regular and overtime)
Col. 4   Gross Pay (amount of gross pay)[2]
Col. 5   FIT (federal income taxes withheld); FUTA (federal unemployment taxes)
Col. 6   SIT (state income taxes withheld); SUTA (state unemployment taxes)
Col. 7   FICA-SS_EE (social security taxes withheld, employee); FICA-SS_ER (social security taxes, employer)
Col. 8   FICA-Med_EE (medicare tax withheld, employee); FICA-Med_ER (medicare tax, employer)
Col. 9   Net pay (Gross pay less amounts withheld from employees)

Net pay for each employee is computed as gross pay minus the items on the first line of columns 5–8. The employer's payroll tax for each employee is computed as the sum of items on the third line of columns 5–8. A payroll register includes all data necessary to record payroll. In some software programs the entries to record payroll are made in a special *payroll journal.*

---

[2] The Gross Pay column shows regular hours worked on the first line multiplied by the regular pay rate—this equals regular pay. Overtime hours multiplied by the overtime premium rate equals overtime premium pay reported on the second line. If employers are engaged in interstate commerce, federal law sets a minimum overtime rate of pay to employees. For this company, workers earn 150% of their regular rate for hours in excess of 40 per week.

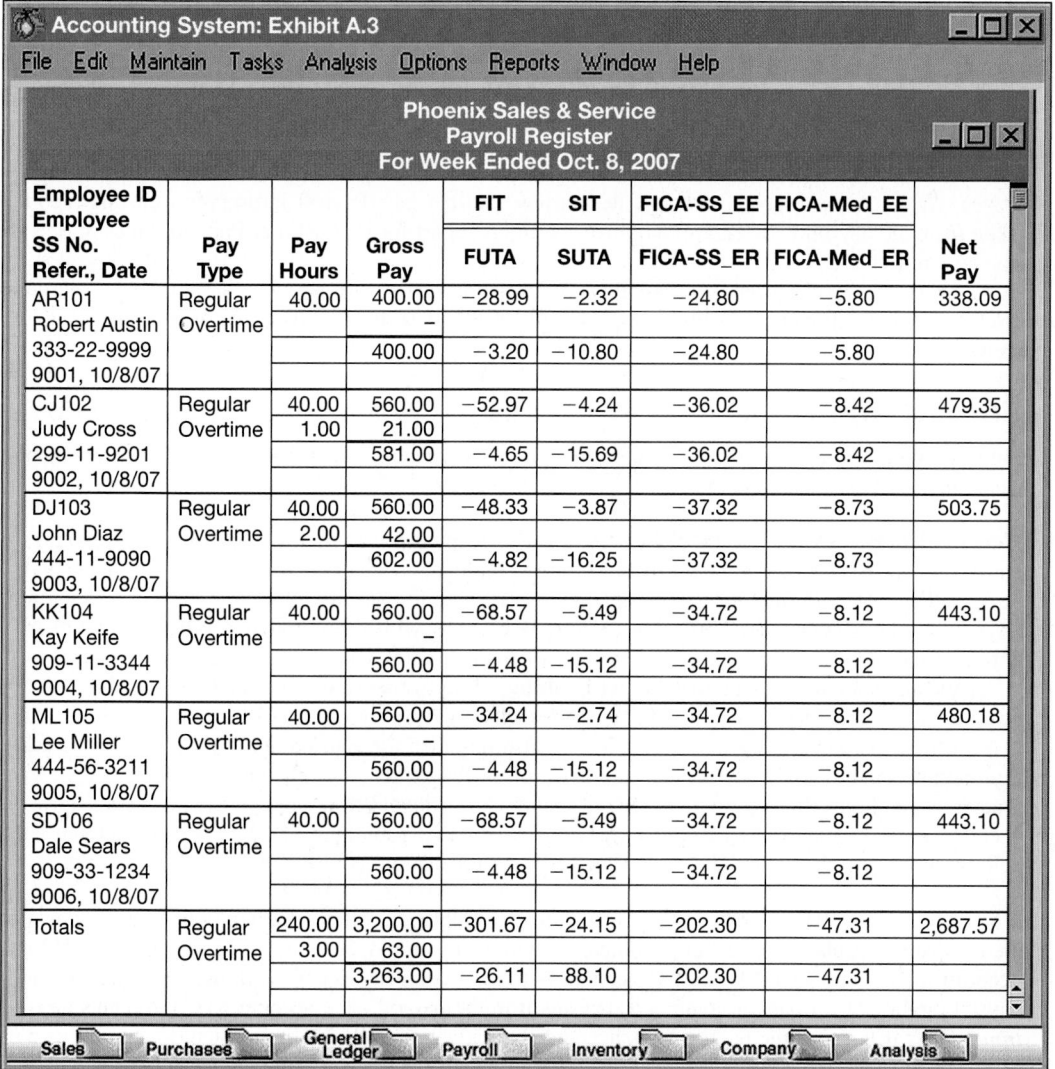

Exhibit 11A.2

Form W-2

Exhibit 11A.3

Payroll Register

Payroll Check   Payment of payroll is usually done by check or electronic funds transfer. Exhibit 11A.4 shows a *payroll check* for a Phoenix employee. This check is accompanied with a detachable *statement of earnings* (at top) showing gross pay, deductions, and net pay.

Exhibit 11A.4

Check and Statement of Earnings

EMPLOYEE NO.	EMPLOYEE NAME		SOCIAL SECURITY NO.	PAY PERIOD END	CHECK DATE
AR101	Robert Austin		333-22-9999	10/8/07	10/8/07

ITEM	RATE	HOURS	TOTAL	ITEM	THIS CHECK	YEAR TO DATE
Regular	10.00	40.00	400.00	Gross	400.00	400.00
Overtime	15.00			Fed. Income tax	-28.99	-28.99
				FICA-Soc. Sec.	-24.80	-24.80
				FICA-Medicare	-5.80	-5.80
				State Income tax	-2.32	-2.32

HOURS WORKED	GROSS THIS PERIOD	GROSS YEAR TO DATE	NET CHECK	CHECK No.
40.00	400.00	400.00	$338.09	9001

(Detach and retain for your records)

PHOENIX SALES & SERVICE   Phoenix Bank and Trust   **9001**
1214 Mill Road   Phoenix, AZ 85621
Phoenix, AZ 85621   3312-87044
602-555-8900

CHECK NO.	DATE	AMOUNT
9001	Oct 8, 2007	***********$338.09*

Three Hundred Thirty–Eight and 9/100 Dollars

PAY TO THE ORDER OF
Robert Austin
18 Roosevelt Blvd., Apt C
Tempe, AZ 86322

Mary Wills
AUTHORIZED SIGNATURE

Employee Earnings Report   An **employee earnings report** is a cumulative record of an employee's hours worked, gross earnings, deductions, and net pay. Payroll information on this report is taken from the payroll register. The employee earnings report for R. Austin at Phoenix Sales & Service is shown in Exhibit 11A.5.

An employee earnings report accumulates information that can show when an employee's earnings reach the tax-exempt points for FICA, FUTA, and SUTA taxes. It also gives data an employer needs to prepare Form W-2.

Payroll Procedures

Employers must be able to compute federal income tax for payroll purposes. This section explains how we compute this tax and how to use a payroll bank account.

Computing Federal Income Taxes   To compute the amount of taxes withheld from each employee's wages, we need to determine both the employee's wages earned and the employee's number of *withholding allowances*. Each employee records the number of withholding allowances claimed on a withholding allowance certificate, **Form W-4,** filed with the employer. When the number of withholding allowances increases, the amount of income taxes withheld decreases.

Employers often use a **wage bracket withholding table** similar to the one shown in Exhibit 11A.6 to compute the federal income taxes withheld from each employee's gross pay. The table in Exhibit 11A.6 is for a single employee paid weekly. Tables are also provided for married employees and for biweekly, semimonthly, and monthly pay periods (most payroll software includes these tables). When using a wage bracket withholding table to compute federal income tax withheld from an employee's gross wages, we need to locate an employee's wage bracket within the first two columns. We then find the amount withheld by looking in the withholding allowance column for that employee.

Payroll Bank Account   Companies with few employees often pay them with checks drawn on the company's regular bank account. Companies with many employees often use a special **payroll bank account** to pay employees. When this account is used, a company either (1) draws one check for total payroll on the regular bank account and deposits it in the payroll bank account or (2) executes an *electronic funds transfer* to the payroll bank account. Individual payroll checks are then drawn on this payroll bank account. Since only one check for the total payroll is drawn on the regular bank account each payday, use of a special payroll bank account helps with internal control. It also helps in reconciling the

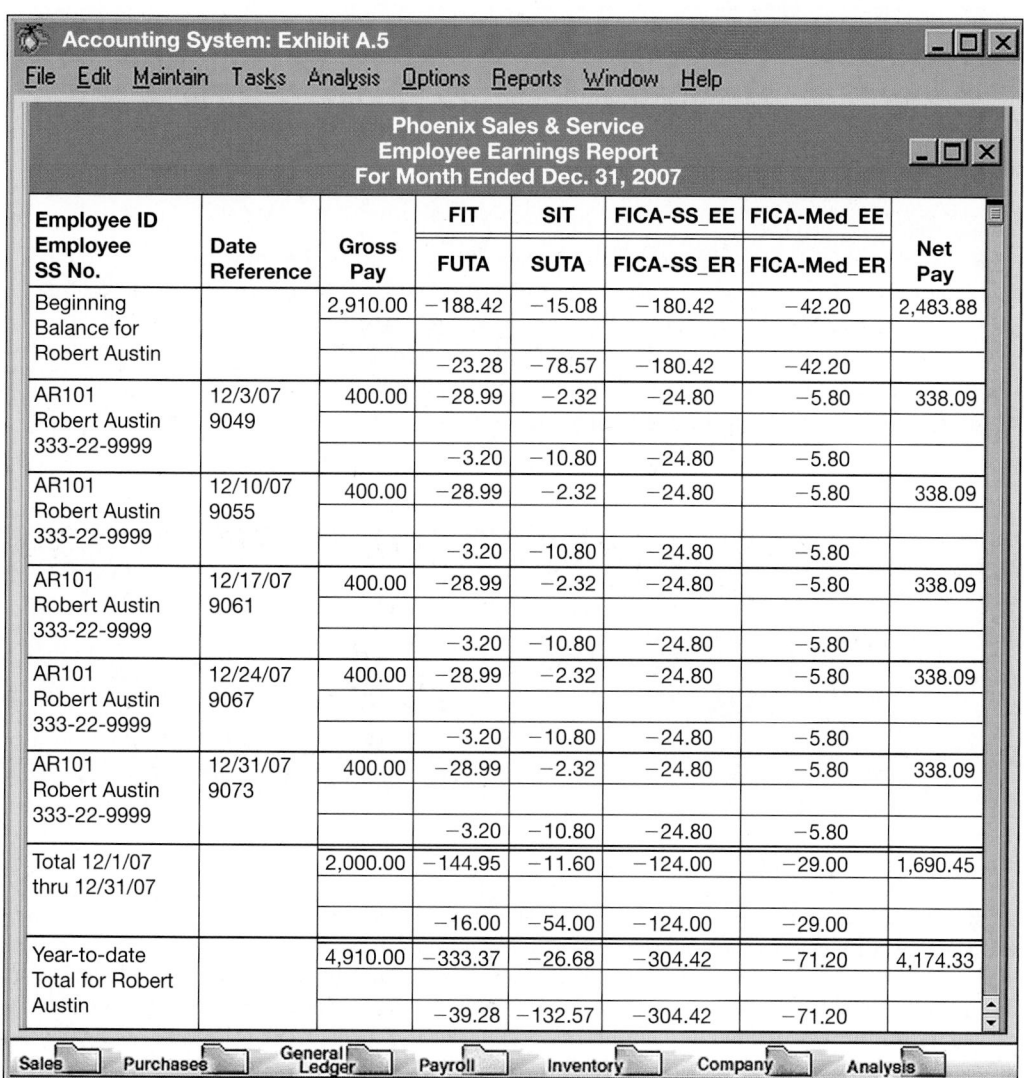

Exhibit 11A.5

Employee Earnings Report

Accounting System: Exhibit A.5

File Edit Maintain Tasks Analysis Options Reports Window Help

Phoenix Sales & Service
Employee Earnings Report
For Month Ended Dec. 31, 2007

Employee ID Employee SS No.	Date Reference	Gross Pay	FIT	SIT	FICA-SS_EE	FICA-Med_EE	Net Pay
			FUTA	SUTA	FICA-SS_ER	FICA-Med_ER	
Beginning Balance for Robert Austin		2,910.00	−188.42	−15.08	−180.42	−42.20	2,483.88
			−23.28	−78.57	−180.42	−42.20	
AR101 Robert Austin 333-22-9999	12/3/07 9049	400.00	−28.99	−2.32	−24.80	−5.80	338.09
			−3.20	−10.80	−24.80	−5.80	
AR101 Robert Austin 333-22-9999	12/10/07 9055	400.00	−28.99	−2.32	−24.80	−5.80	338.09
			−3.20	−10.80	−24.80	−5.80	
AR101 Robert Austin 333-22-9999	12/17/07 9061	400.00	−28.99	−2.32	−24.80	−5.80	338.09
			−3.20	−10.80	−24.80	−5.80	
AR101 Robert Austin 333-22-9999	12/24/07 9067	400.00	−28.99	−2.32	−24.80	−5.80	338.09
			−3.20	−10.80	−24.80	−5.80	
AR101 Robert Austin 333-22-9999	12/31/07 9073	400.00	−28.99	−2.32	−24.80	−5.80	338.09
			−3.20	−10.80	−24.80	−5.80	
Total 12/1/07 thru 12/31/07		2,000.00	−144.95	−11.60	−124.00	−29.00	1,690.45
			−16.00	−54.00	−124.00	−29.00	
Year-to-date Total for Robert Austin		4,910.00	−333.37	−26.68	−304.42	−71.20	4,174.33
			−39.28	−132.57	−304.42	−71.20	

Sales   Purchases   General Ledger   Payroll   Inventory   Company   Analysis

Exhibit 11A.6

Wage Bracket Withholding Table

SINGLE Persons—WEEKLY Payroll Period

If the wages are—		And the number of withholding allowances claimed is—										
At least	But less than	0	1	2	3	4	5	6	7	8	9	10
		The amount of income tax to be withhold is—										
$600	$610	$76	$67	$58	$49	$39	$30	$21	$12	$6	$0	$0
610	620	79	69	59	50	41	32	22	13	7	1	0
620	630	81	70	61	52	42	33	24	15	8	2	0
630	640	84	72	62	53	44	35	25	16	9	3	0
640	650	86	73	64	55	45	36	27	18	10	4	0
650	660	89	75	65	56	47	38	28	19	11	5	0
660	670	91	76	67	58	48	39	30	21	12	6	0
670	680	94	78	68	59	50	41	31	22	13	7	1
680	690	96	81	70	61	51	42	33	24	14	8	2
690	700	99	83	71	62	53	44	34	25	16	9	3
700	710	101	86	73	64	54	45	35	27	17	10	4
710	720	104	88	74	65	56	47	37	28	19	11	5
720	730	106	91	76	67	57	48	39	30	20	12	6
730	740	109	93	78	68	59	50	40	31	22	13	7
740	750	111	96	80	70	60	51	42	33	23	14	8

regular bank account. When companies use a payroll bank account, they usually include check numbers in the payroll register. The payroll register in Exhibit 11A.3 shows check numbers in column 1. For instance, Check No. 9001 is issued to Robert Austin. With this information, the payroll register serves as a supplementary record of wages earned by and paid to employees.

11. What two items determine the amount deducted from an employee's wages for federal income taxes?

12. What amount of income tax is withheld from the salary of an employee who is single with three withholding allowances and earnings of $675 in a week? (*Hint:* Use the wage bracket withholding table in Exhibit 11A.6.)

13. Which of the following steps are executed when a company draws one check for total payroll and deposits it in a special payroll bank account? (*a*) Write a check to the payroll bank account for the total payroll and record it with a debit to Accrued Payroll Payable and a credit to Cash. (*b*) Deposit a check (or transfer funds) for the total payroll in the payroll bank account. (*c*) Issue individual payroll checks drawn on the payroll bank account. (*d*) All of the above.

APPENDIX

11B   Income Taxes

This appendix explains current liabilities involving income taxes for corporations.

Income Tax Liabilities   Corporations are subject to income taxes and must estimate their income tax liability when preparing financial statements. Since income tax expense is created by earning income, a liability is incurred when income is earned. This tax must be paid quarterly under federal regulations. To illustrate, consider a corporation that prepares monthly financial statements. Based on its income in January 2007, this corporation estimates that it owes income taxes of $12,100. The following adjusting entry records this estimate:

Assets = Liabilities + Equity
     +12,100   −12,100

Jan. 31	Income Taxes Expense	12,100	
	Income Taxes Payable.		12,100
	To accrue January income taxes.		

The tax liability is recorded each month until the first quarterly payment is made. If the company's estimated taxes for this first quarter total $30,000, the entry to record its payment is

Assets = Liabilities + Equity
−30,000   −30,000

Apr. 10	Income Taxes Payable	30,000	
	Cash		30,000
	Paid estimated quarterly income taxes based on		
	first quarter income.		

This process of accruing and then paying estimated income taxes continues through the year. When annual financial statements are prepared at year-end, the corporation knows its actual total income and the actual amount of income taxes it must pay. This information allows it to properly record income taxes expense for the fourth quarter so that the total of the four quarters' expense amounts equals the actual taxes paid to the government.

Deferred Income Tax Liabilities   An income tax liability for corporations can arise when the amount of income before taxes that the corporation reports on its income statement is not the same as the amount of income reported on its income tax return. This difference occurs because income tax laws and GAAP measure income differently. (Differences between tax laws and GAAP arise because

Congress uses tax laws to generate receipts, stimulate the economy, and influence behavior, whereas GAAP are intended to provide financial information useful for decision making. Also, tax accounting often follows the cash basis, whereas GAAP follows the accrual basis.)

Some differences between tax laws and GAAP are temporary. *Temporary differences* arise when the tax return and the income statement report a revenue or expense in different years. As an example, companies are often able to deduct higher amounts of depreciation in the early years of an asset's life and smaller amounts in later years for tax reporting in comparison to GAAP. This means that in the early years, depreciation for tax reporting is often more than depreciation on the income statement. In later years, depreciation for tax reporting is often less than depreciation on the income statement. When temporary differences exist between taxable income on the tax return and the income before taxes on the income statement, corporations compute income taxes expense based on the income reported on the income statement. The result is that income taxes expense reported in the income statement is often different from the amount of income taxes payable to the government. This difference is the **deferred income tax liability.**

To illustrate, assume that in recording its usual quarterly income tax payments, a corporation computes $25,000 of income taxes expense. It also determines that only $21,000 is currently due and $4,000 is deferred to future years (a timing difference). The entry to record this end-of-period adjustment is

Dec. 31	Income Taxes Expense	25,000	
	Income Taxes Payable		21,000
	Deferred Income Tax Liability		4,000
	To record tax expense and deferred tax liability.		

Assets = Liabilities + Equity
　　　　　+21,000　−25,000
　　　　　+4,000

The credit to Income Taxes Payable reflects the amount currently due to be paid. The credit to Deferred Income Tax Liability reflects tax payments deferred until future years when the temporary difference reverses.

Temporary differences also can cause a company to pay income taxes *before* they are reported on the income statement as expense. If so, the company reports a *Deferred Income Tax Asset* on its balance sheet.

Summary

C1 **Describe current and long-term liabilities and their characteristics.** Liabilities are probable future payments of assets or services that past transactions or events obligate an entity to make. Current liabilities are due within one year or the operating cycle, whichever is longer. All other liabilities are long term.

C2 **Identify and describe known current liabilities.** Known (determinable) current liabilities are set by agreements or laws and are measurable with little uncertainty. They include accounts payable, sales taxes payable, unearned revenues, notes payable, payroll liabilities, and the current portion of long-term debt.

C3 **Explain how to account for contingent liabilities.** If an uncertain future payment depends on a probable future event and the amount can be reasonably estimated, the payment is recorded as a liability. The uncertain future payment is reported as a contingent liability (in the notes) if (*a*) the future event is reasonably possible but not probable or (*b*) the event is probable but the payment amount cannot be reasonably estimated.

A1 **Compute the times interest earned ratio and use it to analyze liabilities.** Times interest earned is computed by dividing a company's net income before interest expense and income taxes by the amount of interest expense. The times interest earned ratio reflects a company's ability to pay interest obligations.

P1 **Prepare entries to account for short-term notes payable.** Short-term notes payable are current liabilities; most bear

interest. When a short-term note's face value equals the amount borrowed, it identifies a rate of interest to be paid at maturity.

P2 **Compute and record *employee* payroll deductions and liabilities.** Employee payroll deductions include FICA taxes, income taxes, and voluntary deductions such as for pensions and charities. They make up the difference between gross and net pay.

P3 **Compute and record *employer* payroll expenses and liabilities.** An employer's payroll expenses include employees' gross earnings, any employee benefits, and the payroll taxes levied on the employer. Payroll liabilities include employees' net pay amounts, withholdings from employee wages, any employer-promised benefits, and the employer's payroll taxes.

P4 **Account for estimated liabilities, including warranties and bonuses.** Liabilities for health and pension benefits, warranties, and bonuses are recorded with estimated amounts. These items are recognized as expenses when incurred and matched with revenues generated.

P5^A **Identify and describe the details of payroll reports, records, and procedures.** Employers report FICA taxes and federal income tax withholdings using Form 941. FUTA taxes are reported on Form 940. Earnings and deductions are reported to each employee and the federal government on Form W-2. An employer's payroll records often include a payroll register for each pay period, payroll checks and statements of earnings, and individual employee earnings reports.

Web Designer   You need to be concerned about being an accomplice to unlawful payroll activities. Not paying federal and state taxes on wages earned is illegal and unethical. Such payments also will not provide the employee with Social Security and some Medicare credits. The best course of action is to request payment by check. If this fails to change the owner's payment practices, you must consider quitting this job.

Entrepreneur   Risk is partly reflected by the times interest earned ratio. This ratio for the first franchise is 1.5 [($100,000 + $200,000)/$200,000], whereas the ratio for the second franchise is 3.5 [($100,000 + $40,000)/$40,000]. This analysis shows that the first franchise is more at risk of incurring a loss if its sales decline. The second question asks about variability of income. If income greatly varies, this increases the risk an owner will not earn sufficient income to cover interest. Since the first franchise has the greater variability, it is a riskier investment.

Guidance Answers to **Quick Checks**

1. A liability involves a probable future payment of assets or services that an entity is presently obligated to make as a result of past transactions or events.

2. No, an expected future payment is not a liability unless an existing obligation was created by a past event or transaction.

3. In most cases, a liability due in 15 months is classified as long term. It is classified as a current liability if the company's operating cycle is 15 months or longer.

4. A creditor prefers a note payable instead of a past-due account payable so as to (*a*) charge interest and/or (*b*) have evidence of the debt and its terms for potential litigation or disputes.

5. $1,000*(.008) + $1,000*(.04) + $3,000(.062)
    + $3,000(.0145) = $277.50

  * $1,000 of the $3,000 March pay is subject to FUTA and SUTA—the entire $6,000 pay from January and February was subject to them.

6. (*a*) FICA taxes are incurred by both employee and employer.
    (*b*) FUTA taxes are incurred by the employer.
    (*c*) SUTA taxes are incurred by the employer.
    (*d*) Withheld income taxes are incurred by the employee.

7. (*a*)

8. (*a*) Warranty expense was previously estimated and recorded.

9. (*b*)

10. A future payment is reported in the notes as a contingent liability if (*a*) the uncertain future event is probable but the amount of payment cannot be reasonably estimated or (*b*) the uncertain future event is not probable but has a reasonable possibility of occurring.

11. An employee's gross earnings and number of withholding allowances determine the deduction for federal income taxes.

12. $59

13. (*d*)

Key Terms   mhhe.com/wildFAP18e

Key Terms are available at the book's Website for learning and testing in an online Flashcard Format.

Contingent liability (p. 439)

Current liabilities (p. 429)

Current portion of long-term debt (p. 437)

Deferred income tax liability (p. 451)

Employee benefits (p. 437)

Employee earnings report (p. 448)

Estimated liability (p. 437)

Federal depository bank (p. 446)

Federal Insurance Contributions Act (FICA) Taxes (p. 434)

Federal Unemployment Taxes (FUTA) (p. 436)

Form 940 (p. 446)

Form 941 (p. 444)

Form W-2 (p. 446)

Form W-4 (p. 448)

Gross pay (p. 433)

Known liabilities (p. 430)

Long-term liabilities (p. 429)

Merit rating (p. 436)

Net pay (p. 433)

Payroll bank account (p. 448)

Payroll deductions (p. 434)

Payroll register (p. 446)

Short-term note payable (p. 431)

State Unemployment Taxes (SUTA) (p. 436)

Times interest earned (p. 441)

Wage bracket withholding table (p. 448)

Warranty (p. 438)

Multiple Choice Quiz   Answers on p. 469   mhhe.com/wildFAP18e

Multiple Choice Quizzes A and B are available at the book's Website.

1. On December 1, a company signed a $6,000, 90-day, 5% note payable, with principal plus interest due on March 1 of the following year. What amount of interest expense should be accrued at December 31 on the note?
   a. $300
   b. $25
   c. $100
   d. $75
   e. $0

2. An employee earned $50,000 during the year. FICA tax for social security is 6.2% and FICA tax for Medicare is 1.45%. The employer's share of FICA taxes is
   a. Zero, since the employee's pay exceeds the FICA limit.
   b. Zero, since FICA is not an employer tax.
   c. $3,100
   d. $725
   e. $3,825

3. Assume the FUTA tax rate is 0.8% and the SUTA tax rate is 5.4%. Both taxes are applied to the first $7,000 of an employee's pay. What is the total unemployment tax an employer must pay on an employee's annual wages of $40,000?
   a. $2,480
   b. $434
   c. $56
   d. $378
   e. Zero; the employee's wages exceed the $7,000 maximum.

4. A company sells big screen televisions for $3,000 each. Each television has a two-year warranty that covers the replacement of defective parts. It is estimated that 1% of all televisions sold will be returned under warranty at an average cost of $250 each. During July, the company sold 10,000 big screen televisions, and 80 were serviced under the warranty during July at a total cost of $18,000. The credit balance in the Estimated Warranty Liability account at July 1 was $26,000. What is the company's warranty expense for the month of July?
   a. $51,000
   b. $1,000
   c. $25,000
   d. $33,000
   e. $18,000

5. Employees earn vacation pay at the rate of 1 day per month. During October, 150 employees qualify for one vacation day each. Their average daily wage is $175 per day. What is the amount of vacation benefit expense for October?
   a. $26,250
   b. $175
   c. $2,100
   d. $63,875
   e. $150

Superscript letter ^{A} (^{B}) denotes assignments based on Appendix 11A (11B).

Discussion Questions

1. What are the three important questions concerning the uncertainty of liabilities?

2. What is the difference between a current and a long-term liability?

3. What is an estimated liability?

4. If $988 is the total of a sale that includes its sales tax of 4%, what is the selling price of the item only?

5. What is the combined amount (in percent) of the employee and employer Social Security tax rate?

6. What is the current Medicare tax rate? This rate is applied to what maximum level of salary and wages?

7. What determines the amount deducted from an employee's wages for federal income taxes?

8. Which payroll taxes are the employee's responsibility and which are the employer's responsibility?

9. What is an employer's unemployment merit rating? How are these ratings assigned to employers?

10. Why are warranty liabilities usually recognized on the balance sheet as liabilities even when they are uncertain?

11. Suppose that a company has a facility located where disastrous weather conditions often occur. Should it report a probable loss from a future disaster as a liability on its balance sheet? Explain.

12.^{A} What is a wage bracket withholding table?

13.^{A} What amount of income tax is withheld from the salary of an employee who is single with two withholding allowances and earning $725 per week? What if the employee earned $625 and has no withholding allowances? (Use Exhibit 11A.6.)

14. Refer to **Best Buy**'s balance sheet in Appendix A. What payroll-related liability does Best Buy report at February 26, 2005?

15. Refer to **Circuit City**'s balance sheet in Appendix A. What accounts related to income taxes are on its balance

sheet? Explain the meaning of each income tax account you identify.

16. Refer to **Apple**'s balance sheet in Appendix A. List Apple's current liabilities as of September 25, 2004.

 Red numbers denote Discussion Questions that involve decision-making.

QUICK STUDY

QS 11-1

Classifying liabilities   C1

Which of the following items are normally classified as a current liability for a company that has a 15-month operating cycle?

1. Note payable due in 18 months.
2. Note payable maturing in 2 years.
3. Portion of long-term note due in 15 months.
4. Salaries payable.
5. FICA taxes payable.
6. Note payable due in 11 months.

QS 11-2

Unearned revenue   C2

Ticketmaster receives $5,000,000 in advance ticket sales for a four-date tour of the Rolling Stones. Record the advance ticket sales on October 31. Record the revenue earned for the first concert date of November 5, assuming it represents one-fourth of the advance ticket sales.

QS 11-3

Accounting for sales taxes

C2

Dextra Computing sells merchandise for $6,000 cash on September 30 (cost of merchandise is $3,900). The sales tax law requires Dextra to collect 5% sales tax on every dollar of merchandise sold. Record the entry for the $6,000 sale and its applicable sales tax. Also record the entry that shows the remittance of the 5% tax on this sale to the state government on October 15.

QS 11-4

Interest-bearing note transactions

P1

On November 7, 2008, Mura Company borrows $160,000 cash by signing a 90-day, 8% note payable with a face value of $160,000. (1) Compute the accrued interest payable on December 31, 2008, (2) prepare the journal entry to record the accrued interest expense at December 31, 2008, and (3) prepare the journal entry to record payment of the note at maturity.

QS 11-5

Record employer payroll taxes

P2   P3

Major Co. has five employees, each of whom earns $2,500 per month and has been employed since January 1. FICA Social Security taxes are 6.2% of the first $94,200 paid to each employee, and FICA Medicare taxes are 1.45% of gross pay. FUTA taxes are 0.8% and SUTA taxes are 2.8% of the first $7,000 paid to each employee. Prepare the March 31 journal entry to record the March payroll taxes expense.

QS 11-6

Accounting for vacations

P4

Chavez Co.'s salaried employees earn four weeks vacation per year. It pays $312,000 in total employee salaries for 52 weeks but its employees work only 48 weeks. This means Chavez's total weekly expense is $6,500 ($312,000/48 weeks) instead of the $6,000 cash paid weekly to the employees ($312,000/52 weeks). Record Chavez's weekly vacation benefits expense.

QS 11-7

Accounting for bonuses   P4

Noura Company offers an annual bonus to employees if the company meets certain net income goals. Prepare the journal entry to record a $15,000 bonus owed to its workers (to be shared equally) at calendar year-end.

QS 11-8

Recording warranty repairs

P4

On September 11, 2007, Lawn Outfitters sells a mower for $500 with a one-year warranty that covers parts. Warranty expense is estimated at 5% of sales. On July 24, 2008, the mower is brought in for repairs covered under the warranty requiring $55 in materials taken from the Repair Parts Inventory. Prepare the July 24, 2008, entry to record the warranty repairs.

The following legal claims exist for Kewa Co. Identify the accounting treatment for each claim as either (*a*) a liability that is recorded or (*b*) an item described in notes to its financial statements.

1. Kewa (defendant) estimates that a pending lawsuit could result in damages of $1,250,000; it is reasonably possible that the plaintiff will win the case.

2. Kewa faces a probable loss on a pending lawsuit; the amount is not reasonably estimable.

3. Kewa estimates damages in a case at $3,500,000 with a high probability of losing the case.

QS 11-9
Accounting for contingent liabilities
C3

Compute the times interest earned for Park Company, which reports income before interest expense and income taxes of $1,885,000, and interest expense of $145,000. Interpret its times interest earned (assume that its competitors average a times interest earned of 4.0).

QS 11-10
Times interest earned
A1

Sera Corporation has made and recorded its quarterly income tax payments. After a final review of taxes for the year, the company identifies an additional $40,000 of income tax expense that should be recorded. A portion of this additional expense, $6,000, is deferred for payment in future years. Record Sera's year-end adjusting entry for income tax expense.

QS 11-11[B]
Record deferred income tax liability
P4

The following items appear on the balance sheet of a company with a two-month operating cycle. Identify the proper classification of each item as follows: *C* if it is a current liability, *L* if it is a long-term liability, or *N* if it is not a liability.

_____ **1.** Notes payable (due in 120 days).
_____ **2.** Notes payable (mature in five years).
_____ **3.** Notes payable (due in 6 to 12 months).
_____ **4.** Current portion of long-term debt.
_____ **5.** Notes payable (due in 13 to 24 months).
_____ **6.** Sales taxes payable.
_____ **7.** Accounts receivable.
_____ **8.** Wages payable.
_____ **9.** FUTA taxes payable.
_____ **10.** Accrued payroll payable.

EXERCISES

Exercise 11-1
Classifying liabilities
C1

Prepare any necessary adjusting entries at December 31, 2008, for Casco Company's year-end financial statements for each of the following separate transactions and events.

1. During December, Casco Company sold 4,000 units of a product that carries a 60-day warranty. December sales for this product total $150,000. The company expects 8% of the units to need warranty repairs, and it estimates the average repair cost per unit will be $17.

2. A disgruntled employee is suing Casco Company. Legal advisers believe that the company will probably need to pay damages, but the amount cannot be reasonably estimated.

3. Employees earn vacation pay at a rate of one day per month. During December, 20 employees qualify for one vacation day each. Their average daily wage is $150 per employee.

4. Casco Company guarantees the $7,500 debt of a supplier. The supplier will probably not default on the debt.

5. Casco Company records an adjusting entry for $750,000 of previously unrecorded cash sales (costing $500,000) and its sales taxes at a rate of 5%.

6. The company earned $75,000 of $100,000 previously received in advance for services.

Exercise 11-2
Adjusting entries for liabilities
C2 C3 P4

For the year ended December 31, 2008, Lopez Company has implemented an employee bonus program equal to 3% of Lopez's net income, which employees will share equally. Lopez's net income (prebonus) is expected to be $500,000, and bonus expense is deducted in computing net income.

1. Compute the amount of the bonus payable to the employees at year-end (use the method described in the chapter and round to the nearest dollar).

2. Prepare the journal entry at December 31, 2008, to record the bonus due the employees.

3. Prepare the journal entry at January 19, 2009, to record payment of the bonus to employees.

Exercise 11-3
Computing and recording bonuses C2

Check (1) $14,563

Exercise 11-4

Accounting for note payable

P1

Check (2b) Interest expense, $2,080

Ideal Systems borrows $104,000 cash on May 15, 2008, by signing a 60-day, 12% note.

1. On what date does this note mature?

2. Suppose the face value of the note equals $104,000, the principal of the loan. Prepare the journal entries to record (*a*) issuance of the note and (*b*) payment of the note at maturity.

Exercise 11-5

Interest-bearing notes payable with year-end adjustments

P1

Check (2) $3,000
         (3) $1,500

Keesha Co. borrows $200,000 cash on November 1, 2008, by signing a 90-day, 9% note with a face value of $200,000.

1. On what date does this note mature?

2. How much interest expense results from this note in 2008? (Assume a 360-day year.)

3. How much interest expense results from this note in 2009? (Assume a 360-day year.)

4. Prepare journal entries to record (*a*) issuance of the note, (*b*) accrual of interest at the end of 2008, and (*c*) payment of the note at maturity.

Exercise 11-6

Computing payroll taxes

P2 P3

BMX Co. has one employee, and the company is subject to the following taxes:

Tax	Rate	Applied To
FICA—Social Security	6.20%	First $94,200
FICA—Medicare	1.45	All gross pay
FUTA	0.80	First $7,000
SUTA	2.90	First $7,000

Compute BMX's amounts for each of these four taxes as applied to the employee's gross earnings for September under each of three separate situations (*a*), (*b*), and (*c*):

	Gross Pay through August	Gross Pay for September
a.	$ 6,800	$ 900
b.	19,200	2,200
c.	89,200	8,000

Check (*a*) FUTA, $1.60; SUTA, $5.80

Exercise 11-7

Payroll-related journal entries

P2 P3

Using the data in situation *a* of Exercise 11-6, prepare the employer's September 30 journal entries to record (1) salary expense and its related payroll liabilities for this employee and (2) the employer's payroll taxes expense and its related liabilities. The employee's federal income taxes withheld by the employer are $150 for this pay period.

Exercise 11-8

Warranty expense and liability computations and entries

P4

Check (1) $240

(4) $31

Hitzu Co. sold a copier costing $4,800 with a two-year parts warranty to a customer on August 16, 2008, for $6,000 cash. Hitzu uses the perpetual inventory system. On November 22, 2009, the copier requires on-site repairs that are completed the same day. The repairs cost $209 for materials taken from the Repair Parts Inventory. These are the only repairs required in 2009 for this copier. Based on experience, Hitzu expects to incur warranty costs equal to 4% of dollar sales. It records warranty expense with an adjusting entry at the end of each year.

1. How much warranty expense does the company report in 2008 for this copier?

2. How much is the estimated warranty liability for this copier as of December 31, 2008?

3. How much warranty expense does the company report in 2009 for this copier?

4. How much is the estimated warranty liability for this copier as of December 31, 2009?

5. Prepare journal entries to record (*a*) the copier's sale; (*b*) the adjustment on December 31, 2008, to recognize the warranty expense; and (*c*) the repairs that occur in November 2009.

Use the following information from separate companies *a* through *f* to compute times interest earned. Which company indicates the strongest ability to pay interest expense as it comes due?

Exercise 11-9
Computing and interpreting times interest earned

A1

Check (b) 11.00

	Net Income (Loss)	Interest Expense	Income Taxes
a.	$115,000	$44,000	$ 35,000
b.	110,000	16,000	50,000
c.	100,000	12,000	70,000
d.	235,000	14,000	130,000
e.	59,000	14,000	30,000
f.	(5,000)	10,000	0

The payroll records of One Click Software show the following information about Keisha LeShon, an employee, for the weekly pay period ending September 30, 2008. LeShon is single and claims one allowance. Compute her Social Security tax (6.2%), Medicare tax (1.45%), federal income tax withholding, state income tax (0.5%), and net pay for the current pay period. The state income tax is 0.5 percent on the first $9,000 earned. (Use the withholding table in Exhibit 11A.6.)

Exercise 11-10ᴬ
Net pay and tax computations

P5

Total (gross) earnings for current pay period . . . . $ 725
Cumulative earnings of previous pay periods   9,600

Check   Net pay, $578.54

Lucinda Florita, an unmarried employee, works 48 hours in the week ended January 12. Her pay rate is $14 per hour, and her wages are subject to no deductions other than FICA—Social Security, FICA—Medicare, and federal income taxes. She claims two withholding allowances. Compute her regular pay, overtime pay (overtime premium is 50% of the regular rate for hours in excess of 40 per week), and gross pay. Then compute her FICA tax deduction (use 6.2% for the Social Security portion and 1.45% for the Medicare portion), income tax deduction (use the wage bracket withholding table of Exhibit 11A.6), total deductions, and net pay.

Exercise 11-11ᴬ
Gross and net pay computation

P5

Check   Net pay, $596.30

Nishi Corporation prepares financial statements for each month-end. As part of its accounting process, estimated income taxes are accrued each month for 30% of the current month's net income. The income taxes are paid in the first month of each quarter for the amount accrued for the prior quarter. The following information is available for the fourth quarter of year 2008. When tax computations are completed on January 20, 2009, Nishi determines that the quarter's Income Taxes Payable account balance should be $28,300 on December 31, 2008 (its unadjusted balance is $24,690).

Exercise 11-12ᴮ
Accounting for income taxes

P4

October 2008 net income $28,600
November 2008 net income   19,100
December 2008 net income   34,600

1. Determine the amount of the accounting adjustment (dated as of December 31, 2008) to produce the proper ending balance in the Income Taxes Payable account.

Check (1) $3,610

2. Prepare journal entries to record (*a*) the December 31, 2008, adjustment to the Income Taxes Payable account and (*b*) the January 20, 2009, payment of the fourth-quarter taxes.

Tyrell Co. entered into the following transactions involving short-term liabilities in 2007 and 2008.

PROBLEM SET A

2007

Apr. 20   Purchased $40,250 of merchandise on credit from Locust, terms are 1/10, n/30. Tyrell uses the perpetual inventory system.

May 19   Replaced the April 20 account payable to Locust with a 90-day, $35,000 note bearing 10% annual interest along with paying $5,250 in cash.

Problem 11-1A
Short-term notes payable transactions and entries

P1

mhhe.com/wildFAP18e

July   8   Borrowed $80,000 cash from National Bank by signing a 120-day, 9% interest-bearing note with a face value of $80,000.

____?____   Paid the amount due on the note to Locust at the maturity date.

____?____   Paid the amount due on the note to National Bank at the maturity date.

Nov. 28   Borrowed $42,000 cash from Fargo Bank by signing a 60-day, 8% interest-bearing note with a face value of $42,000.

Dec. 31   Recorded an adjusting entry for accrued interest on the note to Fargo Bank.

2008

____?____   Paid the amount due on the note to Fargo Bank at the maturity date.

Required

Check   (2) Locust, $875
(3) $308
(4) $252

1. Determine the maturity date for each of the three notes described.
2. Determine the interest due at maturity for each of the three notes. (Assume a 360-day year.)
3. Determine the interest expense to be recorded in the adjusting entry at the end of 2007.
4. Determine the interest expense to be recorded in 2008.
5. Prepare journal entries for all the preceding transactions and events for years 2007–2008.

Problem 11-2A
Warranty expense and
liability estimation

P4

On October 29, 2007, Lobo Co. began operations by purchasing razors for resale. Lobo uses the perpetual inventory method. The razors have a 90-day warranty that requires the company to replace any nonworking razor. When a razor is returned, the company discards it and mails a new one from Merchandise Inventory to the customer. The company's cost per new razor is $20 and its retail selling price is $75 in both 2007 and 2008. The manufacturer has advised the company to expect warranty costs to equal 8% of dollar sales. The following transactions and events occurred.

2007

Nov. 11   Sold 105 razors for $7,875 cash.
    30   Recognized warranty expense related to November sales with an adjusting entry.
Dec. 9   Replaced 15 razors that were returned under the warranty.
    16   Sold 220 razors for $16,500 cash.
    29   Replaced 30 razors that were returned under the warranty.
    31   Recognized warranty expense related to December sales with an adjusting entry.

2008

Jan. 5   Sold 150 razors for $11,250 cash.
    17   Replaced 50 razors that were returned under the warranty.
    31   Recognized warranty expense related to January sales with an adjusting entry.

Required

Check   (3) $900
(4) $1,050 Cr.
(5) $950 Cr.

1. Prepare journal entries to record these transactions and adjustments for 2007 and 2008.
2. How much warranty expense is reported for November 2007 and for December 2007?
3. How much warranty expense is reported for January 2008?
4. What is the balance of the Estimated Warranty Liability account as of December 31, 2007?
5. What is the balance of the Estimated Warranty Liability account as of January 31, 2008?

Problem 11-3A
Computing and analyzing times
interest earned

A1

Shown here are condensed income statements for two different companies (both are organized as LLCs and pay no income taxes).

Miller Company	
Sales	$1,000,000
Variable expenses (80%)	800,000
Income before interest	200,000
Interest expense (fixed)	60,000
Net income	$ 140,000

Weaver Company	
Sales	$1,000,000
Variable expenses (60%)	600,000
Income before interest	400,000
Interest expense (fixed)	260,000
Net income	$ 140,000

Required

1. Compute times interest earned for Miller Company.

2. Compute times interest earned for Weaver Company.

3. What happens to each company's net income if sales increase by 30%?

4. What happens to each company's net income if sales increase by 50%?

5. What happens to each company's net income if sales increase by 80%?

6. What happens to each company's net income if sales decrease by 10%?

7. What happens to each company's net income if sales decrease by 20%?

8. What happens to each company's net income if sales decrease by 40%?

Check (3) Miller net income, $200,000 (43% increase)

(6) Weaver net income, $100,000 (29% decrease)

Analysis Component

9. Comment on the results from parts 3 through 8 in relation to the fixed-cost strategies of the two companies and the ratio values you computed in parts 1 and 2.

Paloma Co. pays its employees each week. Its employees' gross pay is subject to these taxes:

Tax	Rate	Applied To
FICA—Social Security	6.20%	First $94,200
FICA—Medicare	1.45	All gross pay
FUTA	0.80	First $7,000
SUTA	2.15	First $7,000

Problem 11-4A
Payroll expenses, withholdings, and taxes

P2 P3

mhhe.com/wildFAP18e

The company is preparing its payroll calculations for the week ended August 25. Payroll records show the following information for the company's four employees.

File Edit View Insert Format Tools Data Accounting Window Help

Name	Gross Pay through 8/18	Current Week	
		Gross Pay	Income Tax Withholding
Dahlia	$93,400	$2,800	$284
Trey	31,700	1,000	145
Kiesha	6,850	550	39
Chee	1,250	500	30

Sheet1 / Sheet2 / Sheet3 /

In addition to gross pay, the company must pay one-half of the $34 per employee weekly health insurance; each employee pays the remaining one-half. The company also contributes an extra 8% of each employee's gross pay (at no cost to employees) to a pension fund.

Required

Compute the following for the week ended August 25 (round amounts to the nearest cent):

1. Each employee's FICA withholdings for Social Security.

2. Each employee's FICA withholdings for Medicare.

3. Employer's FICA taxes for Social Security.

4. Employer's FICA taxes for Medicare.

5. Employer's FUTA taxes.

6. Employer's SUTA taxes.

7. Each employee's net (take-home) pay.

8. Employer's total payroll-related expense for each employee.

Check (3) $176.70
(4) $70.33
(5) $5.20

(7) Total net pay, $4,036.97

Problem 11-5A
Entries for payroll transactions

P2   P3

On January 8, the end of the first weekly pay period of the year, Regis Company's payroll register showed that its employees earned $22,760 of office salaries and $65,840 of sales salaries. Withholdings from the employees' salaries include FICA Social Security taxes at the rate of 6.2%, FICA Medicare taxes at the rate of 1.45%, $12,860 of federal income taxes, $1,340 of medical insurance deductions, and $840 of union dues. No employee earned more than $7,000 in this first period.

Required

Check   (1) Cr. Accrued Payroll
             Payable, $66,782.10

            (2) Dr. Payroll Taxes
             Expense, $11,030.70

1. Calculate FICA Social Security taxes payable and FICA Medicare taxes payable. Prepare the journal entry to record Regis Company's January 8 (employee) payroll expenses and liabilities.

2. Prepare the journal entry to record Regis's (employer) payroll taxes resulting from the January 8 payroll. Regis's merit rating reduces its state unemployment tax rate to 4.0% of the first $7,000 paid each employee. The federal unemployment tax rate is 0.8%.

Problem 11-6A[A]
Entries for payroll transactions

P2   P3   P5

Francisco Company has 10 employees, each of whom earns $2,800 per month and is paid on the last day of each month. All 10 have been employed continuously at this amount since January 1. Francisco uses a payroll bank account and special payroll checks to pay its employees. On March 1, the following accounts and balances exist in its general ledger:

a. FICA—Social Security Taxes Payable, $3,472; FICA—Medicare Taxes Payable, $812. (The balances of these accounts represent total liabilities for *both* the employer's and employees' FICA taxes for the February payroll only.)

b. Employees' Federal Income Taxes Payable, $4,000 (liability for February only).

c. Federal Unemployment Taxes Payable, $448 (liability for January and February together).

d. State Unemployment Taxes Payable, $2,240 (liability for January and February together).

During March and April, the company had the following payroll transactions.

Mar. 15   Issued check payable to Swift Bank, a federal depository bank authorized to accept employers' payments of FICA taxes and employee income tax withholdings. The $8,284 check is in payment of the February FICA and employee income taxes.

Check   March 31: Cr. Accrued Payroll
             Payable, $21,858

       31   Recorded the March payroll and transferred funds from the regular bank account to the payroll bank account. Issued checks payable to each employee in payment of the March payroll. The payroll register shows the following summary totals for the March pay period.

Salaries and Wages				Federal	
Office Salaries	Shop Wages	Gross Pay	FICA Taxes*	Income Taxes	Net Pay
$11,200	$16,800	$28,000	$1,736	$4,000	$21,858
			$ 406		

* FICA taxes are Social Security and Medicare, respectively.

March 31: Dr. Payroll Taxes
Expenses, $2,814

       31   Recorded the employer's payroll taxes resulting from the March payroll. The company has a merit rating that reduces its state unemployment tax rate to 4.0% of the first $7,000 paid each employee. The federal rate is 0.8%.

April 15: Cr. Cash, $8,284
(Swift Bank)

Apr. 15   Issued check to Swift Bank in payment of the March FICA and employee income taxes.
      15   Issued check to the State Tax Commission for the January, February, and March state unemployment taxes. Mailed the check and the first quarter tax return to the Commission.
      30   Issued check payable to Swift Bank in payment of the employer's FUTA taxes for the first quarter of the year.
      30   Mailed Form 941 to the IRS, reporting the FICA taxes and the employees' federal income tax withholdings for the first quarter.

Required

Prepare journal entries to record the transactions and events for both March and April.

Warner Co. entered into the following transactions involving short-term liabilities in 2007 and 2008.

2007

Problem 11-1B
Short-term notes payable transactions and entries

P1

Apr. 22   Purchased $5,000 of merchandise on credit from Fox Products, terms are 1/10, n/30. Warner uses the perpetual inventory system.

May 23   Replaced the April 22 account payable to Fox Products with a 60-day, $4,600 note bearing 15% annual interest along with paying $400 in cash.

July 15   Borrowed $12,000 cash from Spring Bank by signing a 120-day, 10% interest-bearing note with a face value of $12,000.

___?___   Paid the amount due on the note to Fox Products at maturity.

___?___   Paid the amount due on the note to Spring Bank at maturity.

Dec. 6   Borrowed $8,000 cash from City Bank by signing a 45-day, 9% interest-bearing note with a face value of $8,000.

31   Recorded an adjusting entry for accrued interest on the note to City Bank.

2008

___?___   Paid the amount due on the note to City Bank at maturity.

Required

1. Determine the maturity date for each of the three notes described.
2. Determine the interest due at maturity for each of the three notes. (Assume a 360-day year.)
3. Determine the interest expense to be recorded in the adjusting entry at the end of 2007.
4. Determine the interest expense to be recorded in 2008.
5. Prepare journal entries for all the preceding transactions and events for years 2007–2008.

Check (2) Fox, $115
(3) $50
(4) $40

On November 10, 2007, Lee Co. began operations by purchasing coffee grinders for resale. Lee uses the perpetual inventory method. The grinders have a 60-day warranty that requires the company to replace any nonworking grinder. When a grinder is returned, the company discards it and mails a new one from Merchandise Inventory to the customer. The company's cost per new grinder is $24 and its retail selling price is $50 in both 2007 and 2008. The manufacturer has advised the company to expect warranty costs to equal 10% of dollar sales. The following transactions and events occurred.

Problem 11-2B
Warranty expense and liability estimation

P4

2007

Nov. 16   Sold 50 grinders for $2,500 cash.

30   Recognized warranty expense related to November sales with an adjusting entry.

Dec. 12   Replaced six grinders that were returned under the warranty.

18   Sold 200 grinders for $10,000 cash.

28   Replaced 17 grinders that were returned under the warranty.

31   Recognized warranty expense related to December sales with an adjusting entry.

2008

Jan. 7   Sold 40 grinders for $2,000 cash.

21   Replaced 36 grinders that were returned under the warranty.

31   Recognized warranty expense related to January sales with an adjusting entry.

Required

1. Prepare journal entries to record these transactions and adjustments for 2007 and 2008.
2. How much warranty expense is reported for November 2007 and for December 2007?
3. How much warranty expense is reported for January 2008?
4. What is the balance of the Estimated Warranty Liability account as of December 31, 2007?
5. What is the balance of the Estimated Warranty Liability account as of January 31, 2008?

Check (3) $200
(4) $698 Cr.
(5) $34 Cr.

Problem 11-3B

Computing and analyzing times interest earned

A1

Shown here are condensed income statements for two different companies (both are organized as LLCs and pay no income taxes).

Ellis Company	
Sales	$240,000
Variable expenses (50%)	120,000
Income before interest	120,000
Interest expense (fixed)	90,000
Net income	$ 30,000

Seidel Company	
Sales	$240,000
Variable expenses (75%)	180,000
Income before interest	60,000
Interest expense (fixed)	30,000
Net income	$ 30,000

Required

1. Compute times interest earned for Ellis Company.
2. Compute times interest earned for Seidel Company.
3. What happens to each company's net income if sales increase by 10%?
4. What happens to each company's net income if sales increase by 40%?
5. What happens to each company's net income if sales increase by 90%?
6. What happens to each company's net income if sales decrease by 20%?
7. What happens to each company's net income if sales decrease by 50%?
8. What happens to each company's net income if sales decrease by 80%?

Check   (4) Ellis net income, $78,000 (160% increase)

(6) Seidel net income, $18,000 (40% decrease)

Analysis Component

9. Comment on the results from parts 3 through 8 in relation to the fixed cost strategies of the two companies and the ratio values you computed in parts 1 and 2.

Problem 11-4B

Payroll expenses, withholdings, and taxes

P2 P3

Fishing Guides Co. pays its employees each week. Employees' gross pay is subject to these taxes.

Tax	Rate	Applied To
FICA—Social Security	6.20%	First $94,200
FICA—Medicare	1.45	All gross pay
FUTA	0.80	First $7,000
SUTA	1.75	First $7,000

The company is preparing its payroll calculations for the week ended September 30. Payroll records show the following information for the company's four employees.

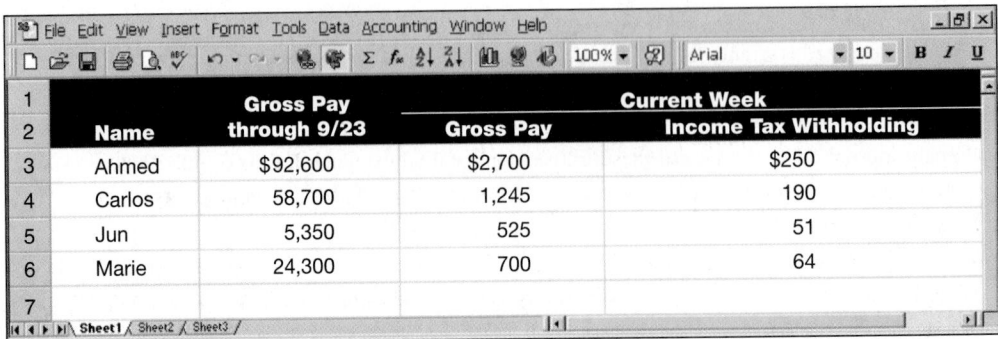

	Name	Gross Pay through 9/23	Current Week Gross Pay	Current Week Income Tax Withholding
3	Ahmed	$92,600	$2,700	$250
4	Carlos	58,700	1,245	190
5	Jun	5,350	525	51
6	Marie	24,300	700	64

In addition to gross pay, the company must pay one-half of the $40 per employee weekly health insurance; each employee pays the remaining one-half. The company also contributes an extra 5% of each employee's gross pay (at no cost to employees) to a pension fund.

Required

Compute the following for the week ended September 30 (round amounts to the nearest cent):

1. Each employee's FICA withholdings for Social Security.
2. Each employee's FICA withholdings for Medicare.
3. Employer's FICA taxes for Social Security.
4. Employer's FICA taxes for Medicare.
5. Employer's FUTA taxes.
6. Employer's SUTA taxes.
7. Each employee's net (take-home) pay.
8. Employer's total payroll-related expense for each employee.

Check (3) $252.34
(4) $74.96
(5) $4.20

(7) Total net pay, $4,207.70

Tavella Company's first weekly pay period of the year ends on January 8. On that date, the column totals in Tavella's payroll register indicate its sales employees earned $34,745, its office employees earned $21,225, and its delivery employees earned $1,030. The employees are to have withheld from their wages FICA Social Security taxes at the rate of 6.2%, FICA Medicare taxes at the rate of 1.45%, $8,625 of federal income taxes, $1,160 of medical insurance deductions, and $138 of union dues. No employee earned more than $7,000 in the first pay period.

Problem 11-5B
Entries for payroll transactions

P2 P3

Required

1. Calculate FICA Social Security taxes payable and FICA Medicare taxes payable. Prepare the journal entry to record Tavella Company's January 8 (employee) payroll expenses and liabilities.
2. Prepare the journal entry to record Tavella's (employer) payroll taxes resulting from the January 8 payroll. Tavella's merit rating reduces its state unemployment tax rate to 3.4% of the first $7,000 paid each employee. The federal unemployment tax rate is 0.8%.

Check (1) Cr. Accrued Payroll
Payable, $42,716.50
(2) Dr. Payroll Taxes
Expense, $6,754.50

MLS Company has five employees, each of whom earns $1,600 per month and is paid on the last day of each month. All five have been employed continuously at this amount since January 1. MLS uses a payroll bank account and special payroll checks to pay its employees. On June 1, the following accounts and balances exist in its general ledger:

Problem 11-6B^A
Entries for payroll transactions

P2 P3 P5

a. FICA—Social Security Taxes Payable, $992; FICA—Medicare Taxes Payable, $232. (The balances of these accounts represent total liabilities for *both* the employer's and employees' FICA taxes for the May payroll only.)
b. Employees' Federal Income Taxes Payable, $1,050 (liability for May only).
c. Federal Unemployment Taxes Payable, $88 (liability for April and May together).
d. State Unemployment Taxes Payable, $440 (liability for April and May together).

During June and July, the company had the following payroll transactions.

June 15 Issued check payable to Security Bank, a federal depository bank authorized to accept employers' payments of FICA taxes and employee income tax withholdings. The $2,274 check is in payment of the May FICA and employee income taxes.

30 Recorded the June payroll and transferred funds from the regular bank account to the payroll bank account. Issued checks payable to each employee in payment of the June payroll. The payroll register shows the following summary totals for the June pay period.

Check June 30: Cr. Accrued Payroll
Payable, $6,338

| Salaries and Wages | | | | Federal | |
Office Salaries	Shop Wages	Gross Pay	FICA Taxes*	Income Taxes	Net Pay
$3,800	$4,200	$8,000	$496	$1,050	$6,338
			$116		

* FICA taxes are Social Security and Medicare, respectively.

30   Recorded the employer's payroll taxes resulting from the June payroll. The company has a merit rating that reduces its state unemployment tax rate to 4.0% of the first $7,000 paid each employee. The federal rate is 0.8%.

July 15   Issued check payable to Security Bank in payment of the June FICA and employee income taxes.

15   Issued check to the State Tax Commission for the April, May, and June state unemployment taxes. Mailed the check and the second quarter tax return to the State Tax Commission.

31   Issued check payable to Security Bank in payment of the employer's FUTA taxes for the second quarter of the year.

31   Mailed Form 941 to the IRS, reporting the FICA taxes and the employees' federal income tax withholdings for the second quarter.

Required

Prepare journal entries to record the transactions and events for both June and July.

PROBLEM SET C

Problem Set C is available at the book's Website to further reinforce and assess your learning.

SERIAL PROBLEM

Success Systems

(This serial problem began in Chapter 1 and continues through most of the book. If previous chapter segments were not completed, the serial problem can begin at this point. It is helpful, but not necessary, for you to use the Working Papers that accompany the book.)

SP 11   Review the February 26 and March 25 transactions for Success Systems (SP 5) from Chapter 5.

Required

1.^AAssume that Michelle Jones is an unmarried employee. Her $1,200 of wages are subject to no deductions other than FICA Social Security taxes, FICA Medicare taxes, and federal income taxes. Her federal income taxes for this pay period total $189. Compute her net pay for the eight days' work paid on February 26.

2. Record the journal entry to reflect the payroll payment to Michelle Jones as computed in part 1.

3. Record the journal entry to reflect the (employer) payroll tax expenses for the February 26 payroll payment. Assume Michelle Jones has not met earnings limits for FUTA and SUTA—the FUTA rate is 0.8% and the SUTA rate is 4% for Success Systems.

4. Record the entry(ies) for the merchandise sold on March 25 if a 4% sales tax rate applies.

COMPREHENSIVE PROBLEM

Bug-Off Exterminators
(Review of Chapters 1–11)

CP 11   Bug-Off Exterminators provides pest control services and sells extermination products manufactured by other companies. The following six-column table contains the company's unadjusted trial balance as of December 31, 2008.

BUG-OFF EXTERMINATORS December 31, 2008				
	Unadjusted Trial Balance		Adjustments	Adjusted Trial Balance
Cash	$ 18,000			
Accounts receivable	5,000			
Allowance for doubtful accounts		$ 928		
Merchandise inventory	12,700			
Trucks	40,000			
Accum. depreciation—Trucks		0		
Equipment	55,000			
Accum. depreciation—Equipment		14,400		
Accounts payable		4,800		

[continued on next page]

[continued from previous page]

Estimated warranty liability		1,400
Unearned services revenue		0
Interest payable		0
Long-term notes payable		15,000
D. Buggs, Capital		62,600
D. Buggs, Withdrawals	10,000	
Extermination services revenue		70,000
Interest revenue		872
Sales (of merchandise)		80,000
Cost of goods sold	57,991	
Depreciation expense—Trucks	0	
Depreciation expense—Equipment	0	
Wages expense	32,500	
Interest expense	0	
Rent expense	10,000	
Bad debts expense	0	
Miscellaneous expense	1,338	
Repairs expense	671	
Utilities expense	6,800	
Warranty expense	0	
Totals	$250,000	$250,000

The following information in *a* through *h* applies to the company at the end of the current year.

a. The bank reconciliation as of December 31, 2008, includes these facts:

Cash balance per bank	$16,100
Cash balance per books	18,000
Outstanding checks	1,800
Deposit in transit	1,450
Interest earned (on bank account)	52
Bank service charges (miscellaneous expense)	15

Reported on the bank statement is a canceled check that the company failed to record. (Information from the bank reconciliation allows you to determine the amount of this check, which is a payment on an account payable.)

b. An examination of customers' accounts shows that accounts totaling $779 should be written off as uncollectible. Using an aging of receivables, the company determines that the ending balance of the Allowance for Doubtful Accounts should be $800.

c. A truck is purchased and placed in service on January 1, 2008. Its cost is being depreciated with the straight-line method using these facts and estimates:

Original cost	$40,000
Expected salvage value	5,000
Useful life (years)	5

d. Two items of equipment (a sprayer and an injector) were purchased and put into service in early January 2006. They are being depreciated with the straight-line method using these facts and estimates:

	Sprayer	Injector
Original cost	$35,000	$20,000
Expected salvage value	3,000	4,000
Useful life (years)	8	5

e. On August 1, 2008, the company is paid $7,680 in advance to provide monthly service for an apartment complex for one year. The company began providing the services in August. When the cash was received, the full amount was credited to the Extermination Services Revenue account.

f. The company offers a warranty for the services it sells. The expected cost of providing warranty service is 2.5% of the extermination services revenue of $65,520 for 2008. No warranty expense has been recorded for 2008. All costs of servicing warranties in 2008 were properly debited to the Estimated Warranty Liability account.

g. The $15,000 long-term note is an 8%, five-year, interest-bearing note with interest payable annually on December 31. The note was signed with First National Bank on December 31, 2008.

h. The ending inventory of merchandise is counted and determined to have a cost of $12,700. Bug-Off uses a perpetual inventory system.

Required

1. Use the preceding information to determine amounts for the following items.

Check (1*a*) Cash bal. $15,750
        (1*b*) $651 credit

    a. Correct (reconciled) ending balance of Cash, and the amount of the omitted check.

    b. Adjustment needed to obtain the correct ending balance of the Allowance for Doubtful Accounts.

    c. Depreciation expense for the truck used during year 2008.

    d. Depreciation expense for the two items of equipment used during year 2008.

    e. The adjusted 2008 ending balances of the Extermination Services Revenue and Unearned Services Revenue accounts.

(1*f*) Estim. warranty liability, $3,038 Cr.

    f. The adjusted 2008 ending balances of the accounts for Warranty Expense and Estimated Warranty Liability.

    g. The adjusted 2008 ending balances of the accounts for Interest Expense and Interest Payable. (Round amounts to nearest whole dollar.)

(2) Adjusted trial balance totals, $263,475

2. Use the results of part 1 to complete the six-column table by first entering the appropriate adjustments for items *a* through *g* and then completing the adjusted trial balance columns. (*Hint:* Item *b* requires two adjustments.)

3. Prepare journal entries to record the adjustments entered on the six-column table. Assume Bug-Off's adjusted balance for Merchandise Inventory matches the year-end physical count.

(4) Net income, $20,640; Total assets, $98,271

4. Prepare a single-step income statement, a statement of owner's equity (cash withdrawals during 2008 were $10,000), and a classified balance sheet.

BEYOND THE NUMBERS

REPORTING IN ACTION

A1 P4

BTN 11-1   Refer to the financial statements of **Best Buy** in Appendix A to answer the following.

1. Compute times interest earned for the fiscal years ended 2005, 2004, and 2003. Comment on Best Buy's ability to cover its interest expense for this period. Assume an industry average of 19.9.

2. Best Buy's current liabilities include "Unredeemed gift card liabilities." Explain how this liability is created and how Best Buy satisfies this liability.

3. Does Best Buy have any commitments or contingencies? Briefly explain them.

Fast Forward

4. Access Best Buy's financial statements for fiscal years ending after February 26, 2005, at its Website (BestBuy.com) or the SEC's EDGAR database (www.SEC.gov). Compute its times interest earned for years ending after February 26, 2005, and compare your results to those in part 1.

COMPARATIVE ANALYSIS

A1

BTN 11-2   Key comparative figures ($ millions) for both **Best Buy** and **Circuit City** follow.

Key Figures	Best Buy			Circuit City		
	Current Year	One Year Prior	Two Years Prior	Current Year	One Year Prior	Two Years Prior
Net income	$984	$705	$ 99	$62	$(89)	$82
Income taxes	509	496	392	36	0	0
Interest expense	44	32	30	2	2	1

Required

1. Compute times interest earned for the three years' data shown for each company.
2. Comment on which company appears stronger in its ability to pay interest obligations if income should decline. Assume an industry average of 19.9.

BTN 11-3 Carmine Bly is a sales manager for an automobile dealership. He earns a bonus each year based on revenue from the number of autos sold in the year less related warranty expenses. Actual warranty expenses have varied over the prior 10 years from a low of 3% of an automobile's selling price to a high of 10%. In the past, Bly has tended to estimate warranty expenses on the high end to be conservative. He must work with the dealership's accountant at year-end to arrive at the warranty expense accrual for cars sold each year.

ETHICS CHALLENGE

P4

1. Does the warranty accrual decision create any ethical dilemma for Bly?
2. Since warranty expenses vary, what percent do you think Bly should choose for the current year? Justify your response.

BTN 11-4 Dustin Clemens is the accounting and finance manager for a manufacturer. At year-end, he must determine how to account for the company's contingencies. His manager, Tom Pretti, objects to Clemens's proposal to recognize an expense and a liability for warranty service on units of a new product introduced in the fourth quarter. Pretti comments, "There's no way we can estimate this warranty cost. We don't owe anyone anything until a product fails and it is returned. Let's report an expense if and when we do any warranty work."

COMMUNICATING IN PRACTICE

C3

Required

Prepare a one-page memorandum for Clemens to send to Pretti defending his proposal.

BTN 11-5 Access the March 4, 2005, filing of the December 31, 2004, annual 10-K report of McDonald's Corporation (Ticker: MCD), which is available from www.sec.gov.

TAKING IT TO THE NET

C1 A1

Required

1. Identify the current liabilities on McDonald's balance sheet as of December 31, 2004.
2. What portion (in percent) of McDonald's long-term debt matures within the next 12 months?
3. Use the consolidated statement of income for the year ended December 31, 2004, to compute McDonald's times interest earned ratio. Comment on the result. Assume an industry average of 7.9.

BTN 11-6 Assume that your team is in business and you must borrow $6,000 cash for short-term needs. You have been shopping banks for a loan, and you have the following two options.
A. Sign a $6,000, 90-day, 10% interest-bearing note dated June 1.
B. Sign a $6,000, 120-day, 8% interest-bearing note dated June 1.

TEAMWORK IN ACTION

C2 P1

Required

1. Discuss these two options and determine the best choice. Ensure that all teammates concur with the decision and understand the rationale.
2. Each member of the team is to prepare *one* of the following journal entries.
   a. Option A—at date of issuance.
   b. Option B—at date of issuance.
   c. Option A—at maturity date.
   d. Option B—at maturity date.
3. In rotation, each member is to explain the entry he or she prepared in part 2 to the team. Ensure that all team members concur with and understand the entries.

4. Assume that the funds are borrowed on December 1 (instead of June 1) and your business operates on a calendar-year reporting period. Each member of the team is to prepare *one* of the following entries.

    a. Option A—the year-end adjustment.

    b. Option B—the year-end adjustment.

    c. Option A—at maturity date.

    d. Option B—at maturity date.

5. In rotation, each member is to explain the entry he or she prepared in part 4 to the team. Ensure that all team members concur with and understand the entries.

BusinessWeek
ACTIVITY

P4

BTN 11-7   Read the article "Lessons from the Vioxx Fiasco" in the November 29, 2004, issue of *BusinessWeek*. (The book's Website provides a free link.)

Required

1. The article reports that Merck & Co. is facing personal-injury lawsuits that could cost billions. How should Merck & Co. account for these potential lawsuits?

2. The article reports that some Vioxx users are threatening to sue to get it back on the market. What would be the effect of these lawsuits on Merck & Co.'s financial statements.

ENTREPRENEURIAL DECISION

A1

BTN 11-8   Review the chapter's opening feature about Youngsong Martin and Wildflower Linens. Assume that Martin is considering expanding her business to open a branch in Hawaii. Assume her current income statement is as follows.

WILDFLOWER LINENS Income Statement For Year Ended December 31, 2008	
Sales	$1,000,000
Cost of goods sold (30%)	300,000
Gross profit	700,000
Operating expenses (25%)	250,000
Net income	$ 450,000

Martin currently has no interest-bearing debt. If Martin expands to open a Hawaiian location, she will require a $300,000 loan. She has found a bank that will loan her the money on a 7% note payable. Martin believes that, at least for the first few years, sales at her Hawaiian location will be $250,000, and that all expenses (including cost of goods sold) will follow the same patterns as her California location.

Required

1. Prepare an income statement (separately for California, Hawaii, and total) for Wildflower Linens assuming that she borrows the funds and expands to Hawaii. Annual revenues at the California location are expected to remain at $1,000,000.

2. Compute Wildflower Linens' times interest earned under the expansion assumptions in part 1.

3. Assume sales at the Hawaii location are $400,000. Prepare an income statement (separately for California, Hawaii, and total) for Wildflower Linens and compute times interest earned.

4. Assume sales at the Hawaii location are $100,000. Prepare an income statement (separately for California, Hawaii, and total) for Wildflower Linens and compute times interest earned.

5. Comment on your results from parts 1 through 4.

HITTING THE ROAD

P2

BTN 11-9 Check your phone book or the Social Security Administration Website (www.ssa.gov) to locate the Social Security office near you. Visit the office to request a personal earnings and estimate form. Fill out the form and mail according to the instructions. You will receive a statement from the Social Security Administration regarding your earnings history and future Social Security benefits you can receive. (Formerly the request could be made online. The online service has been discontinued and is now under review by the Social Security Administration due to security concerns.) It is good to request an earnings and benefit statement every 5 to 10 years to make sure you have received credit for all wages earned and for which you and your employer have paid taxes into the system.

GLOBAL DECISION

A1

BTN 11-10 Dixons, Best Buy, and Circuit City are all competitors in the global marketplace. Key comparative figures for Dixons (Dixons-Group.com), along with selected figures from Best Buy and Circuit City, follow.

Key Figures	Dixons (£ millions) Current Year	Prior Year	Best Buy Current Year	Prior Year	Circuit City Current Year	Prior Year
Net income	243.1	280.4	—	—	—	—
Income taxes	88.1	82.9	—	—	—	—
Interest expense	23.6	34.0	—	—	—	—
Times interest earned	?	?	34.9	38.5	50.0	(43.5)

Required

1. Compute the times interest earned ratio for the most recent two years for Dixons using the data shown.

2. Which company of the three presented provides the best coverage of interest expense? Explain.

ANSWERS TO MULTIPLE CHOICE QUIZ

1. b; $6,000 \times 0.05 \times 30/360 = \$25$

2. e; $\$50,000 \times (.062 + .0145) = \$3,825$

3. b; $\$7,000 \times (.008 + .054) = \$434$

4. c; 10,000 television sets $\times$ .01 $\times$ $250 = \$25,000$

5. a; 150 employees $\times$ $175 per day $\times$ 1 vacation day earned $= \$26,250$

12

Accounting for Partnerships

A Look Back

Chapter 11 focused on how current liabilities are identified, computed, recorded, and reported. Attention was directed at notes, payroll, sales taxes, warranties, employee benefits, and contingencies.

A Look at This Chapter

This chapter explains the partnership form of organization. Important partnership characteristics are described along with the accounting concepts and procedures for its most fundamental transactions.

A Look Ahead

Chapter 13 extends our discussion to the corporate form of organization. We describe the accounting and reporting for stock issuances, dividends, and other equity transactions.

Learning Objectives

CAP

Conceptual

C1 Identify characteristics of partnerships and similar organizations. *(p. 472)*

Analytical

A1 Compute partner return on equity and use it to evaluate partnership performance. *(p. 484)*

Procedural

P1 Prepare entries for partnership formation. *(p. 475)*

P2 Allocate and record income and loss among partners. *(p. 475)*

P3 Account for the admission and withdrawal of partners. *(p. 478)*

P4 Prepare entries for partnership liquidation. *(p. 482)*

"We're just really happy that we can still do what we enjoy doing ... we're lucky as hell"
—Catharine Lyons
(on right; Elska Sandor on left)

Skating Partners

NEW YORK, NY—In a Chinatown loft just off New York's Canal Street, Rookie Skateboards (**RookieSkateboards.com**) creates skateboard decks and apparel. But founders Catharine Lyons and Elska Sandor run a different sort of business. "Although we are women and happen to be the first women owned and operated skateboard company," says Catharine, "we run a company that simply celebrates the art and spirit of skate boarding." Adds Elska, "Tomboy can be chic—although skating is perhaps more difficult in a knee-length skirt."

The partners quickly learned there is more to the skate business than skating. Knowledge of partnerships and their financial implications became important to Rookie's success. "It's been hard for us to catch up with the business side of it," says Catharine. "We don't have much enthusiasm for the unpleasant details of running a business." Yet she stresses the importance of attending to partnership formation, agreements, and financials to stay afloat.

Success is causing their partnership to evolve. "We want to offer a unique route for all skateboarders and especially girls, but at the same time we want to be considered a legitimate skateboard company, not a novelty," says Catharine. "I don't feel the need to make a point of being a woman. What I'm doing is—in the end—about skating." As their skateboards and apparel evolve, the partners have not sold out. "I don't have to have daisies on my board," says Elska. "I can play with the same toys and still be a girl in the end. We are certainly not women trying to be men."

Still, the partners are gaining business savvy. "We're trying to get ourselves as streamlined and efficient as possible," says Catharine. "Rookie embodies an enthusiasm and positive outlook for the future while keeping a 'scrappy' edge."

The partners also know to ask for help. When starting a partnership "it's good to be honest about what you are good at and what you are not, and align yourself with good professionals, like accountants, to fill in the gaps," says Catharine. "Don't take yourself too seriously. Laugh a lot, and at yourself. Know how to enjoy yourself. That helps make it work."

[Sources: *Rookie Skateboards Website*, January 2006; *Koch Entertainment Website*, January 2004; *Entrepreneur*, May 2003; *Newsday*, April 2003; *Billboard*, June 2002]

The three basic types of business organizations are proprietorships, partnerships, and corporations. Partnerships are similar to proprietorships, except they have more than one owner. This chapter explains partnerships and looks at several variations of them such as limited partnerships, limited liability partnerships, S corporations, and limited liability companies. Understanding the advantages and disadvantages of the partnership form of business organization is important for making informed business decisions.

Accounting for Partnerships

Partnership Organization	Basic Partnership Accounting	Partner Admission and Withdrawal	Partnership Liquidation
• Characteristics • Organizations with partnership characteristics • Choice of a business form	• Organizing a partnership • Dividing income or loss • Partnership financial statements	• Admission of partner • Withdrawal of partner • Death of partner	• No capital deficiency • Capital deficiency

Partnership Form of Organization

C1 Identify characteristics of partnerships and similar organizations.

A **partnership** is an unincorporated association of two or more people to pursue a business for profit as co-owners. Many businesses are organized as partnerships. They are especially common in small retail and service businesses. Many professional practitioners, including physicians, lawyers, investors, and accountants, also organize their practices as partnerships.

Characteristics of Partnerships

Partnerships are an important type of organization because they offer certain advantages with their unique characteristics. We describe these characteristics in this section.

Voluntary Association A partnership is a voluntary association between partners. Joining a partnership increases the risk to one's personal financial position. Some courts have ruled that partnerships are created by the actions of individuals even when there is no *express agreement* to form one.

Partnership Agreement Forming a partnership requires that two or more legally competent people (who are of age and of sound mental capacity) agree to be partners. Their agreement becomes a **partnership contract,** also called *articles of copartnership.* Although it should be in writing, the contract is binding even if it is only expressed verbally. Partnership agreements normally include details of the partners' (1) names and contributions, (2) rights and duties, (3) sharing of income and losses, (4) withdrawal arrangement, (5) dispute procedures, (6) admission and withdrawal of partners, and (7) rights and duties in the event a partner dies.

Point: When a new partner is admitted, all parties usually must agree to the admission.

Limited Life The life of a partnership is limited. Death, bankruptcy, or any event taking away the ability of a partner to enter into or fulfill a contract ends a partnership. Any one of the partners can also terminate a partnership at will.

Point: The end of a partnership is referred to as its *dissolution.*

Taxation A partnership is not subject to taxes on its income. The income or loss of a partnership is allocated to the partners according to the partnership agreement, and it is included in determining the taxable income for each partner's tax return. Partnership income or loss is allocated each year whether or not cash is distributed to partners.

Point: Partners are taxed on their share of partnership income, not on their withdrawals.

Mutual Agency   **Mutual agency** implies that each partner is a fully authorized agent of the partnership. As its agent, a partner can commit or bind the partnership to any contract within the scope of the partnership business. For instance, a partner in a merchandising business can sign contracts binding the partnership to buy merchandise, lease a store building, borrow money, or hire employees. These activities are all within the scope of a merchandising firm. A partner in a law firm, acting alone, however, cannot bind the other partners to a contract to buy snowboards for resale or rent an apartment for parties. These actions are outside the normal scope of a law firm's business. Partners also can agree to limit the power of any one or more of the partners to negotiate contracts for the partnership. This agreement is binding on the partners and on outsiders who know it exists. It is not binding on outsiders who do not know it exists. Outsiders unaware of the agreement have the right to assume each partner has normal agency powers for the partnership. Mutual agency exposes partners to the risk of unwise actions by any one partner.

Point: The majority of states adhere to the Uniform Partnership Act for the basic rules of partnership formation, operation, and dissolution.

Unlimited Liability   **Unlimited liability** implies that each partner can be called on to pay a partnership's debts. When a partnership cannot pay its debts, creditors usually can apply their claims to partners' *personal* assets. If a partner does not have enough assets to meet his or her share of the partnership debt, the creditors can apply their claims to the assets of the other partners. A partnership in which all partners have *mutual agency* and *unlimited liability* is called a **general partnership.** Mutual agency and unlimited liability are two main reasons that most general partnerships have only a few members.

Point: Limited life, mutual agency, and unlimited liability are disadvantages of a partnership.

Co-Ownership of Property   Partnership assets are owned jointly by all partners. Any investment by a partner becomes the joint property of all partners. Partners have a claim on partnership assets based on their capital account and the partnership contract.

Organizations with Partnership Characteristics

Organizations exist that combine certain characteristics of partnerships with other forms of organizations. We discuss several of these forms in this section.

Limited Partnerships   Some individuals who want to invest in a partnership are unwilling to accept the risk of unlimited liability. Their needs can be met with a **limited partnership.** This type of organization is identified in its name with the words "Limited Partnership," or

"Ltd.," or "LP." A limited partnership has two classes of partners, general and limited. At least one partner must be a **general partner,** who assumes management duties and unlimited liability for the debts of the partnership. The **limited partners** have no personal liability beyond the amounts they invest in the partnership. Limited partners have no active role except as specified in the partnership agreement. A limited partnership agreement often specifies unique procedures for allocating income and losses between general and limited partners. The accounting procedures are similar for both limited and general partnerships.

<table><tr><td colspan="2">**Decision Insight**</td></tr></table>

Nutty Partners   The Hawaii-based ML Macadamia Orchards LP is one of the world's largest growers of macadamia nuts. It reported the following partners' capital balances ($ 000s) in its balance sheet:

| General Partner . . . . | $ 505 |
| Limited Partners . . . . | $50,037 |

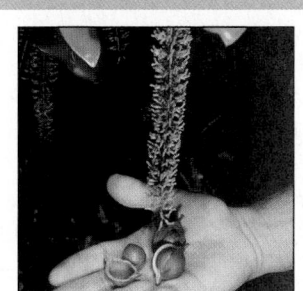

Limited Liability Partnerships   Most states allow individuals to form a **limited liability partnership.** This is identified in its name with the words "Limited Liability Partnership" or by "LLP." This type of partnership is designed to protect innocent partners from malpractice or negligence claims resulting from the acts of another partner. When a partner provides service resulting in a malpractice claim, that partner has personal liability for the claim. The remaining partners who were not responsible for the actions resulting in the claim are not personally liable for it. However, most states hold all partners personally liable for other partnership debts. Accounting for a limited liability partnership is the same as for a general partnership.

Point: Many accounting services firms are set up as LLPs.

S Corporations   Certain corporations with 75 or fewer stockholders can elect to be treated as a partnership for income tax purposes. These corporations are called *Sub-Chapter S* or simply **S corporations.** This distinguishes them from other corporations, called *Sub-Chapter C* or simply **C corporations.** S corporations provide stockholders the same limited liability feature that C corporations do. The advantage of an S corporation is that it does not pay income taxes. If stockholders work for an S corporation, their salaries are treated as expenses of the corporation. The remaining income or loss of the corporation is allocated to stockholders for inclusion on their personal tax returns. Except for C corporations having to account for income tax expenses and liabilities, the accounting procedures are the same for both S and C corporations.

Limited Liability Companies   A relatively new form of business organization is the **limited liability company.** The names of these businesses usually include the words "Limited Liability Company" or an abbreviation such as "LLC" or "LC." This form of business has certain features similar to a corporation and others similar to a limited partnership. The owners, who are called *members,* are protected with the same limited liability feature as owners of corporations. While limited partners cannot actively participate in the management of a limited partnership, the members of a limited liability company can assume an active management role. A limited liability company usually has a limited life. For income tax purposes, a limited liability company is typically treated as a partnership. This treatment depends on factors such as whether the members' equity interests are freely transferable and whether the company has continuity of life. A limited liability company's accounting system is designed to help management comply with the dictates of the articles of organization and company regulations adopted by its members. The accounting system also must provide information to support the company's compliance with state and federal laws, including taxation.

Choosing a Business Form

Choosing the proper business form is crucial. Many factors should be considered, including taxes, liability risk, tax and fiscal year-end, ownership structure, estate planning, business risks, and earnings and property distributions. The following table summarizes several important characteristics of business organizations:

	Proprietorship	Partnership	LLP	LLC	S Corp.	Corporation
Business entity	yes	yes	yes	yes	yes	yes
Legal entity	no	no	no	yes	yes	yes
Limited liability	no	no	limited*	yes	yes	yes
Business taxed	no	no	no	no	no	yes
One owner allowed	yes	no	no	yes	yes	yes

* A partner's personal liability for LLP debts is limited. Most LLPs carry insurance to protect against malpractice.

We must remember that this table is a summary, not a detailed list. Many details underlie each of these business forms, and several details differ across states. Also, state and federal laws change, and a body of law is still developing around LLCs. Business owners should look at these details and consider unique business arrangements such as organizing various parts of their businesses in different forms.

Point: The majority of proprietorships and partnerships that are being organized today are being set up as an LLC.

Point: Accounting for LLCs is similar to that for partnerships (and proprietorships). One difference is that Owner (Partner), Capital is usually called *Members, Capital* for LLCs.

Point: Small Business Administration provides suggestions and information on setting up the proper form for your organization—see **SBA.gov.**

Quick Check
Answers—p. 487

1. A partnership is terminated in the event (*a*) a partnership agreement is not in writing, (*b*) a partner dies, (*c*) a partner exercises mutual agency.
2. What does the term *unlimited liability* mean when applied to a general partnership?
3. Which of the following forms of organization do not provide limited liability to *all* of its owners: (*a*) S corporation, (*b*) limited liability company, (*c*) limited partnership?

Basic Partnership Accounting

Since ownership rights in a partnership are divided among partners, partnership accounting

- ■ Uses a capital account for each partner.
- ■ Uses a withdrawals account for each partner.
- ■ Allocates net income or loss to partners according to the partnership agreement.

This section describes partnership accounting for organizing a partnership, distributing income and loss, and preparing financial statements.

Organizing a Partnership

When partners invest in a partnership, their capital accounts are credited for the invested amounts. Partners can invest both assets and liabilities. Each partner's investment is recorded at an agreed-on value, normally the market values of the contributed assets and liabilities at the date of contribution. To illustrate, Kayla Zayn and Hector Perez organize a partnership on January 11 called BOARDS that offers year-round facilities for skateboarding and snowboarding. Zayn's initial net investment in BOARDS is $30,000, made up of cash ($7,000), boarding facilities ($33,000), and a note payable reflecting a bank loan for the new business ($10,000). Perez's initial investment is cash of $10,000. These amounts are the values agreed on by both partners. The entries to record these investments follow.

P1 Prepare entries for partnership formation.

Zayn's Investment

Jan. 11	Cash....................................	7,000	
	Boarding facilities...........................	33,000	
	Note payable........................		10,000
	K. Zayn, Capital.......................		30,000
	To record the investment of Zayn.		

Assets = Liabilities + Equity
+7,000   +10,000   +30,000
+33,000

Perez's Investment

Jan. 11	Cash....................................	10,000	
	H. Perez, Capital.......................		10,000
	To record the investment of Perez.		

Assets = Liabilities + Equity
+10,000   +10,000

In accounting for a partnership, the following additional relations hold true: (1) Partners' withdrawals are debited to their own separate withdrawals accounts. (2) Partners' capital accounts are credited (or debited) for their shares of net income (or net loss) when closing the accounts at the end of a period. (3) Each partner's withdrawals account is closed to that partner's capital account. Separate capital and withdrawals accounts are kept for each partner.

Point: Both equity and cash are reduced when a partner withdraws cash from a partnership.

Dividing Income or Loss

Partners are not employees of the partnership but are its owners. If partners devote their time and services to their partnership, they are understood to do so for profit, not for salary. This means there are no salaries to partners that are reported as expenses on the partnership income statement.

Decision Insight

Broadway Partners Big River Productions is a partnership that owns the rights to the play *Big River*. The play is performed on tour and periodically on Broadway. For 2004, its Partners' Capital was $58,777 and its partners received no distributions.

However, when net income or loss of a partnership is allocated among partners, the partners can agree to allocate "salary allowances" reflecting the relative value of services provided. Partners also can agree to allocate "interest allowances" based on the amount invested. For instance, since Zayn contributes three times the investment of Perez, it is only fair that this be considered when allocating income between them. Like salary allowances, these interest allowances are not expenses on the income statement.

P2 Allocate and record income and loss among partners.

Partners can agree to any method of dividing income or loss. In the absence of an agreement, the law says that the partners share income or loss of a partnership equally. If partners agree on how to share income but say nothing about losses, they share losses the same way they share income. Three common methods to divide income or loss use (1) a stated ratio basis, (2) the ratio of capital balances, or (3) salary and interest allowances and any remainder according to a fixed ratio. We explain each of these methods in this section.

Allocation on Stated Ratios

The *stated ratio* (also called the *income-and-loss-sharing ratio,* the *profit and loss ratio,* or the *P&L ratio*) method of allocating partnership income or loss gives each partner a fraction of the total. Partners must agree on the fractional share each receives. To illustrate, assume the partnership agreement of K. Zayn and H. Perez says Zayn receives two-thirds and Perez one-third of partnership income and loss. If their partnership's net income is $60,000, it is allocated to the partners when the Income Summary account is closed as follows.

Dec. 31	Income Summary	60,000	
	K. Zayn, Capital		40,000
	H. Perez, Capital		20,000
	To allocate income and close Income Summary.		

Allocation on Capital Balances

The *capital balances* method of allocating partnership income or loss assigns an amount based on the ratio of each partner's relative capital balance. If Zayn and Perez agree to share income and loss on the ratio of their beginning capital balances—Zayn's $30,000 and Perez's $10,000—Zayn receives three-fourths of any income or loss ($30,000/$40,000) and Perez receives one-fourth ($10,000/$40,000). The journal entry follows the same format as that using stated ratios (see preceding entries).

Allocation on Services, Capital, and Stated Ratios

The *services, capital, and stated ratio* method of allocating partnership income or loss recognizes that service and capital contributions of partners often are not equal. Salary allowances can make up for differences in service contributions. Interest allowances can make up for unequal capital contributions. Also, the allocation of income and loss can include *both* salary and interest allowances. To illustrate, assume that the partnership agreement of K. Zayn and H. Perez reflects differences in service and capital contributions as follows: (1) annual salary allowances of $36,000 to Zayn and $24,000 to Perez, (2) annual interest allowances of 10% of a partner's beginning-year capital balance, and (3) equal share of any remaining balance of income or loss. These salaries and interest allowances are *not* reported as expenses on the income statement. They are simply a means of dividing partnership income or loss. The remainder of this section provides two illustrations using this three-point allocation agreement.

Illustration when income exceeds allowance. If BOARDS has first-year net income of $70,000, and Zayn and Perez apply the three-point partnership agreement described in the prior paragraph, income is allocated as shown in Exhibit 12.1. Zayn gets $42,000 and Perez gets $28,000 of the $70,000 total.

Illustration when allowances exceed income. The sharing agreement between Zayn and Perez must be followed even if net income is less than the total of the allowances. For example, if BOARDS' first-year net income is $50,000 instead of $70,000, it is allocated to the partners as shown in Exhibit 12.2. Computations for salaries and interest are identical to those in Exhibit 12.1. However, when we apply the total allowances against income, the balance of income is negative. This $(14,000) negative balance is allocated equally to the partners per their sharing agreement. This means that a negative $(7,000) is allocated to each partner. In this case, Zayn ends up with $32,000 and Perez with $18,000. If BOARDS had experienced a net loss, Zayn and Perez would share it in the same manner as the $50,000 income. The only difference is that they would have begun with a negative amount because of the loss. Specifically, the partners would still have been allocated their salary and interest allowances, further adding

	Zayn	Perez	Total
Net income			$70,000
Salary allowances			
Zayn	$ 36,000		
Perez		$ 24,000	
Interest allowances			
Zayn (10% × $30,000)	3,000		
Perez (10% × $10,000)		1,000	
Total salaries and interest	39,000	25,000	64,000
Balance of income			6,000
Balance allocated equally			
Zayn	3,000 ←		
Perez		3,000 ←	
Total allocated			6,000
Balance of income			$ 0
Income of each partner	$42,000	$28,000	

Exhibit 12.1

Dividing Income When Income Exceeds Allowances

	Zayn	Perez	Total
Net income			$50,000
Salary allowances			
Zayn	$ 36,000		
Perez		$ 24,000	
Interest allowances			
Zayn (10% × $30,000)	3,000		
Perez (10% × $10,000)		1,000	
Total salaries and interest	39,000	25,000	64,000
Balance of income			(14,000)
Balance allocated equally			
Zayn	(7,000) ←		
Perez		(7,000) ←	
Total allocated			(14,000)
Balance of income			$ 0
Income of each partner	$32,000	$18,000	

Exhibit 12.2

Dividing Income When Allowances Exceed Income

to the negative balance of the loss. This *total* negative balance *after* salary and interest allowances would have been allocated equally between the partners. These allocations would have been applied against the positive numbers from any allowances to determine each partner's share of the loss.

Point: When a loss occurs, it is possible for a specific partner's capital to increase (when closing income summary) if that partner's allowance is in excess of his or her share of the negative balance. This implies that decreases to the capital balances of other partners exceed the partnership's loss amount.

Quick Check
Answers—p. 487

4. Denzel and Shantell form a partnership by contributing $70,000 and $35,000, respectively. They agree to an interest allowance equal to 10% of each partner's capital balance at the beginning of the year, with the remaining income shared equally. Allocate first-year income of $40,000 to each partner.

Partnership Financial Statements

Partnership financial statements are similar to those of other organizations. The **statement of partners' equity,** also called *statement of partners' capital,* is one exception. It shows *each* partner's beginning capital balance, additional investments, allocated income or loss, withdrawals, and ending capital balance. To illustrate, Exhibit 12.3 shows the statement of partners' equity for BOARDS prepared using the sharing agreement of Exhibit 12.1. Recall that BOARDS' income was $70,000; also, assume that Zayn withdrew $20,000 and Perez $12,000 at year-end.

The equity section of the balance sheet of a partnership usually shows the separate capital account balance of each partner. In the case of BOARDS, both K. Zayn, Capital, and H. Perez, Capital, are listed in the equity section along with their balances of $52,000 and $26,000, respectively.

Exhibit 12.3

Statement of Partners' Equity

	BOARDS				
	Statement of Partners' Equity				
	For Year Ended December 31, 2008				
		Zayn		**Perez**	**Total**
Beginning capital balances		$ 0		$ 0	$ 0
Plus					
Investments by owners		30,000		10,000	40,000
Net income					
Salary allowances	$36,000		$24,000		
Interest allowances	3,000		1,000		
Balance allocated	3,000		3,000		
Total net income		42,000		28,000	70,000
		72,000		38,000	110,000
Less partners' withdrawals		(20,000)		(12,000)	(32,000)
Ending capital balances		**$52,000**		**$26,000**	**$78,000**

Admission and Withdrawal of Partners

P3   Account for the admission and withdrawal of partners.

A partnership is based on a contract between individuals. When a partner is admitted or withdraws, the present partnership ends. Still, the business can continue to operate as a new partnership consisting of the remaining partners. This section considers how to account for the admission and withdrawal of partners.

Admission of a Partner

A new partner is admitted in one of two ways: by purchasing an interest from one or more current partners or by investing cash or other assets in the partnership.

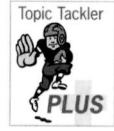

Topic Tackler

PLUS

12-2

Purchase of Partnership Interest The purchase of partnership interest is a *personal transaction between one or more current partners and the new partner.* To become a partner, the current partners must accept the purchaser. Accounting for the purchase of partnership interest involves reallocating current partners' capital to reflect the transaction. To illustrate, at the end of BOARDS' first year, H. Perez sells one-half of his partnership interest to Tyrell Rasheed for $18,000. This means that Perez gives up a $13,000 recorded interest ($26,000 × 1/2) in the partnership (see the ending capital balance in Exhibit 12.3). The partnership records this January 4 transaction as follows.

Assets = Liabilities + Equity			
−13,000	Jan. 4	H. Perez, Capital............................	13,000	
+13,000		T. Rasheed, Capital......................		13,000
		To record admission of Rasheed by purchase.		

After this entry is posted, BOARDS' equity shows K. Zayn, Capital; H. Perez, Capital; and T. Rasheed, Capital, and their respective balances of $52,000, $13,000, and $13,000.

Two aspects of this transaction are important. First, the partnership, does *not* record the $18,000 Rasheed paid Perez. The partnership's assets, liabilities, and *total equity* are unaffected by this transaction among partners. Second, Zayn and Perez must agree that Rasheed is to become a partner. If they agree to accept Rasheed, a new partnership is formed and a new contract with a new income-and-loss-sharing agreement is prepared. If Zayn or Perez refuses to accept Rasheed as a partner, then (under the Uniform Partnership Act) Rasheed gets Perez's sold share of partnership income and loss. If the partnership is liquidated, Rasheed gets Perez's sold share of partnership assets. Rasheed gets no voice in managing the company unless Rasheed is admitted as a partner.

Point: Partners' withdrawals are not constrained by the partnership's annual income or loss.

Investing Assets in a Partnership   Admitting a partner by accepting assets is a *transaction between the new partner and the partnership*. The invested assets become partnership property. To illustrate, if Zayn (with a $52,000 interest) and Perez (with a $26,000 interest) agree to accept Rasheed as a partner in BOARDS after an investment of $22,000 cash, this is recorded as follows.

Jan. 4	Cash..	22,000	
	T. Rasheed, Capital......................		22,000
	To record admission of Rasheed by investment.		

Assets	= Liabilities +	Equity
+22,000		+22,000

After this entry is posted, both assets (cash) and equity (T. Rasheed, Capital) increase by $22,000. Rasheed now has a 22% equity in the assets of the business, computed as $22,000 divided by the entire partnership equity ($52,000 + $26,000 + $22,000). Rasheed does not necessarily have a right to 22% of income. Dividing income and loss is a separate matter on which partners must agree.

Bonus to old partners.   When the current value of a partnership is greater than the recorded amounts of equity, the partners usually require a new partner to pay a bonus for the privilege of joining. To illustrate, assume that Zayn and Perez agree to accept Rasheed as a partner with a 25% interest in BOARDS if Rasheed invests $42,000. Recall the partnership's accounting records show Zayn's recorded equity in the business is $52,000 and Perez's recorded equity is $26,000 (see Exhibit 12.3). Rasheed's equity is determined as follows.

Equities of existing partners ($52,000 + $26,000)	$ 78,000
Investment of new partner	42,000
Total partnership equity	$120,000
Equity of Rasheed (25% × $120,000)	$ 30,000

Although Rasheed invests $42,000, the equity attributed to Rasheed in the new partnership is only $30,000. The $12,000 difference is called a *bonus* and is allocated to existing partners (Zayn and Perez) according to their income-and-loss-sharing agreement. A bonus is shared in this way because it is viewed as reflecting a higher value of the partnership that is not yet reflected in income. The entry to record this transaction follows.

Jan. 4	Cash.....................................	42,000	
	T. Rasheed, Capital......................		30,000
	K. Zayn, Capital ($12,000 × ½)............		6,000
	H. Perez, Capital ($12,000 × ½)...........		6,000
	To record admission of Rasheed and bonus.		

Assets	= Liabilities +	Equity
+42,000		+30,000
		+6,000
		+6,000

Bonus to new partner. Alternatively, existing partners can grant a bonus to a new partner. This usually occurs when they need additional cash or the new partner has exceptional talents. The bonus to the new partner is in the form of a larger share of equity than the amount invested. To illustrate, assume that Zayn and Perez agree to accept Rasheed as a partner with a 25% interest in the partnership, but they require Rasheed to invest only $18,000. Rasheed's equity is determined as follows.

Equities of existing partners ($52,000 + $26,000)	$78,000
Investment of new partner	18,000
Total partnership equity	$96,000
Equity of Rasheed (25% × $96,000)	$24,000

The old partners contribute the $6,000 bonus (computed as $24,000 minus $18,000) to Rasheed according to their income-and-loss-sharing ratio. Moreover, Rasheed's 25% equity does not necessarily entitle Rasheed to 25% of future income or loss. This is a separate matter for agreement by the partners. The entry to record the admission and investment of Rasheed is

Assets	= Liabilities +	Equity
+18,000		−3,000
		−3,000
		+24,000

Jan. 4			
	Cash..................................	18,000	
	K. Zayn, Capital ($6,000 × ½).................	3,000	
	H. Perez, Capital ($6,000 × ½)................	3,000	
	T. Rasheed, Capital......................		24,000
	To record Rasheed's admission and bonus.		

Withdrawal of a Partner

A partner generally withdraws from a partnership in one of two ways. (1) First, the withdrawing partner can sell his or her interest to another person who pays for it in cash or other assets. For this, we need only debit the withdrawing partner's capital account and credit the new partner's capital account. (2) The second case is when cash or other assets of the partnership are distributed to the withdrawing partner in settlement of his or her interest. To illustrate these cases, assume that Perez withdraws from the partnership of BOARDS in some future period. The partnership shows the following capital balances at the date of Perez's withdrawal: K. Zayn, $84,000; H. Perez, $38,000; and T. Rasheed, $38,000. The partners (Zayn, Perez, and Rasheed) share income and loss equally. Accounting for Perez's withdrawal depends on whether a bonus is paid. We describe three possibilities.

No Bonus If Perez withdraws and takes cash equal to Perez's capital balance, the entry is

Assets	= Liabilities +	Equity
−38,000		−38,000

Oct. 31			
	H. Perez, Capital..........................	38,000	
	Cash		38,000
	To record withdrawal of Perez from partnership with no bonus.		

Perez can take any combination of assets to which the partners agree to settle Perez's equity. Perez's withdrawal creates a new partnership between the remaining partners. A new partnership contract and a new income-and-loss-sharing agreement are required.

Bonus to Remaining Partners A withdrawing partner is sometimes willing to take less than the recorded value of his or her equity to get out of the partnership or because the recorded value is overstated. Whatever the reason, when this occurs, the withdrawing partner in effect gives the remaining partners a bonus equal to the equity left behind. The remaining partners share this unwithdrawn equity according to their income-and-loss-sharing ratio. To illustrate, if Perez withdraws and agrees to take $34,000 cash in settlement of Perez's

capital balance, the entry is

Oct. 31	H. Perez, Capital.	38,000	
	Cash		34,000
	K. Zayn, Capital.		2,000
	T. Rasheed, Capital.		2,000
	To record withdrawal of Perez and bonus to remaining partners.		

Assets = Liabilities + Equity
−34,000 −38,000
+2,000
+2,000

Perez withdrew $4,000 less than Perez's recorded equity of $38,000. This $4,000 is divided between Zayn and Rasheed according to their income-and-loss-sharing ratio.

Bonus to Withdrawing Partner A withdrawing partner may be able to receive more than his or her recorded equity for at least two reasons. First, the recorded equity may be understated. Second, the remaining partners may agree to remove this partner by giving assets of greater value than this partner's recorded equity. In either case, the withdrawing partner receives a bonus. The remaining partners reduce their equity by the amount of this bonus according to their income-and-loss-sharing ratio. To illustrate, if Perez withdraws and receives $40,000 cash in settlement of Perez's capital balance, the entry is

Oct. 31	H. Perez, Capital.	38,000	
	K. Zayn, Capital	1,000	
	T. Rasheed, Capital	1,000	
	Cash		40,000
	To record Perez's withdrawal from partnership with a bonus to Perez.		

Assets = Liabilities + Equity
−40,000 −38,000
−1,000
−1,000

Falcon Cable Communications LLC set up a partnership withdrawal agreement. Falcon owns and operates cable television systems and had two managing general partners. The partnership agreement stated that either partner "can offer to sell to the other partner the offering partner's entire partnership interest . . . for a negotiated price. If the partner receiving such an offer rejects it, the offering partner may elect to cause [the partnership] . . . to be liquidated and dissolved."

Death of a Partner

A partner's death dissolves a partnership. A deceased partner's estate is entitled to receive his or her equity. The partnership contract should contain provisions for settlement in this case. These provisions usually require (1) closing the books to determine income or loss since the end of the previous period and (2) determining and recording current market values for both assets and liabilities. The remaining partners and the deceased partner's estate then must agree to a settlement of the deceased partner's equity. This can involve selling the equity to remaining partners or to an outsider, or it can involve withdrawing assets.

> **Decision Ethics**   Answer—p. 487
>
> **Financial Planner** You are hired by the two remaining partners of a three-member partnership after the third partner's death. The partnership agreement states that a deceased partner's estate is entitled to a "share of partnership assets equal to the partner's relative equity balance" (partners' equity balances are equal). The estate argues it is entitled to one-third of the current value of partnership assets. The remaining partners say the distribution should use asset book values, which are 75% of current value. They also point to partnership liabilities, which equal 40% of total asset book value and 30% of current value. How would you resolve this situation?

Liquidation of a Partnership

When a partnership is liquidated, its business ends and four concluding steps are required.

1. Record the sale of noncash assets for cash and any gain or loss from their liquidation.
2. Allocate any gain or loss from liquidation of the assets in step 1 to the partners using their income-and-loss-sharing ratio.

3. Pay or settle all partner liabilities.

4. Distribute any remaining cash to partners based on their capital balances.

Partnership liquidation usually falls into one of two cases, as described in this section.

No Capital Deficiency

P4   Prepare entries for partnership liquidation.

No capital deficiency means that all partners have a zero or credit balance in their capital accounts for final distribution of cash. To illustrate, assume that Zayn, Perez, and Rasheed operate their partnership in BOARDS for several years, sharing income and loss equally. The partners then decide to liquidate. On the liquidation date, the current period's income or loss is transferred to the partners' capital accounts according to the sharing agreement. After that transfer, assume the partners' recorded equity balances (immediately prior to liquidation) are Zayn, $70,000; Perez, $66,000; and Rasheed, $62,000.

Next, assume that BOARDS sells its noncash assets for a net gain of $6,000. In a liquidation, gains or losses usually result from the sale of noncash assets, which are called *losses and gains from liquidation.* Partners share losses and gains from liquidation according to their income-and-loss-sharing agreement (equal for these partners) yielding the partners' revised equity balances of Zayn, $72,000; Perez, $68,000; and Rasheed, $64,000.[1] Then, after partnership assets are sold and any gain or loss is allocated, the liabilities must be paid. After creditors are paid, any remaining cash is divided among the partners according to their capital account balances. BOARDS' only liability at liquidation is $20,000 in accounts payable. The entries to record the payment to creditors and the final distribution of cash to partners follow.

Assets = Liabilities + Equity
−20,000   −20,000

Assets = Liabilities + Equity
−204,000   −72,000
                     −68,000
                     −64,000

Jan. 15	Accounts Payable	20,000	
	Cash		20,000
	To pay claims of creditors.		
Jan. 15	K. Zayn, Capital	72,000	
	H. Perez, Capital.	68,000	
	T. Rasheed, Capital	64,000	
	Cash		204,000
	To distribute remaining cash to partners.		

It is important to remember that the final cash payment is distributed to partners according to their capital account balances, whereas gains and losses from liquidation are allocated according to the income-and-loss-sharing ratio.

---

[1] The concepts behind these entries are not new. For example, assume that BOARDS has two noncash assets recorded as boarding facilities, $15,000, and land, $25,000. The entry to sell these assets for $46,000 is

Jan. 15	Cash	46,000	
	Boarding facilities		15,000
	Land		25,000
	Gain from Liquidation.		6,000
	Sold noncash assets at a gain.		

We then record the allocation of any loss or gain (a gain in this case) from liquidation according to the partners' income-and-loss-sharing agreement as follows.

Jan. 15	Gain from Liquidation	6,000	
	K. Zayn, Capital		2,000
	H. Perez, Capital		2,000
	T. Rasheed, Capital		2,000
	To allocate liquidation gain to partners.		

Capital Deficiency

Capital deficiency means that at least one partner has a debit balance in his or her capital account at the point of final cash distribution. This can arise from liquidation losses, excessive withdrawals before liquidation, or recurring losses in prior periods. A partner with a capital deficiency must, if possible, cover the deficit by paying cash into the partnership.

To illustrate, assume that Zayn, Perez, and Rasheed operate their partnership in BOARDS for several years, sharing income and losses equally. The partners then decide to liquidate. Immediately prior to the final distribution of cash, the partners' recorded capital balances are Zayn, $19,000; Perez, $8,000; and Rasheed, $(3,000). Rasheed's capital deficiency means that Rasheed owes the partnership $3,000. Both Zayn and Perez have a legal claim against Rasheed's personal assets. The final distribution of cash in this case depends on how this capital deficiency is handled. Two possibilities exist.

Partner Pays Deficiency Rasheed is obligated to pay $3,000 into the partnership to cover the deficiency. If Rasheed is willing and able to pay, the entry to record receipt of payment from Rasheed follows.

Jan. 15	Cash	3,000	
	T. Rasheed, Capital.		3,000
	To record payment of deficiency by Rasheed.		

Assets = Liabilities + Equity
+3,000   +3,000

After the $3,000 payment, the partners' capital balances are Zayn, $19,000; Perez, $8,000; and Rasheed, $0. The entry to record the final cash distributions to partners is

Jan. 15	K. Zayn, Capital	19,000	
	H. Perez, Capital.	8,000	
	Cash		27,000
	To distribute remaining cash to partners.		

Assets = Liabilities + Equity
−27,000   −19,000
                          −8,000

Partner Cannot Pay Deficiency The remaining partners with credit balances absorb any partner's unpaid deficiency according to their income-and-loss-sharing ratio. To illustrate, if Rasheed is unable to pay the $3,000 deficiency, Zayn and Perez absorb it. Since they share income and loss equally, Zayn and Perez each absorb $1,500 of the deficiency. This is recorded as follows.

Jan. 15	K. Zayn, Capital	1,500	
	H. Perez, Capital.	1,500	
	T. Rasheed, Capital.		3,000
	To transfer Rasheed deficiency to Zayn and Perez.		

Assets = Liabilities + Equity
                          −1,500
                          −1,500
                          +3,000

After Zayn and Perez absorb Rasheed's deficiency, the capital accounts of the partners are Zayn, $17,500; Perez, $6,500; and Rasheed, $0. The entry to record the final cash distribution to the partners is

Jan. 15	K. Zayn, Capital	17,500	
	H. Perez, Capital.	6,500	
	Cash		24,000
	To distribute remaining cash to partners.		

Assets = Liabilities + Equity
−24,000   −17,500
                          −6,500

Rasheed's inability to cover this deficiency does not relieve Rasheed of the liability. If Rasheed becomes able to pay at a future date, Zayn and Perez can each collect $1,500 from Rasheed.

Decision Analysis   **Partner Return on Equity**

A1   Compute partner return on equity and use it to evaluate partnership performance.

An important role of partnership financial statements is to aid current and potential partners in evaluating partnership success compared with other opportunities. One measure of this success is the **partner return on equity** ratio:

$$\text{Partner return on equity} = \frac{\text{Partner net income}}{\text{Average partner equity}}$$

This measure is separately computed for each partner. To illustrate, Exhibit 12.4 reports selected data from the Boston Celtics LP. The return on equity for the *total* partnership is computed as $216/[($84 + $252)/2] = 128.6\%$. However, return on equity is quite different across the partners. For example, the Boston Celtics LP I partner return on equity is computed as $44/[($122 + $166)/2] = 30.6\%$, whereas the Celtics LP partner return on equity is computed as $111/[($270 + $333)/2] = 36.8\%$. Partner return on equity provides *each* partner an assessment of its return on its equity invested in the partnership. A specific partner often uses this return to decide whether additional investment or withdrawal of resources is best for that partner. Exhibit 12.4 reveals that the year shown produced good returns for all partners (the Boston Celtics LP II return is not computed because its average equity is negative due to an unusual and large distribution in the prior year).

Exhibit 12.4

Selected Data from Boston Celtics LP

($ thousands)	Total*	Boston Celtics LP I	Boston Celtics LP II	Celtics LP
Beginning-year balance	$ 84	$122	$(307)	$270
Net income (loss) for year	216	44	61	111
Cash distribution	(48)	—	—	(48)
Ending-year balance	$252	$166	$(246)	$333
Partner return on equity	128.6%	30.6%	n.a.	36.8%

* Totals may not add up due to rounding.

Demonstration Problem

The following transactions and events affect the partners' capital accounts in several successive partnerships. Prepare a table with six columns, one for each of the five partners along with a total column to show the effects of the following events on the five partners' capital accounts.

Part 1

4/13/2007   Ries and Bax create R&B Company. Each invests $10,000, and they agree to share income and losses equally.

12/31/2007   R&B Co. earns $15,000 in income for its first year. Ries withdraws $4,000 from the partnership, and Bax withdraws $7,000.

1/1/2008   Royce is made a partner in RB&R Company after contributing $12,000 cash. The partners agree that a 10% interest allowance will be given on each partner's beginning-year capital balance. In addition, Bax and Royce are to receive $5,000 salary allowances. The remainder of the income or loss is to be divided evenly.

12/31/2008   The partnership's income for the year is $40,000, and withdrawals at year-end are Ries, $5,000; Bax, $12,500; and Royce, $11,000.

1/1/2009   Ries sells her interest for $20,000 to Murdock, whom Bax and Royce accept as a partner in the new BR&M Co. Income or loss is to be shared equally after Bax and Royce each receives $25,000 salary allowances.

12/31/2009   The partnership's income for the year is $35,000, and year-end withdrawals are Bax, $2,500, and Royce, $2,000.

1/1/2010   Elway is admitted as a partner after investing $60,000 cash in the new Elway & Associates partnership. He is given a 50% interest in capital after the other partners transfer $3,000 to his account from each of theirs. A 20% interest allowance (on the beginning-year capital balances) will be used in sharing any income or loss, there will be no salary allowances, and Elway will receive 40% of the remaining balance—the other three partners will each get 20%.

12/31/2010 Elway & Associates earns $127,600 in income for the year, and year-end withdrawals are Bax, $25,000; Royce, $27,000; Murdock, $15,000; and Elway, $40,000.

1/1/2011 Elway buys out Bax and Royce for the balances of their capital accounts after a revaluation of the partnership assets. The revaluation gain is $50,000, which is divided in using a 1:1:1:2 ratio (Bax:Royce:Murdock:Elway). Elway pays the others from personal funds. Murdock and Elway will share income on a 1:9 ratio.

2/29/2011 The partnership earns $10,000 of income since the beginning of the year. Murdock retires and receives partnership cash equal to her capital balance. Elway takes possession of the partnership assets in his own name, and the company is dissolved.

Part 2

Journalize the events affecting the partnership for the year ended December 31, 2008.

Planning the Solution

- Evaluate each transaction's effects on the capital accounts of the partners.
- Each time a new partner is admitted or a partner withdraws, allocate any bonus based on the income-or-loss-sharing agreement.
- Each time a new partner is admitted or a partner withdraws, allocate subsequent net income or loss in accordance with the new partnership agreement.
- Prepare entries to (1) record Royce's initial investment; (2) record the allocation of interest, salaries, and remainder; (3) show the cash withdrawals from the partnership; and (4) close the withdrawal accounts on December 31, 2008.

Solution to Demonstration Problem

Part 1

Event	Ries	Bax	Royce	Murdock	Elway	Total
4/13/2007						
Initial Investment	$10,000	$10,000				$ 20,000
12/31/2007						
Income (equal)	7,500	7,500				15,000
Withdrawals	(4,000)	(7,000)				(11,000)
Ending balance	$13,500	$10,500				$ 24,000
1/1/2008						
New investment			$12,000			$ 12,000
12/31/2008						
10% interest	1,350	1,050	1,200			3,600
Salaries		5,000	5,000			10,000
Remainder (equal)	8,800	8,800	8,800			26,400
Withdrawals	(5,000)	(12,500)	(11,000)			(28,500)
Ending balance	$18,650	$12,850	$16,000			$ 47,500
1/1/2009						
Transfer interest	(18,650)			$18,650		$ 0
12/31/2009						
Salaries		25,000	25,000			50,000
Remainder (equal)		(5,000)	(5,000)	(5,000)		(15,000)
Withdrawals		(2,500)	(2,000)			(4,500)
Ending balance	$ 0	$30,350	$34,000	$13,650		$ 78,000
1/1/2010						
New investment					$ 60,000	60,000
Bonuses to Elway		(3,000)	(3,000)	(3,000)	9,000	0
Adjusted balance		$27,350	$31,000	$10,650	$ 69,000	$138,000

[continued on next page]

[continued from previous page]

Event	Ries	Bax	Royce	Murdock	Elway	Total
12/31/2010						
20% interest		5,470	6,200	2,130	13,800	27,600
Remainder (1:1:1:2)		20,000	20,000	20,000	40,000	100,000
Withdrawals		(25,000)	(27,000)	(15,000)	(40,000)	(107,000)
Ending Balance		$27,820	$30,200	$17,780	$ 82,800	$158,600
1/1/2011						
Gain (1:1:1:2)		10,000	10,000	10,000	20,000	50,000
Adjusted balance		$37,820	$40,200	$27,780	$102,800	$208,600
Transfer interests		(37,820)	(40,200)		78,020	0
Adjusted balance		$ 0	$ 0	$27,780	$180,820	$208,600
2/29/2011						
Income (1:9)				1,000	9,000	10,000
Adjusted balance				$28,780	$189,820	$218,600
Settlements				(28,780)	(189,820)	(218,600)
Final balance				$ 0	$ 0	$ 0

Part 2

2008				
Jan. 1	Cash		12,000	
	Royce, Capital			12,000
	To record investment of Royce.			
Dec. 31	Income Summary		40,000	
	Ries, Capital			10,150
	Bax, Capital			14,850
	Royce, Capital			15,000
	To allocate interest, salaries, and remainders.			
Dec. 31	Ries, Withdrawals		5,000	
	Bax, Withdrawals		12,500	
	Royce, Withdrawals		11,000	
	Cash			28,500
	To record cash withdrawals by partners.			
Dec. 31	Ries, Capital		5,000	
	Bax, Capital		12,500	
	Royce, Capital		11,000	
	Ries, Withdrawals			5,000
	Bax, Withdrawals			12,500
	Royce, Withdrawals			11,000
	To close withdrawal accounts.			

Summary

C1 **Identify characteristics of partnerships and similar organizations.** Partnerships are voluntary associations, involve partnership agreements, have limited life, are not subject to income tax, include mutual agency, and have unlimited liability. Organizations that combine selected characteristics of partnerships and corporations include limited partnerships, limited liability partnerships, S corporations, and limited liability companies.

A1 **Compute partner return on equity and use it to evaluate partnership performance.** Partner return on equity provides each partner an assessment of his or her return on equity invested in the partnership.

P1 **Prepare entries for partnership formation.** A partner's initial investment is recorded at the market value of the assets contributed to the partnership.

P2 **Allocate and record income and loss among partners.** A partnership agreement should specify how to allocate partnership income or loss among partners. Allocation can be based on a stated ratio, capital balances, or salary and interest allowances to compensate partners for differences in their service and capital contributions.

P3 **Account for the admission and withdrawal of partners.** When a new partner buys a partnership interest directly from one or more existing partners, the amount of cash paid from one partner to another does not affect the partnership total recorded equity. When a new partner purchases equity by investing additional assets in the partnership, the new partner's investment can yield a bonus either to existing partners or to the new partner. The entry to record a withdrawal can involve payment from either (1) the existing partners' personal assets or (2) partnership assets. The latter can yield a bonus to either the withdrawing or remaining partners.

P4 **Prepare entries for partnership liquidation.** When a partnership is liquidated, losses and gains from selling partnership assets are allocated to the partners according to their income-and-loss-sharing ratio. If a partner's capital account has a deficiency that the partner cannot pay, the other partners share the deficit according to their relative income-and-loss-sharing ratio.

Guidance Answer to **Decision Ethics**

Financial Planner The partnership agreement apparently fails to mention liabilities or use the term *net assets*. To give the estate one-third of total assets is not fair to the remaining partners because if the partner had lived and the partners had decided to liquidate, the liabilities would need to be paid out of assets before any liquidation. Also, a settlement based on the deceased partner's recorded equity would fail to recognize excess of current value over book value. This value increase would be realized if the partnership were liquidated. A fair settlement would seem to be a payment to the estate for the balance of the deceased partner's equity based on the *current value of net assets*.

Guidance Answers to **Quick Checks**

1. (*b*)

2. *Unlimited liability* means that the creditors of a partnership require each partner to be personally responsible for all partnership debts.

3. (*c*)

4.

	Denzel	Shantell	Total
Net Income			$40,000
Interest allowance (10%)	$ 7,000	$ 3,500	10,500
Balance of income			$29,500
Balance allocated equally	14,750	14,750	29,500
Balance of income			$ 0
Income of partners	$21,750	$18,250	

Key Terms   mhhe.com/wildFAP18e

Key Terms are available at the book's Website for learning and testing in an online Flashcard Format.

C corporation (p. 474)
General partner (p. 473)
General partnership (p. 473)
Limited liability company (LLC) (p. 474)
Limited liability partnership (p. 473)

Limited partners (p. 473)
Limited partnership (p. 473)
Mutual agency (p. 473)
Partner return on equity (p. 484)
Partnership (p. 472)

Partnership contract (p. 472)
Partnership liquidation (p. 482)
S corporation (p. 474)
Statement of partners' equity (p. 477)
Unlimited liability (p. 473)

Multiple Choice Quiz   Answers on p. 497   mhhe.com/wildFAP18e

Multiple Choice Quizzes A and B are available at the book's Website.

1. Stokely and Leder are forming a partnership. Stokely invests a building that has a market value of $250,000; and the partnership assumes responsibility for a $50,000 note secured by a mortgage on that building. Leder invests $100,000 cash. For the partnership, the amounts recorded for the building and for Stokely's Capital account are:

a. Building, $250,000; Stokely, Capital, $250,000.
b. Building, $200,000; Stokely, Capital, $200,000.
c. Building, $200,000; Stokely, Capital, $100,000.
d. Building, $200,000; Stokely, Capital, $250,000.
e. Building, $250,000; Stokely, Capital, $200,000.

2. Katherine, Alliah, and Paulina form a partnership. Katherine contributes $150,000, Alliah contributes $150,000, and Paulina contributes $100,000. Their partnership agreement calls for the income or loss division to be based on the ratio of capital invested. If the partnership reports income of $90,000 for its first year of operations, what amount of income is credited to Paulina's capital account?
   a. $22,500
   b. $25,000
   c. $45,000
   d. $30,000
   e. $90,000

3. Jamison and Blue form a partnership with capital contributions of $600,000 and $800,000, respectively. Their partnership agreement calls for Jamison to receive $120,000 per year in salary. Also, each partner is to receive an interest allowance equal to 10% of the partner's beginning capital contributions, with any remaining income or loss divided equally. If net income for its initial year is $270,000, then Jamison and Blue's respective shares are:
   a. $135,000; $135,000
   b. $154,286; $115,714
   c. $120,000; $150,000

   d. $185,000; $85,000
   e. $85,000; $185,000

4. Hansen and Fleming are partners and share equally in income or loss. Hansen's current capital balance in the partnership is $125,000 and Fleming's is $124,000. Hansen and Fleming agree to accept Black with a 20% interest. Black invests $75,000 in the partnership. The bonus granted to Hansen and Fleming equals:
   a. $13,000 each.
   b. $5,100 each.
   c. $4,000 each.
   d. $5,285 to Jamison; $4,915 to Blue.
   e. $0; Jamison and Blue grant a bonus to Black.

5. Mee Su is a partner in Hartford Partners, LLC. Her partnership capital balance at the beginning of the current year was $110,000, and her ending balance was $124,000. Her share of the partnership income is $10,500. What is her partner return on equity?
   a. 8.97%
   b. 1060.00%
   c. 9.54%
   d. 1047.00%
   e. 8.47%

Discussion Questions

1. If a partnership contract does not state the period of time the partnership is to exist, when does the partnership end?

2. What does the term *mutual agency* mean when applied to a partnership?

3. Can partners limit the right of a partner to commit their partnership to contracts? Would such an agreement be binding (*a*) on the partners and (*b*) on outsiders?

4. Assume that Amey and Lacey are partners. Lacey dies, and her son claims the right to take his mother's place in the partnership. Does he have this right? Why or why not?

5. Assume that the Barnes and Ardmore partnership agreement provides for a two-third/one-third sharing of income but says nothing about losses. The first year of partnership operation resulted in a loss, and Barnes argues that the loss should be shared equally because the partnership agreement said nothing about sharing losses. Is Barnes correct? Explain.

6. Allocation of partnership income among the partners appears on what financial statement?

7. What does the term *unlimited liability* mean when it is applied to partnership members?

8. How does a general partnership differ from a limited partnership?

9. George, Burton, and Dillman have been partners for three years. The partnership is being dissolved. George is leaving the firm, but Burton and Dillman plan to carry on the business. In the final settlement, George places a $75,000 salary claim against the partnership. He contends that he has a claim for a salary of $25,000 for each year because he devoted all of his time for three years to the affairs of the partnership. Is his claim valid? Why or why not?

10. Kay, Kat, and Kim are partners. In a liquidation, Kay's share of partnership losses exceeds her capital account balance. Moreover, she is unable to meet the deficit from her personal assets, and her partners shared the excess losses. Does this relieve Kay of liability?

11. After all partnership assets have been converted to cash and all liabilities paid, the remaining cash should equal the sum of the balances of the partners' capital accounts. Why?

12. Assume a partner withdraws from a partnership and receives assets of greater value than the book value of his equity. Should the remaining partners share the resulting reduction in their equities in the ratio of their relative capital balances or according to their income-and-loss-sharing ratio?

 Red numbers denote Discussion Questions that involve decision-making.

Amaya and Leon are partners in operating a store. Without consulting Amaya, Leon enters into a contract to purchase merchandise for the store. Amaya contends that she did not authorize the order and refuses to pay for it. The vendor sues the partners for the contract price of the merchandise. (*a*) Must the partnership pay for the merchandise? Why? (*b*) Does your answer differ if Amaya and Leon are partners in a public accounting firm? Explain.

Ann Stolton and Susie Bright are partners in a business they started two years ago. The partnership agreement states that Stolton should receive a salary allowance of $15,000 and that Bright should receive a $20,000 salary allowance. Any remaining income or loss is to be shared equally. Determine each partner's share of the current year's net income of $52,000.

QS 12-2
Partnership income allocation
P2

Blake and Matthai are partners who agree that Blake will receive a $100,000 salary allowance and that any remaining income or loss will be shared equally. If Matthai's capital account is credited for $2,000 as her share of the net income in a given period, how much net income did the partnership earn in that period?

QS 12-3
Partnership income allocation
P2

Frain organized a limited partnership and is the only general partner. Mourlan invested $20,000 in the partnership and was admitted as a limited partner with the understanding that he would receive 10% of the profits. After two unprofitable years, the partnership ceased doing business. At that point, partnership liabilities were $85,000 larger than partnership assets. How much money can the partnership's creditors obtain from Mourlan personal assets to satisfy the unpaid partnership debts?

QS 12-4
Liability in limited partnerships
P1

Stein agrees to pay Choi and Amal $10,000 each for a one-third (33⅓%) interest in the Choi and Amal partnership. Immediately prior to Stein's admission, each partner had a $30,000 capital balance. Make the journal entry to record Stein's purchase of the partners' interest.

QS 12-5
Partner admission
through purchase of interest   P3

Jules and Johnson are partners, each with $40,000 in their partnership capital accounts. Kwon is admitted to the partnership by investing $40,000 cash. Make the entry to show Kwon's admission to the partnership.

QS 12-6
Admission of a partner   P3

Howe and Duley's company is organized as a partnership. At the prior year-end, partnership equity totaled $150,000 ($100,000 from Howe and $50,000 from Duley). For the current year, partnership net income is $25,000 ($20,000 allocated to Howe and $5,000 allocated to Duley), and year-end total partnership equity is $200,000 ($140,000 from Howe and $60,000 from Duley). Compute the total partnership return on equity *and* the individual partner return on equity ratios.

QS 12-7
Partner return on equity
A1

Next to the following list of eight characteristics of business organizations, write a brief description of how each characteristic applies to general partnerships.

EXERCISES

Exercise 12-1
Characteristics of partnerships
C1

Characteristic	Application to General Partnerships
1. Life	
2. Owners' liability	
3. Legal status	
4. Tax status of income	
5. Owners' authority	
6. Ease of formation	
7. Transferability of ownership	
8. Ability to raise large amounts of capital	

Exercise 12-2

Forms of organization

C1

For each of the following separate cases, recommend a form of business organization. With each recommendation, explain how business income would be taxed if the owners adopt the form of organization recommended. Also list several advantages that the owners will enjoy from the form of business organization that you recommend.

a. Sharif, Henry, and Korb are recent college graduates in computer science. They want to start a Website development company. They all have college debts and currently do not own any substantial computer equipment needed to get the company started.

b. Dr. Ward and Dr. Liu are recent graduates from medical residency programs. Both are family practice physicians and would like to open a clinic in an underserved rural area. Although neither has any funds to bring to the new venture, a banker has expressed interest in making a loan to provide start-up funds for their practice.

c. Munson has been out of school for about five years and has become quite knowledgeable about the commercial real estate market. He would like to organize a company that buys and sells real estate. Munson believes he has the expertise to manage the company but needs funds to invest in commercial property.

Exercise 12-3

Journalizing partnership transactions

P2

On March 1, 2008, Eckert and Kelley formed a partnership. Eckert contributed $82,500 cash and Kelley contributed land valued at $60,000 and a building valued at $100,000. The partnership also assumed responsibility for Kelley's $92,500 long-term note payable associated with the land and building. The partners agreed to share income as follows: Eckert is to receive an annual salary allowance of $25,000, both are to receive an annual interest allowance of 10% of their beginning-year capital investment, and any remaining income or loss is to be shared equally. On October 20, 2008, Eckert withdrew $34,000 cash and Kelley withdrew $20,000 cash. After the adjusting and closing entries are made to the revenue and expense accounts at December 31, 2008, the Income Summary account had a credit balance of $90,000.

1. Prepare journal entries to record (*a*) the partners' initial capital investments, (*b*) their cash withdrawals, and (*c*) the December 31 closing of both the Withdrawals and Income Summary accounts.

Check (2) Kelley, $79,250

2. Determine the balances of the partners' capital accounts as of December 31, 2008.

Exercise 12-4

Income allocation in a partnership

P2

Kramer and Knox began a partnership by investing $60,000 and $80,000, respectively. During its first year, the partnership earned $160,000. Prepare calculations showing how the $160,000 income should be allocated to the partners under each of the following three separate plans for sharing income and loss: (1) the partners failed to agree on a method to share income; (2) the partners agreed to share income and loss in proportion to their initial investments (round amounts to the nearest dollar); and (3) the partners agreed to share income by granting a $50,000 per year salary allowance to Kramer, a $40,000 per year salary allowance to Knox, 10% interest on their initial capital investments, and the remaining balance shared equally.

Check Plan 3, Kramer, $84,000

Exercise 12-5

Income allocation in a partnership

P2

Check (2) Kramer, $(4,400)

Assume that the partners of Exercise 12-4 agreed to share net income and loss by granting annual salary allowances of $50,000 to Kramer and $40,000 to Knox, 10% interest allowances on their investments, and any remaining balance shared equally.

1. Determine the partners' shares of Kramer and Knox given a first-year net income of $98,800.

2. Determine the partners' shares of Kramer and Knox given a first-year net loss of $16,800.

Exercise 12-6

Sale of partnership interest   P3

The partners in the Biz Partnership have agreed that partner Mandy may sell her $100,000 equity in the partnership to Brittney, for which Brittney will pay Mandy $85,000. Present the partnership's journal entry to record the sale of Mandy's interest to Brittney on September 30.

Exercise 12-7

Admission of new partner

P3

The Struter Partnership has total partners' equity of $510,000, which is made up of Main, Capital, $400,000, and Frist, Capital, $110,000. The partners share net income and loss in a ratio of 80% to Main and 20% to Frist. On November 1, Madison is admitted to the partnership and given a 15% interest in equity and a 15% share in any income and loss. Prepare the journal entry to record the admission of Madison under each of the following separate assumptions: Madison invests cash of (1) $90,000; (2) $120,000; and (3) $80,000.

Holland, Flowers, and Tulip have been partners while sharing net income and loss in a 5:3:2 ratio. On January 31, the date Tulip retires from the partnership, the equities of the partners are Holland, $150,000; Flowers, $90,000; and Tulip, $60,000. Present journal entries to record Tulip's retirement under each of the following separate assumptions: Tulip is paid for her equity using partnership cash of (1) $60,000; (2) $80,000; and (3) $30,000.

Exercise 12-8
Retirement of partner
P3

The Red, White & Blue partnership was begun with investments by the partners as follows: Red, $180,000; White, $240,000; and Blue, $210,000. The operations did not go well, and the partners eventually decided to liquidate the partnership, sharing all losses equally. On August 31, after all assets were converted to cash and all creditors were paid, only $60,000 in partnership cash remained.

1. Compute the capital account balance of each partner after the liquidation of assets and the payment of creditors.

2. Assume that any partner with a deficit agrees to pay cash to the partnership to cover the deficit. Present the journal entries on August 31 to record (*a*) the cash receipt from the deficient partner(s) and (*b*) the final disbursement of cash to the partners.

3. Assume that any partner with a deficit is not able to reimburse the partnership. Present journal entries (*a*) to transfer the deficit of any deficient partners to the other partners and (*b*) to record the final disbursement of cash to the partners.

Exercise 12-9
Liquidation of partnership
P4

Check (1) Red, $(10,000)

Turner, Roth, and Lowe are partners who share income and loss in a 1:4:5 ratio. After lengthy disagreements among the partners and several unprofitable periods, the partners decided to liquidate the partnership. Immediately before liquidation, the partnership balance sheet shows: total assets, $126,000; total liabilities, $78,000; Turner, Capital, $2,500; Roth, Capital, $14,000; and Lowe, Capital, $31,500. The cash proceeds from selling the assets were sufficient to repay all but $28,000 to the creditors. (*a*) Calculate the loss from selling the assets. (*b*) Allocate the loss to the partners. (*c*) Determine how much of the remaining liability should be paid by each partner.

Exercise 12-10
Liquidation of partnership P4

Check (b) Lowe, Capital after allocation, $(6,500)

Assume that the Turner, Roth, and Lowe partnership of Exercise 12-10 is a limited partnership. Turner and Roth are general partners and Lowe is a limited partner. How much of the remaining $28,000 liability should be paid by each partner?

Exercise 12-11
Liquidation of limited partnership
P4

Hunt Sports Enterprises LP is organized as a limited partnership consisting of two individual partners: Soccer LP and Football LP. Both partners separately operate a minor league soccer team and a semipro football team. Compute partner return on equity for each limited partnership (and the total) for the year ended June 30, 2008, using the following selected data on partner capital balances from Hunt Sports Enterprises LP.

Exercise 12-12
Partner return on equity
A1

	Soccer LP	Football LP	Total
Balance at 6/30/2007	$189,000	$ 758,000	$ 947,000
Annual net income	22,134	445,898	468,032
Cash distribution	—	(50,000)	(50,000)
Balance at 6/30/2008	$211,134	$1,153,898	$1,365,032

Kim Ries, Tere Bax, and Josh Thomas invested $80,000, $112,000, and $128,000, respectively, in a partnership. During its first calendar-year, the firm earned $249,000.

PROBLEM SET A

Required

Prepare the entry to close the firm's Income Summary account as of its December 31 year-end and to allocate the $249,000 net income to the partners under each of the following separate assumptions: The partners (1) have no agreement on the method of sharing income and loss; (2) agreed to share income and loss in the ratio of their beginning capital investments; and (3) agreed to share income and loss by providing annual salary allowances of $66,000 to Ries, $56,000 to Bax, and $80,000 to Thomas; granting 10% interest on the partners' beginning capital investments; and sharing the remainder equally.

Problem 12-1A
Allocating partnership income
P2

Check (3) Thomas, Capital, $97,800

Problem 12-2A

Allocating partnership income and loss; sequential years

P2

mhhe.com/wildFAP18e

Irma Watts and John Lyon are forming a partnership to which Watts will devote one-half time and Lyon will devote full time. They have discussed the following alternative plans for sharing income and loss: (*a*) in the ratio of their initial capital investments, which they have agreed will be $42,000 for Watts and $63,000 for Lyon; (*b*) in proportion to the time devoted to the business; (*c*) a salary allowance of $6,000 per month to Lyon and the balance in accordance with the ratio of their initial capital investments; or (*d*) a salary allowance of $6,000 per month to Lyon, 10% interest on their initial capital investments, and the balance shared equally. The partners expect the business to perform as follows: Year 1, $36,000 net loss; Year 2, $90,000 net income; and Year 3, $150,000 net income.

Required

Prepare three tables with the following column headings.

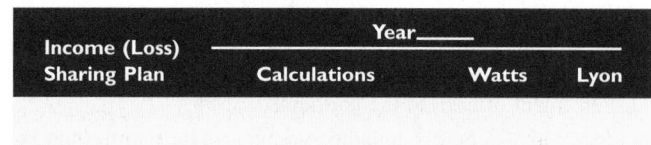

Income (Loss) Sharing Plan	Year_____		
	Calculations	Watts	Lyon

Check　Plan d, Year 1, Lyon's share, $19,050

Complete the tables, one for each of the first three years, by showing how to allocate partnership income or loss to the partners under each of the four plans being considered. (Round answers to the nearest whole dollar.)

Problem 12-3A

Partnership income allocation, statement of partners' equity, and closing entries

P2

mhhe.com/wildFAP18e

Bill Beck, Bruce Beck, and Barb Beck formed the BBB Partnership by making capital contributions of $67,500, $262,500, and $420,000, respectively. They predict annual partnership net income of $450,000 and are considering the following alternative plans of sharing income and loss: (*a*) equally; (*b*) in the ratio of their initial capital investments; or (*c*) salary allowances of $80,000 to Bill, $60,000 to Bruce, and $90,000 to Barb; interest allowances of 10% on their initial capital investments; and the balance shared equally.

Required

1. Prepare a table with the following column headings.

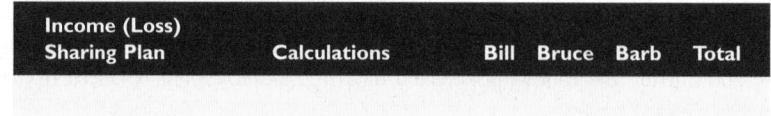

Income (Loss) Sharing Plan	Calculations	Bill	Bruce	Barb	Total

Check　(2) Barb, Ending Capital, $456,000

Use the table to show how to distribute net income of $450,000 for the calendar year under each of the alternative plans being considered. (Round answers to the nearest whole dollar.)

2. Prepare a statement of partners' equity showing the allocation of income to the partners assuming they agree to use plan (*c*), that income earned is $209,000, and that Bill, Bruce, and Barb withdraw $34,000, $48,000, and $64,000, respectively, at year-end.

3. Prepare the December 31 journal entry to close Income Summary assuming they agree to use plan (*c*) and that net income is $209,000. Also close the withdrawals accounts.

Problem 12-4A

Partner withdrawal and admission

P3

Check　(1e) Cr. Lau, Capital, $38,250

Part 1. Meir, Benson, and Lau are partners and share income and loss in a 3:2:5 ratio. The partnership's capital balances are as follows: Meir, $168,000; Benson, $138,000; and Lau, $294,000. Benson decides to withdraw from the partnership, and the partners agree to not have the assets revalued upon Benson's retirement. Prepare journal entries to record Benson's February 1 withdrawal from the partnership under each of the following separate assumptions: Benson (*a*) sells his interest to North for $160,000 after Meir and Lau approve the entry of North as a partner; (*b*) gives his interest to a son-in-law, Schmidt, and thereafter Meir and Lau accept Schmidt as a partner; (*c*) is paid $138,000 in partnership cash for his equity; (*d*) is paid $214,000 in partnership cash for his equity; and (*e*) is paid $30,000 in partnership cash plus equipment recorded on the partnership books at $70,000 less its accumulated depreciation of $23,200.

Part 2. Assume that Benson does not retire from the partnership described in Part 1. Instead, Rhodes is admitted to the partnership on February 1 with a 25% equity. Prepare journal entries to record Rhodes's entry into the partnership under each of the following separate assumptions: Rhodes invests (*a*) $200,000; (*b*) $145,000; and (*c*) $262,000.

(2c) Cr. Benson, Capital, $9,300

Kendra, Cogley, and Mei share income and loss in a 3:2:1 ratio. The partners have decided to liquidate their partnership. On the day of liquidation their balance sheet appears as follows.

Problem 12-5A
Liquidation of a partnership

P4

KENDRA, COGLEY, AND MEI Balance Sheet May 31			
Assets		**Liabilities and Equity**	
Cash	$180,800	Accounts payable	$245,500
Inventory	537,200	Kendra, Capital	93,000
		Cogley, Capital	212,500
		Mei, Capital	167,000
Total assets	$718,000	Total liabilities and equity	$718,000

Required

Prepare journal entries for (*a*) the sale of inventory, (*b*) the allocation of its gain or loss, (*c*) the payment of liabilities at book value, and (*d*) the distribution of cash in each of the following separate cases: Inventory is sold for (1) $600,000; (2) $500,000; (3) $320,000 and any partners with capital deficits pay in the amount of their deficits; and (4) $250,000 and the partners have no assets other than those invested in the partnership. (Round to the nearest dollar.)

Check (4) Cash distribution, Mei, $102,266

Matt Albin, Ryan Peters, and Seth Ramsey invested $164,000, $98,400, and $65,600, respectively, in a partnership. During its first calendar-year, the firm earned $270,000.

PROBLEM SET B

Problem 12-1B
Allocating partnership income

P2

Required

Prepare the entry to close the firm's Income Summary account as of its December 31 year-end and to allocate the $270,000 net income to the partners under each of the following separate assumptions. (Round answers to whole dollars.) The partners (1) have no agreement on the method of sharing income and loss; (2) agreed to share income and loss in the ratio of their beginning capital investments; and (3) agreed to share income and loss by providing annual salary allowances of $96,000 to Albin, $72,000 to Peters, and $50,000 to Ramsey; granting 10% interest on the partners' beginning capital investments; and sharing the remainder equally.

Check (3) Ramsey, Capital, $62,960

Maria Bell and J. R. Green are forming a partnership to which Bell will devote one-third time and Green will devote full time. They have discussed the following alternative plans for sharing income and loss: (*a*) in the ratio of their initial capital investments, which they have agreed will be $104,000 for Bell and $156,000 for Green; (*b*) in proportion to the time devoted to the business; (*c*) a salary allowance of $4,000 per month to Green and the balance in accordance with the ratio of their initial capital investments; or (*d*) a salary allowance of $4,000 per month to Green, 10% interest on their initial capital investments, and the balance shared equally. The partners expect the business to perform as follows: Year 1, $36,000 net loss; Year 2, $76,000 net income; and Year 3, $188,000 net income.

Problem 12-2B
Allocating partnership income and loss; sequential years

P2

Required

Prepare three tables with the following column headings.

Income (Loss) Sharing Plan	Year_____		
	Calculations	Bell	Green

Complete the tables, one for each of the first three years, by showing how to allocate partnership income or loss to the partners under each of the four plans being considered. (Round answers to the nearest whole dollar.)

Problem 12-3B
Partnership income allocation, statement of partners' equity, and closing entries

P2

Sally Cook, Lin Xi, and Ken Schwartz formed the CXS Partnership by making capital contributions of $144,000, $216,000, and $120,000, respectively. They predict annual partnership net income of $240,000 and are considering the following alternative plans of sharing income and loss: (*a*) equally; (*b*) in the ratio of their initial capital investments; or (*c*) salary allowances of $40,000 to Cook, $30,000 to Xi, and $80,000 to Schwartz; interest allowances of 12% on their initial capital investments; and the balance shared equally.

Required

1. Prepare a table with the following column headings.

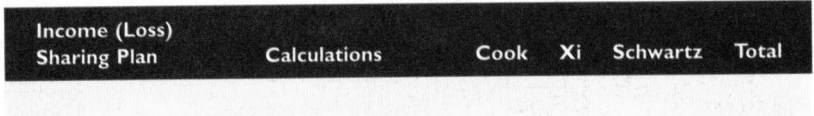

Income (Loss) Sharing Plan	Calculations	Cook	Xi	Schwartz	Total

Use the table to show how to distribute net income of $240,000 for the calendar year under each of the alternative plans being considered. (Round answers to the nearest whole dollar.)

2. Prepare a statement of partners' equity showing the allocation of income to the partners assuming they agree to use plan (*c*), that income earned is $87,600, and that Cook, Xi, and Schwartz withdraw $18,000, $38,000, and $24,000, respectively, at year-end.

3. Prepare the December 31 journal entry to close Income Summary assuming they agree to use plan *c* and that net income is $87,600. Also close the withdrawals accounts.

Problem 12-4B
Partner withdrawal and admission

P3

Part 1. Craig, Cook, and Chan are partners and share income and loss in a 5:1:4 ratio. The partnership's capital balances are as follows: Craig, $606,000; Cook, $148,000; and Chan, $446,000. Craig decides to withdraw from the partnership, and the partners agree not to have the assets revalued upon Craig's retirement. Prepare journal entries to record Craig's April 30 withdrawal from the partnership under each of the following separate assumptions: Craig (*a*) sells her interest to Collin for $250,000 after Cook and Chan approve the entry of Collin as a partner; (*b*) gives her interest to a daughter-in-law, Cam, and thereafter Cook and Chan accept Cam as a partner; (*c*) is paid $606,000 in partnership cash for her equity; (*d*) is paid $350,000 in partnership cash for her equity; and (*e*) is paid $200,000 in partnership cash plus manufacturing equipment recorded on the partnership books at $538,000 less its accumulated depreciation of $336,000.

Part 2. Assume that Craig does not retire from the partnership described in Part 1. Instead, Chip is admitted to the partnership on April 30 with a 20% equity. Prepare journal entries to record the entry of Chip under each of the following separate assumptions: Chip invests (*a*) $300,000; (*b*) $196,000; and (*c*) $426,000.

Problem 12-5B
Liquidation of a partnership

P4

Lasure, Ramirez, and Toney, who share income and loss in a 2:1:2 ratio, plan to liquidate their partnership. At liquidation, their balance sheet appears as follows.

LASURE, RAMIREZ, AND TONEY			
Balance Sheet			
January 18			
Assets		**Liabilities and Equity**	
Cash	$348,600	Accounts payable	$342,600
Equipment	617,200	Lasure, Capital	300,400
		Ramirez, Capital	195,800
		Toney, Capital	127,000
Total assets	$965,800	Total liabilities and equity	$965,800

Required

Prepare journal entries for (*a*) the sale of equipment, (*b*) the allocation of its gain or loss, (*c*) the payment of liabilities at book value, and (*d*) the distribution of cash in each of the following separate cases: Equipment is sold for (1) $650,000; (2) $530,000; (3) $200,000 and any partners with capital deficits pay in the amount of their deficits; and (4) $150,000 and the partners have no assets other than those invested in the partnership.

Check (4) Cash distribution, Lasure, $73,600

 Problem Set C is available at the book's Website to further reinforce and assess your learning.

PROBLEM SET C

(This serial problem began in Chapter 1 and continues through most of the book. If previous chapter segments were not completed, the serial problem can begin at this point. It is helpful, but not necessary, for you to use the Working Papers that accompany the book.)

SERIAL PROBLEM

Success Systems

SP 12 At the start of 2008, Adriana Lopez is considering adding a partner to her business. She envisions the new partner taking the lead in generating sales of both services and merchandise for Success Systems. Lopez's equity in Success Systems as of January 1, 2008, is reflected in the following capital balance.

A. Lopez, Capital $117,435

Required

1. Lopez is evaluating whether the prospective partner should be an equal partner with respect to capital investment and profit sharing (1:1) or whether the agreement should be 3:1 with Lopez retaining three-fourths interest with rights to three-fourths of the net income or loss. What factors should she consider in deciding which partnership agreement to offer?

2. Prepare the January 1, 2008, journal entry(ies) necessary to admit a new partner to Success Systems through the purchase of a partnership interest for each of the following two separate cases (*a*) 1:1 sharing agreement and (*b*) 3:1 sharing agreement.

3. Prepare the January 1, 2008, journal entry(ies) required to admit a new partner if the new partner invests cash of $39,145.

4. After posting the entry in part 3, what would be the new partner's equity percentage?

BEYOND THE NUMBERS

BTN 12-1 Take a step back in time and imagine **Best Buy** in its infancy as a company. The year is 1966.

REPORTING IN ACTION

C1

Required

1. Read the history of Best Buy at **BestBuymedia.tekgroup.com**. Can you determine from the history whether Best Buy was originally organized as a sole proprietorship, partnership, or corporation?

2. Assume that Best Buy was originally organized as a partnership. Best Buy's income statement in Appendix A varies in several key ways from what it would look like for a partnership. Explain how a corporate income statement differs from a partnership income statement.

3. Compare the Best Buy balance sheet in Appendix A to what a partnership balance sheet would have shown. Identify and explain any account differences you would anticipate.

BTN 12-2 Over the years **Best Buy** and **Circuit City** have evolved into large corporations. Today it is difficult to imagine them as fledgling start-ups. Research each company's history online.

COMPARATIVE ANALYSIS

C1

Required

1. Which company is older?

2. Which company started as a partnership?

3. In what years did each company first achieve $1,000,000 in sales?

4. In what years did each company have its first public offering of stock?

**ETHICS
CHALLENGE**

P2

BTN 12-3 Doctors Maben, Orlando, and Clark have been in a group practice for several years. Maben and Orlando are family practice physicians, and Clark is a general surgeon. Clark receives many referrals for surgery from his family practice partners. Upon the partnership's original formation, the three doctors agreed to a two-part formula to share income. Every month each doctor receives a salary allowance of $3,000. Additional income is divided according to a percent of patient charges the doctors generate for the month. In the current month, Maben generated 10% of the billings, Orlando 30%, and Clark 60%. The group's income for this month is $50,000. Clark has expressed dissatisfaction with the income-sharing formula and asks that income be split entirely on patient charge percents.

Required

1. Compute the income allocation for the current month using the original agreement.
2. Compute the income allocation for the current month using Clark's proposed agreement.
3. Identify the ethical components of this partnership decision for the doctors.

**COMMUNICATING
IN PRACTICE**

C1

BTN 12-4 Assume that you are studying for an upcoming accounting exam with a good friend. Your friend says that she has a solid understanding of general partnerships but is less sure that she understands organizations that combine certain characteristics of partnerships with other forms of business organization. You offer to make some study notes for your friend to help her learn about limited partnerships, limited liability partnerships, S Corporations, and limited liability companies. Prepare a one-page set of well-organized, complete study notes on these four forms of business organization.

**TAKING IT TO
THE NET**

P1 P2

BTN 12-5 Access the February 8, 2005, filing of the December 31, 2004, 10-K of **America First Tax Exempt Investors LP**. This company deals with tax-exempt mortgage revenue bonds that, among other things, finance student housing properties.

1. Locate its December 31, 2004, balance sheet and list the account titles reported in the equity section of the balance sheet.
2. Locate its statement of partners' capital and comprehensive income (loss). How many units of limited partnership (known as "beneficial unit certificate holders") are outstanding at December 31, 2004?
3. What is the partnership's largest asset and its amount at December 31, 2004?

**TEAMWORK IN
ACTION**

P2

BTN 12-6 This activity requires teamwork to reinforce understanding of accounting for partnerships.

Required

1. Assume that Baker, Warner, and Rice form the BWR Partnership by making capital contributions of $200,000, $300,000, and $500,000, respectively. BWR predicts annual partnership net income of $600,000. The partners are considering various plans for sharing income and loss. Assign a different team member to compute how the projected $600,000 income would be shared under each of the following separate plans:
   a. Shared equally.
   b. In the ratio of the partners' initial capital investments.
   c. Salary allowances of $50,000 to Baker, $60,000 to Warner, and $70,000 to Rice, with the remaining balance shared equally.
   d. Interest allowances of 10% on the partners' initial capital investments, with the remaining balance shared equally.
2. In sequence, each member is to present his or her income-sharing calculations with the team.
3. As a team, identify and discuss at least one other possible way that income could be shared.

BTN 12-7 Read the article "A Partnership That's Really Limited" in the May 25, 2005, issue of *BusinessWeek*. (This book's Website provides a free link.)

1. Who does the author contend are the winners in a limited partnership such as **Williams Partners**?

2. Why does the author say that the general partner will be better off in Williams Partners than the limited partners?

3. Why do investors invest in limited partnerships if the general partners seem to do better than the limited partners?

BusinessWeek
ACTIVITY

C1

BTN 12-8 Revisit the chapter's opening feature involving Catharine Lyons and Elska Sandor and their company **Rookie Skateboards**. Assume that Lyons and Sandor have decided to expand with the help of general partners.

Required

1. What details should Lyons, Sandor, and their future partners specify in their general partnership agreements?

2. What advantages should Lyons, Sandor, and their future partners be aware of with respect to organizing as general partnerships?

3. What disadvantages should Lyons, Sandor, and their future partners be aware of with respect to organizing as general partnerships?

ENTREPRENEURIAL DECISION

C1

BTN 12-9 Access **Dixons's** Website (Dixons-Group.com) and research the company's history.

1. When was the company founded, and what was its original form of ownership?

2. Why did the company use the name Dixons?

3. What were some of the acquisitions that caused Dixons to become "Dixons Group?"

GLOBAL DECISION

C1

Dixons

ANSWERS TO MULTIPLE CHOICE QUIZ

1. e; Capital = $250,000 − $50,000

2. a; $90,000 × [$100,000/($150,000 + $150,000 + $100,000)] = $22,500

3. d;

	Jamison	Blue	Total
Net income			$ 270,000
Salary allowance	$120,000		(120,000)
Interest allowance.	60,000	$80,000	(140,000)
Balance of income.			10,000
Balance divided equally	5,000	5,000	(10,000)
Totals.	$185,000	$85,000	$ 0

4. b; Total partnership equity = $125,000 + $124,000 + $75,000 = $324,000

Equity of Black = $324,000 × 20% = $64,800

Bonus to old partners = $75,000 − $64,800 = $10,200, split equally

5. a; $10,500/[($110,000 + $124,000)/2] = 8.97%

13

Accounting for Corporations

A Look Back

Chapter 12 focused on the partnership form of organization. We described crucial characteristics of partnerships and the accounting and reporting of their important transactions.

A Look at This Chapter

This chapter emphasizes details of the corporate form of organization. The accounting concepts and procedures for equity transactions are explained. We also describe how to report and analyze income, earnings per share, and retained earnings.

A Look Ahead

Chapter 14 focuses on long-term liabilities. We explain how to value, record, amortize, and report these liabilities in financial statements.

Learning Objectives

CAP

Conceptual

C1 Identify characteristics of corporations and their organization. *(p. 500)*

C2 Describe the components of stockholders' equity. *(p. 503)*

C3 Explain characteristics of common and preferred stock. *(p. 511)*

C4 Explain the items reported in retained earnings. *(p. 516)*

Analytical

A1 Compute earnings per share and describe its use. *(p. 518)*

A2 Compute price-earnings ratio and describe its use in analysis. *(p. 519)*

A3 Compute dividend yield and explain its use in analysis. *(p. 519)*

A4 Compute book value and explain its use in analysis. *(p. 520)*

Procedural

P1 Record the issuance of corporate stock. *(p. 504)*

P2 Record transactions involving cash dividends. *(p. 507)*

P3 Account for stock dividends and stock splits. *(p. 508)*

P4 Distribute dividends between common stock and preferred stock. *(p. 511)*

P5 Record purchases and sales of treasury stock and the retirement of stock. *(p. 514)*

"Keep your eye on the big picture of where you want to be five years from now; don't get lost in the day to day"
—Sundeep Bhan (Top; Sanjay Pingle and Sameer Shariff, middle, left to right; and Rajnish Kapoor, bottom)

Decision Feature

Genesis of a Life-Saving Business

NEW YORK, NY—Sundeep Bhan, Sanjay Pingle, Sameer Shariff, and Rajnish Kapoor are immigrant success stories. Together, they launched **Medsite, Inc. (Medsite.com),** a healthcare marketing and pharmaceutical services company. The genesis for Medsite was Sundeep's frustration with a lack of spell-checking software in the medical field—and the birthplace of their startup was a cramped Manhattan loft. Sundeep says, "I had some furniture, a computer, and together we had about $5,000." But by the time they had sold their first product, the spell-checker, to Mosby, the entrepreneurial spirit had overcome them.

Cofounder, Sanjay Pingle, says they then "set up a few Websites for products... and people started calling in. That's when we realized we were onto something bigger." The friends began providing promotional and educational help to physicians, including continuing education. "We really started out with the physician in mind, and have been able to keep that as a core part of our vision," adds Sundeep.

With limited capital, the four entrepreneurs struggled to get financial backing. Investors wanted to see success, but without cash it was an uphill battle. "We once had to leave a restaurant because they would take only cash, no credit cards," recalls co-founder Sameer Shariff. The four

also faced serious accounting-related corporate issues, including corporate formation, organization form, capital stock, and stock issuance. Yet the friends persisted. "We wanted something of our own," says Sanjay. "We all had the crazy [entrepreneurial] drive."

The four also shared a sense of community and a commitment to helping others. Our educational service "is a great tool to get information to physicians, and a great way for pharmaceuticals to sponsor medical education," says Sundeep. He also credits Medsite's success to an online database of drug products and its online continuing-education courses for physicians. Those services are free for doctors and paid for by Medsite's pharmaceutical clients.

Medsite's success in the business of saving lives has helped it secure financing. Although the company still confronts the realities of a corporate world—such as stock distributions, dividends, and equity reporting—it seems to be worth the effort. Sundeep proudly exclaims, "We want a [company]... where people come in to work looking forward to the day, and leave work in the evening looking forward to coming back the next morning."

[Sources: *Medsite Website,* January 2006; *Rediff.com,* May 1999; *Siliconindia,* July 1999; *Indus Business Journal,* September 2002; *Frost and Sullivan Market Insight,* April 2004]

This chapter focuses on equity transactions. The first part of the chapter describes the basics of the corporate form of organization and explains the accounting for common and preferred stock. We then focus on several special financing transactions, including cash and stock dividends, stock splits, and treasury stock. The final section considers accounting for retained earnings, including prior period adjustments, retained earnings restrictions, and reporting guidelines.

Accounting for Corporations

Corporations
- Characteristics
- Organization and management
- Stockholders
- Stock basics

Common Stock
- Par value
- No-par value
- Stated value
- Stock for noncash assets

Dividends
- Cash dividends
- Stock dividends
- Stock splits

Preferred Stock
- Issuance of preferred
- Dividend preferences
- Convertible preferred
- Callable preferred

Treasury Stock
- Purchasing treasury stock
- Reissuing treasury stock
- Retiring stock

Reporting on Equity
- Statement of retained earnings
- Statement of stockholders' equity
- Stock options

Corporate Form of Organization

A **corporation** is an entity created by law that is separate from its owners. It has most of the rights and privileges granted to individuals. Owners of corporations are called *stockholders* or *shareholders*. Corporations can be separated into two types. A *privately held* (or *closely held*) corporation does not offer its stock for public sale and usually has few stockholders. A *publicly held* corporation offers its stock for public sale and can have thousands of stockholders. *Public sale* usually refers to issuance and trading on an organized stock market.

Characteristics of Corporations

C1 Identify characteristics of corporations and their organization.

Corporations represent an important type of organization. Their unique characteristics offer advantages and disadvantages.

Advantages of Corporate Characteristics

■ **Separate legal entity:** A corporation conducts its affairs with the same rights, duties, and responsibilities of a person. It takes actions through its agents, who are its officers and managers.

■ **Limited liability of stockholders:** Stockholders are neither liable for corporate acts nor corporate debt.

■ **Transferable ownership rights:** The transfer of shares from one stockholder to another usually has no effect on the corporation or its operations except when this causes a change in the directors who control or manage the corporation.

■ **Continuous life:** A corporation's life continues indefinitely because it is not tied to the physical lives of its owners.

■ **Lack of mutual agency for stockholders:** A corporation acts through its agents, who are its officers and managers. Stockholders, who are not its officers and managers, do not have the power to bind the corporation to contracts—referred to as *lack of mutual agency*.

Point: The *business entity principle* requires a corporation to be accounted for separately from its owners (shareholders).

Global: U.S., U.K., and Canadian corporations finance much of their operations with stock issuances, but companies in countries such as France, Germany, and Japan finance mainly with note and bond issuances.

- **Ease of capital accumulation:** Buying stock is attractive to investors because (1) stockholders are not liable for the corporation's acts and debts, (2) stocks usually are transferred easily, (3) the life of the corporation is unlimited, and (4) stockholders are not corporate agents. These advantages enable corporations to accumulate large amounts of capital from the combined investments of many stockholders.

> **Decision Insight**
>
> **Stock Financing**   Marc Andreessen cofounded Netscape at age 22, only four months after earning his degree. One year later, he and friends issued Netscape shares to the public. The stock soared, making Andreessen a multimillionaire.

Disadvantages of Corporate Characteristics

- **Government regulation:** A corporation must meet requirements of a state's incorporation laws, which subject the corporation to state regulation and control. Proprietorships and partnerships avoid many of these regulations and governmental reports.

- **Corporate taxation:** Corporations are subject to the same property and payroll taxes as proprietorships and partnerships plus *additional* taxes. The most burdensome of these are federal and state income taxes that together can take 40% or more of corporate pretax income. Moreover, corporate income is usually taxed a second time as part of stockholders' personal income when they receive cash distributed as dividends. This is called *double taxation.* (The usual dividend tax is 15%; however, it is less than 15% for lower income taxpayers, and in some cases zero.)

Point: Proprietorships and partnerships are not subject to income taxes. Their income is taxed as the personal income of their owners.

Point: Double taxation is less severe when a corporation's owner-manager collects a salary that is taxed only once as part of his or her personal income.

Corporate Organization and Management

This section describes the incorporation, costs, and management of corporate organizations.

Point: A corporation is not required to have an office in its state of incorporation.

Incorporation   A corporation is created by obtaining a charter from a state government. A charter application usually must be signed by the prospective stockholders called *incorporators* or *promoters* and then filed with the proper state official. When the application process is complete and fees paid, the charter is issued and the corporation is formed. Investors then purchase the corporation's stock, meet as stockholders, and elect a board of directors. Directors oversee a corporation's affairs.

> **Decision Insight**
>
> **Seed Money**   Sources for start-up money include (1) "angel" investors such as family, friends, or anyone who believes in a company, (2) employees, investors, and even suppliers who can be paid with stock, and (3) venture capitalists (investors) who have a record of entrepreneurial success. See the National Venture Capital Association (**NVCA.org**) for information.

Organization Expenses   **Organization expenses** (also called *organization costs*) are the costs to organize a corporation; they include legal fees, promoters' fees, and amounts paid to obtain a charter. The corporation records (debits) these costs to an expense account called *Organization Expenses*. Organization costs are expensed as incurred because it is difficult to determine the amount and timing of their future benefits.

Management of a Corporation   The ultimate control of a corporation rests with stockholders who control a corporation by electing its *board of directors,* or simply, *directors.* Each stockholder usually has one vote for each share of stock owned. This control relation is shown in Exhibit 13.1. Directors are responsible for and have final authority for managing corporate activities. A board can act only as a collective body and usually limits its actions to setting general policy.

A corporation usually holds a stockholder meeting at least once a year to elect directors and transact

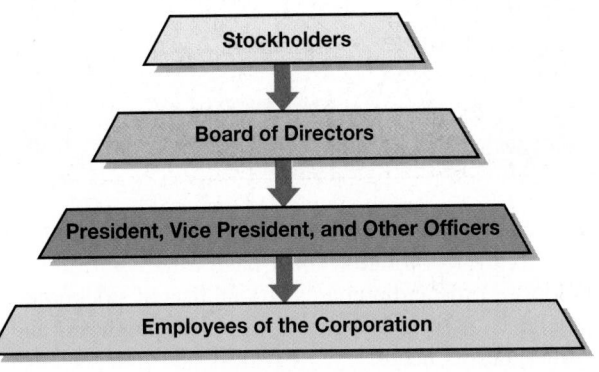

Exhibit 13.1

Corporate Structure

Point: *Bylaws* are guidelines that govern the behavior of individuals employed by and managing the corporation.

Global: Some corporate labels are:

Country	Label
United States	Inc.
France	SA
United Kingdom	
Public	PLC
Private	LTD
Germany	
Public	AG
Private	GmbH
Sweden	AB
Italy	SpA

business as its bylaws require. A group of stockholders owning or controlling votes of more than a 50% share of a corporation's stock can elect the board and control the corporation. Stockholders who do not attend stockholders' meetings must have an opportunity to delegate their voting rights to an agent by signing a **proxy,** a document that gives a designated agent the right to vote the stock.

Day-to-day direction of corporate business is delegated to executive officers appointed by the board. A corporation's chief executive officer (CEO) is often its president. Several vice presidents, who report to the president, are commonly assigned specific areas of management responsibility such as finance, production, and marketing. One person often has the dual role of chairperson of the board of directors and CEO. In this case, the president is usually designated the chief operating officer (COO).

Stockholders of Corporations

This section explains stockholder rights, stock purchases and sales, and the role of registrar and transfer agents.

Rights of Stockholders   When investors buy stock, they acquire all *specific* rights the corporation's charter grants to stockholders. They also acquire *general* rights granted stockholders by the laws of the state in which the company is incorporated. When a corporation has only one class of stock, it is identified as **common stock.** State laws vary, but common stockholders usually have the general right to

1. Vote at stockholders' meetings.
2. Sell or otherwise dispose of their stock.
3. Purchase their proportional share of any common stock later issued by the corporation. This **preemptive right** protects stockholders' proportionate interest in the corporation. For example, a stockholder who owns 25% of a corporation's common stock has the first opportunity to buy 25% of any new common stock issued.
4. Receive the same dividend, if any, on each common share of the corporation.
5. Share in any assets remaining after creditors are paid when, and if, the corporation is liquidated. Each share receives the same amount of remaining liquidated assets.

Stockholders also have the right to receive timely financial reports.

Global: Stockholders' access to financial information varies across countries both in scope and by level of ownership. For instance, stockholders of Mexican companies holding small percent ownership often have difficulty obtaining quality financial information.

Stock Certificates and Transfer   Investors who buy a corporation's stock, sometimes receive a *stock certificate* as proof of share ownership. Many corporations issue only one

Exhibit 13.2

Stock Certificate

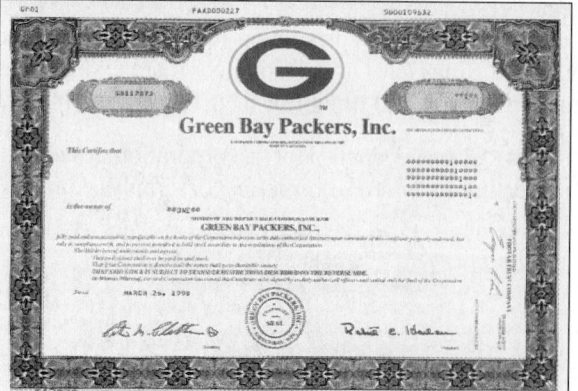

certificate for each block of stock purchased. A certificate can be for any number of shares. Exhibit 13.2 shows a stock certificate of the **Green Bay Packers.** A certificate shows the company name, stockholder name, number of shares, and other crucial information. Issuance of certificates is becoming less common. Instead, many stockholders maintain accounts with the corporation or their stockbrokers and never receive actual certificates.

Registrar and Transfer Agents   If a corporation's stock is traded on a major stock exchange, the corporation must have a registrar and a transfer agent. A *registrar* keeps stockholder records and prepares official lists of stockholders for stockholder meetings and dividend payments. A *transfer agent* assists with purchases and sales of shares by receiving and issuing certificates as necessary. Registrars and transfer agents are usually large banks or trust companies with computer facilities and staff to do this work.

Basics of Capital Stock

Capital stock is a general term that refers to any shares issued to obtain capital (owner financing). This section introduces terminology and accounting for capital stock.

Authorized Stock   **Authorized stock** is the number of shares that a corporation's charter allows it to sell. The number of authorized shares usually exceeds the number of shares issued (and outstanding), often by a large amount. (*Outstanding stock* refers to issued stock held by stockholders.) No formal journal entry is required for stock authorization. A corporation must apply to the state for a change in its charter if it wishes to issue more shares than previously authorized. A corporation discloses the number of shares authorized in the equity section of its balance sheet or notes. Best Buy's balance sheet in Appendix A reports 1 billion shares authorized as of 2005.

C2   Describe the components of stockholders' equity.

Selling (Issuing) Stock   A corporation can sell stock directly or indirectly. To *sell directly,* it advertises its stock issuance to potential buyers. This type of issuance is most common with privately held corporations. To *sell indirectly,* a corporation pays a brokerage house (investment banker) to issue its stock. Some brokerage houses *underwrite* an indirect issuance of stock; that is, they buy the stock from the corporation and take all gains or losses from its resale.

> **Decision Insight**
>
> **Pricing Stock**   A prospectus accompanies a stock's initial public offering (IPO), giving financial information about the company issuing the stock. A prospectus should help answer these questions to price an IPO: (1) Is the underwriter reliable? (2) Is there growth in revenues, profits, and cash flows? (3) What is management's view of operations? (4) Are current owners selling? (5) What are the risks?

Market Value of Stock   **Market value per share** is the price at which a stock is bought and sold. Expected future earnings, dividends, growth, and other company and economic factors influence market value. Traded stocks' market values are available daily in newspapers such as *The Wall Street Journal* and online. The current market value of previously issued shares (for example, the price of stock in trades between investors) does not impact the issuing corporation's stockholders' equity.

Classes of Stock   When all authorized shares have the same rights and characteristics, the stock is called *common stock*. A corporation is sometimes authorized to issue more than one class of stock, including preferred stock and different classes of common stock. American Greetings, for instance, has two types of common stock: Class A stock has 1 vote per share and Class B stock has 10 votes per share.

> **Decision Insight**
>
> **Stock Quote**   The Best Buy stock quote is
>
> | 52 Weeks | | | | Yld | Vol | | | | Net |
> |---|---|---|---|---|---|---|---|---|---|
> | Hi | Lo | Sym | Div | % | PE | 100s | Hi | Lo | Close | Chg |
> | 53.17 | 31.85 | BBY | 0.32 | 0.7 | 22 | 220 | 47.26 | 46.48 | 46.61 | −0.37 |
>
> interpreted as (left to right): **Hi,** highest price in past 52 weeks; **Lo,** lowest price in past 52 weeks; **Sym,** company exchange symbol; **Div,** dividends paid per share in past year; **Yld %,** dividend divided by closing price; **PE,** stock price per share divided by earnings per share; **Vol 100s,** number (in 100s) of shares traded; **Hi,** highest price for the day; **Lo,** lowest price for the day; **Close,** closing price for the day; **Net Chg,** change in closing price from prior day.

Par Value Stock   **Par value stock** is a class of stock assigned a **par value,** which is an amount assigned per share by the corporation in its charter. For example, Best Buy's common stock has a par value of $0.10. Other commonly assigned par values are $10, $5, $1 and $0.01. There is no restriction on the assigned par value. In many states, the par value of a stock establishes **minimum legal capital,** which refers to the least amount that the buyers of stock must contribute to the corporation or be subject to paying at a future date. For example, if a corporation issues 1,000 shares of $10 par value stock, the corporation's minimum legal capital in these states would be $10,000. Minimum legal capital is intended to protect a corporation's creditors. Since creditors cannot demand payment from stockholders' personal assets, their claims are limited to the corporation's assets and any minimum legal capital. At liquidation, creditor claims are paid before any amounts are distributed to stockholders.

Point: Managers are motivated to set a low par value when minimum legal capital or state issuance taxes are based on par value.

Point: Minimum legal capital was intended to protect creditors by requiring a minimum amount of net assets in the corporation. However, such net assets can be lost by unprofitable operations.

No-Par Value Stock   **No-par value stock,** or simply *no-par stock,* is stock *not* assigned a value per share by the corporate charter. Its advantage is that it can be issued at any price without the possibility of a minimum legal capital deficiency.

Point: Par, no-par, and stated value do *not* set the stock's market value.

Exhibit 13.3

Equity Composition

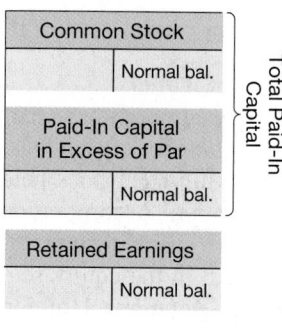

Point: Paid-in capital comes from stock-related transactions, whereas retained earnings comes from operations.

Stated Value Stock   **Stated value stock** is no-par stock to which the directors assign a "stated" value per share. Stated value per share becomes the minimum legal capital per share in this case.

Stockholders' Equity   A corporation's equity is known as **stockholders' equity,** also called *shareholders' equity* or *corporate capital.* Stockholders' equity consists of (1) paid-in (or contributed) capital and (2) retained earnings; see Exhibit 13.3. **Paid-in capital** is the total amount of cash and other assets the corporation receives from its stockholders in exchange for common stock. **Retained earnings** is the cumulative net income (and loss) retained by a corporation.

Quick Check

Answers—p. 525

1. Which of the following is *not* a characteristic of the corporate form of business? (*a*) Ease of capital accumulation, (*b*) Stockholder responsibility for corporate debts, (*c*) Ease in transferability of ownership rights, or (*d*) Double taxation.
2. Why is a corporation's income said to be taxed twice?
3. What is a proxy?

Common Stock

P1 Record the issuance of corporate stock.

Topic Tackler

PLUS

13-1

Accounting for the issuance of common stock affects only paid-in (contributed) capital accounts; no retained earnings accounts are affected.

Issuing Par Value Stock

Par value stock can be issued at par, at a premium (above par), or at a discount (below par). In each case, stock can be exchanged for either cash or noncash assets.

Issuing Par Value Stock at Par   When common stock is issued at par value, we record amounts for both the asset(s) received and the par value stock issued. To illustrate, the entry to record Dillon Snowboards' issuance of 30,000 shares of $10 par value stock for $300,000 cash on June 5, 2008, follows.

Assets   = Liabilities +   Equity
+300,000   +300,000

June 5	Cash	300,000	
	Common Stock, $10 Par Value		300,000
	Issued 30,000 shares of $10 par value		
	common stock at par.		

Exhibit 13.4 shows the stockholders' equity of Dillon Snowboards at year-end 2008 (its first year of operations) after income of $65,000 and no dividend payments.

Exhibit 13.4

Stockholders' Equity for Stock Issued at Par

Stockholders' Equity	
Common Stock—$10 par value; 50,000 shares authorized;	
30,000 shares issued and outstanding	$300,000
Retained earnings	65,000
Total stockholders' equity	$365,000

Issuing Par Value Stock at a Premium A **premium on stock** occurs when a corporation sells its stock for more than par (or stated) value. To illustrate, if Dillon Snowboards issues its $10 par value common stock at $12 per share, its stock is sold at a $2 per share premium. The premium, known as **paid-in capital in excess of par value,** is reported as part of equity; it is not revenue and is not listed on the income statement. The entry to record Dillon Snowboards' issuance of 30,000 shares of $10 par value stock for $12 per share on June 5, 2008, follows

Point: The "Paid-In Capital in Excess of Par Value, Common Stock" account is also called "Additional Paid-In Capital, Common Stock."

June 5	Cash....................................	360,000	
	Common Stock, $10 Par Value.............		300,000
	Paid-In Capital in Excess of Par Value, Common Stock............		60,000
	Sold and issued 30,000 shares of $10 par value common stock at $12 per share.		

Assets	= Liabilities +	Equity
+360,000		+300,000
		+60,000

The Paid-In Capital in Excess of Par Value account is added to the par value of the stock in the equity section of the balance sheet as shown in Exhibit 13.5.

Point: The *Paid-In Capital* terminology is interchangeable with *Contributed Capital.*

Exhibit 13.5

Stockholders' Equity for Stock Issued at a Premium

Stockholders' Equity	
Common Stock—$10 par value; 50,000 shares authorized; 30,000 shares issued and outstanding	$300,000
Paid-in capital in excess of par value, common stock	60,000
Retained earnings	65,000
Total stockholders' equity	$425,000

Issuing Par Value Stock at a Discount A **discount on stock** occurs when a corporation sells its stock for less than par (or stated) value. Most states prohibit the issuance of stock at a discount. In states that allow stock to be issued at a discount, its buyers usually become contingently liable to creditors for the discount. If stock is issued at a discount, the amount by which issue price is less than par is debited to a *Discount on Common Stock* account, a contra to the common stock account, and its balance is subtracted from the par value of stock in the equity section of the balance sheet. This discount is not an expense and does not appear on the income statement.

Point: Retained earnings can be negative, reflecting accumulated losses. Amazon.com had an accumulated deficit of $2.4 billion at the start of 2005.

Issuing No-Par Value Stock

When no-par stock is issued and is not assigned a stated value, the amount the corporation receives becomes legal capital and is recorded as Common Stock. This means that the entire proceeds are credited to a no-par stock account. To illustrate, a corporation records its October 20 issuance of 1,000 shares of no-par stock for $40 cash per share as follows.

Oct. 20	Cash....................................	40,000	
	Common Stock, No-Par Value		40,000
	Issued 1,000 shares of no-par value common stock at $40 per share.		

Assets	= Liabilities +	Equity
+40,000		+40,000

Frequency of Stock Types

Par 88%   Stated 3%   No-Par 9%

Issuing Stated Value Stock

When no-par stock is issued and assigned a stated value, its stated value becomes legal capital and is credited to a stated value stock account. Assuming that stated value stock is issued at an amount in excess of stated value (the usual case), the excess is credited to Paid-In Capital

Point: A *premium* is the amount by which issue price exceeds par (or stated) value. It is recorded in a separate equity account.

in Excess of Stated Value, Common Stock, which is reported in the stockholders' equity section. To illustrate, a corporation that issues 1,000 shares of no-par common stock having a stated value of $40 per share in return for $50 cash per share records this as follows.

Assets = Liabilities + Equity
+50,000   +40,000
                           +10,000

Oct. 20	Cash	50,000	
	Common Stock, $40 Stated Value.............		40,000
	Paid-In Capital in Excess of Stated Value, Common Stock		10,000
	Issued 1,000 shares of $40 per share stated value stock at $50 per share.		

Issuing Stock for Noncash Assets

Point: Stock issued for noncash assets should be recorded at the market value of either the stock or the noncash asset, whichever is more clearly determinable.

A corporation can receive assets other than cash in exchange for its stock. (It can also assume liabilities on the assets received such as a mortgage on property received.) The corporation records the assets received at their market values as of the date of the transaction. The stock given in exchange is recorded at its par (or stated) value with any excess recorded in the Paid-In Capital in Excess of Par (or Stated) Value account. (If no-par stock is issued, the stock is recorded at the assets' market value.) To illustrate, the entry to record receipt of land valued at $105,000 in return for issuance of 4,000 shares of $20 par value common stock on June 10 is

Assets = Liabilities + Equity
+105,000   +80,000
                            +25,000

June 10	Land	105,000	
	Common Stock, $20 Par Value..............		80,000
	Paid-In Capital in Excess of Par Value, Common Stock......................		25,000
	Exchanged 4,000 shares of $20 par value common stock for land.		

Point: Any type of stock can be issued for noncash assets.

A corporation sometimes gives shares of its stock to promoters in exchange for their services in organizing the corporation, which the corporation records as **Organization Expenses.** The entry to record receipt of services valued at $12,000 in organizing the corporation in return for 600 shares of $15 par value common stock on June 5 is

Assets = Liabilities + Equity
                           −12,000
                           +9,000
                           +3,000

June 5	Organization Expenses	12,000	
	Common Stock, $15 Par Value..............		9,000
	Paid-In Capital in Excess of Par Value, Common Stock......................		3,000
	Gave promoters 600 shares of $15 par value common stock in exchange for their services.		

Quick Check
Answers—p. 525

4. A company issues 7,000 shares of its $10 par value common stock in exchange for equipment valued at $105,000. The entry to record this transaction includes a credit to (*a*) Paid-In Capital in Excess of Par Value, Common Stock, for $35,000. (*b*) Retained Earnings for $35,000. (*c*) Common Stock, $10 Par Value, for $105,000.

5. What is a premium on stock?

6. Who is intended to be protected by minimum legal capital?

Dividends

This section describes both cash and stock dividend transactions.

P2 Record transactions involving cash dividends.

Cash Dividends

The decision to pay cash dividends rests with the board of directors and involves more than evaluating the amounts of retained earnings and cash. The directors, for instance, may decide to keep the cash to invest in the corporation's growth, to meet emergencies, to take advantage of unexpected opportunities, or to pay off debt. Alternatively, many corporations pay cash dividends to their stockholders at regular dates. These cash flows provide a return to investors and almost always affect the stock's market value.

Accounting for Cash Dividends Dividend payment involves three important dates: declaration, record, and payment. **Date of declaration** is the date the directors vote to declare and pay a dividend. This creates a legal liability of the corporation to its stockholders. **Date of record** is the future date specified by the directors for identifying those stockholders listed in the corporation's records to receive dividends. The date of record usually follows the date of declaration by at least two weeks. Persons who own stock on the date of record receive dividends. **Date of payment** is the date when the corporation makes payment; it follows the date of record by enough time to allow the corporation to arrange checks, money transfers, or other means to pay dividends.

Percent of Corporations Paying Dividends

Cash Dividend to Common — **75%**

Cash Dividend to Preferred — **22%**

0% 20 40 60 80 100%

Point: A cash dividend reduces a company's assets (and its working capital).

To illustrate, the entry to record a January 9 declaration of a $1 per share cash dividend by the directors of Z-Tech, Inc., with 5,000 outstanding shares is

Date of Declaration

Jan. 9	Retained Earnings...........................	5,000	
	Common Dividend Payable		5,000
	Declared $1 per common share cash dividend.[1]		

Assets = Liabilities + Equity
        +5,000   −5,000

Common Dividend Payable is a current liability. The date of record for the Z-Tech dividend is January 22. *No formal journal entry is needed on the date of record.* The February 1 date of payment requires an entry to record both the settlement of the liability and the reduction of the cash balance, as follows:

Topic Tackler

PLUS

13-2

Date of Payment

Feb. 1	Common Dividend Payable..................	5,000	
	Cash		5,000
	Paid $1 per common share cash dividend.		

Assets = Liabilities + Equity
−5,000   −5,000

Deficits and Cash Dividends A corporation with a debit (abnormal) balance for retained earnings is said to have a **retained earnings deficit,** which arises when a company incurs cumulative losses and/or pays more dividends than total earnings from current and prior years. A deficit is reported as a deduction on the balance sheet, as shown in Exhibit 13.6. Most states prohibit a corporation with a deficit from paying a cash dividend to its stockholders. This legal restriction is designed to protect creditors by preventing distribution of assets to stockholders when the company may be in financial difficulty.

Point: It is often said a dividend is a distribution of retained earnings, but it is more precise to describe a dividend as a distribution of assets to satisfy stockholder claims.

Point: The Retained Earnings Deficit account is also called *Accumulated Deficit.*

---

[1] An alternative entry is to debit Dividends instead of Retained Earnings. The balance in Dividends is then closed to Retained Earnings at the end of the reporting period. The effect is the same: Retained Earnings is decreased and a Dividend Payable is increased. For simplicity, all assignments in this chapter use the Retained Earnings account to record dividend declarations.

Exhibit 13.6

Stockholders' Equity with a Deficit

Common stock—$10 par value, 5,000 shares authorized, issued, and outstanding	$50,000
Retained earnings deficit	(6,000)
Total stockholders' equity	$44,000

Some state laws allow cash dividends to be paid by returning a portion of the capital contributed by stockholders. This type of dividend is called a **liquidating cash dividend,** or simply *liquidating dividend,* because it returns a part of the original investment back to the stockholders. This requires a debit entry to one of the contributed capital accounts instead of Retained Earnings at the declaration date.

Quick Check
Answers—p. 525

7. What type of an account is the Common Dividend Payable account?

8. What three crucial dates are involved in the process of paying a cash dividend?

9. When does a dividend become a company's legal obligation?

Stock Dividends

P3 Account for stock dividends and stock splits.

A **stock dividend,** declared by a corporation's directors, is a distribution of additional shares of the corporation's own stock to its stockholders without the receipt of any payment in return. Stock dividends and cash dividends are different. A stock dividend does not reduce assets and equity but instead transfers a portion of equity from retained earnings to contributed capital.

Reasons for Stock Dividends   Stock dividends exist for at least two reasons. First, directors are said to use stock dividends to keep the market price of the stock affordable. For example, if a corporation continues to earn income but does not issue cash dividends, the price of its common stock likely increases. The price of such a stock may become so high that it discourages some investors from buying the stock (especially in lots of 100 and 1,000). When a corporation has a stock dividend, it increases the number of outstanding shares and lowers the per share stock price. Another reason for a stock dividend is to provide evidence of management's confidence that the company is doing well and will continue to do well.

Point: Berkshire Hathaway has not declared a cash dividend since 1967. Its recent stock price was about $85,000 per share.

Accounting for Stock Dividends   A stock dividend affects the components of equity by transferring part of retained earnings to contributed capital accounts, sometimes described as *capitalizing* retained earnings. Accounting for a stock dividend depends on whether it is a small or large stock dividend. A **small stock dividend** is a distribution of 25% or less of previously outstanding shares. It is recorded by capitalizing retained earnings for an amount equal to the market value of the shares to be distributed. A **large stock dividend** is a distribution of more than 25% of previously outstanding shares. A large stock dividend is recorded by capitalizing retained earnings for the minimum amount required by state law governing the corporation. Most states require capitalizing retained earnings equal to the par or stated value of the stock.

To illustrate stock dividends, we use the equity section of X-Quest's balance sheet shown in Exhibit 13.7 just *before* its declaration of a stock dividend on December 31.

Exhibit 13.7

Stockholders' Equity *before* Declaring a Stock Dividend

Stockholders' Equity (before dividend)	
Common stock—$10 par value, 15,000 shares authorized,	
10,000 shares issued and outstanding	$100,000
Paid-in capital in excess of par value, common stock	8,000
Retained earnings	35,000
Total stockholders' equity	$143,000

Recording a small stock dividend.   Assume that X-Quest's directors declare a 10% stock dividend on December 31. This stock dividend of 1,000 shares, computed as 10% of its 10,000 issued and outstanding shares, is to be distributed on January 20 to the stockholders of record on January 15. Since the market price of X-Quest's stock on December 31 is $15 per share, this small stock dividend declaration is recorded as follows:

Point: Small stock dividends are recorded at market value.

Date of Declaration

Dec. 31	Retained Earnings.............................	15,000	
	Common Stock Dividend Distributable........		10,000
	Paid-In Capital in Excess of Par Value,		
	Common Stock......................		5,000
	Declared a 1,000-share (10%) stock dividend.		

Assets = Liabilities + Equity
−15,000
+10,000
+5,000

The $10,000 credit in the declaration entry equals the par value of the shares and is recorded in *Common Stock Dividend Distributable*. Its balance exists only until the shares are issued. The $5,000 credit equals the amount by which market value exceeds par value. This amount increases the Paid-In Capital in Excess of Par Value account in anticipation of the issue of shares. In general, the balance sheet changes in three ways when a stock dividend is declared. First, the amount of equity attributed to common stock increases; for X-Quest, from $100,000 to $110,000 for 1,000 additional declared shares. Second, paid-in capital in excess of par increases by the excess of market value over par value for the declared shares. Third, retained earnings decreases, reflecting the transfer of amounts to both common stock and contributed capital in excess of par. The stockholders' equity of X-Quest is shown in Exhibit 13.8 *after* its 10% stock dividend is declared on December 31.

Point: The term *Distributable* (not *Payable*) is used for stock dividends.

Point: The credit to Paid-In Capital in Excess of Par Value is recorded when the stock dividend is declared. This account is not affected when stock is later distributed.

Point: A stock dividend is never a liability on a balance sheet because it never reduces assets.

Stockholders' Equity (after dividend)	
Common stock—$10 par value, 15,000 shares authorized,	
10,000 shares issued and outstanding	$100,000
Common stock dividend distributable—1,000 shares	**10,000**
Paid-in capital in excess of par value, common stock	**13,000**
Retained earnings	**20,000**
Total stockholders' equity	$143,000

Exhibit 13.8

Stockholders' Equity *after* Declaring a Stock Dividend

No entry is made on the date of record for a stock dividend. On January 20, the date of payment, X-Quest distributes the new shares to stockholders and records this entry:

Point: A stock dividend does not affect assets (or working capital).

Date of Payment

Jan. 20	Common Stock Dividend Distributable	10,000	
	Common Stock, $10 Par Value..............		10,000
	To record issuance of common stock dividend.		

Assets = Liabilities + Equity
−10,000
+10,000

The combined effect of these stock dividend entries is to transfer (or capitalize) $15,000 of retained earnings to paid-in capital accounts. The amount of capitalized retained earnings equals the market value of the 1,000 issued shares ($15 × 1,000 shares). A stock dividend has no effect on the ownership percent of individual stockholders.

Decision Maker   Answer—p. 525

Entrepreneur A company you cofounded and own stock in announces a 50% stock dividend. Has the value of your stock investment increased, decreased, or remained the same?

Recording a large stock dividend.   A corporation capitalizes retained earnings equal to the minimum amount required by state law for a large stock dividend. For most states, this amount is the par or stated value of the newly issued shares. To illustrate, suppose X-Quest's board declares a stock dividend of 30% instead of 10% on December 31. Since this dividend is more

Point: Large stock dividends are recorded at par or stated value.

than 25%, it is treated as a large stock dividend. Thus, the par value of the 3,000 dividend shares is capitalized at the date of declaration with this entry:

Date of Declaration

Assets = Liabilities + Equity
            −30,000
            +30,000

Dec. 31	Retained Earnings.	30,000	
	Common Stock Dividend Distributable.		30,000
	Declared a 3,000-share (30%) stock dividend.		

This transaction decreases retained earnings and increases contributed capital by $30,000. On the date of payment the company debits Common Stock Dividend Distributable and credits Common Stock for $30,000. The effects from a large stock dividend on balance sheet accounts are similar to those for a small stock dividend except for the absence of any effect on contributed capital in excess of par.

Stock Splits

A **stock split** is the distribution of additional shares to stockholders according to their percent ownership. When a stock split occurs, the corporation "calls in" its outstanding shares and issues more than one new share in exchange for each old share. Splits can be done in any ratio, including 2-for-1, 3-for-1, or higher. Stock splits reduce the par or stated value per share.

To illustrate, CompTec has 100,000 outstanding shares of $20 par value common stock with a current market value of $88 per share. A 2-for-1 stock split cuts par value in half as it replaces 100,000 shares of $20 par value stock with 200,000 shares of $10 par value stock. Market value is reduced from $88 per share to about $44 per share. The split does not affect any equity amounts reported on the balance sheet or any individual stockholder's percent ownership. Both the Paid-In Capital and Retained Earnings accounts are unchanged by a split, and *no journal entry is made*. The only effect on the accounts is a change in the stock account description. CompTec's 2-for-1 split on its $20 par value stock means that after the split, it changes its stock account title to Common Stock, $10 Par Value. This stock's description on the balance sheet also changes to reflect the additional authorized, issued, and outstanding shares and the new par value.

Point: A reverse stock split is the opposite of a stock split. It increases both the market value per share and the par or stated value per share by specifying the split ratio to be less than 1-for-1, such as 1-for-2. A reverse stock split results in fewer shares.

The difference between stock splits and large stock dividends is often blurred. Many companies report stock splits in their financial statements without calling in the original shares by simply changing their par value. This type of "split" is really a large stock dividend and results in additional shares issued to stockholders by capitalizing retained earnings or transferring other paid-in capital to Common Stock. This approach avoids administrative costs of splitting the stock. **Harley-Davidson** recently declared a 2-for-1 stock split executed in the form of a 100% stock dividend.

Quick Check

Answers—p. 525

10. How does a stock dividend impact assets and retained earnings?

11. What distinguishes a large stock dividend from a small stock dividend?

12. What amount of retained earnings is capitalized for a small stock dividend?

Preferred Stock

A corporation can issue two basic kinds of stock, common and preferred. **Preferred stock** has special rights that give it priority (or senior status) over common stock in one or more areas. Special rights typically include a preference for receiving dividends and for the distribution of assets if the corporation is liquidated. Preferred stock carries all rights of common stock unless the corporate charter nullifies them. Most preferred stock, for instance, does not confer the right to vote. Exhibit 13.9 shows that preferred stock is issued by about one-fourth of large corporations. All corporations issue common stock.

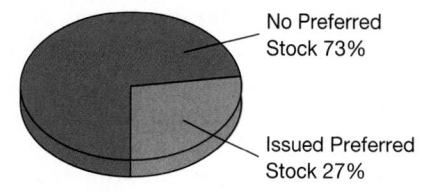

Exhibit 13.9

Corporations and Preferred Stock

Issuance of Preferred Stock

Preferred stock usually has a par value. Like common stock, it can be sold at a price different from par. Preferred stock is recorded in its own separate capital accounts. To illustrate, if Dillon Snowboards issues 50 shares of $100 par value preferred stock for $6,000 cash on July 1, 2008, the entry is

C3 Explain characteristics of common and preferred stock.

July 1	Cash.....................................	6,000	
	Preferred Stock, $100 Par Value.............		5,000
	Paid-In Capital in Excess of Par Value,		
	Preferred Stock......................		1,000
	Issued preferred stock for cash.		

Assets = Liabilities + Equity
+6,000   +5,000
                            +1,000

The equity section of the year-end balance sheet for Dillon Snowboards, including preferred stock, is shown in Exhibit 13.10. (This exhibit assumes that common stock was issued at par.) Issuing no-par preferred stock is similar to issuing no-par common stock. Also, the entries for issuing preferred stock for noncash assets are similar to those for common stock.

Stockholders' Equity

Common stock—$10 par value; 50,000 shares authorized;	
30,000 shares issued and outstanding	$300,000
Preferred stock—$100 par value; 1,000 shares authorized;	
50 shares issued and outstanding	5,000
Paid-in capital in excess of par value, preferred stock	1,000
Retained earnings	65,000
Total stockholders' equity	$371,000

Exhibit 13.10

Stockholders' Equity with Common and Preferred Stock

Dividend Preference of Preferred Stock

Preferred stock usually carries a preference for dividends, meaning that preferred stockholders are allocated their dividends before any dividends are allocated to common stockholders. The dividends allocated to preferred stockholders are usually expressed as a dollar amount per share or a percent applied to par value. A preference for dividends does *not* ensure dividends. If the directors do not declare a dividend, neither the preferred nor the common stockholders receive one.

P4 Distribute dividends between common stock and preferred stock.

Cumulative or Noncumulative Dividend Most preferred stocks carry a cumulative dividend right. **Cumulative preferred stock** has a right to be paid both the current and all prior periods' unpaid dividends before any dividend is paid to common stockholders. When preferred stock is cumulative and the directors either do not declare a dividend to preferred stockholders or declare one that does not cover the total amount of cumulative dividend, the unpaid dividend amount is called **dividend in arrears.** Accumulation of dividends in arrears on cumulative preferred stock does not guarantee they will be paid. **Noncumulative preferred stock** confers no right to prior periods' unpaid dividends if they were not declared in those prior periods.

Point: Dividend preference does not imply that preferred stockholders receive more dividends than common stockholders, nor does it guarantee a dividend.

To illustrate the difference between cumulative and noncumulative preferred stock, assume that a corporation's outstanding stock includes (1) 1,000 shares of $100 par, 9% preferred stock—yielding $9,000 per year in potential dividends, and (2) 4,000 shares of $50 par value common stock. During 2007, the first year of operations, the directors declare cash dividends of $5,000. In year 2008, they declare cash dividends of $42,000. See Exhibit 13.11 for the allocation of dividends for these two years. Allocation of year 2008 dividends depends on whether the preferred stock is noncumulative or cumulative. With noncumulative preferred, the preferred stockholders never receive the $4,000 skipped in 2007. If the preferred stock is cumulative, the $4,000 in arrears is paid in 2008 before any other dividends are paid.

Exhibit 13.11

Allocation of Dividends (noncumulative vs. cumulative preferred stock)

	Preferred	Common
Preferred Stock Is Noncumulative		
Year 2007	$ 5,000	$ 0
Year 2008		
Step 1: Current year's preferred dividend	$ 9,000	
Step 2: Remainder to common		$33,000
Preferred Stock Is Cumulative		
Year 2007	$ 5,000	$ 0
Year 2008		
Step 1: Dividend in arrears	$ 4,000	
Step 2: Current year's preferred dividend	9,000	
Step 3: Remainder to common		$29,000
Totals for year 2008	$13,000	$29,000

A liability for a dividend does not exist until the directors declare a dividend. If a preferred dividend date passes and the corporation's board fails to declare the dividend on its cumulative preferred stock, the dividend in arrears is not a liability. The *full-disclosure principle* requires a corporation to report (usually in a note) the amount of preferred dividends in arrears as of the balance sheet date.

Participating or Nonparticipating Dividend   **Nonparticipating preferred stock** has a feature that limits dividends to a maximum amount each year. This maximum is often stated as a percent of the stock's par value or as a specific dollar amount per share. Once preferred stockholders receive this amount, the common stockholders receive any and all additional dividends. **Participating preferred stock** has a feature allowing preferred stockholders to share with common stockholders in any dividends paid in excess of the percent or dollar amount stated on the preferred stock. This participation feature does not apply until common stockholders receive dividends equal to the preferred stock's dividend percent. Many corporations are authorized to issue participating preferred stock but rarely do, and most managers never expect to issue it.[2]

---

[2] Participating preferred stock is usually authorized as a defense against a possible corporate *takeover* by an "unfriendly" investor (or a group of investors) who intends to buy enough voting common stock to gain control. Taking a term from spy novels, the financial world refers to this type of plan as a *poison pill* that a company swallows if enemy investors threaten its capture. A poison pill usually works as follows: A corporation's common stockholders on a given date are granted the right to purchase a large amount of participating preferred stock at a very low price. This right to purchase preferred shares is *not* transferable. If an unfriendly investor buys a large block of common shares (whose right to purchase participating preferred shares does *not* transfer to this buyer), the board can issue preferred shares at a low price to the remaining common shareholders who retained the right to purchase. Future dividends are then divided between the newly issued participating preferred shares and the common shares. This usually transfers value from common shares to preferred shares, causing the unfriendly investor's common stock to lose much of its value and reduces the potential benefit of a hostile takeover.

Convertible Preferred Stock

Preferred stock is more attractive to investors if it carries a right to exchange preferred shares for a fixed number of common shares. **Convertible preferred stock** gives holders the option to exchange their preferred shares for common shares at a specified rate. When a company prospers and its common stock increases in value, convertible preferred stockholders can share in this success by converting their preferred stock into more valuable common stock.

Callable Preferred Stock

Callable preferred stock gives the issuing corporation the right to purchase (retire) this stock from its holders at specified future prices and dates. Many issues of preferred stock are callable. The amount paid to call and retire a preferred share is its **call price,** or *redemption value,* and is set when the stock is issued. The call price normally includes the stock's par value plus a premium giving holders additional return on their investment. When the issuing corporation calls and retires a preferred stock, the terms of the agreement often require it to pay the call price *and* any dividends in arrears.

Point: The issuing corporation has the right, or option, to retire its callable preferred stock.

Reasons for Issuing Preferred Stock

Corporations issue preferred stock for several reasons. One is to raise capital without sacrificing control. For example, suppose a company's organizers have $100,000 cash to invest and organize a corporation that needs $200,000 of capital to start. If they sell $200,000 worth of common stock (with $100,000 to the organizers), they would have only 50% control and would need to negotiate extensively with other stockholders in making policy. However, if they issue $100,000 worth of common stock to themselves and sell outsiders $100,000 of 8%, cumulative preferred stock with no voting rights, they retain control.

A second reason to issue preferred stock is to boost the return earned by common stockholders. To illustrate, suppose a corporation's organizers expect to earn an annual after-tax income of $24,000 on an investment of $200,000. If they sell and issue $200,000 worth of common stock, the $24,000 income produces a 12% return on the $200,000 of common stockholders' equity. However, if they issue $100,000 of 8% preferred stock to outsiders and $100,000 of common stock to themselves, their own return increases to 16% per year, as shown in Exhibit 13.12.

Net (after-tax) income	$24,000
Less preferred dividends at 8%	(8,000)
Balance to common stockholders	$16,000
Return to common stockholders ($16,000/$100,000)	16%

Exhibit 13.12

Return to Common Stockholders When Preferred Stock Is Issued

Common stockholders earn 16% instead of 12% because assets contributed by preferred stockholders are invested to earn $12,000 while the preferred dividend is only $8,000. Use of preferred stock to increase return to common stockholders is an example of **financial leverage** (also called *trading on the equity*). As a general rule, when the dividend rate on preferred stock is less than the rate the corporation earns on its assets, the effect of issuing preferred stock is to increase (or *lever*) the rate earned by common stockholders.

Other reasons for issuing preferred stock include its appeal to some investors who believe that the corporation's common stock is too risky or that the expected return on common stock is too low.

Point: Financial leverage also occurs when debt is issued and the interest rate paid on it is less than the rate earned from using the assets the creditors lend the company.

Decision Maker   Answer—p. 525

Concert Organizer Assume that you alter your business strategy from organizing concerts targeted at under 1,000 people to those targeted at between 5,000 to 20,000 people. You also incorporate because of increased risk of lawsuits and a desire to issue stock for financing. It is important that you control the company for decisions on whom to schedule. What types of stock do you offer?

13. In what ways does preferred stock often have priority over common stock?

14. Increasing the return to common stockholders by issuing preferred stock is an example of
(*a*) Financial leverage. (*b*) Cumulative earnings. (*c*) Dividend in arrears.

15. A corporation has issued and outstanding (i) 9,000 shares of $50 par value, 10% cumulative, nonparticipating preferred stock and (ii) 27,000 shares of $10 par value common stock. No dividends have been declared for the two prior years. During the current year, the corporation declares $288,000 in dividends. The amount paid to common shareholders is
(*a*) $243,000. (*b*) $153,000. (*c*) $135,000.

Treasury Stock

P5 Record purchases and sales of treasury stock and the retirement of stock.

Corporations acquire shares of their own stock for several reasons: (1) to use their shares to acquire another corporation, (2) to purchase shares to avoid a hostile takeover of the company, (3) to reissue them to employees as compensation, and (4) to maintain a strong market for their stock or to show management confidence in the current price.

A corporation's reacquired shares are called **treasury stock,** which is similar to unissued stock in several ways: (1) neither treasury stock nor unissued stock is an asset, (2) neither receives cash dividends or stock dividends, and (3) neither allows the exercise of voting rights.

Corporations and Treasury Stock

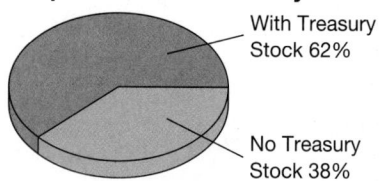

With Treasury Stock 62%

No Treasury Stock 38%

However, treasury stock does differ from unissued stock in one major way: The corporation can resell treasury stock at less than par without having the buyers incur a liability, provided it was originally issued at par value or higher. Treasury stock purchases also require management to exercise ethical sensitivity because funds are being paid to specific stockholders instead of all stockholders. Managers must be sure the purchase is in the best interest of all stockholders. These concerns cause companies to fully disclose treasury stock transactions.

Purchasing Treasury Stock

Purchasing treasury stock reduces the corporation's assets and equity by equal amounts. (We describe the *cost method* of accounting for treasury stock, which is the most widely used method. The *par value* method is another method explained in advanced courses.) To illustrate, Exhibit 13.13 shows Cyber Corporation's account balances *before* any treasury stock purchase (Cyber has no liabilities).

Exhibit 13.13

Account Balances *before* Purchasing Treasury Stock

Assets		Stockholders' Equity	
Cash	$ 30,000	Common stock—$10 par; 10,000 shares	
Other assets	95,000	authorized, issued, and outstanding	$100,000
		Retained earnings	25,000
Total assets	$125,000	Total stockholders' equity	$125,000

Global: Many countries, such as China, Japan, and Singapore, do not permit purchase of treasury stock.

Cyber then purchases 1,000 of its own shares for $11,500 on May 1, which is recorded as follows.

Assets = Liabilities + Equity
−11,500　　　　　　　−11,500

May 1	Treasury Stock, Common	11,500	
	Cash		11,500
	Purchased 1,000 treasury shares at $11.50 per share.		

This entry reduces equity through the debit to the Treasury Stock account, which is a contra equity account. Exhibit 13.14 shows account balances *after* this transaction.

Point: Treasury stock does not carry voting or dividend rights.

Assets		Stockholders' Equity	
Cash	$ 18,500	Common stock—$10 par; 10,000 shares	
Other assets	95,000	authorized and issued; 1,000 shares in treasury	$100,000
		Retained earnings, $11,500 restricted by	
		treasury stock purchase	25,000
		Less cost of treasury stock	(11,500)
Total assets	$113,500	Total stockholders' equity	$113,500

Exhibit 13.14

Account Balances *after* Purchasing Treasury Stock

The treasury stock purchase reduces Cyber's cash, total assets, and total equity by $11,500 but does not reduce the balance of either the Common Stock or the Retained Earnings account. The equity reduction is reported by deducting the cost of treasury stock in the equity section. Also, two disclosures are evident. First, the stock description reveals that 1,000 issued shares are in treasury, leaving only 9,000 shares still outstanding. Second, the description for retained earnings reveals that it is partly restricted.

Point: The Treasury Stock account is *not* an asset. This contra equity account is a subtraction in the equity section.

Point: A treasury stock purchase is also called a *stock buyback*.

Reissuing Treasury Stock

Treasury stock can be reissued by selling it at cost, above cost, or below cost.

Selling Treasury Stock at Cost
If treasury stock is reissued at cost, the entry is the reverse of the one made to record the purchase. For instance, if on May 21 Cyber reissues 100 of the treasury shares purchased on May 1 at the same $11.50 per share cost, the entry is

May 21	Cash	1,150	
	Treasury Stock, Common.		1,150
	Received $11.50 per share for 100 treasury		
	shares costing $11.50 per share.		

Assets = Liabilities + Equity
+1,150   +1,150

Selling Treasury Stock *above* Cost
If treasury stock is sold for more than cost, the amount received in excess of cost is credited to the Paid-In Capital, Treasury Stock account. This account is reported as a separate item in the stockholders' equity section. No gain is ever reported from the sale of treasury stock. To illustrate, if Cyber receives $12 cash per share for 400 treasury shares costing $11.50 per share on June 3, the entry is

Point: Treasury stock does not represent ownership. A company cannot own a part of itself.

June 3	Cash	4,800	
	Treasury Stock, Common.		4,600
	Paid-In Capital, Treasury Stock.		**200**
	Received $12 per share for 400 treasury		
	shares costing $11.50 per share.		

Assets = Liabilities + Equity
+4,800   +4,600
                              +200

Selling Treasury Stock *below* Cost
When treasury stock is sold below cost, the entry to record the sale depends on whether the Paid-In Capital, Treasury Stock account has a credit balance. If it has a zero balance, the excess of cost over the sales price is debited to Retained Earnings. If the Paid-In Capital, Treasury Stock account has a credit balance, it is debited for the excess of the cost over the selling price but not to exceed the balance in this account. When the credit balance in this paid-in capital account is eliminated, any remaining difference between the cost and selling price is debited to Retained Earnings. To illustrate, if Cyber sells its remaining 500 shares of treasury stock at $10 per share on July 10,

Point: The term *treasury stock* is believed to arise from the fact that reacquired stock is held in a corporation's treasury.

Point: The Paid-In Capital, Treasury Stock account can have a zero or credit balance but never a debit balance.

equity is reduced by $750 (500 shares × $1.50 per share excess of cost over selling price), as shown in this entry:

July 10	Cash	5,000	
	Paid-In Capital, Treasury Stock	200	
	Retained Earnings	550	
	Treasury Stock, Common.		5,750
	Received $10 per share for 500 treasury shares costing $11.50 per share.		

This entry eliminates the $200 credit balance in the paid-in capital account created on June 3 and then reduces the Retained Earnings balance by the remaining $550 excess of cost over selling price. A company never reports a loss (or gain) from the sale of treasury stock.

Retiring Stock

Point: Wrigley Company reported that its "Directors adopted a resolution retiring the entire balance of shares of Common Stock held in the corporate treasury."

Point: Recording stock retirement results in canceling the equity from the original issuance of the shares.

A corporation can purchase its own stock and retire it. Retiring stock reduces the number of issued shares. Retired stock is the same as authorized and unissued shares. Purchases and retirements of stock are permissible under state law only if they do not jeopardize the interests of creditors and stockholders. When stock is purchased for retirement, we remove all capital amounts related to the retired shares. If the purchase price exceeds the net amount removed, this excess is debited to Retained Earnings. If the net amount removed from all capital accounts exceeds the purchase price, this excess is credited to the Paid-In Capital from Retirement of Stock account. A company's assets and equity are always reduced by the amount paid for the retiring stock.

Quick Check

Answers—p. 526

16. Purchase of treasury stock (*a*) has no effect on assets; (*b*) reduces total assets and total equity by equal amounts; or (*c*) is recorded with a debit to Retained Earnings.

17. Southern Co. purchases shares of Northern Corp. Should either company classify these shares as treasury stock?

18. How does treasury stock affect the authorized, issued, and outstanding shares?

19. When a company purchases treasury stock, (*a*) retained earnings are restricted by the amount paid; (*b*) Retained Earnings is credited; or (*c*) it is retired.

Reporting of Equity

Statement of Retained Earnings

C4 Explain the items reported in retained earnings.

Retained earnings generally consist of a company's cumulative net income less any net losses and dividends declared since its inception. Retained earnings are part of stockholders' claims on the company's net assets, but this does *not* imply that a certain amount of cash or other assets is available to pay stockholders. For example, **Circuit City** has $1,247 million in retained earnings, but only $880 million in cash. This section describes events and transactions affecting retained earnings and how retained earnings are reported.

Global: Some countries, such as Japan, require companies to set up reserves at specified rates for the protection of creditors.

Restrictions and Appropriations The term **restricted retained earnings** refers to both statutory and contractual restrictions. A common *statutory* (or *legal*) *restriction* is to limit treasury stock purchases to the amount of retained earnings. The balance sheet in Exhibit 13.14 provides an example. A common *contractual restriction* involves loan agreements that restrict paying dividends beyond a specified amount or percent of retained earnings. Restrictions are usually described in the notes. The term **appropriated retained earnings** refers to a voluntary transfer of amounts from the Retained Earnings account to the Appropriated Retained Earnings account to inform users of special activities that require funds.

Prior Period Adjustments **Prior period adjustments** are corrections of material errors in prior period financial statements. These errors include arithmetic mistakes, unacceptable accounting, and missed facts. Prior period adjustments are reported in the *statement of retained earnings* (or the statement of stockholders' equity), net of any income tax effects. Prior period adjustments result in changing the beginning balance of retained earnings for events occurring prior to the earliest period reported in the current set of financial statements. To illustrate, assume that ComUS makes an error in a 2006 journal entry for the purchase of land by incorrectly debiting an expense account. When this is discovered in 2008, the statement of retained earnings includes a prior period adjustment, as shown in Exhibit 13.15. This exhibit also shows the usual format of the statement of retained earnings.

Many items reported in financial statements are based on estimates. Future events are certain to reveal that some of these estimates were inaccurate even when based on the best data avail-

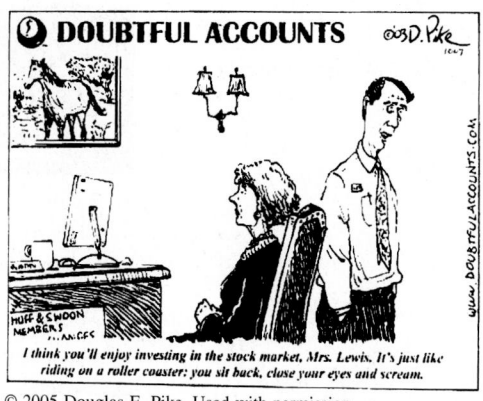

☺ DOUBTFUL ACCOUNTS

I think you'll enjoy investing in the stock market, Mrs. Lewis. It's just like riding on a roller coaster: you sit back, close your eyes and scream.

© 2005 Douglas E. Pike. Used with permission.

Point: If a year 2006 error is discovered in 2007, the company records the adjustment in 2007. But if the financial statements include 2006 and 2007 figures, the statements report the correct amounts for 2006, and a note describes the correction.

Exhibit 13.15

Statement of Retained Earnings with a Prior Period Adjustment

ComUS Statement of Retained Earnings For Year Ended December 31, 2008	
Retained earnings, Dec. 31, 2007, as previously reported	$4,745,000
Prior period adjustment	
Cost of land incorrectly expensed (net of $63,000 income taxes)	**147,000**
Retained earnings, Dec. 31, 2007, as adjusted	4,892,000
Plus net income	1,224,300
Less cash dividends declared	(301,800)
Retained earnings, Dec. 31, 2008	$5,814,500

Point: Accounting for changes in estimates is sometimes criticized as two wrongs to make a right. Consider a change in an asset's life. Depreciation neither before nor after the change is the amount computed if the revised estimate were originally selected. Regulators chose this approach to avoid restating prior period numbers.

able at the time. These inaccuracies are *not* considered errors and are *not* reported as prior period adjustments. Instead, they are identified as **changes in accounting estimates** and are accounted for in current and future periods. To illustrate, we know that depreciation is based on estimated useful lives and salvage values. As time passes and new information becomes available, managers may need to change these estimates and the resulting depreciation expense for current and future periods.

Statement of Stockholders' Equity

Instead of a separate statement of retained earnings, companies commonly report a statement of stockholders' equity that includes changes in retained earnings. A **statement of stockholders' equity** lists the beginning and ending balances of each equity account and describes the changes that occur during the period. The companies in Appendix A report such a statement. The usual format is to provide a column for each component of equity and use the rows to describe events occurring in the period. Exhibit 13.16 shows a condensed statement for Apple Computer.

Reporting Stock Options

The majority of corporations whose shares are publicly traded issue **stock options,** which are

Exhibit 13.16

Statement of Stockholders' Equity

($ millions, shares in thousands)	Common Stock Shares	Common Stock Amount	Retained Earnings	Other	Total Equity
APPLE COMPUTER Statement of Stockholders' Equity					
Balance, Sept. 27, 2003	366,727	$1,926	$2,394	$ (97)	$4,223
Net income	—	—	276	—	276
Issuance of Common Stock	24,717	588	—	—	588
Other	—	—	—	(11)	(11)
Cash Dividends ($0.00 per share)	—	—	—	—	—
Balance, Sept. 25, 2004	391,444	$2,514	$2,670	$(108)	$5,076

rights to purchase common stock at a fixed price over a specified period. As the stock's price rises above the fixed price, the option's value increases. **Starbucks** and **Home Depot** offer stock options to both full- and part-time employees. Stock options are said to motivate managers and employees to (1) focus on company performance, (2) take a long-run perspective, and (3) remain with the company. A stock option is like having an investment with no risk ("a carrot with no stick").

To illustrate, Quantum grants each of its employees the option to purchase 100 shares of its $1 par value common stock at its current market price of $50 per share anytime within the next 10 years. If the stock price rises to $70 per share, an employee can exercise the option at a gain of $20 per share (acquire a $70 stock at the $50 option price). With 100 shares, a single employee would have a total gain of $2,000, computed as $20 × 100 shares. Companies report the cost of stock options in the income statement. Measurement of this cost is explained in advanced courses.

Decision Ethics   Answer—p. 525

Director   The board of Intex is planning its stockholders' meeting. The first item is whether to disclose a contract just signed that will increase future income. One officer argues, "The meeting should focus on actual results." After agreeing not to disclose the contract, the next item is a motion for stockholders to approve a two-year option for managers to buy shares at a price equal to the average stock price over the next 2 weeks. What action (if any) do you take?

Decision Analysis

Earnings per Share, Price-Earnings Ratio, Dividend Yield, and Book Value per Share

Earnings per Share

A1   Compute earnings per share and describe its use.

The income statement reports **earnings per share,** also called *EPS* or *net income per share,* which is the amount of income earned per each share of a company's outstanding common stock. The **basic earnings per share** formula is shown in Exhibit 13.17. When a company has no preferred stock, then preferred dividends are zero. The weighted-average common shares outstanding is measured over the income reporting period; its computation is explained in advanced courses.

Exhibit 13.17

Basic Earnings per Share

$$\text{Basic earnings per share} = \frac{\text{Net income} - \text{Preferred dividends}}{\text{Weighted-average common shares outstanding}}$$

To illustrate, assume that Quantum Co. earns $40,000 net income in 2008 and declares dividends of $7,500 on its noncumulative preferred stock. (If preferred stock is *non*cumulative, the income available [numerator] is the current period net income less any preferred dividends *declared* in that same period. If preferred stock is cumulative, the income available [numerator] is the current period net income less the preferred dividends whether declared or not.) Quantum has 5,000 weighted-average common shares outstanding during 2008. Its basic EPS[3] is

Global: Some countries, such as Japan and Australia, use the number of shares outstanding at the end of the period when computing EPS.

$$\text{Basic earnings per share} = \frac{\$40,000 - \$7,500}{5,000 \text{ shares}} = \$6.50$$

Price-Earnings Ratio

A stock's market value is determined by its *expected* future cash flows. A comparison of a company's EPS and its market value per share reveals information about market expectations. This comparison is traditionally made using a **price-earnings (or PE) ratio,** expressed also as *price earnings, price to earnings,* or *PE.* Some analysts interpret this ratio as what price the market is willing to pay for a company's current earnings stream. Price-earnings ratios can differ across companies that have similar earnings because of either higher or lower expectations of future earnings. The price-earnings ratio is defined in Exhibit 13.18.

A2 Compute price-earnings ratio and describe its use in analysis.

Point: The average PE ratio of stocks in the 1950–2005 period is about 14.

$$\text{Price-earnings ratio} = \frac{\textbf{Market value (price) per share}}{\textbf{Earnings per share}}$$

Exhibit 13.18

Price-Earnings Ratio

Point: Average PE ratios for U.S. stocks increased over the past two decades. Some analysts interpret this as a signal the market is overpriced. But higher ratios can at least partly reflect accounting changes that have reduced reported earnings.

This ratio is often computed using EPS from the most recent period (for Amazon, its PE is 31; for Altria, its PE is 13). However, many users compute this ratio using *expected* EPS for the next period.

Some analysts view stocks with high PE ratios (higher than 20 to 25) as more likely to be overpriced and stocks with low PE ratios (less than 5 to 8) as more likely to be underpriced. These investors prefer to sell or avoid buying stocks with high PE ratios and to buy or hold stocks with low PE ratios. However, investment decision making is rarely so simple as to rely on a single ratio. For instance, a stock with a high PE ratio can prove to be a good investment if its earnings continue to increase beyond current expectations. Similarly, a stock with a low PE ratio can prove to be a poor investment if its earnings decline below expectations.

> **Decision Maker**   Answer—p. 525
>
> **Money Manager** You plan to invest in one of two companies identified as having identical future prospects. One has a PE of 19 and the other a PE of 25. Which do you invest in? Does it matter if your *estimate* of PE for these two companies is 29 as opposed to 22?

Dividend Yield

Investors buy shares of a company's stock in anticipation of receiving a return from either or both cash dividends and stock price increases. Stocks that pay large dividends on a regular basis, called *income stocks,* are attractive to investors who want recurring cash flows from their investments. In contrast, some stocks pay little or no dividends but are still attractive to investors because of their expected stock price increases. The stocks of companies that distribute little or no cash but use their cash to finance expansion are called *growth stocks.* One way to help identify whether a stock is an income stock or a growth stock is to analyze its dividend yield. **Dividend yield,** defined in Exhibit 13.19, shows the annual amount of cash dividends distributed to common shares relative to their market value.

A3 Compute dividend yield and explain its use in analysis.

$$\text{Dividend yield} = \frac{\textbf{Annual cash dividends per share}}{\textbf{Market value per share}}$$

Exhibit 13.19

Dividend Yield

---

[3] A corporation can be classified as having either a simple or complex capital structure. The term **simple capital structure** refers to a company with only common stock and nonconvertible preferred stock outstanding. The term **complex capital structure** refers to companies with dilutive securities. **Dilutive securities** include options, rights to purchase common stock, and any bonds or preferred stock that are convertible into common stock. A company with a complex capital structure must often report two EPS figures: basic and diluted. **Diluted earnings per share** is computed by adding all dilutive securities to the denominator of the basic EPS computation. It reflects the decrease in basic EPS *assuming* that all dilutive securities are converted into common shares.

Dividend yield can be computed for current and prior periods using actual dividends and stock prices and for future periods using expected values. Exhibit 13.20 shows recent dividend and stock price data for **Amazon** and **Altria Group** to compute dividend yield.

Exhibit 13.20

Dividend and Stock Price Information

Company	Cash Dividends per Share	Market Value per Share	Dividend Yield
Amazon	$0.00	$45	0.0%
Altria Group	2.82	55	5.1

Point: The *payout ratio* equals cash dividends declared on common stock divided by net income. A low payout ratio suggests that a company is retaining earnings for future growth.

Dividend yield is zero for Amazon, implying it is a growth stock. An investor in Amazon would look for increases in stock prices (and eventual cash from the sale of stock). Altria has a dividend yield of 5.1%, implying it is an income stock for which dividends are important in assessing its value.

Book Value per Share

A4   Compute book value and explain its use in analysis.

Case 1: Common Stock (Only) Outstanding. **Book value per common share,** defined in Exhibit 13.21, is the recorded amount of stockholders' equity applicable to *common* shares on a per share basis. To illustrate, we use Dillon Snowboards' data from Exhibit 13.4. Dillon has 30,000 outstanding common shares, and the stockholders' equity applicable to common shares is $365,000. Dillon's book value per common share is $12.17, computed as $365,000 divided by 30,000 shares.

Exhibit 13.21

Book Value per Common Share

$$\text{Book value per common share} = \frac{\text{Stockholders' equity applicable to common shares}}{\text{Number of common shares outstanding}}$$

Point: Book value per share is also referred to as *stockholders' claim to assets on a per share basis.*

Case 2: Common and Preferred Stock Outstanding. To compute book value when both common and preferred shares are outstanding, we allocate total stockholders' equity between the two types of shares. The **book value per preferred share** is computed first; its computation is shown in Exhibit 13.22.

Exhibit 13.22

Book Value per Preferred Share

$$\text{Book value per preferred share} = \frac{\text{Stockholders' equity applicable to preferred shares}}{\text{Number of preferred shares outstanding}}$$

The stockholders' equity applicable to preferred shares equals the preferred share's call price (or par value if the preferred is not callable) plus any cumulative dividends in arrears. The remaining stockholders' equity is the portion applicable to common shares. To illustrate, consider LTD's stockholders' equity in Exhibit 13.23. Its preferred stock is callable at $108 per share, and two years of cumulative preferred dividends are in arrears.

Exhibit 13.23

Stockholders' Equity with Preferred and Common Stock

Stockholders' Equity	
Preferred stock—$100 par value, 7% cumulative, 2,000 shares authorized, 1,000 shares issued and outstanding	$100,000
Common stock—$25 par value, 12,000 shares authorized, 10,000 shares issued and outstanding	250,000
Paid-in capital in excess of par value, common stock	15,000
Retained earnings	82,000
Total stockholders' equity	$447,000

The book value computations are in Exhibit 13.24. Equity is first allocated to preferred shares before the book value of common shares is computed.

Exhibit 13.24

Computing Book Value per Preferred and Common Share

Total stockholders' equity		$447,000
Less equity applicable to preferred shares		
Call price (1,000 shares × $108)	$108,000	
Dividends in arrears ($100,000 × 7% × 2 years)	14,000	(122,000)
Equity applicable to common shares		$325,000
Book value per preferred share ($122,000/1,000 shares)		**$122.00**
Book value per common share ($325,000/10,000 shares)		**$ 32.50**

Book value per share reflects the value per share if a company is liquidated at balance sheet amounts. Book value is also the starting point in many stock valuation models, merger negotiations, price setting for public utilities, and loan contracts. The main limitation in using book value is the potential difference between recorded value and market value for assets and liabilities. Investors often adjust their analysis for estimates of these differences.

> ## Decision Maker
> Answer—p. 525
>
> **Investor** You are considering investing in **BMX**, whose book value per common share is $4 and price per common share on the stock exchange is $7. From this information, are BMX's net assets priced higher or lower than its recorded values?

Demonstration Problem 1

Barton Corporation began operations on January 1, 2008. The following transactions relating to stockholders' equity occurred in the first two years of the company's operations.

2008

Jan. 1   Authorized the issuance of 2 million shares of $5 par value common stock and 100,000 shares of $100 par value, 10% cumulative, preferred stock.

Jan. 2   Issued 200,000 shares of common stock for $12 cash per share.

Jan. 3   Issued 100,000 shares of common stock in exchange for a building valued at $820,000 and merchandise inventory valued at $380,000.

Jan. 4   Paid $10,000 cash to the company's founders for organization activities.

Jan. 5   Issued 12,000 shares of preferred stock for $110 cash per share.

2009

June 4   Issued 100,000 shares of common stock for $15 cash per share.

Required

1. Prepare journal entries to record these transactions.

2. Prepare the stockholders' equity section of the balance sheet as of December 31, 2008, and December 31, 2009, based on these transactions.

3. Prepare a table showing dividend allocations and dividends per share for 2008 and 2009 assuming Barton declares the following cash dividends: 2008, $50,000, and 2009, $300,000.

4. Prepare the January 2, 2008, journal entry for Barton's issuance of 200,000 shares of common stock for $12 cash per share assuming

   a. Common stock is no-par stock without a stated value.

   b. Common stock is no-par stock with a stated value of $10 per share.

Planning the Solution

- Record journal entries for the transactions for 2008 and 2009.
- Determine the balances for the 2008 and 2009 equity accounts for the balance sheet.
- Prepare the contributed capital portion of the 2008 and 2009 balance sheets.
- Prepare a table similar to Exhibit 13.11 showing dividend allocations for 2008 and 2009.
- Record the issuance of common stock under both specifications of no-par stock.

Solution to Demonstration Problem I

1. Journal entries.

2008			
Jan. 2	Cash	2,400,000	
	Common Stock, $5 Par Value		1,000,000
	Paid-In Capital in Excess of Par Value, Common Stock		1,400,000
	Issued 200,000 shares of common stock.		

[continued on next page]

[continued from previous page]

Jan. 3	Building	820,000	
	Merchandise Inventory	380,000	
	Common Stock, $5 Par Value.		500,000
	Paid-In Capital in Excess of Par Value,		
	Common Stock.		700,000
	Issued 100,000 shares of common stock.		
Jan. 4	Organization Expenses	10,000	
	Cash		10,000
	Paid founders for organization costs.		
Jan. 5	Cash	1,320,000	
	Preferred Stock, $100 Par Value		1,200,000
	Paid-In Capital in Excess of Par Value,		
	Preferred Stock.		120,000
	Issued 12,000 shares of preferred stock.		
2009			
June 4	Cash	1,500,000	
	Common Stock, $5 Par Value.		500,000
	Paid-In Capital in Excess of Par Value,		
	Common Stock.		1,000,000
	Issued 100,000 shares of common stock.		

2. Balance sheet presentations (at December 31 year-end).

	2008	2009
Stockholders' Equity		
Preferred stock—$100 par value, 10% cumulative, 100,000		
shares authorized, 12,000 shares issued and outstanding	$1,200,000	$1,200,000
Paid-in capital in excess of par value, preferred stock	120,000	120,000
Total paid-in capital by preferred stockholders	1,320,000	1,320,000
Common stock—$5 par value, 2,000,000 shares authorized,		
300,000 shares issued and outstanding in 2008, and		
400,000 shares issued and outstanding in 2009	1,500,000	2,000,000
Paid-in capital in excess of par value, common stock	2,100,000	3,100,000
Total paid-in capital by common stockholders	3,600,000	5,100,000
Total paid-in capital	$4,920,000	$6,420,000

3. Dividend allocation table.

	Common	Preferred
2008 ($50,000)		
Preferred—current year (12,000 shares × $10 = $120,000)	$ 0	$ 50,000
Common—remainder (300,000 shares outstanding)	0	0
Total for the year	$ 0	$ 50,000
2009 ($300,000)		
Preferred—dividend in arrears from 2008 ($120,000 − $50,000)	$ 0	$ 70,000
Preferred—current year	0	120,000
Common—remainder (400,000 shares outstanding)	110,000	0
Total for the year	$110,000	$190,000
Dividends per share		
2008	$ 0.00	$ 4.17
2009	$ 0.28	$ 15.83

4. Journal entries.

a. For 2008:

Jan. 2	Cash	2,400,000	
	Common Stock, No-Par Value		2,400,000
	Issued 200,000 shares of no-par common		
	stock at $12 per share.		

b. For 2008:

Jan. 2	Cash	2,400,000	
	Common Stock, $10 Stated Value.		2,000,000
	Paid-In Capital in Excess of		
	Stated Value, Common Stock		400,000
	Issued 200,000 shares of $10 stated value		
	common stock at $12 per share.		

Demonstration Problem 2

Precision Company began year 2008 with the following balances in its stockholders' equity accounts.

Common stock—$10 par, 500,000 shares authorized,	
200,000 shares issued and outstanding	$2,000,000
Paid-in capital in excess of par, common stock	1,000,000
Retained earnings	5,000,000
Total	$8,000,000

All outstanding common stock was issued for $15 per share when the company was created. Prepare journal entries to account for the following transactions during year 2008.

Jan. 10   The board declared a $0.10 cash dividend per share to shareholders of record Jan. 28.
Feb. 15   Paid the cash dividend declared on January 10.
Mar. 31   Declared a 20% stock dividend. The market value of the stock is $18 per share.
May   1   Distributed the stock dividend declared on March 31.
July 1   Purchased 30,000 shares of treasury stock at $20 per share.
Sept. 1   Sold 20,000 treasury shares at $26 cash per share.
Dec. 1   Sold the remaining 10,000 shares of treasury stock at $7 cash per share.

Planning the Solution

- Calculate the total cash dividend to record by multiplying the cash dividend declared by the number of shares as of the date of record.
- Decide whether the stock dividend is a small or large dividend. Then analyze each event to determine the accounts affected and the appropriate amounts to be recorded.

Solution to Demonstration Problem 2

Jan. 10	Retained Earnings.	20,000	
	Common Dividend Payable		20,000
	Declared a $0.10 per share cash dividend.		
Feb. 15	Common Dividend Payable.	20,000	
	Cash		20,000
	Paid $0.10 per share cash dividend.		

[continued on next page]

[continued from previous page]

Mar. 31	Retained Earnings..........................	720,000	
	Common Stock Dividend Distributable.........		400,000
	Paid-In Capital in Excess of		
	Par Value, Common Stock		320,000
	Declared a small stock dividend of 20% or		
	40,000 shares; market value is $18 per share.		
May 1	Common Stock Dividend Distributable	400,000	
	Common Stock........................		400,000
	Distributed 40,000 shares of common stock.		
July 1	Treasury Stock, Common	600,000	
	Cash		600,000
	Purchased 30,000 common shares at $20 per		
	share.		
Sept. 1	Cash	520,000	
	Treasury Stock, Common.................		400,000
	Paid-In Capital, Treasury Stock		120,000
	Sold 20,000 treasury shares at $26 per share.		
Dec. 1	Cash	70,000	
	Paid-In Capital, Treasury Stock.................	120,000	
	Retained Earnings.........................	10,000	
	Treasury Stock, Common.................		200,000
	Sold 10,000 treasury shares at $7 per share.		

Summary

C1 Identify characteristics of corporations and their organization. Corporations are legal entities whose stockholders are not liable for its debts. Stock is easily transferred, and the life of a corporation does not end with the incapacity of a stock holder. A corporation acts through its agents, who are its officers and managers. Corporations are regulated and subject to income taxes.

C2 Describe the components of stockholders' equity.
Authorized stock is the stock that a corporation's charter authorizes it to sell. Issued stock is the portion of authorized shares sold. Par value stock is a value per share assigned by the charter. No-par value stock is stock *not* assigned a value per share by the charter. Stated value stock is no-par stock to which the directors assign a value per share. Stockholders' equity is made up of (1) paid-in capital and (2) retained earnings. Paid-in capital consists of funds raised by stock issuances. Retained earnings consists of cumulative net income (losses) not distributed.

C3 Explain characteristics of common and preferred stock.
Preferred stock has a priority (or senior status) relative to common stock in one or more areas, usually (1) dividends and (2) assets in case of liquidation. Preferred stock usually does not carry voting rights and can be convertible or callable. Convertibility permits the holder to convert preferred to common. Callability permits the issuer to buy back preferred stock under specified conditions.

C4 Explain the items reported in retained earnings. Many companies face statutory and contractual restrictions on retained earnings. Corporations can voluntarily appropriate retained earnings to inform others about their disposition. Prior period adjustments are corrections of errors in prior financial statements.

A1 Compute earnings per share and describe its use. A company with a simple capital structure computes basic EPS by dividing net income less any preferred dividends by the weighted-average number of outstanding common shares. A company with a complex capital structure must usually report both basic and diluted EPS.

A2 Compute price-earnings ratio and describe its use in analysis. A common stock's price-earnings (PE) ratio is computed by dividing the stock's market value (price) per share by its EPS. A stock's PE is based on expectations that can prove to be better or worse than eventual performance.

A3 Compute dividend yield and explain its use in analysis.
Dividend yield is the ratio of a stock's annual cash dividends per share to its market value (price) per share. Dividend yield can be compared with the yield of other companies to determine whether the stock is expected to be an income or growth stock.

A4 Compute book value and explain its use in analysis. Book value per common share is equity applicable to common shares divided by the number of outstanding common shares. Book value per preferred share is equity applicable to preferred shares divided by the number of outstanding preferred shares.

P1 Record the issuance of corporate stock. When stock is issued, its par or stated value is credited to the stock account and any excess is credited to a separate contributed capital account. If a stock has neither par nor stated value, the entire proceeds are credited to the stock account. Stockholders must contribute assets equal to minimum legal capital or be potentially liable for the deficiency.

P2 Record transactions involving cash dividends. Cash dividends involve three events. On the date of declaration, the directors bind the company to pay the dividend. A dividend declaration reduces retained earnings and creates a current liability. On the date of record, recipients of the dividend are identified. On the date of payment, cash is paid to stockholders and the current liability is removed.

P3 **Account for stock dividends and stock splits.** Neither a stock dividend nor a stock split alters the value of the company. However, the value of each share is less due to the distribution of additional shares. The distribution of additional shares is according to individual stockholders' ownership percent. Small stock dividends (≤25%) are recorded by capitalizing retained earnings equal to the market value of distributed shares. Large stock dividends (>25%) are recorded by capitalizing retained earnings equal to the par or stated value of distributed shares. Stock splits do not yield journal entries but do yield changes in the description of stock.

P4 **Distribute dividends between common stock and preferred stock.** Preferred stockholders usually hold the right

to dividend distributions before common stockholders. When preferred stock is cumulative and in arrears, the amount in arrears must be distributed to preferred before any dividends are distributed to common.

P5 **Record purchases and sales of treasury stock and the retirement of stock.** When a corporation purchases its own previously issued stock, it debits the cost of these shares to Treasury Stock. Treasury stock is subtracted from equity in the balance sheet. If treasury stock is reissued, any proceeds in excess of cost are credited to Paid-In Capital, Treasury Stock. If the proceeds are less than cost, they are debited to Paid-In Capital, Treasury Stock to the extent a credit balance exists. Any remaining amount is debited to Retained Earnings. When stock is retired, all accounts related to the stock are removed.

Guidance Answers to **Decision Maker** and **Decision Ethics**

Entrepreneur The 50% stock dividend provides you no direct income. A stock dividend often reveals management's optimistic expectations about the future and can improve a stock's marketability by making it affordable to more investors. Accordingly, a stock dividend usually reveals "good news" and because of this, it likely increases (slightly) the market value for your stock.

Concert Organizer You have two basic options: (1) different classes of common stock or (2) common and preferred stock. Your objective is to issue to yourself stock that has all or a majority of the voting power. The other class of stock would carry limited or no voting rights. In this way, you maintain control and are able to raise the necessary funds.

Director This case deals with insider trading in a company's stock. The ethical conflict is between your director responsibilities to stockholders (and the public) and your interest in increasing personal wealth from the options. If information about the new contract is kept private until after the option plan is approved and the options are priced, you are likely to make more money. (*Note:* Insider trading laws may make nondisclosure in this case a crime.) You should raise

ethical and legal concerns to the board. You might also consider whether staying on the board of this company is proper since it appears there was some intent to deceive outsiders.

Money Manager Since one company requires a payment of $19 for each $1 of earnings, and the other requires $25, you would prefer the stock with the PE of 19; it is a better deal given identical prospects. You should make sure these companies' earnings computations are roughly the same, for example, no extraordinary items, unusual events, and so forth. Also, your PE estimates for these companies do matter. If you are willing to pay $29 for each $1 of earnings for these companies, you obviously expect both to exceed current market expectations.

Investor Book value reflects recorded values. BMX's book value is $4 per common share. Stock price reflects the market's expectation of net asset value (both tangible and intangible items). BMX's market value is $7 per common share. Comparing these figures suggests BMX's market value of net assets is higher than its recorded values (by an amount of $7 versus $4 per share).

Guidance Answers to **Quick Checks**

1. (*b*)

2. A corporation pays taxes on its income, and its stockholders normally pay personal income taxes (at the 15% rate or lower) on any cash dividends received from the corporation.

3. A proxy is a legal document used to transfer a stockholder's right to vote to another person.

4. (*a*)

5. A stock premium is an amount in excess of par (or stated) value paid by purchasers of newly issued stock.

6. Minimum legal capital intends to protect creditors of a corporation by obligating stockholders to some minimum level of equity financing and by constraining a corporation from excessive payments to stockholders.

7. Common Dividend Payable is a current liability account.

8. The date of declaration, date of record, and date of payment.

9. A dividend is a legal liability at the date of declaration, on which date it is recorded as a liability.

10. A stock dividend does not transfer assets to stockholders, but it does require an amount of retained earnings to be transferred to a contributed capital account(s).

11. A small stock dividend is 25% or less of the previous outstanding shares. A large stock dividend is more than 25%.

12. Retained earnings equal to the distributable shares' market value should be capitalized for a small stock dividend.

13. Typically, preferred stock has a preference in receipt of dividends and in distribution of assets.

14. (*a*)

15. (*b*)

Total cash dividend	$288,000
To preferred shareholders	135,000*
Remainder to common shareholders	$153,000

* 9,000 × $50 × 10% × 3 years = $135,000.

16. (*b*)

17. No. The shares are an investment for Southern Co. and are issued and outstanding shares for Northern Corp.

18. Treasury stock does not affect the number of authorized or issued shares, but it reduces the outstanding shares.

19. (*a*)

Key Terms

mhhe.com/wildFAP18e

Key Terms are available at the book's Website for learning and testing in an online Flashcard Format.

Appropriated retained earnings (p. 517)
Authorized stock (p. 503)
Basic earnings per share (p. 518)
Book value per common share (p. 520)
Book value per preferred share (p. 520)
Call price (p. 513)
Callable preferred stock (p. 513)
Capital stock (p. 503)
Changes in accounting estimates (p. 517)
Common stock (p. 502)
Complex capital structure (p. 519)
Convertible preferred stock (p. 513)
Corporation (p. 500)
Cumulative preferred stock (p. 511)
Date of declaration (p. 507)
Date of payment (p. 507)
Date of record (p. 507)
Diluted earnings per share (p. 519)
Dilutive securities (p. 519)

Discount on stock (p. 505)
Dividend in arrears (p. 511)
Dividend yield (p. 519)
Earnings per share (EPS) (p. 518)
Financial leverage (p. 513)
Large stock dividend (p. 508)
Liquidating cash dividend (p. 508)
Market value per share (p. 503)
Minimum legal capital (p. 503)
Noncumulative preferred stock (p. 511)
Nonparticipating preferred stock (p. 512)
No-par value stock (p. 503)
Organization expenses (p. 501)
Paid-in capital (p. 504)
Paid-in capital in excess of par value (p. 505)
Participating preferred stock (p. 512)
Par value (p. 503)
Par value stock (p. 503)

Preemptive right (p. 502)
Preferred stock (p. 510)
Premium on stock (p. 505)
Price-earnings (PE) ratio (p. 519)
Prior period adjustment (p. 517)
Proxy (p. 502)
Restricted retained earnings (p. 516)
Retained earnings (p. 504)
Retained earnings deficit (p. 507)
Reverse stock split (p. 510)
Simple capital structure (p. 519)
Small stock dividend (p. 508)
Stated value stock (p. 504)
Statement of stockholders' equity (p. 517)
Stock dividend (p. 508)
Stock options (p. 517)
Stock split (p. 510)
Stockholders' equity (p. 504)
Treasury stock (p. 514)

Multiple Choice Quiz

Answers on p. 541   mhhe.com/wildFAP18e

Multiple Choice Quizzes A and B are available at the book's Website.

1. A corporation issues 6,000 shares of $5 par value common stock for $8 cash per share. The entry to record this transaction includes:
   a. A debit to Paid-In Capital in Excess of Par Value for $18,000.
   b. A credit to Common Stock for $48,000.
   c. A credit to Paid-In Capital in Excess of Par Value for $30,000.
   d. A credit to Cash for $48,000.
   e. A credit to Common Stock for $30,000.

2. A company reports net income of $75,000. Its weighted-average common shares outstanding is 19,000. It has no other stock outstanding. Its earnings per share is:
   a. $4.69
   b. $3.95

   c. $3.75
   d. $2.08
   e. $4.41

3. A company has 5,000 shares of $100 par preferred stock and 50,000 shares of $10 par common stock outstanding. Its total stockholders' equity is $2,000,000. Its book value per common share is:
   a. $100.00
   b. $ 10.00
   c. $ 40.00
   d. $ 30.00
   e. $ 36.36

4. A company paid cash dividends of $0.81 per share. Its earnings per share is $6.95 and its market price per share is $45.00. Its dividend yield is:
 a. 1.8%
 b. 11.7%
 c. 15.4%
 d. 55.6%
 e. 8.6%

5. A company's shares have a market value of $85 per share. Its net income is $3,500,000, and its weighted-average common shares outstanding is 700,000. Its price-earnings ratio is:
 a. 5.9
 b. 425.0
 c. 17.0
 d. 10.4
 e. 41.2

Discussion Questions

1. What are organization expenses? Provide examples.
2. How are organization expenses reported?
3. Who is responsible for directing a corporation's affairs?
4. What is the preemptive right of common stockholders?
5. List the general rights of common stockholders.
6. What is the difference between authorized shares and outstanding shares?
7. Why would an investor find convertible preferred stock attractive?
8. What is the difference between the market value per share and the par value per share?
9. What is the difference between the par value and the call price of a share of preferred stock?
10. Identify and explain the importance of the three dates relevant to corporate dividends.
11. Why is the term *liquidating dividend* used to describe cash dividends debited against paid-in capital accounts?
12. How does declaring a stock dividend affect the corporation's assets, liabilities, and total equity? What are the effects of the eventual distribution of that stock?

13. What is the difference between a stock dividend and a stock split?
14. Courts have ruled that a stock dividend is not taxable income to stockholders. What justifies this decision?
15. How does the purchase of treasury stock affect the purchaser's assets and total equity?
16. Why do laws place limits on treasury stock purchases?
17. How are EPS results computed for a corporation with a simple capital structure?
18. What is a stock option?
19. How is book value per share computed for a corporation with no preferred stock? What is the main limitation of using book value per share to value a corporation?
20. Review the balance sheet for **Best Buy** in Appendix A and list the classes of stock that it has issued.
21. Refer to the balance sheet for **Circuit City** in Appendix A. What is the par value per share of its common stock? Suggest a rationale for the amount of par value it assigned.
22. Refer to the financial statements for **Apple** in Appendix A. Did it issue or repurchase any common stock for the year ended September 25, 2004? Explain.

 Red numbers denote Discussion Questions that involve decision-making.

Of the following statements, which are true for the corporate form of organization?
1. Ownership rights cannot be easily transferred.
2. Owners have unlimited liability for corporate debts.
3. Capital is more easily accumulated than with most other forms of organization.
4. Corporate income that is distributed to shareholders is usually taxed twice.
5. It is a separate legal entity.
6. It has a limited life.
7. Owners are not agents of the corporation.

QUICK STUDY

QS 13-1
Characteristics of corporations
C1

Prepare the journal entry to record Zende Company's issuance of 75,000 shares of $5 par value common stock assuming the shares sell for:
a. $5 cash per share.
b. $6 cash per share.

QS 13-2
Issuance of common stock
P1

QS 13-3 Issuance of par and stated value common stock P1	Prepare the journal entry to record Jevonte Company's issuance of 36,000 shares of its common stock assuming the shares have a: **a.** $2 par value and sell for $18 cash per share. **b.** $2 stated value and sell for $18 cash per share.
QS 13-4 Issuance of no-par common stock P1	Prepare the journal entry to record Autumn Company's issuance of 63,000 shares of no-par value common stock assuming the shares: **a.** Sell for $29 cash per share. **b.** Are exchanged for land valued at $1,827,000.
QS 13-5 Issuance of common stock P1	Prepare the issuer's journal entry for each separate transaction. (*a*) On March 1, Atlantic Co. issues 42,500 shares of $4 par value common stock for $297,500 cash. (*b*) On April 1, OP Co. issues no-par value common stock for $70,000 cash. (*c*) On April 6, MPG issues 2,000 shares of $25 par value common stock for $45,000 of inventory, $145,000 of machinery, and acceptance of a $94,000 note payable.
QS 13-6 Issuance of preferred stock C3	**a.** Prepare the journal entry to record Tamasine Company's issuance of 5,000 shares of $100 par value 7% cumulative preferred stock for $102 cash per share. **b.** Assuming the facts in part 1, if Tamasine declares a year-end cash dividend, what is the amount of dividend paid to preferred shareholders? (Assume no dividends in arrears.)
QS 13-7 Accounting for cash dividends P2	Prepare journal entries to record the following transactions for Fletcher Corporation. May 15 Declared a $54,000 cash dividend payable to common stockholders. June 31 Paid the dividend declared on May 15.
QS 13-8 Accounting for small stock dividend C2 P3	The stockholders' equity section of Jun Company's balance sheet as of April 1 follows. On April 2, Jun declares and distributes a 10% stock dividend. The stock's per share market value on April 2 is $20 (prior to the dividend). Prepare the stockholders' equity section immediately after the stock dividend.

Common stock—$5 par value, 375,000 shares authorized, 200,000 shares issued and outstanding	$1,000,000
Paid-in capital in excess of par value, common stock	600,000
Retained earnings	833,000
Total stockholders' equity	$2,433,000

QS 13-9 Dividend allocation between classes of shareholders P4	Stockholders' equity of Ernst Company consists of 80,000 shares of $5 par value, 8% cumulative preferred stock and 250,000 shares of $1 par value common stock. Both classes of stock have been outstanding since the company's inception. Ernst did not declare any dividends in the prior year, but it now declares and pays a $110,000 cash dividend at the current year-end. Determine the amount distributed to each class of stockholders for this two-year-old company.
QS 13-10 Purchase and sale of treasury stock P5	On May 3, Zirbal Corporation purchased 4,000 shares of its own stock for $36,000 cash. On November 4, Zirbal reissued 850 shares of this treasury stock for $8,500. Prepare the May 3 and November 4 journal entries to record Zirbal's purchase and reissuance of treasury stock.
QS 13-11 Accounting for changes in estimates; error adjustments C4	Answer the following questions related to a company's activities for the current year: **1.** A review of the notes payable files discovers that three years ago the company reported the entire amount of a payment (principal and interest) on an installment note payable as interest expense. This mistake had a material effect on the amount of income in that year. How should the correction be reported in the current year financial statements? **2.** After using an expected useful life of seven years and no salvage value to depreciate its office equipment over the preceding three years, the company decided early this year that the equipment will last only two more years. How should the effects of this decision be reported in the current year financial statements?

Murray Company reports net income of $770,000 for the year. It has no preferred stock, and its weighted-average common shares outstanding is 280,000 shares. Compute its basic earnings per share.

QS 13-12
Basic earnings per share A1

Epic Company earned net income of $900,000 this year. The number of common shares outstanding during the entire year was 400,000, and preferred shareholders received a $20,000 cash dividend. Compute Epic Company's basic earnings per share.

QS 13-13
Basic earnings per share A1

Compute Topp Company's price-earnings ratio if its common stock has a market value of $32.60 per share and its EPS is $3.95. Would an analyst likely consider this stock potentially over- or underpriced? Explain.

QS 13-14
Price-earnings ratio A2

Foxboro Company expects to pay a $2.30 per share cash dividend this year on its common stock. The current market value of Foxboro stock is $32.50 per share. Compute the expected dividend yield on the Foxboro stock. Would you classify the Foxboro stock as a growth or an income stock? Explain.

QS 13-15
Dividend yield

A3

The stockholders' equity section of Montaigne Company's balance sheet follows. The preferred stock's call price is $40. Determine the book value per share of the common stock.

QS 13-16
Book value per common share

A4

Preferred stock—5% cumulative, $10 par value, 20,000 shares authorized, issued and outstanding	$ 200,000
Common stock—$5 par value, 200,000 shares authorized, 150,000 shares issued and outstanding	750,000
Retained earnings	890,000
Total stockholders' equity	$1,840,000

Describe how each of the following characteristics of organizations applies to corporations.

EXERCISES

1. Owner authority and control	5. Duration of life
2. Ease of formation	6. Owner liability
3. Transferability of ownership	7. Legal status
4. Ability to raise large capital amounts	8. Tax status of income

Exercise 13-1
Characteristics of corporations
C1

Rodriguez Corporation issues 19,000 shares of its common stock for $152,000 cash on February 20. Prepare journal entries to record this event under each of the following separate situations.
1. The stock has neither par nor stated value.
2. The stock has a $2 par value.
3. The stock has a $5 stated value.

Exercise 13-2
Accounting for par, stated, and no-par stock issuances
P1

Prepare journal entries to record the following four separate issuances of stock.
1. Two thousand shares of no-par common stock are issued to the corporation's promoters in exchange for their efforts, estimated to be worth $40,000. The stock has no stated value.
2. Two thousand shares of no-par common stock are issued to the corporation's promoters in exchange for their efforts, estimated to be worth $40,000. The stock has a $1 per share stated value.
3. Four thousand shares of $5 par value common stock are issued for $35,000 cash.
4. One thousand shares of $50 par value preferred stock are issued for $60,000 cash.

Exercise 13-3
Recording stock issuances
P1

Sudoku Company issues 7,000 shares of $7 par value common stock in exchange for land and a building. The land is valued at $45,000 and the building at $85,000. Prepare the journal entry to record issuance of the stock in exchange for the land and building.

Exercise 13-4
Stock issuance for noncash assets
P1

Exercise 13-5
Identifying characteristics of preferred stock

C2   C3

Match each description 1 through 6 with the characteristic of preferred stock that it best describes by writing the letter of the characteristic in the blank next to each description.

A. Callable   **B.** Convertible   **C.** Cumulative

D. Noncumulative   **E.** Nonparticipating   **F.** Participating

_____ **1.** Holders of the stock are entitled to receive current and all past dividends before common stockholders receive any dividends.

_____ **2.** The issuing corporation can retire the stock by paying a prespecified price.

_____ **3.** Holders of the stock can receive dividends exceeding the stated rate under certain conditions.

_____ **4.** Holders of the stock are not entitled to receive dividends in excess of the stated rate.

_____ **5.** Holders of this stock can exchange it for shares of common stock.

_____ **6.** Holders of the stock lose any dividends that are not declared in the current year.

Exercise 13-6
Stock dividends and splits

P3

On June 30, 2008, Sharper Corporation's common stock is priced at $62 per share before any stock dividend or split, and the stockholders' equity section of its balance sheet appears as follows.

Common stock—$10 par value, 120,000 shares authorized, 50,000 shares issued and outstanding	$ 500,000
Paid-in capital in excess of par value, common stock	200,000
Retained earnings	660,000
Total stockholders' equity	$1,360,000

1. Assume that the company declares and immediately distributes a 50% stock dividend. This event is recorded by capitalizing retained earnings equal to the stock's par value. Answer these questions about stockholders' equity as it exists *after* issuing the new shares.

     a. What is the retained earnings balance?

Check (1*b*) $1,360,000

     b. What is the amount of total stockholders' equity?

     c. How many shares are outstanding?

2. Assume that the company implements a 3-for-2 stock split instead of the stock dividend in part 1. Answer these questions about stockholders' equity as it exists *after* issuing the new shares.

(2*a*) $660,000

     a. What is the retained earnings balance?

     b. What is the amount of total stockholders' equity?

     c. How many shares are outstanding?

3. Explain the difference, if any, to a stockholder from receiving new shares distributed under a large stock dividend versus a stock split.

Exercise 13-7
Stock dividends and per share book values

P3

The stockholders' equity of TVX Company at the beginning of the day on February 5 follows.

Common stock—$10 par value, 150,000 shares authorized, 60,000 shares issued and outstanding	$ 600,000
Paid-in capital in excess of par value, common stock	425,000
Retained earnings	550,000
Total stockholders' equity	$1,575,000

On February 5, the directors declare a 20% stock dividend distributable on February 28 to the February 15 stockholders of record. The stock's market value is $40 per share on February 5 before the stock dividend. The stock's market value is $33.40 per share on February 28.

1. Prepare entries to record both the dividend declaration and its distribution.

Check (2) Book value per share: before, $26.250; after, $21.875

2. One stockholder owned 800 shares on February 5 before the dividend. Compute the book value per share and total book value of this stockholder's shares immediately before and after the stock dividend of February 5.

3. Compute the total market value of the investor's shares in part 2 as of February 5 and February 28.

York's outstanding stock consists of (*a*) 80,000 shares of noncumulative 7.5% preferred stock with a $5 par value and (*b*) 200,000 shares of common stock with a $1 par value. During its first four years of operation, the corporation declared and paid the following total cash dividends.

2006	$ 20,000
2007	28,000
2008	200,000
2009	350,000

Determine the amount of dividends paid each year to each of the two classes of stockholders. Also compute the total dividends paid to each class for the four years combined.

Exercise 13-8
Dividends on common and noncumulative preferred stock

P4

Check   Total paid to preferred, $108,000

Use the data in Exercise 13-8 to determine the amount of dividends paid each year to each of the two classes of stockholders assuming that the preferred stock is cumulative. Also determine the total dividends paid to each class for the four years combined.

Exercise 13-9
Dividends on common and cumulative preferred stock   P4

On October 10, the stockholders' equity of Sherman Systems appears as follows.

Common stock—$10 par value, 72,000 shares authorized, issued, and outstanding	$ 720,000
Paid-in capital in excess of par value, common stock	216,000
Retained earnings	864,000
Total stockholders' equity	$1,800,000

Exercise 13-10
Recording and reporting treasury stock transactions

P5

1. Prepare journal entries to record the following transactions for Sherman Systems.
  a. Purchased 5,000 shares of its own common stock at $25 per share on October 11.
  b. Sold 1,000 treasury shares on November 1 for $31 cash per share.
  c. Sold all remaining treasury shares on November 25 for $20 cash per share.
2. Explain how Sherman's equity section changes after the October 11 treasury stock purchase, and prepare the revised equity section of its balance sheet at that date.

Check   (1c) Dr. Retained Earnings, $14,000

The following information is available for Amos Company for the year ended December 31, 2008.
  a. Balance of retained earnings, December 31, 2007, prior to discovery of error, $1,375,000.
  b. Cash dividends declared and paid during 2008, $43,000.
  c. It neglected to record 2006 depreciation expense of $55,500, which is net of $4,500 in income taxes.
  d. Amos earned $126,000 in 2008 net income.
Prepare a 2008 statement of retained earnings for Amos Company.

Exercise 13-11
Preparing a statement of retained earnings

C4

Ecker Company reports $2,700,000 of net income for 2008 and declares $390,000 of cash dividends on its preferred stock for 2008. At the end of 2008, the company had 678,000 weighted-average shares of common stock.
  1. What amount of net income is available to common stockholders for 2008?
  2. What is the company's basic EPS for 2008?

Exercise 13-12
Earnings per share

A1

Check   (2) $3.41

Kelley Company reports $960,000 of net income for 2008 and declares $130,000 of cash dividends on its preferred stock for 2008. At the end of 2008, the company had 379,000 weighted-average shares of common stock.
  1. What amount of net income is available to common stockholders for 2008?
  2. What is the company's basic EPS for 2008?

Exercise 13-13
Earnings per share

A1

Exercise 13-14
Price-earnings ratio computation and interpretation

A2

Compute the price-earnings ratio for each of these four separate companies. Which stock might an analyst likely investigate as being potentially undervalued by the market? Explain.

Company	Earnings per Share	Market Value per Share
1	$12.00	$176.00
2	10.00	96.00
3	7.50	94.00
4	50.00	250.00

Exercise 13-15
Dividend yield computation and interpretation

A3

Compute the dividend yield for each of these four separate companies. Which company's stock would probably *not* be classified as an income stock? Explain.

Company	Annual Cash Dividend per Share	Market Value per Share
1	$16.00	$220.00
2	14.00	136.00
3	4.00	72.00
4	1.00	80.00

Exercise 13-16
Book value per share

A4

The equity section of Cyril Corporation's balance sheet shows the following.

Preferred stock—6% cumulative, $25 par value, $30 call price, 10,000 shares issued and outstanding	$ 250,000
Common stock—$10 par value, 80,000 shares issued and outstanding	800,000
Retained earnings	535,000
Total stockholders' equity	$1,585,000

Determine the book value per share of the preferred and common stock under two separate situations.

Check (1) Book value of common, $16.06

1. No preferred dividends are in arrears.

2. Three years of preferred dividends are in arrears.

PROBLEM SET A

Problem 13-1A
Stockholders' equity transactions and analysis

C2 C3 P1

Kinkaid Co. is incorporated at the beginning of this year and engages in a number of transactions. The following journal entries impacted its stockholders' equity during its first year of operations.

a.	Cash	300,000	
	Common Stock, $25 Par Value		250,000
	Paid-In Capital in Excess of Par Value, Common Stock		50,000
b.	Organization Expenses	150,000	
	Common Stock, $25 Par Value		125,000
	Paid-In Capital in Excess of Par Value, Common Stock		25,000

[continued on next page]

[continued from previous page]

c.	Cash	43,000	
	Accounts Receivable	15,000	
	Building	81,500	
	Notes Payable		59,500
	Common Stock, $25 Par Value		50,000
	Paid-In Capital in Excess of Par Value, Common Stock		30,000
d.	Cash	120,000	
	Common Stock, $25 Par Value		75,000
	Paid-In Capital in Excess of Par Value, Common Stock		45,000

Required

1. Explain each journal entry (*a*) through (*d*).

2. How many shares of common stock are outstanding at year-end?

3. What is the amount of minimum legal capital (based on par value) at year-end?

4. What is the total paid-in capital at year-end?

5. What is the book value per share of the common stock at year-end if total paid-in capital plus retained earnings equals $695,000?

Check (2) 20,000 shares

(3) $500,000

(4) $650,000

Kohler Corporation reports the following components of stockholders' equity on December 31, 2008.

Problem 13-2A

Cash dividends, treasury stock, and statement of retained earnings

C2 C4 P2 P5

Common stock—$10 par value, 100,000 shares authorized, 40,000 shares issued and outstanding	$400,000
Paid-in capital in excess of par value, common stock	60,000
Retained earnings	270,000
Total stockholders' equity	$730,000

In year 2009, the following transactions affected its stockholders' equity accounts.

Jan.	1	Purchased 4,000 shares of its own stock at $20 cash per share.
Jan.	5	Directors declared a $2 per share cash dividend payable on Feb. 28 to the Feb. 5 stockholders of record.
Feb.	28	Paid the dividend declared on January 5.
July	6	Sold 1,500 of its treasury shares at $24 cash per share.
Aug.	22	Sold 2,500 of its treasury shares at $17 cash per share.
Sept.	5	Directors declared a $2 per share cash dividend payable on October 28 to the September 25 stockholders of record.
Oct.	28	Paid the dividend declared on September 5.
Dec.	31	Closed the $388,000 credit balance (from net income) in the Income Summary account to Retained Earnings.

Required

1. Prepare journal entries to record each of these transactions for 2009.

2. Prepare a statement of retained earnings for the year ended December 31, 2009.

3. Prepare the stockholders' equity section of the company's balance sheet as of December 31, 2009.

Check (2) Retained earnings, Dec. 31, 2009, $504,500.

At September 30, the end of Beijing Company's third quarter, the following stockholders' equity accounts are reported.

Problem 13-3A

Equity analysis—journal entries and account balances

P2 P3

Common stock, $12 par value	$360,000
Paid-in capital in excess of par value, common stock	90,000
Retained earnings	320,000

In the fourth quarter, the following entries related to its equity accounts are recorded.

Oct. 2	Retained Earnings.............................	60,000	
	Common Dividend Payable		60,000
Oct. 25	Common Dividend Payable	60,000	
	Cash		60,000
Oct. 31	Retained Earnings	75,000	
	Common Stock Dividend Distributable		36,000
	Paid-In Capital in Excess of		
	Par Value, Common Stock		39,000
Nov. 5	Common Stock Dividend Distributable	36,000	
	Common Stock, $12 Par Value		36,000
Dec. 1	Memo—Change the title of the common stock account to reflect the new par value of $4.		
Dec. 31	Income Summary	210,000	
	Retained Earnings		210,000

Required

1. Explain each journal entry.

2. Complete the following table showing the equity account balances at each indicated date.

	Oct. 2	Oct. 25	Oct. 31	Nov. 5	Dec. 1	Dec. 31
Common stock	$____	$____	$____	$____	$____	$____
Common stock dividend distributable	____	____	____	____	____	____
Paid-in capital in excess of par, common stock	____	____	____	____	____	____
Retained earnings	____	____	____	____	____	____
Total equity	$____	$____	$____	$____	$____	$____

Check Total equity: Oct. 2, $710,000; Dec. 31, $920,000

Problem 13-4A
Analysis of changes in stockholders' equity accounts

C4 P2 P3 P5

The equity sections from Atticus Group's 2008 and 2009 year-end balance sheets follow.

Stockholders' Equity (December 31, 2008)

Common stock—$4 par value, 100,000 shares authorized, 40,000 shares issued and outstanding	$160,000
Paid-in capital in excess of par value, common stock	120,000
Retained earnings	320,000
Total stockholders' equity	$600,000

Stockholders' Equity (December 31, 2009)

Common stock—$4 par value, 100,000 shares authorized, 47,400 shares issued, 3,000 shares in treasury	$189,600
Paid-in capital in excess of par value, common stock	179,200
Retained earnings ($30,000 restricted by treasury stock)	400,000
	768,800
Less cost of treasury stock	(30,000)
Total stockholders' equity	$738,800

The following transactions and events affected its equity accounts during year 2009.

Jan.   5   Declared a $0.50 per share cash dividend, date of record January 10.
Mar. 20   Purchased treasury stock for cash.
Apr.   5   Declared a $0.50 per share cash dividend, date of record April 10.
July   5   Declared a $0.50 per share cash dividend, date of record July 10.
July 31   Declared a 20% stock dividend when the stock's market value is $12 per share.

Aug. 14   Issued the stock dividend that was declared on July 31.

Oct.   5   Declared a $0.50 per share cash dividend, date of record October 10.

Required

1. How many common shares are outstanding on each cash dividend date?

2. What is the total dollar amount for each of the four cash dividends?

3. What is the amount of the capitalization of retained earnings for the stock dividend?

4. What is the per share cost of the treasury stock purchased?

5. How much net income did the company earn during year 2009?

Check   (3) $88,800

(4) $10

(5) $248,000

Raphael Corporation's common stock is currently selling on a stock exchange at $85 per share, and its current balance sheet shows the following stockholders' equity section.

Problem 13-5A
Computation of book values and dividend allocations

C3   A4   P4

Preferred stock—5% cumulative, $___ par value, 1,000 shares authorized, issued, and outstanding	$ 50,000
Common stock—$___ par value, 4,000 shares authorized, issued, and outstanding	80,000
Retained earnings	150,000
Total stockholders' equity	$280,000

Required

1. What is the current market value (price) of this corporation's common stock?

2. What are the par values of the corporation's preferred stock and its common stock?

3. If no dividends are in arrears, what are the book values per share of the preferred stock and the common stock?

4. If two years' preferred dividends are in arrears, what are the book values per share of the preferred stock and the common stock?

5. If two years' preferred dividends are in arrears and the preferred stock is callable at $55 per share, what are the book values per share of the preferred stock and the common stock?

6. If two years' preferred dividends are in arrears and the board of directors declares cash dividends of $11,500, what total amount will be paid to the preferred and to the common shareholders? What is the amount of dividends per share for the common stock?

Check   (4) Book value of common, $56.25

(5) Book value of common, $55

(6) Dividends per common share, $1.00

Analysis Component

7. What are some factors that can contribute to a difference between the book value of common stock and its market value (price)?

Weiss Company is incorporated at the beginning of this year and engages in a number of transactions. The following journal entries impacted its stockholders' equity during its first year of operations.

PROBLEM SET B

Problem 13-1B
Stockholders' equity transactions and analysis

C2   C3   P1

a.	Cash	120,000	
	Common Stock, $1 Par Value		3,000
	Paid-In Capital in Excess of Par Value, Common Stock		117,000
b.	Organization Expenses	40,000	
	Common Stock, $1 Par Value		1,000
	Paid-In Capital in Excess of Par Value, Common Stock		39,000
c.	Cash	13,300	
	Accounts Receivable	8,000	
	Building	37,000	
	Notes Payable		18,300
	Common Stock, $1 Par Value		800
	Paid-In Capital in Excess of Par Value, Common Stock		39,200

[continued on next page]

[continued from previous page]

d.	Cash	60,000	
	Common Stock, $1 Par Value		1,200
	Paid-In Capital in Excess of Par Value, Common Stock		58,800

Required

1. Explain each journal entry (*a*) through (*d*).
2. How many shares of common stock are outstanding at year-end?
3. What is the amount of minimum legal capital (based on par value) at year-end?
4. What is the total paid-in capital at year-end?
5. What is the book value per share of the common stock at year-end if total paid-in capital plus retained earnings equals $283,000?

Check (2) 6,000 shares
(3) $6,000
(4) $260,000

Problem 13-2B
Cash dividends, treasury stock, and statement of retained earnings

C2 C4 P2 P5

Balthus Corp. reports the following components of stockholders' equity on December 31, 2008.

Common stock—$1 par value, 320,000 shares authorized, 200,000 shares issued and outstanding	$ 200,000
Paid-in capital in excess of par value, common stock	1,400,000
Retained earnings	2,160,000
Total stockholders' equity	$3,760,000

It completed the following transactions related to stockholders' equity in year 2009.

Jan. 10 Purchased 40,000 shares of its own stock at $12 cash per share.
Mar. 2 Directors declared a $1.50 per share cash dividend payable on March 31 to the March 15 stockholders of record.
Mar. 31 Paid the dividend declared on March 2.
Nov. 11 Sold 24,000 of its treasury shares at $13 cash per share.
Nov. 25 Sold 16,000 of its treasury shares at $9.50 cash per share.
Dec. 1 Directors declared a $2.50 per share cash dividend payable on January 2 to the December 10 stockholders of record.
Dec. 31 Closed the $1,072,000 credit balance (from net income) in the Income Summary account to Retained Earnings.

Required

1. Prepare journal entries to record each of these transactions for 2009.
2. Prepare a statement of retained earnings for the year ended December 31, 2009.
3. Prepare the stockholders' equity section of the company's balance sheet as of December 31, 2009.

Check (2) Retained earnings, Dec. 31, 2009, $2,476,000

Problem 13-3B
Equity analysis—journal entries and account balances

P2 P3

At December 31, the end of Chilton Communication's third quarter, the following stockholders' equity accounts are reported.

Common stock, $10 par value	$ 960,000
Paid-in capital in excess of par value, common stock	384,000
Retained earnings	1,600,000

In the fourth quarter, the following entries related to its equity accounts are recorded.

Jan. 17	Retained Earnings	96,000	
	Common Dividend Payable		96,000
Feb. 5	Common Dividend Payable	96,000	
	Cash		96,000

[continued on next page]

[continued from previous page]

Feb. 28	Retained Earnings.	252,000	
	Common Stock Dividend Distributable.		120,000
	Paid-In Capital in Excess of Par Value,		
	Common Stock		132,000
Mar. 14	Common Stock Dividend Distributable	120,000	
	Common Stock, $10 Par Value		120,000
Mar. 25	Memo—Change the title of the common stock		
	account to reflect the new par value of $5.		
Mar. 31	Income Summary	720,000	
	Retained Earnings		720,000

Required

1. Explain each journal entry.

2. Complete the following table showing the equity account balances at each indicated date.

	Jan. 17	Feb. 5	Feb. 28	Mar. 14	Mar. 25	Mar. 31
Common stock	$_____	$_____	$_____	$_____	$_____	$_____
Common stock dividend distributable	_____	_____	_____	_____	_____	_____
Paid-in capital in excess of par, common stock	_____	_____	_____	_____	_____	_____
Retained earnings	_____	_____	_____	_____	_____	_____
Total equity	$_____	$_____	$_____	$_____	$_____	$_____

Check Total equity: Jan. 17, $2,848,000; Mar. 31, $3,568,000

The equity sections from Hovo Corporation's 2008 and 2009 balance sheets follow.

Problem 13-4B
Analysis of changes in stockholders' equity accounts

C4 P2 P3 P5

Stockholders' Equity (December 31, 2008)	
Common stock—$20 par value, 30,000 shares authorized,	
17,000 shares issued and outstanding	$340,000
Paid-in capital in excess of par value, common stock	60,000
Retained earnings	270,000
Total stockholders' equity	$670,000

Stockholders' Equity (December 31, 2009)	
Common stock—$20 par value, 30,000 shares authorized,	
19,000 shares issued, 1,000 shares in treasury	$380,000
Paid-in capital in excess of par value, common stock	104,000
Retained earnings ($40,000 restricted by treasury stock)	295,200
	779,200
Less cost of treasury stock	(40,000)
Total stockholders' equity	$739,200

The following transactions and events affected its equity accounts during year 2009.

Feb. 15	Declared a $0.40 per share cash dividend, date of record five days later.
Mar. 2	Purchased treasury stock for cash.
May 15	Declared a $0.40 per share cash dividend, date of record five days later.
Aug. 15	Declared a $0.40 per share cash dividend, date of record five days later.
Oct. 4	Declared a 12.5% stock dividend when the stock's market value is $42 per share.
Oct. 20	Issued the stock dividend that was declared on October 4.
Nov. 15	Declared a $0.40 per share cash dividend, date of record five days later.

Required

1. How many common shares are outstanding on each cash dividend date?

2. What is the total dollar amount for each of the four cash dividends?

3. What is the amount of the capitalization of retained earnings for the stock dividend?

4. What is the per share cost of the treasury stock purchased?

5. How much net income did the company earn during year 2009?

Problem 13-5B
Computation of book values and
dividend allocations

C3   A4   P4

Soltech Company's common stock is currently selling on a stock exchange at $90 per share, and its current balance sheet shows the following stockholders' equity section.

Preferred stock—8% cumulative, $___ par value, 1,500 shares authorized, issued, and outstanding	$ 375,000
Common stock—$___ par value, 18,000 shares authorized, issued, and outstanding	900,000
Retained earnings	1,125,000
Total stockholders' equity	$2,400,000

Required

1. What is the current market value (price) of this corporation's common stock?

2. What are the par values of the corporation's preferred stock and its common stock?

3. If no dividends are in arrears, what are the book values per share of the preferred stock and the common stock?

4. If two years' preferred dividends are in arrears, what are the book values per share of the preferred stock and the common stock?

5. If two years' preferred dividends are in arrears and the preferred stock is callable at $280 per share, what are the book values per share of the preferred stock and the common stock?

6. If two years' preferred dividends are in arrears and the board of directors declares cash dividends of $100,000, what total amount will be paid to the preferred and to the common shareholders? What is the amount of dividends per share for the common stock?

Analysis Component

7. Discuss why the book value of common stock is not always a good estimate of its market value.

PROBLEM SET C

Problem Set C is available at the book's Website to further reinforce and assess your learning.

SERIAL PROBLEM

Success Systems

(This serial problem began in Chapter 1 and continues through most of the book. If previous chapter segments were not completed, the serial problem can begin at this point. It is helpful, but not necessary, for you to use the Working Papers that accompany the book.)

SP 13   Adriana Lopez created Success Systems on October 1, 2007. The company has been successful, and Adriana plans to expand her business. She believes that an additional $100,000 is needed and is investigating three funding sources.

a. Adriana's sister Cicely is willing to invest $100,000 in the business as a common shareholder. Since Adriana currently has $120,000 invested in the business, Cicely's investment will mean that Adriana will maintain about 55% ownership, and Cicely will have 45% ownership of Success Systems.

b. Adriana's uncle Marcello is willing to invest $100,000 in the business as a preferred shareholder. Marcello would purchase 1,000 shares of $100 par value, 7% preferred stock.

c. Adriana's banker is willing to lend her $100,000 on a 7%, 10-year note payable. Adriana would make monthly payments of $1,160.00 per month for 10 years.

Required

1. Prepare the journal entry to reflect the initial $100,000 investment under each of the options (a), (b), and (c).

2. Evaluate the three proposals for expansion, providing the pros and cons of each option.

3. Which option do you recommend Adriana adopt? Explain.

BEYOND THE NUMBERS

BTN 13-1   Refer to **Best Buy**'s financial statements in Appendix A to answer the following.

1. How many shares of common stock are issued and outstanding at February 26, 2005, and February 28, 2004? How do these numbers compare with the weighted-average common shares outstanding at February 26, 2005 and February 28, 2004?

2. What is the book value of its entire common stock at February 26, 2005?

3. What is the total amount of cash dividends paid to common stockholders for the years ended February 26, 2005, and February 28, 2004?

4. Identify and compare basic EPS amounts across years 2005, 2004, and 2003. Identify and comment on any marked changes.

5. Does Best Buy hold any treasury stock as of February 26, 2005? As of February 28, 2004?

REPORTING IN ACTION

C2 C3 A1 A4

Fast Forward

6. Access Best Buy's financial statements for fiscal years ending after February 26, 2005, from its Website (**BestBuy.com**) or the SEC's EDGAR database (**www.SEC.gov**). Has the number of common shares outstanding increased since February 26, 2005? Has Best Buy increased the total amount of cash dividends paid compared to the total amount for fiscal year 2005?

BTN 13-2   Key comparative figures for both **Best Buy** and **Circuit City** follow.

COMPARATIVE ANALYSIS

A1 A2 A3 A4

Key Figures	Best Buy	Circuit City
Net income (in millions)	$ 984	$ 62
Cash dividends declared per common share	$ 0.42	$ 0.07
Common shares outstanding (in millions)	328	188
Weighted-average common shares outstanding (in mil.)	326	193
Market value (price) per share	$51.69	$15.63
Equity applicable to common shares (in millions)	$4,449	$2,087

Required

1. Compute the book value per common share for each company using these data.

2. Compute the basic EPS for each company using these data.

3. Compute the dividend yield for each company using these data. Does the dividend yield of either company characterize it as an income or growth stock? Explain.

4. Compute, compare, and interpret the price-earnings ratio for each company using these data.

BTN 13-3   Harriet Moore is an accountant for New World Pharmaceuticals. Her duties include tracking research and development spending in the new product development division. Over the course of the past six months, Harriet notices that a great deal of funds have been spent on a particular project for a new drug. She hears "through the grapevine" that the company is about to patent the drug and expects it to be a major advance in antibiotics. Harriet believes that this new drug will greatly improve company performance and will cause the company's stock to increase in value. Harriet decides to purchase shares of New World in order to benefit from this expected increase.

ETHICS CHALLENGE

C4

Required

What are Harriet's ethical responsibilities, if any, with respect to the information she has learned through her duties as an accountant for New World Pharmaceuticals? What are the implications to her planned purchase of New World shares?

COMMUNICATING IN PRACTICE

A1   A2

Hint: Make a transparency of each team's memo for a class discussion.

BTN 13-4   Teams are to select an industry, and each team member is to select a different company in that industry. Each team member then is to acquire the selected company's financial statements (or Form 10-K) from the SEC EDGAR site (www.sec.gov). Use these data to identify basic EPS. Use the financial press (or finance.yahoo.com) to determine the market price of this stock, and then compute the price-earnings ratio. Communicate with teammates via a meeting, e-mail, or telephone to discuss the meaning of this ratio, how companies compare, and the industry norm. The team must prepare a single memorandum reporting the ratio for each company and identifying the team conclusions or consensus of opinion. The memorandum is to be duplicated and distributed to the instructor and teammates.

TAKING IT TO THE NET

C2

BTN 13-5   Access the March 4, 2005, filing of the 2004 calendar-year 10-K report of McDonald's, (ticker MCD) from www.sec.gov.

Required

1. How many classes of stock has McDonald's issued?
2. What are the par values, number of authorized shares, and issued shares of the classes of stock you identified in part 1?
3. What total amount of cash did McDonald's pay in 2004 to purchase treasury stock?
4. What amount did McDonald's pay out in cash dividends for 2004?

TEAMWORK IN ACTION

P5

Hint: Instructor should be sure each team accurately completes part 1 before proceeding.

BTN 13-6   This activity requires teamwork to reinforce understanding of accounting for treasury stock.

1. Write a brief team statement (*a*) generalizing what happens to a corporation's financial position when it engages in a stock "buyback" and (*b*) identifying reasons that a corporation would engage in this activity.
2. Assume that an entity acquires 100 shares of its $100 par value common stock at a cost of $134 cash per share. Discuss the entry to record this acquisition. Next, assign *each* team member to prepare *one* of the following entries (assume each entry applies to all shares):
   a. Reissue treasury shares at cost.
   b. Reissue treasury shares at $150 per share.
   c. Reissue treasury shares at $120 per share; assume the contributed capital account from treasury shares has a $1,500 balance.
   d. Reissue treasury shares at $120 per share; assume the contributed capital account from treasury shares has a $1,000 balance.
   e. Reissue treasury shares at $120 per share; assume the contributed capital account from treasury shares has a zero balance.
3. In sequence, each member is to present his/her entry to the team and explain the *similarities* and *differences* between that entry and the previous entry.

BusinessWeek ACTIVITY

A1   C4

BTN 13-7   Read the commentary "How Tax Reform Drives Growth and Investment" by Robert J. Barro in the January 24, 2005, issue of *BusinessWeek*.

Required

1. How did the 2003 tax cuts related to dividend taxation affect companies' decisions to pay cash dividends? Explain.
2. What kinds of companies increased their dividends following those tax cuts? Why?
3. Why do you believe managers of these companies acted as they did?

BTN 13-8 Assume that Sundeep Bhan's launch of Medsite, Inc. requires $500,000 of start-up capital. Bhan contributes $375,000 of personal assets in return for 15,000 shares of common stock but needs to raise another $125,000 in cash. There are two alternative plans for raising the additional cash. Plan A is to sell 3,750 shares of common stock to one or more investors for $125,000 cash. Plan B is to sell 1,250 shares of cumulative preferred stock to one or more investors for $125,000 cash (this preferred stock would have a $100 par value, an annual 8% dividend rate, and be issued at par).

1. If the business is expected to earn $72,000 of after-tax net income in the first year, what rate of return on beginning equity will Bhan personally earn under each alternative? Which plan will provide the higher expected return to Bhan?

2. If the business is expected to earn $16,800 of after-tax net income in the first year, what rate of return on beginning equity will Bhan personally earn under each alternative? Which plan will provide the higher expected return to Bhan?

3. Analyze and interpret the differences between the results for parts 1 and 2.

ENTREPRENEURIAL DECISION

C2 C3 P2

BTN 13-9 Watch 30 to 60 minutes of financial news on the CNBC television channel. Take notes on companies that are catching analysts' attention. You might hear reference to over- and undervaluation of firm and to reports about PE ratios, dividend yields, and earnings per share. Be prepared to give a brief description to the class of your observations of CNBC.

HITTING THE ROAD

A1 A2 A3

BTN 13-10 Financial information for Dixons (Dixons-Group.com) follows.

Net income (in millions)	£ 283
Cash dividends declared per share	£ 0.07
Number of shares outstanding (in millions)*	1,945
Equity applicable to shares (in millions)	£1,428

* Assume that the year-end number of shares outstanding approximates the weighted-average shares outstanding.

GLOBAL DECISION

A1 C4

Dixons

Required

1. Compute book value per share for Dixons.
2. Compute EPS for Dixons.
3. Compare Dixons' dividends per share with its EPS. Is Dixons paying out a large or small amount of its income as dividends? Explain.

ANSWERS TO MULTIPLE CHOICE QUIZ

1. e; Entry to record this stock issuance is:

Cash (6,000 × $8)	48,000	
Common Stock (6,000 × $5)		30,000
Paid-In Capital in Excess of Par Value, Common Stock		18,000

2. b; $75,000/19,000 shares = $3.95 per share

3. d; Preferred stock = 5,000 × $100 = $500,000
Book value per share = ($2,000,000 − $500,000)/50,000 shares = $30 per common share

4. a; $0.81/$45.00 = 1.8%

5. c; Earnings per share = $3,500,000/700,000 shares = $5 per share
PE ratio = $85/$5 = 17.0

14

Long-Term Liabilities

A Look Back

Chapter 13 focused on corporate equity transactions, including stock issuances and dividends. We also explained how to report and analyze income, earnings per share, and retained earnings.

A Look at This Chapter

This chapter describes the accounting for and analysis of bonds and notes. We explain their characteristics, payment patterns, interest computations, retirement, and reporting requirements. An appendix to this chapter introduces leases and pensions.

A Look Ahead

Chapter 15 focuses on how to classify, account for, and report investments in both debt and equity securities. We also describe accounting for transactions listed in a foreign currency.

Learning Objectives

CAP

Conceptual

C1 Explain the types and payment patterns of notes. (p. 554)

C2 Appendix 14A—Explain and compute the present value of an amount(s) to be paid at a future date(s). (p. 561)

C3 Appendix 14C—Describe the accrual of bond interest when bond payments do not align with accounting periods. (p. 565)

C4 Appendix 14D—Describe accounting for leases and pensions. (p. 567)

Analytical

A1 Compare bond financing with stock financing. (p. 544)

A2 Assess debt features and their implications. (p. 557)

A3 Compute the debt-to-equity ratio and explain its use. (p. 558)

Procedural

P1 Prepare entries to record bond issuance and bond interest expense. (p. 546)

P2 Compute and record amortization of bond discount. (p. 547)

P3 Compute and record amortization of bond premium. (p. 550)

P4 Record the retirement of bonds. (p. 553)

P5 Prepare entries to account for notes. (p. 555)

"We offer individuals the opportunity to realize their dreams of owning their own business"
—Mark Melton
(Holly Melton on left)

Cleaning Up in Business

CARPINTERIA, CA—Mark and Holly Melton always wanted to be entrepreneurs, and a special idea made it happen. The Meltons identified a growing demand for high-quality cleaning services. "Cleaning offices is not glamorous," says Mark. "But it's stable, year-round, and highly sought after [work]. And, no technology is going to make the industry obsolete."

Mark and Holly quickly developed a business plan, partnered with Coverall Cleaning Concepts (**Coverall.com/Locations**), and launched Melton Franchise Systems. Their company operates as a "master franchisor," which means it recruits and organizes smaller, individual franchise owners. It also provides their franchisees with equipment, training, and marketing and billing services in return for royalty fees. The Meltons currently serve over 300 franchise owners—many of whom are immigrants. "[Our company] provides local residents with an opportunity to own or manage their own business, where they might not have had the chance otherwise," Mark says proudly. "We offer individuals the opportunity to realize their dreams."

A key to their success, say the Meltons, is providing long-term financing for each individual franchise owner. Franchise owners typically provide only one-half of their financing up front, and the rest becomes a long-term liability. Mark and Holly must also manage their own company's long-term financing needs. The Meltons took on an SBA loan of over $600,000 in liabilities. Consequently, they are like their franchise owners in that they confront the realities of debt, interest payments, and collateral agreements.

Inc. magazine named the Meltons as heading one of the fastest-growing privately held U.S. companies. Mark humbly recognizes the company's dedicated employees. "Instead of the high turnover associated with low wage and marginally trained employees ... we are able to offer our janitorial customers the services of a highly trained franchise owner who brings the consistency and caring of an owner," says Mark.

The Meltons say they are "thrilled" to continue expanding. Mark adds, "Our rapid growth is evidence that more and more companies are counting on [us]." With continued smart financing and sound management of liabilities, expect them to clean up the competition.

[Sources: *Coverall Website*, January 2006; *Inc.*, April 2005; *SBA.gov Website*, January 2005; *BizJournals*, April 2005; *Franchise News*, May 2004; *Building Services Management*, November 2004]

Individuals, companies, and governments issue bonds to finance their activities. In return for financing, bonds promise to repay the lender with interest. This chapter explains the basics of bonds and the accounting for their issuance and retirement. The chapter also describes long-term notes as another financ-

ing source. We explain how present value concepts impact both the accounting for and reporting of bonds and notes. Appendixes to this chapter discuss present value concepts applicable to liabilities, effective interest amortization, and the accounting for leases and pensions.

Long-Term Liabilities

Bond Basics	Bond Issuances	Bond Retirement	Long-Term Notes
• Bond financing • Bond trading • Issuance procedures	• Issuance at par • Issuance at a discount • Issuance at a premium • Bond pricing	• At maturity • Before maturity • By conversion	• Installment notes • Mortgage terms

Basics of Bonds

This section explains the basics of bonds and a company's motivation for issuing them.

Bond Financing

Projects that demand large amounts of money often are funded from bond issuances. (Both for-profit and nonprofit companies, as well as governmental units, such as nations, states, cities, and school districts, issue bonds.) A **bond** is its issuer's written promise to pay an amount identified as the par value of the bond with interest. The **par value of a bond,** also called the *face amount* or *face value,* is paid at a specified future date known as the bond's *maturity date.* Most bonds also require the issuer to make semiannual interest payments. The amount of interest paid each period is determined by multiplying the par value of the bond by the bond's contract rate of interest. This section explains both advantages and disadvantages of bond financing.

A1   Compare bond financing with stock financing.

Advantages of Bonds   There are three main advantages of bond financing:

1. *Bonds do not affect owner control.* Equity financing reflects ownership in a company, whereas bond financing does not. A person who contributes $1,000 of a company's $10,000 equity financing typically controls one-tenth of all owner decisions. A person who owns a $1,000, 11%, 20-year bond has no ownership right. This person, or bond-holder, is to receive from the bond issuer 11% interest, or $110, each year the bond is outstanding and $1,000 when it matures in 20 years.

2. *Interest on bonds is tax deductible.* Bond interest payments are tax deductible for the issuer, but equity payments (distributions) to owners are not. To illustrate, assume that a corporation with no bond financing earns $15,000 in income *before* paying taxes at a 40% tax rate, which amounts to $6,000 ($15,000 × 40%) in taxes. If a portion of its financing is in bonds, however, the resulting bond interest is deducted in computing taxable income. That is, if bond interest expense is $10,000, the taxes owed would be $2,000 ([$15,000 − $10,000] × 40%), which is less than the $6,000 owed with no bond financing.

3. *Bonds can increase return on equity.* A company that earns a higher return with borrowed funds than it pays in interest on those funds increases its return on equity. This process is called *financial leverage* or *trading on the equity.*

To illustrate the third point, consider Magnum Co., which has $1 million in equity and is planning a $500,000 expansion to meet increasing demand for its product. Magnum predicts the $500,000 expansion will yield $125,000 in additional income before paying any interest. It currently earns $100,000 per year and has no interest expense. Magnum is considering three plans. Plan A is to not expand. Plan B is to expand and raise $500,000 from equity financing. Plan C is to expand and issue $500,000 of bonds that pay 10% annual interest ($50,000). Exhibit 14.1 shows how these three plans affect Magnum's net income, equity, and return on equity (net income/equity). The owner(s) will earn a higher return on equity if expansion occurs. Moreover, the preferred expansion plan is to issue bonds. Projected net income under Plan C ($175,000) is smaller than under Plan B ($225,000), but the return on equity is larger because of less equity investment. Plan C has another advantage if income is taxable. This illustration reflects a general rule: *Return on equity increases when the expected rate of return from the new assets is higher than the rate of interest expense on the debt financing.*

Point: Financial leverage can be achieved by issuing either bonds, notes, or preferred stock.

Example: Compute return on equity for all three plans if Magnum currently earns $150,000 instead of $100,000. *Answer ($ 000s):*
Plan A = 15%   ($150/$1,000)
Plan B = 18.3%   ($275/$1,500)
Plan C = 22.5%   ($225/$1,000)

	Plan A Do Not Expand	Plan B Equity Financing	Plan C Bond Financing
Income before interest expense	$ 100,000	$ 225,000	$ 225,000
Interest expense	—	—	(50,000)
Net income	**$ 100,000**	**$ 225,000**	**$ 175,000**
Equity	$1,000,000	$1,500,000	$1,000,000
Return on equity	**10.0%**	**15.0%**	**17.5%**

Exhibit 14.1

Financing with Bonds versus Equity

Disadvantages of Bonds The two main disadvantages of bond financing are:

1. *Bonds can decrease return on equity.* When a company earns a lower return with the borrowed funds than it pays in interest, it decreases its return on equity. This downside risk of financial leverage is more likely to arise when a company has periods of low income or net losses.
2. *Bonds require payment of both periodic interest and the par value at maturity.* Bond payments can be especially burdensome when income and cash flow are low. Equity financing, in contrast, does not require any payments because cash withdrawals (dividends) are paid at the discretion of the owner (or board).

Point: Debt financing is desirable when interest is tax deductible, when owner control is preferred, and when return on equity is higher than interest rate on debt.

A company must weigh the risks and returns of the disadvantages and advantages of bond financing when deciding whether to issue bonds to finance operations.

Bond Trading

Bonds are securities that can be readily bought and sold. A large number of bonds trade on both the New York Exchange and the American Exchange. A bond *issue* consists of a number of bonds, usually in denominations of $1,000 or $5,000, and is sold to many different lenders.

After bonds are issued, they often are bought and sold by investors, meaning that any particular bond probably has a number of owners before it matures. Since bonds are exchanged (bought and sold) in the market, they have a market value (price). For convenience, bond market values are expressed as a percent of their par (face) value. For example, a company's bonds might be trading at 103½, meaning they can be bought or sold for 103.5% of their par value. Bonds can also trade below par value. For instance, if a company's bonds are trading at 95, they can be bought or sold at 95% of their par value.

Decision Insight

Quotes The bond quote here is interpreted (left to right) as **Bonds,** issuer name; **Rate,** contract interest rate (7%); **Mat,** matures in year 2025 when principal is paid; **Yld,** yield rate (5.9%) of bond at current price; **Vol,** daily dollar worth ($130,000) of trades (in 1,000s); **Close,** closing price (119.25) for the day as percent of par value; **Chg,** change (+1.25) in closing price from prior day's close.

Bonds	Rate	Mat	Yld	Vol	Close	Chg
IBM	7	25	5.9	130	119¼	+1¼

Bond-Issuing Procedures

State and federal laws govern bond issuances. Bond issuers also want to ensure that they do not violate any of their existing contractual agreements when issuing bonds. Authorization of bond issuances includes the number of bonds authorized, their par value, and the contract interest rate.

Exhibit 14.2

Bond Certificate

The legal document identifying the rights and obligations of both the bondholders and the issuer is called the **bond indenture,** which is the legal contract between the issuer and the bondholders. A bondholder may also receive a bond certificate as evidence of the company's debt. A **bond certificate,** such as that shown in Exhibit 14.2, includes specifics such as the issuer's name, the par value, the contract interest rate, and the maturity date. Many companies reduce costs by not issuing paper certificates to bondholders.[1]

Bond Issuances

Topic Tackler
PLUS

14-1

P1   Prepare entries to record bond issuance and bond interest expense.

This section explains accounting for bond issuances at par, below par (discount), and above par (premium). It also describes how to amortize a discount or premium and record bonds issued between interest payment dates.

Issuing Bonds at Par

To illustrate an issuance of bonds at par value, suppose a company receives authorization to issue $800,000 of 9%, 20-year bonds dated January 1, 2008, that mature on December 31, 2027, and pay interest semiannually on each June 30 and December 31. After accepting the bond indenture on behalf of the bondholders, the trustee can sell all or a portion of the bonds to an underwriter. If all bonds are sold at par value, the issuer records the sale as:

Assets = Liabilities + Equity
+800,000   +800,000

2008			
Jan. 1	Cash..	800,000	
	Bonds Payable.........................		800,000
	Sold bonds at par.		

This entry reflects increases in the issuer's cash *and* long-term liabilities.

The issuer records the first semiannual interest payment as follows.

Assets = Liabilities + Equity
−36,000   −36,000

2008			
June 30	Bond Interest Expense......................	36,000	
	Cash.................................		36,000
	Paid semiannual interest (9% × $800,000 × ½ year).		

---

[1] The issuing company normally sells its bonds to an investment firm called an *underwriter,* which resells them to the public. An issuing company can also sell bonds directly to investors. When an underwriter sells bonds to a large number of investors, a *trustee* represents and protects the bondholders' interests. The trustee monitors the issuer to ensure that it complies with the obligations in the bond indenture. Most trustees are large banks or trust companies. The trustee writes and accepts the terms of a bond indenture before it is issued. When bonds are offered to the public, called *floating an issue,* they must be registered with the Securities and Exchange Commission (SEC). SEC registration requires the issuer to file certain financial information. Most company bonds are issued in par value units of $1,000 or $5,000. *A baby bond* has a par value of less than $1,000, such as $100.

The issuer pays and records its semiannual interest obligation every six months until the bonds mature. When they mature, the issuer records its payment of principal as:

2027					Assets = Liabilities + Equity
Dec. 31	Bonds Payable	800,000			−800,000 −800,000
	Cash		800,000		
	Paid bond principal at maturity.				

Bond Discount or Premium

The bond issuer pays the interest rate specified in the indenture, the **contract rate,** also referred to as the *coupon rate, stated rate,* or *nominal rate.* The annual interest paid is determined by multiplying the bond par value by the contract rate. The contract rate is usually stated on an annual basis, even if interest is paid semiannually. For example, if a company issues a $1,000, 8% bond paying interest semiannually, it pays annual interest of $80 (8% × $1,000) in two semiannual payments of $40 each.

The contract rate sets the amount of interest the issuer pays in *cash,* which is not necessarily the *bond interest expense* actually incurred by the issuer. Bond interest expense depends on the bond's market value at issuance, which is determined by market expectations of the risk of lending to the issuer. The bond's **market rate** of interest is the rate that borrowers are willing to pay and lenders are willing to accept for a particular bond and its risk level. As the risk level increases, the rate increases to compensate purchasers for the bonds' increased risk. Also, the market rate is generally higher when the time period until the bond matures is longer due to the risk of adverse events occurring over a longer time period.

Many bond issuers try to set a contract rate of interest equal to the market rate they expect as of the bond issuance date. When the contract rate and market rate are equal, a bond sells at par value, but when they are not equal, a bond does not sell at par value. Instead, it is sold at a *premium* above par value or at a *discount* below par value. Exhibit 14.3 shows the relation between the contract rate, market rate, and a bond's issue price.

> **Decision Insight**
>
> **Ratings Game** Many bond buyers rely on rating services to assess bond risk. The best known are **Standard & Poor's** and **Moody's.** These services focus on the issuer's financial statements and other factors in setting ratings. Standard & Poor's ratings, from best quality to default, are AAA, AA, A, BBB, BB, B, CCC, CC, C, and D. Ratings can include a plus (+) or minus (−) to show relative standing within a category.

Point: Business acquisitions are sometimes financed by issuing "junk bonds" that carry high market rates of interest but offer little security. Bondholders can suffer huge losses if the bond issuers do not generate adequate cash flows to pay interest and principal.

Bond States	Market Sets	Bond Price Determined	
Contract rate	Market rate	Contract rate > Market rate ➡	Bond sells at Premium
		Contract rate = Market rate ➡	Bond sells at Par
		Contract rate < Market rate ➡	Bond sells at Discount

Exhibit 14.3

Relation between Bond Issue Price, Contract Rate, and Market Rate

> ## Quick Check
> Answers—p. 570
>
> 1. Unsecured bonds backed only by the issuer's general credit standing are called (*a*) serial bonds, (*b*) debentures, (*c*) registered bonds, or (*d*) convertible bonds.
> 2. How do you compute the amount of interest a bond issuer pays in cash each year?
> 3. When the contract rate is above the market rate, do bonds sell at a premium or a discount? Do purchasers pay more or less than the par value of the bonds?

Issuing Bonds at a Discount

A **discount on bonds payable** occurs when a company issues bonds with a contract rate less than the market rate. This means that the issue price is less than par value. To illustrate, assume that **Fila** announces an offer to issue bonds with a $100,000 par value, an 8% annual

P2 Compute and record amortization of bond discount.

contract rate (paid semiannually), and a five-year life. Also assume that the market rate for Fila bonds is 10%. These bonds then will sell at a discount since the contract rate is less than the market rate. The exact issue price for these bonds is 92.277 (or 92.277% of par value); we show how to compute this issue price later in the chapter. These bonds obligate the issuer to pay two separate types of future cash flows.

1. Par value of $100,000 cash at the end of the bonds' five-year life.
2. Cash interest payments of $4,000 (4% × $100,000) at the end of each semiannual period during the bonds' five-year life.

The exact pattern of cash flows for the Fila bonds is shown in Exhibit 14.4.

Exhibit 14.4

Cash Flows for Fila Bonds

When Fila accepts $92,277 cash for its bonds on the issue date of December 31, 2008, it records the sale as follows.

Assets = Liabilities + Equity
+92,277   +100,000
          −7,723

Dec. 31	Cash	92,277	
	Discount on Bonds Payable..................	7,723	
	Bonds Payable.........................		100,000
	Sold bonds at a discount on their issue date.		

These bonds are reported in the long-term liability section of the issuer's December 31, 2008, balance sheet as shown in Exhibit 14.5. A discount is deducted from the par value of bonds to yield the **carrying (book) value of bonds.** Discount on Bonds Payable is a contra liability account.

Exhibit 14.5

Balance Sheet Presentation of Bond Discount

Long-term liabilities		
Bonds payable, 8%, due December 31, 2013	$100,000	
Less discount on bonds payable	7,723	$92,277

Amortizing a Bond Discount   Fila receives $92,277 for its bonds; in return it must pay bondholders $100,000 after five years (plus semiannual interest payments). The $7,723 discount is paid to bondholders at maturity and is part of the cost of using the $92,277 for five years. The upper portion of panel A in Exhibit 14.6 shows that total bond interest expense of $47,723 is the difference between the total amount repaid to bondholders ($140,000) and the amount borrowed from bondholders ($92,277). Alternatively, we can compute total bond interest expense as the sum of the 10 interest payments and the bond discount. This alternative computation is shown in the lower portion of panel A.

The total $47,723 bond interest expense must be allocated across the 10 semiannual periods in the bonds' life, and the bonds' carrying value must be updated at each balance sheet date. This is accomplished using the straight-line method (or the effective interest method in Appendix 14B). Both methods systematically reduce the bond discount to zero over the five-year life. This process is called *amortizing a bond discount*.

Straight-Line Method   The **straight-line bond amortization** method allocates an equal portion of the total bond interest expense to each interest period. To apply the straight-line method to Fila's bonds, we divide the total bond interest expense of $47,723 by 10 (the number

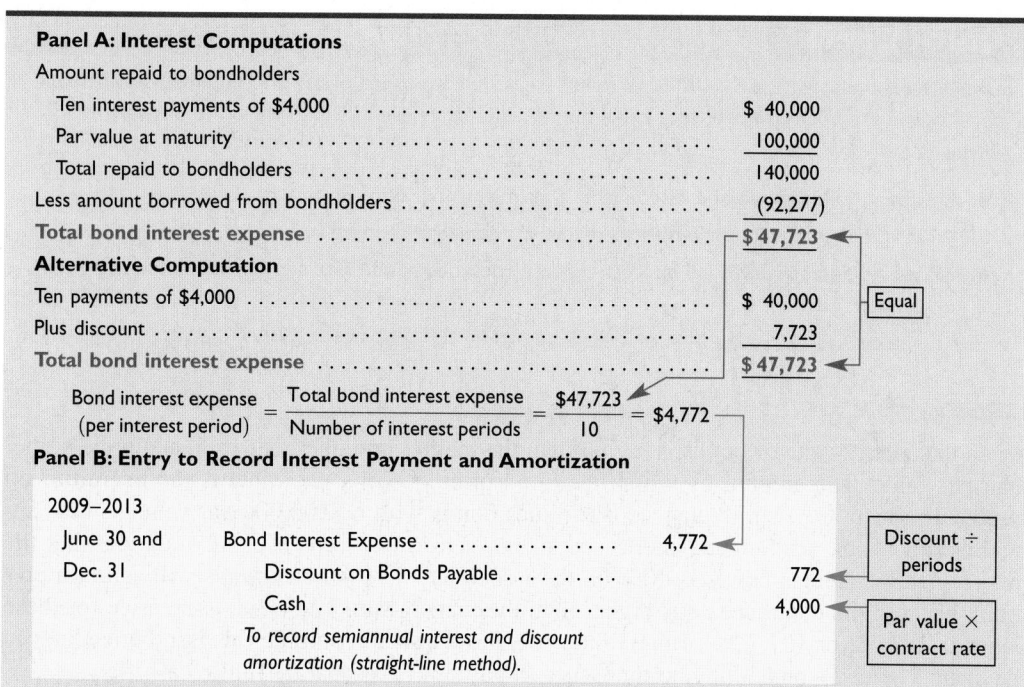

Exhibit 14.6

Interest Computation and Entry for Bonds Issued at a Discount

of semiannual periods in the bonds' life). This gives a bond interest expense of $4,772 per period (all computations, including those for assignments, are rounded to the nearest whole dollar). Alternatively, we can find this number by first dividing the $7,723 discount by 10, which yields the $772 amount of discount to be amortized each interest period. When the $772 is added to the $4,000 cash payment, the bond interest expense for each period is $4,772. Panel B of Exhibit 14.6 shows how the issuer records bond interest expense and updates the balance of the bond liability account at the end of *each* of the 10 semiannual interest periods (June 30, 2009, through December 31, 2013).

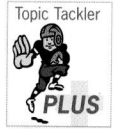

Topic Tackler **PLUS**

14-2

Exhibit 14.7 shows the pattern of decreases in the Discount on Bonds Payable account and the pattern of increases in the bonds' carrying value. The following points summarize the discount bonds' straight-line amortization.

1. At issuance, the $100,000 par value consists of the $92,277 cash received by the issuer plus the $7,723 discount.

2. During the bonds' life, the (unamortized) discount decreases each period by the $772 amortization ($7,723/10), and the carrying value (par value less unamortized discount) increases each period by $772.

3. At maturity, the unamortized discount equals zero, and the carrying value equals the $100,000 par value that the issuer pays the holder.

Notice that the issuer incurs a $4,772 bond interest expense each period but pays only $4,000 cash. The $772 unpaid portion of this expense is added to the bonds' carrying value. (The total $7,723 unamortized discount is "paid" when the bonds mature; $100,000 is paid at maturity but only $92,277 was received at issuance.)

Semiannual Period-End		Unamortized Discount*	Carrying Value†
(0)	12/31/2008	$7,723	$ 92,277
(1)	6/30/2009	6,951	93,049
(2)	12/31/2009	6,179	93,821
(3)	6/30/2010	5,407	94,593
(4)	12/31/2010	4,635	95,365
(5)	6/30/2011	3,863	96,137
(6)	12/31/2011	3,091	96,909
(7)	6/30/2012	2,319	97,681
(8)	12/31/2012	1,547	98,453
(9)	6/30/2013	775	99,225
(10)	**12/31/2013**	0‡	100,000

Exhibit 14.7

Straight-Line Amortization of Bond Discount

The two columns always sum to par value for a discount bond.

* Total bond discount (of $7,723) less accumulated periodic amortization ($772 per semiannual interest period).

† Bond par value (of $100,000) less unamortized discount.

‡ Adjusted for rounding.

Answers—p. 570

Quick Check

Five-year, 6% bonds with a $100,000 par value are issued at a price of $91,893. Interest is paid semi-annually, and the bonds' market rate is 8% on the issue date. Use this information to answer the following questions:

4. Are these bonds issued at a discount or a premium? Explain your answer.

5. What is the issuer's journal entry to record the issuance of these bonds?

6. What is the amount of bond interest expense recorded at the first semiannual period using the straight-line method?

Issuing Bonds at a Premium

P3 Compute and record amortization of bond premium.

When the contract rate of bonds is higher than the market rate, the bonds sell at a price higher than par value. The amount by which the bond price exceeds par value is the **premium on bonds.** To illustrate, assume that **Adidas** issues bonds with a $100,000 par value, a 12% annual contract rate, semiannual interest payments, and a five-year life. Also assume that the market rate for Adidas bonds is 10% on the issue date. The Adidas bonds will sell at a premium because the contract rate is higher than the market rate. The exact issue price for these bonds is 107.72 (or 107.72% of par value); we show how to compute this issue price later in the chapter. These bonds obligate the issuer to pay out two separate future cash flows.

1. Par value of $100,000 cash at the end of the bonds' five-year life.
2. Cash interest payments of $6,000 (6% × $100,000) at the end of each semiannual period during the bonds' five-year life.

The exact pattern of cash flows for the Adidas bonds is shown in Exhibit 14.8.

Exhibit 14.8

Cash Flows for Adidas Bonds

								$100,000
	$6,000	$6,000	$6,000	$6,000		$6,000	$6,000	$6,000
0	6 mo.	12 mo.	18 mo.	24 mo.	...	48 mo.	54 mo.	60 mo.

When Adidas accepts $107,720 cash for its bonds on the issue date of December 31, 2008, it records this transaction as follows.

Assets = Liabilities + Equity
+107,720   +100,000
           +7,720

Dec. 31	Cash	107,720	
	Premium on Bonds Payable		7,720
	Bonds Payable........................		100,000
	Sold bonds at a premium on their issue date.		

These bonds are reported in the long-term liability section of the issuer's December 31, 2008, balance sheet as shown in Exhibit 14.9. A premium is added to par value to yield the carrying (book) value of bonds. Premium on Bonds Payable is an adjunct (also called *accretion*) liability account.

Exhibit 14.9

Balance Sheet Presentation of Bond Premium

Long-term liabilities		
Bonds payable, 12%, due December 31, 2013	$100,000	
Plus premium on bonds payable	7,720	$107,720

Amortizing a Bond Premium   Adidas receives $107,720 for its bonds; in return, it pays bondholders $100,000 after five years (plus semiannual interest payments). The $7,720 premium not repaid to issuer's bondholders at maturity goes to reduce the issuer's expense of using the $107,720 for five years. The upper portion of panel A of Exhibit 14.10 shows that total bond interest expense of $52,280 is the difference between the total amount repaid to bondholders ($160,000) and the amount borrowed from bondholders ($107,720). Alternatively, we can compute total bond interest expense as the sum of the 10 interest payments less the bond premium. The premium is subtracted because it will not be paid to bondholders when the bonds mature; see the lower portion of panel A. Total bond interest expense must be allocated over the 10 semiannual periods using the straight-line method (or the effective interest method in Appendix 14B).

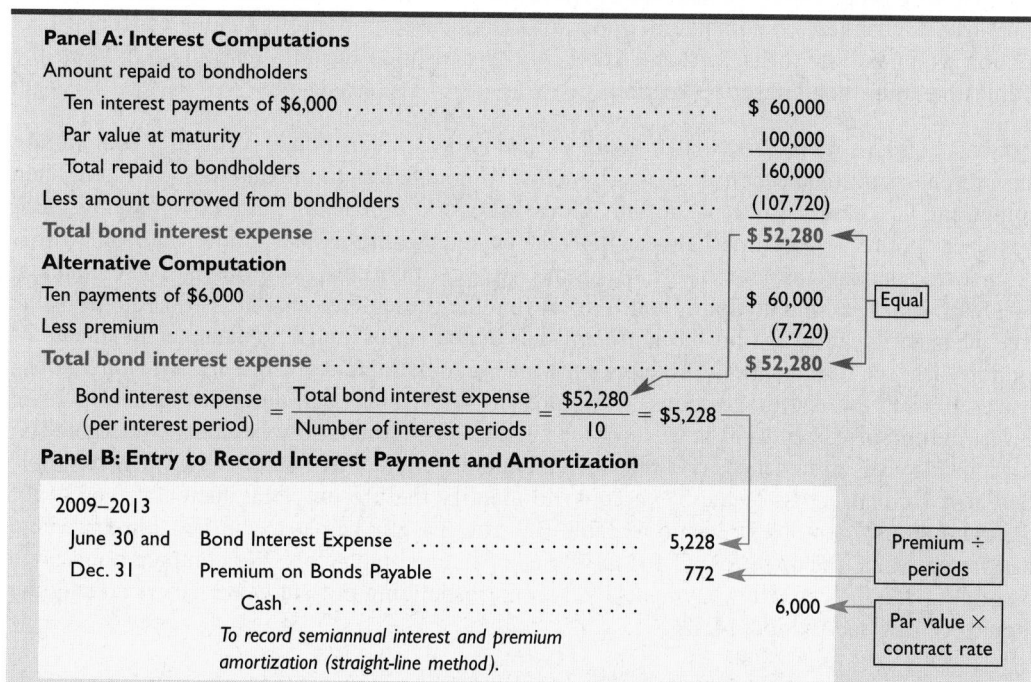

Exhibit 14.10

Interest Computation and Entry for Bonds Issued at a Premium

Straight-Line Method   The straight-line method allocates an equal portion of total bond interest expense to each of the bonds' semiannual interest periods. To apply this method to Adidas bonds, we divide the five years' total bond interest expense of $52,280 by 10 (the number of semiannual periods in the bonds' life). This gives a total bond interest expense of $5,228 per period. Panel B of Exhibit 14.10 shows how the issuer records bond interest expense and updates the balance of the bond liability account for *each* semiannual period (June 30, 2009, through December 31, 2013).

Point: A premium decreases Bond Interest Expense while a discount increases it.

Exhibit 14.11

Straight-Line Amortization of Bond Premium

Semiannual Period-End	Unamortized Premium*	Carrying Value†
(0) 12/31/2008	$7,720	$107,720
(1) 6/30/2009	6,948	106,948
(2) 12/31/2009	6,176	106,176
(3) 6/30/2010	5,404	105,404
(4) 12/31/2010	4,632	104,632
(5) 6/30/2011	3,860	103,860
(6) 12/31/2011	3,088	103,088
(7) 6/30/2012	2,316	102,316
(8) 12/31/2012	1,544	101,544
(9) 6/30/2013	772	100,772
(10) 12/31/2013	0	100,000

Exhibit 14.11 shows the pattern of decreases in the unamortized Premium on Bonds Payable account and in the bonds' carrying value. The following points summarize straight-line amortization of the premium bonds.

* Total bond premium (of $7,720) less accumulated periodic amortization ($772 per semiannual interest period).

† Bond par value (of $100,000) plus unamortized premium.

During the bond life, carrying value is adjusted to par and the amortized premium to zero.

1. At issuance, the $100,000 par value plus the $7,720 premium equals the $107,720 cash received by the issuer.

2. During the bonds' life, the (unamortized) premium decreases each period by the $772 amortization ($7,720/10), and the carrying value decreases each period by the same $772.

3. At maturity, the unamortized premium equals zero, and the carrying value equals the $100,000 par value that the issuer pays the holder.

The next section describes bond pricing. An instructor can choose to cover bond pricing or not. Assignments requiring the next section are: Quick Study 14-4, Exercises 14-6 & 14-7, Problems 14-1A & 14-1B and 14-4A & 14-4B.

Bond Pricing

Prices for bonds traded on an organized exchange are often published in newspapers and through online services. This information normally includes the bond price (called *quote*), its contract rate, and its current market (called *yield*) rate. However, only a fraction of bonds are traded on organized exchanges. To compute the price of a bond, we apply present value concepts. This section explains how to use *present value concepts* to price the Fila discount bond and the Adidas premium bond described earlier.

Present Value of a Discount Bond The issue price of bonds is found by computing the present value of the bonds' cash payments, discounted at the bonds' market rate. When computing the present value of the Fila bonds, we work with *semiannual* compounding periods because this is the time between interest payments; the annual market rate of 10% is considered a semiannual rate of 5%. Also, the five-year bond life is viewed as 10 semiannual periods. The price computation is twofold: (1) find the present value of the $100,000 par value paid at maturity and (2) find the present value of the series of 10 semiannual payments of $4,000 each; see Exhibit 14.4. These present values can be found by using *present value tables*. Appendix B at the end of this book shows present value tables and describes their use. Table B.1 at the end of Appendix B is used for the single $100,000 maturity payment, and Table B.3 in Appendix B is used for the $4,000 series of interest payments. Specifically, we go to Table B.1, row 10, and across to the 5% column to identify the present value factor of 0.6139 for the maturity payment. Next, we go to Table B.3, row 10, and across to the 5% column, where the present value factor is 7.7217 for the series of interest payments. We compute bond price by multiplying the cash flow payments by their corresponding present value factors and adding them together; see Exhibit 14.12.

Exhibit 14.12

Computing Issue Price for the Fila Discount Bonds

Cash Flow	Table	Present Value Factor	Amount	Present Value
$100,000 par (maturity) value	B.1	0.6139	× $100,000 =	$ 61,390
$4,000 interest payments	B.3	7.7217	× 4,000 =	30,887
Price of bond				$92,277

Present Value of a Premium Bond We find the issue price of the Adidas bonds by using the market rate to compute the present value of the bonds' future cash flows. When computing the present value of these bonds, we again work with *semiannual* compounding periods because this is the time between interest payments. The annual 10% market rate is applied as a semiannual rate of 5%, and the five-year bond life is viewed as 10 semiannual periods. The computation is twofold: (1) find the present value of the $100,000 par value paid at maturity and (2) find the present value of the series of 10 payments of $6,000 each; see Exhibit 14.8. These present values can be found by using present value tables. First, go to Table B.1, row 10, and across to the 5% column where the present value factor is 0.6139 for the maturity payment. Second, go to Table B.3, row 10, and across to the 5% column, where the present value factor is 7.7217 for the series of interest payments. The bonds' price is computed by multiplying the cash flow payments by their corresponding present value factors and adding them together; see Exhibit 14.13.

Exhibit 14.13

Computing Issue Price for the Adidas Premium Bonds

Cash Flow	Table	Present Value Factor	Amount	Present Value
$100,000 par (maturity) value	B.1	0.6139	× $100,000 =	$ 61,390
$6,000 interest payments	B.3	7.7217	× 6,000 =	46,330
Price of bond				$107,720

Quick Check

Answers—p. 570

On December 31, 2007, a company issues 16%, 10-year bonds with a par value of $100,000. Interest is paid on June 30 and December 31. The bonds are sold to yield a 14% annual market rate at an issue price of $110,592. Use this information to answer questions 7 through 9:

7. Are these bonds issued at a discount or a premium? Explain your answer.

8. Using the straight-line method to allocate bond interest expense, the issuer records the second interest payment (on December 31, 2008) with a debit to Premium on Bonds Payable in the amount of (a) $7,470, (b) $530, (c) $8,000, or (d) $400.

9. How are these bonds reported in the long-term liability section of the issuer's balance sheet as of December 31, 2008?

Bond Retirement

This section describes the retirement of bonds (1) at maturity, (2) before maturity, and (3) by conversion to stock.

Bond Retirement at Maturity

The carrying value of bonds at maturity always equals par value. For example, both Exhibits 14.7 (a discount) and 14.11 (a premium) show that the carrying value of bonds at the end of their lives equals par value ($100,000). The retirement of these bonds at maturity, assuming interest is already paid and entered, is recorded as follows:

P4 Record the retirement of bonds.

2013			
Dec. 31	Bonds Payable	100,000	
	Cash		100,000
	To record retirement of bonds at maturity.		

Assets = Liabilities + Equity
−100,000 −100,000

Bond Retirement before Maturity

Issuers sometimes wish to retire some or all of their bonds prior to maturity. For instance, if interest rates decline significantly, an issuer may wish to replace high-interest-paying bonds with new low-interest bonds. Two common ways to retire bonds before maturity are to (1) exercise a call option or (2) purchase them on the open market. In the first instance, an issuer can reserve the right to retire bonds early by issuing callable bonds. The bond indenture can give the issuer an option to *call* the bonds before they mature by paying the par value plus a *call premium* to bondholders. In the second case, the issuer retires bonds by repurchasing them on the open market at their current price. Whether bonds are called or repurchased, the issuer is unlikely to pay a price that exactly equals their carrying value. When a difference exists between the bonds' carrying value and the amount paid, the issuer records a gain or loss equal to the difference.

To illustrate the accounting for retiring callable bonds, assume that a company issued callable bonds with a par value of $100,000. The call option requires the issuer to pay a call premium of $3,000 to bondholders in addition to the par value. Next, assume that after the June 30, 2008, interest payment, the bonds have a carrying value of $104,500. Then on July 1, 2008, the issuer calls these bonds and pays $103,000 to bondholders. The issuer recognizes a $1,500 gain from the difference between the bonds' carrying value of $104,500 and the retirement price of $103,000. The issuer records this bond retirement as:

Point: Bond retirement is also referred to as *bond redemption*.

Point: Gains and losses from retiring bonds were *previously* reported as extraordinary items. New standards require that they now be judged by the "unusual and infrequent" criteria for reporting purposes.

July 1	Bonds Payable	100,000	
	Premium on Bonds Payable.................	4,500	
	Gain on Bond Retirement		1,500
	Cash		103,000
	To record retirement of bonds before maturity.		

Assets = Liabilities + Equity
−103,000 −100,000 +1,500
−4,500

An issuer usually must call all bonds when it exercises a call option. However, to retire as many or as few bonds as it desires, an issuer can purchase them on the open market. If it retires less than the entire class of bonds, it recognizes a gain or loss for the difference between the carrying value of those bonds retired and the amount paid to acquire them.

Bond Retirement by Conversion

Convertible Bond

We describe convertible bonds in the Decision Analysis section of this chapter. Holders of convertible bonds have the right to convert their bonds to stock. When conversion occurs, the bonds' carrying value is transferred to equity accounts and no gain or loss is recorded. (The market prices of the bonds and stock are *not* relevant to this entry; the material in Chapter 13 is helpful in understanding this transaction.) To illustrate, assume that on January 1 the $100,000 par value bonds of **Converse**, with a carrying value of $100,000, are converted to 15,000 shares of $2 par value common stock. The entry to record this conversion is:

Assets = Liabilities + Equity
−100,000   +30,000
                       +70,000

Jan. 1	Bonds Payable	100,000	
	Common Stock		30,000
	Paid-In Capital in Excess of Par Value		70,000
	To record retirement of bonds by conversion.		

Quick Check   Answer—p. 570

10. Six years ago, a company issued $500,000 of 6%, eight-year bonds at a price of 95. The current carrying value is $493,750. The company decides to retire 50% of these bonds by buying them on the open market at a price of 102½. What is the amount of gain or loss on retirement of these bonds?

Long-Term Notes Payable

Like bonds, notes are issued to obtain assets such as cash. Unlike bonds, notes are typically transacted with a *single* lender such as a bank. An issuer initially records a note at its selling price; that is, the note's face value minus any discount or plus any premium. Over the note's life, the amount of interest expense allocated to each period is computed by multiplying the market rate (at issuance of the note) by the beginning-of-period note balance. The note's carrying (book) value at any time equals its face value minus any unamortized discount or plus any unamortized premium; carrying value is also computed as the present value of all remaining payments, discounted using the market rate at issuance.

Installment Notes

C1 Explain the types and payment patterns of notes.

An **installment note** is an obligation requiring a series of payments to the lender. Installment notes are common for franchises and other businesses when lenders and borrowers agree to spread payments over several periods. To illustrate, assume that Foghog borrows $60,000 from a bank to purchase equipment. It signs an 8% installment note requiring six annual payments of principal plus interest and it records the note's issuance at January 1, 2008, as follows.

Assets = Liabilities + Equity
+60,000   +60,000

Jan. 1	Cash	60,000	
	Notes Payable		60,000
	Borrowed $60,000 by signing an 8%, six-year installment note.		

Payments on an installment note normally include the accrued interest expense plus a portion of the amount borrowed (the *principal*). This section describes an installment note with equal payments.

The equal total payments pattern consists of changing amounts of both interest and principal. To illustrate, assume that Foghog borrows $60,000 by signing a $60,000 note that requires six *equal payments* of $12,979 at the end of each year. (The present value of an annuity of six annual payments of $12,979, discounted at 8%, equals $60,000; we show this computation in footnote 2 on the next page.) The $12,979 includes both interest and principal, the amounts of which change with each payment. Exhibit 14.14 shows the pattern of equal total payments and its two parts, interest and principal. Column A shows the note's beginning balance. Column B shows accrued interest for each year at 8% of the beginning note balance. Column C shows the impact on the note's principal, which equals the difference between the total payment in column D and the interest expense in column B. Column E shows the note's year-end balance.

P5 Prepare entries to account for notes.

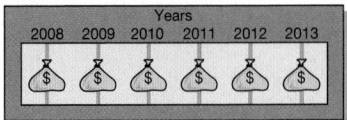

Point: Most consumer notes are installment notes that require equal total payments.

Exhibit 14.14

Installment Note: Equal Total Payments

Period Ending Date	(A) Beginning Balance	(B) Debit Interest Expense 8% × (A)	+	(C) Debit Notes Payable (D) − (B)	=	(D) Credit Cash (computed)	(E) Ending Balance (A) − (C)
				Payments			
(1) 12/31/2008	$60,000	$ 4,800		$ 8,179		$12,979	$51,821
(2) 12/31/2009	51,821	4,146		8,833		12,979	42,988
(3) 12/31/2010	42,988	3,439		9,540		12,979	33,448
(4) 12/31/2011	33,448	2,676		10,303		12,979	23,145
(5) 12/31/2012	23,145	1,852		11,127		12,979	12,018
(6) 12/31/2013	12,018	961		12,018		12,979	0
		$17,874		$60,000		$77,874	

Principal
Interest

Increasing Principal Component
Decreasing Accrued Interest
Equal Total Payments

End of Year		
2013	$12,018	$961
2012	$11,127	$1,852
2011	$10,303	$2,676
2010	$9,540	$3,439
2009	$8,833	$4,146
2008	$8,179	$4,800

0    $2,500 $5,000 $7,500 $10,000 $12,500 $15,000

Cash Payment Pattern

Although the six cash payments are equal, accrued interest decreases each year because the principal balance of the note declines. As the amount of interest decreases each year, the portion of each payment applied to principal increases. This pattern is graphed in the lower part

Point: The Truth-in-Lending Act requires lenders to provide information about loan costs including finance charges and interest rate.

of Exhibit 14.14. Foghog uses the amounts in Exhibit 14.14 to record its first two payments (for years 2008 and 2009) as follows:

Assets = Liabilities + Equity
−12,979　　−8,179　　−4,800

2008			
Dec. 31	Interest Expense	4,800	
	Notes Payable	8,179	
	Cash		12,979
	To record first installment payment.		

Assets = Liabilities + Equity
−12,979　　−8,833　　−4,146

2009			
Dec. 31	Interest Expense	4,146	
	Notes Payable	8,833	
	Cash		12,979
	To record second installment payment.		

Decision Maker

Answer—p. 570

Entrepreneur　You are an electronics retailer planning a holiday sale on a custom stereo system that requires no payments for two years. At the end of two years, buyers must pay the full amount. The system's suggested retail price is $4,100, but you are willing to sell it today for $3,000 cash. What is your holiday sale price if payment will not occur for two years and the market interest rate is 10%?

Foghog records similar entries but with different amounts for each of the remaining four payments. After six years, the Notes Payable account balance is zero.[2]

Mortgage Notes and Bonds

A **mortgage** is a legal agreement that helps protect a lender if a borrower fails to make required payments on notes or bonds. A mortgage gives the lender a right to be paid from the cash proceeds of the sale of a borrower's assets identified in the mortgage. A legal document, called a *mortgage contract,* describes the mortgage terms.

　Mortgage notes carry a mortgage contract pledging title to specific assets as security for the note. Mortgage notes are especially popular in the purchase of homes and the acquisition of plant assets. Less common *mortgage bonds* are backed by the issuer's assets. Accounting for mortgage notes and bonds is similar to that for unsecured notes and bonds, except that the mortgage agreement must be disclosed. For example, Musicland reports that its "mortgage note payable is collateralized by land, buildings and certain fixtures."

Global: Countries vary in the preference given to debtholders vs. stockholders when a company is in financial distress. Some countries such as Germany, France, and Japan give preference to stockholders over debtholders.

Quick Check

Answers—p. 570

11. Which of the following is true for an installment note requiring a series of equal total cash payments? (*a*) Payments consist of increasing interest and decreasing principal; (*b*) Payments consist of changing amounts of principal but constant interest; or (*c*) Payments consist of decreasing interest and increasing principal.

12. How is the interest portion of an installment note payment computed?

13. When a borrower records an interest payment on an installment note, how are the balance sheet and income statement affected?

Example: Suppose the $60,000 installment loan has an 8% interest rate with eight equal annual payments. What is the annual payment? *Answer* (using Table B.3): $60,000/5.7466 = $10,441

---

[2] Table B.3 in Appendix B is used to compute the dollar amount of the six payments that equal the initial note balance of $60,000 at 8% interest. We go to Table B.3, row 6, and across to the 8% column, where the present value factor is 4.6229. The dollar amount is then computed by solving this relation:

Table	Present Value Factor		Dollar Amount		Present Value
B.3	4.6229	×	?	=	$60,000

The dollar amount is computed by dividing $60,000 by 4.6229, yielding $12,979.

| **Debt Features and the Debt-to-Equity Ratio** | **Decision Analysis** |

Collateral agreements can reduce the risk of loss for both bonds and notes. Unsecured bonds and notes are riskier because the issuer's obligation to pay interest and principal has the same priority as all other unsecured liabilities in the event of bankruptcy. If a company is unable to pay its debts in full, the unsecured creditors (including the holders of debentures) lose all or a portion of their balances. These types of legal agreements and other characteristics of long-term liabilities are crucial for effective business decisions. The first part of this section describes the different types of features sometimes included with bonds and notes. The second part explains and applies the debt-to-equity ratio.

Features of Bonds and Notes

This section describes common features of debt securities.

A2   Assess debt features and their implications.

Secured or Unsecured   **Secured bonds** (and notes) have specific assets of the issuer pledged (or *mortgaged*) as collateral. This arrangement gives holders added protection against the issuer's default. If the issuer fails to pay interest or par value, the secured holders can demand that the collateral be sold and the proceeds used to pay the obligation. **Unsecured bonds** (and notes), also called *debentures*, are backed by the issuer's general credit standing. Unsecured debt is riskier than secured debt. *Subordinated debentures* are liabilities that are not repaid until the claims of the more senior, unsecured (and secured) liabilities are settled.

Secured Debt   **Unsecured Debt**

Term or Serial   **Term bonds** (and notes) are scheduled for maturity on one specified date. **Serial bonds** (and notes) mature at more than one date (often in series) and thus are usually repaid over a number of periods. For instance, $100,000 of serial bonds might mature at the rate of $10,000 each year from 6 to 15 years after they are issued. Many bonds are **sinking fund bonds,** which to reduce the holder's risk, require the issuer to create a *sinking fund* of assets set aside at specified amounts and dates to repay the bonds.

Registered or Bearer   Bonds issued in the names and addresses of their holders are **registered bonds.** The issuer makes bond payments by sending checks (or cash transfers) to registered holders. A reg-
istered holder must notify the issuer of any ownership change. Registered bonds offer the issuer the practical advantage of not having to actually issue bond certificates, which protects holders against loss of bonds. Bonds payable to whoever holds them (the *bearer*) are called **bearer bonds** or *unregistered bonds*. Sales or exchanges might not be recorded, so the holder of a bearer bond is presumed to be its rightful owner. As a result, lost bearer bonds are difficult to replace. Many bearer bonds are also **coupon bonds.** This term reflects interest coupons that are attached to the bonds. When each coupon matures, the holder presents it to a bank or bro-

ker for collection. At maturity, the holder follows the same process and presents the bond certificate for collection. Issuers of coupon bonds cannot deduct the related interest expense for taxable income. This is to prevent abuse by taxpayers who own coupon bonds but fail to report interest income on their tax returns.

Convertible Debt   **Callable Debt**

Convertible and/or Callable   **Convertible bonds** (and notes) can be exchanged for a fixed number of shares of the issuing corporation's common stock. Convertible debt of-
fers holders the potential to participate in future increases in stock price. Holders still receive periodic interest while the debt is held and the par value if they hold the debt to maturity. In most cases, the holders decide whether and when to convert debt to stock. **Callable bonds** (and notes) have an option exercisable by the issuer to retire them at a stated dollar amount before maturity.

Debt-to-Equity Ratio

A3 Compute the debt-to-equity ratio and explain its use.

Beyond assessing different characteristics of debt as described above, we want to know the level of debt, especially in relation to total equity. Such knowledge helps us assess the risk of a company's financing structure. A company financed mainly with debt is more risky because liabilities must be repaid—usually with periodic interest—whereas equity financing does not. A measure to assess the risk of a company's financing structure is the **debt-to-equity ratio** (see Exhibit 14.15).

Exhibit 14.15

Debt-to-Equity Ratio

$$\text{Debt-to-equity} = \frac{\text{Total liabilities}}{\text{Total equity}}$$

The debt-to-equity ratio varies across companies and industries. Industries that are more variable tend to have lower ratios, while more stable industries are less risky and tend to have higher ratios. To apply the debt-to-equity ratio, let's look at this measure for Six Flags in Exhibit 14.16.

Exhibit 14.16

Debt-to-Equity Ratio for Six Flags

($ millions)	2004	2003	2002
Total liabilities	$2,816	3,321	3,011
Total equity	826	1,362	1,360
Debt-to-equity	3.4	2.4	2.2
Industry debt-to-equity	0.9	0.8	0.7

Decision Maker

Answer—p. 570

Bond Investor You plan to purchase debenture bonds from one of two companies in the same industry that are similar in size and performance. The first company has $350,000 in total liabilities, and $1,750,000 in equity. The second company has $1,200,000 in total liabilities, and $1,000,000 in equity. Which company's debenture bonds are less risky based on the debt-to-equity ratio?

Six Flags' 2004 debt-to-equity ratio is 3.4, meaning that debtholders contributed $3.4 for each $1 contributed by equityholders. This implies a fairly risky financing structure for Six Flags. A similar concern is drawn from a comparison of Six Flags with its competitors, where the 2004 industry ratio is 0.9. Analysis across the years also shows that Six Flags' financing structure has grown increasingly risky over the past few years. Given its declining revenues and increasing costs over the past few years (see its annual report), Six Flags is increasingly at risk of financial distress.

Demonstration Problem

Water Sports Company (WSC) patented and successfully test-marketed a new product. To expand its ability to produce and market the new product, WSC needs to raise $800,000 of financing. On January 1, 2007, the company obtained the money in two ways:

a. WSC signed a $400,000, 10% installment note to be repaid with five equal annual installments to be made on December 31 of 2007 through 2011.

b. WSC issued five-year bonds with a par value of $400,000. The bonds have a 12% annual contract rate and pay interest on June 30 and December 31. The bonds' annual market rate is 10% as of January 1, 2007.

Required

1. For the installment note, (*a*) compute the size of each annual payment, (*b*) prepare an amortization table such as Exhibit 14.14, and (*c*) prepare the journal entry for the first payment.

2. For the bonds, (*a*) compute their issue price; (*b*) prepare the January 1, 2007, journal entry to record their issuance; (*c*) prepare an amortization table using the straight-line method; (*d*) prepare the June 30, 2007, journal entry to record the first interest payment; and (*e*) prepare a journal entry to record retiring the bonds at a $416,000 call price on January 1, 2009.

3.[B]Redo parts 2(*c*), 2(*d*), and 2(*e*) assuming the bonds are amortized using the effective interest method.

Planning the Solution

- For the installment note, divide the borrowed amount by the annuity factor (from Table B.3) using the 10% rate and five payments to compute the amount of each payment. Prepare a table similar to Exhibit 14.14 and use the numbers in the table's first line for the journal entry.
- Compute the bonds' issue price by using the market rate to find the present value of their cash flows (use tables found in Appendix B). Then use this result to record the bonds' issuance. Next, prepare an amortization table like Exhibit 14.11 (and Exhibit 14B.2) and use it to get the numbers needed for the journal entry. Also use the table to find the carrying value as of the date of the bonds' retirement that you need for the journal entry.

Solution to Demonstration Problem

Part 1: Installment Note

a. Annual payment = Note balance/Annuity factor = $400,000/3.7908 = $105,519 (Note: Annuity factor is for five payments and a rate of 10%.)

b. Amortization table follows.

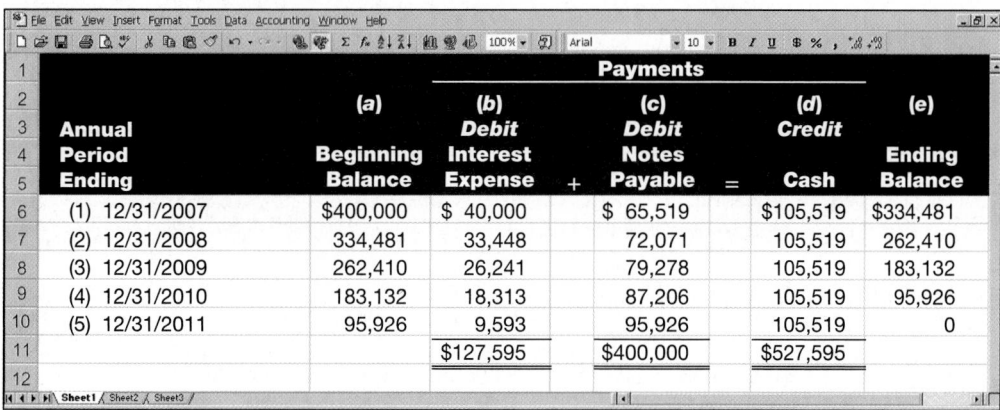

Annual Period Ending	(a) Beginning Balance	(b) Debit Interest Expense	+	(c) Debit Notes Payable	=	(d) Credit Cash	(e) Ending Balance
(1) 12/31/2007	$400,000	$ 40,000		$ 65,519		$105,519	$334,481
(2) 12/31/2008	334,481	33,448		72,071		105,519	262,410
(3) 12/31/2009	262,410	26,241		79,278		105,519	183,132
(4) 12/31/2010	183,132	18,313		87,206		105,519	95,926
(5) 12/31/2011	95,926	9,593		95,926		105,519	0
		$127,595		$400,000		$527,595	

c. Journal entry for December 31, 2007, payment.

Dec. 31	Interest Expense	40,000	
	Notes Payable	65,519	
	Cash		105,519
	To record first installment payment.		

Part 2: Bonds (straight-line amortization)

a. Compute the bonds' issue price.

Cash Flow	Table	Present Value Factor*	Amount	Present Value
Par (maturity) value	B.1 in App. B (PV of 1)	0.6139	× 400,000	= $245,560
Interest payments	B.3 in App. B (PV of annuity)	7.7217	× 24,000	= 185,321
Price of bond				$430,881

* Present value factors are for 10 payments using a semiannual market rate of 5%.

b. Journal entry for January 1, 2007, issuance.

Jan. 1	Cash	430,881	
	Premium on Bonds Payable		30,881
	Bonds Payable		400,000
	Sold bonds at a premium.		

c. Straight-line amortization table for premium bonds.

Semiannual Period-End		Unamortized Premium	Carrying Value
(0)	1/1/2007	$30,881	$430,881
(1)	6/30/2007	27,793	427,793
(2)	12/31/2007	24,705	424,705
(3)	6/30/2008	21,617	421,617
(4)	12/31/2008	18,529	418,529
(5)	6/30/2009	15,441	415,441
(6)	12/31/2009	12,353	412,353
(7)	6/30/2010	9,265	409,265
(8)	12/31/2010	6,177	406,177
(9)	6/30/2011	3,089	403,089
(10)	12/31/2011	0*	400,000

* Adjusted for rounding.

d. Journal entry for June 30, 2007, bond payment.

June 30	Bond Interest Expense	20,912	
	Premium on Bonds Payable	3,088	
	Cash		24,000
	Paid semiannual interest on bonds.		

e. Journal entry for January 1, 2009, bond retirement.

Jan. 1	Bonds Payable	400,000	
	Premium on Bonds Payable	18,529	
	Cash		416,000
	Gain on Retirement of Bonds		2,529
	To record bond retirement (carrying value as of Dec. 31, 2008).		

Part 3: Bonds (effective interest amortization)[B]

c. Effective interest amortization table for premium bonds.

Semiannual Interest Period	(A) Cash Interest Paid 6% × $400,000	(B) Interest Expense 5% × Prior (E)	(C) Premium Amortization (A) − (B)	(D) Unamortized Premium Prior (D) − (C)	(E) Carrying Value $400,000 + (D)
(0) 1/1/2007				$30,881	$430,881
(1) 6/30/2007	$ 24,000	$ 21,544	$ 2,456	28,425	428,425
(2) 12/31/2007	24,000	21,421	2,579	25,846	425,846
(3) 6/30/2008	24,000	21,292	2,708	23,138	423,138
(4) 12/31/2008	24,000	21,157	2,843	20,295	420,295
(5) 6/30/2009	24,000	21,015	2,985	17,310	417,310
(6) 12/31/2009	24,000	20,866	3,134	14,176	414,176
(7) 6/30/2010	24,000	20,709	3,291	10,885	410,885
(8) 12/31/2010	24,000	20,544	3,456	7,429	407,429
(9) 6/30/2011	24,000	20,371	3,629	3,800	403,800
(10) 12/31/2011	24,000	20,200	3,800	0	400,000
	$240,000	$209,119	$30,881		

* Adjusted for rounding.

d. Journal entry for June 30, 2007, bond payment.

June 30	Bond Interest Expense	21,544	
	Premium on Bonds Payable	2,456	
	Cash		24,000
	Paid semiannual interest on bonds.		

e. Journal entry for January 1, 2009, bond retirement.

Jan. 1	Bonds Payable	400,000	
	Premium on Bonds Payable	20,295	
	Cash		416,000
	Gain on Retirement of Bonds		4,295
	To record bond retirement (carrying value as of December 31, 2008).		

APPENDIX

Present Values of Bonds and Notes

14A

This appendix explains how to apply present value techniques to measure a long-term liability when it is created and to assign interest expense to the periods until it is settled. Appendix B at the end of the book provides additional discussion of present value concepts.

Present Value Concepts

The basic present value concept is that cash paid (or received) in the future has less value now than the same amount of cash paid (or received) today. To illustrate, if we must pay $1 one year from now, its present value is less than $1. To see this, assume that we borrow $0.9259 today that must be paid back in one year with 8% interest. Our interest expense for this loan is computed as $0.9259 × 8%, or $0.0741.

When the $0.0741 interest is added to the $0.9259 borrowed, we get the $1 payment necessary to repay our loan with interest. This is formally computed in Exhibit 14A.1. The $0.9259 borrowed is the present value of the $1 future payment. More generally, an amount borrowed equals the present value of the future payment. (This same interpretation applies to an investment. If $0.9259 is invested at 8%, it yields $0.0741 in revenue after one year. This amounts to $1, made up of principal and interest.)

Amount borrowed	**$0.9259**
Interest for one year at 8%	0.0741
Amount owed after 1 year	$ 1.0000

To extend this example, assume that we owe $1 two years from now instead of one year, and the 8% interest is compounded annually. *Compounded* means that interest during the second period is based on the total of the amount borrowed plus the interest accrued from the first period. The second period's interest is then computed as 8% multiplied by the sum of the amount borrowed plus interest earned in the first period. Exhibit 14A.2 shows how we compute the present value of $1 to be paid in two years. This amount is $0.8573. The first year's interest of $0.0686 is added to the principal so that the second year's interest is based on $0.9259. Total interest for this two-year period is $0.1427, computed as $0.0686 plus $0.0741.

Amount borrowed	**$0.8573**
Interest for first year ($0.8573 × 8%)	0.0686
Amount owed after 1 year	0.9259
Interest for second year ($0.9259 × 8%)	0.0741
Amount owed after 2 years	$ 1.0000

C2 Explain and compute the present value of an amount(s) to be paid at a future date(s).

Exhibit 14A.1

Components of a One-Year Loan

Point: Benjamin Franklin is said to have described compounding as "the money, money makes, makes more money."

Exhibit 14A.2

Components of a Two-Year Loan

Present Value Tables

The present value of $1 that we must repay at some future date can be computed by using this formula: $1/(1 + i)^n$. The symbol i is the interest rate per period and n is the number of periods until the future payment must be made. Applying this formula to our two-year loan, we get $1/(1.08)^2$, or $0.8573. This is the same value shown in Exhibit 14A.2. We can use this formula to find any present value. However, a simpler method is to use a *present value table,* which lists present values computed with this formula for various interest rates and time periods. Many people find it helpful in learning present value concepts to first work with the table and then move to using a calculator.

Exhibit 14A.3

Present Value of 1

Periods	6%	8%	10%
		Rate	
1	0.9434	**0.9259**	0.9091
2	0.8900	**0.8573**	0.8264
3	0.8396	0.7938	0.7513
4	0.7921	0.7350	0.6830
5	0.7473	0.6806	0.6209
6	0.7050	0.6302	0.5645
7	0.6651	0.5835	0.5132
8	0.6274	0.5403	0.4665
9	0.5919	0.5002	0.4241
10	0.5584	0.4632	0.3855

Exhibit 14A.3 shows a present value table for a future payment of 1 for up to 10 periods at three different interest rates. Present values in this table are rounded to four decimal places. This table is drawn from the larger and more complete Table B.1 in Appendix B at the end of the book. Notice that the first value in the 8% column is 0.9259, the value we computed earlier for the present value of a $1 loan for one year at 8% (see Exhibit 14A.1). Go to the second row in the same 8% column and find the present value of 1 discounted at 8% for two years, or 0.8573. This $0.8573 is the present value of our obligation to repay $1 after two periods at 8% interest (see Exhibit 14A.2).

Example: Use Exhibit 14A.3 to find the present value of $1 discounted for 2 years at 6%. *Answer:* Present value = $0.8900

Applying a Present Value Table

To illustrate how to measure a liability using a present value table, assume that a company plans to borrow cash and repay it as follows: $2,000 after one year, $3,000 after two years, and $5,000 after three years. How much does this company receive today if the interest rate on this loan is 10%? To answer, we need to compute the present value of the three future payments, discounted at 10%. This computation is shown in Exhibit 14A.4 using present values from Exhibit 14A.3. The company can borrow $8,054 today at 10% interest in exchange for its promise to make these three payments at the scheduled dates.

Exhibit 14A.4

Present Value of a Series of Unequal Payments

Periods	Payments	Present Value of 1 at 10%	Present Value of Payments
1	$2,000	0.9091	$ 1,818
2	3,000	0.8264	2,479
3	5,000	0.7513	3,757
Present value of all payments			**$8,054**

Present Value of an Annuity

The $8,054 present value for the loan in Exhibit 14A.4 equals the sum of the present values of the three payments. When payments are not equal, their combined present value is best computed by adding the individual present values as shown in Exhibit 14A.4. Sometimes payments follow an **annuity,** which is a series of *equal* payments at equal time intervals. The present value of an annuity is readily computed.

To illustrate, assume that a company must repay a 6% loan with a $5,000 payment at each year-end for the next four years. This loan amount equals the present value of the four payments discounted at 6%. Exhibit 14A.5 shows how to compute this loan's present value of $17,326 by multiplying each payment by its matching present value factor taken from Exhibit 14A.3.

However, the series of $5,000 payments is an annuity, so we can compute its present value with either of two shortcuts. First, the third column of Exhibit 14A.5 shows that the sum of the present values of 1 at 6% for periods 1 through 4 equals 3.4651. One shortcut is to multiply this total of 3.4651 by the $5,000 annual payment to get the combined present value of $17,326. It requires one multiplication instead of four.

Exhibit 14A.5

Present Value of a Series of Equal Payments (Annuity) by Discounting Each Payment

Periods	Payments	Present Value of 1 at 6%	Present Value of Payments
1	$5,000	0.9434	$ 4,717
2	5,000	0.8900	4,450
3	5,000	0.8396	4,198
4	5,000	0.7921	3,961
Present value of all payments		**3.4651**	**$17,326**

The second shortcut uses an *annuity table* such as the one shown in Exhibit 14A.6, which is drawn from the more complete Table B.3 in Appendix B. We go directly to the annuity table to get the present value factor for a specific number of payments and interest rate. We then multiply this factor by the amount of the payment to find the present value of the annuity. Specifically, find the row for four periods and go across to the 6% column, where the factor is 3.4651. This factor equals the present value of an annuity with four payments of 1, discounted at 6%. We then multiply 3.4651 by $5,000 to get the $17,326 present value of the annuity.

	Rate		
Periods	**6%**	**8%**	**10%**
1	0.9434	0.9259	0.9091
2	1.8334	1.7833	1.7355
3	2.6730	2.5771	2.4869
4	**3.4651**	3.3121	3.1699
5	4.2124	3.9927	3.7908
6	4.9173	4.6229	4.3553
7	5.5824	5.2064	4.8684
8	6.2098	5.7466	5.3349
9	6.8017	6.2469	5.7590
10	7.3601	6.7101	6.1446

Exhibit 14A.6

Present Value of an Annuity of 1

Example: Use Exhibit 14A.6 to find the present value of an annuity of eight $15,000 payments with an 8% interest rate. *Answer:* Present value = $15,000 × 5.7466 = $86,199

Compounding Periods Shorter than a Year

The present value examples all involved periods of one year. In many situations, however, interest is compounded over shorter periods. For example, the interest rate on bonds is usually stated as an annual rate but interest is often paid every six months (semiannually). This means that the present value of interest payments from such bonds must be computed using interest periods of six months.

Assume that a borrower wants to know the present value of a series of 10 *semiannual payments* of $4,000 made over five years at an *annual interest rate* of 12%. The interest rate is stated as an annual rate of 12%, but it is actually a rate of 6% per semiannual interest period. To compute the present value of this series of $4,000 payments, go to row 10 of Exhibit 14A.6 and across to the 6% column to find the factor 7.3601. The present value of this annuity is $29,440 (7.3601 × $4,000).

Appendix B further describes present value concepts and includes more complete present value tables and assignments.

Example: If this borrower makes five semiannual payments of $8,000, what is the present value of this annuity at a 12% annual rate? *Answer:* 4.2124 × $8,000 = $33,699

Quick Check
Answers—p. 570

14. A company enters into an agreement to make four annual year-end payments of $1,000 each, starting one year from now. The annual interest rate is 8%. The present value of these four payments is (*a*) $2,923, (*b*) $2,940, or (*c*) $3,312.

15. Suppose a company has an option to pay either (*a*) $10,000 after one year or (*b*) $5,000 after six months and another $5,000 after one year. Which choice has the lower present value?

APPENDIX

Effective Interest Amortization

14B

Effective Interest Amortization of a Discount Bond

The straight-line method yields changes in the bonds' carrying value while the amount for bond interest expense remains constant. This gives the impression of a changing interest rate when users divide a constant bond interest expense over a changing carrying value. As a result, accounting standards allow use of the straight-line method only when its results do not differ materially from those obtained using the effective interest method. The **effective interest method,** or simply *interest method,* allocates total bond interest expense over the bonds' life in a way that yields a constant rate of interest. This constant rate of interest is the market rate at the issue date. Thus, bond interest expense for a period equals the carrying value of the bond at the beginning of that period multiplied by the market rate when issued.

Point: The effective interest method consistently computes bond interest expense using the market rate at issuance. This rate is applied to a changing carrying value.

Exhibit 14B.1 shows an effective interest amortization table for the Fila bonds (as described in Exhibit 14.4). The key difference between the effective interest and straight-line methods lies in computing bond interest expense. Instead of assigning an equal amount of bond interest expense to each period, the effective interest method assigns a bond interest expense amount that increases over the life of a discount bond. **Both methods allocate the *same* $47,723 of total bond interest expense to the bonds' life, but in different patterns.** Specifically, the amortization table in Exhibit 10B.1 shows that the balance of the discount (column D) is amortized until it reaches zero. Also, the bonds' carrying value (column E) changes each period until it equals par value at maturity. Compare columns D and E to the corresponding columns in Exhibit 14.7 to see the amortization patterns. Total bond interest expense is $47,723, consisting of $40,000 of semiannual cash payments and $7,723 of the original bond discount, the same for both methods.

Exhibit 14B.1

Effective Interest Amortization of Bond Discount

File Edit View Insert Format Tools Data Accounting Window Help						
Bonds: $100,000 Par Value, Semiannual Interest Payments, Five-Year Life, 4% Semiannual Contract Rate, 5% Semiannual Market Rate						
	(A)	**(B)**	**(C)**	**(D)**	**(E)**
Semiannual Interest Period-End	**Cash Interest Paid**	**Bond Interest Expense**	**Discount Amortization**	**Unamortized Discount**	**Carrying Value**
(0) 12/31/2008				$7,723	$ 92,277
(1) 6/30/2009	$4,000	$4,614	$ 614	7,109	92,891
(2) 12/31/2009	4,000	4,645	645	6,464	93,536
(3) 6/30/2010	4,000	4,677	677	5,787	94,213
(4) 12/31/2010	4,000	4,711	711	5,076	94,924
(5) 6/30/2011	4,000	4,746	746	4,330	95,670
(6) 12/31/2011	4,000	4,784	784	3,546	96,454
(7) 6/30/2012	4,000	4,823	823	2,723	97,277
(8) 12/31/2012	4,000	4,864	864	1,859	98,141
(9) 6/30/2013	4,000	4,907	907	952	99,048
(10) 12/31/2013	4,000	4,952	952	0	100,000
	$40,000	$47,723	$7,723		

Column (**A**) is par value ($100,000) multiplied by the semiannual contract rate (4%).

Column (**B**) is prior period's carrying value multiplied by the semiannual market rate (5%).

Column (**C**) is the difference between interest paid and bond interest expense, or [(B) − (A)].

Column (**D**) is the prior period's unamortized discount less the current period's discount amortization.

Column (**E**) is par value less unamortized discount, or [$100,000 − (D)].

Except for differences in amounts, journal entries recording the expense and updating the liability balance are the same under the effective interest method and the straight-line method. We can use the numbers in Exhibit 14B.1 to record each semiannual entry during the bonds' five-year life (June 30, 2009, through December 31, 2013). For instance, we record the interest payment at the end of the first semiannual period as:

	2009			
Assets = Liabilities + Equity	June 30	Bond Interest Expense	4,614	
−4,000 +614 −4,614		Discount on Bonds Payable		614
		Cash		4,000
		To record semiannual interest and discount amortization (effective interest method).		

Effective Interest Amortization of a Premium Bond

Exhibit 14B.2 shows the amortization table using the effective interest method for the Adidas bonds (as described in Exhibit 14.8). Column A lists the semiannual cash payments. Column B shows the amount of bond interest expense, computed as the 5% semiannual market rate at issuance multiplied by the beginning-of-period carrying value. The amount of cash paid in column A is larger than the bond interest expense because the cash payment is based on the higher 6% semiannual contract rate. The excess cash payment over the interest expense reduces the principal. These amounts are shown in column C. Column E

Exhibit 14B.2

Effective Interest Amortization
of Bond Premium

```
File Edit View Insert Format Tools Data Accounting Window Help                          _ 8 x
```

Bonds: $100,000 Par Value, Semiannual Interest Payments, Five-Year Life, 6% Semiannual Contract Rate, 5% Semiannual Market Rate					
	(A)	**(B)**	**(C)**	**(D)**	**(E)**
Semiannual Interest Period-End	**Cash Interest Paid**	**Bond Interest Expense**	**Premium Amortization**	**Unamortized Premium**	**Carrying Value**
(0) 12/31/2008				$7,720	$107,720
(1) 6/30/2009	$6,000	$5,386	$ 614	7,106	107,106
(2) 12/31/2009	6,000	5,355	645	6,461	106,461
(3) 6/30/2010	6,000	5,323	677	5,784	105,784
(4) 12/31/2010	6,000	5,289	711	5,073	105,073
(5) 6/30/2011	6,000	5,254	746	4,327	104,327
(6) 12/31/2011	6,000	5,216	784	3,543	103,543
(7) 6/30/2012	6,000	5,177	823	2,720	102,720
(8) 12/31/2012	6,000	5,136	864	1,856	101,856
(9) 6/30/2013	6,000	5,093	907	949	100,949
(10) 12/31/2013	6,000	5,051*	949	0	100,000
	$60,000	$52,280	$7,720		

```
Sheet1 Sheet2 Sheet3 Sheet2 Sheet3
```

Column (**A**) is par value ($100,000) multiplied by the semiannual contract rate (6%).

Column (**B**) is prior period's carrying value multiplied by the semiannual market rate (5%).

Column (**C**) is the difference between interest paid and bond interest expense, or [(A) − (B)].

Column (**D**) is the prior period's unamortized premium less the current period's premium amortization.

Column (**E**) is par value plus unamortized premium, or [$100,000 + (D)].

* Adjusted for rounding.

shows the carrying value after deducting the amortized premium in column C from the prior period's carrying value. Column D shows the premium's reduction by periodic amortization. When the issuer makes the first semiannual interest payment, the effect of premium amortization on bond interest expense and bond liability is recorded as follows:

2009			
June 30	Bond Interest Expense	5,386	
	Premium on Bonds Payable.	614	
	Cash		6,000
	To record semiannual interest and premium amortization (effective interest method).		

Assets = Liabilities + Equity
−6,000   −614   −5,386

Similar entries with different amounts are recorded at each payment date until the bond matures at the end of 2013. The effective interest method yields decreasing amounts of bond interest expense and increasing amounts of premium amortization over the bonds' life.

APPENDIX

Issuing Bonds between Interest Dates

14C

An issuer can sell bonds at a date other than an interest payment date. When this occurs, the buyers normally pay the issuer the purchase price plus any interest accrued since the prior interest payment date. This accrued interest is then repaid to these buyers on the next interest payment date. To illustrate, suppose Avia sells $100,000 of its 9% bonds at par on March 1, 2008, sixty days after the stated issue date.

C3 Describe the accrual of bond interest when bond payments do not align with accounting periods.

The interest on Avia bonds is payable semiannually on each June 30 and December 31. Since 60 days have passed, the issuer collects accrued interest from the buyers at the time of issuance. This amount is $1,500 ($100,000 × 9% × $^{60}/_{360}$ year). This case is reflected in Exhibit 14C.1.

Exhibit 14C.1

Accruing Interest between Interest Payment Dates

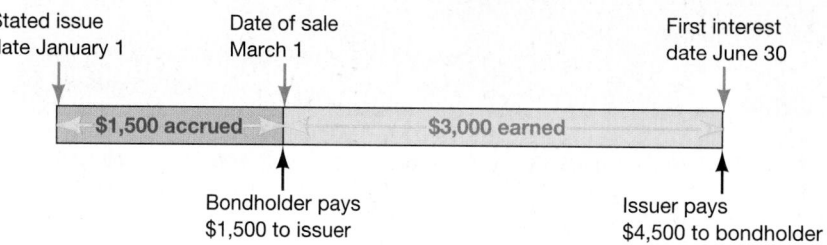

Avia records the issuance of these bonds on March 1, 2008, as follows:

Assets = Liabilities + Equity
+101,500   +100,000
           +1,500

Mar. I	Cash	101,500	
	Interest Payable.		1,500
	Bonds Payable.		100,000
	Sold bonds at par with accrued interest.		

Example: How much interest is collected from a buyer of $50,000 of Avia bonds sold at par 150 days after the contract issue date? *Answer:* $1,875 (computed as $50,000 × 9% × $^{150}/_{360}$ year)

Note that liabilities for interest payable and bonds payable are recorded in separate accounts. When the June 30, 2008, semiannual interest date arrives, Avia pays the full semiannual interest of $4,500 ($100,000 × 9% × ½ year) to the bondholders. This payment includes the four months' interest of $3,000 earned by the bondholders from March 1 to June 30 *plus* the repayment of the 60 days' accrued interest collected by Avia when the bonds were sold. Avia records this first semiannual interest payment as follows:

Assets = Liabilities + Equity
−4,500   −1,500   −3,000

June 30	Interest Payable	1,500	
	Bond Interest Expense	3,000	
	Cash		4,500
	Paid semiannual interest on the bonds.		

Global: In some countries such as Kuwait, Saudi Arabia, and Iran, charging explicit interest for use of money is rare due to Islamic law.

The practice of collecting and then repaying accrued interest with the next interest payment is to simplify the issuer's administrative efforts. To explain, suppose an issuer sells bonds on 15 or 20 different dates between the stated issue date and the first interest payment date. If the issuer does not collect accrued interest from buyers, it needs to pay different amounts of cash to each of them according to the time that passed after purchasing the bonds. The issuer needs to keep detailed records of buyers and the dates they bought bonds. Issuers avoid this recordkeeping by having each buyer pay accrued interest at purchase. Issuers then pay the full semiannual interest to all buyers, regardless of when they bought bonds.

Decision Maker

Answer—p. 570

Bond Rater   You must assign a rating to a bond that reflects its risk to bondholders. Identify factors you consider in assessing bond risk. Indicate the likely levels (relative to the norm) for the factors you identify for a bond that sells at a discount.

Accruing Bond Interest Expense

If a bond's interest period does not coincide with the issuer's accounting period, an adjusting entry is needed to recognize bond interest expense accrued since the most recent interest payment. To illustrate, assume that the Adidas bonds described in Exhibit 14.10 are sold on the stated issue date of September 1, 2008, instead of December 31, 2008. As a result, four months' interest (and premium amortization) accrue before the end of the 2008 calendar year. Interest for this period equals $3,485, or $^{4}/_{6}$ of the first six months' interest of $5,228. Also, the premium amortization is $515, or $^{4}/_{6}$ of the first six months' amortization of $772. The sum of the bond interest expense and the amortization is $4,000 ($3,485 + $515), which equals $^{4}/_{6}$ of the $6,000 cash payment due on February 28, 2009. Adidas records these effects with an adjusting entry at December 31, 2008:

Point: Computation of accrued bond interest may use months instead of days for simplicity purposes. For example, the accrued interest computation for the Adidas bonds is based on months.

Assets = Liabilities + Equity
        −515   −3,485
        +4,000

Dec. 31	Bond Interest Expense	3,485	
	Premium on Bonds Payable.	515	
	Interest Payable.		4,000
	To record four months' accrued interest and premium amortization.		

Similar entries are made on each December 31 throughout the bonds' five-year life. When the $6,000 cash payment occurs on each February 28 interest payment date, Adidas must recognize bond interest expense and amortization for January and February. It must also eliminate the interest payable liability created by the December 31 adjusting entry. For example, Adidas records its payment on February 28, 2009, as:

Feb. 28	Interest Payable	4,000	
	Bond Interest Expense ($5,228 × ⅔)	1,743	
	Premium on Bonds Payable ($772 × ⅔)	257	
	Cash		6,000
	To record 2 months' interest and amortization and		
	eliminate accrued interest liability.		

Assets = Liabilities + Equity
−6,000   −4,000   −1,743
              −257

The interest payments made each August 31 are recorded as usual because the entire six-month interest period is included within this company's calendar-year reporting period.

Quick Check
Answer—p. 570

16. On May 1, a company sells 9% bonds with a $500,000 par value that pay semiannual interest on each January 1 and July 1. The bonds are sold at par plus interest accrued since January 1. The issuer records the first semiannual interest payment on July 1 with (*a*) a debit to Interest Payable for $15,000, (*b*) a debit to Bond Interest Expense for $22,500, or (*c*) a credit to Interest Payable for $7,500.

APPENDIX

Leases and Pensions

14D

This appendix briefly explains the accounting and analysis for both leases and pensions.

Lease Liabilities

A **lease** is a contractual agreement between a *lessor* (asset owner) and a *lessee* (asset renter or tenant) that grants the lessee the right to use the asset for a period of time in return for cash (rent) payments. Nearly one-fourth of all equipment purchases is financed with leases. The advantages of lease financing include the lack of an immediate large cash payment and the potential to deduct rental payments in computing taxable income. From an accounting perspective, leases can be classified as either operating or capital leases.

C4 Describe accounting for leases and pensions.

Operating Leases **Operating leases** are short-term (or cancelable) leases in which the lessor retains the risks and rewards of ownership. Examples include most car and apartment rental agreements. The lessee records such lease payments as expenses; the lessor records them as revenue. The lessee does not report the leased item as an asset or a liability (it is the lessor's asset). To illustrate, if an employee of Amazon leases a car for $300 at an airport while on company business, Amazon (lessee) records this cost as:

Point: Home Depot's annual report indicates that its rental expenses from operating leases total more than $600 million.

July 4	Rental Expense	300	
	Cash		300
	To record lease rental payment.		

Assets = Liabilities + Equity
−300   −300

Capital Leases **Capital leases** are long-term (or noncancelable) leases by which the lessor transfers substantially all risks and rewards of ownership to the lessee.[3] Examples include most leases of airplanes and department store buildings. The lessee records the leased item as its own asset along with a lease liability at the start of the lease term; the amount recorded equals the present value of all lease payments. To illustrate, assume that K2 Co. enters into a six-year lease of a building in which it will sell sporting equipment. The lease transfers all building ownership risks and rewards to K2 (the present value of its $12,979 annual lease payments is $60,000). K2 records this transaction as follows:

Assets = Liabilities + Equity
+60,000   +60,000

2008			
Jan. 1	Leased Asset—Building......................	60,000	
	Lease Liability..........................		60,000
	To record leased asset and lease liability.		

Point: Home Depot reports *"certain retail locations are leased under capital leases."* The net present value of its Lease Liability is about $350 million.

K2 reports the leased asset as a plant asset and the lease liability as a long-term liability. The portion of the lease liability expected to be paid in the next year is reported as a current liability.[4] At each year-end, K2 records depreciation on the leased asset (assume straight-line depreciation, six-year lease term, and no salvage value) as follows:

Assets = Liabilities + Equity
−10,000   −10,000

Dec. 31	Depreciation Expense—Building...............	10,000	
	Accumulated Depreciation—Building.........		10,000
	To record depreciation on leased asset.		

K2 also accrues interest on the lease liability at each year-end. Interest expense is computed by multiplying the remaining lease liability by the interest rate on the lease. Specifically, K2 records its annual interest expense as part of its annual lease payment ($12,979) as follows (for its first year):

Assets = Liabilities + Equity
−12,979   −8,179   −4,800

2008			
Dec. 31	Interest Expense	4,800	
	Lease Liability.............................	8,179	
	Cash		12,979
	To record first annual lease payment.*		

* These numbers are computed from a *lease payment schedule*. For simplicity, we use the same numbers from Exhibit 14.14 for this lease payment schedule—with different headings as follows:

		Payments			
	(A)	(B) *Debit*	(C) *Debit*	(D) *Credit*	(E)
Period Ending Date	Beginning Balance of Lease Liability	Interest on Lease + Liability 8% × (A)	Lease = Liability (D) − (B)	Cash Lease Payment	Ending Balance of Lease Liability (A) − (C)
12/31/2008	$60,000	$ 4,800	$ 8,179	$12,979	$51,821
12/31/2009	51,821	4,146	8,833	12,979	42,988
12/31/2010	42,988	3,439	9,540	12,979	33,448
12/31/2011	33,448	2,676	10,303	12,979	23,145
12/31/2012	23,145	1,852	11,127	12,979	12,018
12/31/2013	12,018	961	12,018	12,979	0
		$17,874	$60,000	$77,874	

[3] A *capital lease* meets any one or more of four criteria: (1) transfers title of leased asset to lessee, (2) contains a bargain purchase option, (3) has a lease term that is 75% or more of the leased asset's useful life, or (4) has a present value of lease payments that is 90% or more of the leased asset's market value.

[4] Most lessees try to keep leased assets and lease liabilities off their balance sheets by failing to meet any one of the four criteria of a capital lease. This is because a lease liability increases a company's total liabilities, making it more difficult to obtain additional financing. The acquisition of assets without reporting any related liabilities (or other asset outflows) on the balance sheet is called **off-balance-sheet financing.**

Pension Liabilities

A **pension plan** is a contractual agreement between an employer and its employees for the employer to provide benefits (payments) to employees after they retire. Most employers pay the full cost of the pension, but sometimes employees pay part of the cost. An employer records its payment into a pension plan with a debit to Pension Expense and a credit to Cash. A *plan administrator* receives payments from the employer, invests them in pension assets, and makes benefit payments to *pension recipients* (retired employees). Insurance and trust companies often serve as pension plan administrators.

Many pensions are known as *defined benefit plans* that define future benefits; the employer's contributions vary, depending on assumptions about future pension assets and liabilities. Several disclosures are necessary in this case. Specifically, a pension liability is reported when the accumulated benefit obligation is *more than* the plan assets, a so-called *underfunded plan*. The accumulated benefit obligation is the present value of promised future pension payments to retirees. *Plan assets* refer to the market value of assets the plan administrator holds. A pension asset is reported when the accumulated benefit obligation is *less than* the plan assets, a so-called *overfunded plan*. An employer reports pension expense when it receives the benefits from the employees' services, which is sometimes decades before it pays pension benefits to employees. (*Other Postretirement Benefits* refer to nonpension benefits such as health care and life insurance benefits. Similar to a pension, costs of these benefits are estimated and liabilities accrued when the employees earn them.)

Point: Fringe benefits are often 40% or more of salaries and wages, and pension benefits make up nearly 15% of fringe benefits.

Point: Two types of pension plans are (1) *defined benefit plan*—the retirement benefit is defined and the employer estimates the contribution necessary to pay these benefits and (2) *defined contribution plan*—the pension contribution is defined and the employer and/or employee contributes amounts specified in the pension agreement.

Summary

C1 **Explain the types and payment patterns of notes.** Notes repaid over a period of time are called *installment notes* and usually follow one of two payment patterns: (1) decreasing payments of interest plus equal amounts of principal or (2) equal total payments. Mortgage notes also are common.

C2[A] **Explain and compute the present value of an amount(s) to be paid at a future date(s).** The basic concept of present value is that an amount of cash to be paid or received in the future is worth less than the same amount of cash to be paid or received today. Another important present value concept is that interest is compounded, meaning interest is added to the balance and used to determine interest for succeeding periods. An annuity is a series of equal payments occurring at equal time intervals. An annuity's present value can be computed using the present value table for an annuity (or a calculator).

C3[C] **Describe the accrual of bond interest when bond payments do not align with accounting periods.** Issuers and buyers of debt record the interest accrued when issue dates or accounting periods do not coincide with debt payment dates.

C4[D] **Describe accounting for leases and pensions.** A lease is a rental agreement between the lessor and the lessee. When the lessor retains the risks and rewards of asset ownership (an *operating lease*), the lessee debits Rent Expense and credits Cash for its lease payments. When the lessor substantially transfers the risks and rewards of asset ownership to the lessee (a *capital lease*), the lessee capitalizes the leased asset and records a lease liability. Pension agreements can result in either pension assets or pension liabilities.

A1 **Compare bond financing with stock financing.** Bond financing is used to fund business activities. Advantages of bond financing versus stock include (1) no effect on owner control, (2) tax savings, and (3) increased earnings due to financial leverage. Disadvantages include (1) interest and principal payments and (2) amplification of poor performance.

A2 **Assess debt features and their implications.** Certain bonds are secured by the issuer's assets; other bonds, called *debentures,* are unsecured. Serial bonds mature at different points in time;

term bonds mature at one time. Registered bonds have each bondholder's name recorded by the issuer; bearer bonds are payable to the holder. Convertible bonds are exchangeable for shares of the issuer's stock. Callable bonds can be retired by the issuer at a set price. Debt features alter the risk of loss for creditors.

A3 **Compute the debt-to-equity ratio and explain its use.** Both creditors and equity holders are concerned about the relation between the amount of liabilities and the amount of equity. A company's financing structure is at less risk when the debt-to-equity ratio is lower, as liabilities must be paid and usually with periodic interest.

P1 **Prepare entries to record bond issuance and bond interest expense.** When bonds are issued at par, Cash is debited and Bonds Payable is credited for the bonds' par value. At bond interest payment dates (usually semiannual), Bond Interest Expense is debited and Cash credited; the latter for an amount equal to the bond par value multiplied by the bond contract rate.

P2 **Compute and record amortization of bond discount.** Bonds are issued at a discount when the contract rate is less than the market rate, making the issue (selling) price less than par. When this occurs, the issuer records a credit to Bonds Payable (at par) and debits both Discount on Bonds Payable and Cash. The amount of bond interest expense assigned to each period is computed using either the straight-line or effective interest method.

P3 **Compute and record amortization of bond premium.** Bonds are issued at a premium when the contract rate is higher than the market rate, making the issue (selling) price greater than par. When this occurs, the issuer records a debit to Cash and credits both Premium on Bonds Payable and Bonds Payable (at par). The amount of bond interest expense assigned to each period is computed using either the straight-line or effective interest method. The Premium on Bonds Payable is allocated to reduce bond interest expense over the life of the bonds.

P4 **Record the retirement of bonds.** Bonds are retired at maturity with a debit to Bonds Payable and a credit to Cash at par value. The issuer can retire the bonds early by exercising a call option or purchasing them in the market. Bondholders can also retire bonds early by exercising a conversion feature on convertible bonds. The issuer recognizes a gain or loss for the difference between the amount paid and the bond carrying value.

P5   **Prepare entries to account for notes.** Interest is allocated to each period in a note's life by multiplying its beginning-

period carrying value by its market rate at issuance. If a note is repaid with equal payments, the payment amount is computed by dividing the borrowed amount by the present value of an annuity factor (taken from a present value table) using the market rate and the number of payments.

Guidance Answers to **Decision Maker**

Entrepreneur   This is a "present value" question. The market interest rate (10%) and present value ($3,000) are known, but the payment required two years later is unknown. This amount ($3,630) can be computed as $3,000 × 1.10 × 1.10. Thus, the sale price is $3,630 when no payments are received for two years. Note that the $3,630 received two years from today is equivalent to $3,000 cash today.

Bond Investor   The debt-to-equity ratio for the first company is 0.2 ($350,000/$1,750,000) and for the second company is 1.2 ($1,200,000/$1,000,000), suggesting that the financing structure of

the second company is more risky than that of the first company. Consequently, as a buyer of unsecured debenture bonds, you prefer the first company (all else equal).

Bond Rater   Bonds with longer repayment periods (life) have higher risk. Also, bonds issued by companies in financial difficulties or facing higher than normal uncertainties have higher risk. Moreover, companies with higher than normal debt and large fluctuations in earnings are considered of higher risk. Discount bonds are more risky on one or more of these factors.

Guidance Answers to **Quick Checks**

1. (*b*)

2. Multiply the bond's par value by its contract rate of interest.

3. Bonds sell at a premium when the contract rate exceeds the market rate and the purchasers pay more than their par value.

4. The bonds are issued at a discount, meaning that issue price is less than par value. A discount occurs because the bond contract rate (6%) is less than the market rate (8%).

5.

Cash	91,893
Discount on Bonds Payable	8,107
Bonds Payable	100,000

6. $3,811 (Total bond interest expense of $38,107 divided by 10 periods; or the $3,000 semiannual cash payment plus the $8,107 discount divided by 10 periods.)

7. The bonds are issued at a premium, meaning issue price is higher than par value. A premium occurs because the bonds' contract rate (16%) is higher than the market rate (14%).

8. (*b*) For each semiannual period: $10,592/20 periods = $530 premium amortization.

9.

Bonds payable, 16%, due 12/31/2017	$100,000
Plus premium on bonds payable	9,532* $109,532

* Original premium balance of $10,592 less $530 and $530 amortized on 6/30/2008 and 12/31/2008, respectively.

10. $9,375 loss. Computed as the difference between the repurchase price of $256,250 [50% of ($500,000 × 102.5%)] and the carrying value of $246,875 (50% of $493,750).

11. (*c*)

12. The interest portion of an installment payment equals the period's beginning loan balance multiplied by the market interest rate at the time of the note's issuance.

13. On the balance sheet, the account balances of the related liability (note payable) and asset (cash) accounts are decreased. On the income statement, interest expense is recorded.

14. (*c*) Computed as 3.3121 × $1,000 = $3,312.

15. The option of paying $10,000 after one year has a lower present value. It postpones paying the first $5,000 by six months. More generally, the present value of a further delayed payment is always lower than a less delayed payment.

16. (*a*) Reflects payment of accrued interest recorded back on May 1; $500,000 × 9% × ⅟₁₂ = $15,000.

Key Terms   mhhe.com/wildFAP18e

Key Terms are available at the book's Website for learning and testing in an online Flashcard Format.

Lease (p. 567)	Par value of a bond (p. 544)	Serial bonds (p. 557)
Market rate (p. 547)	Pension plan (p. 569)	Sinking fund bonds (p. 557)
Mortgage (p. 556)	Premium on bonds (p. 550)	Straight-line bond amortization (p. 548)
Off-balance-sheet financing (p. 568)	Registered bonds (p. 557)	Term bonds (p. 557)
Operating leases (p. 567)	Secured bonds (p. 557)	Unsecured bonds (p. 557)

Multiple Choice Quiz   Answers on p. 583   mhhe.com/wildFAP18e

Multiple Choice Quizzes A and B are available at the book's Website.

1. A bond traded at 97½ means that:
  a. The bond pays 97½% interest.
  b. The bond trades at $975 per $1,000 bond.
  c. The market rate of interest is below the contract rate of interest for the bond.
  d. The bonds can be retired at $975 each.
  e. The bond's interest rate is 2½%.

2. A bondholder that owns a $1,000, 6%, 15-year bond has:
  a. The right to receive $1,000 at maturity.
  b. Ownership rights in the bond issuing entity.
  c. The right to receive $60 per month until maturity.
  d. The right to receive $1,900 at maturity.
  e. The right to receive $600 per year until maturity.

3. A company issues 8%, 20-year bonds with a par value of $500,000. The current market rate for the bonds is 8%. The amount of interest owed to the bondholders for each semiannual interest payment is:
  a. $40,000.
  b. $0.
  c. $20,000.

  d. $800,000.
  e. $400,000.

4. A company issued 5-year, 5% bonds with a par value of $100,000. The company received $95,735 for the bonds. Using the straight-line method, the company's interest expense for the first semiannual interest period is:
  a. $2,926.50.
  b. $5,853.00.
  c. $2,500.00.
  d. $5,000.00.
  e. $9,573.50.

5. A company issued 8-year, 5% bonds with a par value of $350,000. The company received proceeds of $373,745. Interest is payable semiannually. The amount of premium amortized for the first semiannual interest period, assuming straight-line bond amortization, is:
  a. $2,698.
  b. $23,745.
  c. $8,750.
  d. $9,344.
  e. $1,484.

Superscript letter ^{B} ($^{C, D}$) denotes assignments based on Appendix 14B (14C, 14D).

Discussion Questions

1. What is the main difference between a bond and a share of stock?

2. What is the main difference between notes payable and bonds payable?

3. What is the advantage of issuing bonds instead of obtaining financing from the company's owners?

4. What are the duties of a trustee for bondholders?

5. What is a bond indenture? What provisions are usually included in it?

6. What are the *contract* rate and the *market* rate for bonds?

7. What factors affect the market rates for bonds?

8.^{B}Does the straight-line or effective interest method produce an interest expense allocation that yields a constant rate of interest over a bond's life? Explain.

9.^{C}Why does a company that issues bonds between interest dates collect accrued interest from the bonds' purchasers?

10. If you know the par value of bonds, the contract rate, and the market rate, how do you compute the bonds' price?

11. What is the issue price of a $2,000 bond sold at 98¼? What is the issue price of a $6,000 bond sold at 101½?

12. Describe the debt-to-equity ratio and explain how creditors and owners would use this ratio to evaluate a company's risk.

13. What obligation does an entrepreneur (owner) have to investors that purchase bonds to finance the business?

14. Refer to **Best Buy**'s annual report in Appendix A. Is there any indication that Best Buy has issued bonds?

15. Refer to the statement of cash flows for **Circuit City** in Appendix A. For the year ended February 28, 2005, what was the amount of principal payments on long-term debt?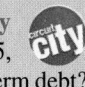

16. Refer to the annual report for **Apple** in Appendix A. For the year ended September 25, 2004, did it raise more cash by issuing stock or debt?

17.^{D}When can a lease create both an asset and a liability for the lessee?

18.^{D}Compare and contrast an operating lease with a capital lease.

19.^{D}Describe the two basic types of pension plans.

 Red numbers denote Discussion Questions that involve decision-making.

QUICK STUDY

QS 14-1
Bond computations—
straight-line   P1 P2

Enviro Company issues 8%, 10-year bonds with a par value of $250,000 and semiannual interest payments. On the issue date, the annual market rate for these bonds is 10%, which implies a selling price of 87½. The straight-line method is used to allocate interest expense.

1. What are the issuer's cash proceeds from issuance of these bonds?

2. What total amount of bond interest expense will be recognized over the life of these bonds?

3. What is the amount of bond interest expense recorded on the first interest payment date?

QS 14-2[B]
Bond computations—
effective interest

P1 P3

Garcia Company issues 10%, 15-year bonds with a par value of $240,000 and semiannual interest payments. On the issue date, the annual market rate for these bonds is 8%, which implies a selling price of 117¼. The effective interest method is used to allocate interest expense.

1. What are the issuer's cash proceeds from issuance of these bonds?

2. What total amount of bond interest expense will be recognized over the life of these bonds?

3. What amount of bond interest expense is recorded on the first interest payment date?

QS 14-3
Journalize bond issuance   P1

Prepare the journal entry for the issuance of the bonds in both QS 14-1 and QS 14-2. Assume that both bonds are issued for cash on January 1, 2008.

QS 14-4
Computing bond price   P2 P3

Using the bond details in both QS 14-1 and QS 14-2, confirm that the bonds' selling prices given in each problem are approximately correct. Use the present value tables B.1 and B.3 in Appendix B.

QS 14-5
Bond retirement by call option

P4

On July 1, 2008, Advocate Company exercises an $8,000 call option (plus par value) on its outstanding bonds that have a carrying value of $416,000 and par value of $400,000. The company exercises the call option after the semiannual interest is paid on June 30, 2008. Record the entry to retire the bonds.

QS 14-6
Bond retirement by stock
conversion   P4

On January 1, 2008, the $2,000,000 par value bonds of Spitz Company with a carrying value of $2,000,000 are converted to 1,000,000 shares of $1.00 par value common stock. Record the entry for the conversion of the bonds.

QS 14-7
Computing payments for
an installment note   C1

Murray Company borrows $340,000 cash from a bank and in return signs an installment note for five annual payments of equal amount, with the first payment due one year after the note is signed. Use Table B.3 in Appendix B to compute the amount of the annual payment for each of the following annual market rates: (a) 4%, (b) 8%, and (c) 12%.

QS 14-8
Bond features and terminology

A2

Enter the letter of the description A through H that best fits each term or phrase 1 through 8.

A. Records and tracks the bondholders' names.

B. Is unsecured; backed only by the issuer's credit standing.

C. Has varying maturity dates for amounts owed.

D. Identifies rights and responsibilities of the issuer and the bondholders.

E. Can be exchanged for shares of the issuer's stock.

F. Is unregistered; interest is paid to whoever possesses them.

G. Maintains a separate asset account from which bondholders are paid at maturity.

H. Pledges specific assets of the issuer as collateral.

1. _____ Registered bond   **5.** _____ Convertible bond

2. _____ Serial bond   **6.** _____ Bond indenture

3. _____ Secured bond   **7.** _____ Sinking fund bond

4. _____ Bearer bond   **8.** _____ Debenture

Compute the debt-to-equity ratio for each of the following companies. Which company appears to have a riskier financing structure? Explain.

QS 14-9
Debt-to-equity ratio

A2

	Atlanta Company	Spokane Company
Total liabilities	$429,000	$ 548,000
Total equity	572,000	1,827,000

Madrid Company plans to issue 8% bonds on January 1, 2008, with a par value of $4,000,000. The company sells $3,600,000 of the bonds on January 1, 2008. The remaining $400,000 sells at par on March 1, 2008. The bonds pay interest semiannually as of June 30 and December 31. Record the entry for the March 1 cash sale of bonds.

QS 14-10^C
Issuing bonds between interest dates

P1

Jin Li, an employee of ETrain.com, leases a car at O'Hare airport for a three-day business trip. The rental cost is $250. Prepare the entry by ETrain.com to record Jin Li's short-term car lease cost.

QS 14-11^D
Recording operating leases   C4

Algoma, Inc., signs a five-year lease for office equipment with Office Solutions. The present value of the lease payments is $15,499. Prepare the journal entry that Algoma records at the inception of this capital lease.

QS 14-12^D
Recording capital leases   C4

Round dollar amounts to the nearest whole dollar. Assume no reversing entries are used.

EXERCISES

On January 1, 2008, Boston Enterprises issues bonds that have a $3,400,000 par value, mature in 20 years, and pay 9% interest semiannually on June 30 and December 31. The bonds are sold at par.

1. How much interest will Boston pay (in cash) to the bondholders every six months?

2. Prepare journal entries to record (*a*) the issuance of bonds on January 1, 2008; (*b*) the first interest payment on June 30, 2008; and (*c*) the second interest payment on December 31, 2008.

3. Prepare the journal entry for issuance assuming the bonds are issued at (*a*) 98 and (*b*) 102.

Exercise 14-1
Recording bond issuance and interest

P1

Tano issues bonds with a par value of $180,000 on January 1, 2008. The bonds' annual contract rate is 8%, and interest is paid semiannually on June 30 and December 31. The bonds mature in three years. The annual market rate at the date of issuance is 10%, and the bonds are sold for $170,862.

1. What is the amount of the discount on these bonds at issuance?

2. How much total bond interest expense will be recognized over the life of these bonds?

3. Prepare an amortization table like the one in Exhibit 14.7 for these bonds; use the straight-line method to amortize the discount.

Exercise 14-2
Straight-line amortization of bond discount

P2

Stanford issues bonds dated January 1, 2008, with a par value of $500,000. The bonds' annual contract rate is 9%, and interest is paid semiannually on June 30 and December 31. The bonds mature in three years. The annual market rate at the date of issuance is 12%, and the bonds are sold for $463,140.

1. What is the amount of the discount on these bonds at issuance?

2. How much total bond interest expense will be recognized over the life of these bonds?

3. Prepare an amortization table like the one in Exhibit 14B.1 for these bonds; use the effective interest method to amortize the discount.

Exercise 14-3^B
Effective interest amortization of bond discount

P2

Quatro Co. issues bonds dated January 1, 2008, with a par value of $400,000. The bonds' annual contract rate is 13%, and interest is paid semiannually on June 30 and December 31. The bonds mature in three years. The annual market rate at the date of issuance is 12%, and the bonds are sold for $409,850.

1. What is the amount of the premium on these bonds at issuance?

2. How much total bond interest expense will be recognized over the life of these bonds?

3. Prepare an amortization table like the one in Exhibit 14.11 for these bonds; use the straight-line method to amortize the premium.

Exercise 14-4
Straight-line amortization of bond premium

P3

Exercise 14-5ᴮ
Effective interest amortization of bond premium P3

Refer to the bond details in Exercise 14-4 and prepare an amortization table like the one in Exhibit 14B.2 for these bonds using the effective interest method to amortize the premium.

Exercise 14-6
Computing bond interest and price; recording bond issuance

P2

Brigham Company issues bonds with a par value of $800,000 on their stated issue date. The bonds mature in 10 years and pay 6% annual interest in semiannual payments. On the issue date, the annual market rate for the bonds is 8%.

1. What is the amount of each semiannual interest payment for these bonds?

2. How many semiannual interest payments will be made on these bonds over their life?

3. Use the interest rates given to determine whether the bonds are issued at par, at a discount, or at a premium.

Check (4) $691,287

4. Compute the price of the bonds as of their issue date.

5. Prepare the journal entry to record the bonds' issuance.

Exercise 14-7
Computing bond interest and price; recording bond issuance

P3

Citywide Company issues bonds with a par value of $150,000 on their stated issue date. The bonds mature in five years and pay 10% annual interest in semiannual payments. On the issue date, the annual market rate for the bonds is 8%.

1. What is the amount of each semiannual interest payment for these bonds?

2. How many semiannual interest payments will be made on these bonds over their life?

3. Use the interest rates given to determine whether the bonds are issued at par, at a discount, or at a premium.

Check (4) $162,172

4. Compute the price of the bonds as of their issue date.

5. Prepare the journal entry to record the bonds' issuance.

Exercise 14-8
Bond computations, straight-line amortization, and bond retirement

P2 P4

On January 1, 2007, Shay issues $700,000 of 10%, 15-year bonds at a price of 97¾. Six years later, on January 1, 2013, Shay retires 20% of these bonds by buying them on the open market at 104½. All interest is accounted for and paid through December 31, 2012, the day before the purchase. The straight-line method is used to amortize any bond discount.

1. How much does the company receive when it issues the bonds on January 1, 2007?

2. What is the amount of the discount on the bonds at January 1, 2007?

3. How much amortization of the discount is recorded on the bonds for the entire period from January 1, 2007, through December 31, 2012?

4. What is the carrying (book) value of the bonds as of the close of business on December 31, 2012? What is the carrying value of the 20% soon-to-be-retired bonds on this same date?

5. How much did the company pay on January 1, 2013, to purchase the bonds that it retired?

Check (6) $8,190 loss

6. What is the amount of the recorded gain or loss from retiring the bonds?

7. Prepare the journal entry to record the bond retirement at January 1, 2013.

Exercise 14-9ᶜ
Recording bond issuance with accrued interest

C4 P1

On May 1, 2008, Brussels Enterprises issues bonds dated January 1, 2008, that have a $3,400,000 par value, mature in 20 years, and pay 9% interest semiannually on June 30 and December 31. The bonds are sold at par plus four months' accrued interest.

1. How much accrued interest do the bond purchasers pay Brussels on May 1, 2008?

Check (1) $102,000

2. Prepare Brussels' journal entries to record (*a*) the issuance of bonds on May 1, 2008; (*b*) the first interest payment on June 30, 2008; and (*c*) the second interest payment on December 31, 2008.

Exercise 14-10
Straight-line amortization and accrued bond interest expense

P1 P2

Duval Co. issues four-year bonds with a $100,000 par value on June 1, 2007, at a price of $95,948. The annual contract rate is 7%, and interest is paid semiannually on November 30 and May 31.

1. Prepare an amortization table like the one in Exhibit 14.7 for these bonds. Use the straight-line method of interest amortization.

2. Prepare journal entries to record the first two interest payments and to accrue interest as of December 31, 2007.

On January 1, 2008, Eagle borrows $100,000 cash by signing a four-year, 7% installment note. The note requires four equal total payments of accrued interest and principal on December 31 of each year from 2008 through 2011.

1. Compute the amount of each of the four equal total payments.

2. Prepare an amortization table for this installment note like the one in Exhibit 14.14.

Exercise 14-11
Installment note with equal total payments   C1 P5
Check (1) $29,523

Use the information in Exercise 14-11 to prepare the journal entries for Eagle to record the loan on January 1, 2008, and the four payments from December 31, 2008, through December 31, 2011.

Exercise 14-12
Installment note entries   P5

Montclair Company is considering a project that will require a $500,000 loan. It presently has total liabilities of $220,000, and total assets of $610,000.

1. Compute Montclair's (a) present debt-to-equity ratio and (b) the debt-to-equity ratio assuming it borrows $500,000 to fund the project.

2. Evaluate and discuss the level of risk involved if Montclair borrows the funds to pursue the project.

Exercise 14-13
Applying debt-to-equity ratio
A3

Indicate whether the company in each separate case 1 through 3 has entered into an operating lease or a capital lease.

1. The lessor retains title to the asset, and the lease term is three years on an asset that has a five-year useful life.

2. The title is transferred to the lessee, the lessee can purchase the asset for $1 at the end of the lease, and the lease term is five years. The leased asset has an expected useful life of six years.

3. The present value of the lease payments is 95% of the leased asset's market value, and the lease term is 70% of the leased asset's useful life.

Exercise 14-14^D
Identifying capital and operating leases
C4

Harbor (lessee) signs a five-year capital lease for office equipment with a $10,000 annual lease payment. The present value of the five annual lease payments is $41,000, based on a 7% interest rate.

1. Prepare the journal entry Harbor will record at inception of the lease.

2. If the leased asset has a 5-year useful life with no salvage value, prepare the journal entry Harbor will record each year to recognize depreciation expense related to the leased asset.

Exercise 14-15^D
Accounting for capital lease
C4

General Motors advertised three alternatives for a 25-month lease on a new Blazer: (1) zero dollars down and a lease payment of $1,750 per month for 25 months, (2) $5,000 down and $1,500 per month for 25 months, or (3) $38,500 down and no payments for 25 months. Use the present value Table B.3 in Appendix B to determine which is the best alternative (assume you have enough cash to accept any alternative and the annual interest rate is 12% compounded monthly).

Exercise 14-16^D
Analyzing lease options
C2 C3 C4

Round dollar amounts to the nearest whole dollar. Assume no reversing entries are used.

Hartford Research issues bonds dated January 1, 2008, that pay interest semiannually on June 30 and December 31. The bonds have a $40,000 par value, an annual contract rate of 10%, and mature in 10 years.

Required

For each of the following three separate situations, (a) determine the bonds' issue price on January 1, 2008, and (b) prepare the journal entry to record their issuance.

1. Market rate at the date of issuance is 8%.

2. Market rate at the date of issuance is 10%.

3. Market rate at the date of issuance is 12%.

PROBLEM SET A

Problem 14-1A
Computing bond price and recording issuance
P1 P2 P3

Check (1) Premium, $4,537

(3) Discount, $4,588

Problem 14-2A
Straight-line amortization of bond discount and bond premium

P1 P2 P3

mhhe.com/wildFAP18e

Check (3) $4,143,552

(4) 12/31/2008 carrying value, $3,528,920

Hillside issues $4,000,000 of 6%, 15-year bonds dated January 1, 2007, that pay interest semiannually on June 30 and December 31. The bonds are issued at a price of $3,456,448.

Required

1. Prepare the January 1, 2007, journal entry to record the bonds' issuance.
2. For each semiannual period, compute (*a*) the cash payment, (*b*) the straight-line discount amortization, and (*c*) the bond interest expense.
3. Determine the total bond interest expense to be recognized over the bonds' life.
4. Prepare the first two years of an amortization table like Exhibit 14.7 using the straight-line method.
5. Prepare the journal entries to record the first two interest payments.
6. Assume that the bonds are issued at a price of $4,895,980. Repeat parts 1 through 5.

Problem 14-3A
Straight-line amortization of bond premium; computing bond price

P1 P3

mhhe.com/wildFAP18e

Check (2) 6/30/2009 carrying value, $252,668

Ellis issues 6.5%, five-year bonds dated January 1, 2007, with a $250,000 par value. The bonds pay interest on June 30 and December 31 and are issued at a price of $255,333. The annual market rate is 6% on the issue date.

Required

1. Calculate the total bond interest expense over the bonds' life.
2. Prepare a straight-line amortization table like Exhibit 14.11 for the bonds' life.
3. Prepare the journal entries to record the first two interest payments.

Problem 14-4A[B]
Effective interest amortization of bond premium; computing bond price P1 P3

Check (2) 6/30/2009 carrying value, $252,865

(4) $252,326

Refer to the bond details in Problem 14-3A.

Required

1. Compute the total bond interest expense over the bonds' life.
2. Prepare an effective interest amortization table like the one in Exhibit 14B.2 for the bonds' life.
3. Prepare the journal entries to record the first two interest payments.
4. Use the market rate at issuance to compute the present value of the remaining cash flows for these bonds as of December 31, 2009. Compare your answer with the amount shown on the amortization table as the balance for that date (from part 2) and explain your findings.

Problem 14-5A
Straight-line amortization of bond discount

P1 P2

Check (2) $97,819

(3) 12/31/2008 carrying value, $308,589

Legacy issues $325,000 of 5%, four-year bonds dated January 1, 2007, that pay interest semiannually on June 30 and December 31. They are issued at $292,181 and their market rate is 8% at the issue date.

Required

1. Prepare the January 1, 2007, journal entry to record the bonds' issuance.
2. Determine the total bond interest expense to be recognized over the bonds' life.
3. Prepare a straight-line amortization table like the one in Exhibit 14.7 for the bonds' first two years.
4. Prepare the journal entries to record the first two interest payments.

Analysis Component

5. Assume the market rate on January 1, 2007, is 4% instead of 8%. Without providing numbers, describe how this change affects the amounts reported on Legacy's financial statements.

Problem 14-6A[B]
Effective interest amortization of bond discount P1 P2

Check (2) $97,819

(3) 12/31/2008 carrying value, $307,308

mhhe.com/wildFAP18e

Refer to the bond details in Problem 14-5A.

Required

1. Prepare the January 1, 2007, journal entry to record the bonds' issuance.
2. Determine the total bond interest expense to be recognized over the bonds' life.
3. Prepare an effective interest amortization table like the one in Exhibit 14B.1 for the bonds' first two years.
4. Prepare the journal entries to record the first two interest payments.

Ike issues $180,000 of 11%, three-year bonds dated January 1, 2007, that pay interest semiannually on June 30 and December 31. They are issued at $184,566. Their market rate is 10% at the issue date.

Required

1. Prepare the January 1, 2007, journal entry to record the bonds' issuance.
2. Determine the total bond interest expense to be recognized over the bonds' life.
3. Prepare an effective interest amortization table like Exhibit 14B.2 for the bonds' first two years.
4. Prepare the journal entries to record the first two interest payments.
5. Prepare the journal entry to record the bonds' retirement on January 1, 2009, at 98.

Analysis Component

6. Assume that the market rate on January 1, 2007, is 12% instead of 10%. Without presenting numbers, describe how this change affects amounts reported on Ike's financial statements.

Problem 14-7A[B]

Effective interest amortization of bond premium; retiring bonds

P1 P3 P4

Check (3) 6/30/2008 carrying value, $182,448

(5) $5,270 gain

mhhe.com/wildFAP18e

On November 1, 2007, Norwood borrows $200,000 cash from a bank by signing a five-year installment note bearing 8% interest. The note requires equal total payments each year on October 31.

Required

1. Compute the total amount of each installment payment.
2. Complete an amortization table for this installment note similar to the one in Exhibit 14.14.
3. Prepare the journal entries in which Norwood (*a*) records accrued interest as of December 31, 2007 (the end of its annual reporting period), and (*b*) the first annual payment on the note.

Problem 14-8A

Installment notes

C1 P5

Check (2) 10/31/2011 ending balance, $46,382

At the end of the current year, the following information is available for both the Pulaski Company and the Scott Company:

	Pulaski Company	Scott Company
Total assets	$900,000	$450,000
Total liabilities	360,000	240,000
Total equity	540,000	210,000

Required

1. Compute the debt-to-equity ratio for both companies.
2. Comment on your results and discuss the riskiness of each company's financing structure.

Problem 14-9A

Applying the debt-to-equity ratio

A3

Rogers Company signs a five-year capital lease with Packer Company for office equipment. The annual lease payment is $10,000, and the interest rate is 8%.

Required

1. Compute the present value of Rogers' five-year lease payments.
2. Prepare the journal entry to record Rogers' capital lease at its inception.
3. Complete a lease payment schedule for the five years of the lease with the following headings. Assume that the beginning balance of the lease liability (present value of lease payments) is $39,927. (*Hint:* To find the amount allocated to interest in year 1, multiply the interest rate by the beginning-of-year lease liability. The amount of the annual lease payment not allocated to interest is allocated to principal. Reduce the lease liability by the amount allocated to principal to update the lease liability at each year-end.)

Problem 14-10A[D]

Capital lease accounting

C4

Check (1) $39,927

(3) Year 3 ending balance, $17,833

Period Ending Date	Beginning Balance of Lease Liability	Interest on Lease Liability	Reduction of Lease Liability	Cash Lease Payment	Ending Balance of Lease Liability

4. Use straight-line depreciation and prepare the journal entry to depreciate the leased asset at the end of year 1. Assume zero salvage value and a five-year life for the office equipment.

PROBLEM SET B

Problem 14-1B
Computing bond price and recording issuance

P1 P2 P3

Check (1) Premium, $6,948

(3) Discount, $6,326

Flagstaff Systems issues bonds dated January 1, 2008, that pay interest semiannually on June 30 and December 31. The bonds have a $90,000 par value, an annual contract rate of 12%, and mature in five years.

Required

For each of the following three separate situations, (a) determine the bonds' issue price on January 1, 2008, and (b) prepare the journal entry to record their issuance.

1. Market rate at the date of issuance is 10%.

2. Market rate at the date of issuance is 12%.

3. Market rate at the date of issuance is 14%.

Problem 14-2B
Straight-line amortization of bond discount and bond premium

P1 P2 P3

Check (3) $3,790,000

(4) 6/30/2008 carrying value, $3,068,500

Romero issues $3,400,000 of 10%, 10-year bonds dated January 1, 2007, that pay interest semiannually on June 30 and December 31. The bonds are issued at a price of $3,010,000.

Required

1. Prepare the January 1, 2007, journal entry to record the bonds' issuance.

2. For each semiannual period, compute (a) the cash payment, (b) the straight-line discount amortization, and (c) the bond interest expense.

3. Determine the total bond interest expense to be recognized over the bonds' life.

4. Prepare the first two years of an amortization table like Exhibit 14.7 using the straight-line method.

5. Prepare the journal entries to record the first two interest payments.

6. Assume that the bonds are issued at a price of $4,192,932. Repeat parts 1 through 5.

Problem 14-3B
Straight-line amortization of bond premium; computing bond price

P1 P3

Check (2) 6/30/2009 carrying value, $326,493

Ripkin Company issues 9%, five-year bonds dated January 1, 2007, with a $320,000 par value. The bonds pay interest on June 30 and December 31 and are issued at a price of $332,988. Their annual market rate is 8% on the issue date.

Required

1. Calculate the total bond interest expense over the bonds' life.

2. Prepare a straight-line amortization table like Exhibit 14.11 for the bonds' life.

3. Prepare the journal entries to record the first two interest payments.

Problem 14-4B^B
Effective interest amortization of bond premium; computing bond price P1 P3

Check (2) 6/30/2009 carrying value, $327,136

(4) $325,807

Refer to the bond details in Problem 14-3B.

Required

1. Compute the total bond interest expense over the bonds' life.

2. Prepare an effective interest amortization table like the one in Exhibit 14B.2 for the bonds' life.

3. Prepare the journal entries to record the first two interest payments.

4. Use the market rate at issuance to compute the present value of the remaining cash flows for these bonds as of December 31, 2009. Compare your answer with the amount shown on the amortization table as the balance for that date (from part 2) and explain your findings.

Problem 14-5B
Straight-line amortization of bond discount

P1 P2

Check (2) $257,506

(3) 6/30/2008 carrying value, $202,646

Gomez issues $240,000 of 6%, 15-year bonds dated January 1, 2007, that pay interest semiannually on June 30 and December 31. They are issued at $198,494, and their market rate is 8% at the issue date.

Required

1. Prepare the January 1, 2007, journal entry to record the bonds' issuance.

2. Determine the total bond interest expense to be recognized over the life of the bonds.

3. Prepare a straight-line amortization table like the one in Exhibit 14.7 for the bonds' first two years.

4. Prepare the journal entries to record the first two interest payments.

Refer to the bond details in Problem 14-5B.

Required

1. Prepare the January 1, 2007, journal entry to record the bonds' issuance.
2. Determine the total bond interest expense to be recognized over the bonds' life.
3. Prepare an effective interest amortization table like the one in Exhibit 14B.1 for the bonds' first two years.
4. Prepare the journal entries to record the first two interest payments.

Problem 14-6B^B

Effective interest amortization of bond discount

P1 P2

Check   (2) $257,506;
(3) 6/30/2008 carrying value, $200,803

Valdez issues $450,000 of 13%, four-year bonds dated January 1, 2007, that pay interest semiannually on June 30 and December 31. They are issued at $493,608, and their market rate is 10% at the issue date.

Required

1. Prepare the January 1, 2007, journal entry to record the bonds' issuance.
2. Determine the total bond interest expense to be recognized over the bonds' life.
3. Prepare an effective interest amortization table like the one in Exhibit 14B.2 for the bonds' first two years.
4. Prepare the journal entries to record the first two interest payments.
5. Prepare the journal entry to record the bonds' retirement on January 1, 2009, at 106.

Analysis Component

6. Assume that the market rate on January 1, 2007, is 14% instead of 10%. Without presenting numbers, describe how this change affects amounts reported on Valdez's financial statements.

Problem 14-7B^B

Effective interest amortization of bond premium; retiring bonds

P1 P3 P4

Check   (3) 6/30/2008 carrying value, $479,202

(5) $3,088 loss

On October 1, 2007, Gordon Enterprises borrows $150,000 cash from a bank by signing a three-year installment note bearing 10% interest. The note requires equal total payments each year on September 30.

Required

1. Compute the total amount of each installment payment.
2. Complete an amortization table for this installment note similar to the one in Exhibit 14.14.
3. Prepare the journal entries in which Gordon records (*a*) accrued interest as of December 31, 2007 (the end of its annual reporting period) and (*b*) the first annual payment on the note.

Problem 14-8B

Installment notes

C1 P5

Check   (2) 9/30/2009 ending balance, $54,836

At the end of the current year, the following information is available for both Atlas Company and Bryan Company.

	Atlas Company	Bryan Company
Total assets	$180,000	$750,000
Total liabilities	81,000	562,500
Total equity	99,000	187,500

Problem 14-9B

Applying the debt-to-equity ratio

A3

Required

1. Compute the debt-to-equity ratio for both companies.
2. Comment on your results and discuss what they imply about the relative riskiness of these companies.

Braun Company signs a five-year capital lease with Verdi Company for office equipment. The annual lease payment is $20,000, and the interest rate is 10%.

Required

1. Compute the present value of Braun's lease payments.
2. Prepare the journal entry to record Braun's capital lease at its inception.

Problem 14-10B^D

Capital lease accounting

C4

Check   (1) $75,816

(3) Year 3 ending balance, $34,712

3. Complete a lease payment schedule for the five years of the lease with the following headings. Assume that the beginning balance of the lease liability (present value of lease payments) is $75,816. (*Hint:* To find the amount allocated to interest in year 1, multiply the interest rate by the beginning-of-year lease liability. The amount of the annual lease payment not allocated to interest is allocated to principal. Reduce the lease liability by the amount allocated to principal to update the lease liability at each year-end.)

Period Ending Date	Beginning Balance of Lease Liability	Interest on Lease Liability	Reduction of Lease Liability	Cash Lease Payment	Ending Balance of Lease Liability

4. Use straight-line depreciation and prepare the journal entry to depreciate the leased asset at the end of year 1. Assume zero salvage value and a five-year life for the office equipment.

PROBLEM SET C

Problem Set C is available at the book's Website to further reinforce and assess your learning.

SERIAL PROBLEM

Success Systems

(This serial problem began in Chapter 1 and continues through most of the book. If previous chapter segments were not completed, the serial problem can begin at this point. It is helpful, but not necessary, for you to use the Working Papers that accompany the book.)

SP 14   Adriana Lopez has consulted with her local banker and is considering financing an expansion of her business by obtaining a long-term bank loan. Selected account balances at March 31, 2008, for Success Systems follow.

Total assets	$147,529	Total liabilities	$1,050	Total equity	$146,479

Required

1. The bank has offered a long-term secured note to Success Systems. The bank's loan procedures require that a client's debt-to-equity ratio not exceed 0.8. As of March 31, 2008, what is the maximum amount that Success Systems could borrow from this bank (rounded to nearest dollar)?

2. If Success Systems borrows the maximum amount allowed from the bank, what percentage of assets would be financed (*a*) by debt, and (*b*) by equity?

3. What are some factors Lopez should consider before borrowing the funds?

BEYOND THE NUMBERS

REPORTING IN ACTION

A1 A2

BTN 14-1   Refer to **Best Buy**'s financial statements in Appendix A to answer the following.

1. Identify the items that make up Best Buy's long-term debt at February 26, 2005? (Hint: See note 4.)

2. How much annual cash interest must Best Buy pay on the 2.25% convertible subordinated debt?

3. Did it have any additions to long-term debt that provided cash for the year-end February 26, 2005?

Fast Forward

4. Access Best Buy's financial statements for the years ending after February 26, 2005, from its Website (BestBuy.com) or the SEC's EDGAR database (www.sec.gov). Has it issued additional long-term debt since the year-end February 26, 2005? If yes, indentify the amount(s).

BTN 14-2 Key comparative figures ($ millions) for both **Best Buy** and **Circuit City** follow.

| Key Figures | Best Buy | | Circuit City | |
	Current Year	Prior Year	Current Year	Prior Year
Total Assets	$10,294	$8,652	$3,789	$3,731
Total Liabilities	5,845	5,230	1,702	1,507
Total Equity	4,449	3,422	2,087	2,224

Required

1. Compute the debt-to-equity ratio for Best Buy and Circuit City for both the current year and the prior year.

2. Use the ratio you computed in part 1 to determine which company's financing structure is less risky. Assume an industry average of 1.1 for debt-to-equity.

BTN 14-3 Brevard County needs a new county government building that would cost $24 million. The politicians feel that voters will not approve a municipal bond issue to fund the building since it would increase taxes. They opt to have a state bank issue $24 million of tax-exempt securities to pay for the building construction. The county then will make yearly lease payments (of principal and interest) to repay the obligation. Unlike conventional municipal bonds, the lease payments are not binding obligations on the county and, therefore, require no voter approval.

Required

1. Do you think the actions of the politicians and the bankers in this situation are ethical?

2. How do the tax-exempt securities used to pay for the building compare in risk to a conventional municipal bond issued by Brevard County?

BTN 14-4 Your business associate mentions that she is considering investing in corporate bonds currently selling at a premium. She says that since the bonds are selling at a premium, they are highly valued and her investment will yield more than the going rate of return for the risk involved. Reply with a memorandum to confirm or correct your associate's interpretation of premium bonds.

BTN 14-5 Access the April 11, 2005, filing of the 10-K report of **Home Depot** for the year ended January 30, 2005, from www.sec.gov (Ticker: HD). Refer to Home Depot's balance sheet, including its Note 2 (on long-term debt).

Required

1. Identify Home Depot's long-term liabilities and the amounts for those liabilities from Home Depot's balance sheet at January 30, 2005.

2. Review Home Depot's Note 2. The note reports that it "issued $1.0 billion of 3¾% senior notes due September 15, 2009, at a discount of $5 million with interest payable semiannually on March 15 and September 15 each year."

  a. Why would Home Depot issue $1 billion of its notes for only $995 million?

  b. How much cash interest must Home Depot pay each March 15 and September 15 on these notes?

BTN 14-6ᴮ Break into teams and complete the following requirements related to effective interest amortization for a premium bond.

1. Each team member is to independently prepare a blank table with proper headings for amortization of a bond premium. When all have finished, compare tables and ensure all are in agreement.

Parts 2 and 3 require use of these facts: On January 1, 2008, BC issues $100,000, 9%, five-year bonds at 104.1. The market rate at issuance is 8%. BC pays interest semiannually on June 30 and December 31.

2. In rotation, *each* team member must explain how to complete *one* line of the bond amortization table, including all computations for his or her line. (Round amounts to the nearest dollar.) All members are to fill in their tables during this process. You need not finish the table; stop after all members have explained a line.

3. In rotation, *each* team member is to identify a separate column of the table and indicate what the final number in that column will be and explain the reasoning.

Hint: Rotate teams to report on parts 4 and 5. Consider requiring entries for issuance and interest payments.

4. Reach a team consensus as to what the total bond interest expense on this bond issue will be if the bond is not retired before maturity.

5. As a team, prepare a list of similarities and differences between the amortization table just prepared and the amortization table if the bond had been issued at a discount.

BusinessWeek ACTIVITY

A2

BTN 14-7   Read the article "A Growing Tide of Risky Mortgages" in the May 18, 2005, issue of *BusinessWeek*. (The book's Website provides a free link.)

Required

1. What is an interest-only mortgage? How is this different from a conventional mortgage? Why would a borrower seek an interest-only mortgage?

2. Refer to the article's example of a conventional $400,000 mortgage with a fixed rate of 4.875% for the first five years yielding monthly payments of $2,120. Determine the monthly payment if this loan were an interest-only loan. What would be the loan balance after the second payment?

3. What would be the loan balance after the second payment if the loan were a conventional mortgage?

4. What are the risks involved in interest-only mortgages?

ENTREPRENEURIAL DECISION

A1

BTN 14-8   Mark and Holly Melton are entrepreneurs and owners of **Melton Franchise Systems.** Assume that Meltons' franchise program currently has $250,000 in equity; and they are considering a $100,000 expansion to meet increased demand. The $100,000 expansion would yield $16,000 in additional annual income before interest expense. Assume that Meltons' franchise program currently earns $40,000 annual income before interest expense of $10,000, yielding a return on equity of 12% ($30,000/$250,000). To fund the expansion, the Meltons are considering the issuance of a 10-year, $100,000 note with annual interest payments (the principal due at the end of 10 years).

Required

1. Using return on equity as the decision criterion, show computations to support or reject Meltons' expansion if interest on the $100,000 note is (*a*) 10%, (*b*) 15%, (*c*) 16%, (*d*) 17%, and (*e*) 20%.

2. What general rule do the results in part 1 illustrate?

HITTING THE ROAD

A1

BTN 14-9   Visit your city or county library. Ask the librarian to help you locate the recent financial records of your city or county government. Examine the records.

Required

1. Determine the amount of long-term bonds and notes currently outstanding.

2. Read the supporting information to your municipality's financial statements and record:
   a. Market interest rate(s) when the bonds and/or notes were issued.
   b. Date(s) when the bonds and/or notes will mature.
   c. Any rating(s) on the bonds and/or notes received from **Moody's, Standard & Poor's,** or another rating agency.

BTN 14-10 Dixons (Dixons-Group.com), Best Buy, and Circuit City are competitors in the global marketplace. Selected results from these companies follow.

Key Figures	Dixons (£ millions)		Best Buy ($ millions)		Circuit City ($ millions)	
	Current Year	Prior Year	Current Year	Prior Year	Current Year	Prior Year
Total assets	£3,874	£4,158	$10,294	$8,652	$3,789	$3,731
Total liabilities	2,406	2,782	5,845	5,230	1,702	1,507
Total equity	1,468	1,376	4,449	3,422	2,087	2,224
Debt-to-equity ratio	?	?	1.3	1.5	0.8	0.7

Required

1. Compute Dixons' debt-to-equity ratio for the current year and the prior year.

2. Use the data provided and the ratios you computed in part 1 to determine which company's financing structure is least risky.

ANSWERS TO MULTIPLE CHOICE QUIZ

1. b

2. a

3. c; $500,000 × 0.08 × ½ year = $20,000

4. a; Cash interest paid = $100,000 × 5% × ½ year = $2,500

   Discount amortization = ($100,000 − $95,735)/10 periods = $426.50

   Interest expense = $2,500.00 + $426.50 = $2,926.50

5. e; ($373,745 − $350,000)/16 periods = $1,484

15

Investments and International Operations

A Look Back

Chapter 14 focused on long-term liabilities—a main part of most companies' financing. We explained how to value, record, amortize, and report these liabilities in financial statements.

A Look at This Chapter

This chapter focuses on investments in securities. We explain how to identify, account for, and report investments in both debt and equity securities. We also explain accounting for transactions listed in a foreign currency.

A Look Ahead

Chapter 16 focuses on reporting and analyzing a company's cash flows. Special emphasis is directed at the statement of cash flows—reported under the indirect method.

Learning Objectives

CAP

Conceptual

C1 Distinguish between debt and equity securities and between short-term and long-term investments. *(p. 586)*

C2 Identify and describe the different classes of investments in securities. *(p. 587)*

C3 Describe how to report equity securities with controlling influence. *(p. 593)*

C4 *Appendix 15A*—Explain foreign exchange rates between currencies. *(p. 599)*

Analytical

A1 Compute and analyze the components of return on total assets. *(p. 594)*

Procedural

P1 Account for trading securities. *(p. 589)*

P2 Account for held-to-maturity securities. *(p. 590)*

P3 Account for available-for-sale securities. *(p. 590)*

P4 Account for equity securities with significant influence. *(p. 591)*

P5 *Appendix 15A*—Record transactions listed in a foreign currency. *(p. 600)*

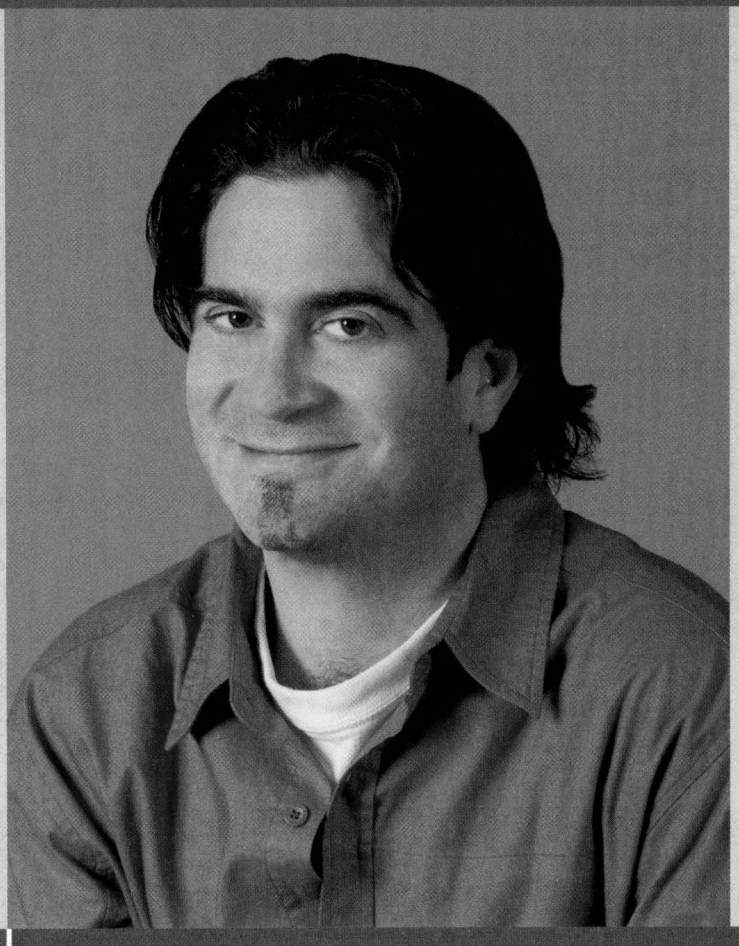

Manga-nificent Entertainment

LOS ANGELES, CA—"I fell in love with the combination of old and new, East and West—sort of a neo-Buddhist modernism—that hooked me the most," says Stu Levy, founder of **TOKYOPOP** (**Tokyopop.com**). The object of Stu's desire is manga (pronounced MAHN-gah), a form of graphic entertainment native to Japan. TOKYOPOP is a leading multimedia company that specializes in publishing manga in English. Manga is described as the Japanese counterpart to comic books, though quicker to read and with a wider range of genres, characters, and layouts.

"The art [of manga] really resonates with this generation of young people, teenagers, and children," explains Stu. "We are putting a lot of time and energy into getting it out there into the hands of the potential audience. I love the ability to merge the visual medium with lyrical storytelling."

The art of running a company that publishes manga involves the business of acquiring and developing material. Stu likens himself to a producer. As he puts it, "A producer gets the team together, handles the finances, but is also totally involved in the creative side. [Yet] acquisitions and development is probably my most enjoyable and largest job. I also handle our capital-raising activities," adds Stu.

TOKYOPOP's acquisition and development activities involve considerable investment in manga. This often means investing in the Japanese rights to material that the company then translates for its U.S. audience. Accordingly, Stu's job requires conducting international transactions and performing currency translations. These tasks demand that he know the accounting and reporting requirements for investments. This chapter focuses on how to account for investments, particularly those in the debt and equity securities of other companies.

"The publishing part of our business is kind of like a platform. . . we are a delivering mechanism," says Stu. "Most people who read manga. . . get hooked. It's addictive," he adds. Revenues should continue to look *manga-nificent* for years to come because the more people experience manga, the larger the market grows. "Our goal at TOKYOPOP is to deliver the most exciting entertainment possible and merging the best cultures in the world to do so," says Stu. "I dove into the Japanese culture and Asian culture. . . but I fell in love with manga."

[Sources: *TOKYOPOP Website,* January 2006, *Entrepreneur,* November 2004; *Japan Today,* February 2004; *License!,* May 2005; *Comic Book Resources,* February 2002; *FSB Magazine,* June 2004]

This chapter's main focus is investments in securities. Many companies have investments, and many of these are in the form of debt and equity securities issued by other companies. We describe investments in these securities and how to account for them. An increasing number of companies also invest in international operations. We explain how to account for and report international transactions listed in foreign currencies.

Investments and International Operations

Basics of Investments
- Motivation for investments
- Short-term versus long-term
- Classification and reporting
- Accounting basics

Noninfluential Investments
- Trading securities
- Held-to-maturity securities
- Available-for-sale securities

Influential Investments
- Securities with significant influence
- Securities with controlling influence
- Accounting summary

Basics of Investments

C1 Distinguish between debt and equity securities and between short-term and long-term investments.

Point: Reporting securities at market value is referred to as *mark-to-market* accounting.

Exhibit 15.1

Investments of Selected Companies

This section describes the motivation for investments, the distinction between short- and long-term investments, and the different classes of investments.

Motivation for Investments

Companies make investments for at least three reasons. First, companies transfer *excess cash* into investments to produce higher income. Second, some entities, such as mutual funds and pension funds, are set up to produce income from investments. Third, companies make investments for strategic reasons. Examples are investments in competitors, suppliers, and even customers.

Exhibit 15.1 shows short-term (S-T) and long-term (L-T) investments as a percent of total assets for several companies.

Short-Term versus Long-Term

Cash equivalents are investments that are both readily converted to known amounts of cash and mature within three months. Many investments, however, mature between 3 and 12 months. These investments are **short-term investments,** also called *temporary investments* and *marketable securities*. Specifically, short-term investments are securities that (1) management intends to convert to cash within one year or the operating cycle, whichever is longer, and (2) are readily convertible to cash. Short-term investments are reported under current assets and serve a purpose similar to cash equivalents.

Long-term investments in securities are defined as those securities that are not readily convertible to cash or are not intended to be converted into cash in the short term. Long-term investments can also include funds earmarked for a special purpose, such as bond sinking funds and investments in land or other assets not used in the company's operations. Long-term investments are reported in the noncurrent section of the balance sheet, often in its own separate line titled *Long-Term Investments*.

Investments in securities can include both debt and equity securities. *Debt securities* reflect a creditor relationship such as investments in notes, bonds, and certificates of deposit; they are

Topic Tackler
PLUS

issued by governments, companies, and individuals. *Equity securities* reflect an owner relationship such as shares of stock issued by companies.

Classification and Reporting

Accounting for investments in securities depends on three factors: (1) security type, either debt or equity, (2) the company's intent to hold the security either short term or long term, and (3) the company's (investor's) percent ownership in the other company's (investee's) equity securities. Exhibit 15.2 identifies five classes of securities using these three factors. It describes each of these five classes of securities and the reporting required under each class.

C2 Identify and describe the different classes of investments in securities.

Exhibit 15.2

Investments in Securities

^a Holding less than 20% of voting stock (equity securities only).   ^b Holding 20% or more, but not more than 50%, of voting stock.
^c Holding more than 50% of voting stock.
[*] Unrealized gains and losses reported on the income statement.
^{**} Unrealized gains and losses reported in the equity section of the balance sheet and in comprehensive income.

Accounting Basics for Debt Securities

This section explains the accounting basics for debt securities, including that for acquisition, disposition, and any interest.

Acquisition. Debt securities are recorded at cost when purchased. Assume that Music City paid $29,500 plus a $500 brokerage fee on September 1, 2008, to buy Dell's 7%, two-year bonds payable with a $30,000 par value. The bonds pay interest semiannually on August 31 and February 28. Music City intends to hold the bonds until they mature on August 31, 2010; consequently, they are classified as held-to-maturity (HTM) securities. The entry to record this purchase follows. (If the maturity of the securities was short term, and management's intent was to hold them until they mature, then they would be classified as Short-Term Investments—HTM.)

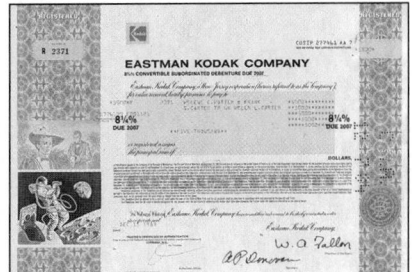

2008			
Sept. 1	Long-Term Investments—HTM (Dell)	30,000	
	Cash		30,000
	Purchased bonds to be held to maturity.		

Assets = Liabilities + Equity
+30,000
−30,000

Interest earned. Interest revenue for investments in debt securities is recorded when earned. On December 31, 2008, at the end of its accounting period, Music City accrues interest receivable as follows.

Dec. 31	Interest Receivable.	700	
	Interest Revenue.		700
	Accrued interest earned ($30,000 × 7% × ⅟₁₂).		

Assets = Liabilities + Equity
+700   +700

The $700 reflects 4/6 of the semiannual cash receipt of interest—the portion Music City earned as of December 31. Relevant sections of Music City's financial statements at December 31, 2008, are shown in Exhibit 15.3.

Exhibit 15.3

Financial Statement Presentation
of Debt Securities

On the income statement for year 2008:	
Interest revenue	$ 700
On the December 31, 2008, balance sheet:	
Long-term investments—Held-to-maturity securities (at amortized cost)	$30,000

On February 28, 2009, Music City records receipt of semiannual interest.

Assets = Liabilities + Equity
+1,050   +350
−700

Feb. 28	Cash	1,050	
	Interest Receivable		700
	Interest Revenue		350
	Received six months' interest on Dell bonds.		

Disposition. When the bonds mature, the proceeds (not including the interest entry) are recorded as:

Assets = Liabilities + Equity
+30,000
−30,000

2010			
Aug. 31	Cash	30,000	
	Long-Term Investments—HTM (Dell)		30,000
	Received cash from matured bonds.		

Example: What is cost per share?
Answer: Cost per share is the total cost of acquisition, including broker fees, divided by number of shares acquired.

The cost of a debt security can be either higher or lower than its maturity value. When the investment is long term, the difference between cost and maturity value is amortized over the remaining life of the security. We assume for ease of computations that the cost of a long-term debt security equals its maturity value.

Accounting Basics for <u>Equity Securities</u>

This section explains the accounting basics for equity securities, including that for acquisition, dividends, and disposition.

Acquisition. Equity securities are recorded at cost when acquired, including commissions or brokerage fees paid. Assume that Music City purchases 1,000 shares of Intex common stock at par value for $86,000 on October 10, 2008. It records this purchase of available-for-sale (AFS) securities as follows.

Assets = Liabilities + Equity
+86,000
−86,000

Oct. 10	Long-Term Investments—AFS (Intex)	86,000	
	Cash		86,000
	Purchased 1,000 shares of Intex.		

Dividend earned. Any cash dividends received are credited to Dividend Revenue and reported in the income statement. On November 2, Music City receives a $1,720 quarterly cash dividend on the Intex shares, which it records as:

Assets = Liabilities + Equity
+1,720   +1,720

Nov. 2	Cash	1,720	
	Dividend Revenue		1,720
	Received dividend of $1.72 per share.		

Disposition. When the securities are sold, sale proceeds are compared with the cost, and any gain or loss is recorded. On December 20, Music City sells 500 of the Intex shares for $45,000 cash and records this sale as:

Assets = Liabilities + Equity
+45,000   +2,000
−43,000

Dec. 20	Cash	45,000	
	Long-Term Investments—AFS (Intex)		43,000
	Gain on Sale of Long-Term Investments		2,000
	Sold 500 Intex shares ($86,000 × 500/1,000).		

Reporting of *Non*influential Investments

Companies must value and report most noninfluential investments at *fair market value,* or simply *market value.* The exact reporting requirements depend on whether the investments are classified as (1) trading, (2) held-to-maturity, or (3) available-for-sale.

P1 Account for trading securities.

Trading Securities

Trading securities are *debt and equity securities* that the company intends to actively manage and trade for profit. Frequent purchases and sales are expected and are made to earn profits on short-term price changes.

Point: Trading securities are *always* reported under current assets.

Valuing and reporting trading securities.   The entire portfolio of trading securities is reported at its market value; this requires a "market adjustment" from the cost of the portfolio. The term *portfolio* refers to a group of securities. Any **unrealized gain (or loss)** from a change in the market value of the portfolio of trading securities is reported on the income statement. Most users believe accounting reports are more useful when changes in market value for trading securities are reported in income.

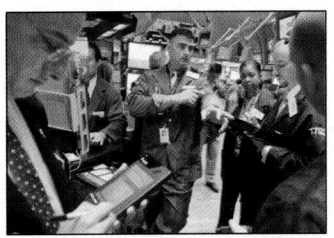

Point: The phrase *unrealized gain (or loss)* refers to a change in market value that is not yet realized through an actual sale.

To illustrate, TechCom's portfolio of trading securities had a total cost of $11,500 and a market value of $13,000 on December 31, 2008, the first year it held trading securities. The difference between the $11,500 cost and the $13,000 market value reflects a $1,500 gain. It is an unrealized gain because it is not yet confirmed by actual sales. The market adjustment for trading securities is recorded with an adjusting entry at the end of each period to equal the difference between the portfolio's cost and its market value. TechCom records this gain as follows.

Point: Market Adjustment—Trading is a *permanent account,* shown as a deduction or addition to Short-Term Investments—Trading.

Dec. 31	Market Adjustment—Trading.................	1,500	
	Unrealized Gain—Income................		1,500
	To reflect an unrealized gain in market values of trading securities.		

Assets = Liabilities + Equity
+1,500   +1,500

The Unrealized Gain (or Loss) is reported in the Other Revenues and Gains (or Expenses and Losses) section on the income statement. Unrealized Gain (or Loss)—Income is a *temporary* account that is closed to Income Summary at the end of each period. Market Adjustment—Trading is a *permanent* account, which adjusts the reported value of the trading securities portfolio from its prior period market value to the current period market value. The total cost of the trading securities portfolio is maintained in one account, and the market adjustment is recorded in a separate account. For example, TechCom's investment in trading securities is reported in the current assets section of its balance sheet as follows.

Example: If TechCom's trading securities have a cost of $14,800 and a market of $16,100 at Dec. 31, 2009, its adjusting entry is
Unrealized Loss—Income 200
  Market Adj.—Trading 200
This is computed as: $1,500 Beg. Dr. bal. + $200 Cr. = $1,300 End. Dr. bal.

Current Assets		
Short-term investments—Trading (at cost)	$11,500	
Market adjustment—Trading	1,500	
Short-term investments—Trading (at market)		$13,000
or simply		
Short-term investments—Trading (at market; cost is $11,500)		$13,000

Selling trading securities.   When individual trading securities are sold, the difference between the net proceeds (sale price less fees) and the cost of the individual trading securities that are sold is recognized as a gain or a loss. Any prior period market adjustment to the portfolio is *not* used to compute the gain or loss from sale of individual trading securities. For example, if TechCom sold some of its trading securities that had cost $1,000 for $1,200 cash on January 9, 2009, it would record the following.

Assets = Liabilities + Equity
+1,200   +200
−1,000

Jan. 9	Cash		1,200	
	Short-Term Investments—Trading			1,000
	Gain on Sale of Short-Term Investments			200
	Sold trading securities costing $1,000 for $1,200 cash.			

A gain is reported in the Other Revenues and Gains section on the income statement, whereas a loss is shown in Other Expenses and Losses. When the period-end market adjustment for the portfolio of trading securities is computed, it excludes the cost and market value of any securities sold.

Held-to-Maturity Securities

P2 Account for held-to-maturity securities.

Point: Only debt securities can be classified as *held-to-maturity*; equity securities have no maturity date.

Held-to-maturity (HTM) securities are *debt* securities a company intends and is able to hold until maturity. They are reported in current assets if their maturity dates are within one year or the operating cycle, whichever is longer. HTM securities are reported in long-term assets when the maturity dates extend beyond one year or the operating cycle, whichever is longer. All HTM securities are recorded at cost when purchased, and interest revenue is recorded when earned.

The portfolio of HTM securities is reported at (amortized) cost, which is explained in advanced courses. There is no market adjustment to the portfolio of HTM securities—neither to the short-term nor long-term portfolios. The basics of accounting for HTM securities were described earlier in this chapter.

Decision Maker   Answer—p. 602

Money Manager   You expect interest rates to sharply fall within a few weeks and remain at this lower rate. What is your strategy for holding investments in fixed-rate bonds and notes?

Available-for-Sale Securities

P3 Account for available-for-sale securities.

Available-for-sale (AFS) securities are *debt and equity securities* not classified as trading or held-to-maturity securities. AFS securities are purchased to yield interest, dividends, or increases in market value. They are not actively managed like trading securities. If the intent is to sell AFS securities within the longer of one year or operating cycle, they are classified as short-term investments. Otherwise, they are classified as long-term.

Valuing and reporting available-for-sale securities.   As with trading securities, companies adjust the cost of the portfolio of AFS securities to reflect changes in market value. This is done with a market adjustment to its total portfolio cost. However, any unrealized gain or loss for the portfolio of AFS securities is *not* reported on the income statement. Instead, it is reported in the equity section of the balance sheet (and is part of *comprehensive income,* explained later). To illustrate, assume that Music City had no prior period investments in available-for-sale securities other than those purchased in the current period. Exhibit 15.4 shows both the cost and market value of those investments on December 31, 2008, the end of its reporting period.

Example: If market value in Exhibit 15.4 is $70,000 (instead of $74,550), what entry is made? *Answer:*
Unreal. Loss—Equity . . . 3,000
  Market Adj.—AFS   3,000

Exhibit 15.4

Cost and Market Value of Available-for-Sale Securities

	Cost	Market Value	Unrealized Gain (Loss)
Improv bonds	$30,000	$29,050	$ (950)
Intex common stock, 500 shares	43,000	45,500	2,500
Total	$73,000	$74,550	$1,550

The year-end adjusting entry to record the market value of these investments follows.

Assets = Liabilities + Equity
+1,550   +1,550

Dec. 31	Market Adjustment—Available-for-Sale (LT)		1,550	
	Unrealized Gain—Equity			1,550
	To record adjustment to market value of available-for-sale securities.			

Point: Unrealized Loss—Equity and Unrealized Gain—Equity are *permanent* (balance sheet) *accounts* reported in the equity section.

Exhibit 15.5 shows the December 31, 2008, balance sheet presentation—it assumes these investments are long term, but they can also be short term. It is also common to combine the cost of investments with the balance in the Market Adjustment account and report the net as a single amount.

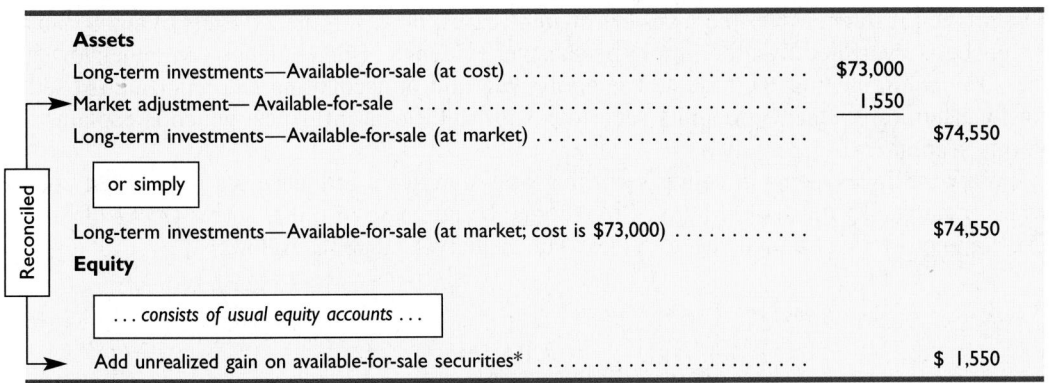

Exhibit 15.5

Balance Sheet Presentation of Available-for-Sale Securities

Assets	
Long-term investments—Available-for-sale (at cost)	$73,000
Market adjustment— Available-for-sale	1,550
Long-term investments—Available-for-sale (at market)	$74,550
or simply	
Long-term investments—Available-for-sale (at market; cost is $73,000)	$74,550
Equity	
. . . consists of usual equity accounts . . .	
Add unrealized gain on available-for-sale securities*	$ 1,550

Reconciled

* Often included under the caption Accumulated Other Comprehensive Income.

Let's extend this illustration and assume that at the end of its next calendar year (December 31, 2009), Music City's portfolio of long-term AFS securities has an $81,000 cost and an $82,000 market value. It records the adjustment to market value as follows.

Dec. 31	Unrealized Gain—Equity.	550	
	Market Adjustment—Available-for-Sale (LT).		550
	To record adjustment to market value of available-for-sale securities.		

Assets = Liabilities + Equity
−550   −550

The effects of the 2008 and 2009 securities transactions are reflected in the following T-accounts.

Market Adjustment—Available-for-Sale (LT)			
Bal. 12/31/08	1,550	Adj. 12/31/09	550
Bal. 12/31/09	1,000		

Unrealized Gain—Equity			
Adj. 12/31/09	550	Bal. 12/31/08	1,550
		Bal. 12/31/09	1,000

Amounts reconcile.

Selling available-for-sale securities.   Accounting for the sale of individual AFS securities is identical to that described for the sale of trading securities. When individual AFS securities are sold, the difference between the cost of the individual securities sold and the net proceeds (sale price less fees) is recognized as a gain or loss.

Quick Check   Answers—p. 602

1. How are short-term held-to-maturity securities reported (valued) on the balance sheet?

2. How are trading securities reported (valued) on the balance sheet?

3. Where are unrealized gains and losses on available-for-sale securities reported?

4. Where are unrealized gains and losses on trading securities reported?

Alert   The FASB released a 2006 Exposure Draft that would permit companies to use market value in reporting financial assets (referred to as the fair value option). This option would allow companies to report any financial asset at fair market value and recognize value changes in income. This method was previously reserved only for trading securities, but would now be an option for available-for-sale and held-to-maturity securities. It is unclear whether many companies will choose that option—stay tuned...

Reporting of Influential Investments

Investment in Securities with Significant Influence

A long-term investment classified as **equity securities with significant influence** implies that the investor can exert significant influence over the investee. An investor that owns 20% or more (but not more than 50%) of a company's voting stock is usually presumed to have

P4   Account for equity securities with significant influence.

a significant influence over the investee. In some cases, however, the 20% test of significant influence is overruled by other, more persuasive, evidence. This evidence can either lower the 20% requirement or increase it. The **equity method** of accounting and reporting is used for long-term investments in equity securities with significant influence, which is explained in this section.

Long-term investments in equity securities with significant influence are recorded at cost when acquired. To illustrate, Micron Co. records the purchase of 3,000 shares (30%) of Star Co. common stock at a total cost of $70,650 on January 1, 2008, as follows.

Assets = Liabilities + Equity
+70,650
−70,650

Jan. 1	Long-Term Investments—Star.................	70,650	
	Cash		70,650
	To record purchase of 3,000 Star shares.		

The investee's (Star) earnings increase both its net assets and the claim of the investor (Micron) on the investee's net assets. Thus, when the investee reports its earnings, the investor records its share of those earnings in its investment account. To illustrate, assume that Star reports net income of $20,000 for 2008. Micron then records its 30% share of those earnings as follows.

Assets = Liabilities + Equity
+6,000   +6,000

Dec. 31	Long-Term Investments—Star.................	6,000	
	Earnings from Long-Term Investment		6,000
	To record 30% equity in investee earnings.		

The debit reflects the increase in Micron's equity in Star. The credit reflects 30% of Star's net income. Earnings from Long-Term Investment is a *temporary* account (closed to Income Summary at each period-end) and is reported on the investor's (Micron's) income statement. If the investee incurs a net loss instead of a net income, the investor records its share of the loss and reduces (credits) its investment account. The investor closes this earnings or loss account to Income Summary.

The receipt of cash dividends is not revenue under the equity method because the investor has already recorded its share of the investee's earnings. Instead, cash dividends received by an investor from an investee are viewed as a conversion of one asset to another; that is, dividends reduce the balance of the investment account. To illustrate, Star declares and pays $10,000 in cash dividends on its common stock. Micron records its 30% share of these dividends received on January 9, 2009, as:

Assets = Liabilities + Equity
+3,000
−3,000

Jan. 9	Cash....................................	3,000	
	Long-Term Investments—Star..............		3,000
	To record share of dividend paid by Star.		

The book value of an investment under the equity method equals the cost of the investment plus (minus) the investor's equity in the *undistributed* (*distributed*) earnings of the investee. Once Micron records these transactions, its Long-Term Investments account appears as in Exhibit 15.6.

Exhibit 15.6

Investment in Star Common Stock (Ledger Account)

Date	Explanation	Debit	Credit	Balance
2008				
Jan. 1	Investment acquisition	70,650		70,650
Dec. 31	Share of earnings	6,000		76,650
2009				
Jan. 9	Share of dividend		3,000	73,650

Micron's account balance on January 9, 2009, for its investment in Star is $73,650. This is the investment's cost *plus* Micron's equity in Star's earnings since its purchase *less* Micron's equity in Star's cash dividends since its purchase. When an investment in equity securities is sold, the gain or loss is computed by comparing proceeds from the sale with the book value of the investment on the date of sale. If Micron sells its Star stock for $80,000 on January 10, 2009, it records the sale as:

Jan. 10	Cash	80,000	
	Long-Term Investments—Star		73,650
	Gain on Sale of Investment		6,350
	Sold 3,000 shares of stock for $80,000.		

Assets = Liabilities + Equity
+80,000 +6,350
−73,650

Investment in Securities with Controlling Influence

A long-term investment classified as **equity securities with controlling influence** implies that the investor can exert a controlling influence over the investee. An investor who owns more than 50% of a company's voting stock has control over the investee. This investor can dominate all other shareholders in electing the corporation's board of directors and has control over the investee's management. In some cases, controlling influence can extend to situations of less than 50% ownership. Exhibit 15.7 summarizes the accounting for investments in equity securities based on an investor's ownership in the stock.

Exhibit 15.7

Accounting for Equity Investments by Percent of Ownership

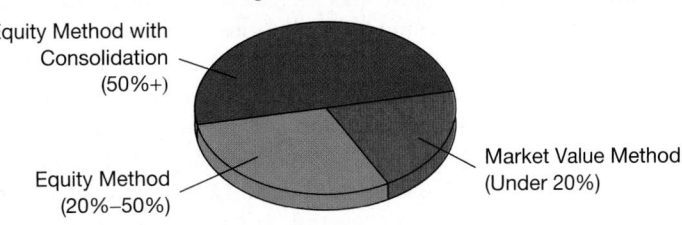

Equity Method with Consolidation (50%+)

Equity Method (20%–50%)

Market Value Method (Under 20%)

The *equity method with consolidation* is used to account for long-term investments in equity securities with controlling influence. The investor reports *consolidated financial statements* when owning such securities. The controlling investor is called the **parent,** and the investee is called the **subsidiary.** Many companies are parents with subsidiaries. Examples are (1) McGraw-Hill, the parent of *Business Week,* Standard & Poor's, and Compustat; (2) Gap, Inc., the parent of Gap, Old Navy, and Banana Republic; and (3) Brunswick, the parent of Mercury Marine, Sea Ray, and U.S. Marine. A company owning all the outstanding stock of a subsidiary can, if it desires, take over the subsidiary's assets, retire the subsidiary's stock, and merge the subsidiary into the parent. However, there often are financial, legal, and tax advantages if a business operates as a parent controlling one or more subsidiaries. When a company operates as a parent with subsidiaries, each entity maintains separate accounting records. From a legal viewpoint, the parent and each subsidiary are separate entities with all rights, duties, and responsibilities of individual companies.

Consolidated financial statements show the financial position, results of operations, and cash flows of all entities under the parent's control, including all subsidiaries. These statements are prepared as if the business were organized as one entity. The parent uses the equity method in its accounts, but the investment account is *not* reported on the parent's financial statements. Instead, the individual assets and liabilities of the parent and its subsidiaries are combined on one balance sheet. Their revenues and expenses also are combined on one income statement, and their cash flows are combined on one statement of cash flows. The procedures for preparing consolidated financial statements are in advanced courses.

Accounting Summary for Investments in Securities

Exhibit 15.8 summarizes the accounting for investments in securities. Recall that many investment securities are classified as either short term or long term depending on management's intent and ability to convert them in the future. Understanding the accounting for these investments enables us to draw better conclusions from financial statements in making business decisions.

Comprehensive Income The term **comprehensive income** refers to all changes in equity for a period except those due to investments and distributions to owners. This means that it includes (1) the revenues, gains, expenses, and losses reported in net income *and* (2) the gains and losses that bypass net income but affect equity. An example of an item that bypasses net income is unrealized gains and losses on available-for-sale securities. These items make up *other*

Exhibit 15.8

Accounting for Investments in Securities

Classification	Accounting
Short-Term Investment in Securities	
Held-to-maturity (debt) securities	**Cost** (without any discount or premium amortization)
Trading (debt and equity) securities	**Market value** (with market adjustment to income)
Available-for-sale (debt and equity) securities	**Market value** (with market adjustment to equity)
Long-Term Investment in Securities	
Held-to-maturity (debt) securities	**Cost** (with any discount or premium amortization)
Available-for-sale (debt and equity) securities	**Market value** (with market adjustment to equity)
Equity securities with significant influence	Equity method
Equity securities with controlling influence	Equity method (with consolidation)

Point: Many users believe that since AFS securities are not actively traded, reporting market value changes in income would unnecessarily increase income variability and decrease usefulness.

comprehensive income and are usually reported as a part of the statement of stockholders' equity. (Two other options are as a second separate income statement or as a combined income statement of comprehensive income; these less common options are described in advanced courses.) Most often this simply requires one additional column for Other Comprehensive Income in the usual columnar form of the statement of stockholders' equity (the details of this are left for advanced courses). The FASB encourages, but does *not* require, other comprehensive income items to be grouped under the caption *Accumulated Other Comprehensive Income* in the equity section of the balance sheet, which would include unrealized gains and losses on available-for-sale securities. For instructional benefits, we use actual account titles for these items in the equity section instead of this general, less precise caption.

Quick Check

Answers—p. 602

5. Give at least two examples of assets classified as long-term investments.

6. What are the requirements for an equity security to be listed as a long-term investment?

7. Identify similarities and differences in accounting for long-term investments in debt securities that are held-to-maturity versus those available-for-sale.

8. What are the three possible classifications of long-term equity investments? Describe the criteria for each class and the method used to account for each.

Decision Analysis

Components of Return on Total Assets

A1   Compute and analyze the components of return on total assets.

A company's **return on total assets** (or simply *return on assets*) is important in assessing financial performance. The return on total assets can be separated into two components, profit margin and total asset turnover, for additional analyses. Exhibit 15.9 shows how these two components determine return on total assets.

Exhibit 15.9

Components of Return on Total Assets

$$\text{Return on total assets} = \text{Profit margin} \times \text{Total asset turnover}$$

$$\frac{\text{Net income}}{\text{Average total assets}} = \frac{\text{Net income}}{\text{Net sales}} \times \frac{\text{Net sales}}{\text{Average total assets}}$$

Profit margin reflects the percent of net income in each dollar of net sales. Total asset turnover reflects a company's ability to produce net sales from total assets. All companies desire a high return on total assets. By considering these two components, we can often discover strengths and weaknesses not revealed by return on total assets alone. This improves our ability to assess future performance and company strategy.

To illustrate, consider return on total assets and its components for Gap Inc. in Exhibit 15.10.

Fiscal Year	Return on Total Assets	=	Profit Margin	×	Total Asset Turnover
2005	11.1%	=	7.1%	×	1.57
2004	9.8%	=	6.5%	×	1.51
2003	5.2%	=	3.3%	×	1.57

Exhibit 15.10

Gap's Components of Return on Total Assets

At least three findings emerge. First, Gap's return on total assets steadily improved from 2003 through 2005. Second, total asset turnover has remained steady at 1.5 to 1.6. Third, Gap's profit margin sharply rose between 2003 and 2005. These components reveal the dual role of profit margin and total asset turnover in determining return on total assets. They also reveal that the driver of Gap's rebound is not total asset turnover but profit margin.

Generally, if a company is to maintain or improve its return on total assets, it must meet any decline in either profit margin or total asset turnover with an increase in the other. If not, return on assets will decline. Companies consider these components in planning strategies. A component analysis can also reveal where a company is weak and where changes are needed, especially in a competitor analysis. If asset turnover is lower than the industry norm, for instance, a company should focus on raising asset turnover at least to the norm. The same applies to profit margin.

Decision Maker   Answer—p. 602

Retailer You are an entrepreneur and owner of a retail sporting goods store. The store's recent annual performance reveals (industry norms in parentheses): return on total assets = 11% (11.2%); profit margin = 4.4% (3.5%); and total asset turnover = 2.5 (3.2). What does your analysis of these figures reveal?

Demonstration Problem—1

Garden Company completes the following selected transactions related to its short-term investments during 2008.

May 8   Purchased 300 shares of FedEx stock as a short-term investment in available-for-sale securities at $40 per share plus $975 in broker fees.
Sept. 2 Sold 100 shares of its investment in FedEx stock at $47 per share and held the remaining 200 shares; broker's commission was $225.
Oct. 2   Purchased 400 shares of Ajay stock for $60 per share plus $1,600 in commissions. The stock is held as a short-term investment in available-for-sale securities.

Required

1. Prepare journal entries for the above transactions of Garden Company for 2008.
2. Prepare an adjusting journal entry as of December 31, 2008, if the market prices of the equity securities held by Garden Company are $48 per share for FedEx and $55 per share for Ajay. (Year 2008 is the first year Garden Company acquired short-term investments.)

Solution to Demonstration Problem—1

1.

May 8	Short-Term Investments—AFS (FedEx)	12,975	
	Cash		12,975

Purchased 300 shares of FedEx stock
(300 × $40) + $975.

[continued on next page]

[continued from previous page]

Sept. 2	Cash	4,475	
	Gain on Sale of Short-Term Investment		150
	Short-Term Investments—AFS (FedEx)		4,325
	Sold 100 shares of FedEx for $47 per share less		
	a $225 commission. The original cost is		
	($12,975 × 100/300).		
Oct. 2	Short-Term Investments—AFS (Ajay)............	25,600	
	Cash		25,600
	Purchased 400 shares of Ajay for $60 per share		
	plus $1,600 in commissions.		

2. Computation of unrealized gain or loss follows.

Short-Term Investments in Available-for-Sale Securities	Shares	Cost per Share	Total Cost	Market Value per Share	Total Market Value	Unrealized Gain (Loss)
FedEx	200	$43.25	$ 8,650	$48.00	$ 9,600	
Ajay	400	64.00	25,600	55.00	22,000	
Totals			$34,250		$31,600	$(2,650)

The adjusting entry follows.

Dec. 31	Unrealized Loss—Equity......................	2,650	
	Market Adjustment—Available-for-Sale (ST)		2,650
	To reflect an unrealized loss in market values		
	of available-for-sale securities.		

Demonstration Problem—2

The following transactions relate to Brown Company's long-term investments during 2008 and 2009. Brown did not own any long-term investments prior to 2008. Show (1) the appropriate journal entries and (2) the relevant portions of each year's balance sheet and income statement that reflect these transactions for both 2008 and 2009.

2008

Sept. 9   Purchased 1,000 shares of Packard, Inc., common stock for $80,000 cash. These shares represent 30% of Packard's outstanding shares.

Oct.   2   Purchased 2,000 shares of AT&T common stock for $60,000 cash. These shares represent less than a 1% ownership in AT&T.

       17   Purchased as a long-term investment 1,000 shares of Apple Computer common stock for $40,000 cash. These shares are less than 1% of Apple's outstanding shares.

Nov. 1   Received $5,000 cash dividend from Packard.

       30   Received $3,000 cash dividend from AT&T.

Dec. 15   Received $1,400 cash dividend from Apple.

       31   Packard's net income for this year is $70,000.

       31   Market values for the investments in equity securities are Packard, $84,000; AT&T, $48,000; and Apple Computer, $45,000.

       31   For preparing financial statements, note the following post-closing account balances: Common Stock, $500,000, and Retained Earnings, $350,000.

2009

Jan.   1   Sold Packard, Inc., shares for $108,000 cash.

May 30   Received $3,100 cash dividend from AT&T.

June 15   Received $1,600 cash dividend from Apple.

Aug. 17   Sold the AT&T stock for $52,000 cash.

     19   Purchased 2,000 shares of Coca-Cola common stock for $50,000 cash as a long-term investment. The stock represents less than a 5% ownership in Coca-Cola.

Dec. 15   Received $1,800 cash dividend from Apple.

     31   Market values of the investments in equity securities are Apple, $39,000, and Coca-Cola, $48,000.

     31   For preparing financial statements, note the following post-closing account balances: Common Stock, $500,000, and Retained Earnings, $410,000.

Planning the Solution

- Account for the investment in Packard under the equity method.
- Account for the investments in AT&T, Apple, and Coca-Cola as long-term investments in available-for-sale securities.
- Prepare the information for the two years' balance sheets by including the appropriate asset and equity accounts.

Solution to Demonstration Problem—2

1. Journal entries for 2008.

Sept. 9	Long-Term Investments—Packard	80,000	
	Cash		80,000
	Acquired 1,000 shares, representing a 30% equity in Packard.		
Oct. 2	Long-Term Investments—AFS (AT&T)	60,000	
	Cash		60,000
	Acquired 2,000 shares as a long-term investment in available-for-sale securities.		
Oct. 17	Long-Term Investments—AFS (Apple)	40,000	
	Cash		40,000
	Acquired 1,000 shares as a long-term investment in available-for-sale securities.		
Nov. 1	Cash	5,000	
	Long-Term Investments—Packard.		5,000
	Received dividend from Packard.		
Nov. 30	Cash	3,000	
	Dividend Revenue		3,000
	Received dividend from AT&T.		
Dec. 15	Cash	1,400	
	Dividend Revenue		1,400
	Received dividend from Apple.		
Dec. 31	Long-Term Investments—Packard	21,000	
	Earnings from Investment (Packard)		21,000
	To record 30% share of Packard's annual earnings of $70,000.		
Dec. 31	Unrealized Loss—Equity.	7,000	
	Market Adjustment—Available-for-Sale (LT)*. . . .		7,000
	To record change in market value of long-term available-for-sale securities.		

* Market adjustment computations:

	Cost	Market Value	Unrealized Gain (Loss)
AT&T	$ 60,000	$48,000	$(12,000)
Apple	40,000	45,000	5,000
Total	$100,000	$93,000	$ (7,000)

Required balance of the Market Adjustment—Available-for-Sale (LT) account (credit) . . . . $(7,000)
Existing balance 0
Necessary adjustment (credit) . . . . . $(7,000)

2. The December 31, 2008, selected balance sheet items appear as follows.

Assets	
Long-term investments	
Available-for-sale securities (at market; cost is $100,000)	$ 93,000
Investment in equity securities	96,000
Total long-term investments	189,000
Stockholders' Equity	
Common stock	500,000
Retained earnings	350,000
Unrealized loss—Equity	(7,000)

The relevant income statement items for the year ended December 31, 2008, follow.

Dividend revenue	$ 4,400
Earnings from investment	21,000

1. Journal entries for 2009.

Jan. 1	Cash	108,000	
	Long-Term Investments—Packard.		96,000
	Gain on Sale of Long-Term Investments		12,000
	Sold 1,000 shares for cash.		
May 30	Cash	3,100	
	Dividend Revenue		3,100
	Received dividend from AT&T.		
June 15	Cash	1,600	
	Dividend Revenue		1,600
	Received dividend from Apple.		
Aug. 17	Cash	52,000	
	Loss on Sale of Long-Term Investments	8,000	
	Long-Term Investments—AFS (AT&T).		60,000
	Sold 2,000 shares for cash.		
Aug. 19	Long-Term Investments—AFS (Coca-Cola)	50,000	
	Cash		50,000
	Acquired 2,000 shares as a long-term investment in available-for-sale securities.		
Dec. 15	Cash	1,800	
	Dividend Revenue		1,800
	Received dividend from Apple.		
Dec. 31	Market Adjustment—Available-for-Sale (LT)*	4,000	
	Unrealized Loss—Equity		4,000
	To record change in market value of long-term available-for-sale securities.		

* Market adjustment computations:

	Cost	Market Value	Unrealized Gain (Loss)
Apple	$40,000	$39,000	$(1,000)
Coca-Cola	50,000	48,000	(2,000)
Total	$90,000	$87,000	$(3,000)

Required balance of the Market Adjustment—Available-for-Sale (LT) account (credit)	$(3,000)
Existing balance (credit)	(7,000)
Necessary adjustment (debit)	$ 4,000

2. The December 31, 2009, balance sheet items appear as follows.

Assets	
Long-term investments	
Available-for-sale securities (at market; cost is $90,000)	$ 87,000
Stockholders' Equity	
Common stock	500,000
Retained earnings	410,000
Unrealized loss—Equity	(3,000)

The relevant income statement items for the year ended December 31, 2009, follow.

Dividend revenue	$ 6,500
Gain on sale of long-term investments	12,000
Loss on sale of long-term investments	(8,000)

APPENDIX

Investments in International Operations

15A

Many entities from small entrepreneurs to large corporations conduct business internationally. Some entities' operations occur in so many different countries that the companies are called **multinationals.** Many of us think of Coca-Cola and McDonald's, for example, as primarily U.S. companies, but most of their sales occur outside the United States. Exhibit 15A.1 shows the percent of international sales and income for selected U.S. companies. Managing and accounting for multinationals present challenges. This section describes some of these challenges and how to account for and report these activities.

Two major accounting challenges that arise when companies have international operations relate to transactions that involve more than one currency. The first is to account for sales and purchases listed in a foreign currency. The second is to prepare consolidated financial statements with international subsidiaries. For ease in this discussion, we use companies with a U.S. base of operations and assume the need to prepare financial statements in U.S. dollars. This means the *reporting currency* of these companies is the U.S. dollar.

Exhibit 15A.1

International Sales and Income as a Percent of Their Totals

Topic Tackler

PLUS

15-2

Point: Transactions *listed* or *stated* in a foreign currency are said to be *denominated* in that currency.

Exchange Rates between Currencies

Markets for the purchase and sale of foreign currencies exist all over the world. In these markets, U.S. dollars can be exchanged for Canadian dollars, British pounds, Japanese yen, Euros, or any other legal currencies. The price of one currency stated in terms of another currency is called a **foreign exchange rate.** Exhibit 15A.2 lists recent exchange rates for selected currencies. The exchange rate for British pounds and U.S. dollars is $1.8054, meaning 1 British pound could be purchased for $1.8054. On that same day, the exchange rate between Mexican pesos and U.S. dollars is $0.0925, or 1 Mexican peso can be purchased for

C4 Explain foreign exchange rates between currencies.

Decision Insight

Rush to Russia Investors are still eager to buy Russian equities even in the face of rampant crime, corruption, and slow economic growth. Why? Many argue Russia remains a bargain-priced, if risky, bet on future growth. Some analysts argue that natural-resource-rich Russia is one of the least expensive emerging markets.

Exhibit 15A.2

Foreign Exchange Rates for
Selected Currencies*

Source (unit)	Price in $U.S.	Source (unit)	Price in $U.S.
Britain (pound)	$1.8054	Canada (dollar)	$0.8439
Mexico (peso)	0.0925	Japan (yen)	0.0090
Taiwan (dollar)	0.0305	Europe (Euro)	1.2219

* Rates will vary over time based on economic, political, and other changes.

Point: For currency conversion, see XE.com

$0.0925. Exchange rates fluctuate due to changing economic and political conditions, including the supply and demand for currencies and expectations about future events.

Sales and Purchases Listed in a Foreign Currency

P5   Record transactions listed in a foreign currency.

When a U.S. company makes a credit sale to an international customer, accounting for the sale and the account receivable is straightforward if sales terms require the international customer's payment in U.S. dollars. If sale terms require (or allow) payment in a foreign currency, however, the U.S. company must account for the sale and the account receivable in a different manner.

Decision Insight

Global Greenback What do changes in foreign exchange rates mean? A decline in the price of the U.S. dollar against other currencies usually yields increased international sales for U.S. companies, without hiking prices or cutting costs, and puts them on a stronger competitive footing abroad. At home, they can raise prices without fear that foreign rivals will undercut them.

To illustrate, consider the case of the U.S.-based manufacturer Boston Company, which makes credit sales to London Outfitters, a British retail company. A sale occurs on December 12, 2008, for a price of £10,000 with payment due on February 10, 2009. Boston Company keeps its accounting records in U.S. dollars. To record the sale, Boston Company must translate the sales price from pounds to dollars. This is done using the exchange rate on the date of the sale. Assuming the exchange rate on December 12, 2008, is $1.80, Boston records this sale as follows.

Assets = Liabilities + Equity	Dec. 12	Accounts Receivable—London Outfitters	18,000	
+18,000 +18,000		Sales*		18,000
		To record a sale at £10,000, when the exchange rate equals $1.80. * (£10,000 × $1.80)		

When Boston Company prepares its annual financial statements on December 31, 2008, the current exchange rate is $1.84. Thus, the current dollar value of Boston Company's receivable is $18,400 (10,000 × $1.84). This amount is $400 higher than the amount recorded on December 12. Accounting principles require a receivable to be reported in the balance sheet at its current dollar value. Thus, Boston Company must make the following entry to record the increase in the dollar value of this receivable at year-end.

Assets = Liabilities + Equity	Dec. 31	Accounts Receivable—London Outfitters	400	
+400 +400		Foreign Exchange Gain		400
		To record the increased value of the British pound for the receivable.		

Point: Foreign exchange gains are credits, and foreign exchange losses are debits.

On February 10, 2009, Boston Company receives London Outfitters' payment of £10,000. It immediately exchanges the pounds for U.S. dollars. On this date, the exchange rate for pounds is $1.78. Thus, Boston Company receives only $17,800 (£10,000 × $1.78). It records the cash receipt and the loss associated with the decline in the exchange rate as follows.

Assets = Liabilities + Equity	Feb. 10	Cash.....................................	17,800	
+17,800 −600		Foreign Exchange Loss	600	
−18,400		Accounts Receivable—London Outfitters		18,400
		Received foreign currency payment of an account and converted it into dollars.		

Gains and losses from foreign exchange transactions are accumulated in the Foreign Exchange Gain (or Loss) account. After year-end adjustments, the balance in the Foreign Exchange Gain (or Loss) account is reported on the income statement and closed to the Income Summary account.

Accounting for credit purchases from an international seller is similar to the case of a credit sale to an international customer. In particular, if the U.S. company is required to make payment in a foreign currency, the account payable must be translated into dollars before the U.S. company can record it. If the exchange rate is different when preparing financial statements and when paying for the purchase, the U.S. company must recognize a foreign exchange gain or loss at those dates. To illustrate, assume NC Imports, a U.S. company, purchases products costing €20,000 (euros) from Hamburg Brewing on January 15, when the exchange rate is $1.20 per euro. NC records this transaction as follows.

Example: Assume that a U.S. company makes a credit purchase from a British company for £10,000 when the exchange rate is $1.62. At the balance sheet date, this rate is $1.72. Does this imply a gain or loss for the U.S. company? *Answer:* A loss.

Jan. 15	Inventory.	24,000	
	Accounts Payable—Hamburg Brewing.		24,000
	To record a €20,000 purchase when exchange rate *is $1.20 (€20,000 × $1.20)*		

Assets = Liabilities + Equity
+24,000   +24,000

NC Imports makes payment in full on February 14 when the exchange rate is $1.25 per euro, which is recorded as follows.

Feb. 14	Accounts Payable—Hamburg Brewing	24,000	
	Foreign Exchange Loss	1,000	
	Cash		25,000
	To record cash payment towards €20,000 account *when exchange rate is $1.25 (€20.000 × $1.25).*		

Assets = Liabilities + Equity
−25,000   −24,000   −1,000

Consolidated Statements with International Subsidiaries

A second challenge in accounting for international operations involves preparing consolidated financial statements when the parent company has one or more international subsidiaries. Consider a U.S.-based company that owns a controlling interest in a French subsidiary. The reporting currency of the U.S. parent is the dollar. The French subsidiary maintains its financial records in euros. Before preparing consolidated statements, the parent must translate financial statements of the French company into U.S. dollars. After this translation is complete (including that for accounting differences), it prepares consolidated statements the same as for domestic subsidiaries. Procedures for translating an international subsidiary's account balances depend on the nature of the subsidiary's operations. The process requires the parent company to select appropriate foreign exchange rates and to apply those rates to the foreign subsidiary's account balances. This is described in advanced courses.

Global: A weaker U.S. dollar often increases global sales for U.S. companies.

Decision Maker   Answer—p. 602

Entrepreneur   You are a U.S. home builder that purchases lumber from mills in both the U.S. and Canada. The price of the Canadian dollar in terms of the U.S. dollar jumps from US$0.70 to US$0.80. Are you now more or less likely to buy lumber from Canadian or U.S. mills?

Summary

C1 **Distinguish between debt and equity securities and between short-term and long-term investments.** *Debt securities* reflect a creditor relationship and include investments in notes, bonds, and certificates of deposit. *Equity securities* reflect an owner relationship and include shares of stock issued by other companies. Short-term investments in securities are current assets that meet two criteria: (1) They are expected to be converted into cash within one year or the current operating cycle of the business, whichever is longer and (2) they are readily convertible to cash, or *marketable*. All other investments in securities are long-term. Long-term investments also include assets not used in operations and those held for special purposes, such as land for expansion.

C2 **Identify and describe the different classes of investments in securities.** Investments in securities are classified into

one of five groups: (1) trading securities, which are always short-term, (2) debt securities held-to-maturity, (3) debt and equity securities available-for-sale, (4) equity securities in which an investor has a significant influence over the investee, and (5) equity securities in which an investor has a controlling influence over the investee.

C3 **Describe how to report equity securities with controlling influence.** If an investor owns more than 50% of another company's voting stock and controls the investee, the investor's financial reports are prepared on a consolidated basis. These reports are prepared as if the company were organized as one entity.

C4^A **Explain foreign exchange rates between currencies.** A foreign exchange rate is the price of one currency stated in terms of another. An entity with transactions in a foreign currency when the exchange rate changes between the transaction dates and their settlement will experience exchange gains or losses.

A1 Compute and analyze the components of return on total assets. Return on total assets has two components: profit margin and total asset turnover. A decline in one component must be met with an increase in another if return on assets is to be maintained. Component analysis is helpful in assessing company performance compared to that of competitors and its own past.

P1 Account for trading securities. Investments are initially recorded at cost, and any dividend or interest from these investments is recorded in the income statement. Investments classified as trading securities are reported at market value. Unrealized gains and losses on trading securities are reported in income. When investments are sold, the difference between the net proceeds from the sale and the cost of the securities is recognized as a gain or loss.

P2 Account for held-to-maturity securities. Debt securities held-to-maturity are reported at cost when purchased. Interest revenue is recorded as it accrues. The cost of long-term held-to-maturity securities is adjusted for the amortization of any difference between cost and maturity value.

P3 Account for available-for-sale securities. Debt and equity securities available-for-sale are recorded at cost when pur-

chased. Available-for-sale securities are reported at their market values on the balance sheet with unrealized gains or losses shown in the equity section. Gains and losses realized on the sale of these investments are reported in the income statement.

P4 Account for equity securities with significant influence. The equity method is used when an investor has a significant influence over an investee. This usually exists when an investor owns 20% or more of the investee's voting stock but not more than 50%. The equity method means an investor records its share of investee earnings with a debit to the investment account and a credit to a revenue account. Dividends received reduce the investment account balance.

P5ᴬ Record transactions listed in a foreign currency. When a company makes a credit sale to a foreign customer and sales terms call for payment in a foreign currency, the company must translate the foreign currency into dollars to record the receivable. If the exchange rate changes before payment is received, exchange gains or losses are recognized in the year they occur. The same treatment is used when a company makes a credit purchase from a foreign supplier and is required to make payment in a foreign currency.

Guidance Answers to **Decision Maker**

Money Manager   If you have investments in fixed-rate bonds and notes when interest rates fall, the value of your investments increases. This is so because the bonds and notes you hold continue to pay the same (high) rate while the market is demanding a new lower interest rate. Your strategy is to continue holding your investments in bonds and notes, and, potentially, to increase these holdings through additional purchases.

Retailer   Your store's return on assets is 11%, which is similar to the industry norm of 11.2%. However, disaggregation of return on assets reveals that your store's profit margin of 4.4% is much higher than the norm of 3.5%, but your total asset turnover of 2.5 is much lower than the norm of 3.2. These results suggest that, as compared with competitors, you are less efficient in using assets. You need to focus on increasing sales or reducing as-

sets. You might consider reducing prices to increase sales, provided such a strategy does not reduce your return on assets. For instance, you could reduce your profit margin to 4% to increase sales. If total asset turnover increases to more than 2.75 when profit margin is lowered to 4%, your overall return on assets is improved.

Entrepreneur   You are now less likely to buy Canadian lumber because it takes more U.S. money to buy a Canadian dollar (and lumber). For instance, the purchase of lumber from a Canadian mill with a $1,000 (Canadian dollars) price would have cost the U.S. builder $700 (U.S. dollars, computed as C$1,000 × US$0.70) before the rate change, and $800 (US dollars, computed as C$1,000 × US$0.80) after the rate change.

Guidance Answers to **Quick Checks**

1. Short-term held-to-maturity securities are reported at cost.

2. Trading securities are reported at market value.

3. The equity section of the balance sheet (and in comprehensive income).

4. The income statement.

5. Long-term investments include (1) long-term funds earmarked for a special purpose, (2) debt and equity securities that do not meet current asset requirements, and (3) long-term assets not used in the regular operations of the business.

6. An equity investment is classified as long term if it is not marketable or, if marketable, it is not held as an available source of cash to meet the needs of current operations.

7. Debt securities held-to-maturity and debt securities available-for-sale are both recorded at cost. Also, interest on both is accrued as earned. However, only long-term securities held-to-maturity require amortization of the difference between cost and maturity value. In addition, only securities available-for-sale require a period-end adjustment to market value.

8. Long-term equity investments are placed in one of three categories and accounted for as follows: (a) **available-for-sale** (noninfluential, less than 20% of outstanding stock)—market value; (b) **significant influence** (20% to 50% of outstanding stock)—equity method; and (c) **controlling influence** (holding more than 50% of outstanding stock)—equity method with consolidation.

Key Terms

mhhe.com/wildFAP18e

Key Terms are available at the book's Website for learning and testing in an online Flashcard Format.

Available-for-sale (AFS) securities (p. 590)

Comprehensive income (p. 593)

Consolidated financial statements (p. 593)

Equity method (p. 592)

Equity securities with controlling influence (p. 593)

Equity securities with significant influence (p. 591)

Foreign exchange rate (p. 599)

Held-to-maturity (HTM) securities (p. 590)

Long-term investments (p. 586)

Multinational (p. 599)

Parent (p. 593)

Return on total assets (p. 594)

Short-term investments (p. 586)

Subsidiary (p. 593)

Trading securities (p. 589)

Unrealized gain (loss) (p. 589)

Multiple Choice Quiz

Answers on p. 619   mhhe.com/wildFAP18e

Multiple Choice Quizzes A and B are available at the book's Website.

1. A company purchased $30,000 of 5% bonds for investment purposes on May 1. The bonds pay interest on February 1 and August 1. The amount of interest revenue accrued at December 31 (the company's year-end) is:
   a. $1,500
   b. $1,375
   c. $1,000
   d. $625
   e. $300

2. Earlier this period, Amadeus Co. purchased its only available-for-sale investment in the stock of Bach Co. for $83,000. The period-end market value of this stock is $84,500. Amadeus records a:
   a. Credit to Unrealized Gain—Equity for $1,500
   b. Debit to Unrealized Loss—Equity for $1,500
   c. Debit to Investment Revenue for $1,500
   d. Credit to Market Adjustment—Available-for-Sale for $3,500
   e. Credit to Cash for $1,500

3. Mozart Co. owns 35% of Melody Inc. Melody pays $50,000 in cash dividends to its shareholders for the period. Mozart's entry to record the Melody dividend includes a:
   a. Credit to Investment Revenue for $50,000.
   b. Credit to Long-Term Investments for $17,500.
   c. Credit to Cash for $17,500.

   d. Debit to Long-Term Investments for $17,500.
   e. Debit to Cash for $50,000.

4. A company has net income of $300,000, net sales of $2,500,000, and total assets of $2,000,000. Its return on total assets equals:
   a. 6.7%
   b. 12.0%
   c. 8.3%
   d. 80.0%
   e. 15.0%

5. A company had net income of $80,000, net sales of $600,000, and total assets of $400,000. Its profit margin and total asset turnover are:

	Profit Margin	Total Asset Turnover
a.	1.5%	13.3
b.	13.3%	1.5
c.	13.3%	0.7
d.	7.0%	13.3
e.	10.0%	26.7

Superscript ^A^ denotes assignments based on Appendix 15A.

Discussion Questions

1. Under what two conditions should investments be classified as current assets?

2. On a balance sheet, what valuation must be reported for short-term investments in trading securities?

3. If a short-term investment in available-for-sale securities costs $6,780 and is sold for $7,500, how should the difference between these two amounts be recorded?

4. Identify the three classes of noninfluential and two classes of influential investments in securities.

5. Under what conditions should investments be classified as current assets? As long-term assets?

6. If a company purchases its only long-term investments in available-for-sale debt securities this period and their market value

is below cost at the balance sheet date, what entry is required to recognize this unrealized loss?

7. On a balance sheet, what valuation must be reported for debt securities classified as available-for-sale?

8. Under what circumstances are long-term investments in debt securities reported at cost and adjusted for amortization of any difference between cost and maturity value?

9. For investments in available-for-sale securities, how are unrealized (holding) gains and losses reported?

10. In accounting for investments in equity securities, when should the equity method be used?

11. Under what circumstances does a company prepare consolidated financial statements?

12.ᴬWhat are two major challenges in accounting for international operations?

13.ᴬAssume a U.S. company makes a credit sale to a foreign customer that is required to make payment in its foreign currency. In the current period, the exchange rate is $1.40 on

the date of the sale and is $1.30 on the date the customer pays the receivable. Will the U.S. company record an exchange gain or loss?

14.ᴬIf a U.S. company makes a credit sale to a foreign customer required to make payment in U.S. dollars, can the U.S. company have an exchange gain or loss on this sale?

15. Refer to **Best Buy**'s statement of changes in stockholders' equity in Appendix A. What is the amount of foreign currency translation adjustment for the year ended February 26, 2005? Is this adjustment an unrealized gain or an unrealized loss?

16. Refer to the balance sheet of **Circuit City** in Appendix A. How can you tell that Circuit City uses the consolidated method of accounting?

17. Refer to the financial statements of **Apple** in Appendix A. Compute its return on total assets for the year ended September 25, 2004.

Red numbers denote Discussion Questions that involve decision-making.

QUICK STUDY

QS 15-1

Short-term equity
investments   C2 P1

On April 18, Riley Co. made a short-term investment in 300 common shares of XLT Co. The purchase price is $42 per share and the broker's fee is $250. The intent is to actively manage these shares for profit. On May 30, Riley Co. receives $1 per share from XLT in dividends. Prepare the April 18 and May 30 journal entries to record these transactions.

QS 15-2

Available-for-sale securities

C2 P3

Journ Co. purchased short-term investments in available-for-sale securities at a cost of $50,000 on November 25, 2008. At December 31, 2008, these securities had a market value of $47,000. This is the first and only time the company has purchased such securities.

1. Prepare the December 31, 2008, year-end adjusting entry for the securities' portfolio.

2. For each account in the entry for part 1, explain how it is reported in financial statements.

3. Prepare the April 6, 2009, entry when Journ sells one-half of these securities for $26,000.

QS 15-3

Available-for-sale securities

C2 P3

Prepare Hertog Company's journal entries to reflect the following transactions for the current year.

May 7   Purchases 200 shares of Kraft stock as a short-term investment in available-for-sale securities at a cost of $50 per share plus $300 in broker fees.

June 6   Sells 200 shares of its investment in Kraft stock at $56 per share. The broker's commission on this sale is $150.

QS 15-4

Available-for-sale securities

C2 P3

Hiker Company completes the following transactions during the current year.

May 9   Purchases 200 shares of Higo stock as a short-term investment in available-for-sale securities at a cost of $25 per share plus $150 in broker fees.

June 2   Sells 100 shares of its investment in Higo stock at $28 per share. The broker's commission on this sale is $90.

Dec. 31   The closing market price of the Higo stock is $23 per share.

Prepare the May 9 and June 2 journal entries and the December 31 adjusting entry. This is the first and only time the company purchased such securities.

QS 15-5

Identifying long-term investments

C1

Which of the following statements are true of long-term investments?

a. They are held as an investment of cash available for current operations.

b. They can include funds earmarked for a special purpose, such as bond sinking funds.

c. They can include investments in trading securities.

d. They can include debt securities held-to-maturity.

e. They are always easily sold and therefore qualify as being marketable.

f. They can include debt and equity securities available-for-sale.

g. They can include bonds and stocks not intended to serve as a ready source of cash.

Complete the following descriptions by filling in the blanks.

1. Accrual of interest on bonds held as long-term investments requires a credit to _____ _____.

2. Equity securities giving an investor significant influence are accounted for using the _____ _____.

3. Available-for-sale debt securities are reported on the balance sheet at _____ _____.

4. Trading securities are classified as _____ assets.

5. The controlling investor (more than 50% ownership) is called the _____, and the investee company is called the _____.

QS 15-6
Describing investments in securities

C1   C2   C3

On February 1, 2008, Garzon purchased 6% bonds issued by PBS Utilities at a cost of $40,000, which is their par value. The bonds pay interest semiannually on July 31 and January 31. For 2008, prepare entries to record Garzon's July 31 receipt of interest and its December 31 year-end interest accrual.

QS 15-7
Debt securities transactions

C2   P2

On May 20, 2008, Montero Co. paid $1,000,000 to acquire 25,000 common shares (10%) of ORD Corp. as a long-term investment. On August 5, 2009, Montero sold one-half of these shares for $625,000. What valuation method should be used to account for this stock investment? Prepare entries to record both the acquisition and the sale of these shares.

QS 15-8
Recording equity securities

C2   P3

Assume the same facts as in QS 15-8 except that the stock acquired represents 40% of ORD Corp.'s outstanding stock. Also assume that ORD Corp. paid a $100,000 dividend on November 1, 2008, and reported a net income of $700,000 for 2008. Prepare the entries to record (*a*) the receipt of the dividend and (*b*) the December 31, 2008, year-end adjustment required for the investment account.

QS 15-9
Equity method transactions

C2   P4

During the current year, Reed Consulting Group acquired long-term available-for-sale securities at a $70,000 cost. At its December 31 year-end, these securities had a market value of $58,000. This is the first and only time the company purchased such securities.

1. Prepare the necessary year-end adjusting entry related to these securities.

2. Explain how each account used in part 1 is reported in the financial statements.

QS 15-10
Recording market adjustment for securities

P3

How is the return on total assets computed? What does this important ratio reflect?

QS 15-11
Return on total assets   A1

Write the formula to separate the return on total assets into its two basic components. Explain how these components of the return on total assets are helpful to financial statement users for business decisions.

QS 15-12
Component return on total assets   A1

A U.S. company sells a product to a British company with the transaction listed in British pounds. On the date of the sale, the transaction total of $14,500 is billed as £10,000, reflecting an exchange rate of 1.45 (that is, $1.45 per pound). Prepare the entry to record (1) the sale and (2) the receipt of payment in pounds when the exchange rate is 1.35.

QS 15-13^A
Foreign currency transactions

P5

On March 1, 2008, a U.S. company made a credit sale requiring payment in 30 days from a Malaysian company, Hamac Sdn. Bhd., in 20,000 Malaysian ringgits. Assuming the exchange rate between Malaysian ringgits and U.S. dollars is $0.4538 on March 1 and $0.4899 on March 31, prepare the entries to record the sale on March 1 and the cash receipt on March 31.

QS 15-14^A
Foreign currency transactions

P5

EXERCISES

Exercise 15-1
Accounting for transactions in short-term securities

C2 P1 P2 P3

Check (c) Dr. Cash $122,400

(f) Dr. Cash $11,760

Prepare journal entries to record the following transactions involving the short-term securities investments of Blake Co., all of which occurred during year 2008.

a. On February 15, paid $120,000 cash to purchase RTF's 90-day short-term debt securities ($120,000 principal), dated February 15, that pay 8% interest (categorized as held-to-maturity securities).

b. On March 22, purchased 700 shares of XIF Company stock at $27.50 per share plus a $150 brokerage fee. These shares are categorized as trading securities.

c. On May 16, received a check from RTF in payment of the principal and 90 days' interest on the debt securities purchased in transaction *a*.

d. On August 1, paid $80,000 cash to purchase Flash Co.'s 10% debt securities ($80,000 principal), dated July 30, 2008, and maturing January 30, 2009 (categorized as available-for-sale securities).

e. On September 1, received a $1.00 per share cash dividend on the XIF Company stock purchased in transaction *b*.

f. On October 8, sold 350 shares of XIF Co. stock for $34 per share, less a $140 brokerage fee.

g. On October 30, received a check from Flash Co. for 90 days' interest on the debt securities purchased in transaction *d*.

Exercise 15-2
Accounting for trading securities

C1 P1

Check (3) Gain, $2,000

Brooks Co. purchases various investments in trading securities at a cost of $66,000 on December 27, 2008. (This is its first and only purchase of such securities.) At December 31, 2008, these securities had a market value of $72,000.

1. Prepare the December 31, 2008, year-end adjusting entry for the trading securities' portfolio.

2. Explain how each account in the entry of part 1 is reported in financial statements.

3. Prepare the January 3, 2009, entry when Brooks sells a portion of its trading securities (that had originally cost $33,000) for $35,000.

Exercise 15-3
Adjusting available-for-sale securities to market

C2 P3

Check Unrealized loss, $9,100

On December 31, 2008, Reggit Company held the following short-term investments in its portfolio of available-for-sale securities. Reggit had no short-term investments in its prior accounting periods. Prepare the December 31, 2008, adjusting entry to report these investments at market value.

	Cost	Market Value
Verrizano Corporation bonds payable	$89,600	$91,600
Preble Corporation notes payable	70,600	62,900
Lucerne Company common stock	86,500	83,100

Exercise 15-4
Transactions in short-term and long-term investments

C1 C2

Prepare journal entries to record the following transactions involving both the short-term and long-term investments of Cancun Corp., all of which occurred during calendar year 2008. Use the account Short-Term Investments for any transactions that you determine are short term.

a. On February 15, paid $160,000 cash to purchase American General's 90-day short-term notes at par, which are dated February 15 and pay 10% interest (classified as held-to-maturity).

b. On March 22, bought 700 shares of Fran Industries common stock at $51 cash per share plus a $150 brokerage fee (classified as long-term available-for-sale securities).

c. On May 15, received a check from American General in payment of the principal and 90 days' interest on the notes purchased in transaction *a*.

d. On July 30, paid $100,000 cash to purchase MP3 Electronics' 8% notes at par, dated July 30, 2008, and maturing on January 30, 2009 (classified as trading securities).

e. On September 1, received a $1 per share cash dividend on the Fran Industries common stock purchased in transaction *b*.

f. On October 8, sold 350 shares of Fran Industries common stock for $64 cash per share, less a $125 brokerage fee.

g. On October 30, received a check from MP3 Electronics for three months' interest on the notes purchased in transaction *d*.

On December 31, 2008, Lujack Co. held the following short-term available-for-sale securities.

	Cost	Market Value
Nintendo Co. common stock	$44,450	$48,900
Atlantic Richfield Co. bonds payable	49,000	47,000
Kellogg Co. notes payable	25,000	23,200
McDonald's Corp. common stock	46,300	44,800

Lujack had no short-term investments prior to the current period. Prepare the December 31, 2008, year-end adjusting entry to record the market adjustment for these securities.

Exercise 15-5
Market adjustment to available-for-sale securities

P3

Pilsen Co. began operations in 2007. The cost and market values for its long-term investments portfolio in available-for-sale securities are shown below. Prepare Pilsen's December 31, 2008, adjusting entry to reflect any necessary market adjustment for these investments.

	Cost	Market Value
December 31, 2007	$87,855	$80,293
December 31, 2008	89,980	90,980

Exercise 15-6
Market adjustment to available-for-sale securities

P3

Ticker Services began operations in 2006 and maintains long-term investments in available-for-sale securities. The year-end cost and market values for its portfolio of these investments follow. Prepare journal entries to record each year-end market adjustment for these securities.

	Cost	Market Value
December 31, 2006	$372,000	$360,860
December 31, 2007	428,500	455,800
December 31, 2008	600,200	700,500
December 31, 2009	876,900	780,200

Exercise 15-7
Multi-year market adjustments to available-for-sale securities

P3

Information regarding Central Company's individual investments in securities during its calendar-year 2008, along with the December 31, 2008, market values, follows.

a. Investment in Beeman Company bonds: $420,500 cost, $457,000 market value. Central intends to hold these bonds until they mature in 2011.

b. Investment in Baybridge common stock: 29,500 shares; $362,450 cost; $391,375 market value. Central owns 32% of Baybridge's voting stock and has a significant influence over Baybridge.

c. Investment in Carroll common stock: 12,000 shares; $165,500 cost; $178,000 market value. This investment amounts to 3% of Carroll's outstanding shares, and Central's goal with this investment is to earn dividends over the next few years.

d. Investment in Newtech common stock: 3,500 shares; $90,300 cost; $88,625 market value. Central's goal with this investment is to reap an increase in market value of the stock over the next three to five years. Newtech has 30,000 common shares outstanding.

e. Investment in Flock common stock: 16,300 shares; $100,860 cost; $111,210 market value. This stock is marketable and is held as an investment of cash available for operations.

Required

1. Identify whether each investment should be classified as a short-term or long-term investment. For each long-term investment, indicate in which of the long-term investment classifications it should be placed.

2. Prepare a journal entry dated December 31, 2008, to record the market value adjustment of the long-term investments in available-for-sale securities. Central had no long-term investments prior to year 2008.

Exercise 15-8
Classifying investments in securities; recording market values

C1 C2 P2 P3 P4

Check Unrealized gain, $10,825

Exercise 15-9

Securities transactions; equity method

P4   C2

Prepare journal entries to record the following transactions and events of Kodan Company.

2008

Jan.   2   Purchased 30,000 shares of Goreten Co. common stock for $408,000 cash plus a broker's fee of $3,000 cash. Goreten has 90,000 shares of common stock outstanding and its policies will be significantly influenced by Kodan.

Sept. 1   Goreten declared and paid a cash dividend of $1.50 per share.

Dec. 31   Goreten announced that net income for the year is $486,900.

2009

June   1   Goreten declared and paid a cash dividend of $2.10 per share.

Dec. 31   Goreten announced that net income for the year is $702,750.

Dec. 31   Kodan sold 10,000 shares of Goreten for $320,000 cash.

Exercise 15-10

Return on total assets

A1

The following information is available from the financial statements of Regae Industries. Compute Regae's return on total assets for 2008 and 2009. (Round returns to one-tenth of a percent.) Comment on the company's efficiency in using its assets in 2008 and 2009.

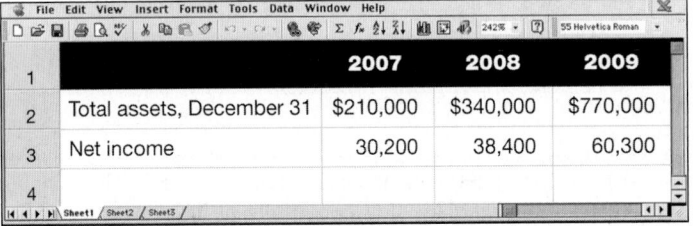

	2007	2008	2009
Total assets, December 31	$210,000	$340,000	$770,000
Net income	30,200	38,400	60,300

Exercise 15-11^A

Foreign currency transactions

P5

Leigh of New York sells its products to customers in the United States and the United Kingdom. On December 16, 2008, Leigh sold merchandise on credit to Bronson Ltd. of London at a price of 17,000 pounds. The exchange rate on that day for £1 was $1.4583. On December 31, 2008, when Leigh prepared its financial statements, the rate was £1 for $1.4382. Bronson paid its bill in full on January 15, 2009, at which time the exchange rate was £1 for $1.4482. Leigh immediately exchanged the 17,000 pounds for U.S. dollars. Prepare Leigh's journal entries on December 16, December 31, and January 15 (round to the nearest dollar).

Exercise 15-12^A

Computing foreign exchange gains and losses on receivables

C4   P5

On May 8, 2008, Jett Company (a U.S. company) made a credit sale to Lopez (a Mexican company). The terms of the sale required Lopez to pay 800,000 pesos on February 10, 2009. Jett prepares quarterly financial statements on March 31, June 30, September 30, and December 31. The exchange rates for pesos during the time the receivable is outstanding follow.

May 8, 2008	$0.1323
June 30, 2008	0.1352
September 30, 2008	0.1368
December 31, 2008	0.1335
February 10, 2009	0.1386

Compute the foreign exchange gain or loss that Jett should report on each of its quarterly income statements for the last three quarters of 2008 and the first quarter of 2009. Also compute the amount reported on Jett's balance sheets at the end of each of its last three quarters of 2008.

PROBLEM SET A

Problem 15-1A

Recording transactions and market adjustments for trading securities

C2   P1

Carlsville Company, which began operations in 2008, invests its idle cash in trading securities. The following transactions are from its short-term investments in its trading securities.

2008

Jan. 20   Purchased 800 shares of Ford Motor Co. at $26 per share plus a $125 commission.

Feb. 9   Purchased 2,200 shares of Lucent at $44.25 per share plus a $578 commission.

Oct. 12   Purchased 750 shares of Z-Seven at $7.50 per share plus a $200 commission.

2009

Apr. 15   Sold 800 shares of Ford Motor Co. at $29 per share less a $285 commission.
July   5   Sold 750 shares of Z-Seven at $10.25 per share less a $102.50 commission.
July 22   Purchased 1,600 shares of Hunt Corp. at $30 per share plus a $444 commission.
Aug. 19   Purchased 1,800 shares of Donna Karan at $18.25 per share plus a $290 commission.

2010

Feb. 27   Purchased 3,400 shares of HCA at $34 per share plus a $420 commission.
Mar.   3   Sold 1,600 shares of Hunt at $25 per share less a $250 commission.
June 21   Sold 2,200 shares of Lucent at $42 per share less a $420 commission.
June 30   Purchased 1,200 shares of Black & Decker at $47.50 per share plus a $595 commission.
Nov.   1   Sold 1,800 shares of Donna Karan at $18.25 per share less a $309 commission.

Required

1. Prepare journal entries to record these short-term investment activities for the years shown. (Ignore any year-end adjusting entries.)
2. On December 31, 2010, prepare the adjusting entry to record any necessary market adjustment for the portfolio of trading securities when HCA's share price is $36 and Black & Decker's share price is $43.50. (Assume the Market Adjustment—Trading account had an unadjusted balance of zero.)

Check (2) Dr. Market Adjustment—Trading $985

Rose Company had no short-term investments prior to year 2008. It had the following transactions involving short-term investments in available-for-sale securities during 2008.

Apr. 16   Purchased 4,000 shares of Gem Co. stock at $24.25 per share plus a $180 brokerage fee.
May   1   Paid $100,000 to buy 90-day U.S. Treasury bills (debt securities): $100,000 principal amount, 6% interest, securities dated May 1.
July   7   Purchased 2,000 shares of PepsiCo stock at $49.25 per share plus a $175 brokerage fee.
      20   Purchased 1,000 shares of Xerox stock at $16.75 per share plus a $205 brokerage fee.
Aug.   3   Received a check for principal and accrued interest on the U.S. Treasury bills that matured on July 29.
      15   Received an $0.85 per share cash dividend on the Gem Co. stock.
      28   Sold 2,000 shares of Gem Co. stock at $30 per share less a $225 brokerage fee.
Oct.   1   Received a $1.90 per share cash dividend on the PepsiCo shares.
Dec. 15   Received a $1.05 per share cash dividend on the remaining Gem Co. shares.
      31   Received a $1.30 per share cash dividend on the PepsiCo shares.

Problem 15-2A
Recording, adjusting, and reporting short-term available-for-sale securities

C2 P3

Required

1. Prepare journal entries to record the preceding transactions and events.
2. Prepare a table to compare the year-end cost and market values of Rose's short-term investments in available-for-sale securities. The year-end market values per share are: Gem Co., $26.50; PepsiCo, $46.50; and Xerox, $13.75.
3. Prepare an adjusting entry, if necessary, to record the year-end market adjustment for the portfolio of short-term investments in available-for-sale securities.

Check (2) Cost = $164,220

(3) Dr. Unrealized Loss—Equity $4,470

Analysis Component

4. Explain the balance sheet presentation of the market adjustment for Rose's short-term investments.
5. How do these short-term investments affect Rose's (*a*) income statement for year 2008 and (*b*) the equity section of its balance sheet at year-end 2008?

Grass Security, which began operations in 2008, invests in long-term available-for-sale securities. Following is a series of transactions and events determining its long-term investment activity.

2008

Jan. 20   Purchased 1,000 shares of Johnson & Johnson at $20.50 per share plus a $240 commission.
Feb.   9   Purchased 1,200 shares of Sony at $46.20 per share plus a $225 commission.
June 12   Purchased 1,500 shares of Mattel at $27.00 per share plus a $195 commission.
Dec. 31   Per share market values for stocks in the portfolio are Johnson & Johnson, $21.50; Mattel, $30.90; Sony, $38.00.

Problem 15-3A
Recording, adjusting, and reporting long-term available-for-sale securities

C2 P3

2009

Apr. 15   Sold 1,000 shares of Johnson & Johnson at $23.50 per share less a $525 commission.
July   5   Sold 1,500 shares of Mattel at $23.90 per share less a $235 commission.
July 22   Purchased 600 shares of Sara Lee at $22.50 per share plus a $480 commission.
Aug. 19   Purchased 900 shares of Eastman Kodak at $17.00 per share plus a $198 commission.
Dec. 31   Per share market values for stocks in the portfolio are: Kodak, $19.25; Sara Lee, $20.00; Sony, $35.00.

2010

Feb. 27   Purchased 2,400 shares of Microsoft at $67.00 per share plus a $525 commission.
June 21   Sold 1,200 shares of Sony at $48.00 per share less an $880 commission.
June 30   Purchased 1,400 shares of Black & Decker at $36.00 per share plus a $435 commission.
Aug.   3   Sold 600 shares of Sara Lee at $16.25 per share less a $435 commission.
Nov.   1   Sold 900 shares of Eastman Kodak at $22.75 per share less a $625 commission.
Dec. 31   Per share market values for stocks in the portfolio are: Black & Decker, $39.00; Microsoft, $69.00.

Required

1. Prepare journal entries to record these transactions and events and any year-end market adjustments to the portfolio of long-term available-for-sale securities.

Check   (2b) Market adjustment bal.: 12/31/08, $(3,650); 12/31/09; $(13,818)

2. Prepare a table that summarizes the (*a*) total cost, (*b*) total market adjustment, and (*c*) total market value of the portfolio of long-term available-for-sale securities at each year-end.

     (3b) Unrealized Gain at 12/31/2010, $8,040

3. Prepare a table that summarizes (*a*) the realized gains and losses and (*b*) the unrealized gains or losses for the portfolio of long-term available-for-sale securities at each year-end.

Problem 15-4A

Long-term investment transactions; unrealized and realized gains and losses

C2   C3   P3   P4

Stoll Co.'s long-term available-for-sale portfolio at December 31, 2007, consists of the following.

Available-for-Sale Securities	Cost	Market Value
40,000 shares of Company A common stock	$535,300	$490,000
7,000 shares of Company B common stock	159,380	154,000
17,500 shares of Company C common stock	662,750	640,938

Stoll enters into the following long-term investment transactions during year 2008.

Jan. 29   Sold 3,500 shares of Company B common stock for $79,188 less a brokerage fee of $1,500.
Apr. 17   Purchased 10,000 shares of Company W common stock for $197,500 plus a brokerage fee of $2,400. The shares represent a 30% ownership in Company W.
July   6   Purchased 4,500 shares of Company X common stock for $126,562 plus a brokerage fee of $1,750. The shares represent a 10% ownership in Company X.
Aug. 22   Purchased 50,000 shares of Company Y common stock for $375,000 plus a brokerage fee of $1,200. The shares represent a 51% ownership in Company Y.
Nov. 13   Purchased 8,500 shares of Company Z common stock for $267,900 plus a brokerage fee of $2,450. The shares represent a 5% ownership in Company Z.
Dec.   9   Sold 40,000 shares of Company A common stock for $515,000 less a brokerage fee of $4,100.

The market values of its investments at December 31, 2008, are: B, $81,375; C, $610,312; W, $191,250; X, $118,125; Y, $531,250; and Z, $278,800.

Required

1. Determine the amount Stoll should report on its December 31, 2008, balance sheet for its long-term investments in available-for-sale securities.

Check   (2) Cr. Unrealized Loss— Equity, $20,002

2. Prepare any necessary December 31, 2008, adjusting entry to record the market value adjustment for the long-term investments in available-for-sale securities.

3. What amount of gains or losses on transactions relating to long-term investments in available-for-sale securities should Stoll report on its December 31, 2008, income statement?

Selk Steel Co., which began operations on January 4, 2008, had the following subsequent transactions and events in its long-term investments.

Problem 15-5A
Accounting for long-term investments in securities; with and without significant influence

C2   P3   P4

2008

Jan.   5   Selk purchased 60,000 shares (20% of total) of Kildaire's common stock for $1,560,000.
Oct. 23   Kildaire declared and paid a cash dividend of $3.20 per share.
Dec. 31   Kildaire's net income for 2008 is $1,164,000, and the market value of its stock at December 31 is $30.00 per share.

2009

Oct. 15   Kildaire declared and paid a cash dividend of $2.60 per share.
Dec. 31   Kildaire's net income for 2009 is $1,476,000, and the market value of its stock at December 31 is $32.00 per share.

2010

Jan.   2   Selk sold all of its investment in Kildaire for $1,894,000 cash.

Part 1

Assume that Selk has a significant influence over Kildaire with its 20% share of stock.

Required

1. Prepare journal entries to record these transactions and events for Selk.
2. Compute the carrying (book) value per share of Selk's investment in Kildaire common stock as reflected in the investment account on January 1, 2010.
3. Compute the net increase or decrease in Selk's equity from January 5, 2008, through January 2, 2010, resulting from its investment in Kildaire.

Check (2) Carrying value per share, $29

Part 2

Assume that although Selk owns 20% of Kildaire's outstanding stock, circumstances indicate that it does not have a significant influence over the investee and that it is classified as an available-for-sale security investment.

Required

1. Prepare journal entries to record the preceding transactions and events for Selk. Also prepare an entry dated January 2, 2010, to remove any balance related to the market adjustment.
2. Compute the cost per share of Selk's investment in Kildaire common stock as reflected in the investment account on January 1, 2010.
3. Compute the net increase or decrease in Selk's equity from January 5, 2008, through January 2, 2010, resulting from its investment in Kildaire.

(1) 1/2/10 Dr. Unrealized Gain—Equity $360,000

(3) Net increase, $682,000

Doering Company, a U.S. corporation with customers in several foreign countries, had the following selected transactions for 2008 and 2009.

Problem 15-6A[A]
Foreign currency transactions

C4   P5

2008

Apr.   8   Sold merchandise to Salinas & Sons of Mexico for $5,938 cash. The exchange rate for pesos is $0.1043 on this day.
July 21   Sold merchandise on credit to Sumito Corp. in Japan. The price of 1.5 million yen is to be paid 120 days from the date of sale. The exchange rate for yen is $0.0094 on this day.
Oct. 14   Sold merchandise for 19,000 pounds to Smithers Ltd. of Great Britain, payment in full to be received in 90 days. The exchange rate for pounds is $1.4566 on this day.
Nov. 18   Received Sumito's payment in yen for its July 21 purchase and immediately exchanged the yen for dollars. The exchange rate for yen is $0.0092 on this day.
Dec. 20   Sold merchandise for 17,000 ringgits to Hamid Albar of Malaysia, payment in full to be received in 30 days. On this day, the exchange rate for ringgits is $0.4501.

Dec. 31   Recorded adjusting entries to recognize exchange gains or losses on Doering's annual financial statements. Rates for exchanging foreign currencies on this day follow.

Pesos (Mexico)	$0.1055
Yen (Japan)	0.0093
Pounds (Britain)	1.4620
Ringgits (Malaysia)	0.4456

2009

Jan. 12   Received full payment in pounds from Smithers for the October 14 sale and immediately exchanged the pounds for dollars. The exchange rate for pounds is $1.4699 on this day.

Jan. 19   Received Hamid Albar's full payment in ringgits for the December 20 sale and immediately exchanged the ringgits for dollars. The exchange rate for ringgits is $0.4420 on this day.

Required

1. Prepare journal entries for the Doering transactions and adjusting entries (round amounts to the nearest dollar).

Check (2) 2008 total foreign exchange loss, $274

2. Compute the foreign exchange gain or loss to be reported on Doering's 2008 income statement.

Analysis Component

3. What actions might Doering consider to reduce its risk of foreign exchange gains or losses?

PROBLEM SET B

Problem 15-1B
Recording transactions and market adjustments for trading securities

C2   P1

Harris Company, which began operations in 2008, invests its idle cash in trading securities. The following transactions relate to its short-term investments in its trading securities.

2008

Mar. 10   Purchased 2,400 shares of AOL at $59.15 per share plus a $1,545 commission.
May   7   Purchased 5,000 shares of MTV at $36.25 per share plus a $2,855 commission.
Sept. 1   Purchased 1,200 shares of UPS at $57.25 per share plus a $1,250 commission.

2009

Apr. 26   Sold 5,000 shares of MTV at $34.50 per share less a $2,050 commission.
Apr. 27   Sold 1,200 shares of UPS at $60.50 per share less a $1,788 commission.
June   2   Purchased 3,600 shares of SPW at $172 per share plus a $3,250 commission.
June 14   Purchased 900 shares of Wal-Mart at $50.25 per share plus a $1,082 commission.

2010

Jan. 28   Purchased 2,000 shares of PepsiCo at $43 per share plus a $2,890 commission.
Jan. 31   Sold 3,600 shares of SPW at $168 per share less a $2,040 commission.
Aug. 22   Sold 2,400 shares of AOL at $56.75 per share less a $2,480 commission.
Sept. 3   Purchased 1,500 shares of Vodaphone at $40.50 per share plus a $1,680 commission.
Oct.   9   Sold 900 shares of Wal-Mart at $53.75 per share less a $1,220 commission.

Required

1. Prepare journal entries to record these short-term investment activities for the years shown. (Ignore any year-end adjusting entries.)

Check (2) Cr. Market Adjustment—Trading $13,820

2. On December 31, 2010, prepare the adjusting entry to record any necessary market adjustment for the portfolio of trading securities when PepsiCo's share price is $41 and Vodaphone's share price is $37. (Assume the Market Adjustment—Trading account had an unadjusted balance of zero.)

Slip Systems had no short-term investments prior to 2008. It had the following transactions involving short-term investments in available-for-sale securities during 2008.

Feb. 6   Purchased 3,400 shares of Nokia stock at $41.25 per share plus a $3,000 brokerage fee.
     15   Paid $20,000 to buy six-month U.S. Treasury bills (debt securities): $20,000 principal amount, 6% interest, securities dated February 15.
Apr. 7   Purchased 1,200 shares of Dell Co. stock at $39.50 per share plus a $1,255 brokerage fee.
June 2   Purchased 2,500 shares of Merck stock at $72.50 per share plus a $2,890 brokerage fee.
     30   Received a $0.19 per share cash dividend on the Nokia shares.
Aug. 11   Sold 850 shares of Nokia stock at $46 per share less a $1,050 brokerage fee.
     16   Received a check for principal and accrued interest on the U.S. Treasury bills purchased February 15.
     24   Received a $0.10 per share cash dividend on the Dell shares.
Nov. 9   Received a $0.20 per share cash dividend on the remaining Nokia shares.
Dec. 18   Received a $0.15 per share cash dividend on the Dell shares.

Problem 15-2B
Recording, adjusting, and reporting short-term available-for-sale securities

C2 P3

Required

1. Prepare journal entries to record the preceding transactions and events.

2. Prepare a table to compare the year-end cost and market values of the short-term investments in available-for-sale securities. The year-end market values per share are: Nokia, $40.25; Dell, $40.50; and Merck, $59.

3. Prepare an adjusting entry, if necessary, to record the year-end market adjustment for the portfolio of short-term investments in available-for-sale securities.

Check   (2) Cost = $340,232

(3) Dr. Unrealized Loss—Equity, $41,494

Analysis Component

4. Explain the balance sheet presentation of the market adjustment to Slip's short-term investments.

5. How do these short-term investments affect (*a*) its income statement for year 2008 and (*b*) the equity section of its balance sheet at the 2008 year-end?

Paris Enterprises, which began operations in 2008, invests in long-term available-for-sale securities. Following is a series of transactions and events involving its long-term investment activity.

Problem 15-3B
Recording, adjusting, and reporting long-term available-for-sale securities

C2 P3

2008

Mar. 10   Purchased 1,200 shares of Apple Computer at $25.50 per share plus $800 commission.
Apr. 7   Purchased 2,500 shares of Ford at $22.50 per share plus $1,033 commission.
Sept. 1   Purchased 600 shares of Polaroid at $47.00 per share plus $890 commission.
Dec. 31   Per share market values for stocks in the portfolio are: Apple, $27.50; Ford, $21.00; Polaroid, $49.00.

2009

Apr. 26   Sold 2,500 shares of Ford at $20.50 per share less a $1,207 commission.
June 2   Purchased 1,800 shares of Duracell at $19.25 per share plus a $1,050 commission.
June 14   Purchased 1,200 shares of Sears at $21.00 per share plus a $280 commission.
Nov. 27   Sold 600 shares of Polaroid at $51 per share less an $845 commission.
Dec. 31   Per share market values for stocks in the portfolio are: Apple, $29.00; Duracell, $18.00; Sears, $23.00.

2010

Jan. 28   Purchased 1,000 shares of Coca-Cola Co. at $40 per share plus a $1,480 commission.
Aug. 22   Sold 1,200 shares of Apple at $21.50 per share less a $1,850 commission.
Sept. 3   Purchased 3,000 shares of Motorola at $28.00 per share plus a $780 commission.
Oct. 9   Sold 1,200 shares of Sears at $24.00 per share less a $599 commission.
Oct. 31   Sold 1,800 shares of Duracell at $15.00 per share less an $898 commission.
Dec. 31   Per share market values for stocks in the portfolio are: Coca-Cola, $48.00; Motorola, $24.00.

Required

1. Prepare journal entries to record these transactions and events and any year-end market adjustments to the portfolio of long-term available-for-sale securities.

2. Prepare a table that summarizes the (a) total cost, (b) total market adjustment, and (c) total market value for the portfolio of long-term available-for-sale securities at each year-end.

3. Prepare a table that summarizes (a) the realized gains and losses and (b) the unrealized gains or losses for the portfolio of long-term available-for-sale securities at each year-end.

Problem 15-4B
Long-term investment
transactions; unrealized and
realized gains and losses

C2   C3   P3   P4

Troyer's long-term available-for-sale portfolio at December 31, 2007, consists of the following.

Available-for-Sale Securities	Cost	Market Value
27,500 shares of Company R common stock	$559,125	$599,063
8,500 shares of Company S common stock	308,380	293,250
11,000 shares of Company T common stock	147,295	151,800

Troyer enters into the following long-term investment transactions during year 2008.

Jan. 13   Sold 2,125 shares of Company S common stock for $72,250 less a brokerage fee of $1,195.
Mar. 24   Purchased 15,500 shares of Company U common stock for $282,875 plus a brokerage fee of $1,980. The shares represent a 62% ownership in Company U.
Apr. 5   Purchased 42,500 shares of Company V common stock for $133,875 plus a brokerage fee of $1,125. The shares represent a 10% ownership in Company V.
Sept. 2   Sold 11,000 shares of Company T common stock for $156,750 less a brokerage fee of $2,700.
Sept. 27   Purchased 2,500 shares of Company W common stock for $50,500 plus a brokerage fee of $1,050. The shares represent a 25% ownership in Company W.
Oct. 30   Purchased 5,000 shares of Company X common stock for $48,750 plus a brokerage fee of $1,170. The shares represent a 13% ownership in Company X.

The market values of its investments at December 31, 2008, are: R, $568,125; S, $210,375; U, $272,800; V, $134,938; W, $54,689; and X, $45,625.

Required

1. Determine the amount Troyer should report on its December 31, 2008, balance sheet for its long-term investments in available-for-sale securities.

2. Prepare any necessary December 31, 2008, adjusting entry to record the market value adjustment of the long-term investments in available-for-sale securities.

3. What amount of gains or losses on transactions relating to long-term investments in available-for-sale securities should Troyer report on its December 31, 2008, income statement?

Problem 15-5B
Accounting for long-term
investments in securities; with
and without significant influence

C2   P3   P4

Brinkley Company, which began operations on January 3, 2008, had the following subsequent transactions and events in its long-term investments.

2008

Jan. 5   Brinkley purchased 20,000 shares (25% of total) of Bloch's common stock for $200,500.
Aug. 1   Bloch declared and paid a cash dividend of $1.05 per share.
Dec. 31   Bloch's net income for 2008 is $82,000, and the market value of its stock is $11.90 per share.

2009

Aug. 1   Bloch declared and paid a cash dividend of $1.35 per share.
Dec. 31   Bloch's net income for 2009 is $78,000, and the market value of its stock is $13.65 per share.

2010

Jan. 8   Brinkley sold all of its investment in Bloch for $375,000 cash.

Part 1

Assume that Brinkley has a significant influence over Bloch with its 25% share.

Required

1. Prepare journal entries to record these transactions and events for Brinkley.

2. Compute the carrying (book) value per share of Brinkley's investment in Bloch common stock as reflected in the investment account on January 7, 2010.

Check   (2) Carrying value per share, $9.63

3. Compute the net increase or decrease in Brinkley's equity from January 5, 2008, through January 8, 2010, resulting from its investment in Bloch.

Part 2

Assume that although Brinkley owns 25% of Bloch's outstanding stock, circumstances indicate that it does not have a significant influence over the investee and that it is classified as an available-for-sale security investment.

Required

1. Prepare journal entries to record these transactions and events for Brinkley. Also prepare an entry dated January 8, 2010, to remove any balance related to the market adjustment.

(1) 1/8/10 Dr. Unrealized Gain—Equity $72,500

2. Compute the cost per share of Brinkley's investment in Bloch common stock as reflected in the investment account on January 7, 2010.

3. Compute the net increase or decrease in Brinkley's equity from January 5, 2008, through January 8, 2010, resulting from its investment in Bloch.

(3) Net increase, $222,500

Datamix, a U.S. corporation with customers in several foreign countries, had the following selected transactions for 2008 and 2009.

Problem 15-6B[A]
Foreign currency transactions

C4   P5

2008

May 26   Sold merchandise for 6.5 million yen to Fuji Company of Japan, payment in full to be received in 60 days. On this day, the exchange rate for yen is $0.0093.

June 1   Sold merchandise to Fordham Ltd. of Great Britain for $64,800 cash. The exchange rate for pounds is $1.4498 on this day.

July 25   Received Fuji's payment in yen for its May 26 purchase and immediately exchanged the yen for dollars. The exchange rate for yen is $0.0092 on this day.

Oct. 15   Sold merchandise on credit to Martinez Brothers of Mexico. The price of 378,000 pesos is to be paid 90 days from the date of sale. On this day, the exchange rate for pesos is $0.1020.

Dec. 6   Sold merchandise for 250,000 yuans to Chi-Ying Company of China, payment in full to be received in 30 days. The exchange rate for yuans is $0.1439 on this day.

Dec. 31   Recorded adjusting entries to recognize exchange gains or losses on Datamix's annual financial statements. Rates of exchanging foreign currencies on this day follow.

Yen (Japan)	$0.0094
Pounds (Britain)	1.4580
Pesos (Mexico)	0.1060
Yuans (China)	0.1450

2009

Jan. 5   Received Chi-Ying's full payment in yuans for the December 6 sale and immediately exchanged the yuans for dollars. The exchange rate for yuans is $0.1580 on this day.

Jan. 13   Received full payment in pesos from Martinez for the October 15 sale and immediately exchanged the pesos for dollars. The exchange rate for pesos is $0.1039 on this day.

Required

1. Prepare journal entries for the Datamix transactions and adjusting entries.

2. Compute the foreign exchange gain or loss to be reported on Datamix's 2008 income statement.

Check   2008 total foreign exchange gain, $1,137

Analysis Component

3. What actions might Datamix consider to reduce its risk of foreign exchange gains or losses?

    Problem Set C is available at the book's Website to reinforce and assess your learning.   **PROBLEM SET C**

SERIAL PROBLEM

Success Systems

(This serial problem began in Chapter 1 and continues through most of the book. If previous chapter segments were not completed, the serial problem can begin at this point. It is helpful, but not necessary, for you to use the Working Papers that accompany the book.)

SP 15   While reviewing the March 31, 2008, balance sheet of Success Systems, Adriana Lopez notes that the business has built a large cash balance of $87,171. Its most recent bank money market statement shows that the funds are earning an annualized return of 0.75%. Lopez decides to make several investments with the desire to earn a higher return on the idle cash balance. Accordingly, in April 2008, Success Systems makes the following investments in trading securities:

April 16   Purchases 400 shares of Johnson & Johnson stock at $55 per share plus $300 commission.
April 30   Purchases 200 shares of Starbucks Corporation at $27 per share plus $250 commission.

On June 30, 2008, the per share market price of the Johnson & Johnson shares is $60 and the Starbucks shares is $24.

Required

1. Prepare journal entries to record the April purchases of trading securities by Success Systems.
2. On June 30, 2008, prepare the adjusting entry to record any necessary market adjustment to its portfolio of trading securities.

BEYOND THE NUMBERS

REPORTING IN ACTION

C3 C4 A1

BTN 15-1   Refer to Best Buy's financial statements in Appendix A to answer the following.

1. Are Best Buy's financial statements consolidated? How can you tell?
2. What is Best Buy's *comprehensive income* for the year ended February 26, 2005?
3. Does Best Buy have any foreign operations? How can you tell?
4. Compute Best Buy's return on total assets for the year ended February 26, 2005.

Fast Forward

5. Access Best Buy's annual report for a fiscal year ending after February 26, 2005, from either its Website (BestBuy.com) or the SEC's EDGAR database (www.SEC.gov). Recompute Best Buy's return on total assets for the years subsequent to February 26, 2005.

COMPARATIVE ANALYSIS

A1

BTN 15-2   Key comparative figures ($ millions) for Best Buy and Circuit City follow.

Key Figures	Best Buy			Circuit City		
	Current Year	1 Year Prior	2 Years Prior	Current Year	1 Year Prior	2 Years Prior
Net income	$ 984	$ 705	$ 99	$ 62	$ (89)	$ 82
Net sales	27,433	24,548	20,943	10,472	9,857	10,055
Total assets	10,294	8,652	7,694	3,789	3,731	3,841

Required

1. Compute return on total assets for Best Buy and Circuit City for the two most recent years.
2. Separate the return on total assets computed in part 1 into its components for both companies and both years according to the formula in Exhibit 15.9.
3. Which company has the higher total return on assets? The higher profit margin? The higher total asset turnover? What does this comparative analysis reveal? (Assume an industry average of 6.5% for return on assets.)

BTN 15-3 Kendra Wecker is the controller for Wildcat Company, which has numerous long-term investments in debt securities. Wildcat's investments are mainly in 10-year bonds. Wecker is preparing its year-end financial statements. In accounting for long-term debt securities, she knows that each long-term investment must be designated as a held-to-maturity or an available-for-sale security. Interest rates rose sharply this past year causing the portfolio's market value to substantially decline. The company does not intend to hold the bonds for the entire 10 years. Wecker also earns a bonus each year, which is computed as a percent of net income.

ETHICS
CHALLENGE
C2 P2 P3

Required

1. Will Wecker's bonus depend in any way on the classification of the debt securities? Explain.
2. What criteria must Wecker use to classify the securities as held-to-maturity or available-for-sale?
3. Is there likely any company oversight of Wecker's classification of the securities? Explain.

BTN 15-4 Assume that you are Jackson Company's accountant. Company owner Abel Terrio has reviewed the 2009 financial statements you prepared and questions the $6,000 loss reported on the sale of its investment in Blackhawk Co. common stock. Jackson acquired 50,000 shares of Blackhawk's common stock on December 31, 2007, at a cost of $500,000. This stock purchase represented a 40% interest in Blackhawk. The 2008 income statement reported that earnings from all investments were $126,000. On January 3, 2009, Jackson Company sold the Blackhawk stock for $575,000. Blackhawk did not pay any dividends during 2008 but reported a net income of $202,500 for that year. Terrio believes that because the Blackhawk stock purchase price was $500,000 and was sold for $575,000, the 2009 income statement should report a $75,000 gain on the sale.

COMMUNICATING
IN PRACTICE
C2 P4

Required

Draft a one-half page memorandum to Terrio explaining why the $6,000 loss on sale of Blackhawk stock is correctly reported.

BTN 15-5 Access the August 26, 2005, 10-K filing (for year-end June 30, 2005) of Microsoft (MSFT) at www.sec.gov. Review its footnote 3, "Investments."

TAKING IT TO
THE NET
C1 C2

Required

1. How does the cost-basis total for cash and securities as of June 30, 2005, compare to the prior year–end amount?
2. Identify at least eight types of short-term investments held by Microsoft as of June 30, 2005.
3. What were Microsoft's unrealized gains and its unrealized losses from cash and securities for 2005?
4. Was the cost or market (recorded) value of the investments higher as of June 30, 2005?

BTN 15-6 Each team member is to become an expert on a specific classification of long-term investments. This expertise will be used to facilitate other teammates' understanding of the concepts and procedures relevent to the classification chosen.

TEAMWORK IN
ACTION
C1 C2 C3 P1 P2 P3 P4

1. Each team member must select an area for expertise by choosing one of the following classifications of long-term investments.
  a. Held-to-maturity debt securities
  b. Available-for-sale debt and equity securities
  c. Equity securities with significant influence
  d. Equity securities with controlling influence
2. Learning teams are to disburse and expert teams are to be formed. Expert teams are made up of those who select the same area of expertise. The instructor will identify the location where each expert team will meet.
3. Expert teams will collaborate to develop a presentation based on the following requirements. Students must write the presentation in a format they can show to their learning teams in part (4).

Requirements for Expert Presentation

    a. Write a transaction for the acquisition of this type of investment security. The transaction description is to include all necessary data to reflect the chosen classification.

    b. Prepare the journal entry to record the acquisition.

    [*Note:* The expert team on equity securities with controlling influence will substitute requirements (*d*) and (*e*) with a discussion of the reporting of these investments.]

    c. Identify information necessary to complete the end-of-period adjustment for this investment.

    d. Assuming that this is the only investment owned, prepare any necessary year-end entries.

    e. Present the relevant balance sheet section(s).

4. Re-form learning teams. In rotation, experts are to present to their teams the presentations they developed in part 3. Experts are to encourage and respond to questions.

BusinessWeek
ACTIVITY

C2

BTN 15-7   Read the article "Accounting: Bringing the Future into Play" in the March 11, 2002, issue of *BusinessWeek*. (This book's Website provides a free link.)

Required

1. On what types of data do accountants focus? How does this compare with the data desired by investors?

2. Explain the phrase "marking to market."

3. What ideas have been proposed to allow marking to market that will also limit fraud by insiders?

4. How do accountants respond to the economists' argument that mark-to-market accounting will result in "asymmetrical" information for investors?

5. What is the best argument for mark-to-market accounting?

ENTREPRENEURIAL DECISION

C4 P5

BTN 15-8ᴬ   Refer to the opening feature in this chapter about Stu Levy and **TOKYOPOP**. Stu must acquire the Japanese rights to material that is then translated for the U.S. audience. Assume that on January 1, 2008, Stu acquires the rights to manga material from a Japanese distributor and agrees to pay 12,000,000 yen per year for those rights. Quarterly payments are due March 31, June 30, September 30, and December 31 each year. On January 1, 2008, the yen is worth $0.00891.

Required

1. Prepare the journal entry to record the publishing rights purchased on January 1, 2008.

2. Prepare the journal entries to record the payments on March 31, June 30, September 30, and December 31, 2008. The value of the yen on those dates follows.

March 31	$0.00893
June 30	0.00901
September 30	0.00902
December 31	0.00897

3. How can Stu protect himself from unanticipated gains and losses from currency translation if all of his payments are specified to be paid in yen?

HITTING THE ROAD C4

BTN 15-9ᴬ   Assume that you are planning a spring break trip to Europe. Identify three locations where you can find exchange rates for the dollar relative to the Euro or other currencies.

BTN 15-10 Dixons, Best Buy, and Circuit City are competitors in the global marketplace. Following are selected data from each company.

| Key Figure | Dixons (£ millions) | | | Best Buy | | Circuit City | |
	Current Year	One Year Prior	Two Years Prior	Current Year	Prior Year	Current Year	Prior Year
Net income	£ 284	£ 209	£ 211	—	—	—	—
Total assets	3,874	4,158	3,577	—	—	—	—
Net sales	6,492	5,758	4,868	—	—	—	—
Profit margin	?	?	—	3.6%	2.9%	0.6%	(0.9)%
Total asset turnover	?	?	—	2.9	3.0	2.8	2.6

Required

1. Compute Dixons' return on total assets for the most recent two years using the data provided.

2. Which of these three companies has the highest return on total assets? Highest profit margin? Highest total asset turnover?

ANSWERS TO MULTIPLE CHOICE QUIZ

1. d; $30,000 × 5% × 5/12 = $625
2. a; Unrealized gain = $84,500 − $83,000 = $1,500
3. b; $50,000 × 35% = $17,500

4. e; $300,000/$2,000,000 = 15%
5. b; Profit margin = $80,000/$600,000 = 13.3%
     Total asset turnover = $600,000/$400,000 = 1.5

16

Reporting the Statement of Cash Flows

A Look Back

Chapter 15 focused on how to identify, account for, and report investments in securities. We also accounted for transactions listed in a foreign currency.

A Look at This Chapter

This chapter focuses on reporting and analyzing cash inflows and cash outflows. We emphasize how to prepare and interpret the statement of cash flows.

A Look Ahead

Chapter 17 focuses on tools to help us analyze financial statements. We also describe comparative analysis and the application of ratios for financial analysis.

Learning Objectives

CAP

Conceptual

C1 Explain the purpose and importance of cash flow information. *(p. 622)*

C2 Distinguish between operating, investing, and financing activities. *(p. 623)*

C3 Identify and disclose noncash investing and financing activities. *(p. 625)*

C4 Describe the format of the statement of cash flows. *(p. 625)*

Analytical

A1 Analyze the statement of cash flows. *(p. 639)*

A2 Compute and apply the cash flow on total assets ratio. *(p. 640)*

Procedural

P1 Prepare a statement of cash flows. *(p. 626)*

P2 Compute cash flows from operating activities using the indirect method. *(p. 629)*

P3 Determine cash flows from both investing and financing activities. *(p. 635)*

P4 *Appendix 16A*—Illustrate use of a spreadsheet to prepare a statement of cash flows. *(p. 643)*

P5 *Appendix 16B*—Compute cash flows from operating activities using the direct method. *(p. 646)*

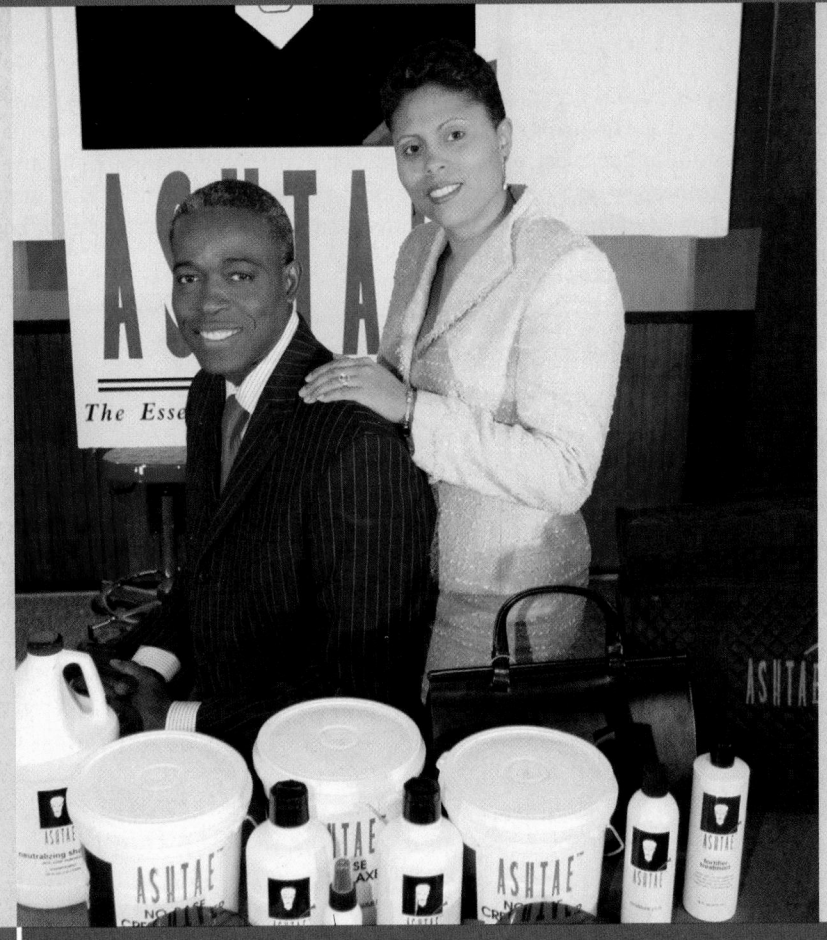

"We don't sell products. . . we sell relationships"
—Michael Woods
(Ramona Woods on right)

Hair-Raising Cash Flows

GREENSBORO, NC—Although cash may not be king, it certainly improves the King's health. Just ask Michael and Ramona Woods, entrepreneurial cofounders of **Ashtae Products (ASHTAE.com),** a multicultural hair-care products and services company. The husband-and-wife team opened Ashtae, named after daughters Ashley and Taylore, in 1995—and revenues now exceed $5 million per year.

But early on, all was not well in the kingdom. "We did everything wrong when we started our business," says Ramona. Cash flow was a constant battle for fledgling Ashtae, as cash flows ran short despite growing profits. "Our mortgage went into foreclosure. Our cars were repossessed," recalls Ramona. "I had to take the bus with two little kids. Sometimes I didn't have the money for the bus. . . we did so much wrong."

Michael and Ramona learned the importance of cash flows the hard way. "We failed to realize that knowing how to sell and make money doesn't mean you know how to keep it," says Michael. Cash outflows for inventory and asset growth yielded negative cash flows for Ashtae in spite of growing sales and profits.

Managing cash was a constant struggle. The couple eventually learned how to monitor and control cash flows associated with each of its operating, investing, and financing activities. They discovered, says Michael, how "to plan for the various stages of growth" and to manage cash flows.

This chapter focuses on cash flows—its measurement, presentation, analysis, and interpretation. It describes how to analyze separately the cash flows related to operating, investing, and financing activities. Michael and Ramona know first-hand the importance of scrutinizing and overseeing cash flows. Says Ramona, "We had to learn to draw the line. . . [to achieve] a profitable business." With healthy cash flows today, the outlook for King Michael and Queen Ramona is good. As Michael puts it, "WOW! That is the only word that can describe our performance."

[Sources: *Ashtae Website,* May 2006; *The Business Journal,* July 2005, January 2005, and December 2004; *SCORE.org Website,* September 2005; *Age Venture News,* February 2003]

Profitability is a main goal of most managers, but not the only goal. A company cannot achieve or maintain profits without carefully managing cash. Managers and other users of information pay close attention to a company's cash position and the events and transactions affecting cash. This chapter explains how we prepare, analyze, and interpret a statement of cash flows. It also discusses the importance of cash flow information for predicting future performance and making managerial decisions. More generally, effectively using the statement of cash flows is crucial for managing and analyzing the operating, investing, and financing activities of businesses.

Reporting the Statement of Cash Flows

Basics of Cash Flow Reporting	Cash Flows from Operating	Cash Flows from Investing	Cash Flows from Financing
• Purpose • Importance • Measurement • Classification • Noncash activities • Format • Preparation	• Indirect and direct methods of reporting • Application of indirect method of reporting • Summary of indirect method adjustments	• Three-stage process of analysis • Analysis of noncurrent assets • Analysis of other assets	• Three-stage process of analysis • Analysis of noncurrent liabilities • Analysis of equity

Basics of Cash Flow Reporting

This section describes the basics of cash flow reporting, including its purpose, measurement, classification, format, and preparation.

Purpose of the Statement of Cash Flows

C1 Explain the purpose and importance of cash flow information.

The purpose of the **statement of cash flows** is to report all major cash receipts (inflows) and cash payments (outflows) during a period. This includes separately identifying the cash flows related to operating, investing, and financing activities. The statement of cash flows does more than simply report changes in cash. It is the detailed disclosure of individual cash flows that makes this statement useful to users. Information in this statement helps users answer questions such as these:

■ How does a company obtain its cash?
■ Where does a company spend its cash?
■ What explains the change in the cash balance?

The statement of cash flows addresses important questions such as these by summarizing, classifying, and reporting a company's cash inflows and cash outflows for each period.

Point: Internal users rely on the statement of cash flows to make investing and financing decisions. External users rely on this statement to assess the amount and timing of a company's cash flows.

Topic Tackler
PLUS

Importance of Cash Flows

Information about cash flows can influence decision makers in important ways. For instance, we look more favorably at a company that is financing its expenditures with cash from operations than one that does it by selling its assets. Information about cash flows helps users decide whether a company has enough cash to pay its existing debts as they mature. It is also relied upon to evaluate a company's ability to meet unexpected obligations and pursue unexpected opportunities. External information users especially want to assess a company's ability to take advantage of new business opportunities. Internal users such as managers use cash flow information to plan day-to-day operating activities and make long-term investment decisions.

Macy's striking turnaround is an example of how analysis and management of cash flows can lead to improved financial stability. Several years ago Macy's obtained temporary protection from bankruptcy, at which time it desperately needed to improve its cash flows. It did so by engaging in aggressive cost-cutting measures. As a result, Macy's annual cash flow rose to $210 million, up from a negative cash flow of $38.9 million in the prior year. Macy's eventually met its financial obligations and then successfully merged with **Federated Department Stores**.

The case of **W. T. Grant Co.** is a classic example of the importance of cash flow information in predicting a company's future performance and financial strength. Grant reported net income of more than $40 million per year for three consecutive years. At that same time, it was experiencing an alarming decrease in cash provided by operations. For instance, net cash outflow was more than $90 million by the end of that three-year period. Grant soon went bankrupt. Users who relied solely on Grant's income numbers were unpleasantly surprised. This reminds us that cash flows as well as income statement and balance sheet information are crucial in making business decisions.

> **Decision Insight**
>
> **Cash Multiple** Some experts who value private companies do so on the basis of a multiple of operating cash flow. Medium-sized private companies usually sell for five to seven times their operating cash flows. Larger companies often command higher multiples.

Measurement of Cash Flows

Cash flows are defined to include both *cash* and *cash equivalents*. The statement of cash flows explains the difference between the beginning and ending balances of cash and cash equivalents. We continue to use the phrases *cash flows* and the *statement of cash flows,* but we must remember that both phrases refer to cash and cash equivalents. Recall that a cash equivalent must satisfy two criteria: (1) be readily convertible to a known amount of cash and

Cash and Cash Equivalents

(2) be sufficiently close to its maturity so its market value is unaffected by interest rate changes. In most cases, a debt security must be within three months of its maturity to satisfy these criteria. Companies must disclose and follow a clear policy for determining cash and cash equivalents and apply it consistently from period to period. **American Express**, for example, defines its cash equivalents as "time deposits and other highly liquid investments with original maturities of 90 days or less."

> **Decision Insight**
>
> **Cash Flow** "A lender must have a complete understanding of a borrower's cash flows to assess both the borrowing needs and repayment sources. This requires information about the major types of cash inflows and outflows. I have seen many companies, whose financial statements indicate good profitability, experience severe financial problems because the owners or managers lacked a good understanding of cash flows."—Mary E. Garza, **Bank of America**.

Classification of Cash Flows

Since cash and cash equivalents are combined, the statement of cash flows does not report transactions between cash and cash equivalents such as cash paid to purchase cash equivalents and cash received from selling cash equivalents. However, all other cash receipts and cash payments are classified and reported on the statement as operating, investing, or financing activities. Individual cash receipts and payments for each of these three categories are labeled to identify their originating transactions or events. A net cash inflow (source) occurs when the receipts in a category exceed the payments. A net cash outflow (use) occurs when the payments in a category exceed the receipts.

C2 Distinguish between operating, investing, and financing activities.

Operating Investing Financing

Operating Activities **Operating activities** include those transactions and events that determine net income. Examples are the production and purchase of merchandise, the sale of goods and services to customers, and the expenditures to administer the business. Not all items in income, such as unusual gains and losses, are operating activities (we discuss these exceptions later in the chapter). Exhibit 16.1 lists the more common cash inflows and outflows from operating activities. (Although cash receipts and cash payments from buying and selling trading securities are often reported under operating activities, new standards require that these receipts and payments be classified based on the nature and purpose of those securities.)

Exhibit 16.1

Cash Flows from Operating Activities

Investing Activities   **Investing activities** generally include those transactions and events that affect long-term assets, namely, the purchase and sale of long-term assets. They also include the (1) purchase and sale of short-term investments other than cash equivalents and trading securities and (2) lending and collecting money for notes receivable. Exhibit 16.2 lists examples of cash flows from investing activities. Proceeds from collecting the principal amounts of notes deserve special mention. If the note results from sales to customers, its cash receipts are classed as operating activities whether short term or long term. If the note results from a loan to another party apart from sales, however, the cash receipts from collecting the note principal are classed as an investing activity. The FASB requires the collection of interest on loans be reported as an operating activity.

Point: Common errors include misclassification of *cash dividends received* and *cash interest received* as investing activities and *cash interest paid* as financing. The FASB requires these cash flows be reported as operating activities.

Exhibit 16.2

Cash Flows from Investing Activities

Financing Activities   **Financing activities** include those transactions and events that affect long-term liabilities and equity. Examples are (1) obtaining cash from issuing debt and repaying the amounts borrowed and (2) receiving cash from or distributing cash to owners. These activities involve transactions with a company's owners and creditors. They also often involve borrowing and repaying principal amounts relating to both short- and long-term debt. Notice that payments of interest expense are classified as operating activities. Also, cash payments to settle credit purchases of merchandise, whether on account or by note, are operating activities. Exhibit 16.3 lists examples of cash flows from financing activities.

Point: Interest payments on a loan are classified as operating activities, but payments of loan principal are financing activities.

Exhibit 16.3

Cash Flows from Financing Activities

Noncash Investing and Financing

When important investing and financing activities do not affect cash receipts or payments, they are still disclosed at the bottom of the statement of cash flows or in a note to the statement because of their importance and the *full-disclosure principle*. One example of such a transaction is the purchase of long-term assets using a long-term note payable. This transaction involves both investing and financing activities but does not affect any cash inflow or outflow and is not reported in any of the three sections of the statement of cash flows. This disclosure rule also extends to transactions with partial cash receipts or payments.

To illustrate, assume that Goorin purchases land for $12,000 by paying $5,000 cash and trading in used equipment with a $7,000 market value. The investing section of the statement of cash flows reports only the $5,000 cash outflow for the land purchase. The $12,000 investing transaction is only partially described in the body of the statement of cash flows, yet this information is potentially important to users because it changes the makeup of assets. Goorin could either describe the transaction in a note or include a small schedule at the bottom of its statement that lists the $12,000 land purchase along with the cash financing of $5,000 and a $7,000 trade-in of used equipment. As another example, Borg Co. acquired $900,000 of assets in exchange for $200,000 cash and a $700,000 long-term note, which is reported as follows:

C3 Identify and disclose noncash investing and financing activities.

Point: A stock dividend transaction involving a transfer from retained earnings to common stock or a credit to contributed capital is *not* considered a noncash investing and financing activity because the company receives no consideration for shares issued.

Decision Maker	Answer—p. 652

Entrepreneur You are considering purchasing a start-up business that recently reported a $110,000 annual net loss and a $225,000 annual net cash inflow. How are these results possible?

Fair value of assets acquired	$900,000
Less cash paid	200,000
Liabilities incurred or assumed	$700,000

Exhibit 16.4 lists transactions commonly disclosed as noncash investing and financing activities.

- Retirement of debt by issuing equity stock.
- Conversion of preferred stock to common stock.
- Lease of assets in a capital lease transaction.
- Purchase of long-term assets by issuing a note or bond.
- Exchange of noncash assets for other noncash assets.
- Purchase of noncash assets by issuing equity or debt.

Exhibit 16.4

Examples of Noncash Investing and Financing Activities

Format of the Statement of Cash Flows

Accounting standards require companies to include a statement of cash flows in a complete set of financial statements. This statement must report information about a company's cash receipts and cash payments during the period. Exhibit 16.5 shows the usual format. A company must report cash flows from three activities: operating, investing, and financing. The statement explains how transactions and events impact the prior period-end cash (and cash equivalents) balance to produce its current period-end balance.

C4 Describe the format of the statement of cash flows.

Exhibit 16.5

Format of the Statement of Cash Flows

COMPANY NAME Statement of Cash Flows For *period* Ended *date*	
Cash flows from operating activities	
[List of individual inflows and outflows]	
Net cash provided (used) by operating activities	$ #
Cash flows from investing activities	
[List of individual inflows and outflows]	
Net cash provided (used) by investing activities	#
Cash flows from financing activities	
[List of individual inflows and outflows]	
Net cash provided (used) by financing activities	#
Net increase (decrease) in cash	$ #
Cash (and equivalents) balance at prior period-end	#
Cash (and equivalents) balance at current period-end	$ #

Separate schedule or note disclosure of any "noncash investing and financing transactions" is required.

Global: International standards also require a statement of cash flows separated into operating, investing, and financing activities.

Quick Check
Answers—p. 652

1. Does a statement of cash flows report the cash payments to purchase cash equivalents? Does it report the cash receipts from selling cash equivalents?

2. Identify the categories of cash flows reported separately on the statement of cash flows.

3. Identify the cash activity category for each transaction: (*a*) purchase equipment for cash, (*b*) cash payment of wages, (*c*) sale of common stock for cash, (*d*) receipt of cash dividends from stock investment, (*e*) cash collection from customers, (*f*) bonds issuance for cash.

Preparing the Statement of Cash Flows

P1   Prepare a statement of cash flows.

Step 1: Compute net increase or decrease in cash

Step 2: Compute net cash from operating activities

Step 3: Compute net cash from investing activities

Step 4: Compute net cash from financing activities

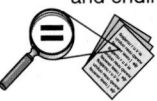

Step 5: Prove and report beginning and ending cash balances

Preparing a statement of cash flows involves five steps: (1) compute the net increase or decrease in cash; (2) compute and report net cash provided (used) by operating activities (using either the direct or indirect method; both are explained); (3) compute and report net cash provided (used) by investing activities; (4) compute and report net cash provided (used) by financing activities; and (5) compute net cash flow by combining net cash provided (used) by operating, investing, and financing activities and then *prove it* by adding it to the beginning cash balance to show that it equals the ending cash balance. Important noncash investing and financing activities are disclosed in either a note or a separate schedule to the statement.

Computing the net increase or net decrease in cash is a simple but crucial computation. It equals the current period's cash balance minus the prior period's cash balance. This is the *bottom-line* figure for the statement of cash flows and is a check on the accuracy of one's work. The information we need to prepare a statement of cash flows comes from various sources including comparative balance sheets at the beginning and end of the period, and an income statement for the period. There are two alternative approaches to preparing the statement: (1) analyzing the Cash account and (2) analyzing noncash accounts.

Analyzing the Cash Account   A company's cash receipts and cash payments are recorded in the Cash account in its general ledger. The Cash account is therefore a natural place to look for information about cash flows from operating, investing, and financing activities. To illustrate, review the summarized Cash T-account of Genesis, Inc., in Exhibit 16.6. Individual cash transactions are summarized in this Cash account according to the major types of cash receipts and cash payments. For instance, only the total of cash receipts from all customers is listed. Individual cash transactions underlying these totals can number in the thousands. Accounting software programs are available to provide summarized cash accounts.

Preparing a statement of cash flows from Exhibit 16.6 requires determining whether an individual cash inflow or outflow is an operating, investing, or financing activity, and then listing each by activity. This yields the statement shown in Exhibit 16.7. However, preparing

```
Accounting System:                                                        _ □ ×
File  Edit  Maintain  Tasks  Analysis  Options  Reports  Window  Help
┌──────────────────────────────── Cash ──────────────────────────── _ □ × ┐
│ Balance, Dec. 31, 2007 ............  12,000                                │
│ Receipts from customers .........  570,000 │ Payments for merchandise ................................  319,000 │
│ Receipts from asset sales .......  12,000 │ Payments for wages and operating expenses .....  218,000 │
│ Receipts from stock issuance ..  15,000 │ Payments for interest .........................................  8,000 │
│                                            │ Payments for taxes ............................................  5,000 │
│                                            │ Payments for assets ..........................................  10,000 │
│                                            │ Payments for bond retirement ...........................  18,000 │
│                                            │ Payments for dividends ....................................  14,000 │
│ Balance, Dec. 31, 2008 ............  17,000 │                                                          │
└────────────────────────────────────────────────────────────────────────┘
  Sales     Purchases    General    Payroll    Inventory    Company    Analysis
                         Ledger
```

Exhibit 16.6

Summarized Cash Account

the statement of cash flows from an analysis of the summarized Cash account has two limitations. First, most companies have many individual cash receipts and payments, making it difficult to review them all. Accounting software minimizes this burden, but it is still a task requiring professional judgment for many transactions. Second, the Cash account does not usually carry an adequate description of each cash transaction, making assignment of all cash transactions according to activity difficult.

Point: View the change in cash as a *target* number that you will fully explain and prove in the statement of cash flows.

GENESIS Statement of Cash Flows For Year Ended December 31, 2008		
Cash flows from operating activities		
Cash received from customers	$570,000	
Cash paid for merchandise	(319,000)	
Cash paid for wages and other operating expenses	(218,000)	
Cash paid for interest	(8,000)	
Cash paid for taxes	(5,000)	
Net cash provided by operating activities		$20,000
Cash flows from investing activities		
Cash received from sale of plant assets	12,000	
Cash paid for purchase of plant assets	(10,000)	
Net cash provided by investing activities		2,000
Cash flows from financing activities		
Cash received from issuing stock	15,000	
Cash paid to retire bonds	(18,000)	
Cash paid for dividends	(14,000)	
Net cash used in financing activities		(17,000)
Net increase in cash		$ 5,000
Cash balance at prior year-end		12,000
Cash balance at current year-end		$17,000

Exhibit 16.7

Statement of Cash Flows—
Direct Method

Analyzing Noncash Accounts A second approach to preparing the statement of cash flows is analyzing noncash accounts. This approach uses the fact that when a company records cash inflows and outflows with debits and credits to the Cash account (see Exhibit 16.6), it also records credits and debits in noncash accounts (reflecting double-entry accounting). Many of these noncash accounts are balance sheet accounts, for instance, from the sale of land for cash. Others are revenue and expense accounts that are closed to equity. For instance, the sale of services for cash yields a credit to Services Revenue that is closed to Retained Earnings for a corporation. In sum, *all cash transactions eventually affect noncash balance sheet accounts.* Thus, we can determine cash inflows and outflows by analyzing changes in noncash balance sheet accounts.

Exhibit 16.8 uses the accounting equation to show the relation between the Cash account and the noncash balance sheet accounts. This exhibit starts with the accounting equation at the top. It is then expanded in line (2) to separate cash from noncash asset accounts. Line (3) moves noncash asset accounts to the right-hand side of the equality where they are subtracted. This

Global: Some countries require a statement of funds flow instead of a statement of cash flows; *funds* are often defined as *working capital* (current assets minus current liabilities).

Exhibit 16.8

Relation between Cash and Noncash Accounts

shows that cash equals the sum of the liability and equity accounts *minus* the noncash asset accounts. Line (4) points out that *changes* on one side of the accounting equation equal *changes* on the other side. It shows that we can explain changes in cash by analyzing changes in the noncash accounts consisting of liability accounts, equity accounts, and noncash assets accounts. By analyzing noncash balance sheet accounts and any related income statement accounts, we can prepare a statement of cash flows.

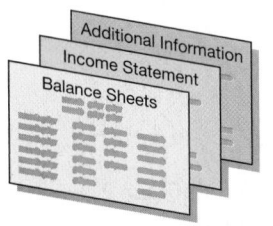

Information to Prepare the Statement　Information to prepare the statement of cash flows usually comes from three sources: (1) comparative balance sheets, (2) current income statement, and (3) additional information. Comparative balance sheets are used to compute changes in noncash accounts from the beginning to the end of the period. The current income statement is used to help compute cash flows from operating activities. Additional information often includes details on transactions and events that help explain both the cash flows and noncash investing and financing activities.

Decision Insight

e-Cash　Every credit transaction on the Net leaves a trail that a hacker or a marketer can pick up. Enter e-cash—or digital money. The encryption of e-cash protects your money from snoops and thieves and cannot be traced, even by the issuing bank.

Cash Flows from Operating

Indirect and Direct Methods of Reporting

Cash flows provided (used) by operating activities are reported in one of two ways: the *direct method* or the *indirect method*. **These two different methods apply only to the operating activities section.**

The **direct method** separately lists each major item of operating cash receipts (such as cash received from customers) and each major item of operating cash payments (such as cash paid

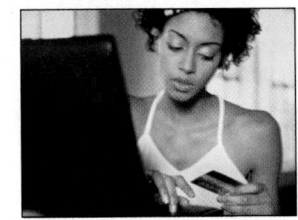

for merchandise). The cash payments are subtracted from cash receipts to determine the net cash provided (used) by operating activities. The operating activities section of Exhibit 16.7 reflects the direct method of reporting operating cash flows.

The **indirect method** reports net income and then adjusts it for items necessary to obtain net cash provided (used) by operating activities. It does *not* report individual items of cash inflows and cash outflows from operating activities. Instead, the indirect method reports the necessary adjustments to reconcile net income to net cash provided (used) by operating activities. The operating activities section for Genesis prepared under the indirect method is shown in Exhibit 16.9.

Cash flows from operating activities		
Net income	$ 38,000	
Adjustments to reconcile net income to net cash provided by operating activities		
Increase in accounts receivable	(20,000)	
Increase in merchandise inventory	(14,000)	
Increase in prepaid expenses	(2,000)	
Decrease in accounts payable	(5,000)	
Decrease in interest payable	(1,000)	
Increase in income taxes payable	10,000	
Depreciation expense	24,000	
Loss on sale of plant assets	6,000	
Gain on retirement of bonds	(16,000)	
Net cash provided by operating activities		**$20,000**

Exhibit 16.9

Operating Activities Section—
Indirect Method

The net cash amount provided by operating activities is *identical* **under both the direct and indirect methods.** This equality always exists. The difference in these methods is with the computation and presentation of this amount. The FASB recommends the direct method, but because it is not required and the indirect method is arguably easier to compute, nearly all companies report operating cash flows using the indirect method.

Point: To better understand the direct and indirect methods of reporting operating cash flows, identify similarities and differences between Exhibits 16.7 and 16.11.

To illustrate, we prepare the operating activities section of the statement of cash flows for Genesis. Exhibit 16.10 shows the December 31, 2007 and 2008, balance sheets of Genesis along with its 2008 income statement. We use this information to prepare a statement of cash flows that explains the $5,000 increase in cash for 2008 as reflected in its balance sheets. This $5,000 is computed as Cash of $17,000 at the end of 2008 minus Cash of $12,000 at the end of 2007. Genesis discloses additional information about 2008 transactions:

a. The accounts payable balances result from merchandise inventory purchases.

b. Purchased plant assets costing $70,000 by paying $10,000 cash and issuing $60,000 of bonds payable.

c. Sold plant assets with an original cost of $30,000 and accumulated depreciation of $12,000 for $12,000 cash, yielding a $6,000 loss.

d. Received cash of $15,000 from issuing 3,000 shares of common stock.

e. Paid $18,000 cash to retire bonds with a $34,000 book value, yielding a $16,000 gain.

f. Declared and paid cash dividends of $14,000.

> The next section describes the indirect method. Appendix 16B describes the direct method. An instructor can choose to cover either one or both methods. Neither section depends on the other.

Topic Tackler

PLUS

16-2

Application of the Indirect Method of Reporting

Net income is computed using accrual accounting, which recognizes revenues when earned and expenses when incurred. Revenues and expenses do not necessarily reflect the receipt and payment of cash. The indirect method of computing and reporting net cash flows from operating activities involves adjusting the net income figure to obtain the net cash provided (used) by operating activities. This includes subtracting noncash increases (credits) from net income and adding noncash charges (debits) back to net income.

P2 Compute cash flows from operating activities using the indirect method.

To illustrate, the indirect method begins with Genesis's net income of $38,000 and adjusts it to obtain net cash provided (used) by operating activities of $20,000. Exhibit 16.11 shows the results of the indirect method of reporting operating cash flows, which adjusts net income for three types of adjustments. There are adjustments ① to reflect changes in noncash current assets and current liabilities related to operating activities, ② to income statement items involving operating activities that do not affect cash inflows or outflows, and ③ to eliminate gains and losses resulting from investing and financing activities (not part of operating activities). This section describes each of these adjustments.

Point: *Noncash credits refer to revenue amounts reported on the income statement that are not collected in cash this period. Noncash charges refer to expense amounts reported on the income statement that are not paid this period.*

Exhibit 16.10

Financial Statements

GENESIS Income Statement For Year Ended December 31, 2008		
Sales		$590,000
Cost of goods sold	$300,000	
Wages and other operating expenses	216,000	
Interest expense	7,000	
Depreciation expense	24,000	(547,000)
		43,000
Other gains (losses)		
Gain on retirement of bonds	16,000	
Loss on sale of plant assets	(6,000)	10,000
Income before taxes		53,000
Income taxes expense		(15,000)
Net income		$ 38,000

GENESIS Balance Sheets December 31, 2008 and 2007		
	2008	**2007**
Assets		
Current assets		
Cash	$ 17,000	$ 12,000
Accounts receivable	60,000	40,000
Merchandise inventory	84,000	70,000
Prepaid expenses	6,000	4,000
Total current assets	167,000	126,000
Long-term assets		
Plant assets	250,000	210,000
Accumulated depreciation	(60,000)	(48,000)
Total assets	$357,000	$288,000
Liabilities		
Current liabilities		
Accounts payable	$ 35,000	$ 40,000
Interest payable	3,000	4,000
Income taxes payable	22,000	12,000
Total current liabilities	60,000	56,000
Long-term bonds payable	90,000	64,000
Total liabilities	150,000	120,000
Equity		
Common stock, $5 par	95,000	80,000
Retained earnings	112,000	88,000
Total equity	207,000	168,000
Total liabilities and equity	$357,000	$288,000

① **Adjustments for Changes in Current Assets and Current Liabilities**   This section describes adjustments for changes in noncash current assets and current liabilities.

Adjustments for changes in noncash current assets.   Changes in noncash current assets are normally the result of operating activities. Examples are sales affecting accounts receivable and asset usage affecting prepaid rent. Decreases in noncash current assets yield the following adjustment:

Decreases in noncash current assets are added to net income.

To see the logic for this adjustment, consider that a decrease in a noncash current asset such as accounts receivable suggests more available cash at the end of the period compared to the beginning. This is so because a decrease in accounts receivable implies higher cash receipts than reflected in sales. We add these higher cash receipts (from decreases in noncash current assets) to net income when computing cash flow from operations.

In contrast, an increase in noncash current assets such as accounts receivable implies less cash receipts than reflected in sales. As another example, an increase in prepaid rent indicates that more cash is paid for rent than is deducted as rent expense. Increases in noncash current assets yield the following adjustment:

Increases in noncash current assets are subtracted from net income.

To illustrate, these adjustments are applied to the noncash current assets in Exhibit 16.10.

Accounts receivable. Accounts Receivable *increase* $20,000, from a beginning balance of $40,000 to an ending balance of $60,000. This increase implies that Genesis collects less cash than is reported in sales. That is, some of these sales were in the form of accounts receivable and that amount increased during the period. To see this it is helpful to use *account analysis.* This usually involves setting up a T-account and reconstructing its major entries to compute cash receipts or payments. The following reconstructed Accounts Receivable T-account reveals the lower amount of cash receipts compared to sales:

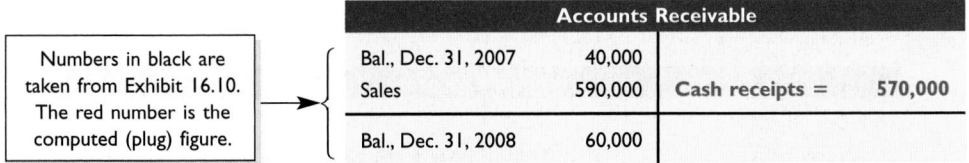

		Accounts Receivable		
Bal., Dec. 31, 2007	40,000			
Sales	590,000	Cash receipts =	570,000
Bal., Dec. 31, 2008	60,000			

Numbers in black are taken from Exhibit 16.10. The red number is the computed (plug) figure.

Notice that sales are $20,000 greater than the cash receipts. This $20,000—as reflected in the $20,000 increase in Accounts Receivable—is subtracted from net income when computing cash provided by operating activities (see Exhibit 16.11).

Merchandise inventory. Merchandise inventory *increases* by $14,000, from a $70,000 beginning balance to an $84,000 ending balance. This increase implies that Genesis had a larger amount of cash purchases than cost of goods sold. This larger amount of cash purchases is in the form of inventory, as reflected in the following account analysis:

		Merchandise Inventory	
Bal., Dec. 31, 2007	70,000		
Purchases =	314,000	Cost of goods sold	300,000
Bal., Dec. 31, 2008	84,000		

Exhibit 16.11

Statement of Cash Flows—Indirect Method

GENESIS	
Statement of Cash Flows	
For Year Ended December 31, 2008	
Cash flows from operating activities	
Net income	$ 38,000
Adjustments to reconcile net income to net	
cash provided by operating activities	
① Increase in accounts receivable	(20,000)
Increase in merchandise inventory	(14,000)
Increase in prepaid expenses	(2,000)
Decrease in accounts payable	(5,000)
Decrease in interest payable	(1,000)
Increase in income taxes payable	10,000
② Depreciation expense	24,000
③ Loss on sale of plant assets	6,000
Gain on retirement of bonds	(16,000)
Net cash provided by operating activities	$20,000
Cash flows from investing activities	
Cash received from sale of plant assets	12,000
Cash paid for purchase of plant assets	(10,000)
Net cash provided by investing activities	2,000
Cash flows from financing activities	
Cash received from issuing stock	15,000
Cash paid to retire bonds	(18,000)
Cash paid for dividends	(14,000)
Net cash used in financing activities	(17,000)
Net increase in cash	$ 5,000
Cash balance at prior year-end	12,000
Cash balance at current year-end	$17,000

Point: Refer to Exhibit 16.10 and identify the $5,000 change in cash. This change is what the statement of cash flows explains; it serves as a check figure.

The amount by which purchases exceed cost of goods sold—as reflected in the $14,000 increase in inventory—is subtracted from net income when computing cash provided by operating activities (see Exhibit 16.11).

Prepaid expenses. Prepaid expenses *increase* $2,000, from a $4,000 beginning balance to a $6,000 ending balance, implying that Genesis's cash payments exceed its recorded prepaid expenses. These higher cash payments increase the amount of Prepaid Expenses, as reflected in its reconstructed T-account:

Prepaid Expenses			
Bal., Dec. 31, 2007	4,000		
Cash payments =	218,000	Wages and other operating exp.	216,000
Bal., Dec. 31, 2008	6,000		

The amount by which cash payments exceed the recorded operating expenses—as reflected in the $2,000 increase in Prepaid Expenses—is subtracted from net income when computing cash provided by operating activities (see Exhibit 16.11).

Adjustments for changes in current liabilities.   Changes in current liabilities are normally the result of operating activities. An example is a purchase that affects accounts payable. Increases in current liabilities yield the following adjustment to net income when computing operating cash flows:

Increases in current liabilities are added to net income.

To see the logic for this adjustment, consider that an increase in the Accounts Payable account suggests that cash payments are less than the related (cost of goods sold) expense. As another example, an increase in wages payable implies that cash paid for wages is less than the recorded wages expense. Since the recorded expense is greater than the cash paid, we add the increase in wages payable to net income to compute net cash flow from operations.

Conversely, when current liabilities decrease, the following adjustment is required:

Decreases in current liabilities are subtracted from net income.

To illustrate, this adjustment is applied to the current liabilities in Exhibit 16.10.

Accounts payable. Accounts Payable *decrease* $5,000, from a beginning balance of $40,000 to an ending balance of $35,000. This decrease implies that cash payments to suppliers exceed purchases by $5,000 for the period, which is reflected in the reconstructed Accounts Payable T-account:

Accounts Payable			
		Bal., Dec. 31, 2007	40,000
Cash payments =	319,000	Purchases	314,000
		Bal., Dec. 31, 2008	35,000

The amount by which cash payments exceed purchases—as reflected in the $5,000 decrease in Accounts Payable—is subtracted from net income when computing cash provided by operating activities (see Exhibit 16.11).

Interest payable. Interest Payable *decreases* $1,000, from a $4,000 beginning balance to a $3,000 ending balance. This decrease indicates that cash paid for interest exceeds interest expense by $1,000, which is reflected in the Interest Payable T-account:

Interest Payable			
		Bal., Dec. 31, 2007	4,000
Cash paid for interest =	8,000	Interest expense	7,000
		Bal., Dec. 31, 2008	3,000

The amount by which cash paid exceeds recorded expense—as reflected in the $1,000 decrease in Interest Payable—is subtracted from net income (see Exhibit 16.11).

Income taxes payable. Income Taxes Payable *increase* $10,000, from a $12,000 beginning balance to a $22,000 ending balance. This increase implies that reported income taxes exceed the cash paid for taxes, which is reflected in the Income Taxes Payable T-account:

Income Taxes Payable			
		Bal., Dec. 31, 2007	12,000
Cash paid for taxes =	5,000	Income taxes expense	15,000
		Bal., Dec. 31, 2008	22,000

The amount by which cash paid falls short of the reported taxes expense—as reflected in the $10,000 increase in Income Taxes Payable—is added to net income when computing cash provided by operating activities (see Exhibit 16.11).

② **Adjustments for Operating Items Not Providing or Using Cash** The income statement usually includes some expenses that do not reflect cash outflows in the period. Examples are depreciation, amortization, depletion, and bad debts expense. The indirect method for reporting operating cash flows requires that

Expenses with no cash outflows are added back to net income.

To see the logic of this adjustment, recall that items such as depreciation, amortization, depletion, and bad debts originate from debits to expense accounts and credits to noncash accounts. These entries have *no* cash effect, and we add them back to net income when computing net cash flows from operations. Adding them back cancels their deductions.

Similarly, when net income includes revenues that do not reflect cash inflows in the period, the indirect method for reporting operating cash flows requires that

Revenues with no cash inflows are subtracted from net income.

We apply these adjustments to the Genesis operating items that do not provide or use cash.

Depreciation. Depreciation expense is the only Genesis operating item that has no effect on cash flows in the period. We must add back the $24,000 depreciation expense to net income when computing cash provided by operating activities. (We later explain that the cash outflow to acquire a plant asset is reported as an investing activity.)

③ **Adjustments for Nonoperating Items** Net income often includes losses that are not part of operating activities but are part of either investing or financing activities. Examples are a loss from the sale of a plant asset and a loss from retirement of a bond payable. The indirect method for reporting operating cash flows requires that

Nonoperating losses are added back to net income.

To see the logic, consider that items such as a plant asset sale and a bond retirement are normally recorded by recognizing the cash, removing all plant asset or bond accounts, and recognizing any loss or gain. The cash received or paid is not part of operating activities but is part of either investing or financing activities. *No* operating cash flow effect occurs. However, because the nonoperating loss is a deduction in computing net income, we need to add it back to net income when computing cash flow from operations. Adding it back cancels the deduction.

Similarly, when net income includes gains not part of operating activities, the indirect method for reporting operating cash flows requires that

Nonoperating gains are subtracted from net income.

To illustrate these adjustments, we consider the nonoperating items of Genesis.

Adjustments for Changes in Current Assets and Current Liabilities

Account	Increases	Decreases
Noncash current assets	Deduct from NI	Add to NI
Current liabilities	Add to NI	Deduct from NI

Point: An income statement reports revenues, gains, expenses, and losses on an accrual basis. The statement of cash flows reports cash received and cash paid for operating, financing, and investing activities.

Loss on sale of plant assets. Genesis reports a $6,000 loss on sale of plant assets as part of net income. This loss is a proper deduction in computing income, but it is *not part of operating activities*. Instead, a sale of plant assets is part of investing activities. Thus, the $6,000 nonoperating loss is added back to net income (see Exhibit 16.11). Adding it back cancels the loss. We later explain how to report the cash inflow from the asset sale in investing activities.

Gain on retirement of debt. A $16,000 gain on retirement of debt is properly included in net income, but it is *not part of operating activities*. This means the $16,000 nonoperating gain must be subtracted from net income to obtain net cash provided by operating activities (see Exhibit 16.11). Subtracting it cancels the recorded gain. We later describe how to report the cash outflow to retire debt.

Decision Insight

Cash or Income The difference between net income and operating cash flows can be large and reflect on the quality of earnings. This bar chart shows net income and operating cash flows of four companies. Operating cash flows can be either higher or lower than net income.

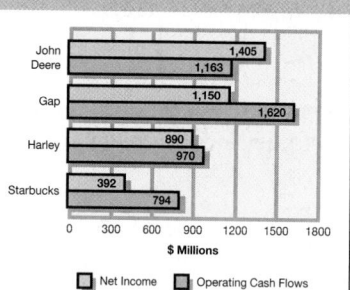

Summary of Adjustments for Indirect Method

Exhibit 16.12 summarizes the most common adjustments to net income when computing net cash provided (used) by operating activities under the indirect method.

Exhibit 16.12

Summary of Selected Adjustments for Indirect Method

Net Income	
+Decrease in noncash current asset	
−Increase in noncash current asset	① Adjustments for changes in current assets and current liabilities
+Increase in current liability*	
−Decrease in current liability*	
+Depreciation, depletion, and amortization	
+Accrued expenses reported in income	② Adjustments for operating items not providing or using cash
−Accrued revenues reported in income	
+Loss on disposal of long-term asset	
+Loss on retirement of debt	③ Adjustments for nonoperating items
−Gain on disposal of long-term asset	
−Gain on retirement of debt	
Net cash provided (used) by operating activities	

* Excludes current portion of long-term debt and any (nonsales-related) short-term notes payable—both are financing activities.

The computations in determining cash provided (used) by operating activities are different for the indirect and direct methods, but the result is identical. Both methods yield the same $20,000 figure for cash from operating activities for Genesis; see Exhibits 16.7 and 16.11.

Quick Check

Answers—p. 652

4. Determine net cash provided (used) by operating activities using the following data: net income, $74,900; decrease in accounts receivable, $4,600; increase in inventory, $11,700; decrease in accounts payable, $1,000; loss on sale of equipment, $3,400; payment of cash dividends, $21,500.

5. Why are expenses such as depreciation and amortization added to net income when cash flow from operating activities is computed by the indirect method?

6. A company reports net income of $15,000 that includes a $3,000 gain on the sale of plant assets. Why is this gain subtracted from net income in computing cash flow from operating activities using the indirect method?

Cash Flows from Investing

The third major step in preparing the statement of cash flows is to compute and report cash flows from investing activities. We normally do this by identifying changes in (1) all noncurrent asset accounts and (2) the current accounts for both notes receivable and investments in securities (excluding trading securities). We then analyze changes in these accounts to determine their effect, if any, on cash and report the cash flow effects in the investing activities section of the statement of cash flows. **Reporting of investing activities is identical under the direct method and indirect method.**

Three-Stage Process of Analysis

Information to compute cash flows from investing activities is usually taken from beginning and ending balance sheets and the income statement. We use a three-stage process to determine cash provided (used) by investing activities: (1) identify changes in investing-related accounts, (2) explain these changes using reconstruction analysis, and (3) report their cash flow effects.

Analysis of Noncurrent Assets

Information about the Genesis transactions provided earlier reveals that the company both purchased and sold plant assets during the period. Both transactions are investing activities and are analyzed for their cash flow effects in this section.

P3 Determine cash flows from both investing and financing activities.

Plant Asset Transactions The first stage in analyzing the Plant Assets account and its related Accumulated Depreciation is to identify any changes in these accounts from comparative balance sheets in Exhibit 16.10. This analysis reveals a $40,000 increase in plant assets from $210,000 to $250,000 and a $12,000 increase in accumulated depreciation from $48,000 to $60,000.

Point: Investing activities include (1) purchasing and selling long-term assets, (2) lending and collecting on notes receivable, and (3) purchasing and selling short-term investments other than cash equivalents and trading securities.

The second stage is to explain these changes. Items *b* and *c* of the additional information for Genesis (page 629) are relevant in this case. Recall that the Plant Assets account is affected by both asset purchases and sales, while its Accumulated Depreciation account is normally increased from depreciation and decreased from the removal of accumulated depreciation in asset sales. To explain changes in these accounts and to identify their cash flow effects, we prepare *reconstructed entries* from prior transactions; *they are not the actual entries by the preparer.*

Point: Financing and investing info is available in ledger accounts to help explain changes in comparative balance sheets. Post references lead to relevant entries and explanations.

To illustrate, item *b* reports that Genesis purchased plant assets of $70,000 by issuing $60,000 in bonds payable to the seller and paying $10,000 in cash. The reconstructed entry for analysis of item *b* follows:

Reconstruction	Plant Assets	70,000	
	Bonds Payable		60,000
	Cash		**10,000**

Assets = Liabilities + Equity
+70,000   +60,000
−10,000

This entry reveals a $10,000 cash outflow for plant assets and a $60,000 noncash investing and financing transaction involving bonds exchanged for plant assets.

Next, item *c* reports that Genesis sold plant assets costing $30,000 (with $12,000 of accumulated depreciation) for $12,000 cash, resulting in a $6,000 loss. The reconstructed entry for analysis of item *c* follows:

Reconstruction	**Cash**	**12,000**	
	Accumulated Depreciation	12,000	
	Loss on Sale of Plant Assets	6,000	
	Plant Assets		30,000

Assets = Liabilities + Equity
+12,000   −6,000
−30,000
+12,000

This entry reveals a $12,000 cash inflow from assets sold. The $6,000 loss is computed by comparing the asset book value to the cash received and does not reflect any cash inflow or outflow. We also reconstruct the entry for Depreciation Expense using information from the income statement:

Assets = Liabilities + Equity
−24,000   −24,000

| Reconstruction | Depreciation Expense .... | 24,000 | |
| | Accumulated Depreciation .... | | 24,000 |

This entry shows that Depreciation Expense results in no cash flow effect. These three reconstructed entries are reflected in the following plant asset and related T-accounts.

Plant Assets			
Bal., Dec. 31, 2007	210,000		
Purchase	70,000	Sale	30,000
Bal., Dec. 31, 2008	250,000		

Accumulated Depreciation—Plant Assets			
		Bal., Dec. 31, 2007	48,000
Sale	12,000	Depr. expense	24,000
		Bal., Dec. 31, 2008	60,000

This reconstruction analysis is complete in that the change in plant assets from $210,000 to $250,000 is fully explained by the $70,000 purchase and the $30,000 sale. Also, the change in accumulated depreciation from $48,000 to $60,000 is fully explained by depreciation expense of $24,000 and the removal of $12,000 in accumulated depreciation from an asset sale. (*Note:* Preparers of the statement of cash flows have the entire ledger and additional information at their disposal, but for brevity reasons only the information needed for reconstructing accounts is given.)

The third stage looks at the reconstructed entries for identification of cash flows. The two identified cash flow effects are reported in the investing section of the statement as follows (also see Exhibit 16.7 or 16.11):

Example: If a plant asset costing $40,000 with $37,000 of accumulated depreciation is sold at a $1,000 loss, what is the cash flow? What is the cash flow if this asset is sold at a gain of $3,000? *Answers:* +$2,000; +$6,000.

Cash flows from investing activities	
Cash received from sale of plant assets	$12,000
Cash paid for purchase of plant assets	(10,000)

Also, the $60,000 portion of the purchase described in item *b* and financed by issuing bonds is a noncash investing and financing activity. It is reported in a note or in a separate schedule to the statement as follows:

Noncash investing and financing activity	
Purchased plant assets with issuance of bonds	$60,000

Analysis of Other Assets

Many other asset transactions (including those involving current notes receivable and investments in certain securities) are considered investing activities and can affect a company's cash flows. Since Genesis did not enter into other investing activities impacting assets, we do not need to extend our analysis to these other assets. If such transactions did exist, we would analyze them using the same three-stage process illustrated for plant assets.

Quick Check
Answer—p. 652

7. Equipment costing $80,000 with accumulated depreciation of $30,000 is sold at a loss of $10,000. What is the cash receipt from this sale? In what section of the statement of cash flows is this transaction reported?

Cash Flows from Financing

The fourth major step in preparing the statement of cash flows is to compute and report cash flows from financing activities. We normally do this by identifying changes in all noncurrent liability accounts (including the current portion of any notes and bonds) and the equity accounts. These accounts include long-term debt, notes payable, bonds payable, common stock, and retained earnings. Changes in these accounts are then analyzed using available information to determine their effect, if any, on cash. Results are reported in the financing activities section of the statement. **Reporting of financing activities is identical under the direct method and indirect method.**

Three-Stage Process of Analysis

We again use a three-stage process to determine cash provided (used) by financing activities: (1) identify changes in financing-related accounts, (2) explain these changes using reconstruction analysis, and (3) report their cash flow effects.

Analysis of Noncurrent Liabilities

Information about Genesis provided earlier reveals two transactions involving noncurrent liabilities. We analyzed one of those, the $60,000 issuance of bonds payable to purchase plant assets. This transaction is reported as a significant noncash investing and financing activity in a note or a separate schedule to the statement of cash flows. The other remaining transaction involving noncurrent liabilities is the cash retirement of bonds payable.

Point: Financing activities generally refer to changes in the noncurrent liability and the equity accounts. Examples are (1) receiving cash from issuing debt or repaying amounts borrowed and (2) receiving cash from or distributing cash to owners.

Bonds Payable Transactions   The first stage in analysis of bonds is to review the comparative balance sheets from Exhibit 16.10. This analysis reveals an increase in bonds payable from $64,000 to $90,000.

The second stage explains this change. Item *e* of the additional information for Genesis (page 629) reports that bonds with a carrying value of $34,000 are retired for $18,000 cash, resulting in a $16,000 gain. The reconstructed entry for analysis of item *e* follows:

Reconstruction	Bonds Payable	34,000	
	Gain on retirement of debt		16,000
	Cash		**18,000**

Assets	= Liabilities +	Equity
−18,000	−34,000	+16,000

This entry reveals an $18,000 cash outflow for retirement of bonds and a $16,000 gain from comparing the bonds payable carrying value to the cash received. This gain does not reflect any cash inflow or outflow. Also, item *b* of the additional information reports that Genesis purchased plant assets costing $70,000 by issuing $60,000 in bonds payable to the seller and paying $10,000 in cash. We reconstructed this entry when analyzing investing activities: It showed a $60,000 increase to bonds payable that is reported as a noncash investing and financing transaction. The Bonds Payable account reflects (and is fully explained by) these reconstructed entries as follows:

	Bonds Payable		
		Bal., Dec. 31, 2007	64,000
Retired bonds	34,000	**Issued bonds**	60,000
		Bal., Dec. 31, 2008	90,000

The third stage is to report the cash flow effect of the bond retirement in the financing section of the statement as follows (also see Exhibit 16.7 or 16.11):

Cash flows from financing activities
Cash paid to retire bonds . . . . $(18,000)

Analysis of Equity

The Genesis information reveals two transactions involving equity accounts. The first is the issuance of common stock for cash. The second is the declaration and payment of cash dividends. We analyze both.

Common Stock Transactions   The first stage in analyzing common stock is to review the comparative balance sheets from Exhibit 16.10, which reveals an increase in common stock from $80,000 to $95,000.

The second stage explains this change. Item *d* of the additional information (page 629) reports that 3,000 shares of common stock are issued at par for $5 per share. The reconstructed entry for analysis of item *d* follows:

Assets = Liabilities + Equity
+15,000   +15,000

Reconstruction	**Cash**	**15,000**	
	Common Stock		15,000

This entry reveals a $15,000 cash inflow from stock issuance and is reflected in (and explains) the Common Stock account as follows:

Common Stock		
	Bal., Dec. 31, 2007	80,000
	Issued stock	**15,000**
	Bal., Dec. 31, 2008	95,000

The third stage discloses the cash flow effect from stock issuance in the financing section of the statement as follows (also see Exhibit 16.7 or 16.11):

Cash flows from financing activities	
Cash received from issuing stock	$15,000

Retained Earnings Transactions   The first stage in analyzing the Retained Earnings account is to review the comparative balance sheets from Exhibit 16.10. This reveals an increase in retained earnings from $88,000 to $112,000.

The second stage explains this change. Item *f* of the additional information (page 629) reports that cash dividends of $14,000 are paid. The reconstructed entry follows:

Assets = Liabilities + Equity
−14,000   −14,000

Reconstruction	Retained Earnings............................	14,000	
	Cash		**14,000**

This entry reveals a $14,000 cash outflow for cash dividends. Also note that the Retained Earnings account is impacted by net income of $38,000. (Net income was analyzed under the operating section of the statement of cash flows.) The reconstructed Retained Earnings account follows:

Retained Earnings			
		Bal., Dec. 31, 2007	88,000
Cash dividend	**14,000**	**Net income**	**38,000**
		Bal., Dec. 31, 2008	112,000

The third stage reports the cash flow effect from the cash dividend in the financing section of the statement as follows (also see Exhibit 16.7 or 16.11):

Cash flows from financing activities
Cash paid for dividends . . . . $(14,000)

We now have identified and explained all of the Genesis cash inflows and cash outflows and one noncash investing and financing transaction. Specifically, our analysis has reconciled changes in all noncash balance sheet accounts.

Proving Cash Balances

The fifth and final step in preparing the statement is to report the beginning and ending cash balances and prove that the *net change in cash* is explained by operating, investing, and financing cash flows. This step is shown here for Genesis.

Net cash provided by operating activities	$20,000
Net cash provided by investing activities	2,000
Net cash used in financing activities	(17,000)
Net increase in cash	**$ 5,000**
Cash balance at 2007 year-end	12,000
Cash balance at 2008 year-end	$17,000

The preceding table shows that the $5,000 net increase in cash, from $12,000 at the beginning of the period to $17,000 at the end, is reconciled by net cash flows from operating ($20,000 inflow), investing ($2,000 inflow), and financing ($17,000 outflow) activities. This is formally reported at the bottom of the statement of cash flows as shown in both Exhibits 16.7 and 16.11.

Point: Financing activities not affecting cash flow include *declaration* of a cash dividend, *declaration* of a stock dividend, payment of a stock dividend, and a stock split.

Global: There are no requirements to separate domestic and international cash flows, leading some users to ask "Where in the world is cash flow?"

Point: The following ratio helps assess whether operating cash flow is adequate to meet long-term obligations:
Cash coverage of debt = Cash flow from operations divided by noncurrent liabilities.
A low ratio suggests a higher risk of insolvency; a high ratio suggests a greater ability to meet long-term obligations.

Decision Maker   Answer—p. 652

Reporter   Management is in labor contract negotiations and grants you an interview. It highlights a recent $600,000 net loss that involves a $930,000 extraordinary loss and a total net cash outflow of $550,000 (which includes net cash outflows of $850,000 for investing activities and $350,000 for financing activities). What is your assessment of this company?

Cash Flow Analysis   **Decision Analysis**

Analyzing Cash Sources and Uses

Most managers stress the importance of understanding and predicting cash flows for business decisions. Creditors evaluate a company's ability to generate cash before deciding whether to lend money. Investors also assess cash inflows and outflows before buying and selling stock. Information in the statement of cash flows helps address these and other questions such as (1) How much cash is generated from or used in operations? (2) What expenditures are made with cash from operations? (3) What is the source of cash for debt payments? (4) What is the source of cash for distributions to owners? (5) How is the increase in investing activities financed? (6) What is the source of cash for new plant assets? (7) Why is cash flow from operations different from income? (8) How is cash from financing used?

To effectively answer these questions, it is important to separately analyze investing, financing, and operating activities. To illustrate, consider data from three different companies in Exhibit 16.13. These companies operate in the same industry and have been in business for several years.

A1 Analyze the statement of cash flows.

Decision Insight

Free Cash Flows   Cash-based valuation of a company is theoretically equal to earnings-based valuation, but it usually yields a different value due to practical limitations. One limitation is the measurement of cash flows that are "free" for distribution to shareholders. These *free cash flows* are defined as cash flows available to shareholders after operating asset reinvestments and debt payments. Growth and financial flexibility depend on adequate free cash flow.

Exhibit 16.13

Cash Flows of Competing Companies

($ thousands)	BMX	ATV	Trex
Cash provided (used) by operating activities	$90,000	$40,000	$(24,000)
Cash provided (used) by investing activities			
Proceeds from sale of plant assets			26,000
Purchase of plant assets	(48,000)	(25,000)	
Cash provided (used) by financing activities			
Proceeds from issuance of debt			13,000
Repayment of debt	(27,000)		
Net increase (decrease) in cash	$15,000	$15,000	$ 15,000

Each company generates an identical $15,000 net increase in cash, but its sources and uses of cash flows are very different. BMX's operating activities provide net cash flows of $90,000, allowing it to purchase plant assets of $48,000 and repay $27,000 of its debt. ATV's operating activities provide $40,000 of cash flows, limiting its purchase of plant assets to $25,000. Trex's $15,000 net cash increase is due to selling plant assets and incurring additional debt. Its operating activities yield a net cash outflow of $24,000. Overall, analysis of these cash flows reveals that BMX is more capable of generating future cash flows than is ATV or Trex.

Cash Flow on Total Assets

A2 Compute and apply the cash flow on total assets ratio.

Cash flow information has limitations, but it can help measure a company's ability to meet its obligations, pay dividends, expand operations, and obtain financing. Users often compute and analyze a cash-based ratio similar to return on total assets except that its numerator is net cash flows from operating activities. The **cash flow on total assets** ratio is in Exhibit 16.14.

Exhibit 16.14

Cash Flow on Total Assets

$$\text{Cash flow on total assets} = \frac{\text{Cash flow from operations}}{\text{Average total assets}}$$

Exhibit 16.15

Nike's Cash Flow on Total Assets

Year	Cash Flow on Total Assets	Return on Total Assets
2005	18.8%	14.5%
2004	20.6	12.8
2003	13.9	7.1
2002	17.6	10.8
2001	11.2	10.1

This ratio reflects actual cash flows and is not affected by accounting income recognition and measurement. It can help business decision makers estimate the amount and timing of cash flows when planning and analyzing operating activities.

To illustrate, the 2005 cash flow on total assets ratio for **Nike** is 18.8%—see Exhibit 16.15. Is an 18.8% ratio good or bad? To answer this question, we compare this ratio with the ratios of prior years (we could also compare its ratio with those of its competitors and the market). Nike's cash flow on total assets ratio for several prior years is in the second column of Exhibit 16.15. Results show that its 18.8% return is higher than each of the prior years' returns except 2004.

As an indicator of *earnings quality,* some analysts compare the cash flow on total assets ratio to the return on total assets ratio. Nike's return on total assets is provided in the third column of Exhibit 16.15. Nike's cash flow on total assets ratio exceeds its return on total assets in each of the five years, leading some analysts to infer that Nike's earnings quality is high for that period because more earnings are realized in the form of cash.

Decision Insight

Cash Flow Ratios Analysts use various other cash-based ratios:

(1) $$\text{Cash coverage of growth} = \frac{\text{Operating cash flow}}{\text{Cash outflow for plant assets}}$$

where a low ratio (less than 1) implies cash inadequacy to meet asset growth, whereas a high ratio implies cash adequacy for asset growth.

(2) $$\text{Operating cash flow to sales} = \frac{\text{Operating cash flow}}{\text{Net sales}}$$

when this ratio substantially and consistently differs from the operating income to net sales ratio, the risk of accounting improprieties increases.

Demonstration Problem

Umlauf's comparative balance sheets, income statement, and additional information follow.

UMLAUF COMPANY
Balance Sheets
December 31, 2008 and 2007

	2008	2007
Assets		
Cash	$ 43,050	$ 23,925
Accounts receivable	34,125	39,825
Merchandise inventory	156,000	146,475
Prepaid expenses	3,600	1,650
Equipment	135,825	146,700
Accum. depreciation—Equipment	(61,950)	(47,550)
Total assets	$310,650	$311,025
Liabilities and Equity		
Accounts payable	$ 28,800	$ 33,750
Income taxes payable	5,100	4,425
Dividends payable	0	4,500
Bonds payable	0	37,500
Common stock, $10 par	168,750	168,750
Retained earnings	108,000	62,100
Total liabilities and equity	$310,650	$311,025

UMLAUF COMPANY
Income Statement
For Year Ended December 31, 2008

Sales		$446,100
Cost of goods sold	$222,300	
Other operating expenses	120,300	
Depreciation expense	25,500	(368,100)
		78,000
Other gains (losses)		
Loss on sale of equipment	3,300	
Loss on retirement of bonds	825	(4,125)
Income before taxes		73,875
Income taxes expense		(13,725)
Net income		$ 60,150

Additional Information

a. Equipment costing $21,375 with accumulated depreciation of $11,100 is sold for cash.

b. Equipment purchases are for cash.

c. Accumulated Depreciation is affected by depreciation expense and the sale of equipment.

d. The balance of Retained Earnings is affected by dividend declarations and net income.

e. All sales are made on credit.

f. All merchandise inventory purchases are on credit.

g. Accounts Payable balances result from merchandise inventory purchases.

h. Prepaid expenses relate to "other operating expenses."

Required

1. Prepare a statement of cash flows using the indirect method for year 2008.

2.[B] Prepare a statement of cash flows using the direct method for year 2008.

Planning the Solution

- Prepare two blank statements of cash flows with sections for operating, investing, and financing activities using the (1) indirect method format and (2) direct method format.
- Compute the cash paid for equipment and the cash received from the sale of equipment using the additional information provided along with the amount for depreciation expense and the change in the balances of equipment and accumulated depreciation. Use T-accounts to help chart the effects of the sale and purchase of equipment on the balances of the Equipment account and the Accumulated Depreciation account.
- Compute the effect of net income on the change in the Retained Earnings account balance. Assign the difference between the change in retained earnings and the amount of net income to dividends declared. Adjust the dividends declared amount for the change in the Dividends Payable balance.
- Compute cash received from customers, cash paid for merchandise, cash paid for other operating expenses, and cash paid for taxes as illustrated in the chapter.
- Enter the cash effects of reconstruction entries to the appropriate section(s) of the statement.
- Total each section of the statement, determine the total net change in cash, and add it to the beginning balance to get the ending balance of cash.

Solution to Demonstration Problem

Supporting computations for cash receipts and cash payments.

(1)	*Cost of equipment sold	$ 21,375
	Accumulated depreciation of equipment sold	(11,100)
	Book value of equipment sold	10,275
	Loss on sale of equipment	(3,300)
	Cash received from sale of equipment	$ 6,975
	Cost of equipment sold	$ 21,375
	Less decrease in the equipment account balance	(10,875)
	Cash paid for new equipment	$ 10,500
(2)	Loss on retirement of bonds	$ 825
	Carrying value of bonds retired	37,500
	Cash paid to retire bonds	$ 38,325
(3)	Net income	$ 60,150
	Less increase in retained earnings	45,900
	Dividends declared	14,250
	Plus decrease in dividends payable	4,500
	Cash paid for dividends	$ 18,750
(4)B	Sales	$ 446,100
	Add decrease in accounts receivable	5,700
	Cash received from customers	$451,800
(5)B	Cost of goods sold	$ 222,300
	Plus increase in merchandise inventory	9,525
	Purchases	231,825
	Plus decrease in accounts payable	4,950
	Cash paid for merchandise	$236,775
(6)B	Other operating expenses	$ 120,300
	Plus increase in prepaid expenses	1,950
	Cash paid for other operating expenses	$122,250
(7)B	Income taxes expense	$ 13,725
	Less increase in income taxes payable	(675)
	Cash paid for income taxes	$ 13,050

* Supporting T-account analysis for part 1 follows:

Equipment				
Bal., Dec. 31, 2007	146,700			
Cash purchase	10,500	Sale		21,375
Bal., Dec. 31, 2008	135,825			

Accumulated Depreciation—Equipment				
			Bal., Dec. 31, 2007	47,550
Sale	11,100		Depr. expense	25,500
			Bal., Dec. 31, 2008	61,950

UMLAUF COMPANY
Statement of Cash Flows (Indirect Method)
For Year Ended December 31, 2008

Cash flows from operating activities		
Net income		$60,150
Adjustments to reconcile net income to net cash provided by operating activities		
Decrease in accounts receivable		5,700
Increase in merchandise inventory		(9,525)
Increase in prepaid expenses		(1,950)
Decrease in accounts payable		(4,950)
Increase in income taxes payable		675
Depreciation expense		25,500

[continued on next page]

[continued from previous page]

Loss on sale of plant assets	3,300	
Loss on retirement of bonds	825	
Net cash provided by operating activities		$79,725
Cash flows from investing activities		
Cash received from sale of equipment	6,975	
Cash paid for equipment	(10,500)	
Net cash used in investing activities		(3,525)
Cash flows from financing activities		
Cash paid to retire bonds payable	(38,325)	
Cash paid for dividends	(18,750)	
Net cash used in financing activities		(57,075)
Net increase in cash		$19,125
Cash balance at prior year-end		23,925
Cash balance at current year-end		$43,050

UMLAUF COMPANY
Statement of Cash Flows (Direct Method)
For Year Ended December 31, 2008

Cash flows from operating activities		
Cash received from customers	$451,800	
Cash paid for merchandise	(236,775)	
Cash paid for other operating expenses	(122,250)	
Cash paid for income taxes	(13,050)	
Net cash provided by operating activities		$79,725
Cash flows from investing activities		
Cash received from sale of equipment	6,975	
Cash paid for equipment	(10,500)	
Net cash used in investing activities		(3,525)
Cash flows from financing activities		
Cash paid to retire bonds payable	(38,325)	
Cash paid for dividends	(18,750)	
Net cash used in financing activities		(57,075)
Net increase in cash		$19,125
Cash balance at prior year-end		23,925
Cash balance at current year-end		$43,050

APPENDIX

Spreadsheet Preparation of the Statement of Cash Flows

16A

This appendix explains how to use a spreadsheet to prepare the statement of cash flows under the indirect method.

Preparing the Indirect Method Spreadsheet

Analyzing noncash accounts can be challenging when a company has a large number of accounts and many operating, investing, and financing transactions. A *spreadsheet,* also called *work sheet* or *working paper,* can help us organize the information needed to prepare a statement of cash flows. A spreadsheet also makes it easier to check the accuracy of our work. To illustrate, we return to the comparative balance sheets and

P4 Illustrate use of a spreadsheet to prepare a statement of cash flows.

income statement shown in Exhibit 16.10. Information needed for the spreadsheet in preparing the statement of cash flows along with identifying letters *a* through *m* follow:

a. Net income is $38,000.

b. Accounts receivable increase by $20,000.

c. Merchandise inventory increases by $14,000.

d. Prepaid expenses increase by $2,000.

e. Accounts payable decrease by $5,000.

f. Interest payable decreases by $1,000.

g. Income taxes payable increase by $10,000.

h. Depreciation expense is $24,000.

i. Plant assets costing $30,000 with accumulated depreciation of $12,000 are sold for $12,000 cash. This yields a loss on sale of assets of $6,000.

j. Bonds with a book value of $34,000 are retired with a cash payment of $18,000, yielding a $16,000 gain on retirement.

k. Plant assets costing $70,000 are purchased with a cash payment of $10,000 and an issuance of bonds payable for $60,000.

l. Issued 3,000 shares of common stock for $15,000 cash.

m. Paid cash dividends of $14,000.

Exhibit 16A.1 shows the indirect method spreadsheet for Genesis. We enter both beginning and ending balance sheet amounts on the spreadsheet. We also enter information in the Analysis of Changes columns (keyed to the additional information items *a* through *m*) to explain changes in the accounts and determine the cash flows for operating, investing, and financing activities. Information about noncash investing and financing activities is reported near the bottom.

Entering the Analysis of Changes on the Spreadsheet

The following sequence of procedures is used to complete the spreadsheet after the beginning and ending balances of the balance sheet accounts are entered:

① Enter net income as the first item in the Statement of Cash Flows section for computing operating cash inflow (debit) and as a credit to Retained Earnings.

② In the Statement of Cash Flows section, adjustments to net income are entered as debits if they increase cash flows and as credits if they decrease cash flows. Applying this same rule, adjust net income for the change in each noncash current asset and current liability account related to operating activities. For each adjustment to net income, the offsetting debit or credit must help reconcile the beginning and ending balances of a current asset or current liability account.

③ Enter adjustments to net income for income statement items not providing or using cash in the period. For each adjustment, the offsetting debit or credit must help reconcile a noncash balance sheet account.

④ Adjust net income to eliminate any gains or losses from investing and financing activities. Because the cash from a gain must be excluded from operating activities, the gain is entered as a credit in the operating activities section. Losses are entered as debits. For each adjustment, the related debit and/or credit must help reconcile balance sheet accounts and involve reconstructed entries to show the cash flow from investing or financing activities.

⑤ After reviewing any unreconciled balance sheet accounts and related information, enter the remaining reconciling entries for investing and financing activities. Examples are purchases of plant assets, issuances of long-term debt, stock issuances, and dividend payments. Some of these may require entries in the noncash investing and financing section of the spreadsheet (reconciled).

⑥ Check accuracy by totaling the Analysis of Changes columns and by determining that the change in each balance sheet account has been explained (reconciled).

Point: Analysis of the changes on the spreadsheet are summarized as:

1. Cash flows from operating activities generally affect net income, current assets, and current liabilities.

2. Cash flows from investing activities generally affect noncurrent asset accounts.

3. Cash flows from financing activities generally affect noncurrent liability and equity accounts.

We illustrate these steps in Exhibit 16A.1 for Genesis:

Step	Entries
① · · · · · · · ·	(*a*)
② · · · · · · · ·	(*b*) through (*g*)
③ · · · · · · · ·	(*h*)
④ · · · · · · · ·	(*i*) through (*j*)
⑤ · · · · · · · ·	(*k*) through (*m*)

Exhibit 16A.1

Spreadsheet for Preparing Statement of Cash Flows—Indirect Method

	File Edit View Insert Format Tools Data Accounting Window Help					

GENESIS
Spreadsheet for Statement of Cash Flows–Indirect Method
For Year Ended December 31, 2008

		Dec. 31, 2007	Analysis of Changes Debit		Analysis of Changes Credit	Dec. 31, 2008
8	**Balance Sheet—Debits**					
9	Cash	$ 12,000				$ 17,000
10	Accounts receivable	40,000	(b)	$ 20,000		60,000
11	Merchandise inventory	70,000	(c)	14,000		84,000
12	Prepaid expenses	4,000	(d)	2,000		6,000
13	Plant assets	210,000	(k1)	70,000	(i) $ 30,000	250,000
14		$336,000				$417,000
16	**Balance Sheet—Credits**					
17	Accumulated depreciation	$ 48,000	(i)	12,000	(h) 24,000	$ 60,000
18	Accounts payable	40,000	(e)	5,000		35,000
19	Interest payable	4,000	(f)	1,000		3,000
20	Income taxes payable	12,000			(g) 10,000	22,000
21	Bonds payable	64,000	(j)	34,000	(k2) 60,000	90,000
22	Common stock, $5 par value	80,000			(l) 15,000	95,000
23	Retained earnings	88,000	(m)	14,000	(a) 38,000	112,000
24		$336,000				$417,000
26	**Statement of Cash Flows**					
27	Operating activities					
28	Net income		(a)	38,000		
29	Increase in accounts receivable				(b) 20,000	
30	Increase in merchandise inventory				(c) 14,000	
31	Increase in prepaid expenses				(d) 2,000	
32	Decrease in accounts payable				(e) 5,000	
33	Decrease in interest payable				(f) 1,000	
34	Increase in income taxes payable		(g)	10,000		
35	Depreciation expense		(h)	24,000		
36	Loss on sale of plant assets		(i)	6,000		
37	Gain on retirement of bonds				(j) 16,000	
38	Investing activities					
39	Receipts from sale of plant assets		(i)	12,000		
40	Payment for purchase of plant assets				(k1) 10,000	
41	Financing activities					
42	Payment to retire bonds				(j) 18,000	
43	Receipts from issuing stock		(l)	15,000		
44	Payment of cash dividends				(m) 14,000	
46	**Noncash Investing and Financing Activities**					
47	Purchase of plant assets with bonds		(k2)	60,000	(k1) 60,000	
48				$337,000	$337,000	

Since adjustments *i, j,* and *k* are more challenging, we show them in the following debit and credit format. These entries are for purposes of our understanding; they are *not* the entries actually made in the journals. Changes in the Cash account are identified as sources or uses of cash.

i.	Loss from sale of plant assets	6,000	
	Accumulated depreciation	12,000	
	Receipt from sale of plant assets **(source of cash)**	12,000	
	Plant assets		30,000
	To describe sale of plant assets.		

[continued on next page]

[continued from previous page]

j.	Bonds payable..	34,000		
	Payments to retire bonds **(use of cash)**.................		18,000	
	Gain on retirement of bonds		16,000	
	To describe retirement of bonds.			
k1.	Plant assets...	70,000		
	Payment to purchase plant assets **(use of cash)**		10,000	
	Purchase of plant assets financed by bonds		60,000	
	To describe purchase of plant assets.			
k2.	Purchase of plant assets financed by bonds..................	60,000		
	Bonds payable		60,000	
	To issue bonds for purchase of assets.			

APPENDIX

16B Direct Method of Reporting Operating Cash Flows

P5 Compute cash flows from operating activities using the direct method.

We compute cash flows from operating activities under the direct method by adjusting accrual-based income statement items to the cash basis. The usual approach is to adjust income statement accounts related to operating activities for changes in their related balance sheet accounts as follows:

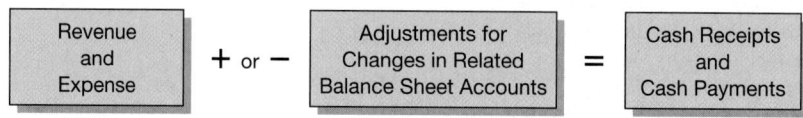

The framework for reporting cash receipts and cash payments for the operating section of the cash flow statement under the direct method is as in Exhibit 16B.1. We consider cash receipts first and then cash payments.

Exhibit 16B.1

Major Classes of Operating Cash Flows

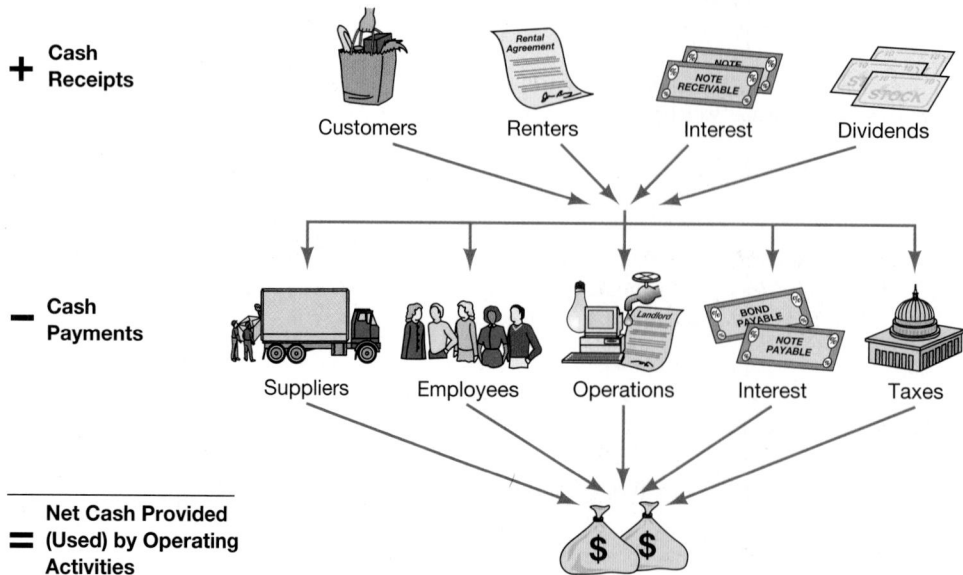

Operating Cash Receipts

A review of Exhibit 16.10 and the additional information reported by Genesis suggests only one potential cash receipt: sales to customers. This section, therefore, starts with sales to customers as reported on the income statement and then adjusts it as necessary to obtain cash received from customers to report on the statement of cash flows.

Cash Received from Customers If all sales are for cash, the amount received from customers equals the sales reported on the income statement. When some or all sales are on account, however, we must adjust the amount of sales for the change in Accounts Receivable. It is often helpful to use *account analysis* to do this. This usually involves setting up a T-account and reconstructing its major entries, with emphasis on cash receipts and payments. To illustrate, we use a T-account that includes accounts receivable balances for Genesis on December 31, 2007 and 2008. The beginning balance is $40,000 and the ending balance is $60,000. Next, the income statement shows sales of $590,000, which we enter on the debit side of this account. We now can reconstruct the Accounts Receivable account to determine the amount of cash received from customers as follows:

Point: An accounts receivable increase implies cash received from customers is less than sales (the converse is also true).

Accounts Receivable			
Bal., Dec. 31, 2007	40,000		
Sales	590,000	Cash receipts =	570,000
Bal., Dec. 31, 2008	60,000		

This T-account shows that the Accounts Receivable balance begins at $40,000 and increases to $630,000 from sales of $590,000, yet its ending balance is only $60,000. This implies that cash receipts from customers are $570,000, computed as $40,000 + $590,000 − [?] = $60,000. This computation can be rearranged to express cash received as equal to sales of $590,000 minus a $20,000 increase in accounts receivable. This computation is summarized as a general rule in Exhibit 16B.2. The statement of cash flows in Exhibit 16.7 reports the $570,000 cash received from customers as a cash inflow from operating activities.

Example: If the ending balance of accounts receivable is $20,000 (instead of $60,000), what is cash received from customers? *Answer:* $610,000

$$\text{Cash received from customers} = \text{Sales} - \begin{bmatrix} + \text{ Decrease in accounts receivable} \\ \text{or} \\ - \text{ Increase in accounts receivable} \end{bmatrix}$$

Exhibit 16B.2

Formula to Compute Cash Received from Customers—Direct Method

Other Cash Receipts While Genesis's cash receipts are limited to collections from customers, we often see other types of cash receipts, most commonly cash receipts involving rent, interest, and dividends. We compute cash received from these items by subtracting an increase in their respective receivable or adding a decrease. For instance, if rent receivable increases in the period, cash received from renters is less than rent revenue reported on the income statement. If rent receivable decreases, cash received is more than reported rent revenue. The same logic applies to interest and dividends. The formulas for these computations are summarized later in this appendix.

Point: Net income and cash flows from operations are different. Net income is measured using accrual accounting. Cash flows from operations are measured using cash basis accounting.

Operating Cash Payments

A review of Exhibit 16.10 and the additional Genesis information shows four operating expenses: cost of goods sold; wages and other operating expenses; interest expense; and taxes expense. We analyze each expense to compute its cash amounts for the statement of cash flows. (We then examine depreciation and the other losses and gains.)

Cash Paid for Merchandise We compute cash paid for merchandise by analyzing both cost of goods sold and merchandise inventory. If all merchandise purchases are for cash and the ending balance of Merchandise Inventory is unchanged from the beginning balance, the amount of cash paid for merchandise equals cost of goods sold—an uncommon situation. Instead, there normally is some change in the Merchandise Inventory balance. Also, some or all merchandise purchases are often made on credit, and this yields changes in the Accounts Payable balance. When the balances of both Merchandise Inventory and Accounts Payable change, we must adjust the cost of goods sold for changes in both accounts to compute cash paid for merchandise. This is a two-step adjustment.

First, we use the change in the account balance of Merchandise Inventory, along with the cost of goods sold amount, to compute cost of purchases for the period. An increase in merchandise inventory implies that we bought more than we sold, and we add this inventory increase to cost of goods sold to compute cost of purchases. A decrease in merchandise inventory implies that we bought less than we sold, and we subtract the inventory decrease from cost of goods sold to compute purchases. We illustrate the *first step* by reconstructing the Merchandise Inventory account of Genesis:

Merchandise Inventory			
Bal., Dec. 31, 2007	70,000		
Purchases =	314,000	Cost of goods sold	300,000
Bal., Dec. 31, 2008	84,000		

The beginning balance is $70,000, and the ending balance is $84,000. The income statement shows that cost of goods sold is $300,000, which we enter on the credit side of this account. With this information, we determine the amount for cost of purchases to be $314,000. This computation can be rearranged to express cost of purchases as equal to cost of goods sold of $300,000 plus the $14,000 increase in inventory.

The second step uses the change in the balance of Accounts Payable, and the amount of cost of purchases, to compute cash paid for merchandise. A decrease in accounts payable implies that we paid for more goods than we acquired this period, and we would then add the accounts payable decrease to cost of purchases to compute cash paid for merchandise. An increase in accounts payable implies that we paid for less than the amount of goods acquired, and we would subtract the accounts payable increase from purchases to compute cash paid for merchandise. The *second step* is applied to Genesis by reconstructing its Accounts Payable account:

Accounts Payable			
		Bal., Dec. 31, 2007	40,000
Cash payments =	319,000	Purchases	314,000
		Bal., Dec. 31, 2008	35,000

Example: If the ending balances of Inventory and Accounts Payable are $60,000 and $50,000, respectively (instead of $84,000 and $35,000), what is cash paid for merchandise? *Answer:* $280,000

Its beginning balance of $40,000 plus purchases of $314,000 minus an ending balance of $35,000 yields cash paid of $319,000 (or $40,000 + $314,000 − [?] = $35,000). Alternatively, we can express cash paid for merchandise as equal to purchases of $314,000 plus the $5,000 decrease in accounts payable. The $319,000 cash paid for merchandise is reported on the statement of cash flows in Exhibit 16.7 as a cash outflow under operating activities.

We summarize this two-step adjustment to cost of goods sold to compute cash paid for merchandise inventory in Exhibit 16B.3.

Exhibit 16B.3

Two Steps to Compute Cash Paid for Merchandise—Direct Method

Cash Paid for Wages and Operating Expenses (excluding depreciation)

The income statement of Genesis shows wages and other operating expenses of $216,000 (see Exhibit 16.10). To compute cash paid for wages and other operating expenses, we adjust this amount for any changes in their related balance sheet accounts. We begin by looking for any prepaid expenses and accrued liabilities related to wages and other operating expenses in the balance sheets of Genesis in

Exhibit 16.10. The balance sheets show prepaid expenses but no accrued liabilities. Thus, the adjustment is limited to the change in prepaid expenses. The amount of adjustment is computed by assuming that all cash paid for wages and other operating expenses is initially debited to Prepaid Expenses. This assumption allows us to reconstruct the Prepaid Expenses account:

Prepaid Expenses			
Bal., Dec. 31, 2007	4,000		
Cash payments =	218,000	Wages and other operating exp.	216,000
Bal., Dec. 31, 2008	6,000		

Prepaid Expenses increase by $2,000 in the period, meaning that cash paid for wages and other operating expenses exceeds the reported expense by $2,000. Alternatively, we can express cash paid for wages and other operating expenses as equal to its reported expenses of $216,000 plus the $2,000 increase in prepaid expenses.[1]

Point: A decrease in prepaid expenses implies that reported expenses include an amount(s) that did not require a cash outflow in the period.

Exhibit 16B.4 summarizes the adjustments to wages (including salaries) and other operating expenses. The Genesis balance sheet did not report accrued liabilities, but we include them in the formula to explain the adjustment to cash when they do exist. A decrease in accrued liabilities implies that we paid cash for more goods or services than received this period, so we add the decrease in accrued liabilities to the expense amount to obtain cash paid for these goods or services. An increase in accrued liabilities implies that we paid cash for less than what was acquired, so we subtract this increase in accrued liabilities from the expense amount to get cash paid.

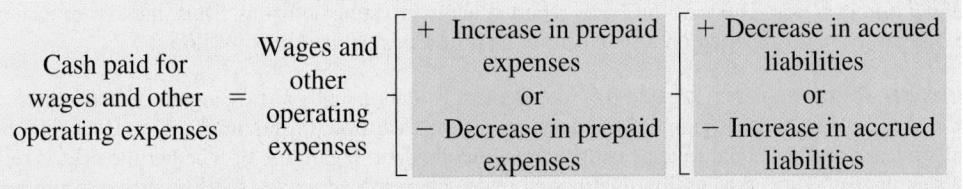

Exhibit 16B.4

Formula to Compute Cash Paid for Wages and Operating Expenses—Direct Method

Cash Paid for Interest and Income Taxes   Computing operating cash flows for interest and taxes is similar to that for operating expenses. Both require adjustments to their amounts reported on the income statement for changes in their related balance sheet accounts. We begin with the Genesis income statement showing interest expense of $7,000 and income taxes expense of $15,000. To compute the cash paid, we adjust interest expense for the change in interest payable and then the income taxes expense for the change in income taxes payable. These computations involve reconstructing both liability accounts:

Interest Payable			
		Bal., Dec. 31, 2007	4,000
Cash paid for interest =	8,000	Interest expense	7,000
		Bal., Dec. 31, 2008	3,000

Income Taxes Payable			
		Bal., Dec. 31, 2007	12,000
Cash paid for taxes =	5,000	Income taxes expense	15,000
		Bal., Dec. 31, 2008	22,000

These accounts reveal cash paid for interest of $8,000 and cash paid for income taxes of $5,000. The formulas to compute these amounts are in Exhibit 16B.5. Both of these cash payments are reported as operating cash outflows on the statement of cash flows in Exhibit 16.7.

---

[1] The assumption that all cash payments for wages and operating expenses are initially debited to Prepaid Expenses is not necessary for our analysis to hold. If cash payments are debited directly to the expense account, the total amount of cash paid for wages and other operating expenses still equals the $216,000 expense plus the $2,000 increase in Prepaid Expenses (which arise from end-of-period adjusting entries).

Exhibit 16B.5

Formulas to Compute Cash Paid for Both Interest and Taxes—Direct Method

Analysis of Additional Expenses, Gains, and Losses

Genesis has three additional items reported on its income statement: depreciation, loss on sale of assets, and gain on retirement of debt. We must consider each for its potential cash effects.

Depreciation Expense

Depreciation expense is $24,000. It is often called a *noncash expense* because depreciation has no cash flows. Depreciation expense is an allocation of an asset's depreciable cost. The cash outflow with a plant asset is reported as part of investing activities when it is paid for. Thus, depreciation expense is *never* reported on a statement of cash flows using the direct method, nor is depletion or amortization expense.

Loss on Sale of Assets

Sales of assets frequently result in gains and losses reported as part of net income, but the amount of recorded gain or loss does *not* reflect any cash flows in these transactions. Asset sales result in cash inflow equal to the cash amount received, regardless of whether the asset was sold at a gain or a loss. This cash inflow is reported under investing activities. Thus, the loss or gain on a sale of assets is *never* reported on a statement of cash flows using the direct method.

Point: The direct method is usually viewed as *user friendly* because less accounting knowledge is required to understand and use it.

Gain on Retirement of Debt

Retirement of debt usually yields a gain or loss reported as part of net income, but that gain or loss does *not* reflect cash flow in this transaction. Debt retirement results in cash outflow equal to the cash paid to settle the debt, regardless of whether the debt is retired at a gain or loss. This cash outflow is reported under financing activities; the loss or gain from retirement of debt is *never* reported on a statement of cash flows using the direct method.

Summary of Adjustments for Direct Method

Exhibit 16B.6 summarizes common adjustments for net income to yield net cash provided (used) by operating activities under the direct method.

Exhibit 16B.6

Summary of Selected Adjustments for Direct Method

Item	From Income Statement	Adjustments to Obtain Cash Flow Numbers
Receipts		
From sales	Sales Revenue	⌈ +Decrease in Accounts Receivable ⌊ −Increase in Accounts Receivable
From rent	Rent Revenue	⌈ +Decrease in Rent Receivable ⌊ −Increase in Rent Receivable
From interest	Interest Revenue	⌈ +Decrease in Interest Receivable ⌊ −Increase in Interest Receivable
From dividends	Dividend Revenue	⌈ +Decrease in Dividends Receivable ⌊ −Increase in Dividends Receivable
Payments		
To suppliers	Cost of Goods Sold	⌈ +Increase in Inventory ⌈ +Decrease in Accounts Payable ⌊ −Decrease in Inventory ⌊ −Increase in Accounts Payable
For operations	Operating Expense	⌈ +Increase in Prepaids ⌈ +Decrease in Accrued Liabilities ⌊ −Decrease in Prepaids ⌊ −Increase in Accrued Liabilities
To employees	Wages (Salaries) Expense	⌈ +Decrease in Wages (Salaries) Payable ⌊ −Increase in Wages (Salaries) Payable
For interest	Interest Expense	⌈ +Decrease in Interest Payable ⌊ −Increase in Interest Payable
For taxes	Income Tax Expense	⌈ +Decrease in Income Tax Payable ⌊ −Increase in Income Tax Payable

Direct Method Format of Operating Activities Section

Exhibit 16.7 shows the Genesis statement of cash flows using the direct method. Major items of cash inflows and cash outflows are listed separately in the operating activities section. The format requires that operating cash outflows be subtracted from operating cash inflows to get net cash provided (used) by operating activities. The FASB recommends that the operating activities section of the statement of cash flows be reported using the direct method, which is considered more useful to financial statement users. *However, the FASB requires a reconciliation of net income to net cash provided (used) by operating activities when the direct method is used* (which can be reported in the notes). This reconciliation is similar to preparation of the operating activities section of the statement of cash flows using the indirect method.

Point: Some preparers argue that it is easier to prepare a statement of cash flows using the indirect method. This likely explains its greater frequency in financial statements.

Quick Check

Answers—p. 652

8. Net sales in a period are $590,000, beginning accounts receivable are $120,000, and ending accounts receivable are $90,000. What cash amount is collected from customers in the period?

9. The Merchandise Inventory account balance decreases in the period from a beginning balance of $32,000 to an ending balance of $28,000. Cost of goods sold for the period is $168,000. If the Accounts Payable balance increases $2,400 in the period, what is the cash amount paid for merchandise inventory?

10. Wages and other operating expenses total $112,000. Beginning-of-period prepaid expenses totaled $1,200, and its ending balance is $4,200. The end-of-period wages payable equal $5,600, whereas there were no accrued liabilities at period-end. How much cash is paid for wages and other operating expenses?

Summary

C1 Explain the purpose and importance of cash flow information. The main purpose of the statement of cash flows is to report the major cash receipts and cash payments for a period. This includes identifying cash flows as relating to either operating, investing, or financing activities. Most business decisions involve evaluating activities that provide or use cash.

C2 Distinguish between operating, investing, and financing activities. Operating activities include transactions and events that determine net income. Investing activities include transactions and events that mainly affect long-term assets. Financing activities include transactions and events that mainly affect long-term liabilities and equity.

C3 Identify and disclose noncash investing and financing activities. Noncash investing and financing activities must be disclosed either in a note or a separate schedule to the statement of cash flows. Examples are the retirement of debt by issuing equity and the exchange of a note payable for plant assets.

C4 Describe the format of the statement of cash flows. The statement of cash flows separates cash receipts and payments into operating, investing, or financing activities.

A1 Analyze the statement of cash flows. To understand and predict cash flows, users stress identification of the sources and uses of cash flows by operating, investing, and financing activities. Emphasis is on operating cash flows since they derive from continuing operations.

A2 Compute and apply the cash flow on total assets ratio. The cash flow on total assets ratio is defined as operating cash flows divided by average total assets. Analysis of current and past values for this ratio can reflect a company's ability to yield regular and positive cash flows. It is also viewed as a measure of earnings quality.

P1 Prepare a statement of cash flows. Preparation of a statement of cash flows involves five steps: (1) Compute the net increase or decrease in cash; (2) compute net cash provided (used) by operating activities (*using either the direct or indirect method*); (3) compute net cash provided (used) by investing activities; (4) compute net cash provided (used) by financing activities; and (5) report the beginning and ending cash balance and prove that it is explained by net cash flows. Noncash investing and financing activities are also disclosed.

P2 Compute cash flows from operating activities using the indirect method. The indirect method for reporting net cash provided (used) by operating activities starts with net income and then adjusts it for three items: (1) changes in noncash current assets and current liabilities related to operating activities, (2) revenues and expenses not providing (using) cash, and (3) gains and losses from investing and financing activities.

P3 Determine cash flows from both investing and financing activities. Cash flows from both investing and financing activities are determined by identifying the cash flow effects of transactions and events affecting each balance sheet account related to these activities. All cash flows from these activities are identified when we can explain changes in these accounts from the beginning to the end of the period.

P4^A Illustrate use of a spreadsheet to prepare a statement of cash flows. A spreadsheet is a useful tool in preparing a statement of cash flows. Six key steps (see appendix) are applied when using the spreadsheet to prepare the statement.

P5^B Compute cash flows from operating activities using the direct method. The direct method for reporting net cash provided (used) by operating activities lists major operating cash inflows less cash outflows to yield net cash inflow or outflow from operations.

Entrepreneur   Several factors might explain an increase in net cash flows when a net loss is reported, including (1) early recognition of expenses relative to revenues generated (such as research and development), (2) cash advances on long-term sales contracts not yet recognized in income, (3) issuances of debt or equity for cash to finance expansion, (4) cash sale of assets, (5) delay of cash payments, and (6) cash prepayment on sales. Analysis needs to focus on the components of both the net loss and the net cash flows and their implications for future performance.

Reporter   Your initial reaction based on the company's $600,000 loss with a $550,000 decrease in net cash flows is not positive. However, closer scrutiny reveals a more positive picture of this company's performance. Cash flow from operating activities is $650,000, computed as [?] − $850,000 − $350,000 = $(550,000). You also note that net income *before* the extraordinary loss is $330,000, computed as [?] − $930,000 = $(600,000).

Guidance Answers to **Quick Checks**

1. No to both. The statement of cash flows reports changes in the sum of cash plus cash equivalents. It does not report transfers between cash and cash equivalents.

2. The three categories of cash inflows and outflows are operating activities, investing activities, and financing activities.

3. **a.** Investing   **c.** Financing   **e.** Operating
   b. Operating   **d.** Operating   **f.** Financing

4. $74,900 + $4,600 − $11,700 − $1,000 + $3,400 = $70,200

5. Expenses such as depreciation and amortization do not require current cash outflows. Therefore, adding these expenses back to net income eliminates these noncash items from the net income number, converting it to a cash basis.

6. A gain on the sale of plant assets is subtracted from net income because a sale of plant assets is not an operating activity; it is an investing activity for the amount of cash received from its sale. Also, such a gain yields no cash effects.

7. $80,000 − $30,000 − $10,000 = $40,000 cash receipt. The $40,000 cash receipt is reported as an investing activity.

8. $590,000 + ($120,000 − $90,000) = $620,000

9. $168,000 − ($32,000 − $28,000) − $2,400 = $161,600

10. $112,000 + ($4,200 − $1,200) − $5,600 = $109,400

Key Terms   mhhe.com/wildFAP18e

Key Terms are available at the book's Website for learning and testing in an online Flashcard Format.

Cash flow on total assets (p. 640)   Indirect method (p. 628)   Operating activities (p. 623)
Direct method (p. 628)   Investing activities (p. 624)   Statement of cash flows (p. 622)
Financing activities (p. 624)

Multiple Choice Quiz   Answers on p. 671   mhhe.com/wildFAP18e

Multiple Choice Quizzes A and B are available at the book's Website.

1. A company uses the indirect method to determine its cash flows from operating activities. Use the following information to determine its net cash provided or used by operating activities.

Net income	$15,200
Depreciation expense	10,000
Cash payment on note payable	8,000
Gain on sale of land	3,000
Increase in inventory	1,500
Increase in accounts payable	2,850

   a. $23,550 used by operating activities
   b. $23,550 provided by operating activities

   c. $15,550 provided by operating activities
   d. $42,400 provided by operating activities
   e. $20,850 provided by operating activities

2. A machine with a cost of $175,000 and accumulated depreciation of $94,000 is sold for $87,000 cash. The amount reported as a source of cash under cash flows from investing activities is:
   a. $81,000.
   b. $6,000.
   c. $87,000.
   d. Zero; this is a financing activity.
   e. Zero; this is an operating activity.

3. A company settles a long-term note payable plus interest by paying $68,000 cash toward the principal amount and $5,440

cash for interest. The amount reported as a use of cash under cash flows from financing activities is:

a. Zero; this is an investing activity.
b. Zero; this is an operating activity.
c. $73,440.
d. $68,000.
e. $5,440.

4. The following information is available regarding a company's annual salaries and wages. What amount of cash is paid for salaries and wages?

Salaries and wages expense	$255,000
Salaries and wages payable, prior year-end	8,200
Salaries and wages payable, current year-end	10,900

a. $252,300
b. $257,700

c. $255,000
d. $274,100
e. $235,900

5. The following information is available for a company. What amount of cash is paid for merchandise for the current year?

Cost of goods sold	$545,000
Merchandise inventory, prior year-end	105,000
Merchandise inventory, current year-end	112,000
Accounts payable, prior year-end	98,500
Accounts payable, current year-end	101,300

a. $545,000
b. $554,800
c. $540,800
d. $535,200
e. $549,200

Superscript letter ^{A}(^{B}) denotes assignments based on Appendix 16A (16B).

Discussion Questions

1. What is the reporting purpose of the statement of cash flows? Identify at least two questions that this statement can answer.

2. Describe the direct method of reporting cash flows from operating activities.

3. When a statement of cash flows is prepared using the direct method, what are some of the operating cash flows?

4. Describe the indirect method of reporting cash flows from operating activities.

5. What are some investing activities reported on the statement of cash flows?

6. What are some financing activities reported on the statement of cash flows?

7. Where on the statement of cash flows is the payment of cash dividends reported?

8. Assume that a company purchases land for $100,000, paying $20,000 cash and borrowing the remainder with a long-term note payable. How should this transaction be reported on a statement of cash flows?

9. On June 3, a company borrows $50,000 cash by giving its bank a 160-day, interest-bearing note. On the statement of cash flows, where should this be reported?

10. If a company reports positive net income for the year, can it also show a net cash outflow from operating activities? Explain.

11. Is depreciation a source of cash flow?

12. Refer to **Best Buy**'s statement of cash flows in Appendix A. (*a*) Which method is used to compute its net cash provided by operating activities? (*b*) While its balance sheet shows an increase in receivables from fiscal years 2004 to 2005, why is this increase in receivables subtracted when computing net cash provided by operating activities for the year ended February 26, 2005?

13. Refer to **Circuit City**'s statement of cash flows in Appendix A. What are its cash flows from financing activities for the year ended February 28, 2005? List items and amounts.

14. Refer to **Apple**'s statement of cash flows in Appendix A. What investing activities result in cash outflows for the year ended September 25, 2004? List items and amounts.

 Red numbers denote Discussion Questions that involve decision-making.

The statement of cash flows is one of the four primary financial statements.

1. Describe the content and layout of a statement of cash flows, including its three sections.

2. List at least three transactions classified as investing activities in a statement of cash flows.

3. List at least three transactions classified as financing activities in a statement of cash flows.

4. List at least three transactions classified as significant noncash financing and investing activities in the statement of cash flows.

QUICK STUDY

QS 16-1
Statement of cash flows

C1 C2 C3

QS 16-2

Transaction classification
by activity

C2

Classify the following cash flows as operating, investing, or financing activities.

1. Sold long-term investments for cash.

2. Received cash payments from customers.

3. Paid cash for wages and salaries.

4. Purchased inventories for cash.

5. Paid cash dividends.

6. Issued common stock for cash.

7. Received cash interest on a note.

8. Paid cash interest on outstanding bonds.

9. Received cash from sale of land at a loss.

10. Paid cash for property taxes on building.

QS 16-3

Computing cash from operations
(indirect)

P2

Use the following information to determine this company's cash flows from operating activities using the indirect method.

KATAHN COMPANY Selected Balance Sheet Information December 31, 2008 and 2007		
	2008	**2007**
Current assets		
Cash	$84,650	$26,800
Accounts receivable	25,000	32,000
Inventory	60,000	54,100
Current liabilities		
Accounts payable	30,400	25,700
Income taxes payable	2,050	2,200

KATAHN COMPANY Income Statement For Year Ended December 31, 2008		
Sales		$515,000
Cost of goods sold		331,600
Gross profit		183,400
Operating expenses		
Depreciation expense	$ 36,000	
Other expenses	121,500	157,500
Income before taxes		25,900
Income taxes expense		7,700
Net income		$ 18,200

QS 16-4

Computing cash from asset sales

P3

The following selected information is from Ellerby Company's comparative balance sheets.

At December 31	2008	2007
Furniture	$132,000	$ 184,500
Accumulated depreciation—Furniture	(88,700)	(110,700)

The income statement reports depreciation expense for the year of $18,000. Also, furniture costing $52,500 was sold for its book value. Compute the cash received from the sale of the furniture.

QS 16-5

Computing financing cash flows

P3

The following selected information is from the Princeton Company's comparative balance sheets.

At December 31	2008	2007
Common stock, $10 par value	$105,000	$100,000
Paid-in capital in excess of par	567,000	342,000
Retained earnings	313,500	287,500

Princeton's net income for the year ended December 31, 2008, was $48,000.

1. Compute the cash received from the sale of its common stock during 2008.

2. Compute the cash paid for dividends during 2008.

QS 16-6

Computing cash from
operations (indirect) P2

Use the following balance sheets and income statement to answer QS 16-6 through QS 16-11.

Use the indirect method to prepare the cash provided (used) from operating activities section only of the statement of cash flows.

CRUZ, INC.
Comparative Balance Sheets
December 31, 2008

	2008	2007
Assets		
Cash	$ 94,800	$ 24,000
Accounts receivable, net	41,000	51,000
Inventory	85,800	95,800
Prepaid expenses	5,400	4,200
Furniture	109,000	119,000
Accum. depreciation—Furniture	(17,000)	(9,000)
Total assets	$319,000	$285,000
Liabilities and Equity		
Accounts payable	$ 15,000	$ 21,000
Wages payable	9,000	5,000
Income taxes payable	1,400	2,600
Notes payable (long-term)	29,000	69,000
Common stock, $5 par value	229,000	179,000
Retained earnings	35,600	8,400
Total liabilities and equity	$319,000	$285,000

CRUZ, INC.
Income Statement
For Year Ended December 31, 2008

Sales		$488,000
Cost of goods sold		314,000
Gross profit		174,000
Operating expenses		
Depreciation expense	$37,600	
Other expenses	89,100	126,700
Income before taxes		47,300
Income taxes expense		17,300
Net income		$ 30,000

Refer to the data in QS 16-6.

Furniture costing $55,000 is sold at its book value in 2008. Acquisitions of furniture total $45,000 cash, on which no depreciation is necessary because it is acquired at year-end. What is the cash inflow related to the sale of furniture?

QS 16-7
Computing cash
from asset sales   P3

Refer to the data in QS 16-6.

1. Assume that all common stock is issued for cash. What amount of cash dividends is paid during 2008?

2. Assume that no additional notes payable are issued in 2008. What cash amount is paid to reduce the notes payable balance in 2008?

QS 16-8
Computing financing
cash outflows   P3

Refer to the data in QS 16-6.

1. How much cash is received from sales to customers for year 2008?

2. What is the net increase or decrease in cash for year 2008?

QS 16-9ᴮ
Computing cash received
from customers   P5

Refer to the data in QS 16-6.

1. How much cash is paid to acquire merchandise inventory during year 2008?

2. How much cash is paid for operating expenses during year 2008?

QS 16-10ᴮ
Computing operating
cash outflows   P5

Refer to the data in QS 16-6.

Use the direct method to prepare the cash provided (used) from operating activities section only of the statement of cash flows.

QS 16-11ᴮ
Computing cash from
operations (direct)   P5

Financial data from three competitors in the same industry follow.

1. Which of the three competitors is in the strongest position as shown by its statement of cash flows?

2. Analyze and discuss the strength of Peña's cash flow on total assets ratio to that of Garcia.

QS 16-12
Analyses of sources
and uses of cash   A1 A2

($ thousands)	Peña	Garcia	Piniella
Cash provided (used) by operating activities	$ 70,000	$ 60,000	$ (24,000)
Cash provided (used) by investing activities			
Proceeds from sale of operating assets			26,000
Purchase of operating assets	(28,000)	(34,000)	
Cash provided (used) by financing activities			
Proceeds from issuance of debt			23,000
Repayment of debt	(6,000)		
Net increase (decrease) in cash	$ 36,000	$ 26,000	$ 25,000
Average total assets	$ 790,000	$ 625,000	$ 300,000

QS 16-13^A
Noncash accounts
on a spreadsheet   P4

When a spreadsheet for a statement of cash flows is prepared, all changes in noncash balance sheet accounts are fully explained on the spreadsheet. Explain how these noncash balance sheet accounts are used to fully account for cash flows on a spreadsheet.

QS 16-14
Computing cash flows from operations (indirect)

P2

For each of the following separate cases, compute cash flows from operations. The list includes all balance sheet accounts related to operating activities.

	Case A	Case B	Case C
Net income	$ 4,000	$100,000	$72,000
Depreciation expense	30,000	8,000	24,000
Accounts receivable increase (decrease)	40,000	20,000	(4,000)
Inventory increase (decrease)	(20,000)	(10,000)	10,000
Accounts payable increase (decrease)	24,000	(22,000)	14,000
Accrued liabilities increase (decrease)	(44,000)	12,000	(8,000)

QS 16-15
Computing cash flows from investing

P3

Compute cash flows from investing activities using the following information.

Sale of short-term investments	$ 6,000
Cash collections from customers	16,000
Purchase of used equipment	5,000
Depreciation expense	2,000

QS 16-16
Computing cash flows from financing

P3

Compute cash flows from financing activities using the following information.

Additional short-term borrowings	$20,000
Purchase of short-term investments	5,000
Cash dividends paid	16,000
Interest paid	8,000

EXERCISES

Exercise 16-1
Cash flow from operations (indirect)

P2

Salud Company reports net income of $400,000 for the year ended December 31, 2008. It also reports $80,000 depreciation expense and a $20,000 gain on the sale of machinery. Its comparative balance sheets reveal a $40,000 increase in accounts receivable, $6,000 increase in accounts payable, $12,000 decrease in prepaid expenses, and $2,000 decrease in wages payable.

Required

Prepare only the operating activities section of the statement of cash flows for 2008 using the *indirect method*.

The following transactions and events occurred during the year. Assuming that this company uses the *indirect method* to report cash provided by operating activities, indicate where each item would appear on its statement of cash flows by placing an *x* in the appropriate column.

Exercise 16-2
Cash flow classification
(indirect) C2 C3 P2

	Statement of Cash Flows			Noncash Investing and Financing Activities	Not Reported on Statement or in Notes
	Operating Activities	**Investing Activities**	**Financing Activities**		
a. Paid cash to purchase inventory.	___	___	___	___	___
b. Purchased land by issuing common stock.	___	___	___	___	___
c. Accounts receivable decreased in the year.	___	___	___	___	___
d. Sold equipment for cash, yielding a loss.	___	___	___	___	___
e. Recorded depreciation expense.	___	___	___	___	___
f. Income taxes payable increased in the year.	___	___	___	___	___
g. Declared and paid a cash dividend.	___	___	___	___	___
h. Accounts payable decreased in the year	___	___	___	___	___
i. Paid cash to settle bond payable	___	___	___	___	___
j. Prepaid expenses increased in the year	___	___	___	___	___

The following transactions and events occurred during the year. Assuming that this company uses the *direct method* to report cash provided by operating activities, indicate where each item would appear on the statement of cash flows by placing an *x* in the appropriate column.

Exercise 16-3[B]
Cash flow classification
(direct) C2 C3 P5

	Statement of Cash Flows			Noncash Investing and Financing Activities	Not Reported on Statement or in Notes
	Operating Activities	**Investing Activities**	**Financing Activities**		
a. Retired long-term bonds payable by issuing common stock	___	___	___	___	___
b. Recorded depreciation expense.	___	___	___	___	___
c. Paid cash dividend that was declared in a prior period.	___	___	___	___	___
d. Sold inventory for cash.	___	___	___	___	___
e. Borrowed cash from bank by signing a 9-month note payable.	___	___	___	___	___
f. Paid cash to purchase a patent.	___	___	___	___	___
g. Accepted six-month note receivable in exchange for plant assets.	___	___	___	___	___
h. Paid cash toward accounts payable.	___	___	.	___	___
i. Collected cash from sales.	___	___	___	___	___
j. Paid cash to acquire treasury stock.	___	___	___	___	___

Olhstead Company's calendar-year 2008 income statement shows the following: Net Income, $374,000; Depreciation Expense, $44,000; Amortization Expense, $7,200; Gain on Sale of Plant Assets, $6,000. An examination of the company's current assets and current liabilities reveals the following changes (all from operating activities): Accounts Receivable decrease, $17,100; Merchandise Inventory decrease, $42,000; Prepaid Expenses increase, $4,700; Accounts Payable decrease, $8,200; Other Payables increase, $1,200. Use the *indirect method* to compute cash flow from operating activities.

Exercise 16-4
Cash flows from operating
activities (indirect)

P2

Exercise 16-5[B]
Computation of cash
flows (direct)

P5

For each of the following three separate cases, use the information provided about the calendar-year 2008 operations of Alberto Company to compute the required cash flow information.

Case A: Compute cash received from customers:

Sales	$515,000
Accounts receivable, December 31, 2007	27,200
Accounts receivable, December 31, 2008	33,600

Case B: Compute cash paid for rent:

Rent expense	$139,800
Rent payable, December 31, 2007	7,800
Rent payable, December 31, 2008	6,200

Case C: Compute cash paid for merchandise:

Cost of goods sold	$525,000
Merchandise inventory, December 31, 2007	158,600
Accounts payable, December 31, 2007	66,700
Merchandise inventory, December 31, 2008	130,400
Accounts payable, December 31, 2008	82,000

Exercise 16-6
Cash flows from operating
activities (indirect)

P2

Use the following income statement and information about changes in noncash current assets and current liabilities to prepare only the cash flows from operating activities section of the statement of cash flows using the *indirect* method.

ABBECK COMPANY
Income Statement
For Year Ended December 31, 2008

Sales		$1,828,000
Cost of goods sold		991,000
Gross profit		837,000
Operating expenses		
Salaries expense	$245,535	
Depreciation expense	44,200	
Rent expense	49,600	
Amortization expenses—Patents	4,200	
Utilities expense	18,125	361,660
		475,340
Gain on sale of equipment		6,200
Net income		$ 481,540

Changes in current asset and current liability accounts for the year that relate to operations follow.

Accounts receivable	$30,500 increase		Accounts payable	$12,500 decrease
Merchandise inventory	25,000 increase		Salaries payable	3,500 decrease

---

Exercise 16-7[B]
Cash flows from operating
activities (direct)   P5

Refer to the information about Abbeck Company in Exercise 16-6.
Use the *direct method* to prepare only the cash provided (used) by operating activities section of the statement of cash flows.

Exercise 16-8
Cash flows from investing
activities

P3

Use the following information to determine a company's cash flows from investing activities.
a. Equipment with a book value of $65,300 and an original cost of $133,000 was sold at a loss of $14,000.
b. Paid $89,000 cash for a new truck.
c. Sold land costing $154,000 for $198,000 cash, yielding a gain of $44,000.
d. Long-term investments in stock were sold for $60,800 cash, yielding a gain of $4,150.

Use the following information to determine a company's cash flows from financing activities.

a. Net income was $35,000.

b. Issued common stock for $64,000 cash.

c. Paid cash dividend of $14,600.

d. Paid $50,000 cash to settle a bond payable at its $50,000 maturity value.

e. Paid $12,000 cash to acquire its treasury stock.

f. Purchased equipment for $39,000 cash.

Exercise 16-9
Cash flows from financing activities

P3

Use the following financial statements and additional information to (1) prepare a statement of cash flows for the year ended June 30, 2008, using the *indirect method,* and (2) compute the cash flow on total assets ratio for Ikiban for its fiscal year 2008.

Exercise 16-10
Preparation of statement of cash flows (indirect)

C2 A2 P1 P2 P3

IKIBAN INC. Comparative Balance Sheets June 30, 2008 and 2007		
	2008	**2007**
Assets		
Cash	$ 87,500	$ 44,000
Accounts receivable, net	65,000	51,000
Inventory	63,800	86,500
Prepaid expenses	4,400	5,400
Equipment	124,000	115,000
Accum. depreciation—Equipment	(27,000)	(9,000)
Total assets	$317,700	$292,900
Liabilities and Equity		
Accounts payable	$ 25,000	$ 30,000
Wages payable	6,000	15,000
Income taxes payable	3,400	3,800
Notes payable (long term)	30,000	60,000
Common stock, $5 par value	220,000	160,000
Retained earnings	33,300	24,100
Total liabilities and equity	$317,700	$292,900

IKIBAN INC. Income Statement For Year Ended June 30, 2008		
Sales		$678,000
Cost of goods sold		411,000
Gross profit		267,000
Operating expenses		
Depreciation expense	$58,600	
Other expenses	67,000	
Total operating expenses		125,600
		141,400
Other gains (losses)		
Gain on sale of equipment		2,000
Income before taxes		143,400
Income taxes expense		43,890
Net income		$ 99,510

Additional Information

a. A $30,000 note payable is retired at its carrying (book) value in exchange for cash.

b. The only changes affecting retained earnings are net income and cash dividends paid.

c. New equipment is acquired for $57,600 cash.

d. Received cash for the sale of equipment that had cost $48,600, yielding a $2,000 gain.

e. Prepaid Expenses and Wages Payable relate to Other Expenses on the income statement.

f. All purchases and sales of merchandise inventory are on credit.

Refer to the data in Exercise 16-10.

Using the *direct method,* prepare the statement of cash flows for the year ended June 30, 2008.

Exercise 16-11[B]
Preparation of statement of cash flows (direct) C2 P1 P3 P5

Exercise 16-12^B

Preparation of statement of
cash flows (direct) and
supporting note

C2 C3 C4 P1

Use the following information about the cash flows of Ferron Company to prepare a complete statement of cash flows (*direct method*) for the year ended December 31, 2008. Use a note disclosure for any non-cash investing and financing activities.

Cash and cash equivalents balance, December 31, 2007	$ 40,000
Cash and cash equivalents balance, December 31, 2008	148,000
Cash received as interest	3,500
Cash paid for salaries	76,500
Bonds payable retired by issuing common stock (no gain or loss on retirement)	185,500
Cash paid to retire long-term notes payable	100,000
Cash received from sale of equipment	60,250
Cash received in exchange for six-month note payable	35,000
Land purchased by issuing long-term note payable	105,250
Cash paid for store equipment	24,750
Cash dividends paid	10,000
Cash paid for other expenses	20,000
Cash received from customers	495,000
Cash paid for merchandise	254,500

Exercise 16-13^B

Preparation of statement of
cash flows (direct) from
Cash T-account

C2 A1 P1 P3 P5

The following summarized Cash T-account reflects the total debits and total credits to the Cash account of Thomas Corporation for calendar year 2008.

(1) Use this information to prepare a complete statement of cash flows for year 2008. The cash provided (used) by operating activities should be reported using the *direct method.*

(2) Refer to the statement of cash flows prepared for part 1 to answer the following questions *a* through *d*: (*a*) Which section—operating, investing, or financing—shows the largest cash (i) inflow and (ii) outflow? (*b*) What is the largest individual item among the investing cash outflows? (*c*) Are the cash proceeds larger from issuing notes or issuing stock? (*d*) Does the company have a net cash inflow or outflow from borrowing activities?

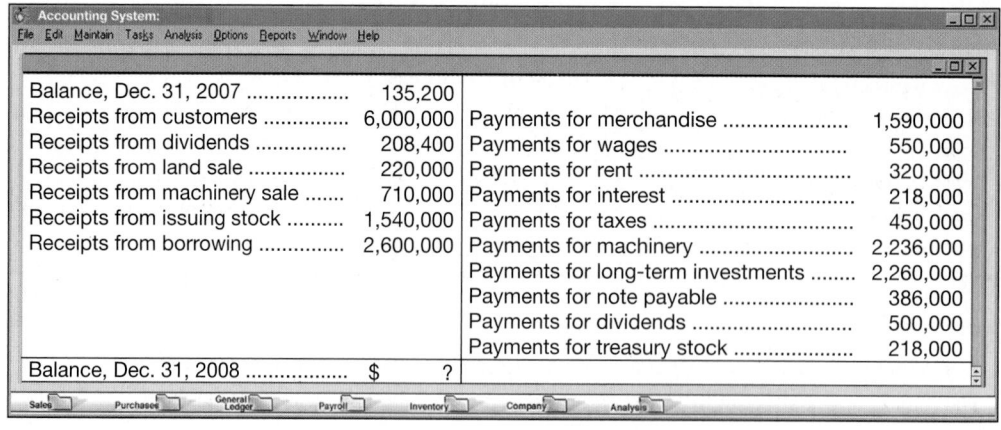

Exercise 16-14

Reporting cash flows from
operations (indirect)

C4 P2

Hampton Company reports the following information.

Sales		$160,000
Expenses		
Cost of goods sold		100,000
Salaries expense		24,000
Depreciation expense		12,000
Net income		$ 24,000
Accounts receivable increase		$ 10,000
Inventory decrease		16,000
Salaries payable increase		1,000

Required

Prepare the operating activities section of the statement of cash flows for Hampton Company using the indirect method.

Arundel Company disclosed the following income statement and balance sheet information.

Exercise 16-15
Reporting and interpreting cash flows from operations (indirect)

C4 P2

Revenues	$100,000
Expenses	
Salaries expense	84,000
Utilities expense	14,000
Depreciation expense	14,600
Other expenses	3,400
Net loss	$(16,000)
Accounts receivable decrease	$ 24,000
Purchased a machine	10,000
Salaries payable increase	18,000
Other accrued liabilities decrease	8,000

Required

1. Prepare the operating activities section of the statement of cash flows for Arundel Company using the indirect method.

2. What were the major reasons that Arundel Company was able to report a net loss but positive cash flow from operations?

3. Of the potential causes of differences between cash flow from operations and net income, which are the most important to investors?

Forten Company, a merchandiser, recently completed its calendar-year 2008 operations. For the year, (1) all sales are credit sales, (2) all credits to Accounts Receivable reflect cash receipts from customers, (3) all purchases of inventory are on credit, (4) all debits to Accounts Payable reflect cash payments for inventory, and (5) Other Expenses are paid in advance and are initially debited to Prepaid Expenses. Forten's balance sheets and income statement follow:

PROBLEM SET A

Problem 16-1A
Statement of cash flows (indirect method)

C2 C3 A1 P1 P2 P3

FORTEN COMPANY
Comparative Balance Sheets
December 31, 2008 and 2007

	2008	2007
Assets		
Cash	$ 49,800	$ 73,500
Accounts receivable	65,810	50,625
Merchandise inventory	275,656	251,800
Prepaid expenses	1,250	1,875
Equipment	157,500	108,000
Accum. depreciation—Equipment	(36,625)	(46,000)
Total assets	$513,391	$439,800
Liabilities and Equity		
Accounts payable	$ 53,141	$114,675
Short-term notes payable	10,000	6,000
Long-term notes payable	65,000	48,750
Common stock, $5 par value	162,750	150,250
Paid-in capital in excess		
of par, common stock	37,500	0
Retained earnings	185,000	120,125
Total liabilities and equity	$513,391	$439,800

FORTEN COMPANY
Income Statement
For Year Ended December 31, 2008

Sales		$582,500
Cost of goods sold		285,000
Gross profit		297,500
Operating expenses		
Depreciation expense	$ 20,750	
Other expenses	132,400	153,150
Other gains (losses)		
Loss on sale of equipment		5,125
Income before taxes		139,225
Income taxes expense		24,250
Net income		$114,975

Additional Information on Year 2008 Transactions

a. The loss on the cash sale of equipment was $5,125 (details in *b*).

b. Sold equipment costing $46,875, with accumulated depreciation of $30,125, for $11,625 cash.

c. Purchased equipment costing $96,375 by paying $30,000 cash and signing a long-term note payable for the balance.

d. Borrowed $4,000 cash by signing a short-term note payable.

e. Paid $50,125 cash to reduce the long-term notes payable.

f. Issued 2,500 shares of common stock for $20 cash per share.

g. Declared and paid cash dividends of $50,100.

Required

Check Cash from operating activities, $40,900

1. Prepare a complete statement of cash flows; report its operating activities using the *indirect method.* Disclose any noncash investing and financing activities in a note.

Analysis Component

2. Analyze and discuss the statement of cash flows prepared in part 1, giving special attention to the wisdom of the cash dividend payment.

Problem 16-2A^A

Cash flows spreadsheet (indirect method)

P1 P2 P3 P4

Refer to the information reported about Forten Company in Problem 16-1A.

Required

Prepare a complete statement of cash flows using a spreadsheet as in Exhibit 16A.1; report its operating activities using the indirect method. Identify the debits and credits in the Analysis of Changes columns with letters that correspond to the following list of transactions and events.

a. Net income was $114,975.

b. Accounts receivable increased.

c. Merchandise inventory increased.

d. Prepaid expenses decreased.

e. Accounts payable decreased.

f. Depreciation expense was $20,750.

g. Sold equipment costing $46,875, with accumulated depreciation of $30,125, for $11,625 cash. This yielded a loss of $5,125.

h. Purchased equipment costing $96,375 by paying $30,000 cash and **(i.)** by signing a long-term note payable for the balance.

j. Borrowed $4,000 cash by signing a short-term note payable.

k. Paid $50,125 cash to reduce the long-term notes payable.

l. Issued 2,500 shares of common stock for $20 cash per share.

Check Analysis of Changes column totals, $600,775

m. Declared and paid cash dividends of $50,100.

Problem 16-3A^B

Statement of cash flows (direct method) C3 P1 P3 P5

Check Cash used in financing activities, $(46,225)

Refer to Forten Company's financial statements and related information in Problem 16-1A.

Required

Prepare a complete statement of cash flows; report its operating activities according to the *direct method.* Disclose any noncash investing and financing activities in a note.

Problem 16-4A

Statement of cash flows (indirect method) C3 P1 P2 P3

mhhe.com/wildFAP18e

Golden Corp., a merchandiser, recently completed its 2008 operations. For the year, (1) all sales are credit sales, (2) all credits to Accounts Receivable reflect cash receipts from customers, (3) all purchases of inventory are on credit, (4) all debits to Accounts Payable reflect cash payments for inventory, (5) Other Expenses are all cash expenses, and (6) any change in Income Taxes Payable reflects the accrual and cash payment of taxes. Golden's balance sheets and income statement follow.

GOLDEN CORPORATION Comparative Balance Sheets December 31, 2008 and 2007		
	2008	**2007**
Assets		
Cash	$ 164,000	$107,000
Accounts receivable	83,000	71,000
Merchandise inventory	601,000	526,000
Equipment	335,000	299,000
Accum. depreciation—Equipment	(158,000)	(104,000)
Total assets	$1,025,000	$899,000
Liabilities and Equity		
Accounts payable	$ 87,000	$ 71,000
Income taxes payable	28,000	25,000
Common stock, $2 par value	592,000	568,000
Paid-in capital in excess		
of par value, common stock	196,000	160,000
Retained earnings	122,000	75,000
Total liabilities and equity	$1,025,000	$899,000

GOLDEN CORPORATION Income Statement For Year Ended December 31, 2008		
Sales		$1,792,000
Cost of goods sold		1,086,000
Gross profit		706,000
Operating expenses		
Depreciation expense	$ 54,000	
Other expenses	494,000	548,000
Income before taxes		158,000
Income taxes expense		22,000
Net income		$ 136,000

Additional Information on Year 2008 Transactions

a. Purchased equipment for $36,000 cash.

b. Issued 12,000 shares of common stock for $5 cash per share.

c. Declared and paid $89,000 in cash dividends.

Required

Prepare a complete statement of cash flows; report its cash inflows and cash outflows from operating activities according to the *indirect method*.

Check Cash from operating activities, $122,000

Refer to the information reported about Golden Corporation in Problem 16-4A.

Required

Prepare a complete statement of cash flows using a spreadsheet as in Exhibit 16A.1; report operating activities under the indirect method. Identify the debits and credits in the Analysis of Changes columns with letters that correspond to the following list of transactions and events.

a. Net income was $136,000.

b. Accounts receivable increased.

c. Merchandise inventory increased.

d. Accounts payable increased.

e. Income taxes payable increased.

f. Depreciation expense was $54,000.

g. Purchased equipment for $36,000 cash.

h. Issued 12,000 shares at $5 cash per share.

i. Declared and paid $89,000 of cash dividends.

Problem 16-5A[A]

Cash flows spreadsheet (indirect method)

P1 P2 P3 P4

mhhe.com/wildFAP18e

Check Analysis of Changes column totals, $481,000

Refer to Golden Corporation's financial statements and related information in Problem 16-4A.

Required

Prepare a complete statement of cash flows; report its cash flows from operating activities according to the *direct method*.

Problem 16-6A[B]

Statement of cash flows (direct method) P1 P3 P5

mhhe.com/wildFAP18e

Check Cash used in financing activities, $(29,000)

Problem 16-7A
Computing cash flows from operations (indirect)

C4　P2

Lansing Company's 2008 income statement and selected balance sheet data at December 31, 2007 and 2008, follow ($ thousands).

LANSING COMPANY Selected Balance Sheet Accounts		
At Decmber 31	2008	2007
Accounts receivable	$560	$580
Inventory	198	154
Accounts payable	440	460
Salaries payable	88	70
Utilities payable	22	16
Prepaid insurance	26	28
Prepaid rent	22	18

LANSING COMPANY Income Statement	
Sales revenue	$97,200
Expenses	
Cost of goods sold	42,000
Depreciation expense	12,000
Salaries expense	18,000
Rent expense	9,000
Insurance expense	3,800
Interest expense	3,600
Utilities expense	2,800
Net income	$ 6,000

Required

Check Cash from operating activities, $17,978

Prepare the cash flows from operating activities section of the company's 2008 statement of cash flows using the indirect method.

Problem 16-8A[B]
Computing cash flows from operations (direct)

C4　P5

Refer to the information in Problem 16-7A.

Required

Prepare the cash flows from operating activities section of the company's 2008 statement of cash flows using the direct method.

PROBLEM SET B

Problem 16-1B
Statement of cash flows (indirect method)

C2　C3　A1　P1　P2　P3

Gazelle Corporation, a merchandiser, recently completed its calendar-year 2008 operations. For the year, (1) all sales are credit sales, (2) all credits to Accounts Receivable reflect cash receipts from customers, (3) all purchases of inventory are on credit, (4) all debits to Accounts Payable reflect cash payments for inventory, and (5) Other Expenses are paid in advance and are initially debited to Prepaid Expenses. Gazelle's balance sheets and income statement follow.

GAZELLE CORPORATION Income Statement For Year Ended December 31, 2008		
Sales		$1,185,000
Cost of goods sold		595,000
Gross profit		590,000
Operating expenses		
Depreciation expense	$ 38,600	
Other expenses	362,850	
Total operating expenses		401,450
		188,550
Other gains (losses)		
Loss on sale of equipment		2,100
Income before taxes		186,450
Income taxes expense		28,350
Net income		$ 158,100

GAZELLE CORPORATION Comparative Balance Sheets December 31, 2008 and 2007		
	2008	2007
Assets		
Cash	$123,450	$ 61,550
Accounts receivable	77,100	80,750
Merchandise inventory	240,600	250,700
Prepaid expenses	15,100	17,000
Equipment	262,250	200,000
Accum. depreciation—Equipment	(110,750)	(95,000)
Total assets	$607,750	$515,000
Liabilities and Equity		
Accounts payable	$17,750	$102,000
Short-term notes payable	15,000	10,000
Long-term notes payable	100,000	77,500
Common stock, $5 par	215,000	200,000
Paid-in capital in excess of par, common stock	30,000	0
Retained earnings	230,000	125,500
Total liabilities and equity	$607,750	$515,000

Additional Information on Year 2008 Transactions

a. The loss on the cash sale of equipment was $2,100 (details in *b*).

b. Sold equipment costing $51,000, with accumulated depreciation of $22,850, for $26,050 cash.

c. Purchased equipment costing $113,250 by paying $43,250 cash and signing a long-term note payable for the balance.

d. Borrowed $5,000 cash by signing a short-term note payable.

e. Paid $47,500 cash to reduce the long-term notes payable.

f. Issued 3,000 shares of common stock for $15 cash per share.

g. Declared and paid cash dividends of $53,600.

Required

1. Prepare a complete statement of cash flows; report its operating activities using the *indirect method*. Disclose any noncash investing and financing activities in a note.

Check Cash from operating activities, $130,200

Analysis Component

2. Analyze and discuss the statement of cash flows prepared in part 1, giving special attention to the wisdom of the cash dividend payment.

Refer to the information reported about Gazelle Corporation in Problem 16-1B.

Problem 16-2B[A]
Cash flows spreadsheet
(indirect method)
P1 P2 P3 P4

Required

Prepare a complete statement of cash flows using a spreadsheet as in Exhibit 16A.1; report its operating activities using the *indirect method*. Identify the debits and credits in the Analysis of Changes columns with letters that correspond to the following list of transactions and events.

a. Net income was $158,100.

b. Accounts receivable decreased.

c. Merchandise inventory decreased.

d. Prepaid expenses decreased.

e. Accounts payable decreased.

f. Depreciation expense was $38,600.

g. Sold equipment costing $51,000, with accumulated depreciation of $22,850, for $26,050 cash. This yielded a loss of $2,100.

h. Purchased equipment costing $113,250 by paying $43,250 cash and **(i.)** by signing a long-term note payable for the balance.

j. Borrowed $5,000 cash by signing a short-term note payable.

k. Paid $47,500 cash to reduce the long-term notes payable.

l. Issued 3,000 shares of common stock for $15 cash per share.

Check Analysis of Changes column totals, $681,950

m. Declared and paid cash dividends of $53,600.

Refer to Gazelle Corporation's financial statements and related information in Problem 16-1B.

Problem 16-3B[B]
Statement of cash flows (direct method) C3 P1 P3 P5

Required

Prepare a complete statement of cash flows; report its operating activities according to the *direct method*. Disclose any noncash investing and financing activities in a note.

Check Cash used in financing activities, $51,100

Problem 16-4B
Statement of cash flows
(indirect method)

C3 P1 P2 P3

Satu Co., a merchandiser, recently completed its 2008 operations. For the year, (1) all sales are credit sales, (2) all credits to Accounts Receivable reflect cash receipts from customers, (3) all purchases of inventory are on credit, (4) all debits to Accounts Payable reflect cash payments for inventory, (5) Other Expenses are cash expenses, and (6) any change in Income Taxes Payable reflects the accrual and cash payment of taxes. Satu's balance sheets and income statement follow.

SATU COMPANY
Comparative Balance Sheets
December 31, 2008 and 2007

	2008	2007
Assets		
Cash	$ 58,750	$ 28,400
Accounts receivable	20,222	25,860
Merchandise inventory	165,667	140,320
Equipment	107,750	77,500
Accum. depreciation—Equipment	(46,700)	(31,000)
Total assets	$305,689	$241,080
Liabilities and Equity		
Accounts payable	$ 20,372	$157,530
Income taxes payable	2,100	6,100
Common stock, $5 par value	40,000	25,000
Paid-in capital in excess of par, common stock	68,000	20,000
Retained earnings	175,217	32,450
Total liabilities and equity	$305,689	$241,080

SATU COMPANY
Income Statement
For Year Ended December 31, 2008

Sales		$750,800
Cost of goods sold		269,200
Gross profit		481,600
Operating expenses		
Depreciation expense	$ 15,700	
Other expenses	173,933	189,633
Income before taxes		291,967
Income taxes expense		89,200
Net income		$202,767

Additional Information on Year 2008 Transactions

a. Purchased equipment for $30,250 cash.

b. Issued 3,000 shares of common stock for $21 cash per share.

c. Declared and paid $60,000 of cash dividends.

Required

Check Cash from operating activities, $57,600

Prepare a complete statement of cash flows; report its cash inflows and cash outflows from operating activities according to the *indirect method*.

Problem 16-5B[A]
Cash flows spreadsheet
(indirect method)

P1 P2 P3 P4

Refer to the information reported about Satu Company in Problem 16-4B.

Required

Prepare a complete statement of cash flows using a spreadsheet as in Exhibit 16A.1; report operating activities under the *indirect method*. Identify the debits and credits in the Analysis of Changes columns with letters that correspond to the following list of transactions and events.

a. Net income was $202,767.

b. Accounts receivable decreased.

c. Merchandise inventory increased.

d. Accounts payable decreased.

e. Income taxes payable decreased.

f. Depreciation expense was $15,700.

g. Purchased equipment for $30,250 cash.

h. Issued 3,000 shares at $21 cash per share.

i. Declared and paid $60,000 of cash dividends.

Check Analysis of Changes column totals, $543,860

Refer to Satu Company's financial statements and related information in Problem 16-4B.

Required

Prepare a complete statement of cash flows; report its cash flows from operating activities according to the *direct method.*

Problem 16-6B[B]
Statement of cash flows
(direct method)   P1   P3   P5

Check   Cash provided by financing
activities, $3,000

Salt Lake Company's 2008 income statement and selected balance sheet data at December 31, 2007 and 2008, follow ($ thousands).

Problem 16-7B
Computing cash flows from
operations (indirect)

C4   P2

SALT LAKE COMPANY Income Statement	
Sales revenue	$156,000
Expenses	
Cost of goods sold	72,000
Depreciation expense	32,000
Salaries expense	20,000
Rent expense	5,000
Insurance expense	2,600
Interest expense	2,400
Utilities expense	2,000
Net income	$ 20,000

SALT LAKE COMPANY Selected Balance Sheet Accounts		
At December 31	2008	2007
Accounts receivable	$360	$300
Inventory	86	98
Accounts payable	240	260
Salaries payable	90	60
Utilities payable	20	0
Prepaid insurance	14	18
Prepaid rent	10	20

Required

Prepare the cash flows from operating activities section of the company's 2008 statement of cash flows using the indirect method.

Check   Cash from operating
activities, $51,996

Refer to the information in Problem 16-7B.

Required

Prepare the cash flows from operating activities section of the company's 2008 statement of cash flows using the direct method.

Problem 16-8B[B]
Computing cash flows from
operations (direct)

C4   P5

Problem Set C is available at the book's Website to further reinforce and assess your learning.

PROBLEM SET C

(This serial problem began in Chapter 1 and continues through most of the book. If previous chapter segments were not completed, the serial problem can begin at this point. It is helpful, but not necessary, for you to use the Working Papers that accompany the book.)

SERIAL PROBLEM

Success Systems

SP 16   Adriana Lopez, owner of Success Systems, decides to prepare a statement of cash flows for her business. (Although the serial problem allowed for various ownership changes in earlier chapters, we will prepare the statement of cash flows using the following financial data.)

SUCCESS SYSTEMS
Income Statement
For Three Months Ended March 31, 2008

Computer services revenue		$31,850
Net sales		20,345
Total revenue		52,195
Cost of goods sold	$14,272	
Depreciation expense—		
Office equipment	625	
Depreciation expense—		
Computer equipment	1,250	
Wages expense	3,900	
Insurance expense	600	
Rent expense	2,625	
Computer supplies expense	2,075	
Advertising expense	800	
Mileage expense	512	
Repairs expense—Computer	1,200	
Total expenses		27,859
Net income		$24,336

SUCCESS SYSTEMS
Comparative Balance Sheets
December 31, 2007, and March 31, 2008

	2008	2007
Assets		
Cash	$ 87,266	$ 80,260
Accounts receivable	24,400	5,800
Merchandise Inventory	680	0
Computer supplies	1,950	775
Prepaid insurance	1,200	1,800
Prepaid rent	875	875
Office equipment	10,000	10,000
Accumulated depreciation—Office		
equipment	(1,250)	(625)
Computer equipment	25,000	25,000
Accumulated depreciation—		
Computer equipment	(2,500)	(1,250)
Total assets	$147,621	$122,635
Liabilities and Equity		
Accounts payable	$ 0	$ 2,100
Wages payable	1,050	600
Unearned computer service revenue	0	2,500
Common stock	120,000	110,000
Retained earnings	26,571	7,435
Total liabilities and equity	$147,621	$122,635

Required

Prepare a statement of cash flows for Success Systems using the *indirect method* for the three months ended March 31, 2008. Recall that the owner Adriana Lopez contributed $10,000 to the business in exchange for additional stock in the first quarter of 2008 and has received $5,200 in cash dividends.

BEYOND THE NUMBERS

REPORTING IN ACTION

C4 A1

BTN 16-1   Refer to Best Buy's financial statements in Appendix A to answer the following.

1. Is Best Buy's statement of cash flows prepared under the direct method or the indirect method? How do you know?

2. For each fiscal year 2005, 2004, and 2003, is the amount of cash provided by operating activities more or less than the cash paid for dividends?

3. What is the largest amount in reconciling the difference between net income and cash flow from operating activities in 2005? In 2004? In 2003?

4. Identify the largest cash flows for investing and for financing activities in 2005 and in 2004.

Fast Forward

5. Obtain Best Buy's financial statements for a fiscal year ending after February 26, 2005, from either its Website (BestBuy.com) or the SEC's EDGAR database (www.sec.gov). Since February 26, 2005, what are Best Buy's largest cash outflows and cash inflows in the investing and in the financing sections of its statement of cash flow?

BTN 16-2 Key comparative figures ($ millions) for **Best Buy** and **Circuit City** follow.

Key Figures	Best Buy			Circuit City		
	Current Year	I Year Prior	2 Years Prior	Current Year	I Year Prior	2 Years Prior
Operating cash flows	$ 1,841	$1,369	$ 778	$ 456	$ (126)	$ (163)
Total assets	10,294	8,652	7,694	3,789	3,731	3,841

Required

1. Compute the recent two years' cash flow on total assets ratios for both Best Buy and Circuit City.
2. What does the cash flow on total assets ratio measure?
3. Which company has the higher cash flow on total assets ratio for the periods shown?
4. Does the cash flow on total assets ratio reflect on the quality of earnings? Explain.

BTN 16-3 Lisa Gish is preparing for a meeting with her banker. Her business is finishing its fourth year of operations. In the first year, it had negative cash flows from operations. In the second and third years, cash flows from operations were positive. However, inventory costs rose significantly in year 4, and cash flows from operations will probably be down 25%. Gish wants to secure a line of credit from her banker as a financing buffer. From experience, she knows the banker will scrutinize operating cash flows for years 1 through 4 and will want a projected number for year 5. Gish knows that a steady progression upward in operating cash flows for years 1 through 4 will help her case. She decides to use her discretion as owner and considers several business actions that will turn her operating cash flow in year 4 from a decrease to an increase over year 3.

Required

1. Identify two business actions Gish might take to improve cash flows from operations.
2. Comment on the ethics and possible consequences of Gish's decision to pursue these actions.

BTN 16-4 Your friend, Jessica Willard, recently completed the second year of her business and just received annual financial statements from her accountant. Willard finds the income statement and balance sheet informative but does not understand the statement of cash flows. She says the first section is especially confusing because it contains a lot of additions and subtractions that do not make sense to her. Willard adds, "The income statement tells me the business is more profitable than last year and that's most important. If I want to know how cash changes, I can look at comparative balance sheets."

Required

Write a half-page memorandum to your friend explaining the purpose of the statement of cash flows. Speculate as to why the first section is so confusing and how it might be rectified.

BTN 16-5 Access the April 29, 2005, filing of the 10-K report (for fiscal year ending January 29, 2005) of **J. Crew Group, Inc.**, at www.sec.gov.

Required

1. Does J. Crew use the direct or indirect method to construct its consolidated statement of cash flows?
2. For the fiscal year ended January 29, 2005, what is the largest item in reconciling the net loss to cash flow provided by operations?
3. In recent years J. Crew has recorded several net losses. Has the company been more successful in generating operating cash flows over this time period than in generating net income?
4. In the year ended January 29, 2005, what was the largest cash outflow for investing activities and for financing activities?
5. What items does J. Crew report as supplementary cash flow information?
6. Does J. Crew report any noncash financing activities?

TEAMWORK IN ACTION

C1 C4 A1 P2 P5

BTN 16-6   Team members are to coordinate and independently answer one question within each of the following three sections. Team members should then report to the team and confirm or correct team-mates' answers.

1. Answer *one* of the following questions about the statement of cash flows.
    a. What are this statement's reporting objectives?
    b. What two methods are used to prepare it? Identify similarities and differences between them.
    c. What steps are followed to prepare the statement?
    d. What types of analyses are often made from this statement's information?
2. Identify and explain the adjustment from net income to obtain cash flows from operating activities using the indirect method for *one* of the following items.
    a. Noncash operating revenues and expenses.
    b. Nonoperating gains and losses.
    c. Increases and decreases in noncash current assets.
    d. Increases and decreases in current liabilities.
3.[B]Identify and explain the formula for computing cash flows from operating activities using the direct method for *one* of the following items.
    a. Cash receipts from sales to customers.
    b. Cash paid for merchandise inventory.
    c. Cash paid for wages and operating expenses.
    d. Cash paid for interest and taxes.

Note: For teams of more than four, some pairing within teams is necessary. Use as an in-class activity or as an assignment. If used in class, specify a time limit on each part. Conclude with reports to the entire class, using team rotation. Each team can prepare responses on a transparency.

***BusinessWeek* ACTIVITY**

A1

BTN 16-7   Read the article "Amazon.com's Split Personality" by Nicholas G. Carr in the June 9, 2005, issue of *BusinessWeek*. (The book's Website provides a free link.) Also, access **Amazon.com**'s most recent financial statements from www.sec.gov.

Required

1. In what order does Amazon.com present its financial statements? How does this ordering compare to other companies' financial statements that you have seen?
2. Why do you believe Amazon.com presents its financial statements in the order it does?
3. What is Jeff Bezo's perception of the relative importance of the cash flow statement and the income statement? Explain.

ENTREPRENEURIAL DECISION

C1 A1

BTN 16-8   Review the chapter's opener involving **Ashtae Products, Inc.**

Required

1. In a business such as Ashtae Products, monitoring cash flow is always a priority. Even though Ashtae has about $5 million in annual sales and earns a positive net income, explain how cash flow can lag behind earnings?
2. Ashtae is a closely held corporation. What are potential sources of financing for its future expansion?

C2 A1

BTN 16-9   Jenna and Matt Wilder are completing their second year operating Mountain High, a downhill ski area and resort. Mountain High reports a net loss of $(10,000) for its second year, which includes an $85,000 extraordinary loss from fire. This past year also involved major purchases of plant assets for renovation and expansion, yielding a year-end total asset amount of $800,000. Mountain High's net cash outflow for its second year is $(5,000); a summarized version of its statement of cash flows follows:

Net cash flow provided by operating activities	$295,000
Net cash flow used by investing activities	(310,000)
Net cash flow provided by financing activities	10,000

Required

Write a one-page memorandum to the Wilders evaluating Mountain High's current performance and assessing its future. Give special emphasis to cash flow data and their interpretation.

BTN 16-10   Visit **The Motley Fool**'s Website (Fool.com). Click on the sidebar link titled *Fool's School*. Identify and select the link *How to Value Stocks*.

HITTING THE ROAD

C1

Required

1. How does the Fool's school define cash flow?

2. Per the school's instruction, why do analysts focus on earnings before interest and taxes (EBIT)?

3. Visit other links at this Website that interest you such as "A Journey through the Balance Sheet," or find out what the "Fool's Ratio" is. Write a half-page report on what you find.

BTN 16-11   Key comparative information for **Dixons** (Dixons-Group.com) follows.

GLOBAL DECISION

C1 C2 C4

(£ millions)	Current Year	1 Year Prior	2 Years Prior
Operating cash flows	£ 328	£ 340	£ 340
Total assets	3,874	4,158	4,081

Required

1. Compute the recent two years' cash flow on total assets ratio for Dixons.

2. How does Dixons' ratio compare to Best Buy and Circuit City's ratios from BTN 16-2?

ANSWERS TO MULTIPLE CHOICE QUIZ

1. b;

Net income	$15,200
Depreciation expense	10,000
Gain on sale of land	(3,000)
Increase in inventory	(1,500)
Increase in accounts payable	2,850
Net cash provided by operations	$23,550

2. c; cash received from sale of machine is reported as an investing activity.

3. d; FASB requires cash interest paid to be reported under operating.

4. a; Cash paid for salaries and wages = $255,000 + $8,200 − $10,900 = $252,300

5. e; Increase in inventory = $112,000 − $105,000 = $7,000
Increase in accounts payable = $101,300 − $98,500 = $2,800
Cash paid for merchandise = $545,000 + $7,000 − $2,800 = $549,200

17

Analysis of Financial Statements

A Look Back

Chapter 16 focused on reporting and analyzing cash inflows and cash outflows. We explained how to prepare, analyze, and interpret the statement of cash flows.

A Look at This Chapter

This chapter emphasizes the analysis and interpretation of financial statement information. We learn to apply horizontal, vertical, and ratio analyses to better understand company performance and financial condition.

A Look Ahead

Chapter 18 introduces us to managerial accounting. We discuss its purposes, concepts, and roles in helping managers gather and organize information for decisions. We also explain basic management principles.

Learning Objectives

CAP

Conceptual

C1 Explain the purpose of analysis. (p. 674)

C2 Identify the building blocks of analysis. (p. 675)

C3 Describe standards for comparisons in analysis. (p. 676)

C4 Identify the tools of analysis. (p. 676)

Analytical

A1 Summarize and report results of analysis. (p. 694)

A2 Appendix 17A—Explain the form and assess the content of a complete income statement. (p. 697)

Procedural

P1 Explain and apply methods of horizontal analysis. (p. 676)

P2 Describe and apply methods of vertical analysis. (p. 681)

P3 Define and apply ratio analysis. (p. 685)

> "What goes on at The Motley Fool every day is similar to what goes on in a library"
> —Tom Gardner
> (David Gardner on left)

Fools and Their Money

ALEXANDRIA, VA—In Shakespeare's Elizabethan comedy *As You Like It*, only the fool could speak truthfully to the King without getting his head lopped off. Inspired by Shakespeare's stage character, Tom and David Gardner vowed to become modern-day fools who tell it like it is. With under $10,000 in startup money, the brothers launched **The Motley Fool (Fool.com)**. And befitting of a Shakespearean play, the two say they are "dedicated to educating, amusing, and enriching individuals in search of the truth."

The Gardners do not fear the wrath of any King, real or fictional. They are intent on exposing the truth, as they see it, "that the financial world preys on ignorance and fear." As Tom explains, "There is such a great need in the general populace for financial information." Who can argue, given their brilliant success through practically every medium; including their Website, radio shows, newspaper columns, online store, investment newsletters, and global expansion.

Despite the brothers' best efforts, however, ordinary people still do not fully use information contained in financial statements. For instance, discussions keep appearing on The Motley Fool's online bulletin board that can be easily resolved using reliable and available accounting data. So, it would seem that the Fools must continue their work of "educating and enriching" individuals.

Resembling The Motley Fools' objectives, this chapter introduces horizontal and vertical analyses—tools used to reveal crucial trends and insights from financial information. It also expands on ratio analysis, which gives insight into a company's financial condition and performance. By arming ourselves with the information contained in this chapter and the investment advice of The Motley Fool, *we* can be sure to not play the fool in today's financial world.

[Sources: *Motley Fool Website*, May 2006; *Entrepreneur*, July 1997; *What to do with Your Money Now*, June 2002; *USA Weekend*, July 2004]

This chapter shows how to use information in financial statements to evaluate a company's financial performance and condition. We describe the purpose of financial statement analysis, its basic building blocks, the information available, standards for comparisons, and tools of analysis. The chapter emphasizes three major analysis tools: horizontal analysis, vertical analysis, and ratio analysis. We illustrate the application of each of these tools using **Best Buy**'s financial statements. We also introduce comparative analysis using **Circuit City**'s financial statements. This chapter expands and organizes the ratio analyses introduced at the end of each chapter.

Analysis of Financial Statements

Basics of Analysis
- Purpose
- Building blocks
- Information
- Standards for comparisons
- Tools

Horizontal Analysis
- Comparative balance sheets
- Comparative income statements
- Trend analysis

Vertical Analysis
- Common-size balance sheet
- Common-size income statement
- Common-size graphics

Ratio Analysis
- Liquidity and efficiency
- Solvency
- Profitability
- Market prospects
- Ratio summary

Basics of Analysis

Financial statement analysis applies analytical tools to general-purpose financial statements and related data for making business decisions. It involves transforming accounting data into more useful information. Financial statement analysis reduces our reliance on hunches, guesses, and intuition as well as our uncertainty in decision making. It does not lessen the need for expert judgment; instead, it provides us an effective and systematic basis for making business decisions. This section describes the purpose of financial statement analysis, its information sources, the use of comparisons, and some issues in computations.

Purpose of Analysis

C1 Explain the purpose of analysis.

Internal users of accounting information are those involved in strategically managing and operating the company. They include managers, officers, internal auditors, consultants, budget directors, and market researchers. The purpose of financial statement analysis for these users is to provide strategic information to improve company efficiency and effectiveness in providing products and services.

External users of accounting information are *not* directly involved in running the company. They include shareholders, lenders, directors, customers, suppliers, regulators, lawyers, brokers, and the press. External users rely on financial statement analysis to make better and more informed decisions in pursuing their own goals.

Point: Financial statement analysis tools are also used for personal financial investment decisions.

We can identify other uses of financial statement analysis. Shareholders and creditors assess company prospects to make investing and lending decisions. A board of directors analyzes financial statements in monitoring management's decisions. Employees and unions use financial statements in labor negotiations. Suppliers use financial statement information in establishing credit terms. Customers analyze financial statements in deciding whether to establish supply relationships. Public utilities set customer rates by analyzing financial statements. Auditors use financial statements in assessing the "fair presentation" of their clients' financial

Point: Financial statement analysis is a topic on the CPA, CMA, CIA, and CFA exams.

reports. Analyst services such as **Dun & Bradstreet, Moody's,** and **Standard & Poor's** use financial statements in making buy-sell recommendations and in setting credit ratings. The common goal of these users is to evaluate company performance and financial condition. This includes evaluating (1) past and current performance, (2) current financial position, and (3) future performance and risk.

Building Blocks of Analysis

Financial statement analysis focuses on one or more elements of a company's financial condition or performance. Our analysis emphasizes four areas of inquiry—with varying degrees of importance. These four areas are described and illustrated in this chapter and are considered the *building blocks* of financial statement analysis:

C2 Identify the building blocks of analysis.

- **Liquidity** and **efficiency**—ability to meet short-term obligations and to efficiently generate revenues.
- **Solvency**—ability to generate future revenues and meet long-term obligations.
- **Profitability**—ability to provide financial rewards sufficient to attract and retain financing.
- **Market prospects**—ability to generate positive market expectations.

Applying the building blocks of financial statement analysis involves determining (1) the objectives of analysis and (2) the relative emphasis among the building blocks. We distinguish among these four building blocks to emphasize the different aspects of a company's financial condition or performance, yet we must remember that these areas of analysis are interrelated. For instance, a company's operating performance is affected by the availability of financing and short-term liquidity conditions. Similarly, a company's credit standing is not limited to satisfactory short-term liquidity but depends also on its profitability and efficiency in using assets. Early in our analysis, we need to determine the relative emphasis of each building block. Emphasis and analysis can later change as a result of evidence collected.

Decision Insight

Chips and Brokers   The phrase *blue chips* refers to stock of big, profitable companies. The phrase comes from poker; where the most valuable chips are blue. The term *brokers* refers to those who execute orders to buy or sell stock. The term comes from wine retailers—individuals who broach (break) wine casks.

Information for Analysis

Some users, such as managers and regulatory authorities, are able to receive special financial reports prepared to meet their analysis needs. However, most users must rely on **general-purpose financial statements** that include the (1) income statement, (2) balance sheet, (3) statement of stockholders' equity (or statement of retained earnings), (4) statement of cash flows, and (5) notes to these statements.

Financial reporting refers to the communication of financial information useful for making investment, credit, and other business decisions. Financial reporting includes not only general-purpose financial statements but also information from SEC 10-K or other filings, press releases, shareholders' meetings, forecasts, management letters, auditors' reports, and Webcasts.

Management's Discussion and Analysis (MD&A) is one example of useful information outside traditional financial statements. **Best Buy**'s MD&A (available at <u>BestBuy.com</u>), for example, begins with an overview and strategic initiatives. It then discusses operating results followed by liquidity and capital resources—roughly equivalent to investing and financing. The final few parts discuss special financing arrangements, key accounting policies, interim results, and the next year's outlook. The MD&A is an excellent starting point in understanding a company's business activities.

Decision Insight

Analysis Online   Many Websites offer free access and screening of companies by key numbers such as earnings, sales, and book value. For instance, **Standard & Poor's** has information for more than 10,000 stocks (<u>StandardPoor.com</u>) that is accessible by its programs.

Standards for Comparisons

C3 Describe standards for comparisons in analysis.

When interpreting measures from financial statement analysis, we need to decide whether the measures indicate good, bad, or average performance. To make such judgments, we need standards (benchmarks) for comparisons that include the following:

■ *Intracompany*—The company under analysis can provide standards for comparisons based on its own prior performance and relations between its financial items. **Best Buy**'s current net income, for instance, can be compared with its prior years' net income and in relation to its revenues or total assets.

■ *Competitor*—One or more direct competitors of the company being analyzed can provide standards for comparisons. **Coca-Cola**'s profit margin, for instance, can be compared with **PepsiCo**'s profit margin.

■ *Industry*—Industry statistics can provide standards of comparisons. Such statistics are available from services such as **Dun & Bradstreet**, **Standard & Poor's**, and **Moody's**.

■ *Guidelines (rules of thumb)*—General standards of comparisons can develop from experience. Examples are the 2:1 level for the current ratio or 1:1 level for the acid-test ratio. Guidelines, or rules of thumb, must be carefully applied because context is crucial.

Point: Each chapter's *Reporting in Action* problems engage students in *intracompany* analysis, whereas *Comparative Analysis* problems require competitor analysis (Best Buy vs. Circuit City).

All of these comparison standards are useful when properly applied, yet measures taken from a selected competitor or group of competitors are often best. Intracompany and industry measures are also important. Guidelines or rules of thumb should be applied with care, and then only if they seem reasonable given past experience and industry norms.

Quick Check   Answers—p. 700

1. Who are the intended users of general-purpose financial statements?
2. General-purpose financial statements consist of what information?
3. Which of the following is *least* useful as a basis for comparison when analyzing ratios?
   (*a*) Company results from a different economic setting. (*b*) Standards from past experience.
   (*c*) Rule-of-thumb standards. (*d*) Industry averages.
4. What is the preferred basis of comparison for ratio analysis?

Tools of Analysis

C4 Identify the tools of analysis.

Three of the most common tools of financial statement analysis are

1. **Horizontal analysis**—Comparison of a company's financial condition and performance across time.
2. **Vertical analysis**—Comparison of a company's financial condition and performance to a base amount.
3. **Ratio analysis**—Measurement of key relations between financial statement items.

The remainder of this chapter describes these analysis tools and how to apply them.

Horizontal Analysis

Analysis of any single financial number is of limited value. Instead, much of financial statement analysis involves identifying and describing relations between numbers, groups of numbers, and changes in those numbers. Horizontal analysis refers to examination of financial statement data *across time*. [The term *horizontal analysis* arises from the left-to-right (or right-to-left) movement of our eyes as we review comparative financial statements across time.]

Comparative Statements

P1 Explain and apply methods of horizontal analysis.

Comparing amounts for two or more successive periods often helps in analyzing financial statements. **Comparative financial statements** facilitate this comparison by showing financial amounts in side-by-side columns on a single statement, called a *comparative format*. Using figures from **Best Buy**'s financial statements, this section explains how to compute dollar changes and percent changes for comparative statements.

Topic Tackler

PLUS

17-1

Computation of Dollar Changes and Percent Changes   Comparing financial statements over relatively short time periods—two to three years—is often done by analyzing changes in line items. A change analysis usually includes analyzing absolute dollar amount changes and percent changes. Both analyses are relevant because dollar changes can yield large percent changes inconsistent with their importance. For instance, a 50% change from a base figure of $100 is less important than the same percent change from a base amount of $100,000 in the same statement. Reference to dollar amounts is necessary to retain a proper perspective and to assess the importance of changes. We compute the *dollar change* for a financial statement item as follows:

Example: What is a more significant change, a 70% increase on a $1,000 expense or a 30% increase on a $400,000 expense? *Answer:* The 30% increase.

$$\text{Dollar change} = \text{Analysis period amount} - \text{Base period amount}$$

Analysis period is the point or period of time for the financial statements under analysis, and *base period* is the point or period of time for the financial statements used for comparison purposes. The prior year is commonly used as a base period. We compute the *percent change* by dividing the dollar change by the base period amount and then multiplying this quantity by 100 as follows:

$$\text{Percent change (\%)} = \frac{\text{Analysis period amount} - \text{Base period amount}}{\text{Base period amount}} \times 100$$

We can always compute a dollar change, but we must be aware of a few rules in working with percent changes. To illustrate, look at four separate cases in this chart:

Case	Analysis Period	Base Period	Change Analysis Dollar	Change Analysis Percent
A	$ 1,500	$(4,500)	$ 6,000	—
B	(1,000)	2,000	(3,000)	—
C	8,000	—	8,000	—
D	0	10,000	(10,000)	(100%)

When a negative amount appears in the base period and a positive amount in the analysis period (or vice versa), we cannot compute a meaningful percent change; see cases A and B. Also, when no value is in the base period, no percent change is computable; see case C. Finally, when an item has a value in the base period and zero in the analysis period, the decrease is 100 percent; see case D.

It is common when using horizontal analysis to compare amounts to either average or median values from prior periods (average and median values smooth out erratic or unusual fluctuations).[1] We also commonly round percents and ratios to one or two decimal places, but practice on this matter is not uniform. Computations are as

Example: When there is a value in the base period and zero in the analysis period, the decrease is 100%. Why isn't the reverse situation an increase of 100%? *Answer:* A 100% increase of zero is still zero.

Decision Insight

Ticker Prices   *Ticker prices* refer to a band of moving data on a monitor carrying up-to-the-minute stock prices. The phrase comes from *ticker tape*, a 1-inch-wide strip of paper spewing stock prices from a printer that ticked as it ran. Most of today's investors have never seen actual ticker tape, but the phrase survives.

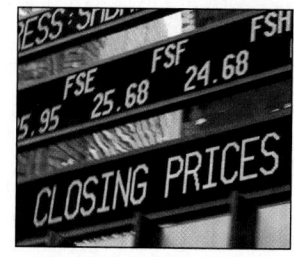

---

[1] *Median* is the middle value in a group of numbers. For instance, if five prior years' incomes are (in 000s) $15, $19, $18, $20, and $22, the median value is $19. When there are two middle numbers, we can take their average. For instance, if four prior years' sales are (in 000s) $84, $91, $96, and $93, the median is $92 (computed as the average of $91 and $93).

detailed as necessary, which is judged by whether rounding potentially affects users' decisions. Computations should not be excessively detailed so that important relations are lost among a mountain of decimal points and digits.

Comparative Balance Sheets   Comparative balance sheets consist of balance sheet amounts from two or more balance sheet dates arranged side by side. Its usefulness is often improved by showing each item's dollar change and percent change to highlight large changes.

Analysis of comparative financial statements begins by focusing on items that show large dollar or percent changes. We then try to identify the reasons for these changes and, if possible, determine whether they are favorable or unfavorable. We also follow up on items with small changes when we expected the changes to be large.

Exhibit 17.1 shows comparative balance sheets for **Best Buy**. A few items stand out. All asset categories substantially increase, which is probably not surprising because Best Buy is a growth company. At least part of the increase in liquid assets is from the 10.2% increase in current liabilities and the cash inflows from employee stock options; see the financing activities

Point: Spreadsheet programs can help with horizontal, vertical, and ratio analyses, including graphical depictions of financial relations. The key is using this information effectively for business decisions.

Point: Business consultants use comparative statement analysis to provide management advice.

Exhibit 17.1

Comparative Balance Sheets

BEST BUY **Comparative Balance Sheets** **February 26, 2005, and February 28, 2004**				
(in millions)	2005	2004	Dollar Change	Percent Change
Assets				
Cash and cash equivalents	$ 470	$ 245	$ 225	91.8%
Short-term investments	2,878	2,355	523	22.2
Receivables, net	375	343	32	9.3
Merchandise inventories	2,851	2,607	244	9.4
Other current assets	329	174	155	89.1
Total current assets	6,903	5,724	1,179	20.6
Property and equipment	4,192	3,574	618	17.3
Less accumulated depreciation	1,728	1,330	398	29.9
Net property and equipment	2,464	2,244	220	9.8
Goodwill	513	477	36	7.5
Tradename	40	37	3	8.1
Long-term investments	148	—	148	—
Other long-term assets	226	170	56	32.9
Total assets	$10,294	$8,652	$1,642	19.0
Liabilities				
Accounts payable	$ 2,824	$2,460	364	14.8
Unredeemed gift card liabilities	410	300	110	36.7
Accrued compensation and related expenses	234	269	(35)	(13.0)
Accrued liabilities	844	724	120	16.6
Accrued income taxes	575	380	195	51.3
Current portion of long-term debt	72	368	(296)	(80.4)
Total current liabilities	4,959	4,501	458	10.2
Long-term liabilities	358	247	111	44.9
Long-term debt	528	482	46	9.5
Shareholders' equity				
Common stock	33	32	1	3.1
Additional paid-in capital	952	836	116	13.9
Retained earnings	3,315	2,468	847	34.3
Accumulated other comprehensive income	149	86	63	73.3
Total shareholders' equity	4,449	3,422	1,027	30.0
Total liabilities and shareholders' equity	$10,294	$8,652	$1,642	19.0

section of the statement of cash flows. Of course, substantial asset growth (19.0%) must be accompanied by future income to validate Best Buy's growth strategy.

We likewise see substantial increases on the financing side, the most notable ones being current and long-term liabilities totaling about $569 million. Much of this is reflected in the increase in current assets and property and equipment. Best Buy also reinvested much of its income as reflected in the $847 million increase in retained earnings. Again, we must monitor the increases in investing and financing activities to be sure they are reflected in increased operating performance.

Comparative Income Statements   Comparative income statements are prepared similarly to comparative balance sheets. Amounts for two or more periods are placed side by side, with additional columns for dollar and percent changes. Exhibit 17.2 shows Best Buy's comparative income statements.

Exhibit 17.2
Comparative Income Statements

BEST BUY **Comparative Income Statements** **For Years Ended February 26, 2005, and February 28, 2004**				
(in millions, except per share data)	2005	2004	Dollar Change	Percent Change
Revenues	$27,433	$24,548	$2,885	11.8%
Cost of goods sold	20,938	18,677	2,261	12.1
Gross profit	6,495	5,871	624	10.6
Selling, general & administrative expenses	5,053	4,567	486	10.6
Operating income	1,442	1,304	138	10.6
Net interest income (expense)	1	(8)	9	—
Earnings from continuing operations before income taxes	1,443	1,296	147	11.3
Income tax expense	509	496	13	2.6
Earnings from continuing operations	934	800	134	16.8
Loss from discontinued operations, net of tax	—	(29)	29	(100.0)
Gain (loss) on disposal of discontinued operations	50	(66)	116	—
Net earnings	$ 984	$ 705	$ 279	39.6
Basic earnings per share	$ 3.02	$ 2.18	0.84	38.5
Diluted earnings per share	$ 2.94	$ 2.13	0.81	38.0

Best Buy has substantial revenue growth of 11.8% in 2005. This finding helps support management's growth strategy as reflected in the comparative balance sheets. Equally impressive is its ability to control cost of sales and general and administrative expenses, which increased 12.1% and 10.6%, respectively. Best Buy's net income growth of 39.6% on revenue growth of 11.8% is impressive.

Trend Analysis

Trend analysis, also called *trend percent analysis* or *index number trend analysis,* is a form of horizontal analysis that can reveal patterns in data across successive periods. It involves computing trend percents for a series of financial numbers and is a variation on the use of percent changes. The difference is that trend analysis does not subtract the base period amount in the numerator. To compute trend percents, we do the following:

1. Select a *base period* and assign each item in the base period a weight of 100%.
2. Express financial numbers as a percent of their base period number.

Specifically, a *trend percent,* also called an *index number,* is computed as follows:

$$\text{Trend percent (\%)} = \frac{\text{Analysis period amount}}{\text{Base period amount}} \times 100$$

Point: Percent change can also be computed by dividing the current period by the prior period and subtracting 1.0. For example, the 11.8% revenue increase of Exhibit 17.2 is computed as: ($27,433/$24,548) − 1.

Point: *Index* refers to the comparison of the analysis period to the base period. Percents determined for each period are called *index numbers.*

To illustrate trend analysis, we use the **Best Buy** data in Exhibit 17.3.

Exhibit 17.3

Revenues and Expenses

(in millions)	2005	2004	2003	2002	2001
Revenues	$27,433	$24,548	$20,943	$17,711	$15,189
Cost of goods sold	20,938	18,677	15,998	13,941	12,177
Selling, general & administrative expenses	5,053	4,567	3,935	2,862	2,401

These data are from Best Buy's *Selected Financial Data* section. The base period is 2001 and the trend percent is computed in each subsequent year by dividing that year's amount by its 2001 amount. For instance, the revenue trend percent for 2005 is 180.6%, computed as $27,433/$15,189. The trend percents—using the data from Exhibit 17.3—are shown in Exhibit 17.4.

Exhibit 17.4

Trend Percents for Revenues and Expenses

	2005	2004	2003	2002	2001
Revenues	180.6%	161.6%	137.9%	116.6%	100%
Cost of goods sold	171.9	153.4	131.4	114.5	100%
Selling, general & administrative expenses	210.5	190.2	163.9	119.2	100%

Point: Trend analysis expresses a percent of base, not a percent of change.

Exhibit 17.5

Trend Percent Lines for Revenues and Expenses of Best Buy

Graphical depictions often aid analysis of trend percents. Exhibit 17.5 shows the trend percents from Exhibit 17.4 in a *line graph,* which can help us identify trends and detect changes in direction or magnitude. It reveals that the trend line for revenues consistently exceeds that for cost of goods sold. Moreover, the magnitude of that difference has consistently grown. This result bodes well for Best Buy because its cost of goods sold are by far its largest cost, and the company shows an ability to control these expenses as it expands. The line graph also reveals a consistent increase in each of these accounts, which is typical of growth companies. The trend line for selling, general and administrative expenses is troubling because it exceeds the revenue trend line in all years. The good news is that nearly all of that upward shift in costs occured in one year (2003). In other years, management appears to have limited those costs to not exceed revenue growth.

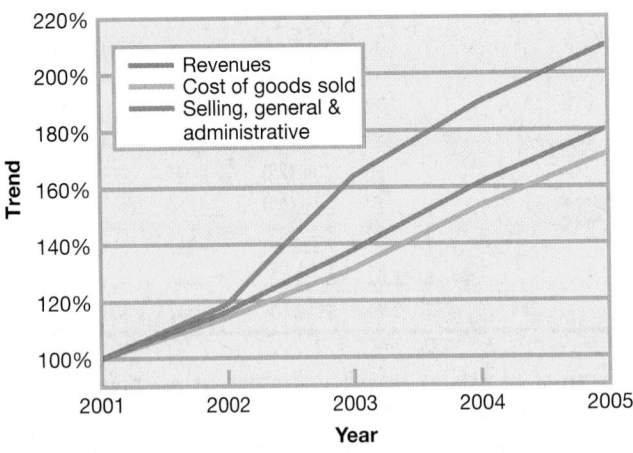

Exhibit 17.6 compares **Best Buy**'s revenue trend line to that of **Circuit City** for this same period. Best Buy's revenues sharply increased over this time period while those of Circuit City were flat. These data indicate that Best Buy's products and services have met with considerable consumer acceptance.

Exhibit 17.6

Trend Percent Lines—Best Buy vs. Circuit City

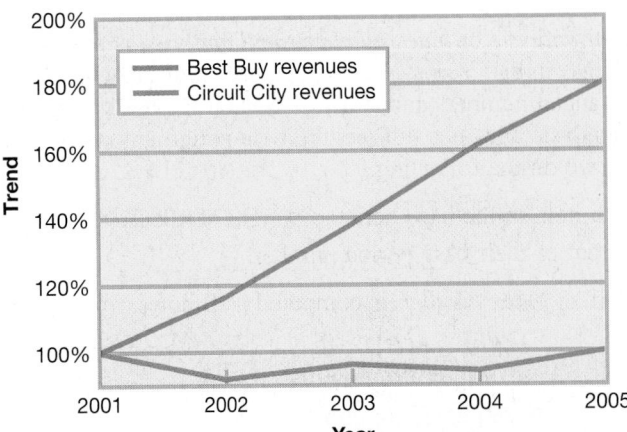

Trend analysis of financial statement items can include comparisons of relations between items on different financial statements. For instance, Exhibit 17.7 compares Best Buy's revenues and total assets. The rate of increase in total assets (212.7%) is greater than the increase in revenues (180.6%) since 2001. Is this result favorable or not? It suggests that Best Buy was less efficient in using its assets in 2005. Management apparently is expecting future years' revenues to compensate for this asset growth.

($ millions)	2005	2001	Trend Percent (2005 vs. 2001)
Revenues	$27,433	$15,189	180.6%
Total assets	10,294	4,840	212.7

Exhibit 17.7

Revenue and Asset Data for Best Buy

Overall we must remember that an important role of financial statement analysis is identifying questions and areas of interest, which often direct us to important factors bearing on a company's future. Accordingly, financial statement analysis should be seen as a continuous process of refining our understanding and expectations of company performance and financial condition.

Decision Maker   Answer—p. 700

Auditor Your tests reveal a 3% increase in sales from $200,000 to $206,000 and a 4% decrease in expenses from $190,000 to $182,400. Both changes are within your "reasonableness" criterion of ±5%, and thus you don't pursue additional tests. The audit partner in charge questions your lack of follow-up and mentions the *joint relation* between sales and expenses. To what is the partner referring?

Vertical Analysis

Vertical analysis is a tool to evaluate individual financial statement items or a group of items in terms of a specific base amount. We usually define a key aggregate figure as the base, which for an income statement is usually revenue and for a balance sheet is usually total assets. This section explains vertical analysis and applies it to Best Buy. [The term *vertical analysis* arises from the up-down (or down-up) movement of our eyes as we review common-size financial statements. Vertical analysis is also called *common-size analysis*.]

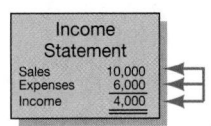

Common-Size Statements

The comparative statements in Exhibits 17.1 and 17.2 show the change in each item over time, but they do not emphasize the relative importance of each item. We use **common-size financial statements** to reveal changes in the relative importance of each financial statement item. All individual amounts in common-size statements are redefined in terms of common-size percents. A *common-size percent* is measured by dividing each individual financial statement amount under analysis by its base amount:

P2 Describe and apply methods of vertical analysis.

$$\text{Common-size percent } (\%) = \frac{\text{Analysis amount}}{\text{Base amount}} \times 100$$

Common-Size Balance Sheets Common-size statements express each item as a percent of a *base amount,* which for a common-size balance sheet is usually total assets. The base amount is assigned a value of 100%. (This implies that the total amount of liabilities plus equity equals 100% since this amount equals total assets.) We then compute a common-size percent for each asset, liability, and equity item using total assets as the base amount. When we present a company's successive balance sheets in this way, changes in the mixture of assets, liabilities, and equity are apparent.

Exhibit 17.8 shows common-size comparative balance sheets for Best Buy. Some relations that stand out on both a magnitude and percentage basis include (1) a nearly twofold increase in cash and equivalents, (2) a 2.4% decline in inventories as a percentage of assets, (3) a 2%

Point: The *base* amount in common-size analysis is an *aggregate* amount from the same period's financial statement.

Point: Common-size statements often are used to compare two or more companies in the same industry.

Exhibit 17.8

Common-Size Comparative
Balance Sheets

			Common-Size Percents*	
BEST BUY **Common-Size Comparative Balance Sheets** **February 26, 2005, and February 28, 2004**				
($ millions)	2005	2004	2005	2004
Assets				
Cash and cash equivalents	$ 470	$ 245	4.6%	2.8%
Short-term investments	2,878	2,355	28.0	27.2
Receivables, net	375	343	3.6	4.0
Merchandise inventories	2,851	2,607	27.7	30.1
Other current assets	329	174	3.2	2.0
Total current assets	6,903	5,724	67.1	66.2
Property and equipment	4,192	3,574	40.7	41.3
Less accumulated depreciation	1,728	1,330	16.8	15.4
Net property and equipment	2,464	2,244	23.9	25.9
Goodwill	513	477	5.0	5.5
Tradename	40	37	0.4	0.4
Long-term investments	148	—	1.4	0.0
Other long-term assets	226	170	2.2	2.0
Total assets	$10,294	$8,652	100.0%	100.0%
Liabilities				
Accounts payable	$ 2,824	$2,460	27.4%	28.4%
Unredeemed gift card liabilities	410	300	4.0	3.5
Accrued compensation and related expenses	234	269	2.3	3.1
Accrued liabilities	844	724	8.2	8.4
Accrued income taxes	575	380	5.6	4.4
Current portion of long-term debt	72	368	0.7	4.3
Total current liabilities	4,959	4,501	48.2	52.0
Long-term liabilities	358	247	3.5	2.9
Long-term debt	528	482	5.1	5.6
Shareholders' equity				
Common stock	33	32	0.3	0.4
Additional paid-in capital	952	836	9.2	9.7
Retained earnings	3,315	2,468	32.2	28.5
Accumulated other comprehensive income	149	86	1.4	1.0
Total shareholders' equity	4,449	3,422	43.2	39.6
Total liabilities and shareholders' equity	$10,294	$8,652	100.0%	100.0%

* Percents are rounded to tenths and thus may not exactly sum to totals and subtotals.

decrease in net property and equipment as a percentage of assets, (4) a decline in the current portion of long-term debt, and (5) a marked increase in retained earnings. Most of these changes are characteristic of a successful growth/stable company. The concern, if any, is whether Best Buy can continue to generate sufficient revenues and income to support its asset buildup within a very competitive industry.

Point: Common-size statements are also useful in comparing firms that report in different currencies.

Global: International companies sometimes disclose "convenience" financial statements, which are statements translated in other languages and currencies. However, these statements rarely adjust for differences in accounting principles across countries.

Common-Size Income Statements   Analysis also benefits from use of a common-size income statement. Revenues is usually the base amount, which is assigned a value of 100%. Each common-size income statement item appears as a percent of revenues. If we think of the 100% revenues amount as representing one sales dollar, the remaining items show how each revenue dollar is distributed among costs, expenses, and income.

Exhibit 17.9 shows common-size comparative income statements for each dollar of Best Buy's revenues. The past two years' common-size numbers are similar. The good news is that Best Buy

BEST BUY Common-Size Comparative Income Statements For Years Ended February 26, 2005, and February 28, 2004			Common-Size Percents*	
($ millions)	2005	2004	2005	2004
Revenues	$27,433	$24,548	100.0%	100.0%
Cost of goods sold	20,938	18,677	76.3	76.1
Gross profit	6,495	5,871	23.7	23.9
Selling, general & administrative expenses	5,053	4,567	18.4	18.6
Operating income	1,442	1,304	5.3	5.3
Net interest income (expense)	1	(8)	0.0	(0.0)
Earnings from continuing operations before income taxes	1,443	1,296	5.3	5.3
Income tax expense	509	496	1.9	2.0
Earnings from continuing operations	934	800	3.4	3.3
Loss from discontinued operations, net of tax	—	(29)	—	(0.1)
Gain (loss) on disposal of discontinued operations	50	(66)	0.2	(0.3)
Net earnings	$ 984	$ 705	3.6%	2.9%

Exhibit 17.9

Common-Size Comparative
Income Statements

* Percents are rounded to tenths and thus may not exactly sum to totals and subtotals.

has been able to squeeze an extra 0.7 cent in earnings per revenue dollar—evidenced by the 2.9% to 3.6% rise in earnings as a percentage of revenues. This implies that management is effectively controlling costs and/or the company is reaping growth benefits, so-called *economies of scale*. The bad news is that gross profit lost 0.2 cent per revenue dollar—evidenced by the 23.9% to 23.7% decline in gross profit as a percentage of revenues. This is a concern given the price-competitive electronics market. Analysis here shows that common-size percents for successive income statements can uncover potentially important changes in a company's expenses. Evidence of no changes, especially when changes are expected, is also informative.

Common-Size Graphics

Two of the most common tools of common-size analysis are trend analysis of common-size statements and graphical analysis. The trend analysis of common-size statements is similar to that of comparative statements discussed under vertical analysis. It is not illustrated here because the only difference is the substitution of common-size percents for trend percents. Instead, this section discusses graphical analysis of common-size statements.

An income statement readily lends itself to common-size graphical analysis. This is so because revenues affect nearly every item in an income statement. Exhibit 17.10 shows **Best Buy**'s 2005 common-size income statement in graphical form. This pie chart highlights the contribution of each component of revenues for *earnings from continuing operations*.

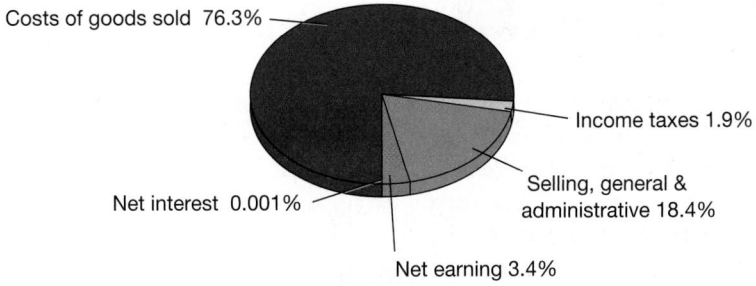

Exhibit 17.10

Common-Size Graphic of
Income Statement

Exhibit 17.11 previews more complex graphical analyses available and the insights they provide. The data for this exhibit are taken from **Best Buy**'s *Segments* footnote. Best Buy has two reportable segments: domestic and international.

Exhibit 17.11

Revenue and Operating Income
Breakdown by Segment

The upper bar in Exhibit 17.11 shows the percent of revenues from each segment. The major revenue source is Domestic (89.7%). The lower bar shows the percent of operating income from each segment. Although International provides 10.3% of revenues, it provides only 3.4% of operating income. This type of information can help users in determining strategic analyses and actions.

Graphical analysis is also useful in identifying (1) sources of financing including the distribution among current liabilities, noncurrent liabilities, and equity capital and (2) focuses of investing activities, including the distribution among current and noncurrent assets. As illustrative, Exhibit 17.12 shows a common-size graphical display of Best Buy's assets. Common-size balance sheet analysis can be extended to examine the composition of these subgroups. For instance, in assessing liquidity of current assets, knowing what proportion of current assets consists of inventories is usually important, and not simply what proportion inventories are of total assets.

Common-size financial statements are also useful in comparing different companies. Exhibit 17.13 shows common-size graphics of both Best Buy and Circuit City on financing sources. This graphic highlights the much larger percent of equity financing (and less current liability financing) for Circuit City than for Best Buy. Comparison of a company's common-size statements with competitors' or industry common-size statistics alerts us to differences in the structure or distribution of its financial statements but not to their dollar magnitude.

Exhibit 17.12

Common-Size Graphic of
Asset Components

Exhibit 17.13

Common-Size Graphic of
Financing Sources—
Competitor Analysis

Quick Check

Answers—p. 700

5. Which of the following is true for common-size comparative statements? (*a*) Each item is expressed as a percent of a base amount. (*b*) Total assets often are assigned a value of 100%. (*c*) Amounts from successive periods are placed side by side. (*d*) All are true. (*e*) None is true.

6. What is the difference between the percents shown on a comparative income statement and those shown on a common-size comparative income statement?

7. Trend percents are (*a*) shown on comparative income statements and balance sheets, (*b*) shown on common-size comparative statements, or (*c*) also called *index numbers*.

Ratio Analysis

Ratios are among the more widely used tools of financial analysis because they provide clues to and symptoms of underlying conditions. A ratio can help us uncover conditions and trends difficult to detect by inspecting individual components making up the ratio. Ratios, like other analysis tools, are usually future oriented; that is, they are often adjusted for their probable future trend and magnitude, and their usefulness depends on skillful interpretation.

A ratio expresses a mathematical relation between two quantities. It can be expressed as a percent, rate, or proportion. For instance, a change in an account balance from $100 to $250 can be expressed as (1) 150%, (2) 2.5 times, or (3) 2.5 to 1 (or 2.5:1). Computation of a ratio is a simple arithmetic operation, but its interpretation is not. To be meaningful, a ratio must refer to an economically important relation. For example, a direct and crucial relation exists between an item's sales price and its cost. Accordingly, the ratio of cost of goods sold to sales is meaningful. In contrast, no obvious relation exists between freight costs and the balance of long-term investments.

This section describes an important set of financial ratios and its application. The selected ratios are organized into the four building blocks of financial statement analysis: (1) liquidity and efficiency, (2) solvency, (3) profitability, and (4) market prospects. All of these ratios were explained at relevant points in prior chapters. The purpose here is to organize and apply them under a summary framework. We use four common standards, in varying degrees, for comparisons: intracompany, competitor, industry, and guidelines.

P3 Define and apply ratio analysis.

17-2

Point: Some sources for industry norms are *Annual Statement Studies* by Robert Morris Associates, *Industry Norms & Key Business Ratios* by Dun & Bradstreet, *Standard & Poor's Industry Surveys*, and MarketGuide.com.

Liquidity and Efficiency

Liquidity refers to the availability of resources to meet short-term cash requirements. It is affected by the timing of cash inflows and outflows along with prospects for future performance. Analysis of liquidity is aimed at a company's funding requirements. *Efficiency* refers to how productive a company is in using its assets. Efficiency is usually measured relative to how much revenue is generated from a certain level of assets.

Both liquidity and efficiency are important and complementary. If a company fails to meet its current obligations, its continued existence is doubtful. Viewed in this light, all other measures of analysis are of secondary importance. Although accounting measurements assume the company's continued existence, our analysis must always assess the validity of this assumption using liquidity measures. Moreover, inefficient use of assets can cause liquidity problems. A lack of liquidity often precedes lower profitability and fewer opportunities. It can foretell a loss of owner control or of investment. To a company's creditors, lack of liquidity can yield delays in collecting interest and principal payments or the loss of amounts due them. A company's customers and suppliers of goods and services also are affected by short-term liquidity problems. Implications include a company's inability to execute contracts and potential damage to important customer and supplier relationships. This section describes and illustrates key ratios relevant to assessing liquidity and efficiency.

Working Capital and Current Ratio   The amount of current assets less current liabilities is called **working capital,** or *net working capital.* A company needs adequate working capital to meet current debts, to carry sufficient inventories, and to take advantage of cash discounts. A company that runs low on working capital is less likely to meet current obligations or to continue operating. When evaluating a company's working capital, we must not only look at the dollar amount of current assets less current liabilities, but also at their ratio. Chapter 3 defined the *current ratio* as follows:

$$\text{Current ratio} = \frac{\text{Current assets}}{\text{Current liabilities}}$$

Drawing on information in Exhibit 17.1, **Best Buy**'s working capital and current ratio for both 2005 and 2004 are shown in Exhibit 17.14. **Circuit City**'s (and the Industry) current ratio of 2.13 (1.8) is shown in the margin. Best Buy's ratio (1.39) is lower than either of the comparison

Exhibit 17.14

Best Buy's Working Capital and Current Ratio

($ millions)	2005	2004
Current assets	$ 6,903	$ 5,724
Current liabilities	4,959	4,501
Working capital	$1,944	$1,223
Current ratio		
$6,903/$4,959	1.39 to 1	
$5,724/$4,501		1.27 to 1

Circuit City (Industry)
Current ratio = 2.13 (1.8)

ratios, but it does not appear in danger of defaulting on loan payments. A high current ratio suggests a strong liquidity position and an ability to meet current obligations. A company can, however, have a current ratio that is too high. An excessively high current ratio means that the company has invested too much in current assets compared to its current obligations. An excessive investment in current assets is not an efficient use of funds because current assets normally generate a low return on investment (compared with long-term assets).

Many users apply a guideline of 2:1 (or 1.5:1) for the current ratio in helping evaluate a company's debt-paying ability. A company with a 2:1 or higher current ratio is generally thought to be a good credit risk in the short run. Such a guideline or any analysis of the current ratio must recognize at least three additional factors: (1) type of business, (2) composition of current assets, and (3) turnover rate of current asset components.

Type of business. A service company that grants little or no credit and carries few inventories can probably operate on a current ratio of less than 1:1 if its revenues generate enough cash to pay its current liabilities. On the other hand, a company selling high-priced clothing or furniture requires a higher ratio because of difficulties in judging customer demand and cash receipts. For instance, if demand falls, inventory may not generate as much cash as expected. Accordingly, analysis of the current ratio should include a comparison with ratios from successful companies in the same industry and from prior periods. We must also recognize that a company's accounting methods, especially choice of inventory method, affect the current ratio. For instance, when costs are rising, a company using LIFO tends to report a smaller amount of current assets than when using FIFO.

Point: When a firm uses LIFO in a period of rising costs, the standard for an adequate current ratio usually is lower than if it used FIFO.

Composition of current assets. The composition of a company's current assets is important to an evaluation of short-term liquidity. For instance, cash, cash equivalents, and short-term investments are more liquid than accounts and notes receivable. Also, short-term receivables normally are more liquid than inventory. Cash, of course, can be used to immediately pay current debts. Items such as accounts receivable and inventory, however, normally must be converted into cash before payment is made. An excessive amount of receivables and inventory weakens a company's ability to pay current liabilities. The acid-test ratio (see below) can help with this assessment.

Turnover rate of assets. Asset turnover measures a company's efficiency in using its assets. One relevant measure of asset efficiency is the revenue generated. A measure of total asset turnover is revenues divided by total assets, but evaluation of turnover for individual assets is also useful. We discuss both receivables turnover and inventory turnover on the next page.

Decision Maker

Answer—p. 700

Banker A company requests a one-year, $200,000 loan for expansion. This company's current ratio is 4:1, with current assets of $160,000. Key competitors carry a current ratio of about 1.9:1. Using this information, do you approve the loan application? Does your decision change if the application is for a 10-year loan?

Acid-Test Ratio Quick assets are cash, short-term investments, and current receivables. These are the most liquid types of current assets. The *acid-test ratio,* also called *quick ratio,* was introduced in Chapter 5 and it reflects on short-term liquidity.

$$\text{Acid-test ratio} = \frac{\text{Cash} + \text{Short-term investments} + \text{Current receivables}}{\text{Current liabilities}}$$

Global: Ratio analysis helps overcome most currency translation problems, but it does *not* overcome differences in accounting principles.

Best Buy's acid-test ratio is computed in Exhibit 17.15. Best Buy's 2005 acid-test ratio (0.75) is slightly less than that for both Circuit City (0.93) and the 1:1 common guideline for an acceptable acid-test ratio, but it is greater than the industry 0.7. Similar to analysis of the current ratio, we need to consider other factors. For instance, the frequency with which a company converts its current assets into cash affects its working capital requirements. This implies that analysis of short-term liquidity should also include an analysis of receivables and inventories, which we consider next.

($ millions)	2005	2004
Cash and equivalents	$ 470	$ 245
Short-term investments	2,878	2,355
Current receivables	375	343
Total quick assets	$3,723	$2,943
Current liabilities	$4,959	$4,501
Acid-test ratio		
$3,723/$4,959	0.75 to 1	
$2,943/$4,501		0.65 to 1

Exhibit 17.15

Acid-Test Ratio

Circuit City (Industry)
Acid-test ratio = 0.93 (0.7)

Accounts Receivable Turnover   We can measure how frequently a company converts its receivables into cash by computing the *accounts receivable turnover*. As explained in Chapter 9, it is computed as follows.

$$\text{Accounts receivable turnover} = \frac{\text{Net sales}}{\text{Average accounts receivable}}$$

Short-term receivables from customers are often included in the denominator along with accounts receivable. Also, accounts receivable turnover is more precise if credit sales are used for the numerator, but external users generally use net sales (or net revenues) because information about credit sales is typically not reported. Best Buy's 2005 accounts receivable turnover is computed as follows ($ millions).

Point: Some users prefer using gross accounts receivable (before subtracting the allowance for doubtful accounts) to avoid the influence of a manager's bad debts estimates.

$$\frac{\$27,433}{(\$375 + \$343)/2} = 76.4 \text{ times}$$

Circuit City
Accounts receivable turnover = 61.0

Best Buy's value of 76.4 is larger than Circuit City's 61.0. Accounts receivable turnover is high when accounts receivable are quickly collected. A high turnover is favorable because it means the company need not commit large amounts of funds to accounts receivable. However, an accounts receivable turnover can be too high; this can occur when credit terms are so restrictive that they negatively affect sales volume.

Point: Ending accounts receivable can be substituted for the average balance in computing accounts receivable turnover if the difference between ending and average receivables is small.

Inventory Turnover   How long a company holds inventory before selling it affects working capital requirements. One measure of this effect is *inventory turnover,* also called *merchandise turnover* or *merchandise inventory turnover,* which is defined in Chapter 6 as:

$$\text{Inventory turnover} = \frac{\text{Cost of goods sold}}{\text{Average inventory}}$$

Using Best Buy's cost of goods sold and inventories information, we compute its inventory turnover for 2005 as follows (if the beginning and ending inventories for the year do not represent the usual inventory amount, an average of quarterly or monthly inventories can be used).

$$\frac{\$20,938}{(\$2,851 + \$2,607)/2} = 7.67 \text{ times}$$

Circuit City (Industry)
Inventory turnover = 5.31 (5.0)

Best Buy's inventory turnover of 7.67 is higher than Circuit City's 5.31. A company with a high turnover requires a smaller investment in inventory than one producing the same sales with a lower turnover. Inventory turnover can be too high, however, if the inventory a company keeps is so small that it restricts sales volume.

Days' Sales Uncollected   Accounts receivable turnover provides insight into how frequently a company collects its accounts. Days' sales uncollected is one measure of this activity, which is defined in Chapter 8 as:

$$\text{Days' sales uncollected} = \frac{\text{Accounts receivable}}{\text{Net sales}} \times 365$$

Any short-term notes receivable from customers are normally included in the numerator. Best Buy's 2005 days' sales uncollected follows.

Circuit City
Day's sales uncollected = 6.03

$$\frac{\$375}{\$27,433} \times 365 = 4.99 \text{ days}$$

Circuit City's days' sales uncollected of 6.03 days is longer than the 4.99 days for Best Buy. Days' sales uncollected is more meaningful if we know company credit terms. A rough guideline states that days' sales uncollected should not exceed $1\frac{1}{3}$ times the days in its (1) credit period, *if* discounts are not offered or (2) discount period, *if* favorable discounts are offered.

Days' Sales in Inventory   Chapter 6 explained how *days' sales in inventory* is a useful measure in evaluating inventory liquidity. Days' sales in inventory is linked to inventory in a way that days' sales uncollected is linked to receivables. We compute days' sales in inventory as follows.

$$\text{Days' sales in inventory} = \frac{\text{Ending inventory}}{\text{Cost of goods sold}} \times 365$$

Best Buy's days' sales in inventory for 2005 follows.

Circuit City
Days' sales in inventory = 67.4

$$\frac{\$2,851}{\$20,938} \times 365 = 49.7 \text{ days}$$

Point: *Average collection period is estimated by dividing 365 by the accounts receivable turnover ratio. For example, 365 divided by an accounts receivable turnover of 6.1 indicates a 60-day average collection period.*

If the products in Best Buy's inventory are in demand by customers, this formula estimates that its inventory will be converted into receivables (or cash) in 49.7 days. If all of Best Buy's sales were credit sales, the conversion of inventory to receivables in 49.7 days *plus* the conversion of receivables to cash in 4.99 days implies that inventory will be converted to cash in about 54.69 days (49.7 + 4.99).

Total Asset Turnover   *Total asset turnover* reflects a company's ability to use its assets to generate sales and is an important indication of operating efficiency. We explained in Chapter 10 the computation of this ratio as follows.

$$\text{Total asset turnover} = \frac{\text{Net sales}}{\text{Average total assets}}$$

Best Buy's total asset turnover for 2005 follows and is better than Circuit City's.

Circuit City
Total asset turnover = 2.79

$$\frac{\$27,433}{(\$10,294 + \$8,652)/2} = 2.90 \text{ times}$$

Quick Check   Answers—p. 700

8. Information from Paff Co. at Dec. 31, 2007, follows: cash, $820,000; accounts receivable, $240,000; inventories, $470,000; plant assets, $910,000; accounts payable, $350,000; and income taxes payable, $180,000. Compute its (a) current ratio and (b) acid-test ratio.

9. On Dec. 31, 2008, Paff Company (see question 8) had accounts receivable of $290,000 and inventories of $530,000. During 2008, net sales amounted to $2,500,000 and cost of goods sold was $750,000. Compute (a) accounts receivable turnover, (b) days' sales uncollected, (c) inventory turnover, and (d) days' sales in inventory.

Solvency

Solvency refers to a company's long-run financial viability and its ability to cover long-term obligations. All of a company's business activities—financing, investing, and operating—affect its solvency. Analysis of solvency is long term and uses less precise but more encompassing measures than liquidity. One of the most important components of solvency analysis is the composition of a company's capital structure. *Capital structure* refers to a company's financing sources. It ranges from relatively permanent equity financing to riskier or more temporary short-term financing. Assets represent security for financiers, ranging from loans secured by specific assets to the assets available as general security to unsecured creditors. This section describes the tools of solvency analysis. Our analysis focuses on a company's ability to both meet its obligations and provide security to its creditors *over the long run*. Indicators of this ability include *debt* and *equity* ratios, the relation between *pledged assets and secured liabilities,* and the company's capacity to earn sufficient income to *pay fixed interest charges.*

Debt and Equity Ratios   One element of solvency analysis is to assess the portion of a company's assets contributed by its owners and the portion contributed by creditors. This relation is reflected in the debt ratio described in Chapter 2. The *debt ratio* expresses total liabilities as a percent of total assets. The **equity ratio** provides complementary information by expressing total equity as a percent of total assets. **Best Buy**'s debt and equity ratios follow.

Point: For analysis purposes, Minority Interest is usually added to equity.

($ millions)	2005	Ratios	
Total liabilities	$ 5,845	56.8%	[Debt ratio]
Total equity	4,449	43.2	[Equity ratio]
Total liabilities and equity	$10,294	100.0%	

Circuit City
Debt ratio = 44.9%
Equity ratio = 55.1%

Best Buy's financial statements reveal more debt than equity. A company is considered less risky if its capital structure (equity and long-term debt) contains more equity. One risk factor is the required payment for interest and principal when debt is outstanding. Another factor is the greater the stockholder financing, the more losses a company can absorb through equity before the assets become inadequate to satisfy creditors' claims. From the stockholders' point of view, if a company earns a return on borrowed capital that is higher than the cost of borrowing, the difference represents increased income to stockholders. The inclusion of debt is described as *financial leverage* because debt can have the effect of increasing the return to stockholders. Companies are said to be highly leveraged if a large portion of their assets is financed by debt.

Point: Bank examiners from the FDIC and other regulatory agencies use debt and equity ratios to monitor compliance with regulatory capital requirements imposed on banks and S&Ls.

Debt-to-Equity Ratio   We explained in Chapter 14 how to use the ratio of total liabilities to equity as another measure of solvency. We compute the ratio as follows.

$$\text{Debt-to-equity ratio} = \frac{\text{Total liabilities}}{\text{Total equity}}$$

Best Buy's debt-to-equity ratio for 2005 is

$$\$5,845/\$4,449 = 1.31$$

Best Buy's 1.31 debt-to-equity ratio is larger than the 0.82 ratio for Circuit City and the industry ratio of 0.99. Consistent with our inferences from the debt ratio, Best Buy's capital structure has more debt than equity, which increases risk. Recall that debt must be repaid with interest, while equity does not. These debt requirements can be burdensome when the industry and/or the economy experience a downturn. The larger debt-to-equity ratio also implies less opportunity to expand through use of debt financing.

Decision Insight

Bears and Bulls   A *bear market* is a declining market. The phrase comes from bear-skin jobbers who often sold the skins before the bears were caught. The term *bear* was then used to describe investors who sold shares they did not own in anticipation of a price decline. A *bull market* is a rising market. This phrase comes from the once popular sport of bear and bull baiting. The term *bull* came to mean the opposite of *bear*.

Times Interest Earned   The amount of income before deductions for interest expense and income taxes is the amount available to pay interest expense. Chapter 11 explained that the following *times interest earned* ratio reflects the creditors' risk of loan repayments with interest.

Point: The times interest earned ratio and the debt and equity ratios are of special interest to bank lending officers.

$$\text{Times interest earned} = \frac{\text{Income before interest expense and income taxes}}{\text{Interest expense}}$$

The larger this ratio, the less risky is the company for creditors. One guideline says that creditors are reasonably safe if the company earns its fixed interest expense two or more times each year. Best Buy's times interest earned ratio follows; its value suggests that its creditors have little risk of nonrepayment.

$$\frac{\$934 + \$44\ (\text{see Best Buy note \#6}) + \$509}{\$44} = 33.8$$

Profitability

We are especially interested in a company's ability to use its assets efficiently to produce profits (and positive cash flows). *Profitability* refers to a company's ability to generate an adequate return on invested capital. Return is judged by assessing earnings relative to the level and sources of financing. Profitability is also relevant to solvency. This section describes key profitability measures and their importance to financial statement analysis.

Profit Margin   A company's operating efficiency and profitability can be expressed by two components. The first is *profit margin,* which Chapter 3 explained reflects a company's ability to earn net income from sales. It is measured by expressing net income as a percent of sales (*sales* and *revenues* are similar terms). **Best Buy's** profit margin follows.

$$\text{Profit margin} = \frac{\text{Net income}}{\text{Net sales}} = \frac{\$984}{\$27,433} = 3.6\%$$

To evaluate profit margin, we must consider the industry. For instance, an appliance company might require a profit margin between 10% and 15%; whereas a retail supermarket might require a profit margin of 1% or 2%. Both profit margin and *total asset turnover* make up the two basic components of operating efficiency. These ratios reflect on management because managers are ultimately responsible for operating efficiency. The next section explains how we use both measures to analyze return on total assets.

Return on Total Assets *Return on total assets* is defined as follows.

$$\text{Return on total assets} = \frac{\text{Net income}}{\text{Average total assets}}$$

Best Buy's 2005 return on total assets is

$$\frac{\$984}{(\$10,294 + \$8,652)/2} = 10.4\%$$

Circuit City (Industry)
Return on total assets = 1.6% (3.1)

Best Buy's 10.4% return on total assets is lower than that for many businesses but is higher than Circuit City's return of 1.6% and the industry's 3.1% return. We also should evaluate any trend in the rate of return.

Point: Many analysts add back *Interest expense* × (*1 − Tax rate*) to net income in computing return on total assets.

The following equation shows the important relation between profit margin, total asset turnover, and return on total assets.

$$\text{Profit margin} \times \text{Total asset turnover} = \text{Return on total assets}$$

or

$$\frac{\text{Net income}}{\text{Net sales}} \times \frac{\text{Net sales}}{\text{Average total assets}} = \frac{\text{Net income}}{\text{Average total assets}}$$

Both profit margin and total asset turnover contribute to overall operating efficiency, as measured by return on total assets. If we apply this formula to Best Buy, we get

$$3.6\% \times 2.90 = 10.4\%$$

Circuit City: 0.6% × 2.79 = 1.6%
(with rounding)

This analysis shows that Best Buy's superior return on assets to that of Circuit City is driven by its higher profit margin.

Return on Common Stockholders' Equity Perhaps the most important goal in operating a company is to earn net income for its owner(s). *Return on common stockholders' equity* measures a company's success in reaching this goal and is defined as follows.

$$\text{Return on common stockholders' equity} = \frac{\text{Net income} - \text{Preferred dividends}}{\text{Average common stockholders' equity}}$$

Best Buy's 2005 return on common stockholders' equity is computed as follows:

$$\frac{\$984 - \$0}{(\$4,449 + \$3,422)/2} = 25.0\%$$

Circuit City
Return on common stockholders' equity = 2.9%

The denominator in this computation is the book value of common equity (including any minority interest). In the numerator, the dividends on cumulative preferred stock are subtracted whether they are declared or are in arrears. If preferred stock is noncumulative, its dividends are subtracted only if declared.

> ### Decision Insight
>
> **Wall Street** *Wall Street* is synonymous with financial markets, but its name comes from the street location of the original New York Stock Exchange. The street's name derives from stockades built by early settlers to protect New York from pirate attacks.

Market Prospects

Market measures are useful for analyzing corporations with publicly traded stock. These market measures use stock price, which reflects the market's (public's) expectations for the company. This includes expectations of both company return and risk—as the market perceives it.

Price-Earnings Ratio   Computation of the *price-earnings ratio* was explained in Chapter 13 as follows.

$$\text{Price-earnings ratio} = \frac{\text{Market price per common share}}{\text{Earnings per share}}$$

Point: PE ratio can be viewed as an indicator of the market's expected growth and risk for a stock. High expected risk suggests a low PE ratio. High expected growth suggests a high PE ratio.

Predicted earnings per share for the next period is often used in the denominator of this computation. Reported earnings per share for the most recent period is also commonly used. In both cases, the ratio is used as an indicator of the future growth and risk of a company's earnings as perceived by the stock's buyers and sellers.

The market price of Best Buy's common stock at the start of fiscal year 2006 was $51.69. Using Best Buy's $3.02 basic earnings per share, we compute its price-earnings ratio as follows (some analysts compute this ratio using the median of the low and high stock price).

Circuit City
PE (year-end) = 48.8

$$\frac{\$51.69}{\$3.02} = 17.1$$

Point: Some investors avoid stocks with high PE ratios under the belief they are "overpriced." Alternatively, some investors *sell these stocks short*—hoping for price declines.

Best Buy's price-earnings ratio is slightly higher than the norm. (Circuit City's ratio is high due to its abnormally low earnings.) Best Buy's middle-of-the-pack ratio likely reflects investors' expectations of continued growth but normal earnings.

Dividend Yield   *Dividend yield* is used to compare the dividend-paying performance of different investment alternatives. We compute dividend yield as explained in Chapter 13 as follows.

$$\text{Dividend yield} = \frac{\text{Annual cash dividends per share}}{\text{Market price per share}}$$

Best Buy's dividend yield, based on its fiscal year-end market price per share of $51.69 and its policy of $0.42 cash dividends per share, is computed as follows.

Circuit City
Dividend yield = 0.4%

$$\frac{\$0.42}{\$51.69} = 0.8\%$$

Some companies do not declare and pay dividends because they wish to reinvest the cash.

Point: Corporate PE ratios and dividend yields are found in daily stock market quotations listed in *The Wall Street Journal, Investor's Business Daily,* or other publications and Web services.

Summary of Ratios

Exhibit 17.16 summarizes the major financial statement analysis ratios illustrated in this chapter and throughout the book. This summary includes each ratio's title, its formula, and the purpose for which it is commonly used.

Quick Check	Answers—p. 700

10. Which ratio best reflects a company's ability to meet immediate interest payments? (*a*) Debt ratio. (*b*) Equity ratio. (*c*) Times interest earned.

11. Which ratio best measures a company's success in earning net income for its owner(s)? (*a*) Profit margin. (*b*) Return on common stockholders' equity. (*c*) Price-earnings ratio. (*d*) Dividend yield.

12. If a company has net sales of $8,500,000, net income of $945,000, and total asset turnover of 1.8 times, what is its return on total assets?

Exhibit 17.16

Financial Statement Analysis Ratios*

Ratio	Formula	Measure of
Liquidity and Efficiency		
Current ratio	$= \dfrac{\text{Current assets}}{\text{Current liabilities}}$	Short-term debt-paying ability
Acid-test ratio	$= \dfrac{\text{Cash} + \text{Short-term investments} + \text{Current receivables}}{\text{Current liabilities}}$	Immediate short-term debt-paying ability
Accounts receivable turnover	$= \dfrac{\text{Net sales}}{\text{Average accounts receivable}}$	Efficiency of collection
Inventory turnover	$= \dfrac{\text{Cost of goods sold}}{\text{Average inventory}}$	Efficiency of inventory management
Days' sales uncollected	$= \dfrac{\text{Accounts receivable}}{\text{Net sales}} \times 365$	Liquidity of receivables
Days' sales in inventory	$= \dfrac{\text{Ending inventory}}{\text{Cost of goods sold}} \times 365$	Liquidity of inventory
Total asset turnover	$= \dfrac{\text{Net sales}}{\text{Average total assets}}$	Efficiency of assets in producing sales
Solvency		
Debt ratio	$= \dfrac{\text{Total liabilities}}{\text{Total assets}}$	Creditor financing and leverage
Equity ratio	$= \dfrac{\text{Total equity}}{\text{Total assets}}$	Owner financing
Debt-to-equity ratio	$= \dfrac{\text{Total liabilities}}{\text{Total equity}}$	Debt versus equity financing
Times interest earned	$= \dfrac{\text{Income before interest expense and income taxes}}{\text{Interest expense}}$	Protection in meeting interest payments
Profitability		
Profit margin ratio	$= \dfrac{\text{Net income}}{\text{Net sales}}$	Net income in each sales dollar
Gross margin ratio	$= \dfrac{\text{Net sales} - \text{Cost of goods sold}}{\text{Net sales}}$	Gross margin in each sales dollar
Return on total assets	$= \dfrac{\text{Net income}}{\text{Average total assets}}$	Overall profitability of assets
Return on common stockholders' equity	$= \dfrac{\text{Net income} - \text{Preferred dividends}}{\text{Average common stockholders' equity}}$	Profitability of owner investment
Book value per common share	$= \dfrac{\text{Shareholders' equity applicable to common shares}}{\text{Number of common shares outstanding}}$	Liquidation at reported amounts
Basic earnings per share	$= \dfrac{\text{Net income} - \text{Preferred dividends}}{\text{Weighted-average common shares outstanding}}$	Net income per common share
Market Prospects		
Price-earnings ratio	$= \dfrac{\text{Market price per common share}}{\text{Earnings per share}}$	Market value relative to earnings
Dividend yield	$= \dfrac{\text{Annual cash dividends per share}}{\text{Market price per share}}$	Cash return per common share

* Additional ratios also examined in previous chapters included credit risk ratio; plant asset useful life; plant asset age; days' cash expense coverage; cash coverage of growth; cash coverage of debt; free cash flow; cash flow on total assets; and payout ratio. Many of these are defined on the back inside cover of the book.

Decision Analysis   **Analysis Reporting**

A1   Summarize and report
     results of analysis.

Understanding the purpose of financial statement analysis is crucial to the usefulness of any analysis. This understanding leads to efficiency of effort, effectiveness in application, and relevance in focus. The purpose of most financial statement analyses is to reduce uncertainty in business decisions through a rigorous and sound evaluation. A *financial statement analysis report* helps by directly addressing the building blocks of analysis and by identifying weaknesses in inference by requiring explanation: It forces us to organize our reasoning and to verify its flow and logic. A report also serves as a communication link with readers, and the writing process reinforces our judgments and vice versa. Finally, the report helps us (re)evaluate evidence and refine conclusions on key building blocks. A good analysis report usually consists of six sections:

1. **Executive summary**—brief focus on important analysis results and conclusions.
2. **Analysis overview**—background on the company, its industry, and its economic setting.
3. **Evidential matter**—financial statements and information used in the analysis, including ratios, trends, comparisons, statistics, and all analytical measures assembled; often organized under the building blocks of analysis.
4. **Assumptions**—identification of important assumptions regarding a company's industry and economic environment, and other important assumptions for estimates.
5. **Key factors**—list of important favorable and unfavorable factors, both quantitative and qualitative, for company performance; usually organized by areas of analysis.
6. **Inferences**—forecasts, estimates, interpretations, and conclusions drawing on all sections of the report.

Decision Insight

Short Selling   *Short selling* refers to selling stock before you buy it. Here's an example: You borrow 100 shares of Nike stock, sell them in the market at $40 each, and receive money from their sale. You then wait. You hope that Nike's stock price falls to, say, $35 each and you can replace the borrowed stock for less money than you sold it for, reaping a profit of $5 each less any transaction costs.

We must remember that the user dictates relevance, meaning that the analysis report should include a brief table of contents to help readers focus on those areas most relevant to their decisions. All irrelevant matter must be eliminated. For example, decades-old details of obscure transactions and detailed miscues of the analysis are irrelevant. Ambiguities and qualifications to avoid responsibility or hedging inferences must be eliminated. Finally, writing is important. Mistakes in grammar and errors of fact compromise the report's credibility.

Demonstration Problem

Use the following financial statements of Precision Co. to complete these requirements.

1. Prepare comparative income statements showing the percent increase or decrease for year 2009 in comparison to year 2008.
2. Prepare common-size comparative balance sheets for years 2009 and 2008.
3. Compute the following ratios as of December 31, 2009, or for the year ended December 31, 2009, and identify its building block category for financial statement analysis.

    a. Current ratio   **g.** Debt-to-equity ratio
    b. Acid-test ratio   **h.** Times interest earned
    c. Accounts receivable turnover   **i.** Profit margin ratio
    d. Days' sales uncollected   **j.** Total asset turnover
    e. Inventory turnover   **k.** Return on total assets
    f. Debt ratio   **l.** Return on common stockholders' equity

PRECISION COMPANY Comparative Balance Sheets December 31, 2009 and 2008		
	2009	**2008**
Assets		
Current assets		
Cash	$ 79,000	$ 42,000
Short-term investments	65,000	96,000
Accounts receivable, net	120,000	100,000
Merchandise inventory	250,000	265,000
Total current assets	514,000	503,000
Plant assets		
Store equipment, net	400,000	350,000
Office equipment, net	45,000	50,000
Buildings, net	625,000	675,000
Land	100,000	100,000
Total plant assets	1,170,000	1,175,000
Total assets	$1,684,000	$1,678,000
Liabilities		
Current liabilities		
Accounts payable	$ 164,000	$ 190,000
Short-term notes payable	75,000	90,000
Taxes payable	26,000	12,000
Total current liabilities	265,000	292,000
Long-term liabilities		
Notes payable (secured by		
mortgage on buildings)	400,000	420,000
Total liabilities	665,000	712,000
Stockholders' Equity		
Common stock, $5 par value	475,000	475,000
Retained earnings	544,000	491,000
Total stockholders' equity	1,019,000	966,000
Total liabilities and equity	$1,684,000	$1,678,000

PRECISION COMPANY Comparative Income Statements For Years Ended December 31, 2009 and 2008		
	2009	**2008**
Sales	$2,486,000	$2,075,000
Cost of goods sold	1,523,000	1,222,000
Gross profit	963,000	853,000
Operating expenses		
Advertising expense	145,000	100,000
Sales salaries expense	240,000	280,000
Office salaries expense	165,000	200,000
Insurance expense	100,000	45,000
Supplies expense	26,000	35,000
Depreciation expense	85,000	75,000
Miscellaneous expenses	17,000	15,000
Total operating expenses	778,000	750,000
Operating income	185,000	103,000
Interest expense	44,000	46,000
Income before taxes	141,000	57,000
Income taxes	47,000	19,000
Net income	$ 94,000	$ 38,000
Earnings per share	$ 0.99	$ 0.40

Planning the Solution

- Set up a four-column income statement; enter the 2009 and 2008 amounts in the first two columns and then enter the dollar change in the third column and the percent change from 2008 in the fourth column.
- Set up a four-column balance sheet; enter the 2009 and 2008 year-end amounts in the first two columns and then compute and enter the amount of each item as a percent of total assets.
- Compute the required ratios using the data provided. Use the average of beginning and ending amounts when appropriate (see Exhibit 17.16 for definitions).

Solution to Demonstration Problem

1.

PRECISION COMPANY Comparative Income Statements For Years Ended December 31, 2009 and 2008				
			Increase (Decrease) in 2009	
	2009	**2008**	**Amount**	**Percent**
Sales	$2,486,000	$2,075,000	$411,000	19.8%
Cost of goods sold	1,523,000	1,222,000	301,000	24.6
Gross profit	963,000	853,000	110,000	12.9
Operating expenses				
Advertising expense	145,000	100,000	45,000	45.0
Sales salaries expense	240,000	280,000	(40,000)	(14.3)
Office salaries expense	165,000	200,000	(35,000)	(17.5)

[continued on next page]

[continued from previous page]

Insurance expense	100,000	45,000	55,000	122.2
Supplies expense	26,000	35,000	(9,000)	(25.7)
Depreciation expense	85,000	75,000	10,000	13.3
Miscellaneous expenses	17,000	15,000	2,000	13.3
Total operating expenses	778,000	750,000	28,000	3.7
Operating income	185,000	103,000	82,000	79.6
Interest expense	44,000	46,000	(2,000)	(4.3)
Income before taxes	141,000	57,000	84,000	147.4
Income taxes	47,000	19,000	28,000	147.4
Net income	$ 94,000	$ 38,000	$ 56,000	147.4
Earnings per share	$ 0.99	$ 0.40	$ 0.59	147.5

2.

PRECISION COMPANY
Common-Size Comparative Balance Sheets
December 31, 2009 and 2008

	December 31		Common-Size Percents	
	2009	2008	2009*	2008*
Assets				
Current assets				
Cash	$ 79,000	$ 42,000	4.7%	2.5%
Short-term investments	65,000	96,000	3.9	5.7
Accounts receivable, net	120,000	100,000	7.1	6.0
Merchandise inventory	250,000	265,000	14.8	15.8
Total current assets	514,000	503,000	30.5	30.0
Plant Assets				
Store equipment, net	400,000	350,000	23.8	20.9
Office equipment, net	45,000	50,000	2.7	3.0
Buildings, net	625,000	675,000	37.1	40.2
Land	100,000	100,000	5.9	6.0
Total plant assets	1,170,000	1,175,000	69.5	70.0
Total assets	$1,684,000	$1,678,000	100.0	100.0
Liabilities				
Current liabilities				
Accounts payable	$ 164,000	$ 190,000	9.7%	11.3%
Short-term notes payable	75,000	90,000	4.5	5.4
Taxes payable	26,000	12,000	1.5	0.7
Total current liabilities	265,000	292,000	15.7	17.4
Long-term liabilities				
Notes payable (secured by mortgage on buildings)	400,000	420,000	23.8	25.0
Total liabilities	665,000	712,000	39.5	42.4
Stockholders' Equity				
Common stock, $5 par value	475,000	475,000	28.2	28.3
Retained earnings	544,000	491,000	32.3	29.3
Total stockholders' equity	1,019,000	966,000	60.5	57.6
Total liabilities and equity	$1,684,000	$1,678,000	100.0	100.0

* Columns do not always exactly add to 100 due to rounding.

3. **Ratios for 2009:**

   a. Current ratio: $514,000/$265,000 = 1.9:1 (liquidity and efficiency)

   b. Acid-test ratio: ($79,000 + $65,000 + $120,000)/$265,000 = 1.0:1 (liquidity and efficiency)

   c. Average receivables: ($120,000 + $100,000)/2 = $110,000
   Accounts receivable turnover: $2,486,000/$110,000 = 22.6 times (liquidity and efficiency)

   d. Days' sales uncollected: ($120,000/$2,486,000) × 365 = 17.6 days (liquidity and efficiency)

   e. Average inventory: ($250,000 + $265,000)/2 = $257,500
   Inventory turnover: $1,523,000/$257,500 = 5.9 times (liquidity and efficiency)

f. Debt ratio: $665,000/$1,684,000 = 39.5% (solvency)

g. Debt-to-equity ratio: $665,000/$1,019,000 = 0.65 (solvency)

h. Times interest earned: $185,000/$44,000 = 4.2 times (solvency)

i. Profit margin ratio: $94,000/$2,486,000 = 3.8% (profitability)

j. Average total assets: ($1,684,000 + $1,678,000)/2 = $1,681,000
    Total asset turnover: $2,486,000/$1,681,000 = 1.48 times (liquidity and efficiency)

k. Return on total assets: $94,000/$1,681,000 = 5.6% or 3.8% × 1.48 = 5.6% (profitability)

l. Average total common equity: ($1,019,000 + $966,000)/2 = $992,500
    Return on common stockholders' equity: $94,000/$992,500 = 9.5% (profitability)

Sustainable Income

When a company's revenue and expense transactions are from normal, continuing operations, a simple income statement is usually adequate. When a company's activities include income-related events not part of its normal, continuing operations, it must disclose information to help users understand these events and predict future performance. To meet these objectives, companies separate the income statement into continuing operations, discontinued segments, extraordinary items, comprehensive income, and earnings per share. For illustration, Exhibit 17A.1 shows such an income statement for ComUS. These separate distinctions help us measure *sustainable income,* which is the income level most likely to continue into the future. Sustainable income is commonly used in PE ratios and other market-based measures of performance.

Continuing Operations

The first major section (①) shows the revenues, expenses, and income from continuing operations. Users especially rely on this information to predict future operations. Many users view this section as the most important. Earlier chapters explained the items comprising income from continuing operations.

A2 Explain the form and assess the content of a complete income statement.

Discontinued Segments

A **business segment** is a part of a company's operations that serves a particular line of business or class of customers. A segment has assets, liabilities, and financial results of operations that can be distinguished from those of other parts of the company. A company's gain or loss from selling or closing down a segment is separately reported. Section ② of Exhibit 17A.1 reports both (1) income from operating the discontinued segment for the current period prior to its disposal and (2) the loss from disposing of the segment's net assets. The income tax effects of each are reported separately from the income taxes expense in section ①.

Extraordinary Items

Section ③ reports **extraordinary gains and losses,** which are those that are *both unusual* and *infrequent.* An **unusual gain or loss** is abnormal or otherwise unrelated to the company's regular activities and environment. An **infrequent gain or loss** is not expected to recur given the company's operating environment. Reporting extraordinary items in a separate category helps users predict future performance, absent the effects of extraordinary items. Items usually considered extraordinary include (1) expropriation (taking away) of property by a foreign government, (2) condemning of property by a domestic government body, (3) prohibition against using an asset by a newly enacted law, and (4) losses and gains from an unusual and infrequent calamity ("act of God"). Items *not* considered extraordinary include (1) write-downs

Exhibit 17A.1

Income Statement (all-inclusive)
for a Corporation

ComUS Income Statement For Year Ended December 31, 2008		
Net sales		$8,478,000
Operating expenses		
Cost of goods sold	$5,950,000	
Depreciation expense	35,000	
Other selling, general, and administrative expenses ...	515,000	
Interest expense	20,000	
① Total operating expenses		(6,520,000)
Other gains (losses)		
Loss on plant relocation		(45,000)
Gain on sale of surplus land		72,000
Income from continuing operations before taxes		1,985,000
Income taxes expense		(595,500)
Income from continuing operations		1,389,500
Discontinued segment		
② Income from operating Division A (net of $180,000 taxes)	420,000	
Loss on disposal of Division A (net of $66,000 tax benefit)	(154,000)	266,000
Income before extraordinary items		1,655,500
Extraordinary items		
③ Gain on land expropriated by state (net of $61,200 taxes)	198,800	
Loss from earthquake damage (net of $270,000 tax benefit)	(630,000)	(431,200)
Net income		$1,224,300
Earnings per common share (200,000 outstanding shares)		
Income from continuing operations		$ 6.95
④ Discontinued operations		1.33
Income before extraordinary items		8.28
Extraordinary items		(2.16)
Net income (basic earnings per share)		$ 6.12

of inventories and write-offs of receivables, (2) gains and losses from disposing of segments, and (3) financial effects of labor strikes.

Gains and losses that are neither unusual nor infrequent are reported as part of continuing operations. Gains and losses that are *either* unusual *or* infrequent, but *not* both, are reported as part of continuing operations *but* after the normal revenues and expenses.

Earnings per Share

The final section ④ of the income statement in Exhibit 17A.1 reports earnings per share for each of the three subcategories of income (continuing operations, discontinued segments, and extraordinary items) when they exist. Earnings per share is discussed in Chapter 13.

Changes in Accounting Principles

Point: Changes in principles are sometimes required when new accounting standards are issued.

The *consistency principle* directs a company to apply the same accounting principles across periods. Yet a company can change from one acceptable accounting principle (such as FIFO, LIFO, or weighted-average) to another as long as the change improves the usefulness of information in its financial statements. A footnote would describe the accounting change and why it is an improvement.

Changes in accounting principles require retrospective application to prior periods' financial statements. *Retrospective application* involves applying a different accounting principle to prior periods as if that principle had always been used. Retrospective application

Decision Maker   Answer—p. 700

Small Business Owner   You own an orange grove near Jacksonville, Florida. A bad frost destroys about one-half of your oranges. You are currently preparing an income statement for a bank loan. Can you claim the loss of oranges as extraordinary?

enhances the consistency of financial information between periods, which improves the usefulness of information, especially with comparative analyses. (Prior to 2005, the cumulative effect of changes in accounting principles was recognized in net income in the period of the change.) Accounting standards also require that *a change in depreciation, amortization, or depletion method for long-term operating assets is accounted for as a change in accounting estimate*—that is, prospectively over current and future periods. This reflects the notion that an entity should change its depreciation, amortization, or depletion method only with changes in estimated asset benefits, the pattern of benefit usage, or information about those benefits.

Comprehensive Income

Comprehensive income is net income plus certain gains and losses that bypass the income statement. These items are recorded directly to equity. Specifically, comprehensive income equals the change in equity for the period, excluding investments from and distributions (dividends) to its stockholders. For **Best Buy**, it is computed as follows:

Net income	$ 984
Accumulated other comprehensive income	63
Comprehensive income	$1,047

The most common items included in *accumulated other comprehensive income,* or *AOCI*, are unrealized gains and losses on available-for-sale securities, foreign currency translation adjustments, and minimum pension liability adjustments. (Detailed computations for these items are in advanced courses.) Analysts disagree on how to treat these items. Some analysts believe that AOCI items should not be considered when predicting future performance, and some others believe AOCI items should be considered as they reflect on company and managerial performance. Whatever our position, we must be familiar with what AOCI items are as they are commonly reported in financial statements. Best Buy reports its comprehensive income in its statement of shareholders' equity (see Appendix A).

Quick Check
Answers—p. 700

13. Which of the following is an extraordinary item? (*a*) a settlement paid to a customer injured while using the company's product, (*b*) a loss to a plant from damages caused by a meteorite, or (*c*) a loss from selling old equipment.

14. Identify the four major sections of an income statement that are potentially reportable.

15. A company using FIFO for the past 15 years decides to switch to LIFO. The effect of this event on prior years' net income is (*a*) reported as if the new method had always been used; (*b*) ignored because it is a change in an accounting estimate; or (*c*) reported on the current year income statement.

Summary

C1 **Explain the purpose of analysis.** The purpose of financial statement analysis is to help users make better business decisions. Internal users want information to improve company efficiency and effectiveness in providing products and services. External users want information to make better and more informed decisions in pursuing their goals. The common goals of all users are to evaluate a company's (1) past and current performance, (2) current financial position, and (3) future performance and risk.

C2 **Identify the building blocks of analysis.** Financial statement analysis focuses on four "building blocks" of analysis: (1) liquidity and efficiency—ability to meet short-term obligations and efficiently generate revenues; (2) solvency—ability to generate future revenues and meet long-term obligations; (3) profitability—ability to provide financial rewards sufficient to attract and retain

financing; and (4) market prospects—ability to generate positive market expectations.

C3 **Describe standards for comparisons in analysis.** Standards for comparisons include (1) intracompany—prior performance and relations between financial items for the company under analysis; (2) competitor—one or more direct competitors of the company; (3) industry—industry statistics; and (4) guidelines (rules of thumb)—general standards developed from past experiences and personal judgments.

C4 **Identify the tools of analysis.** The three most common tools of financial statement analysis are (1) horizontal analysis—comparing a company's financial condition and performance across time; (2) vertical analysis—comparing a company's financial condition and performance to a base amount such as revenues or total assets; and (3) ratio analysis—using and quantifying key relations among financial statement items.

A1 **Summarize and report results of analysis.** A financial statement analysis report is often organized around the building blocks of analysis. A good report separates interpretations and conclusions of analysis from the information underlying them. An analysis report often consists of six sections: (1) executive summary, (2) analysis overview, (3) evidential matter, (4) assumptions, (5) key factors, and (6) inferences.

A2ᴬ **Explain the form and assess the content of a complete income statement.** An income statement has four *potential* sections: (1) continuing operations, (2) discontinued segments, (3) extraordinary items, and (4) earnings per share.

P1 **Explain and apply methods of horizontal analysis.** Horizontal analysis is a tool to evaluate changes in data across time. Two important tools of horizontal analysis are comparative statements and trend analysis. Comparative statements show amounts for two or more successive periods, often with changes

disclosed in both absolute and percent terms. Trend analysis is used to reveal important changes occurring from one period to the next.

P2 **Describe and apply methods of vertical analysis.** Vertical analysis is a tool to evaluate each financial statement item or group of items in terms of a base amount. Two tools of vertical analysis are common-size statements and graphical analyses. Each item in common-size statements is expressed as a percent of a base amount. For the balance sheet, the base amount is usually total assets, and for the income statement, it is usually sales.

P3 **Define and apply ratio analysis.** Ratio analysis provides clues to and symptoms of underlying conditions. Ratios, properly interpreted, identify areas requiring further investigation. A ratio expresses a mathematical relation between two quantities such as a percent, rate, or proportion. Ratios can be organized into the building blocks of analysis: (1) liquidity and efficiency, (2) solvency, (3) profitability, and (4) market prospects.

Guidance Answers to **Decision Maker**

Auditor The *joint relation* referred to is the combined increase in sales and the decrease in expenses yielding more than a 5% increase in income. Both *individual* accounts (sales and expenses) yield percent changes within the ±5% acceptable range. However, a joint analysis suggests a different picture. For example, consider a joint analysis using the profit margin ratio. The client's profit margin is 11.46% ($206,000 − $182,400/$206,000) for the current year compared with 5.0% ($200,000 − $190,000/$200,000) for the prior year—yielding a 129% increase in profit margin! This is what concerns the partner, and it suggests expanding audit tests to verify or refute the client's figures.

Banker Your decision on the loan application is positive for at least two reasons. First, the current ratio suggests a strong ability to meet short-term obligations. Second, current assets of $160,000 and

a current ratio of 4:1 imply current liabilities of $40,000 (one-fourth of current assets) and a working capital excess of $120,000. This working capital excess is 60% of the loan amount. However, if the application is for a 10-year loan, our decision is less optimistic. The current ratio and working capital suggest a good safety margin, but indications of inefficiency in operations exist. In particular, a 4:1 current ratio is more than double its key competitors' ratio. This is characteristic of inefficient asset use.

Small Business Owner The frost loss is probably not extraordinary. Jacksonville experiences enough recurring frost damage to make it difficult to argue this event is both unusual and infrequent. Still, you want to highlight the frost loss and hope the bank views this uncommon event separately from continuing operations.

Guidance Answers to **Quick Checks**

1. General-purpose financial statements are intended for a variety of users interested in a company's financial condition and performance—users without the power to require specialized financial reports to meet their specific needs.

2. General-purpose financial statements include the income statement, balance sheet, statement of stockholders' (owner's) equity, and statement of cash flows plus the notes related to these statements.

3. *a*

4. Data from one or more direct competitors are usually preferred for comparative purposes.

5. *d*

6. Percents on comparative income statements show the increase or decrease in each item from one period to the next. On common-size comparative income statements, each item is shown as a percent of net sales for that period.

7. *c*

8. (*a*) ($820,000 + $240,000 + $470,000)/
    ($350,000 + $180,000) = 2.9 to 1.

(*b*) ($820,000 + $240,000)/($350,000 + $180,000) = 2:1.

9. (*a*) $2,500,000/[($290,000 + $240,000)/2] = 9.43 times.
   (*b*) ($290,000/$2,500,000) × 365 = 42 days.
   (*c*) $750,000/[($530,000 + $470,000)/2] = 1.5 times.
   (*d*) ($530,000/$750,000) × 365 = 258 days.

10. *c*

11. *b*

12. Profit margin × $\dfrac{\text{Total asset}}{\text{turnover}}$ = $\dfrac{\text{Return on}}{\text{total assets}}$

$$\frac{\$945,000}{\$8,500,000} \times 1.8 = 20\%$$

13. (*b*)

14. The four (potentially reportable) major sections are income from continuing operations, discontinued segments, extraordinary items, and earnings per share.

15. (*a*); known as retrospective application.

Key Terms

mhhe.com/wildFAP18e

Key Terms are available at the book's Website for learning and testing in an online Flashcard Format.

Business segment (p. 697)
Common-size financial statement (p. 681)
Comparative financial statements (p. 676)
Efficiency (p. 675)
Equity ratio (p. 689)
Extraordinary gains and losses (p. 697)
Financial reporting (p. 675)

Financial statement analysis (p. 674)
General-purpose financial statements (p. 675)
Horizontal analysis (p. 676)
Infrequent gain or loss (p. 697)
Liquidity (p. 675)
Market prospects (p. 675)

Profitability (p. 675)
Ratio analysis (p. 676)
Solvency (p. 675)
Unusual gain or loss (p. 697)
Vertical analysis (p. 676)
Working capital (p. 685)

Multiple Choice Quiz

Answers on p. 717   mhhe.com/wildFAP18e

Multiple Choice Quizzes A and B are available at the book's Website.

1. A company's sales in 2007 were $300,000 and in 2008 were $351,000. Using 2007 as the base year, the sales trend percent for 2008 is:
   a. 17%
   b. 85%
   c. 100%
   d. 117%
   e. 48%

Use the following information for questions 2 through 5.

GALLOWAY COMPANY
Balance Sheet
December 31, 2008

Assets	
Cash	$ 86,000
Accounts receivable	76,000
Merchandise inventory	122,000
Prepaid insurance	12,000
Long-term investments	98,000
Plant assets, net	436,000
Total assets	$830,000
Liabilities and Equity	
Current liabilities	$124,000
Long-term liabilities	90,000
Common stock	300,000
Retained earnings	316,000
Total liabilities and equity	$830,000

2. What is Galloway Company's current ratio?
   a. 0.69
   b. 1.31
   c. 3.88
   d. 6.69
   e. 2.39

3. What is Galloway Company's acid-test ratio?
   a. 2.39
   b. 0.69
   c. 1.31
   d. 6.69
   e. 3.88

4. What is Galloway Company's debt ratio?
   a. 25.78%
   b. 100.00%
   c. 74.22%
   d. 137.78%
   e. 34.74%

5. What is Galloway Company's equity ratio?
   a. 25.78%
   b. 100.00%
   c. 34.74%
   d. 74.22%
   e. 137.78%

Superscript letter ^A *denotes assignments based on Appendix 17A.*

Discussion Questions

1. What is the difference between comparative financial statements and common-size comparative statements?

2. Which items are usually assigned a 100% value on (*a*) a common-size balance sheet and (*b*) a common-size income statement?

3. Explain the difference between financial reporting and financial statements.

4. What three factors would influence your evaluation as to whether a company's current ratio is good or bad?

5. Suggest several reasons why a 2:1 current ratio may not be adequate for a particular company.

6. Why is working capital given special attention in the process of analyzing balance sheets?

7. What does the number of days' sales uncollected indicate?

8. What does a relatively high accounts receivable turnover indicate about a company's short-term liquidity?

9. Why is a company's capital structure, as measured by debt and equity ratios, important to financial statement analysts?

10. How does inventory turnover provide information about a company's short-term liquidity?

11. What ratios would you compute to evaluate management performance?

12. Why must the ratio of pledged assets to secured liabilities be interpreted with caution?

13. Why would a company's return on total assets be different from its return on common stockholders' equity?

14. Where on the income statement does a company report an unusual gain not expected to occur more often than once every two years or so?

15. Use **Best Buy**'s financial statements in Appendix A to compute its return on total assets for the years ended February 26, 2005, and February 28, 2004. Total assets at March, 2003, were $7,694 (in millions).

16. Refer to **Circuit City**'s financial statements in Appendix A to compute its equity ratio as of February 28, 2005 and February 29, 2004.

17. Refer to **Apple**'s financial statements in Appendix A. Compute its profit margin for the fiscal year ended September 25, 2004.

 Red numbers denote Discussion Questions that involve decision-making.

QUICK STUDY

QS 17-1
Financial reporting   C1

Which of the following items (1) through (9) are part of financial reporting but are *not* included as part of general-purpose financial statements? (1) stock price information and analysis, (2) statement of cash flows, (3) management discussion and analysis of financial performance, (4) income statement, (5) company news releases, (6) balance sheet, (7) financial statement notes, (8) statement of shareholders' equity, (9) prospectus.

QS 17-2
Standard of comparison   C3

What are four possible standards of comparison used to analyze financial statement ratios? Which of these is generally considered to be the most useful? Which one is least likely to provide a good basis for comparison?

QS 17-3
Common-size and trend percents
P1   P2

Use the following information for Ciolino Corporation to determine (1) the 2007 and 2008 common-size percents for cost of goods sold using net sales as the base and (2) the 2007 and 2008 trend percents for net sales using 2007 as the base year.

($ thousands)	2008	2007
Net sales	$202,800	$116,200
Cost of goods sold	110,600	61,400

QS 17-4
Horizontal analysis

P1

Compute the annual dollar changes and percent changes for each of the following accounts.

	2008	2007
Short-term investments	$220,000	$160,000
Accounts receivable	38,000	44,000
Notes payable	60,000	0

QS 17-5
Building blocks of analysis

C2   C4   P3

Match the ratio to the building block of financial statement analysis to which it best relates.

A. Liquidity and efficiency   **C.** Profitability

B. Solvency   **D.** Market prospects

1. _____ Book value per common share

2. _____ Days' sales in inventory

3. _____ Accounts receivable turnover

4. _____ Debt-to-equity

5. _____ Times interest earned

6. _____ Gross margin ratio

7. _____ Acid-test ratio

8. _____ Equity ratio

9. _____ Return on total assets

10. _____ Dividend yield

1. Which two short-term liquidity ratios measure how frequently a company collects its accounts?

2. What measure reflects the difference between current assets and current liabilities?

3. Which two ratios are key components in measuring a company's operating efficiency? Which ratio summarizes these two components?

QS 17-6
Identifying financial ratios

C4 P3

For each ratio listed, identify whether the change in ratio value from 2007 to 2008 is usually regarded as favorable or unfavorable.

QS 17-7
Ratio interpretation

P3

Ratio	2008	2007	Ratio	2008	2007
1. Profit margin	9%	8%	5. Accounts receivable turnover	5.5	6.7
2. Debt ratio	47%	42%	6. Basic earnings per share	$1.25	$1.10
3. Gross margin	34%	46%	7. Inventory turnover	3.6	3.4
4. Acid-test ratio	1.00	1.15	8. Dividend yield	2%	1.2%

A review of the notes payable files discovers that three years ago the company reported the entire amount of a payment (principal and interest) on an installment note payable as interest expense. This mistake had a material effect on the amount of income in that year. How should the correction be reported in the current year financial statements?

QS 17-8[A]
Error adjustments

A2

Compute trend percents for the following financial items, using 2006 as the base year. State whether the situation as revealed by the trends appears to be favorable or unfavorable for each item.

EXERCISES

Exercise 17-1
Computation and analysis of trend percents

P1

	2010	2009	2008	2007	2006
Sales	$282,880	$270,800	$252,600	$234,560	$150,000
Cost of goods sold	128,200	122,080	115,280	106,440	67,000
Accounts receivable	18,100	17,300	16,400	15,200	9,000

Common-size and trend percents for Skelton Company's sales, cost of goods sold, and expenses follow. Determine whether net income increased, decreased, or remained unchanged in this three-year period.

Exercise 17-2
Determination of income effects from common-size and trend percents

P1 P2

	Common-Size Percents			Trend Percents		
	2009	2008	2007	2009	2008	2007
Sales	100.0%	100.0%	100.0%	105.4%	104.2%	100.0%
Cost of goods sold	63.4	61.9	59.1	103.0	101.1	100.0
Total expenses	15.3	14.8	15.1	95.0	91.0	100.0

Express the following comparative income statements in common-size percents and assess whether or not this company's situation has improved in the most recent year.

Exercise 17-3
Common-size percent computation and interpretation

P2

MACHIKO CORPORATION Comparative Income Statements For Years Ended December 31, 2008 and 2007		
	2008	2007
Sales	$740,000	$625,000
Cost of goods sold	560,300	290,800
Gross profit	179,700	334,200
Operating expenses	128,200	218,500
Net income	$ 51,500	$115,700

Exercise 17-4
Analysis of short-term financial condition

A1 P3

Team Project: Assume that the two companies apply for a one-year loan from the team. Identify additional information the companies must provide before the team can make a loan decision.

The following information is available for Morgan Company and Parker Company, similar firms operating in the same industry. Write a half-page report comparing Morgan and Parker using the available information. Your discussion should include their ability to meet current obligations and to use current assets efficiently.

Microsoft Excel - Book1
File Edit View Insert Format Tools Data Accounting Window Help

	Morgan			Parker		
	2009	2008	2007	2009	2008	2007
3 Current ratio	1.7	1.6	2.1	3.2	2.7	1.9
4 Acid-test ratio	1.0	1.1	1.2	2.8	2.5	1.6
5 Accounts receivable turnover	30.5	25.2	29.2	16.4	15.2	16.0
6 Merchandise inventory turnover	24.2	21.9	17.1	14.5	13.0	12.6
7 Working capital	$70,000	$58,000	$52,000	$131,000	$103,000	$78,000

Exercise 17-5
Analysis of efficiency and financial leverage

A1 P3

Roak Company and Clay Company are similar firms that operate in the same industry. Clay began operations in 2008 and Roak in 2005. In 2010, both companies pay 7% interest on their debt to creditors. The following additional information is available.

	Roak Company			Clay Company		
	2010	2009	2008	2010	2009	2008
Total asset turnover	3.1	2.8	3.0	1.7	1.5	1.2
Return on total assets	9.0%	9.6%	8.8%	5.9%	5.6%	5.3%
Profit margin ratio	2.4%	2.5%	2.3%	2.8%	3.0%	2.9%
Sales	$410,000	$380,000	$396,000	$210,000	$170,000	$110,000

Write a half-page report comparing Roak and Clay using the available information. Your analysis should include their ability to use assets efficiently to produce profits. Also comment on their success in employing financial leverage in 2010.

Exercise 17-6
Common-size percents

P2

Simeon Company's year-end balance sheets follow. Express the balance sheets in common-size percents. Round amounts to the nearest one-tenth of a percent. Analyze and comment on the results.

At December 31	2009	2008	2007
Assets			
Cash	$ 31,800	$ 35,625	$ 37,800
Accounts receivable, net	89,500	62,500	50,200
Merchandise inventory	112,500	82,500	54,000
Prepaid expenses	10,700	9,375	5,000
Plant assets, net	278,500	255,000	230,500
Total assets......................	$523,000	$445,000	$377,500
Liabilities and Equity			
Accounts payable	$129,900	$ 75,250	$ 51,250
Long-term notes payable secured by mortgages on plant assets	98,500	101,500	83,500
Common stock, $10 par value	163,500	163,500	163,500
Retained earnings	131,100	104,750	79,250
Total liabilities and equity	$523,000	$445,000	$377,500

Refer to Simeon Company's balance sheets in Exercise 17-6. Analyze its year-end short-term liquidity position at the end of 2009, 2008, and 2007 by computing (1) the current ratio and (2) the acid-test ratio. Comment on the ratio results.

Exercise 17-7
Liquidity analysis

P3

Refer to the Simeon Company information in Exercise 17-6. The company's income statements for the years ended December 31, 2009 and 2008, follow. Assume that all sales are on credit and then compute: (1) days' sales uncollected, (2) accounts receivable turnover, (3) inventory turnover, and (4) days' sales in inventory. Comment on the changes in the ratios from 2008 to 2009.

Exercise 17-8
Liquidity analysis and interpretation

P3

For Year Ended December 31		2009		2008
Sales		$673,500		$532,000
Cost of goods sold	$411,225		$345,500	
Other operating expenses	209,550		134,980	
Interest expense	12,100		13,300	
Income taxes	9,525		8,845	
Total costs and expenses		642,400		502,625
Net income		$ 31,100		$ 29,375
Earnings per share		$ 1.90		$ 1.80

Refer to the Simeon Company information in Exercises 17-6 and 17-8. Compare the company's long-term risk and capital structure positions at the end of 2009 and 2008 by computing these ratios: (1) debt and equity ratios, (2) debt-to-equity ratio, and (3) times interest earned. Comment on these ratio results.

Exercise 17-9
Risk and capital structure analysis

P3

Refer to Simeon Company's financial information in Exercises 17-6 and 17-8. Evaluate the company's efficiency and profitability by computing the following for 2009 and 2008: (1) profit margin ratio, (2) total asset turnover, and (3) return on total assets. Comment on these ratio results.

Exercise 17-10
Efficiency and profitability analysis   P3

Refer to Simeon Company's financial information in Exercises 17-6 and 17-8. Additional information about the company follows. To help evaluate the company's profitability, compute and interpret the following ratios for 2009 and 2008: (1) return on common stockholders' equity, (2) price-earnings ratio on December 31, and (3) dividend yield.

Exercise 17-11
Profitability analysis

P3

Common stock market price, December 31, 2009	$30.00
Common stock market price, December 31, 2008	28.00
Annual cash dividends per share in 2009	0.29
Annual cash dividends per share in 2008	0.24

In 2008, Randa Merchandising, Inc., sold its interest in a chain of wholesale outlets, taking the company completely out of the wholesaling business. The company still operates its retail outlets. A listing of the major sections of an income statement follows:

A. Income (loss) from continuing operations

B. Income (loss) from operating, or gain (loss) from disposing, a discontinued segment

C. Extraordinary gain (loss)

Indicate where each of the following income-related items for this company appears on its 2008 income statement by writing the letter of the appropriate section in the blank beside each item.

Exercise 17-12ᴬ
Income statement categories

A2

Section	Item	Debit	Credit
_____	1. Net sales		$2,900,000
_____	2. Gain on state's condemnation of company property (net of tax)		230,000
_____	3. Cost of goods sold	$1,480,000	
_____	4. Income taxes expense	217,000	
_____	5. Depreciation expense	232,500	
_____	6. Gain on sale of wholesale business segment (net of tax)		775,000
_____	7. Loss from operating wholesale business segment (net of tax)	444,000	
_____	8. Salaries expense	640,000	

Exercise 17-13[A]

Income statement presentation

A2

Use the financial data for Randa Merchandising, Inc., in Exercise 17-12 to prepare its income statement for calendar year 2008. (Ignore the earnings per share section.)

PROBLEM SET A

Selected comparative financial statements of Korbin Company follow.

Problem 17-1A

Ratios, common-size statements, and trend percents

P1 P2 P3

mhhe.com/wildFAP18e

KORBIN COMPANY Comparative Income Statements For Years Ended December 31, 2009, 2008, and 2007			
	2009	**2008**	**2007**
Sales	$555,000	$340,000	$278,000
Cost of goods sold	283,500	212,500	153,900
Gross profit	271,500	127,500	124,100
Selling expenses	102,900	46,920	50,800
Administrative expenses	50,668	29,920	22,800
Total expenses	153,568	76,840	73,600
Income before taxes	117,932	50,660	50,500
Income taxes	40,800	10,370	15,670
Net income	$ 77,132	$ 40,290	$ 34,830

KORBIN COMPANY Comparative Balance Sheets December 31, 2009, 2008, and 2007			
	2009	**2008**	**2007**
Assets			
Current assets	$ 52,390	$ 37,924	$ 51,748
Long-term investments	0	500	3,950
Plant assets, net	100,000	96,000	60,000
Total assets	$152,390	$134,424	$115,698
Liabilities and Equity			
Current liabilities	$ 22,800	$ 19,960	$ 20,300
Common stock	72,000	72,000	60,000
Other paid-in capital	9,000	9,000	6,000
Retained earnings	48,590	33,464	29,398
Total liabilities and equity	$152,390	$134,424	$115,698

Required

1. Compute each year's current ratio.

2. Express the income statement data in common-size percents.

3. Express the balance sheet data in trend percents with 2007 as the base year.

Check (3) 2009, Total assets trend, 131.71%

Analysis Component

4. Comment on any significant relations revealed by the ratios and percents computed.

Selected comparative financial statements of Haroun Company follow.

Problem 17-2A

Calculation and analysis of trend percents

A1 P1

HAROUN COMPANY Comparative Income Statements ($000) For Years Ended December 31, 2009–2003							
	2009	**2008**	**2007**	**2006**	**2005**	**2004**	**2003**
Sales	$1,694	$1,496	$1,370	$1,264	$1,186	$1,110	$928
Cost of goods sold	1,246	1,032	902	802	752	710	586
Gross profit	448	464	468	462	434	400	342
Operating expenses	330	256	234	170	146	144	118
Net income	$ 118	$ 208	$ 234	$ 292	$ 288	$ 256	$224

HAROUN COMPANY Comparative Balance Sheets ($000) December 31, 2009–2003							
	2009	**2008**	**2007**	**2006**	**2005**	**2004**	**2003**
Assets							
Cash	$ 58	$ 78	$ 82	$ 84	$ 88	$ 86	$ 89
Accounts receivable, net	490	514	466	360	318	302	216
Merchandise inventory	1,838	1,364	1,204	1,032	936	810	615
Other current assets	36	32	14	34	28	28	9
Long-term investments	0	0	0	146	146	146	146
Plant assets, net	2,020	2,014	1,752	944	978	860	725
Total assets	$4,442	$4,002	$3,518	$2,600	$2,494	$2,232	$1,800
Liabilities and Equity							
Current liabilities	$1,220	$1,042	$ 718	$ 614	$ 546	$ 522	$ 282
Long-term liabilities	1,294	1,140	1,112	570	580	620	400
Common stock	1,000	1,000	1,000	850	850	650	650
Other paid-in capital	250	250	250	170	170	150	150
Retained earnings	678	570	438	396	348	290	318
Total liabilities and equity	$4,442	$4,002	$3,518	$2,600	$2,494	$2,232	$1,800

Required

1. Compute trend percents for all components of both statements using 2003 as the base year.

Check (1) 2009, Total assets trend, 246.8%

Analysis Component

2. Analyze and comment on the financial statements and trend percents from part 1.

Plum Corporation began the month of May with $700,000 of current assets, a current ratio of 2.50:1, and an acid-test ratio of 1.10:1. During the month, it completed the following transactions (the company uses a perpetual inventory system).

May 2   Purchased $50,000 of merchandise inventory on credit.
    8   Sold merchandise inventory that cost $55,000 for $110,000 cash.
    10   Collected $20,000 cash on an account receivable.
    15   Paid $22,000 cash to settle an account payable.

Problem 17-3A

Transactions, working capital, and liquidity ratios

P3

mhhe.com/wildFAP18e

Check May 22: Current ratio, 2.19;
Acid-test, 1.11

     May 29: Current ratio, 1.80;
Working capital, $325,000

17 Wrote off a $5,000 bad debt against the Allowance for Doubtful Accounts account.
22 Declared a $1 per share cash dividend on the 50,000 shares of outstanding common stock.
26 Paid the dividend declared on May 22.
27 Borrowed $100,000 cash by giving the bank a 30-day, 10% note.
28 Borrowed $80,000 cash by signing a long-term secured note.
29 Used the $180,000 cash proceeds from the notes to buy new machinery.

Required

Prepare a table showing Plum's (1) current ratio, (2) acid-test ratio, and (3) working capital, after each transaction. Round ratios to hundredths.

Problem 17-4A

Calculation of financial
statement ratios

P3

mhhe.com/wildFAP18e

Selected year-end financial statements of Cabot Corporation follow. (All sales were on credit; selected balance sheet amounts at December 31, 2007, were inventory, $48,900; total assets, $189,400; common stock, $90,000; and retained earnings, $22,748.)

CABOT CORPORATION Income Statement For Year Ended December 31, 2008	
Sales	$448,600
Cost of goods sold	297,250
Gross profit	151,350
Operating expenses	98,600
Interest expense	4,100
Income before taxes	48,650
Income taxes	19,598
Net income	$ 29,052

CABOT CORPORATION Balance Sheet December 31, 2008			
Assets		**Liabilities and Equity**	
Cash	$ 10,000	Accounts payable	$ 17,500
Short-term investments	8,400	Accrued wages payable	3,200
Accounts receivable, net	29,200	Income taxes payable	3,300
Notes receivable (trade)*	4,500	Long-term note payable, secured	
Merchandise inventory	32,150	by mortgage on plant assets	63,400
Prepaid expenses	2,650	Common stock	90,000
Plant assets, net	153,300	Retained earnings	62,800
Total assets	$240,200	Total liabilities and equity	$240,200

* These are short-term notes receivable arising from customer (trade) sales.

Required

Check Acid-test ratio, 2.2 to 1;
Inventory turnover, 7.3

Compute the following: (1) current ratio, (2) acid-test ratio, (3) days' sales uncollected, (4) inventory turnover, (5) days' sales in inventory, (6) debt-to-equity ratio, (7) times interest earned, (8) profit margin ratio, (9) total asset turnover, (10) return on total assets, and (11) return on common stockholders' equity.

Problem 17-5A

Comparative ratio
analysis   A1   P3

Summary information from the financial statements of two companies competing in the same industry follows.

	Barco Company	Kyan Company		Barco Company	Kyan Company
Data from the current year-end balance sheets			**Data from the current year's income statement**		
Assets			Sales	$770,000	$880,200
Cash	$ 19,500	$ 34,000	Cost of goods sold	585,100	632,500
Accounts receivable, net	37,400	57,400	Interest expense	7,900	13,000
Current notes receivable (trade)	9,100	7,200	Income tax expense	14,800	24,300
Merchandise inventory	84,440	132,500	Net income	$162,200	$210,400
Prepaid expenses	5,000	6,950	Basic earnings per share	$ 4.51	$ 5.11
Plant assets, net	290,000	304,400			
Total assets	$445,440	$542,450			
			Beginning-of-year balance sheet data		
Liabilities and Equity			Accounts receivable, net	$ 29,800	$ 54,200
Current liabilities	$ 61,340	$ 93,300	Current notes receivable (trade)	0	0
Long-term notes payable	80,800	101,000	Merchandise inventory	55,600	107,400
Common stock, $5 par value	180,000	206,000	Total assets	398,000	382,500
Retained earnings	123,300	142,150	Common stock, $5 par value	180,000	206,000
Total liabilities and equity	$445,440	$542,450	Retained earnings	98,300	93,600

Required

1. For both companies compute the (*a*) current ratio, (*b*) acid-test ratio, (*c*) accounts (including notes) receivable turnover, (*d*) inventory turnover, (*e*) days' sales in inventory, and (*f*) days' sales uncollected. Identify the company you consider to be the better short-term credit risk and explain why.

2. For both companies compute the (*a*) profit margin ratio, (*b*) total asset turnover, (*c*) return on total assets, and (*d*) return on common stockholders' equity. Assuming that each company paid cash dividends of $3.80 per share and each company's stock can be purchased at $75 per share, compute their (*e*) price-earnings ratios and (*f*) dividend yields. Identify which company's stock you would recommend as the better investment and explain why.

Check (1) Kyan: Accounts receivable turnover, 14.8; Inventory turnover, 5.3

(2) Barco: Profit margin, 21.1%; PE, 16.6

Selected account balances from the adjusted trial balance for Olinda Corporation as of its calendar year-end December 31, 2005, follow.

Problem 17-6A[A]

Income statement computations and format

A2

	Debit	Credit
a. Interest revenue		$ 14,000
b. Depreciation expense—Equipment	$ 34,000	
c. Loss on sale of equipment	25,850	
d. Accounts payable		44,000
e. Other operating expenses	106,400	
f. Accumulated depreciation—Equipment		71,600
g. Gain from settlement of lawsuit		44,000
h. Accumulated depreciation—Buildings		174,500
i. Loss from operating a discontinued segment (pretax)	18,250	
j. Gain on insurance recovery of tornado damage (pretax and extraordinary)		29,120
k. Net sales		998,500
l. Depreciation expense—Buildings	52,000	
m. Correction of overstatement of prior year's sales (pretax)	16,000	
n. Gain on sale of discontinued segment's assets (pretax)		34,000
o. Loss from settlement of lawsuit	23,750	
p. Income taxes expense		
q. Cost of goods sold	482,500	

Required

Answer each of the following questions by providing supporting computations.

1. Assume that the company's income tax rate is 30% for all items. Identify the tax effects and after-tax amounts of the four items labeled pretax.

2. What is the amount of income from continuing operations before income taxes? What is the amount of the income taxes expense? What is the amount of income from continuing operations?

Check   (3) $11,025

(4) $221,375

(5) $241,759

3. What is the total amount of after-tax income (loss) associated with the discontinued segment?

4. What is the amount of income (loss) before the extraordinary items?

5. What is the amount of net income for the year?

PROBLEM SET B

Selected comparative financial statement information of Bluegrass Corporation follows.

Problem 17-1B

Ratios, common-size statements, and trend percents

P1 P2 P3

BLUEGRASS CORPORATION Comparative Income Statements For Years Ended December 31, 2009, 2008, and 2007			
	2009	2008	2007
Sales	$198,800	$166,000	$143,800
Cost of goods sold	108,890	86,175	66,200
Gross profit	89,910	79,825	77,600
Selling expenses	22,680	19,790	18,000
Administrative expenses	16,760	14,610	15,700
Total expenses	39,440	34,400	33,700
Income before taxes	50,470	45,425	43,900
Income taxes	6,050	5,910	5,300
Net income	$ 44,420	$ 39,515	$ 38,600

BLUEGRASS CORPORATION Comparative Balance Sheets December 31, 2009, 2008, and 2007			
	2009	2008	2007
Assets			
Current assets	$ 54,860	$ 32,660	$ 36,300
Long-term investments	0	1,700	10,600
Plant assets, net	112,810	113,660	79,000
Total assets	$167,670	$148,020	$125,900
Liabilities and Equity			
Current liabilities	$ 22,370	$ 19,180	$ 16,500
Common stock	46,500	46,500	37,000
Other paid-in capital	13,850	13,850	11,300
Retained earnings	84,950	68,490	61,100
Total liabilities and equity	$167,670	$148,020	$125,900

Required

1. Compute each year's current ratio.

2. Express the income statement data in common-size percents.

3. Express the balance sheet data in trend percents with 2007 as the base year.

Check   (3) 2009, Total assets trend, 133.18%

Analysis Component

4. Comment on any significant relations revealed by the ratios and percents computed.

Selected comparative financial statements of Tripoly Company follow.

TRIPOLY COMPANY Comparative Income Statements ($000) For Years Ended December 31, 2009–2003							
	2009	2008	2007	2006	2005	2004	2003
Sales	$560	$610	$630	$680	$740	$770	$860
Cost of goods sold	276	290	294	314	340	350	380
Gross profit	284	320	336	366	400	420	480
Operating expenses	84	104	112	126	140	144	150
Net income	$200	$216	$224	$240	$260	$276	$330

TRIPOLY COMPANY Comparative Balance Sheets ($000) December 31, 2009–2003							
	2009	2008	2007	2006	2005	2004	2003
Assets							
Cash	$ 44	$ 46	$ 52	$ 54	$ 60	$ 62	$ 68
Accounts receivable, net	130	136	140	144	150	154	160
Merchandise inventory	166	172	178	180	186	190	208
Other current assets	34	34	36	38	38	40	40
Long-term investments	36	30	26	110	110	110	110
Plant assets, net	510	514	520	412	420	428	454
Total assets	$920	$932	$952	$938	$964	$984	$1,040
Liabilities and Equity							
Current liabilities	$148	$156	$186	$190	$210	$260	$ 280
Long-term liabilities	92	120	142	148	194	214	260
Common stock	160	160	160	160	160	160	160
Other paid-in capital	70	70	70	70	70	70	70
Retained earnings	450	426	394	370	330	280	270
Total liabilities and equity	$920	$932	$952	$938	$964	$984	$1,040

Problem 17-2B
Calculation and analysis of trend percents

A1   P1

Required

1. Compute trend percents for all components of both statements using 2003 as the base year.

Analysis Component

2. Analyze and comment on the financial statements and trend percents from part 1.

Check (1) 2009, Total assets trend, 88.5%

Koto Corporation began the month of June with $300,000 of current assets, a current ratio of 2.5:1, and an acid-test ratio of 1.4:1. During the month, it completed the following transactions (the company uses a perpetual inventory system).

June 1 Sold merchandise inventory that cost $75,000 for $120,000 cash.
        3 Collected $88,000 cash on an account receivable.
        5 Purchased $150,000 of merchandise inventory on credit.
        7 Borrowed $100,000 cash by giving the bank a 60-day, 10% note.
       10 Borrowed $120,000 cash by signing a long-term secured note.
       12 Purchased machinery for $275,000 cash.
       15 Declared a $1 per share cash dividend on the 80,000 shares of outstanding common stock.
       19 Wrote off a $5,000 bad debt against the Allowance for Doubtful Accounts account.
       22 Paid $12,000 cash to settle an account payable.
       30 Paid the dividend declared on June 15.

Problem 17-3B
Transactions, working capital, and liquidity ratios

P3

Check June 1: Current ratio, 2.88; Acid-test, 2.40

June 30: Working capital, $(10,000); Current ratio, 0.97

Required

Prepare a table showing the company's (1) current ratio, (2) acid-test ratio, and (3) working capital after each transaction. Round ratios to hundredths.

Problem 17-4B
Calculation of financial
statement ratios

P3

Selected year-end financial statements of Overton Corporation follow. (All sales were on credit; selected balance sheet amounts at December 31, 2007, were inventory, $17,400; total assets, $94,900; common stock, $35,500; and retained earnings, $18,800.)

OVERTON CORPORATION
Income Statement
For Year Ended December 31, 2008

Sales	$315,500
Cost of goods sold	236,100
Gross profit	79,400
Operating expenses	49,200
Interest expense	2,200
Income before taxes	28,000
Income taxes	4,200
Net income	$ 23,800

OVERTON CORPORATION
Balance Sheet
December 31, 2008

Assets		Liabilities and Equity	
Cash	$ 6,100	Accounts payable	$ 11,500
Short-term investments	6,900	Accrued wages payable	3,300
Accounts receivable, net	12,100	Income taxes payable	2,600
Notes receivable (trade)*	3,000	Long-term note payable, secured	
Merchandise inventory	13,500	by mortgage on plant assets	30,000
Prepaid expenses	2,000	Common stock, $5 par value	35,000
Plant assets, net	73,900	Retained earnings	35,100
Total assets	$117,500	Total liabilities and equity	$117,500

* These are short-term notes receivable arising from customer (trade) sales.

Required

Check   Acid-test ratio, 1.6 to 1;
Inventory turnover, 15.3

Compute the following: (1) current ratio, (2) acid-test ratio, (3) days' sales uncollected, (4) inventory turnover, (5) days' sales in inventory, (6) debt-to-equity ratio, (7) times interest earned, (8) profit margin ratio, (9) total asset turnover, (10) return on total assets, and (11) return on common stockholders' equity.

Problem 17-5B
Comparative
ratio analysis   A1   P3

Summary information from the financial statements of two companies competing in the same industry follows.

	Fargo Company	Ball Company		Fargo Company	Ball Company
Data from the current year-end balance sheets			**Data from the current year's income statement**		
Assets			Sales	$393,600	$667,500
Cash	$ 20,000	$ 36,500	Cost of goods sold	290,600	480,000
Accounts receivable, net	77,100	70,500	Interest expense	5,900	12,300
Current notes receivable (trade)	11,600	9,000	Income tax expense	5,700	12,300
Merchandise inventory	86,800	82,000	Net income	33,850	61,700
Prepaid expenses	9,700	10,100	Basic earnings per share	1.27	2.19
Plant assets, net	176,900	252,300			
Total assets	$382,100	$460,400			
			Beginning-of-year balance sheet data		
Liabilities and Equity			Accounts receivable, net	$ 72,200	$ 73,300
Current liabilities	$ 90,500	$ 97,000	Current notes receivable (trade)	0	0
Long-term notes payable	93,000	93,300	Merchandise inventory	105,100	80,500
Common stock, $5 par value	133,000	141,000	Total assets	383,400	443,000
Retained earnings	65,600	129,100	Common stock, $5 par value	133,000	141,000
Total liabilities and equity	$382,100	$460,400	Retained earnings	49,100	109,700

Required

1. For both companies compute the (*a*) current ratio, (*b*) acid-test ratio, (*c*) accounts (including notes) receivable turnover, (*d*) inventory turnover, (*e*) days' sales in inventory, and (*f*) days' sales uncollected. Identify the company you consider to be the better short-term credit risk and explain why.

2. For both companies compute the (*a*) profit margin ratio, (*b*) total asset turnover, (*c*) return on total assets, and (*d*) return on common stockholders' equity. Assuming that each company paid cash dividends of $1.50 per share and each company's stock can be purchased at $25 per share, compute their (*e*) price-earnings ratios and (*f*) dividend yields. Identify which company's stock you would recommend as the better investment and explain why.

Check (1) Fargo: Accounts receivable turnover, 4.9; Inventory turnover, 3.0

(2) Ball: Profit margin, 9.2%; PE, 11.4

Selected account balances from the adjusted trial balance for Harbor Corp. as of its calendar year-end December 31, 2008, follow.

Problem 17-6B[A]

Income statement computations and format

A2

	Debit	Credit
a. Accumulated depreciation—Buildings		$ 400,000
b. Interest revenue		20,000
c. Net sales.....		2,640,000
d. Income taxes expense	$?	
e. Loss on hurricane damage (pretax and extraordinary)	64,000	
f. Accumulated depreciation—Equipment		220,000
g. Other operating expenses	328,000	
h. Depreciation expense—Equipment	100,000	
i. Loss from settlement of lawsuit	36,000	
j. Gain from settlement of lawsuit		68,000
k. Loss on sale of equipment	24,000	
l. Loss from operating a discontinued segment (pretax)	120,000	
m. Depreciation expense—Buildings	156,000	
n. Correction of overstatement of prior year's expense (pretax)		48,000
o. Cost of goods sold	1,040,000	
p. Loss on sale of discontinued segment's assets (pretax)	180,000	
q. Accounts payable		132,000

Required

Answer each of the following questions by providing supporting computations.

1. Assume that the company's income tax rate is 25% for all items. Identify the tax effects and after-tax amounts of the four items labeled pretax.

2. What is the amount of income from continuing operations before income taxes? What is the amount of income taxes expense? What is the amount of income from continuing operations?

3. What is the total amount of after-tax income (loss) associated with the discontinued segment?

4. What is the amount of income (loss) before the extraordinary items?

5. What is the amount of net income for the year?

Check (3) $(225,000)

(4) $558,000

(5) $510,000

 Problem Set C is available at the book's Website to reinforce and assess your learning.

PROBLEM SET C

(This serial problem began in Chapter 1 and continues through most of the book. If previous chapter segments were not completed, the serial problem can begin at this point. It is helpful, but not necessary, for you to use the Working Papers that accompany the book.)

SERIAL PROBLEM

Success Systems

SP 17   Use the following selected data from Success Systems' income statement for the three months ended March 31, 2008, and from its March 31, 2008, balance sheet to complete the requirements below: computer services revenue, $31,850; net (goods) sales, $20,345; total sales and revenue, $52,195; cost of goods sold, $14,272; net income, $24,336; quick assets, $111,666; current assets, $116,371; total assets, $147,621; current liabilities, $1,050; total liabilities, $1,050; and total equity, $146,571.

Required

1. Compute the gross margin ratio (both with and without services revenue) and net profit margin ratio.
2. Compute the current ratio and acid-test ratio.
3. Compute the debt ratio and equity ratio.
4. What percent of its assets are current? What percent are long term?

BEYOND THE NUMBERS

REPORTING IN ACTION

A1   P1   P2

BTN 17-1   Refer to Best Buy's financial statements in Appendix A to answer the following.

1. Using 2003 as the base year, compute trend percents for fiscal years 2003, 2004, and 2005 for revenues, cost of sales, selling general and administrative expenses, income taxes, and net income. (Round to the nearest whole percent.)
2. Compute common-size percents for fiscal years 2005 and 2004 for the following categories of assets: (*a*) total current assets, (*b*) property and equipment, net, and (*c*) intangible assets. (Round to the nearest tenth of a percent.)
3. Comment on any significant changes across the years for the income statement trends computed in part 1 and the balance sheet percents computed in part 2.

Fast Forward

4. Access Best Buy's financial statements for fiscal years ending after February 26, 2005, from Best Buy's Website (BestBuy.com) or the SEC database (www.SEC.gov). Update your work for parts 1, 2, and 3 using the new information accessed.

COMPARATIVE ANALYSIS

C3   P2

BTN 17-2   Key comparative figures ($ millions) for both Best Buy and Circuit City follow.

Key Figures	Best Buy	Circuit City
Cash and equivalents	$ 470	$ 880
Accounts receivable, net	375	173
Inventories	2,851	1,460
Retained earnings	3,315	1,247
Costs of sales	20,938	7,904
Revenues	27,433	10,472
Total assets	10,294	3,789

Required

1. Compute common-size percents for both companies using the data provided.
2. Which company retains a higher portion of cumulative net income in the company?
3. Which company has a higher gross margin ratio on sales?
4. Which company holds a higher percent of its total assets as inventory?

ETHICS CHALLENGE

A1

BTN 17-3   As Beacon Company controller, you are responsible for informing the board of directors about its financial activities. At the board meeting, you present the following information.

	2009	2008	2007
Sales trend percent	147.0%	135.0%	100.0%
Selling expenses to sales	10.1%	14.0%	15.6%
Sales to plant assets ratio	3.8 to 1	3.6 to 1	3.3 to 1
Current ratio	2.9 to 1	2.7 to 1	2.4 to 1
Acid-test ratio	1.1 to 1	1.4 to 1	1.5 to 1
Inventory turnover	7.8 times	9.0 times	10.2 times
Accounts receivable turnover	7.0 times	7.7 times	8.5 times
Total asset turnover	2.9 times	2.9 times	3.3 times
Return on total assets	10.4%	11.0%	13.2%
Return on stockholders' equity	10.7%	11.5%	14.1%
Profit margin ratio	3.6%	3.8%	4.0%

After the meeting, the company's CEO holds a press conference with analysts in which she mentions the following ratios.

	2009	2008	2007
Sales trend percent	147.0%	135.0%	100.0%
Selling expenses to sales	10.1%	14.0%	15.6%
Sales to plant assets ratio	3.8 to 1	3.6 to 1	3.3 to 1
Current ratio	2.9 to 1	2.7 to 1	2.4 to 1

Required

1. Why do you think the CEO decided to report 4 ratios instead of the 11 prepared?

2. Comment on the possible consequences of the CEO's reporting of the ratios selected.

BTN 17-4 Each team is to select a different industry, and each team member is to select a different company in that industry and acquire its financial statements. Use those statements to analyze the company, including at least one ratio from each of the four building blocks of analysis. When necessary, use the financial press to determine the market price of its stock. Communicate with teammates via a meeting, e-mail, or telephone to discuss how different companies compare to each other and to industry norms. The team is to prepare a single one-page memorandum reporting on its analysis and the conclusions reached.

COMMUNICATING IN PRACTICE

C2 A1 P3

BTN 17-5 Access the March 7, 2005, filing of the 2004 10-K report of the Hershey Foods Corporation (ticker HSY) at www.sec.gov and complete the following requirements.

TAKING IT TO THE NET

C4 P3

Required

Compute or identify the following profitability ratios of Hershey for its years ending December 31, 2004, *and* December 31, 2003. Interpret its profitability using the following ratio results.

1. Profit margin ratio

2. Gross profit ratio

3. Return on total assets (*Note:* Total assets in 2002 were $3,480,551,000.)

4. Return on common stockholders' equity (*Note:* Total shareholders' equity in 2002 was $1,371,703,000.)

5. Basic earnings per share

BTN 17-6 A team approach to learning financial statement analysis is often useful.

TEAMWORK IN ACTION

C2 P1 P2 P3

Required

1. Each team should write a description of horizontal and vertical analysis that all team members agree with and understand. Illustrate each description with an example.

2. *Each* member of the team is to select *one* of the following categories of ratio analysis. Explain what the ratios in that category measure. Choose one ratio from the category selected, present its formula, and explain what it measures.

    a. Liquidity and efficiency   **c.** Profitability

    b. Solvency   **d.** Market prospects

3. Each team member is to present his or her notes from part 2 to teammates. Team members are to confirm or correct other teammates' presentation.

Hint: Pairing within teams may be necessary for part 2. Use as an in-class activity or as an assignment. Consider presentations to the entire class using team rotation with transparencies.

BTN 17-7 Read the article "Hollinger's Troubles, in Black and White," by Louis Lavelle in the September 2, 2004, issue of *BusinessWeek*. (The book's Website provides a free link.)

BusinessWeek **ACTIVITY**

C1 C4

Required

What are the suggestions that Lavelle has for stockholders to identify a potentially troubled company?

ENTREPRENEURIAL DECISION

A1 P1 P2 P3

BTN 17-8   Assume that David and Tom Gardner of The Motley Fool (Fool.com) have impressed you since you first heard of their rather improbable rise to prominence in financial circles. You learn of a staff opening at The Motley Fool and decide to apply for it. Your resume is successfully screened from the thousands received and you advance to the interview process. You learn that the interview consists of analyzing the following financial facts and answering analysis questions. (*Note:* The data are taken from a small merchandiser in outdoor recreational equipment.)

	2008	2007	2006
Sales trend percents	137.0%	125.0%	100.0%
Selling expenses to sales	9.8%	13.7%	15.3%
Sales to plant assets ratio	3.5 to 1	3.3 to 1	3.0 to 1
Current ratio	2.6 to 1	2.4 to 1	2.1 to 1
Acid-test ratio	0.8 to 1	1.1 to 1	1.2 to 1
Merchandise inventory turnover	7.5 times	8.7 times	9.9 times
Accounts receivable turnover	6.7 times	7.4 times	8.2 times
Total asset turnover	2.6 times	2.6 times	3.0 times
Return on total assets	8.8%	9.4%	11.1%
Return on equity	9.75%	11.50%	12.25%
Profit margin ratio	3.3%	3.5%	3.7%

Required

Use these data to answer each of the following questions with explanations.

1. Is it becoming easier for the company to meet its current liabilities on time and to take advantage of any available cash discounts? Explain.
2. Is the company collecting its accounts receivable more rapidly? Explain.
3. Is the company's investment in accounts receivable decreasing? Explain.
4. Is the company's investment in plant assets increasing? Explain.
5. Is the owner's investment becoming more profitable? Explain.
6. Did the dollar amount of selling expenses decrease during the three-year period? Explain.

HITTING THE ROAD

C1 P3

BTN 17-9   You are to devise an investment strategy to enable you to accumulate $1,000,000 by age 65. Start by making some assumptions about your salary. Next compute the percent of your salary that you will be able to save each year. If you will receive any lump-sum monies, include those amounts in your calculations. Historically, stocks have delivered average annual returns of 10–11%. Given this history, you should probably not assume that you will earn above 10% on the money you invest. It is not necessary to specify exactly what types of assets you will buy for your investments; just assume a rate you expect to earn. Use the future value tables in Appendix B to calculate how your savings will grow. Experiment a bit with your figures to see how much less you have to save if you start at, for example, age 25 versus age 35 or 40. (For this assignment, do not include inflation in your calculations.)

GLOBAL DECISION

A1

BTN 17-10   Dixons, Best Buy, and Circuit City are competitors in the global marketplace. Visit the Dixons' Website (Dixons-Group.com) and access its most recent annual report.

Required

Review Dixons' Website and skim through its annual report. Compare its annual report to one of its U.S. competitor's reports (Best Buy or Circuit City) presented in Appendix A. Identify five ways that the U.K. company's report or its Website differs from that of its U.S. competitors.

ANSWERS TO MULTIPLE CHOICE QUIZ

1. d; ($351,000/$300,000) × 100 = 117%

2. e; ($86,000 + $76,000 + $122,000 + $12,000)/$124,000 = 2.39

3. c; ($86,000 + $76,000)/$124,000 = 1.31

4. a; ($124,000 + $90,000)/$830,000 = 25.78%

5. d; ($300,000 + $316,000)/$830,000 = 74.22%

18

Managerial Accounting Concepts and Principles

A Look Back

Chapter 17 described the analysis and interpretation of financial statement information. We applied horizontal, vertical, and ratio analyses to better understand company performance and financial condition.

A Look at This Chapter

We begin our study of managerial accounting by explaining its purpose and describing its major characteristics. We also discuss cost concepts and describe how they help managers gather and organize information for making decisions. The reporting of manufacturing activities is also discussed.

A Look Ahead

The remaining chapters discuss the types of decisions managers must make and how managerial accounting helps with those decisions. The first of these chapters, Chapter 19, considers how we measure costs assigned to certain types of projects.

Learning Objectives

CAP

Conceptual

C1 Explain the purpose and nature of managerial accounting. *(p. 720)*

C2 Describe the lean business model. *(p. 723)*

C3 Describe accounting concepts useful in classifying costs. *(p. 725)*

C4 Define product and period costs and explain how they impact financial statements. *(p. 726)*

C5 Explain how balance sheets and income statements for manufacturing and merchandising companies differ. *(p. 728)*

C6 Explain manufacturing activities and the flow of manufacturing costs. *(p. 732)*

Analytical

A1 Compute cycle time and cycle efficiency, and explain their importance to production management *(p. 735)*

Procedural

P1 Compute cost of goods sold for a manufacturer. *(p. 730)*

P2 Prepare a manufacturing statement and explain its purpose and links to financial statements. *(p. 733)*

> *"I've transitioned from being a fan of the guitar, to a guitar builder, to being a guitar CEO"*
> —Chris Griffiths

Good Vibrations

ST. JOHN'S, NEWFOUNDLAND—"I've always had a mechanical curiosity," admits Chris Griffiths. "I was always one of those kids who took apart the alarm clock and spread out all the pieces. I was always really curious as to what made things work." In his curiosity Chris found his passion: guitars and what makes them tick. "If I was home and unemployed, I'd just be playing guitar anyway!"

Says Chris of his early start building guitars, "I've got my little chisel, and I've got my little stack of sandpaper, and I'm going to do it. I thought, well, that's great, man." But Chris had bigger dreams. "I wanted to do something really, really different, and really innovative. I was looking for a competitive advantage." Chris' innovation was a one-piece injection-molded structure he called *Griffiths Active Bracing System*™ that would be encased in the guitar body. "I didn't know what I was doing," admits Chris. "I was making it up as I was going along."

What Chris did was revolutionize the way to make guitars, and make them better. "Because all the braces are made out of one piece they vibrate as a single unit," explains Chris. "All of a sudden, it comes alive acoustically." His startup, **Garrison Guitars**

(GarrisonGuitars.com), manufactures guitars using Chris's bracing system. "Whether you bake pies or you build guitars or you cut hair," explains Chris, "[you build] a business infrastructure around that. It

was the best thing that ever happened to me." It is also the best thing for Chris' customers. "It's all about adding value for the consumer. We offer exceptional value by building quality instruments and by providing outstanding service and support," says Chris.

Chris believes basic managerial principles, product and period costs, and manufacturing statements are like another language to most people. But he also realizes entrepreneurial success often depends on embracing, understanding, and applying these concepts. Knowing your manufacturing activities and cost flows is not easy, notes Chris, but the cost of not understanding those concepts is far greater. "In a typical guitar factory it would take you about two and a half hours to make [the bracing] components," says Chris. "We make this component in 45 seconds. I'm no accountant, but apparently that's pretty good!"

Chris believes entrepreneurs fill a void by creating a niche, and then monitoring and controlling production while meeting customer needs. But Chris strikes a cautionary note for any would-be entrepreneur in his line of work. Without applying managerial accounting principles and lean manufacturing, says Chris, "It's just a building, a bunch of machines, and a pile of wood." Now there's advice that sounds really great, man.

[Sources: *Garrison Guitars Website*, May 2006; *Entrepreneur*, December 2005; *Innovation Strategy Website*, March 2003; *Association for Manufacturing Excellence Website*, March 2006; *Composites News Supersite*, January 2005]

Managerial accounting, like financial accounting, provides information to help users make better decisions. However, managerial accounting and financial accounting differ in important ways, which this chapter explains. This chapter also compares the accounting and reporting practices used by manufacturing and merchandising companies. A merchandising company sells products without changing their condition. A manufacturing company buys raw materials and turns them into finished products for sale to customers. A third type of company earns revenues by providing services rather than products. The skills, tools, and techniques developed for measuring a manufacturing company's activities apply to service companies as well. The chapter concludes by explaining the flow of manufacturing activities and preparing the manufacturing statement.

Managerial Accounting Concepts and Principles

Managerial Accounting Basics	Managerial Cost Concepts	Reporting Manufacturing Activities
• Purpose of managerial accounting • Nature of managerial accounting • Managerial decisions • Managerial accounting in business	• Types of cost classifications • Identification of cost classifications • Cost concepts for service companies	• Balance sheet • Income statement • Flow of activities • Manufacturing statement

Managerial Accounting Basics

Managerial accounting is an activity that provides financial and nonfinancial information to an organization's managers and other internal decision makers. This section explains the purpose of managerial accounting (also called *management accounting*) and compares it with financial accounting. The main purpose of the financial accounting system is to prepare general-purpose financial statements. That information is incomplete for internal decision makers who manage organizations.

Purpose of Managerial Accounting

C1 Explain the purpose and nature of managerial accounting.

The purpose of both managerial accounting and financial accounting is providing useful information to decision makers. They do this by collecting, managing, and reporting information in demand by their users. Both areas of accounting also share the common practice of reporting monetary information, although managerial accounting includes the reporting of nonmonetary information. They even report some of the same information. For instance, a company's financial statements contain information useful for both its managers (insiders) and other persons interested in the company (outsiders).

The remainder of this book looks carefully at managerial accounting information, how to gather it, and how managers use it. We consider the concepts and procedures used to determine the costs of products and services as well as topics such as budgeting, break-even analysis, product costing, profit planning, and cost analysis. Information about the costs of products and services is important for many decisions that managers make. These decisions include predicting the future costs of a product or service. Predicted costs are used in product pricing, profitability analysis, and in deciding whether to make or buy a product or component. More generally, much of managerial accounting involves gathering information about costs for planning and control decisions.

Planning is the process of setting goals and making plans to achieve them. Companies formulate long-term strategic plans that usually span a 5- to 10-year horizon and then refine them with medium-term and short-term plans. Strategic plans usually set a firm's long-term direction by developing a road map based on opportunities such as new products, new markets, and capital investments. A strategic plan's goals and objectives are broadly defined given its long-term orientation. Medium- and short-term plans are more operational in nature. They translate the strategic plan into actions. These plans are more concrete and consist of better defined objectives and goals. A short-term plan often covers a one-year period that, when translated in monetary terms, is known as a budget.

Point: Costs are important to managers because they impact both the financial position and profitability of a business. Managerial accounting assists in analysis, planning, and control of costs.

Control is the process of monitoring planning decisions and evaluating an organization's activities and employees. It includes the measurement and evaluation of actions, processes, and outcomes. Feedback provided by the control function allows managers to revise their plans. Measurement of actions and processes also allows managers to take corrective actions to avoid undesirable outcomes. For example, managers periodically compare actual results with planned results. Exhibit 18.1 portrays the important management functions of planning and control.

Exhibit 18.1
Planning and Control

Monitoring

Feedback

Planning
• Strategic aims
• Long- & short-term
• Annual budgets

Control
• Measurement
• Evaluation
• Oversight

Managers use information to plan and control business activities. In later chapters, we explain how managers also use this information to direct and improve business operations.

Nature of Managerial Accounting

Managerial accounting has its own special characteristics. To understand these characteristics, we compare managerial accounting to financial accounting; they differ in at least seven important ways. These differences are summarized in Exhibit 18.2. This section discusses each of these characteristics.

Exhibit 18.2
Key Differences between Managerial Accounting and Financial Accounting

"This company's outlook is good. I'll buy its shares."

"This department is doing well. We'll expand its product line."

	Financial Accounting	**Managerial Accounting**
1. Users and decision makers	Investors, creditors, and other users external to the organization	Managers, employees, and decision makers internal to the organization
2. Purpose of information	Assist external users in making investment, credit, and other decisions	Assist managers in making planning and control decisions
3. Flexibility of practice	Structured and often controlled by GAAP	Relatively flexible (no GAAP constraints)
4. Timeliness of information	Often available only after an audit is complete	Available quickly without the need to wait for an audit
5. Time dimension	Focus on historical information with some predictions	Many projections and estimates; historical information also presented
6. Focus of information	Emphasis on whole organization	Emphasis on an organization's projects, processes, and subdivisions
7. Nature of information	Monetary information	Mostly monetary; but also nonmonetary information

Point: It is desirable to accumulate information for management reports in a database separate from financial accounting records.

Users and Decision Makers   Companies accumulate, process, and report financial accounting and managerial accounting information for different groups of decision makers. Financial accounting information is primarily provided to external users including investors, creditors, analysts, and regulators. External users rarely have a major role in managing a company's daily activities. Managerial accounting information is primarily provided to internal users who are responsible for making and implementing decisions about a company's business activities.

Purpose of Information   Investors, creditors, and other external users of financial accounting information must often decide whether to invest in or lend to a company. If they have already done so, they must decide whether to continue owning the company or carrying the loan. Internal decision makers must plan a company's future. They seek to take advantage of opportunities or to overcome obstacles. They also try to control activities and ensure their effective and efficient implementation. Managerial accounting information helps these internal users make both planning and control decisions.

Point: The *Institute of Management Accountants* issues statements that govern the practice of managerial accounting. Accountants who pass a qualifying exam are awarded the CMA.

Flexibility of Practice   External users compare companies by using financial reports and need protection against false or misleading information. Accordingly, financial accounting relies on accepted principles that are enforced through an extensive set of rules and guidelines, or GAAP. Internal users need managerial accounting information for planning and controlling their company's activities rather than for external comparisons. They require different types of information depending on the activity. This makes standardizing managerial accounting systems across companies difficult. Instead, managerial accounting systems are flexible. The design of a company's managerial accounting system largely depends on the nature of the business and the arrangement of its internal operations. Managers can decide for themselves what information they want and how they want it reported. Even within a single company, different managers often design their own systems to meet their special needs. The important question a manager must ask is whether the information being collected and reported is useful for planning, decision making, and control purposes.

Point: Financial statements are usually issued several weeks after the period-end. GAAP requires the reporting of important events that occur while the statements are being prepared. These events are called *subsequent events*.

Point: Independent auditors test the integrity of managerial accounting records when they are used in preparing financial statements.

Timeliness of Information   Formal financial statements reporting past transactions and events are not immediately available to outside parties. Independent certified public accountants often must *audit* a company's financial statements before it provides them to external users. Thus, because audits often take several weeks to complete, financial reports to outsiders usually are not available until well after the period-end. However, managers can quickly obtain managerial accounting information. External auditors need not review it. Estimates and projections are acceptable. To get information quickly, managers often accept less precision in reports. As an example, an early internal report to management prepared right after the year-end could report net income for the year between $4.2 and $4.8 million. An audited income statement could later show net income for the year at $4.6 million. The internal report is not precise, but its information can be more useful because it is available earlier.

Internal auditing plays an important role in managerial accounting. Internal auditors evaluate the flow of information not only inside but also outside the company. Managers are responsible for preventing and detecting fraudulent activities in their companies.

Time Dimension   To protect external users from false expectations, financial reports deal primarily with results of both past activities and current conditions. While some predictions such as service lives and salvage values of plant assets are necessary, financial accounting avoids predictions whenever possible. Managerial accounting regularly includes predictions of conditions and events. As an example, one important managerial

---

Production Manager   You invite three friends to a restaurant. When the dinner check arrives, David, a self-employed entrepreneur, picks it up saying, "Here, let me pay. I'll deduct it as a business expense on my tax return." Denise, a salesperson, takes the check from David's hand and says, "I'll put this on my company's credit card. It won't cost us anything." Derek, a factory manager for a company, laughs and says, "Neither of you understands. I'll put this on my company's credit card and call it overhead on a cost-plus contract my company has with a client." (*A cost-plus contract means the company receives its costs plus a percent of those costs.*) Adds Derek, "That way, my company pays for dinner *and* makes a profit." Who should pay the bill? Why?

accounting report is a budget, which predicts revenues, expenses, and other items. If managerial accounting reports were restricted to the past and present, managers would be less able to plan activities and less effective in managing and evaluating current activities.

Focus of Information   Companies often organize into divisions and departments, but investors rarely can buy shares in one division or department. Nor do creditors lend money to a company's single division or department. Instead, they own shares in or make loans to the entire company. Financial accounting focuses primarily on a company as a whole as depicted in Exhibit 18.3. The focus of managerial accounting is different. While top-level managers are responsible for managing the whole company, most other managers are responsible for much smaller sets of activities. These middle-level and lower-level managers need managerial accounting reports dealing with specific activities, projects, and subdivisions for which they are responsible. For instance, division sales managers are directly responsible only for the results achieved in their divisions. Accordingly, division sales managers need information about results achieved in their own divisions to improve their performance. This information includes the level of success achieved by each individual or department in each division as depicted in Exhibit 18.4.

Nature of Information   Both financial and managerial accounting systems report monetary information. Managerial accounting systems also report considerable nonmonetary information. Monetary information is an important part of managerial decisions, and nonmonetary information plays a crucial role, especially when monetary effects are difficult to measure. Common examples of nonmonetary information are the quality and delivery criteria of purchasing decisions.

Exhibit 18.3

Focus of External Reports

Exhibit 18.4

Focus of Internal Reports

Managerial Decision Making

The previous section emphasized differences between financial and managerial accounting, but they are not entirely separate. Similar information is useful to both external and internal users. For instance, information about costs of manufacturing products is useful to all users in making decisions. Also, both financial and managerial accounting affect peoples' actions. For example, Trek's design of a sales compensation plan affects the behavior of its salesforce. It also must estimate the dual effects of promotion and sales compensation plans on buying patterns of customers. These estimates impact the equipment purchase decisions for manufacturing and can affect the supplier selection criteria established by purchasing. Thus, financial and managerial accounting systems do more than measure; they also affect people's decisions and actions.

Managerial Accounting in Business

We have explained the importance of managerial accounting for internal decision making. Although the analytical tools and techniques of managerial accounting have always been useful, their relevance and importance continue to increase. This is so because of changes in the business environment. This section describes some of these changes and their impact on managerial accounting.

C2   Describe the lean business model.

Lean Business Model   Two important factors have encouraged companies to be more effective and efficient in running their operations. First, there is an increased emphasis on *customers* as the most important constituent of a business. Customers expect to derive a certain value for the money they spend to buy products and services. Specifically, they expect that their suppliers will offer them the right service (or product) at the right time and the right price. This implies that companies accept the notion of **customer orientation,** which means that employees understand the changing needs and wants of their customers and align their management and operating practices accordingly.

Second, our *global economy* expands competitive boundaries, thereby providing customers more choices. The global economy also produces changes in business activities. One notable case that reflects these changes in customer demand and global competition is auto manufacturing. The top three Japanese auto manufacturers (**Honda**, **Nissan**, and **Toyota**) once controlled more than 40% of the U.S. auto market. Customers perceived that Japanese auto manufacturers provided value not available from other manufacturers. Many European and North American auto manufacturers responded to this challenge and regained much of the lost market share.

Companies must be alert to these and other factors. Many companies have responded by adopting the **lean business model,** whose goal is to *eliminate waste* while "satisfying the customer" and "providing a positive return" to the company.

Lean Practices   **Continuous improvement** rejects the notions of "good enough" or "acceptable" and challenges employees and managers to continuously experiment with new and improved business practices. This has led companies to adopt practices such as total quality management (TQM) and just-in-time (JIT) manufacturing. The philosophy underlying both practices is continuous improvement; the difference is in the focus.

Point: Goals of a TQM process include reduced waste, better inventory control, fewer defects, and continuous improvement. Just-in-time concepts have similar goals.

Total quality management focuses on quality improvement and applies this standard to all aspects of business activities. In doing so, managers and employees seek to uncover waste in business activities including accounting activities such as payroll and disbursements. To encourage an emphasis on quality, the U.S. Congress established the Malcolm Baldrige National Quality Award (MBQNA). Entrants must conduct a thorough analysis and evaluation of their business using guidelines from the Baldrige committee. **Ritz Carlton Hotel** is a recipient of the Baldrige award in the service category. The company applies a core set of values, collectively called *The Gold Standards,* to improve customer service.

Point: The time between buying raw materials and selling finished goods is called *throughput time.*

Just-in-time manufacturing is a system that acquires inventory and produces only when needed. An important aspect of JIT is that companies manufacture products only after they receive an order (a *demand-pull* system) and then deliver the customer's requirements on time. This means that processes must be aligned to eliminate any delays and inefficiencies including inferior inputs and outputs. Companies must also establish good relations and communications with their suppliers. On the downside, JIT is more susceptible to disruption than traditional systems. As one example, several **General Motors** plants were

Point: Many industries can benefit from a JIT system.

temporarily shut down due to a strike at an assembly division; the plants supplied components *just in time* to the assembly division.

Implications for Managerial Accounting   Adopting the lean business model can be challenging because to foster its implementation, all systems and procedures that a company follows must be realigned. Managerial accounting has an important role to play by providing accurate cost and performance information. Companies must understand the nature and sources of cost and must develop systems that capture costs accurately. Developing such a system is important to measuring the "value" provided to customers. The price that customers pay for acquiring goods and services is an important determinant of value. In turn, the costs a company incurs are key determinants of price. All else being equal, the better a company is at controlling its costs, the better its performance.

Managerial Cost Concepts

An organization incurs many different types of costs that are classified differently, depending on management needs (different costs for different purposes). We can classify costs on the basis of their (1) behavior, (2) traceability, (3) controllability, (4) relevance, and (5) function. This section explains each concept for assigning costs to products and services.

C3 Describe accounting concepts useful in classifying costs.

Types of Cost Classifications

Classification by Behavior At a basic level, a cost can be classified as fixed or variable. A **fixed cost** does not change with changes in the volume of activity (within a range of activity known as an activity's *relevant range*). For example, straight-line depreciation on equipment is a fixed cost. A **variable cost** changes in proportion to changes in the volume of activity. Sales commissions computed as a percent of sales revenue are variable costs. Additional examples of fixed and variable costs for a bike manufacturer are provided in Exhibit 18.5. When cost items are combined, total cost can be fixed, variable, or mixed. *Mixed* refers to a combination of fixed and variable costs. Equipment rental often includes a fixed cost for some minimum amount and a variable cost based on amount of usage. Classification of costs by behavior is helpful in cost-volume-profit analyses and short-term decision making. We discuss these in Chapters 22 and 25.

Topic Tackler

PLUS

18-1

Fixed Cost: Rent for Rocky Mountain Bikes' building is $22,000, and doesn't change with the number of bikes produced.

Variable Cost: Cost of bicycle tires is variable with the number of bikes produced—this cost is $15 per pair.

Exhibit 18.5

Fixed and Variable Costs

Classification by Traceability A cost is often traced to a **cost object,** which is a product, process, department, or customer to which costs are assigned. **Direct costs** are those traceable to a single cost object. For example, if a product is a cost object, its material and labor costs are usually directly traceable. **Indirect costs** are those that cannot be traced to a single cost object. An example of an indirect cost is a maintenance plan that benefits two or more departments. Exhibit 18.6 identifies examples of both direct and indirect costs for the maintenance department in a manufacturing plant. Classification of costs by traceability is useful for cost allocation. This is discussed in Chapter 21.

Exhibit 18.6

Direct and Indirect Costs of a Maintenance Department

Direct Costs
- Salaries of maintenance department employees
- Equipment purchased by maintenance department
- Materials purchased by maintenance department
- Maintenance department equipment depreciation

Indirect Costs
- Factory accounting
- Factory administration
- Factory rent
- Factory managers' salary
- Factory light and heat
- Factory internal audit
- Factory intranet

Exhibit 18.7

Controllability of Costs

Senior Manager
Controls costs of investment in land, buildings, and equipment.

Supervisor
Controls daily expenses such as supplies, maintenance, and overtime.

Point: Opportunity costs are not recorded by the accounting system.

C4 Define product and period costs and explain how they impact financial statements.

Point: Only costs of production and purchases are classed as product costs.

Point: Product costs are either in the income statement as part of cost of goods sold or in the balance sheet as inventory. Period costs appear only on the income statement under operating expenses. See Exhibit 18.8.

Classification by Controllability A cost can be defined as **controllable** or **not controllable.** Whether a cost is controllable or not depends on the employee's responsibilities, as shown in Exhibit 18.7. This is referred to as *hierarchical levels* in management, or *pecking order.* For example, investments in machinery are controllable by upper-level managers but not lower-level managers. Many daily operating expenses such as overtime often are controllable by lower-level managers. Classification of costs by controllability is especially useful for assigning responsibility to and evaluating managers.

Classification by Relevance A cost can be classified by relevance by identifying it as either a sunk cost or an out-of-pocket cost. A **sunk cost** has already been incurred and cannot be avoided or changed. It is irrelevant to future decisions. One example is the cost of a company's office equipment previously purchased. An **out-of-pocket cost** requires a future outlay of cash and is relevant for decision making. Future purchases of equipment involve out-of-pocket costs. A discussion of relevant costs must also consider opportunity costs. An **opportunity cost** is the potential benefit lost by choosing a specific action from two or more alternatives. One example is a student giving up wages from a job to attend evening classes. Consideration of opportunity cost is important when, for example, an insurance company must decide whether to outsource its payroll function or maintain it internally. This is discussed in Chapter 25.

Classification by Function Another cost classification (for manufacturers) is capitalization as inventory or to expense as incurred. Costs capitalized as inventory are called **product costs,** which refer to expenditures necessary and integral to finished products. They include direct materials, direct labor, and indirect manufacturing costs called *overhead costs*. Product costs pertain to activities carried out to manufacture the product. Costs expensed are called **period costs,** which refer to expenditures identified more with a time period than with finished products. They include selling and general administrative expenses. Period costs pertain to activities that are not part of the manufacturing process. A distinction between product and period costs is important because period costs are expensed in the income statement and product costs are assigned to inventory on the balance sheet until that inventory is sold. An ability to understand and identify product costs and period costs is crucial to using and interpreting a *manufacturing statement* described later in this chapter.

Exhibit 18.8 shows the different effects of product and period costs. Period costs flow directly to the current income statement as expenses. They are not reported as assets. Product costs are first assigned to inventory. Their final treatment depends on when inventory is sold or disposed of. Product costs assigned to finished goods that are sold in year 2007 are reported on the 2007 income statement as part of cost of goods sold. Product costs assigned to unsold inventory are carried forward on the balance sheet at the end of year 2007. If this inventory is sold in year 2008, product costs assigned to it are reported as part of cost of goods sold in that year's income statement.

The difference between period and product costs explains why the year 2007 income statement does not report operating expenses related to either factory workers' wages or depreciation on factory buildings and equipment. Instead, both costs are combined with the cost of raw materials to compute the product cost of finished goods. A portion of these manufacturing costs

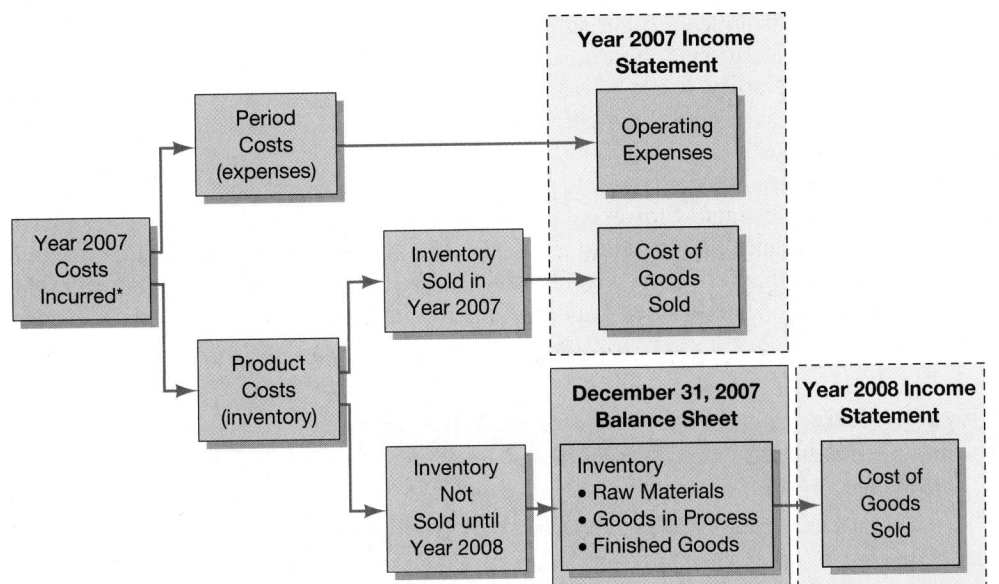

Exhibit 18.8

Period and Product Costs in Financial Statements

* This diagram excludes costs to acquire assets other than inventory.

(related to the goods sold) is reported in the year 2007 income statement as part of Cost of Goods Sold. The other portion is reported on the balance sheet at the end of that year as part of Inventory. The portion assigned to inventory could be included in any or all of raw materials, goods in process, or finished goods inventories.

Point: For a team approach to identifying period and product costs, see *Teamwork in Action* in the *Beyond the Numbers* section.

Identification of Cost Classification

It is important to understand that a cost can be classified using any one (or combination) of the five different means described here. To do this we must understand costs and operations. Specifically, for the five classifications, we must be able to identify the *activity* for behavior, *cost object* for traceability, *management hierarchical level* for controllability, *opportunity cost* for relevance, and *benefit period* for function. Factory rent, for instance, can be classified as a product cost; it is fixed with respect to number of units produced, it is indirect with respect to the product, and it is not controllable by a production supervisor. Potential multiple classifications are shown in Exhibit 18.9 using different cost items incurred in manufacturing mountain bikes. The finished bike is the cost object. Proper allocation of these costs and the managerial decisions based on cost data depend on a correct cost classification.

Point: All expenses of service companies are period costs because these companies do not have inventory.

Cost Item	By Behavior	By Traceability	By Function
Bicycle tires	Variable	Direct	Product
Wages of assembly worker*	Variable	Direct	Product
Advertising	Fixed	Indirect	Period
Production manager's salary	Fixed	Indirect	Product
Office depreciation	Fixed	Indirect	Period

Exhibit 18.9

Examples of Multiple Cost Classifications

* Although an assembly worker's wages are classified as variable costs, their actual behavior depends on how workers are paid and whether their wages are based on a union contract (such as piece rate or monthly wages).

Cost Concepts for Service Companies

The cost concepts described are generally applicable to service organizations. For example, consider **Southwest Airlines**. Its cost of beverages for passengers is a variable cost based on number of passengers. The cost of leasing an aircraft is fixed with respect to number of

Service Costs

- Beverages and snacks
- Cleaning fees
- Pilot and co-pilot salaries
- Attendant salaries
- Fuel and oil costs
- Travel agent fees
- Ground crew salaries

passengers. We can also trace a flight crew's salary to a specific flight whereas we likely cannot trace wages for the ground crew to a specific flight. Classification by function (such as product versus period costs) is not relevant to service companies because services are not inventoried. Instead, costs incurred by a service firm are expensed in the reporting period when incurred.

Managers in service companies must understand and apply cost concepts. They seek and rely on accurate cost estimates for many decisions. For example, an airline manager must often decide between canceling or rerouting flights. The manager must also be able to estimate costs saved by canceling a flight versus rerouting. Knowledge of fixed costs is equally important. We explain more about the cost requirements for these and other managerial decisions in Chapter 25.

Quick Check

Answers—p. 741

5. Which type of cost behavior increases total costs when volume of activity increases?

6. How could traceability of costs improve managerial decisions?

Reporting Manufacturing Activities

Companies with manufacturing activities differ from both merchandising and service companies. The main difference between merchandising and manufacturing companies is that merchandisers buy goods ready for sale while manufacturers produce goods from materials and labor. **Payless** is an example of a merchandising company. It buys and sells shoes without physically changing them. **Adidas** is primarily a manufacturer of shoes, apparel, and accessories. It purchases materials such as leather, cloth, dye, plastic, rubber, glue, and laces and then uses employees' labor to convert these materials to products. **Southwest Airlines** is a service company that transports people and items.

Manufacturing activities differ from both selling merchandise and providing services. Also, the financial statements for manufacturing companies differ slightly. This section considers some of these differences and compares them to accounting for a merchandising company.

Manufacturer's Balance Sheet

C5 Explain how balance sheets and income statements for manufacturing and merchandising companies differ.

Manufacturers carry several unique assets and usually have three inventories instead of the single inventory that merchandisers carry. Exhibit 18.10 shows three different inventories in the current asset section of the balance sheet for Rocky Mountain Bikes, a manufacturer. The three inventories are raw materials, goods in process, and finished goods.

Point: Reducing the size of inventories saves storage costs and frees money for other uses.

Raw Materials Inventory   **Raw materials inventory** refers to the goods a company acquires to use in making products. It uses raw materials in two ways: directly and indirectly. Most raw materials physically become part of a product and are identified with specific units or batches of a product. Raw materials used directly in a product are called *direct materials*. Other materials used to support production processes are sometimes not as clearly identified with specific units or batches of product. These materials are called **indirect materials** because they are not clearly identified with specific product units or batches. Items used as indirect materials often appear on a balance sheet as factory supplies or are included in raw materials. Some direct materials are classified as indirect materials when their costs are low (insignificant). Examples include screws and nuts used in assembling mountain bikes and staples and glue used in manufacturing shoes. Using the *materiality principle,* individually tracing the costs of each of these materials and classifying them separately as direct materials does not make much economic sense. For

Inventories of Rocky Mountain Bikes

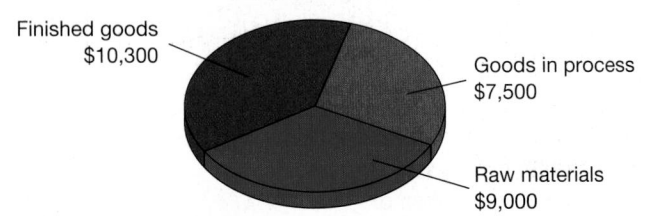

Finished goods $10,300

Goods in process $7,500

Raw materials $9,000

Exhibit 18.10

Balance Sheet for a Manufacturer

ROCKY MOUNTAIN BIKES			
Balance Sheet			
December 31, 2008			
Assets		**Liabilities and Equity**	
Current assets		Current liabilities	
Cash	$ 11,000	Accounts payable	$ 14,000
Accounts receivable, net	30,150	Wages payable	540
Raw materials inventory	9,000	Interest payable	2,000
Goods in process inventory	7,500	Income taxes payable	32,600
Finished goods inventory	10,300	Total current liabilities	49,140
Factory supplies	350	Long-term liabilities	
Prepaid insurance	300	Long-term notes payable	50,000
Total current assets	68,600	Total liabilities	99,140
Plant assets			
Small tools	1,100	Stockholders' equity	
Delivery equipment, net	5,000	Common stock, $1.2 par	24,000
Office equipment, net	1,300	Paid-in capital	76,000
Factory machinery, net	65,500	Retained earnings	49,760
Factory building, net	86,700	Total stockholders' equity	149,760
Land	9,500	Total liabilities and equity	$248,900
Total plant assets, net	169,100		
Intangible assets (patents), net	11,200		
Total assets	$248,900		

instance, keeping detailed records of the amount of glue used to manufacture one shoe is not cost beneficial.

Goods in Process Inventory   Another inventory held by manufacturers is **goods in process inventory,** also called *work in process inventory.* It consists of products in the process of being manufactured but not yet complete. The amount of goods in process inventory depends on the type of production process. If the time required to produce a unit of product is short, the goods in process inventory is likely small, but if weeks or months are needed to produce a unit, the goods in process inventory is usually larger.

Finished Goods Inventory   A third inventory owned by a manufacturer is **finished goods inventory,** which consists of completed products ready for sale. This inventory is similar to merchandise inventory owned by a merchandising company. Manufacturers also often own unique plant assets such as small tools, factory buildings, factory equipment, and patents to manufacture products. The balance sheet in Exhibit 18.10 shows that Rocky Mountain Bikes owns all of these assets. Some manufacturers invest millions or even billions of dollars in production facilities and patents. Briggs & Stratton's recent balance sheet shows about $500 million net investment in land, buildings, machinery and equipment, much of which involves production facilities. It manufactures more racing engines than any other company in the world.

Manufacturer's Income Statement

The main difference between the income statement of a manufacturer and that of a merchandiser involves the items making up cost of goods sold. Exhibit 18.11 compares the components of cost of goods sold for a manufacturer and a merchandiser. A merchandiser adds cost of

Exhibit 18.11

Cost of Goods Sold
Computation

goods purchased to beginning merchandise inventory and then subtracts ending merchandise inventory to get cost of goods sold. A manufacturer adds cost of goods manufactured to beginning finished goods inventory and then subtracts ending finished goods inventory to get cost of goods sold.

A merchandiser often uses the term *merchandise* inventory; a manufacturer often uses the term *finished goods* inventory. A manufacturer's inventories of raw materials and goods in process are not included in finished goods because they are not available for sale. A manufacturer also shows cost of goods *manufactured* instead of cost of goods *purchased.* This difference occurs because a manufacturer produces its goods instead of purchasing them ready for sale. We show later in this chapter how to derive cost of goods manufactured from the manufacturing statement.

The Cost of Goods Sold section for both a merchandiser (Tele-Mart) and a manufacturer (Rocky Mountain Bikes) is shown in Exhibit 18.12 to highlight these differences. The remaining income statement sections are similar.

Exhibit 18.12

Cost of Goods Sold for a
Merchandiser and Manufacturer

Merchandising Company		Manufacturing Company	
Cost of goods sold		Cost of goods sold	
Beginning *merchandise* inventory	$ 14,200	Beginning *finished goods* inventory	$ 11,200
Cost of merchandise *purchased*	234,150	Cost of goods *manufactured**	170,500
Goods available for sale	248,350	Goods available for sale	181,700
Less ending *merchandise* inventory	12,100	Less ending *finished goods* inventory	10,300
Cost of goods sold	$236,250	Cost of goods sold	$171,400

* Cost of goods manufactured is reported in the income statement of Exhibit 18.14.

Topic Tackler
PLUS

18-2

Although the cost of goods sold computations are similar, the numbers in these computations reflect different activities. A merchandiser's cost of goods purchased is the cost of buying products to be sold. A manufacturer's cost of goods manufactured is the sum of direct materials, direct labor, and factory overhead costs incurred in producing products. The remainder of this section further explains these three manufacturing costs and describes prime and conversion costs.

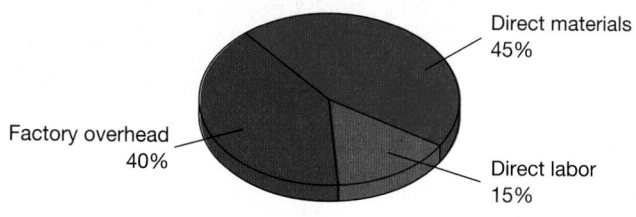

Typical Manufacturing Costs in Today's Products

Direct materials 45%

Factory overhead 40%

Direct labor 15%

Direct Materials   **Direct materials** are tangible components of a finished product. **Direct material costs** are the expenditures for direct materials that are separately and readily traced through the manufacturing process to finished goods. Examples of direct materials in manufacturing a mountain bike include its tires, seat, frame, pedals, brakes, cables, gears, and handlebars. The chart in the margin shows that direct materials generally make up about 45% of manufacturing costs in today's products, but this amount varies across industries and companies.

Direct Labor   **Direct labor** refers to the efforts of employees who physically convert materials to finished product. **Direct labor costs** are the wages and salaries for direct labor that are separately and readily traced through the manufacturing process to finished goods. Examples of direct labor in manufacturing a mountain bike include operators directly involved in converting raw materials into finished products (welding, painting, forming) and assembly workers who attach materials such as tires, seats, pedals, and brakes to the bike frames. Costs of other workers on the assembly line who assist direct laborers are classified as **indirect labor costs**. **Indirect labor** refers to manufacturing workers' efforts not linked to specific units or batches of the product.

Point: Indirect labor costs are part of factory overhead.

Factory Overhead   **Factory overhead** consists of all manufacturing costs that are not direct materials or direct labor. **Factory overhead costs** cannot be separately or readily traced to finished goods. These costs include indirect materials and indirect labor, costs not directly traceable to the product. Overtime paid to direct laborers is also included in overhead because overtime is due to delays, interruptions, or constraints not necessarily identifiable to a specific product or batches of product. Factory overhead costs also include maintenance of the mountain bike factory, supervision of its employees, repairing manufacturing equipment, factory utilities (water, gas, electricity), production manager's salary, factory rent, depreciation on factory buildings and equipment, factory insurance, property taxes on factory buildings and equipment, and factory accounting and legal services. Factory overhead does *not* include selling and administrative expenses because they are not incurred in manufacturing products. These expenses are called *period costs* and are recorded as expenses on the income statement when incurred.

Point: Factory overhead is also called *manufacturing overhead.*

Prime and Conversion Costs   Direct material costs and direct labor costs are also called **prime costs**—expenditures directly associated with the manufacture of finished goods. Direct labor costs and overhead costs are called **conversion costs**—expenditures incurred in the process of converting raw materials to finished goods. Direct labor costs are considered both prime costs and conversion costs. Exhibit 18.13 conveys the relation between prime and conversion costs and their components of direct material, direct labor, and factory overhead.

Exhibit 18.13

Prime and Conversion Costs and Their Makeup

Point: Prime costs = Direct materials + Direct labor. Conversion costs = Direct labor + Factory overhead.

Reporting Performance   Exhibit 18.14 shows the income statement for Rocky Mountain Bikes. Its operating expenses include sales salaries, office salaries, and depreciation of delivery and office equipment. Operating expenses do not include manufacturing costs such as factory workers' wages and depreciation of production equipment and the factory buildings. These manufacturing costs are reported as part of cost of goods manufactured and included in cost of goods sold. We explained why and how this is done in the section Classification by Function.

Point: Manufacturers treat costs such as depreciation and rent as product costs if they are related to manufacturing.

Quick Check   Answers—p. 741

7. What are the three types of inventory on a manufacturing company's balance sheet?

8. How does cost of goods sold differ for merchandising versus manufacturing companies?

Exhibit 18.14

Income Statement for a
Manufacturer

ROCKY MOUNTAIN BIKES
Income Statement
For Year Ended December 31, 2008

Sales		$310,000
Cost of goods sold		
Finished goods inventory, Dec. 31, 2007	$ 11,200	
Cost of goods manufactured	170,500	
Goods available for sale	181,700	
Less finished goods inventory, Dec. 31, 2008	10,300	
Cost of goods sold		171,400
Gross profit		138,600
Operating expenses		
Selling expenses		
Sales salaries expense	18,000	
Advertising expense	5,500	
Delivery wages expense	12,000	
Shipping supplies expense	250	
Insurance expense—Delivery equipment	300	
Depreciation expense—Delivery equipment	2,100	
Total selling expenses		38,150
General and administrative expenses		
Office salaries expense	15,700	
Miscellaneous expense	200	
Bad debts expense	1,550	
Office supplies expense	100	
Depreciation expense—Office equipment	200	
Interest expense	4,000	
Total general and administrative expenses		21,750
Total operating expenses		59,900
Income before income taxes		78,700
Income taxes expense		32,600
Net income		$ 46,100
Net income per common share (20,000 shares)		$ 2.31

Flow of Manufacturing Activities

C6 Explain manufacturing activities and the flow of manufacturing costs.

To understand manufacturing and its reports, we must first understand the flow of manufacturing activities and costs. Exhibit 18.15 shows the flow of manufacturing activities for a manufacturer. This exhibit has three important sections: *materials activity, production activity,* and *sales activity.* We explain each activity in this section.

Materials Activity   The far left side of Exhibit 18.15 shows the flow of raw materials. Manufacturers usually start a period with some beginning raw materials inventory carried over from the previous period. The company then acquires additional raw materials in the current period. Adding these purchases to beginning inventory gives total raw materials available for use in production. These raw materials are then either used in production in the current period or remain in inventory at the end of the period for use in future periods.

Point: Knowledge of managerial accounting provides us a means of measuring manufacturing costs and is a sound foundation for studying advanced business topics.

Production Activity   The middle section of Exhibit 18.15 describes production activity. Four factors come together in production: beginning goods in process inventory, direct materials, direct labor, and overhead. Beginning goods in process inventory consists of partly assembled products from the previous period. Production activity results in products that are either finished or remain unfinished. The cost of finished products makes up the cost of goods manufactured for the current period. Unfinished products are identified as ending goods in

Point: The series of activities that add value to a company's products or services is called a **value chain.**

Exhibit 18.15

Activities and Cost Flows in Manufacturing

process inventory. The cost of unfinished products consists of direct materials, direct labor, and factory overhead, and is reported on the current period's balance sheet. The costs of both finished goods manufactured and goods in process are *product costs.*

Sales Activity   The company's sales activity is portrayed in the far right side of Exhibit 18.15. Newly completed units are combined with beginning finished goods inventory to make up total finished goods available for sale in the current period. The cost of finished products sold is reported on the income statement as cost of goods sold. The cost of products not sold is reported on the current period's balance sheet as ending finished goods inventory.

Manufacturing Statement

A company's manufacturing activities are described in a **manufacturing statement,** also called the *schedule of manufacturing activities* or the *schedule of cost of goods manufactured.* The manufacturing statement summarizes the types and amounts of costs incurred in a company's manufacturing process. Exhibit 18.16 shows the manufacturing statement for Rocky Mountain Bikes. The statement is divided into four parts: *direct materials, direct labor, overhead,* and *computation of cost of goods manufactured.* We describe each of these parts in this section.

P2 Prepare a manufacturing statement and explain its purpose and links to financial statements.

① The manufacturing statement begins by computing direct materials used. We start by adding beginning raw materials inventory of $8,000 to the current period's purchases of $86,500. This yields $94,500 of total raw materials available for use. A physical count of inventory shows $9,000 of ending raw materials inventory. This implies a total cost of raw materials used during the period of $85,500 ($94,500 total raw materials available for use − $9,000 ending inventory). (*Note:* All raw materials are direct materials for Rocky Mountain Bikes.)

② The second part of the manufacturing statement reports direct labor costs. Rocky Mountain Bikes had total direct labor costs of $60,000 for the period. This amount includes payroll taxes and fringe benefits.

"My boss wants us to appeal to a younger and hipper crowd. So, I'd like to get a tattoo that says-- 'Accounting rules!'"

Exhibit 18.16

Manufacturing Statement

ROCKY MOUNTAIN BIKES		
Manufacturing Statement		
For Year Ended December 31, 2008		
Direct materials		
① Raw materials inventory, Dec. 31, 2007	$ 8,000	
Raw materials purchases	86,500	
Raw materials available for use	94,500	
Less raw materials inventory, Dec. 31, 2008	9,000	
Direct materials used		$ 85,500
② Direct labor		60,000
Factory overhead		
Indirect labor	9,000	
Factory supervision	6,000	
Factory utilities	2,600	
Repairs—Factory equipment	2,500	
Property taxes—Factory building	1,900	
③ Factory supplies used	600	
Factory insurance expired	1,100	
Small tools written off	200	
Depreciation expense—Factory equipment	3,500	
Depreciation expense—Factory building	1,800	
Amortization expense—Patents	800	
Total factory overhead		30,000
Total manufacturing costs		175,500
Add goods in process inventory, Dec. 31, 2007		2,500
④ Total cost of goods in process		178,000
Less goods in process inventory, Dec. 31, 2008		7,500
Cost of goods manufactured		$170,500

Point: Direct material and direct labor costs increase with increases in production volume and are called *variable costs.* Overhead can be both variable and fixed. When overhead costs vary with production, they are called *variable overhead.* When overhead costs don't vary with production, they are called *fixed overhead.*

③ The third part of the manufacturing statement reports overhead costs. The statement lists each important factory overhead item and its cost. Total factory overhead cost for the period is $30,000. Some companies report only *total* factory overhead on the manufacturing statement and attach a separate schedule listing individual overhead costs.

④ The final section of the manufacturing statement computes and reports the *cost of goods manufactured.* (Total manufacturing costs for the period are $175,500 [$85,500 + $60,000 + $30,000], the sum of direct materials used and direct labor and overhead costs incurred.) This amount is first added to beginning goods in process inventory. This gives the total goods in process inventory of $178,000 ($175,500 + $2,500). We then compute the current period's cost of goods manufactured of $170,500 by taking the $178,000 total goods in process and subtracting the $7,500 cost of ending goods in process inventory that consists of direct materials, direct labor, and factory overhead. The cost of goods manufactured amount is also called *net cost of goods manufactured* or *cost of goods completed.* Exhibit 18.14 shows that this item and amount are listed in the Cost of Goods Sold section of Rocky Mountain Bikes' income statement.

Point: Manufacturers sometimes report variable and fixed overhead separately in the manufacturing statement to provide more information to managers about cost behavior.

A managerial accounting system records costs and reports them in various reports that eventually determine financial statements. Exhibit 18.17 shows how overhead costs flow through the system: from an initial listing of specific costs, to a section of the manufacturing statement, to the reporting on the income statement.

Management uses information in the manufacturing statement to plan and control the company's manufacturing activities. To provide timely information for decision making, the statement is often prepared monthly, weekly, or even daily. In anticipation of its Xbox 360 release, **Microsoft** grew its finished goods inventories from $271 million in 2004 to $422 million in

Exhibit 18.17

Overhead Cost Flows across Accounting Reports

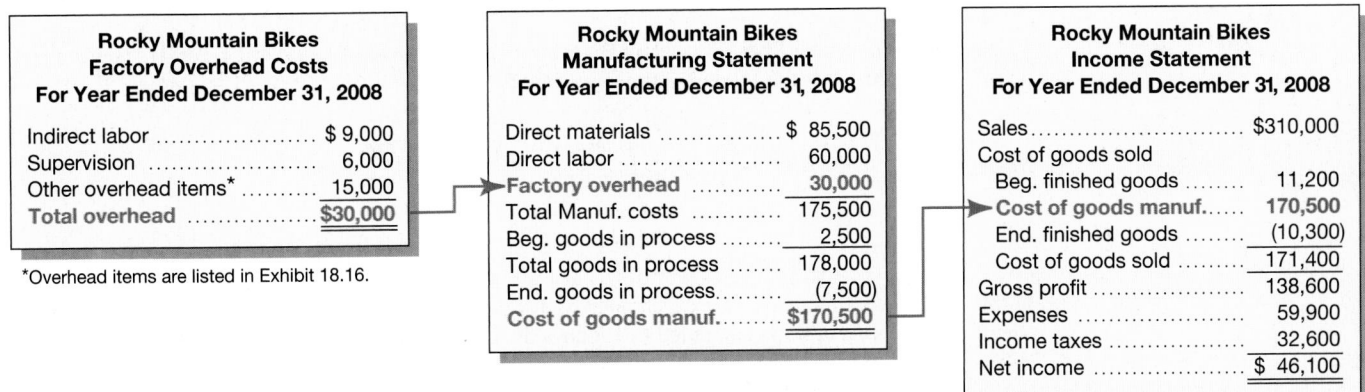

Rocky Mountain Bikes **Factory Overhead Costs** **For Year Ended December 31, 2008**	
Indirect labor	$ 9,000
Supervision	6,000
Other overhead items*	15,000
Total overhead	$30,000

*Overhead items are listed in Exhibit 18.16.

Rocky Mountain Bikes **Manufacturing Statement** **For Year Ended December 31, 2008**	
Direct materials	$ 85,500
Direct labor	60,000
Factory overhead	30,000
Total Manuf. costs	175,500
Beg. goods in process	2,500
Total goods in process	178,000
End. goods in process	(7,500)
Cost of goods manuf.	$170,500

Rocky Mountain Bikes **Income Statement** **For Year Ended December 31, 2008**	
Sales	$310,000
Cost of goods sold	
Beg. finished goods	11,200
Cost of goods manuf.	170,500
End. finished goods	(10,300)
Cost of goods sold	171,400
Gross profit	138,600
Expenses	59,900
Income taxes	32,600
Net income	$ 46,100

2005. The manufacturing statement contains information useful to external users but is not a general-purpose financial statement. Companies rarely publish the manufacturing statement because managers view this information as proprietary and potentially harmful to them if released to competitors.

Quick Check

Answers—p. 741

9. A manufacturing statement (*a*) computes cost of goods manufactured for the period, (*b*) computes cost of goods sold for the period, or (*c*) reports operating expenses incurred for the period.

10. Are companies required to report a manufacturing statement?

11. How are both beginning and ending goods in process inventories reported on a manufacturing statement?

Cycle Time and Cycle Efficiency

Decision Analysis

As lean manufacturing practices help companies move toward just-in-time manufacturing, it is important for these companies to reduce the time to manufacture their products and to improve manufacturing efficiency. One metric that measures that time element is **cycle time (CT)**. A definition of cycle time is in Exhibit 18.18.

A1 Compute cycle time and cycle efficiency, and explain their importance to production management.

$$\text{Cycle time} = \text{Process time} + \text{Inspection time} + \text{Move time} + \text{Wait time}$$

Exhibit 18.18

Cycle Time

Process time is the time spent producing the product. *Inspection time* is the time spent inspecting (1) raw materials when received, (2) goods in process while in production, and (3) finished goods prior to shipment. *Move time* is the time spent moving (1) raw materials from storage to production and (2) goods in process from factory location to another factory location. *Wait time* is the time that an order or job sits with no production applied to it; this can be due to order delays, bottlenecks in production, and poor scheduling.

Process time is considered **value-added time** because it is the only activity in cycle time that adds value to the product from the customer's perspective. The other three time activities are considered **non-value-added time** because they add no value to the customer.

Companies strive to reduce non-value-added time to improve **cycle efficiency (CE).** Cycle efficiency is the ratio of value-added time to total cycle time—see Exhibit 18.19.

Exhibit 18.19

Cycle Efficiency

$$\text{Cycle efficiency} = \frac{\text{Value-added time}}{\text{Cycle time}}$$

To illustrate, assume that Rocky Mountain Bikes receives and produces an order for 500 Tracker® mountain bikes. Assume that the following times were measured during production of this order.

Process time	1.8 days
Inspection time	0.5 days
Move time	0.7 days
Wait time	3.0 days

In this case, cycle time is 6.0 days, computed as 1.8 days + 0.5 days + 0.7 days + 3.0 days. Also, cycle efficiency is 0.3, or 30%, computed as 1.8 days divided by 6.0 days. This means that Rocky Mountain Bikes spends 30% of its time working on the product (value-added time). The other 70% is spent on non-value-added activities.

If a company has a CE of 1, it means that its time is spent entirely on value-added activities. If the CE is low, the company should evaluate its production process to see if it can identify ways to reduce non-value-added activities. The 30% CE for Rocky Mountain Bikes is low and its management should look for ways to reduce non-value-added activities.

Demonstration Problem 1: Cost Behavior and Classification

Understanding the classification and assignment of costs is important. Consider a company that manufactures computer chips. It incurs the following costs in manufacturing chips and in operating the company.

1. Plastic board used to mount the chip, $3.50 each.
2. Assembly worker pay of $15 per hour to attach chips to plastic board.
3. Salary for factory maintenance workers who maintain factory equipment.
4. Factory supervisor pay of $55,000 per year to supervise employees.
5. Real estate taxes paid on the factory, $14,500.
6. Real estate taxes paid on the company office, $6,000.
7. Depreciation costs on machinery used by workers, $30,000.
8. Salary paid to the chief financial officer, $95,000.
9. Advertising costs of $7,800 paid to promote products.
10. Salespersons' commissions of $0.50 for each assembled chip sold.
11. Management has the option to rent the manufacturing plant to six local hospitals to store medical records instead of producing and assembling chips.

Classify each cost in the following table according to the categories listed in the table header. A cost can be classified under more than one category. For example, the plastic board used to mount chips is classified as a direct material product cost and as a direct unit cost.

Cost	Period Costs — Selling and Administrative	Product Costs — Direct Material (prime cost)	Product Costs — Direct Labor (prime and conversion)	Product Costs — Factory Overhead (conversion cost)	Unit Cost Classification — Direct	Unit Cost Classification — Indirect	Sunk Cost	Opportunity Cost
1. Plastic board used to mount the chip, $3.50 each		✔			✔			

Solution to Demonstration Problem 1

Cost*	Period Costs — Selling and Administrative	Product Costs — Direct Material (prime cost)	Product Costs — Direct Labor (prime and conversion)	Product Costs — Factory Overhead (conversion cost)	Unit Cost Classification — Direct	Unit Cost Classification — Indirect	Sunk Cost	Opportunity Cost
1.		✔			✔			
2.			✔		✔			
3.				✔		✔		
4.				✔		✔		
5.				✔		✔		
6.	✔							
7.				✔		✔	✔	
8.	✔							
9.	✔							
10.	✔							
11.								✔

* Costs 1 through 11 refer to the 11 cost items described at the beginning of the problem.

Demonstration Problem 2: Reporting for Manufacturers

A manufacturing company's balance sheet and income statement differ from those for a merchandising or service company.

Required

1. Fill in the [BLANK] descriptors on the partial balance sheets for both the manufacturing company and the merchandising company. Explain why a different presentation is required.

Manufacturing Company

ADIDAS GROUP
Partial Balance Sheet
December 31, 2008

Current assets	
Cash	$10,000
[BLANK]	8,000
[BLANK]	5,000
[BLANK]	7,000
Supplies	500
Prepaid insurance	500
Total current assets	$31,000

Merchandising Company

PAYLESS SHOE OUTLET
Partial Balance Sheet
December 31, 2008

Current assets	
Cash	$ 5,000
[BLANK]	12,000
Supplies	500
Prepaid insurance	500
Total current assets	$18,000

2. Fill in the [BLANK] descriptors on the income statements for the manufacturing company and the merchandising company. Explain why a different presentation is required.

Manufacturing Company

ADIDAS GROUP
Partial Income Statement
For Year Ended December 31, 2008

Sales	$200,000
Cost of goods sold	
Finished goods inventory, Dec. 31, 2007	10,000
[BLANK]	120,000
Goods available for sale	130,000
Finished goods inventory, Dec. 31, 2008	(7,000)
Cost of goods sold	123,000
Gross profit	$ 77,000

Merchandising Company

PAYLESS SHOE OUTLET
Partial Income Statement
For Year Ended December 31, 2008

Sales	$190,000
Cost of goods sold	
Merchandise inventory, Dec. 31, 2007	8,000
[BLANK]	108,000
Goods available for sale	116,000
Merchandise inventory, Dec. 31, 2008	(12,000)
Cost of goods sold	104,000
Gross profit	$ 86,000

3. The manufacturer's cost of goods manufactured is the sum of (a) _____, (b) _____, and (c) _____ costs incurred in producing the product.

Solution to Demonstration Problem 2

1. Inventories for a manufacturer and for a merchandiser.

Manufacturing Company

ADIDAS GROUP
Partial Balance Sheet
December 31, 2008

Current assets	
Cash	$10,000
Raw materials inventory	8,000
Goods in process inventory	5,000
Finished goods inventory	7,000
Supplies	500
Prepaid insurance	500
Total current assets	$31,000

Merchandising Company

PAYLESS SHOE OUTLET
Partial Balance Sheet
December 31, 2008

Current assets	
Cash	$ 5,000
Merchandise inventory	12,000
Supplies	500
Prepaid insurance	500
Total current assets	$18,000

Explanation: A manufacturing company must control and measure three types of inventories: raw materials, goods in process, and finished goods. In the sequence of making a product, the raw materials move into production—called *goods in process inventory*—and then to finished goods. All raw materials and goods in process inventory at the end of each accounting period are considered current assets. All unsold finished inventory is considered a current asset at the end of each accounting period. The merchandising company must control and measure only one type of inventory, purchased goods.

2. Cost of goods sold for a manufacturer and for a merchandiser.

Manufacturing Company

ADIDAS GROUP
Partial Income Statement
For Year Ended December 31, 2008

Sales	$200,000
Cost of goods sold	
Finished goods inventory, Dec. 31, 2007	10,000
Cost of goods manufactured	120,000
Goods available for sale	130,000
Finished goods inventory, Dec. 31, 2008	(7,000)
Cost of goods sold	123,000
Gross profit	$ 77,000

Merchandising Company

PAYLESS SHOE OUTLET
Partial Income Statement
For Year Ended December 31, 2008

Sales	$190,000
Cost of goods sold	
Merchandise inventory, Dec. 31, 2007	8,000
Cost of purchases	108,000
Goods available for sale	116,000
Merchandise inventory, Dec. 31, 2008	(12,000)
Cost of goods sold	104,000
Gross profit	$ 86,000

Explanation: Manufacturing and merchandising companies use different reporting terms. In particular, the terms *finished goods* and *cost of goods manufactured* are used to reflect the production of goods, yet the concepts and techniques of reporting cost of goods sold for a manufacturing company and merchandising company are similar.

3. A manufacturer's cost of goods manufactured is the sum of (a) *direct material,* (b) *direct labor,* and (c) *factory overhead* costs incurred in producing the product.

Demonstration Problem 3: Manufacturing Statement

The following account balances and other information are from SUNN Corporation's accounting records for year-end December 31, 2008. Use this information to prepare (1) a table listing factory overhead costs, (2) a manufacturing statement (show only the total factory overhead cost), and (3) an income statement.

Advertising expense	$ 85,000	Goods in process inventory, Dec. 31, 2007	$ 8,000
Amortization expense—Patents	16,000	Goods in process inventory, Dec. 31, 2008	9,000
Bad debts expense	28,000	Income taxes	53,400
Depreciation expense—Office equipment	37,000	Indirect labor	26,000
Depreciation expense—Factory building	133,000	Interest expense	25,000
Depreciation expense—Factory equipment	78,000	Miscellaneous expense	55,000
Direct labor	250,000	Property taxes on factory equipment	14,000
Factory insurance expired	62,000	Raw materials inventory, Dec. 31, 2007	60,000
Factory supervision	74,000	Raw materials inventory, Dec. 31, 2008	78,000
Factory supplies used	21,000	Raw materials purchases	313,000
Factory utilities	115,000	Repairs expense—Factory equipment	31,000
Finished goods inventory, Dec. 31, 2007	15,000	Salaries expense	150,000
Finished goods inventory, Dec. 31, 2008	12,500	Sales	1,630,000

Planning the Solution

- Analyze the account balances and select those that are part of factory overhead costs.
- Arrange these costs in a table that lists factory overhead costs for the year.
- Analyze the remaining costs and select those related to production activity for the year; selected costs should include the materials and goods in process inventories and direct labor.
- Prepare a manufacturing statement for the year showing the calculation of the cost of materials used in production, the cost of direct labor, and the total factory overhead cost. When presenting overhead cost on this statement, report only total overhead cost from the table of overhead costs for the year. Show the costs of beginning and ending goods in process inventory to determine cost of goods manufactured.
- Organize the remaining revenue and expense items into the income statement for the year. Combine cost of goods manufactured from the manufacturing statement with the finished goods inventory amounts to compute cost of goods sold for the year.

Solution to Demonstration Problem 3

SUNN CORPORATION Factory Overhead Costs For Year Ended December 31, 2008	
Amortization expense—Patents	$ 16,000
Depreciation expense—Factory building	133,000
Depreciation expense—Factory equipment	78,000
Factory insurance expired	62,000
Factory supervision	74,000
Factory supplies used	21,000

SUNN CORPORATION Manufacturing Statement For Year Ended December 31, 2008		
Direct materials		
Raw materials inventory, Dec. 31, 2007		$ 60,000
Raw materials purchase		313,000
Raw materials available for use		373,000
Less raw materials inventory, Dec. 31, 2008		78,000
Direct materials used		295,000

[continued on next page]

[continued from previous page]

Factory utilities	115,000
Indirect labor	26,000
Property taxes on factory equipment	14,000
Repairs expense—Factory equipment	31,000
Total factory overhead	$570,000

Direct labor	250,000
Factory overhead	570,000
Total manufacturing costs	1,115,000
Goods in process inventory, Dec. 31, 2007	8,000
Total cost of goods in process	1,123,000
Less goods in process inventory, Dec. 31, 2008	9,000
Cost of goods manufactured	$1,114,000

SUNN CORPORATION
Income Statement
For Year Ended December 31, 2008

Sales		$1,630,000
Cost of goods sold		
Finished goods inventory, Dec. 31, 2007	$ 15,000	
Cost of goods manufactured	1,114,000	
Goods available for sale	1,129,000	
Less finished goods inventory, Dec. 31, 2008	12,500	
Cost of goods sold		1,116,500
Gross profit		513,500
Operating expenses		
Advertising expense	85,000	
Bad debts expense	28,000	
Depreciation expense—Office equipment	37,000	
Interest expense	25,000	
Miscellaneous expense	55,000	
Salaries expense	150,000	
Total operating expenses		380,000
Income before income taxes		133,500
Income taxes		53,400
Net income		$ 80,100

Summary

C1 Explain the purpose and nature of managerial accounting.
The purpose of managerial accounting is to provide useful information to management and other internal decision makers. It does this by collecting, managing, and reporting both monetary and nonmonetary information in a manner useful to internal users. Major characteristics of managerial accounting include (1) focus on internal decision makers, (2) emphasis on planning and control, (3) flexibility, (4) timeliness, (5) reliance on forecasts and estimates, (6) focus on segments and projects, and (7) reporting both monetary and nonmonetary information.

C2 Describe the lean business model. The main purpose of the lean business model is the elimination of waste. Concepts such as total quality management and just-in-time production often aid in effective application of the model.

C3 Describe accounting concepts useful in classifying costs.
We can classify costs on the basis of their (1) behavior—fixed vs. variable, (2) traceability—direct vs. indirect, (3) controllability—controllable vs. uncontrollable, (4) relevance—sunk vs. out of pocket, and (5) function—product vs. period. A cost can be classified in more than one way, depending on the purpose for which the cost is being determined. These classifications help to understand cost patterns, analyze performance, and plan operations.

C4 Define product and period costs and explain how they impact financial statements. Costs that are capitalized because they are expected to have future value are called *product costs;* costs that are expensed are called *period costs.* This classification is important because it affects the amount of costs expensed in the income statement and the amount of costs assigned to inventory on the balance sheet. Product costs are commonly made up of direct materials, direct labor, and overhead. Period costs include selling and administrative expenses.

C5 Explain how balance sheets and income statements for manufacturing and merchandising companies differ. The main difference is that manufacturers usually carry three inventories on their balance sheets—raw materials, goods in process, and finished goods—instead of one inventory that merchandisers carry. The main difference between income statements of manufacturers and merchandisers is the items making up cost of goods sold. A merchandiser adds beginning merchandise inventory to cost of goods purchased and then subtracts ending merchandise inventory to get cost of goods sold. A manufacturer adds beginning finished goods inventory to cost of goods manufactured and then subtracts ending finished goods inventory to get cost of goods sold.

C6 **Explain manufacturing activities and the flow of manufacturing costs.** Manufacturing activities consist of materials, production, and sales activities. The materials activity consists of the purchase and issuance of materials to production. The production activity consists of converting materials into finished goods. At this stage in the process, the materials, labor, and overhead costs have been incurred and the manufacturing statement is prepared. The sales activity consists of selling some or all of finished goods available for sale. At this stage, the cost of goods sold is determined.

A1 **Compute cycle time and cycle efficiency, and explain their importance to production management.** It is important for companies to reduce the time to produce their products and to

improve manufacturing efficiency. One measure of that time is cycle time (CT), defined as Process time + Inspection time + Move time + Wait time. Process time is value-added time, the others are non-value-added time. Cycle efficiency (CE) is the ratio of value-added time to total cycle time. If CE is low, management should evaluate its production process to see if it can reduce non-value-added activities.

P1 **Compute cost of goods sold for a manufacturer.** A manufacturer adds beginning finished goods inventory to cost of goods manufactured and then subtracts ending finished goods inventory to get cost of goods sold.

P2 **Prepare a manufacturing statement and explain its purpose and links to financial statements.** The manufacturing statement reports computation of cost of goods manufactured for the period. It begins by showing the period's costs for direct materials, direct labor, and overhead and then adjusts these numbers for the beginning and ending inventories of the goods in process to yield cost of goods manufactured.

Guidance Answers to **Decision Maker** and **Decision Ethics**

Production Manager It appears that all three friends want to pay the bill with someone else's money. David is using money belonging to the tax authorities, Denise is taking money from her company, and Derek is defrauding the client. To prevent such practices, companies have internal audit mechanisms. Many companies also adopt ethical codes of conduct to help guide employees. We must recognize that some entertainment expenses are justifiable and even encouraged. For example, the tax law allows certain deductions for entertainment that have a business purpose. Corporate policies also sometimes allow and encourage reimbursable spending for social activities, and contracts can include entertainment as allowable costs. Nevertheless, without further details, payment for this bill should be made from personal accounts.

Entrepreneur Tracing all costs directly to cost objects is always desirable, but you need to be able to do so in an economically feasible

manner. In this case, you are able to trace 90% of the assembly department's direct costs. It may not be economical to spend more money on a new software to trace the final 10% of costs. You need to make a cost-benefit trade-off. If the software offers benefits beyond tracing the remaining 10% of the assembly department's costs, your decision should consider this.

Purchase Manager Opportunity costs relate to the potential quality and delivery benefits given up by not choosing supplier (A). Selecting supplier (B) might involve future costs of poor-quality seats (inspection, repairs, and returns). Also, potential delivery delays could interrupt work and increase manufacturing costs. Your company could also incur sales losses if the product quality of supplier (B) is low. As purchase manager, you are responsible for these costs and must consider them in making your decision.

Guidance Answers to **Quick Checks**

1. *d*

2. Financial accounting information is intended for users external to an organization such as investors, creditors, and government authorities. Managerial accounting focuses on providing information to managers, officers, and other decision makers within the organization.

3. No, GAAP do not control the practice of managerial accounting. Unlike external users, the internal users need managerial accounting information for planning and controlling business activities rather than for external comparison. Different types of information are required, depending on the activity. Therefore it is difficult to standardize managerial accounting.

4. Under TQM, all managers and employees should strive toward higher standards in their work and in the products and services they offer to customers.

5. Variable costs increase when volume of activity increases.

6. By being able to trace costs to cost objects (say, to products and departments), managers better understand the total costs

associated with a cost object. This is useful when managers consider making changes to the cost object (such as when dropping the product or expanding the department).

7. Raw materials inventory, goods in process inventory, and finished goods inventory.

8. The cost of goods sold for merchandising companies includes all costs of acquiring the merchandise; the cost of goods sold for manufacturing companies includes the three costs of manufacturing: direct materials, direct labor, and overhead.

9. *a*

10. No; companies rarely report a manufacturing statement.

11. Beginning goods in process inventory is added to total manufacturing costs to yield total goods in process. Ending goods in process inventory is subtracted from total goods in process to yield cost of goods manufactured for the period.

Key Terms

mhhe.com/wildFAP18e

Key Terms are available at the book's Website for learning and testing in an online Flashcard Format.

Continuous improvement (p. 724)
Control (p. 721)
Controllable or not controllable cost (p. 726)
Conversion costs (p. 731)
Cost object (p. 725)
Customer orientation (p. 723)
Cycle efficiency (CE) (p. 735)
Cycle time (CT) (p. 735)
Direct costs (p. 725)
Direct labor (p. 731)
Direct labor costs (p. 731)
Direct material (p. 730)
Direct material costs (p. 730)

Factory overhead (p. 731)
Factory overhead costs (p. 731)
Finished goods inventory (p. 729)
Fixed cost (p. 725)
Goods in process inventory (p. 729)
Indirect costs (p. 725)
Indirect labor (p. 731)
Indirect labor costs (p. 731)
Indirect material (p. 728)
Just-in-time (JIT) manufacturing (p. 724)
Lean business model (p. 724)
Managerial accounting (p. 720)
Manufacturing statement (p. 733)
Non-value-added time (p. 735)

Opportunity cost (p. 726)
Out-of-pocket cost (p. 726)
Period costs (p. 726)
Planning (p. 721)
Prime costs (p. 731)
Product costs (p. 726)
Raw materials inventory (p. 728)
Sunk cost (p. 726)
Total quality management (TQM) (p. 724)
Value-added time (p. 735)
Value chain (p. 732)
Variable cost (p.725)

Multiple Choice Quiz

Answers on p. 759   mhhe.com/wildFAP18e

Personal Interactive Quizzes A and B are available at the book's Website.

1. Continuous improvement
  a. Is used to reduce inventory levels.
  b. Is applicable only in service businesses.
  c. Rejects the notion of "good enough."
  d. Is used to reduce ordering costs.
  e. Is applicable only in manufacturing businesses.

2. A direct cost is one that is
  a. Variable with respect to the cost object.
  b. Traceable to the cost object.
  c. Fixed with respect to the cost object.
  d. Allocated to the cost object.
  e. A period cost.

3. Costs that are incurred as part of the manufacturing process, but are not clearly traceable to the specific unit of product or batches of product are called
  a. Period costs.
  b. Factory overhead.
  c. Sunk costs.
  d. Opportunity costs.
  e. Fixed costs.

4. The three major cost components of manufacturing a product are
  a. Direct materials, direct labor, and factory overhead.
  b. Period costs, product costs, and sunk costs.
  c. Indirect labor, indirect materials, and fixed expenses.
  d. Variable costs, fixed costs, and period costs.
  e. Opportunity costs, sunk costs, and direct costs.

5. A company reports the following for the current year.

Finished goods inventory, beginning year	$6,000
Finished goods inventory, ending year	3,200
Cost of goods sold	7,500

Its cost of goods manufactured for the current year is
  a. $1,500.
  b. $1,700.
  c. $7,500.
  d. $2,800.
  e. $4,700.

Discussion Questions

1. Describe the managerial accountant's role in business planning, control, and decision making.

2. Distinguish between managerial and financial accounting on
  a. Users and decision makers   **b.** Purpose of information

  c. Flexibility of practice   **e.** Focus of information
  d. Time dimension   **f.** Nature of information

3. Identify the usual changes that a company must make when it adopts a customer orientation.

4. Distinguish between direct material and indirect material.

5. Distinguish between direct labor and indirect labor.

6. Distinguish between (*a*) factory overhead and (*b*) selling and administrative overhead.

7. What product cost is listed as both a prime cost and a conversion cost?

8. Assume that you tour **Apple**'s factory where it makes its products. List three direct costs and three indirect costs that you are likely to see.

9. Should we evaluate a manager's performance on the basis of controllable or noncontrollable costs? Why?

10. Explain why knowledge of cost behavior is useful in product performance evaluation.

11. Explain why product costs are capitalized but period costs are expensed in the current accounting period.

12. Explain how business activities and inventories for a manufacturing company, a merchandising company, and a service company differ.

13. Why does managerial accounting often involve working with numerous predictions and estimates?

14. How do an income statement and a balance sheet for a manufacturing company and a merchandising company differ?

15. Besides inventories, what other assets often appear on manufacturers' balance sheets but not on merchandisers' balance sheets?

16. Why does a manufacturing company require three different inventory categories?

17. Manufacturing activities of a company are described in the _____. This statement summarizes the types and amounts of costs incurred in its manufacturing _____.

18. What are the three categories of manufacturing costs?

19. List several examples of factory overhead.

20. List the four components of a manufacturing statement and provide specific examples of each for **Apple**.

21. Prepare a proper title for the annual "manufacturing statement" of **Apple**. Does the date match the balance sheet or income statement? Why?

22. Describe the relations among the income statement, the manufacturing statement, and a detailed listing of factory overhead costs.

23. Define and describe *cycle time* and identify the components of cycle time.

24. Explain the difference between value-added time and non-value-added time.

25. Define and describe *cycle efficiency*.

26. Can management of a company such as **Best Buy** use cycle time and cycle efficiency as useful measures of performance? Explain.

27. Access **Anheuser-Busch**'s 2004 annual report (10-K) for fiscal year ended December 31, 2004, at the SEC's EDGAR database (**SEC.gov**) or its Website (**Anheuser-Busch.com**). From its balance sheet, identify the titles and amounts of its inventory components.

 Red numbers denote Discussion Questions that involve decision-making.

Managerial accounting (choose one):

1. Provides information to aid management in planning and controlling business activities.

2. Provides information that is widely available to all interested parties.

3. Is directed at reporting aggregate data on the company as a whole.

4. Must follow generally accepted accounting principles.

QUICK STUDY

QS 18-1
Managerial accounting defined
C1

Identify whether each description most likely applies to managerial or financial accounting.

1. _____ It is directed at external users in making investment, credit, and other decisions.

2. _____ Its information is often available only after an audit is complete.

3. _____ Its primary focus is on the organization as a whole.

4. _____ Its principles and practices are very flexible.

5. _____ Its primary users are company managers.

QS 18-2
Managerial accounting versus financial accounting
C1

Match each lean business concept with its best description by entering its letter in the blank.

1. _____ Just-in-time manufacturing

2. _____ Continuous improvements

3. _____ Customer orientation

4. _____ Total quality management

A. Inventory is acquired or produced only as needed.

B. Flexible product designs can be modified to accommodate customer choices.

C. Every manager and employee constantly looks for ways to improve company operations.

D. Focuses on quality throughout the production process.

QS 18-3
Lean business concepts
C2

QS 18-4
Fixed and variable costs

C3

Which of these statements is true regarding fixed and variable costs?

1. Fixed costs stay the same and variable costs increase in total as activity volume increases.

2. Fixed costs increase and variable costs decrease in total as activity volume decreases.

3. Both fixed and variable costs stay the same in total as activity volume increases.

4. Both fixed and variable costs increase as activity volume increases.

QS 18-5
Direct and indirect costs

C3

Verdi Company produces sporting equipment, including leather footballs. Identify each of the following costs as direct or indirect if the cost object is a football produced by Verdi.

1. Electricity used in the production plant.

2. Labor used on the football production line.

3. Salary of manager who supervises the entire plant.

4. Depreciation on equipment used to produce footballs.

5. Leather used to produce footballs.

QS 18-6
Product and period costs

C4

Which of these statements is true regarding product and period costs?

1. Sales commission is a product cost and depreciation on factory equipment is a product cost.

2. Factory maintenance is a product cost and sales commission is a period cost.

3. Sales commission is a product cost and factory rent is a period cost.

4. Factory wages is a product cost and direct material is a period cost.

QS 18-7
Inventory reporting for manufacturers

C5

Three inventory categories are reported on a manufacturing company's balance sheet: (*a*) raw materials, (*b*) goods in process, and (*c*) finished goods. Identify the usual order in which these inventory items are reported on the balance sheet.

1. (*b*)(*c*)(*a*)   **2.** (*c*)(*b*)(*a*)   **3.** (*a*)(*b*)(*c*)   **4.** (*b*)(*a*)(*c*)

QS 18-8
Cost of goods sold   P1

A company has year-end cost of goods manufactured of $4,000, beginning finished goods inventory of $500, and ending finished goods inventory of $750. Its cost of goods sold is

1. $4,250   **2.** $4,000   **3.** $3,750   **4.** $3,900

QS 18-9
Manufacturing flows identified

C6

Identify the usual sequence of manufacturing activities by filling in the blank (1, 2, or 3) corresponding to its order: _____ Production activities; _____ Sales activities; _____ Materials activities.

QS 18-10
Cost of goods manufactured

P2

Prepare the manufacturing statement for Briton Company using the following information.

Direct materials	$190,500
Direct labor	63,150
Factory overhead costs	24,000
Goods in process, Dec. 31, 2007	157,600
Goods in process, Dec. 31, 2008	142,750

QS 18-11
Manufacturing cycle time and efficiency

A1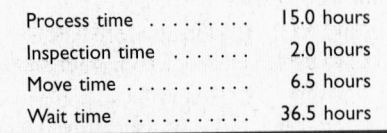

Compute and interpret (*a*) manufacturing cycle time and (*b*) manufacturing cycle efficiency using the following information.

Process time	15.0 hours
Inspection time	2.0 hours
Move time	6.5 hours
Wait time	36.5 hours

Compute cost of goods sold for year 2008 using the following information.

Finished goods inventory, Dec. 31, 2007	$345,000
Goods in process inventory, Dec. 31, 2007	83,500
Goods in process inventory, Dec. 31, 2008	72,300
Cost of goods manufactured, year 2008	918,700
Finished goods inventory, Dec. 31, 2008	283,600

QS 18-12
Cost of goods sold

P1

Both managerial accounting and financial accounting provide useful information to decision makers. Indicate in the following chart the most likely source of information for each business decision (a decision can require major input from both sources).

EXERCISES

Exercise 18-1
Sources of accounting information

C1

	Primary Information Source	
Business Decision	Managerial	Financial
Report financial performance to board of directors	____	____
Estimate product cost for a new line of shoes	____	____
Plan the budget for next quarter	____	____
Measure profitability of all individual stores	____	____
Prepare financial reports according to GAAP	____	____
Determine amount of dividends to pay stockholders	____	____
Determine location and size for a new plant	____	____
Evaluate a purchasing department's performance	____	____

Complete the following statements by filling in the blanks.

1. _____ is the process of setting goals and making plans to achieve them.
2. _____ is the process of monitoring planning decisions and evaluating an organization's activities and employees.
3. _____ _____ usually covers a period of 5 to 10 years.
4. _____ _____ usually covers a period of one year.

Exercise 18-2
Planning and control descriptions

C1

In the following chart, compare financial accounting and managerial accounting by describing how each differs for the items listed. Be specific in your responses.

Exercise 18-3
Characteristics of financial accounting and managerial accounting

C1

	Financial Accounting	Managerial Accounting
1. Users and decision makers		
2. Purpose of information		
3. Flexibility of practice		
4. Timeliness of information		
5. Time dimension		
6. Focus of information		
7. Nature of information		

Customer orientation means that a company's managers and employees respond to customers' changing wants and needs. A manufacturer of plastic fasteners has created a customer satisfaction survey that it asks each of its customers to complete. The survey asks about the following factors: (A) lead time; (B) delivery; (C) price; (D) product performance. Each factor is to be rated as unsatisfactory, marginal, average, satisfactory, very satisfied.

Exercise 18-4
Customer orientation in practice

C2

a. Match the competitive forces 1 through 4 to the factors on the survey. A factor can be matched to more than one competitive force.

Survey Factor	Competitive Force
A. Lead time	_____ **1.** Time
B. Delivery	_____ **2.** Quality
C. Price	_____ **3.** Cost
D. Product performance	_____ **4.** Flexibility of service

b. How can managers of this company use the information from this customer satisfaction survey to better meet competitive forces and satisfy their customers?

Exercise 18-5

Management concepts

C2

Following are three separate events affecting the managerial accounting systems for different companies. Match the management concept(s) that the company is likely to adopt for the event identified. There is some overlap in the meaning of customer orientation and total quality management and, therefore, some responses can include more than one concept.

Event	Management Concept
_____ 1. The company starts reporting measures on customer complaints and product returns from customers.	a. Total quality management (TQM)
_____ 2. The company starts reporting measures such as the percent of defective products and the number of units scrapped.	b. Just-in-time (JIT) system c. Continuous improvement (CI)
_____ 3. The company starts measuring inventory turnover and discontinues elaborate inventory records. Its new focus is to pull inventory through the system.	d. Customer orientation (CO)

Exercise 18-6

Cost analysis and identification

C3 C4

Georgia Pacific, a manufacturer, incurs the following costs. (1) Classify each cost as either a product or a period cost. If a product cost, identify it as a prime and/or conversion cost. (2) Classify each product cost as either a direct cost or an indirect cost using the product as the cost object.

Cost	Product Cost Prime	Product Cost Conversion	Period Cost	Direct Cost	Indirect Cost
Direct materials used	____	____	____	____	____
State and federal income taxes	____	____	____	____	____
Payroll taxes for production supervisor	____	____	____	____	____
Amortization of patents on factory machine	____	____	____	____	____
Accident insurance on factory workers	____	____	____	____	____
Wages to assembly workers	____	____	____	____	____
Factory utilities	____	____	____	____	____
Small tools used	____	____	____	____	____
Bad debts expense	____	____	____	____	____
Depreciation—Factory building	____	____	____	____	____
Advertising	____	____	____	____	____
Office supplies used	____	____	____	____	____

Exercise 18-7

Cost classifications   C3

(1) Identify each of the five cost classifications discussed in the chapter. (2) List two purposes of identifying these separate cost classifications.

Exercise 18-8

Cost analysis and classification

C3

Listed here are product costs for the production of soccer balls. (1) Classify each cost (a) as either fixed or variable and (b) as either direct or indirect. (2) What pattern do you see regarding the relation between costs classified by behavior and costs classified by traceability?

Product Cost	Cost by Behavior		Cost by Traceability	
	Variable	Fixed	Direct	Indirect
Annual flat fee paid for office security	——	——	——	——
Leather cover for soccer balls	——	——	——	——
Lace to hold leather together	——	——	——	——
Wages of assembly workers	——	——	——	——
Taxes on factory	——	——	——	——
Coolants for machinery	——	——	——	——
Machinery depreciation	——	——	——	——

Current assets for two different companies at calendar year-end 2008 are listed here. One is a manufacturer, Salomon Skis Mfg., and the other, Sun Fresh Foods, is a grocery distribution company. (1) Identify which set of numbers relates to the manufacturer and which to the merchandiser. (2) Prepare the current asset section for each company from this information. Discuss why the current asset section for these two companies is different.

Exercise 18-9
Balance sheet identification and preparation
C5

Account	Company 1	Company 2
Cash	$ 7,000	$ 5,000
Raw materials inventory	—	42,000
Merchandise inventory	45,000	—
Goods in process inventory	—	30,000
Finished goods inventory	—	50,000
Accounts receivable, net	62,000	75,000
Prepaid expenses	1,500	900

Compute cost of goods sold for each of these two companies for the year ended December 31, 2008.

Exercise 18-10
Cost of goods sold computation
C5   P1

	Viking Retail	Log Homes Manufacturing
3 Beginning inventory		
4 Merchandise	$275,000	
5 Finished goods		$450,000
6 Cost of purchases	500,000	
7 Cost of goods manufactured		900,000
8 Ending inventory		
9 Merchandise	115,000	
10 Finished goods		375,000

Check   Viking COGS, $660,000

Using the following data, compute (1) the cost of goods manufactured and (2) the cost of goods sold for both Garcia Company and Culpepper Company.

Exercise 18-11
Cost of goods manufactured and cost of goods sold computation
P1   P2

	Garcia Company	Culpepper Company
Beginning finished goods inventory	$12,000	$16,450
Beginning goods in process inventory	14,500	19,950
Beginning raw materials inventory	7,250	9,000
Rental cost on factory equipment	27,000	22,750
Direct labor	19,000	35,000
Ending finished goods inventory	17,650	13,300
Ending goods in process inventory	22,000	16,000

[continued on next page]

[continued from previous page]

Ending raw materials inventory	5,300	7,200
Factory utilities	9,000	12,000
Factory supplies used	8,200	3,200
General and administrative expenses	21,000	43,000
Indirect labor	1,250	7,660
Repairs—Factory equipment	4,780	1,500
Raw materials purchases	33,000	52,000
Sales salaries	50,000	46,000

Check   Garcia COGS, $91,030

Exercise 18-12
Components of accounting reports

C6   P2

For each of the following account balances for a manufacturing company, place a ✔ in the appropriate column indicating that it appears on the balance sheet, the income statement, the manufacturing statement, and/or a detailed listing of factory overhead costs. Assume that the income statement shows the calculation of cost of goods sold and the manufacturing statement shows only the total amount of factory overhead. (An account balance can appear on more than one report.)

File Edit View Insert Format Tools Data Window Help

	Account	Balance Sheet	Income Statement	Manufacturing Statement	Overhead Report
3	Accounts receivable				
4	Computer supplies used in office				
5	Beginning finished goods inventory				
6	Beginning goods in process inventory				
7	Beginning raw materials inventory				
8	Cash				
9	Depreciation expense—Factory building				
10	Depreciation expense—Factory equipment				
11	Depreciation expense—Office building				
12	Depreciation expense—Office equipment				
13	Direct labor				
14	Ending finished goods inventory				
15	Ending goods in process inventory				
16	Ending raw materials inventory				
17	Factory maintenance wages				
18	Computer supplies used in factory				
19	Income taxes				
20	Insurance on factory building				
21	Rent cost on office building				
22	Office supplies used				
23	Property taxes on factory building				
24	Raw materials purchases				
25	Sales				

Sheet1 / Sheet2 / Sheet3 /

Exercise 18-13
Manufacturing statement preparation   P2

Given the following selected account balances of Shanta Company, prepare its manufacturing statement for the year ended on December 31, 2008. Include a listing of the individual overhead account balances in this statement.

Sales	$1,250,000
Raw materials inventory, Dec. 31, 2007	37,000
Goods in process inventory, Dec. 31, 2007	53,900
Finished goods inventory, Dec. 31, 2007	62,750
Raw materials purchases	175,600
Direct labor	225,000
Factory computer supplies used	17,840
Indirect labor	47,000
Repairs—Factory equipment	5,250
Rent cost of factory building	57,000
Advertising expense	94,000
General and administrative expenses	129,300
Raw materials inventory, Dec. 31, 2008	42,700
Goods in process inventory, Dec. 31, 2008	41,500
Finished goods inventory, Dec. 31, 2008	67,300

Check   Cost of goods manufactured, $534,390

Use the information in Exercise 18-13 to prepare an income statement for Shanta Company (a manufacturer). Assume that its cost of goods manufactured is $534,390.

Exercise 18-14
Income statement
preparation   P2

The following chart shows how costs flow through a business as a product is manufactured. Some boxes
in the flowchart show cost amounts. Compute the cost amounts for boxes that contain question marks.

Exercise 18-15
Cost flows in manufacturing

C6   P2

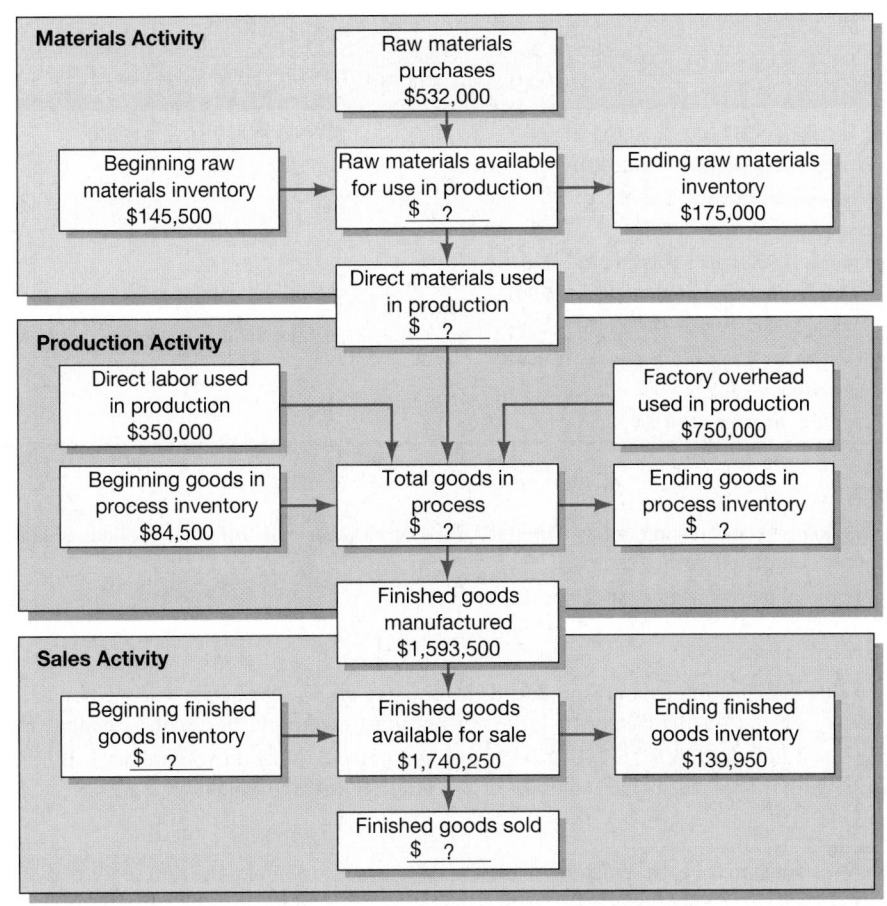

This chapter explained the purpose of managerial accounting in the context of the current business environment. Review the *automobile* section of your local newspaper; the Sunday paper is often best.
Review advertisements of sport utility vehicles and identify the manufacturers that offer these products
and the factors on which they compete.

PROBLEM SET A

Problem 18-1A
Managerial accounting role

C1   C2

Required

Discuss the potential contributions and responsibilities of the managerial accounting professional in helping an automobile manufacturer succeed. (*Hint:* Think about information and estimates that a managerial accountant might provide new entrants into the sports utility market.)

Many fast food restaurants compete on lean business concepts. Match each of the following activities at
a fast food restaurant with the lean business concept it strives to achieve.

Problem 18-2A
Lean business concepts

C2

_____ **1.** Courteous employees	**a.** Total quality management (TQM)
_____ **2.** Food produced to order	**b.** Just-in-time (JIT)
_____ **3.** New product development	**c.** Continuous improvement (CI)
_____ **4.** Clean tables and floors	
_____ **5.** Orders filled within 3 minutes	
_____ **6.** Standardized food making processes	
_____ **7.** Customer satisfaction surveys	

[continued on next page]

_____ **8.** Continually changing menus

_____ **9.** Drive-through windows

_____ **10.** Standardized menus from location to location

Problem 18-3A

Cost computation, classification, and analysis

C3

Listed here are the total costs associated with the production of 1,000 drum sets manufactured by DrumBeat. The drum sets sell for $500 each.

Costs	Cost by Behavior		Cost by Function	
	Variable	Fixed	Product	Period
Plastic for casing—$17,000	$17,000		$17,000	
Wages of assembly workers—$82,000				
Property taxes on factory—$5,000				
Accounting staff salaries—$35,000				
Drum stands (1,000 stands outsourced)—$26,000				
Rent cost of equipment for sales staff—$10,000				
Upper management salaries—$125,000				
Annual flat fee for maintenance service—$10,000				
Sales commissions—$15 per unit				
Machinery depreciation—$40,000				

Required

Check   (1) Total variable cost, $125,000

1. Classify each cost and its amount as (*a*) either fixed or variable and (*b*) either product or period (the first cost is completed as an example).

2. Compute the manufacturing cost per drum set.

Analysis Component

3. Assume that 1,200 drum sets are produced in the next month. What do you predict will be the total cost of plastic for the casings and the per-unit cost of the plastic for the casings? Explain.

4. Assume that 1,200 drum sets are produced in the next month. What do you predict will be the total cost of property taxes and the per-unit cost of the property taxes? Explain.

Problem 18-4A

Cost classification and explanation

C3 C4

Assume that you must make a presentation to the marketing staff explaining the difference between product and period costs. Your supervisor tells you the marketing staff would also like clarification regarding prime and conversion costs and an explanation of how these terms fit with product and period cost. You are told that many on the staff are unable to classify costs in their merchandising activities.

Required

Prepare a one-page memorandum to your supervisor outlining your presentation to the marketing staff.

Problem 18-5A

Opportunity cost estimation and application

C1 C3

Refer to *Decision Maker,* **Purchase Manager,** in this chapter. Assume that you are the motorcycle manufacturer's managerial accountant. The purchasing manager asks you about preparing an estimate of the related costs for buying motorcycle seats from supplier (B). She tells you this estimate is needed because unless dollar estimates are attached to nonfinancial factors, such as lost production time, her supervisor will not give it full attention. The manager also shows you the following information.

● Production output is 1,000 motorcycles per year based on 250 production days a year.

● Production time per day is 8 hours at a cost of $2,000 per hour to run the production line.

● Lost production time due to poor quality is 1%.

● Satisfied customers purchase, on average, three motorcycles during a lifetime.

● Satisfied customers recommend the product, on average, to 5 other people.

● Marketing predicts that using seat (B) will result in 5 lost customers per year from repeat business and referrals.

● Average contribution margin per motorcycle is $3,000.

Required

Estimate the costs (including opportunity costs) of buying motorcycle seats from supplier (B). This problem requires that you think creatively and make reasonable estimates and, therefore, there could be more than one correct answer. (*Hint:* Reread the answer to *Decision Maker* and compare the cost savings for buying from supplier [B] to the sum of lost customer revenue from repeat business and referrals and the cost of lost production time.)

Check Estimated cost of lost production time, $40,000

Notaro's Boot Company makes specialty boots for the rodeo circuit. On December 31, 2007, the company had (*a*) 300 pairs of boots in finished goods inventory and (*b*) 1,200 heels at a cost of $8 each in raw materials inventory. During 2008, the company purchased 35,000 additional heels at $8 each and manufactured 16,600 pairs of boots.

Problem 18-6A
Ending inventory computation and evaluation

C2 C5

Required

1. Determine the unit and dollar amounts of raw materials inventory in heels at December 31, 2008.

Check (1) Ending (heel) inventory, $24,000 (3,000 units)

Analysis Component

2. Write a one-half page memorandum to the production manager explaining why a just-in-time inventory system for heels should be considered. Include the amount of working capital that can be reduced at December 31, 2008, if the ending heel raw material inventory is cut in half.

Shown here are annual financial data at December 31, 2008, taken from two different companies.

Problem 18-7A
Inventory computation and reporting

C3 C5 P1

mhhe.com/wildFAP18e

	Sports World Retail	Sno-Board Manufacturing
Beginning inventory		
Merchandise	$200,000	
Finished goods		$500,000
Cost of purchases	300,000	
Cost of goods manufactured		875,000
Ending inventory		
Merchandise	175,000	
Finished goods		225,000

Required

1. Compute the cost of goods sold section of the income statement at December 31, 2008, for each company. Include proper title and format in the solution.

2. Write a half-page memorandum to your instructor (*a*) identifying the inventory accounts and (*b*) describing where each is reported on the income statement and balance sheet for both companies.

Check (1) Sno-Board's cost of goods sold, $1,150,000

The following calendar year-end information is taken from the December 31, 2008, adjusted trial balance and other records of DeLeon Company.

Problem 18-8A
Manufacturing and income statements; inventory analysis P2

Advertising expense	$ 28,750	Direct labor	675,480
Depreciation expense—Office equipment	7,250	Income taxes expense	233,725
Depreciation expense—Selling equipment	8,600	Indirect labor	56,875
Depreciation expense—Factory equipment	33,550	Miscellaneous production costs	8,425
Factory supervision	102,600	Office salaries expense	63,000
Factory supplies used	7,350	Raw materials purchases	925,000
Factory utilities	33,000	Rent expense—Office space	22,000
Inventories		Rent expense—Selling space	26,100
Raw materials, December 31, 2007	166,850	Rent expense—Factory building	76,800
Raw materials, December 31, 2008	182,000	Maintenance expense—Factory equipment	35,400
Goods in process, December 31, 2007	15,700	Sales	4,525,000
Goods in process, December 31, 2008	19,380	Sales discounts	62,500
Finished goods, December 31, 2007	167,350	Sales salaries expense	392,560
Finished goods, December 31, 2008	136,490		

Required

1. Prepare the company's 2008 manufacturing statement.

2. Prepare the company's 2008 income statement that reports separate categories for (*a*) selling expenses
and (*b*) general and administrative expenses.

Analysis Component

3. Compute the (*a*) inventory turnover and (*b*) days' sales in inventory for both its raw materials inventory and its finished goods inventory (see Chapter 6). Discuss some possible reasons for differences
between these ratios for the two types of inventories.

Problem 18-9A
Manufacturing cycle time and
efficiency

A1

Oakwood Company produces oak bookcases to customer order. Oakwood received an order from a
customer to produce 5,000 bookcases. The following information is available for the production of the
bookcases.

Process time	6.0 days
Inspection time	0.8 days
Move time	3.2 days
Wait time	5.0 days

Required

1. Compute the company's manufacturing cycle time.

2. Compute the company's manufacturing cycle efficiency. Interpret your answer.

Analysis Component

3. Assume that Oakwood wishes to increase its manufacturing cycle efficiency to 0.75. What are some
ways that Oakwood can accomplish this?

PROBLEM SET B

Problem 18-1B
Managerial accounting role

C1 C2

This chapter described the purpose of managerial accounting in the context of the current business
environment. Review the *home electronics* section of your local newspaper; the Sunday paper is often
best. Review advertisements of home electronics and identify the manufacturers that offer these products and the factors on which they compete.

Required

Discuss the potential contributions and responsibilities of the managerial accounting professional in helping a home electronics manufacturer succeed. (*Hint:* Think about information and estimates that a managerial accountant might provide new entrants into the home electronics market.)

Problem 18-2B
Lean business concepts

C2

Eastman-Kodak manufactures digital cameras and must compete on lean manufacturing concepts. Match
each of the following activities that it engages in with the lean manufacturing concept it strives to achieve.

_____ **1.** Lenses are received daily based on customer
orders.

_____ **2.** Customers receive a satisfaction survey with
each camera purchased.

_____ **3.** The manufacturing process is standardized and
documented.

_____ **4.** Cameras are produced in small lots, and only
to customer order.

_____ **5.** Manufacturing facilities are arranged to reduce
move time and wait time.

_____ **6.** Kodak conducts focus groups to determine
new features that customers want in digital
cameras.

a. Total quality management (TQM)

b. Just-in-time (JIT)

c. Continuous improvement (CI)

[continued on next page]

_____ **7.** Orders received are filled within two business days.

_____ **8.** Kodak works with suppliers to reduce inspection time of incoming materials.

_____ **9.** Kodak monitors the market to determine what features its competitors are offering on digital cameras.

_____ **10.** Kodak asks production workers for ideas to improve production.

Listed here are the total costs associated with the production of 15,000 CDs manufactured by Hip-Hop. The CDs sell for $18 each.

Problem 18-3B
Cost computation, classification, and analysis

C3

Costs	Cost by Behavior		Cost by Function	
	Variable	Fixed	Product	Period
Plastic for CDs—$1,500	$1,500		$1,500	
Wages of assembly workers—$30,000				
Cost of factory rent—$6,750				
Systems staff salaries—$15,000				
Labeling (12,000 outsourced)—$3,750				
Cost of office equipment rent—$1,050				
Upper management salaries—$120,000				
Annual fixed fee for cleaning service—$4,520				
Sales commissions—$0.50 per CD				
Machinery depreciation—$18,000				

Required

1. Classify each cost and its amount as (_a_) either fixed or variable and (_b_) either product or period.

2. Compute the manufacturing cost per CD.

Check   (2) Total variable manufacturing cost, $35,250

Analysis Component

3. Assume that 10,000 CDs are produced in the next month. What do you predict will be the total cost of plastic for the CDs and the per-unit cost of the plastic for the CDs? Explain.

4. Assume that 10,000 CDs are produced in the next month. What do you predict will be the total cost of factory rent and the per-unit cost of the factory rent? Explain.

Assume that you must make a presentation to a client explaining the difference between prime and conversion costs. The client makes and sells 200,000 cookies per week. The client tells you that her sales staff also would like a clarification regarding product and period costs. She tells you that most of the staff lack training in managerial accounting.

Problem 18-4B
Cost classification and explanation

C3 C4

Required

Prepare a one-page memorandum to your client outlining your planned presentation to her sales staff.

Refer to _Decision Maker,_ **Purchase Manager,** in this chapter. Assume that you are the motorcycle manufacturer's managerial accountant. The purchasing manager asks you about preparing an estimate of the related costs for buying motorcycle seats from supplier (B). She tells you this estimate is needed because unless dollar estimates are attached to nonfinancial factors such as lost production time, her supervisor will not give it full attention. The manager also shows you the following information.

Problem 18-5B
Opportunity cost estimation and application

C1 C3

- Production output is 1,000 motorcycles per year based on 250 production days a year.
- Production time per day is 8 hours at a cost of $500 per hour to run the production line.
- Lost production time due to poor quality is 1%.
- Satisfied customers purchase, on average, three motorcycles during a lifetime.
- Satisfied customers recommend the product, on average, to four other people.
- Marketing predicts that using seat (B) will result in four lost customers per year from repeat business and referrals.
- Average contribution margin per motorcycle is $4,000.

Required

Estimate the costs (including opportunity costs) of buying motorcycle seats from supplier (B). This problem requires that you think creatively and make reasonable estimates and, therefore, there could be more than one correct answer. (*Hint:* Reread the answer to *Decision Maker,* and compare the cost savings for buying from supplier [B] to the sum of lost customer revenue from repeat business and referrals and the cost of lost production time.)

Problem 18-6B
Ending inventory computation
and evaluation

C2 C5

Check   (1) Ending (blade) inventory,
$120,000 (6,000 units)

Sharp Edges makes specialty skates for the ice skating circuit. On December 31, 2007, the company had (a) 1,500 skates in finished goods inventory and (b) 2,500 blades at a cost of $20 each in raw materials inventory. During 2008, Sharp Edges purchased 45,000 additional blades at $20 each and manufactured 20,750 pairs of skates.

Required

1. Determine the unit and dollar amounts of raw materials inventory in blades at December 31, 2008.

Analysis Component

2. Write a one-half page memorandum to the production manager explaining why a just-in-time inventory system for blades should be considered. Include the amount of working capital that can be reduced at December 31, 2008, if the ending blade raw material inventory is cut in half.

Problem 18-7B
Inventory computation
and reporting

C3 C5   P1

Shown here are annual financial data at December 31, 2008, taken from two different companies.

	Badger Retail	Naima Manufacturing
Beginning inventory		
Merchandise	$100,000	
Finished goods		$300,000
Cost of purchases	250,000	
Cost of goods manufactured		586,000
Ending inventory		
Merchandise	150,000	
Finished goods		200,000

Required

Check   (1) Badger cost of goods
sold, $200,000

1. Compute the cost of goods sold section of the income statement at December 31, 2008, for each company. Include proper title and format in the solution.

2. Write a half-page memorandum to your instructor (a) identifying the inventory accounts and (b) identifying where each is reported on the income statement and balance sheet for both companies.

Problem 18-8B
Manufacturing and income
statements; analysis of inventories

P2

The following calendar year-end information is taken from the December 31, 2008, adjusted trial balance and other records of Elegant Furniture.

Advertising expense	$ 20,250		Direct labor	562,500
Depreciation expense—Office equipment	8,440		Income taxes expense	136,700
Depreciation expense—Selling equipment	10,125		Indirect labor	59,000
Depreciation expense—Factory equipment	35,400		Miscellaneous production costs	8,440
Factory supervision	121,500		Office salaries expense	70,875
Factory supplies used	6,060		Raw materials purchases	894,375
Factory utilities	37,500		Rent expense—Office space	23,625
Inventories			Rent expense—Selling space	27,000
Raw materials, December 31, 2007	40,375		Rent expense—Factory building	93,500
Raw materials, December 31, 2008	70,430		Maintenance expense—Factory equipment	30,375
Goods in process, December 31, 2007	12,500		Sales	5,000,000
Goods in process, December 31, 2008	14,100		Sales discounts	57,375
Finished goods, December 31, 2007	177,200		Sales salaries expense	295,300
Finished goods, December 31, 2008	141,750			

Required

1. Prepare the company's 2008 manufacturing statement.

2. Prepare the company's 2008 income statement that reports separate categories for (*a*) selling expenses and (*b*) general and administrative expenses.

Check (1) Cost of goods manufactured, $1,816,995

Analysis Component

3. Compute the (*a*) inventory turnover and (*b*) days' sales in inventory for both its raw materials inventory and its finished goods inventory (see Chapter 6). Discuss some possible reasons for differences between these ratios for the two types of inventories.

Best Ink produces ink-jet printers for personal computers. Best Ink received an order for 500 printers from a customer. The following information is available for this order.

Problem 18-9B
Manufacturing cycle time and efficiency

A1

Process time	16.0 hours
Inspection time	3.5 hours
Move time	9.0 hours
Wait time	21.5 hours

Required

1. Compute the company's manufacturing cycle time.

2. Compute the company's manufacturing cycle efficiency. Interpret your answer.

Analysis Component

3. Assume that Best Ink wishes to increase its manufacturing cycle efficiency to 0.80. What are some ways that Best Ink can accomplish this?

 Problem Set C is available at the book's Website to reinforce and assess your learning.   **PROBLEM SET C**

(This serial problem began in Chapter 1 and continues through most of the book. If previous chapter segments were not completed, the serial problem can begin at this point. It is helpful, but not necessary, for you to use the Working Papers that accompany the book.)

SERIAL PROBLEM

Success Systems

SP 18   Adriana Lopez, owner of Success Systems, decides to diversify her business by also manufacturing computer workstation furniture.

Required

1. Classify the following manufacturing costs of Success Systems by behavior and traceability.

Product Costs	Cost by Behavior		Cost by Traceability	
	Variable	Fixed	Direct	Indirect
Glue to assemble workstation component parts	____	____	____	____
Laminate coverings for desktops	____	____	____	____
Wages of desk assembler	____	____	____	____
Taxes on assembly workshop	____	____	____	____
Depreciation on tools	____	____	____	____
Electricity for workshop	____	____	____	____
Monthly flat fee to clean workshop	____	____	____	____

2. Prepare a manufacturing statement for Success Systems for the month ended January 31, 2009. Assume the following manufacturing costs:

Direct materials: $2,125

Factory overhead: $460

Direct labor: $852

Beginning goods in process: none (December 31, 2008)

Ending goods in process: $1,796 (January 31, 2009)

Beginning finished goods inventory: none (December 31, 2008)

Ending finished goods inventory: $344 (January 31, 2009)

Check   (3) COGS, $1,297

3. Prepare the cost of goods sold section of a partial income statement for Success Systems for the month ended January 31, 2009.

BEYOND THE NUMBERS

REPORTING IN ACTION

C1   C2

BTN 18-1   Managerial accounting is more than recording, maintaining, and reporting financial results. Managerial accountants must provide managers with both financial and nonfinancial information including estimates, projections, and forecasts. There are many accounting estimates that management accountants must make, and **Best Buy** must notify shareholders of these estimates.

Required

1. Access and read Best Buy's "Critical Accounting Estimates" section (5 pages), which is part of its *Management's Discussion and Analysis of Financial Condition and Results of Operations* section, from either its annual report or its 10-K for the year ended February 26, 2005 [BestBuy.com]. What are some of the accounting estimates that Best Buy made in preparing its financial statements? What are some of the effects if the actual results of Best Buy differ from its assumptions?

2. What is the management accountant's role in determining those estimates?

Fast Forward

3. Access **Best Buy**'s annual report for a fiscal year ending after February 26, 2005, from either its Website [BestBuy.com] or the SEC's EDGAR database [www.sec.gov]. Answer the questions in parts (1) and (2) after reading the current MD&A section. Identify any major changes.

COMPARATIVE ANALYSIS

C1   C2

BTN 18-2   **Best Buy** and **Circuit City** are both merchandisers that rely on customer satisfaction. Access and read (1) Best Buy's "Strategic Initiatives" section [1 page] and (2) Circuit City's "Fiscal 2006 Outlook" section [2 pages]. Both sections are located in the respective company's *Management Discussion and Analysis of Financial Condition and Results of Operations* section from the annual report or 10-K. The Best Buy report is for the year ended February 26, 2005, and the Circuit City report is for the year ended February 28, 2005.

Required

1. Identify the strategic initiatives that each company put forward in its desire to better compete and succeed in the marketplace.

2. For each of these strategic initiatives for both companies, explain how it reflects (or does not reflect) a customer satisfaction focus.

BTN 18-3   Assume that you are the managerial accountant at Infostore, a manufacturer of hard drives, CDs, and diskettes. Its reporting year-end is December 31. The chief financial officer is concerned about having enough cash to pay the expected income tax bill because of poor cash flow management. On November 15, the purchasing department purchased excess inventory of CD raw materials in anticipation of rapid growth of this product beginning in January. To decrease the company's tax liability, the chief financial officer tells you to record the purchase of this inventory as part of supplies and expense it in the current year; this would decrease the company's tax liability by increasing expenses.

ETHICS CHALLENGE

C1   C3   C4

Required

1. In which account should the purchase of CD raw materials be recorded?

2. How should you respond to this request by the chief financial officer?

BTN 18-4   Write a one-page memorandum to a prospective college student about salary expectations for graduates in business. Compare and contrast the expected salaries for accounting (including different subfields such as public, corporate, tax, audit, and so forth), marketing, management, and finance majors. Prepare a graph showing average starting salaries (and those for experienced professionals in those fields if available). To get this information, stop by your school's career services office; libraries also have this information. The Website JobStar.org (click on *Salary Info*) also can get you started.

COMMUNICATING IN PRACTICE

BTN 18-5   Managerial accounting professionals follow a code of ethics. As a member of the Institute of Management Accountants, the managerial accountant must comply with Standards of Ethical Conduct.

TAKING IT TO THE NET

C1   C2

Required

Identify, print, and read the *Ethical Standards* posted at www.IMAnet.org. (Search using "ethical standards.")

BTN 18-6   The following calendar-year information is taken from the December 31, 2008, adjusted trial balance and other records of Dahlia Company.

TEAMWORK IN ACTION

C6   P2

Advertising expense	$ 19,125	Direct labor	650,750
Depreciation expense—Office equipment	8,750	Indirect labor	60,000
Depreciation expense—Selling equipment	10,000	Miscellaneous production costs	8,500
Depreciation expense—Factory equipment	32,500	Office salaries expense	100,875
Factory supervision	122,500	Raw materials purchases	872,500
Factory supplies used	15,750	Rent expense—Office space	21,125
Factory utilities	36,250	Rent expense—Selling space	25,750
Inventories		Rent expense—Factory building	79,750
Raw materials, December 31, 2007	177,500	Maintenance expense—Factory equipment	27,875
Raw materials, December 31, 2008	168,125	Sales	3,275,000
Goods in process, December 31, 2007	15,875	Sales discounts	57,500
Goods in process, December 31, 2008	14,000	Sales salaries expense	286,250
Finished goods, December 31, 2007	164,375		
Finished goods, December 31, 2008	129,000		

Required

1. *Each* team member is to be responsible for computing **one** of the following amounts. You are not to duplicate your teammates' work. Get any necessary amounts from teammates. Each member is to explain the computation to the team in preparation for reporting to class.

   a. Materials used.   **d.** Total cost of goods in process.

   b. Factory overhead.   **e.** Cost of goods manufactured.

   c. Total manufacturing costs.

2. Check your cost of goods manufactured with the instructor. If it is correct, proceed to part (3).

3. *Each* team member is to be responsible for computing **one** of the following amounts. You are not to duplicate your teammates' work. Get any necessary amounts from teammates. Each member is to explain the computation to the team in preparation for reporting to class.

   a. Net sales.   **d.** Total operating expenses.

   b. Cost of goods sold.   **e.** Net income or loss before taxes.

   c. Gross profit.

Point: Provide teams with transparencies and markers for presentation purposes.

BusinessWeek
ACTIVITY

C1   C2

BTN 18-7   Read the article "A CEO Explains 'the Concept of Lean'" in the July 19, 2005, issue of *BusinessWeek*. (The book's Website provides a free link.)

Required

1. What advantages does Donald E. Washkewicz see in **Parker Hannifin**'s change to a lean manufacturing environment? Explain.

2. Explain why the lean manufacturing environment does not reduce operating efficiencies.

ENTREPRENEURIAL DECISION

C1   C3

BTN 18-8   Chris Griffiths of **Garrison Guitars** must understand his manufacturing costs to effectively operate and succeed as a profitable and efficient company.

Required

1. What are the three main categories of manufacturing costs that Chris must monitor and control? Provide examples of each.

2. How can Chris make the Garrison Guitars' manufacturing process more cost effective? Provide examples of two useful managerial measures of time and efficiency.

HITTING THE ROAD

C1   C4

BTN 18-9   Visit your favorite fast-food restaurant. Observe its business operations.

Required

1. Describe all business activities from the time a customer arrives to the time that customer departs.

2. List all costs you can identify with the separate activities described in part 1.

3. Classify each cost from part 2 as fixed or variable, and explain your classification.

GLOBAL DECISION

Dixons

BTN 18-10   Access **Dixons**' annual report for the year ended May 1, 2004 (<u>Dixons-Group.com</u>). Read the section "Corporate Governance" dealing with the responsibilities of the board of directors.

Required

1. Identify the responsibilities of Dixons' board of directors.

2. How would management accountants be involved in assisting the board of directors in carrying out their responsibilities? Explain.

ANSWERS TO MULTIPLE CHOICE QUIZ

1. c
2. b
3. b
4. a
5. Beginning finished goods + Cost of goods manufactured (COGM) −
Ending finished goods = Cost of goods sold
$6,000 + COGM − $3,200 = $7,500
COGM = $4,700

19

Job Order Cost Accounting

A Look Back

Chapter 18 introduced managerial accounting and explained basic cost concepts. We also described the lean business model and the reporting of manufacturing activities, including the manufacturing statement.

A Look at This Chapter

We begin this chapter by describing a cost accounting system. We then explain the procedures used to determine costs using a job order costing system. We conclude with a discussion of over- and underapplied overhead.

A Look Ahead

Chapter 20 focuses on measuring costs in process production companies. We explain process production, describe how to assign costs to processes, and compute and analyze cost per equivalent unit.

Learning Objectives

CAP

Conceptual

C1 Explain the cost accounting system. *(p. 762)*

C2 Describe important features of job order production. *(p. 762)*

C3 Explain job cost sheets and how they are used in job order cost accounting. *(p. 764)*

Analytical

A1 Apply job order costing in pricing services. *(p. 774)*

Procedural

P1 Describe and record the flow of materials costs in job order cost accounting. *(p. 765)*

P2 Describe and record the flow of labor costs in job order cost accounting. *(p. 767)*

P3 Describe and record the flow of overhead costs in job order cost accounting. *(p. 769)*

P4 Determine adjustments for overapplied and underapplied factory overhead. *(p. 773)*

"We're saving lives ... it's awesome"
—Sandra Johnson
(Marco Johnson on left)

Business of Saving Lives

LANCASTER, CA—Witnessing needless injury and death, firefighter Marco Johnson began teaching first aid and CPR courses. Although he was performing a valuable community service, Marco wanted to do more. "I wish someone would start CPR or first aid before we get on the scene," says Marco of the anguish he sometimes feels at the site of an accident. "I think maybe a few more lives could be saved," he says. "Knowing the basics of CPR and first aid saves lives."

So Marco and his wife, Sandra, started Antelope Valley Medical College (AVMedicalCollege.com), a company devoted to training people in life-saving procedures. Sandra's tasks were to find clients and set times and places for instruction. "We made simple fliers and went right to daycare providers," says Marco. "[Then] we went to large corporations because we knew there were OSHA laws that had to be met."

But the early days brought several challenges. Marco and Sandra needed to monitor and control job costs for their training programs. Success depended not only on securing clients, but also on maintaining cost controls and emphasizing quality instruction. "There were times," says Marco, "when we looked at each other and said, 'What did we get ourselves into?' My wife would schedule appointments and

I would teach classes between shifts and on my days off," recalls Marco. Yet the couple carefully handled labor and overhead costs and soon grew profitable.

Today, the company uses state-of-the-art job order cost accounting to track program costs. This includes tracking the costs of labor and overhead, and managing those expenses. Cost accounting procedures help Marco and Sandra avoid the mistakes made by startups that fail to use costing techniques and then experience run-away costs. Recruiting top-notch personnel also controls labor costs. "[We] make sure they have a passion for what they're doing," insists Marco. "We want people at our institutions and our schools to care."

"We're saving lives," says Sandra. "It's awesome to know I was part of that with my husband." The public clearly agrees with their cause. After just eight years in business, annual revenues of Antelope Valley Medical College is projected to be over $7 million. Yet Marco and Sandra have never lost sight of their core mission. "Do whatever it takes," say Marco and Sandra. "It can mean the difference between life and death."

[Sources: *Antelope Valley Medical College Website,* May 2006; *Entrepreneur,* November and October 2004; *Black Enterprise,* 2003; *Kiplinger,* February 2005; *Making It!,* April 2005]

This chapter introduces a cost accounting system for assigning costs to the flow of goods through a production process. We then describe the details of a *job order cost accounting system.* Job order costing is frequently used by manufacturers of custom products or providers of custom services.

Manufacturers that use job order costing typically base it on a perpetual inventory system, which provides a continuous record of materials, goods in process, and finished goods inventories.

Job Order Cost Accounting

This section describes a cost accounting system and job order production and costing.

Cost Accounting System

An ever-increasing number of companies use a cost accounting system to generate timely and accurate inventory information. A **cost accounting system** records manufacturing activities using a *perpetual* inventory system, which continuously updates records for costs of materials, goods in process, and finished goods inventories. A cost accounting system also provides timely information about inventories and manufacturing costs per unit of product. This is especially helpful for managers' efforts to control costs and determine selling prices. (A **general accounting system** records manufacturing activities using a *periodic* inventory system. Some companies still use a general accounting system, but its use is declining as competitive forces and customer demands have increased pressures on companies to better manage inventories.)

Point: Cost accounting systems accumulate costs and then assign them to products and services.

The two basic types of cost accounting systems are *job order cost accounting* and *process cost accounting.* We describe job order cost accounting in this chapter. Process cost accounting is explained in Chapter 20.

Job Order Production

C2   Describe important features of job order production.

Many companies produce products individually designed to meet the needs of a specific customer. Each customized product is manufactured separately and its production is called **job order production,** or *job order manufacturing* (also called *customized production,* which is the production of products in response to special orders). Examples of such products include special-order machines, a factory building, custom jewelry, wedding invitations, and artwork.

Topic Tackler

PLUS

The production activities for a customized product represent a **job.** The principle of customization is equally applicable to both manufacturing *and* service companies. Most service companies meet customers' needs by performing a custom service for a specific customer. Examples of such services include an accountant auditing a client's financial statements, an interior designer remodeling an office, a wedding consultant planning and supervising a reception, and a lawyer defending a client. Whether the setting is manufacturing or services, job order operations involve meeting the needs of customers by producing or performing custom jobs.

Boeing's aerospace division is one example of a job order production system. Its primary business is twofold: (1) design, develop, and integrate space carriers and (2) provide systems engineering and integration of Department of Defense (DoD) systems. Many of its orders are customized and produced through job order operations.

When a job involves producing more than one unit of a custom product, it is often called a **job lot.** Products produced as job lots could include benches for a church, imprinted T-shirts for a 10K race or company picnic, or advertising signs for a chain of stores. Although these orders involve more than one unit, the volume of production is typically low, such as 50 benches, 200 T-shirts, or 100 signs. Another feature of job order production is the diversity, often called *heterogeneity,* of the products produced. Namely, each customer order is likely to differ from another in some important respect. These variations can be minor or major.

Point: Many professional examinations including the CPA and CMA exams require knowledge of job order and process cost accounting.

Events in Job Order Costing

The initial event in a normal job order operation is the receipt of a customer order for a custom product. This causes the company to begin work on a job. A less common case occurs when management decides to begin work on a job before it has a signed contract. This is referred to as *jobs produced on speculation.*

The first step in both cases is to predict the cost to complete the job. This cost depends on the product design prepared by either the customer or the producer. The second step is to negotiate a sales price and decide whether to pursue the job. Other than for government or other cost-plus contracts, the selling price is determined by market factors. Producers evaluate the market price, compare it to cost, and determine whether the profit on the job is reasonable. If the profit is not reasonable, the producer would determine a desired **target cost.** The third step is for the producer to schedule production of the job to meet the customer's needs and to fit within its own production constraints. Preparation of this work schedule should consider workplace facilities including equipment, personnel, and supplies. Once this schedule is complete, the producer can place orders for raw materials. Production occurs as materials and labor are applied to the job.

An overview of job order production activity is shown in Exhibit 19.1. This exhibit shows the March production activity of Road Warriors, which manufactures security-equipped cars and trucks. The company converts any vehicle by giving it a diversity of security items such as alarms, reinforced exterior, bulletproof glass, and bomb detectors. The company began by catering to high-profile celebrities, but it now caters to anyone who desires added security in a vehicle.

Job order production for Road Warriors requires materials, labor, and overhead costs. Recall that direct materials are goods used in manufacturing that are clearly identified with a particular job. Similarly, direct labor is effort devoted to a particular job. Overhead costs support production of more than one job. Common overhead items are depreciation on factory buildings and equipment, factory supplies, supervision, maintenance, cleaning, and utilities.

Exhibit 19.1 shows that materials, labor, and overhead are added to Jobs B15, B16, B17, B18, and B19 during March. Road Warriors completed Jobs B15, B16, and B17 in March and delivered Jobs B15 and B16 to customers. At the end of March, Jobs B18 and B19 remain in goods in process inventory and Job B17 is in finished goods

Point: Some jobs are priced on a *cost-plus basis:* The customer pays the manufacturer for costs incurred on the job plus a negotiated amount or rate of profit.

Decision Insight

Custom Design Managers once saw companies as the center of a solar system orbited by suppliers and customers. Now the customer has become the center of the business universe. Companies such as **Dell** encourage consumers to customize products. Soon consumers may be able to personalize almost any product, from cellular phones to appliances to furniture.

Decision Insight

Target Costing Many producers determine a target cost for their jobs. Target cost is determined as follows: Expected selling price − Desired profit = Target cost. If the projected target cost of the job as determined by job costing is too high, the producer can apply *value engineering,* which is a method of determining ways to reduce job cost until the target cost is met.

Exhibit 19.1

Job Order Production Activities

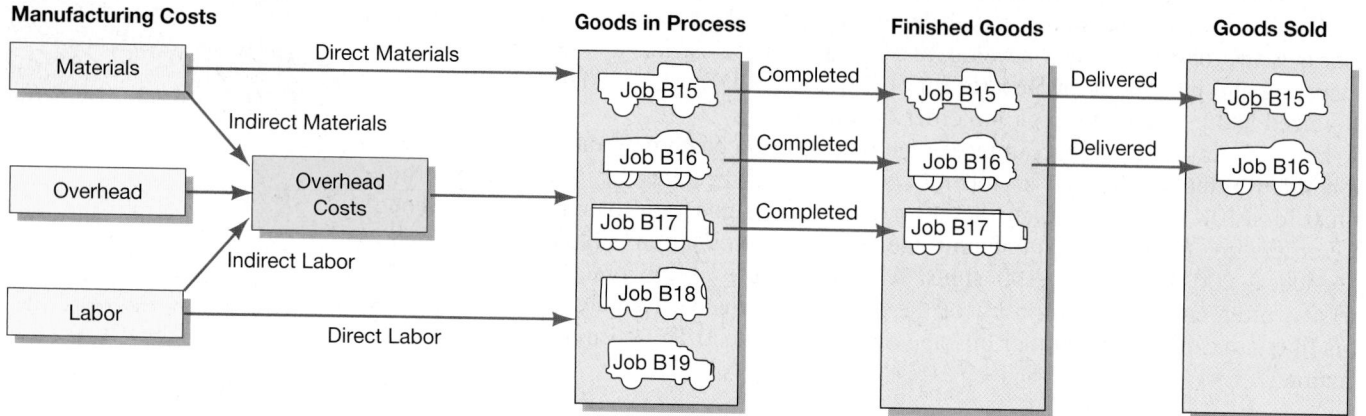

Management Consultant   One of your tasks is to control and manage costs for a consulting company. At the end of a recent month, you find that three consulting jobs were completed and two are 60% complete. Each unfinished job is estimated to cost $10,000 and to earn a revenue of $12,000. You are unsure how to recognize goods in process inventory and record costs and revenues. Do you recognize any inventory? If so, how much? How much revenue is recorded for unfinished jobs this month?

inventory. Both labor and materials costs are also separated into their direct and indirect components. Their indirect amounts are added to overhead. Total overhead cost is then allocated to the various jobs.

Job Cost Sheet

C3   Explain job cost sheets and how they are used in job order cost accounting.

General ledger accounts usually do not provide the accounting information that managers of job order cost operations need to plan and control production activities. This is so because the needed information often requires more detailed data. Such detailed data are usually stored in subsidiary records controlled by general ledger accounts. Subsidiary records store information about raw materials, overhead costs, jobs in process, finished goods, and other items. This section describes the use of these records.

A major aim of a **job order cost accounting system** is to determine the cost of producing each job or job lot. In the case of a job lot, the system also aims to compute the cost per unit. The accounting system must include separate records for each job to accomplish this, and it must capture information about costs incurred and charge these costs to each job.

A **job cost sheet** is a separate record maintained for each job. Exhibit 19.2 shows a job cost sheet for an alarm system that Road Warriors produced for a customer. This job cost sheet identifies the customer, the job number assigned, the product, and key dates. Costs incurred on the job are immediately recorded on this sheet. When each job is complete, the supervisor enters the date of completion, records any remarks, and signs the sheet. The job cost sheet in Exhibit 19.2 classifies costs as direct materials, direct labor, or overhead. It shows that a total of $600 in direct materials is added to Job B15 on four different dates. It also shows seven entries for direct labor costs that total $1,000. Road Warriors *allocates* (also termed *applies, assigns,* or *charges*) factory overhead costs of $1,600 to this job using an allocation rate of 160% of direct labor cost (160% × $1,000)—we discuss overhead allocation later in this chapter.

Point: Factory overhead consists of costs (other than direct materials and direct labor) that ensure the production activities are carried out.

While a job is being produced, its accumulated costs are kept in **Goods in Process Inventory.** The collection of job cost sheets for all jobs in process makes up a subsidiary ledger controlled by the Goods in Process Inventory account in the general ledger. Managers use job cost sheets to monitor costs incurred to date and to predict and control costs for each job.

When a job is finished, its job cost sheet is completed and moved from the jobs in process file to the finished jobs file. This latter file acts as a subsidiary ledger controlled by the **Finished**

Exhibit 19.2

Job Cost Sheet

Goods Inventory account. When a finished job is delivered to a customer, the job cost sheet is moved to a permanent file supporting the total cost of goods sold. This permanent file contains records from both current and prior periods.

Point: Documents (electronic and paper) are crucial in a job order system, and the job cost sheet is a cornerstone. Understanding it aids in grasping concepts of capitalizing product costs and product cost flow.

Quick Check

Answers—p. 779

1. Which of these products is likely to involve job order production? (a) inexpensive watches, (b) racing bikes, (c) bottled soft drinks, or (d) athletic socks.

2. What is the difference between a job and a job lot?

3. Which of these statements is correct? (a) The collection of job cost sheets for unfinished jobs makes up a subsidiary ledger controlled by the Goods in Process Inventory account, (b) Job cost sheets are financial statements provided to investors, or (c) A separate job cost sheet is maintained in the general ledger for each job in process.

4. What three costs are normally accumulated on job cost sheets?

Job Order Cost Flows and Reports

Materials Cost Flows and Documents

This section focuses on the flow of materials costs and the related documents in a job order cost accounting system. We begin analysis of the flow of materials costs by examining Exhibit 19.3. When materials are first received from suppliers, the employees count and inspect them and record the items' quantity and cost on a receiving report. The receiving report serves as the *source document* for recording materials received in both a materials ledger card and in the general ledger. In nearly all job order cost systems, **materials ledger cards** (or files) are perpetual records that are updated each time units are purchased and each time units are issued for use in production.

P1 Describe and record the flow of materials costs in job order cost accounting.

Materials

Point: Some companies certify certain suppliers based on the quality of their materials. Goods received from these suppliers are not always inspected by the purchaser to save costs.

Exhibit 19.3

Materials Cost Flows through
Subsidiary Records

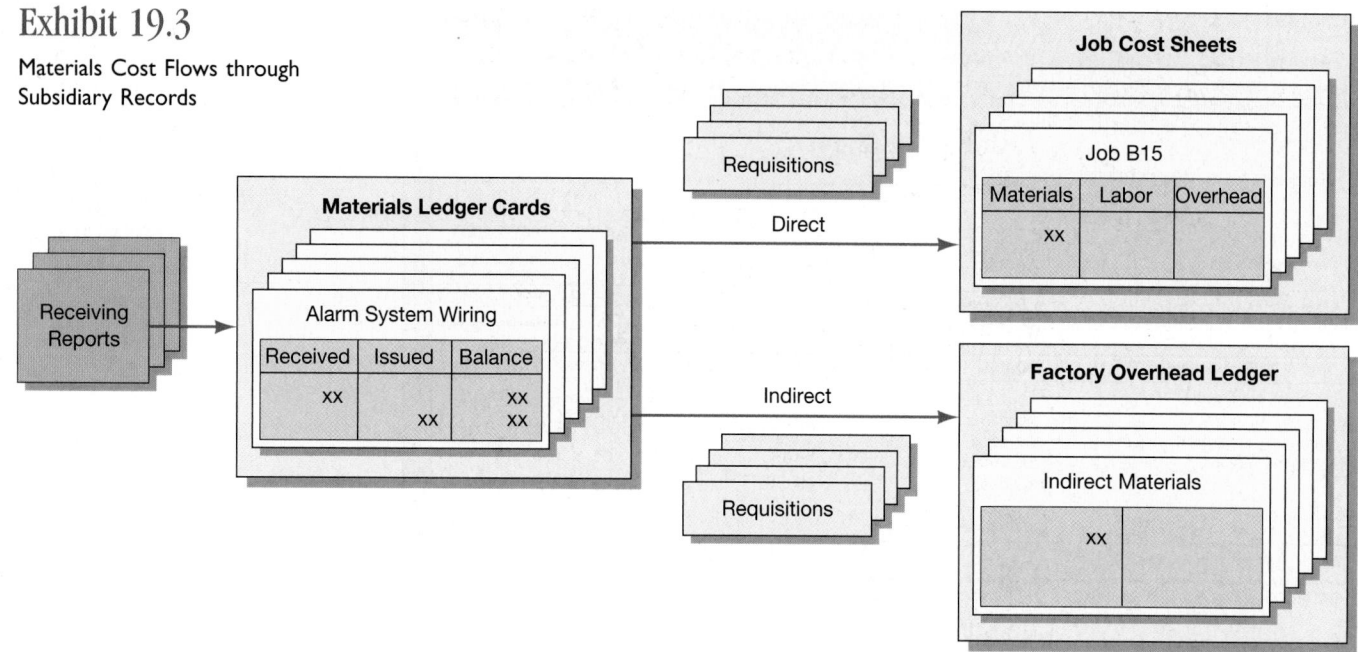

To illustrate the purchase of materials, Road Warriors acquired $450 of wiring and related materials on March 7, 2008. This purchase is recorded as follows.

Assets = Liabilities + Equity
+450   +450

Mar. 4	Raw Materials Inventory—M-347.	450	
	Accounts Payable		450
	To record purchase of materials for production.		

Exhibit 19.3 shows that materials can be requisitioned for use either on a specific job (direct materials) or as overhead (indirect materials). Cost of direct materials flows from the materials ledger card to the job cost sheet. The cost of indirect materials flows from the materials ledger card to the Indirect Materials account in the factory overhead ledger, which is a subsidiary ledger controlled by the Factory Overhead account in the general ledger.

Exhibit 19.4 shows a materials ledger card for material received and issued by Road Warriors. The card identifies the item as alarm system wiring and shows the item's stock number, its location in the storeroom, information about the maximum and minimum quantities that should be available, and the reorder quantity. For example, alarm system wiring is issued and recorded on March 7, 2008. The job cost sheet in Exhibit 19.2 showed that Job B15 used this wiring.

Exhibit 19.4

Materials Ledger Card

Road Warriors

Item ___Alarm system wiring___   Stock No. __M–347__   Location in Storeroom __Bin 137__

Maximum quantity __5 units__   Minimum quantity __1 unit__   Quantity to reorder __2 units__

	Received				Issued				Balance		
Date	Receiving Report Number	Units	Unit Price	Total Price	Requi-sition Number	Units	Unit Price	Total Price	Units	Unit Price	Total Price
									1	225.00	225.00
3/ 4/2008	C-7117	2	225.00	450.00					3	225.00	675.00
3/ 7/2008					R–4705	1	225.00	225.00	2	225.00	450.00

When materials are needed in production, a production manager prepares a **materials requisition** and sends it to the materials manager. The requisition shows the job number, the type of material, the quantity needed, and the signature of the manager authorized to make the requisition. Exhibit 19.5 shows the materials requisition for alarm system wiring for Job B15. To see how this requisition ties to the flow of costs, compare the information on the requisition with the March 7, 2008, data in Exhibits 19.2 and 19.4.

Exhibit 19.5

Materials Requisition

Road Warriors

MATERIALS REQUISITION NUMBER R–4705

Job No. _____ B15 _____   Date _____ 3/7/2008 _____

Material Stock No. ____ M–347 ____   Material Description ___ Alarm system wiring ___

Quantity Requested _____ 1 _____   Requested By _____ C. Luther _____

Quantity Provided _____ 1 _____   Date Provided ___ 3/7/2008 ___

Filled By ____ M. Bateman ____   Material Received By ____ C. Luther ____

Remarks _____

The use of alarm system wiring on Job B15 yields the following entry (locate this cost item in the job cost sheet shown in Exhibit 19.2).

Mar. 7	Goods in Process Inventory—Job B15............	225	
	Raw Materials Inventory—M-347............		225
	To record use of material on Job B15.		

Assets = Liabilities + Equity
+225
−225

This entry is posted both to its general ledger accounts and to subsidiary records. Posting to subsidiary records includes a debit to a job cost sheet and a credit to a materials ledger card. (*Note:* An entry to record use of indirect materials is the same as that for direct materials *except* the debit is to Factory Overhead. In the subsidiary factory overhead ledger, this entry is posted to Indirect Materials.)

Point: Requisitions are often accumulated and recorded in one entry. The frequency of entries depends on the job, the industry, and management procedures.

Labor Cost Flows and Documents

Exhibit 19.6 shows the flow of labor costs from clock cards and the Factory Payroll account to subsidiary records of the job order cost accounting system. Recall that costs in subsidiary records give detailed information needed to manage and control operations.

Labor

The flow of costs in Exhibit 19.6 begins with **clock cards.** Employees commonly use these cards to record the number of hours worked, and they serve as source documents for entries to record labor costs. Clock card data on the number of hours worked is used at the end of each pay period to determine total labor cost. This amount is then debited to the Factory Payroll account, a temporary account containing the total payroll cost (both direct and indirect). Payroll cost is later allocated to both specific jobs and overhead.

According to clock card data, workers earned $1,500 for the week ended March 5. Illustrating the flow of labor costs, the accrual and payment of these wages are recorded as follows.

P2 Describe and record the flow of labor costs in job order cost accounting.

Point: Indirect materials are included in overhead on the job cost sheet. Assigning overhead costs to products is described in the next section.

Mar. 6	Factory payroll.............................	1,500	
	Cash		1,500
	To record the weekly payroll.		

Assets = Liabilities + Equity
−1,500   −1,500

Exhibit 19.6

Labor Cost Flows through Subsidiary Records

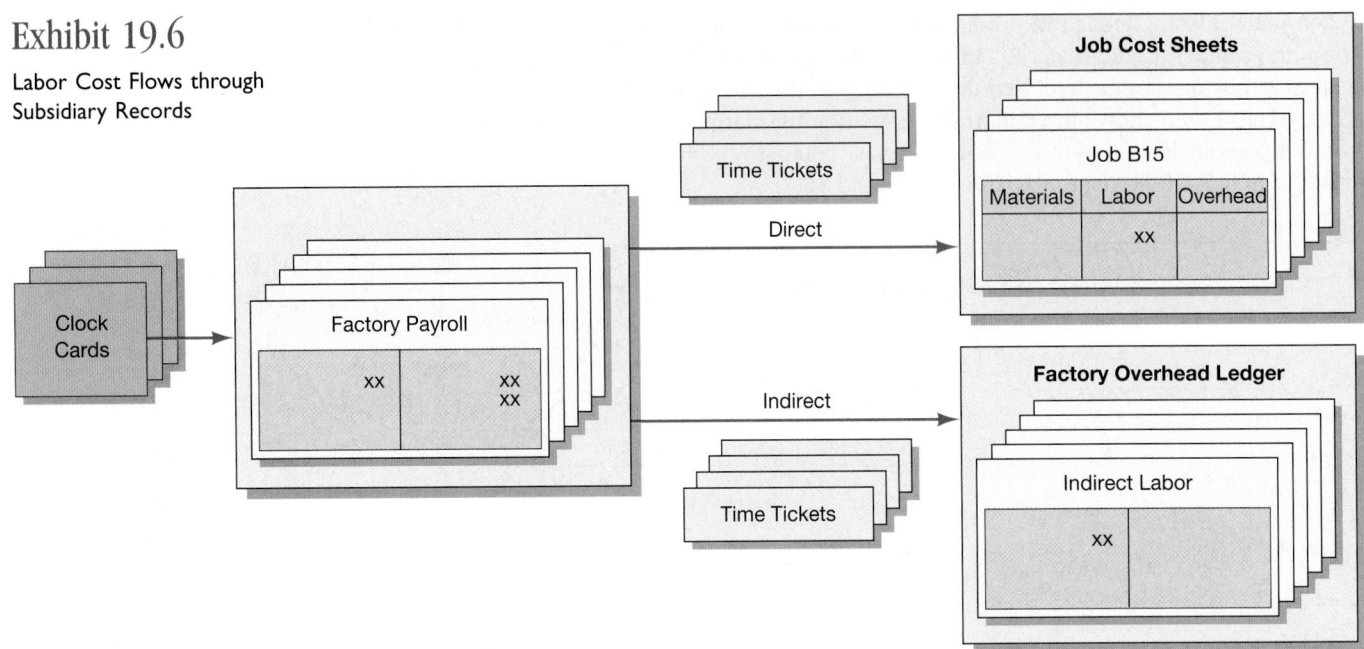

To assign labor costs to specific jobs and to overhead, we must know how each employee's time is used and its costs. Source documents called **time tickets** usually capture these data. Employees regularly fill out time tickets to report how much time they spent on each job. An employee who works on several jobs during a day completes a separate time ticket for each job. Tickets are also prepared for time charged to overhead as indirect labor. A supervisor signs an employee's time ticket to confirm its accuracy.

Exhibit 19.7 shows a time ticket reporting the time a Road Warrior employee spent working on Job B15. The employee's supervisor signed the ticket to confirm its accuracy. The hourly rate and total labor cost are computed after the time ticket is turned in. To see the effect of this time ticket on the job cost sheet, look at the entry dated March 8, 2008, in Exhibit 19.2.

"It's on Corporate Standard Time...
It loses an hour of your pay every day."

Exhibit 19.7

Time Ticket

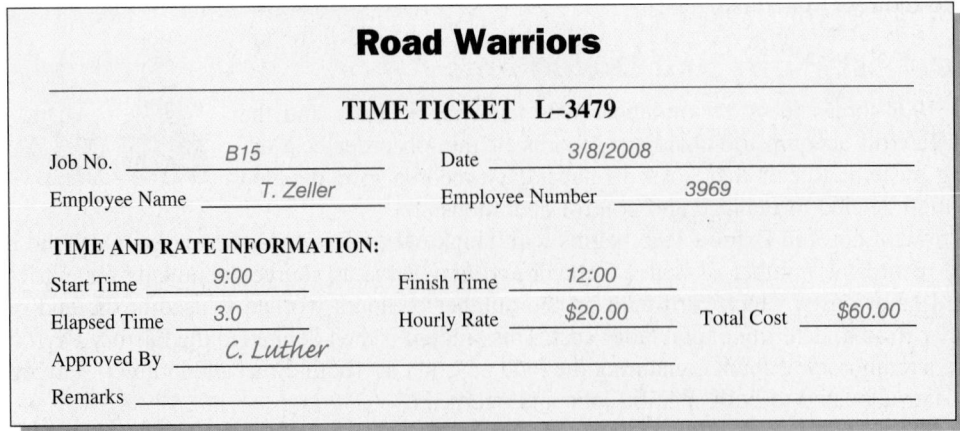

When time tickets report labor used on a specific job, this cost is recorded as direct labor. The following entry records the data from the time ticket in Exhibit 19.7.

Assets = Liabilities + Equity			
+60	+60		

Mar. 8	Goods in Process Inventory—Job B15	60	
	Factory Payroll		60
	To record direct labor used on Job B15.		

The debit in this entry is posted both to the general ledger account and to the appropriate job cost sheet. (*Note:* An entry to record indirect labor is the same as for direct labor *except* that it debits Factory Overhead and credits Factory Payroll. In the subsidiary factory overhead ledger, the debit in this entry is posted to the Indirect Labor account.)

Point: In the accounting equation, we treat accounts such as Factory Overhead and Factory Payroll as temporary accounts, which hold various expenses until they are allocated to balance sheet or income statement accounts.

Overhead Cost Flows and Documents

Factory overhead (or simply overhead) cost flows are shown in Exhibit 19.8. Factory overhead includes all production costs other than direct materials and direct labor. Two sources of overhead costs are indirect materials and indirect labor. These costs are recorded from requisitions for indirect materials and time tickets for indirect labor. Two other sources of overhead are (1) vouchers authorizing payments for items such as supplies or utilities and (2) adjusting entries for costs such as depreciation.

Overhead

P3 Describe and record the flow of overhead costs in job order cost accounting.

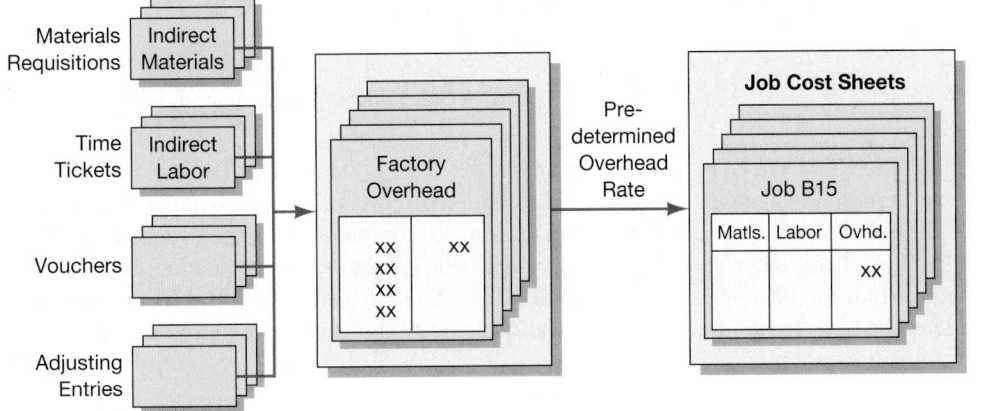

Exhibit 19.8

Overhead Cost Flows through Subsidiary Records

Factory overhead usually includes many different costs and, thus, a separate account for each is often maintained in a subsidiary factory overhead ledger. This ledger is controlled by the Factory Overhead account in the general ledger. Factory Overhead is a temporary account that accumulates costs until they are allocated to jobs.

Topic Tackler PLUS

19-2

Recall that overhead costs are recorded with debits to the Factory Overhead account and with credits to other accounts such as Cash, Accounts Payable, and Accumulated Depreciation—Equipment. In the subsidiary factory overhead ledger, the debits are posted to their respective accounts such as Depreciation Expense—Equipment, Insurance Expense—Warehouse, or Amortization Expense—Patents.

To illustrate the recording of overhead, the following two entries reflect the depreciation of factory equipment and the accrual of utilities, respectively, for the week ended March 6.

Mar. 6	Factory Overhead	600	
	Accumulated Depreciation—Equipment		600
	To record depreciation on factory equipment.		
Mar. 6	Factory Overhead	250	
	Utilities Payable.		250
	To record the accrual of factory utilities.		

Assets = Liabilities + Equity
−600   −600

Assets = Liabilities + Equity
          +250   −250

Exhibit 19.8 shows that overhead costs flow from the Factory Overhead account to job cost sheets. Because overhead is made up of costs not directly associated with specific jobs or job lots, we cannot determine the dollar amount incurred on a specific job. We know, however, that overhead costs represent a necessary part of business activities. If a job cost is to include all costs needed to complete the job, some amount of overhead must be included. Given the difficulty in determining the overhead amount for a specific job, however, we allocate overhead to individual jobs in some reasonable manner.

We generally allocate overhead by linking it to another factor used in production, such as direct labor or machine hours. The factor to which overhead costs are linked is known as the

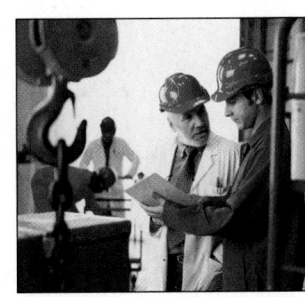

allocation base. A manager must think carefully about how many and which allocation bases to use. This managerial decision influences the accuracy with which overhead costs are allocated to individual jobs. In Exhibit 19.2, overhead is expressed as 160% of direct labor. We then allocate overhead by multiplying 160% by the estimated amount of direct labor on the jobs.

Point: The predetermined overhead rate is computed at the start of the period and is used throughout the period to allocate overhead to jobs.

Point: Predetermined overhead rates can be estimated using mathematical equations, statistical analysis, or professional experience.

We cannot wait until the end of a period to allocate overhead to jobs because perpetual inventory records are part of the job order costing system (demanding up-to-date costs). Instead, we must predict overhead in advance and assign it to jobs so that a job's total costs can be estimated prior to its completion. This estimated cost is useful for managers in many decisions including setting prices. Being able to estimate overhead in advance requires a **predetermined overhead rate,** also called *predetermined overhead allocation* (or *application*) *rate.* This rate requires an estimate of total overhead cost and an allocation factor such as total direct labor cost before the start of the period. Exhibit 19.9 shows the usual formula for computing a predetermined overhead rate (estimates are commonly based on annual amounts). This rate is used during the period to allocate overhead to jobs. It is common for companies to use multiple activity (allocation) bases and multiple predetermined overhead rates for different types of products and services.

Exhibit 19.9

Predetermined Overhead Allocation Rate Formula

$$\text{Predetermined overhead rate} = \frac{\text{Estimated overhead costs}}{} \div \frac{\text{Estimated activity base}}{}$$

Example: If management predicts total direct labor costs of $100,000 and total overhead costs of $200,000, what is its predetermined overhead rate? *Answer:* 200% of direct labor cost.

To illustrate, Road Warriors allocates overhead by linking it to direct labor. At the start of the current period, management predicts total direct labor costs of $125,000 and total overhead costs of $200,000. Using these estimates, management computes its predetermined overhead rate as 160% of direct labor cost ($200,000 ÷ $125,000). Specifically, reviewing the job order cost sheet in Exhibit 19.2, we see that $1,000 of direct labor went into Job B15. We then use the predetermined overhead rate of 160% to allocate $1,600 of overhead to this job. The entry to record this allocation is

Assets = Liabilities + Equity
+1,600   +1,600

Mar. 11	Goods in Process Inventory—Job B15.	1,600	
	Factory Overhead.		1,600
	To assign overhead to Job B15.		

Since the allocation rate for overhead is estimated at the start of a period, the total amount assigned to jobs during a period rarely equals the amount actually incurred. We explain how this difference is treated later in this chapter.

Summary of Cost Flows

We showed journal entries for charging Goods in Process Inventory (Job B15) with the cost of (1) direct materials requisitions, (2) direct labor

Point: Study the flow of manufacturing costs through general ledger accounts and job cost sheets. Use Exhibit 19.11 as reinforcement.

time tickets, and (3) factory overhead. We made separate entries for each of these costs, but they are usually recorded in one entry. Specifically, materials requisitions are often collected for a day or a week and recorded with a single entry summarizing them. The same is done with labor time tickets. When summary entries are made, supporting schedules of the jobs charged and the types of materials used provide the basis for postings to subsidiary records.

To show all production cost flows for a period and their related entries, we again look at Road Warriors' activities. Exhibit 19.10 shows costs linked to all of Road Warriors' production activities for March. Road Warriors did not have any jobs in process at the beginning of March, but it did apply materials, labor, and overhead costs to five new jobs in March. Jobs B15 and B16 are completed and delivered to customers in March, Job B17 is completed but not delivered, and Jobs B18 and B19 are still in process. Exhibit 19.10 also shows purchases of raw materials for $2,750, labor costs incurred for $5,300, and overhead costs of $6,720.

The upper part of Exhibit 19.11 shows the flow of these costs through general ledger accounts and the end-of-month balances in key subsidiary records. Arrow lines are numbered

Exhibit 19.10

Job Order Costs of All Production Activities

Explanation	Materials	Labor	Overhead Incurred	Overhead Allocated	Goods in Process	Finished Goods	Cost of Goods Sold
ROAD WARRIORS							
Job Order Manufacturing Costs							
For Month Ended March 31, 2008							
Job B15	$ 600	$1,000		$1,600			$3,200
Job B16	300	800		1,280			2,380
Job B17	500	1,100		1,760		$3,360	
Job B18	150	700		1,120	$1,970		
Job B19	250	600		960	1,810		
Total job costs	1,800	4,200		$6,720	$3,780	$3,360	$5,580
Indirect materials	550		$ 550				
Indirect labor		1,100	1,100				
Other overhead			5,070				
Total costs used in production	2,350	$5,300	$6,720				
Ending materials inventory	1,400						
Materials available	3,750						
Less beginning materials inventory	(1,000)						
Materials purchased	$2,750						

Exhibit 19.11

Job Order Cost Flows and Ending Job Cost Sheets

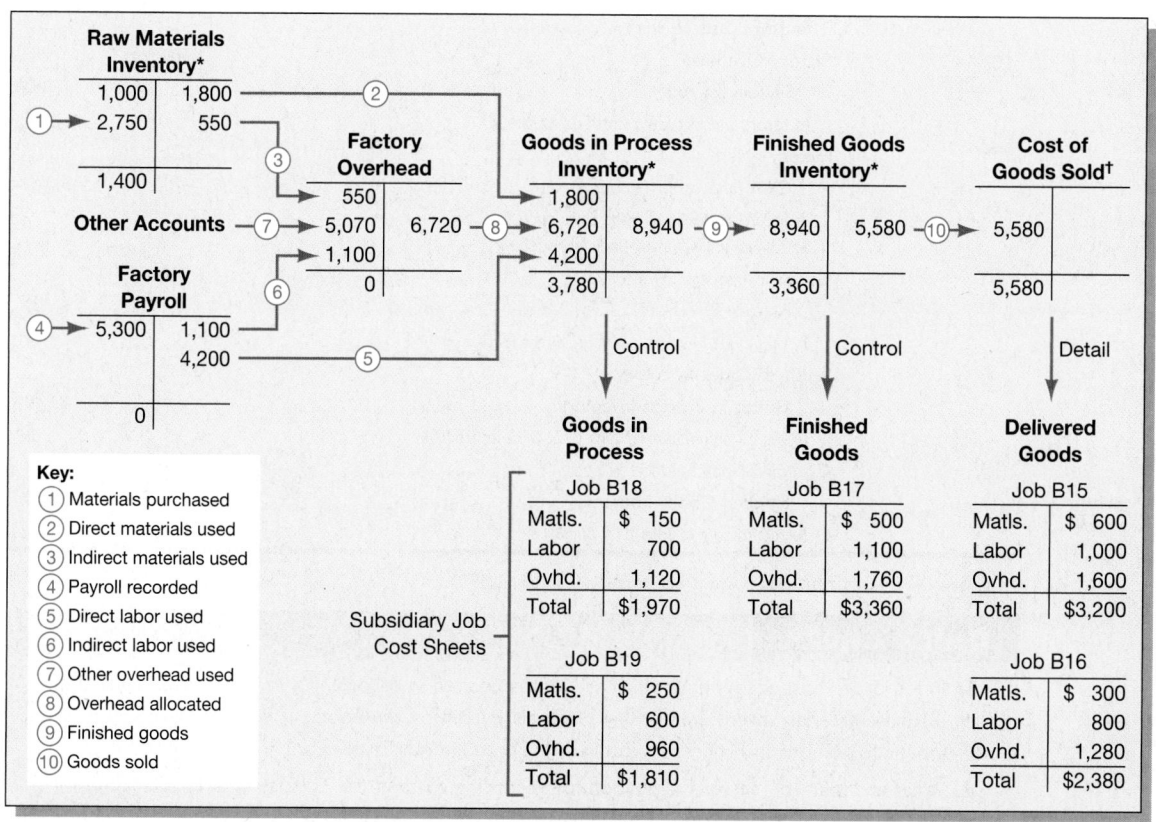

* The ending balances in the inventory accounts are carried to the balance sheet.
† The Cost of Goods Sold balance is carried to the income statement.

Decision Maker Answer—p. 779

Entrepreneur Competitors' prices on one of your product segments are lower than yours. Of the total product cost used in setting your prices, 53% is overhead allocated using direct labor hours. You believe that product costs are distorted and wonder whether there is a better way to allocate overhead and to set product price. What do you suggest?

to show the flows of costs for March. Each numbered cost flow reflects several entries made in March. The lower part of Exhibit 19.11 shows summarized job cost sheets and their status at the end of March. The sum of costs assigned to the jobs in process ($1,970 + $1,810) equals the $3,780 balance in Goods in Process Inventory shown in Exhibit 19.10. Also, costs assigned to Job B17 equal the $3,360 balance in Finished Goods Inventory. The sum of costs assigned to Jobs B15 and B16 ($3,200 + $2,380) equals the $5,580 balance in Cost of Goods Sold.

Exhibit 19.12 shows each cost flow with a single entry summarizing the actual individual entries made in March. Each entry is numbered to link with the arrow lines in Exhibit 19.11.

Exhibit 19.12

Entries for Job Order Production Costs*

①	Raw Materials Inventory..........................	2,750	
	Accounts Payable		2,750
	Acquired materials on credit for factory use.		
②	Goods in Process Inventory	1,800	
	Raw Materials Inventory		1,800
	To assign costs of direct materials used.		
③	Factory Overhead	550	
	Raw Materials Inventory		550
	To record use of indirect materials.		
④	Factory Payroll	5,300	
	Cash (and other accounts)		5,300
	To record salaries and wages of factory workers (including various payroll liabilities).		
⑤	Goods in Process Inventory	4,200	
	Factory Payroll		4,200
	To assign costs of direct labor used.		
⑥	Factory Overhead	1,100	
	Factory Payroll		1,100
	To record indirect labor costs as overhead.		
⑦	Factory Overhead	5,070	
	Cash (and other accounts)		5,070
	To record factory overhead costs such as insurance, utilities, rent, and depreciation.		
⑧	Goods in Process Inventory	6,720	
	Factory Overhead...........................		6,720
	To apply overhead at 160% of direct labor.		
⑨	Finished Goods Inventory........................	8,940	
	Goods in Process Inventory....................		8,940
	To record completion of Jobs B15, B16, and B17.		
⑩	Cost of Goods Sold............................	5,580	
	Finished Goods Inventory		5,580
	To record sale of Jobs B15 and B16.		

Point: *Actual* overhead is debited to Factory Overhead. *Allocated* overhead is credited to Factory Overhead.

* Transactions are numbered to be consistent with arrow lines in Exhibit 19.11.

Quick Check Answers—p. 779

5. In job order cost accounting, which account is debited in recording a raw materials requisition? (a) Raw Materials Inventory, (b) Raw Materials Purchases, (c) Goods in Process Inventory if for a job, or (d) Goods in Process Inventory if they are indirect materials.

6. What are four sources of information for recording costs in the Factory Overhead account?

7. Why does job order cost accounting require a predetermined overhead rate?

8. What events result in a debit to Factory Payroll? What events result in a credit?

Adjustment of Overapplied or Underapplied Overhead

Refer to the debits in the Factory Overhead account in Exhibit 19.11 (or Exhibit 19.12). The total cost of factory overhead incurred during March is $6,720 ($550 + $5,070 + $1,100). The $6,720 exactly equals the amount assigned to goods in process inventory (see arrow line ⑧). Therefore, the overhead incurred equals the overhead applied in March. The amount of overhead incurred rarely equals the amount of overhead applied, however, because a job order cost accounting system uses a predetermined overhead rate in applying factory overhead costs to jobs. This rate is determined using estimated amounts before the period begins, and estimates rarely equal the exact amounts actually incurred. This section explains what we do when too much or too little overhead is applied to jobs.

Underapplied Overhead

When less overhead is applied than is actually incurred, the remaining debit balance in the Factory Overhead account at the end of the period is called **underapplied overhead.** To illustrate, assume that Road Warriors actually incurred *other overhead costs* of $5,550 instead of the $5,070 shown in Exhibit 19.11. This yields an actual total overhead cost of $7,200 in March. Since the amount of overhead applied was only $6,720, the Factory Overhead account is left with a $480 debit balance as shown in the ledger account in Exhibit 19.13.

P4   Determine adjustments for overapplied and underapplied factory overhead.

Factory Overhead				Acct. No. 540
Date	Explanation	Debit	Credit	Balance
Mar. 31	Indirect materials cost	550		550 Dr.
31	Indirect labor cost	1,100		1,650 Dr.
31	Other overhead cost	5,550		7,200 Dr.
31	Overhead costs applied to jobs		6,720	480 Dr.

Exhibit 19.13

Underapplied Overhead in the Factory Overhead Ledger Account

The $480 debit balance reflects manufacturing costs not assigned to jobs. This means that the balances in Goods in Process Inventory, Finished Goods Inventory, and Cost of Goods Sold do not include all production costs incurred. When the underapplied overhead amount is immaterial, it is allocated (closed) to the Cost of Goods Sold account with the following adjusting entry.[1]

Example: If we do not adjust for underapplied overhead, will net income be overstated or understated? *Answer:* Overstated.

Mar. 31	Cost of Goods Sold.............................	480	
	Factory Overhead.........................		480
	To adjust for underapplied overhead costs.		

Assets = Liabilities + Equity
−480
+480

The $480 debit (increase) to Cost of Goods Sold reduces income by $480.

---

[1] When the underapplied (or overapplied) overhead is significant, the amount is normally allocated to the Cost of Goods Sold, Finished Goods Inventory, and Goods in Process Inventory accounts. The preferred method of allocating underapplied (or overapplied) overhead in this case is one consistent with the allocation method used in the period. For Road Warriors, underapplied overhead is allocated to jobs based on direct labor. Jobs B15 and B16, which are sold, account for 42.8% of the total direct labor cost in March. Also, 26.2% of direct labor was consumed by B17, which is in Finished Goods inventory, and the remaining 31% was consumed by Jobs B18 and B19, which are in Goods in Process inventory. These percents are multiplied by $480 to compute the amount of underapplied overhead allocated to each account (for example, 42.8% of $480, or $205, is allocated to the Cost of Goods Sold account). The following adjusting entry records this allocation.

Mar. 31	Goods in Process Inventory......................	149	
	Finished Goods Inventory	126	
	Cost of Goods Sold............................	205	
	Factory Overhead...........................		480
	To adjust for underapplied overhead costs.		

Decision Insight

Job Order Education Many companies invest in their employees, and the demand for executive education is strong. Annual spending on training and education exceeds $20 billion. Annual revenues for providers of executive education continue to rise, with about 40% of revenues coming from custom programs designed for one or a select group of companies.

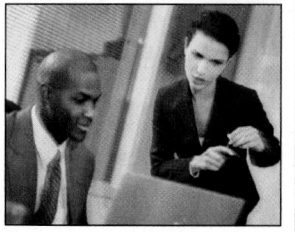

Overapplied Overhead

When the overhead applied in a period exceeds the overhead incurred, the resulting credit balance in the Factory Overhead account is called **overapplied overhead.** We treat overapplied overhead at the end of the period in the same way we treat underapplied overhead, except that we debit Factory Overhead and credit Cost of Good Sold for the amount.

Quick Check

Answers—p. 779

9. In a job order cost accounting system, why does the Factory Overhead account usually have an overapplied or underapplied balance at period-end?

10. When the Factory Overhead account has a debit balance at period-end, does this reflect overapplied or underapplied overhead?

Decision Analysis

Pricing for Services

A1 Apply job order costing in pricing services.

The chapter described job order costing mainly using a manufacturing setting. However, these concepts and procedures are applicable to a service setting. Consider AdWorld, an advertising agency that develops Web-based ads for small firms. Each of its customers has unique requirements, so costs for each individual job must be tracked separately.

AdWorld uses two types of labor: Web designers ($65 per hour) and computer staff ($50 per hour). It also incurs overhead costs that it assigns using two different predetermined overhead allocation rates: $125 per designer hour and $96 per staff hour. For each job, AdWorld must estimate the number of designer and staff hours needed. Then total costs pertaining to each job are determined using the procedures in the chapter. (*Note:* Most service firms have neither the category of materials cost nor inventory.)

To illustrate, a manufacturer of golf balls requested a quote from AdWorld for an advertising engagement. AdWorld estimates that the job will require 43 designer hours and 61 staff hours, with the following total estimated cost for this job.

Direct Labor		
Designers (43 hours × $65)	$ 2,795	
Staff (61 hours × $50)	3,050	
Total direct labor		$ 5,845
Overhead		
Designer related (43 hours × $125)	5,375	
Staff related (61 hours × $96)	5,856	
Total overhead		11,231
Total estimated job cost		$17,076

Decision Maker

Answer—p. 779

Sales Manager As AdWorld's sales manager, assume that you estimate costs pertaining to a proposed job as $17,076. Your normal pricing policy is to apply a markup of 18% from total costs. However, you learn that three other agencies are likely to bid for the same job, and that their quotes will range from $16,500 to $22,000. What price should you quote? What factors other than cost must you consider?

AdWorld can use this cost information to help determine the price quote for the job (see *Decision Maker, Sales Manager,* scenario in the margin).

Another source of information that AdWorld must consider is the market, that is, how much competitors will quote for this job. Competitor information is often unavailable; therefore, AdWorld's managers must use estimates based on their assessment of the competitive environment.

Demonstration Problem—Job Order Costing

The following information reflects Walczak Company's job order production activities for May.

Raw materials purchases	$16,000
Factory payroll cost	15,400
Overhead costs incurred	
Indirect materials	5,000
Indirect labor	3,500
Other factory overhead	9,500

Walczak's predetermined overhead rate is 150% of direct labor cost. Costs are allocated to the three jobs worked on during May as follows.

	Job 401	Job 402	Job 403
In-process balances on April 30			
Direct materials	$3,600		
Direct labor	1,700		
Applied overhead	2,550		
Costs during May			
Direct materials	3,550	$3,500	$1,400
Direct labor	5,100	6,000	800
Applied overhead	?	?	?
Status on May 31	Finished (sold)	Finished (unsold)	In process

Required

1. Determine the total cost of:
   a. The April 30 inventory of jobs in process.
   b. Materials used during May.
   c. Labor used during May.
   d. Factory overhead incurred and applied during May and the amount of any over- or underapplied overhead on May 31.
   e. Each job as of May 31, the May 31 inventories of both goods in process and finished goods, and the goods sold during May.

2. Prepare summarized journal entries for the month to record:
   a. Materials purchases (on credit), the factory payroll (paid with cash), indirect materials, indirect labor, and the other factory overhead (paid with cash).
   b. Assignment of direct materials, direct labor, and overhead costs to the Goods in Process Inventory account. (Use separate debit entries for each job.)
   c. Transfer of each completed job to the Finished Goods Inventory account.
   d. Cost of goods sold.
   e. Removal of any underapplied or overapplied overhead from the Factory Overhead account. (Assume the amount is not material.)

3. Prepare a manufacturing statement for May.

Planning the Solution

- Determine the cost of the April 30 goods in process inventory by totaling the materials, labor, and applied overhead costs for Job 401.
- Compute the cost of materials used and labor by totaling the amounts assigned to jobs and to overhead.

- Compute the total overhead incurred by summing the amounts for the three components. Compute the amount of applied overhead by multiplying the total direct labor cost by the predetermined overhead rate. Compute the underapplied or overapplied amount as the difference between the actual cost and the applied cost.
- Determine the total cost charged to each job by adding the costs incurred in April (if any) to the cost of materials, labor, and overhead applied during May.
- Group the costs of the jobs according to their completion status.
- Record the direct materials costs assigned to the three jobs, using a separate Goods in Process Inventory account for each job; do the same for the direct labor and the applied overhead.
- Transfer costs of Jobs 401 and 402 from Goods in Process Inventory to Finished Goods.
- Record the costs of Job 401 as cost of goods sold.
- Record the transfer of underapplied overhead from the Factory Overhead account to the Cost of Goods Sold account.
- On the manufacturing statement, remember to include the beginning and ending goods in process inventories and to deduct the underapplied overhead.

Solution to Demonstration Problem

1. Total cost of

a. April 30 inventory of jobs in process (Job 401).

Direct materials	$3,600
Direct labor	1,700
Applied overhead	2,550
Total cost	$7,850

b. Materials used during May.

Direct materials		
Job 401		$ 3,550
Job 402		3,500
Job 403		1,400
Total direct materials		8,450
Indirect materials		5,000
Total materials used		$13,450

c. Labor used during May.

Direct labor		
Job 401		$ 5,100
Job 402		6,000
Job 403		800
Total direct labor		11,900
Indirect labor		3,500
Total labor used		$15,400

d. Factory overhead incurred in May.

Actual overhead		
Indirect materials		$ 5,000
Indirect labor		3,500
Other factory overhead		9,500
Total actual overhead		18,000
Overhead applied (150% × $11,900)		17,850
Underapplied overhead		$ 150

e. Total cost of each job.

	401	402	403
In-process costs from April			
Direct materials	$ 3,600		
Direct labor	1,700		
Applied overhead*	2,550		
Cost incurred in May			
Direct materials	3,550	$ 3,500	$1,400
Direct labor	5,100	6,000	800
Applied overhead*	7,650	9,000	1,200
Total costs	$24,150	$18,500	$3,400

* Equals 150% of the direct labor cost.

Total cost of the May 31 inventory of goods in process (Job 403) = $3,400

Total cost of the May 31 inventory of finished goods (Job 402) = $18,500

Total cost of goods sold during May (Job 401) = $24,150

2. Journal entries.

a.

Raw Materials Inventory	16,000	
Accounts Payable		16,000
To record materials purchases.		
Factory Payroll	15,400	
Cash		15,400
To record factory payroll.		
Factory Overhead	5,000	
Raw Materials Inventory		5,000
To record indirect materials.		
Factory Overhead	3,500	
Factory Payroll		3,500
To record indirect labor.		
Factory Overhead	9,500	
Cash		9,500
To record other factory overhead.		

b. Assignment of costs to Goods in Process Inventory.

Goods in Process Inventory (Job 401)	3,550	
Goods in Process Inventory (Job 402)	3,500	
Goods in Process Inventory (Job 403)	1,400	
Raw Materials Inventory		8,450
To assign direct materials to jobs.		
Goods in Process Inventory (Job 401)	5,100	
Goods in Process Inventory (Job 402)	6,000	
Goods in Process Inventory (Job 403)	800	
Factory Payroll		11,900
To assign direct labor to jobs.		
Goods in Process Inventory (Job 401)	7,650	
Goods in Process Inventory (Job 402)	9,000	
Goods in Process Inventory (Job 403)	1,200	
Factory Overhead		17,850
To apply overhead to jobs.		

c. Transfer of completed jobs to Finished Goods Inventory.

Finished Goods Inventory	42,650	
Goods in Process Inventory (Job 401)		24,150
Goods in Process Inventory (Job 402)		18,500
To record completion of jobs.		

d.

Cost of Goods Sold	24,150	
Finished Goods Inventory		24,150
To record sale of Job 401.		

e.

Cost of Goods Sold	150	
Factory Overhead		150
To assign underapplied overhead.		

3.

WALCZAK COMPANY Manufacturing Statement For Month Ended May 31		
Direct materials		$ 8,450
Direct labor		11,900
Factory overhead		
Indirect materials	$5,000	
Indirect labor	3,500	
Other factory overhead	9,500	18,000
Total production costs		38,350
Add goods in process, April 30		7,850
Total cost of goods in process		46,200
Less goods in process, May 31		3,400
Less underapplied overhead		150
Cost of goods manufactured		$42,650

> Note how underapplied overhead is reported. Overapplied overhead is similarly reported, but is added.

Summary

C1 Explain the cost accounting system. A cost accounting system records production activities using a perpetual inventory system, which continuously updates records for transactions and events that affect inventory costs.

C2 Describe important features of job order production.
Certain companies called *job order manufacturers* produce custom-made products for customers. These customized products are produced in response to a customer's orders. A job order manufacturer produces products that usually are different and, typically, produced in low volumes. The production systems of job order companies are flexible and are not highly standardized.

C3 Explain job cost sheets and how they are used in job order cost accounting. In a job order cost accounting system, the costs of producing each job are accumulated on a separate job cost sheet. Costs of direct materials, direct labor, and overhead are accumulated separately on the job cost sheet and then added to determine the total cost of a job. Job cost sheets for jobs in process, finished jobs, and jobs sold make up subsidiary records controlled by general ledger accounts.

A1 Apply job order costing in pricing services. Job order costing can usefully be applied to a service setting. The resulting job cost estimate can then be used to help determine a price for services.

P1 Describe and record the flow of materials costs in job order cost accounting. Costs of materials flow from receiving reports to materials ledger cards and then to either job cost sheets or the Indirect Materials account in the factory overhead ledger.

P2 Describe and record the flow of labor costs in job order cost accounting. Costs of labor flow from clock cards to the Factory Payroll account and then to either job cost sheets or the Indirect Labor account in the factory overhead ledger.

P3 Describe and record the flow of overhead costs in job order cost accounting. Overhead costs are accumulated in the Factory Overhead account that controls the subsidiary factory overhead ledger. Then, using a predetermined overhead rate, overhead costs are charged to jobs.

P4 Determine adjustments for overapplied and underapplied factory overhead. At the end of each period, the Factory Overhead account usually has a residual debit (underapplied overhead) or credit (overapplied overhead) balance. If the balance is not material, it is transferred to Cost of Goods Sold, but if it is material, it is allocated to Goods in Process Inventory, Finished Goods Inventory, and Cost of Goods Sold.

Guidance Answers to **Decision Maker** and **Decision Ethics**

Management Consultant Service companies (such as this consulting firm) do not recognize goods in process inventory or finished goods inventory—an important difference between service and manufacturing companies. For the two jobs that are 60% complete, you could recognize revenues and costs at 60% of the total expected amounts. This means you could recognize revenue of $7,200 (0.60 × $12,000) and costs of $6,000 (0.60 × $10,000), yielding net income of $1,200 from each job.

Web Consultant The partner has a monetary incentive to *manage* the numbers and assign more costs to the two cost-plus engagements. This also would reduce costs on the fixed-price engagements. To act in such a manner is unethical. As a professional and an honest person, it is your responsibility to engage in ethical behavior. You must not comply with the partner's instructions. If the partner insists you act in an unethical manner, you should report the matter to a higher authority in the organization.

Entrepreneur An inadequate cost system can distort product costs. You should review overhead costs in detail. Once you know the different cost elements in overhead, you can classify them into groups such as material related, labor related, or machine related. Other groups can also be formed (we discuss this in Chapter 21). Once you have classified overhead items into groups, you can better establish overhead allocation bases and use them to compute predetermined overhead rates. These multiple rates and bases can then be used to assign overhead costs to products. This will likely improve product pricing.

Sales Manager The price based on AdWorld's normal pricing policy is $20,150 ($17,076 × 1.18), which is within the price range offered by competitors. One option is to apply normal pricing policy and quote a price of $20,150. On the other hand, assessing the competition, particularly in terms of their service quality and other benefits they might offer, would be useful. Although price is an input customers use to select suppliers, factors such as quality and timeliness (responsiveness) of suppliers are important. Accordingly, your price can reflect such factors.

Guidance Answers to **Quick Checks**

1. *b*

2. A job is a special order for a custom product. A job lot consists of a quantity of identical, special-order items.

3. *a*

4. Three costs normally accumulated on a job cost sheet are direct materials, direct labor, and factory overhead.

5. *c*

6. Four sources of factory overhead are materials requisitions, time tickets, vouchers, and adjusting entries.

7. Since a job order cost accounting system uses perpetual inventory records, overhead costs must be assigned to jobs before the

end of a period. This requires the use of a predetermined overhead rate.

8. Debits are recorded when wages and salaries of factory employees are paid or accrued. Credits are recorded when direct labor costs are assigned to jobs and when indirect labor costs are transferred to the Factory Overhead account.

9. Overapplied or underapplied overhead usually exists at the end of a period because application of overhead is based on estimates of overhead and another variable such as direct labor. Estimates rarely equal actual amounts incurred.

10. A debit balance reflects underapplied factory overhead.

Key Terms
mhhe.com/wildFAP18e

Key Terms are available at the book's Website for learning and testing in an online Flashcard Format.

Clock card (p. 767)	Job cost sheet (p. 764)	Materials requisition (p. 767)
Cost accounting system (p. 762)	Job lot (p. 763)	Overapplied overhead (p. 774)
Finished Goods Inventory (p. 764)	Job order cost accounting	Predetermined overhead rate (p. 770)
General accounting system (p. 762)	system (p. 764)	Target cost (p. 763)
Goods in Process Inventory (p. 764)	Job order production (p. 762)	Time ticket (p. 768)
Job (p. 762)	Materials ledger card (p. 765)	Underapplied overhead (p. 773)

Multiple Choice Quiz
Answers on p. 795   mhhe.com/wildFAP18e

Multiple Choice Quizzes A and B are available at the book's Website.

1. A company's predetermined overhead allocation rate is 150% of its direct labor costs. How much overhead is applied to a job that requires total labor costs of $30,000?
   a. $15,000
   b. $30,000
   c. $45,000
   d. $60,000
   e. $75,000

2. A company's cost accounting system uses direct labor costs to apply overhead to goods in process and finished goods inventories. Its production costs for the period are: direct

materials, $45,000; direct labor, $35,000; and overhead applied, $38,500. What is its predetermined overhead allocation rate?
   a. 10%
   b. 110%
   c. 86%
   d. 91%
   e. 117%

3. A company's ending inventory of finished goods has a total cost of $10,000 and consists of 500 units. If the overhead applied to these goods is $4,000, and the predetermined overhead rate is 80% of direct labor costs, how much direct materials cost was incurred in producing these 500 units?

a. $10,000
b. $ 6,000
c. $ 4,000
d. $ 5,000
e. $ 1,000

4. A company's Goods in Process Inventory T-account follows.

Goods in Process Inventory			
Beginning balance	9,000		
Direct materials	94,200		
Direct labor	59,200	?	Finished goods
Overhead applied	31,600		
Ending balance	17,800		

The cost of units transferred to Finished Goods inventory is

a. $193,000
b. $211,800
c. $185,000
d. $144,600
e. $176,200

5. At the end of its current year, a company learned that its overhead was underapplied by $1,500 and that this amount is not considered material. Based on this information, the company should

a. Close the $1,500 to Finished Goods Inventory.
b. Close the $1,500 to Cost of Goods Sold.
c. Carry the $1,500 to the next period.
d. Do nothing about the $1,500 because it is not material and it is likely that overhead will be overapplied by the same amount next year.
e. Carry the $1,500 to the Income Statement as "Other Expense."

Discussion Questions

1. Why must a company estimate the amount of factory overhead assigned to individual jobs or job lots?

2. The chapter used a percent of labor cost to assign factory overhead to jobs. Identify another factor (or base) a company might reasonably use to assign overhead costs.

3. What information is recorded on a job cost sheet? How do management and employees use job cost sheets?

4. In a job order cost accounting system, what records serve as a subsidiary ledger for Goods in Process Inventory? For Finished Goods Inventory?

5. What journal entry is recorded when a materials manager receives a materials requisition and then issues materials (both direct and indirect) for use in the factory?

6. How does the materials requisition help safeguard a company's assets?

7. What is the difference between a clock card and a time ticket?

8. What events cause debits to be recorded in the Factory Overhead account? What events cause credits to be recorded in the Factory Overhead account?

9. What account(s) is(are) used to eliminate overapplied or underapplied overhead from the Factory Overhead account, assuming the amount is not material?

10. Assume that **Apple** produces a batch of 1,000 iPods. Does it account for this as 1,000 individual jobs or as a job lot? Explain (consider costs and benefits).

11. Why must a company prepare a predetermined overhead rate when using job order cost accounting?

12. How would a hospital apply job order costing? Explain.

13. **Harley-Davidson** manufactures 30 luxury-model motorcycles. Does it account for these motorcycles as 30 individual jobs or as a job lot? Explain. **Harley-Davidson**

 Red numbers denote Discussion Questions that involve decision-making.

QUICK STUDY

QS 19-1
Factory overhead rates P3

A company incurred the following manufacturing costs this period: direct labor, $468,000; direct materials, $354,500; and factory overhead, $117,000. Compute overhead cost as a percent of (1) direct labor and (2) direct materials. Round percents to the nearest whole number.

QS 19-2
Jobs and job lots
C2

Determine which products are most likely to be manufactured as a job and which as a job lot.
1. A hand-crafted table.
2. A 90-foot motor yacht.
3. Wedding dresses for a chain of stores.
4. A custom-designed home.
5. Hats imprinted with company logo.
6. Little League trophies.

QS 19-3
Job cost computation
C3

The following information is from the materials requisitions and time tickets for Job 9-1005 completed by Great Bay Boats. The requisitions are identified by code numbers starting with the letter Q and the time tickets start with W. At the start of the year, management estimated that overhead cost would equal 110% of direct labor cost for each job. Determine the total cost on the job cost sheet for Job 9-1005.

Date		Document	Amount
7/1/2008	....	Q-4698	$1,250
7/1/2008	....	W-3393	600
7/5/2008	....	Q-4725	1,000
7/5/2008	....	W-3479	450
7/10/2008	....	W-3559	300

During the current month, a company that uses a job order cost accounting system purchases $50,000 in raw materials for cash. It then uses $12,000 of raw materials indirectly as factory supplies and uses $32,000 of raw materials as direct materials. Prepare entries to record these three transactions.

QS 19-4
Direct materials journal entries
P1

During the current month, a company that uses a job order cost accounting system incurred a monthly factory payroll of $80,000, paid in cash. Of this amount, $40,000 is classified as indirect labor and the remainder as direct. Prepare entries to record these transactions.

QS 19-5
Direct labor journal entries   P2

During the current month, a company that uses a job order cost accounting system incurred a monthly factory payroll of $175,000, paid in cash. Of this amount, $44,000 is classified as indirect labor and the remainder as direct for the production of a job lot. Factory overhead is applied at 90% of direct labor. Prepare the entry to apply factory overhead to this job lot.

QS 19-6
Factory overhead journal entries
P3

A company allocates overhead at a rate of 150% of direct labor cost. Actual overhead cost for the current period is $950,000, and direct labor cost is $600,000. Prepare the entry to close over- or underapplied overhead to cost of goods sold.

QS 19-7
Entry for over- or underapplied overhead   P4

The left column lists the titles of documents and accounts used in job order cost accounting. The right column presents short descriptions of the purposes of the documents. Match each document in the left column to its numbered description in the right column.

EXERCISES

Exercise 19-1
Documents in job order cost accounting

C2 C3 P1 P2 P3

A. Factory Payroll account
B. Materials ledger card
C. Time ticket
D. Voucher
E. Materials requisition
F. Factory Overhead account
G. Clock card

_____ **1.** Shows amount of time an employee works on a job.
_____ **2.** Temporarily accumulates incurred labor costs until they are assigned to specific jobs or to overhead.
_____ **3.** Shows only total time an employee works each day.
_____ **4.** Perpetual inventory record of raw materials received, used, and available for use.
_____ **5.** Shows amount approved for payment of an overhead or other cost.
_____ **6.** Temporarily accumulates the cost of incurred overhead until the cost is assigned to specific jobs.
_____ **7.** Communicates the need for materials to complete a job.

As of the end of June, the job cost sheets at Racing Wheels, Inc., show the following total costs accumulated on three custom jobs.

Exercise 19-2
Analysis of cost flows

C2 P1 P2 P3

	Job 102	Job 103	Job 104
Direct materials	$15,000	$33,000	$27,000
Direct labor	8,000	14,200	21,000
Overhead	4,000	7,100	10,500

Job 102 was started in production in May and the following costs were assigned to it in May: direct materials, $6,000; direct labor, $1,800; and overhead, $900. Jobs 103 and 104 are started in June. Overhead cost is applied with a predetermined rate based on direct labor cost. Jobs 102 and 103 are finished in June, and Job 104 is expected to be finished in July. No raw materials are used indirectly in June. Using this information, answer the following questions.

1. What is the cost of the raw materials requisitioned in June for each of the three jobs?
2. How much direct labor cost is incurred during June for each of the three jobs?
3. What predetermined overhead rate is used during June?
4. How much total cost is transferred to finished goods during June?

Check (4) $81,300

Exercise 19-3

Overhead rate; costs
assigned to jobs

P3

Check   (2) $22,710

In December 2007, Shire Computer's management establishes the year 2008 predetermined overhead rate based on direct labor cost. The information used in setting this rate includes estimates that the company will incur $747,500 of overhead costs and $575,000 of direct labor cost in year 2008. During March 2008, Shire began and completed Job No. 13-56.

1. What is the predetermined overhead rate for year 2008?

2. Use the information on the following job cost sheet to determine the total cost of the job.

JOB COST SHEET

Customer's Name   Keiser Co.   **Job No.**   13-56

Job Description   5 plasma monitors—61 inch

	Direct Materials			Direct Labor		Overhead Costs Applied	
Date	Requisition No.	Amount	Time-Ticket No.	Amount	Rate	Amount
Mar. 8	4-129	$5,000	T-306	$ 700		
Mar. 11	4-142	7,020	T-432	1,250		
Mar. 18	4-167	3,330	T-456	1,250		
Totals						

Exercise 19-4

Analysis of costs assigned to
goods in process

P3

Lorenzo Company uses a job order cost accounting system that charges overhead to jobs on the basis of direct material cost. At year-end, the Goods in Process Inventory account shows the following.

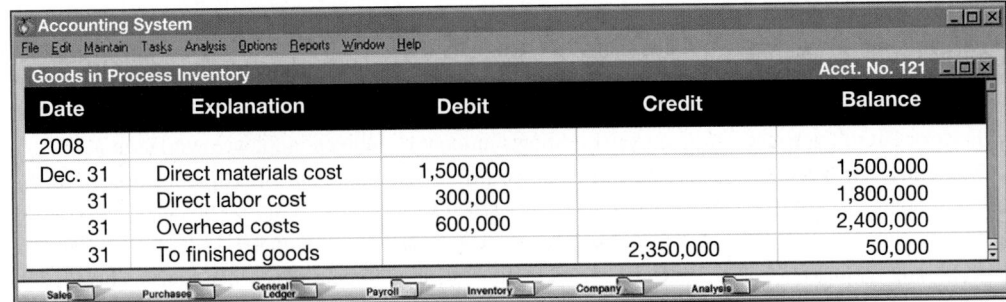

Date	Explanation	Debit	Credit	Balance
2008				
Dec. 31	Direct materials cost	1,500,000		1,500,000
31	Direct labor cost	300,000		1,800,000
31	Overhead costs	600,000		2,400,000
31	To finished goods		2,350,000	50,000

1. Determine the overhead rate used (based on direct material cost).

Check   (2) Direct labor cost, $8,000

2. Only one job remained in the goods in process inventory at December 31, 2008. Its direct materials cost is $30,000. How much direct labor cost and overhead cost are assigned to it?

Exercise 19-5

Cost flows in a job order
cost system

C3   P3

The following information is available for Lock-Safe Company, which produces special-order security products and uses a job order cost accounting system.

	April 30	May 31
Inventories		
Raw materials	$43,000	$ 52,000
Goods in process	10,200	21,300
Finished goods	63,000	35,600
Activities and information for May		
Raw materials purchases (paid with cash)		210,000
Factory payroll (paid with cash)		345,000
Factory overhead		
Indirect materials		15,000
Indirect labor		80,000
Other overhead costs		120,000
Sales (received in cash)		1,400,000
Predetermined overhead rate based on direct labor cost		70%

Compute the following amounts for the month of May.

1. Cost of direct materials used.   **4.** Cost of goods sold.*

2. Cost of direct labor used.   **5.** Gross profit.

3. Cost of goods manufactured.   **6.** Overapplied or underapplied overhead.

Check   (3) $625,400

*Do not consider any underapplied or overapplied overhead.

Use information in Exercise 19-5 to prepare journal entries for the following events in May.

1. Raw materials purchases for cash.

2. Direct materials usage.

3. Indirect materials usage.

4. Factory payroll costs in cash.

5. Direct labor usage.

6. Indirect labor usage.

7. Factory overhead excluding indirect materials and indirect labor (record credit to Other Accounts).

8. Application of overhead to goods in process.

9. Transfer of finished jobs to the finished goods inventory.

10. Sale and delivery of finished goods to customers for cash (record unadjusted cost of sales).

11. Allocation (closing) of overapplied or underapplied overhead to Cost of Goods Sold.

Exercise 19-6
Journal entries for a job order cost accounting system

P1 P2 P3 P4

In December 2007, Infovision established its predetermined overhead rate for movies produced during year 2008 by using the following cost predictions: overhead costs, $1,680,000, and direct labor costs, $480,000. At year end 2008, the company's records show that actual overhead costs for the year are $1,652,000. Actual direct labor cost had been assigned to jobs as follows.

Exercise 19-7
Factory overhead computed, applied, and adjusted

P3 P4

Movies completed and released	$425,000
Movies still in production	50,000
Total actual direct labor cost	$475,000

1. Determine the predetermined overhead rate for year 2008.

2. Set up a T-account for overhead and enter the overhead costs incurred and the amounts applied to movies during the year using the predetermined overhead rate.

3. Determine whether overhead is overapplied or underapplied (and the amount) during the year.

4. Prepare the adjusting entry to allocate any over- or underapplied overhead to Cost of Goods Sold.

Check   (3) $10,500 overapplied

In December 2007, Cardozo Company established its predetermined overhead rate for jobs produced during year 2008 by using the following cost predictions: overhead costs, $750,000, and direct labor costs, $625,000. At year end 2008, the company's records show that actual overhead costs for the year are $830,000. Actual direct labor cost had been assigned to jobs as follows.

Exercise 19-8
Factory overhead computed, applied, and adjusted

P3 P4

Jobs completed and sold	$513,750
Jobs in finished goods inventory	102,750
Jobs in goods in process inventory	68,500
Total actual direct labor cost	$685,000

1. Determine the predetermined overhead rate for year 2008.

2. Set up a T-account for Factory Overhead and enter the overhead costs incurred and the amounts applied to jobs during the year using the predetermined overhead rate.

3. Determine whether overhead is overapplied or underapplied (and the amount) during the year.

4. Prepare the adjusting entry to allocate any over- or underapplied overhead to Cost of Goods Sold.

5. Prepare the adjusting entry to allocate any over- or underapplied overhead to Cost of Goods Sold, Finished Goods Inventory, and Goods in Process Inventory.

Check   (3) $8,000 underapplied

Sunrise Company applies factory overhead based on direct labor costs. The company incurred the following costs during 2008: direct materials costs, $650,000; direct labor costs, $3,000,000; and factory overhead costs applied, $1,800,000.

Exercise 19-9
Overhead rate calculation, allocation, and analysis P3

1. Determine the company's predetermined overhead rate for year 2008.

2. Assuming that the company's $71,000 ending Goods in Process Inventory account for year 2008 had $20,000 of direct labor costs, determine the inventory's direct materials costs.

3. Assuming that the company's $490,000 ending Finished Goods Inventory account for year 2008 had $250,000 of direct materials costs, determine the inventory's direct labor costs and its overhead costs.

Exercise 19-10

Costs allocated to ending inventories

P3

Deschamps Company's ending Goods in Process Inventory account consists of 5,000 units of partially completed product, and its Finished Goods Inventory account consists of 12,000 units of product. The factory manager determines that Goods in Process Inventory includes direct materials cost of $10 per unit and direct labor cost of $7 per unit. Finished goods are estimated to have $12 of direct materials cost per unit and $9 of direct labor cost per unit. The company established the predetermined overhead rate using the following predictions: estimated direct labor cost, $300,000, and estimated factory overhead, $375,000. The company allocates factory overhead to its goods in process and finished goods inventories based on direct labor cost. During the period, the company incurred these costs: direct materials, $535,000; direct labor, $290,000; and factory overhead applied, $362,500.

1. Determine the predetermined overhead rate.

2. Compute the total cost of the two ending inventories.

3. Compute cost of goods sold for the year (assume no beginning inventories and no underapplied or overapplied overhead).

Exercise 19-11

Cost-based pricing

A1

Hansel Corporation has requested bids from several architects to design its new corporate headquarters. Frey Architects is one of the firms bidding on the job. Frey estimates that the job will require the following direct labor.

	Labor	Estimated Hours	Hourly Rate
1			
2	Architects	150	$300
3	Staff	300	75
4	Clerical	500	20
5			

Frey applies overhead to jobs at 175% of direct labor cost. Frey would like to earn at least $80,000 profit on the architectural job. Based on past experience and market research, it estimates that the competition will bid between $285,000 and $350,000 for the job.

1. What is Frey's estimated cost of the architectural job?

2. What bid would you suggest that Frey submit?

PROBLEM SET A

Problem 19-1A

Production costs computed and recorded; reports prepared

C3 P1 P2 P3 P4

Ciolino Co.'s March 31 inventory of raw materials is $80,000. Raw materials purchases in April are $500,000, and factory payroll cost in April is $363,000. Overhead costs incurred in April are: indirect materials, $50,000; indirect labor, $23,000; factory rent, $32,000; factory utilities, $19,000; and factory equipment depreciation, $51,000. The predetermined overhead rate is 50% of direct labor cost. Job 306 is sold for $635,000 cash in April. Costs of the three jobs worked on in April follow.

	Job 306	Job 307	Job 308
Balances on March 31			
Direct materials	$ 29,000	$ 35,000	
Direct labor	20,000	18,000	
Applied overhead	10,000	9,000	
Costs during April			
Direct materials	135,000	220,000	$100,000
Direct labor	85,000	150,000	105,000
Applied overhead	?	?	?
Status on April 30	Finished (sold)	Finished (unsold)	In process

Required

1. Determine the total of each production cost incurred for April (direct labor, direct materials, and applied overhead), and the total cost assigned to each job (including the balances from March 31).

2. Prepare journal entries for the month of April to record the following.

   a. Materials purchases (on credit), factory payroll (paid in cash), and actual overhead costs including indirect materials and indirect labor. (Factory rent and utilities are paid in cash.)

   b. Assignment of direct materials, direct labor, and applied overhead costs to the Goods in Process Inventory.

   c. Transfer of Jobs 306 and 307 to the Finished Goods Inventory.

   d. Cost of goods sold for Job 306.

   e. Revenue from the sale of Job 306.

   f. Assignment of any underapplied or overapplied overhead to the Cost of Goods Sold account. (The amount is not material.)

Check (2f) $5,000 underapplied

3. Prepare a manufacturing statement for April (use a single line presentation for direct materials and show the details of overhead cost).

(3) Cost of goods manufactured, $828,500

4. Compute gross profit for April. Show how to present the inventories on the April 30 balance sheet.

Analysis Component

5. The over- or underapplied overhead is closed to Cost of Goods Sold. Discuss how this adjustment impacts business decision-making regarding individual jobs or batches of jobs.

Farina Bay's computer system generated the following trial balance on December 31, 2008. The company's manager knows something is wrong with the trial balance because it does not show any balance for Goods in Process Inventory but does show balances for the Factory Payroll and Factory Overhead accounts.

Problem 19-2A
Source documents, journal entries, overhead, and financial reports

P1 P2 P3 P4

	Debit	Credit
Cash	$102,000	
Accounts receivable	75,000	
Raw materials inventory	80,000	
Goods in process inventory	0	
Finished goods inventory	15,000	
Prepaid rent	3,000	
Accounts payable		$ 17,000
Notes payable		25,000
Common stock		50,000
Retained earnings		271,000
Sales		373,000
Cost of goods sold	218,000	
Factory payroll	68,000	
Factory overhead	115,000	
Operating expenses	60,000	
Totals	$736,000	$736,000

After examining various files, the manager identifies the following six source documents that need to be processed to bring the accounting records up to date.

Materials requisition 21-3010:	$10,200 direct materials to Job 402
Materials requisition 21-3011:	$18,600 direct materials to Job 404
Materials requisition 21-3012:	$5,600 indirect materials
Labor time ticket 6052:	$36,000 direct labor to Job 402
Labor time ticket 6053:	$23,800 direct labor to Job 404
Labor time ticket 6054:	$8,200 indirect labor

Jobs 402 and 404 are the only units in process at year-end. The predetermined overhead rate is 200% of direct labor cost.

Required

1. Use information on the six source documents to prepare journal entries to assign the following costs.

   a. Direct materials costs to Goods in Process Inventory.

   b. Direct labor costs to Goods in Process Inventory.

   c. Overhead costs to Goods in Process Inventory.

d. Indirect materials costs to the Factory Overhead account.

e. Indirect labor costs to the Factory Overhead account.

2. Determine the revised balance of the Factory Overhead account after making the entries in part 1. Determine whether there is any under- or overapplied overhead for the year. Prepare the adjusting entry to allocate any over- or underapplied overhead to Cost of Goods Sold, assuming the amount is not material.

3. Prepare a revised trial balance.

4. Prepare an income statement for year 2008 and a balance sheet as of December 31, 2008.

Analysis Component

5. Assume that the $5,600 on materials requisition 21-3012 should have been direct materials charged to Job 404. Without providing specific calculations, describe the impact of this error on the income statement for 2008 and the balance sheet at December 31, 2008.

Problem 19-3A

Source documents, journal entries, and accounts in job order cost accounting

P1 P2 P3

Widmer Watercraft's predetermined overhead rate for year 2008 is 200% of direct labor. Information on the company's production activities during May 2008 follows.

a. Purchased raw materials on credit, $200,000.

b. Paid $126,000 cash for factory wages.

c. Paid $15,000 cash to a computer consultant to reprogram factory equipment.

d. Materials requisitions record use of the following materials for the month.

Job 136	$ 48,000
Job 137	32,000
Job 138	19,200
Job 139	22,400
Job 140	6,400
Total direct materials	128,000
Indirect materials	19,500
Total materials used	$147,500

e. Time tickets record use of the following labor for the month.

Job 136	$ 12,000
Job 137	10,500
Job 138	37,500
Job 139	39,000
Job 140	3,000
Total direct labor	102,000
Indirect labor	24,000
Total	$126,000

f. Applied overhead to Jobs 136, 138, and 139.

g. Transferred Jobs 136, 138, and 139 to Finished Goods.

h. Sold Jobs 136 and 138 on credit at a total price of $525,000.

i. The company incurred the following overhead costs during the month (credit Prepaid Insurance for expired factory insurance).

Depreciation of factory building	$68,000
Depreciation of factory equipment	36,500
Expired factory insurance	10,000
Accrued property taxes payable	35,000

j. Applied overhead at month-end to the Goods in Process (Jobs 137 and 140) using the predetermined overhead rate of 200% of direct labor cost.

Required

1. Prepare a job cost sheet for each job worked on during the month. Use the following simplified form.

```
┌─────────────────────────────────────────┐
│  Job No. _____                        │
│                                           │
│  Materials . . . . . . .   $ _____    │
│                                           │
│  Labor . . . . . . . . .     _____    │
│                                           │
│  Overhead . . . . . . .      _____    │
│                                           │
│  Total cost . . . . . . .  $ ═════════    │
└─────────────────────────────────────────┘
```

2. Prepare journal entries to record the events and transactions *a* through *j*.

3. Set up T-accounts for each of the following general ledger accounts, each of which started the month with a zero balance: Raw Materials Inventory; Goods in Process Inventory; Finished Goods Inventory; Factory Payroll; Factory Overhead; Cost of Goods Sold. Then post the journal entries to these T-accounts and determine the balance of each account.

4. Prepare a report showing the total cost of each job in process and prove that the sum of their costs equals the Goods in Process Inventory account balance. Prepare similar reports for Finished Goods Inventory and Cost of Goods Sold.

Check   (2f) Cr. Factory Overhead, $177,000

Check   (4) Finished Goods Inventory, $139,400

In December 2007, Yerbury Company's manager estimated next year's total direct labor cost assuming 50 persons working an average of 2,000 hours each at an average wage rate of $25 per hour. The manager also estimated the following manufacturing overhead costs for year 2008.

Problem 19-4A
Overhead allocation and adjustment using a predetermined overhead rate

C3   P3   P4

mhhe.com/wildFAP18e

Indirect labor	$ 319,200
Factory supervision	240,000
Rent on factory building	140,000
Factory utilities	88,000
Factory insurance expired	68,000
Depreciation—Factory equipment	480,000
Repairs expense—Factory equipment	60,000
Factory supplies used	68,800
Miscellaneous production costs	36,000
Total estimated overhead costs	$1,500,000

At the end of 2008, records show the company incurred $1,520,000 of actual overhead costs. It completed and sold five jobs with the following direct labor costs: Job 201, $604,000; Job 202, $563,000; Job 203, $298,000; Job 204, $716,000; and Job 205, $314,000. In addition, Job 206 is in process at the end of 2008 and had been charged $17,000 for direct labor. No jobs were in process at the end of 2007. The company's predetermined overhead rate is based on direct labor cost.

Required

1. Determine the following.

   a. Predetermined overhead rate for year 2008.

   b. Total overhead cost applied to each of the six jobs during year 2008.

   c. Over- or underapplied overhead at year-end 2008.

2. Assuming that any over- or underapplied overhead is not material, prepare the adjusting entry to allocate any over- or underapplied overhead to Cost of Goods Sold at the end of year 2008.

Check   (1c) $12,800 underapplied

(2) Cr. Factory Overhead $12,800

If the working papers that accompany this book are unavailable, do not attempt to solve this problem.
Sager Company manufactures variations of its product, a technopress, in response to custom orders from its customers. On May 1, the company had no inventories of goods in process or finished goods but held the following raw materials.

Problem 19-5A
Production transactions; subsidiary records; and source documents

P1   P2   P3   P4

Material M	. . . .	200 units @	$250	=	$50,000
Material R	. . . .	95 units @	180	=	17,100
Paint	. . . .	55 units @	75	=	4,125
Total cost	. . . .				$71,225

On May 4, the company began working on two technopresses: Job 102 for Worldwide Company and Job 103 for Reuben Company.

Required

Follow the instructions in this list of activities and complete the sheets provided in the working papers.

a. Purchased raw materials on credit and recorded the following information from receiving reports and invoices.

> Receiving Report No. 426, Material M, 250 units at $250 each.
> Receiving Report No. 427, Material R, 90 units at $180 each.

Instructions: Record these purchases with a single journal entry and post it to general ledger T-accounts, using the transaction letter *a* to identify the entry. Enter the receiving report information on the materials ledger cards.

b. Requisitioned the following raw materials for production.

> Requisition No. 35, for Job 102, 135 units of Material M.
> Requisition No. 36, for Job 102, 72 units of Material R.
> Requisition No. 37, for Job 103, 70 units of Material M.
> Requisition No. 38, for Job 103, 38 units of Material R.
> Requisition No. 39, for 15 units of paint.

Instructions: Enter amounts for direct materials requisitions on the materials ledger cards and the job cost sheets. Enter the indirect material amount on the materials ledger card and record a debit to the Indirect Materials account in the subsidiary factory overhead ledger. Do not record a journal entry at this time.

c. Received the following employee time tickets for work in May.

> Time tickets Nos. 1 to 10 for direct labor on Job 102, $90,000.
> Time tickets Nos. 11 to 30 for direct labor on Job 103, $65,000.
> Time tickets Nos. 31 to 36 for equipment repairs, $19,250.

Instructions: Record direct labor from the time tickets on the job cost sheets and then debit indirect labor to the Indirect Labor account in the subsidiary factory overhead ledger. Do not record a journal entry at this time.

d. Paid cash for the following items during the month: factory payroll, $174,250, and miscellaneous overhead items, $102,000.

Instructions: Record these payments with journal entries and then post them to the general ledger accounts. Also record a debit in the Miscellaneous Overhead account in the subsidiary factory overhead ledger.

e. Finished Job 102 and transferred it to the warehouse. The company assigns overhead to each job with a predetermined overhead rate equal to 80% of direct labor cost.

Instructions: Enter the allocated overhead on the cost sheet for Job 102, fill in the cost summary section of the cost sheet, and then mark the cost sheet "Finished." Prepare a journal entry to record the job's completion and its transfer to Finished Goods and then post it to the general ledger accounts.

f. Delivered Job 102 and accepted the customer's promise to pay $400,000 within 30 days.

Instructions: Prepare journal entries to record the sale of Job 102 and the cost of goods sold. Post them to the general ledger accounts.

g. Applied overhead to Job 103 based on the job's direct labor to date.

Instructions: Enter overhead on the job cost sheet but do not make a journal entry at this time.

Check (h) Dr. Goods in Process Inventory, $71,050

h. Recorded the total direct and indirect materials costs as reported on all the requisitions for the month.

Instructions: Prepare a journal entry to record these costs and post it to general ledger accounts.

i. Recorded the total direct and indirect labor costs as reported on all time tickets for the month.

Instructions: Prepare a journal entry to record these costs and post it to general ledger accounts.

j. Recorded the total overhead costs applied to jobs.

Check Balance in Factory Overhead, $1,625 Cr., overapplied

Instructions: Prepare a journal entry to record the allocation of these overhead costs and post it to general ledger accounts.

Tavella Co.'s August 31 inventory of raw materials is $150,000. Raw materials purchases in September are $400,000, and factory payroll cost in September is $220,000. Overhead costs incurred in September are: indirect materials, $30,000; indirect labor, $14,000; factory rent, $20,000; factory utilities, $12,000; and factory equipment depreciation, $30,000. The predetermined overhead rate is 50% of direct labor cost. Job 114 is sold for $380,000 cash in September. Costs for the three jobs worked on in September follow.

PROBLEM SET B

Problem 19-1B
Production costs computed and recorded; reports prepared

C3   P1   P2   P3   P4

	Job 114	Job 115	Job 116
Balances on August 31			
Direct materials	$14,000	$18,000	
Direct labor	18,000	16,000	
Applied overhead	9,000	8,000	
Costs during September			
Direct materials	100,000	170,000	$80,000
Direct labor	30,000	68,000	120,000
Applied overhead	?	?	?
Status on September 30	Finished (sold)	Finished (unsold)	In process

Required

1. Determine the total of each production cost incurred for September (direct labor, direct materials, and applied overhead), and the total cost assigned to each job (including the balances from August 31).

2. Prepare journal entries for the month of September to record the following.

   a. Materials purchases (on credit), factory payroll (paid in cash), and actual overhead costs including indirect materials and indirect labor. (Factory rent and utilities are paid in cash.)

   b. Assignment of direct materials, direct labor, and applied overhead costs to Goods in Process Inventory.

   c. Transfer of Jobs 114 and 115 to the Finished Goods Inventory.

   d. Cost of Job 114 in the Cost of Goods Sold account.

   e. Revenue from the sale of Job 114.

   f. Assignment of any underapplied or overapplied overhead to the Cost of Goods Sold account. (The amount is not material.)

3. Prepare a manufacturing statement for September (use a single line presentation for direct materials and show the details of overhead cost).

4. Compute gross profit for September. Show how to present the inventories on the September 30 balance sheet.

Check   (2f) $3,000 overapplied

(3) Cost of goods manufactured, $500,000

Analysis Component

5. The over- or underapplied overhead adjustment is closed to Cost of Goods Sold. Discuss how this adjustment impacts business decision making regarding individual jobs or batches of jobs.

Swisher Company's computer system generated the following trial balance on December 31, 2008. The company's manager knows that the trial balance is wrong because it does not show any balance for Goods in Process Inventory but does show balances for the Factory Payroll and Factory Overhead accounts.

Problem 19-2B
Source documents, journal entries, overhead, and financial reports

P1   P2   P3   P4

	Debit	Credit
Cash	$48,000	
Accounts receivable	42,000	
Raw materials inventory	26,000	
Goods in process inventory	0	
Finished goods inventory	9,000	
Prepaid rent	3,000	
Accounts payable		$10,500
Notes payable		13,500
Common stock		30,000
Retained earnings		87,000
Sales		180,000
Cost of goods sold	105,000	

[continued on next page]

[continued from previous page]

Factory payroll	16,000	
Factory overhead	27,000	
Operating expenses	45,000	
Totals	$321,000	$321,000

After examining various files, the manager identifies the following six source documents that need to be processed to bring the accounting records up to date.

Materials requisition 94-231:	$4,600 direct materials to Job 603
Materials requisition 94-232:	$7,600 direct materials to Job 604
Materials requisition 94-233:	$2,100 indirect materials
Labor time ticket 765:	$5,000 direct labor to Job 603
Labor time ticket 766:	$8,000 direct labor to Job 604
Labor time ticket 777:	$3,000 indirect labor

Jobs 603 and 604 are the only units in process at year-end. The predetermined overhead rate is 200% of direct labor cost.

Required

1. Use information on the six source documents to prepare journal entries to assign the following costs.
   a. Direct materials costs to Goods in Process Inventory.
   b. Direct labor costs to Goods in Process Inventory.
   c. Overhead costs to Goods in Process Inventory.
   d. Indirect materials costs to the Factory Overhead account.
   e. Indirect labor costs to the Factory Overhead account.

2. Determine the revised balance of the Factory Overhead account after making the entries in part 1. Determine whether there is under- or overapplied overhead for the year. Prepare the adjusting entry to allocate any over- or underapplied overhead to Cost of Goods Sold, assuming the amount is not material.

3. Prepare a revised trial balance.

4. Prepare an income statement for year 2008 and a balance sheet as of December 31, 2008.

Analysis Component

5. Assume that the $2,100 indirect materials on materials requisition 94-233 should have been direct materials charged to Job 604. Without providing specific calculations, describe the impact of this error on the income statement for 2008 and the balance sheet at December 31, 2008.

Problem 19-3B

Source documents, journal entries, and accounts in job order cost accounting

P1 P2 P3

Prescott Company's predetermined overhead rate is 200% of direct labor. Information on the company's production activities during September 2008 follows.
   a. Purchased raw materials on credit, $125,000.
   b. Paid $84,000 cash for factory wages.
   c. Paid $11,000 cash for miscellaneous factory overhead costs.
   d. Materials requisitions record use of the following materials for the month.

Job 487	$30,000
Job 488	20,000
Job 489	12,000
Job 490	14,000
Job 491	4,000
Total direct materials	80,000
Indirect materials	12,000
Total materials used	$92,000

   e. Time tickets record use of the following labor for the month.

Job 487	$ 8,000
Job 488	7,000
Job 489	25,000
Job 490	26,000
Job 491	2,000
Total direct labor	68,000
Indirect labor	16,000
Total	$84,000

f. Allocated overhead to Jobs 487, 489, and 490.

g. Transferred Jobs 487, 489, and 490 to Finished Goods.

h. Sold Jobs 487 and 489 on credit for a total price of $340,000.

i. The company incurred the following overhead costs during the month (credit Prepaid Insurance for expired factory insurance).

Depreciation of factory building	$37,000
Depreciation of factory equipment	21,000
Expired factory insurance	7,000
Accrued property taxes payable	31,000

j. Applied overhead at month-end to the Goods in Process (Jobs 488 and 491) using the predetermined overhead rate of 200% of direct labor cost.

Required

1. Prepare a job cost sheet for each job worked on in the month. Use the following simplified form.

Job No. _____	
Materials	$ _____
Labor	_____
Overhead	_____
Total cost	$ _____

2. Prepare journal entries to record the events and transactions *a* through *j*.

3. Set up T-accounts for each of the following general ledger accounts, each of which started the month with a zero balance: Raw Materials Inventory, Goods in Process Inventory, Finished Goods Inventory, Factory Payroll, Factory Overhead, Cost of Goods Sold. Then post the journal entries to these T-accounts and determine the balance of each account.

4. Prepare a report showing the total cost of each job in process and prove that the sum of their costs equals the Goods in Process Inventory account balance. Prepare similar reports for Finished Goods Inventory and Cost of Goods Sold.

Check (2f) Cr. Factory Overhead, $118,000

(4) Finished Goods Inventory, $92,000

In December 2007, Pavelka Company's manager estimated next year's total direct labor cost assuming 50 persons working an average of 2,000 hours each at an average wage rate of $15 per hour. The manager also estimated the following manufacturing overhead costs for year 2008.

Problem 19-4B
Overhead allocation and adjustment using a predetermined overhead rate

C3   P3   P4

Indirect labor	$159,600
Factory supervision	120,000
Rent on factory building	70,000
Factory utilities	44,000
Factory insurance expired	34,000
Depreciation—Factory equipment	240,000
Repairs expense—Factory equipment	30,000
Factory supplies used	34,400
Miscellaneous production costs	18,000
Total estimated overhead costs	$750,000

At the end of 2008, records show the company incurred $725,000 of actual overhead costs. It completed and sold five jobs with the following direct labor costs: Job 625, $354,000; Job 626, $330,000; Job 627, $175,000; Job 628, $420,000; and Job 629, $184,000. In addition, Job 630 is in process at the end of 2008 and had been charged $10,000 for direct labor. No jobs were in process at the end of 2007. The company's predetermined overhead rate is based on direct labor cost.

Required

1. Determine the following.

    a. Predetermined overhead rate for year 2008.

    b. Total overhead cost applied to each of the six jobs during year 2008.

    c. Over- or underapplied overhead at year-end 2008.

2. Assuming that any over- or underapplied overhead is not material, prepare the adjusting entry to allocate any over- or underapplied overhead to Cost of Goods Sold at the end of year 2008.

Check (1c) $11,500 overapplied

(2) Dr. Factory Overhead, $11,500

Problem 19-5B

Production transactions; subsidiary records; and source documents

P1 P2 P3 P4

If the working papers that accompany this book are unavailable, do not attempt to solve this problem. King Company produces variations of its product, a megatron, in response to custom orders from its customers. On June 1, the company had no inventories of goods in process or finished goods but held the following raw materials.

Material M	120 units @ $200 =	$24,000
Material R	80 units @ 160 =	12,800
Paint	44 units @ 72 =	3,168
Total cost		$39,968

On June 3, the company began working on two megatrons: Job 450 for Encinita Company and Job 451 for Fargo, Inc.

Required

Follow instructions in this list of activities and complete the sheets provided in the working papers.

a. Purchased raw materials on credit and recorded the following information from receiving reports and invoices.

> Receiving Report No. 20, Material M, 150 units at $200 each.
>
> Receiving Report No. 21, Material R, 70 units at $160 each.

Instructions: Record these purchases with a single journal entry and post it to general ledger T-accounts, using the transaction letter *a* to identify the entry. Enter the receiving report information on the materials ledger cards.

b. Requisitioned the following raw materials for production.

> Requisition No. 223, for Job 450, 80 units of Material M.
>
> Requisition No. 224, for Job 450, 60 units of Material R.
>
> Requisition No. 225, for Job 451, 40 units of Material M.
>
> Requisition No. 226, for Job 451, 30 units of Material R.
>
> Requisition No. 227, for 12 units of paint.

Instructions: Enter amounts for direct materials requisitions on the materials ledger cards and the job cost sheets. Enter the indirect material amount on the materials ledger card and record a debit to the Indirect Materials account in the subsidiary factory overhead ledger. Do not record a journal entry at this time.

c. Received the following employee time tickets for work in June.

> Time tickets Nos. 1 to 10 for direct labor on Job 450, $40,000.
>
> Time tickets Nos. 11 to 20 for direct labor on Job 451, $32,000.
>
> Time tickets Nos. 21 to 24 for equipment repairs, $12,000.

Instructions: Record direct labor from the time tickets on the job cost sheets and then debit indirect labor to the Indirect Labor account in the subsidiary factory overhead ledger. Do not record a journal entry at this time.

d. Paid cash for the following items during the month: factory payroll, $84,000, and miscellaneous overhead items, $36,800.

Instructions: Record these payments with journal entries and post them to the general ledger accounts. Also record a debit in the Miscellaneous Overhead account in the subsidiary factory overhead ledger.

e. Finished Job 450 and transferred it to the warehouse. The company assigns overhead to each job with a predetermined overhead rate equal to 70% of direct labor cost.

Instructions: Enter the allocated overhead on the cost sheet for Job 450, fill in the cost summary section of the cost sheet, and then mark the cost sheet "Finished." Prepare a journal entry to record the job's completion and its transfer to Finished Goods and then post it to the general ledger accounts.

f. Delivered Job 450 and accepted the customer's promise to pay $290,000 within 30 days.

Instructions: Prepare journal entries to record the sale of Job 450 and the cost of goods sold. Post them to the general ledger accounts.

g. Applied overhead cost to Job 451 based on the job's direct labor used to date.

Instructions: Enter overhead on the job cost sheet but do not make a journal entry at this time.

h. Recorded the total direct and indirect materials costs as reported on all the requisitions for the month.

Instructions: Prepare a journal entry to record these costs and post it to general ledger accounts.

Check (h) Dr. Goods in Process Inventory, $38,400

i. Recorded the total direct and indirect labor costs as reported on all time tickets for the month.

Instructions: Prepare a journal entry to record these costs and post it to general ledger accounts.

j. Recorded the total overhead costs applied to jobs.

Instructions: Prepare a journal entry to record the allocation of these overhead costs and post it to general ledger accounts.

Check Balance in Factory Overhead, $736 Cr., overapplied

 Problem Set C is available at the book's Website to reinforce and assess your learning.   **PROBLEM SET C**

(This serial problem began in Chapter 1 and continues through most of the book. If previous chapter segments were not completed, the serial problem can begin at this point. It is helpful, but not necessary, for you to use the Working Papers that accompany the book.)

SERIAL PROBLEM

Success Systems

SP 19 The computer workstation furniture manufacturing that Adriana Lopez started in January 2009, is progressing well. As of the end of June, Success Systems' job cost sheets show these total costs accumulated on three furniture jobs.

	Job 6.02	Job 6.03	Job 6.04
Direct materials	$3,000	$6,600	$5,400
Direct labor	1,600	2,840	4,200
Overhead	800	1,420	2,100

Job 6.02 was started in production in May, and these costs were assigned to it in May: direct materials, $1,200; direct labor, $360; and overhead, $180. Jobs 6.03 and 6.04 were started in June. Overhead cost is applied with a predetermined rate based on direct labor costs. Jobs 6.02 and 6.03 are finished in June, and Job 6.04 is expected to be finished in July. No raw materials are used indirectly in June.

Required

1. What is the cost of the raw materials used in June for each of the three jobs and in total?

2. How much total direct labor cost is incurred in June?

3. What predetermined overhead rate is used in June?

4. How much cost is transferred to finished goods inventory in June?

Check (1) Total materials, $13,800

(3) 50%

BEYOND THE NUMBERS

BTN 19-1 Best Buy's financial statements and notes in Appendix A provide evidence of growth potential in its domestic sales.

REPORTING IN ACTION

C2

Required

1. Identify at least two types of costs that will predictably increase as a percent of sales with growth in domestic sales.

2. Explain why you believe the types of costs identified for part 1 will increase, and describe how you might assess Best Buy's success with these costs. (*Hint:* You might consider the gross margin ratio.)

Fast Forward

3. Access Best Buy's annual report for a fiscal year ending after February 26, 2005, from its Website [BestBuy.com] or the SEC's EDGAR database [www.sec.gov]. Review and report its growth in sales along with its cost and income levels (including its gross margin ratio).

COMPARATIVE ANALYSIS

C1

BTN 19-2   Retailers as well as manufacturers can apply just-in-time (JIT) to their inventory management. Both **Best Buy** and **Circuit City** want to know the impact of a JIT inventory system for their operating cash flows. Review each company's statement of cash flows in Appendix A to answer the following.

Required

1. Identify the impact on operating cash flows (increase or decrease) for changes in inventory levels (increase or decrease) for both companies for each of the three most recent years.

2. What impact would a JIT inventory system have on both Best Buy's and Circuit City's operating income? Link the answer to your response for part 1.

3. Would the move to a JIT system have a one-time or recurring impact on operating cash flow?

ETHICS CHALLENGE

P3

Point: Students could compare responses and discuss differences in concerns with allocating overhead.

BTN 19-3   An accounting professional requires at least two skill sets. The first is to be technically competent. Knowing how to capture, manage, and report information is a necessary skill. Second, the ability to assess manager and employee actions and biases for accounting analysis is another skill. For instance, knowing how a person is compensated helps anticipate information biases. Draw on these skills and write a one-half page memo to the financial officer on the following practice of allocating overhead.

Background: Assume that your company sells portable housing to both general contractors and the government. It sells jobs to contractors on a bid basis. A contractor asks for three bids from different manufacturers. The combination of low bid and high quality wins the job. However, jobs sold to the government are bid on a cost-plus basis. This means price is determined by adding all costs plus a profit based on cost at a specified percent, such as 10%. You observe that the amount of overhead allocated to government jobs is higher than that allocated to contract jobs. These allocations concern you and motivate your memo.

COMMUNICATING IN PRACTICE

C2 C3

Point: Have students present a mock interview, one assuming the role of the president of the company and the other the applicant.

BTN 19-4   Assume that you are preparing for a second interview with a manufacturing company. The company is impressed with your credentials but has indicated that it has several qualified applicants. You anticipate that in this second interview, you must show what you offer over other candidates. You learn the company currently uses a periodic inventory system and is not satisfied with the timeliness of its information and its inventory management. The company manufactures custom-order holiday decorations and display items. To show your abilities, you plan to recommend that it use a cost accounting system.

Required

In preparation for the interview, prepare notes outlining the following:

1. Your cost accounting system recommendation and why it is suitable for this company.

2. A general description of the documents that the proposed cost accounting system requires.

3. How the documents in part 2 facilitate the operation of the cost accounting system.

TAKING IT TO THE NET

C2

BTN 19-5   Many contractors work on custom jobs that require a job order costing system.

Required

Access the Website **AEC.Geac.com** and under *Job Cost Accounting* click on *The Construction Manager*. Prepare a one-page memorandum for the CEO of a construction company providing information about the job order costing software this company offers. Would you recommend that the company purchase this software?

TEAMWORK IN ACTION

C2

BTN 19-6   Consider the activities undertaken by a medical clinic in your area.

Required

1. Do you consider a job order cost accounting system appropriate for the clinic?

2. Identify as many factors as possible to lead you to conclude that it uses a job order system.

BTN 19-7 Read the article "Ikea—How the Swedish Retailer Became a Global Cult Brand" in the November 14, 2005, issue of *BusinessWeek*.

BusinessWeek **ACTIVITY**

C1   C2

Required

Identify the reasons why Ikea can offer low-cost products to its customers.

BTN 19-8 Refer to the chapter opener regarding Marco and Sandra Johnson and their company, Antelope Valley Medical College. All successful businesses track their costs. It is especially important for a startup business to monitor and control its costs. Marco and Sandra hope to track all costs associated with each training course taught at their college.

ENTREPRENEURIAL DECISION

C2

Required

1. How can Marco and Sandra apply a job order costing system for Antelope Valley Medical College to monitor the costs of each course? Can they apply the same system to monitor the profitability of each course taught? Explain.
2. Assume that Marco and Sandra use a job order costing system at Antelope Valley Medical College. Identify the three basic cost categories. List at least two typical costs that will fall into each cost category.

BTN 19-9 Job order cost accounting is frequently used by home builders.

HITTING THE ROAD

C3   P2   P3   P4

Required

1. You (or your team) are to prepare a job cost sheet for a single-family home under construction. List four items of both direct materials and direct labor. Explain how you think overhead should be applied.
2. Contact a builder and compare your job cost sheet to this builder's job cost sheet. If possible, speak to that company's accountant. Write your findings in a short report.

BTN 19-10 Dixons, Circuit City, and Best Buy are competitors in the global marketplace. Access Dixons' annual report (Dixons-Group.com) for the year ended May 1, 2004. The following information is available for Dixons.

GLOBAL DECISION

C1

(£ millions)	Current Year	One Year Prior	Two Years Prior
Inventories	£777.7	£699.9	£615.7

Required

1. Determine the change in Dixons' inventories for the last two years. Then identify the impact on net resources generated by operating activities (increase or decrease) for changes in inventory levels (increase or decrease) for Dixons for the last two years.
2. Would a move to a JIT system likely impact Dixons more than it would Best Buy or Circuit City? Explain.

ANSWERS TO MULTIPLE CHOICE QUIZ

1. c; $30,000 \times 150\% = \$45,000$
2. b; $\$38,500/\$35,000 = \underline{110\%}$
3. e; Direct materials + Direct labor + Overhead = Total cost;
   Direct materials + ($4,000/.80) + $4,000 = $10,000
   Direct materials = $\underline{\$1,000}$

4. e; $9,000 + $94,200 + $59,200 + $31,600 − Finished goods = $17,800
   Thus, finished goods = $\underline{\$176,200}$
5. b

20

Process Cost Accounting

A Look Back

Chapter 18 introduced managerial accounting and described cost concepts and the reporting of manufacturing activities. Chapter 19 explained job order costing—an important cost accounting system for customized products and services.

A Look at This Chapter

This chapter focuses on how to measure and account for costs in process operations. We explain process production, describe how to assign costs to processes, and compute cost per equivalent unit for a process.

A Look Ahead

Chapter 21 explains how to allocate factory overhead costs to different products and introduces the activity-based costing method of overhead allocation. It also explains responsibility accounting and measures of departmental performance.

Learning Objectives

CAP

Conceptual

C1 Explain process operations and the way they differ from job order operations. (p. 798)

C2 Define equivalent units and explain their use in process cost accounting. (p. 805)

C3 Explain the four steps in accounting for production activity in a period. (p. 806)

C4 Define a process cost summary and describe its purposes. (p. 809)

C5 Appendix 20A—Explain and illustrate the four steps in accounting for production activity using FIFO. (p. 816)

Analytical

A1 Compare process cost accounting and job order cost accounting. (p. 799)

A2 Explain and illustrate a hybrid costing system. (p. 813)

Procedural

P1 Record the flow of direct materials costs in process cost accounting. (p. 802)

P2 Record the flow of direct labor costs in process cost accounting. (p. 802)

P3 Record the flow of factory overhead costs in process cost accounting. (p. 803)

P4 Compute equivalent units produced in a period. (p. 805)

P5 Prepare a process cost summary. (p. 809)

P6 Record the transfer of completed goods to Finished Goods Inventory and Cost of Goods Sold. (p. 811)

Decision Feature

Styling to the DuWop Tune

GLENDALE, CA—A few years ago, Cristina Bartolucci and Laura DeLuisa were making their livings as hair and makeup artists on Hollywood movie sets. They had no idea they would soon become makeup moguls. "We had this problem," explains Cristina. "Stars would go out late, eat too much . . . drink too much . . . and arrive on the set at 5 AM with tired, puffy eyes, and then expect us to make them look flawless and wide awake." So the pair headed into Laura's kitchen and developed *I Gels*—naturally cool gel discs filled with botanicals that, when placed on the eyes, are soothing and help with dark circles and puffiness. Cristina and Laura promptly started their makeup company called DuWop (**DuWop.com**), meaning "two Italian girls."

"If it weren't for *I Gels*, I don't know if we'd be here," says Laura. Although *I Gels* were an instant hit, it took a lot of hard work. Cristina and Laura had to learn about production operations and suppliers. A big part of their success, they say, was learning the skills needed to monitor and control the costs of materials, labor, and overhead applied to production processes. Cristina and Laura also adopted a hands-on managerial style. "The UPS truck would arrive and we'd start flinging parcels," jokes Laura. But they feel their highly involved approach to production management is necessary. "[If] you make a

mistake that costs you a lot of money, you risk losing your company," says Cristina.

Cristina and Laura also developed their abilities to prepare and interpret process cost summaries on their production activities. Sales are important, they admit, but without cost controls, income is quickly eaten away. "[We] fix problems right away," says Cristina. Suppliers of materials presented special challenges, explains Laura. "I'd actually gotten bullied by a few suppliers. [And] they'd talk us into things that we really didn't need," she says. Yet the pair's focus on cost management helped curtail the risks of making bad decisions, and they stayed committed to improving process operations and tracking all costs.

DuWop began with the advantage of having a natural research lab. "On the packaging it says, 'Not tested on animals, only on actors,' and that's the truth," says Laura. They also focused on satisfying customers. "Some of our most devoted customers are people who have had suggestions about how to make a product better," says Cristina. The DuWop duo listens intently to its actor-customers to grow their beloved business. "I don't believe in giving up," says Laura. Adds Cristina, "I love what I'm doing."

[Sources: *DuWop Website,* May 2006; *Entrepreneur,* November and October 2004; *CPC Packaging,* February 2005; *Health and Beauty,* November 2001; *Factio,* July 2005; *Oprah Winfrey Show,* 2003]

The type of product or service a company offers determines its cost accounting system. Job order costing is used to account for custom products and services that meet the demands of a particular customer. Not all products are manufactured in this way; many carry standard designs so that one unit is no different than any other unit. Such a system often produces large numbers of units on a continuous basis, all of which pass through similar processes. This chapter describes how to use a process cost accounting system to account for these types of products. It also explains how costs are accumulated for each process and then assigned to units passing through those processes. This information helps to understand and estimate the cost of each process as well as find ways to reduce costs and improve processes.

Process Cost Accounting

Process Operations
- Comparison of job order and process operations
- Organization of process operations
- GenX Company— An Illustration

Process Cost Accounting
- Direct and indirect costs
- Accounting for materials costs
- Accounting for labor costs
- Accounting for factory overhead

Equivalent Units of Production (EUP)
- Accounting for goods in process
- Differences between EUP for materials and that for labor and overhead

Process Costing Illustration
- Physical flow of units
- EUP
- Cost per EUP
- Cost reconciliation
- Process cost summary
- Transfers to finished goods and to cost of goods sold

Process Operations

C1 Explain process operations and the way they differ from job order operations.

Process operations, also called *process manufacturing* or *process production,* is the mass production of products in a continuous flow of steps. This means that products pass through a series of sequential processes. Petroleum refining is a common example of process operations. Crude oil passes through a series of steps before it is processed into different grades of petroleum. **Exxon Mobil**'s oil activities reflect a process operation. An important characteristic of process operations is the high level of standardization necessary if the system is to produce large volumes of products. Process operations also extend to services. Examples include mail sorting in large post offices and order processing in large mail-order firms such as **L.L. Bean.** The common feature in these service organizations is that operations are performed in a sequential manner using a series of standardized processes. Other companies using process operations include **Kellogg** (cereals), **Pfizer** (drugs), **Procter & Gamble** (household products), **Xerox** (copiers), **Coca-Cola** (softdrinks), **Heinz** (ketchup), and **Hershey** (chocolate).

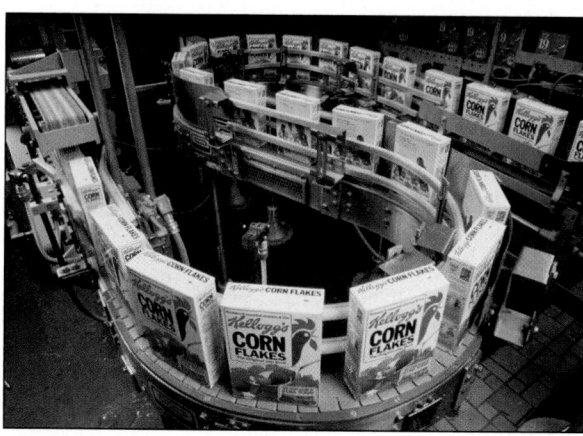

Each of these examples of products and services involves operations having a series of *processes,* or steps. Each process involves a different set of activities. A production operation that processes chemicals, for instance, might include the four steps shown in Exhibit 20.1. Understanding such processes for companies with process operations is crucial for measuring their costs.

Exhibit 20.1

Process Operations: Chemicals

| Preparing the chemicals | Mixing the chemicals | Bottling the chemical mix | Packaging the bottles |

Comparing Job Order and Process Operations

Job order and process operations can be considered as two ends of a continuum. Important features of both systems are shown in Exhibit 20.2. We often describe job order and process operations with manufacturing examples, but they both apply to service companies. In a job order costing system, the measurement focus is on the individual job or batch. In a process costing system, the measurement focus is on the process itself and the standardized units produced.

A1 Compare process cost accounting and job order cost accounting.

Exhibit 20.2

Comparing Job Order and Process Operations

Job Order Systems	Process Systems
• Custom orders	• Repetitive operations
• Heterogeneous products and services	• Homogeneous products and services
• Low production volume	• High production volume
• High product flexibility	• Low product flexibility
• Low to medium standardization	• High standardization

Organization of Process Operations

In a process operation, each process is identified as a separate *production department, workstation,* or *work center.* With the exception of the first process or department, each receives the output from the prior department as a partially processed product. Depending on the nature of the process, a company applies direct labor, overhead, and, perhaps, additional direct materials to move the product toward completion. Only the final process or department in the series produces finished goods ready for sale to customers.

Tracking costs for several related departments can seem complex. Yet because process costing procedures are applied to the activity of each department or process separately, we need only consider one process at a time. This simplifies the procedures.

When the output of one department becomes an input to another department, as is the case in sequential processing, we simply transfer the costs associated with those units from the first department into the next. We repeat these steps from department to department until the final process is complete. At that point the accumulated costs are transferred with the product from Goods in Process Inventory to Finished Goods Inventory. The next section illustrates a company with a single process, but the methods illustrated apply to a multiprocess scenario as each department's costs are handled separately for each department.

GenX Company— An Illustration

The GenX Company illustrates process operations. It produces Profen®, an over-the-counter pain reliever for athletes. GenX sells Profen to wholesale distributors who in turn sell it to retailers. Profen is produced by mixing its active

Decision Insight

Accounting for Health Many service companies use process departments to perform specific tasks for consumers. Hospitals, for instance, have radiology and physical therapy facilities with special equipment and trained employees. When patients need services, they are processed through departments to receive prescribed care. Service companies need process cost accounting information as much as manufacturers to estimate costs of services, to plan future operations, to control costs, and to determine customer charges.

ingredient, Profelene, with flavorings and preservatives, molding it into Profen tablets, and packaging the tablets. Exhibit 20.3 shows a summary floor plan of the GenX factory, which has five areas.

1̲ *Storeroom*—materials are received and then distributed when requisitioned.

2̲ *Production support offices*—used by administrative and maintenance employees who support manufacturing operations.

3̲ *Locker rooms*—workers change from street clothes into sanitized uniforms before working in the factory.

4̲ *Production floor*—area where the powder is processed into tablets.

5̲ *Warehouse*—finished products are stored before being shipped to wholesalers.

Point: Robots, computers, and online information are common in today's factory.

Exhibit 20.3

Floor Plan of GenX's Factory

The first step in process manufacturing is to decide when to produce a product. Management determines the types and quantities of materials and labor needed and then schedules the work. Based on these plans, production begins. The flowchart in Exhibit 20.4 shows the production steps for GenX. The following sections explain how GenX uses a process cost accounting system to compute these costs. Many of the explanations refer to this exhibit and its numbered cost flows ① through ⑩. (*Hint:* The amounts for the numbered cost flows in Exhibit 20.4 are summarized in Exhibit 20.21. Those amounts are explained in the following pages, but it can help to refer to Exhibit 20.21 as we proceed through the explanations.)

Exhibit 20.4

Process Operations and Costs: GenX

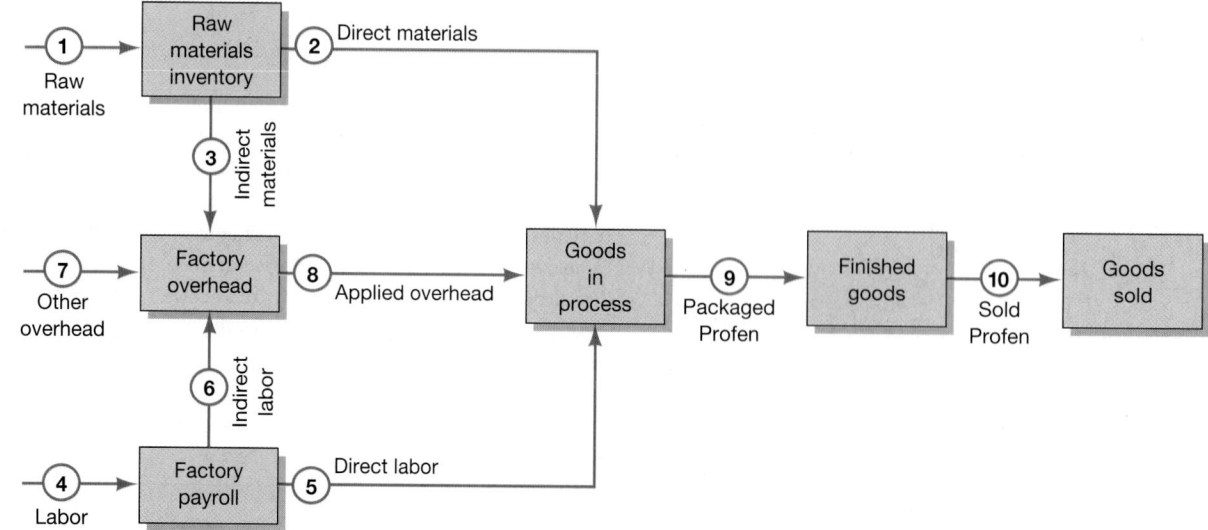

Process Cost Accounting

Process and job order operations are similar in that both combine materials, labor, and overhead in the process of producing products. They differ in how they are organized and managed. The measurement focus in a job order costing system is on the individual job or batch, whereas in a process costing system, it is on the individual process. Regardless of the measurement focus, we are ultimately interested in determining the cost per unit of product (or service) resulting from either system.

Specifically, the **job order cost accounting system** assigns direct materials, direct labor, and overhead to jobs. The total job cost is then divided by the number of units to compute a cost per unit for that job. The **process cost accounting system** assigns direct materials, direct labor, and overhead to specific processes (or departments). The total costs associated with each process are then divided by the number of units passing through that process to determine the cost per equivalent unit (defined later in the chapter) for that process. Differences in the way these two systems apply materials, labor, and overhead costs are highlighted in Exhibit 20.5.

Point: The cost object in a job order system is the specific job; the cost object in a process costing system is the process.

Job order operations / Process operations

Exhibit 20.5

Comparing Job Order and Process Cost Accounting Systems

Direct and Indirect Costs

Point: If a cost can be traced to the cost object, it is direct; if it cannot, it is indirect.

Like job order operations, process cost accounting systems use the concepts of direct and indirect costs. Materials and labor that can be traced to specific processes are assigned to those processes as direct costs. Materials and labor that cannot be traced to a specific process are indirect costs and are assigned to overhead. Some costs classified as overhead in a job order system may be classified as direct costs in process cost accounting. For example, depreciation of a machine used entirely by one process is a direct cost of that process.

Decision Insight

JIT Boon to Process Operations   Companies that adopt JIT manufacturing often organize their production system as a series of sequential processes. One survey found 60% of companies that converted to JIT used process operations; this compares to only 20% before converting to JIT.

Accounting for Materials Costs

P1 Record the flow of direct materials costs in process cost accounting.

In Exhibit 20.4, arrow line ① reflects the arrival of materials at GenX's factory. These materials include Profelene, flavorings, preservatives, and packaging. They also include supplies for the production support office. GenX uses a perpetual inventory system and makes all purchases on credit. The summary entry for receipts of raw materials in April follows (dates in journal entries numbered ① through ⑩ are omitted because they are summary entries, often reflecting two or more transactions or events).

Assets = Liabilities + Equity
+11,095   +11,095

①	Raw Materials Inventory	11,095	
	Accounts Payable		11,095
	Acquired materials on credit for factory use.		

Arrow line ② in Exhibit 20.4 reflects the flow of direct materials to production, where they are used to produce Profen. Most direct materials are physically combined into the finished product; the remaining direct materials include those used and clearly linked with a specific process. The manager of a process usually obtains materials by submitting a *materials requisition* to the materials storeroom manager. In some situations, materials move continuously from raw materials inventory through the manufacturing process. **Pepsi Bottling**, for instance, uses a process in which inventory moves continuously through the system. In these cases, a **materials consumption report** summarizes the materials used by a department during a reporting period and replaces materials requisitions. The entry to record the use of direct materials by GenX's production department in April follows.

Assets = Liabilities + Equity
+9,900
−9,900

②	Goods in Process Inventory	9,900	
	Raw Materials Inventory		9,900
	To assign costs of direct materials used in production.		

This entry transfers costs from one asset account to another asset account. (When two or more production departments exist, a company uses two or more Goods in Process Inventory accounts to separately accumulate costs incurred by each.)

In Exhibit 20.4, the arrow line ③ reflects the flow of indirect materials from the storeroom to factory overhead. These materials are not clearly linked with any specific production process or department but are used to support overall production activity. The following entry records the cost of indirect materials used by GenX in April.

Example: What types of materials might the flow of arrow line ③ in Exhibit 20.4 reflect? *Answer:* Goggles, gloves, protective clothing, recordkeeping supplies, and cleaning supplies.

Assets = Liabilities + Equity
−1,195   −1,195

③	Factory Overhead	1,195	
	Raw Materials Inventory		1,195
	To record indirect materials used in April.		

After the entries for both direct and indirect materials are posted, the Raw Materials Inventory account appears as shown in Exhibit 20.6. The April 30 balance sheet reports the $4,000 Raw Materials Inventory account as a current asset.

Exhibit 20.6

Raw Materials Inventory

Raw Materials Inventory				Acct. No. 132		
Date		Explanation	Debit	Credit	Balance
Mar.	31	Balance			4,000
Apr.	30	Materials purchases	11,095		15,095
	30	Direct materials usage		9,900	5,195
	30	Indirect materials usage		1,195	4,000

Accounting for Labor Costs

P2 Record the flow of direct labor costs in process cost accounting.

Exhibit 20.4 shows GenX factory payroll costs as reflected in arrow line ④. Total labor costs of $8,920 are paid in cash and are recorded in the Factory Payroll account.

④	Factory Payroll.	8,920		
	Cash		8,920	
	To record factory wages for April.			

Assets = Liabilities + Equity
−8,920   −8,920

Time reports from the production department and the production support office triggered this entry. (For simplicity, we do not separately identify withholdings and additional payroll taxes for employees.) In a process operation, the direct labor of a production department includes all labor used exclusively by that department. This is the case even if the labor is not applied to the product itself. If a production department in a process operation, for instance, has a full-time manager and a full-time maintenance worker, their salaries are direct labor costs of that process and are not factory overhead.

Arrow line ⑤ in Exhibit 20.4 shows GenX's use of direct labor in the production department. The following entry transfers April's direct labor costs from the Factory Payroll account to the Goods in Process Inventory account.

⑤	Goods in Process Inventory	5,700	
	Factory Payroll		5,700
	To assign costs of direct labor used in production.		

Assets = Liabilities + Equity
+5,700   +5,700

Arrow line ⑥ in Exhibit 20.4 reflects GenX's indirect labor costs. These employees provide clerical, maintenance, and other services that help produce Profen efficiently. For example, they order materials, deliver them to the factory floor, repair equipment, operate and program computers used in production, keep payroll and other production records, clean up, and move the finished goods to the warehouse. The following entry charges these indirect labor costs to factory overhead.

Point: A department's indirect labor cost might include an allocated portion of the salary of a manager who supervises two or more departments. Allocation of costs between departments is discussed in Chapter 21.

⑥	Factory Overhead	3,220	
	Factory Payroll		3,220
	To record indirect labor as overhead.		

Assets = Liabilities + Equity
                                          −3,220
                                          +3,220

After these entries for both direct and indirect labor are posted, the Factory Payroll account appears as shown in Exhibit 20.7. The Factory Payroll account is now closed and ready to receive entries for May.

Factory Payroll			Acct. No. 530			
Date		Explanation		Debit	Credit	Balance
Mar.	31	Balance				0
Apr.	30	Total payroll for April		8,920		8,920
	30	Direct labor costs			5,700	3,220
	30	Indirect labor costs			3,220	0

Exhibit 20.7

Factory Payroll

Accounting for Factory Overhead

Overhead costs other than indirect materials and indirect labor are reflected by arrow line ⑦ in Exhibit 20.4. These overhead items include the costs of insuring production assets, renting the factory building, using factory utilities, and depreciating equipment not directly related to a specific process. The following entry records overhead costs for April.

P3 Record the flow of factory overhead costs in process cost accounting.

⑦	Factory Overhead	2,425	
	Prepaid Insurance		180
	Utilities Payable		645
	Cash		750
	Accumulated Depreciation—Factory Equipment . .		850
	To record overhead items incurred in April.		

Assets = Liabilities + Equity
−180   +645   −2,425
−750
−850

After this entry is posted, the Factory Overhead account balance is $6,840, comprising indirect materials of $1,195, indirect labor of $3,220, and $2,425 of other overhead.

Point: The time it takes to process (cycle) products through a process is sometimes used to allocate costs.

Arrow line ⑧ in Exhibit 20.4 reflects the application of factory overhead to production. Factory overhead is applied to processes by relating overhead cost to another variable such as direct labor hours or machine hours used. In some situations, a single allocation basis such as direct labor hours (or a single rate for the entire plant) fails to provide useful allocations. As a result, management can use different rates for different production departments. Based on an analysis of its operations, GenX applies its April overhead at a rate of 120% of direct labor cost, as shown in Exhibit 20.8.

Exhibit 20.8

Applying Factory Overhead

	Direct Labor Cost	Predetermined Rate	Overhead Applied
Production Department	$5,700	120%	$6,840

GenX records its applied overhead with the following entry.

Assets = Liabilities + Equity
+6,840   +6,840

⑧	Goods in Process Inventory	6,840	
	Factory Overhead.		6,840
	Allocated overhead costs to production at 120% of direct labor cost.		

Decision Ethics   Answer—p. 821

Budget Officer You are working to identify the direct and indirect costs of a new processing department that has several machines. This department's manager instructs you to classify a majority of the costs as indirect to take advantage of the direct labor-based overhead allocation method so it will be charged a lower amount of overhead (because of its small direct labor cost). This would penalize other departments with higher allocations. It also will cause the performance ratings of managers in these other departments to suffer. What action do you take?

After posting this entry, the Factory Overhead account appears as shown in Exhibit 20.9. For GenX, the amount of overhead applied equals the actual overhead incurred during April. In most cases, using a predetermined overhead rate leaves an over-applied or underapplied balance in the Factory Overhead account. At the end of the period, this overapplied or underapplied balance should be either closed to the Cost of Goods Sold account or allocated among the Cost of Goods Sold, the Goods in Process Inventory, and the Finished Goods Inventory. Procedures for this allocation are the same as that described in Chapter 19 for job order cost accounting systems.

Exhibit 20.9

Factory Overhead

Example: If applied overhead results in a $6,940 credit to the factory overhead account, does it yield an over- or underapplied overhead amount?
Answer: $100 overapplied overhead

		Factory Overhead			Acct. No. 540
Date		**Explanation**	**Debit**	**Credit**	**Balance**
Mar.	31	Balance			0
Apr.	30	Indirect materials usage	1,195		1,195
	30	Indirect labor costs	3,220		4,415
	30	Other overhead costs	2,425		6,840
	30	Applied to production departments		6,840	0

Quick Check

Answers—p. 822

1. A process operation (a) is another name for a job order operation, (b) does not use the concepts of direct materials or direct labor, or (c) typically produces large quantities of homogenous products or services.

2. Under what conditions is a process cost accounting system more suitable for measuring production costs than a job order cost accounting system?

3. When direct materials are assigned and used in production, the entry to record their use includes (a) a credit to Goods in Process Inventory, (b) a debit to Goods in Process Inventory, or (c) a debit to Raw Materials Inventory.

4. What are the three cost categories incurred by both job order and process operations?

5. How many Goods in Process Inventory accounts are needed in a process cost system?

Equivalent Units of Production

We explained how materials, labor, and overhead costs for a period are accumulated in the Goods in Process Inventory account, but we have not explained the arrow lines labeled ⑨ and ⑩ in Exhibit 20.4. These lines reflect the transfer of products from the production department to finished goods inventory, and from finished goods inventory to cost of goods sold. To determine the costs recorded for these flows, we must first determine the cost per unit of product and then apply this result to the number of units transferred.

C2 Define equivalent units and explain their use in process cost accounting.

20-1

Accounting for Goods in Process

If a process has *no beginning and no ending goods in process inventory,* the unit cost of goods transferred out of a process is computed as follows.

Total cost assigned to the process (direct materials, direct labor, and overhead)
Total number of units started and finished in the period

If a process has a beginning or ending inventory of partially processed units (or both), then the total cost assigned to the process must be allocated to all completed and incomplete units worked on during the period. Therefore, the denominator must measure the entire production activity of the process for the period, called **equivalent units of production** (or **EUP**), a phrase that refers to the number of units that could have been started *and* completed given the cost incurred during a period. This measure is then used to compute the cost per equivalent unit and to assign costs to finished goods and goods in process inventory.

To illustrate, assume that GenX adds (or introduces) 100 units into its process during a period. Suppose at the end of that period, the production supervisor determines that those 100 units are 60% of the way through the process. Therefore, equivalent units of production for that period total 60 EUP (100 units × 60%). This means that with the resources used to put 100 units 60% of the way through the process we could have started and completed 60 whole units.

Differences in Equivalent Units for Materials, Labor, and Overhead

In many processes, the equivalent units of production for direct materials are not the same with respect to direct labor and overhead. To illustrate, consider a 5-step process operation shown in Exhibit 20.10.

P4 Compute equivalent units produced in a period.

Exhibit 20.10

An Illustrative 5-Step Process Operation

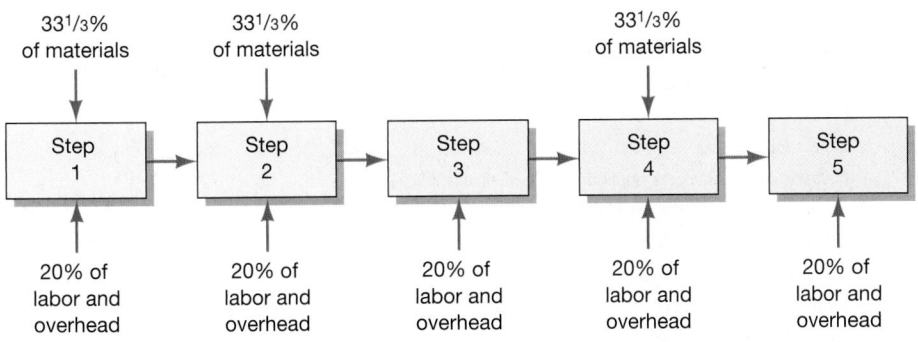

This exhibit shows that one-third of the direct material cost is added at each of three steps: 1, 2, and 4. One-fifth of the direct labor cost is added at each of the five steps. One-fifth of the overhead also is added at each step because overhead is applied as a percent of direct labor for this company.

When units finish step 1, they are one-third complete with respect to direct materials but only one-fifth complete with respect to direct labor and overhead. When they finish step 2,

Process Services Customer-interaction software is a hot item in customer-service processes. Whether in insurance, delivery, or technology services, companies are finding that this software can turn their customer-service process into an asset. How does it work? For starters, it cuts time spent on service calls because a customer describes a problem only once. It also yields a database of customer questions and complaints that gives insights into needed improvements. It also recognizes incoming phone numbers and accesses previous dealings.

they are two-thirds complete with respect to direct materials but only two-fifths complete with respect to direct labor and overhead. When they finish step 3, they remain two-thirds complete with respect to materials but are now three-fifths complete with respect to labor and overhead. When they finish step 4, they are 100% complete with respect to materials (all direct materials have been added) but only four-fifths complete with respect to labor and overhead.

For example, if 300 units of product are started and processed through step 1 of Exhibit 20.10, they are said to be one-third complete *with respect to materials*. Expressed in terms of equivalent finished units, the processing of these 300 units is equal to finishing 100 EUP with respect to materials (300 units × 33⅓%). However, only one-fifth of direct labor and overhead has been applied to the 300 units at the end of step 1. This means that the equivalent units of production *with respect to labor and overhead* total 60 EUP (300 units × 20%).

Process Costing Illustration

This section applies process costing concepts and procedures to GenX. **This illustration uses the weighted average method for inventory costs. The FIFO method is illustrated in Appendix 20A.** (Assume a weighted average cost flow for all computations and assignments in this chapter unless explicitly stated differently. When using a just-in-time inventory system, different inventory methods yield similar results because inventories are immaterial.)

C3 Explain the four steps in accounting for production activity in a period.

Exhibit 20.11 shows selected information from the production department for the month of April. Accounting for a department's activity for a period includes four steps involving analysis of (1) physical flow, (2) equivalent units, (3) cost per equivalent unit, and (4) cost assignment and reconciliation. The next sections describe each step.

Exhibit 20.11

Production Data

Beginning goods in process inventory (March 31)	
Units of product	30,000
Percentage of completion—Direct materials	100%
Percentage of completion—Direct labor	65%
Direct materials costs	$ 3,300
Direct labor costs	$ 600
Factory overhead costs applied (120% of direct labor)	$ 720
Activities during the current period (April)	
Units started this period	90,000
Units transferred out (completed)	100,000
Direct materials costs	$ 9,900
Direct labor costs	$ 5,700
Factory overhead costs applied (120% of direct labor)	$ 6,840
Ending goods in process inventory (April 30)	
Units of product	20,000
Percentage of completion—Direct materials	100%
Percentage of completion—Direct labor	25%

Step 1: Determine Physical Flow of Units

A *physical flow reconciliation* is a report that reconciles (1) the physical units started in a period with (2) the physical units completed in that period. A physical flow reconciliation for GenX is shown in Exhibit 20.12 for April.

Units to Account For		Units Accounted For	
Beginning goods in process inventory	30,000 units	Units completed and transferred out	100,000 units
Units started this period	90,000 units	Ending goods in process inventory	20,000 units
Total units to account for	**120,000 units**	Total units accounted for	**120,000 units**

reconciled

Exhibit 20.12

Physical Flow Reconciliation

The weighted average method does not require us to separately track the units in beginning work in process from those units started this period. Instead, the units are treated as part of a large pool with an average cost per unit.

Step 2: Compute Equivalent Units of Production

The second step is to compute *equivalent units of production* for direct materials, direct labor, and factory overhead for April. Overhead is applied using direct labor as the allocation base for GenX. This also implies that equivalent units are the same for both labor and overhead.

GenX used its direct materials, direct labor, and overhead to make finished units of Profen and to begin processing some units that are not yet complete. We must convert the physical units measure to equivalent units based on how each input has been used. Equivalent units are computed by multiplying the number of physical units by the percentage of completion for each input—see Exhibit 20.13.

Equivalent Units of Production	Direct Materials	Direct Labor	Factory Overhead
Equivalent units completed and transferred out (100,000 × 100%)	100,000 EUP	100,000 EUP	100,000 EUP
Equivalent units for ending goods in process			
Direct materials (20,000 × 100%)	20,000		
Direct labor (20,000 × 25%)		5,000	
Factory overhead (20,000 × 25%)			5,000
Equivalent units of production	120,000 EUP	105,000 EUP	105,000 EUP

Exhibit 20.13

Equivalent Units of Production—Weighted Average

The first row of Exhibit 20.13 reflects units transferred out in April. The production department entirely completed its work on the 100,000 units transferred out. These units have 100% of the materials, labor, and overhead required, or 100,000 equivalent units of each input (100,000 × 100%).

The second row references the ending goods in process, and rows three, four, and five break it down by materials, labor, and overhead. For direct materials, the units in ending goods in process inventory (20,000 physical units) include all materials required, so there are 20,000 equivalent units (20,000 × 100%) of materials in the unfinished physical units. Regarding labor, the units in ending goods in process inventory include 25% of the labor required, which implies 5,000 equivalent units of labor (20,000 × 25%). These units are only 25% complete and labor is used uniformly through the process. Overhead is applied on the basis of direct labor for GenX, so equivalent units for overhead is computed identically to labor (20,000 × 25%).

The final row reflects the whole units of product that could have been manufactured with the amount of inputs used to create some complete and some incomplete units. For GenX, the amount of inputs used to produce 100,000 complete units and to start 20,000 additional units is equivalent to the amount of direct materials in 120,000 whole units, the amount of direct labor in 105,000 whole units, the amount of overhead in 105,000 whole units.

Step 3: Compute Cost per Equivalent Unit

Equivalent units of production for each product (from step 2) is used to compute the average cost per equivalent unit. Under the **weighted average method,** the computation of EUP does not separate the units in beginning inventory from those started this period; similarly, this method combines the costs of beginning goods in process inventory with the costs incurred in the current period. This process is illustrated in Exhibit 20.14.

Exhibit 20.14

Cost per Equivalent Unit of Production—Weighted Average

Cost per Equivalent Unit of Production	Direct Materials	Direct Labor	Factory Overhead
Costs of beginning goods in process inventory	$ 3,300	$ 600	$ 720
Costs incurred this period	9,900	5,700	6,840
Total costs	$13,200	$6,300	$7,560
÷ Equivalent units of production (from Step 2)	120,000 EUP	105,000 EUP	105,000 EUP
= Cost per equivalent unit of production	$0.11 per EUP*	$0.06 per EUP†	$0.072 per EUP‡

*$13,200 ÷ 120,000 EUP   †$6,300 ÷ 105,000 EUP   ‡$7,560 ÷ 105,000 EUP

For direct materials, the cost averages $0.11 per EUP, computed as the sum of direct materials cost from beginning goods in process inventory ($3,300) and the direct materials cost incurred in April ($9,900), and this sum ($13,200) is then divided by the 120,000 EUP for materials (from step 2). The costs per equivalent unit for labor and overhead are similarly computed. Specifically, direct labor cost averages $0.06 per EUP, computed as the sum of labor cost in beginning goods in process inventory ($600) and the labor costs incurred in April ($5,700), and this sum ($6,300) divided by 105,000 EUP for labor. Overhead costs averages $0.072 per EUP, computed as the sum of overhead cost in the beginning goods in process inventory ($720) and the overhead costs applied in April ($6,840), and this sum ($7,560) divided by 105,000 EUP for overhead.

Topic Tackler
PLUS
20-2

Step 4: Assign and Reconcile Costs

The EUP from Step 2 and the cost per EUP from Step 3 are used in Step 4 to assign costs to (a) units that production completed and transferred to finished goods and (b) units that remain in process. This is illustrated in Exhibit 20.15.

Exhibit 20.15

Report of Costs Accounted For—Weighted Average

Cost of units completed and transferred out		
Direct materials (100,000 EUP × $0.11 per EUP)	$11,000	
Direct labor (100,000 EUP × $0.06 per EUP)	6,000	
Factory overhead (100,000 EUP × $0.072 per EUP)	7,200	
Cost of units completed this period		$ 24,200
Cost of ending goods in process inventory		
Direct materials (20,000 EUP × $0.11 per EUP)	2,200	
Direct labor (5,000 EUP × $0.06 per EUP)	300	
Factory overhead (5,000 EUP × $0.072 per EUP)	360	
Cost of ending goods in process inventory		2,860
Total costs accounted for		$27,060

Cost of Units Completed and Transferred   The 100,000 units completed and transferred to finished goods inventory required 100,000 EUP of direct materials. Thus, we assign $11,000 (100,000 EUP × $0.11 per EUP) of direct materials cost to those units. Similarly, those units had received 100,000 EUP of direct labor and 100,000 EUP of factory overhead (recall Exhibit 20.13). Thus, we assign $6,000 (100,000 EUP × $0.06 per EUP) of direct labor and $7,200 (100,000 EUP × $0.072 per EUP) of overhead to those units. The total cost of the 100,000 completed and transferred units is $24,200 ($11,000 + $6,000 + $7,200) and their average cost per unit is $0.242 ($24,200 ÷ 100,000 units).

Cost of Units for Ending Goods in Process   There are 20,000 incomplete units in goods in process inventory at period-end. For direct materials, those units have 20,000 EUP of material (from step 2) at a cost of $0.11 per EUP (from step 3), which yields the materials cost of goods in process inventory of $2,200 (20,000 EUP × $0.11 per EUP). For direct labor, the in-process units have 25% of the required labor, or 5,000 EUP (from step 2). Using the $0.06 labor cost per EUP (from step 3) we obtain the labor cost of goods in process inventory of $300 (5,000 EUP × $0.06 per EUP). For overhead, the in-process units reflect 5,000 EUP (from step 2). Using the $0.072 overhead cost per EUP (from step 3) we obtain overhead costs with in-process inventory of $360 (5,000 EUP × $0.072 per EUP). Total cost of goods in process inventory at period-end is $2,860 ($2,200 + $300 + $360).

As a check, management verifies that total costs assigned to those units completed and transferred plus the costs of those in process (from Exhibit 20.15) equal the costs incurred by production. Exhibit 20.16 shows the costs incurred by production this period. We then reconcile the *costs accounted for* in Exhibit 20.15 with the *costs to account for* in Exhibit 20.16.

Exhibit 20.16

Report of Costs to Account For—Weighted Average

Cost of beginning goods in process inventory		
Direct materials	$3,300	
Direct labor	600	
Factory overhead	720	$ 4,620
Cost incurred this period		
Direct materials	9,900	
Direct labor	5,700	
Factory overhead	6,840	22,440
Total costs to account for		**$27,060**

At GenX, the production department manager is responsible for $27,060 in costs: $4,620 that is assigned to the goods in process at the start of the period plus $22,440 of materials, labor, and overhead incurred in the period. At period-end, that manager must show where these costs are assigned. The manager for GenX reports that $2,860 are assigned to units in process and $24,200 are assigned to units completed (per Exhibit 20.15). The sum of these amounts equals $27,060. Thus, the total *costs to account for* equals the total *costs accounted for* (minor differences can sometimes occur from rounding).

Process Cost Summary   An important managerial accounting report for a process cost accounting system is the **process cost summary** (also called *production report*), which is prepared separately for each process or production department. Three reasons for the summary are to (1) help department managers control and monitor their departments, (2) help factory managers evaluate department managers' performances, and (3) provide cost information for financial statements. A process cost summary achieves these purposes by describing the costs charged to each department, reporting the equivalent units of production achieved by each department, and determining the costs assigned to each department's output. For our purposes, it is prepared using a combination of Exhibits 20.13, 20.14, 20.15, and 20.16.

C4 Define a process cost summary and describe its purposes.

The process cost summary for GenX is shown in Exhibit 20.17. The report is divided into three sections. Section ① lists the total costs charged to the department, including direct materials, direct labor, and overhead costs incurred, as well as the cost of the beginning goods in process inventory. Section ② describes the equivalent units of production for the department. Equivalent units for materials, labor, and overhead are in separate columns. It also reports direct materials, direct labor, and overhead costs per equivalent unit. Section ③ allocates total costs among units worked on in the period. The $24,200 is the total cost of goods transferred out of the department, and the $2,860 is the cost of partially processed ending inventory units. The assigned costs are then added to show that the total $27,060 cost charged to the department in section ① is now assigned to the units in section ③.

P5 Prepare a process cost summary.

Exhibit 20.17

Process Cost Summary

GenX COMPANY
Process Cost Summary
For Month Ended April 30, 2008

① Costs Charged to Production

Costs of beginning goods in process

Direct materials	$3,300	
Direct labor	600	
Factory overhead	720	$ 4,620

Costs incurred this period

Direct materials	9,900	
Direct labor	5,700	
Factory overhead	6,840	22,440
Total costs to account for		$27,060

Unit Cost Information

Units to account for:		Units accounted for:	
Beginning goods in process	30,000	Completed and transferred out	100,000
Units started this period	90,000	Ending goods in process	20,000
Total units to account for	120,000	Total units accounted for	120,000

② Equivalent Units of Production (EUP)

	Direct Materials	Direct Labor	Factory Overhead
Units completed and transferred out	100,000 EUP	100,000 EUP	100,000 EUP
Units of ending goods in process			
Direct materials (20,000 × 100%)	20,000		
Direct labor (20,000 × 25%)		5,000	
Factory overhead (20,000 × 25%)			5,000
Equivalent units of production	120,000 EUP	105,000 EUP	105,000 EUP

Cost per EUP

	Direct Materials	Direct Labor	Factory Overhead
Costs of beginning goods in process	$ 3,300	$ 600	$ 720
Costs incurred this period	9,900	5,700	6,840
Total costs	$13,200	$6,300	$7,560
÷EUP	120,000 EUP	105,000 EUP	105,000 EUP
Cost per EUP	$0.11 per EUP	$0.06 per EUP	$0.072 per EUP

③ Cost Assignment and Reconciliation

Costs transferred out (cost of goods manufactured)

Direct materials (100,000 EUP × $0.11 per EUP)	$11,000	
Direct labor (100,000 EUP × $0.06 per EUP)	6,000	
Factory overhead (100,000 EUP × $0.072 per EUP)	7,200	$ 24,200

Costs of ending goods in process

Direct materials (20,000 EUP × $0.11 per EUP)	2,200	
Direct labor (5,000 EUP × $0.06 per EUP)	300	
Factory overhead (5,000 EUP × $0.072 per EUP)	360	2,860
Total costs accounted for		$27,060

reconciled

Quick Check
Answers—p. 822

6. Equivalent units are (a) a measure of a production department's productivity in using direct materials, direct labor, or overhead; (b) units of a product produced by a foreign competitor that are similar to units produced by a domestic company; or (c) generic units of a product similar to brand name units of a product.

7. Interpret the meaning of a department's equivalent units with respect to direct labor.

8. A department began the period with 8,000 units that were one-fourth complete with respect to direct labor. It completed 58,000 units, and ended with 6,000 units that were one-third complete with respect to direct labor. What were its direct labor equivalent units for the period using the weighted average method?

9. A process cost summary for a department has three sections. What information is presented in each of them?

Transfers to Finished Goods Inventory and Cost of Goods Sold

Arrow line ⑨ in Exhibit 20.4 reflects the transfer of completed products from production to finished goods inventory. The process cost summary shows that the 100,000 units of finished Profen are assigned a cost of $24,200. The entry to record this transfer is:

P6 Record the transfer of completed goods to Finished Goods Inventory and Cost of Goods Sold.

⑨	Finished Goods Inventory......................	24,200	
	Goods in Process Inventory.................		24,200
	To record transfer of completed units.		

Assets = Liabilities + Equity
+24,200
−24,200

The credit to Goods in Process Inventory reduces that asset balance to reflect that 100,000 units are no longer in production. The cost of these units has been transferred to Finished Goods Inventory, which is recognized as a $24,200 increase in this asset. After this entry is posted, there remains a balance of $2,860 in the Goods in Process Inventory account, which is the amount computed in Step 4 previously. The cost of units transferred from Goods in Process Inventory to Finished Goods Inventory is called the **cost of goods manufactured.** Exhibit 20.18 reveals the activities in the Goods in Process Inventory account for this period. The ending balance of this account equals the cost assigned to the partially completed units in section ③ of Exhibit 20.17.

Goods in Process Inventory					Acct. No. 134
Date		**Explanation**	**Debit**	**Credit**	**Balance**
Mar.	31	Balance			4,620
Apr.	30	Direct materials usage	9,900		14,520
	30	Direct labor costs incurred	5,700		20,220
	30	Factory overhead applied	6,840		27,060
	30	Transfer completed product to warehouse		24,200	2,860

Exhibit 20.18

Goods in Process Inventory

Arrow line ⑩ in Exhibit 20.4 reflects the sale of finished goods. Assume that GenX sold 106,000 units of Profen this period, and that its beginning inventory of finished goods consisted of 26,000 units with a cost of $6,292. Also assume that its ending finished goods inventory consists of 20,000 units at a cost of $4,840. Using this information, we can compute its cost of goods sold for April as shown in Exhibit 20.19.

Beginning finished goods inventory	$ 6,292
+ Cost of goods manufactured this period	24,200
= Cost of goods available for sale	$30,492
− Ending finished goods inventory	4,840
= Cost of goods sold	$25,652

Exhibit 20.19

Cost of Goods Sold

The summary entry to record cost of goods sold for this period follows.

⑩	Cost of Goods Sold..........................	25,652	
	Finished Goods Inventory		25,652
	To record cost of goods sold for April.		

Assets = Liabilities + Equity
−25,652   −25,652

The Finished Goods Inventory account now appears as shown in Exhibit 20.20.

Finished Goods Inventory					Acct. No. 135
Date		**Explanation**	**Debit**	**Credit**	**Balance**
Mar.	31	Balance			6,292
Apr.	30	Transfer in cost of goods manufactured	24,200		30,492
	30	Cost of goods sold		25,652	4,840

Exhibit 20.20

Finished Goods Inventory

Summary of Cost Flows   Exhibit 20.21 shows GenX's manufacturing cost flows for April. Each of these cost flows and the entries to record them have been explained. The flow of costs through the accounts reflects the flow of production activities and products.

Exhibit 20.21*

Cost Flows through GenX

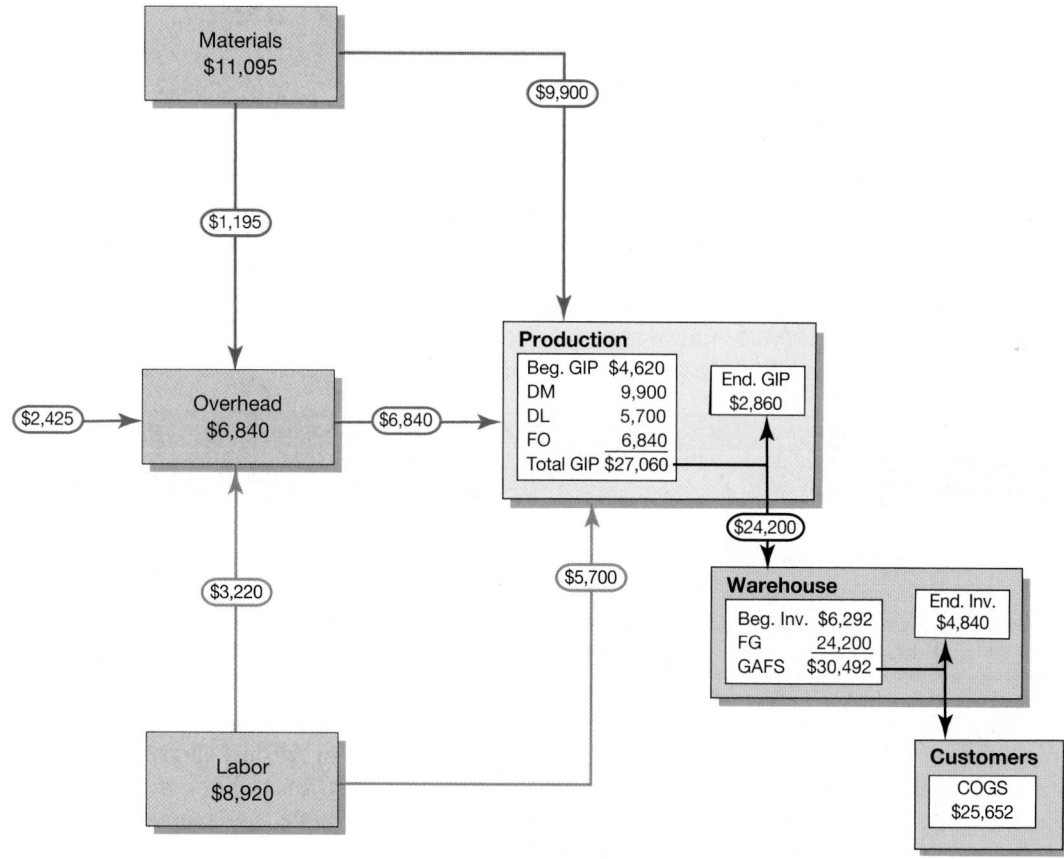

*Abbreviations: GIP (goods in process); DM (direct materials); DL (direct labor); FO (factory overhead); FG (finished goods); GAFS (goods available for sale); COGS (cost of goods sold).

Effect of Lean Business Model on Process Operations

Adopting lean business practices often yields changes in process operations. Management concerns with throughput and just-in-time manufacturing, for instance, cause boundary lines between departments to blur. In some cases, higher quality and better efficiency are obtained by entirely reorganizing production processes. For example, instead of producing different types of computers in a series of departments, a separate work center for each computer can be established in one department. When such a re-arrangement occurs, the process cost accounting system is changed to account for each work center's costs.

To illustrate, when a company adopts a just-in-time inventory system, its inventories can be minimal. If raw materials are not ordered or received until needed, a Raw Materials Inventory

Decision Insight

Lean Machine   Attention to customer orientation has led to improved processes for companies. A manufacturer of control devices improved quality and reduced production time by forming teams to study processes and suggest improvements. Another company set up project groups to evaluate its production processes.

account may be unnecessary. Instead, materials cost is immediately debited to the Goods in Process Inventory account. Similarly, a Finished Goods Inventory account may not be needed. Instead, cost of finished goods may be immediately debited to the Cost of Goods Sold account.

Decision Insight

Best of Both Customer orientation demands both flexibility and standardization. Flexibility allows companies to supply products or services to a customer's specifications as in a job order setting, and standardization helps achieve efficiencies and lower costs as in a process operation.

Hybrid Costing System | Decision Analysis

This chapter explained the process costing system and contrasted it with the job order costing system. Many organizations use a *hybrid system* that contains features of both process and job order operations. A recent survey of manufacturers revealed that a majority use hybrid systems.

A2 Explain and illustrate a hybrid costing system.

To illustrate, consider a car manufacturer's assembly line. On one hand, the line resembles a process operation in that the assembly steps for each car are nearly identical. On the other hand, the specifications of most cars have several important differences. At the Ford Mustang plant, each car assembled on a given day can be different from the previous car and the next car. This means that the costs of materials (subassemblies or components) for each car can differ. Accordingly, while the conversion costs (direct labor and overhead) can be accounted for using a process costing system, the component costs (direct materials) are accounted for using a job order system (separately for each car or type of car).

A hybrid system of processes requires a *hybrid costing system* to properly cost products or services. In the Ford plant, the assembly costs per car are readily determined using process costing. The costs of additional components can then be added to the assembly costs to determine each car's total cost (as in job order costing). To illustrate, consider the following information for a daily assembly process at Ford.

Assembly process costs	
Direct materials	$10,600,000
Direct labor	$5,800,000
Factory overhead	$6,200,000
Number of cars assembled	1,000
Costs of three different types of steering wheels	$240, $330, $480
Costs of three different types of seats	$620, $840, $1,360

The assembly process costs $22,600 per car. Depending on the type of steering wheel and seats the customer requests, the cost of a car can range from $23,460 to $24,440 (a $980 difference).

Today companies are increasingly trying to standardize processes while attempting to meet individual customer needs. To the extent that differences among individual customers' requests are large, understanding the costs to satisfy those requests is important. Thus, monitoring and controlling both process and job order costs are important.

Decision Ethics

Answer—p. 821

Entrepreneur You operate a process production company making similar products for three different customers. One customer demands 100% quality inspection of products at your location before shipping. The added costs of that inspection are spread across all customers, not just the one demanding it. If you charge the added costs to that customer, you could lose that customer and experience a loss. Moreover, your other two customers have agreed to pay 110% of full costs. What actions (if any) do you take?

Demonstration Problem

Pennsylvania Company produces a product that passes through a single production process. Then, completed products are transferred to finished goods in its warehouse. Information related to its manufacturing activities for July follows.

Raw Materials

Beginning inventory	$100,000
Raw materials purchased on credit	211,400
Direct materials used	(190,000)
Indirect materials used	(51,400)
Ending inventory	$ 70,000

Factory Payroll

Direct labor incurred	$ 55,500
Indirect labor incurred	50,625
Total payroll (paid in cash)	$106,125

Factory Overhead

Indirect materials used	$ 51,400
Indirect labor used	50,625
Other overhead costs	71,725
Total factory overhead incurred	$173,750

Factory Overhead Applied

Overhead applied (200% of direct labor)	$111,000

Production Department

Beginning goods in process inventory (units)	5,000
Percentage completed—Materials	100%
Percentage completed—Labor and overhead	60%
Beginning goods in process inventory (costs)	
Direct materials used	$ 20,000
Direct labor incurred	9,600
Overhead applied (200% of direct labor)	19,200
Total costs of beginning goods in process	$ 48,800
Units started this period	20,000
Units completed this period	17,000
Ending goods in process inventory (units)	8,000
Percentage completed—Materials	100%
Percentage completed—Labor and overhead	20%

Finished Goods Inventory

Beginning finished goods inventory	$ 96,400
Cost transferred in from production	321,300
Cost of goods sold	(345,050)
Ending finished goods inventory	$ 72,650

Required

1. Prepare a physical flow reconciliation for July as illustrated in Exhibit 20.12.
2. Compute the equivalent units of production in July for direct materials, direct labor, and factory overhead.
3. Compute the costs per equivalent units of production in July for direct materials, direct labor, and factory overhead.
4. Prepare a report of costs accounted for and a report of costs to account for.
5. Prepare summary journal entries to record the transactions and events of July for (a) raw materials purchases, (b) direct materials usage, (c) indirect materials usage, (d) factory payroll costs, (e) direct labor usage, (f) indirect labor usage, (g) other overhead costs (credit Other Accounts), (h) application of overhead to production, (i) transfer of finished goods from production, and (j) the cost of goods sold.

Planning the Solution

- Track the physical flow to determine the number of units completed in July.
- Compute the equivalent unit of production for direct materials, direct labor, and factory overhead.
- Compute the costs per equivalent unit of production with respect to direct materials, direct labor, and overhead; and determine the cost per unit for each.
- Compute the total cost of the goods transferred to production by using the equivalent units and unit costs. Determine (a) the cost of the beginning in-process inventory, (b) the materials, labor, and overhead costs added to the beginning in-process inventory, and (c) the materials, labor, and overhead costs added to the units started and completed in the month.
- Determine cost of goods sold using balances in finished goods and cost of units completed this period.
- Use the information to record the summary journal entries for July.

Solution to Demonstration Problem

1. Physical Flow Reconciliation

Units to Account For		Units Accounted For	
Beginning goods in process inventory	5,000 units	Units completed and transferred out	17,000 units
Units started this period	20,000 units	Ending goods in process inventory	8,000 units
Total units to account for	25,000 units	Total units accounted for	25,000 units

reconciled

2. Equivalent Units of Production

Equivalent Units of Production	Direct Materials	Direct Labor	Factory Overhead
Equivalent units completed and transferred out	17,000 EUP	17,000 EUP	17,000 EUP
Equivalent units in ending goods in process			
Direct materials (8,000 × 100%)	8,000		
Direct labor (8,000 × 20%)		1,600	
Factory overhead (8,000 × 20%)			1,600
Equivalent units of production	25,000 EUP	18,600 EUP	18,600 EUP

3. Costs per Equivalent Unit of Production

Costs per Equivalent Unit of Production	Direct Materials	Direct Labor	Factory Overhead
Costs of beginning goods in process	$ 20,000	$ 9,600	$ 19,200
Costs incurred this period	190,000	55,500	111,000**
Total costs	$210,000	$65,100	$130,200
÷ Equivalent units of production (from part 2) .	25,000 EUP	18,600 EUP	18,600 EUP
= Costs per equivalent unit of production	$8.40 per EUP	$3.50 per EUP	$7.00 per EUP

**Factory overhead applied

4. Reports of *Costs Accounted For* and of *Costs to Account For*

Report of Costs Accounted For

Cost of units transferred out (cost of goods manufactured)
Direct materials ($8.40 per EUP × 17,000 EUP)	$142,800	
Direct labor ($3.50 per EUP × 17,000 EUP)	59,500	
Factory overhead ($7.00 per EUP × 17,000 EUP)	119,000	
Cost of units completed this period		$ 321,300

Cost of ending goods in process inventory
Direct materials ($8.40 per EUP × 8,000 EUP)	67,200	
Direct labor ($3.50 per EUP × 1,600 EUP)	5,600	
Factory overhead ($7.00 per EUP × 1,600 EUP)	11,200	
Cost of ending goods in process inventory		84,000
Total costs accounted for		**$405,300**

Report of Costs to Account For

Cost of beginning goods in process inventory
Direct materials	$ 20,000	
Direct labor	9,600	
Factory overhead	19,200	$ 48,800

Cost incurred this period
Direct materials	190,000	
Direct labor	55,500	
Factory overhead	111,000	356,500
Total costs to account for		**$405,300**

reconciled

5. Summary journal entries for the transactions and events in July.

a.	Raw Materials Inventory	211,400	
	Accounts Payable		211,400
	To record raw materials purchases.		
b.	Goods in Process Inventory	190,000	
	Raw Materials Inventory		190,000
	To record direct materials usage.		
c.	Factory Overhead	51,400	
	Raw Materials Inventory		51,400
	To record indirect materials usage.		

[continued on next page]

[continued from previous page]

d.	Factory Payroll.............................	106,125	
	Cash..................................		106,125
	To record factory payroll costs.		
e.	Goods in Process Inventory...................	55,500	
	Factory Payroll..........................		55,500
	To record direct labor usage.		
f.	Factory Overhead...........................	50,625	
	Factory Payroll.........................		50,625
	To record indirect labor usage.		
g.	Factory Overhead...........................	71,725	
	Other Accounts.........................		71,725
	To record other overhead costs.		
h.	Goods in Process Inventory...................	111,000	
	Factory Overhead.......................		111,000
	To record application of overhead.		
i.	Finished Goods Inventory.....................	321,300	
	Goods in Process Inventory................		321,300
	To record transfer of finished goods		
	from production.		
j.	Cost of Goods Sold..........................	345,050	
	Finished Goods Inventory		345,050
	To record cost of goods sold.		

20A   FIFO Method of Process Costing

C5   Explain and illustrate the four steps in accounting for production activity using FIFO

The **FIFO method** of process costing assigns costs to units assuming a first-in, first-out flow of product. The objectives, concepts, and journal entries (not amounts) are the same as for the weighted average method, but computation of equivalent units of production and cost assignment are slightly different.

Exhibit 20A.1 shows selected information from GenX's production department for the month of April. Accounting for a department's activity for a period includes four steps: (1) determine physical flow, (2) compute equivalent units, (3) compute cost per equivalent unit, and (4) determine cost assignment and reconciliation. This appendix describes each of these steps using the FIFO method for process costing.

Exhibit 20A.1

Production Data

Beginning goods in process inventory (March 31)	
Units of product.....................................	30,000
Percentage of completion—Direct materials...............	100%
Percentage of completion—Direct labor	65%
Direct materials costs...............................	$ 3,300
Direct labor costs..................................	$ 600
Factory overhead costs applied (120% of direct labor)	$ 720
Activities during the current period (April)	
Units started this period	90,000
Units transferred out (completed)	100,000
Direct materials costs...............................	$ 9,900
Direct labor costs..................................	$ 5,700
Factory overhead costs applied (120% of direct labor)	$ 6,840
Ending goods in process inventory (April 30)	
Units of product....................................	20,000
Percentage of completion—Direct materials...............	100%
Percentage of completion—Direct labor	25%

Step 1: Determine Physical Flow of Units

A *physical flow reconciliation* is a report that reconciles (1) the physical units started in a period with (2) the physical units completed in that period. The physical flow reconciliation for GenX is shown in Exhibit 20A.2 for April.

Units to Account For		Units Accounted For	
Beginning goods in process inventory	30,000 units	Units completed and transferred out	100,000 units
Units started this period	90,000 units	Ending goods in process inventory . . .	20,000 units
Total units to account for . . .	**120,000 units**	Total units accounted for	**120,000 units**

reconciled

Exhibit 20A.2

Physical Flow Reconciliation

FIFO assumes that the 100,000 units transferred to finished goods during April include the 30,000 units from the beginning goods in process inventory. The remaining 70,000 units transferred out are from units started in April. Of the total 90,000 units started in April, 70,000 were completed, leaving 20,000 units unfinished at period-end.

Step 2: Compute Equivalent Units of Production—FIFO

GenX used its direct materials, direct labor, and overhead both to make complete units of Profen and to start some units that are not yet complete. We need to convert the physical measure of units to equivalent units based on how much of each input has been used. We do this by multiplying the number of physical units by the percentage of processing applied to those units in the current period; this is done for each input (materials, labor, and overhead). The FIFO method accounts for cost flow in a sequential manner—earliest costs are the first to flow out. (This is different from the weighted average method, which combines prior period costs—those in beginning Goods in Process Inventory—with costs incurred in the current period.)

Three distinct groups of units must be considered in determining the equivalent units of production under the FIFO method: (a) units in beginning Goods in Process Inventory that were completed this period, (b) units started *and* completed this period, and (c) units in ending Goods in Process Inventory. We must determine how much material, labor, and overhead are used for each of these unit groups. These computations are shown in Exhibit 20A.3. The remainder of this section explains these computations.

Equivalent Units of Production	Direct Materials	Direct Labor	Factory Overhead
(a) Equivalent units to complete beginning goods in process			
Direct materials (30,000 × 0%)	0 EUP		
Direct labor (30,000 × 35%)		10,500 EUP	
Factory overhead (30,000 × 35%)			10,500 EUP
(b) Equivalent units started and completed*	70,000	70,000	70,000
(c) Equivalent units in ending goods in process			
Direct materials (20,000 × 100%)	20,000		
Direct labor (20,000 × 25%)		5,000	
Factory overhead (20,000 × 25%)			5,000
Equivalent units of production	90,000 EUP	85,500 EUP	85,500 EUP

Exhibit 20A.3

Equivalent Units of Production—FIFO

*Units completed this period . . . . 100,000 units
Less units in beginning goods in process 30,000
Units started and completed this period . . . . 70,000 units

(a) Beginning Goods in Process   Under FIFO, we assume that production first completes any units started in the prior period. There were 30,000 physical units in beginning goods in process inventory. Those units were 100% complete with respect to direct materials as of the end of the prior period. This means that no materials (0%) are needed in April to complete those 30,000 units. So, the equivalent units of *materials* to complete beginning goods in process are zero (30,000 × 0%)—see first row under row "(a)" in Exhibit 20A.3. The units in process as of April 1 had already been through

65% of production prior to this period and need only go through the remaining 35% of production. The equivalent units of *labor* to complete the beginning goods in process are 10,500 (30,000 × 35%)—see second row under row "(a)." This implies that the amount of labor required this period to complete the 30,000 units started in the prior period is the amount of labor needed to make 10,500 units, start-to-finish. Finally, overhead is applied based on direct labor costs, so GenX computes equivalent units for overhead as it would for direct labor.

(b) Units Started and Completed This Period   After completing any beginning goods in process, FIFO assumes that production begins on newly started units. GenX began work on 90,000 new units this period. Of those units, 20,000 remain incomplete at period-end. This means that 70,000 of the units started in April were completed in April. These complete units have received 100% of materials, labor, and overhead. Exhibit 20A.3 reflects this by including 70,000 equivalent units (70,000 × 100%) of materials, labor, and overhead in its equivalent units of production—see row "(b)."

(c) Ending Goods in Process   The 20,000 units started in April that GenX was not able to complete by period-end consumed materials, labor, and overhead. Specifically, those 20,000 units received 100% of materials and, therefore, the equivalent units of materials in ending goods in process inventory are 20,000 (20,000 × 100%)—see first row under row "(c)." For labor and overhead, the units in ending goods in process were 25% complete in production. This means the equivalent units of labor and overhead for those units is 5,000 (20,000 × 25%) as GenX incurs labor and overhead costs uniformly throughout its production process. Finally, for each input (direct materials, direct labor, and factory overhead), the equivalent units for each of the unit groups (a), (b), and (c) are added to determine the total equivalent units of production with respect to each—see final row in Exhibit 20A.3.

Step 3: Compute Cost per Equivalent Unit—FIFO

To compute cost per equivalent unit, we take the product costs (for each of direct materials, direct labor, and factory overhead from Exhibit 20A.1) added in April and divide by the equivalent units of production from Step 2. Exhibit 20A.4 illustrates these computations.

Exhibit 20A.4

Cost per Equivalent Unit of Production—FIFO

Cost per Equivalent Unit of Production	Direct Materials	Direct Labor	Factory Overhead
Costs incurred this period	$9,900	$5,700	$6,840
÷ Equivalent units of production (from Step 2)	90,000 EUP	85,500 EUP	85,500 EUP
Cost per equivalent unit of production	$0.11 per EUP	$0.067 per EUP	$0.08 per EUP

It is essential to compute costs per equivalent unit for *each* input because production inputs are added at different times in the process. The FIFO method computes the cost per equivalent unit based solely on this period's EUP and costs (unlike the weighted average method which adds in the costs of the beginning goods in process inventory).

Step 4: Assign and Reconcile Costs

The equivalent units determined in Step 2 and the cost per equivalent unit computed in Step 3 are both used to assign costs (1) to units that the production department completed and transferred to finished goods and (2) to units that remain in process at period-end.

In Exhibit 20A.5, under the section for cost of units transferred out, we see that the cost of units completed in April includes the $4,620 cost carried over from March for work already applied to the 30,000 units that make up beginning Goods in Process Inventory, plus the $1,544 incurred in April to complete those units. This section also includes the $17,990 of cost assigned to the 70,000 units started and completed this period. Thus, the total cost of goods manufactured in April is $24,154 ($4,620 + $1,544 + $17,990). The average cost per unit for goods completed in April is $0.242 ($24,154 ÷ 100,000 completed units).

The computation for cost of ending goods in process inventory is in the lower part of Exhibit 20A.5. The cost of units in process includes materials, labor, and overhead costs corresponding to the percentage of these resources applied to those incomplete units in April. That cost of $2,935 ($2,200 + $335 + $400) also is the ending balance for the Goods in Process Inventory account.

Exhibit 20A.5

Report of Costs Accounted
For—FIFO

Cost of units transferred out (cost of goods manufactured)

Cost of beginning goods in process inventory			$ 4,620
Cost to complete beginning goods in process			
Direct materials ($0.11 per EUP × 0 EUP)		$ 0	
Direct labor ($0.067 per EUP × 10,500 EUP)		704	
Factory overhead ($0.08 per EUP × 10,500 EUP)		840	1,544
Cost of units started and completed this period			
Direct materials ($0.11 per EUP × 70,000 EUP)		7,700	
Direct labor ($0.067 per EUP × 70,000 EUP)		4,690	
Factory overhead ($0.08 per EUP × 70,000 EUP)		5,600	17,990
Total cost of units finished this period			24,154
Cost of ending goods in process inventory			
Direct materials ($0.11 per EUP × 20,000 EUP)		2,200	
Direct labor ($0.067 per EUP × 5,000 EUP)		335	
Factory overhead ($0.08 per EUP × 5,000 EUP)		400	
Total cost of ending goods in process inventory			2,935
Total costs accounted for			**$27,089**

Management verifies that the total costs assigned to units transferred out and units still in process equal the total costs incurred by production. We reconcile the costs accounted for (in Exhibit 20A.5) to the costs that production was charged for as shown in Exhibit 20A.6.

Exhibit 20A.6

Report of Costs to
Account—FIFO

Cost of beginning goods in process inventory		
Direct materials	$3,300	
Direct labor	600	
Factory overhead	720	$ 4,620
Costs incurred this period		
Direct materials	9,900	
Direct labor	5,700	
Factory overhead	6,840	22,440
Total costs to account for		**$27,060**

The production manager is responsible for $27,060 in costs: $4,620 that had been assigned to the department's Goods in Process Inventory as of April 1 plus $22,440 of materials, labor, and overhead costs the department incurred in April. At period-end, the manager must identify where those costs were assigned. The production manager can report that there was $24,154 of cost assigned to units completed in April and $2,935 assigned to units still in process at period-end. The sum of these amounts is $29 different from the $27,060 total costs incurred by production due to rounding in Step 3—rounding errors are common and not a concern.

The final report is the process cost summary, which summarizes key information from Exhibits 20A.3, 20A.4, 20A.5, and 20A.6. Reasons for the summary are to (1) help managers control and monitor costs, (2) help upper management assess department manager performance, and (3) provide cost information for financial reporting. The process cost summary, using FIFO, for GenX is in Exhibit 20A.7. Section ① lists the total costs charged to the department, including direct materials, direct labor, and overhead costs incurred, as well as the cost of the beginning goods in process inventory. Section ② describes the equivalent units of production for the department. Equivalent units for materials, labor, and overhead are in separate columns. It also reports direct materials, direct labor, and overhead costs per equivalent unit. Section ③ allocates total costs among units worked on in the period.

Decision Maker   Answer—p. 822

Cost Manager As cost manager for an electronics manufacturer, you apply a process costing system using FIFO. Your company plans to adopt a just-in-time system and eliminate inventories. What is the impact of the use of FIFO (versus the weighted-average method) given these plans?

Exhibit 20A.7

Process Cost Summary

GenX COMPANY
Process Cost Summary
For Month Ended April 30, 2008

Costs charged to production

Costs of beginning goods in process inventory

Direct materials	$3,300	
Direct labor	600	
Factory overhead	720	$ 4,620

Costs incurred this period

Direct materials	9,900	
Direct labor	5,700	
Factory overhead	6,840	22,440
Total costs to account for		$27,060

Unit cost information

Units to account for		Units accounted for	
Beginning goods in process	30,000	Transferred out	100,000
Units started this period	90,000	Ending goods in process	20,000
Total units to account for	120,000	Total units accounted for	120,000

Equivalent units of production	Direct Materials	Direct Labor	Factory Overhead
Equivalent units to complete beginning goods in process			
Direct materials (30,000 × 0%)	0 EUP		
Direct labor (30,000 × 35%)		10,500 EUP	
Factory overhead (30,000 × 35%)			10,500 EUP
Equivalent units started and completed	70,000	70,000	70,000
Equivalent units in ending goods in process			
Direct materials (20,000 × 100%)	20,000		
Direct labor (20,000 × 25%)		5,000	
Factory overhead (20,000 × 25%)			5000
Equivalent units of production	90,000 EUP	85,500 EUP	85,500 EUP

Cost per equivalent unit of production	Direct Materials	Direct Labor	Factory Overhead
Costs incurred this period	$9,900	$5,700	$6,840
÷ Equivalent units of production	90,000 EUP	85,500 EUP	85,500 EUP
Cost per equivalent unit of production	$0.11 per EUP	$0.067 per EUP	$0.08 per EUP

Cost assignment and reconciliation

(cost of units completed and transferred out)

Cost of beginning goods in process		$ 4,620
Cost to complete beginning goods in process		
Direct materials ($0.11 per EUP × 0 EUP)	$ 0	
Direct labor ($0.067 per EUP × 10,500 EUP)	704	
Factory overhead ($0.08 per EUP × 10,500 EUP)	840	1,544
Cost of units started and completed this period		
Direct Materials ($0.11 per EUP × 70,000 EUP)	7,700	
Direct Labor ($0.067 per EUP × 70,000 EUP)	4,690	
Factory overhead ($0.08 per EUP × 70,000 EUP)	5,600	17,990
Total cost of units finished this period		24,154
Cost of ending goods in process		
Direct materials ($0.11 per EUP × 20,000 EUP)	2,200	
Direct labor ($0.067 per EUP × 5,000 EUP)	335	
Factory overhead ($0.08 per EUP × 5,000 EUP)	400	
Total cost of ending goods in process		2,935
Total costs accounted for		$27,089*

reconciled

* $29 difference due to rounding

Summary

C1 **Explain process operations and the way they differ from job order operations.** Process operations produce large quantities of similar products or services by passing them through a series of processes, or steps, in production. Like job order operations, they combine direct materials, direct labor, and overhead in the operations. Unlike job order operations that assign the responsibility for each job to a manager, process operations assign the responsibility for each *process* to a manager.

C2 **Define equivalent units and explain their use in process cost accounting.** Equivalent units of production measure the activity of a process as the number of units that would be completed in a period if all effort had been applied to units that were started and finished. This measure of production activity is used to compute the cost per equivalent unit and to assign costs to finished goods and goods in process inventory.

C3 **Explain the four steps in accounting for production activity in a period.** The four steps involved in accounting for production activity in a period are (1) recording the physical flow of units, (2) computing the equivalent units of production, (3) computing the cost per equivalent unit of production, and (4) reconciling costs. The last step involves assigning costs to finished goods and goods in process inventory for the period.

C4 **Define a process cost summary and describe its purposes.** A process cost summary reports on the activities of a production process or department for a period. It describes the costs charged to the department, the equivalent units of production for the department, and the costs assigned to the output. The report aims to (1) help managers control their departments, (2) help factory managers evaluate department managers' performances, and (3) provide cost information for financial statements.

C5 **Explain and illustrate the four steps in accounting for production activity using FIFO.** The FIFO method for process costing is applied and illustrated to (1) report the physical flow of units, (2) compute the equivalent units of production, (3) compute the cost per equivalent unit of production, and (4) assign and reconcile costs.

A1 **Compare process cost accounting and job order cost accounting.** Process and job order manufacturing operations are similar in that both combine materials, labor, and factory overhead to produce products or services. They differ in the way they are organized and managed. In job order operations, the job order cost accounting system assigns materials, labor, and overhead to specific jobs. In process operations, the process cost accounting system assigns materials, labor, and overhead to specific processes. The total costs associated with each process are then divided by the number of units passing through that process to get cost per

equivalent unit. The costs per equivalent unit for all processes are added to determine the total cost per unit of a product or service.

A2 **Explain and illustrate a hybrid costing system.** A hybrid costing system contains features of both job order and process costing systems. Generally, certain direct materials are accounted for by individual products as in job order costing, but direct labor and overhead costs are accounted for similar to process costing.

P1 **Record the flow of direct materials costs in process cost accounting.** Materials purchased are debited to a Raw Materials Inventory account. As direct materials are issued to processes, they are separately accumulated in a Goods in Process Inventory account for that process.

P2 **Record the flow of direct labor costs in process cost accounting.** Direct labor costs are initially debited to the Factory Payroll account. The total amount in it is then assigned to the goods in process inventory account pertaining to each process.

P3 **Record the flow of factory overhead costs in process cost accounting.** The different factory overhead items are first accumulated in the Factory Overhead account and are then allocated, using a predetermined overhead rate, to the different processes. The allocated amount is debited to the goods in process inventory account pertaining to each process.

P4 **Compute equivalent units produced in a period.** To compute equivalent units, determine the number of units that would have been finished if all materials (or labor or overhead) had been used to produce units that were started and completed during the period. The costs incurred by a process are divided by its equivalent units to yield cost per unit.

P5 **Prepare a process cost summary.** A process cost summary includes the physical flow of units, equivalent units of production, costs per equivalent unit, and a cost reconciliation. It reports the units and costs to account for during the period and how they were accounted for during the period. In terms of units, the summary includes the beginning goods in process inventory and the units started during the month. These units are accounted for in terms of the goods completed and transferred out, and the ending goods in process inventory. With respect to costs, the summary includes materials, labor, and overhead costs assigned to the process during the period. It shows how these costs are assigned to goods completed and transferred out, and to ending goods in process inventory.

P6 **Record the transfer of completed goods to Finished Goods Inventory and Cost of Goods Sold.** As units complete the final process and are eventually sold, their accumulated cost is transferred to Finished Goods Inventory and finally to Cost of Goods Sold.

Guidance Answers to **Decision Maker** and **Decision Ethics**

Budget Officer By instructing you to classify a majority of costs as indirect, the manager is passing some of his department's costs to a common overhead pool that other departments will partially absorb. Since overhead costs are allocated on the basis of direct labor for this company and the new department has a relatively low direct labor cost, the new department will be assigned less overhead. Such action

suggests unethical behavior by this manager. You must object to such reclassification. If this manager refuses to comply, you must inform someone in a more senior position.

Entrepreneur By spreading the added quality-related costs across three customers, the entrepreneur is probably trying to remain competitive with respect to the customer that demands the 100% quality inspection. Moreover, the entrepreneur is partly covering the added costs by recovering 2/3 of them from the other two customers who are paying 110% of total costs. This act likely breaches the trust placed by the two customers in this entrepreneur's application of its costing system. The costing system should be changed, and the entrepreneur should consider renegotiating the pricing and/or quality-test agreement with this one customer (at the risk of losing this currently loss-producing customer).

Cost Manager Differences between the FIFO and weighted-average methods are greatest when large work in process inventories exist and when costs fluctuate. The method used if inventories are eliminated does not matter; both produce identical costs.

Guidance Answers to **Quick Checks**

1. *c*

2. When a company produces large quantities of similar products/services, a process cost system is often more suitable.

3. *b*

4. The costs are direct materials, direct labor, and overhead.

5. A goods in process inventory account is needed for *each* production department.

6. *a*

7. Equivalent units with respect to direct labor are the number of units that would have been produced if all labor had been used on units that were started and finished during the period.

8.

Units completed and transferred out	58,000 EUP
Units of ending goods in process	
Direct labor (6,000 × 1/3)	2,000 EUP
Units of production	60,000 EUP

9. The first section shows the costs charged to the department. The second section describes the equivalent units produced by the department. The third section shows the assignment of total costs to units worked on during the period.

Key Terms   mhhe.com/wildFAP18e

Key Terms are available at the book's Website for learning and testing in an online Flashcard Format.

Cost of goods manufactured (p. 811)

Equivalent units of production (EUP) (p. 805)

FIFO method (p. 816)

Job order cost accounting system (p. 801)

Materials consumption report (p. 802)

Process cost accounting system (p. 801)

Process cost summary (p. 809)

Process operations (p. 798)

Weighted average method (p. 808)

Multiple Choice Quiz   Answers on p. 839   mhhe.com/wildFAP18e

Multiple Choice Quizzes A and B are available at the book's Website.

1. Equivalent units of production are equal to
   a. Physical units that were completed this period from all effort being applied to them.
   b. The number of units introduced into the process this period.
   c. The number of finished units actually completed this period.
   d. The number of units that could have been started and completed given the cost incurred.
   e. The number of units in the process at the end of the period.

2. Recording the cost of raw materials purchased for use in a process costing system includes a
   a. Credit to Raw Materials Inventory.
   b. Debit to Goods in Process Inventory.
   c. Debit to Factory Overhead.
   d. Credit to Factory Overhead.
   e. Debit to Raw Materials Inventory.

3. The production department started the month with a beginning goods in process inventory of $20,000. During the month, it was assigned the following costs: direct materials, $152,000; direct labor, $45,000; overhead applied at the rate of 40% of direct labor cost. Inventory with a cost of $218,000 was transferred to finished goods. The ending balance of goods in process inventory is
   a. $330,000
   b. $ 17,000
   c. $220,000
   d. $112,000
   e. $118,000

4. A company's beginning work in process inventory consists of 10,000 units that are 20% complete with respect to direct labor costs. A total of 40,000 units are completed this period.

There are 15,000 units in goods in process, one-third complete for direct labor, at period-end. The equivalent units of production (EUP) with respect to direct labor at period-end, assuming the weighted average method, are

a. 45,000 EUP
b. 40,000 EUP
c. 5,000 EUP
d. 37,000 EUP
e. 43,000 EUP

5. Assume the same information as in question 4. Also assume that beginning work in process had $6,000 in direct labor cost; and that $84,000 in direct labor is added during this period. What is the cost per EUP for labor?

a. $0.50 per EUP
b. $1.87 per EUP
c. $2.00 per EUP
d. $2.10 per EUP
e. $2.25 per EUP

Assume weighted-average inventory method is used for all assignments unless stated differently.
Superscript letter [A] denotes assignments based on Appendix 20A.

Discussion Questions

1. Can services be delivered by means of process operations? Support your answer with an example.
2. What is the main factor for a company in choosing between the job order costing and process costing accounting systems? Give two likely applications of each system.
3. Identify the control document for materials flow when a materials requisition slip is not used.
4. The focus in a job order costing system is the job or batch. Identify the main focus in process costing.
5. Are the journal entries that match cost flows to product flows in process costing primarily the same or much different than those in job order costing? Explain.
6. Explain in simple terms the notion of equivalent units of production (EUP). Why is it necessary to use EUP in process costing?
7. What are the two main inventory methods used in process costing? What are the differences between these methods?
8. Why is it possible for direct labor in process operations to include the labor of employees who do not work directly on products or services?

9. Assume that a company produces a single product by processing it first through a single production department. Direct labor costs flow through what accounts in this company's process cost system?
10. After all labor costs for a period are allocated, what balance should remain in the Factory Payroll account?
11. Is it possible to have under- or overapplied overhead costs in a process cost accounting system? Explain.
12. Explain why equivalent units of production for both direct labor and overhead can be the same as, and why they can be different from, equivalent units for direct materials.
13. List the four steps in accounting for production activity in a reporting period (for process operations).
14. What purposes does a process cost summary serve?
15. Are there situations where **Best Buy** can use process costing? Identify at least one and explain it.
16. **Apple** produces iMacs with a multiple production line. Identify and list some of its production processing steps and departments.

Red numbers denote Discussion Questions that involve decision-making.

For each of the following products and services, indicate whether it is most likely produced in a process operation or in a job order operation.

1. Door hinges
2. Cut flower arrangements
3. House paints
4. Concrete swimming pools
5. Custom tailored suits
6. Grand pianos
7. Wall clocks
8. Sport shirts
9. Bolts and nuts
10. Folding chairs

QUICK STUDY

QS 20-1
Matching of product to cost accounting system

C1

Blanche's Boxes makes cardboard shipping cartons in a single operation. This period, Blanche purchased $62,000 in raw materials. Its production department requisitioned $50,000 of those materials for use in producing cartons. Prepare journal entries to record its (1) purchase of raw materials and (2) requisition of direct materials.

QS 20-2
Recording costs of direct materials

P1

Refer to information in QS 20-2. Blanche's Boxes incurred $135,000 in factory payroll costs, of which $125,000 was direct labor. Prepare journal entries to record its (1) total factory payroll incurred and (2) direct labor used in production.

QS 20-3
Recording costs of direct labor

P2

QS 20-4
Recording costs of factory overhead

P3

Refer to information in QS 20-2 and QS 20-3. Blanche's Boxes requisitions $9,000 of indirect materials from its raw materials and used $10,000 of indirect labor in its production of boxes. Also, it incurred $156,000 of other factory overhead costs. It applies factory overhead at the rate of 140% of direct labor costs. Prepare journal entries to record its (1) indirect materials requisitioned, (2) indirect labor used in production, (3) other factory overhead costs incurred, and (4) application of overhead to production.

QS 20-5
Recording transfer of costs to finished goods   P5

Refer to information in QS 20-2, QS 20-3, and QS 20-4. Blanche's Boxes completed 20,000 boxes costing $275,000 and transferred them to finished goods. Prepare its journal entry to record the transfer of the boxes from production to finished goods inventory.

QS 20-6
Computing equivalent units of production

P4

The following refers to units processed in Sunflower Printing's binding department in March. Compute the total equivalent units of production with respect to labor for March using the weighted average inventory method.

	Units of Product	Percent of Labor Added
Beginning goods in process	150,000	80%
Goods started	310,000	100
Goods completed	340,000	100
Ending goods in process	120,000	25

QS 20-7
Computing EUP cost   C4   P5

The cost of beginning inventory plus the costs added during the period should equal the cost of units _____ plus the cost of _____.

QS 20-8
Hybrid costing system   A2

Explain a hybrid costing system. Identify a product or service operation that might well fit a hybrid costing system.

QS 20-9[A]
Computing equivalent units—FIFO   C2   P4

Refer to QS 20-6 and compute the total equivalent units of production with respect to labor for March using the FIFO inventory method.

EXERCISES

Exercise 20-1
Terminology in process cost accounting

C1   A1   P1   P2   P3

Match each of the following items A through G with the best numbered description of its purpose.

A. Factory Overhead account   **E.** Raw Materials Inventory account
B. Process cost summary   **F.** Materials requisition
C. Equivalent units of production   **G.** Finished Goods Inventory account
D. Goods in Process Inventory

_____ **1.** Notifies the materials manager to send materials to a production department.
_____ **2.** Holds costs of indirect materials, indirect labor, and similar costs until assigned to production.
_____ **3.** Holds costs of direct materials, direct labor, and applied overhead until products are transferred from production to finished goods (or another department).
_____ **4.** Standardizes partially completed units into equivalent completed units.
_____ **5.** Holds costs of finished products until sold to customers.
_____ **6.** Describes the activity and output of a production department for a period.
_____ **7.** Holds costs of materials until they are used in production or as factory overhead.

Exercise 20-2
Journal entries in process cost accounting

P1   P2   P3

Wooden Toy Company manufactures toy trucks. Prepare journal entries to record its following production activities for January.
 1. Purchased $80,000 of raw materials on credit.
 2. Used $42,000 of direct materials in production.
 3. Used $22,500 of indirect materials.

4. Incurred total labor cost of $95,000, which is paid in cash.

5. Used $75,000 of direct labor in production.

6. Used $20,000 of indirect labor.

7. Incurred overhead costs of $38,750 (paid in cash).

8. Applied overhead at 110% of direct labor costs.

9. Transferred completed products with a cost of $135,600 to finished goods inventory.

10. Sold $315,000 of products on credit. Their cost is $175,000.

Check (8) Cr. Factory Overhead, $82,500

The following journal entries are recorded in Kiesha Co.'s process cost accounting system. Kiesha produces apparel and accessories. Overhead is applied to production based on direct labor cost for the period. Prepare a brief explanation (including any overhead rates applied) for each journal entry *a* through *j*.

Exercise 20-3

Interpretation of journal entries in process cost accounting

P1   P2   P3   P6

a.	Raw Materials Inventory	52,000	
	Accounts Payable		52,000
b.	Goods in Process Inventory	42,000	
	Raw Materials Inventory		42,000
c.	Goods in Process Inventory	26,000	
	Factory Payroll		26,000
d.	Factory Payroll	32,000	
	Cash		32,000
e.	Factory Overhead	10,000	
	Cash		10,000
f.	Factory Overhead	10,000	
	Raw Materials Inventory		10,000
g.	Factory Overhead	6,000	
	Factory Payroll		6,000
h.	Goods in Process Inventory	32,500	
	Factory Overhead		32,500
i.	Finished Goods Inventory	88,000	
	Goods in Process Inventory		88,000
j.	Accounts Receivable	250,000	
	Sales		250,000
	Cost of Goods Sold	100,000	
	Finished Goods Inventory		100,000

Laffer Lumber produces bagged bark for use in landscaping. Production involves packaging bark chips in plastic bags in a bagging department. The following information describes production operations for October.

Exercise 20-4

Recording cost flows in a process cost system

P1   P2   P3   P6

	Bagging Department
3 Direct materials used	$ 522,000
4 Direct labor used	$ 130,000
5 Predetermined overhead rate (based on direct labor)	175%
6 Goods transferred from bagging to finished goods	$(595,000)

The company's revenue for the month totaled $950,000 from credit sales, and its cost of goods sold for the month is $540,000. Prepare summary journal entries dated October 31 to record its October production activities for (1) direct material usage, (2) direct labor usage, (3) overhead allocation, (4) goods transfer from production to finished goods, and (5) sales.

Check (3) Cr. Factory Overhead, $227,500

Exercise 20-5

Computing equivalent units of production—weighted average

C2   P4

During April, the production department of a process manufacturing system completed a number of units of a product and transferred them to finished goods. Of these transferred units, 60,000 were in process in the production department at the beginning of April and 240,000 were started and completed in April. April's beginning inventory units were 60% complete with respect to materials and 40% complete with respect to labor. At the end of April, 82,000 additional units were in process in the production department and were 80% complete with respect to materials and 30% complete with respect to labor.

Check (2) EUP for materials, 365,600

1. Compute the number of units transferred to finished goods.

2. Compute the number of equivalent units with respect to both materials used and labor used in the production department for April using the weighted-average method.

Exercise 20-6

Costs assigned to output and inventories—weighted average

C3   P4   P5

The production department described in Exercise 20-5 had $850,000 of direct materials and $650,000 of direct labor cost charged to it during April. Also, its beginning inventory included $118,840 of direct materials cost and $47,890 of direct labor.

1. Compute the direct materials cost and the direct labor cost per equivalent unit for the department.

Check (2) Costs accounted for, $1,666,730

2. Using the weighted average method, assign April's costs to the department's output; specifically, its units transferred to finished goods and its ending goods in process inventory.

Exercise 20-7[A]

Computing equivalent units of production—FIFO

C5   P4

Refer to the information in Exercise 20-5 to compute the number of equivalent units with respect to both materials used and labor used in the production department for April using the FIFO method.

Exercise 20-8[A]

Costs assigned to output—FIFO

C5   P4   P5

Refer to the information in Exercise 20-6 and complete its parts (1) and (2) using the FIFO method.

Exercise 20-9

Equivalent units computed—weighted average

C2   P4   P5

The production department in a process manufacturing system completed 80,000 units of product and transferred them to finished goods during a recent period. Of these units, 24,000 were in process at the beginning of the period. The other 56,000 units were started and completed during the period. At period-end, 16,000 units were in process. Compute the department's equivalent units of production with respect to direct materials under each of three separate assumptions:

1. All direct materials are added to products when processing begins.

2. Direct materials are added to products evenly throughout the process. Beginning goods in process inventory was 50% complete, and ending goods in process inventory was 75% complete.

Check (3) EUP for materials, 88,000

3. One-half of direct materials is added to products when the process begins and the other half is added when the process is 75% complete as to direct labor. Beginning goods in process inventory is 40% complete as to direct labor and ending goods in process inventory is 60% complete as to direct labor.

Exercise 20-10[A]

Equivalent units computed—FIFO

C5

Check (3) EUP for materials, 76,000

Refer to the information in Exercise 20-9 and complete it for each of the 3 separate assumptions using the FIFO method for process costing.

Exercise 20-11

Flowchart of costs for a process operation   P1   P2   P3   P6

The following flowchart shows the August production activity of the Spalding Company. Use the amounts shown on the flowchart to compute the missing four numbers identified by blanks.

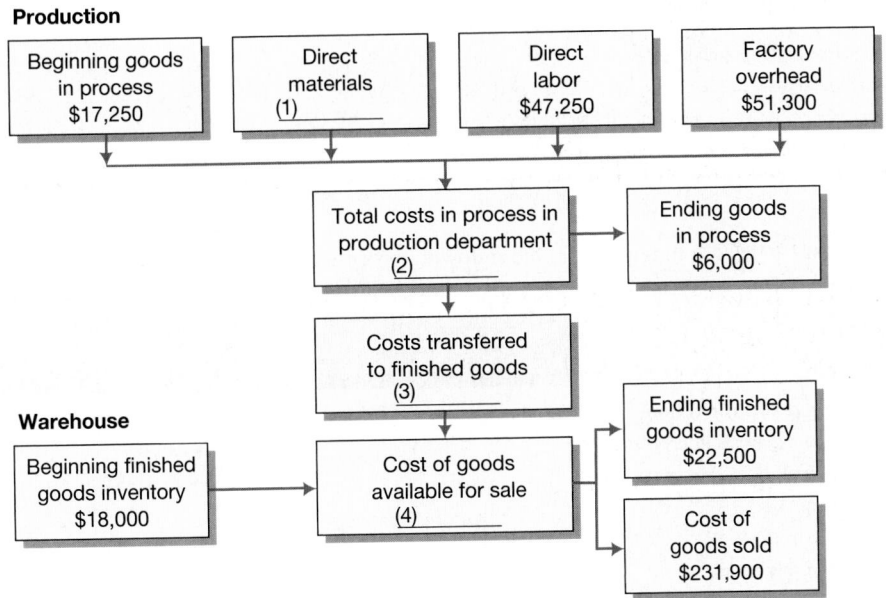

Production

| Beginning goods in process $17,250 | Direct materials (1) ____ | Direct labor $47,250 | Factory overhead $51,300 |

Total costs in process in production department (2) ____

Ending goods in process $6,000

Costs transferred to finished goods (3) ____

Ending finished goods inventory $22,500

Warehouse

Beginning finished goods inventory $18,000

Cost of goods available for sale (4) ____

Cost of goods sold $231,900

The following partially completed process cost summary describes the July production activities of Ashad Company. Its production output is sent to its warehouse for shipping. Prepare its process cost summary using the weighted average method.

Exercise 20-12
Completing a process cost summary

P5

Equivalent Units of Production	Direct Materials	Direct Labor	Factory Overhead
Units transferred out	32,000	32,000	32,000
Units of ending goods in process	2,500	1,500	1,500
Equivalent units of production	34,500	33,500	33,500

Costs per EUP	Direct Materials	Direct Labor	Factory Overhead
Costs of beginning goods in process	$ 18,550	$ 760	$ 1,520
Costs incurred this period	357,500	62,890	125,780
Total costs	$376,050	$63,650	$127,300

Units in beginning goods in process	2,000
Units started this period	32,500
Units completed and transferred out	32,000
Units in ending goods in process	2,500

Hi-Test Company uses the weighted average method of process costing to assign production costs to its products. Information for September follows. Assume that all materials are added at the beginning of its production process, and that direct labor and factory overhead are added uniformly throughout the process.

Exercise 20-13
Process costing—weighted average

P1 P2 P6

Goods in process inventory, September 1 (2,000 units, 100% complete with respect to direct materials, 80% complete with respect to direct labor and overhead; includes $45,000 of direct material cost, $25,600 in direct labor cost, $30,720 overhead cost)	$101,320
Units started in September	28,000
Units completed and transferred to finished goods inventory	23,000
Goods in process inventory, September 30 (__?__ units, 100% complete with respect to direct materials, 40% complete with respect to direct labor and overhead)	?

[continued on next page]

[continued from previous page]

Costs incurred in September	
Direct materials	$375,000
Direct labor	$155,000
Overhead applied at 120% of direct labor cost	?

Required

Fill in the blanks labeled *a* through *uu* in the following process cost summary.

HI-TEST COMPANY
Process Cost Summary
For Month Ended September 30

Costs Charged to Production

Costs of beginning goods in process

Direct materials	$ 45,000		
Direct labor	25,600		
Factory overhead	30,720	$101,320	

Costs incurred this period

Direct materials	$375,000		
Direct labor	155,000		
Factory overhead	(a)_____	(b)_____	
Total costs to account for		(c)_____	

Check (c) $817,320

Unit Cost Information

Units to account for

Beginning goods in process	2,000	Completed and transferred out	23,000
Units started this period	28,000	Ending goods in process	(d)_____
Total units to account for	(e)_____	Total units accounted for	(f)_____

Equivalent Units of Production (EUP)			**Direct Materials**	**Direct Labor**	**Factory Overhead**
Units completed and transferred out			(g)_____ EUP	(h)_____ EUP	(i)_____ EUP
Units of ending goods in process					
Materials	(j)_____	× 100%	(k)_____ EUP		
Direct labor	(l)_____	× 40%		(m)_____ EUP	
Factory overhead	(n)_____	× 40%	_____	_____	(o)_____ EUP
Equivalent units of production (EUP)			(p)_____ EUP	(q)_____ EUP	(r)_____ EUP

Cost per EUP	**Direct Materials**	**Direct Labor**	**Factory Overhead**
Costs of beginning goods in process	$ 45,000	$ 25,600	$30,720
Costs incurred this period	375,000	155,000	(s)_____
Total costs	$420,000	$180,600	(t)_____
÷ EUP	(u)_____	(v)_____	(w)_____
Cost per EUP	(x)_____	(y)_____	(z)_____

(z) $8.40 per EUP

Cost Assignment and Reconciliation

Costs transferred out	Cost/EUP	×	EUP		
Direct materials	(aa)_____	×	(bb)_____	(cc)_____	
Direct labor	(dd)_____	×	(ee)_____	(ff)_____	
Factory overhead	(gg)_____	×	(hh)_____	(ii)_____	
Costs of goods completed and transferred out					(jj)_____
Costs of ending goods in process					
Direct materials	(kk)_____	×	(ll)_____	(mm)_____	
Direct labor	(nn)_____	×	(oo)_____	(pp)_____	
Factory overhead	(qq)_____	×	(rr)_____	(ss)_____	
Costs of ending goods in process					(tt)_____
Total costs accounted for					(uu)_____

Sierra Company manufactures woven blankets and accounts for product costs using process costing. The following information is available regarding its May inventories.

	Beginning Inventory	Ending Inventory
Raw materials inventory	$ 60,000	$ 92,500
Goods in process inventory	435,000	515,000
Finished goods inventory	633,000	605,000

PROBLEM SET A

Problem 20-1A
Production cost flow and measurement; journal entries

P1 P2 P3 P6

The following additional information describes the company's production activities for May.

Raw materials purchases (on credit)	$ 250,000
Factory payroll cost (paid in cash)	1,530,000
Other overhead cost (Other Accounts credited)	87,000
Materials used	
Direct	$ 157,500
Indirect	60,000
Labor used	
Direct	$ 780,000
Indirect	750,000
Overhead rate as a percent of direct labor	115%
Sales (on credit)	$2,500,000

Required

1. Compute the cost of (a) products transferred from production to finished goods, and (b) goods sold.
2. Prepare summary journal entries dated May 31 to record the following production activities during May: (a) raw materials purchases, (b) direct materials usage, (c) indirect materials usage, (d) payroll costs, (e) direct labor costs, (f) indirect labor costs, (g) other overhead costs, (h) overhead applied, (i) goods transferred from production to finished goods, and (j) sale of finished goods.

Check (1b) Cost of goods sold $1,782,500

Victory Company uses weighted-average process costing to account for its production costs. Direct labor is added evenly throughout the process. Direct materials are added at the beginning of the process. During November, Victory transferred 700,000 units of product to finished goods. At the end of November, the goods in process inventory consists of 180,000 units that are 30% complete with respect to labor. Beginning inventory had $420,000 of direct materials and $139,000 of direct labor cost. The direct labor cost added in November is $2,220,000, and the direct materials cost added is $3,254,000.

Required

1. Determine the equivalent units of production with respect to (a) direct labor and (b) direct materials.
2. Compute both the direct labor cost and the direct materials cost per equivalent unit.
3. Compute both direct labor cost and direct materials cost assigned to (a) units completed and transferred out, and (b) ending goods in process inventory.

Analysis Component

4. Victory sells and ships all units to customers as soon as they are completed. Assume that an error is made in determining the percentage of completion for units in ending inventory. Instead of being 30% complete with respect to labor, they are actually 60% complete. Write a one-page memo to the plant manager describing how this error affects its November financial statements.

Problem 20-2A
Cost per equivalent unit; costs assigned to products

P4 P5

mhhe.com/wildFAP18e

Check (2) Direct labor cost per equivalent unit, $4.50

(3b) $783,000

Problem 20-3A

Journalizing in process costing; equivalent units and costs

P1 P2 P3 P4 P6

Elliott Company produces large quantities of a standardized product. The following information is available for its production activities for March.

Raw materials	
Beginning inventory	$ 16,000
Raw materials purchased (on credit)	250,000
Direct materials used	(168,000)
Indirect materials used	(70,000)
Ending inventory	$ 28,000

Factory payroll	
Direct labor used	$199,850
Indirect labor used	45,000
Total payroll cost (paid in cash)	$244,850

Factory overhead incurred	
Indirect materials used	$ 70,000
Indirect labor used	45,000
Other overhead costs	164,790
Total factory overhead incurred	$279,790

Factory overhead applied (140% of direct labor cost)	
Total factory overhead applied	$279,790

Additional information about units and costs of production activities follows.

Units	
Beginning goods in process inventory	2,000
Started	20,000
Ending goods in process inventory	5,000
Status of ending goods in process inventory	
Materials—Percent complete	100%
Labor and overhead—Percent complete	35%

Costs		
Beginning goods in process inventory		
Direct materials	$2,500	
Direct labor	2,650	
Factory overhead	3,710	$ 8,860
Direct materials added		168,000
Direct labor added		199,850
Overhead applied (140% of direct labor)		279,790
Total costs		$656,500
Ending goods in process inventory		$ 84,110

During March, 10,000 units of finished goods are sold for $120 cash each. Cost information regarding finished goods follows.

Beginning finished goods inventory	$150,000
Cost transferred in	572,390
Cost of goods sold	(592,390)
Ending finished goods inventory	$130,000

Required

1. Prepare journal entries dated March 31 to record the following March activities: (a) purchase of raw materials, (b) direct materials usage, (c) indirect materials usage, (d) factory payroll costs, (e) direct labor costs used in production, (f) indirect labor costs, (g) other overhead costs—credit Other Accounts, (h) overhead applied, (i) goods transferred to finished goods, and (j) sale of finished goods.

Check (2) Cost per equivalent unit: materials, $7.75; labor, $10.80; overhead, $15.12

2. Prepare a process cost summary report for this company, showing costs charged to production, units cost information, equivalent units of production, cost per EUP, and its cost assignment and reconciliation.

Analysis Component

3. Elliott provides incentives to its department managers by paying monthly bonuses based on their success in controlling costs per equivalent unit of production. Assume that the production department underestimates the percentage of completion for units in ending inventory with the result that its equivalent units of production in ending inventory for March are understated. What impact does this error have on the March bonuses paid to the production managers? What impact, if any, does this error have on April bonuses?

Fast Co. produces its product through a single processing department. Direct materials are added at the start of production, and direct labor and overhead are added evenly throughout the process. The company uses monthly reporting periods for its weighted-average process cost accounting system. Its Goods in Process Inventory account follows after entries for direct materials, direct labor, and overhead costs for October.

Problem 20-4A
Process cost summary;
equivalent units

P4 P5 P6

mhhe.com/wildFAP18e

Goods in Process Inventory				Acct. No. 133
Date	Explanation	Debit	Credit	Balance
Oct. 1	Balance			335,930
31	Direct materials	102,050		437,980
31	Direct labor	408,200		846,180
31	Applied overhead	244,920		1,091,100

Its beginning goods in process consisted of $59,450 of direct materials, $172,800 of direct labor, and $103,680 of factory overhead. During October, the company started 140,000 units and transferred 150,000 units to finished goods. At the end of the month, the goods in process inventory consisted of 20,000 units that were 80% complete.

Required

1. Prepare the company's process cost summary for October using the weighted average method.
2. Prepare the journal entry dated October 31 to transfer the cost of the completed units to finished goods inventory.

Check   (1) Costs transferred to
finished goods, $982,500

Tamar Co. manufactures a single product in one department. All direct materials are added at the beginning of the manufacturing process. Direct labor and overhead are added evenly throughout the process. Tamar uses monthly reporting periods for its weighted average process cost accounting. During May, the company completed and transferred 22,200 units of product to finished goods inventory. Its 3,000 units of beginning goods in process consisted of $19,800 of direct materials, $123,300 of direct labor, and $98,640 of factory overhead. It has 2,400 units (100% complete with respect to direct materials and 80% complete with respect to direct labor and overhead) in process at month-end. After entries to record direct materials, direct labor, and overhead for May, the company's Goods in Process Inventory account follows.

Problem 20-5A
Process cost summary;
equivalent units; cost estimates

P4 P5

Goods in Process Inventory				Acct. No. 133
Date	Explanation	Debit	Credit	Balance
May 1	Balance			241,740
31	Direct materials	496,800		738,540
31	Direct labor	1,203,300		1,941,840
31	Applied overhead	962,640		2,904,480

Required

1. Prepare the company's process cost summary for May.
2. Prepare the journal entry dated May 31 to transfer the cost of completed units to finished goods inventory.

Check   (1) EUP for labor and
overhead, 24,120 EUP

(2) Cost transferred to
finished goods, $2,664,000

Analysis Components

3. The cost accounting process depends on numerous estimates.
   a. Identify two major estimates that determine the cost per equivalent unit.
   b. In what direction might you anticipate a bias from management for each estimate in part 3a (assume that management compensation is based on maintaining low inventory amounts)? Explain your answer.

Refer to the data in Problem 20-5A. Assume that Tamar uses the FIFO method to account for its process costing system. The following additional information is available:

- Beginning goods in process consisted of 3,000 units that were 100% complete with respect to direct materials and 40% complete with respect to direct labor and overhead.
- Of the 22,200 units completed, 3,000 were from beginning goods in process. The remaining 19,200 were units started and completed during May.

Problem 20-6A[A]
Process cost summary; equivalent
units; and cost estimates

C5   P5   P6

Required

1. Prepare the company's process cost summary for May using FIFO.

2. Prepare the journal entry dated May 31 to transfer the cost of completed units to finished goods inventory.

PROBLEM SET B

Problem 20-1B
Production cost flow and measurement; journal entries

P1 P2 P3 P6

Dream Toys Company manufactures dolls and accounts for product costs using process costing. The following information is available regarding its June inventories.

	Beginning Inventory	Ending Inventory
Raw materials inventory	$ 72,000	$110,000
Goods in process inventory	156,000	250,000
Finished goods inventory	160,000	198,000

The following additional information describes the company's production activities for June.

Raw materials purchases (on credit)	$ 200,000
Factory payroll cost (paid in cash)	400,000
Other overhead cost (Other Accounts credited)	170,500
Materials used	
Direct	$ 120,000
Indirect	42,000
Labor used	
Direct	$ 350,000
Indirect	50,000
Overhead rate as a percent of direct labor	75%
Sales (on credit)	$1,000,000

Required

1. Compute the cost of (a) products transferred from production to finished goods, and (b) goods sold.

2. Prepare journal entries dated June 30 to record the following production activities during June: (a) raw materials purchases, (b) direct materials usage, (c) indirect materials usage, (d) payroll costs, (e) direct labor costs, (f) indirect labor costs, (g) other overhead costs, (h) overhead applied, (i) goods transferred from production to finished goods, and (j) sale of finished goods.

Problem 20-2B
Cost per equivalent unit; costs assigned to products

P4 P5

Abraham Company uses process costing to account for its production costs. Direct labor is added evenly throughout the process. Direct materials are added at the beginning of the process. During September, the production department transferred 80,000 units of product to finished goods. Beginning goods in process had $58,000 of direct materials and $86,400 of direct labor cost. At the end of September, the goods in process inventory consists of 8,000 units that are 25% complete with respect to labor. The direct materials cost added in September is $712,000, and direct labor cost added is $1,980,000.

Required

1. Determine the equivalent units of production with respect to (a) direct labor and (b) direct materials.

2. Compute both the direct labor cost and the direct materials cost per equivalent unit.

3. Compute both direct labor cost and direct materials cost assigned to (a) units completed and transferred out, and (b) ending goods in process inventory.

Analysis Component

4. Abraham sells and ships all units to customers as soon as they are completed. Assume that an error is made in determining the percentage of completion for units in ending inventory. Instead of being 25% complete with respect to labor, they are actually 75% complete. Write a one-page memo to the plant manager describing how this error affects its September financial statements.

Oslo Company produces large quantities of a standardized product. The following information is available for its production activities for May.

Problem 20-3B
Journalizing in process costing;
equivalent units and costs

P1   P2   P3   P4   P6

Raw materials		**Factory overhead incurred**	
Beginning inventory	$ 32,000	Indirect materials used	$ 40,560
Raw materials purchased (on credit)	221,120	Indirect labor used	36,320
Direct materials used	(197,120)	Other overhead costs	34,432
Indirect materials used	(40,560)	Total factory overhead incurred	$111,312
Ending inventory	$ 15,440		
		Factory overhead applied	
Factory payroll		**(90% of direct labor cost)**	
Direct labor used	$123,680	Total factory overhead applied	$111,312
Indirect labor used	36,320		
Total payroll cost (paid in cash)	$160,000		

Additional information about units and costs of production activities follows.

Units		**Costs**		
Beginning goods in process inventory	4,000	Beginning goods in process inventory		
Started	12,000	Direct materials	$2,880	
Ending goods in process inventory	3,000	Direct labor	2,820	
		Factory overhead	2,538	$ 8,238
Status of ending goods in process inventory		Direct materials added		197,120
Materials—Percent complete	100%	Direct labor added		123,680
Labor and overhead—Percent complete	25%	Overhead applied (90% of direct labor)		111,312
		Total costs		$440,350
		Ending goods in process inventory		$ 50,610

During May, 10,000 units of finished goods are sold for $120 cash each. Cost information regarding finished goods follows.

Beginning finished goods inventory	$148,400
Cost transferred in from production	389,740
Cost of goods sold	(474,540)
Ending finished goods inventory	$ 63,600

Required

1. Prepare journal entries dated May 31 to record the following May activities: (a) purchase of raw materials, (b) direct materials usage, (c) indirect materials usage, (d) factory payroll costs, (e) direct labor costs used in production, (f) indirect labor costs, (g) other overhead costs—credit Other Accounts, (h) overhead applied, (i) goods transferred to finished goods, and (j) sale of finished goods.

2. Prepare a process cost summary report for this company, showing costs charged to production, units cost information, equivalent units of production, cost per EUP, and its cost assignment and reconciliation.

Check   (2) Cost per equivalent unit:
materials, $12.50; labor, $9.20;
overhead, $8.28

Analysis Component

3. Oslo provides incentives to its department managers by paying monthly bonuses based on their success in controlling costs per equivalent unit of production. Assume that production overestimates the percentage of completion for units in ending inventory with the result that its equivalent units of production in ending inventory for May are overstated. What impact does this error have on bonuses paid to the managers of the production department? What impact, if any, does this error have on these managers' June bonuses?

Problem 20-4B
Process cost summary; equivalent units

P4 P5 P6

Braun Company produces its product through a single processing department. Direct materials are added at the beginning of the process. Direct labor and overhead are added to the product evenly throughout the process. The company uses monthly reporting periods for its weighted-average process cost accounting. Its Goods in Process Inventory account follows after entries for direct materials, direct labor, and overhead costs for November.

Goods in Process Inventory			Acct. No. 133		
Date		Explanation	Debit	Credit	Balance
Nov.	1	Balance			21,300
	30	Direct materials	116,400		137,700
	30	Direct labor	426,800		564,500
	30	Applied overhead	640,200		1,204,700

The 7,500 units of beginning goods in process consisted of $6,800 of direct materials, $5,800 of direct labor, and $8,700 of factory overhead. During November, the company finished and transferred 100,000 units of its product to finished goods. At the end of the month, the goods in process inventory consisted of 12,000 units that were 25% complete with respect to direct labor and factory overhead and 100% complete with respect to direct materials.

Required

1. Prepare the company's process cost summary for November using the weighted average method.
2. Prepare the journal entry dated November 30 to transfer the cost of the completed units to finished goods inventory.

Problem 20-5B
Process cost summary; equivalent units; cost estimates

P4 P5

Switch Co. manufactures a single product in one department. Direct labor and overhead are added evenly throughout the process. Direct materials are added as needed. The company uses monthly reporting periods for its weighted average process cost accounting. During January, Switch completed and transferred 220,000 units of product to finished goods inventory. Its 10,000 units of beginning goods in process consisted of $7,500 of direct materials, $14,240 of direct labor, and $35,600 of factory overhead. 40,000 units (50% complete with respect to direct materials and 30% complete with respect to direct labor and overhead) are in process at month-end. After entries for direct materials, direct labor, and overhead for January, the company's Goods in Process Inventory account follows.

Goods in Process Inventory			Acct. No. 133		
Date		Explanation	Debit	Credit	Balance
Jan.	1	Balance			57,340
	31	Direct materials	112,500		169,840
	31	Direct labor	176,000		345,840
	31	Applied overhead	440,000		785,840

Required

1. Prepare the company's process cost summary for January.
2. Prepare the journal entry dated January 31 to transfer the cost of completed units to finished goods inventory.

Analysis Components

3. The cost accounting process depends on several estimates.
   a. Identify two major estimates that affect the cost per equivalent unit.
   b. In what direction might you anticipate a bias from management for each estimate in part 3a (assume that management compensation is based on maintaining low inventory amounts)? Explain your answer.

Refer to information in Problem 20-5B. Assume that Switch uses the FIFO method to account for its process costing system. The following additional information is available.

- Beginning goods in process consists of 10,000 units that were 75% complete with respect to direct materials and 60% complete with respect to direct labor and overhead.
- Of the 220,000 units completed, 10,000 were from beginning goods in process; the remaining 210,000 were units started and completed during January.

Problem 20-6B[A]

Process cost summary; equivalent units; and cost estimates

C5 P5 P6

Required

1. Prepare the company's process cost summary for January using FIFO. Round cost per EUP to one-tenth of a cent.

2. Prepare the journal entry dated January 31 to transfer the cost of completed units to finished goods inventory.

Check (1) Labor and overhead EUP, 226,000

(2) Cost transferred, $743,554

 Problem Set C is available at the book's Website to further reinforce and assess your learning.

PROBLEM SET C

(This serial problem began in Chapter 1 and continues through most of the book. If previous chapter segments were not completed, the serial problem can begin at this point.)

SERIAL PROBLEM

Success Systems

C1

SP 20 The computer workstation furniture manufacturing that Adriana Lopez started is progressing well. At this point, Adriana is using a job order costing system to account for the production costs of this product line. Adriana has heard about process costing and is wondering whether process costing might be a better method for her to keep track of and monitor her production costs.

Required

1. What are the features that distinguish job order costing from process costing?

2. Do you believe that Adriana should continue to use job order costing or switch to process costing for her workstation furniture manufacturing? Explain.

CP 20 Corked Bat Company manufactures baseball bats. In addition to its goods in process inventories, Corked Bat maintains inventories of raw materials and finished goods. It uses raw materials as direct materials in production and as indirect materials. Its factory payroll costs include direct labor for production and indirect labor. All materials are added at the beginning of the process, and direct labor and factory overhead are applied uniformly throughout the production process.

COMPREHENSIVE PROBLEM

Corked Bat Company
(Review of Chapters 2, 5, 18, 20)

Required

You are to maintain records and produce measures of inventories to reflect the July events of this company. All computations of unit costs are rounded to the nearest penny and all other dollar amounts to the nearest whole dollar. Set up the following general ledger accounts and enter the June 30 balances: Raw Materials Inventory, $50,000; Goods in Process Inventory, $16,270 ($5,320 of direct materials, $7,300 of direct labor, and $3,650 of overhead); Finished Goods Inventory, $220,000; Sales, $0; Cost of Goods Sold, $0; Factory Payroll, $0; and Factory Overhead, $0.

1. Prepare journal entries to record the following July transactions and events.

   a. Purchased raw materials for $250,000 cash (the company uses a perpetual inventory system).

   b. Used raw materials as follows: direct materials, $104,880; and indirect materials, $20,000.

   c. Incurred factory payroll cost of $454,500 paid in cash (ignore taxes).

   d. Assigned factory payroll costs as follows: direct labor, $404,500; and indirect labor, $50,000.

   e. Incurred additional factory overhead costs of $160,000 paid in cash.

   f. Allocated factory overhead to production at 50% of direct labor costs.

Check (1f) Cr. Factory Overhead, $202,250

Check (2) EUP for overhead,
28,400

2. Information about the July inventories follows. Use this information with that from part 1 to prepare a process cost summary, assuming the weighted average method is used.

Units	
Beginning inventory	10,000 units
Started	28,000 units
Ending inventory	16,000 units
Beginning inventory	
Materials—Percent complete	100%
Labor and overhead—Percent complete	75%
Ending inventory	
Materials—Percent complete	100%
Labor and overhead—Percent complete	40%

(3a) $542,300

3. Using results from part 2 and the available information, make computations and prepare journal entries to record the following:

  a. Total costs transferred to finished goods for July (label entry g).

  b. Sale of finished goods costing $531,400 for $1,250,000 in cash (label entry h).

4. Post entries from parts 1 and 3 to the ledger accounts set up at the beginning of the problem.

5. Compute the amount of gross profit from the sales in July. (*Note:* Add any underapplied overhead to, or deduct any overapplied overhead from, cost of goods sold. Ignore the corresponding journal entry.)

BEYOND THE NUMBERS

**REPORTING IN
ACTION**

C2

BTN 20-1   Best Buy reports in notes to its financial statements that, in addition to its merchandise sold, it includes the following costs (among others) in cost of goods sold: freight expenses associated with moving inventories from vendors to distribution centers, costs of services provided, customer shipping and handling expenses, costs associated with operating their distribution network, and freight expenses associated with moving merchandise from distribution centers to retail stores.

Required

1. Why do you believe Best Buy includes these costs in its cost of goods sold?

2. What effect does this cost accounting policy for its cost of goods sold have on Best Buy's financial statements and any analysis of these statements? Explain.

Fast Forward

3. Access Best Buy's financial statements for fiscal years after February 26, 2005, from its Website (BestBuy.com) or the SEC's EDGAR Website (sec.gov). Review its footnote relating to Cost of Goods Sold and Selling, General, and Administrative Expense. Has Best Buy changed its policy with respect to what costs are included in cost of goods sold? Explain.

**COMPARATIVE
ANALYSIS**

C1

BTN 20-2   Retailers such as Best Buy and Circuit City usually work to maintain a high-quality and low-cost operation. One ratio routinely computed for this assessment is the cost of goods sold divided by total expenses. A decline in this ratio can mean that the company is spending too much on selling and administrative activities. An increase in this ratio beyond a reasonable level can mean that the company is not spending enough on selling activities. (Assume for this analysis that total expenses equal cost of goods sold plus selling, general, and administrative expenses.)

Required

1. For both Best Buy and Circuit City, refer to Appendix A and compute the ratio of cost of goods sold to total expenses for their two most recent fiscal years.

2. Comment on the similarities or differences in the ratio results across both years and companies.

BTN 20-3 Many accounting and accounting-related professionals are skilled in financial analysis, but most are not skilled in manufacturing. This is especially the case for process manufacturing environments (for example, a bottling plant or chemical factory). To provide professional accounting and financial services, one must understand the industry, product, and processes. We have an ethical responsibility to develop this understanding before offering services to clients in these areas.

Required

Write a one-page action plan, in memorandum format, on how you would obtain an understanding of key business processes of a company that hires you to provide financial services. The memorandum should specify an industry, a product, and one selected process and should draw on at least one reference, such as a professional journal or industry magazine.

BTN 20-4 You hire a new assistant production manager whose prior experience is with a company that produced goods to order. Your company engages in continuous production of homogeneous products that go through various production processes. Your new assistant e-mails you questioning some cost classifications on an internal report, specifically why the costs of some materials that do not actually become part of the finished product, including some labor costs not directly associated with producing the product, are classified as direct costs. Respond to this concern via memorandum.

BTN 20-5 Many companies acquire software to help them monitor and control their costs and as an aid to their accounting systems. One company that supplies such software is **proDacapo** (**prodacapo.com**). There are many other such vendors. Access proDacapo's Website, click on "Process Management" and review the information displayed.

Required

How is process management software helpful to businesses? Explain with reference to costs, efficiency, and examples, if possible.

BTN 20-6 The purpose of this team activity is to ensure that each team member understands process operations and the related accounting entries. Find the activities and flows identified in Exhibit 20.4 with numbers ①–⑩. Pick a member of the team to start by describing activity number ① in this exhibit, then verbalizing the related journal entry, and describing how the amounts in the entry are computed. The other members of the team are to agree or disagree; discussion is to continue until all members express understanding. Rotate to the next numbered activity and next team member until all activities and entries have been discussed. If at any point a team member is uncertain about an answer, the team member may pass and get back in the rotation when he or she can contribute to the team's discussion.

BTN 20-7 Read the article "Global or Local? Make it Both," from the August 22, 2005, issue of *BusinessWeek*. (The book's Website provides a free link to the article.)

Required

1. How does Gianfranco Zaccai define *global* products? Does he imply that the products must be the same the world over? Explain.
2. How do global product choices depend on flexibility of mass production?
3. What are some examples of companies who found that their assumptions about international customers were incorrect? Identify and briefly discuss them.

**ENTREPRENEURIAL
DECISION**

C4

BTN 20-8   Read the chapter opener regarding DuWop. Cristina Bartolucci commented that some suppliers tried to bully them and talk them into buying items that they did not really need.

Required

How do unnecessary raw materials inventories affect profitability? If the items are not used in production, how can they affect profits? Explain.

**HITTING THE
ROAD**

C3

Point: The class can compare and discuss the different processes studied and the answers provided.

BTN 20-9   In process costing, the process is analyzed first and then a unit measure is computed in the form of equivalent units for direct materials, direct labor, overhead, and all three combined. The same analysis applies to both manufacturing and service processes.

Required

Visit your local **U.S. Mail** center. Look into the backroom and you will see several ongoing processes. Select one process, such as sorting, and list the costs associated with this process. Your list should include materials, labor, and overhead; be specific. Classify each cost as fixed or variable. At the bottom of your list, outline how overhead should be assigned to your identified process. The following format (with an example) is suggested.

Cost Description	Direct Material	Direct Labor	Overhead	Variable Cost	Fixed Cost
Manual sorting		X		X	
⋮					
Overhead allocation suggestions:					

GLOBAL DECISION

C1

BTN 20-10   Dixons, Best Buy, and Circuit City are competitors in the global marketplace. Selected data for each of these companies follow.

	Dixons*		Best Buy†		Circuit City†	
	Current Year	Prior Year	Current Year	Prior Year	Current Year	Prior Year
Cost of goods sold	£5,806	£5,127	$20,938	$18,677	$ 7,904	$7,573
General, selling, and administrative expenses	378	365	5,053	4,567	2,457	2,277
Total expenses	£6,184	£5,492	$25,991	$23,244	$10,361	$9,850

* millions of pounds
† millions of dollars

Required

1. Review the discussion of the importance of the cost of goods sold divided by total expenses ratio in BTN 20-2. Compute the cost of goods sold to total expenses ratio for all three companies for the two years of data provided.

2. Comment on the similarities or differences in the ratio results across years and companies.

ANSWERS TO MULTIPLE CHOICE QUIZ

1. d

2. e

3. b; $20,000 + $152,000 + $45,000 + $18,000 − $218,000 = $\underline{\underline{\$17,000}}$

4. a; $40,000 + (15,000 \times 1/3) = \underline{\underline{45,000 \text{ EUP}}}$

5. c; $(\$6,000 + \$84,000) \div 45,000 \text{ EUP} = \$2 \text{ per EUP}$

21

Cost Allocation and Performance Measurement

A Look Back

Chapter 20 focused on how to measure and account for costs in process operations. It explained process production, described how to assign costs to processes, and computed cost per equivalent unit.

A Look at This Chapter

This chapter describes cost allocation and activity-based costing. It identifies managerial reports useful in directing a company's activities. It also describes responsibility accounting, measuring departmental performance, and allocating common costs across departments.

A Look Ahead

Chapter 22 looks at cost behavior and explains how its identification is useful to managers in performing cost-volume-profit analyses. It also shows how to apply cost-volume-profit analysis for managerial decisions.

Learning Objectives

CAP

Conceptual

C1 Explain departmentalization and the role of departmental accounting. (p. 848)

C2 Distinguish between direct and indirect expenses. (p. 849)

C3 Identify bases for allocating indirect expenses to departments. (p. 850)

C4 Explain controllable costs and responsibility accounting. (p. 855)

C5 *Appendix 21A*—Describe allocation of joint costs across products. (p. 861)

Analytical

A1 Analyze investment centers using return on total assets. (p. 858)

Procedural

P1 Assign overhead costs using two-stage cost allocation. (p. 842)

P2 Assign overhead costs using activity-based costing. (p. 844)

P3 Prepare departmental income statements. (p. 851)

P4 Prepare departmental contribution reports. (p. 854)

> *"If you put enough energy into your dream, you can make anything happen"*
> —Jim Bonaminio

The Wizard of Odd

FAIRFIELD, OH—Jim Bonaminio built his roadside produce stand while living in an abandoned gas station. "I would get up and leave at 4 in the morning to buy everything fresh [and] my wife opened the market at 8 a.m.," recalls Jim. "By 10 o'clock at night, we'd be sitting on the bed balancing the register receipts . . . we worked seven days a week." The fruit of those early efforts is **Jungle Jim's International Market (JungleJim.com).** Jim and his wife now serve more than 50,000 customers (Jim calls them "Foodies" and his store "Foodieland") each week, and annual sales are near $100 million.

Jungle Jim's is no Wal-Mart wannabe, but it is arguably America's wackiest supermarket. Yet there is a plan to Jim's madness. Instead of trying to beat the big chains at the price-squeezing game, Jim's is a funhouse maze of a store. A seven-foot Elvis lion sings "Jailhouse Rock," an antique fire engine rests atop cases of hot sauce, port-a-potties lead to fancy restrooms, and Robin Hood greets customers with English food set within a 30-foot-tall Sherwood Forest. This is just a sampling. Jim is already working on a plan to install the old monorail acquired from Paramount's Kings Island.

"If you don't go out on a limb, then you're just like everybody else," insists Jim. "The stuff I've collected—all sorts of weird stuff—gets reused. We make it fit into the craziness." Despite the wackiness, his store's defining trait is specialty food departments reflecting nearly 100 countries. Jungle Jim's stocks more than 140,000 items, including 1,600 cheeses, 8,500 wines, 800 beers, 1,000 hot sauces, and an entire acre of produce! More than several dozen ethnic departments make up his 300,000 square foot Foodieland.

This diversity of departments requires cost management. Jim is first and foremost a businessman. "I hire professional people to run the departments," says Jim. "I offer suggestions. They run with the ball. I block and add my creative craziness." Jim has successfully merged cost controls and departmental and individual responsibility into his store. He closely monitors direct, indirect, and controllable costs and allocates them to departments and products. Jim knows how departments and products are performing and their contribution margins. Says Jim about his employees, "[they're] always looking for ways to make money . . . [I want them] to be the best in each food department."

Yet cost management has not curtailed Jim's fun-loving approach to business. "I'm trying to create something that has never been done," says Jim. "I just want to see if I can do it and have fun."

[Sources: *Jungle Jim's Website,* May 2006; *BusinessWeek,* April 2005; *Country Living,* November 2004; *Miamian,* Summer 2004; *Design,* May 2004; *Smithsonian,* October 2000; *Plain Dealer,* November 2004]

This chapter describes how to allocate costs shared by more than one product across those different products and how to allocate indirect costs of shared items such as utilities, advertising, and rent. The chapter also describes activity-based costing and how it traces the costs of individual activities. This knowledge helps managers better understand how to assign costs and assess company performance. The chapter also introduces additional managerial accounting reports useful in managing a company's activities and explains how and why management divides companies into departments.

Cost Allocation and Performance Measurement

Overhead Cost Allocation Methods	Departmental Accounting	Departmental Expense Allocation	Responsibility Accounting
• Two-stage cost allocation • Activity-based cost allocation • Comparison of allocation methods	• Motivation for departmentalization • Departmental evaluation • Departmental reporting and analysis	• Direct and indirect expenses • Allocation of indirect expenses • Departmental income statements • Departmental contribution to overhead	• Controllable versus direct costs • Responsibility accounting system

Section 1—Allocating Costs for Product Costing

This first of two sections in this chapter focuses on alternatives for allocation of costs to products and services. We explain and illustrate two basic methods: (1) traditional two-state cost allocation and (2) activity-based cost allocation. The second section describes and illustrates the allocation of costs for performance evaluation.

Overhead Cost Allocation Methods

P1 Assign overhead costs using two-stage cost allocation.

Point: Use of a single overhead allocation rate is known as using a *plantwide rate*.

We previously explained how to assign overhead costs to jobs (and processes) by using a predetermined overhead rate per unit of an allocation base such as direct labor cost. When a single overhead rate is used on a companywide basis, all overhead is lumped together, and a predetermined overhead rate per unit of an allocation base is computed and used to assign overhead to jobs (and processes). The use of a single predetermined overhead rate suggests that this allocation process is simple. In reality, it can be complicated. This chapter explains the traditional two-stage cost allocation procedure and then introduces the activity-based cost allocation procedure.

Two-Stage Cost Allocation

An organization incurs overhead costs in many activities. These activities can be identified with various departments, which can be broadly classified as either operating or service departments.

Operating departments perform an organization's main functions. For example, an accounting firm's main functions usually include auditing, tax, and advisory services. Similarly, the production and selling departments of a manufacturing firm perform its main functions and serve as operating departments. *Service departments* provide support to an organization's operating departments. Examples of service departments are payroll, human resource management, accounting, and executive management. Service departments do not engage in activities that generate revenues, yet their support is crucial for the operating departments' success. In this section, we apply a two-stage cost allocation procedure to assign (1) service department costs to operating departments and (2) operating department costs, including those assigned from service departments, to the organization's output.

Illustration of Two-Stage Cost Allocation Exhibit 21.1 shows the two-stage cost allocation procedure. This exhibit uses data from **AutoGrand**, a custom automobile manufacturer. AutoGrand has five manufacturing-related departments: janitorial, maintenance, factory accounting, machining, and assembly. Expenses incurred by each of these departments are considered product costs. There are three service departments—janitorial, maintenance, and factory accounting; each incurs expenses of $10,000, $15,000 and $8,000, respectively. As shown in Exhibit 21.1, the first stage of the two-stage procedure involves allocating the costs of the three service departments to the two operating departments (machining and assembly). The two operating departments use the resources of these service departments.

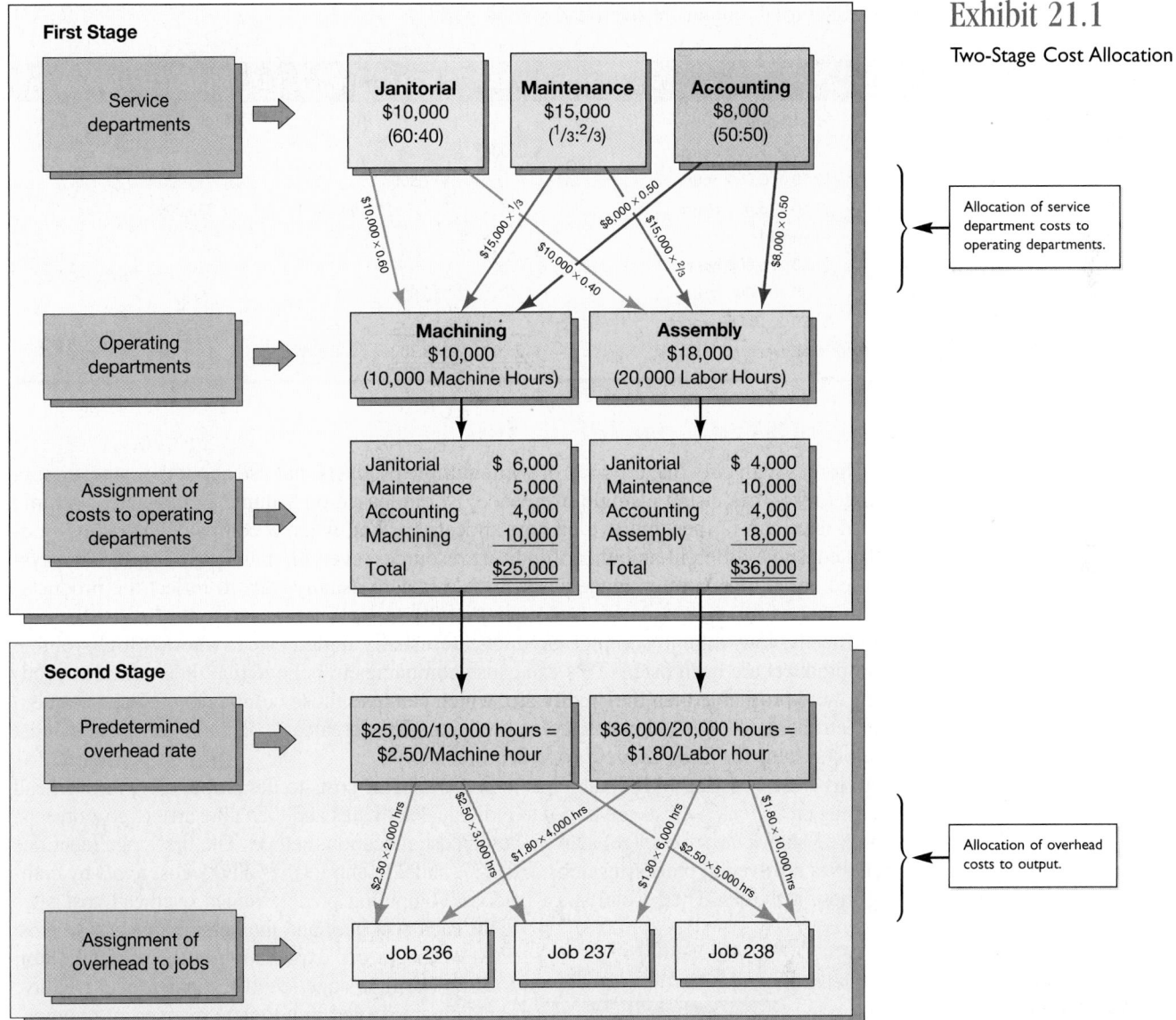

Exhibit 21.1

Two-Stage Cost Allocation

Allocation of service department costs to operating departments.

Allocation of overhead costs to output.

To illustrate the first stage of cost allocation, we use the janitorial department. Its costs are allocated to machining and assembly in the ratio 60 : 40. This means that 60%, or $6,000, of janitorial costs are assigned to the machining department and 40%, or $4,000, to the assembly department. The expenses incurred by the maintenance and factory accounting departments are similarly assigned to machining and assembly. We then add the expenses directly incurred by each operating department to these assigned costs to determine the total expenses for each operating department. This yields total costs of $25,000 for machining and $36,000 for assembly.

In the second stage, predetermined overhead rates are computed for each operating department. The allocation base is machine hours for machining and labor hours for assembly. The

Point: Use of a separate overhead allocation rate for each department is known as using *departmental rates*.

predetermined overhead rate is $2.50 per machine hour for the machining department and $1.80 per labor hour for the assembly department. These predetermined overhead rates are then used to assign overhead to output.

To illustrate this second stage, assume that three jobs were started and finished in a recent month. These jobs consumed resources as follows: Job 236—2,000 machine hours in machining and 4,000 labor hours in assembly; Job 237—3,000 machine hours and 6,000 labor hours; Job 238—5,000 machine hours and 10,000 labor hours. The overhead assigned to these three jobs is shown with the arrow lines in the bottom row of Exhibit 21.1.

Exhibit 21.2 summarizes these allocations. Total overhead allocated to Jobs 236, 237, and 238, is $12,200, $18,300, and $30,500, respectively. These allocated costs sum to $61,000, which is the total amount of overhead started with.

Exhibit 21.2

Assignment of Overhead Costs to Output

	Job 236	Job 237	Job 238	Department Totals
Machining				
$2.50 × 2,000 hours	$ 5,000			
$2.50 × 3,000 hours		$ 7,500		
$2.50 × 5,000 hours			$12,500	$25,000
Assembly				
$1.80 × 4,000 hours	7,200			
$1.80 × 6,000 hours		10,800		
$1.80 × 10,000 hours			18,000	36,000
Total overhead assigned	$12,200	$18,300	$30,500	$61,000

Activity-Based Cost Allocation

P2 Assign overhead costs using activity-based costing.

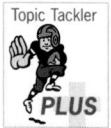

Topic Tackler
PLUS

21-1

Point: A survey found that most respondents believe that activity-based costing is worth the investment because of improved management decisions.

For companies with only one product, or with multiple products that use about the same amount of indirect resources, using a single overhead cost rate based on volume is adequate. Multiple overhead rates can further improve on cost allocations. Yet, when a company has many products that consume different amounts of indirect resources, even the multiple overhead rate system based on volume is often inadequate. Such a system usually fails to reflect the products' different uses of indirect resources and often distorts products costs.

Specifically, low-volume complex products are usually undercosted, whereas high-volume simpler products are overcosted. This can cause companies to believe that their complex products are more profitable than they really are, which can lead those companies to focus on them to the detriment of high-volume simpler products. This creates a demand for a better cost allocation system for these indirect (overhead) costs.

Activity-based costing (ABC) attempts to better allocate costs to the proper users of overhead by focusing on *activities.* Costs are traced to individual activities and then allocated to cost objects. Exhibit 21.3 shows the (two-stage) activity-based cost allocation method. The first stage identifies the activities involved in processing Jobs 236, 237, and 238 and forms activity cost *pools* by combining those activities. The second stage involves computing predetermined overhead cost rates for each cost pool and then assigning costs to jobs.

We begin our explanation at the top of Exhibit 21.3. The first stage identifies individual activities, which are pooled in a logical manner into homogenous groups, or *cost pools.* A homogenous cost pool consists of activities that belong to the same process and/or are caused by the same cost driver. An **activity cost driver,** or simply *cost driver,* is a factor that causes the cost of an activity to go up or down. For example, preparing an invoice, checking it, and dispatching it are activities of the "invoicing" process and can therefore be grouped in a single cost pool. Moreover, the number of invoices processed likely drives the costs of these activities.

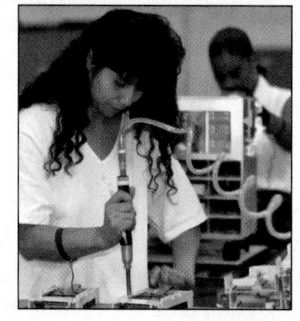

Exhibit 21.3

Activity-Based Cost Allocation

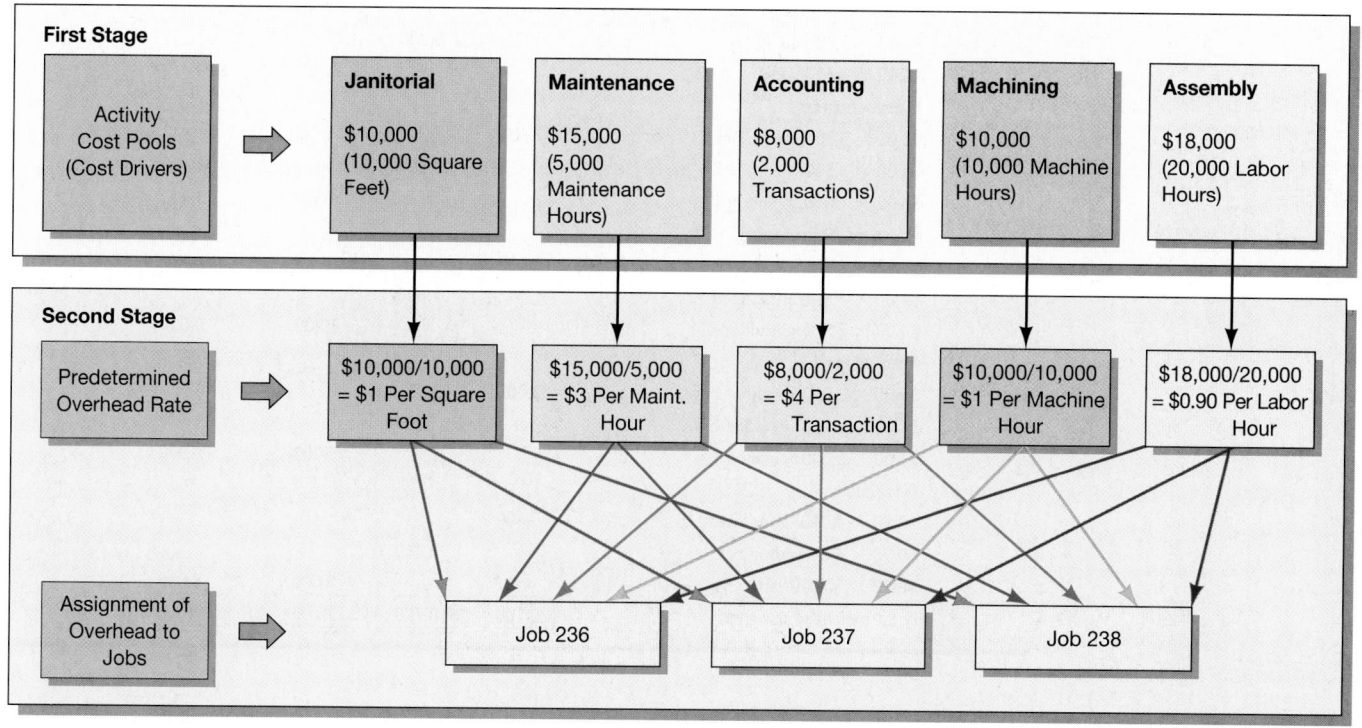

An **activity cost pool** is a temporary account accumulating the costs a company incurs to support an identified set of activities. Costs accumulated in an activity cost pool include the variable and fixed costs of the activities in the pool. Variable costs pertain to resources acquired as needed (such as materials); fixed costs pertain to resources acquired in advance (such as equipment). An activity cost pool account is handled like a factory overhead account.

In the second stage, after all activity costs are accumulated in an activity cost pool account, overhead rates are computed. Then, costs are allocated to cost objects (users) based on cost drivers (allocation bases).

Point: A cost driver is different from an allocation base. An allocation base is used as a basis for assigning overhead but need not have a cause-effect relation with the costs assigned. However, a cost driver has a cause-effect relation with the cost assigned.

Illustration of Activity-Based Costing To illustrate, let's return to AutoGrand's three jobs. Assume that resources used to complete Jobs 236, 237, and 238 are shown in Exhibit 21.4.

Resources Used	Job 236	Job 237	Job 238
Square feet of space	5,000	3,000	2,000
Maintenance hours	2,500	1,500	1,000
Number of transactions	500	700	800
Machine hours	2,000	3,000	5,000
Direct labor hours	4,000	6,000	10,000

Exhibit 21.4

Activity Resource Use

The $61,000 of total costs are assigned to these three jobs using activity-based costing as shown in Exhibit 21.5 (rates are taken from the second stage of Exhibit 21.3). Comparing Exhibits 21.2 and 21.5, we see that the costs assigned to the three jobs vary markedly depending on whether two-stage (departmental) cost allocation or activity-based costing is used. Costs assigned to Job 236 go from $12,200 using two-stage cost allocation to $20,100 under activity-based costing. Costs assigned to Job 238 decline from $30,500 to $22,200. These differences in assigned amounts result from more accurately tracing costs to each job using activity-based costing where the allocation bases reflect actual cost drivers.

Exhibit 21.5

Activity-Based Assignment of Overhead to Output

	Job 236	Job 237	Job 238	Activity Totals
Janitorial				
$1.00 × 5,000 sq. ft.	$ 5,000			
$1.00 × 3,000 sq. ft.		$ 3,000		
$1.00 × 2,000 sq. ft.			$ 2,000	$10,000
Maintenance				
$3.00 × 2,500 maint. hrs.	7,500			
$3.00 × 1,500 maint. hrs.		4,500		
$3.00 × 1,000 maint. hrs.			3,000	15,000
Factory Accounting				
$4.00 × 500 transactions	2,000			
$4.00 × 700 transactions		2,800		
$4.00 × 800 transactions			3,200	8,000
Machining				
$1.00 × 2,000 machine hrs.	2,000			
$1.00 × 3,000 machine hrs.		3,000		
$1.00 × 5,000 machine hrs.			5,000	10,000
Assembly				
$0.90 × 4,000 labor hrs.	3,600			
$0.90 × 6,000 labor hrs.		5,400		
$0.90 × 10,000 labor hrs.			9,000	18,000
Total overhead assigned	$20,100	$18,700	$22,200	$61,000

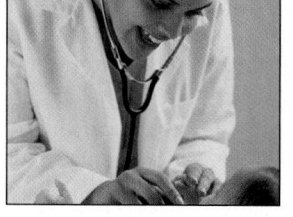
Comparison of Two-Stage and Activity-Based Cost Allocation

Traditional cost systems capture overhead costs by individual department (or function) and accumulate these costs in one or more overhead accounts. Companies then assign these overhead costs using a single allocation base such as direct labor or multiple volume-based allocation bases. Unfortunately, traditional cost systems have tended to use allocation bases that are often not closely related to the way these costs are actually incurred.

In contrast, activity-based cost systems capture costs by individual activity. These activities and their costs are then accumulated into activity cost pools. A company selects a cost driver (allocation base) for each activity pool. It uses this cost driver to assign the accumulated activity costs to cost objects (such as jobs or products) benefiting from the activity.

An activity-based costing system commonly consists of more allocation bases as compared to a traditional cost system. For example, a Chicago-based manufacturer currently uses nearly 20 different activity cost drivers to assign overhead costs to its products. Exhibit 21.6 lists common examples of overhead cost pools and their usual cost drivers.

Activity-based costing is especially effective when the same department or departments produce many different types of products. For instance, more complex products often require more help from service departments such as engineering, maintenance, and materials handling. If the same amount of direct labor is applied to the complex and simple products, a traditional overhead allocation system assigns the same overhead cost to both. With activity-based costing, however, the complex products are assigned a larger portion of overhead. The difference in overhead assigned can affect product pricing, make-or-buy, and other managerial decisions.

Activity-based costing encourages managers to focus on *activities* as well as the use of those

Decision Maker

Answer—p. 863

Director of Operations Two department managers at your ad agency complain to you that overhead costs assigned to them are too high. Overhead is assigned on the basis of labor hours for designers. These managers argue that overhead depends not only on designers' hours but on many activities unrelated to these hours. What is your response?

Activity Cost Pool	Cost Driver
Materials purchasing	Number of purchase orders
Materials handling	Number of materials requisitions
Personnel processing	Number of employees hired or laid off
Equipment depreciation	Number of products produced or hours of use
Quality inspection	Number of units inspected
Indirect labor in setting up equipment	Number of setups required
Engineering costs for product modifications	Number of modifications (engineering change orders)

Exhibit 21.6

Cost Pools and Cost Drivers in Activity-Based Costing

activities. For instance, assume AutoGrand can reduce the number of transactions processed in Factory Accounting to 1,500 (375 transactions for Job 236, 525 transactions for Job 237, and 600 transactions for Job 238) and that through continuous improvement it can reduce costs of processing those transactions to $4,500. The resulting rate to process a transaction is $3 per transaction ($4,500/1,500 transactions—down from $4 per Exhibit 21.3). The cost of transaction processing is reduced for all jobs (Job 236, $1,125; Job 237, $1,575; Job 238, $1,800). However, if those accounting costs were grouped in a single overhead cost pool, it is more difficult to identify cost savings and understand their effects on product costs.

Activity-based costing requires managers to look at each item and encourages them to manage each cost to increase the benefit from each dollar spent. It also encourages managers to cooperate because it shows how their efforts are interrelated. This results in *activity-based management.*

Decision Ethics

Answer—p. 863

Accounting Officer Your company produces expensive garments, whose production involves many complex and specialized activities. Your general manager recently learned about activity-based costing (ABC) and asks your advice. However, your supervisor does not want to disturb the existing cost system and instructs you to prepare a report stating that "implementation of ABC is a complicated process involving too many steps and not worth the effort." You believe ABC will actually help the company identify sources of costs and control them. What action do you take?

Quick Check

Answers—p. 863

1. What is a cost driver?
2. When activity-based costing is used rather than traditional allocation methods, (a) managers must identify cost drivers for various items of overhead cost, (b) individual cost items in service departments are allocated directly to products or services, (c) managers can direct their attention to the activities that drive overhead cost, or (d) all of the above.

Section 2—Allocating Costs for Performance Evaluation

This second section of the chapter describes and illustrates allocation of costs for performance evaluation. We begin with departmental accounting and expense allocations and conclude with responsibility accounting.

Departmental Accounting

Companies are divided into *departments,* also called *subunits,* when they are too large to be managed effectively as a single unit. Managerial accounting for departments has two main goals. The first is to set up a **departmental accounting system** to provide information for managers to evaluate the profitability or cost effectiveness of each department's activities. The second goal is to set up a **responsibility accounting system** to control costs and expenses and evaluate managers' performances by assigning costs and expenses to the managers responsible for controlling them. Departmental and responsibility accounting systems are related and share much information.

Motivation for Departmentalization

C1 Explain departmentalization and the role of departmental accounting.

Many companies are so large and complex that they are broken into separate divisions for efficiency and/or effectiveness purposes. Divisions then are usually organized into separate departments. When a company is departmentalized, each department is often placed under the direction of a manager. As a company grows, management often divides departments into new departments so that responsibilities for a department's activities do not overwhelm the manager's ability to oversee and control them. A company also creates departments to take advantage of the skills of individual managers. Departments are broadly classified as either operating or service departments.

Departmental Evaluation

Point: To improve profitability, **Sears, Roebuck & Co.** eliminated several departments, including its catalog division.

21-2

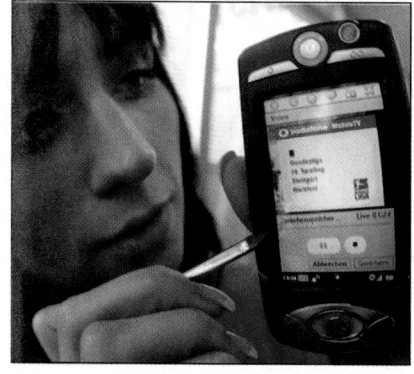

Point: Selling departments are often treated as *revenue centers;* their managers are responsible for maximizing sales revenues.

When a company is divided into departments, managers need to know how each department is performing. The accounting system must supply information about resources used and outputs achieved by each department. This requires a system to measure and accumulate revenue and expense information for each department whenever possible.

Departmental information is rarely distributed publicly because of its potential usefulness to competitors. Information about departments is prepared for internal managers to help control operations, appraise performance, allocate resources, and plan strategy. If a department is highly profitable, management may decide to expand its operations, or if a department is performing poorly, information about revenues or expenses can suggest useful changes.

More companies are emphasizing customer satisfaction as a main responsibility of many departments. This has led to changes in the measures reported. Increasingly, financial measurements are being supplemented with quality and customer satisfaction indexes. **Motorola**, for instance, uses two key measures: the number of defective parts per million parts produced and the percent of orders delivered on time to customers. (Note that some departments have only "internal customers.")

Financial information used to evaluate a department depends on whether it is evaluated as a profit center or a cost center. A **profit center** incurs costs and generates revenues; selling departments are often evaluated as profit centers. A **cost center** incurs costs without directly generating revenues. The manufacturing departments of a manufacturer and its service departments such as accounting, advertising, and purchasing, are all cost centers.

Evaluating managers' performance depends on whether they are responsible for profit centers or cost centers. Profit center managers are judged on their abilities to generate revenues in excess of the department's costs. They are assumed to influence both revenue generation and cost incurrence. Cost center managers are judged on their abilities to control costs by keeping them within a satisfactory range under an assumption that only they influence costs.

Departmental Reporting and Analysis

Companies use various measures (financial and nonfinancial) and reporting formats to evaluate their departments. The type and form of information depend on management's focus and philosophy. **Hewlett-Packard**'s statement of corporate objectives, for instance, indicates that its goal is to satisfy customer needs. Its challenge is to set up managerial accounting systems to provide relevant feedback for evaluating performance in terms of its stated objectives. Also, the means used to obtain information about departments depend on how extensively a company uses computer and information technology.

When accounts are not maintained separately in the general ledger by department, a company can create departmental information by using a *departmental spreadsheet analysis*. For example, after recording sales in its usual manner, a company can compute daily total sales by department and enter these totals on a sales spreadsheet. At period-end, column totals of the spreadsheet show sales by department. The combined total of all columns equals the balance of the Sales account. A merchandiser that uses a spreadsheet analysis of department sales often uses separate spreadsheets to accumulate sales, sales returns, purchases, and purchases returns by department. If each department keeps a count of its inventory, it can also compute its gross profit (assuming it's a profit center).

Point: Many retailers use a point-of-sales system capturing sales data and creating requests to release inventory from the warehouse and order more merchandise. **Wal-Mart's** sales system not only collects data for internal use but also is used by **Procter & Gamble** to plan its production and product deliveries to **Wal-Mart**.

Point: Link Wood Products, a manufacturer of lawn and garden products, records each sale by department on a spreadsheet. Daily totals are accumulated in another spreadsheet to obtain monthly totals by department.

Quick Check

Answers—p. 863

3. What is the difference between a departmental accounting system and a responsibility accounting system?

4. Service departments (*a*) manufacture products, (*b*) make sales directly to customers, (*c*) produce revenues, (*d*) assist operating departments.

5. Explain the difference between a cost center and a profit center. Cite an example of each.

Departmental Expense Allocation

When a company computes departmental profits, it confronts some accounting challenges that involve allocating its expenses across its operating departments.

Direct and Indirect Expenses

Direct expenses are costs readily traced to a department because they are incurred for that department's sole benefit. They require no allocation across departments. For example, the salary of an employee who works in only one department is a direct expense of that one department.

Indirect expenses are costs that are incurred for the joint benefit of more than one department and cannot be readily traced to only one department. For example, if two or more departments share a single building, all enjoy the benefits of the expenses for rent, heat, and light. Indirect expenses are allocated across departments benefiting from them when we need information about departmental profits. Ideally, we allocate indirect expenses by using a cause-effect relation. When we cannot identify cause-effect relations, we allocate each indirect expense on a basis approximating the relative benefit each department receives. Measuring the benefit for each department from an indirect expense can be difficult.

C2 Distinguish between direct and indirect expenses.

Point: Utility expense has elements of both direct and indirect expenses.

Illustration of Indirect Expense Allocation To illustrate how to allocate an indirect expense, we consider a retail store that purchases janitorial services from an outside company. Management allocates this cost across the store's three departments according to the floor space each occupies. Costs of janitorial services for a recent month are $300. Exhibit 21.7 shows the square feet of floor space each department occupies. The store computes the percent of total square feet allotted to each department and uses it to allocate the $300 cost.

Department	Square Feet	Percent of Total	Allocated Cost
Jewelry	2,400	60%	$180
Watch repair	600	15	45
China and silver	1,000	25	75
Totals	4,000	100%	$300

Exhibit 21.7

Indirect Expense Allocation

Specifically, because the jewelry department occupies 60% of the floor space, 60% of the total $300 cost is assigned to it. The same procedure is applied to the other departments. When the allocation process is complete, these and other allocated costs are deducted from the gross profit for each department to determine net income for each. One consideration in allocating costs is to motivate managers and employees to behave as desired. As a result, a cost incurred in one department might be best allocated to other departments when one of the other departments caused the cost.

Allocation of Indirect Expenses

C3 Identify bases for allocating indirect expenses to departments.

This section describes how to identify the bases used to allocate indirect expenses across departments. No standard rule identifies the best basis because expense allocation involves several factors, and the relative importance of these factors varies across departments and organizations. Judgment is required, and people do not always agree. In our discussion, note the parallels between activity-based costing and the departmental expense allocation procedures described here.

Point: Expense allocations cannot always avoid some arbitrariness.

Wages and Salaries Employee wages and salaries can be either direct or indirect expenses. If their time is spent entirely in one department, their wages are direct expenses of that department. However, if employees work for the benefit of more than one department, their wages are indirect expenses and must be allocated across the departments benefited. An employee's contribution to a department usually depends on the number of hours worked in contributing to that department. Thus, a reasonable basis for allocating employee wages and salaries is the *relative amount of time spent in each department*. In the case of a supervisor who manages more than one department, recording the time spent in each department may not always be practical. Instead, a company can allocate the supervisor's salary to departments on the basis of the number of employees in each department—a reasonable basis if a supervisor's main task is managing people. Another basis of allocation is on sales across departments, also a reasonable basis if a supervisor's job reflects on departmental sales.

Point: Some companies ask supervisors to estimate time spent supervising specific departments for purposes of expense allocation.

Rent and Related Expenses Rent expense for a building is reasonably allocated to a department on the basis of floor space it occupies. Location can often make some floor space more valuable than other space. Thus, the allocation method can charge departments that occupy more valuable space a higher expense per square foot. Ground floor retail space, for instance, is often more valuable than basement or upper-floor space because all customers pass departments near the entrance but fewer go beyond the first floor. When no precise measures of floor space values exist, basing allocations on data such as customer traffic and real estate assessments is helpful. When a company owns its building, its expenses for depreciation, taxes, insurance, and other related building expenses are allocated like rent expense.

Advertising Expenses Effective advertising of a department's products increases its sales and customer traffic. Moreover, advertising products for some departments usually helps other departments' sales because customers also often buy unadvertised products. Thus, many stores treat advertising as an indirect expense allocated on the basis of each department's proportion of total sales. For example, a department with 10% of a store's total sales is assigned 10% of advertising expense. Another method is to analyze each advertisement to compute the Web/newspaper space or TV/radio time devoted to the products of a department and charge that department for the proportional costs of advertisements. Management must consider whether this more detailed and costly method is justified.

Point: Employee morale suffers when allocations are perceived as unfair. Thus, it is important to carefully design and explain the allocation of service department costs.

Equipment and Machinery Depreciation Depreciation on equipment and machinery used only in one department is a direct expense of that department. Depreciation on equipment and machinery used by more than one department is an indirect expense to be allocated across departments. Accounting for each department's depreciation expense requires a company to keep records showing which departments use specific assets. The number of hours that a department uses equipment and machinery is a reasonable basis for allocating depreciation.

Utilities Expenses   Utilities expenses such as heating and lighting are usually allocated on the basis of floor space occupied by departments. This practice assumes their use is uniform across departments. When this is not so, a more involved allocation can be necessary, although there is often a trade-off between the usefulness of more precise allocations and the effort to compute them.

Point: Manufacturers often allocate electricity cost to departments on the basis of the horsepower of equipment located in each department.

Service Department Expenses   To generate revenues, operating departments require support services provided by departments such as personnel, payroll, advertising, and purchasing. Such service departments are typically evaluated as cost centers because they do not produce revenues. (Evaluating them as profit centers requires the use of a system that "charges" user departments a price that then serves as the "revenue" generated by service departments.) A departmental accounting system can accumulate and report costs incurred directly by each service department for this purpose. The system then allocates a service department's expenses to operating departments benefiting from them. This is often done, for example, using traditional two-stage cost allocation (see Exhibit 21.1). Exhibit 21.8 shows some commonly used bases for allocating service department expenses to operating departments.

Point: When a service department "charges" its user departments within a company, a *transfer pricing system* must be set up to determine the "revenue" from its services provided.

Service Department	Common Allocation Bases
Office expenses	Number of employees or sales in each department
Personnel expenses	Number of employees in each department
Payroll expenses	Number of employees in each department
Advertising expenses	Sales or amount of advertising charged directly to each department
Purchasing costs	Dollar amounts of purchases or number of purchase orders processed
Cleaning expenses	Square feet of floor space occupied
Maintenance expenses	Square feet of floor space occupied

Exhibit 21.8

Bases for Allocating Service Department Expenses

Departmental Income Statements

An income statement can be prepared for each operating department once expenses have been assigned to it. Its expenses include both direct expenses and its share of indirect expenses. For this purpose, compiling all expenses incurred in service departments before assigning them to operating departments is useful. We illustrate the steps to prepare departmental income statements using **A-1 Hardware** and its five departments. Two of them (office and purchasing) are service departments and the other three (hardware, housewares, and appliances) are operating (selling) departments. Allocating costs to operating departments and preparing departmental income statements involves four steps.

P3   Prepare departmental income statements.

Step 1   Step 1 accumulates direct expenses for each service and operating department as shown in Exhibit 21.9. Direct expenses include salaries, wages, and other expenses that each department incurs but does not share with any other department. This information is accumulated in departmental expense accounts.

Direct Expenses	Direct Expenses	Direct Expenses	Direct Expenses	Direct Expenses
General office	Purchasing	Hardware	Housewares	Appliances

Exhibit 21.9

Step 1: Direct Expense Accumulation

Step 2   Step 2 allocates indirect expenses across all departments using the allocation base identified for each expense as shown in Exhibit 21.10. Indirect expenses can include items such as depreciation, rent, advertising, and any other expenses that cannot be directly assigned to a department. Indirect expenses are recorded in expense accounts, and costs are allocated using a *departmental expense allocation spreadsheet* described in step 3.

Point: We sometimes allocate service department costs across other service departments before allocating them to operating departments. This "step-wise" process is in advanced courses.

Exhibit 21.10

Step 2: Indirect Expense Allocation

Step 3   Step 3 allocates expenses of the service departments (office and purchasing) to the operating departments. Exhibit 21.11 reflects the allocation of service department expenses using the allocation base(s).

Exhibit 21.11

Step 3: Service Department Expense Allocation to Operating Departments

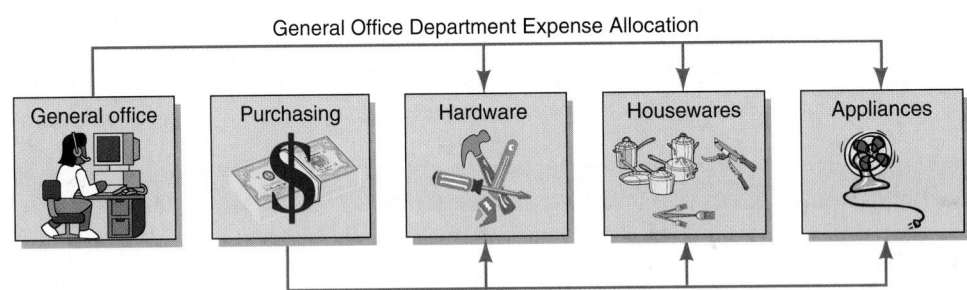

Exhibit 21.12

Departmental Expense Allocation Spreadsheet

Computations for both steps 2 and 3 are commonly made using a departmental expense allocation spreadsheet as shown in Exhibit 21.12.[1] The first two sections of this spreadsheet list direct expenses and indirect expenses by department. The third section lists the service

	Allocation Base	Expense Account Balance	General Office Dept.	Purchasing Dept.	Hardware Dept.	House-wares Dept.	Appliances Dept.
A-1 HARDWARE Departmental Expense Allocations For Year Ended December 31, 2008							
			Allocation of Expenses to Departments				
Direct expenses							
Salaries expense..................	Payroll records	$51,900	$13,300	$8,200	$15,600	$ 7,000	$ 7,800
Depreciation—Equipment......	Depreciation records	1,500	500	300	400	100	200
Supplies expense...................	Requisitions.............................	900	200	100	300	200	100
Indirect expenses							
Rent expense	Amount and value of space..	12,000	600	600	4,860	3,240	2,700
Utilities expense.....................	Floor space.............................	2,400	300	300	810	540	450
Advertising expense..............	Sales..	1,000			500	300	200
Insurance expense................	Value of insured assets	2,500	400	200	900	600	400
Total department expenses		72,200	15,300	9,700	23,370	11,980	11,850
Service department expenses							
General office department.....	Sales..		(15,300)		7,650	4,590	3,060
Purchasing department	Purchase orders.....................			(9,700)	3,880	2,630	3,190
Total expenses allocated to operating departments..		$72,200	$ 0	$ 0	$34,900	$19,200	$18,100

[1] In some cases we allocate a service department's expenses to other service departments when they use its services. For example, expenses of a payroll office benefit all service and operating departments and can be assigned to all departments. Nearly all examples and assignment materials in this book allocate service expenses only to operating departments for simplicity.

department expenses and their allocations to operating departments. The allocation bases are identified in the second column, and total expense amounts are reported in the third column.

The departmental expense allocation spreadsheet is useful in implementing the first three steps. To illustrate, first (step 1) the three direct expenses of salaries, depreciation, and supplies are accumulated in each of the five departments.

Second (step 2), the four indirect expenses of rent, utilities, advertising, and insurance are allocated to all departments using the allocation bases identified. For example, consider rent allocation. Exhibit 21.13 lists the five departments' square footage of space occupied. The two service departments (office and purchasing) occupy 25% of the total space (3,000 sq. feet/12,000 sq. feet). However, they are located near the back of the building, which is of lower value than space near the front that is occupied by operating departments. Management estimates that space near the back accounts for $1,200 of the total rent expense of $12,000. Exhibit 21.14 shows how we allocate the $1,200 rent expense between these two service departments in proportion to their

Exhibit 21.13

Departments' Square Footages

General office	1,500 sq. ft.
Purchasing	1,500 sq. ft.
Hardware	4,050 sq. ft.
Housewares	2,700 sq. ft.
Appliances	2,250 sq. ft.
Total	12,000 sq. ft.

Exhibit 21.14

Allocating Indirect (Rent) Expense to Service Departments

Department	Square Feet	Percent of Total	Allocated Cost
General office	1,500	50.0%	$ 600
Purchasing	1,500	50.0	600
Totals	3,000	100.0%	$1,200

square footage. We then allocate the remaining $10,800 of rent expense to the three operating departments as shown in Exhibit 21.15. We continue step 2 by allocating the $2,400 of utilities expense to all departments based on the square footage occupied as shown in

Exhibit 21.15

Allocating Indirect (Rent) Expense to Operating Departments

Department	Square Feet	Percent of Total	Allocated Cost
Hardware	4,050	45.0%	$ 4,860
Housewares	2,700	30.0	3,240
Appliances	2,250	25.0	2,700
Totals	9,000	100.0%	$10,800

Exhibit 21.16. The rows in Exhibit 21.12 for rent and utilities expenses show the amounts from Exhibits 21.14, 21.15, and 21.16. The allocations of the two other indirect expenses of advertising and insurance are similarly computed. Note that because advertising expense is allocated on the basis of sales and because service departments do not have sales, it is allocated only to the three operating departments.

Exhibit 21.16

Allocating Indirect (Utilities) Expense to All Departments

Department	Square Feet	Percent of Total	Allocated Cost
General office	1,500	12.50%	$ 300
Purchasing	1,500	12.50	300
Hardware	4,050	33.75	810
Housewares	2,700	22.50	540
Appliances	2,250	18.75	450
Totals	12,000	100.00%	$2,400

Third (step 3), total expenses of the two service departments are allocated to the three operating departments using the allocation bases shown in the final three rows of Exhibit 21.12.

Step 4 When the departmental expense spreadsheet is complete, the amounts in the operating department columns are used to prepare departmental income statements as shown in Exhibit 21.17. This exhibit uses the spreadsheet for its operating expenses; information on sales and cost of goods sold comes from departmental records.

Exhibit 21.17

Departmental Income Statements

A-I HARDWARE Departmental Income Statements For Year Ended December 31, 2008				
	Hardware Department	Housewares Department	Appliances Department	Combined
Sales	$119,500	$71,700	$47,800	$239,000
Cost of goods sold	73,800	43,800	30,200	147,800
Gross profit	45,700	27,900	17,600	91,200
Operating expenses				
Salaries expense	15,600	7,000	7,800	30,400
Depreciation expense—Equipment	400	100	200	700
Supplies expense	300	200	100	600
Rent expense	4,860	3,240	2,700	10,800
Utilities expense	810	540	450	1,800
Advertising expense	500	300	200	1,000
Insurance expense	900	600	400	1,900
Share of general office expenses	7,650	4,590	3,060	15,300
Share of purchasing expenses	3,880	2,630	3,190	9,700
Total operating expenses	34,900	19,200	18,100	72,200
Net income (loss)	**$10,800**	**$8,700**	**$ (500)**	**$19,000**

Departmental Contribution to Overhead

Data from departmental income statements are not always best for evaluating each department's performance, especially when indirect expenses are a large portion of total expenses and when weaknesses in assumptions and decisions in allocating indirect expenses can markedly affect net income. In these and other cases, we might better evaluate department performance using the **departmental contribution to overhead,** which is a report of the amount of sales less *direct* expenses.[2]

The upper half of Exhibit 21.18 shows a departmental contribution to overhead as part of an expanded income statement. This format is common when reporting departmental contributions to overhead. Using the information in Exhibits 21.17 and 21.18, we can evaluate the profitability of the three operating departments. For instance, let's compare the performance of the appliances department as described in these two exhibits. Exhibit 21.17 shows a $500 net loss resulting from this department's operations, but Exhibit 21.18 shows a $9,500 positive contribution to overhead, which is 19.9% of sales. The contribution of the appliances department is not as large as that of the other selling departments, but a $9,500 contribution to overhead is better than a $500 loss. This tells us that the appliances department is not a money loser. On the contrary, it is contributing $9,500 toward defraying total indirect expenses of $40,500.

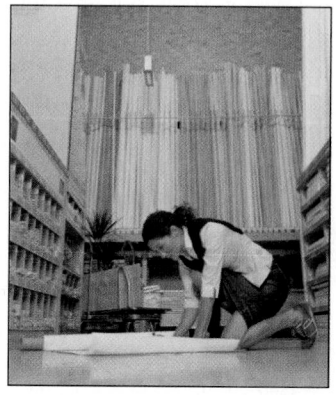

---

[2] A department's contribution is said to be "to overhead" because of the practice of considering all indirect expenses as overhead. Thus, the excess of a department's sales over direct expenses is a contribution toward at least a portion of its total overhead.

Exhibit 21.18

Departmental Contribution to Overhead

A-1 HARDWARE Income Statement Showing Departmental Contribution to Overhead For Year Ended December 31, 2008				
	Hardware Department	Housewares Department	Appliances Department	Combined
Sales	$119,500	$ 71,700	$47,800	$239,000
Cost of goods sold	73,800	43,800	30,200	147,800
Gross profit	45,700	27,900	17,600	91,200
Direct expenses				
Salaries expense	15,600	7,000	7,800	30,400
Depreciation expense—Equipment	400	100	200	700
Supplies expense	300	200	100	600
Total direct expenses	16,300	7,300	8,100	31,700
Departmental contributions to overhead	$ 29,400	$20,600	$ 9,500	$ 59,500
Indirect expenses				
Rent expense				10,800
Utilities expense				1,800
Advertising expense				1,000
Insurance expense				1,900
General office department expense				15,300
Purchasing department expense				9,700
Total indirect expenses				40,500
Net income				$ 19,000
Contribution as percent of sales	24.6%	28.7%	19.9%	24.9%

Quick Check

Answers—p. 863

6. If a company has two operating (selling) departments (shoes and hats) and two service departments (payroll and advertising), which of the following statements is correct? (a) Wages incurred in the payroll department are direct expenses of the shoe department, (b) Wages incurred in the payroll department are indirect expenses of the operating departments, or (c) Advertising department expenses are allocated to the other three departments.

7. Which of the following bases can be used to allocate supervisors' salaries across operating departments? (a) Hours spent in each department, (b) number of employees in each department, (c) sales achieved in each department, or (d) any of the above, depending on which information is most relevant and accessible.

8. What three steps are used to allocate expenses to operating departments?

9. An income statement showing departmental contribution to overhead, (a) subtracts indirect expenses from each department's revenues, (b) subtracts only direct expenses from each department's revenues, or (c) shows net income for each department.

Responsibility Accounting

Departmental accounting reports often provide data used to evaluate a department's performance, but are they useful in assessing how well a department *manager* performs? Neither departmental income nor its contribution to overhead may be useful because many expenses can be outside a manager's control. Instead, we often evaluate a manager's performance using responsibility accounting reports that describe a department's activities in terms of **controllable costs.**[3] A cost is controllable if a manager has the power to determine or at least significantly

C4 Explain controllable costs and responsibility accounting.

---

[3] The terms *cost* and *expense* are often used interchangeably in managerial accounting, but they are not necessarily the same. *Cost* often refers to the monetary outlay to acquire some resource that can have present and future benefit. *Expense* usually refers to an expired cost. That is, as the benefit of a resource expires, a portion of its cost is written off as an expense.

affect the amount incurred. **Uncontrollable costs** are not within the manager's control or influence.

Controllable versus Direct Costs

Controllable costs are not always the same as direct costs. Direct costs are readily traced to a department, but the department manager might or might not control their amounts. For example, department managers often have little or no control over depreciation expense because they cannot affect the amount of equipment assigned to their departments. Also, department managers rarely control their own salaries. However, they can control or influence items such as the cost of supplies used in their department. When evaluating managers' performances, we should use data reflecting their departments' outputs along with their controllable costs and expenses.

Distinguishing between controllable and uncontrollable costs depends on the particular manager and time period under analysis. For example, the cost of property insurance is usually not controllable at the department manager's level but by the executive responsible for obtaining the company's insurance coverage. Likewise, this executive might not control costs resulting from insurance policies already in force. However, when a policy expires, this executive can renegotiate a replacement policy and then controls these costs. Therefore, all costs are controllable at some management level if the time period is sufficiently long. We must use good judgment in identifying controllable costs.

Responsibility Accounting System

A *responsibility accounting system* uses the concept of controllable costs to assign managers the responsibility for costs and expenses under their control. Prior to each reporting period, a company prepares plans that identify costs and expenses under each manager's control. These plans are called **responsibility accounting budgets.** To ensure the cooperation of managers and the reasonableness of budgets, managers should be involved in preparing their budgets.

Exhibit 21.19

Organizational Responsibility Chart

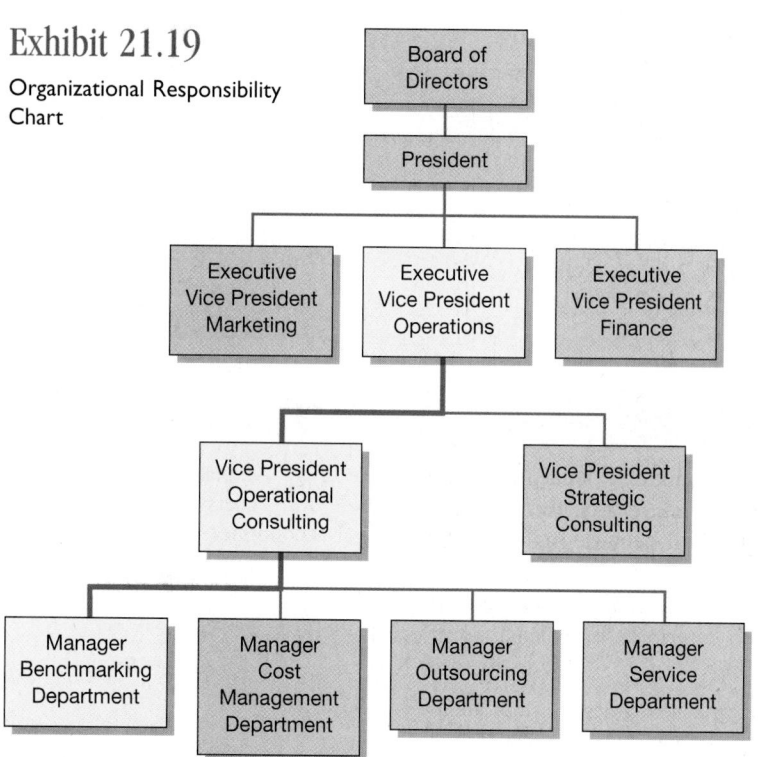

A responsibility accounting system also involves performance reports. A **responsibility accounting performance report** accumulates and reports costs and expenses that a manager is responsible for and their budgeted amounts. Management's analysis of differences between budgeted amounts and actual costs and expenses often results in corrective or strategic managerial actions. Upper-level management uses performance reports to evaluate the effectiveness of lower-level managers in controlling costs and expenses and keeping them within budgeted amounts.

A responsibility accounting system recognizes that control over costs and expenses belongs to several levels of management. We illustrate this by considering the organization chart in Exhibit 21.19. The lines in this chart connecting the managerial positions reflect channels of authority. For example, the four department managers of this consulting firm (benchmarking, cost management, outsourcing, and service) are responsible for controllable costs and expenses incurred in their departments, but these same costs are subject to the overall control of the vice president (VP) for operational consulting. Similarly, this VP's costs are subject to the control of the executive vice president (EVP) for operations, the president, and, ultimately, the board of directors.

At lower levels, managers have limited responsibility and relatively little control over costs and expenses. Performance reports for low-level management typically cover few controllable costs. Responsibility and control broaden for higher-level managers; therefore, their reports span a wider range of costs. However, reports to higher-level managers seldom contain the details reported to their subordinates but are summarized for two reasons: (1) lower-level managers are often responsible for these detailed costs and (2) detailed reports can obscure broader, more important issues facing a company.

Exhibit 21.20 shows summarized performance reports for the three management levels identified in Exhibit 21.19. Exhibit 21.20 shows that costs under the control of the benchmarking department manager are totaled and included among controllable costs of the VP for operational consulting. Also, costs under the control of the VP are totaled and included among controllable costs of the EVP for operations. In this way, a responsibility accounting system provides relevant information for each management level.

Point: Responsibility accounting does not place blame. Instead, responsibility accounting is used to identify opportunities for improving performance.

Exhibit 21.20

Responsibility Accounting Performance Reports

Executive Vice President, Operations

Controllable Costs	For July		
	Budgeted Amount	Actual Amount	Over (Under) Budget
Salaries, VPs	$ 80,000	$ 80,000	$ 0
Quality control costs	21,000	22,400	1,400
Office costs	29,500	28,800	(700)
Operational consulting	276,700	279,500	2,800 ←
Strategic consulting	390,000	380,600	(9,400)
Totals	$ 797,200	$ 791,300	$(5,900)

Vice President, Operational Consulting

Controllable Costs	For July		
	Budgeted Amount	Actual Amount	Over (Under) Budget
Salaries, department managers	$ 75,000	$ 78,000	$ 3,000
Depreciation	10,600	10,600	0
Insurance	6,800	6,300	(500)
→ Benchmarking department	79,600	79,900	300
Cost management department	61,500	60,200	(1,300)
Outsourcing department	24,300	24,700	400
Service department	18,900	19,800	900
Totals	$276,700	$279,500	$2,800

Manager, Benchmarking Department

Controllable Costs	For July		
	Budgeted Amount	Actual Amount	Over (Under) Budget
Salaries	$ 51,600	$ 52,500	$ 900
Supplies	8,000	7,800	(200)
Other controllable costs	20,000	19,600	(400)
Totals	$ 79,600	$ 79,900	$ 300

Technological advances increase our ability to produce vast amounts of information that often exceeds our ability to use it. Good managers select relevant data for planning and controlling the areas under their responsibility. A good responsibility accounting system makes every effort to provide relevant information to the right person (the one who controls the cost) at the right time (before a cost is out of control).

Point: A responsibility accounting system usually divides a company into subunits called *responsibility centers*. The manager of each center is evaluated on how well the center performs, as reported in responsibility accounting reports.

Decision Analysis

Investment Center Return on Total Assets

A1 Analyze investment centers using return on total assets.

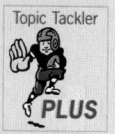

Topic Tackler

PLUS

21-3

We discussed the classification of departments and divisions as profit centers or cost centers. Another way is to classify (and evaluate) a department as an **investment center.** An investment center manager is responsible for effectively using the center's assets to generate income for the center.

A measure often used to evaluate the performance of an investment center manager is the **investment center return on total assets,** also called *return on investment.* This measure is computed as a **center's net income divided by the center's average total assets.** To illustrate, if a center with an average investment of $1 million yields a net income of $210,000, its return on total assets is 21%.

Top management can use a center's return on total assets to assess how well its manager has utilized the center's assets to generate returns for the company. Top management can also compare performance across departments and/or divisions using this measure. Many companies establish a center's target return on total assets and reward managers based on whether they meet targets. In addition, center managers often use the center's return on total assets to decide whether to invest additional resources in the center.

Decision Maker

Answer—p. 863

Center Manager   Your center's usual return on total assets is 19%. You are considering two new investments for your center. The first requires a $250,000 average investment and is expected to yield annual net income of $50,000. The second requires a $1 million average investment with an expected annual net income of $175,000. Do you pursue either?

Demonstration Problem

Management requests departmental income statements for Hacker's Haven, a computer store that has five departments. Three are operating departments (hardware, software, and repairs) and two are service departments (general office and purchasing).

	General Office	Purchasing	Hardware	Software	Repairs
Sales	—	—	$960,000	$600,000	$840,000
Cost of goods sold	—	—	500,000	300,000	200,000
Direct expenses					
Payroll	$60,000	$45,000	80,000	25,000	325,000
Depreciation	6,000	7,200	33,000	4,200	9,600
Supplies	15,000	10,000	10,000	2,000	25,000

The departments incur several indirect expenses. To prepare departmental income statements, the indirect expenses must be allocated across the five departments. Then the expenses of the two service departments must be allocated to the three operating departments. Total cost amounts and the allocation bases for each indirect expense follow.

Indirect Expense	Total Cost	Allocation Basis
Rent	$150,000	Square footage occupied
Utilities	50,000	Square footage occupied
Advertising	125,000	Dollars of sales
Insurance	30,000	Value of assets insured
Service departments		
General office	?	Number of employees
Purchasing	?	Dollars of cost of goods sold

The following additional information is needed for indirect expense allocations.

Department	Square Feet	Sales	Insured Assets	Employees	Cost of Goods Sold
General office	500		$ 60,000		
Purchasing	500		72,000		
Hardware	4,000	$ 960,000	330,000	5	$ 500,000
Software	3,000	600,000	42,000	5	300,000
Repairs	2,000	840,000	96,000	10	200,000
Totals	10,000	$2,400,000	$600,000	20	$1,000,000

Required

1. Prepare a departmental expense allocation spreadsheet for Hacker's Haven.
2. Prepare a departmental income statement reporting net income for each operating department and for all operating departments combined.

Planning the Solution

- Set up and complete four tables to allocate the indirect expenses—one each for rent, utilities, advertising, and insurance.
- Allocate the departments' indirect expenses using a spreadsheet like the one in Exhibit 21.12. Enter the given amounts of the direct expenses for each department. Then enter the allocated amounts of the indirect expenses that you computed.
- Complete two tables for allocating the general office and purchasing department costs to the three operating departments. Enter these amounts on the spreadsheet and determine the total expenses allocated to the three operating departments.
- Prepare departmental income statements like the one in Exhibit 21.17. Show sales, cost of goods sold, gross profit, individual expenses, and net income for each of the three operating departments and for the combined company.

Solution to Demonstration Problem

Allocations of the four indirect expenses across the five departments.

Rent	Square Feet	Percent of Total	Allocated Cost
General office	500	5.0%	$ 7,500
Purchasing	500	5.0	7,500
Hardware	4,000	40.0	60,000
Software	3,000	30.0	45,000
Repairs	2,000	20.0	30,000
Totals	10,000	100.0%	$150,000

Utilities	Square Feet	Percent of Total	Allocated Cost
General office	500	5.0%	$ 2,500
Purchasing	500	5.0	2,500
Hardware	4,000	40.0	20,000
Software	3,000	30.0	15,000
Repairs	2,000	20.0	10,000
Totals	10,000	100.0%	$50,000

Advertising	Sales Dollars	Percent of Total	Allocated Cost
Hardware	$ 960,000	40.0%	$ 50,000
Software	600,000	25.0	31,250
Repairs	840,000	35.0	43,750
Totals	$2,400,000	100.0%	$125,000

Insurance	Assets Insured	Percent of Total	Allocated Cost
General office	$ 60,000	10.0%	$ 3,000
Purchasing	72,000	12.0	3,600
Hardware	330,000	55.0	16,500
Software	42,000	7.0	2,100
Repairs	96,000	16.0	4,800
Totals	$600,000	100.0%	$30,000

1. Allocations of service department expenses to the three operating departments.

General Office Allocations to	Employees	Percent of Total	Allocated Cost
Hardware	5	25.0%	$23,500
Software	5	25.0	23,500
Repairs	10	50.0	47,000
Totals	20	100.0%	$94,000

Purchasing Allocations to	Cost of Goods Sold	Percent of Total	Allocated Cost
Hardware	$ 500,000	50.0%	$37,900
Software	300,000	30.0	22,740
Repairs	200,000	20.0	15,160
Totals	$1,000,000	100.0%	$75,800

HACKER'S HAVEN
Departmental Expense Allocations
For Year Ended December 31, 2008

	Allocation Base	Expense Account Balance	General Office Dept.	Purchasing Dept.	Hardware Dept.	Software Dept.	Repairs Dept.
Direct Expenses							
Payroll		$ 535,000	$ 60,000	$ 45,000	$ 80,000	$ 25,000	$ 325,000
Depreciation		60,000	6,000	7,200	33,000	4,200	9,600
Supplies		62,000	15,000	10,000	10,000	2,000	25,000
Indirect Expenses							
Rent	Square ft.	150,000	7,500	7,500	60,000	45,000	30,000
Utilities	Square ft.	50,000	2,500	2,500	20,000	15,000	10,000
Advertising	Sales	125,000	—	—	50,000	31,250	43,750
Insurance	Assets	30,000	3,000	3,600	16,500	2,100	4,800
Total expenses		1,012,000	94,000	75,800	269,500	124,550	448,150
Service Department Expenses							
General office	Employees		(94,000)		23,500	23,500	47,000
Purchasing	Goods sold			(75,800)	37,900	22,740	15,160
Total expenses allocated to operating departments		$1,012,000	$ 0	$ 0	$330,900	$170,790	$510,310

2. Departmental income statements for Hacker's Haven.

HACKER'S HAVEN
Departmental Income Statements
For Year Ended December 31, 2008

	Hardware	Software	Repairs	Combined
Sales	$ 960,000	$ 600,000	$ 840,000	$2,400,000
Cost of goods sold	500,000	300,000	200,000	1,000,000
Gross profit	460,000	300,000	640,000	1,400,000
Expenses				
Payroll	80,000	25,000	325,000	430,000
Depreciation	33,000	4,200	9,600	46,800
Supplies	10,000	2,000	25,000	37,000
Rent	60,000	45,000	30,000	135,000
Utilities	20,000	15,000	10,000	45,000
Advertising	50,000	31,250	43,750	125,000
Insurance	16,500	2,100	4,800	23,400
Share of general office	23,500	23,500	47,000	94,000
Share of purchasing	37,900	22,740	15,160	75,800
Total expenses	330,900	170,790	510,310	1,012,000
Net income	$129,100	$129,210	$129,690	$ 388,000

Joint Costs and Their Allocation

21A

Most manufacturing processes involve **joint costs,** which refer to costs incurred to produce or purchase two or more products at the same time. A joint cost is like an indirect expense in the sense that more than one cost object share it. For example, a sawmill company incurs a joint cost when it buys logs that it cuts into lumber as shown in Exhibit 21A.1. The joint cost includes the logs (raw material) and its cutting (conversion) into boards classified as Clear, Select, No. 1 Common, No. 2 Common, No. 3 Common, and other types of lumber and by-products.

C5   Describe allocation of joint costs across products.

When a joint cost is incurred, a question arises as to whether to allocate it to different products resulting from it. The answer is that when management wishes to estimate the costs of individual products, joint costs are included and must be allocated to these joint products. However, when management needs information to help decide whether to sell a product at a certain point in the production process or to process it further, the joint costs are ignored.

Exhibit 21A.1

Joint Products from Logs

Financial statements prepared according to GAAP must assign joint costs to products. To do this, management must decide how to allocate joint costs across products benefiting from these costs. If some products are sold and others remain in inventory, allocating joint costs involves assigning costs to both cost of goods sold and ending inventory.

The two usual methods to allocate joint costs are the (1) *physical basis* and (2) the *value basis.* The physical basis typically involves allocating joint cost using physical characteristics such as the ratio of pounds, cubic feet, or gallons of each joint product to the total pounds, cubic feet, or gallons of all joint products flowing from the cost. This method is not preferred because the resulting cost allocations do not reflect the relative market values the joint cost generates. The preferred approach is the value basis, which allocates joint cost in proportion to the sales value of the output produced by the process at the "split-off point"; see Exhibit 21A.1.

Physical Basis Allocation of Joint Cost   To illustrate the physical basis of allocating a joint cost, we consider a sawmill that bought logs for $30,000. When cut, these logs produce 100,000 board feet of lumber in the grades and amounts shown in Exhibit 21A.2. The logs produce 20,000 board feet of No. 3 Common lumber, which is 20% of the total. With physical allocation, the No. 3 Common lumber is assigned 20% of the $30,000 cost of the logs, or $6,000 ($30,000 × 20%). Because this low-grade lumber sells for $4,000, this allocation gives a $2,000 loss from its production and sale. The physical basis for allocating joint costs does not reflect the extra value flowing into some products or the inferior value flowing into others. That is, the portion of a log that produces Clear and Select grade lumber is worth more than the portion used to produce the three grades of common lumber, but the physical basis fails to reflect this.

Exhibit 21A.2

Allocating Joint Costs on a Physical Basis

Grade of Lumber	Board Feet Produced	Percent of Total	Allocated Cost	Sales Value	Gross Profit
Clear and Select	10,000	10.0%	$ 3,000	$12,000	$ 9,000
No. 1 Common	30,000	30.0	9,000	18,000	9,000
No. 2 Common	40,000	40.0	12,000	16,000	4,000
No. 3 Common	20,000	20.0	6,000	4,000	(2,000)
Totals	100,000	100.0%	$30,000	$50,000	$20,000

Value Basis Allocation of Joint Cost   Exhibit 21A.3 illustrates the value basis method of allocation. It determines the percents of the total costs allocated to each grade by the ratio of each grade's sales value to the total sales value of $50,000 (sales value is the unit selling price multiplied by the number of units produced). The Clear and Select lumber grades receive 24% of the total cost ($12,000/$50,000) instead of the 10% portion using a physical basis. The No. 3 Common lumber receives only 8% of the total cost, or $2,400, which is much less than the $6,000 assigned to it using the physical basis.

Exhibit 21A.3

Allocating Joint Costs on a Value Basis

Grade of Lumber	Sales Value	Percent of Total	Allocated Cost	Gross Profit
Clear and Select	$12,000	24.0%	$ 7,200	$ 4,800
No. 1 Common	18,000	36.0	10,800	7,200
No. 2 Common	16,000	32.0	9,600	6,400
No. 3 Common	4,000	8.0	2,400	1,600
Totals	$50,000	100.0%	$30,000	$20,000

Example: Refer to Exhibit 21A.3. If the sales value of Clear and Select lumber is changed to $10,000, what is the revised ratio of the market value of No. 1 Common to the total? *Answer:* $18,000/$48,000 = 37.5%

An outcome of value basis allocation is that *each* grade produces exactly the same 40% gross profit at the split-off point. This 40% rate equals the gross profit rate from selling all the lumber made from the $30,000 logs for a combined price of $50,000.

Quick Check
Answer—p. 863

12. A company produces three products, B1, B2, and B3. The joint cost incurred for the current month for these products is $180,000. The following data relate to this month's production:

Product	Units Produced	Unit Sales Value
B1	96,000	$3.00
B2	64,000	6.00
B3	32,000	9.00

The amount of joint cost allocated to product B3 using the value basis allocation is (*a*) $30,000, (*b*) $54,000, or (*c*) $90,000.

Summary

C1   Explain departmentalization and the role of departmental accounting. Companies are divided into departments when they are too large to be effectively managed as a single unit. Operating departments carry out an organization's main functions. Service departments support the activities of operating departments. Departmental accounting systems provide information for evaluating departmental performance.

C2   Distinguish between direct and indirect expenses. Direct expenses are traced to a specific department and are incurred for the sole benefit of that department. Indirect expenses benefit more than one department. Indirect expenses are allocated to departments when computing departmental net income.

C3   Identify bases for allocating indirect expenses to departments. Ideally, we allocate indirect expenses by using a cause-effect relation for the allocation base. When a cause-effect relation is not identifiable, each indirect expense is allocated on a basis reflecting the relative benefit received by each department.

C4   Explain controllable costs and responsibility accounting. A controllable cost is one that is influenced by a specific management level. The total expenses of operating a department often include some items a department manager does not control.

Responsibility accounting systems provide information for evaluating the performance of department managers. A responsibility accounting system's performance reports for evaluating department managers should include only the expenses (and revenues) that each manager controls.

C5   Describe allocation of joint costs across products. A joint cost refers to costs incurred to produce or purchase two or more products at the same time. When income statements are prepared, joint costs are usually allocated to the resulting joint products using either a physical or value basis.

A1   Analyze investment centers using return on total assets. A measure often used to evaluate an investment center manager is the *investment center return on total assets,* also called *return on investment.* This measure is computed as the center's net income divided by the center's average total assets.

P1   Assign overhead costs using two-stage cost allocation. In the traditional two-stage cost allocation procedure, service department costs are first assigned to operating departments. Then, in the second stage, a predetermined overhead allocation rate is computed for each operating department and is used to assign overhead to output.

P2   **Assign overhead costs using activity-based costing.** In activity-based costing, the costs of related activities are collected and then pooled in some logical manner into activity cost pools. After all activity costs have been accumulated in an activity cost pool account, users of the activity, termed *cost objects,* are assigned a portion of the total activity cost using a cost driver (allocation base).

P3   **Prepare departmental income statements.** Each profit center (department) is assigned its expenses to yield its own income statement. These costs include its direct expenses and its share of indirect expenses. The departmental income statement lists its revenues and costs of goods sold to determine gross profit. Its operating expenses (direct expenses and its indirect expenses allocated to the department) are deducted from gross profit to yield departmental net income.

P4   **Prepare departmental contribution reports.** The departmental contribution report is similar to the departmental income statement in terms of computing the gross profit for each department. Then the direct operating expenses for each department are deducted from gross profit to determine the contribution generated by each department. Indirect operating expenses are deducted *in total* from the company's combined contribution.

Guidance Answers to **Decision Maker** and **Decision Ethics**

Director of Operations   You should collect details on overhead items and review them to see whether direct labor drives these costs. If it does not, overhead might be improperly assigned to departments. The situation also provides an opportunity to consider other overhead allocation bases, including use of activity-based costing.

Accounting Officer   You should not author a report that you disagree with. You are responsible for ascertaining all the facts of ABC (implementation procedures, advantages and disadvantages, and costs). You should then approach your supervisor with these facts and suggest that you would like to modify the report to request, for example, a pilot test. The pilot test will allow you to further assess the suitability of ABC. Your suggestion might be rejected, at which time you may wish to speak with a more senior-level manager.

Center Manager   We must first realize that the two investment opportunities are not comparable on the basis of absolute dollars of income or on assets. For instance, the second investment provides a higher income in absolute dollars but requires a higher investment. Accordingly, we need to compute return on total assets for each alternative: (1) $50,000 ÷ $250,000 = 20%, and (2) $175,000 ÷ $1 million = 17.5%. Alternative 1 has the higher return and is preferred over alternative 2. Do you pursue one, both, or neither? Because alternative 1's return is higher than the center's usual return of 19%, it should be pursued, assuming its risks are acceptable. Also, since alternative 1 requires a small investment, top management is likely to be more agreeable to pursuing it. Alternative 2's return is lower than the usual 19% and is not likely to be acceptable.

Guidance Answers to **Quick Checks**

1. Cost drivers are the factors that have a cause-effect relation with costs (or activities that pertain to costs).

2. *d*

3. A departmental accounting system provides information used to evaluate the performance of *departments.* A responsibility accounting system provides information used to evaluate the performance of *department managers.*

4. *d*

5. A cost center, such as a service department, incurs costs without directly generating revenues. A profit center, such as a product division, incurs costs but also generates revenues.

6. *b*

7. *d*

8. (1) Assign the direct expenses to each department. (2) Allocate indirect expenses to all departments. (3) Allocate the service department expenses to the operating departments.

9. *b*

10. No, because many expenses that enter into these calculations are beyond the manager's control, and managers should not be evaluated using costs they do not control.

11. *c*

12. *b*; $180,000 × ([32,000 × $9]/[96,000 × $3 + 64,000 × $6 + 32,000 × $9]) = $54,000.

Key Terms

mhhe.com/wildFAP18e

Key Terms are available at the book's Website for learning and testing in an online Flashcard Format.

Activity-based costing (ABC) (p. 844)
Activity cost driver (p. 844)
Activity cost pool (p. 845)
Controllable costs (p. 855)
Cost center (p. 848)
Departmental accounting system (p. 847)
Departmental contribution to overhead (p. 854)

Direct expenses (p. 849)
Indirect expenses (p. 849)
Investment center (p. 858)
Investment center return on total assets (p. 858)
Joint cost (p. 861)
Profit center (p. 848)

Responsibility accounting budget (p. 856)
Responsibility accounting performance report (p. 856)
Responsibility accounting system (p. 848)
Uncontrollable costs (p. 856)

Multiple Choice Quiz   Answers on p. 879   mhhe.com/wildFAP18e

Multiple Choice Quizzes A and B are available at the book's Website.

1. A retailer has three departments—housewares, appliances, and clothing—and buys advertising that benefits all departments. Advertising expense is $150,000 for the year, and departmental sales for the year follow: housewares, $356,250; appliances, $641,250; clothing, $427,500. How much advertising expense is allocated to appliances if allocation is based on departmental sales?
  a. $37,500
  b. $67,500
  c. $45,000
  d. $150,000
  e. $641,250

2. An activity-based costing system
  a. Does not require the level of detail that a traditional costing system requires.
  b. Does not enable the calculation of unit cost data.
  c. Allocates costs to products on the basis of activities performed on them.
  d. Cannot be used by a service company.
  e. Allocates costs to products based on the number of direct labor hours used.

3. A company produces two products, Grey and Red. The following information is available relating to those two products. Assume that the company's total setup cost is $162,000. Using activity-based costing, how much setup cost is allocated to each unit of Grey?

	Grey	Red
Units produced	500	40,000
Number of setups	50	100
Direct labor hours per unit	15	15

  a. $1,080
  b. $ 72
  c. $ 162
  d. $2,000
  e. $ 108

4. A company operates three retail departments as profit centers, and the following information is available for each. Which department has the largest dollar amount of departmental contribution to overhead and what is the dollar amount contributed?

Department	Sales	Cost of Goods Sold	Direct Expenses	Allocated Indirect Expenses
X	$500,000	$350,000	$50,000	$40,000
Y	200,000	75,000	20,000	50,000
Z	350,000	150,000	75,000	10,000

  a. Department Y, $ 55,000
  b. Department Z, $125,000
  c. Department X, $500,000
  d. Department Z, $200,000
  e. Department X, $ 60,000

5. Using the data in question 4, Department X's contribution to overhead as a percentage of sales is
  a. 20%
  b. 30%
  c. 12%
  d. 48%
  e. 32%

Superscript letter ^{A} denotes assignments based on Appendix 21A.

Discussion Questions

1. Why are many companies divided into departments?

2. Complete the following for a traditional two-stage allocation system: In the first stage, service department costs are assigned to _____ departments. In the second stage, a predetermined overhead rate is computed for each operating department and used to assign overhead to _____.

3. What is the difference between operating departments and service departments?

4. What is activity-based costing? What is its goal?

5. Identify at least four typical cost pools for activity-based costing in most organizations.

6. In activity-based costing, costs in a cost pool are allocated to _____ using predetermined overhead rates.

7. What company circumstances especially encourage use of activity-based costing?

8. What are two main goals in managerial accounting for reporting on and analyzing departments?

9. Is it possible to evaluate a cost center's profitability? Explain.

10. What is the difference between direct and indirect expenses?

11. Suggest a reasonable basis for allocating each of the following indirect expenses to departments: (a) salary of a supervisor who manages several departments, (b) rent, (c) heat, (d) electricity for lighting, (e) janitorial services, (f) advertising, (g) expired insurance on equipment, and (h) property taxes on equipment.

12. How is a department's contribution to overhead measured?

13. What are controllable costs?

14. Controllable and uncontrollable costs must be identified with a particular _____ and a definite _____ period.

15. Why should managers be closely involved in preparing their responsibility accounting budgets?

16. In responsibility accounting, who receives timely cost reports and specific cost information? Explain.

17.^AWhat is a joint cost? How are joint costs usually allocated among the products produced from them?

18.^AGive two examples of products with joint costs.

19. Each retail store of **Best Buy** has several departments. Why is it useful for its management to (a) collect accounting information about each department and (b) treat each department as a profit center?

20. **Apple** delivers its products to locations around the world. List three controllable and three uncontrollable costs for its delivery department.

 Red numbers denote Discussion Questions that involve decision-making.

In each blank next to the following terms, place the identifying letter of its best description.

1. _____ Cost center
2. _____ Investment center
3. _____ Departmental accounting system
4. _____ Operating department
5. _____ Profit center
6. _____ Responsibility accounting system
7. _____ Service department

A. Incurs costs without directly yielding revenues.

B. Provides information used to evaluate the performance of a department manager.

C. Holds manager responsible for revenues, costs, and investments.

D. Engages directly in manufacturing or in making sales directly to customers.

E. Does not directly manufacture products but contributes to profitability of the entire company.

F. Incurs costs and also generates revenues.

G. Provides information used to evaluate the performance of a department.

QUICK STUDY

QS 21-1

Allocation and measurement terms

C1 C2 C3 C4 A1

For each of the following types of indirect expenses and service department expenses, identify one allocation basis that could be used to distribute it to the departments indicated.

1. Computer service expenses of production scheduling for operating departments.
2. General office department expenses of the operating departments.
3. Maintenance department expenses of the operating departments.
4. Electric utility expenses of all departments.

QS 21-2

Basis for cost allocation

C3

The following is taken from Antuan Co.'s internal records of its factory with two operating departments. The cost driver for indirect labor and supplies is direct labor costs, and the cost driver for the remaining overhead items is number of hours of machine use. Compute the total amount of overhead cost allocated to Operating Department 1 using activity-based costing.

QS 21-3

Activity-based costing and overhead cost allocation

P2

	Direct Labor	Machine Use Hours
Operating department 1	$ 9,400	1,200
Operating department 2	6,600	2,000
Totals	$16,000	3,200
Factory overhead costs		
Rent and utilities	$ 6,100	
Indirect labor	2,700	
General office expense	2,000	
Depreciation—Equipment	1,500	
Supplies	1,300	
Total factory overhead	$13,600	

Check Dept. 1 allocation, $5,950

QS 21-4
Departmental contribution
to overhead
P4

Use the information in the following table to compute each department's contribution to overhead (both in dollars and as a percent). Which department contributes the largest dollar amount to total overhead? Which contributes the highest percent (as a percent of sales)?

	Dept. A	Dept. B	Dept. C
Sales	$53,000	$180,000	$84,000
Cost of goods sold	34,185	103,700	49,560
Gross profit	18,815	76,300	34,440
Total direct expenses	3,660	37,060	7,386
Contribution to overhead	$	$	$
Contribution percent	%	%	%

QS 21-5
Investment center analysis
A1

Compute return on assets for each of these **Best Buy** divisions (each is an investment center). Comment on the relative performance of each investment center.

Investment Center	Net Income	Average Assets	Return on Assets
Cameras and camcorders	$4,500,000	$20,000,000	_____
Phones and communications	1,500,000	12,500,000	_____
Computers and accessories	800,000	10,000,000	_____

QS 21-6ᴬ
Joint cost allocation
C5

A company purchases a 10,020 square foot commercial building for $325,000 and spends an additional $50,000 to divide the space into two separate rental units and prepare it for rent. Unit A, which has the desirable location on the corner and contains 3,340 square feet, will be rented for $1.00 per square foot. Unit B contains 6,680 square feet and will be rented for $0.75 per square foot. How much of the joint cost should be assigned to Unit B using the value basis of allocation?

EXERCISES

Exercise 21-1
Departmental expense allocations
P1 C3

Woh Che Co. has four departments: materials, personnel, manufacturing, and packaging. In a recent month, the four departments incurred three shared indirect expenses. The amounts of these indirect expenses and the bases used to allocate them follow.

Indirect Expense	Cost	Allocation Base
Supervision	$ 82,500	Number of employees
Utilities	50,000	Square feet occupied
Insurance	22,500	Value of assets in use
Total	$155,000	

Departmental data for the company's recent reporting period follow.

Department	Employees	Square Feet	Asset Values
Materials	27	25,000	$ 6,000
Personnel	9	5,000	1,200
Manufacturing	63	55,000	37,800
Packaging	51	15,000	15,000
Total	150	100,000	$60,000

(1) Use this information to allocate each of the three indirect expenses across the four departments. (2) Prepare a summary table that reports the indirect expenses assigned to each of the four departments.

Check (2) Total of $29,600 assigned to Materials Dept.

Provo Company produces two types of glass shelving, rounded edge and squared edge, on the same production line. For the current period, the company reports the following data.

Exercise 21-2
Activity-based costing
of overhead

P2

	Rounded Edge	Squared Edge	Total
Direct materials	$ 9,500	$21,600	$ 31,100
Direct labor	6,100	11,900	18,000
Overhead (300% of direct labor cost)	18,300	35,700	54,000
Total cost	$33,900	$69,200	$103,100
Quantity produced	10,500 ft.	14,100 ft.	
Average cost per ft.	$ 3.23	$ 4.91	

Provo's controller wishes to apply activity-based costing (ABC) to allocate the $54,000 of overhead costs incurred by the two product lines to see whether cost per foot would change markedly from that reported above. She has collected the following information.

Overhead Cost Category (Activity Cost Pool)	Cost
Supervision	$ 2,700
Depreciation of machinery	28,300
Assembly line preparation	23,000
Total overhead	$54,000

She has also collected the following information about the cost drivers for each category (cost pool) and the amount of each driver used by the two product lines.

Overhead Cost Category (Activity Cost Pool)	Driver	Usage		
		Rounded Edge	Squared Edge	Total
Supervision	Direct labor cost($)	$6,100	$11,900	$18,000
Depreciation of machinery	Machine hours	250 hours	750 hours	1,000 hours
Assembly line preparation	Setups (number)	20 times	105 times	125 times

Use this information to (1) assign these three overhead cost pools to each of the two products using ABC, (2) determine average cost per foot for each of the two products using ABC, and (3) compare the average cost per foot under ABC with the average cost per foot under the current method for each product. For part 3, explain why a difference between the two cost allocation methods exists.

Check (2) Rounded edge, $2.60; Squared edge, $5.38

Truck Market pays $130,000 rent each year for its two-story building. The space in this building is occupied by five departments as specified here.

Exercise 21-3
Rent expense allocated
to departments

P1 C3

Paint department	1,440 square feet of first-floor space
Engine department	3,360 square feet of first-floor space
Window department	2,016 square feet of second-floor space
Electrical department	960 square feet of second-floor space
Accessory department	1,824 square feet of second-floor space

The company allocates 65% of total rent expense to the first floor and 35% to the second floor, and then allocates rent expense for each floor to the departments occupying that floor on the basis of space occupied. Determine the rent expense to be allocated to each department. (Round percents to the nearest one-tenth and dollar amounts to the nearest whole dollar.)

Check Allocated to Paint Dept., $25,350

Exercise 21-4

Departmental expense
allocation spreadsheet

C3   P1

Overland Cycle Shop has two service departments (advertising and administration) and two operating departments (cycles and clothing). During 2008, the departments had the following direct expenses and occupied the following amount of floor space.

Department	Direct Expenses	Square Feet
Advertising	$ 18,000	1,120
Administrative	25,000	1,400
Cycles	103,000	7,140
Clothing	15,000	4,340

The advertising department developed and distributed 120 advertisements during the year. Of these, 90 promoted cycles and 30 promoted clothing. The store sold $350,000 of merchandise during the year. Of this amount, $273,000 is from the cycles department, and $77,000 is from the clothing department. The utilities expense of $64,000 is an indirect expense to all departments. Prepare a departmental expense allocation spreadsheet for Overland Cycle Shop. The spreadsheet should assign (1) direct expenses to each of the four departments, (2) the $64,000 of utilities expense to the four departments on the basis of floor space occupied, (3) the advertising department's expenses to the two operating departments on the basis of the number of ads placed that promoted a department's products, and (4) the administrative department's expenses to the two operating departments based on the amount of sales. Provide supporting computations for the expense allocations.

Check   Total expenses allocated to
Cycles Dept., $177,472

Exercise 21-5

Service department
expenses allocated to
operating departments   P3

The following is a partially completed lower section of a departmental expense allocation spreadsheet for Cozy Bookstore. It reports the total amounts of direct and indirect expenses allocated to its five departments. Complete the spreadsheet by allocating the expenses of the two service departments (advertising and purchasing) to the three operating departments.

File Edit View Insert Format Tools Data Window Help

		Allocation of Expenses to Departments					
	Allocation Base	Expense Account Balance	Advertising Dept.	Purchasing Dept.	Books Dept.	Magazines Dept.	Newspapers Dept.
5 Total department expenses..........		$698,000	$24,000	$34,000	$425,000	$90,000	$125,000
6 **Service department expenses**							
7 Advertising department.............Sales			?		?	?	?
8 Purchasing department.............Purch. orders				?	?	?	?
9 Total expenses allocated to							
10 operating departments..............		?	$ 0	$ 0	?	?	?

Advertising and purchasing department expenses are allocated to operating departments on the basis of dollar sales and purchase orders, respectively. Information about the allocation bases for the three operating departments follows.

Department	Sales	Purchase Orders
Books	$495,000	516
Magazines	198,000	360
Newspapers	207,000	324
Total	$900,000	1,200

Check   Total expenses allocated to
Books Dept., $452,820

Exercise 21-6

Indirect payroll expense allocated
to departments

C3

Jessica Porter works in both the jewelry department and the hosiery department of a retail store. Porter assists customers in both departments and arranges and stocks merchandise in both departments. The store allocates Porter's $30,000 annual wages between the two departments based on a sample of the time worked in the two departments. The sample is obtained from a diary of hours worked that Porter kept in a randomly chosen two-week period. The diary showed the following hours and activities spent in the two departments. Allocate Porter's annual wages between the two departments.

Selling in jewelry department	51 hours
Arranging and stocking merchandise in jewelry department	6 hours
Selling in hosiery department	12 hours
Arranging and stocking merchandise in hosiery department	7 hours
Idle time spent waiting for a customer to enter one of the selling departments	4 hours

Check   Assign $7,500 to Hosiery

Maryanne Dinardo manages an auto dealership's service department. The recent month's income statement for her department follows. (1) Analyze the items on the income statement and identify those that definitely should be included on a performance report used to evaluate Dinardo's performance. List them and explain why you chose them. (2) List and explain the items that should definitely be excluded. (3) List the items that are not definitely included or excluded and explain why they fall into that category.

Exercise 21-7
Managerial performance evaluation

C4

Revenues		
Sales of parts	$ 72,000	
Sales of services	105,000	$177,000
Costs and expenses		
Cost of parts sold	30,000	
Building depreciation	9,300	
Income taxes allocated to department	8,700	
Interest on long-term debt	7,500	
Manager's salary	12,000	
Payroll taxes	8,100	
Supplies	15,900	
Utilities	4,400	
Wages (hourly)	16,000	
Total costs and expenses		111,900
Departmental net income		$ 65,100

You must prepare a return on investment analysis for the regional manager of Fast & Great Burgers. This growing chain is trying to decide which outlet of two alternatives to open. The first location (A) requires a $1,000,000 investment and is expected to yield annual net income of $160,000. The second location (B) requires a $600,000 investment and is expected to yield annual net income of $108,000. Compute the return on investment for each Fast & Great Burgers alternative and then make your recommendation in a one-half page memorandum to the regional manager. (The chain currently generates an 18% return on total assets.)

Exercise 21-8
Investment center analysis

A1

Heart & Home Properties is developing a subdivision that includes 600 home lots. The 450 lots in the Canyon section are below a ridge and do not have views of the neighboring canyons and hills; the 150 lots in the Hilltop section offer unobstructed views. The expected selling price for each Canyon lot is $55,000 and for each Hilltop lot is $110,000. The developer acquired the land for $4,000,000 and spent another $3,500,000 on street and utilities improvements. Assign the joint land and improvement costs to the lots using the value basis of allocation and determine the average cost per lot.

Exercise 21-9^A
Joint real estate costs assigned

C5

Check   Total Hilltop cost, $3,000,000

Pirate Seafood Company purchases lobsters and processes them into tails and flakes. It sells the lobster tails for $21 per pound and the flakes for $14 per pound. On average, 100 pounds of lobster are processed into 52 pounds of tails and 22 pounds of flakes, with 26 pounds of waste. Assume that Pirate purchased 2,400 pounds of lobster for $4.50 per pound and processed the lobsters with an additional labor cost of $1,800. No materials or labor costs are assigned to the waste. If 1,096 pounds of tails and 324 pounds of flakes are sold, what is (1) the allocated cost of the sold items and (2) the allocated cost of the ending inventory? Pirate allocates joint costs on a value basis. (Round the dollar cost per pound to the nearest thousandth.)

Exercise 21-10^A
Joint product costs assigned

C5

Check   (2) Inventory cost, $2,268

PROBLEM SET A

Problem 21-1A
Allocation of building occupancy costs to departments

C3 P1

mhhe.com/wildFAP18e

National Bank has several departments that occupy both floors of a two-story building. The departmental accounting system has a single account, Building Occupancy Cost, in its ledger. The types and amounts of occupancy costs recorded in this account for the current period follow.

Depreciation—Building	$18,000
Interest—Building mortgage	27,000
Taxes—Building and land	9,000
Gas (heating) expense	3,000
Lighting expense	3,000
Maintenance expense	6,000
Total occupancy cost	$66,000

The building has 4,000 square feet on each floor. In prior periods, the accounting manager merely divided the $66,000 occupancy cost by 8,000 square feet to find an average cost of $8.25 per square foot and then charged each department a building occupancy cost equal to this rate times the number of square feet that it occupied.

Diane Linder manages a first-floor department that occupies 1,000 square feet, and Juan Chiro manages a second-floor department that occupies 1,800 square feet of floor space. In discussing the departmental reports, the second-floor manager questions whether using the same rate per square foot for all departments makes sense because the first-floor space is more valuable. This manager also references a recent real estate study of average local rental costs for similar space that shows first-floor space worth $30 per square foot and second-floor space worth $20 per square foot (excluding costs for heating, lighting, and maintenance).

Required

1. Allocate all occupancy costs to the Linder and Chiro departments using the current allocation method.

Check (2) Total occupancy cost to Linder, $9,600

2. Allocate the depreciation, interest, and taxes occupancy costs to the Linder and Chiro departments in proportion to the relative market values of the floor space. Allocate the heating, lighting, and maintenance costs to the Linder and Chiro departments in proportion to the square feet occupied (ignoring floor space market values).

Analysis Component

3. Which allocation method would you prefer if you were a manager of a second-floor department? Explain.

Problem 21-2A
Activity-based costing

P2

Patient Health is an outpatient surgical clinic that was profitable for many years, but Medicare has cut its reimbursements by as much as 50%. As a result, the clinic wants to better understand its costs. It decides to prepare an activity-based cost analysis, including an estimate of the average cost of both general surgery and orthopedic surgery. The clinic's three cost centers and their cost drivers follow.

Cost Center	Cost	Cost Driver	Driver Quantity
Professional salaries	$2,000,000	Professional hours	10,000
Patient services and supplies	37,500	Number of patients	500
Building cost	300,000	Square feet	2,000

The two main surgical units and their related data follow.

Service	Hours	Square Feet*	Patients
General surgery	2,500	720	400
Orthopedic surgery	7,500	1,280	100

* Orthopedic surgery requires more space for patients, supplies, and equipment.

Required

1. Compute the cost per cost driver for each of the three cost centers.

Check (2) Average cost of general (orthopedic) surgery, $1,595 ($16,995) per patient

2. Use the results from part 1 to allocate costs from each of the three cost centers to both the general surgery and the orthopedic surgery units. Compute total cost and average cost per patient for both the general surgery and the orthopedic surgery units.

Analysis Component

3. Without providing computations, would the average cost of general surgery be higher or lower if all center costs were allocated based on the number of patients? Explain.

Williams Co. began operations in January 2008 with two operating (selling) departments and one service (office) department. Its departmental income statements follow.

Problem 21-3A
Departmental income statements; forecasts

P3

mhhe.com/wildFAP18e

WILLIAMS COMPANY Departmental Income Statements For Year Ended December 31, 2008			
	Clock	Mirror	Combined
Sales	$130,000	$55,000	$185,000
Cost of goods sold	63,700	34,100	97,800
Gross profit	66,300	20,900	87,200
Direct expenses			
Sales salaries	20,000	7,000	27,000
Advertising	1,200	500	1,700
Store supplies used	900	400	1,300
Depreciation—Equipment	1,500	300	1,800
Total direct expenses	23,600	8,200	31,800
Allocated expenses			
Rent expense	7,020	3,780	10,800
Utilities expense	2,600	1,400	4,000
Share of office department expenses	10,500	4,500	15,000
Total allocated expenses	20,120	9,680	29,800
Total expenses	43,720	17,880	61,600
Net income	$ 22,580	$ 3,020	$ 25,600

Williams plans to open a third department in January 2009 that will sell paintings. Management predicts that the new department will generate $50,000 in sales with a 55% gross profit margin and will require the following direct expenses: sales salaries, $8,000; advertising, $800; store supplies, $500; and equipment depreciation, $200. It will fit the new department into the current rented space by taking some square footage from the other two departments. When opened the new painting department will fill one-fifth of the space presently used by the clock department and one-fourth used by the mirror department. Management does not predict any increase in utilities costs, which are allocated to the departments in proportion to occupied space (or rent expense). The company allocates office department expenses to the operating departments in proportion to their sales. It expects the painting department to increase total office department expenses by $7,000. Since the painting department will bring new customers into the store, management expects sales in both the clock and mirror departments to increase by 8%. No changes for those departments' gross profit percents or their direct expenses are expected except for store supplies used, which will increase in proportion to sales.

Required

Prepare departmental income statements that show the company's predicted results of operations for calendar year 2009 for the three operating (selling) departments and their combined totals. (Round percents to the nearest one-tenth and dollar amounts to the nearest whole dollar.)

Check 2009 forecasted combined net income (sales), $43,472 ($249,800)

Billie Whitehorse, the plant manager of Travel Free's Indiana plant, is responsible for all of that plant's costs other than her own salary. The plant has two operating departments and one service department. The camper and trailer operating departments manufacture different products and have their own managers. The office department, which Whitehorse also manages, provides services equally to the two operating departments. A budget is prepared for each operating department and the office department. The company's responsibility accounting system must assemble information to present budgeted and actual costs in performance reports for each operating department manager and the plant manager. Each performance report includes only those costs that a particular operating department manager can control: raw materials, wages, supplies used, and equipment depreciation. The plant manager is responsible for the department managers' salaries, utilities, building rent, office salaries other than her own, and other

Problem 21-4A
Responsibility accounting performance reports; controllable and budgeted costs

C4 P4

office costs plus all costs controlled by the two operating department managers. The annual departmental budgets and actual costs for the two operating departments follow.

	Budget			Actual		
	Campers	Trailers	Combined	Campers	Trailers	Combined
Raw materials	$195,000	$275,000	$ 470,000	$194,200	$273,200	$ 467,400
Employee wages	104,000	205,000	309,000	106,600	206,400	313,000
Dept. manager salary	43,000	52,000	95,000	44,000	53,500	97,500
Supplies used	33,000	90,000	123,000	31,700	91,600	123,300
Depreciation—Equip.	60,000	125,000	185,000	60,000	125,000	185,000
Utilities	3,600	5,400	9,000	3,300	5,000	8,300
Building rent	5,700	9,300	15,000	5,300	8,700	14,000
Office department costs	68,750	68,750	137,500	67,550	67,550	135,100
Totals	$513,050	$830,450	$1,343,500	$512,650	$830,950	$1,343,600

The office department's annual budget and its actual costs follow.

	Budget	Actual
Plant manager salary	$ 80,000	$ 82,000
Other office salaries	32,500	30,100
Other office costs	25,000	23,000
Totals	$137,500	$135,100

Required

1. Prepare responsibility accounting performance reports like those in Exhibit 21.20 that list costs controlled by the following:

Check (1a) $500 total over budget

    a. Manager of the camper department.

    b. Manager of the trailer department.

(1c) Indiana plant controllable costs, $1,900 total under budget

    c. Manager of the Indiana plant.

In each report, include the budgeted and actual costs and show the amount that each actual cost is over or under the budgeted amount.

Analysis Component

2. Did the plant manager or the operating department managers better manage costs? Explain.

Problem 21-5A[A]
Allocation of joint costs

C5

Georgia Orchards produced a good crop of peaches this year. After preparing the following income statement, Georgia believes it should have given its No. 3 peaches to charity and saved its efforts.

GEORGIA ORCHARDS Income Statement For Year Ended December 31, 2008				
	No. 1	No. 2	No. 3	Combined
Sales (by grade)				
No. 1: 300,000 lbs. @ $1.50/lb	$450,000			
No. 2: 300,000 lbs. @ $1.00/lb		$300,000		
No. 3: 750,000 lbs. @ $0.25/lb			$ 187,500	
Total sales				$937,500
Costs				
Tree pruning and care @ $0.30/lb	90,000	90,000	225,000	405,000
Picking, sorting, and grading @ $0.15/lb	45,000	45,000	112,500	202,500
Delivery costs	15,000	15,000	37,500	67,500
Total costs	150,000	150,000	375,000	675,000
Net income (loss)	$300,000	$150,000	$(187,500)	$262,500

In preparing this statement, Georgia allocated joint costs among the grades on a physical basis as an equal amount per pound. Georgia's delivery cost records show that $30,000 of the $67,500 relates to crating the No. 1 and No. 2 peaches and hauling them to the buyer. The remaining $37,500 of delivery costs is for crating the No. 3 peaches and hauling them to the cannery.

Required

1. Prepare reports showing cost allocations on a sales value basis to the three grades of peaches. Separate the delivery costs into the amounts directly identifiable with each grade. Then allocate any shared delivery costs on the basis of the relative sales value of each grade.

2. Using your answers to part 1, prepare an income statement using the joint costs allocated on a sales value basis.

Check (1) $129,600 tree pruning and care costs allocated to No. 2

(2) Net income from No. 1 & No. 2 peaches, $140,400 & $93,600

Analysis Component

3. Do you think delivery costs fit the definition of a joint cost? Explain.

Harmon's has several departments that occupy all floors of a two-story building that includes a basement floor. Harmon rented this building under a long-term lease negotiated when rental rates were low. The departmental accounting system has a single account, Building Occupancy Cost, in its ledger. The types and amounts of occupancy costs recorded in this account for the current period follow.

PROBLEM SET B

Problem 21-1B
Allocation of building occupancy costs to departments

C3   P1

Building rent	$400,000
Lighting expense	25,000
Cleaning expense	40,000
Total occupancy cost	$465,000

The building has 7,500 square feet on each of the upper two floors but only 5,000 square feet in the basement. In prior periods, the accounting manager merely divided the $465,000 occupancy cost by 20,000 square feet to find an average cost of $23.25 per square foot and then charged each department a building occupancy cost equal to this rate times the number of square feet that it occupies.

Jordan Style manages a department that occupies 2,000 square feet of basement floor space. In discussing the departmental reports with other managers, she questions whether using the same rate per square foot for all departments makes sense because different floor space has different values. Style checked a recent real estate report of average local rental costs for similar space that shows first-floor space worth $40 per square foot, second-floor space worth $20 per square foot, and basement space worth $10 per square foot (excluding costs for lighting and cleaning).

Required

1. Allocate all occupancy costs to Style's department using the current allocation method.

2. Allocate the building rent cost to Style's department in proportion to the relative market value of the floor space. Allocate to Style's department the lighting and heating costs in proportion to the square feet occupied (ignoring floor space market values).

Check (2) Total costs allocated to Style's Dept., $22,500

Analysis Component

3. Which allocation method would you prefer if you were a manager of a basement department?

Wooddale Landscaping has enjoyed profits for many years, but new competition has cut service revenue by as much as 30%. As a result, the company wants to better understand its costs. It decides to prepare an activity-based cost analysis, including an estimate of the average cost of both general landscaping services and custom design landscaping services. The company's three cost centers and their cost drivers follow.

Problem 21-2B
Activity-based costing

P2

Cost Center	Cost	Cost Driver	Driver Quantity
Professional salaries	$600,000	Professional hours	10,000
Customer supplies	150,000	Number of customers	800
Building cost	240,000	Square feet	2,500

The two main landscaping units and their related data follow.

Service	Hours	Square Feet*	Customers
General landscaping	2,500	1,000	600
Custom design landscaping	7,500	1,500	200

* Custom design landscaping requires more space for equipment, supplies, and planning.

Required

1. Compute the cost per cost driver for each of the three cost centers.

2. Use the results from part 1 to allocate costs from each of the three cost centers to both the general landscaping and the custom design landscaping units. Compute total cost and average cost per customer for both the general landscaping and the custom design landscaping units.

Analysis Component

3. Without providing computations, would the average cost of general landscaping be higher or lower if all center costs were allocated based on the number of customers? Explain.

Problem 21-3B
Departmental income statements; forecasts

P3

Bonanza Entertainment began operations in January 2008 with two operating (selling) departments and one service (office) department. Its departmental income statements follow.

BONANZA ENTERTAINMENT Departmental Income Statements For Year Ended December 31, 2008			
	Movies	Video Games	Combined
Sales	$600,000	$200,000	$800,000
Cost of goods sold	420,000	154,000	574,000
Gross profit	180,000	46,000	226,000
Direct expenses			
Sales salaries	37,000	15,000	52,000
Advertising	12,500	6,000	18,500
Store supplies used	4,000	1,000	5,000
Depreciation—Equipment	4,500	3,000	7,500
Total direct expenses	58,000	25,000	83,000
Allocated expenses			
Rent expense	41,000	9,000	50,000
Utilities expense	7,380	1,620	9,000
Share of office department expenses	56,250	18,750	75,000
Total allocated expenses	104,630	29,370	134,000
Total expenses	162,630	54,370	217,000
Net income (loss)	$ 17,370	$ (8,370)	$ 9,000

Bonanza plans to open a third department in January 2009 that will sell compact discs. Management predicts that the new department will generate $300,000 in sales with a 35% gross profit margin and will require the following direct expenses: sales salaries, $18,000; advertising, $10,000; store supplies, $2,000; and equipment depreciation, $1,200. The company will fit the new department into the current rented space by taking some square footage from the other two departments. When opened, the new compact disc department will fill one-fourth of the space presently used by the movie department and one-third of the space used by the video game department. Management does not predict any increase in utilities costs, which are allocated to the departments in proportion to occupied space (or rent expense). The company allocates office department expenses to the operating departments in proportion to their sales. It expects the compact disc department to increase total office department expenses by $10,000. Since the compact disc department will bring new customers into the store, management expects sales in both the movie and video game departments to increase by 8%. No changes for those departments' gross profit percents or for their direct expenses are expected, except for store supplies used, which will increase in proportion to sales.

Required

Prepare departmental income statements that show the company's predicted results of operations for calendar year 2009 for the three operating (selling) departments and their combined totals. (Round percents to the nearest one-tenth and dollar amounts to the nearest whole dollar.)

Check   2009 forecasted movies net income (sales), $52,450 ($648,000)

Britney Brown, the plant manager of LMN Co.'s Chicago plant, is responsible for all of that plant's costs other than her own salary. The plant has two operating departments and one service department. The refrigerator and dishwasher operating departments manufacture different products and have their own managers. The office department, which Brown also manages, provides services equally to the two operating departments. A monthly budget is prepared for each operating department and the office department. The company's responsibility accounting system must assemble information to present budgeted and actual costs in performance reports for each operating department manager and the plant manager. Each performance report includes only those costs that a particular operating department manager can control: raw materials, wages, supplies used, and equipment depreciation. The plant manager is responsible for the department managers' salaries, utilities, building rent, office salaries other than her own, and other office costs plus all costs controlled by the two operating department managers. The April departmental budgets and actual costs for the two operating departments follow.

Problem 21-4B
Responsibility accounting performance reports; controllable and budgeted costs

C4   P4

	Budget			Actual		
	Refrigerators	Dishwashers	Combined	Refrigerators	Dishwashers	Combined
Raw materials	$400,000	$200,000	$ 600,000	$385,000	$202,000	$ 587,000
Employee wages	170,000	80,000	250,000	174,700	81,500	256,200
Dept. manager salary	55,000	49,000	104,000	55,000	46,500	101,500
Supplies used	15,000	9,000	24,000	14,000	9,700	23,700
Depreciation—Equip.	53,000	37,000	90,000	53,000	37,000	90,000
Utilities	30,000	18,000	48,000	34,500	20,700	55,200
Building rent	63,000	17,000	80,000	65,800	16,500	82,300
Office department costs	70,500	70,500	141,000	75,000	75,000	150,000
Totals	$856,500	$480,500	$1,337,000	$857,000	$488,900	$1,345,900

The office department's budget and its actual costs for April follow.

	Budget	Actual
Plant manager salary	$ 80,000	$ 85,000
Other office salaries	40,000	35,200
Other office costs	21,000	29,800
Totals	$141,000	$150,000

Required

1. Prepare responsibility accounting performance reports like those in Exhibit 21.20 that list costs controlled by the following:

   a. Manager of the refrigerator department.

   b. Manager of the dishwasher department.

   c. Manager of the Chicago plant.

   In each report, include the budgeted and actual costs for the month and show the amount by which each actual cost is over or under the budgeted amount.

Check   (1a) $11,300 total under budget

(1c) Chicago plant controllable costs, $3,900 total over budget

Analysis Component

2. Did the plant manager or the operating department managers better manage costs? Explain.

Problem 21-5B[A]
Allocation of joint costs

C5

Rita and Rick Redding own and operate a tomato grove. After preparing the following income statement, Rita believes they should have offered the No. 3 tomatoes to the public for free and saved themselves time and money.

RITA AND RICK REDDING Income Statement For Year Ended December 31, 2008				
	No. 1	**No. 2**	**No. 3**	**Combined**
Sales (by grade)				
No. 1: 500,000 lbs. @ $1.80/lb	$900,000			
No. 2: 400,000 lbs. @ $1.25/lb		$500,000		
No. 3: 100,000 lbs. @ $0.40/lb			$ 40,000	
Total sales				$1,440,000
Costs				
Land preparation, seeding, and cultivating @ $0.70/lb	350,000	280,000	70,000	700,000
Harvesting, sorting, and grading @ $0.04/lb	20,000	16,000	4,000	40,000
Delivery costs	10,000	7,000	3,000	20,000
Total costs	380,000	303,000	77,000	760,000
Net income (loss)	$520,000	$197,000	$(37,000)	$680,000

In preparing this statement, Rita and Rick allocated joint costs among the grades on a physical basis as an equal amount per pound. Also, their delivery cost records show that $17,000 of the $20,000 relates to crating the No. 1 and No. 2 tomatoes and hauling them to the buyer. The remaining $3,000 of delivery costs is for crating the No. 3 tomatoes and hauling them to the cannery.

Required

Check (1) $1,120 harvesting, sorting
and grading costs allocated to No. 3

1. Prepare reports showing cost allocations on a sales value basis to the three grades of tomatoes. Separate the delivery costs into the amounts directly identifiable with each grade. Then allocate any shared delivery costs on the basis of the relative sales value of each grade. (Round percents to the nearest one-tenth and dollar amounts to the nearest whole dollar.)

(2) Net income from No. 1 &
No. 2 tomatoes, $426,569 & $237,151

2. Using your answers to part 1, prepare an income statement using the joint costs allocated on a sales value basis.

Analysis Component

3. Do you think delivery costs fit the definition of a joint cost? Explain.

PROBLEM SET C   **Problem Set C is available at the book's Website to further reinforce and assess your learning.**

BEYOND THE NUMBERS

REPORTING IN ACTION

C4

BTN 21-1   Review Best Buy's income statement in Appendix A and identify its revenues for the years ended February 26, 2005, February 28, 2004, and March 1, 2003. For the year ended February 26, 2005, Best Buy reports the following product revenue mix. (Assume that its product revenue mix is the same for each of the three years reported when answering the requirements.)

Home Office	Entertainment Software	Consumer Electronics	Appliances
34%	21%	39%	6%

Required

1. Compute the amount of revenue from each of its product lines for the years ended February 26, 2005, February 28, 2004, and March 1, 2003.

2. If Best Buy wishes to evaluate each of its product lines, how can it allocate its operating expenses to each of them to determine each product line's profitability?

Fast Forward

3. Access Best Buy's annual report for a fiscal year ending after February 26, 2005, from its Website (BestBuy.com) or the SEC's EDGAR database (sec.gov). Compute its revenues for its product lines for the most recent year(s). Compare those results to those from part 1. How has its product mix changed?

BTN 21-2   **Best Buy** and **Circuit City** compete across the country in several markets. The most common competitive markets for these two companies are by location.

COMPARATIVE ANALYSIS

P3

Required

1. Design a three-tier responsibility accounting organizational chart assuming that you have available internal information for both companies. Use Exhibit 21.19 as an example. The goal of this assignment is to design a reporting framework for the companies; numbers are not required. Limit your reporting framework to sales activity only.

2. Explain why it is important to have similar performance reports when comparing performance within a company (and across different companies). Be specific in your response.

BTN 21-3   Senior Security Co. offers a range of security services for senior citizens. Each type of service is considered within a separate department. Mary Pincus, the overall manager, is compensated partly on the basis of departmental performance by staying within the quarterly cost budget. She often revises operations to make sure departments stay within budget. Says Pincus, "I will not go over budget even if it means slightly compromising the level and quality of service. These are minor compromises that don't significantly affect my clients, at least in the short term."

ETHICS CHALLENGE

P3

Required

1. Is there an ethical concern in this situation? If so, which parties are affected? Explain.

2. Can Mary Pincus take action to eliminate or reduce any ethical concerns? Explain.

3. What is Senior Security's ethical responsibility in offering professional services?

BTN 21-4   Improvement Station is a national home improvement chain with more than 100 stores throughout the country. The manager of each store receives a salary plus a bonus equal to a percent of the store's net income for the reporting period. The following net income calculation is on the Denver store manager's performance report for the recent monthly period.

COMMUNICATING IN PRACTICE

C4 C5 P3

Sales	$2,500,000
Cost of goods sold	800,000
Wages expense	500,000
Utilities expense	200,000
Home office expense	75,000
Net income	$925,000
Manager's bonus (0.5%)	$ 4,625

In previous periods, the bonus had also been 0.5%, but the performance report had not included any charges for the home office expense, which is now assigned to each store as a percent of its sales.

Required

Assume that you are the national office manager. Write a one-half page memorandum to your store managers explaining why home office expense is in the new performance report.

TAKING IT TO THE NET

A1

BTN 21-5   This chapter described and used spreadsheets to prepare various managerial reports (see Exhibit 21-12). You can download from Websites various tutorials showing how spreadsheets are used in managerial accounting and other business applications.

Required

1. Check out the Website <u>Lacher.com</u>. Scroll down and open its table of contents. Select "Business Solutions Tutorials" and identify and list three tutorials for review.
2. Describe in a one-half page memorandum to your instructor how the applications described in each tutorial are helpful in business and managerial decision making.

TEAMWORK IN ACTION

C1 C2

BTN 21-6   Activity-based costing (ABC) is increasingly popular as a useful managerial tool to (1) measure the cost of resources consumed and (2) assign cost to products and services. This managerial tool has been available to accounting and business decision makers for more than 25 years.

Required

Break into teams and identify at least three likely reasons that activity-based costing has gained popularity in recent years. Be prepared to present your answers in a class discussion. (*Hint:* What changes have occurred in products and services over the past 25 years?)

***BusinessWeek* ACTIVITY**

C4

BTN 21-7   Read the article "The Easiest Commute of All" from the December 12, 2005, issue of *BusinessWeek*. (The book's Website provides free access to the article.)

Required

1. Why are many workers becoming remote workers?
2. Are there advantages for a company to have these remote workers?
3. How can a manager assess a worker's productivity if the worker is not on site?

ENTREPRENEURIAL DECISION

P3

BTN 21-8   **Jungle Jim's International Market** has grown considerably since Jim Bonaminio began with his roadside produce stand. Jim now operates a gigantic supermarket with many departments and activities.

Required

1. How can Jim Bonaminio use departmental income statements to assist him in understanding and controlling his supermarket operations?
2. Are departmental income statements always the best measure of a department's performance? Explain.

HITTING THE ROAD

P3

BTN 21-9   Visit a local movie theater and check out both its concession area and its showing areas. The manager of a theater must confront questions such as:

• How much return do we earn on concessions?
• What types of movies generate the greatest sales?
• What types of movies generate the greatest net income?

Required

Assume that you are the new accounting manager for a 16-screen movie theater. You are to set up a responsibility accounting reporting framework for the theater.

1. Recommend how to segment the different departments of a movie theater for responsibility reporting.
2. Propose an expense allocation system for heat, rent, insurance, and maintenance costs of the theater.

BTN 21-10   Key segment data from Dixons (Dixons-Group.com) follow.

Segment, for Year Ended (£ millions)	Net Sales May 1, 2004	Net Sales May 3, 2003	Operating Income May 1, 2004	Operating Income May 3, 2003
United Kingdom retail	£4,697.9	£4,524.5	£254.2	£238.0
International retail	1,760.1	1,195.3	63.6	40.1
Totals	£6,458.0	£5,719.8	£317.8	£278.1

Dixons

Required

1. Compute the growth (in percent) for Dixons' total net sales from fiscal year 2003 to 2004.

2. Compute the growth (in percent) for each segment's net sales from fiscal year 2003 to 2004.

3. Which segment's net sales grew the fastest?

4. Which segment was most profitable?

5. How can Dixons' managers use this information?

ANSWERS TO MULTIPLE CHOICE QUIZ

1. b; [$641,250/($356,250 + $641,250 + $427,500)] × $150,000 = $67,500

2. c;

3. e; $162,000 × 50/150 setups = $54,000; $54,000/500 units = $108 per Grey unit. (Red is $2.70 per unit.)

4. b;

	Department X	Department Y	Department Z
Sales	$500,000	$200,000	$350,000
Cost of goods sold	350,000	75,000	150,000
Gross profit	150,000	125,000	200,000
Direct expenses	50,000	20,000	75,000
Departmental contribution	$100,000	$105,000	$125,000

5. a; $100,000/$500,000 = 20%

22

Cost-Volume-Profit Analysis

A Look Back

Chapter 21 focused on cost allocation, activity-based costing, and performance measurement. We identified ways to measure and analyze company activities, its departments, and its managers.

A Look at This Chapter

This chapter shows how information on both costs and sales behavior is useful to managers in performing cost-volume-profit analysis. This analysis is an important part of successful management and sound business decisions.

A Look Ahead

Chapter 23 introduces and describes the budgeting process and its importance to management. It also explains the master budget and its usefulness to the planning of future company activities.

Learning Objectives

CAP

Conceptual

C1 Describe different types of cost behavior in relation to production and sales volume. *(p. 882)*

C2 Identify assumptions in cost-volume-profit analysis and explain their impact. *(p. 890)*

C3 Describe several applications of cost-volume-profit analysis. *(p. 892)*

Analytical

A1 Compare the scatter diagram, high-low, and regression methods of estimating costs. *(p. 887)*

A2 Compute contribution margin and describe what it reveals about a company's cost structure. *(p. 888)*

A3 Analyze changes in sales using the degree of operating leverage. *(p. 896)*

Procedural

P1 Determine cost estimates using three different methods. *(p. 885)*

P2 Compute break-even point for a single product company. *(p. 888)*

P3 Graph costs and sales for a single product company. *(p. 890)*

P4 Compute break-even point for a multiproduct company. *(p. 895)*

> *"There is no store in any of the Chinatowns across the U.S. that carries our products"*
> —Xiaoning Wang

Sprouting Fruits of China

NEW YORK, NY—Xiaoning Wang launched Brooklyn-based **ChinaSprout** (**ChinaSprout.com**) to provide the best educational and cultural products and community services to people interested in Chinese culture. It all began when Wang and her husband wanted to educate their own son, Simon, about the culture of Chinese people. The couple soon grew frustrated, however, by a lack of quality educational products and services. They also discovered many friends and neighbors who were similarly dismayed.

With $6,000 and a dream, Wang and her husband started their merchandising business of buying and distributing products from China. They promoted their Website by printing flyers and passing them out at cultural events. Word quickly spread and business soared.

"When I started ChinaSprout," says Wang, "I never dreamed that it would grow as fast as it did and develop such an enormous following." The business quickly required cost controls to maintain the quality and service that loyal customers expected. Wang focused on cost behavior and on identifying variable and fixed costs. She says this type of analysis is crucial to understanding break-even points and maintaining the right product mix. "This wonderful mix allows us to expand our categories of products offered," says Wang. "That selection has grown to over 3,000 products in more than 150 different shopping categories."

Wang's keen sense for business and Chinese culture gives her unique insight into how product costs relate to sales volume and profits. As a result, ChinaSprout does not only achieve its break-even point, it markedly exceeds it. Wang also tracks individual products in her multiproduct offerings. With a focus on cost-volume-profit analysis, Wang says she is able to expand and continually look for "culturally relevant products and services to an increasing number of Chinese American families, schools, museums, and stores."

"ChinaSprout has become the most popular destination for Chinese cultural and educational products," says Wang. Each product must pass a cost-volume-profit and break-even analysis. This yields a unique product offering. "There is no store in any of the Chinatowns across the U.S. that carries our products," says Wang proudly. Moreover, "most of our products are sourced directly from China."

Customer satisfaction is equally important. Wang explains how ChinaSprout constantly draws on feedback collected from its customers. "A key success factor . . . is to keep in contact with your customers," says Wang. It has been a "great pleasure and joy to serve such an open-hearted and multicultural community. *Xiexie and Xin Nian Kuai Le!*" she exclaims.

[Sources: *ChinaSprout Website,* May 2006; *Earnshaw's Magazine,* August 2003; *National Association of Women Business Owners,* March 2003; *Multichannel Merchant,* June 2002; *ShopSite Website,* 2006]

This chapter describes different types of costs and shows how changes in a company's operating volume affect these costs. The chapter also analyzes a company's costs and sales to understand how different operating strategies affect profit or loss. Managers use this type of analysis to forecast what will happen if changes are made to costs, sales volume, selling prices, or product mix. They then use these forecasts to select the best business strategy for the company.

Cost-Volume-Profit Analysis

Identifying Cost Behavior
- Fixed costs
- Variable costs
- Mixed costs
- Step-wise costs
- Curvilinear costs

Measuring Cost Behavior
- Scatter diagrams
- High-low method
- Least-squares regression
- Comparison of cost estimation methods

Using Break-Even Analysis
- Computing break-even
- Preparing a cost-volume-profit chart
- Making assumptions in cost-volume-profit analysis

Applying Cost-Volume-Profit Analysis
- Computing income from sales and costs
- Computing sales for target income
- Computing margin of safety
- Using sensitivity analysis
- Computing multiproduct break-even

Identifying Cost Behavior

Planning a company's future activities and events is a crucial phase in successful management. One of the first steps in planning is to predict the volume of activity, the costs to be incurred, sales to be made, and profit to be received. An important tool to help managers carry out this step is **cost-volume-profit (CVP) analysis,** which helps them predict how changes in costs and sales levels affect income. In its basic form, CVP analysis involves computing the sales level at which a company neither earns an income nor incurs a loss, called the *break-even point.* For this reason, this basic form of cost-volume-profit analysis is often called *break-even analysis.* Managers use variations of CVP analysis to answer questions such as these:

Point: *Profit* is another term for income.

- What sales volume is needed to earn a target income?
- What is the change in income if selling prices decline and sales volume increases?
- How much does income increase if we install a new machine to reduce labor costs?
- What is the income effect if we change the sales mix of our products or services?

Consequently, cost-volume-profit analysis is useful in a wide range of business decisions.

Conventional cost-volume-profit analysis requires management to classify all costs as either *fixed* or *variable* with respect to production or sales volume. The remainder of this section discusses the concepts of fixed and variable cost behavior as they relate to CVP analysis.

Topic Tackler

PLUS

22-1

C1 Describe different types of cost behavior in relation to production and sales volume.

Fixed Costs

A *fixed cost* remains unchanged in amount when the volume of activity varies from period to period within a relevant range. For example, $5,000 in monthly rent paid for a factory building remains the same whether the factory operates with a single eight-hour shift or around the clock with three shifts. This means that rent cost is the same each month at any level of output from zero to the plant's full productive capacity. Notice that while *total* fixed cost does not change as the level of production changes the fixed cost *per unit* of output decreases as volume increases. For instance, if 20 units are produced when monthly rent is $5,000, the average rent cost per unit is $250 (computed as $5,000/20 units). When production increases to 100 units per month, the average cost per unit decreases to $50 (computed as $5,000/100 units). The average cost decreases to $10 per unit if production increases to 500 units per month. Common examples of fixed costs include depreciation, property taxes, office salaries, and many service department costs.

Point: Fixed costs do not change when volume changes, but the per unit cost declines as volume increases.

Decision Insight

Cost Driven   Fixed costs were a driving force behind the **Daimler-Benz** and **Chrysler** merger. The auto business has huge fixed costs, mainly in plant and equipment. This means that with higher sales volume, fixed costs can be spread over more units. This yields lower fixed costs (and price) per auto.

When production volume and costs are graphed, units of product are usually plotted on the *horizontal axis* and dollars of cost are plotted on the *vertical axis*. Fixed costs then are represented as a horizontal line because they remain constant at all levels of production. To illustrate, the graph in Exhibit 22.1 shows that fixed costs remain at $32,000 at all production levels up to the company's monthly capacity of 2,000 units of output. The *relevant range* for fixed costs in Exhibit 22.1 is 0 to 2,000 units. If the relevant range changes (that is, production capacity extends beyond this range), the amount of fixed costs will likely change.

Example: If the fixed cost line in Exhibit 22.1 is shifted upward, does the total cost line shift up, down, or remain in the same place? *Answer:* It shifts up by the same amount.

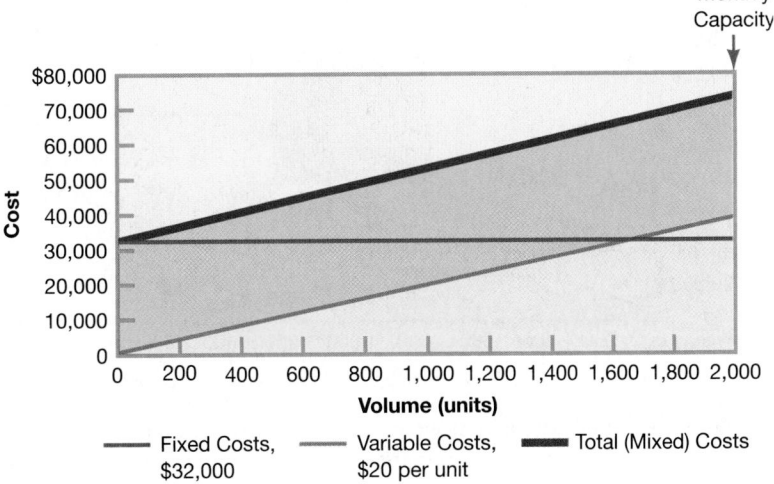

Exhibit 22.1

Relations of Fixed and Variable Costs to Volume

Example: If the level of fixed costs in Exhibit 22.1 changes, does the slope of the total cost line change? *Answer:* No, the slope doesn't change. The total cost line is simply shifted upward or downward.

Variable Costs

A *variable cost* changes in proportion to changes in volume of activity. The direct materials cost of a product is one example of a variable cost. If one unit of product requires materials costing $20, total materials costs are $200 when 10 units of product are manufactured, $400 for 20 units, $600 for 30 units, and so on. Notice that variable cost *per unit* remains constant but the *total* amount of variable cost changes with the level of production. In addition to direct materials, common variable costs include direct labor (if employees are paid per unit), sales commissions, shipping costs, and some overhead costs.

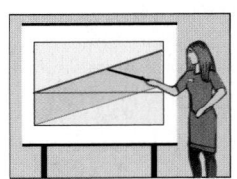

When variable costs are plotted on a graph of cost and volume, they appear as a straight line starting at the zero cost level. This straight line is upward (positive) sloping. The line rises as volume of activity increases. A variable cost line using a $20 per unit cost is graphed in Exhibit 22.1.

Point: Fixed costs are constant in total but vary (decline) per unit as more units are produced. Variable costs vary in total but are fixed per unit.

Mixed Costs

A **mixed cost** includes both fixed and variable cost components. For example, compensation for sales representatives often includes a fixed monthly salary and a variable commission based on sales. The total cost line in Exhibit 22.1 is a mixed cost. Like a fixed cost, it is greater than zero when volume is zero, but unlike a fixed cost, it increases steadily in proportion to increases in volume. The mixed cost line in Exhibit 22.1 starts on the vertical axis at the $32,000 fixed cost point. Thus, at the zero volume level, total cost equals the fixed costs. As the activity level increases, the mixed cost line increases at an amount equal to the variable cost per unit. This line is highest when volume of activity is at 2,000 units (the end point of the relevant range). In CVP analysis, mixed costs are often separated into fixed and variable components. The fixed component is added to other fixed costs, and the variable component is added to other variable costs.

Step-Wise Costs

A **step-wise cost** reflects a step pattern in costs. Salaries of production supervisors often behave in a step-wise manner in that their salaries are fixed within a *relevant range* of the current production volume. However, if production volume expands significantly (for example, with the addition of another shift), additional supervisors must be hired. This means that the total cost for supervisory salaries goes up by a lump-sum amount. Similarly, if volume takes another significant step up, supervisory salaries will increase by another lump sum. This behavior reflects a step-wise cost, also known as *stair-step costs,* which is graphed in Exhibit 22.2. See how it is flat within ranges (steps). Then, when volume significantly changes, it shifts to another level for that range (step).

Exhibit 22.2

Step-Wise and
Curvilinear Costs

In a conventional CVP analysis, a step-wise cost is usually treated as either a fixed cost or a variable cost. This treatment involves manager judgment and depends on the width of the range and the expected volume. To illustrate, suppose after the production of every 25 snowboards, an operator lubricates the finishing machine. The cost of this lubricant reflects a step-wise pattern. Also, suppose that after the production of every 1,000 units, the snowboard cutting tool is replaced. Again, this is a step-wise cost. Note that the range of 25 snowboards is much narrower than the range of 1,000 snowboards. Some managers might treat the lubricant cost as a variable cost and the cutting tool cost as a fixed cost.

Curvilinear Costs

A variable cost, as explained, is a *linear* cost; that is, it increases at a constant rate as volume of activity increases. A **curvilinear cost,** also called *nonlinear cost,* increases at a nonconstant rate as volume increases. When graphed, curvilinear costs appear as a curved line. Exhibit 22.2 shows a curvilinear cost beginning at zero when production is zero and then increasing at different rates.

An example of a curvilinear cost is total direct labor cost when workers are paid by the hour. At low to medium levels of production, adding more employees allows each of them to specialize by doing certain tasks repeatedly instead of doing several different tasks. This often yields additional units of output at lower costs. A point is eventually reached at which adding more employees creates inefficiencies. For instance, a large crew demands more time and effort in communicating and coordinating their efforts. While adding employees in this case increases

Point: Computer spreadsheets are important and effective tools for CVP analysis and for analyzing alternative "what-if" strategies.

Point: Cost-volume-profit analysis helped Rod Canion, Jim Harris, and Bill Murto raise start-up capital of $20 million to launch **Compaq Computer.** They showed that break-even volumes were attainable within the first year.

output, the labor cost per unit increases, and the total labor cost goes up at a steeper slope. This pattern is seen in Exhibit 22.2 where the curvilinear cost curve starts at zero, rises, flattens out, and then increases at a faster rate as output nears the maximum.

Quick Check
Answers—p. 899

1. Which of the following statements is typically true? (*a*) Variable cost per unit increases as volume increases, (*b*) fixed cost per unit decreases as volume increases, or (*c*) a curvilinear cost includes both fixed and variable elements.

2. Describe the behavior of a fixed cost.

3. If cost per unit of activity remains constant (fixed), why is it called a variable cost?

Measuring Cost Behavior

Identifying and measuring cost behavior requires careful analysis and judgment. An important part of this process is to identify costs that can be classified as either fixed or variable, which often requires analysis of past cost behavior. Three methods are commonly used to analyze past costs: scatter diagrams, high-low method, and least-squares regression. Each method is discussed in this section using the unit and cost data shown in Exhibit 22.3, which is taken from a start-up company that uses units produced as the activity base in estimating cost behavior.

P1 Determine cost estimates using three different methods.

Scatter Diagrams

Scatter diagrams display past cost and unit data in graphical form. In preparing a scatter diagram, units are plotted on the horizontal axis and cost is plotted on the vertical axis. Each individual point on a scatter diagram reflects the cost and number of units for a prior period. In Exhibit 22.4, the prior 12 months' cost and number of units are graphed. Each point reflects total costs incurred and units produced for one of those months. For instance, the point labeled March had units produced of 25,000 and costs of $25,000.

Month	Units Produced	Total Cost
January	17,500	$20,500
February	27,500	21,500
March	25,000	25,000
April	35,000	21,500
May	47,500	25,500
June	22,500	18,500
July	30,000	23,500
August	52,500	28,500
September	37,500	26,000
October	57,500	26,000
November	62,500	31,000
December	67,500	29,000

Exhibit 22.3

Data for Estimating Cost Behavior

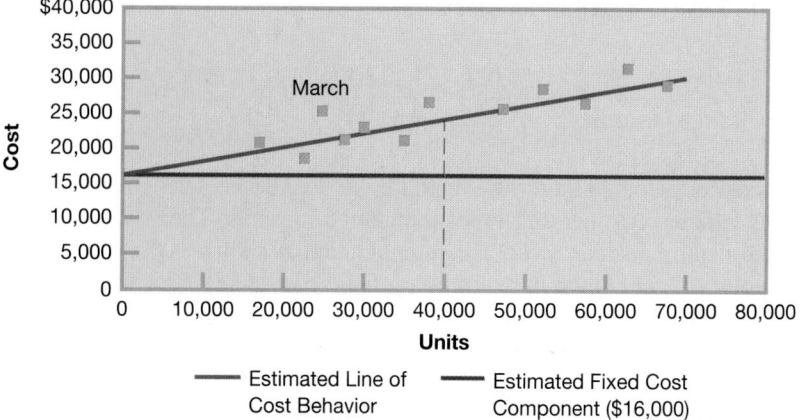

Exhibit 22.4

Scatter Diagram

The **estimated line of cost behavior** is drawn on a scatter diagram to reflect the relation between cost and unit volume. This line best visually "fits" the points in a scatter diagram. Fitting this line demands judgment. The line drawn in Exhibit 22.4 intersects the vertical axis at approximately $16,000, which reflects fixed cost. To compute variable cost per unit, or the slope, we perform three steps. First, we select any two points on the horizontal axis (units), say 0 and 40,000. Second, we draw a vertical line from each of these points to intersect the estimated line of cost behavior. The point on the vertical axis (cost) corresponding to the 40,000 units point that intersects the estimated line is roughly $24,000. Similarly, the cost corresponding to zero units is $16,000 (the fixed cost point). Third, we compute the slope of the line, or variable cost, as the change in cost divided by the change in units. Exhibit 22.5 shows this computation.

Exhibit 22.5

Variable Cost per Unit
(Scatter Diagram)

Example: In Exhibits 22.4 and 22.5, if units are projected at 30,000, what is predicted cost?
Answer: Approximately $22,000.

$$\frac{\textbf{Change in cost}}{\textbf{Change in units}} = \frac{\$24,000 - \$16,000}{40,000 - 0} = \frac{\$8,000}{40,000} = \$0.20 \text{ per unit}$$

Variable cost is $0.20 per unit. Thus, the cost equation that management will use to estimate costs for different unit levels is **$16,000 plus $0.20 per unit**.

High-Low Method

The **high-low method** is a way to estimate the cost equation by graphically connecting the two cost amounts at the highest and lowest unit volumes. In our case, the lowest number of units is 17,500, and the highest is 67,500. The costs corresponding to these unit volumes are $20,500 and $29,000, respectively (see data in Exhibit 22.3). The estimated line of cost behavior for the high-low method is then drawn by connecting these two points on the scatter diagram corresponding to the lowest and highest unit volumes as follows.

Point: Note that the high-low method identifies the high and low points of the volume (activity) base, and the costs linked with those extremes—which may not be the highest and lowest costs.

The variable cost per unit is determined as the change in cost divided by the change in units and uses the data from the high and low unit volumes. This results in a slope, or variable cost per unit, of $0.17 as computed in Exhibit 22.6.

Exhibit 22.6

Variable Cost per Unit
(High-Low Method)

$$\frac{\textbf{Change in cost}}{\textbf{Change in units}} = \frac{\$29,000 - \$20,500}{67,500 - 17,500} = \frac{\$8,500}{50,000} = \$0.17 \text{ per unit}$$

To estimate fixed cost for the high-low method, we use the knowledge that total cost equals fixed cost plus variable cost per unit times the number of units. Then, we pick either the high or low point to determine fixed cost. This computation is shown in Exhibit 22.7—where we use the high point (67,500 units) in determining fixed cost of $17,525. By coincidence, use of the low point (17,500 units) yields the same fixed cost estimate: $20,500 = Fixed cost + ($0.17 per unit × 17,500), or Fixed cost = $17,525.

Exhibit 22.7

Fixed Cost (High-Low Method)

Total cost = Fixed cost + (Variable cost × Units)
$29,000 = Fixed cost + ($0.17 per unit × 67,500 units)
Then,
Fixed cost = $17,525

Thus, the cost equation used to estimate costs at different units is **$17,525 plus $0.17 per unit**. This cost equation differs slightly from that determined from the scatter diagram method. A deficiency of the high-low method is that it ignores all cost points except the highest and lowest. The result is less precision because the high-low method uses the most extreme points rather than the more usual conditions likely to recur.

Least-Squares Regression

Least-squares regression is a statistical method for identifying cost behavior. For our purposes, we use the cost equation estimated from this method but leave the computational details for more advanced courses. Such computations for least-squares regression are readily done using most spreadsheet programs or calculators.

The regression cost equation for the data presented in Exhibit 22.3 is **$16,947 plus $0.19 per unit**; that is, fixed cost is estimated as $16,947 and variable cost at $0.19 per unit. Both costs are reflected in the following graph.

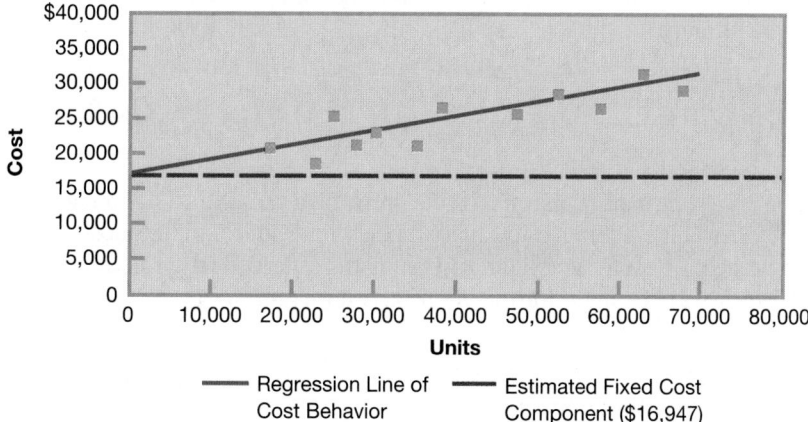

———— Regression Line of   ———— Estimated Fixed Cost
        Cost Behavior   Component ($16,947)

Comparison of Cost Estimation Methods

The three cost estimation methods result in slightly different estimates of fixed and variable costs as summarized in Exhibit 22.8. Estimates from the scatter diagram are based on a visual fit of the cost line and are subject to interpretation. Estimates from the high-low method use only two sets of values corresponding to the lowest and highest unit volumes. Estimates from least-squares regression use a statistical technique and all available data points.

A1   Compare the scatter diagram, high-low, and regression methods of estimating costs.

Estimation Method	Fixed Cost	Variable Cost
Scatter diagram	$16,000	$0.20 per unit
High-low method	17,525	0.17 per unit
Least-squares regression	16,947	0.19 per unit

Exhibit 22.8

Comparison of Cost Estimation Methods

We must remember that all three methods use *past data*. Thus, cost estimates resulting from these methods are only as good as the data used for estimation. Managers must establish that the data are reliable in deriving cost estimates for the future.

Quick Check   Answers—p. 899

4. Which of the following methods is likely to yield the most precise estimated line of cost behavior? (*a*) high-low, (*b*) least-squares regression, or (*c*) scatter diagram.

5. What is the primary weakness of the high-low method?

6. Using conventional CVP analysis, a mixed cost should be (*a*) disregarded, (*b*) treated as a fixed cost, or (*c*) separated into fixed and variable components.

Using Break-Even Analysis

Break-even analysis is a special case of cost-volume-profit analysis. This section describes break-even analysis by computing the break-even point and preparing a CVP (or break-even) chart.

Contribution Margin and Its Measures

A2 Compute contribution margin and describe what it reveals about a company's cost structure.

We explained how managers classify costs by behavior. This often refers to classifying costs as being fixed or variable with respect to volume of activity. In manufacturing companies, volume of activity usually refers to the number of units produced. We then classify a cost as either fixed or variable, depending on whether total cost changes as the number of units produced changes. Once we separate costs by behavior, we can then compute a product's contribution margin. **Contribution margin per unit,** or *unit contribution margin,* is the amount a product's unit selling price exceeds its total unit variable cost. This excess amount contributes to covering fixed costs and generating profits on a per unit basis. Exhibit 22.9 shows the contribution margin per unit formula.

Exhibit 22.9

Contribution Margin per Unit

> **Contribution margin per unit = Sales price per unit − Total variable cost per unit**

Users often use contribution margin in the form of a **contribution margin ratio,** which is the percent of a unit's selling price that exceeds total unit variable cost. It can be interpreted as the percent of each sales dollar that remains after deducting total unit variable cost. Exhibit 22.10 shows the formula for the contribution margin ratio.

Exhibit 22.10

Contribution Margin Ratio

$$\text{Contribution margin ratio} = \frac{\text{Contribution margin per unit}}{\text{Sales price per unit}}$$

To illustrate the use of contribution margin, let's consider **Rydell,** which sells footballs for $100 per unit and incurs variable costs of $70 per unit sold. Its fixed costs are $24,000 per month with monthly capacity of 1,800 units (footballs). Rydell's contribution margin per unit is $30, which is computed as follows.

Topic Tackler
PLUS
22-2

Selling price per unit	$100
Variable cost per unit	70
Contribution margin per unit	$ 30

Answer—p. 899

Decision Maker

Sales Manager You are evaluating orders from two customers but can accept only one of the orders because of your company's limited capacity. The first order is for 100 units of a product with a contribution margin ratio of 60% and a selling price of $1,000. The second order is for 500 units of a product with a contribution margin ratio of 20% and a selling price of $800. The incremental fixed costs are the same for both orders. Which order do you accept?

Its contribution margin ratio is 30%, computed as $30/$100. This reveals that for each unit sold, Rydell has $30 that contribute to covering fixed cost and profit. If we consider sales in dollars, a contribution margin of 30% implies that for each $1 in sales, Rydell has $0.30 that contributes to fixed cost and profit.

Computing Break-Even Point

P2 Compute break-even point for a single product company.

The **break-even point** is the sales level at which a company neither earns a profit nor incurs a loss. The concept of break-even is applicable to nearly all organizations, activities, and events. One of the most important items of information when launching a project is whether it will break even, that is, whether sales will at least cover total costs. The break-even point can be expressed in either units or dollars of sales.

To illustrate the computation of break-even analysis, let's again look at Rydell, which sells footballs for $100 per unit and incurs $70 of variable costs per unit sold. Its fixed costs are $24,000 per month. Rydell breaks even for the month when it sells 800 footballs (sales volume of $80,000). We compute this break-even point using the formula in Exhibit 22.11. This formula uses the contribution margin per unit, which for Rydell is $30 ($100 − $70). From this we can compute break-even sales volume as $24,000/$30, or 800 units per month.

$$\text{Break-even point in units} = \frac{\text{Fixed costs}}{\text{Contribution margin per unit}}$$

Exhibit 22.11

Formula for Computing Break-Even Sales (in units)[1]

At a price of $100 per unit, monthly sales of 800 units yields sales dollars of $80,000 (called *break-even sales dollars*). This $80,000 break-even sales can be computed directly using the formula in Exhibit 22.12.

$$\text{Break-even point in dollars} = \frac{\text{Fixed costs}}{\text{Contribution margin ratio}}$$

Point: The break-even point is where total expenses equal total sales and the profit is zero.

Exhibit 22.12

Formula for Computing Break-Even Sales (in dollars)[2]

Rydell's break-even point in dollars is computed as $24,000/0.30, or $80,000 of monthly sales. To verify that Rydell's break-even point equals $80,000 (or 800 units), we prepare a simplified income statement in Exhibit 22.13. It shows that the $80,000 revenue from sales of 800 units exactly equals the sum of variable and fixed costs.

Point: Even if a company operates at a level in excess of its break-even point, management may decide to stop operating because it is not earning a reasonable return on investment.

Exhibit 22.13

Contribution Margin Income Statement for Break-Even Sales

RYDELL COMPANY	
Contribution Margin Income Statement (at Break-even)	
For Month Ended January 31, 2008	
Sales (800 units at $100 each)	$80,000
Variable costs (800 units at $70 each)	56,000
Contribution margin	24,000
Fixed costs	24,000
Net income	$ 0

The statement in Exhibit 22.13 is called a *contribution margin income statement*. It differs in format from a conventional income statement in two ways. First, it separately classifies costs and expenses as variable or fixed. Second, it reports contribution margin (Sales − Variable costs). The contribution margin income statement format is used in this chapter's assignment materials because of its usefulness in CVP analysis.

Point: A *contribution margin income statement* groups variable and fixed expenses separately and reports the contribution margin.

Point: A contribution margin income statement is also referred to as a *variable costing income statement.* This differs from the traditional *absorption costing* approach where all product costs are assigned to units sold and to units in ending inventory. Recall that variable costing expenses all fixed product costs. Thus, income for the two approaches differs depending on the level of finished goods inventory; the lower is inventory, the more similar the two approaches.

---

[1] To obtain this formula, we define S = Sales in units; R = Revenue per unit; F = Fixed costs per period; V = Variable cost per unit; $S \times R$ = Dollar sales; $S \times V$ = Total variable cost; and contribution margin per unit = $R - V$. At break-even, net income is zero, so therefore,

$$\text{Sales} = \text{Fixed costs} + \text{Variable costs}$$
$$(S \times R) = F + (S \times V)$$
$$(S \times R) - (S \times V) = F$$
$$S \times (R - V) = F$$
$$S = F/(R - V)$$
$$S = F/\text{Contribution margin per unit}$$

[2] To obtain this formula, recall that: Contribution margin ratio = $(R - V)/R$. Then, at break-even,

$$S = F/(R - V) \text{ [from footnote 1]}$$
$$S \times R = (F \times R)/(R - V)$$
$$S \times R = F \times [R/(R - V)]$$
$$S \times R = F/[(R - V)/R]$$
$$S \times R = F/\text{Contribution margin ratio}$$

Preparing a Cost-Volume-Profit Chart

P3 Graph costs and sales for a single product company.

Exhibit 22.14 is a graph of Rydell's cost-volume-profit relations. This graph is called a **cost-volume-profit (CVP) chart,** or a *break-even chart* or *break-even graph.* The horizontal axis is the number of units produced and sold and the vertical axis is dollars of sales and costs. The lines in the chart depict both sales and costs at different output levels.

Exhibit 22.14

Cost-Volume-Profit Chart

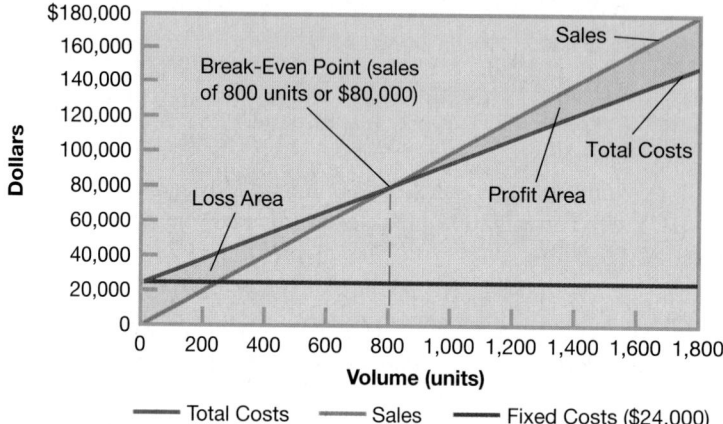

We follow three steps to prepare a CVP chart, which can also be drawn with computer programs that convert numeric data to graphs:

1. Plot fixed costs on the vertical axis ($24,000 for Rydell). Draw a horizontal line at this level to show that fixed costs remain unchanged regardless of output volume (drawing this fixed cost line is not essential to the chart).

2. Draw the total (variable plus fixed) costs line for a relevant range of volume levels. This line starts at the fixed costs level on the vertical axis because total costs equal fixed costs at zero volume. The slope of the total cost line equals the variable cost per unit ($70). To draw the line, compute the total costs for any volume level, and connect this point with the vertical axis intercept ($24,000). Do not draw this line beyond the productive capacity for the planning period (1,800 units for Rydell).

3. Draw the sales line. Start at the origin (zero units and zero dollars of sales) and make the slope of this line equal to the selling price per unit ($100). To sketch the line, compute dollar sales for any volume level and connect this point with the origin. Do not extend this line beyond the productive capacity. Total sales will be at the highest level at maximum capacity.

Example: In Exhibit 22.14, the sales line intersects the total cost line at 800 units. At what point would the two lines intersect if selling price is increased by 20% to $120 per unit? *Answer:* $24,000/ ($120 − $70) = 480 units

The total costs line and the sales line intersect at 800 units in Exhibit 22.14, which is the break-even point, the point where total dollar sales of $80,000 equals the sum of both fixed and variable costs ($80,000).

On either side of the break-even point, the vertical distance between the sales line and the total costs line at any specific volume reflects the profit or loss expected at that point. At volume levels to the left of the break-even point, this vertical distance is the amount of the expected loss because the total costs line is above the total sales line. At volume levels to the right of the break-even point, the vertical distance represents the expected profit because the total sales line is above the total costs line.

Making Assumptions in Cost-Volume-Profit Analysis

C2 Identify assumptions in cost-volume-profit analysis and explain their impact.

Cost-volume-profit analysis assumes that relations can normally be expressed as simple lines similar to those in Exhibits 22.4 and 22.14. Such assumptions allow users to answer several important questions, but the usefulness of the answers depends on the validity of three assumptions: (1) constant selling price per unit, (2) constant variable costs per unit, and (3) constant total fixed costs. These assumptions are not always realistic, but they do not necessarily limit the usefulness of CVP analysis as a way to better understand costs and sales. This section discusses these assumptions and other issues for CVP analysis.

Working with Assumptions The behavior of individual costs and sales often is not perfectly consistent with CVP assumptions. If the expected costs and sales behavior differ from the assumptions, the results of CVP analysis can be limited. Still, we can perform useful analyses in spite of limitations with these assumptions for several reasons.

Summing costs can offset individual deviations. Deviations from assumptions with individual costs are often minor when these costs are summed. That is, individual variable cost items may not be perfectly variable, but when we sum these variable costs, their individual deviations can offset each other. This means the assumption of variable cost behavior can be proper for total variable costs. Similarly, an assumption that total fixed costs are constant can be proper even when individual fixed cost items are not exactly constant.

Point: CVP analysis can be very useful for business decision making even when its assumptions are not strictly met.

CVP is applied to a relevant range of operations. Sales, variable costs, and fixed costs often are reasonably reflected in straight lines on a graph when the assumptions are applied over a relevant range. The **relevant range of operations** is the normal operating range for a business. Except for unusually difficult or prosperous times, management typically plans for operations within a range of volume neither close to zero nor at maximum capacity. The relevant range excludes extremely high and low operating levels that are unlikely to occur. The validity of assuming that a specific cost is fixed or variable is more acceptable when operations are within the relevant range. As shown in Exhibit 22.2, a curvilinear cost can be treated as variable and linear if the relevant range covers volumes where it has a nearly constant slope. If the normal range of activity changes, some costs might need reclassification.

CVP analysis yields estimates. CVP analysis yields approximate answers to questions about costs, volumes, and profits. These answers do not have to be precise because the analysis makes rough estimates about the future. As long as managers understand that CVP analysis gives estimates, it can be a useful tool for starting the planning process. Other qualitative factors also must be considered.

Working with Output Measures CVP analysis usually describes the level of activity in terms of *sales volume,* which can be expressed in terms of either units sold or dollar sales. However, other measures of output exist. For instance, a manufacturer can use the number of units produced as a measure of output. Also, to simplify analysis, we sometimes assume that production level is the same as the sales level. That is, inventory levels do not change. This often is justified by arguing that CVP analysis provides only approximations.

Example: If selling price declines, what happens to the break-even point? *Answer:* It increases.

Quick Check
Answers—p. 899

7. Fixed cost divided by the contribution margin ratio yields the (*a*) break-even point in dollars, (*b*) contribution margin per unit, or (*c*) break-even point in units.

8. A company sells a product for $90 per unit with variable costs of $54 per unit. What is the contribution margin ratio?

9. Refer to Quick Check (8). If fixed costs for the period are $90,000, what is the break-even point in dollars?

10. What three basic assumptions are used in CVP analysis?

Applying Cost-Volume-Profit Analysis

Managers consider a variety of strategies in planning business operations. Cost-volume-profit analysis is useful in helping managers evaluate the likely effects of these strategies, which is the focus of this section.

Computing Income from Sales and Costs

C3   Describe several applications of cost-volume-profit analysis.

An important question managers often need an answer to is "What is the predicted income from a predicted level of sales?" To answer this, we look at four variables in CVP analysis. These variables and their relations to income (pretax) are shown in Exhibit 22.15. We use these relations to compute expected income from predicted sales and cost levels.

Exhibit 22.15

Income Relations in CVP Analysis

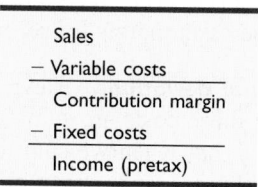

Sales
− Variable costs
Contribution margin
− Fixed costs
Income (pretax)

To illustrate, let's assume that Rydell's management expects to sell 1,500 units in January 2008. What is the amount of income if this sales level is achieved? Following Exhibit 22.15, we compute Rydell's expected income in Exhibit 22.16.

Exhibit 22.16

Computing Expected Pretax Income from Expected Sales

RYDELL COMPANY	
Contribution Margin Income Statement	
For Month Ended January 31, 2008	
Sales (1,500 units at $100 each)	$150,000
Variable costs (1,500 units at $70 each)	105,000
Contribution margin	45,000
Fixed costs	24,000
Income (pretax)	$ 21,000

The $21,000 income is pretax. To find the amount of *after-tax* income from selling 1,500 units, management must apply the proper tax rate. Assume that the tax rate is 25%. Then, we can prepare the after-tax income statement shown in Exhibit 22.17. We can also compute pretax income as after-tax income divided by $(1 - \text{tax rate})$; for Rydell, this is $15,750/(1 − 0.25), or $21,000.

Exhibit 22.17

Computing Expected After-Tax Income from Expected Sales

RYDELL COMPANY	
Contribution Margin Income Statement	
For Month Ended January 31, 2008	
Sales (1,500 units at $100 each)	$150,000
Variable costs (1,500 units at $70 each)	105,000
Contribution margin	45,000
Fixed costs	24,000
Pretax income	21,000
Income taxes (25%)	5,250
Net income (after tax)	$ 15,750

Management then assesses whether this income is an adequate return on assets invested. Management should also consider whether sales and income can be increased by raising or lowering prices. CVP analysis is a good tool for addressing these kinds of "what-if" questions.

Computing Sales for a Target Income

"How many units must I sell to earn $50,000?"

Many companies' annual plans are based on certain income targets (sometimes called *budgets*). Rydell's income target for this year is to increase income by 10% over the prior year. When prior year income is known, Rydell easily computes its target income. CVP analysis helps to determine the sales level needed to achieve the target income. Computing this sales level is important because planning for the year is then based on this level. We use the formula shown in Exhibit 22.18 to compute sales for a target *after-tax* income.

$$\text{Dollar sales at target after-tax income} = \frac{\text{Fixed costs} + \text{Target pretax income}}{\text{Contribution margin ratio}}$$

Exhibit 22.18

Computing Sales (dollars) for a Target After-Tax Income[3]

To illustrate, Rydell has monthly fixed costs of $24,000 and a 30% contribution margin ratio. Assume that it sets a target monthly after-tax income of $9,000 when the tax rate is 25%. This means the pretax income is targeted at $12,000 [$9,000/(1 − 0.25)] with a tax expense of $3,000. Using the formula in Exhibit 22.18, we find that $120,000 of sales is needed to produce a $9,000 after-tax income as shown in Exhibit 22.19.

Example: If variable costs decline, what happens to the break-even point? *Answer:* It decreases.

$$\text{Dollar sales at target after-tax income} = \frac{\$24,000 + \$12,000}{30\%} = \$120,000$$

Exhibit 22.19

Rydell's Dollar Sales for a Target Income

We can alternatively compute *unit sales* instead of dollar sales. To do this, we substitute *contribution margin per unit* for the contribution margin ratio in the denominator. This gives the number of units to sell to reach the target after-tax income. Exhibit 22.20 illustrates this for Rydell. The two computations in Exhibits 22.19 and 22.20 are equivalent because sales of 1,200 units at $100 per unit equals $120,000 of sales.

Point: Break-even is a special case of the formulas in Exhibits 22.18 and 22.20; simply set target pretax income to $0 and the formulas reduce to those in Exhibits 22.11 and 22.12.

$$\text{Unit sales at target after-tax income} = \frac{\text{Fixed costs} + \text{Target pretax income}}{\text{Contribution margin per unit}}$$
$$= \frac{\$24,000 + \$12,000}{\$30} = 1{,}200 \text{ units}$$

Exhibit 22.20

Computing Sales (units) for a Target After-Tax Income

Computing the Margin of Safety

All companies wish to sell more than the break-even number of units. The excess of expected sales over the break-even sales level is called a company's **margin of safety,** the amount that sales can drop before the company incurs a loss. It can be expressed in units, dollars, or even as a percent of the predicted level of sales. To illustrate, if Rydell's expected sales are $100,000, the margin of safety is $20,000 above break-even sales of $80,000. As a percent, the margin of safety is 20% of expected sales as shown in Exhibit 22.21.

Decision Ethics   Answer—p. 899

Supervisor   Your team is conducting a cost-volume-profit analysis for a new product. Different sales projections have different incomes. One member suggests picking numbers yielding favorable income because any estimate is "as good as any other." Another member points to a scatter diagram of 20 months' production on a comparable product and suggests dropping unfavorable data points for cost estimation. What do you do?

---

[3] To obtain this formula, we define S = Sales in units; R = Revenue per unit; F = Fixed costs per period; V = Variable cost per unit; N = Target net income; T = Income taxes; $S \times R$ = Dollar sales; $S \times V$ = Total variable cost; and the Contribution margin ratio = $(R - V)/R$. The after-tax target net income is then defined as:

$$(S \times R) - F - (S \times V) - T = N$$
$$(S \times R) - (S \times V) = F + N + T$$
$$S \times (R - V) = F + N + T$$
$$S = (F + N + T)/(R - V)$$
$$S \times R = [(F + N + T) \times R]/(R - V)$$
$$S \times R = (F + N + T) \times [R/(R - V)]$$
$$S \times R = (F + N + T)/[(R - V)/R]$$
$$S \times R = (F + N + T)/\text{Contribution margin ratio}$$

Exhibit 22.21

Computing Margin of Safety (in percent)

$$\text{Margin of safety (in percent)} = \frac{\text{Expected sales} - \text{Break-even sales}}{\text{Expected sales}}$$

$$= \frac{\$100,000 - \$80,000}{\$100,000} = 20\%$$

Management must assess whether the margin of safety is adequate in light of factors such as sales variability, competition, consumer tastes, and economic conditions.

Using Sensitivity Analysis

Knowing the effects of changing some estimates used in CVP analysis is often useful because they are *estimates,* not actual values. For instance, we might want to know what happens if we reduce a product's selling price to increase sales. Or we might want to know what happens to income if we automate a currently manual process. We can use CVP analysis to predict income if we can describe how these changes affect a company's fixed costs, variable costs, selling price, and volume.

To illustrate, assume that Rydell Company is looking into buying a new machine that would increase monthly fixed costs from $24,000 to $30,000 but decrease variable costs from $70 per unit to $60 per unit. The machine is used to produce output whose selling price will remain unchanged at $100. This results in increases in both the unit contribution margin and the contribution margin ratio. The revised contribution margin per unit is $40 ($100 − $60), and the revised contribution margin ratio is 40% of selling price ($40/$100). Using CVP analysis, Rydell's revised break-even point in dollars would be $75,000 as computed in Exhibit 22.22.

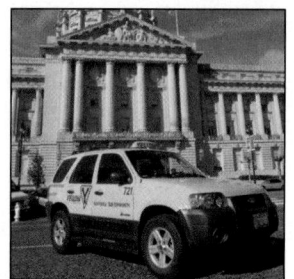
Example: If fixed costs decline, what happens to the break-even point? *Answer:* It decreases.

Exhibit 22.22

Revising Breakeven When Changes Occur

$$\text{Revised break-even point in dollars} = \frac{\text{Revised fixed costs}}{\text{Revised contribution margin ratio}} = \frac{\$30,000}{40\%} = \$75,000$$

Point: Price competition led paging companies to give business to resellers—companies that lease services at a discount and then resell to subscribers. **Paging Network** charged some resellers under $1 per month, less than a third of what is needed to break even. Its CEO now admits the low-price strategy was flawed.

The revised fixed costs and the revised contribution margin ratio can be used to address other issues including computation of (1) expected income for a given sales level and (2) the sales level needed to earn a target income. Another use of sensitivity analysis is to generate different sets of revenue and cost estimates that are *optimistic, pessimistic,* and *most likely.* Different CVP analyses based on these estimates provide different scenarios that management can analyze and use in planning business strategy.

Quick Check   Answers—pp. 899–900

11. A company has fixed costs of $50,000 and a 25% contribution margin ratio. What dollar sales are necessary to achieve an after-tax net income of $120,000 if the tax rate is 20%? (a) $800,000, (b) $680,000, or (c) $600,000.

12. If a company's contribution margin ratio decreases from 50% to 25%, what can be said about unit sales needed to achieve the same target income level?

13. What is a company's margin of safety?

Computing Multiproduct Break-Even Point

To this point, we have looked only at cases where the company sells a single product or service. This was to keep the basic CVP analysis simple. However, many companies sell multiple products or services, and we can modify the CVP analysis for use in these cases. An important assumption in a multiproduct setting is that the sales mix of different products is known and remains constant during the planning period. **Sales mix** is the ratio (proportion) of the sales volumes for the various products. For instance, if a company normally sells 10,000 footballs, 5,000 softballs, and 4,000 basketballs per month, its sales mix can be expressed as 10:5:4 for footballs, softballs, and basketballs.

P4 Compute break-even point for a multiproduct company.

To apply multiproduct CVP analysis, we need to estimate the break-even point by using a **composite unit,** which consists of a specific number of units of each product in proportion to their expected sales mix. Multiproduct CVP analysis treats this composite unit as a single product. To illustrate, let's look at **Hair-Today,** a styling salon that offers three cuts: basic, ultra, and budget in the ratio of 4 basic units to 2 ultra units to 1 budget unit (expressed as 4:2:1). Management wants to estimate its break-even point for next year. Unit selling prices for these three cuts are basic, $10; ultra, $16; and budget, $8. Using the 4:2:1 sales mix, the selling price of a composite unit of the three products is computed as follows.

4 units of basic @ $10 per unit	$40
2 units of ultra @ $16 per unit	32
1 unit of budget @ $8 per unit	8
Selling price of a composite unit	**$80**

Hair-Today's fixed costs are $96,000 per year, and its variable costs of the three products are basic, $6.50; ultra, $9.00; and budget, $4.00. Variable costs for a composite unit of these products follow.

Point: Selling prices and variable costs are usually expressed in per unit amounts. Fixed costs are usually expressed in total amounts.

4 units of basic @ $6.50 per unit	$26
2 units of ultra @ $9.00 per unit	18
1 unit of budget @ $4.00 per unit	4
Variable costs of a composite unit	**$48**

Hair-Today's $32 contribution margin for a composite unit is computed by subtracting the variable costs of a composite unit ($48) from its selling price ($80). We then use the contribution margin to determine Hair-Today's break-even point in composite units in Exhibit 22.23.

$$\text{Break-even point in composite units} = \frac{\text{Fixed costs}}{\text{Contribution margin per composite unit}}$$
$$= \frac{\$96,000}{\$32} = 3,000 \text{ composite units}$$

Exhibit 22.23

Break-Even Point in Composite Units

This computation implies that Hair-Today breaks even when it sells 3,000 composite units. To determine how many units of each product it must sell to break even, we multiply the number of units of each product in the composite by 3,000 as follows.

Point: The break-even point in dollars for Exhibit 22.23 is: $96,000/($32/$80) = $240,000.

Basic:	4 × 3,000	. . . .	12,000 units
Ultra:	2 × 3,000	. . . .	6,000 units
Budget:	1 × 3,000	. . . .	3,000 units

Exhibit 22.24 verifies these results by showing Hair-Today's sales and costs at this break-even point using a contribution margin income statement.

Exhibit 22.24

Multiproduct Break-Even
Income Statement

HAIR-TODAY Forecasted Contribution Margin Income Statement (at Breakeven)				
	Basic	**Ultra**	**Budget**	**Totals**
Sales				
Basic (12,000 @ $10)	$120,000			
Ultra (6,000 @ $16)		$96,000		
Budget (3,000 @ $8)			$24,000	
Total sales				$240,000
Variable costs				
Basic (12,000 @ $6.50)	78,000			
Ultra (6,000 @ $9)		54,000		
Budget (3,000 @ $4)			12,000	
Total variable costs				144,000
Contribution margin	$ 42,000	$42,000	$12,000	96,000
Fixed costs				96,000
Net income				$ 0

Decision Maker

Answer—p. 899

Entrepreneur   A CVP analysis indicates that your start-up, which markets electronic products, will break even with the current sales mix and price levels. You have a target income in mind. What analysis might you perform to assess likelihood for achieving this income?

A CVP analysis using composite units can be used to answer a variety of planning questions. Once a product mix is set, all answers are based on the assumption that the mix remains constant at all relevant sales levels as other factors in the analysis do. We also can vary the sales mix to see what happens under alternative strategies.

Quick Check

Answers—p. 900

14. The sales mix of a company's two products, X and Y, is 2:1. Unit variable costs for both products are $2, and unit sales price is $5 for X and $4 for Y. What is the contribution margin per composite unit? (a) $5, (b) $10, or (c) $8.

15. What additional assumption about sales mix must be made in doing a conventional CVP analysis for a company that produces and sells more than one product?

Decision Analysis   **Degree of Operating Leverage**

A3   Analyze changes in sales using the degree of operating leverage.

CVP analysis is especially useful when management begins the planning process and wishes to predict outcomes of alternative strategies. These strategies can involve changes in selling prices, fixed costs, variable costs, sales volume, and product mix. Managers are interested in seeing the effects of changes in some or all of these factors.

One goal of all managers is to get maximum benefits from their fixed costs. Managers would like to use 100% of their output capacity so that fixed costs are spread over the largest number of units. This would decrease fixed cost per unit and increase income. The extent, or relative size, of fixed costs in the total cost structure is known as **operating leverage.** Companies having a higher proportion of fixed costs in their total cost structure are said to have higher operating leverage. An example of this is a company that chooses to automate its processes instead of using direct labor, increasing its fixed costs and lowering its variable costs. A useful managerial measure to help assess the effect of changes in the level of sales on income is the **degree of operating leverage (DOL)** defined as:

DOL = Total contribution margin (in dollars)/Pretax income

To illustrate, let's return to Rydell Company. At a sales level of 1,200 units, Rydell's total contribution margin is $36,000 (1,200 units × $30 contribution margin per unit). Its pretax income, after subtracting fixed costs of $24,000, is $12,000 ($36,000 − $24,000). Rydell's degree of operating leverage at this sales level is 3.0, computed as contribution margin divided by pretax income ($36,000/$12,000). We then use DOL to measure the effect of changes in the level of sales on pretax income. For instance, suppose Rydell expects sales to increase by 10%. If this increase is within the relevant range of operations, we can expect this 10% increase in sales to result in a 30% increase in pretax income computed as DOL multiplied by the increase in sales (3.0 × 10%). Similar analyses can be done for expected decreases in sales.

Demonstration Problem

Sport Caps Co. manufactures and sells caps for different sporting events. The fixed costs of operating the company are $150,000 per month, and the variable costs for caps are $5 per unit. The caps are sold for $8 per unit. The fixed costs provide a production capacity of up to 100,000 caps per month.

Required

1. Use the formulas in the chapter to compute the following:
   a. Contribution margin per cap.
   b. Break-even point in terms of the number of caps produced and sold.
   c. Amount of net income at 30,000 caps sold per month (ignore taxes).
   d. Amount of net income at 85,000 caps sold per month (ignore taxes).
   e. Number of caps to be produced and sold to provide $45,000 of after-tax income, assuming an income tax rate of 25%.

2. Draw a CVP chart for the company, showing cap output on the horizontal axis. Identify (a) the break-even point and (b) the amount of pretax income when the level of cap production is 70,000. (Omit the fixed cost line.)

3. Use the formulas in the chapter to compute the
   a. Contribution margin ratio.
   b. Break-even point in terms of sales dollars.
   c. Amount of net income at $250,000 of sales per month (ignore taxes).
   d. Amount of net income at $600,000 of sales per month (ignore taxes).
   e. Dollars of sales needed to provide $45,000 of after-tax income, assuming an income tax rate of 25%.

Planning the Solution

- Identify the formulas in the chapter for the required items expressed in units and solve them using the data given in the problem.
- Draw a CVP chart that reflects the facts in the problem. The horizontal axis should plot the volume in units up to 100,000, and the vertical axis should plot the total dollars up to $800,000. Plot the total cost line as upward sloping, starting at the fixed cost level ($150,000) on the vertical axis and increasing until it reaches $650,000 at the maximum volume of 100,000 units. Verify that the break-even point (where the two lines cross) equals the amount you computed in part 1.
- Identify the formulas in the chapter for the required items expressed in dollars and solve them using the data given in the problem.

Solution to Demonstration Problem

1. a. Contribution margin per cap   = Selling price per unit − Variable cost per unit
   = $8 − $5 = $\underline{\underline{\$3}}$

   b. Break-even point in caps $= \dfrac{\text{Fixed costs}}{\text{Contribution margin per cap}} = \dfrac{\$150,000}{\$3} = \underline{\underline{50,000 \text{ caps}}}$

   c. Net income at 30,000 caps sold   = (Units × Contribution margin per unit) − Fixed costs
   = (30,000 × $3) − $150,000 = $\underline{\$(60,000) \text{ loss}}$

   d. Net income at 85,000 caps sold   = (Units × Contribution margin per unit) − Fixed costs
   = (85,000 × $3) − $150,000 = $\underline{\$105,000 \text{ profit}}$

e. Pretax income $= \$45,000/(1 - 0.25) = \$60,000$
Income taxes $= \$60,000 \times 25\% = \$15,000$

$$\text{Units needed for \$45,000 income} = \frac{\text{Fixed costs} + \text{Target pretax income}}{\text{Contribution margin per cap}}$$

$$= \frac{\$150,000 + \$60,000}{\$3} = \underline{70,000 \text{ caps}}$$

2. CVP chart.

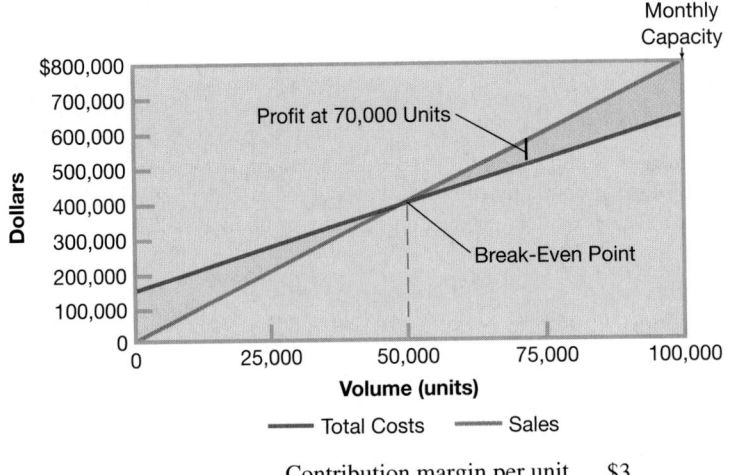

3. a. Contribution margin ratio $= \dfrac{\text{Contribution margin per unit}}{\text{Selling price per unit}} = \dfrac{\$3}{\$8} = \underline{0.375, \text{ or } 37.5\%}$

b. Break-even point in dollars $= \dfrac{\text{Fixed costs}}{\text{Contribution margin ratio}} = \dfrac{\$150,000}{37.5\%} = \underline{\$400,000}$

c. Net income at sales of $250,000 $= (\text{Sales} \times \text{Contribution margin ratio}) - \text{Fixed costs}$
$= (\$250,000 \times 37.5\%) - \$150,000 = \underline{\$(56,250) \text{ loss}}$

d. Net income at sales of $600,000 $= (\text{Sales} \times \text{Contribution margin ratio}) - \text{Fixed costs}$
$= (\$600,000 \times 37.5\%) - \$150,000 = \underline{\$75,000 \text{ income}}$

e. Dollars of sales to yield
$45,000 after-tax income $= \dfrac{\text{Fixed costs} + \text{Target pretax income}}{\text{Contribution margin ratio}}$

$= \dfrac{\$150,000 + \$60,000}{37.5\%} = \underline{\$560,000}$

Summary

C1 Describe different types of cost behavior in relation to production and sales volume. Cost behavior is described in terms of how its amount changes in relation to changes in volume of activity within a relevant range. Fixed costs remain constant to changes in volume. Total variable costs change in direct proportion to volume changes. Mixed costs display the effects of both fixed and variable components. Step-wise costs remain constant over a small volume range, then change by a lump sum and remain constant over another volume range, and so on. Curvilinear costs change in a nonlinear relation to volume changes.

C2 Identify assumptions in cost-volume-profit analysis and explain their impact. Conventional cost-volume-profit analysis is based on assumptions that the product's selling price remains constant and that variable and fixed costs behave in a manner consistent with their variable and fixed classifications.

C3 Describe several applications of cost-volume-profit analysis. Cost-volume-profit analysis can be used to predict what can happen under alternative strategies concerning sales volume, selling prices, variable costs, or fixed costs. Applications include "what-if" analysis, computing sales for a target income, and break-even analysis.

A1 Compare the scatter diagram, high-low, and regression methods of estimating costs. Cost estimates from a scatter diagram are based on a visual fit of the cost line. Estimates from the high-low method are based only on costs corresponding to the lowest and highest sales. The least-squares regression method is a statistical technique and uses all data points.

A2 Compute contribution margin and describe what it reveals about a company's cost structure. Contribution margin per unit is a product's sales price less its total variable costs. Contribution margin ratio is a product's contribution margin per unit divided by its sales price. Unit contribution margin is the amount received from each sale that contributes to fixed costs and income. The contribution margin ratio reveals what portion of each sales dollar is available as contribution to fixed costs and income.

A3 **Analyze changes in sales using the degree of operating leverage.** The extent, or relative size, of fixed costs in a company's total cost structure is known as *operating leverage*. One tool useful in assessing the effect of changes in sales on income is the degree of operating leverage, or DOL. DOL is the ratio of the contribution margin divided by pretax income. This ratio can be used to determine the expected percent change in income given a percent change in sales.

P1 **Determine cost estimates using three different methods.** Three different methods used to estimate costs are the scatter diagram, the high-low method, and least-squares regression. All three methods use past data to estimate costs.

P2 **Compute break-even point for a single product company.** A company's break-even point for a period is the sales volume at

which total revenues equal total costs. To compute a break-even point in terms of sales units, we divide total fixed costs by the contribution margin per unit. To compute a break-even point in terms of sales dollars, divide total fixed costs by the contribution margin ratio.

P3 **Graph costs and sales for a single product company.** The costs and sales for a company can be graphically illustrated using a CVP chart. In this chart, the horizontal axis represents the number of units sold and the vertical axis represents dollars of sales or costs. Straight lines are used to depict both costs and sales on the CVP chart.

P4 **Compute break-even point for a multiproduct company.** CVP analysis can be applied to a multiproduct company by expressing sales volume in terms of composite units. A composite unit consists of a specific number of units of each product in proportion to their expected sales mix. Multiproduct CVP analysis treats this composite unit as a single product.

Guidance Answers to **Decision Maker** and **Decision Ethics**

Sales Manager The contribution margin per unit for the first order is $600 (60% of $1,000); the contribution margin per unit for the second order is $160 (20% of $800). You are likely tempted to accept the first order based on its high contribution margin per unit, but you must compute total contribution margin based on the number of units sold for each order. Total contribution margin is $60,000 ($600 per unit × 100 units) and $80,000 ($160 per unit × 500 units) for the two orders, respectively. The second order provides the largest return in absolute dollars and is the order you would accept. Another factor to consider in your selection is the potential for a long-term relationship with these customers including repeat sales and growth.

Operations Manager Without the availability of past data, none of the three methods described in the chapter can be used to measure cost behavior. Instead, the manager must investigate whether data from similar manufacturers can be accessed. This is likely difficult due to the sensitive nature of such data. In the absence of data, the manager should develop a list of the different production inputs and identify input-output relations. This provides guidance to the manager in measuring cost behavior. After several months, actual cost data will be available for analysis.

Supervisor Your dilemma is whether to go along with the suggestions to "manage" the numbers to make the project look like it will achieve sufficient profits. You should not succumb to these suggestions. Many people will likely be affected negatively if you manage the predicted numbers and the project eventually is unprofitable. Moreover, if it does fail, an investigation would likely reveal that data in the proposal were "fixed" to make it look good. Probably the only benefit from managing the numbers is the short-term payoff of pleasing those who proposed the product. One way to deal with this dilemma is to prepare several analyses showing results under different assumptions and then let senior management make the decision.

Entrepreneur You must first compute the level of sales required to achieve the desired net income. Then you must conduct sensitivity analysis by varying the price, sales mix, and cost estimates. Results from the sensitivity analysis provide information you can use to assess the possibility of reaching the target sales level. For instance, you might have to pursue aggressive marketing strategies to push the high-margin products, or you might have to cut prices to increase sales and profits, or another strategy might emerge.

Guidance Answers to **Quick Checks**

1. *b*

2. A fixed cost remains unchanged in total amount regardless of output levels. However, fixed *cost per unit* declines with increased output.

3. Such a cost is considered variable because the *total* cost changes in proportion to volume changes.

4. *b*

5. The high-low method ignores all costs and sales (activity-base) volume data points except the costs corresponding to the highest and lowest (most extreme) sales (activity-base) volume.

6. *c*

7. *a*

8. ($90 − $54)/$90 = 40%

9. $90,000/40% = $225,000

10. Three basic CVP assumptions are that (1) selling price per unit is constant, (2) variable costs per unit are constant, and (3) total fixed costs are constant.

11. a; Two steps are required for explanation:
(1) Pretax income = $120,000/(1 − 0.20) = $150,000
(2) $\dfrac{\$50,000 + \$150,000}{25\%} = \$800,000$

12. If the contribution margin ratio decreases from 50% to 25%, unit sales would have to double.

13. A company's margin of safety is the excess of the predicted sales level over its break-even sales level.

14. *c*; Selling price of a composite unit:

2 units of X @ $5 per unit	$10
1 unit of Y @ $4 per unit	4
Selling price of a composite unit	$14

Variable costs of a composite unit:

2 units of X @ $2 per unit	$4
1 unit of Y @ $2 per unit	2
Variable costs of a composite unit	$6

Therefore, contribution margin per composite unit is $8.

15. It must be assumed that the sales mix remains unchanged at all sales levels in the relevant range.

Key Terms

Key Terms are available at the book's Website for learning and testing in an online Flashcard Format.

Break-even point (p. 888)
Composite unit (p. 895)
Contribution margin per unit (p. 888)
Contribution margin ratio (p. 888)
Cost-volume-profit (CVP) analysis (p. 882)
Cost-volume-profit (CVP) chart (p. 890)

Curvilinear cost (p. 884)
Degree of operating leverage (DOL) (p. 896)
Estimated line of cost behavior (p. 885)
High-low method (p. 886)
Least-squares regression (p. 887)
Margin of safety (p. 893)

Mixed cost (p. 883)
Operating leverage (p. 896)
Relevant range of operations (p. 891)
Sales mix (p. 895)
Scatter diagram (p. 885)
Step-wise cost (p. 884)

Multiple Choice Quiz   Answers on p. 913   mhhe.com/wildFAP18e

Multiple Choice Quizzes A and B are available at the book's Website.

1. A company's only product sells for $150 per unit. Its variable costs per unit are $100, and its fixed costs total $75,000. What is its contribution margin per unit?
  a. $50
  b. $250
  c. $100
  d. $150
  e. $25

2. Using information from question 1, what is the company's contribution margin ratio?
  a. 66⅔%
  b. 100%
  c. 50%
  d. 0%
  e. 33⅓%

3. Using information from question 1, what is the company's break-even point in units?
  a. 500 units
  b. 750 units

  c. 1,500 units
  d. 3,000 units
  e. 1,000 units

4. A company's forecasted sales are $300,000 and its sales at break-even are $180,000. Its margin of safety in dollars is:
  a. $180,000
  b. $120,000
  c. $480,000
  d. $60,000
  e. $300,000

5. A product sells for $400 per unit and its variable costs per unit are $260. The company's fixed costs are $840,000. If the company desires $70,000 pretax income, what is the required dollar sales?
  a. $2,400,000
  b. $200,000
  c. $2,600,000
  d. $2,275,000
  e. $1,400,000

Discussion Questions

1. How is cost-volume-profit analysis useful?

2. What is a variable cost? Identify two variable costs.

3. When output volume increases, do variable costs per unit increase, decrease, or stay the same within the relevant range of activity? Explain.

4. When output volume increases, do fixed costs per unit increase, decrease, or stay the same within the relevant range of activity? Explain.

5. How do step-wise costs and curvilinear costs differ?

6. Define and describe *contribution margin* per unit.

7. Define and explain the *contribution margin ratio*.

8. Describe the contribution margin ratio in layperson's terms.

9. In performing CVP analysis for a manufacturing company, what simplifying assumption is usually made about the volume of production and the volume of sales?

10. What two arguments tend to justify classifying all costs as either fixed or variable even though individual costs might not behave exactly as classified?

11. How does assuming that operating activity occurs within a relevant range affect cost-volume-profit analysis?

12. List three methods to measure cost behavior.

13. How is a scatter diagram used to identify and measure the behavior of a company's costs?

14. In cost-volume-profit analysis, what is the estimated profit at the break-even point?

15. Assume that a straight line on a CVP chart intersects the vertical axis at the level of fixed costs and has a positive slope that rises with each additional unit of volume by the amount of the variable costs per unit. What does this line represent?

16. Why are fixed costs depicted as a horizontal line on a CVP chart?

17. Each of two similar companies has sales of $20,000 and total costs of $15,000 for a month. Company A's total costs include $10,000 of variable costs and $5,000 of fixed costs. If Company B's total costs include $4,000 of variable costs and $11,000 of fixed costs, which company will enjoy more profit if sales double?

18. _____ of _____ reflects expected sales in excess of the level of break-even sales.

19. Apple produces iPods for sale. Identify some of the variable and fixed product costs associated with that production. [*Hint:* Limit costs to product costs.]

20. Should Best Buy use single product or multiproduct break-even analysis? Explain.

21. Apple is thinking of expanding sales of its most popular MacIntosh model by 65%. Do you expect its variable and fixed costs for this model to stay within the relevant range? Explain.

 Red numbers denote Discussion Questions that involve decision-making.

Determine whether each of the following is best described as a fixed, variable, or mixed cost with respect to product units.

1. Rubber used to manufacture athletic shoes.

2. Maintenance of factory machinery.

3. Packaging expense.

4. Wages of an assembly-line worker paid on the basis of acceptable units produced.

5. Factory supervisor's salary.

6. Taxes on factory building.

7. Depreciation expense of warehouse.

QUICK STUDY

QS 22-1
Cost behavior identification

C1

Listed here are four series of separate costs measured at various volume levels. Examine each series and identify whether it is best described as a fixed, variable, step-wise, or curvilinear cost. (It can help to graph the cost series.)

QS 22-2
Cost behavior identification

C1

Volume (Units)	Series 1	Series 2	Series 3	Series 4
0	$ 0	$450	$ 800	$100
100	800	450	800	105
200	1,600	450	800	120
300	2,400	450	1,600	145
400	3,200	450	1,600	190
500	4,000	450	2,400	250
600	4,800	450	2,400	320

This scatter diagram reflects past maintenance hours and their corresponding maintenance costs.

QS 22-3
Cost behavior estimation

C1   P1

[Scatter diagram: Maintenance Costs (vertical axis, $0 to $12,000) vs. Maintenance Hours (horizontal axis, 0 to 5,000)]

1. Draw an estimated line of cost behavior.

2. Estimate the fixed and variable components of maintenance costs.

QS 22-4
Cost behavior estimation—
high-low method

C1 P1

The following information is available for a company's maintenance cost over the last seven months. Using the high-low method, estimate both the fixed and variable components of its maintenance cost.

Month	Maintenance Hours	Maintenance Cost
June	9	$5,450
July	18	6,900
August	12	5,100
September	15	6,000
October	21	6,900
November	24	8,100
December	6	3,600

QS 22-5
Contribution margin ratio

A2

Compute and interpret the contribution margin ratio using the following data: sales, $5,000; total variable cost, $3,000.

QS 22-6
Contribution margin per unit
and break-even units   A2 P2

SBD Phone Company sells its cordless phone for $90 per unit. Fixed costs total $162,000, and variable costs are $36 per unit. Determine (1) contribution margin per unit and (2) break-even point in units.

QS 22-7
Contribution margin ratio
and break-even dollars   P2

Refer to QS 22-6. Determine (1) contribution margin ratio and (2) break-even point in dollars.

QS 22-8
CVP analysis and target income

C3 P2

Refer to QS 22-6. Assume that SBD Phone Co. is subject to a 30% income tax rate. Compute the units of product that must be sold to earn after-tax income of $140,000.

QS 22-9
CVP assumptions

C2

Which one of the following is an assumption that underlies cost-volume-profit analysis?
1. Selling price per unit must change in proportion to the number of units sold.
2. All costs have approximately the same relevant range.
3. For costs classified as variable, the costs per unit of output must change constantly.
4. For costs classified as fixed, the costs per unit of output must remain constant.

QS 22-10
Operating leverage analysis   A3

A high proportion of Company A's total costs are variable with respect to units sold; a high proportion of Company B's total costs are fixed with respect to units sold. Which company is likely to have a higher degree of operating leverage (DOL)? Explain.

QS 22-11
Multiproduct break-even   P4

Page-Me-Now Company manufactures and sells two products, green beepers and gold beepers, in the ratio of 5:3. Fixed costs are $85,000, and the contribution margin per composite unit is $125. What number of both green and gold beepers is sold at the break-even point?

EXERCISES

Exercise 22-1
Measurement of cost behavior
using a scatter diagram

P1

A company reports the following information about its sales and its cost of sales. Each unit of its product sells for $500. Use these data to prepare a scatter diagram. Draw an estimated line of cost behavior and determine whether the cost appears to be variable, fixed, or mixed.

Period	Sales	Cost of Sales
1	$22,500	$15,150
2	17,250	11,250
3	15,750	10,500
4	11,250	8,250
5	13,500	9,000
6	18,750	14,250

Following are five graphs representing various cost behaviors. (1) Identify whether the cost behavior in each graph is mixed, step-wise, fixed, variable, or curvilinear. (2) Identify the graph (by number) that best illustrates each cost behavior: (a) Factory policy requires one supervisor for every 30 factory workers; (b) real estate taxes on factory; (c) electricity charge that includes the standard monthly charge plus a charge for each kilowatt hour; (d) commissions to salespersons; and (e) costs of hourly paid workers that provide substantial gains in efficiency when a few workers are added but gradually smaller gains in efficiency when more workers are added.

Exercise 22-2
Cost behavior in graphs

C1

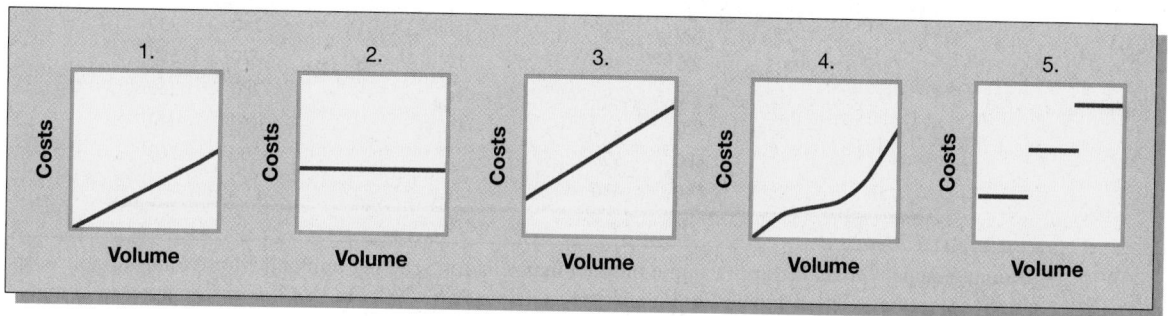

The left column lists several cost classifications. The right column presents short definitions of those costs. In the blank space beside each of the numbers in the right column, write the letter of the cost best described by the definition.

Exercise 22-3
Cost behavior defined

C1

A. Total cost

B. Mixed cost

C. Variable cost

D. Curvilinear cost

E. Step-wise cost

F. Fixed cost

———— **1.** This cost is the combined amount of all the other costs.

———— **2.** This cost remains constant over a limited range of volume; when it reaches the end of its limited range, it changes by a lump sum and remains at that level until it exceeds another limited range.

———— **3.** This cost has a component that remains the same over all volume levels and another component that increases in direct proportion to increases in volume.

———— **4.** This cost increases when volume increases, but the increase is not constant for each unit produced.

———— **5.** This cost remains constant over all volume levels within the productive capacity for the planning period.

———— **6.** This cost increases in direct proportion to increases in volume; its amount is constant for each unit produced.

Following are five series of costs A through E measured at various volume levels. Examine each series and identify which is fixed, variable, mixed, step-wise, or curvilinear.

Exercise 22-4
Cost behavior identification

C1

	Volume (Units)	Series A	Series B	Series C	Series D	Series E
1	0	$ 0	$2,500	$ 0	$1,000	$5,000
2	400	3,600	3,100	6,000	1,000	5,000
3	800	7,200	3,700	6,600	2,000	5,000
4	1,200	10,800	4,300	7,200	2,000	5,000
5	1,600	14,400	4,900	8,200	3,000	5,000
6	2,000	18,000	5,500	9,600	3,000	5,000
7	2,400	21,600	6,100	13,500	4,000	5,000

Bloom Company management predicts that it will incur fixed costs of $160,000 and earn pretax income of $164,000 in the next period. Its expected contribution margin ratio is 25%. Use this information to compute the amounts of (1) total dollar sales and (2) total variable costs.

Exercise 22-5
Predicting sales and variable costs using contribution margin   C3

Exercise 22-6

Scatter diagram and measurement of cost behavior

P1

Use the following information about sales and costs to prepare a scatter diagram. Draw a cost line that reflects the behavior displayed by this cost. Determine whether the cost is variable, step-wise, fixed, mixed, or curvilinear.

Period	Sales	Costs	Period	Sales	Costs
1	$760	$590	9	$580	$390
2	800	560	10	320	240
3	200	230	11	240	230
4	400	400	12	720	550
5	480	390	13	280	260
6	620	550	14	440	410
7	680	590	15	380	260
8	540	430			

Exercise 22-7

Contribution margin, break-even, and CVP chart

P2 P3 A2

Bloom Company manufactures a single product that sells for $180 per unit and whose total variable costs are $135 per unit. The company's annual fixed costs are $562,500. (1) Use this information to compute the company's (a) contribution margin, (b) contribution margin ratio, (c) break-even point in units, and (d) break-even point in dollars of sales. (2) Draw a CVP chart for the company.

Exercise 22-8

Income reporting and break-even analysis C3

Refer to Exercise 22-7. (1) Prepare a contribution margin income statement for Bloom Company showing sales, variable costs, and fixed costs at the break-even point. (2) If Bloom's fixed costs increase by $135,000, what amount of sales (in dollars) is needed to break even? Explain.

Exercise 22-9

Computing sales to achieve target income C3

Bloom Company management (in Exercise 22-7) targets an annual after-tax income of $810,000. The company is subject to a 20% income tax rate. Assume that fixed costs remain at $562,500. Compute the (1) unit sales to earn the target after-tax net income and (2) dollar sales to earn the target after-tax net income.

Exercise 22-10

Forecasted income statement

C3

Bloom Company sales manager (in Exercise 22-7) predicts that annual sales of the company's product will soon reach 40,000 units and its price will increase to $200 per unit. According to the production manager, the variable costs are expected to increase to $140 per unit but fixed costs will remain at $562,500. The income tax rate is 20%. What amounts of pretax and after-tax income can the company expect to earn from these predicted changes? (*Hint:* Prepare a forecasted contribution margin income statement as in Exhibit 22.17.)

Check Forecast income, $1,470,000

Exercise 22-11

Predicting unit and dollar sales

C3

Nombre Company management predicts $390,000 of variable costs, $430,000 of fixed costs, and a pre-tax income of $155,000 in the next period. Management also predicts that the contribution margin per unit will be $9. Use this information to compute the (1) total expected dollar sales for next period and (2) number of units expected to be sold next period.

Exercise 22-12

Computation of variable and fixed costs; CVP chart P3

Cooper Company expects to sell 200,000 units of its product next year, which would generate total sales of $17 million. Management predicts that pretax net income for next year will be $1,250,000 and that the contribution margin per unit will be $25. (1) Use this information to compute next year's total expected (a) variable costs and (b) fixed costs. (2) Prepare a CVP chart from this information.

Exercise 22-13

Operating leverage computed and applied

A3

Company A is a manufacturer with current sales of $3,000,000 and a 60% contribution margin. Its fixed costs equal $1,300,000. Company B is a consulting firm with current service revenues of $3,000,000 and a 25% contribution margin. Its fixed costs equal $250,000. Compute the degree of operating leverage (DOL) for each company. Identify which company benefits more from a 20% increase in sales and explain why.

Exercise 22-14

CVP analysis using composite units P4

Handy Home sells windows and doors in the ratio of 8:2 (windows:doors). The selling price of each window is $200 and of each door is $500. The variable cost of a window is $125 and of a door is $350. Fixed costs are $900,000. Use this information to determine the (1) selling price per composite unit, (2) variable costs per composite unit, (3) break-even point in composite units, and (4) number of units of each product that will be sold at the break-even point.

Check (3) 1,000 units

The following costs result from the production and sale of 1,000 drum sets manufactured by Tom Thompson Company for the year ended December 31, 2008. The drum sets sell for $500 each. The company has a 25% income tax rate.

Variable production costs	
Plastic for casing	$ 17,000
Wages of assembly workers	82,000
Drum stands	26,000
Variable selling costs	
Sales commissions	15,000
Fixed manufacturing costs	
Taxes on factory	5,000
Factory maintenance	10,000
Factory machinery depreciation	40,000
Fixed selling and administrative costs	
Lease of equipment for sales staff	10,000
Accounting staff salaries	35,000
Administrative management salaries	125,000

PROBLEM SET A

Problem 22-1A
Contribution margin income statement and contribution margin ratio

A2

Check (1) Net income, $101,250

Required

1. Prepare a contribution margin income statement for the company.
2. Compute its contribution margin per unit and its contribution margin ratio.

Analysis Component

3. Interpret the contribution margin and contribution margin ratio from part 2.

Xcite Equipment Co. manufactures and markets a number of rope products. Management is considering the future of Product XT, a special rope for hang gliding, that has not been as profitable as planned. Since Product XT is manufactured and marketed independently of the other products, its total costs can be precisely measured. Next year's plans call for a $200 selling price per 100 yards of XT rope. Its fixed costs for the year are expected to be $270,000, up to a maximum capacity of 700,000 yards. Forecasted variable costs are $140 per 100 yards of XT rope.

Problem 22-2A
CVP analysis and charting

P2 P3

mhhe.com/wildFAP18e

Check (1) Break-even sales, 4,500 units or $900,000

Required

1. Estimate Product XT's break-even point in terms of (a) sales units and (b) sales dollars.
2. Prepare a CVP chart for Product XT like that in Exhibit 22.14. Use 700,000 yards as the maximum number of sales units on the horizontal axis of the graph, and $1,400,000 as the maximum dollar amount on the vertical axis.
3. Prepare a contribution margin income statement showing sales, variable costs, and fixed costs for Product XT at the break-even point.

Alden Co.'s monthly sales and cost data for its operating activities of the past year follow. Management wants to use these data to predict future fixed and variable costs.

Problem 22-3A
Scatter diagram and cost behavior estimation

P1

Period	Sales	Total Cost	Period	Sales	Total Cost
1	$320,000	$160,000	7	$340,000	$220,000
2	160,000	100,000	8	280,000	160,000
3	280,000	220,000	9	80,000	64,000
4	200,000	100,000	10	160,000	140,000
5	300,000	230,000	11	100,000	100,000
6	200,000	120,000	12	110,000	80,000

Required

1. Prepare a scatter diagram for these data with sales volume (in $) plotted on the horizontal axis and total cost plotted on the vertical axis.

2. Estimate both the variable costs per sales dollar and the total monthly fixed costs using the high-low method. Draw the total costs line on the scatter diagram in part 1.

Check (3) Variable costs, $0.60 per sales dollar; Fixed costs, $16,000

3. Use the estimated line of cost behavior and results from part 2 to predict future total costs when sales volume is (a) $200,000 and (b) $300,000.

Problem 22-4A

Break-even analysis; income targeting and forecasting

C3 P2

Astro Co. sold 20,000 units of its only product and incurred a $50,000 loss (ignoring taxes) for the current year as shown below. During a planning session for year 2009's activities, the production manager notes that variable costs can be reduced 50% by installing a machine that automates several operations. To obtain these savings, the company must increase its annual fixed costs by $200,000. The maximum output capacity of the company is 40,000 units per year.

ASTRO COMPANY	
Contribution Margin Income Statement	
For Year Ended December 31, 2008	
Sales	$1,000,000
Variable costs	800,000
Contribution margin	200,000
Fixed costs	250,000
Net loss	$ (50,000)

Required

1. Compute the break-even point in dollar sales for year 2008.

2. Compute the predicted break-even point in dollar sales for year 2009 assuming the machine is installed and there is no change in unit sales price.

Check (3) Net income, $150,000

3. Prepare a forecasted contribution margin income statement for 2009 that shows the expected results with the machine installed. Assume that the unit sales price and the number of units sold will not change and no income taxes.

(4) Required sales, $1,083,333 or 21,667 units

4. Compute the sales level required in both dollars and units to earn $140,000 of after-tax income in 2009 with the machine installed and no change in unit sales price. Assume that the income tax rate is 30%. (*Hint:* Use procedures in Exhibits 22.18 and 22.20.)

(5) Net income, $140,000 (rounded)

5. Prepare a forecasted contribution margin income statement that shows the results at the sales level computed in part 4. Assume an income tax rate of 30%.

Problem 22-5A

Break-even analysis, different cost structures, and income calculations

C3

Vanna Co. produces and sells two products, T and O. It manufactures these products in separate factories and markets them through different channels. They have no shared costs. This year, Vanna sold 50,000 units of each product. Sales and costs for each product follow.

	Product T	Product O
Sales	$2,000,000	$2,000,000
Variable costs	1,600,000	250,000
Contribution margin	400,000	1,750,000
Fixed costs	125,000	1,475,000
Income before taxes	275,000	275,000
Income taxes (32% rate)	88,000	88,000
Net income	$ 187,000	$ 187,000

Required

1. Compute the break-even point in dollar sales for each product.

2. Assume that the company expects sales of each product to decline to 30,000 units next year with no change in unit sales price. Prepare forecasted financial results for next year following the format of the contribution margin income statement as shown above with columns for each of the two products (assume a 32% tax rate). Also, assume that any loss before taxes yields a 32% tax savings.

Check (2) After-tax income: T, $78,200; O, $(289,000)

3. Assume that the company expects sales of each product to increase to 60,000 units next year with no change in unit sales price. Prepare forecasted financial results for next year following the format of the contribution margin income statement as shown above with columns for each of the two products (assume a 32% tax rate).

(3) After-tax income: T, $241,400; O, $425,000

Analysis Component

4. If sales greatly decrease, which product would experience a greater loss? Explain.

5. Describe some factors that might have created the different cost structures for these two products.

This year Bertrand Company sold 40,000 units of its only product for $25 per unit. Manufacturing and selling the product required $200,000 of fixed manufacturing costs and $325,000 of fixed selling and administrative costs. Its per unit variable costs follow.

Problem 22-6A
Analysis of price, cost, and volume changes for contribution margin and net income

C3 P2

mhhe.com/wildFAP18e

Material	$8.00
Direct labor (paid on the basis of completed units)	5.00
Variable overhead costs	1.00
Variable selling and administrative costs	0.50

Next year the company will use new material, which will reduce material costs by 50% and direct labor costs by 60% and will not affect product quality or marketability. Management is considering an increase in the unit sales price to reduce the number of units sold because the factory's output is nearing its annual output capacity of 45,000 units. Two plans are being considered. Under plan 1, the company will keep the price at the current level and sell the same volume as last year. This plan will increase income because of the reduced costs from using the new material. Under plan 2, the company will increase price by 20%. This plan will decrease unit sales volume by 10%. Under both plans 1 and 2, the total fixed costs and the variable costs per unit for overhead and for selling and administrative costs will remain the same.

Required

1. Compute the break-even point in dollar sales for both (a) plan 1 and (b) plan 2.

Check (1) Break-even: Plan 1, $750,000; Plan 2, $700,000

2. Prepare a forecasted contribution margin income statement with two columns showing the expected results of plan 1 and plan 2. The statements should report sales, total variable costs, contribution margin, total fixed costs, income before taxes, income taxes (30% rate), and net income.

(2) Net income: Plan 1, $122,500; Plan 2, $199,500

Patriot Co. manufactures and sells three products: red, white, and blue. Their unit sales prices are red, $20; white, $35; and blue, $65. The per unit variable costs to manufacture and sell these products are red, $12; white, $22; and blue, $50. Their sales mix is reflected in a ratio of 5:4:2 (red:white:blue). Annual fixed costs shared by all three products are $250,000. One type of raw material has been used to manufacture all three products. The company has developed a new material of equal quality for less cost. The new material would reduce variable costs per unit as follows: red, by $6; white, by $12; and blue, by $10. However, the new material requires new equipment, which will increase annual fixed costs by $50,000. (Round answers to whole composite unit.)

Problem 22-7A
Break-even analysis with composite units

P4 C3

Required

1. If the company continues to use the old material, determine its break-even point in both sales units and sales dollars of each individual product.

Check (1) Old plan break-even, 2,050 composite units

2. If the company uses the new material, determine its new break-even point in both sales units and sales dollars of each individual product.

(2) New plan break-even, 1,364 composite units

Analysis Component

3. What insight does this analysis offer management for long-term planning?

PROBLEM SET B

Problem 22-1B
Contribution margin income statement and contribution margin ratio

A2

The following costs result from the production and sale of 12,000 CD sets manufactured by Gilmore Company for the year ended December 31, 2008. The CD sets sell for $18 each. The company has a 25% income tax rate.

Variable manufacturing costs	
Plastic for CD sets	$ 1,500
Wages of assembly workers	30,000
Labeling	3,000
Variable selling costs	
Sales commissions	6,000
Fixed manufacturing costs	
Rent on factory	6,750
Factory cleaning service	4,520
Factory machinery depreciation	20,000
Fixed selling and administrative costs	
Lease of office equipment	1,050
Systems staff salaries	15,000
Administrative management salaries	120,000

Required

Check (1) Net income, $6,135

1. Prepare a contribution margin income statement for the company.
2. Compute its contribution margin per unit and its contribution margin ratio.

Analysis Component

3. Interpret the contribution margin and contribution margin ratio from part 2.

Problem 22-2B
CVP analysis and charting

P2 P3

Hip-Hop Co. manufactures and markets several products. Management is considering the future of one product, electronic keyboards, that has not been as profitable as planned. Since this product is manufactured and marketed independently of the other products, its total costs can be precisely measured. Next year's plans call for a $350 selling price per unit. The fixed costs for the year are expected to be $42,000, up to a maximum capacity of 700 units. Forecasted variable costs are $210 per unit.

Required

Check (1) Break-even sales, 300 units or $105,000

1. Estimate the keyboards' break-even point in terms of (a) sales units and (b) sales dollars.
2. Prepare a CVP chart for keyboards like that in Exhibit 22.14. Use 700 keyboards as the maximum number of sales units on the horizontal axis of the graph, and $250,000 as the maximum dollar amount on the vertical axis.
3. Prepare a contribution margin income statement showing sales, variable costs, and fixed costs for keyboards at the break-even point.

Problem 22-3B
Scatter diagram and cost behavior estimation

P1

Kyo Co.'s monthly sales and costs data for its operating activities of the past year follow. Management wants to use these data to predict future fixed and variable costs.

Period	Sales	Total Cost	Period	Sales	Total Cost
1	$195	$ 97	7	$145	$ 93
2	125	87	8	185	105
3	105	73	9	135	85
4	155	89	10	85	58
5	95	81	11	175	95
6	215	110	12	115	79

Required

1. Prepare a scatter diagram for these data with sales volume (in $) plotted on the horizontal axis and total costs plotted on the vertical axis.

2. Estimate both the variable costs per sales dollar and the total monthly fixed costs using the high-low method. Draw the total costs line on the scatter diagram in part 1.

3. Use the estimated line of cost behavior and results from part 2 to predict future total costs when sales volume is (a) $100 and (b) $170.

Check (3) Variable costs, $0.40 per sales dollar; Fixed costs, $24

Rivera Co. sold 20,000 units of its only product and incurred a $50,000 loss (ignoring taxes) for the current year as shown below. During a planning session for year 2009's activities, the production manager notes that variable costs can be reduced 50% by installing a machine that automates several operations. To obtain these savings, the company must increase its annual fixed costs by $150,000. The maximum output capacity of the company is 40,000 units per year.

Problem 22-4B
Break-even analysis; income targeting and forecasting

C3   P2

RIVERA COMPANY	
Contribution Margin Income Statement	
For Year Ended December 31, 2008	
Sales	$750,000
Variable costs	600,000
Contribution margin	150,000
Fixed costs	200,000
Net loss	$ (50,000)

Required

1. Compute the break-even point in dollar sales for year 2008.

2. Compute the predicted break-even point in dollar sales for year 2009 assuming the machine is installed and no change in unit sales price. (Round the change in variable costs to a whole number.)

3. Prepare a forecasted contribution margin income statement for 2009 that shows the expected results with the machine installed. Assume that the unit sales price and the number of units sold will not change and no income taxes.

Check (3) Net income, $100,000

4. Compute the sales level required in both dollars and units to earn $140,000 of after-tax income in 2009 with the machine installed and no change in unit sales price. Assume that the income tax rate is 30%. (*Hint:* Use procedures in Exhibits 22.18 and 22.20.)

(4) Required sales, $916,667 or 24,445 units

5. Prepare a forecasted contribution margin income statement that shows the results at the sales level computed in part 4. Assume an income tax rate of 30%.

(5) Net income, $140,000 (rounded)

Mingei Co. produces and sells two products, BB and TT. It manufactures these products in separate factories and markets them through different channels. They have no shared costs. This year, Mingei Co. sold 50,000 units of each product. Sales and costs for each product follow.

Problem 22-5B
Break-even analysis, different cost structures, and income calculations

C3

	Product BB	Product TT
Sales	$800,000	$800,000
Variable costs	560,000	100,000
Contribution margin	240,000	700,000
Fixed costs	100,000	560,000
Income before taxes	140,000	140,000
Income taxes (32% rate)	44,800	44,800
Net income	$ 95,200	$ 95,200

Required

1. Compute the break-even point in dollar sales for each product.

2. Assume that the company expects sales of each product to decline to 33,000 units next year with no change in unit sales price. Prepare forecasted financial results for next year following the format of the contribution margin income statement as shown above with columns for each of the two products (assume a 32% tax rate, and that any loss before taxes yields a 32% tax savings).

Check (2) After-tax income: BB, $39,712; TT, $(66,640)

3. Assume that the company expects sales of each product to increase to 64,000 units next year with no change in unit sales price. Prepare forecasted financial results for next year following the format of the contribution margin income statement as shown above with columns for each of the two products (assume a 32% tax rate).

(3) After-tax income: BB, $140,896; TT, $228,480

Analysis Component

4. If sales greatly increase, which product would experience a greater increase in profit? Explain.

5. Describe some factors that might have created the different cost structures for these two products.

Problem 22-6B

Analysis of price, cost, and volume changes for contribution margin and net income

C3   P2

This year Best Company earned a disappointing 5.6% after-tax return on sales from marketing 100,000 units of its only product. The company buys its product in bulk and repackages it for resale at the price of $20 per unit. Best incurred the following costs this year.

Total variable unit costs	$800,000
Total variable packaging costs	$100,000
Fixed costs	$950,000
Income tax rate	25%

The marketing manager claims that next year's results will be the same as this year's unless some changes are made. The manager predicts the company can increase the number of units sold by 80% if it reduces the selling price by 20% and upgrades the packaging. This change would increase variable packaging costs by 20%. Increased sales would allow the company to take advantage of a 25% quantity purchase discount on the cost of the bulk product. Neither the packaging change nor the volume discount would affect fixed costs, which provide an annual output capacity of 200,000 units.

Required

Check (1) Break-even for new strategy, $1,727,273

  (2) Net income: Existing strategy, $112,500; New strategy, $475,500

1. Compute the break-even point in dollar sales under the (a) existing business strategy and (b) new strategy that alters both unit sales price and variable costs.

2. Prepare a forecasted contribution margin income statement with two columns showing the expected results of (a) the existing strategy and (b) changing to the new strategy. The statements should report sales, total variable costs (unit and packaging), contribution margin, fixed costs, income before taxes, income taxes, and net income. Also determine the after-tax return on sales for these two strategies.

Problem 22-7B

Break-even analysis with composite units

P4   C3

Milano Co. manufactures and sells three products: product 1, product 2, and product 3. Their unit sales prices are product 1, $40; product 2, $30; and product 3, $20. The per unit variable costs to manufacture and sell these products are product 1, $30; product 2, $15; and product 3, $8. Their sales mix is reflected in a ratio of 6:4:2. Annual fixed costs shared by all three products are $270,000. One type of raw material has been used to manufacture products 1 and 2. The company has developed a new material of equal quality for less cost. The new material would reduce variable costs per unit as follows: product 1 by $10, and product 2, by $5. However, the new material requires new equipment, which will increase annual fixed costs by $50,000.

Required

Check (1) Old plan break-even, 1,875 composite units

  (2) New plan break-even, 1,429 composite units

1. If the company continues to use the old material, determine its break-even point in both sales units and sales dollars of each individual product.

2. If the company uses the new material, determine its new break-even point in both sales units and sales dollars of each individual product.

Analysis Component

3. What insight does this analysis offer management for long-term planning?

PROBLEM SET C

 Problem Set C is available at the book's Website to further reinforce and assess your learning.

SERIAL PROBLEM

Success Systems

(This serial problem began in Chapter 1 and continues through most of the book. If previous chapter segments were not completed, the serial problem can begin at this point. It is helpful, but not necessary, for you to use the Working Papers that accompany the book.)

SP 22 Success Systems sells upscale modular desk units and office chairs in the ratio of 2:1 (desk unit: chair). The selling price is $1,250 per desk unit and $500 per chair. The variable cost is $750 per desk unit and $250 per chair. Fixed costs are $60,000.

Required

1. Compute the selling price per composite unit.

2. Compute the variable costs per composite unit.

3. Compute the break-even point in composite units.

4. Compute the number of units of each product that would be sold at the break-even point.

Check   (3) 48 composite units

BEYOND THE NUMBERS

BTN 22-1   **Best Buy** offers services to customers that help them use products they purchase from Best Buy. One of these services is its Geek Squad, which is Best Buy's 24-Hour Computer Support Task Force. As you complete the following requirements, assume that the Geek Squad uses many of Best Buy's existing resources such as its purchasing department and its buildings and equipment.

REPORTING IN ACTION

C1

Required

1. Identify several of the variable, mixed, and fixed costs that the Geek Squad is likely to incur in carrying out its services.

2. Assume that Geek Squad revenues are expected to grow by 25% in the next year. How do you expect the costs identified in part 1 to change, if at all?

3. How is your answer to part 2 different from many of the examples discussed in the chapter? (*Hint:* Consider how the contribution margin ratio changes as volume—sales or customers served—increases.)

BTN 22-2   Both **Best Buy** and **Circuit City** sell numerous consumer products, and each of these companies has a different product mix.

COMPARATIVE ANALYSIS

P2 C3 A2

Required

1. Assume the following data are available for both companies. Compute each company's break-even point in unit sales. (Each company sells many products at many different selling prices, and each has its own variable costs. This assignment assumes an *average* selling price per unit and an *average* cost per item.)

	Best Buy	Circuit City
Average selling price per item sold	$45	$20
Average variable cost per item sold	$34	$15
Total fixed costs	$5,053 million	$2,457 million

2. If unit sales were to decline, which company would experience the larger decline in operating profit? Explain.

BTN 22-3   Labor costs of an auto repair mechanic are seldom based on actual hours worked. Instead, the amount paid a mechanic is based on an industry average of time estimated to complete a repair job. The repair shop bills the customer for the industry average amount of time at the repair center's billable cost per hour. This means a customer can pay, for example, $120 for two hours of work on a car when the actual time worked was only one hour. Many experienced mechanics can complete repair jobs well under the industry average. The average data are compiled by engineering studies and surveys conducted in the auto repair business. Assume that you are asked to complete such a survey for a repair center. The survey calls for objective input, and many questions require detailed cost data and analysis. The mechanics and owners know you have the survey and encourage you to complete it in a way that increases the average billable hours for repair work.

ETHICS CHALLENGE

C1

Required

Write a one-page memorandum to the mechanics and owners that describes the direct labor analysis you will undertake in completing this survey.

COMMUNICATING IN PRACTICE
C2

BTN 22-4   Several important assumptions underlie CVP analysis. Assumptions often help simplify and focus our analysis of sales and costs. A common application of CVP analysis is as a tool to forecast sales, costs, and income.

Required

Assume that you are actively searching for a job. Prepare a one-half page report identifying (1) three assumptions relating to your expected revenue (salary) and (2) three assumptions relating to your expected costs for the first year of your new job. Be prepared to discuss your assumptions in class.

TAKING IT TO THE NET
C1   C3

BTN 22-5   Access and review the entrepreneurial information at **Business Owner's Toolkit** [Toolkit.cch.com]. Access and review its *New Business Cash Needs Estimate* under the **Business Tools** menu bar or similar worksheets related to controls of cash and costs.

Required

Write a one-half page report that describes the information and resources available at the Business Owner's Toolkit to help the owner of a start-up business to control and monitor its costs.

TEAMWORK IN ACTION
C2

BTN 22-6   A local movie theater owner explains to you that ticket sales on weekends and evenings are strong, but attendance during the weekdays, Monday through Thursday, is poor. The owner proposes to offer a contract to the local grade school to show educational materials at the theater for a set charge per student during school hours. The owner asks your help to prepare a CVP analysis listing the cost and sales projections for the proposal. The owner must propose to the school's administration a charge per child. At a minimum, the charge per child needs to be sufficient for the theater to break even.

Required

Your team is to prepare two separate lists of questions that enable you to complete a reliable CVP analysis of this situation. One list is to be answered by the school's administration, the other by the owner of the movie theater.

BusinessWeek ACTIVITY
C3

BTN 22-7   Read the article, "McNealy: Why Sun Is Back," in the December 2, 2005, issue of *BusinessWeek*. (The book's Website provides free access to the article.)

Required

1. What has been **Sun Microsystems'** business model over the past years?
2. How has their business model changed recently?
3. How can a company profit by giving its product away?

ENTREPRENEURIAL DECISION
C1

BTN 22-8   Xiaoning Wang is a diligent businesswoman. She continually searches for new product additions to further increase the profitability of **ChinaSprout**. She discusses broadly a method she applies for deciding what products to add and not add to her product lines.

Required

1. What information should Wang search for to help her decide whether to add or not add new products to her existing product lines?
2. What managerial tools are available to her to help make the decisions in part 1?

HITTING THE ROAD
P4

BTN 22-9   Multiproduct break-even analysis is often viewed differently when actually applied in practice. You are to visit a local fast-food restaurant and count the number of items on the menu. To apply multiproduct break-even analysis to the restaurant, similar menu items must often be fit into groups. A reasonable approach is to classify menu items into approximately five groups, for example, drink group. We then estimate average selling price and average variable cost to compute average contribution margin. (*Hint:* The contribution margin ratio on drinks is about 90%.)

Required

1. Prepare a one-year multiproduct break-even analysis for the restaurant you visit. Begin by establishing groups. Next, estimate each group's volume and contribution margin. These estimates are necessary to compute each group's contribution margin. Assume that annual fixed costs in total are $500,000 per year. (*Hint:* You must develop your own estimates on volume and contribution margin for each group to obtain the break-even point and sales.)

2. Prepare a one-page report on the results of your analysis. Comment on the volume of sales necessary to break even at a fast-food restaurant.

BTN 22-10   Access and review **Dixons'** Website (Dixons-Group.com) to answer the following questions.

GLOBAL DECISION

C3

Dixons

1. Do you believe that Dixons' managers use single product CVP analysis or multiproduct break-even point analysis? Explain.

2. How does the addition of a new product line affect Dixons' CVP analysis?

3. How does the addition of a new store affect Dixons' CVP analysis?

ANSWERS TO MULTIPLE CHOICE QUIZ

1. a; $150 − $100 = $50
2. e; ($150 − $100)/$150 = 33⅓%
3. c; $75,000/$50 CM per unit = 1,500 units
4. b; $300,000 − $180,000 = $120,000
5. c; Contribution margin ratio = ($400 − $260)/$400 = 0.35
   Targeted sales = ($840,000 + $70,000)/0.35 = $2,600,000

23

Master Budgets and Planning

A Look Back

Chapter 22 looked at cost behavior and its use by managers in performing cost-volume-profit analysis. It also illustrated the application of cost-volume-profit analysis.

A Look at This Chapter

This chapter explains the importance of budgeting and describes the master budget and its preparation. It also discusses the value of the master budget to the planning of future business activities.

A Look Ahead

Chapter 24 focuses on flexible budgets, standard costs, and variance reporting. It explains the usefulness of these procedures and reports for business decisions.

Learning Objectives

CAP

Conceptual

C1 Describe the importance and benefits of budgeting. (p. 916)

C2 Explain the process of budget administration. (p. 918)

C3 Describe a master budget and the process of preparing it. (p. 920)

Analytical

A1 Analyze expense planning using activity-based budgeting. (p. 929)

Procedural

P1 Prepare each component of a master budget and link each to the budgeting process. (p. 922)

P2 Link both operating and capital expenditures budgets to budgeted financial statements. (p. 926)

P3 *Appendix 23A*—Prepare production and manufacturing budgets. (p. 935)

"We were making a unique new product . . . into a category that had a lot of potential for growth"
—Stephen Sullivan (on right; on left is Brian Cousins)

Reaching for the Clouds

JACKSON, WY—It all started when Stephen Sullivan got a pair of pants as a gift. The pants were made of Schoeller® fabric, which is durable, lightweight, and comfortable. "I wore those pants for three years," Stephen recalls. "They reminded me of my Mom's old stretch ski pants and how much she wore them and loved them." Stephen and his friend, Brian Cousins, were working for an outdoor retailer when they devised a plan to develop and market high-performance, multisport mountain apparel called Cloudveil (**Cloudveil.com**)—Cloudveil Dome is a peak in the Tetons.

Stephen quit his day job to research outdoor apparel and learn everything about marketing and operating their new business. While Stephen bartended during evenings to make ends meet, Brian went to work for an apparel manufacturer to learn the production and financial side of the business. "One of the smartest things we did early on was realize we didn't know everything," explains Stephen. "Then we set out to find others who did."

With their plans and dreams came budgets. In the early stages, however, the pair admits their budgeting process and planning were not ideal. "The thinking was, 'Let's be a clothing company and go buy some sewing machines.' [We now know] that style of thinking is archaic," says Stephen. "I can't even sew!" confesses Brian.

The friends now attend more seriously to master budgets and the budgeting process. They say budgets help formalize business expectations and objectives. They also help direct employees and put everyone on the same page. "We did not want the investment in labor or overhead," explains Stephen. Consequently, the pair budgeted for that type of operation and planned accordingly. They also communicated their expectations and plans to employees. To make such a system successful requires trust, an understanding of the process, and knowledge of how decisions impact the budgeted financial statements, says Stephen.

As Cloudveil continues to expand, master budgets and planning remain integral to decisions. Stephen explains that the company must "continue to innovate through design that benefits the discerning outdoor consumer . . . while nurturing and servicing the growing demand." Cloudveil's budgeting and planning process led them to obtain additional funds to expand. "That is so huge for our business," says Stephen. "Bringing this money into the business has really freed up our minds to do what we do best." These friends believe in their tag line: *Live Close to Your Dreams!*

[Sources: *Cloudveil Website*, May 2006; *Entrepreneur*, November 2002; *Outdoor Retailer Magazine*, 2001; *Denver Post*, 2005; *Northwestern Magazine*, Fall 2004]

Management seeks to turn its strategies into action plans. These action plans include financial details that are compiled in a master budget. The budgeting process serves several purposes, including motivating employees and communicating with them. The budget process also helps coordinate a company's activities toward common goals and is useful in evaluating results and management performance. This chapter explains how to prepare a master budget and use it as a formal plan of a company's future activities. The ability to prepare this type of plan is of enormous help in starting and operating a company. Such planning gives managers a glimpse into the future, and it can help translate ideas into actions.

Master Budgets and Planning

Budget Process
- Strategic budgeting
- Benchmarking budgets
- Budgeting and human behavior
- Budgeting as a management tool
- Budgeting communication

Budget Administration
- Budget committee
- Budget reporting
- Budget timing

Master Budget
- Master budget components
- Operating budgets
- Capital expenditures budget
- Financial budgets

Budget Process

Strategic Budgeting

Most companies prepare long-term strategic plans spanning 5 to 10 years. They then fine-tune them in preparing medium-term and short-term plans. Strategic plans usually set a company's long-term direction. They provide a road map for the future about potential opportunities such as new products, markets, and investments. The strategic plan can be inexact, given its long-term focus. Medium- and short-term plans are more operational and translate strategic plans into actions. These action plans are fairly concrete and consist of defined objectives and goals.

C1 Describe the importance and benefits of budgeting.

Short-term financial plans are called *budgets* and typically cover a one-year period. A **budget** is a formal statement of a company's future plans. It is usually expressed in monetary terms because the economic or financial aspects of the business are the primary factors driving management's decisions. All managers should be involved in **budgeting,** the process of planning future business actions and expressing them as formal plans. Managers who plan carefully and formalize plans in a budgeting process increase the likelihood of both personal and company success. (Although most firms prepare annual budgets, it is not unusual for organizations to prepare three-year and five-year budgets that are revised at least annually.)

The relevant focus of a budgetary analysis is the future. Management must focus on future transactions and events and the opportunities available. A focus on the future is important because the pressures of daily operating problems often divert management's attention and take precedence over planning. A good budgeting system counteracts this tendency by formalizing the planning process and demanding relevant input. Budgeting makes planning an explicit management responsibility.

Companies Performing Annual Budgeting

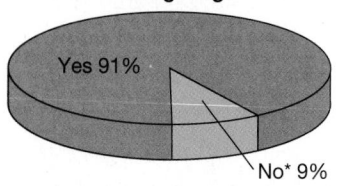

Yes 91%

No* 9%

*Most of the 9% have eliminated annual budgeting in favor of rolling or continual budgeting.

Benchmarking Budgets

The control function requires management to evaluate (benchmark) business operations against some norm. Evaluation involves comparing actual results against one of two usual alternatives: (1) past performance or (2) expected performance.

An evaluation assists management in identifying problems and taking corrective actions if necessary. Evaluation using expected, or budgeted, performance is potentially superior to using past performance to decide whether actual results trigger a need for corrective actions. This is so because past performance fails to consider several changes that can affect current and future activities. Changes in economic conditions, shifts in competitive advantages within the industry, new product developments, increased or decreased advertising, and other factors reduce the usefulness of comparisons with past results. In hi-tech industries, for instance, increasing competition, technological advances, and other innovations often reduce the usefulness of performance comparisons across years.

Budgeted performance is computed after careful analysis and research that attempts to anticipate and adjust for changes in important company, industry, and economic factors. Therefore, budgets usually provide management an effective control and monitoring system.

Point: Managers can evaluate performance by preparing reports that compare actual results to budgeted plans.

Budgeting and Human Behavior

Budgeting provides standards for evaluating performance and can affect the attitudes of employees evaluated by them. It can be used to create a positive effect on employees' attitudes, but it can also create negative effects if not properly applied. Budgeted levels of performance, for instance, must be realistic to avoid discouraging employees. Personnel who will be evaluated should be consulted and involved in preparing the budget to increase their commitment to meeting it. Performance evaluations must allow the affected employees to explain the reasons for apparent performance deficiencies.

The budgeting process has three important guidelines: (1) Employees affected by a budget should be consulted when it is prepared (*participatory budgeting*), (2) goals reflected in a budget should be attainable, and (3) evaluations should be made carefully with opportunities to explain any failures. Budgeting can be a positive motivating force when these guidelines are followed. Budgeted performance levels can provide goals for employees to attain or even exceed as they carry out their responsibilities. This is especially important in organizations that consider the annual budget a "sacred" document.

Point: The practice of involving employees in the budgeting process is known as *participatory budgeting*.

Decision Insight

Budgets Exposed When companies go public and trade their securities on an organized exchange, management usually develops specific future plans and budgets. For this purpose, companies often develop detailed six- to twelve-month budgets and less-detailed budgets spanning 2 to 5 years.

Budgeting as a Management Tool

An important management objective in large companies is to ensure that activities of all departments contribute to meeting the company's overall goals. This requires coordination. Budgeting provides a way to achieve this coordination.

We describe later in this chapter that a company's budget, or operating plan, is based on its objectives. This operating plan starts with the sales budget, which drives all other budgets including production, materials, labor, and overhead. The budgeting process coordinates the activities of these various departments to meet the company's overall goals.

Budgeting Communication

Managers of small companies can adequately explain business plans directly to employees through conversations and other informal communications. However, conversations can create uncertainty and confusion if not supported by clear documentation of the plans. A written budget is preferred and can inform employees in all types of organizations about management's plans. The budget can also communicate management's specific action plans for the employees in the budget period.

Decision Ethics

Answer—p. 937

Budget Staffer Your company's earnings for the current period will be far below the budgeted amount reported in the press. One of your superiors, who is aware of the upcoming earnings shortfall, has accepted a management position with a competitor. This superior is selling her shares of the company. What are your ethical concerns, if any?

Budget Administration

Budget Committee

C2   Explain the process of
budget administration.

The task of preparing a budget should not be the sole responsibility of any one department. Similarly, the budget should not be simply handed down as top management's final word. Instead, budget figures and budget estimates developed through a *bottom-up* process usu-

ally are more useful. This includes, for instance, involving the sales department in preparing sales estimates. Likewise, the production department should have initial responsibility for preparing its own expense budget. Without active employee involvement in preparing budget figures, there is a risk these employees will feel that the numbers fail to reflect their special problems and needs.

Most budgets should be developed by a bottom-up process, but the budgeting system requires central guidance. This guidance is supplied by a budget committee of department heads and other

Point: In a large company, developing a budget through a bottom-up process can involve hundreds of employees and take several weeks to finalize.

executives responsible for seeing that budgeted amounts are realistic and coordinated. If a department submits initial budget figures not reflecting efficient performance, the budget committee should return them with explanatory comments on how to improve them. Then the originating department must either adjust its proposals or explain why they are acceptable. Communication between the originating department and the budget committee should continue as needed to ensure that both parties accept the budget as reasonable, attainable, and desirable.

The concept of continuous improvement applies to budgeting as well as production. **BP**, one of the world's largest energy companies, streamlined its monthly budget report from a one-inch-thick stack of monthly control reports to a tidy, two-page flash report on monthly earnings and key production statistics. The key to this efficiency gain was the integration of new budgeting and cost allocation processes with its strategic planning process. BP's controller explained the new role of the finance department with respect to the budgetary control process as follows: "there's less of an attitude that finance's job is to control. People really have come to see that our job is to help attain business objectives."

Budget Reporting

The budget period usually coincides with the accounting period. Most companies prepare at least an annual budget, which reflects the objectives for the next year. To provide specific guidance, the annual budget usually is separated into quarterly or monthly budgets. These short-term budgets allow management to periodically evaluate performance and take needed corrective action.

Managers can compare actual results to budgeted amounts in a report such as that shown in Exhibit 23.1. This report shows actual amounts, budgeted amounts, and their differences. A difference is called a *variance*. Management examines variances to identify areas for improvement and corrective action.

Budget Timing

The time period required for the annual budgeting process can vary considerably. For example, budgeting for 2009 can begin as early as January 2008 or as late as December 2008. Large, complex organizations usually require a longer time to prepare their budgets than do smaller organizations. This is so because considerable effort is required to coordinate the different units (departments) within large organizations.

Many companies apply **continuous budgeting** by preparing **rolling budgets.** As each monthly or quarterly budget period goes by, these companies revise their entire set of budgets for the months or quarters remaining and add new monthly or quarterly budgets to replace the ones that have lapsed. At any point in time, monthly or quarterly budgets are available for the

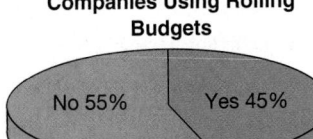

Companies Using Rolling Budgets

No 55%   Yes 45%

ECCENTRIC MUSIC Income Statement with Variations from Budget For Month Ended April 30, 2008			
	Actual	**Budget**	**Variance**
Net sales	$60,500	$57,150	$+3,350
Cost of goods sold	41,350	39,100	+2,250
Gross profit	19,150	18,050	+1,100
Operating expenses			
Selling expenses			
Sales salaries	6,250	6,000	+250
Advertising	900	800	+100
Store supplies	550	500	+50
Depreciation—Store equipment	1,600	1,600	
Total selling expenses	9,300	8,900	+400
General and administrative expenses			
Office salaries	2,000	2,000	
Office supplies used	165	150	+15
Rent	1,100	1,100	
Insurance	200	200	
Depreciation—Office equipment	100	100	
Total general and administrative expenses	3,565	3,550	+15
Total operating expenses	12,865	12,450	+415
Net income	$ 6,285	$ 5,600	$ +685

Exhibit 23.1

Comparing Actual Performance with Budgeted Performance

next 12 months or four quarters. Exhibit 23.2 shows rolling budgets prepared at the end of five consecutive periods. The first set (at top) is prepared in December 2007 and covers the four calendar quarters of 2008. In March 2008, the company prepares another rolling budget for the next four quarters through March 2009. This same process is repeated every three months. As a result, management is continuously planning ahead.

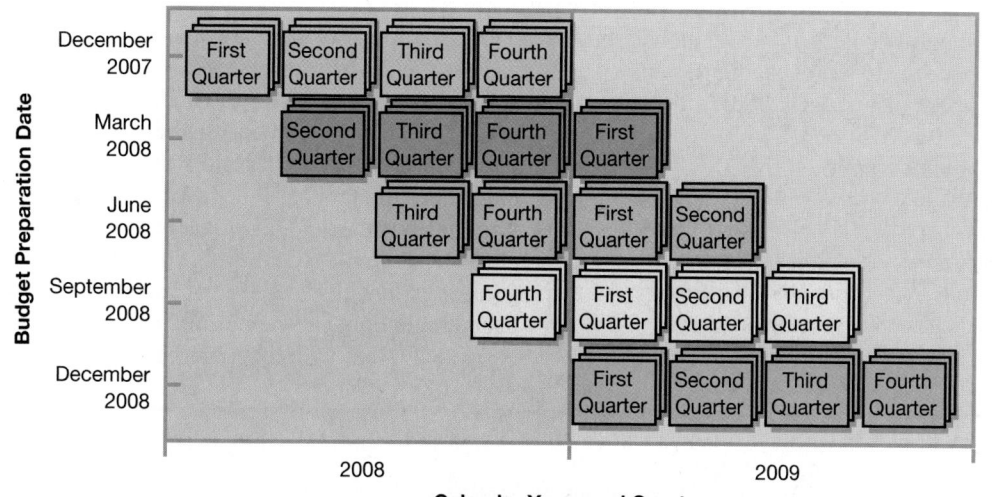

Exhibit 23.2

Rolling Budgets

Exhibit 23.2 reflects an annual budget composed of four quarters prepared four times per year using the most recent information available. For example, the budget for the fourth quarter of 2008 is prepared in December 2007 and revised in March, June, and September of 2008. When continuous budgeting is not used, the fourth-quarter budget is nine months old and perhaps out of date when applied.

Decision Insight

Budget Calendar Many companies use long-range operating budgets. For large companies, three groups usually determine or influence the budgets: creditors, directors, and management. All three are interested in the companies' future cash flows and earnings. The annual budget process often begins six months or more before the budget is due to the board of directors. A typical budget calendar, shown here, provides insight into the budget process during a typical calendar year.

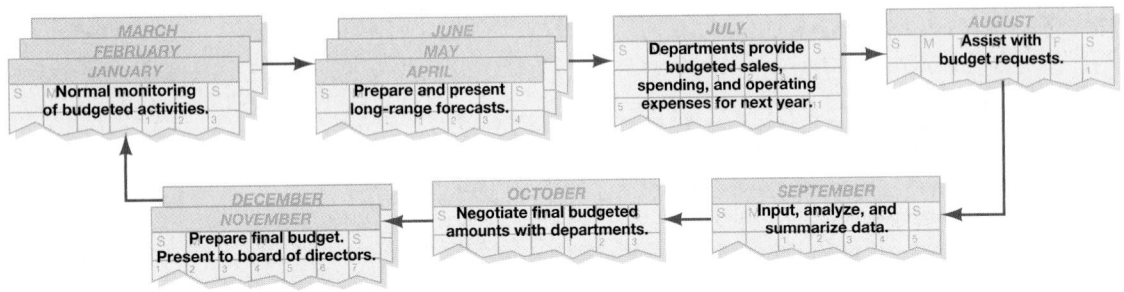

Quick Check

Answers—p. 937

1. What are the major benefits of budgeting?
2. What is the main responsibility of the budget committee?
3. What is the usual time period covered by a budget?
4. What are rolling budgets?

Master Budget

C3 Describe a master budget and the process of preparing it.

A **master budget** is a formal, comprehensive plan for a company's future. It contains several individual budgets that are linked with each other to form a coordinated plan.

Master Budget Components

The master budget typically includes individual budgets for sales, purchases, production, various expenses, capital expenditures, and cash. Managers often express the expected financial results of these planned activities with both a budgeted income statement for the budget period and a budgeted balance sheet for the end of the budget period. The usual number and types of budgets included in a master budget depend on the company's size and complexity. A master budget should include, at a minimum, the budgets listed in Exhibit 23.3. In addition to these individual budgets, managers often include supporting calculations and additional tables with the master budget.

Decision Insight

Budgeting Targets Budgeting is a crucial part of any acquisition. Analysis begins by projecting annual sales volume and prices. It then estimates cost of sales, expenses, and income for the next several years. Using the present value of this projected income stream, buyers determine an offer price.

Exhibit 23.3

Basic Components of a Master Budget

- ■ **Operating budgets**
  - ■ *Sales budget*
  - ■ For merchandisers add: *Merchandise purchases budget* (units to be purchased)
  - ■ For manufacturers add: *Production budget* (units to be produced)
    - *Manufacturing budget* (manufacturing costs)
  - ■ *Selling expense budget*
  - ■ *General and administrative expense budget*
- ■ **Capital expenditures budget** (expenditures for plant assets)
- ■ **Financial budgets**
  - ■ *Cash budget* (cash receipts and disbursements)
  - ■ *Budgeted income statement*
  - ■ *Budgeted balance sheet*

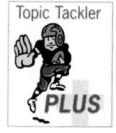

Topic Tackler

PLUS

23-1

Some budgets require the input of other budgets. For example, the merchandise purchases budget cannot be prepared until the sales budget has been prepared because the number of units to be purchased depends on how many units are expected to be sold. As a result, we often must sequentially prepare budgets within the master budget.

A typical sequence for a quarterly budget consists of the five steps in Exhibit 23.4. Any stage in this budgeting process might reveal undesirable outcomes, so changes often must be made to prior budgets by repeating the previous steps. For instance, an early version of the cash budget could show an insufficient amount of cash unless cash outlays are reduced. This could yield a reduction in planned equipment purchases. A preliminary budgeted balance sheet could also reveal too much debt from an ambitious capital expenditures budget. Findings such as these often result in revised plans and budgets.

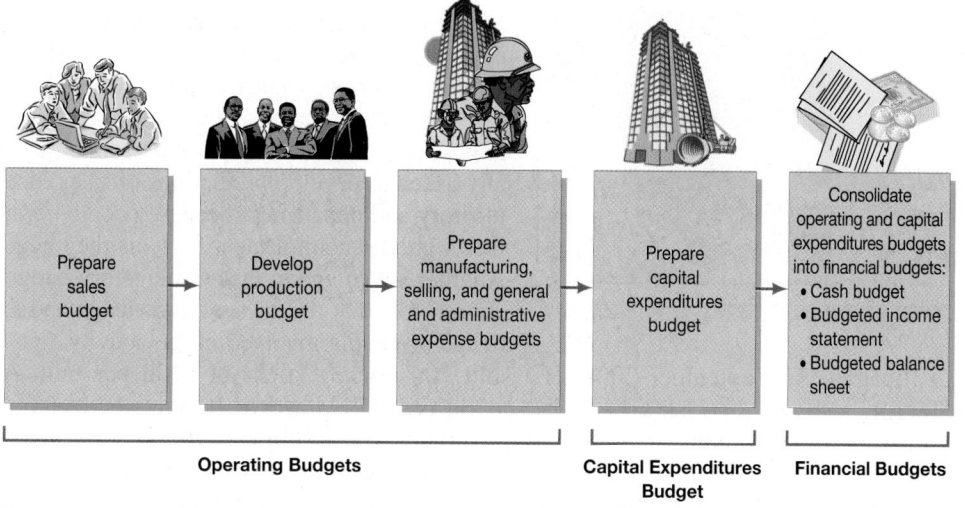

Exhibit 23.4

Master Budget Sequence

The remainder of this section explains how Hockey Den (HD), a retailer of youth hockey sticks, prepares its master budget. Its master budget includes operating, capital expenditures, and cash budgets for each month in each quarter. It also includes a budgeted income statement for each quarter and a budgeted balance sheet as of the last day of each quarter. We show how HD prepares budgets for October, November, and December 2008. Exhibit 23.5 presents HD's balance sheet at the start of this budgeting period, which we often refer to as we prepare the component budgets.

Exhibit 23.5

Balance Sheet Prior to the Budgeting Periods

HOCKEY DEN
Balance Sheet
September 30, 2008

Assets

Cash		$ 20,000
Accounts receivable		42,000
Inventory (900 units @ $60)		54,000
Equipment*	$200,000	
Less accumulated depreciation	36,000	164,000
Total assets		$280,000

Liabilities and Equity

Liabilities		
Accounts payable	$ 58,200	
Income taxes payable (due 10/31/2008)	20,000	
Note payable to bank	10,000	$ 88,200
Stockholders' equity		
Common stock	150,000	
Retained earnings	41,800	191,800
Total liabilities and equity		$280,000

* Equipment is depreciated on a straight-line basis over 10 years (salvage value is $20,000).

Operating Budgets

P1 Prepare each component of a master budget and link each to the budgeting process.

This section explains HD's preparation of operating budgets. Its operating budgets consist of the sales budget, merchandise purchases budget, selling expense budget, and general and administrative expense budget. HD does not prepare production and manufacturing budgets because it is a merchandiser. (The preparation of production budgets and manufacturing budgets is described in Appendix 23A.)

Sales Budget   The first step in preparing the master budget is planning the **sales budget,** which shows the planned sales units and the expected dollars from these sales. The sales budget is the starting point in the budgeting process because plans for most departments are linked to sales.

The sales budget should emerge from a careful analysis of forecasted economic and market conditions, business capacity, proposed selling expenses (such as advertising), and predictions of unit sales. A company's sales personnel are usually asked to develop predictions of sales for each territory and department because people normally feel a greater commitment to goals they help set. Another advantage to this participatory budgeting approach is that it draws on knowledge and experience of people involved in the activity.

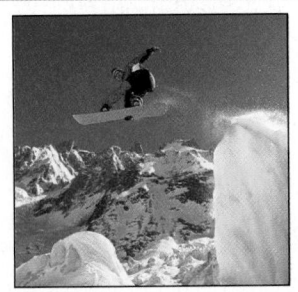
Example: Assume a company's sales force receives a bonus when sales exceed the budgeted amount. How would this arrangement affect the bottom-up process of sales forecasts? *Answer:* Sales reps may understate their budgeted sales.

To illustrate, in September 2008, HD sold 700 hockey sticks at $100 per unit. After considering sales predictions and market conditions, HD prepares its sales budget for the next quarter (three months) plus one extra month (see Exhibit 23.6). The sales budget includes January 2009 because the purchasing department relies on estimated January sales to decide on December 2008 inventory purchases. The sales budget in Exhibit 23.6 includes forecasts of both unit sales and unit prices. Some sales budgets are expressed only in total sales dollars, but most are more detailed. Management finds it useful to know budgeted units and unit prices for many different products, regions, departments, and sales representatives.

Exhibit 23.6

Sales Budget for Planned Unit and Dollar Sales

HOCKEY DEN Monthly Sales Budget October 2008–January 2009			
	Budgeted Unit Sales	Budgeted Unit Price	Budgeted Total Sales
September 2008 (actual)	700	$100	$ 70,000
October 2008	1,000	$100	$100,000
November 2008	800	100	80,000
December 2008	1,400	100	140,000
Totals for the quarter	3,200	100	$320,000
January 2009	900	100	$ 90,000

Merchandise Purchases Budget   Companies use various methods to help managers make inventory purchasing decisions. These methods recognize that the number of units added to inventory depends on budgeted sales volume. Whether a company manufactures or purchases the product it sells, budgeted future sales volume is the primary factor in most inventory management decisions. A company must also consider its inventory system and other factors that we discuss next.

Decision Maker

Answer—p. 937

Entrepreneur   You run a start-up that manufactures designer clothes. Business is seasonal, and fashions and designs quickly change. How do you prepare reliable annual sales budgets?

Just-in-time inventory systems. Managers of *just-in-time* (JIT) inventory systems use sales budgets for short periods (often as few as one or two days) to order just enough merchandise or materials to satisfy the immediate sales demand. This keeps the amount of inventory to a minimum (or zero in an ideal situation). A JIT system minimizes the costs of maintaining inventory, but it is practical only if customers are content to order in advance or if managers can accurately determine short-term sales demand. Suppliers also must be able and willing to ship small quantities regularly and promptly.

Safety stock inventory systems. Market conditions and manufacturing processes for some products do not allow use of a just-in-time system. Companies in these cases maintain sufficient inventory to reduce the risk and cost of running short. This practice requires enough purchases to satisfy the budgeted sales amounts and to maintain a **safety stock,** a quantity of inventory that provides protection against lost sales caused by unfulfilled demands from customers or delays in shipments from suppliers.

Merchandise purchases budget preparation. A merchandiser usually expresses a **merchandise purchases budget** in both units and dollars. Exhibit 23.7 shows the general layout for this budget in equation form. If this formula is expressed in units and only one product is involved, we can compute the number of dollars of inventory to be purchased for the budget by multiplying the units to be purchased by the cost per unit.

Point: Accurate estimates of future sales are crucial in a JIT system.

Topic Tackler

PLUS

23-2

Exhibit 23.7

General Formula for a Merchandise Purchases Budget

To illustrate, after assessing the cost of keeping inventory along with the risk and cost of inventory shortages, HD decided that the number of units in its inventory at each month-end should equal 90% of next month's predicted sales. For example, inventory at the end of October should equal 90% of budgeted November sales, and the November ending inventory should equal 90% of budgeted December sales, and so on. Also, HD's suppliers expect the September 2008 per unit cost of $60 to remain unchanged through January 2009. This information along with knowledge of 900 units in inventory at September 30 (see Exhibit 23.5) allows the company to prepare the merchandise purchases budget shown in Exhibit 23.8.

Example: Assume Hockey Den adopts a JIT system in purchasing merchandise. How will its sales budget differ from its merchandise purchases budget? *Answer:* The two budgets will be similar because future inventory should be near zero.

Exhibit 23.8

Merchandise Purchases Budget

HOCKEY DEN Merchandise Purchases Budget October 2008–December 2008	October	November	December
Next month's budgeted sales (units)	800	1,400	900
Ratio of inventory to future sales	× 90%	× 90%	× 90%
Budgeted ending inventory (units)	720	1,260	810
Add budgeted sales (units)	1,000	800	1,400
Required units of available merchandise	1,720	2,060	2,210
Deduct beginning inventory (units)	900	720	1,260
Units to be purchased	820	1,340	950
Budgeted cost per unit	$ 60	$ 60	$ 60
Budgeted cost of merchandise purchases	$49,200	$80,400	$57,000

The first three lines of HD's merchandise purchases budget determine the required ending inventories (in units). Budgeted unit sales are then added to the desired ending inventory to give the required units of available merchandise. We then subtract beginning inventory to determine the budgeted number of units to be purchased. The last line is the budgeted cost of the purchases, computed by multiplying the number of units to be purchased by the predicted cost per unit.

Example: If ending inventory in Exhibit 23.8 is required to equal 80% of next month's predicted sales, how many units must be purchased each month? *Answer:* Budgeted ending inventory: Oct. = 640 units; Nov. = 1,120 units; Dec. = 720 units. Required purchases: Oct. = 740 units; Nov. = 1,280 units; Dec. = 1,000 units.

We already indicated that some budgeting systems describe only the total dollars of budgeted sales. Likewise, a system can express a merchandise purchases budget only in terms of the total cost of merchandise to be purchased, omitting the number of units to be purchased. This method assumes a constant relation between sales and cost of goods sold. HD, for instance, might assume the expected cost of goods sold to be 60% of sales, computed from the budgeted unit cost of $60 and the budgeted sales price of $100. However, it still must consider the effects of changes in beginning and ending inventories in determining the amounts to be purchased.

Selling Expense Budget   The **selling expense budget** is a plan listing the types and amounts of selling expenses expected during the budget period. Its initial responsibility usually rests with the vice president of marketing or an equivalent sales manager. The selling expense budget is normally created to provide sufficient selling expenses to meet sales goals reflected in the sales budget. Predicted selling expenses are based on both the sales budget and the experience of previous periods. After some or all of the master budget is prepared, management might decide that projected sales volume is inadequate. If so, subsequent adjustments in the sales budget can require corresponding adjustments in the selling expense budget.

To illustrate, HD's selling expense budget is in Exhibit 23.9. The firm's selling expenses consist of commissions paid to sales personnel and a $2,000 monthly salary paid to the sales manager. Sales commissions equal 10% of total sales and are paid in the month sales occur. Sales commissions are variable with respect to sales volume, but the sales manager's salary is fixed. No advertising expenses are budgeted for this particular quarter.

Exhibit 23.9

Selling Expense Budget

HOCKEY DEN **Selling Expense Budget** **October 2008–December 2008**				
	October	**November**	**December**	**Totals**
Budgeted sales	$100,000	$80,000	$140,000	$320,000
Sales commission percent	× 10%	× 10%	× 10%	× 10%
Sales commissions	10,000	8,000	14,000	32,000
Salary for sales manager	2,000	2,000	2,000	6,000
Total selling expenses	$ 12,000	$10,000	$ 16,000	$ 38,000

Example: If sales commissions in Exhibit 23.9 are increased, which budgets are affected? *Answer:* Selling expenses budget, cash budget, and budgeted income statement.

General and Administrative Expense Budget   The **general and administrative expense budget** plans the predicted operating expenses not included in the selling expenses budget. General and administrative expenses can be either variable or fixed with respect to sales volume. The office manager responsible for general administration often is responsible for preparing the initial general and administrative expense budget.

Interest expense and income tax expense are often classified as general and administrative expenses in published income statements, but normally cannot be planned at this stage of the budgeting process. The prediction of interest expense follows the preparation of the cash budget and the decisions regarding debt. The predicted income tax expense depends on the budgeted amount of pretax income. Both interest and income taxes are usually beyond the control of the office manager. As a result, they are not used in comparison to the budget to evaluate that person's performance.

Exhibit 23.10 shows HD's general and administrative expense budget. It includes salaries of $54,000 per year, or $4,500 per month (paid each month when they are earned). Using information in Exhibit 23.5, the depreciation on equipment is computed as $18,000 per year [($200,000 − $20,000)/10 years], or $1,500 per month ($18,000/12 months).

HOCKEY DEN General and Administrative Expense Budget October 2008–December 2008				
	October	November	December	Totals
Administrative salaries	$4,500	$4,500	$4,500	$13,500
Depreciation of equipment	1,500	1,500	1,500	4,500
Total general and administrative expenses	$6,000	$6,000	$6,000	$18,000

Exhibit 23.10

General and Administrative Expense Budget

Example: In Exhibit 23.10, how would a rental agreement of $5,000 per month plus 1% of sales affect the general and administrative expense budget? (Budgeted sales are in Exhibit 23.6.) *Answer: Rent expense:* Oct. = $6,000; Nov. = $5,800; Dec. = $6,400; Total = $18,200; *Revised total general and administrative expenses:* Oct. = $12,000; Nov. = $11,800; Dec. = $12,400; Total = $36,200.

Quick Check

Answers—p. 937

5. What is a master budget?

6. A master budget (*a*) always includes a manufacturing budget specifying the units to be produced; (*b*) is prepared with a process starting with the operating budgets and continues with the capital expenditures budget and then financial budgets; or (*c*) is prepared with a process ending with the sales budget.

7. What are the three primary categories of budgets in the master budget?

8. In preparing monthly budgets for the third quarter, a company budgeted sales of 120 units for July and 140 units for August. Management wants each month's ending inventory to be 60% of next month's sales. The June 30 inventory consists of 50 units. How many units of product for July acquisition should the merchandise purchases budget specify for the third quarter? (*a*) 84, (*b*) 120, (*c*) 154, or (*d*) 204.

9. How do the operating budgets for merchandisers and manufacturers differ?

10. How does a just-in-time inventory system differ from a safety stock system?

Capital Expenditures Budget

The **capital expenditures budget** lists dollar amounts to be both received from plant asset disposals and spent to purchase additional plant assets to carry out the budgeted business activities. It is usually prepared after the operating budgets. Since a company's plant assets determine its productive capacity, this budget is usually affected by long-range plans for the business. Yet the process of preparing a sales or purchases budget can reveal that the company requires more (or less) capacity, which implies more (or less) plant assets.

Capital budgeting is the process of evaluating and planning for capital (plant asset) expenditures. This is an important management task because these expenditures often involve long-run commitments of large amounts, affect predicted cash flows, and impact future debt and equity financing. This means that the capital expenditures budget is often linked with management's evaluation of the company's ability to take on more debt. We describe capital budgeting in Chapter 25.

Hockey Den does not anticipate disposal of any plant assets through December 2008, but it does plan to acquire additional equipment for $25,000 cash near the end of December 2008. This is the only budgeted capital expenditure from October 2008 through January 2009. Thus, no separate budget is shown. The cash budget in Exhibit 23.11 reflects this $25,000 planned expenditure.

Exhibit 23.11

Cash Budget

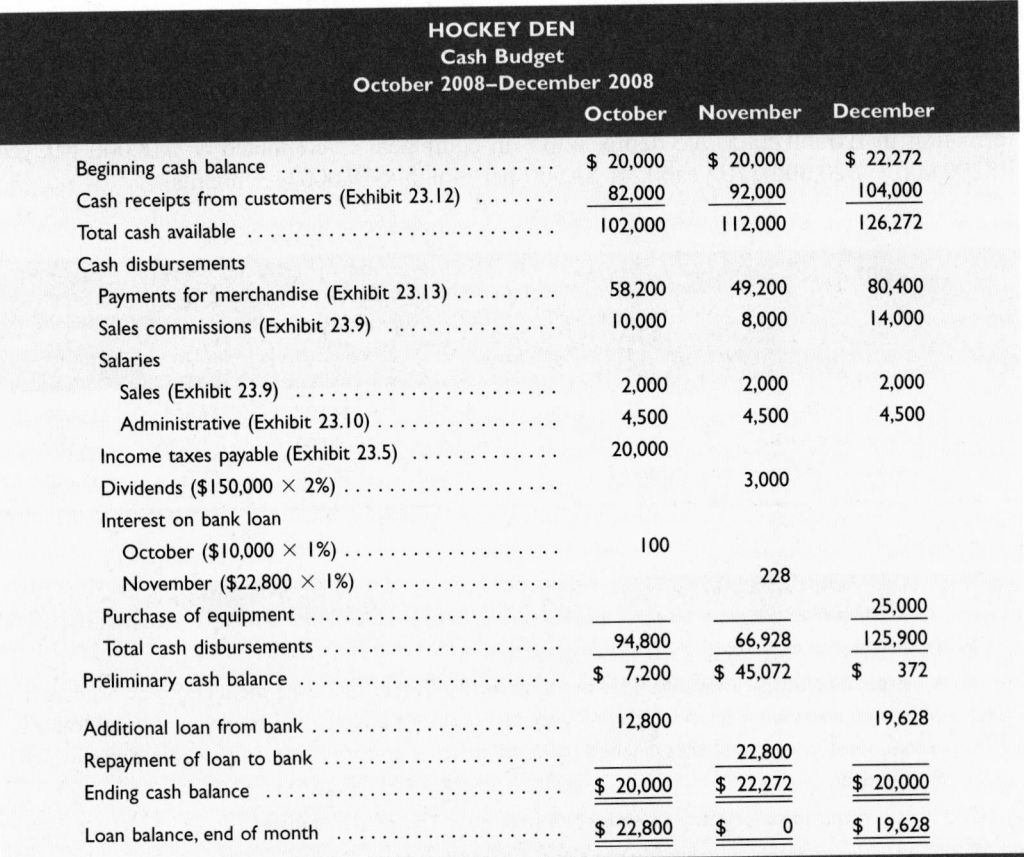

HOCKEY DEN Cash Budget October 2008–December 2008	October	November	December
Beginning cash balance	$ 20,000	$ 20,000	$ 22,272
Cash receipts from customers (Exhibit 23.12)	82,000	92,000	104,000
Total cash available	102,000	112,000	126,272
Cash disbursements			
Payments for merchandise (Exhibit 23.13)	58,200	49,200	80,400
Sales commissions (Exhibit 23.9)	10,000	8,000	14,000
Salaries			
Sales (Exhibit 23.9)	2,000	2,000	2,000
Administrative (Exhibit 23.10)	4,500	4,500	4,500
Income taxes payable (Exhibit 23.5)	20,000		
Dividends ($150,000 × 2%)		3,000	
Interest on bank loan			
October ($10,000 × 1%)	100		
November ($22,800 × 1%)		228	
Purchase of equipment			25,000
Total cash disbursements	94,800	66,928	125,900
Preliminary cash balance	$ 7,200	$ 45,072	$ 372
Additional loan from bank	12,800		19,628
Repayment of loan to bank		22,800	
Ending cash balance	$ 20,000	$ 22,272	$ 20,000
Loan balance, end of month	$ 22,800	$ 0	$ 19,628

Example: If the minimum ending cash balance in Exhibit 23.11 is changed to $25,000 for each month, what is the projected loan balance at Dec. 31, 2008?

Answer:

Loan balance, Oct. 31	$27,800
November interest	278
November payment	25,022
Loan balance, Nov. 30	2,778
December interest	28
Additional loan in Dec.	21,928
Loan balance, Dec. 31	24,706

P2   Link both operating and capital expenditures budgets to budgeted financial statements.

Financial Budgets

After preparing its operating and capital expenditures budgets, a company uses information from these budgets to prepare at least three financial budgets: the cash budget, budgeted income statement, and budgeted balance sheet.

Cash Budget   After developing budgets for sales, merchandise purchases, expenses, and capital expenditures, the next step is to prepare the **cash budget,** which shows expected cash inflows and outflows during the budget period. It is especially important to maintain a cash balance necessary to meet ongoing obligations. By preparing a cash budget, management can prearrange loans to cover anticipated cash shortages before they are needed. A cash budget also helps management avoid a cash balance that is too large. Too much cash is undesirable because it earns a relatively low (if any) return.

When preparing a cash budget, we add expected cash receipts to the beginning cash balance and deduct expected cash disbursements. If the expected ending cash balance is inadequate, additional cash requirements appear in the budget as planned increases from short-term loans. If the expected ending cash balance exceeds the desired balance, the excess is used to repay loans or to acquire short-term investments. Information for preparing the cash budget is mainly taken from the operating and capital expenditures budgets.

To illustrate, Exhibit 23.11 presents HD's cash budget. The beginning cash balance for October is taken from the September 30, 2008, balance sheet in Exhibit 23.5. The remainder of this section describes the computations in the cash budget.

We begin with reference to HD's budgeted sales (Exhibit 23.6). Analysis of past sales indicates that 40% of the firm's sales are for cash. The remaining 60% are credit sales; these customers are expected to pay in full in the month following the sales. We now can compute the budgeted cash receipts from customers as shown in Exhibit 23.12. October's budgeted cash receipts consist of $40,000 from expected cash sales ($100,000 × 40%) plus the anticipated

	September	October	November	December
Sales	$70,000	$100,000	$80,000	$140,000
Less ending accounts receivable (60%)	42,000	60,000	48,000	84,000
Cash receipts from				
Cash sales (40% of sales)		40,000	32,000	56,000
Collections of prior month's receivables		42,000	60,000	48,000
Total cash receipts		$ 82,000	$92,000	$104,000

Exhibit 23.12

Computing Budgeted Cash Receipts

collection of $42,000 of accounts receivable from the end of September. Each month's cash receipts from customers are transferred to the second line of Exhibit 23.11.

Next, we see that HD's merchandise purchases are entirely on account. It makes full payment during the month following its purchases. Therefore, cash disbursements for purchases can be computed from the September 30, 2008, balance sheet (Exhibit 23.5) and the merchandise purchases budget (Exhibit 23.8). This computation is shown in Exhibit 23.13.

October payments (September 30 balance)	$58,200
November payments (October purchases)	49,200
December payments (November purchases)	80,400

Exhibit 23.13

Computing Cash Disbursements for Purchases

The monthly budgeted cash disbursements for sales commissions and salaries are taken from the selling expense budget (Exhibit 23.9) and the general and administrative expense budget (Exhibit 23.10). The cash budget is unaffected by depreciation as reported in the general and administrative expenses budget.

Income taxes are due and payable in October as shown in the September 30, 2008, balance sheet (Exhibit 23.5). The cash budget in Exhibit 23.11 shows this $20,000 expected payment in October. Predicted income tax expense for the quarter ending December 31 is 40% of net income and is due in January 2009. It is therefore not reported in the October–December 2008 cash budget but in the budgeted income statement as income tax expense and on the budgeted balance sheet as income tax liability.

Hockey Den also pays a cash dividend equal to 2% of the par value of common stock in the second month of each quarter. The cash budget in Exhibit 23.11 shows a November payment of $3,000 for this purpose (2% of $150,000; see Exhibit 23.5).

Hockey Den has an agreement with its bank that promises additional loans at each month-end, if necessary, to keep a minimum cash balance of $20,000. If the cash balance exceeds $20,000 at a month-end, HD uses the excess to repay loans. Interest is paid at each month-end at the rate of 1% of the beginning balance of these loans. For October, this payment is 1% of the $10,000 amount reported in the balance sheet of Exhibit 23.5. For November, HD expects to pay interest of $228, computed as 1% of the $22,800 expected loan balance at October 31. No interest is budgeted for December because the company expects to repay the loans in full at the end of November. Exhibit 23.11 shows that the October 31 cash balance declines to $7,200 (before any loan-related activity). This amount is less than the $20,000 minimum. Hockey Den will bring this balance up to the minimum by borrowing $12,800 with a short-term note. At the end of November, the budget shows an expected cash balance of $45,072 before any loan activity. This means that HD expects to repay $22,800 of debt. The equipment purchase budgeted for December reduces the expected

Decision Insight

Netting Cash   The Hockey Company—whose brands include CCM, JOFA, and KOHO—reported net cash outflows for investing activities of $32 million. Much of this amount was a prepayment to the NHL for a 10-year license agreement.

Plan Ahead Most companies allocate dollars based on budgets submitted by department managers. These managers verify the numbers and monitor the budget. Managers must remember, however, that a budget is judged by its success in helping achieve the company's mission. One analogy is that a hiker must know the route to properly plan a hike and monitor hiking progress.

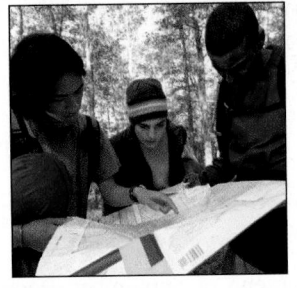

cash balance to $372, far below the $20,000 minimum. The company expects to borrow $19,628 in that month to reach the minimum desired ending balance.

Budgeted Income Statement One of the final steps in preparing the master budget is to summarize the income effects. The **budgeted income statement** is a managerial accounting report showing predicted amounts of sales and expenses for the budget period. Information needed for preparing a budgeted income statement is primarily taken from already prepared budgets. The volume of information summarized in the budgeted income statement is so large for some companies that they often use spreadsheets to accumulate the budgeted transactions and classify them by their effects on income. We condense HD's budgeted income statement and show it in Exhibit 23.14. All information in this exhibit is taken from earlier budgets. Also, we now can predict the amount of income tax expense for the quarter, computed as 40% of the budgeted pretax income. This amount is included in the cash budget and/or the budgeted balance sheet as necessary.

Exhibit 23.14

Budgeted Income Statement

HOCKEY DEN Budgeted Income Statement For Three Months Ended December 31, 2008		
Sales (Exhibit 23.6, 3,200 units @ $100)		$320,000
Cost of goods sold (3,200 units @ $60)		192,000
Gross profit		128,000
Operating expenses		
Sales commissions (Exhibit 23.9)	$32,000	
Sales salaries (Exhibit 23.9)	6,000	
Administrative salaries (Exhibit 23.10)	13,500	
Depreciation on equipment (Exhibit 23.10)	4,500	
Interest expense (Exhibit 23.11)	328	56,328
Income before income taxes		71,672
Income tax expense ($71,672 × 40%)		28,669
Net income		$ 43,003

Point: Lending institutions often require potential borrowers to provide cash budgets, budgeted income statements, and budgeted balance sheets, as well as data on past performance.

Budgeted Balance Sheet The final step in preparing the master budget is summarizing the company's financial position. The **budgeted balance sheet** shows predicted amounts for the company's assets, liabilities, and equity as of the end of the budget period. HD's budgeted balance sheet in Exhibit 23.15 is prepared using information from the other budgets. The sources of amounts are reported in the notes to the budgeted balance sheet.[1]

---

[1] An eight-column spreadsheet, or work sheet, can be used to prepare a budgeted balance sheet (and income statement). The first two columns show the ending balance sheet amounts from the period prior to the budget period. The budgeted transactions and adjustments are entered in the third and fourth columns in the same manner as adjustments are entered on an ordinary work sheet. After all budgeted transactions and adjustments have been entered, the amounts in the first two columns are combined with the budget amounts in the third and fourth columns and sorted to the proper Income Statement (fifth and sixth columns) and Balance Sheet columns (seventh and eighth columns). Amounts in these columns are used to prepare the budgeted income statement and balance sheet.

Exhibit 23.15

Budgeted Balance Sheet

HOCKEY DEN
Budgeted Balance Sheet
December 31, 2008

Assets

Cash[a]		$ 20,000
Accounts receivable[b]		84,000
Inventory[c]		48,600
Equipment[d]	$225,000	
Less accumulated depreciation[e]	40,500	184,500
Total assets		$337,100

Liabilities and Equity

Liabilities		
Accounts payable[f]	$ 57,000	
Income taxes payable[g]	28,669	
Bank loan payable[h]	19,628	$105,297
Stockholders' equity		
Common stock[i]	150,000	
Retained earnings[j]	81,803	231,803
Total liabilities and equity		$337,100

[a] Ending balance for December from the cash budget in Exhibit 23.11.

[b] 60% of $140,000 sales budgeted for December from the sales budget in Exhibit 23.6.

[c] 810 units in budgeted December ending inventory at the budgeted cost of $60 per unit (from the purchases budget in Exhibit 23.8).

[d] September 30 balance of $200,000 from the beginning balance sheet in Exhibit 23.5 plus $25,000 cost of new equipment from the cash budget in Exhibit 23.11.

[e] September 30 balance of $36,000 from the beginning balance sheet in Exhibit 23.5 plus $4,500 expense from the general and administrative expense budget in Exhibit 23.10.

[f] Budgeted cost of purchases for December from the purchases budget in Exhibit 23.8.

[g] Income tax expense from the budgeted income statement for the fourth quarter in Exhibit 23.14.

[h] Budgeted December 31 balance from the cash budget in Exhibit 23.11.

[i] Unchanged from the beginning balance sheet in Exhibit 23.5.

[j] September 30 balance of $41,800 from the beginning balance sheet in Exhibit 23.5 plus budgeted net income of $43,003 from the budgeted income statement in Exhibit 23.14 minus budgeted cash dividends of $3,000 from the cash budget in Exhibit 23.11.

Quick Check

Answers—p. 937

11. In preparing a budgeted balance sheet, (*a*) plant assets are determined by analyzing the capital expenditures budget and the balance sheet from the beginning of the budget period, (*b*) liabilities are determined by analyzing the general and administrative expense budget, or (*c*) retained earnings are determined from information contained in the cash budget and the balance sheet from the beginning of the budget period.

12. What sequence is followed in preparing the budgets that constitute the master budget?

Activity-Based Budgeting

Decision Analysis

Activity-based budgeting (ABB) is a budget system based on expected activities. Knowledge of expected activities and their levels for the budget period enables management to plan for resources required to perform the activities. To illustrate, we consider the budget of a company's accounting department. Traditional budgeting systems list items such as salaries, supplies, equipment, and utilities. Such an itemized budget informs management of the use of the funds budgeted (for example, salaries), but management cannot assess the basis for increases or decreases in budgeted amounts as compared to prior periods. Accordingly, management often makes across-the-board cuts or increases. In contrast, ABB requires management to list activities performed by, say, the accounting department such as auditing, tax reporting, financial reporting, and cost accounting. Exhibit 23.16 contrasts a

A1 Analyze expense planning using activity-based budgeting.

Exhibit 23.16

Activity-Based Budgeting versus Traditional Budgeting (for an accounting department)

Activity-Based Budget		Traditional Budget	
Auditing	$ 58,000	Salaries	$152,000
Tax reporting	71,000	Supplies	22,000
Financial reporting	63,000	Depreciation	36,000
Cost accounting	32,000	Utilities	14,000
Total	$224,000	Total	$224,000

traditional budget with an activity-based budget for a company's accounting department. An understanding of the resources required to perform the activities, the costs associated with these resources, and the way resource use changes with changes in activity levels allows management to better assess how expenses will change to accommodate changes in activity levels. Moreover, by knowing the relation between activities and costs, management can attempt to reduce costs by eliminating nonvalue-added activities.

Decision Maker

Answer—p. 937

Environmental Manager You hold the new position of environmental control manager for a chemical company. You are asked to develop a budget for your job and identify job responsibilities. How do you proceed?

Demonstration Problem

Wild Wood Company's management asks you to prepare its master budget using the following information. The budget is to cover the months of April, May, and June of 2008.

WILD WOOD COMPANY
Balance Sheet
March 31, 2008

Assets		Liabilities and Equity	
Cash	$ 50,000	Accounts payable	$156,000
Accounts receivable	175,000	Short-term notes payable	12,000
Inventory	126,000	Total current liabilities	168,000
Total current assets	351,000	Long-term note payable	200,000
Equipment, gross	480,000	Total liabilities	368,000
Accumulated depreciation	(90,000)	Common stock	235,000
Equipment, net	390,000	Retained earnings	138,000
		Total stockholders' equity	373,000
Total assets	$741,000	Total liabilities and equity	$741,000

Additional Information

a. Sales for March total 10,000 units. Each month's sales are expected to exceed the prior month's results by 5%. The product's selling price is $25 per unit.

b. Company policy calls for a given month's ending inventory to equal 80% of the next month's expected unit sales. The March 31 inventory is 8,400 units, which complies with the policy. The purchase price is $15 per unit.

c. Sales representatives' commissions are 12.5% of sales and are paid in the month of the sales. The sales manager's monthly salary will be $3,500 in April and $4,000 per month thereafter.

d. Monthly general and administrative expenses include $8,000 administrative salaries, $5,000 depreciation, and 0.9% monthly interest on the long-term note payable.

e. The company expects 30% of sales to be for cash and the remaining 70% on credit. Receivables are collected in full in the month following the sale (none is collected in the month of the sale).

f. All merchandise purchases are on credit, and no payables arise from any other transactions. One month's purchases are fully paid in the next month.

g. The minimum ending cash balance for all months is $50,000. If necessary, the company borrows enough cash using a short-term note to reach the minimum. Short-term notes require an interest payment of 1% at each month-end (before any repayment). If the ending cash balance exceeds the minimum, the excess will be applied to repaying the short-term notes payable balance.

h. Dividends of $100,000 are to be declared and paid in May.

i. No cash payments for income taxes are to be made during the second calendar quarter. Income taxes will be assessed at 35% in the quarter.

j. Equipment purchases of $55,000 are scheduled for June.

Required

Prepare the following budgets and other financial information as required:

1. Sales budget, including budgeted sales for July.
2. Purchases budget, the budgeted cost of goods sold for each month and quarter, and the cost of the June 30 budgeted inventory.
3. Selling expense budget.
4. General and administrative expense budget.
5. Expected cash receipts from customers and the expected June 30 balance of accounts receivable.
6. Expected cash payments for purchases and the expected June 30 balance of accounts payable.
7. Cash budget.
8. Budgeted income statement.
9. Budgeted statement of retained earnings.
10. Budgeted balance sheet.

Planning the Solution

- The sales budget shows expected sales for each month in the quarter. Start by multiplying March sales by 105% and then do the same for the remaining months. July's sales are needed for the purchases budget. To complete the budget, multiply the expected unit sales by the selling price of $25 per unit.

- Use these results and the 80% inventory policy to budget the size of ending inventory for April, May, and June. Add the budgeted sales to these numbers and subtract the actual or expected beginning inventory for each month. The result is the number of units to be purchased each month. Multiply these numbers by the per unit cost of $15. Find the budgeted cost of goods sold by multiplying the unit sales in each month by the $15 cost per unit. Compute the cost of the June 30 ending inventory by multiplying the expected units available at that date by the $15 cost per unit.

- The selling expense budget has only two items. Find the amount of the sales representatives' commissions by multiplying the expected dollar sales in each month by the 12.5% commission rate. Then include the sales manager's salary of $3,500 in April and $4,000 in May and June.

- The general and administrative expense budget should show three items. Administrative salaries are fixed at $8,000 per month, and depreciation is $5,000 per month. Budget the monthly interest expense on the long-term note by multiplying its $200,000 balance by the 0.9% monthly interest rate.

- Determine the amounts of cash sales in each month by multiplying the budgeted sales by 30%. Add to this amount the credit sales of the prior month (computed as 70% of prior month's sales). April's cash receipts from collecting receivables equals the March 31 balance of $175,000. The expected June 30 accounts receivable balance equals 70% of June's total budgeted sales.

- Determine expected cash payments on accounts payable for each month by making them equal to the merchandise purchases in the prior month. The payments for April equal the March 31 balance of accounts payable shown on the beginning balance sheet. The June 30 balance of accounts payable equals merchandise purchases for June.

- Prepare the cash budget by combining the given information and the amounts of cash receipts and cash payments on account that you computed. Complete the cash budget for each month by either borrowing enough to raise the preliminary balance to the minimum or paying off short-term debt as much as the balance allows without falling below the minimum. Show the ending balance of the short-term note in the budget.

- Prepare the budgeted income statement by combining the budgeted items for all three months. Determine the income before income taxes and multiply it by the 35% rate to find the quarter's income tax expense.

- The budgeted statement of retained earnings should show the March 31 balance plus the quarter's net income minus the quarter's dividends.

- The budgeted balance sheet includes updated balances for all items that appear in the beginning balance sheet and an additional liability for unpaid income taxes. Amounts for all asset, liability, and equity accounts can be found either in the budgets, other calculations, or by adding amounts found there to the beginning balances.

Solution to Demonstration Problem

1. Sales budget

	April	May	June	July
Prior period's unit sales	10,000	10,500	11,025	11,576
Plus 5% growth	500	525	551	579
Projected unit sales	10,500	11,025	11,576	12,155

	April	May	June	Quarter
Projected unit sales	10,500	11,025	11,576	
Selling price per unit	× $25	× $25	× $25	
Projected sales	$262,500	$275,625	$289,400	$827,525

2. Purchases budget

	April	May	June	Quarter
Next period's unit sales (part 1)	11,025	11,576	12,155	
Ending inventory percent	× 80%	× 80%	× 80%	
Desired ending inventory	8,820	9,261	9,724	
Current period's unit sales (part 1)	10,500	11,025	11,576	
Units to be available	19,320	20,286	21,300	
Less beginning inventory	8,400	8,820	9,261	
Units to be purchased	10,920	11,466	12,039	
Budgeted cost per unit	× $15	× $15	× $15	
Projected purchases	$163,800	$171,990	$180,585	$516,375

Budgeted cost of goods sold

	April	May	June	Quarter
This period's unit sales (part 1)	10,500	11,025	11,576	
Budgeted cost per unit	× $15	× $15	× $15	
Projected cost of goods sold	$157,500	$165,375	$173,640	$496,515

Budgeted inventory for June 30

Units (part 2)	9,724
Cost per unit	× $15
Total	$145,860

3. Selling expense budget

	April	May	June	Quarter
Budgeted sales (part 1)	$262,500	$275,625	$289,400	$827,525
Commission percent	× 12.5%	× 12.5%	× 12.5%	× 12.5%
Sales commissions	32,813	34,453	36,175	103,441
Manager's salary	3,500	4,000	4,000	11,500
Projected selling expenses	$ 36,313	$ 38,453	$ 40,175	$114,941

4. General and administrative expense budget

	April	May	June	Quarter
Administrative salaries	$ 8,000	$ 8,000	$ 8,000	$24,000
Depreciation	5,000	5,000	5,000	15,000
Interest on long-term note payable (0.9% × $200,000)	1,800	1,800	1,800	5,400
Projected expenses	$14,800	$14,800	$14,800	$44,400

5. Expected cash receipts from customers

	April	May	June	Quarter
Budgeted sales (part 1)	$262,500	$275,625	$289,400	
Ending accounts receivable (70%)	$183,750	$192,938	$202,580	
Cash receipts				
Cash sales (30%)	$ 78,750	$ 82,687	$ 86,820	$248,257
Collections of prior period's receivables	175,000	183,750	192,938	551,688
Total cash to be collected	$253,750	$266,437	$279,758	$799,945

6. Expected cash payments to suppliers

	April	May	June	Quarter
Cash payments (equal to prior period's purchases)	$156,000	$163,800	$171,990	$491,790
Expected June 30 balance of accounts payable (June purchases)			$180,585	

7. Cash budget

	April	May	June
Beginning cash balance	$ 50,000	$ 89,517	$ 50,000
Cash receipts (part 5)	253,750	266,437	279,758
Total cash available	303,750	355,954	329,758
Cash payments			
Payments for merchandise (part 6)	156,000	163,800	171,990
Sales commissions (part 3)	32,813	34,453	36,175
Salaries			
Sales (part 3)	3,500	4,000	4,000
Administrative (part 4)	8,000	8,000	8,000
Interest on long-term note (part 4)	1,800	1,800	1,800
Dividends		100,000	
Equipment purchase			55,000
Interest on short-term notes			
April ($12,000 × 1.0%)	120		
June ($6,099 × 1.0%)			61
Total cash payments	202,233	312,053	277,026
Preliminary balance	101,517	43,901	52,732
Additional loan		6,099	
Loan repayment	(12,000)		(2,732)
Ending cash balance	$ 89,517	$ 50,000	$ 50,000
Ending short-term notes	$ 0	$ 6,099	$ 3,367

8.

WILD WOOD COMPANY
Budgeted Income Statement
For Quarter Ended June 30, 2008

Sales (part 1)		$ 827,525
Cost of goods sold (part 2)		496,515
Gross profit		331,010
Operating expenses		
Sales commissions (part 3)	$103,441	
Sales salaries (part 3)	11,500	
Administrative salaries (part 4)	24,000	
Depreciation (part 4)	15,000	
Interest on long-term note (part 4)	5,400	
Interest on short-term notes (part 7)	181	
Total operating expenses		159,522
Income before income taxes		171,488
Income taxes (35%)		60,021
Net income		$ 111,467

9.

WILD WOOD COMPANY
Budgeted Statement of Retained Earnings
For Quarter Ended June 30, 2008

Beginning retained earnings (given)	$138,000
Net income (part 8)	111,467
	249,467
Less cash dividends (given)	100,000
Ending retained earnings	$149,467

10.

WILD WOOD COMPANY
Budgeted Balance Sheet
June 30, 2008

Assets

Cash (part 7)		$ 50,000
Accounts receivable (part 5)		202,580
Inventory (part 2)		145,860
Total current assets		398,440
Equipment (given plus purchase)	$535,000	
Less accumulated depreciation (given plus expense)	105,000	430,000
Total assets		$828,440

Liabilities and Equity

Accounts payable (part 6)	$180,585
Short-term notes payable (part 7)	3,367
Income taxes payable (part 8)	60,021
Total current liabilities	243,973
Long-term note payable (given)	200,000
Total liabilities	443,973
Common stock (given)	235,000
Retained earnings (part 9)	149,467
Total stockholders' equity	384,467
Total liabilities and equity	$828,440

Production and Manufacturing Budgets

23A

Unlike a merchandising company, a manufacturer must prepare a **production budget** instead of a merchandise purchases budget. A production budget, which shows the number of units to be produced each month, is similar to merchandise purchases budgets except that the number of units to be purchased each month (as shown in Exhibit 23.8) is replaced by the number of units to be manufactured each month. A production budget does not show costs; it is *always expressed in units of product*. Exhibit 23A.1 shows the production budget for **Toronto Sticks Company** (**TSC**), a manufacturer of hockey sticks. TSC is an exclusive supplier of hockey sticks to Hockey Den, meaning that TSC uses HD's budgeted sales figures (Exhibit 23.6) to determine its production and manufacturing budgets.

P3 Prepare production and manufacturing budgets.

TSC Production Budget October 2008–December 2008	October	November	December
Next period's budgeted sales (units)	800	1,400	900
Ratio of inventory to future sales	× 90%	× 90%	× 90%
Budgeted ending inventory (units)	720	1,260	810
Add budgeted sales for the period (units)	1,000	800	1,400
Required units of available production	1,720	2,060	2,210
Deduct beginning inventory (units)	(900)	(720)	(1,260)
Units to be produced	820	1,340	950

Exhibit 23A.1

Production Budget

A **manufacturing budget** shows the budgeted costs for direct materials, direct labor, and overhead. It is based on the budgeted production volume from the production budget. The manufacturing budget for most companies consists of three individual budgets: direct materials budget, direct labor budget, and overhead budget. Exhibits 23A.2–23A.4 show these three manufacturing budgets for TSC. These budgets yield the total expected cost of goods to be manufactured in the budget period.

The *direct materials budget* is driven by the budgeted materials needed to satisfy each month's production requirement. To this we must add the desired ending inventory requirements. The desired ending inventory of direct materials as shown in Exhibit 23A.2 is 50% of next month's budgeted materials requirements of wood. For instance, in October 2008, an ending inventory of 335 units of material is desired (50% of November's 670 units). The desired ending inventory for December 2008 is 225 units,

TSC Direct Materials Budget October 2008–December 2008	October	November	December
Budget production (units)	820	1,340	950
Materials requirements per unit	× 0.5	× 0.5	× 0.5
Materials needed for production (units)	410	670	475
Add budgeted ending inventory (units)	335	237.5	225
Total materials requirements (units)	745	907.5	700
Deduct beginning inventory (units)	(205)	(335)	(237.5)
Materials to be purchased (units)	540	572.5	462.5
Material price per unit	$ 20	$ 20	$ 20
Total cost of direct materials purchases	$10,800	$11,450	$9,250

Exhibit 23A.2

Direct Materials Budget

computed from the direct material requirement of 450 units for a production level of 900 units in January 2009. The total materials requirements are computed by adding the desired ending inventory figures to that month's budgeted production material requirements. For October 2008, the total materials requirement is 745 units (335 + 410). From the total materials requirement, we then subtract the units of materials available in beginning inventory. For October 2008, the materials available from September 2008 are computed as 50% of October's materials requirements to satisfy production, or 205 units (50% of 410). Therefore, direct materials purchases in October 2008 are budgeted at 540 units (745 − 205). See Exhibit 23A.2.

TSC's *direct labor budget* is shown in Exhibit 23A.3. About 15 minutes of labor time is required to produce one unit. Labor is paid at the rate of $12 per hour. Budgeted labor hours are computed by multiplying the budgeted production level for each month by one-quarter (0.25) of an hour. Direct labor cost is then computed by multiplying budgeted labor hours by the labor rate of $12 per hour.

Exhibit 23A.3

Direct Labor Budget

				TSC **Direct Labor Budget** October 2008–December 2008		
				October	**November**	**December**
Budgeted production (units)				820	1,340	950
Labor requirements per unit (hours)				× 0.25	× 0.25	× 0.25
Total labor hours needed				205	335	237.5
Labor rate (per hour)				$ 12	$ 12	$ 12
Labor dollars				$2,460	$4,020	$2,850

TSC's *factory overhead budget* is shown in Exhibit 23A.4. The variable portion of overhead is assigned at the rate of $2.50 per unit of production. The fixed portion stays constant at $1,500 per month. The budget in Exhibit 23A.4 is in condensed form; most overhead budgets are more detailed, listing each overhead cost item.

Exhibit 23A.4

Factory Overhead Budget

			TSC **Factory Overhead Budget** October 2008–December 2008		
			October	**November**	**December**
Budgeted production (units)			820	1,340	950
Variable factory overhead rate			× $2.50	× $2.50	× $2.50
Budgeted variable overhead			2,050	3,350	2,375
Budgeted fixed overhead			1,500	1,500	1,500
Budgeted total overhead			$3,550	$4,850	$3,875

Summary

C1 Describe the importance and benefits of budgeting.
Planning is a management responsibility of critical importance to business success. Budgeting is the process management uses to formalize its plans. Budgeting promotes management analysis and focuses its attention on the future. Budgeting also provides a basis for evaluating performance, serves as a source of motivation, is a means of coordinating activities, and communicates management's plans and instructions to employees.

C2 Explain the process of budget administration. Budgeting is a detailed activity that requires administration. At least three aspects are important: budget committee, budget reporting, and budget timing. A budget committee oversees the budget preparation. The budget period pertains to the time period for which the budget is prepared such as a year or month.

C3 Describe a master budget and the process of preparing it.
A master budget is a formal overall plan for a company. It consists of plans for business operations and capital expenditures, plus the financial results of those activities. The budgeting process begins with a sales budget. Based on expected sales volume, companies can budget purchases, selling expenses, and administrative expenses. Next, the capital expenditures budget is prepared, followed by the cash budget and budgeted financial statements. Manufacturers also must budget production quantities, materials purchases, labor costs, and overhead.

A1 Analyze expense planning using activity-based budgeting.
Activity-based budgeting requires management to identify activities performed by departments, plan necessary activity levels, identify resources required to perform these activities, and budget the resources.

P1 **Prepare each component of a master budget and link each to the budgeting process.** The term *master budget* refers to a collection of individual component budgets. Each component budget is designed to guide persons responsible for activities covered by that component. A master budget must reflect the components of a company and their interaction in pursuit of company goals.

P2 **Link both operating and capital expenditures budgets to budgeted financial statements.** The operating budgets, capital expenditures budget, and cash budget contain much of the infor-

mation to prepare a budgeted income statement for the budget period and a budgeted balance sheet at the end of the budget period. Budgeted financial statements show the expected financial consequences of the planned activities described in the budgets.

P3A **Prepare production and manufacturing budgets.** A manufacturer must prepare a *production budget* instead of a purchases budget. A *manufacturing budget* shows the budgeted production costs for direct materials, direct labor, and overhead.

Guidance Answers to **Decision Maker** and **Decision Ethics**

Budget Staffer Your superior's actions appear unethical because she is using private information for personal gain. As a budget staffer, you are low in the company's hierarchical structure and probably unable to confront this superior directly. You should inform an individual with a position of authority within the organization about your concerns.

Entrepreneur You must deal with two issues. First, because fashions and designs frequently change, you cannot heavily rely on previous budgets. As a result, you must carefully analyze the market to understand what designs are in vogue. This will help you plan the product mix and estimate demand. The second issue is the

budgeting period. An annual sales budget may be unreliable because tastes can quickly change. Your best bet might be to prepare monthly and quarterly sales budgets that you continuously monitor and revise.

Environmental Manager You are unlikely to have data on this new position to use in preparing your budget. In this situation, you can use activity-based budgeting. This requires developing a list of activities to conduct, the resources required to perform these activities, and the expenses associated with these resources. You should challenge yourself to be absolutely certain that the listed activities are necessary and that the listed resources are required.

Guidance Answers to **Quick Checks**

1. Major benefits include promoting a focus on the future; providing a basis for evaluating performance; providing a source of motivation; coordinating the departments of a business; and communicating plans and instructions.

2. The budget committee's responsibility is to provide guidance to ensure that budget figures are realistic and coordinated.

3. Budget periods usually coincide with accounting periods and therefore cover a month, quarter, or a year. Budgets can also be prepared for longer time periods, such as five years.

4. Rolling budgets are budgets that are periodically revised in the ongoing process of continuous budgeting.

5. A master budget is a comprehensive or overall plan for the company that is generally expressed in monetary terms.

6. *b*

7. The master budget includes operating budgets, the capital expenditures budget, and financial budgets.

8. *c*; Computed as $(60\% \times 140) + 120 - 50 = 154$.

9. Merchandisers prepare merchandise purchases budgets; manufacturers prepare production and manufacturing budgets.

10. A just-in-time system keeps the level of inventory to a minimum and orders merchandise or materials to meet immediate sales demand. A safety stock system maintains an inventory that is large enough to meet sales demands plus an amount to satisfy unexpected sales demands and an amount to cover delayed shipments from suppliers.

11. *a*

12. (a) Operating budgets (such as sales, selling expense, and administrative budgets), (b) capital expenditures budget, (c) financial budgets: cash budget, budgeted income statement, and budgeted balance sheet.

Key Terms

mhhe.com/wildFAP18e

Key Terms are available at the book's Website for learning and testing in an online Flashcard Format.

Activity-based budgeting (ABB) (p. 929)
Budget (p. 916)
Budgeted balance sheet (p. 928)
Budgeted income statement (p. 928)
Budgeting (p. 916)
Capital expenditures budget (p. 925)

Cash budget (p. 926)
Continuous budgeting (p. 918)
General and administrative expense budget (p. 924)
Manufacturing budget (p. 935)
Master budget (p. 920)

Merchandise purchases budget (p. 923)
Production budget (p. 935)
Rolling budgets (p. 918)
Safety stock (p. 923)
Sales budget (p. 922)
Selling expense budget (p. 924)

Multiple Choice Quiz   Answers on p. 951   mhhe.com/wildFAP18e

Multiple Choice Quizzes A and B are available at the book's Website.

1. A plan that reports the units or costs of merchandise to be purchased by a merchandising company during the budget period is called a
   a. Capital expenditures budget.
   b. Cash budget.
   c. Merchandise purchases budget.
   d. Selling expenses budget.
   e. Sales budget.

2. A hardware store has budgeted sales of $36,000 for its power tool department in July. Management wants to have $7,000 in power tool inventory at the end of July. Its beginning inventory of power tools is expected to be $6,000. What is the budgeted dollar amount of merchandise purchases?
   a. $36,000
   b. $43,000
   c. $42,000
   d. $35,000
   e. $37,000

3. A store has the following budgeted sales for the next five months.

May	$210,000
June	186,000
July	180,000
August	220,000
September	240,000

   Cash sales are 25% of total sales and all credit sales are expected to be collected in the month following the sale. The total amount of cash expected to be received from customers in September is

   a. $240,000
   b. $225,000
   c. $ 60,000
   d. $165,000
   e. $220,000

4. A plan that shows the expected cash inflows and cash outflows during the budget period, including receipts from loans needed to maintain a minimum cash balance and repayments of such loans, is called
   a. A rolling budget.
   b. An income statement.
   c. A balance sheet.
   d. A cash budget.
   e. An operating budget.

5.^A The following sales are predicted for a company's next four months.

	September	October	November	December
Unit sales ..	480	560	600	480

Each month's ending inventory of finished goods should be 30% of the next month's sales. At September 1, the finished goods inventory is 140 units. The budgeted production of units for October is
   a. 572 units.
   b. 560 units.
   c. 548 units.
   d. 600 units.
   e. 180 units.

Superscript letter ^A *denotes assignments based on Appendix 23A.*

Discussion Questions

1. Identify at least three roles that budgeting plays in helping managers control and monitor a business.

2. What two common benchmarks can be used to evaluate actual performance? Which of the two is generally more useful?

3. What is the benefit of continuous budgeting?

4. Identify three usual time horizons for short-term planning and budgets.

5. Why should each department participate in preparing its own budget?

6. How does budgeting help management coordinate and plan business activities?

7. Why is the sales budget so important to the budgeting process?

8. What is a selling expense budget? What is a capital expenditures budget?

9. Budgeting promotes good decision making by requiring managers to conduct _____ and by focusing their attention on the _____.

10. What is a cash budget? Why must operating budgets and the capital expenditures budget be prepared before the cash budget?

11.^A What is the difference between a production budget and a manufacturing budget?

12. Would a manager of a **Best Buy** retail store participate more in budgeting than a manager at the corporate offices? Explain.

13. Does the manager of a local **Circuit City** retail store participate in long-term budgeting? Explain.

14. Assume that **Apple**'s iMac division is charged with preparing a master budget. Identify the participants—for example, the sales manager for the sales budget—and describe the information each person provides in preparing the master budget.

Red numbers denote Discussion Questions that involve decision-making.

Which one of the following sets of items are all necessary components of the master budget?

1. Operating budgets, historical income statement, and budgeted balance sheet.

2. Prior sales reports, capital expenditures budget, and financial budgets.

3. Sales budget, operating budgets, and historical financial budgets.

4. Operating budgets, financial budgets, and capital expenditures budget.

QUICK STUDY

QS 23-1
Components of a master budget
C3

The motivation of employees is one goal of budgeting. Identify three guidelines that organizations should follow if budgeting is to serve effectively as a source of motivation for employees.

QS 23-2
Budget motivation   C1

Montel Company's July sales budget calls for sales of $600,000. The store expects to begin July with $50,000 of inventory and to end the month with $40,000 of inventory. Gross margin is typically 40% of sales. Determine the budgeted cost of merchandise purchases for July.

QS 23-3
Purchases budget   P1

Good management includes good budgeting. (1) Explain why the bottom-up approach to budgeting is considered a more successful management technique than a top-down approach. (2) Provide an example of implementation of the bottom-up approach to budgeting.

QS 23-4
Budgeting process   C2

Lighthouse Company anticipates total sales for June and July of $420,000 and $398,000, respectively. Cash sales are normally 60% of total sales. Of the credit sales, 20% are collected in the same month as the sale, 70% are collected during the first month after the sale, and the remaining 10% are collected in the second month. Determine the amount of accounts receivable reported on Lighthouse's budgeted balance sheet as of July 31.

QS 23-5
Computing budgeted accounts receivable
P2

Use the following information to prepare a cash budget for the month ended on March 31 for Gado Company. The budget should show expected cash receipts and cash disbursements for the month of March and the balance expected on March 31.

a. Beginning cash balance on March 1, $72,000.

b. Cash receipts from sales, $300,000.

c. Budgeted cash disbursements for purchases, $140,000.

d. Budgeted cash disbursements for salaries, $80,000.

e. Other budgeted cash expenses, $45,000.

f. Cash repayment of bank loan, $20,000.

QS 23-6
Cash budget
P1   P2

Activity-based budgeting is a budget system based on *expected activities*. (1) Describe activity-based budgeting, and explain its preparation of budgets. (2) How does activity-based budgeting differ from traditional budgeting?

QS 23-7
Activity-based budgeting
A1

Forrest Company manufactures watches and has a JIT policy that ending inventory must equal 10% of the next month's sales. It estimates that October's actual ending inventory will consist of 40,000 watches. November and December sales are estimated to be 400,000 and 350,000 watches, respectively. Compute the number of watches to be produced that would appear on Forrest's production budget for the month of November.

QS 23-8^A
Production budget
P3

Walker Company prepares monthly budgets. The current budget plans for a September ending inventory of 30,000 units. Company policy is to end each month with merchandise inventory equal to a specified percent of budgeted sales for the following month. Budgeted sales and merchandise purchases for the three most recent months follow. (1) Prepare the merchandise purchases budget for the months of July, August, and September. (2) Compute the ratio of ending inventory to the next month's sales for each budget prepared in part 1. (3) How many units are budgeted for sale in October?

EXERCISES

Exercise 23-1
Preparation of merchandise purchases budgets (for three periods)

C3   P1

	Sales (Units)	Purchases (Units)
July	180,000	200,250
August	315,000	308,250
September	270,000	259,500

Check July budgeted ending inventory, $47,250

Exercise 23-2
Preparation of cash budgets (for three periods)

C3   P2

Kayak Co. budgeted the following cash receipts and cash disbursements for the first three months of next year.

	Cash Receipts	Cash Disbursements
January	$525,000	$475,000
February	400,000	350,000
March	450,000	525,000

Check   January ending cash balance, $30,000

According to a credit agreement with the company's bank, Kayak promises to have a minimum cash balance of $30,000 at each month-end. In return, the bank has agreed that the company can borrow up to $150,000 at an annual interest rate of 12%, paid on the last day of each month. The interest is computed based on the beginning balance of the loan for the month. The company has a cash balance of $30,000 and a loan balance of $60,000 at January 1. Prepare monthly cash budgets for each of the first three months of next year.

Exercise 23-3
Preparation of a cash budget

C3   P2

Use the following information to prepare the July cash budget for Acco Co. It should show expected cash receipts and cash disbursements for the month and the cash balance expected on July 31.

a. Beginning cash balance on July 1: $50,000.

b. Cash receipts from sales: 30% is collected in the month of sale, 50% in the next month, and 20% in the second month after sale (uncollectible accounts are negligible and can be ignored). Sales amounts are: May (actual), $1,720,000; June (actual), $1,200,000; and July (budgeted), $1,400,000.

c. Payments on merchandise purchases: 60% in the month of purchase and 40% in the month following purchase. Purchases amounts are: June (actual), $700,000; and July (budgeted), $750,000.

d. Budgeted cash disbursements for salaries in July: $275,000.

e. Budgeted depreciation expense for July: $36,000.

f. Other cash expenses budgeted for July: $200,000.

g. Accrued income taxes due in July: $80,000.

Check   Ending cash balance, $122,400

h. Bank loan interest due in July: $6,600.

Exercise 23-4
Preparing a budgeted income statement and balance sheet

C3   P2

Use the information in Exercise 23-3 and the following additional information to prepare a budgeted income statement for the month of July and a budgeted balance sheet for July 31.

a. Cost of goods sold is 55% of sales.

b. Inventory at the end of June is $80,000 and at the end of July is $60,000.

c. Salaries payable on June 30 are $50,000 and are expected to be $60,000 on July 31.

d. The equipment account balance is $1,600,000 on July 31. On June 30, the accumulated depreciation on equipment is $280,000.

e. The $6,600 cash payment of interest represents the 1% monthly expense on a bank loan of $660,000.

f. Income taxes payable on July 31 are $30,720, and the income tax rate applicable to the company is 30%.

Check   Net income, $71,680; Total assets, $2,686,400

g. The only other balance sheet accounts are: Common Stock, with a balance of $600,000 on June 30; and Retained Earnings, with a balance of $964,000 on June 30.

Exercise 23-5
Computing budgeted cash payments for purchases

C3   P2

Hardy Company's cost of goods sold is consistently 60% of sales. The company plans to carry ending merchandise inventory for each month equal to 20% of the next month's budgeted cost of goods sold. All merchandise is purchased on credit, and 50% of the purchases made during a month is paid for in that month. Another 35% is paid for during the first month after purchase, and the remaining 15% is paid for during the second month after purchase. Expected sales are: August (actual), $325,000; September (actual), $320,000; October (estimated), $250,000; November (estimated), $310,000. Use this information to determine October's expected cash payments for purchases. (*Hint:* Use the layout of Exhibit 23.8, but revised for the facts given here.)

Check   Budgeted purchases: August, $194,400; October, $157,200

Exercise 23-6
Computing budgeted purchases and costs of goods sold

C3   P1   P2

Quick Dollar Company purchases all merchandise on credit. It recently budgeted the following month-end accounts payable balances and merchandise inventory balances. Cash payments on accounts payable during each month are expected to be: May, $1,600,000; June, $1,490,000; July, $1,425,000; and August, $1,495,000. Use the available information to compute the budgeted amounts of (1) merchandise purchases for June, July, and August, and (2) cost of goods sold for June, July, and August.

	Accounts Payable	Merchandise Inventory
May 31	$150,000	$250,000
June 30	200,000	400,000
July 31	235,000	300,000
August 31	195,000	330,000

Check   June purchases, $1,540,000; June cost of goods sold, $1,390,000

Big Sound, a merchandising company specializing in home computer speakers, budgets its monthly cost of goods sold to equal 70% of sales. Its inventory policy calls for ending inventory in each month to equal 20% of the next month's budgeted cost of goods sold. All purchases are on credit, and 25% of the purchases in a month is paid for in the same month. Another 60% is paid for during the first month after purchase, and the remaining 15% is paid for in the second month after purchase. The following sales budgets are set: July, $350,000; August, $290,000; September, $320,000; October, $275,000; and November, $265,000. Compute the following: (1) budgeted merchandise purchases for July, August, September, and October; (2) budgeted payments on accounts payable for September and October; and (3) budgeted ending balances of accounts payable for September and October.

Exercise 23-7
Computing budgeted accounts payable and purchases   P1   P2

Check   July purchases, $236,600; Sept. payments on accts. pay., $214,235

Electro Company manufactures an innovative automobile transmission for electric cars. Management predicts that ending inventory for the first quarter will be 75,000 units. The following unit sales of the transmissions are expected during the rest of the year: second quarter, 450,000 units; third quarter, 525,000 units; and fourth quarter, 475,000 units. Company policy calls for the ending inventory of a quarter to equal 20% of the next quarter's budgeted sales. Prepare a production budget for both the second and third quarters that shows the number of transmissions to manufacture.

Exercise 23-8^A
Preparing production budgets (for two periods)   P3

Check   Second quarter production, 480,000

Kegler's Supply is a merchandiser of three different products. The company's February 28 inventories are footwear, 20,000 units; sports equipment, 80,000 units; and apparel, 50,000 units. Management believes that excessive inventories have accumulated for all three products. As a result, a new policy dictates that ending inventory in any month should equal 30% of the expected unit sales for the following month. Expected sales in units for March, April, May, and June follow.

PROBLEM SET A

Problem 23-1A
Preparation and analysis of merchandise purchases budgets

C3   P1

mhhe.com/wildFAP18e

	Budgeted Sales in Units			
	March	April	May	June
Footwear	15,000	25,000	32,000	35,000
Sports equipment	70,000	90,000	95,000	90,000
Apparel	40,000	38,000	37,000	25,000

Required

1. Prepare a merchandise purchases budget (in units) for each product for each of the months of March, April, and May.

Check   (1) March budgeted purchases Footwear, 2,500; Sports equip., 17,000; Apparel, 1,400

Analysis Component

2. The purchases budgets in part 1 should reflect fewer purchases of all three products in March compared to those in April and May. What factor caused fewer purchases to be planned? Suggest business conditions that would cause this factor to both occur and impact the company in this way.

During the last week of August, Oneida Company's owner approaches the bank for a $100,000 loan to be made on September 2 and repaid on November 30 with annual interest of 12%, for an interest cost of $3,000. The owner plans to increase the store's inventory by $80,000 during September and needs the loan to pay for inventory acquisitions. The bank's loan officer needs more information about Oneida's ability to repay the loan and asks the owner to forecast the store's November 30 cash position. On September 1, Oneida is expected to have a $5,000 cash balance, $148,000 of accounts receivable, and $125,000 of accounts payable. Its budgeted sales, merchandise purchases, and various cash disbursements for the next three months follow.

Problem 23-2A
Preparation of cash budgets (for three periods)

C3   P2

mhhe.com/wildFAP18e

Budgeted Figures*	September	October	November
1			
2 Sales	$250,000	$375,000	$400,000
3 Merchandise purchases	240,000	225,000	200,000
4 Cash disbursements			
5 Payroll	20,000	22,000	24,000
6 Rent	10,000	10,000	10,000
7 Other cash expenses	35,000	30,000	20,000
8 Repayment of bank loan			100,000
9 Interest on the bank loan			3,000
10			

* Operations began in August; August sales were $215,000 and purchases were $125,000.

The budgeted September merchandise purchases include the inventory increase. All sales are on account. The company predicts that 25% of credit sales is collected in the month of the sale, 45% in the month following the sale, 20% in the second month, 9% in the third, and the remainder is uncollectible. Applying these percents to the August credit sales, for example, shows that $96,750 of the $215,000 will be collected in September, $43,000 in October, and $19,350 in November. All merchandise is purchased on credit; 80% of the balance is paid in the month following a purchase, and the remaining 20% is paid in the second month. For example, of the $125,000 August purchases, $100,000 will be paid in September and $25,000 in October.

Check Budgeted cash balance:
September, $99,250; October, $69,500;
November, $22,600

Required

Prepare a cash budget for September, October, and November for Oneidia Company. Show supporting calculations as needed.

Problem 23-3A
Preparation and analysis of cash budgets with supporting inventory and purchases budgets

C3 P2

Aztec Company sells its product for $180 per unit. Its actual and projected sales follow.

	Units	Dollars
April (actual)	4,000	$ 720,000
May (actual)	2,000	360,000
June (budgeted)	6,000	1,080,000
July (budgeted)	5,000	900,000
August (budgeted)	3,800	684,000

All sales are on credit. Recent experience shows that 20% of credit sales is collected in the month of the sale, 50% in the month after the sale, 28% in the second month after the sale, and 2% proves to be uncollectible. The product's purchase price is $110 per unit. All purchases are payable within 12 days. Thus, 60% of purchases made in a month is paid in that month and the other 40% is paid in the next month. Aztec has a policy to maintain an ending monthly inventory of 20% of the next month's unit sales plus a safety stock of 100 units. The April 30 and May 31 actual inventory levels are consistent with this policy. Selling and administrative expenses for the year are $1,320,000 and are paid evenly throughout the year in cash. The company's minimum cash balance at month-end is $100,000. This minimum is maintained, if necessary, by borrowing cash from the bank. If the balance exceeds $100,000, the company repays as much of the loan as it can without going below the minimum. This type of loan carries an annual 12% interest rate. On May 31, the loan balance is $25,000, and the company's cash balance is $100,000.

Required

Check (1) Cash collections: June,
$597,600; July, $820,800

1. Prepare a table that shows the computation of cash collections of its credit sales (accounts receivable) in each of the months of June and July.

2. Prepare a table that shows the computation of budgeted ending inventories (in units) for April, May, June, and July.

**(3) Budgeted purchases: May,
$308,000; June, $638,000

3. Prepare the merchandise purchases budget for May, June, and July. Report calculations in units and then show the dollar amount of purchases for each month.

4. Prepare a table showing the computation of cash payments on product purchases for June and July.

**(5) Budgeted ending loan
balance: June, $43,650; July, $0

5. Prepare a cash budget for June and July, including any loan activity and interest expense. Compute the loan balance at the end of each month.

Analysis Component

6. Refer to your answer to part 5. Aztec's cash budget indicates the company will need to borrow more than $18,000 in June and will be able to pay it back in July. Suggest some reasons that knowing this information in May would be helpful to management.

Merline, a one-product mail-order firm, buys its product for $75 per unit and sells it for $150 per unit. The sales staff receives a 10% commission on the sale of each unit. Its December income statement follows.

Problem 23-4A
Preparation and analysis of budgeted income statements

C3   P2

MERLINE COMPANY	
Income Statement	
For Month Ended December 31, 2008	
Sales	$2,250,000
Cost of goods sold	1,125,000
Gross profit	1,125,000
Expenses	
Sales commissions (10%)	225,000
Advertising	250,000
Store rent	30,000
Administrative salaries	45,000
Depreciation	50,000
Other expenses	10,000
Total expenses	610,000
Net income	$ 515,000

Management expects December's results to be repeated in January, February, and March of 2009 without any changes in strategy. Management, however, has an alternative plan. It believes that unit sales will increase at a rate of 10% *each* month for the next three months (beginning with January) if the item's selling price is reduced to $125 per unit and advertising expenses are increased by 15% and remain at that level for all three months. The cost of its product will remain at $75 per unit, the sales staff will continue to earn a 10% commission, and the remaining expenses will stay the same.

Required

1. Prepare budgeted income statements for each of the months of January, February, and March that show the expected results from implementing the proposed changes. Use a three-column format, with one column for each month.

Check (1) Budgeted net income: January, $196,250; February, $258,125; March, $326,187

Analysis Component

2. Use the budgeted income statements from part 1 to recommend whether management should implement the proposed changes. Explain.

Near the end of 2008, the management of Dimsdale Sports Co., a merchandising company, prepared the following estimated balance sheet for December 31, 2008.

Problem 23-5A
Preparation of a complete master budget

C2   C3   P1   P2

DIMSDALE SPORTS COMPANY		
Estimated Balance Sheet		
December 31, 2008		
Assets		
Cash		$ 36,000
Accounts receivable		525,000
Inventory		150,000
Total current assets		711,000
Equipment	$540,000	
Less accumulated depreciation	67,500	472,500
Total assets		$1,183,500

[continued on next page]

[continued from previous page]

Liabilities and Equity		
Accounts payable	$360,000	
Bank loan payable	15,000	
Taxes payable (due 3/15/2009)	90,000	
Total liabilities		$ 465,000
Common stock	472,500	
Retained earnings	246,000	
Total stockholders' equity		718,500
Total liabilities and equity		$1,183,500

To prepare a master budget for January, February, and March of 2009, management gathers the following information.

a. Dimsdale Sports' single product is purchased for $30 per unit and resold for $55 per unit. The expected inventory level of 5,000 units on December 31, 2008, is more than management's desired level for 2009, which is 20% of the next month's expected sales (in units). Expected sales are: January, 7,000 units; February, 9,000 units; March, 11,000 units; and April, 10,000 units.

b. Cash sales and credit sales represent 25% and 75%, respectively, of total sales. Of the credit sales, 60% is collected in the first month after the month of sale and 40% in the second month after the month of sale. For the December 31, 2008, accounts receivable balance, $125,000 is collected in January and the remaining $400,000 is collected in February.

c. Merchandise purchases are paid for as follows: 20% in the first month after the month of purchase and 80% in the second month after the month of purchase. For the December 31, 2008, accounts payable balance, $80,000 is paid in January and the remaining $280,000 is paid in February.

d. Sales commissions equal to 20% of sales are paid each month. Sales salaries (excluding commissions) are $60,000 per year.

e. General and administrative salaries are $144,000 per year. Maintenance expense equals $2,000 per month and is paid in cash.

f. Equipment reported in the December 31, 2008, balance sheet was purchased in January 2008. It is being depreciated over eight years under the straight-line method with no salvage value. The following amounts for new equipment purchases are planned in the coming quarter: January, $36,000; February, $96,000; and March, $28,800. This equipment will be depreciated under the straight-line method over eight years with no salvage value. A full month's depreciation is taken for the month in which equipment is purchased.

g. The company plans to acquire land at the end of March at a cost of $150,000, which will be paid with cash on the last day of the month.

h. Dimsdale Sports has a working arrangement with its bank to obtain additional loans as needed. The interest rate is 12% per year, and interest is paid at each month-end based on the beginning balance. Partial or full payments on these loans can be made on the last day of the month. The company has agreed to maintain a minimum ending cash balance of $25,000 in each month.

i. The income tax rate for the company is 40%. Income taxes on the first quarter's income will not be paid until April 15.

Required

Prepare a master budget for each of the first three months of 2009; include the following component budgets (show supporting calculations as needed, and round amounts to the nearest dollar):

1. Monthly sales budgets (showing both budgeted unit sales and dollar sales).

2. Monthly merchandise purchases budgets.

3. Monthly selling expense budgets.

4. Monthly general and administrative expense budgets.

5. Monthly capital expenditures budgets.

6. Monthly cash budgets.

7. Budgeted income statement for the entire first quarter (not for each month).

8. Budgeted balance sheet as of March 31, 2009.

Check   (2) Budgeted purchases: January, $114,000; February, $282,000

          (3) Budgeted selling expenses: January, $82,000; February, $104,000

          (6) Ending cash bal.: January, $30,100; February, $210,300

          (8) Budgeted total assets at March 31, $1,568,650

Black Diamond Company produces snow skis. Each ski requires 2 pounds of carbon fiber. The company's management predicts that 5,000 skis and 6,000 pounds of carbon fiber will be in inventory on June 30 of the current year and that 150,000 skis will be sold during the next (third) quarter. Management wants to end the third quarter with 3,500 skis and 4,000 pounds of carbon fiber in inventory. Carbon fiber can be purchased for $15 per pound.

Problem 23-6A[A]

Preparing production and direct materials budgets

C3 P3

Required

1. Prepare the third-quarter production budget for skis.

2. Prepare the third-quarter direct materials (carbon fiber) budget; include the dollar cost of purchases.

Check (1) Units manuf., 148,500;
(2) Cost of carbon fiber purchases, $4,425,000

H2O Sports Corp. is a merchandiser of three different products. The company's March 31 inventories are water skis, 40,000 units; tow ropes, 90,000 units; and life jackets, 150,000 units. Management believes that excessive inventories have accumulated for all three products. As a result, a new policy dictates that ending inventory in any month should equal 10% of the expected unit sales for the following month. Expected sales in units for April, May, June, and July follow.

PROBLEM SET B

Problem 23-1B

Preparation and analysis of merchandise purchases budgets

C3 P1

	Budgeted Sales in Units			
	April	May	June	July
Water skis	70,000	90,000	130,000	100,000
Tow ropes	100,000	90,000	110,000	100,000
Life jackets	160,000	190,000	200,000	120,000

Required

1. Prepare a merchandise purchases budget (in units) for each product for each of the months of April, May, and June.

Analysis Component

2. The purchases budgets in part 1 should reflect fewer purchases of all three products in April compared to those in May and June. What factor caused fewer purchases to be planned? Suggest business conditions that would cause this factor to both occur and affect the company as it has.

Check (1) April budgeted purchases:
Water skis, 39,000; Tow ropes, 19,000;
Life jackets, 29,000

During the last week of March, Sony Stereo's owner approaches the bank for an $80,000 loan to be made on April 1 and repaid on June 30 with annual interest of 12%, for an interest cost of $2,400. The owner plans to increase the store's inventory by $60,000 in April and needs the loan to pay for inventory acquisitions. The bank's loan officer needs more information about Sony Stereo's ability to repay the loan and asks the owner to forecast the store's June 30 cash position. On April 1, Sony Stereo is expected to have a $3,000 cash balance, $135,000 of accounts receivable, and $100,000 of accounts payable. Its budgeted sales, merchandise purchases, and various cash disbursements for the next three months follow.

Problem 23-2B

Preparation of cash budgets (for three periods)

C3 P2

File Edit View Insert Format Tools Data Window Help			
Budgeted Figures*	**April**	**May**	**June**
Sales	$220,000	$300,000	$380,000
Merchandise purchases	210,000	180,000	220,000
Cash disbursements			
Payroll	16,000	17,000	18,000
Rent	6,000	8,000	6,000
Other cash expenses	64,000	8,000	7,000
Repayment of bank loan			80,000
Interest on the bank loan			2,400

* Operations began in March; March sales were $180,000 and purchases were $100,000.

The budgeted April merchandise purchases include the inventory increase. All sales are on account. The company predicts that 25% of credit sales is collected in the month of the sale, 45% in the month following the sale, 20% in the second month, 9% in the third, and the remainder is uncollectible. Applying these percents to the March credit sales, for example, shows that $81,000 of the $180,000 will be collected in April, $36,000 in May, and $16,200 in June. All merchandise is purchased on credit; 80% of the balance is paid in the month following a purchase and the remaining 20% is paid in the second month. For example, of the $100,000 March purchases, $80,000 will be paid in April and $20,000 in May.

Required

Prepare a cash budget for April, May, and June for Sony Stereo. Show supporting calculations as needed.

Problem 23-3B
Preparation and analysis of cash budgets with supporting inventory and purchases budgets

C3   P2

Connick Company sells its product for $22 per unit. Its actual and projected sales follow.

	Units	Dollars
January (actual)	18,000	$396,000
February (actual)	22,500	495,000
March (budgeted)	19,000	418,000
April (budgeted)	18,750	412,500
May (budgeted)	21,000	462,000

All sales are on credit. Recent experience shows that 40% of credit sales is collected in the month of the sale, 35% in the month after the sale, 23% in the second month after the sale, and 2% proves to be uncollectible. The product's purchase price is $12 per unit. All purchases are payable within 21 days. Thus, 30% of purchases made in a month is paid in that month and the other 70% is paid in the next month. Connick has a policy to maintain an ending monthly inventory of 20% of the next month's unit sales plus a safety stock of 100 units. The January 31 and February 28 actual inventory levels are consistent with this policy. Selling and administrative expenses for the year are $1,920,000 and are paid evenly throughout the year in cash. The company's minimum cash balance for month-end is $50,000. This minimum is maintained, if necessary, by borrowing cash from the bank. If the balance exceeds $50,000, the company repays as much of the loan as it can without going below the minimum. This type of loan carries an annual 12% interest rate. At February 28, the loan balance is $12,000, and the company's cash balance is $50,000.

Required

1. Prepare a table that shows the computation of cash collections of its credit sales (accounts receivable) in each of the months of March and April.

2. Prepare a table showing the computations of budgeted ending inventories (units) for January, February, March, and April.

3. Prepare the merchandise purchases budget for February, March, and April. Report calculations in units and then show the dollar amount of purchases for each month.

4. Prepare a table showing the computation of cash payments on product purchases for March and April.

5. Prepare a cash budget for March and April, including any loan activity and interest expense. Compute the loan balance at the end of each month.

Analysis Component

6. Refer to your answer to part 5. Connick's cash budget indicates whether the company must borrow additional funds at the end of March. Suggest some reasons that knowing this information in February would be helpful to management.

Problem 23-4B
Preparation and analysis of budgeted income statements

C3   P2

Comp-Media buys its product for $60 and sells it for $130 per unit. The sales staff receives a 10% commission on the sale of each unit. Its June income statement follows.

COMP-MEDIA COMPANY Income Statement For Month Ended June 30, 2008	
Sales	$1,300,000
Cost of goods sold	600,000
Gross profit	700,000
Expenses	
Sales commissions (10%)	130,000
Advertising	200,000

[continued on next page]

[continued from previous page]

Store rent	24,000
Administrative salaries	40,000
Depreciation	50,000
Other expenses	12,000
Total expenses	456,000
Net income	$ 244,000

Management expects June's results to be repeated in July, August, and September without any changes in strategy. Management, however, has another plan. It believes that unit sales will increase at a rate of 10% *each* month for the next three months (beginning with July) if the item's selling price is reduced to $115 per unit and advertising expenses are increased by 25% and remain at that level for all three months. The cost of its product will remain at $60 per unit, the sales staff will continue to earn a 10% commission, and the remaining expenses will stay the same.

Required

1. Prepare budgeted income statements for each of the months of July, August, and September that show the expected results from implementing the proposed changes. Use a three-column format, with one column for each month.

Check Budgeted net income: July, $102,500; August, $150,350; September, $202,985

Analysis Component

2. Use the budgeted income statements from part 1 to recommend whether management should implement the proposed plan. Explain.

Near the end of 2008, the management of Isle Corp., a merchandising company, prepared the following estimated balance sheet for December 31, 2008.

Problem 23-5B
Preparation of a complete master budget

C2 C3 P1 P2

ISLE CORPORATION
Estimated Balance Sheet
December 31, 2008

Assets		
Cash		$ 36,000
Accounts receivable		525,000
Inventory		150,000
Total current assets		711,000
Equipment	$540,000	
Less accumulated depreciation	67,500	472,500
Total assets		$1,183,500
Liabilities and Equity		
Accounts payable	$360,000	
Bank loan payable	15,000	
Taxes payable (due 3/15/2009)	90,000	
Total liabilities		$ 465,000
Common stock	472,500	
Retained earnings	246,000	
Total stockholders' equity		718,500
Total liabilities and equity		$1,183,500

To prepare a master budget for January, February, and March of 2009, management gathers the following information.

a. Isle Corp.'s single product is purchased for $30 per unit and resold for $45 per unit. The expected inventory level of 5,000 units on December 31, 2008, is more than management's desired level for 2009, which is 25% of the next month's expected sales (in units). Expected sales are: January, 6,000 units; February, 8,000 units; March, 10,000 units; and April, 9,000 units.

b. Cash sales and credit sales represent 25% and 75%, respectively, of total sales. Of the credit sales, 60% is collected in the first month after the month of sale and 40% in the second month after the month of sale. For the $525,000 accounts receivable balance at December 31, 2008, $315,000 is collected in January 2009 and the remaining $210,000 is collected in February 2009.

c. Merchandise purchases are paid for as follows: 20% in the first month after the month of purchase and 80% in the second month after the month of purchase. For the $360,000 accounts payable balance at December 31, 2008, $72,000 is paid in January 2009 and the remaining $288,000 is paid in February 2009.

d. Sales commissions equal to 20% of sales are paid each month. Sales salaries (excluding commissions) are $90,000 per year.

e. General and administrative salaries are $144,000 per year. Maintenance expense equals $3,000 per month and is paid in cash.

f. Equipment reported in the December 31, 2008, balance sheet was purchased in January 2008. It is being depreciated over 8 years under the straight-line method with no salvage value. The following amounts for new equipment purchases are planned in the coming quarter: January, $72,000; February, $96,000; and March, $28,800. This equipment will be depreciated using the straight-line method over 8 years with no salvage value. A full month's depreciation is taken for the month in which equipment is purchased.

g. The company plans to acquire land at the end of March at a cost of $150,000, which will be paid with cash on the last day of the month.

h. Isle Corp. has a working arrangement with its bank to obtain additional loans as needed. The interest rate is 12% per year, and interest is paid at each month-end based on the beginning balance. Partial or full payments on these loans can be made on the last day of the month. Isle has agreed to maintain a minimum ending cash balance of $36,000 in each month.

i. The income tax rate for the company is 40%. Income taxes on the first quarter's income will not be paid until April 15.

Required

Prepare a master budget for each of the first three months of 2009; include the following component budgets (show supporting calculations as needed, and round amounts to the nearest dollar):

1. Monthly sales budgets (showing both budgeted unit sales and dollar sales).

2. Monthly merchandise purchases budgets.

3. Monthly selling expense budgets.

4. Monthly general and administrative expense budgets.

5. Monthly capital expenditures budgets.

6. Monthly cash budgets.

7. Budgeted income statement for the entire first quarter (not for each month).

8. Budgeted balance sheet as of March 31, 2009.

Check (2) Budgeted purchases:
January, $90,000; February, $255,000;
    (3) Budgeted selling expenses:
January, $61,500; February, $79,500

    (6) Ending cash bal.: January,
$182,850; February, $107,850
    (8) Budgeted total assets at
March 31, $1,346,875

Problem 23-6B[A]
Preparing production and direct materials budgets

C3   P3

NSA Company produces baseball bats. Each bat requires 3 pounds of aluminum alloy. Management predicts that 8,000 bats and 15,000 pounds of aluminum alloy will be in inventory on March 31 of the current year and that 250,000 bats will be sold during this year's second quarter. Management wants to end the second quarter with 6,000 finished bats and 12,000 pounds of aluminum alloy in inventory. Aluminum alloy can be purchased for $4 per pound.

Required

1. Prepare the second-quarter production budget for bats.

2. Prepare the second-quarter direct materials (aluminum alloy) budget; include the dollar cost of purchases.

Check (1) Units manuf., 248,000;
    (2) Cost of aluminum
purchases, $2,964,000

PROBLEM SET C

Problem Set C is available at the book's Website to further reinforce and assess your learning.

SERIAL PROBLEM

Success Systems

(This serial problem began in Chapter 1 and continues through most of the book. If previous chapter segments were not completed, the serial problem can begin at this point. It is helpful, but not necessary, for you to use the Working Papers that accompany the book.)

SP 23 Adriana Lopez expects second quarter 2009 sales of her new line of computer furniture to be the same as the first quarter's sales (reported below) without any changes in strategy. Monthly sales averaged 40 desk units (sales price of $1,250) and 20 chairs (sales price of $500).

SUCCESS SYSTEMS
Segment Income Statement*
For Quarter Ended March 31, 2009

Sales[†]	$180,000
Cost of goods sold[‡]	105,000
Gross profit	75,000
Expenses	
Sales commissions (10%)	18,000
Advertising expenses	9,000
Other fixed expenses	18,000
Total expenses	45,000
Net income	$ 30,000

* Reflects revenue and expense activity only related to the computer furniture segment.

[†] Revenue: (120 desks $\times$ $1,250) + (60 chairs $\times$ $500) = $150,000 + $30,000 = $180,000

[‡] Cost of goods sold: (120 desks $\times$ $750) + (60 chairs $\times$ $250) = $90,000 + $15,000 = $105,000

Lopez believes that sales will increase each month for the next three months (April, 44 desks, 22 chairs; May, 48 desks, 24 chairs; June, 52 desks, 26 chairs) *if* selling prices are reduced to $1,125 for desks and $375 for chairs, and advertising expenses are increased by 25% and remain at that level for all three months. The products' cost will remain at $750 for desks and $250 for chairs. The sales staff will continue to earn a 10% commission, and the fixed costs per month will remain at $5,000.

Required

1. Prepare budgeted income statements for each of the months of April, May, and June that show the expected results from implementing the proposed changes. Use a three-column format, with one column for each month.

2. Use the budgeted income statements from part 1 to recommend whether Lopez should implement the proposed changes. Explain.

Check (1) Budgeted income: April, $3,725; May, $4,950

BEYOND THE NUMBERS

BTN 23-1   Financial statements often serve as a starting point in formulating budgets. You are assigned to review **Best Buy**'s financial statements to determine its cash paid for dividends in the current year and the budgeted cash needed to pay its next year's dividend.

REPORTING IN ACTION

P2 C2 C3

Required

1. Which financial statement(s) reports the amount of (a) cash dividends paid and (b) annual cash dividends declared? Explain where on the statement(s) this information is reported.

2. Indicate the amount of cash dividends (a) paid in the year ended February 26, 2005, and (b) to be paid (budgeted for) next year under the assumption that annual cash dividends equal 20% of the prior year's net income.

Fast Forward

3. Access Best Buy's financial statements for a fiscal year ending after February 26, 2005, from either its Website [BestBuy.com] or the SEC's EDGAR database [www.sec.gov]. Compare your answer for part 2 with actual cash dividends paid for its fiscal year ended 2006. Compute the error, if any, in your estimate. Speculate as to why dividends were higher or lower than budgeted.

COMPARATIVE ANALYSIS

P2

BTN 23-2 One source of cash savings for a company is improved management of inventory. To illustrate, assume that **Best Buy** and **Circuit City** both have $250,000 per month in sales in the Virginia area, and both forecast this level of sales per month for the next 24 months. Also assume that both Best Buy and Circuit City have a 20% contribution margin and equal fixed costs, and that cost of goods sold is the only variable cost. Assume that the main difference between Best Buy and Circuit City is the distribution system. Best Buy uses a just-in-time system and requires ending inventory of only 10% of next month's sales in inventory at each month-end. However, Circuit City is building an improved distribution system and currently requires 40% of next month's sales in inventory at each month-end.

Required

1. Compute the amount by which Circuit City can reduce its inventory level if it can match Best Buy's system of maintaining an inventory equal to 10% of next month's sales. (*Hint:* Focus on the facts given and only on the Virginia area.)

2. Explain how the analysis in part 1 that shows ending inventory levels for both the 40% and 10% required inventory policies can help justify a just-in-time inventory system. You can assume a 15% interest cost for resources that are tied up in ending inventory.

ETHICS CHALLENGE

C1   C2

BTN 23-3 Both the budget process and budgets themselves can impact management actions, both positively and negatively. For instance, a common practice among not-for-profit organizations and government agencies is for management to spend any amounts remaining in a budget at the end of the budget period, a practice often called "use it or lose it." The view is that if a department manager does not spend the budgeted amount, top management will reduce next year's budget by the amount not spent. To avoid losing budget dollars, department managers often spend all budgeted amounts regardless of the value added to products or services. All of us pay for the costs associated with this budget system.

Required

Write a one-half page report to a local not-for-profit organization or government agency offering a solution to the "use it or lose it" budgeting problem.

COMMUNICATING IN PRACTICE

P1

BTN 23-4 The sales budget is usually the first and most crucial of the component budgets in a master budget because all other budgets usually rely on it for planning purposes.

Required

Assume that your company's sales staff provides information on expected sales and selling prices for items making up the sales budget. Prepare a one-page memorandum to your supervisor outlining concerns with the sales staff's input in the sales budget when its compensation is at least partly tied to these budgets. More generally, explain the importance of assessing any potential bias in information provided to the budget process.

TAKING IT TO THE NET

C2   P1   P2

BTN 23-5 Access an e-budgets Website at **HelmsmanGroup.com** (by **FRx Corporation**). Review the information at this site; click on the link *CFO Tour* and examine the information provided.

Required

1. Assume the role of a senior manager in a large, multidivision company. What are the benefits of using e-budgets?

2. As a senior manager, what concerns do you have with the concept and application of e-budgets?

TEAMWORK IN ACTION

A1

BTN 23-6 Your team is to prepare a budget report outlining the costs of attending college (full-time) for the next two semesters (30 hours) or three quarters (45 hours). This budget's focus is solely on attending college; do not include personal items in the team's budget. Your budget must include tuition, books, supplies, club fees, food, housing, and all costs associated with travel to and from college. This budgeting exercise is similar to the initial phase in activity-based budgeting. Include a list of any assumptions you use in completing the budget. Be prepared to present your budget in class.

BTN 23-7   Read the article "Get Thee to a Budget" from the March 14, 2005, issue of *BusinessWeek*. (This book's Website provides free access to this article.)

BusinessWeek **ACTIVITY**

C2   A1

Required

What advantages do new business owners who prepare budgets have over those who do not?

BTN 23-8   **Cloudveil** currently produces high-performance, multisport mountain apparel. Assume that Stephen Sullivan and Brian Cousins are considering producing a new line of apparel for high-altitude camping. They plan on meeting with a financial institution for potential funding and have been asked by its loan officers for their business plan.

ENTREPRENEURIAL DECISION

C1

Required

1. What should Cloudveil's business plan include?

2. How can budgeting help the owners efficiently develop and operate their business?

BTN 23-9   To help understand the factors impacting a sales budget, you are to visit three businesses with the same ownership or franchise membership. Record the selling prices of two identical products at each location, such as regular and premium gas sold at **Chevron** stations. You are likely to find a difference in prices for at least one of the three locations you visit.

HITTING THE ROAD

C3   P1

Required

1. Identify at least three external factors that must be considered when setting the sales budget. (*Note:* There is a difference between internal and external factors that impact the sales budget.)

2. What factors might explain any differences identified in the prices of the businesses you visited?

BTN 23-10   Access **Dixons'** income statement (Dixons-Group.com) for the year ended May 1, 2004.

GLOBAL DECISION

Dixons

Required

1. Is Dixons' administrative expense budget likely to be an important budget in its master budgeting process? Explain.

2. Identify three types of expenses that would be reported as administrative expenses on Dixons' income statement.

3. Who likely has the initial responsibility for Dixons' administrative expense budget? Explain.

ANSWERS TO MULTIPLE CHOICE QUIZ

1. c

2. e; Budgeted purchases = $36,000 + $7,000 − $6,000 = $37,000

3. b; Cash collected = 25% of September sales + 75% of August sales =
(0.25 × $240,000) + (0.75 × $220,000) = $225,000

4. d

5. a; 560 units + (0.30 × 600 units) − (0.30 × 560 units) = 572 units

24

Flexible Budgets and Standard Costs

A Look Back

Chapter 23 explained the master budget and its component budgets as well as their usefulness for planning and monitoring company activities.

A Look at This Chapter

This chapter describes flexible budgets, variance analysis, and standard costs. It explains how each is used for purposes of better controlling and monitoring business activities.

A Look Ahead

Chapter 25 focuses on capital budgeting decisions. It also explains and illustrates several procedures used in evaluating short-term managerial decisions.

Learning Objectives

CAP

Conceptual

C1 Define *standard costs* and explain their computation and uses. *(p. 959)*

C2 Describe variances and what they reveal about performance. *(p. 961)*

C3 Explain how standard cost information is useful for management by exception. *(p. 970)*

Analytical

A1 Compare fixed and flexible budgets. *(p. 956)*

A2 Analyze changes in sales from expected amounts. *(p. 972)*

Procedural

P1 Prepare a flexible budget and interpret a flexible budget performance report. *(p. 957)*

P2 Compute materials and labor variances. *(p. 962)*

P3 Compute overhead variances. *(p. 966)*

P4 Prepare journal entries for standard costs and account for price and quantity variances. *(p. 971)*

Decision Feature

Standards for Performance Apparel

BALTIMORE, MD—Kevin Plank's company, Under Armour (**UnderArmour.com**), manufactures a polyester blend fabric that whisks perspiration away from the skin. "There was a void in apparel and I decided to fill it," says Kevin. He invested his life savings of $20,000 and began working out of his grandma's basement. In the process, Kevin launched an entirely new sportswear category from sweaty undergarments.

As sales grew, Kevin partnered with a factory in Ohio that had excess capacity and hit it off with the factory manager, Sal Fasciana. Sal spent many evenings and weekends teaching Kevin about manufacturing, cost management, and accounting. It was Sal who introduced Kevin to budgets and variances. "I said, 'OK, kid. This is the way it's going to be done,'" recalls Sal. To save money for investing in his new company, Kevin even moved into a spare room in Sal and his wife's home, living on Sal's lasagna and Froot Loops.

Kevin applied what Sal taught him. He ensured the budgeted numbers were sensible and focused on meeting quality standards regarding materials, labor, and overhead. "We can only be concerned about ourselves and the job [that] we do," insists Kevin. The company adheres to tight standards variances. For instance, when a new product failed to meet standards, Kevin quickly pulled it and Under Armour took a $600,000 hit

in inventory. Says Kevin, "It's hard to take a $600,000 hit [but] money can be replaced." Kevin adheres to strict budgets and standards because, as he puts it, "The best product we manufacture is our story." Lose the story, and a company's edge is next.

A commitment to performance reporting and quality standards is propelling Under Armour's sales toward $300 million and shattering Kevin's most optimistic budget goals. "It's about educating consumers . . . investing in the product." Kevin also applies cost analysis and variances, flexible and fixed budgets, and performance reports. Sales variances are especially crucial to production pricing because the polyester-blend fabric that Kevin uses costs two to three times as much as cotton.

"When I first started. . . I was a young punk who thought he knew everything," explains Kevin. Although Kevin admits that insight and ingenuity are vital, he knows accounting reports must show profits for long-term success. "Most people out there are saying we're going to trip up at some point," says Kevin. "Our job is to prove them wrong." He might also prove Thomas Edison right: genius is 99 percent perspiration and 1 percent inspiration.

[Sources: *Under Armour Website,* May 2006; *Entrepreneur,* November 2003; *FastCompany,* 2005 and 2002; *USA Today,* December 2004; *Inc.com,* 2003 and 2004; *All Headline News,* August 2005; *Baltimore Business Journal,* February 2006]

Budgeting helps organize and formalize management's planning activities. This chapter extends the study of budgeting to look more closely at the use of budgets to evaluate performance. Evaluations are important for controlling and monitoring business activities. This chapter also describes and illustrates the use of standard costs and variance analyses. These managerial tools are useful for both evaluating and controlling organizations and for the planning of future activities.

Section 1—Flexible Budgets

This section introduces fixed budgets and fixed budget performance reports. It then introduces flexible budgets and flexible budget performance reports and illustrates their advantages.

Budgetary Process

A master budget reflects management's planned objectives for a future period. The preparation of a master budget is based on a predicted level of activity such as sales volume for the budget period. This section discusses the effects on the usefulness of budget reports when the actual level of activity differs from the predicted level.

Budgetary Control and Reporting

Budgetary control refers to management's use of budgets to monitor and control a company's operations. This includes using budgets to see that planned objectives are met. **Budget reports** contain relevant information that compares actual results to planned activities. This comparison is motivated by a need to both monitor performance and control activities. Budget reports are sometimes viewed as progress reports, or *report cards,* on management's performance in achieving planned objectives. These reports can be prepared at any time and for any period. Three common periods for a budget report are a month, quarter, and year.

Point: Budget reports are often used as a base to determine bonuses of managers.

The budgetary control process involves at least four steps: (1) develop the budget from planned objectives, (2) compare actual results to budgeted amounts and analyze any differences, (3) take corrective and strategic actions, and (4) establish new planned objectives and prepare a new budget. Exhibit 24.1 shows this continual process of budgetary control. Budget

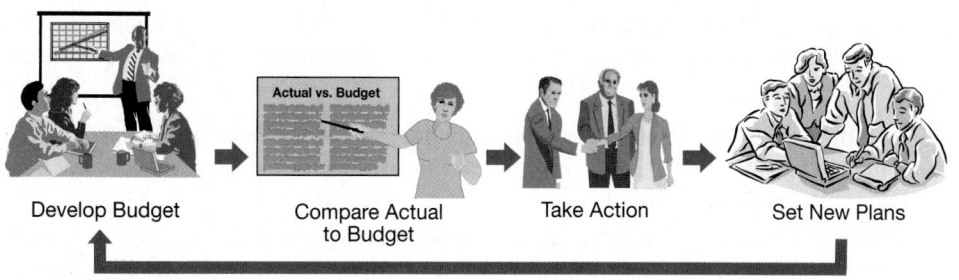

Exhibit 24.1

Process of Budgetary Control

reports and related documents are effective tools for managers to obtain the greatest benefits from this budgetary process.

Fixed Budget Performance Report

In a fixed budgetary control system, the master budget is based on a single prediction for sales volume or other activity level. The budgeted amount for each cost essentially assumes that a specific (or *fixed*) amount of sales will occur. A **fixed budget,** also called *static budget,* is based on a single predicted amount of sales or other measure of activity.

One benefit of a budget is its usefulness in comparing actual results with planned activities. Information useful for analysis is often presented for comparison in a performance report. As shown in Exhibit 24.2, a **fixed budget performance report** for Optel compares actual results for January 2008 with the results expected under its fixed budget that predicted 10,000 (composite) units of sales. Optel manufactures inexpensive eyeglasses, frames, contact lens, and related supplies. For this report, its production volume equals sales volume (its inventory level did not change).

OPTEL Fixed Budget Performance Report For Month Ended January 31, 2008	Fixed Budget	Actual Results	Variances*
Sales (in units)	10,000	12,000	
Sales (in dollars)	$100,000	$125,000	$25,000 F
Cost of goods sold			
Direct materials	10,000	13,000	3,000 U
Direct labor	15,000	20,000	5,000 U
Overhead			
Factory supplies	2,000	2,100	100 U
Utilities	3,000	4,000	1,000 U
Depreciation—Machinery	8,000	8,000	0
Supervisory salaries	11,000	11,000	0
Selling expenses			
Sales commissions	9,000	10,800	1,800 U
Shipping expenses	4,000	4,300	300 U
General and administrative expenses			
Office supplies	5,000	5,200	200 U
Insurance expenses	1,000	1,200	200 U
Depreciation—Office equipment	7,000	7,000	0
Administrative salaries	13,000	13,000	0
Total expenses	88,000	99,600	11,600 U
Income from operations	$ 12,000	$ 25,400	$13,400 F

Exhibit 24.2

Fixed Budget Performance Report

* F = Favorable variance; and U = Unfavorable variance.

This type of performance report designates differences between budgeted and actual results as variances. We see the letters *F* and *U* located beside the numbers in the third number column of this report. Their meanings are as follows:

F = **Favorable variance**   When compared to budget, the actual cost or revenue contributes to a *higher* income. That is, actual revenue is higher than budgeted revenue, or actual cost is lower than budgeted cost.

Example: How is it that the favorable sales variance in Exhibit 24.2 is linked with so many unfavorable cost and expense variances? *Answer:* Costs have increased with the increase in sales.

U = **Unfavorable variance**   When compared to budget, the actual cost or revenue contributes to a *lower* income; actual revenue is lower than budgeted revenue, or actual cost is higher than budgeted cost.

This convention is common in practice and is used throughout this chapter.

Budget Reports for Evaluation

A primary use of budget reports is as a tool for management to monitor and control operations. Evaluation by Optel management is likely to focus on a variety of questions that might include these:

■ Why is actual income from operations $13,400 higher than budgeted?
■ Are amounts paid for each expense item too high?
■ Is manufacturing using too much direct material?
■ Is manufacturing using too much direct labor?

The performance report in Exhibit 24.2 provides little help in answering these questions because actual sales volume is 2,000 units higher than budgeted. A manager does not know if this higher level of sales activity is the cause of variations in total dollar sales and expenses or if other factors have influenced these amounts. This inability of fixed budget reports to adjust for changes in activity levels is a major limitation of a fixed budget performance report. That is, it fails to show whether actual costs are out of line due to a change in actual sales volume or some other factor.

Decision Insight

Green Budget   Budget reporting and evaluation are used at the **Environmental Protection Agency (EPA)**. It regularly prepares performance plans and budget requests that describe performance goals, measure outcomes, and analyze variances.

Flexible Budget Reports

Purpose of Flexible Budgets

A1   Compare fixed and flexible budgets.

Topic Tackler

PLUS

24-1

To help address limitations with the fixed budget performance report, particularly from the effects of changes in sales volume, management can use a flexible budget. A **flexible budget,** also called a *variable budget,* is a report based on predicted amounts of revenues and expenses corresponding to the actual level of output. Flexible budgets are useful both before and after the period's activities are complete.

A flexible budget prepared before the period is often based on several levels of activity. Budgets for those different levels can provide a "what if" look at operations. The different levels often include both a best case and worst case scenario. This allows management to make adjustments to avoid or lessen the effects of the worst case scenario.

A flexible budget prepared after the period helps management evaluate past performance. It is especially useful for such an evaluation because it reflects budgeted revenues and costs based on the actual level of activity. Thus, comparisons of actual results with budgeted performance are more likely to identify the causes of any differences. This can help managers focus attention on real problem areas and implement corrective actions. This is in contrast to a fixed budget, whose primary purpose is to assist managers in planning future activities and whose numbers are based on a single predicted amount of budgeted sales or production.

Preparation of Flexible Budgets

A flexible budget is designed to reveal the effects of volume of activity on revenues and costs. To prepare a flexible budget, management relies on the distinctions between fixed and variable costs. Recall that the cost per unit of activity remains constant for variable costs so that the total amount of a variable cost changes in direct proportion to a change in activity level. The total amount of fixed cost remains unchanged regardless of changes in the level of activity within a relevant (normal) operating range. (Assume that costs can be reasonably classified as variable or fixed within a relevant range.)

When we create the numbers constituting a flexible budget, we express each variable cost as either a constant amount per unit of sales or as a percent of a sales dollar. In the case of a fixed cost, we express its budgeted amount as the total amount expected to occur at any sales volume within the relevant range.

Exhibit 24.3 shows a set of flexible budgets for Optel in January 2008. Seven of its expenses are classified as variable costs. Its remaining five expenses are fixed costs. These classifications result from management's investigation of each expense. Variable and fixed expense categories are *not* the same for every company, and we must avoid drawing conclusions from specific cases. For example, depending on the nature of a company's operations, office supplies expense can be either fixed or variable with respect to sales.

P1 **Prepare a flexible budget and interpret a flexible budget performance report.**

Point: Usefulness of a flexible budget depends on valid classification of variable and fixed costs. Some costs are mixed and must be analyzed to determine their variable and fixed portions.

OPTEL Flexible Budgets For Month Ended January 31, 2008	Flexible Budget Variable Amount per Unit	Flexible Budget Total Fixed Cost	Flexible Budget for Unit Sales of 10,000	Flexible Budget for Unit Sales of 12,000	Flexible Budget for Unit Sales of 14,000
Sales	$10.00		$100,000	$120,000	$140,000
Variable costs					
Direct materials	1.00		10,000	12,000	14,000
Direct labor	1.50		15,000	18,000	21,000
Factory supplies	0.20		2,000	2,400	2,800
Utilities	0.30		3,000	3,600	4,200
Sales commissions	0.90		9,000	10,800	12,600
Shipping expenses	0.40		4,000	4,800	5,600
Office supplies	0.50		5,000	6,000	7,000
Total variable costs	4.80		48,000	57,600	67,200
Contribution margin	$ 5.20		$ 52,000	$ 62,400	$ 72,800
Fixed costs					
Depreciation—Machinery		$ 8,000	8,000	8,000	8,000
Supervisory salaries		11,000	11,000	11,000	11,000
Insurance expense		1,000	1,000	1,000	1,000
Depreciation—Office equipment		7,000	7,000	7,000	7,000
Administrative salaries		13,000	13,000	13,000	13,000
Total fixed costs		$40,000	40,000	40,000	40,000
Income from operations			$ 12,000	$ 22,400	$ 32,800

Exhibit 24.3

Flexible Budgets

The layout for the flexible budgets in Exhibit 24.3 follows a *contribution margin format—* beginning with sales followed by variable costs and then fixed costs. Both the expected individual and total variable costs are reported and then subtracted from sales. The difference between sales and variable costs equals contribution margin. The expected amounts of fixed costs are listed next, followed by the expected income from operations before taxes.

Example: Using Exhibit 24.3, what is the budgeted income from operations for unit sales of (a) 11,000 and (b) 13,000? *Answers:* $17,200 for unit sales of 11,000. $27,600 for unit sales of 13,000.

The first and second number columns of Exhibit 24.3 show the flexible budget amounts for variable costs per unit and each fixed cost for any volume of sales in the relevant range. The third, fourth, and fifth columns show the flexible budget amounts computed for three different sales volumes. For instance, the third column's flexible budget is based on 10,000 units. These numbers are the same as those in the fixed budget of Exhibit 24.2 because the expected volumes are the same for these two budgets.

Recall that Optel's actual sales volume for January is 12,000 units. This sales volume is 2,000 units more than the 10,000 units originally predicted in the master budget. When differences between actual and predicted volume arise, the usefulness of a flexible budget is apparent. For instance, compare the flexible budget for 10,000 units in the third column (which is the same as the fixed budget in Exhibit 24.2) with the flexible budget for 12,000 units in the fourth column. The higher levels for both sales and variable costs reflect nothing more than the increase in sales activity. Any budget analysis comparing actual with planned results that ignores this information is less useful to management.

To illustrate, when we evaluate Optel's performance, we need to prepare a flexible budget showing actual and budgeted values at 12,000 units. As part of a complete profitability analysis, managers could compare the actual income of $25,400 (from Exhibit 24.2) with the $22,400 income expected at the actual sales volume of 12,000 units (from Exhibit 24.3). This results in a total income variance of $3,000 to be explained and interpreted. This variance is markedly different from the $13,400 variance identified in Exhibit 24.2 using a fixed budget. After receiving the flexible budget based on January's actual volume, management must determine what caused this $3,000 difference. The next section describes a flexible budget performance report that provides guidance in this analysis.

Point: Flexible budgeting allows a budget to be prepared at the *actual* output level. Performance reports are then prepared comparing the flexible budget to actual revenues and costs.

Point: A flexible budget yields an "apples to apples" comparison because budgeted activity levels are the same as the actual.

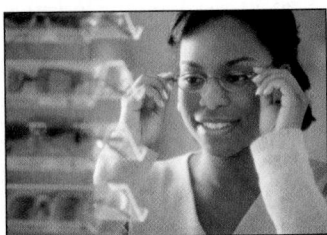

Flexible Budget Performance Report

A **flexible budget performance report** lists differences between actual performance and budgeted performance based on actual sales volume or other activity level. This report helps direct management's attention to those costs or revenues that differ substantially from budgeted amounts. Exhibit 24.4 shows Optel's flexible budget performance report for January. We prepare this report after the actual volume is known to be 12,000 units. This report shows a $5,000 favorable variance in total dollar sales. Because actual and budgeted volumes are both 12,000 units, the $5,000 sales variance must have resulted from a higher than expected selling price. Further analysis of the facts surrounding this $5,000 sales variance reveals a favorable sales variance per unit of nearly $0.42 as shown here:

Actual average price per unit (rounded to cents)	$125,000/12,000 = $10.42
Budgeted price per unit	$120,000/12,000 = 10.00
Favorable sales variance per unit	$5,000/12,000 = $ 0.42

The other variances in Exhibit 24.4 also direct management's attention to areas where corrective actions can help control Optel's operations. Each expense variance is analyzed as the sales variance was. We can think of each expense as the joint result of using a given number of units of input and paying a specific price per unit of input.

Each variance in Exhibit 24.4 is due in part to a difference between *actual price* per unit of input and *budgeted price* per unit of input. This is a **price variance.** Each variance also can be due in part to a difference between *actual quantity* of input used and *budgeted quantity* of input. This is a **quantity variance.** We explain more about this breakdown, known as **variance analysis,** later in the standard costs section.

OPTEL Flexible Budget Performance Report For Month Ended January 31, 2008	Flexible Budget	Actual Results	Variances*
Sales (12,000 units)	$120,000	$125,000	$5,000 F
Variable costs			
Direct materials	12,000	13,000	1,000 U
Direct labor	18,000	20,000	2,000 U
Factory supplies	2,400	2,100	300 F
Utilities	3,600	4,000	400 U
Sales commissions	10,800	10,800	0
Shipping expenses	4,800	4,300	500 F
Office supplies	6,000	5,200	800 F
Total variable costs	57,600	59,400	1,800 U
Contribution margin	62,400	65,600	3,200 F
Fixed costs			
Depreciation—Machinery	8,000	8,000	0
Supervisory salaries	11,000	11,000	0
Insurance expense	1,000	1,200	200 U
Depreciation—Office equipment	7,000	7,000	0
Administrative salaries	13,000	13,000	0
Total fixed costs	40,000	40,200	200 U
Income from operations	$ 22,400	$ 25,400	$3,000 F

Exhibit 24.4

Flexible Budget Performance Report

* F = Favorable variance; and U = Unfavorable variance.

Quick Check

Answers—p. 978

1. A flexible budget (a) shows fixed costs as constant amounts of cost per unit of activity, (b) shows variable costs as constant amounts of cost per unit of activity, or (c) is prepared based on one expected amount of budgeted sales or production.
2. What is the initial step in preparing a flexible budget?
3. What is the main difference between a fixed and a flexible budget?
4. What is contribution margin?

Section 2—Standard Costs

Standard costs are preset costs for delivering a product or service under normal conditions. These costs are established by personnel, engineering, and accounting studies using past experiences and data. Management uses these costs to assess the reasonableness of actual costs incurred for producing the product or service. When actual costs vary from standard costs, management follows up to identify potential problems and take corrective actions.

Standard costs are often used in preparing budgets because they are the anticipated costs incurred under normal conditions. Terms such as *standard materials cost, standard labor cost,* and *standard overhead cost* are often used to refer to amounts budgeted for direct materials, direct labor, and overhead.

C1 Define *standard costs* and explain their computation and uses.

Point: Since standard costs are often budgeted costs, they can be used to prepare both fixed budgets and flexible budgets.

Materials and Labor Standards

This section explains how to set materials and labor standards and how to prepare a standard cost card.

Identifying Standard Costs

Managerial accountants, engineers, personnel administrators, and other managers combine their efforts to set standard costs. To identify standards for direct labor costs, we can conduct time and motion studies for each labor operation in the process of providing a product or service. From these studies, management can learn the best way to perform the operation and then set the standard labor time required for the operation under normal conditions. Similarly, standards for materials are set by studying the quantity, grade, and cost of each material used. Standards for overhead costs are explained later in the chapter.

Point: Business practice often uses the word *budget* when speaking of total amounts and *standard* when discussing per unit amounts.

Regardless of the care used in setting standard costs and in revising them as conditions change, actual costs frequently differ from standard costs, often as a result of one or more factors. For instance, the actual quantity of material used can differ from the standard, or the price paid per unit of material can differ from the standard. Quantity and price differences from standard amounts can also occur for labor. That is, the actual labor time and actual labor rate can vary from what was expected. The same analysis applies to overhead costs.

Decision Insight

Cruis'n Standards   The **Corvette** consists of hundreds of parts for which engineers set standards. Various types of labor are also involved in its production, including machining, assembly, painting, and welding, and standards are set for each. Actual results are periodically compared with standards to assess performance.

Setting Standard Costs

To illustrate the setting of a standard cost, we consider a professional league baseball bat manufactured by ProBat. Its engineers have determined that manufacturing one bat requires 0.90 kgs. of high-grade wood. They also expect some loss of material as part of the process because of inefficiencies and waste. This results in adding an *allowance* of 0.10 kgs., making the standard requirement 1.0 kg. of wood for each bat.

Example: What factors might be considered when deciding whether to revise standard costs? *Answer:* Changes in the processes and/or resources needed to carry out the processes.

The 0.90 kgs. portion is called an *ideal standard;* it is the quantity of material required if the process is 100% efficient without any loss or waste. Reality suggests that some loss of material usually occurs with any process. The standard of 1.0 kg. is known as the *practical standard,* the quantity of material required under normal application of the process.

Point: Companies promoting continuous improvement strive to achieve ideal standards by eliminating inefficiencies and waste.

High-grade wood can be purchased at a standard price of $25 per kg. The purchasing department sets this price as the expected price for the budget period. To determine this price, the purchasing department considers factors such as the quality of materials, future economic conditions, supply factors (shortages and excesses), and any available discounts. The engineers also decide that two hours of labor time (after including allowances) are required to manufacture a bat. The wage rate is $20 per hour (better than average skilled labor is required). ProBat assigns all overhead at the rate of $10 per labor hour. The standard costs of direct materials, direct labor, and overhead for one bat are as shown in Exhibit 24.5 in what is called a *standard cost card.* These cost amounts are then used to prepare manufacturing budgets for a budgeted level of production.

Exhibit 24.5

Standard Cost Card

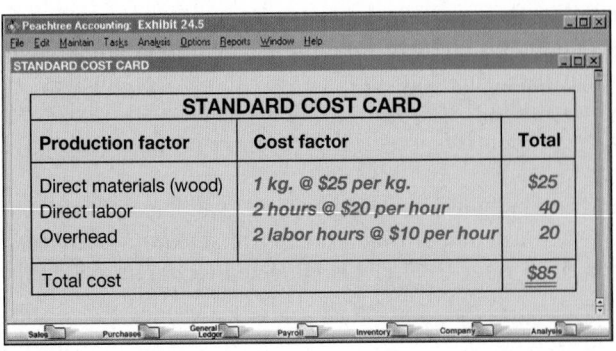

STANDARD COST CARD		
Production factor	**Cost factor**	**Total**
Direct materials (wood)	*1 kg. @ $25 per kg.*	$25
Direct labor	*2 hours @ $20 per hour*	40
Overhead	*2 labor hours @ $10 per hour*	20
Total cost		$85

Cost Variances

A **cost variance,** also simply called a *variance,* is the difference between actual and standard costs. A cost variance can be favorable or unfavorable. A variance from standard cost is considered favorable if actual cost is less than standard cost. It is considered unfavorable if actual cost is more than standard cost.[1] This section discusses variance analysis.

C2 Describe variances and what they reveal about performance.

Cost Variance Analysis

Variances are usually identified in performance reports. When a variance occurs, management wants to determine the factors causing it. This often involves analysis, evaluation, and explanation. The results of these efforts should enable management to assign responsibility for the variance and then to take actions to correct the situation.

To illustrate, Optel's standard materials cost for producing 12,000 units of its product is $12,000. Its actual materials cost for January proved to be $13,000. The $1,000 unfavorable variance raises questions that call for answers that, in turn, can lead to changes to correct the situation and eliminate this variance in the next period. A performance report often identifies the existence of a problem, but we must follow up with further investigation to see what can be done to improve future performance.

Exhibit 24.6 shows the flow of events in the effective management of variance analysis. It shows four steps: (1) preparing a standard cost performance report, (2) computing and analyzing variances, (3) identifying questions and their explanations, and (4) taking corrective and strategic actions. These variance analysis steps are interrelated and are frequently applied in good organizations.

Prepare Reports → **Analyze Variances** → **Questions and Answers** → **Take Action**

Exhibit 24.6

Variance Analysis

Cost Variance Computation

Management needs information about the factors causing a cost variance, but first it must properly compute the variance. In its most simple form, a cost variance (CV) is computed as the difference between actual cost (AC) and standard cost (SC) as shown in Exhibit 24.7.

> **Cost Variance (CV) = Actual Cost (AC) − Standard Cost (SC)**
> where:
> **Actual Cost (AC) = Actual Quantity (AQ) × Actual Price (AP)**
> **Standard Cost (SC) = Standard Quantity (SQ) × Standard Price (SP)**

Exhibit 24.7

Cost Variance Formulas

A cost variance is further defined by its components. Actual quantity (AQ) is the input (material or labor) used to manufacture the quantity of output. Standard quantity (SQ) is the expected input for the quantity of output. Actual price (AP) is the amount paid to acquire the input (material or labor), and standard price (SP) is the expected price.

---

[1] Short-term favorable variances can sometimes lead to long-term unfavorable variances. For instance, if management spends less than the budgeted amount on maintenance or insurance, the performance report would show a favorable variance. Cutting these expenses can lead to major losses in the long run if machinery wears out prematurely or insurance coverage proves inadequate.

Two main factors cause a cost variance: (1) the difference between actual price and standard price results in a *price* (or rate) *variance* and (2) the difference between actual quantity and standard quantity results in a *quantity* (or usage or efficiency) *variance*. To assess the impacts of these two factors on a cost variance, we use the formula in Exhibit 24.8.

Exhibit 24.8
Price Variance and Quantity Variance Formulas

These formulas identify the sources of the cost variance. Managers sometimes find it useful to apply an alternative (but equivalent) computation for the price and quantity variances as shown in Exhibit 24.9.

Exhibit 24.9
Alternative Price Variance and Quantity Variance Formulas

> **Price Variance (PV)** = [**Actual Price (AP)** − **Standard Price (SP)**] × **Actual Quantity (AQ)**
>
> **Quantity Variance (QV)** = [**Actual Quantity (AQ)** − **Standard Quantity (SQ)**] × **Standard Price (SP)**

The results from applying the formulas in Exhibits 24.8 and 24.9 are identical.

Materials and Labor Variances

We illustrate the computation of the materials and labor cost variances using data from **G-Max,** a company that makes specialty golf equipment and accessories for individual customers. This company has set the following standard quantities and prices for materials and labor per unit for one of its hand-crafted golf clubheads:

Direct materials (1 lb. per unit at $1 per lb.)	$1.00
Direct labor (1 hr. per unit at $8 per hr.)	8.00
Total standard direct cost per unit	$9.00

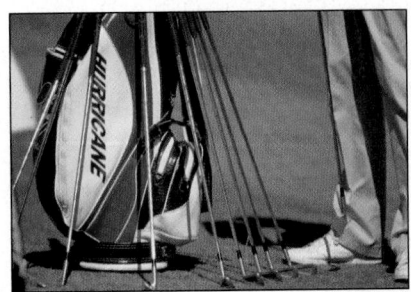

Materials Cost Variances   During May 2008, G-Max budgeted to produce 4,000 clubheads (units). It actually produced only 3,500 units. It used 3,600 pounds of direct materials (titanium) costing $1.05 per pound, meaning its total materials cost was $3,780. This information allows us to compute both actual and standard direct materials costs for G-Max's 3,500 units and its direct materials cost variance as follows:

Actual cost	3,600 lbs. @ $1.05 per lb.	= $3,780
Standard cost	3,500 lbs. @ $1.00 per lb.	= 3,500
Direct materials cost variance (unfavorable)		= $ 280

The materials price and quantity variances for these G-Max clubheads are computed and shown in Exhibit 24.10.

Actual Cost		Standard Cost
AQ × AP	AQ × SP	SQ × SP
3,600 lbs. × $1.05	3,600 lbs. × $1.00	3,500 lbs. × $1.00
$3,780	$3,600	$3,500

$180 U — Price Variance

$100 U — Quantity Variance

$280 U — Total Direct Materials Variance

Exhibit 24.10

Materials Price and Quantity Variances

The $180 unfavorable price variance results from paying 5 cents more than the standard price, computed as 3,600 lbs. × $0.05. The $100 unfavorable quantity variance is due to using 100 lbs. more materials than the standard quantity, computed as 100 lbs. × $1. The total direct materials variance is $280 and is unfavorable. This information allows management to ask the responsible individuals for explanations and corrective actions.

The purchasing department is usually responsible for the price paid for materials. Responsibility for explaining the price variance in this case rests with the purchasing manager if a price higher than standard caused the variance. The production department is usually responsible for the amount of material used and in this case is responsible for explaining why the process used more than the standard amount of materials.

Variance analysis presents challenges. For instance, the production department could have used more than the standard amount of material because its quality did not meet specifications and led to excessive waste. In this case, the purchasing manager is responsible for explaining why inferior materials were acquired. However, the production manager is responsible for explaining what happened if analysis shows that waste was due to inefficiencies, not poor quality material.

In evaluating price variances, managers must recognize that a favorable price variance can indicate a problem with poor product quality. **Redhook Ale**, a micro brewery in the Pacific Northwest, can probably save 10% to 15% in material prices by buying six-row barley malt instead of the better two-row from Washington's Yakima valley. Attention to quality, however, has helped Redhook Ale become the only craft brewer to be "kosher" certified. Redhook's purchasing activities are judged on both the quality of the materials and the purchase price variance. This stand on quality has helped Redhook report increases in both sales and gross margin.

Labor Cost Variances   Labor cost for a specific product or service depends on the number of hours worked (quantity) and the wage rate paid to employees (price). When actual amounts for a task differ from standard, the labor cost variance can be divided into a rate (price) variance and an efficiency (quantity) variance.

To illustrate, G-Max's direct labor standard for 3,500 units of its hand-crafted clubheads is one hour per unit, or 3,500 hours at $8 per hour. Since only 3,400 hours at $8.30 per hour were actually used to complete the units, the actual and standard labor costs are

Actual cost	3,400 hrs. @ $8.30 per hr.	= $28,220
Standard cost	3,500 hrs. @ $8.00 per hr.	= 28,000
Direct labor cost variance (unfavorable)		= $ 220

This analysis shows that actual cost is merely $220 over the standard and suggests no immediate concern. Computing both the labor rate and efficiency variances reveals a different picture, however, as shown in Exhibit 24.11.

Exhibit 24.11

Labor Rate and
Efficiency Variances*

* AH is actual direct labor hours: AR is actual wage rate; SH is standard direct labor hours allowed for actual output; SR is standard wage rate.

Example: Compute the rate variance and the efficiency variance for Exhibit 24.11 if 3,700 actual hours are used at an actual price of $7.50 per hour. *Answer:* $1,850 favorable labor rate variance and $1,600 unfavorable labor efficiency variance.

The analysis in Exhibit 24.11 shows that an $800 favorable efficiency variance results from using 100 fewer direct labor hours than standard for the units produced, but this favorable variance is more than offset by a wage rate that is $0.30 higher than standard. The personnel administrator or possibly the production manager needs to explain why the wage rate is higher than expected. The production manager should also explain how the labor hours were reduced. If this experience can be repeated and transferred to other departments, more savings are possible.

One possible explanation of these labor rate and efficiency variances is the use of workers with different skill levels. If this is the reason, senior management must discuss the implications with the production manager who has the responsibility to assign workers to tasks with the appropriate skill level. In this case, an investigation might show that higher skilled workers were used to produce 3,500 units of hand-crafted clubheads. As a result, fewer labor hours might be required for the work, but the wage rate paid these workers is higher than standard because of their greater skills. The effect of this strategy is a higher than standard total cost, which would require actions to remedy the situation or adjust the standard.

Decision Maker

Answer—p. 978

Human Resource Manager You receive the manufacturing variance report for June and discover a large unfavorable labor efficiency (quantity) variance. What factors do you investigate to identify its possible causes?

Quick Check

Answers—p. 978

5. A standard cost (*a*) changes in direct proportion to changes in the level of activity, (*b*) is an amount incurred at the actual level of production for the period, or (*c*) is an amount incurred under normal conditions to provide a product or service.

6. What is a cost variance?

7. The following information is available for York Company.

Actual direct labor hours per unit	2.5 hours
Standard direct labor hours per unit	2.0 hours
Actual production (units)	2,500 units
Budgeted production (units)	3,000 units
Actual rate per hour	$3.10
Standard rate per hour	$3.00

The labor efficiency variance is (*a*) $3,750 U, (*b*) $3,750 F, or (*c*) $3,875 U.

8. Refer to Quick Check 7; the labor rate variance is (*a*) $625 F or (*b*) $625 U.

9. If a materials quantity variance is favorable and a materials price variance is unfavorable, can the total materials cost variance be favorable?

Overhead Standards and Variances

When standard costs are used, a predetermined overhead rate is used to assign standard overhead costs to products or services produced. This predetermined rate is often based on some overhead allocation base (such as standard labor cost, standard labor hours, or standard machine hours).

Setting Overhead Standards

Standard overhead costs are the amounts expected to occur at a certain activity level. Unlike direct materials and direct labor, overhead includes fixed costs and variable costs. This results in the average overhead cost per unit changing as the predicted volume changes. Since standard costs are also budgeted costs, they must be established before the reporting period begins. Standard overhead costs are therefore average per unit costs based on the predicted activity level.

To establish the standard overhead cost rate, management uses the same cost structure it used to construct a flexible budget at the end of a period. This cost structure identifies the different overhead cost components and classifies them as variable or fixed. To get the standard overhead rate, management selects a level of activity (volume) and predicts total overhead cost. It then divides this total by the allocation base to get the standard rate. Standard direct labor hours expected to be used to produce the predicted volume is a common allocation base and is used in this section.

Point: Managers consider the types of overhead costs when choosing the basis for assigning overhead costs to products.

To illustrate, Exhibit 24.12 shows the overhead cost structure used to develop G-Max's flexible overhead budgets for May 2008. The predetermined standard overhead rate for May is set before the month begins. The first two number columns list the per unit amounts of variable costs and the monthly amounts of fixed costs. The four right-most columns show the costs expected to occur at four different levels of activity. The predetermined overhead rate per labor hour is smaller as volume of activity increases because fixed costs remain constant.

G-Max managers predicted an 80% activity level for May, or a production volume of 4,000 clubheads. At this volume, they budget $8,000 as the May total overhead. This choice implies a $2 per unit (labor hour) average overhead cost ($8,000/4,000 units). Since G-Max has a standard of one direct labor hour per unit, the predetermined standard overhead rate for May is $2 per standard direct labor hour. The variable overhead rate remains constant at $1 per direct labor hour regardless of the budgeted production level. The fixed overhead rate changes according to the budgeted production volume. For instance, for the predicted level of 4,000 units of production, the fixed rate is $1 per hour ($4,000 fixed costs/4,000 units). For a production level of 5,000 units, however, the fixed rate is $0.80 per hour.

Point: Variable costs per unit remain constant, but fixed costs per unit decline with increases in volume. This means the average total overhead cost per unit declines with increases in volume.

When choosing the predicted activity level, management considers many factors. The level can be set as high as 100% of capacity, but this is rare. Factors causing the activity level to be less than full capacity include difficulties in scheduling work, equipment under repair or maintenance, and insufficient product demand. Good long-run management practices often call for some plant capacity in excess of current operating needs to allow for special opportunities and demand changes.

Decision Insight

Measuring Up In the spirit of continuous improvement, competitors compare their processes and performance standards against benchmarks established by industry leaders. Those that use **benchmarking** include Precision Lube, Jiffy Lube, All Tune and Lube, and Speedee Oil Change and Tune-Up.

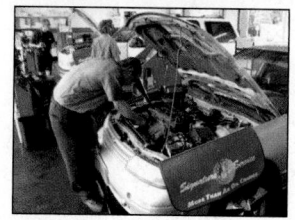

Exhibit 24.12

Flexible Overhead Budgets

	Flexible Budget		Flexible Budget at 70% Capacity	Flexible Budget at 80% Capacity	Flexible Budget at 90% Capacity	Flexible Budget at 100% Capacity
G-MAX Flexible Overhead Budgets For Month Ended May 31, 2008	Variable Amount per Unit	Total Fixed Cost				
Production (in units)	I unit		3,500	4,000	4,500	5,000
Factory overhead						
Variable costs						
Indirect labor	$0.40/unit		$1,400	$1,600	$1,800	$2,000
Indirect materials	0.30/unit		1,050	1,200	1,350	1,500
Power and lights	0.20/unit		700	800	900	1,000
Maintenance	0.10/unit		350	400	450	500
Total variable overhead costs	$1.00/unit		3,500	4,000	4,500	5,000
Fixed costs (per month)						
Building rent		$1,000	1,000	1,000	1,000	1,000
Depreciation—Machinery		1,200	1,200	1,200	1,200	1,200
Supervisory salaries		1,800	1,800	1,800	1,800	1,800
Total fixed overhead costs		$4,000	4,000	4,000	4,000	4,000
Total factory overhead			$7,500	$8,000	$8,500	$9,000
Standard direct labor hours	I hr./unit		3,500 hrs.	4,000 hrs.	4,500 hrs.	5,000 hrs.
Predetermined overhead rate per standard direct labor hour			$ 2.14	$ 2.00	$ 1.89	$ 1.80

P3   Compute overhead variances.

Using Overhead Cost Variance Analysis

When standard costs are used, the cost accounting system applies overhead to the good units produced using the predetermined standard overhead rate. At period-end, the difference between the total overhead cost applied to products and the total overhead cost actually incurred is called an **overhead cost variance,** which is defined in Exhibit 24.13.

Exhibit 24.13

Overhead Cost Variance

Overhead cost variance (OCV) = Actual overhead incurred (AOI) − Standard overhead applied (SOA)

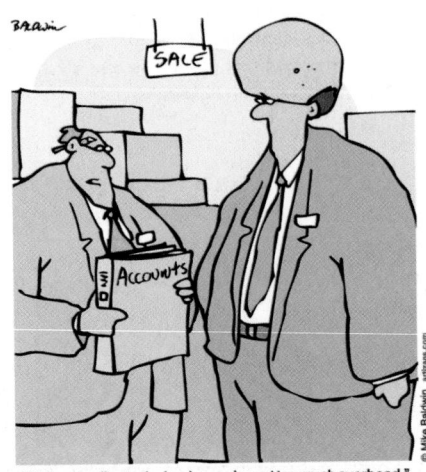

"Well, according to the books, you've got too much overhead."

To help identify factors causing the overhead cost variance, managers analyze this variance separately for variable and fixed overhead. The results provide information useful for taking strategic actions to improve company performance. Similar to analysis of direct materials and direct labor variances, both the variable and fixed overhead variances can be separated into useful components as shown in Exhibit 24.14.

A **spending variance** occurs when management pays an amount different than the standard price to acquire an item. For instance, the actual wage rate paid to indirect labor might be higher than the standard rate. Similarly, actual supervisory salaries might be different than expected. Spending variances such as these cause management to investigate the reasons that the amount paid differs from the standard. Both variable and fixed overhead costs can yield their own spending variances. Analyzing variable overhead includes computing an **efficiency variance,** which occurs when standard direct labor hours (the allocation base) expected for actual production differ from the actual direct labor hours used. This efficiency

Exhibit 24.14

Variable and Fixed
Overhead Variances

* AH = actual direct labor hours; AVR = actual variable overhead rate; SH = standard direct labor hours; SVR = standard variable overhead rate.

variance reflects on the cost-effectiveness in using the overhead allocation base (such as direct labor).

A **volume variance** occurs when a difference occurs between the actual volume of production and the standard volume of production. The budgeted fixed overhead amount is the same regardless of the volume of production (within the relevant range). This budgeted amount is computed based on standard direct labor hours that the budgeted production volume allows. The applied overhead is based, however, on the standard direct labor hours allowed for the actual volume of production. A difference between budgeted and actual production volumes results in a difference in the standard direct labor hours allowed for these two production levels. This situation yields a volume variance different from zero.

We can combine the variable overhead spending variance, the fixed overhead spending variance, and the variable overhead efficiency variance to get **controllable variance;** see Exhibit 24.15. The controllable variance is so named because it refers to activities usually under management control.

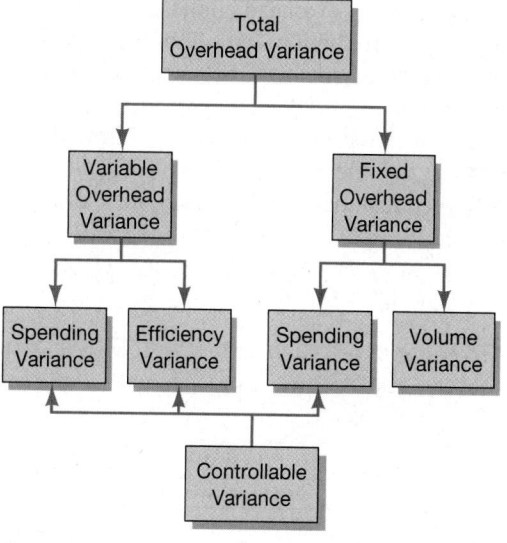

Exhibit 24.15

Framework for Understanding
Total Overhead Variance

Computing Overhead Cost Variances

To illustrate how to compute overhead cost variances, return to the G-Max data. We know that it actually produced 3,500 units when 4,000 units were budgeted. Additional G-Max data show that actual overhead cost incurred is $7,650 (variable portion of $3,650; fixed portion of $4,000). Using this information, we can compute overhead variances for both variable and fixed overhead.

Variable Overhead Cost Variances Recall that G-Max applies overhead based on direct labor hours as the allocation base. We know that it used 3,400 direct labor hours to produce 3,500 units. This compares favorably to the standard requirement of 3,500 direct labor hours at one labor hour per unit. We compute and separate G-Max's variable overhead cost variances as shown in Exhibit 24.16.

Exhibit 24.16

Computing Variable Overhead Cost Variances

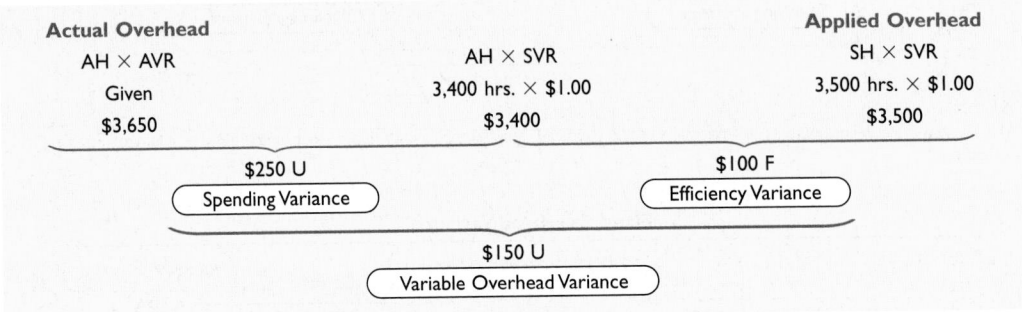

The $3,650 actual variable overhead from G-Max's cost records is used to compute the actual variable overhead rate of $1.07 per direct labor hour ($3,650/3,400 direct labor hours). This reveals that, on average, G-Max incurred $0.07 more per direct labor hour in variable overhead than the standard rate. The middle column of Exhibit 24.16 is computed by multiplying the 3,400 actual direct labor hours by the $1 standard rate per direct labor hour. The applied overhead is computed by multiplying the 3,500 standard hours allowed for actual production by the $1 standard rate per direct labor hour.

Fixed Overhead Cost Variances   G-Max reports that it incurred $4,000 in actual fixed overhead; this amount equals the budgeted fixed overhead for May (see Exhibit 24.12). G-Max's budgeted fixed overhead application rate is $1 per hour ($4,000/4,000 direct labor hours), but the actual production level is only 3,500 units. Using this information, we can compute the fixed overhead cost variances shown in Exhibit 24.17. The applied fixed overhead is computed by multiplying 3,500 standard hours allowed for the actual production by the $1 fixed overhead allocation rate. Exhibit 24.17 reveals that the fixed overhead spending variance is zero and the volume variance is $500. The volume variance occurs because 500 fewer units are produced than budgeted; namely, 80% of the manufacturing capacity is budgeted but only 70% is used.

Exhibit 24.17

Computing Fixed Overhead Cost Variances

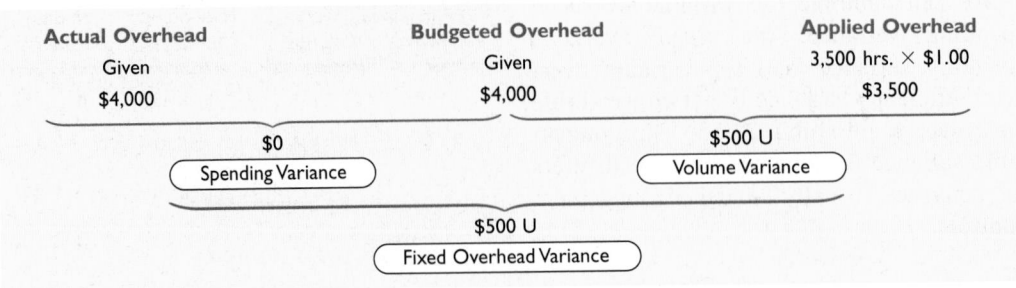

We show this volume variance graphically in Exhibit 24.18. The upward-sloping line reflects the amount of fixed overhead costs applied to the units produced in May using the predetermined fixed overhead rate. The uppermost horizontal line reflects the $4,000 of total fixed costs budgeted for May. These two lines cross at the planned operating volume of 4,000 units. When unit volume is 3,500 units, the overhead-costs-applied line falls $500 below the budgeted fixed overhead line. This shortfall is the volume variance.

An unfavorable volume variance implies that the company did not reach its predicted operating level. Management needs to know why the actual level of performance differs from the

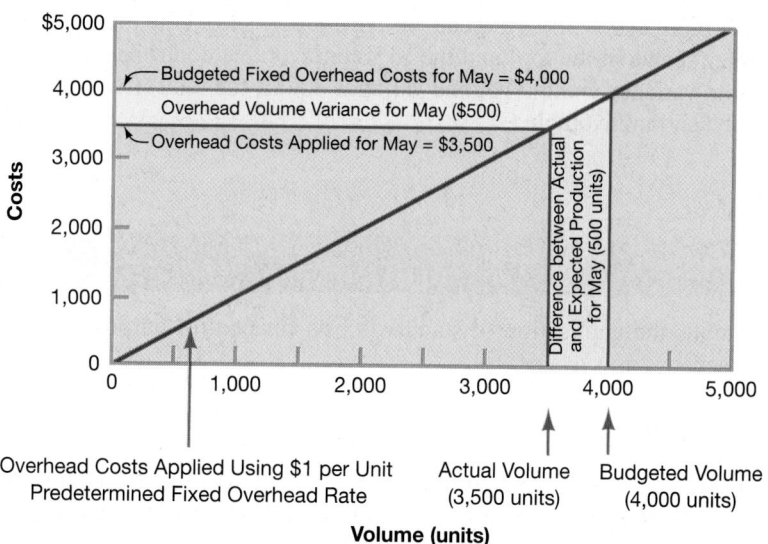

Exhibit 24.18

Fixed Overhead Volume Variance

expected level. The main purpose of the volume variance is to identify what portion of the total variance is caused by failing to meet the expected volume level. This information permits management to focus on the controllable variance.

A complete overhead variance report provides managers information about specific overhead costs and how they differ from budgeted amounts. Exhibit 24.19 shows G-Max's overhead variance report for May. It reveals that (1) fixed costs and maintenance cost were incurred as expected, (2) costs for indirect labor and power and lights were higher than expected, and (3) indirect materials cost was less than expected.

Using information from Exhibits 24.16 and 24.17, we can compute the total controllable overhead variance as $150 unfavorable ($250 U + $100 F + $0). This amount is also readily

Exhibit 24.19

Overhead Variance Report

G-MAX Overhead Variance Report For Month Ended May 31, 2008			
Volume Variance			
Expected production level	80% of capacity		
Production level achieved	70% of capacity		
Volume variance	$500 (unfavorable)		
	Flexible	**Actual**	
Controllable Variance	**Budget**	**Results**	**Variances***
Variable overhead costs			
Indirect labor	$1,400	$1,525	$125 U
Indirect materials	1,050	1,025	25 F
Power and lights	700	750	50 U
Maintenance	350	350	0
Total variable overhead costs	3,500	3,650	150 U†
Fixed overhead costs			
Building rent	1,000	1,000	0
Depreciation—Machinery	1,200	1,200	0
Supervisory salaries	1,800	1,800	0
Total fixed overhead costs	4,000	4,000	0‡
Total overhead costs	$7,500	$7,650	$150 U

* F = Favorable variance; and U = Unfavorable variance.

† Total variable overhead (spending and efficiency) variance.

‡ Fixed overhead spending variance.

available from Exhibit 24.19. The overhead variance report shows the total volume variance as $500 unfavorable (shown at the top) and the $150 unfavorable controllable variance. The sum of the controllable variance and the volume variance equals the total (fixed and variable) overhead variance of $650 unfavorable.

Extensions of Standard Costs

This section extends the application of standard costs for control purposes, for service companies, and for accounting systems.

Standard Costs for Control

C3 Explain how standard cost information is useful for management by exception.

To control business activities, top management must be able to affect the actions of lower-level managers responsible for the company's revenues and costs. After preparing a budget and establishing standard costs, management should take actions to gain control when actual costs differ from standard or budgeted amounts.

Reports such as the ones illustrated in this chapter call management's attention to variances from business plans and other standards. When managers use these reports to focus on problem areas, the budgeting process contributes to the control function. In using budgeted performance reports, practice of management by exception is often useful. **Management by exception** means that managers focus attention on the most significant variances and give less attention to areas where performance is reasonably close to the standard. This practice leads management to concentrate on the exceptional or irregular situations. Management by exception is especially useful when directed at controllable items.

Standard Costs for Services

Many managers use standard costs and variance analysis to investigate manufacturing costs. Many managers also recognize that standard costs and variances can help them control *non*manufacturing costs. Companies providing services instead of products can benefit from the use of standard costs. Application of standard costs and variances can be readily adapted to nonmanufacturing situations. To illustrate, many service providers use standard costs to help control expenses. First, they use standard costs as a basis for budgeting all services. Second, they use periodic performance reports to compare actual results to standards. Third, they use these reports to identify significant variances within specific areas of responsibility. Fourth, they implement the appropriate control procedures.

Standard Cost Accounting System

We have shown how companies use standard costs in management reports. Most standard cost systems also record these costs and variances in accounts. This practice simplifies recordkeeping and helps in preparing reports. Although we do not need knowledge of standard cost accounting practices to understand standard costs and their use, we must know how to interpret the accounts in which standard costs and variances are recorded. The entries in this section briefly illustrate the important aspects of this process for G-Max's standard costs and variances for May.

The first of these entries records standard materials cost incurred in May in the Goods in Process Inventory account. This part of the entry is similar to the usual accounting entry, but the amount of the debit equals the standard cost ($3,500) instead of the actual cost ($3,780). This entry credits Raw Materials Inventory for actual cost. The difference between standard and actual costs is recorded with debits to two separate materials variance accounts (recall Exhibit 24.10). Both the materials price and quantity variances are recorded as debits because they reflect additional costs higher than the standard cost (if actual costs were less than the standard, they are recorded as credits). This treatment (debit) reflects their unfavorable effect because they represent higher costs and lower income.

May 31	Goods in Process Inventory	3,500	
	Direct Materials Price Variance*	**180**	
	Direct Materials Quantity Variance	**100**	
	Raw Materials Inventory		3,780
	To charge production for standard quantity of materials used (3,500 lbs.) at the standard price ($1 per lb.), and to record material price and material quantity variances.		

Assets = Liabilities + Equity
+3,500   −100
−3,780   −180

* Many companies record the materials price variance when materials are purchased. For simplicity, we record both the materials price and quantity variances when materials are issued to production.

The second entry debits Goods in Process Inventory for the standard labor cost of the goods manufactured during May ($28,000). Actual labor cost ($28,220) is recorded with a credit to the Factory Payroll account. The difference between standard and actual labor costs is explained by two variances (see Exhibit 24.11). The direct labor rate variance is unfavorable and is debited to that account. The direct labor efficiency variance is favorable and is credited. The direct labor efficiency variance is favorable because it represents a lower cost and a higher net income.

May 31	Goods in Process Inventory	28,000	
	Direct Labor Rate Variance	**1,020**	
	Direct Labor Efficiency Variance		**800**
	Factory Payroll		28,220
	To charge production with 3,500 standard hours of direct labor at the standard $8 per hour rate, and to record the labor rate and efficiency variances.		

Assets = Liabilities + Equity
+28,000   +28,220
                     − 1,020
                     +   800

The entry to assign standard predetermined overhead to the cost of goods manufactured must debit the $7,000 predetermined amount to the Goods in Process Inventory account. The $7,650 actual overhead costs are debited to the Factory Overhead account. Thus, when Factory Overhead is applied to Goods in Process Inventory, the amount applied is debited to the Goods in Process Inventory account and credited to the Factory Overhead account. To account for the difference between actual and standard costs, the entry includes a $250 debit to the Variable Overhead Spending Variance, a $100 credit to the Variable Overhead Efficiency Variance, and a $500 debit to the Volume Variance (recall Exhibits 24.16 and 24.17). An alternative (simpler) approach, shown here, is to record the difference with a $150 debit to the Controllable Variance account and a $500 debit to the Volume Variance account (recall from Exhibit 24.15 that controllable variance is the sum of both variable overhead variances and the fixed overhead spending variance).

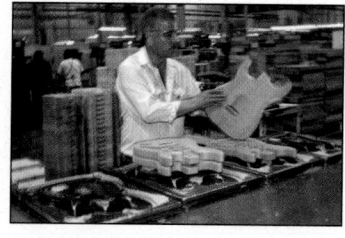

Assets = Liabilities + Equity
+7,000   +7,650
                 − 150
                 − 500

May 31	Goods in Process Inventory	7,000	
	Controllable Variance......................	150	
	Volume Variance.........................	500	
	Factory Overhead......................		7,650

To apply overhead at the standard rate of
$2 per standard direct labor hour (3,500 hours),
and to record overhead variances.

The balances of these six different variance accounts accumulate until the end of the accounting period. As a result, the unfavorable variances of some months offset the favorable variances of others.

These variance account balances, which reflect results of the period's various transactions
and events, are closed at period-end. If the variances are *material,* they are added to or subtracted from the balances of the Goods in Process Inventory, the Finished Goods Inventory,
and the Cost of Goods Sold accounts. If the amounts are *immaterial,* they are added to or subtracted from the balance of the Cost of Goods Sold account. This process is similar to that
shown in Chapter 19 for eliminating an underapplied or overapplied balance in the Factory
Overhead account. (*Note:* These variance balances, which represent differences between actual and standard costs, must be added to or subtracted from the materials, labor, and overhead
costs recorded. In this way, the recorded costs equal the actual costs incurred in the period; a
company must use actual costs in external financial statements prepared in accordance with
generally accepted accounting principles.)

Quick Check

Answers—p. 978

10. Under what conditions is an overhead volume variance considered favorable?

11. To use management by exception with standard costs, a company (*a*) must record standard
costs in its accounting, (*b*) should compute variances from flexible budget amounts to allow
management to focus its attention on significant differences between actual and budgeted
results, or (*c*) should analyze only variances for direct materials and direct labor.

12. A company uses a standard cost accounting system. Prepare the journal entry to record these
direct materials variances:

Direct materials cost actually incurred	$73,200
Direct materials quantity variance (favorable)	3,800
Direct materials price variance (unfavorable)	1,300

13. If standard costs are recorded in the manufacturing accounts, how are recorded variances
treated at the end of an accounting period?

Decision Analysis   Sales Variances

A2   Analyze changes in
      sales from expected
amounts.

This chapter explained the computation and analysis of cost variances. A similar variance analysis can
be applied to sales. To illustrate, consider the following sales data from G-Max for two of its golf products, Excel golf balls and Big Bert® drivers.

	Budgeted	Actual
Sales of Excel golf balls (units)	1,000 units	1,100 units
Sales price per Excel golf ball	$ 10	$ 10.50
Sales of Big Bert® drivers (units)	150 units	140 units
Sales price per Big Bert® driver	$ 200	$ 190

Using this information, we compute both the *sales price variance* and the *sales volume variance* as shown in Exhibit 24.20. The total sales price variance is $850 unfavorable, and the total sales volume variance is $1,000 unfavorable. Neither variance implies anything positive about these two products. Further analysis of these total sales variances reveals that both the sales price and sales volume variances for Excel golf balls are favorable, meaning that both the unfavorable total sales price variance and the unfavorable total sales volume variance are due to the Big Bert driver.

Exhibit 24.20

Computing Sales Variances

Managers use sales variances for planning and control purposes. The sales variance information is used to plan future actions to avoid unfavorable variances. G-Max sold 90 total combined units (both balls and drivers) more than planned, but these 90 units were not sold in the proportion budgeted. G-Max sold fewer than the budgeted quantity of the higher priced driver, which contributed to the unfavorable total sales variances. Managers use such detail to question what caused the company to sell more golf balls and fewer drivers. Managers also use this information to evaluate and even reward their salespeople. Extra compensation is paid to salespeople who contribute to a higher profit margin. Finally, with multiple products, the sales volume variance can be separated into a *sales mix variance* and a *sales quantity variance*. The sales mix variance is the difference between the actual and budgeted sales mix of the products. The sales quantity variance is the difference between the total actual and total budgeted quantity of units sold.

Decision Maker

Answer—p. 978

Sales Manager The current performance report reveals a large favorable sales volume variance but an unfavorable sales price variance. You did not expect to see a large increase in sales volume. What steps do you take to analyze this situation?

Demonstration Problem

Pacific Company provides the following information about its budgeted and actual results for June 2008. Although the expected June volume was 25,000 units produced and sold, the company actually produced and sold 27,000 units as detailed here:

	Budget (25,000 units)	Actual (27,000 units)
Selling price	$5.00 per unit	$5.23 per unit
Variable costs (per unit)		
Direct materials	1.24 per unit	1.12 per unit
Direct labor	1.50 per unit	1.40 per unit
Factory supplies*	0.25 per unit	0.37 per unit
Utilities*	0.50 per unit	0.60 per unit
Selling costs	0.40 per unit	0.34 per unit

[continued on next page]

[continued from previous page]

Fixed costs (per month)		
Depreciation—Machinery*	$3,750	$3,710
Depreciation—Building*	2,500	2,500
General liability insurance	1,200	1,250
Property taxes on office equipment	500	485
Other administrative expense	750	900

* Indicates factory overhead item; $0.75 per unit or $3 per direct labor hour for variable overhead, and $0.25 per unit or $1 per direct labor hour for fixed overhead.

Standard costs based on expected output of 25,000 units

	Per Unit of Output	Quantity to Be Used	Total Cost
Direct materials, 4 oz. @ $0.31/oz.	$1.24/unit	100,000 oz.	$31,000
Direct labor, 0.25 hrs. @ $6.00/hr.	1.50/unit	6,250 hrs.	37,500
Overhead	1.00/unit		25,000

Actual costs incurred to produce 27,000 units

	Per Unit of Output	Quantity Used	Total Cost
Direct materials, 4 oz. @ $0.28/oz.	$1.12/unit	108,000 oz.	$30,240
Direct labor, 0.20 hrs. @ $7.00/hr.	1.40/unit	5,400 hrs.	37,800
Overhead	1.20/unit		32,400

Standard costs based on expected output of 27,000 units

	Per Unit of Output	Quantity to Be Used	Total Cost
Direct materials, 4 oz. @ $0.31/oz.	$1.24/unit	108,000 oz.	$33,480
Direct labor, 0.25 hrs. @ $6.00/hr.	1.50/unit	6,750 hrs.	40,500
Overhead			26,500

Required

1. Prepare June flexible budgets showing expected sales, costs, and net income assuming 20,000, 25,000, and 30,000 units of output produced and sold.
2. Prepare a flexible budget performance report that compares actual results with the amounts budgeted if the actual volume had been expected.
3. Apply variance analysis for direct materials, for direct labor, and for overhead.

Planning the Solution

- Prepare a table showing the expected results at the three specified levels of output. Compute the variable costs by multiplying the per unit variable costs by the expected volumes. Include fixed costs at the given amounts. Combine the amounts in the table to show total variable costs, contribution margin, total fixed costs, and income from operations.
- Prepare a table showing the actual results and the amounts that should be incurred at 27,000 units. Show any differences in the third column and label them with an *F* for favorable if they increase income or a *U* for unfavorable if they decrease income.
- Using the chapter's format, compute these total variances and the individual variances requested:
  - Total materials variance (including the direct materials quantity variance and the direct materials price variance).

- Total direct labor variance (including the direct labor efficiency variance and rate variance).
- Total overhead variance (including both variable and fixed overhead variances and their component variances).

Solution to Demonstration Problem

1.

PACIFIC COMPANY
Flexible Budgets
For Month Ended June 30, 2008

	Flexible Budget		Flexible Budget for Unit Sales of 20,000	Flexible Budget for Unit Sales of 25,000	Flexible Budget for Unit Sales of 30,000
	Variable Amount per Unit	Total Fixed Cost			
Sales	$5.00		$100,000	$125,000	$150,000
Variable costs					
Direct materials	1.24		24,800	31,000	37,200
Direct labor	1.50		30,000	37,500	45,000
Factory supplies	0.25		5,000	6,250	7,500
Utilities	0.50		10,000	12,500	15,000
Selling costs	0.40		8,000	10,000	12,000
Total variable costs	3.89		77,800	97,250	116,700
Contribution margin	$1.11		22,200	27,750	33,300
Fixed costs					
Depreciation—Machinery		$3,750	3,750	3,750	3,750
Depreciation—Building		2,500	2,500	2,500	2,500
General liability insurance		1,200	1,200	1,200	1,200
Property taxes on office equipment		500	500	500	500
Other administrative expense		750	750	750	750
Total fixed costs		$8,700	8,700	8,700	8,700
Income from operations			$ 13,500	$ 19,050	$ 24,600

2.

PACIFIC COMPANY
Flexible Budget Performance Report
For Month Ended June 30, 2008

	Flexible Budget	Actual Results	Variance*
Sales (27,000 units)	$135,000	$141,210	$6,210 F
Variable costs			
Direct materials	33,480	30,240	3,240 F
Direct labor	40,500	37,800	2,700 F
Factory supplies	6,750	9,990	3,240 U
Utilities	13,500	16,200	2,700 U
Selling costs	10,800	9,180	1,620 F
Total variable costs	105,030	103,410	1,620 F
Contribution margin	29,970	37,800	7,830 F
Fixed costs			
Depreciation—Machinery	3,750	3,710	40 F
Depreciation—Building	2,500	2,500	0
General liability insurance	1,200	1,250	50 U
Property taxes on office equipment	500	485	15 F
Other administrative expense	750	900	150 U
Total fixed costs	8,700	8,845	145 U
Income from operations	$ 21,270	$ 28,955	$7,685 F

* F = Favorable variance; and U = Unfavorable variance.

3. Variance analysis of materials, labor, and overhead costs.

Materials cost variances

Actual cost	108,000 oz. @ $0.28	$30,240
Standard cost	108,000 oz. @ $0.31	33,480
Direct materials cost variance (favorable)		$ 3,240

Price and quantity variances (based on formulas in Exhibit 24.10):

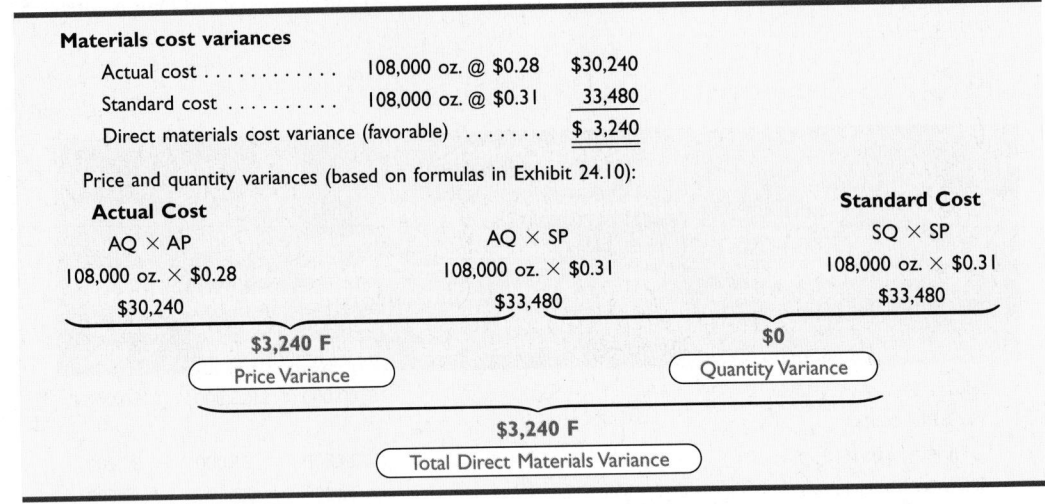

Actual Cost		**Standard Cost**
AQ × AP	AQ × SP	SQ × SP
108,000 oz. × $0.28	108,000 oz. × $0.31	108,000 oz. × $0.31
$30,240	$33,480	$33,480

$3,240 F
Price Variance

$0
Quantity Variance

$3,240 F
Total Direct Materials Variance

Labor cost variances

Actual cost	5,400 hrs. @ $7.00	$37,800
Standard cost	6,750 hrs. @ $6.00	40,500
Direct labor cost variance (favorable)		$ 2,700

Rate and efficiency variances (based on formulas in Exhibit 24.11):

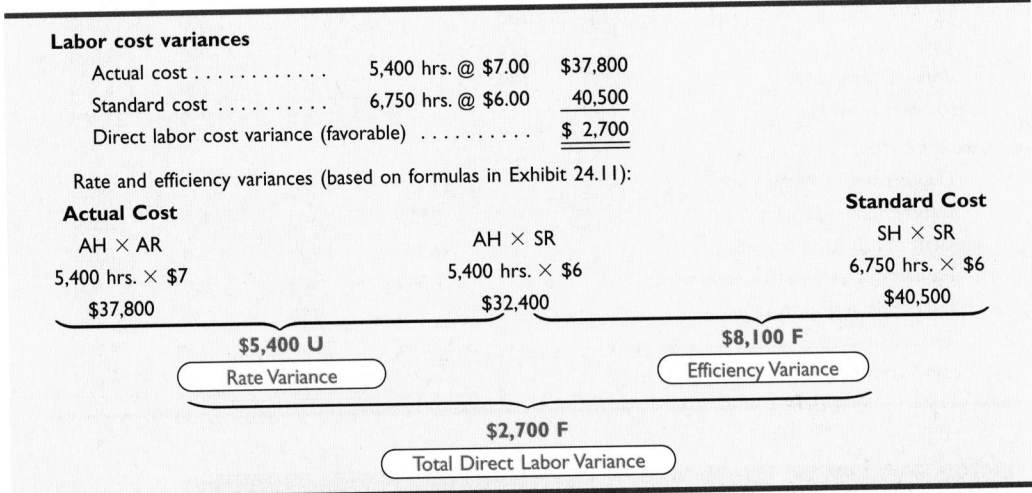

Actual Cost		**Standard Cost**
AH × AR	AH × SR	SH × SR
5,400 hrs. × $7	5,400 hrs. × $6	6,750 hrs. × $6
$37,800	$32,400	$40,500

$5,400 U
Rate Variance

$8,100 F
Efficiency Variance

$2,700 F
Total Direct Labor Variance

Overhead cost variances

Total overhead cost incurred	27,000 units @ $1.20	$32,400
Total overhead applied	27,000 units @ $1.00	27,000
Overhead cost variance (unfavorable)		$ 5,400

Variable overhead variance (factory supplies and utilities)

Variable overhead cost incurred	(given)	$26,190
Variable overhead cost applied	6,750 hrs. @ $3/hr.	20,250
Variable overhead cost variance (unfavorable)		$ 5,940

Spending and efficiency variances (based on formulas in Exhibit 24.14):

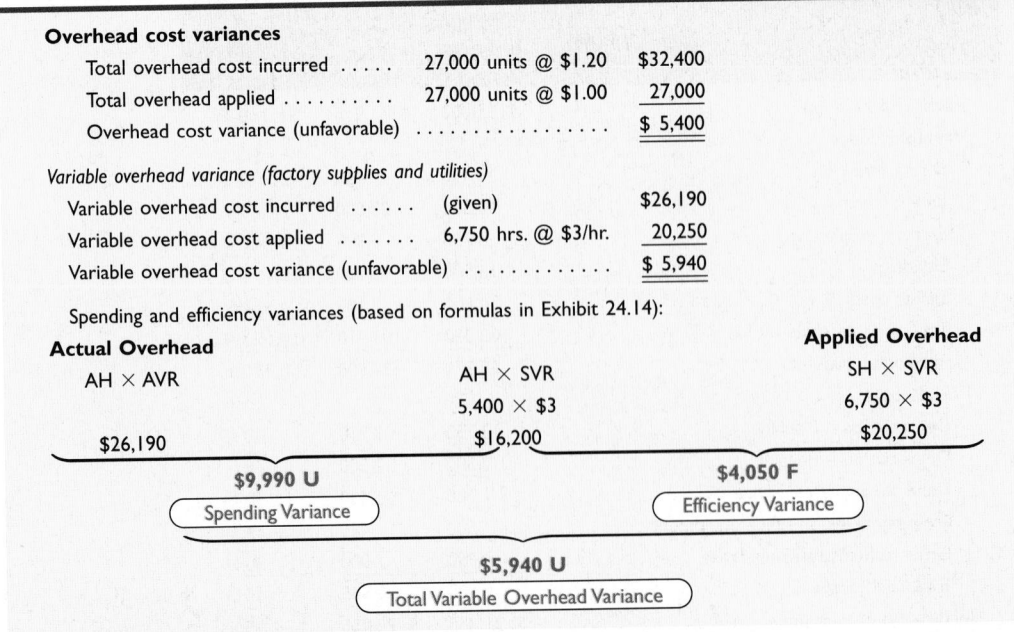

Actual Overhead		**Applied Overhead**
AH × AVR	AH × SVR	SH × SVR
	5,400 × $3	6,750 × $3
$26,190	$16,200	$20,250

$9,990 U
Spending Variance

$4,050 F
Efficiency Variance

$5,940 U
Total Variable Overhead Variance

[continued on next page]

[continued from previous page]

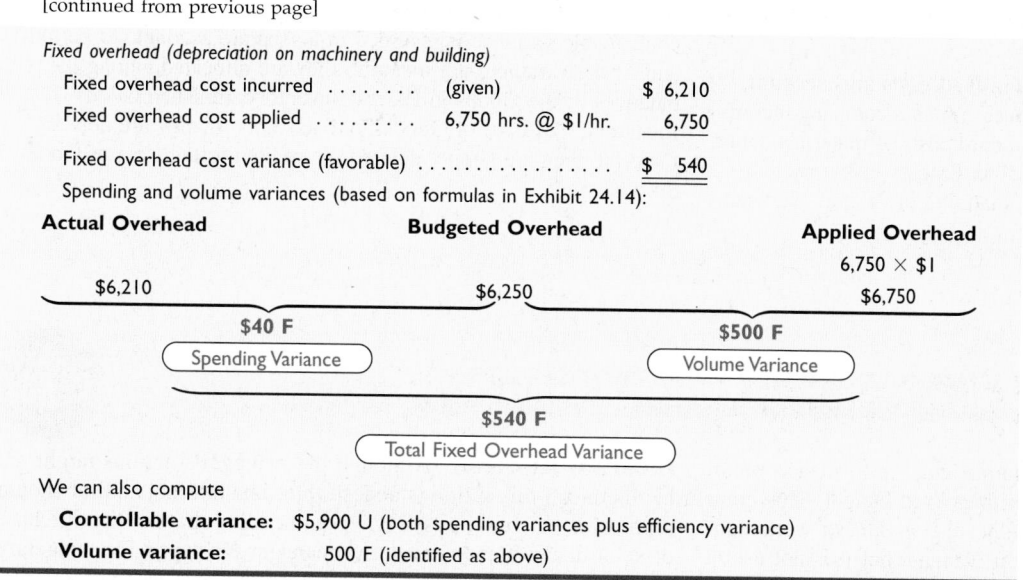

Fixed overhead (depreciation on machinery and building)

Fixed overhead cost incurred	(given)	$ 6,210
Fixed overhead cost applied	6,750 hrs. @ $1/hr.	6,750
Fixed overhead cost variance (favorable)		$ 540

Spending and volume variances (based on formulas in Exhibit 24.14):

Actual Overhead   **Budgeted Overhead**   **Applied Overhead**
                                                                      6,750 × $1
$6,210 $6,250 $6,750

$40 F   **$500 F**
(Spending Variance)   (Volume Variance)

$540 F
(Total Fixed Overhead Variance)

We can also compute

Controllable variance: $5,900 U (both spending variances plus efficiency variance)

Volume variance: 500 F (identified as above)

Summary

C1 **Define *standard costs* and explain their computation and uses.** Standard costs are the normal costs that should be incurred to produce a product or perform a service. They should be based on a careful examination of the processes used to produce a product or perform a service as well as the quantities and prices that should be incurred in carrying out those processes. On a performance report, standard costs (which are flexible budget amounts) are compared to actual costs, and the differences are presented as variances.

C2 **Describe variances and what they reveal about performance.** Management can use variances to monitor and control activities. Total cost variances can be broken into price and quantity variances to direct management's attention to those responsible for quantities used and prices paid.

C3 **Explain how standard cost information is useful for management by exception.** Standard cost accounting provides management information about costs that differ from budgeted (expected) amounts. Performance reports disclose the costs or areas of operations that have significant variances from budgeted amounts. This allows managers to focus attention on the exceptions and less attention on areas proceeding normally.

A1 **Compare fixed and flexible budgets.** A fixed budget shows the revenues and costs expected to occur at a specified volume level. If actual volume is at some other level, the amounts in the fixed budget do not provide a reasonable basis for evaluating actual performance. A flexible budget expresses variable costs in per unit terms so that it can be used to develop budgeted amounts for any volume level within the relevant range. Thus, managers compute budgeted amounts for evaluation after a period for the volume that actually occurred.

A2 **Analyze changes in sales from expected amounts.** Actual sales can differ from budgeted sales, and managers can inves-

tigate this difference by computing both the sales price and sales volume variances. The *sales price variance* refers to that portion of total variance resulting from a difference between actual and budgeted selling prices. The *sales volume variance* refers to that portion of total variance resulting from a difference between actual and budgeted sales quantities.

P1 **Prepare a flexible budget and interpret a flexible budget performance report.** To prepare a flexible budget, we express each variable cost as a constant amount per unit of sales (or as a percent of sales dollar). In contrast, the budgeted amount of each fixed cost is expressed as a total amount expected to occur at any sales volume within the relevant range. The flexible budget is then determined using these computations and amounts for fixed and variable costs at the expected sales volume.

P2 **Compute materials and labor variances.** Materials and labor variances are due to differences between the actual costs incurred and the budgeted costs. The price (or rate) variance is computed by comparing the actual cost with the flexible budget amount that should have been incurred to acquire the actual quantity of resources. The quantity (or efficiency) variance is computed by comparing the flexible budget amount that should have been incurred to acquire the actual quantity of resources with the flexible budget amount that should have been incurred to acquire the standard quantity of resources.

P3 **Compute overhead variances.** Overhead variances are due to differences between the actual overhead costs incurred and the overhead applied to production. An overhead spending variance arises when the actual amount incurred differs from the budgeted amount of overhead. An overhead efficiency (or volume) variance arises when the flexible overhead budget amount differs from the overhead applied to production. It is important to realize that overhead is assigned using an overhead allocation base, meaning that an efficiency variance (in the case of variable overhead) is a result of the overhead application base being used more or less efficiently than planned.

P4   **Prepare journal entries for standard costs and account for price and quantity variances.** When a company records standard costs in its accounts, the standard costs of materials, labor, and overhead are debited to the Goods in Process Inventory account. Based on an analysis of the material, labor, and overhead

costs, each quantity variance, price variance, volume variance, and controllable variance is recorded in a separate account. At period-end, if the variances are material, they are allocated among the balances of the Goods in Process Inventory, Finished Goods Inventory, and Cost of Goods Sold accounts. If they are not material, they are simply debited or credited to the Cost of Goods Sold account.

Guidance Answers to **Decision Maker** and **Decision Ethics**

Entrepreneur   From the complaints, this performance report appears to compare actual results with a fixed budget. This comparison is useful in determining whether the amount of work actually performed was more or less than planned, but it is not useful in determining whether the divisions were more or less efficient than planned. If the two consulting divisions worked on more assignments than expected, some costs will certainly increase. Therefore, you should prepare a flexible budget using the actual number of consulting assignments and then compare actual performance to the flexible budget.

Human Resource Manager   As HR manager, you should investigate the causes for any labor-related variances although you may not be responsible for them. An unfavorable labor efficiency variance occurs because more labor hours than standard were used during the period. There are at least three possible reasons for this: (1) materials quality could be poor, resulting in more labor consumption due to rework, (2) unplanned interruptions (strike, breakdowns, accidents) could have occurred during the period, and (3) the production manager could have used a different labor mix to expedite orders. This new labor mix could have consisted of a larger proportion of untrained labor, which resulted in more labor hours.

Internal Auditor   Although the manager's actions might not be unethical, this action is undesirable. The internal auditor should report this behavior, possibly recommending that for the purchase of such discretionary items, the manager must provide budgetary requests using an activity-based budgeting process. The internal auditor would then be given full authority to verify this budget request.

Sales Manager   The unfavorable sales price variance suggests that actual prices were lower than budgeted prices. As the sales manager, you want to know the reasons for a lower than expected price. Perhaps your salespeople lowered the price of certain products by offering quantity discounts. You then might want to know what prompted them to offer the quantity discounts (perhaps competitors were offering discounts). You want to break the sales volume variance into both the sales mix and sales quantity variances. You could find that although the sales quantity variance is favorable, the sales mix variance is not. Then you need to investigate why actual sales mix differs from budgeted sales mix.

Guidance Answers to **Quick Checks**

1. *b*

2. The first step is classifying each cost as variable or fixed.

3. A fixed budget is prepared using an expected volume of sales or production. A flexible budget is prepared using the actual volume of activity.

4. Contribution margin equals sales less variable costs.

5. *c*

6. It is the difference between actual cost and standard cost.

7. *a*; Total actual hours: 2,500 × 2.5 = 6,250
        Total standard hours: 2,500 × 2.0 = 5,000
        Efficiency variance = (6,250 − 5,000) × $3.00
                            = $3,750 U

8. *b*; Rate variance = ($3.10 − $3.00) × 6,250 = $625 U

9. Yes, this will occur when the materials quantity variance is more than the materials price variance.

10. The overhead volume variance is favorable when the actual operating level is higher than the expected level.

11. *b*

12.

Goods in Process Inventory	75,700	
Direct Materials Price Variance	1,300	
Direct Materials Quantity Variance		3,800
Raw Materials Inventory		73,200

13. If the variances are material, they should be prorated among the Goods in Process Inventory, Finished Goods Inventory, and Cost of Goods Sold accounts. If they are not material, they can be closed to Cost of Goods Sold.

Key Terms

Key Terms are available at the book's Website for learning and testing in an online Flashcard Format.

Budgetary control (p. 954)
Budget report (p. 954)
Controllable variance (p. 967)
Cost variance (p. 961)
Efficiency variance (p. 966)
Favorable variance (p. 956)
Fixed budget (p. 955)

Fixed budget performance report (p. 955)
Flexible budget (p. 956)
Flexible budget performance report (p. 958)
Management by exception (p. 970)
Overhead cost variance (p. 966)
Price variance (p. 958)

Quantity variance (p. 958)
Spending variance (p. 966)
Standard costs (p. 959)
Unfavorable variance (p. 956)
Variance analysis (p. 958)
Volume variance (p. 967)

Multiple Choice Quiz

Answers on p. 995

Multiple Choice Quizzes A and B are available at the book's Website.

1. A company predicts its production and sales will be 24,000 units. At that level of activity, its fixed costs are budgeted at $300,000, and its variable costs are budgeted at $246,000. If its activity level declines to 20,000 units, what will be its fixed costs and its variable costs?
  a. Fixed, $300,000; Variable, $246,000
  b. Fixed, $250,000; Variable, $205,000
  c. Fixed, $300,000; Variable, $205,000
  d. Fixed, $250,000; Variable, $246,000
  e. Fixed, $300,000; Variable, $300,000

2. Using the following information about a single-product company, compute its total actual cost of direct materials used.
  • Direct materials standard cost: 5 lbs. × $2 per lb. = $10.
  • Total direct materials cost variance: $15,000 unfavorable.
  • Actual direct materials used: 300,000 lbs.
  • Actual units produced: 60,000 units.
  a. $585,000
  b. $600,000
  c. $300,000
  d. $315,000
  e. $615,000

3. A company uses four hours of direct labor to produce a product unit. The standard direct labor cost is $20 per hour. This period the company produced 20,000 units and used 84,160 hours of direct labor at a total cost of $1,599,040. What is its labor rate variance for the period?
  a. $83,200 F
  b. $84,160 U

  c. $84,160 F
  d. $83,200 U
  e. $ 960 F

4. A company's standard for a unit of its single product is $6 per unit in variable overhead (4 hours × $1.50 per hour). Actual data for the period shows variable overhead costs of $150,000 and production of 24,000 units. Its total variable overhead cost variance is
  a. $ 6,000 F
  b. $ 6,000 U
  c. $114,000 U
  d. $114,000 F
  e. $ 0

5. A company's standard for a unit of its single product is $4 per unit in fixed overhead ($24,000 total/6,000 units budgeted). Actual data for the period shows total actual fixed overhead of $24,100 and production of 4,800 units. Its volume variance is
  a. $4,800 U
  b. $4,800 F
  c. $ 100 U
  d. $ 100 F
  e. $4,900 U

Discussion Questions

1. What limits the usefulness to managers of fixed budget performance reports?

2. Identify the main purpose of a flexible budget for managers.

3. Prepare a flexible budget performance report title (in proper form) for Spalding Company for the calendar year 2008. Why is a proper title important for this or any report?

4. What type of analysis does a flexible budget performance report help management perform?

5. In what sense can a variable cost be considered constant?

6. What department is usually responsible for a direct labor rate variance? What department is usually responsible for a direct labor efficiency variance? Explain.

7. What is a price variance? What is a quantity variance?

8. What is the purpose of using standard costs?

9. In an analysis of fixed overhead cost variances, what is the volume variance?

10. What is the predetermined standard overhead rate? How is it computed?

11. In general, variance analysis is said to provide information about _____ and _____ variances.

12. In an analysis of overhead cost variances, what is the controllable variance and what causes it?

13. What is the relation among standard costs, flexible budgets, variance analysis, and management by exception?

14. How can the manager of a music department of a Best Buy retail store use flexible budgets to enhance performance?

15. Is it possible for a retail store such as Circuit City to use variances in analyzing its operating performance? Explain.

16. Assume that Apple is budgeted to operate at 80% of capacity but actually operates at 75% of capacity. What effect will the 5% deviation have on its controllable variance? Its volume variance?

 Red numbers denote Discussion Questions that involve decision-making.

QUICK STUDY

QS 24-1
Flexible budget performance report

P1

Beech Company reports the following selected financial results for May. For the level of production achieved in May, the budgeted amounts would be: sales, $1,300,000; variable costs, $750,000; and fixed costs, $300,000. Prepare a flexible budget performance report for May.

Sales (150,000 units)	$1,275,000
Variable costs	712,500
Fixed costs	300,000

QS 24-2
Labor cost variances

C2   P2

Frontera Company's output for the current period results in a $20,000 unfavorable direct labor rate variance and a $10,000 unfavorable direct labor efficiency variance. Production for the current period was assigned a $400,000 standard direct labor cost. What is the actual total direct labor cost for the current period?

QS 24-3
Materials cost variances

C2   P2

Juan Company's output for the current period was assigned a $150,000 standard direct materials cost. The direct materials variances included a $12,000 favorable price variance and a $2,000 favorable quantity variance. What is the actual total direct materials cost for the current period?

QS 24-4
Materials cost variances

C2   P2

For the current period, Kayenta Company's manufacturing operations yield a $4,000 unfavorable price variance on its direct materials usage. The actual price per pound of material is $78; the standard price is $77.50. How many pounds of material are used in the current period?

QS 24-5
Management by exception

C3

Managers use *management by exception* for control purposes. (1) Describe the concept of management by exception. (2) Explain how standard costs help managers apply this concept to monitor and control costs.

QS 24-6
Overhead cost variances   P3

Alvarez Company's output for the current period yields a $20,000 favorable overhead volume variance and a $60,400 unfavorable overhead controllable variance. Standard overhead charged to production for the period is $225,000. What is the actual total overhead cost incurred for the period?

Refer to the information in QS 24-6. Alvarez records standard costs in its accounts. Prepare the journal entry to charge overhead costs to the Goods in Process Inventory account and to record any variances.

QS 24-7
Preparing overhead entries   P4

Farad Company specializes in selling used SUVs. During the first six months of 2008, the dealership sold 50 SUVs at an average price of $9,000 each. The budget for the first six months of 2008 was to sell 45 SUVs at an average price of $9,500 each. Compute the dealership's sales price variance and sales volume variance for the first six months of 2008.

QS 24-8
Computing sales price and volume variances

A2

Tempo Company's fixed budget for the first quarter of calendar year 2008 reveals the following. Prepare flexible budgets following the format of Exhibit 24.3 that show variable costs per unit, fixed costs, and three different flexible budgets for sales volumes of 6,000, 7,000, and 8,000 units.

EXERCISES

Exercise 24-1
Preparation of flexible budgets

P1

Sales (7,000 units)		$2,800,000
Cost of goods sold		
Direct materials	$280,000	
Direct labor	490,000	
Production supplies	175,000	
Plant manager salary	65,000	1,010,000
Gross profit		1,790,000
Selling expenses		
Sales commissions	140,000	
Packaging	154,000	
Advertising	125,000	419,000
Administrative expenses		
Administrative salaries	85,000	
Depreciation—Office equip.	35,000	
Insurance	20,000	
Office rent	36,000	176,000
Income from operations		$1,195,000

Check   Income (at 6,000 units), $972,000

JPAK Company manufactures and sells mountain bikes. It normally operates eight hours a day, five days a week. Using this information, classify each of the following costs as fixed or variable. If additional information would affect your decision, describe the information.

a. Depreciation on tools   **e.** Management salaries   **i.** Gas used for heating

b. Pension cost   **f.** Incoming shipping expenses   **j.** Direct labor

c. Bike frames   **g.** Office supplies   **k.** Repair expense for tools

d. Screws for assembly   **h.** Taxes on property

Exercise 24-2
Classification of costs as fixed or variable

P1

Solitaire Company's fixed budget performance report for June follows. The $315,000 budgeted expenses include $294,000 variable expenses and $21,000 fixed expenses. Actual expenses include $27,000 fixed expenses. Prepare a flexible budget performance report that shows any variances between budgeted results and actual results. List fixed and variable expenses separately.

Exercise 24-3
Preparation of a flexible budget performance report

A1

	Fixed Budget	Actual Results	Variances
Sales (in units)	8,400	10,800	
Sales (in dollars)	$420,000	$540,000	$120,000 F
Total expenses	315,000	378,000	63,000 U
Income from operations	$105,000	$162,000	$ 57,000 F

Check   Income variance, $21,000 F

Exercise 24-4

Preparation of a flexible budget performance report

A1

Bay City Company's fixed budget performance report for July follows. The $647,500 budgeted expenses include $487,500 variable expenses and $160,000 fixed expenses. Actual expenses include $158,000 fixed expenses. Prepare a flexible budget performance report showing any variances between budgeted and actual results. List fixed and variable expenses separately.

	Fixed Budget	Actual Results	Variances
Sales (in units)	7,500	7,200	
Sales (in dollars)	$750,000	$737,000	$13,000 U
Total expenses	647,500	641,000	6,500 F
Income from operations	$102,500	$ 96,000	$ 6,500 U

Check Income variance, $4,000 F

Exercise 24-5

Computation and interpretation of labor variances

C2 P2

Check October rate variance, $3,250 U

After evaluating Null Company's manufacturing process, management decides to establish standards of 3 hours of direct labor per unit of product and $15 per hour for the labor rate. During October, the company uses 16,250 hours of direct labor at a $247,000 total cost to produce 5,600 units of product. In November, the company uses 22,000 hours of direct labor at a $335,500 total cost to produce 6,000 units of product. (1) Compute the rate variance, the efficiency variance, and the total direct labor cost variance for each of these two months. (2) Interpret the October direct labor variances.

Exercise 24-6

Computation and interpretation of overhead variances

C2 P3

Sedona Company set the following standard costs for one unit of its product for 2008.

Direct material (20 lbs. @ $2.50 per lb.)	$ 50.00
Direct labor (10 hrs. @ $8.00 per hr.)	80.00
Factory variable overhead (10 hrs. @ $4.00 per hr.)	40.00
Factory fixed overhead (10 hrs. @ $1.60 per hr.)	16.00
Standard cost	$186.00

The $5.60 ($4.00 + $1.60) total overhead rate per direct labor hour is based on an expected operating level equal to 75% of the factory's capacity of 50,000 units per month. The following monthly flexible budget information is also available.

	Operating Levels		
	70%	75%	80%
Budgeted output (units)	35,000	37,500	40,000
Budgeted labor (standard hours)	350,000	375,000	400,000
Budgeted overhead (dollars)			
Variable overhead	$1,400,000	$1,500,000	$1,600,000
Fixed overhead	600,000	600,000	600,000
Total overhead	$2,000,000	$2,100,000	$2,200,000

During the current month, the company operated at 70% of capacity, employees worked 340,000 hours, and the following actual overhead costs are incurred.

Variable overhead costs	$1,375,000
Fixed overhead costs	628,600
Total overhead costs	$2,003,600

(1) Show how the company computed its predetermined overhead application rate per hour for total overhead, variable overhead, and fixed overhead. (2) Compute and interpret the variable overhead spending and efficiency variances. (3) Compute and interpret the fixed overhead spending and volume variances.

Hart Company made 3,000 bookshelves using 22,000 board feet of wood costing $266,200. The company's direct materials standards for one bookshelf are 8 board feet of wood at $12 per board foot. (1) Compute the direct materials variances incurred in manufacturing these bookshelves. (2) Interpret the direct materials variances.

Exercise 24-7
Computation and interpretation of materials variances

C2 P2

Check Price variance, $2,200 U

Refer to Exercise 24-7. Hart Company records standard costs in its accounts and its material variances in separate accounts when it assigns materials costs to the Goods in Process Inventory account. (1) Show the journal entry that both charges the direct materials costs to the Goods in Process Inventory account and records the materials variances in their proper accounts. (2) Assume that Hart's material variances are the only variances accumulated in the accounting period and that they are immaterial. Prepare the adjusting journal entry to close the variance accounts at period-end. (3) Identify the variance that should be investigated according to the management by exception concept. Explain.

Exercise 24-8
Materials variances recorded and closed

C3 P4

Check (2) Cr. to cost of goods sold, $21,800

World Company expects to operate at 80% of its productive capacity of 50,000 units per month. At this planned level, the company expects to use 25,000 standard hours of direct labor. Overhead is allocated to products using a predetermined standard rate based on direct labor hours. At the 80% capacity level, the total budgeted cost includes $50,000 fixed overhead cost and $275,000 variable overhead cost. In the current month, the company incurred $305,000 actual overhead and 22,000 actual labor hours while producing 35,000 units. Compute the (1) total overhead variance, (2) overhead volume variance, and (3) overhead controllable variance.

Exercise 24-9
Computation of volume and controllable overhead variances

P3

Check (3) $14,375 U

Comp Wiz sells computers. During May 2008, it sold 350 computers at a $1,200 average price each. The May 2008 budget included sales of 365 computers at an average price of $1,100 each. (1) Compute the sales price variance and the sales volume variance for May 2008. (2) Interpret the findings.

Exercise 24-10
Computing and interpreting sales variances A2

Trico Company set the following standard unit costs for its single product.

PROBLEM SET A

Problem 24-1A
Computation of materials, labor, and overhead variances

C2 P2 P3

mhhe.com/wildFAP18e

Direct materials (30 lbs. @ $4 per lb.)	$120.00
Direct labor (5 hrs. @ $14 per hr.)	70.00
Factory overhead—Variable (5 hrs. @ $8 per hr.)	40.00
Factory overhead—Fixed (5 hrs. @ $10 per hr.)	50.00
Total standard cost	$280.00

The predetermined overhead rate is based on a planned operating volume of 80% of the productive capacity of 60,000 units per quarter. The following flexible budget information is available.

	Operating Levels		
	70%	**80%**	**90%**
Production in units	42,000	48,000	54,000
Standard direct labor hours	210,000	240,000	270,000
Budgeted overhead			
Fixed factory overhead	$2,400,000	$2,400,000	$2,400,000
Variable factory overhead	$1,680,000	$1,920,000	$2,160,000

During the current quarter, the company operated at 90% of capacity and produced 54,000 units of product; actual direct labor totaled 265,000 hours. Units produced are assigned the following standard costs:

Direct materials (1,620,000 lbs. @ $4 per lb.)	$ 6,480,000
Direct labor (270,000 hrs. @ $14 per hr.)	3,780,000
Factory overhead (270,000 hrs. @ $18 per hr.)	4,860,000
Total standard cost	$15,120,000

Actual costs incurred during the current quarter follow:

Direct materials (1,615,000 lbs. @ $4.10)	$ 6,621,500
Direct labor (265,000 hrs. @ $13.75)	3,643,750
Fixed factory overhead costs	2,350,000
Variable factory overhead costs	2,200,000
Total actual costs	$14,815,250

Required

Check (1) Materials variances:
Price, $161,500 U; Quantity, $20,000 F.

(2) Labor variances: Rate,
$66,250 F; Efficiency, $70,000 F

1. Compute the direct materials cost variance, including its price and quantity variances.

2. Compute the direct labor variance including its rate and efficiency variances.

3. Compute these variances: (a) variable overhead spending and efficiency, (b) fixed overhead spending and volume, and (c) total overhead controllable.

Problem 24-2A
Preparation and analysis
of a flexible budget

P1 A1

Phoenix Company's 2008 master budget included the following fixed budget report. It is based on an expected production and sales volume of 15,000 units.

PHOENIX COMPANY
Fixed Budget Report
For Year Ended December 31, 2008

Sales		$3,000,000
Cost of goods sold		
Direct materials	$975,000	
Direct labor	225,000	
Machinery repairs (variable cost)	60,000	
Depreciation—Plant equipment	300,000	
Utilities ($45,000 is variable)	195,000	
Plant management salaries	200,000	1,955,000
Gross profit		1,045,000
Selling expenses		
Packaging	75,000	
Shipping	105,000	
Sales salary (fixed annual amount)	250,000	430,000
General and administrative expenses		
Advertising expense	125,000	
Salaries	241,000	
Entertainment expense	90,000	456,000
Income from operations		$ 159,000

Required

1. Classify all items listed in the fixed budget as variable or fixed. Also determine their amounts per unit or their amounts for the year, as appropriate.

Check (2) Budgeted income at
16,000 units, $260,000

2. Prepare flexible budgets (see Exhibit 24.3) for the company at sales volumes of 14,000 and 16,000 units.

3. The company's business conditions are improving. One possible result is a sales volume of approximately 18,000 units. The company president is confident that this volume is within the relevant range of existing capacity. How much would operating income increase over the 2008 budgeted amount of $159,000 if this level is reached without increasing capacity?

(4) Potential operating loss,
$(144,000)

4. An unfavorable change in business is remotely possible; in this case, production and sales volume for 2008 could fall to 12,000 units. How much income (or loss) from operations would occur if sales volume falls to this level?

Refer to information in Problem 24-2A. Phoenix Company's actual income statement for 2008 follows.

Problem 24-3A
Preparation and analysis of a flexible budget performance report

P1 A2

e**X**cel

mhhe.com/wildFAP18e

PHOENIX COMPANY		
Statement of Income from Operations		
For Year Ended December 31, 2008		
Sales (18,000 units)		$3,648,000
Cost of goods sold		
Direct materials	$1,185,000	
Direct labor	278,000	
Machinery repairs (variable cost)	63,000	
Depreciation—Plant equipment	300,000	
Utilities (fixed cost is $147,500)	200,500	
Plant management salaries	210,000	2,236,500
Gross profit		1,411,500
Selling expenses		
Packaging	87,500	
Shipping	118,500	
Sales salary (annual)	268,000	474,000
General and administrative expenses		
Advertising expense	132,000	
Salaries	241,000	
Entertainment expense	93,500	466,500
Income from operations		$ 471,000

Required

1. Prepare a flexible budget performance report for 2008.

Check (1) Variances: Fixed costs, $36,000 U; Income, $9,000 F

Analysis Component

2. Analyze and interpret both the (a) sales variance and (b) direct materials variance.

Antuan Company set the following standard costs for one unit of its product.

Problem 24-4A
Flexible budget preparation; computation of materials, labor, and overhead variances; and overhead variance report

P1 P2 P3 C2

Direct materials (6 lbs. @ $5 per lb.)	$ 30
Direct labor (2 hrs. @ $17 per hr.)	34
Overhead (2 hrs. @ $18.50 per hr.)	37
Total standard cost	$101

The predetermined overhead rate ($18.50 per direct labor hour) is based on expected volume of 75% of the factory's capacity of 20,000 units per month. Following are the company's budgeted overhead costs per month at the 75% level.

Overhead Budget (75% capacity)		
Variable overhead costs		
Indirect materials	$ 45,000	
Indirect labor	180,000	
Power	45,000	
Repairs and maintenance	90,000	
Total variable overhead costs		$360,000
Fixed overhead costs		
Depreciation—Building	24,000	
Depreciation—Machinery	80,000	
Taxes and insurance	12,000	
Supervision	79,000	
Total fixed overhead costs		195,000
Total overhead costs		$555,000

The company incurred the following actual costs when it operated at 75% of capacity in October.

Direct materials (91,000 lbs. @ $5.10 per lb.)		$ 464,100
Direct labor (30,500 hrs. @ $17.25 per hr.)		526,125
Overhead costs		
Indirect materials	$ 44,250	
Indirect labor	177,750	
Power	43,000	
Repairs and maintenance	96,000	
Depreciation—Building	24,000	
Depreciation—Machinery	75,000	
Taxes and insurance	11,500	
Supervision	89,000	560,500
Total costs		$1,550,725

Required

Check (2) Budgeted total overhead at 13,000 units, $507,000.

(3) Materials variances: Price, $9,100 U; Quantity, $5,000 U.

(4) Labor variances: Rate, $7,625 U; Efficiency, $8,500 U

1. Examine the monthly overhead budget to (a) determine the costs per unit for each variable overhead item and its total per unit costs, and (b) identify the total fixed costs per month.

2. Prepare flexible overhead budgets (as in Exhibit 24.12) for October showing the amounts of each variable and fixed cost at the 65%, 75%, and 85% capacity levels.

3. Compute the direct materials cost variance, including its price and quantity variances.

4. Compute the direct labor cost variance, including its rate and efficiency variances.

5. Compute the (a) variable overhead spending and efficiency variances, (b) fixed overhead spending and volume variances, and (c) total overhead controllable variance.

6. Prepare a detailed overhead variance report (as in Exhibit 24.19) that shows the variances for individual items of overhead.

Problem 24-5A

Materials, labor, and overhead variances; and overhead variance report

C2 P2 P3

Kegler Company has set the following standard costs per unit for the product it manufactures.

Direct materials (15 lbs. @ $4 per lb.)	$ 60.00
Direct labor (3 hrs. @ $15 per hr.)	45.00
Overhead (3 hrs. @ $3.85 per hr.)	11.55
Total standard cost	$116.55

The predetermined overhead rate is based on a planned operating volume of 80% of the productive capacity of 10,000 units per month. The following flexible budget information is available.

	Operating Levels		
	70%	**80%**	**90%**
Production in units	7,000	8,000	9,000
Standard direct labor hours	21,000	24,000	27,000
Budgeted overhead			
Variable overhead costs			
Indirect materials	$13,125	$ 15,000	$16,875
Indirect labor	21,000	24,000	27,000
Power	5,250	6,000	6,750
Maintenance	2,625	3,000	3,375
Total variable costs	42,000	48,000	54,000
Fixed overhead costs			
Rent of factory building	15,000	15,000	15,000
Depreciation—Machinery	10,000	10,000	10,000
Supervisory salaries	19,400	19,400	19,400
Total fixed costs	44,400	44,400	44,400
Total overhead costs	$86,400	$ 92,400	$98,400

During May, the company operated at 90% of capacity and produced 9,000 units, incurring the following actual costs.

Direct materials (138,000 lbs. @ $3.75 per lb.)		$ 517,500
Direct labor (31,000 hrs. @ $15.10 per hr.)		468,100
Overhead costs		
Indirect materials	$15,000	
Indirect labor	26,500	
Power	6,750	
Maintenance	4,000	
Rent of factory building	15,000	
Depreciation—Machinery	10,000	
Supervisory salaries	22,000	99,250
Total costs		$1,084,850

Required

1. Compute the direct materials variance, including its price and quantity variances.
2. Compute the direct labor variance, including its rate and efficiency variances.
3. Compute these variances: (a) variable overhead spending and efficiency, (b) fixed overhead spending and volume, and (c) total overhead controllable.
4. Prepare a detailed overhead variance report (as in Exhibit 24.19) that shows the variances for individual items of overhead.

Check (1) Materials variances:
Price, $34,500 F; Quantity, $12,000 U.
(2) Labor variances: Rate, $3,100 U;
Efficiency, $60,000 U.

Boss Company's standard cost accounting system recorded this information from its December operations.

Problem 24-6A
Materials, labor, and overhead variances recorded and analyzed

C3 P4

Standard direct materials cost	$100,000
Direct materials quantity variance (unfavorable)	3,000
Direct materials price variance (favorable)	500
Actual direct labor cost	90,000
Direct labor efficiency variance (favorable)	7,000
Direct labor rate variance (unfavorable)	1,200
Actual overhead cost	375,000
Volume variance (unfavorable)	12,000
Controllable variance (unfavorable)	9,000

Required

1. Prepare December 30 journal entries to record the company's costs and variances for the month.

Check (1) Dr. Goods in Process Inventory (for overhead), $354,000

Analysis Component

2. Identify the areas that would attract the attention of a manager who uses management by exception. Explain what action(s) the manager should consider.

Kryll Company set the following standard unit costs for its single product.

PROBLEM SET B

Problem 24-1B
Computation of materials, labor, and overhead variances

C2 P2 P3

Direct materials (25 lbs. @ $4 per lb.)	$100.00
Direct labor (6 hrs. @ $8 per hr.)	48.00
Factory overhead—Variable (6 hrs. @ $5 per hr.)	30.00
Factory overhead—Fixed (6 hrs. @ $7 per hr.)	42.00
Total standard cost	$220.00

The predetermined overhead rate is based on a planned operating volume of 80% of the productive capacity of 60,000 units per quarter. The following flexible budget information is available.

	Operating Levels		
	70%	**80%**	**90%**
Production in units	42,000	48,000	54,000
Standard direct labor hours	252,000	288,000	324,000
Budgeted overhead			
Fixed factory overhead	$2,016,000	$2,016,000	$2,016,000
Variable factory overhead	1,260,000	1,440,000	1,620,000

During the current quarter, the company operated at 70% of capacity and produced 42,000 units of product; direct labor hours worked were 250,000. Units produced are assigned the following standard costs:

Direct materials (1,050,000 lbs. @ $4 per lb.)	$4,200,000
Direct labor (252,000 hrs. @ $8 per hr.)	2,016,000
Factory overhead (252,000 hrs. @ $12 per hr.)	3,024,000
Total standard cost	$9,240,000

Actual costs incurred during the current quarter follow:

Direct materials (1,000,000 lbs. @ $4.25)	$4,250,000
Direct labor (250,000 hrs. @ $7.75)	1,937,500
Fixed factory overhead costs	1,960,000
Variable factory overhead costs	1,200,000
Total actual costs	$9,347,500

Required

Check (1) Materials variances:
Price, $250,000 U; Quantity, $200,000 F.
(2) Labor variances: Rate, $62,500 F;
Efficiency, $16,000 F

1. Compute the direct materials cost variance, including its price and quantity variances.

2. Compute the direct labor variance, including its rate and efficiency variances.

3. Compute these variances: (a) variable overhead spending and efficiency, (b) fixed overhead spending and volume, and (c) total overhead controllable.

Problem 24-2B
Preparation and analysis of a flexible budget

P1 A1

Tohono Company's 2008 master budget included the following fixed budget report. It is based on an expected production and sales volume of 20,000 units.

TOHONO COMPANY
Fixed Budget Report
For Year Ended December 31, 2008

Sales		$3,000,000
Cost of goods sold		
Direct materials	$1,200,000	
Direct labor	260,000	
Machinery repairs (variable cost)	57,000	
Depreciation—Machinery	250,000	
Utilities (25% is variable cost)	200,000	
Plant manager salaries	140,000	2,107,000
Gross profit		893,000
Selling expenses		
Packaging	80,000	
Shipping	116,000	
Sales salary (fixed annual amount)	160,000	356,000
General and administrative expenses		
Advertising	81,000	
Salaries	241,000	
Entertainment expense	90,000	412,000
Income from operations		$ 125,000

Required

1. Classify all items listed in the fixed budget as variable or fixed. Also determine their amounts per unit or their amounts for the year, as appropriate.

2. Prepare flexible budgets (see Exhibit 24.3) for the company at sales volumes of 18,000 and 24,000 units.

3. The company's business conditions are improving. One possible result is a sales volume of approximately 28,000 units. The company president is confident that this volume is within the relevant range of existing capacity. How much would operating income increase over the 2008 budgeted amount of $125,000 if this level is reached without increasing capacity?

4. An unfavorable change in business is remotely possible; in this case, production and sales volume for 2008 could fall to 14,000 units. How much income (or loss) from operations would occur if sales volume falls to this level?

Check (2) Budgeted income at 24,000 units, $372,400

(4) Potential operating loss, $(246,100)

Refer to information in Problem 24-2B. Tohono Company's actual income statement for 2008 follows.

Problem 24-3B
Preparation and analysis of a flexible budget performance report

P1   A2

TOHONO COMPANY Statement of Income from Operations For Year Ended December 31, 2008		
Sales (24,000 units)		$3,648,000
Cost of goods sold		
Direct materials	$1,400,000	
Direct labor	360,000	
Machinery repairs (variable cost)	60,000	
Depreciation—Machinery	250,000	
Utilities (variable cost, $64,000)	218,000	
Plant manager salaries	155,000	2,443,000
Gross profit		1,205,000
Selling expenses		
Packaging	90,000	
Shipping	124,000	
Sales salary (annual)	162,000	376,000
General and administrative expenses		
Advertising expense	104,000	
Salaries	232,000	
Entertainment expense	100,000	436,000
Income from operations		$ 393,000

Required

1. Prepare a flexible budget performance report for 2008.

Check (1) Variances: Fixed costs, $45,000 U; Income, $20,600 F

Analysis Component

2. Analyze and interpret both the (a) sales variance and (b) direct materials variance.

SunCoast Company set the following standard costs for one unit of its product.

Problem 24-4B
Flexible budget preparation; computation of materials, labor, and overhead variances; and overhead variance report

P1 P2 P3 C2

Direct materials (4.5 lb. @ $6 per lb.)	$27
Direct labor (1.5 hrs. @ $12 per hr.)	18
Overhead (1.5 hrs. @ $16 per hr.)	24
Total standard cost	$69

The predetermined overhead rate ($16.00 per direct labor hour) is based on an expected volume of 75% of the factory's capacity of 20,000 units per month. Following are the company's budgeted overhead costs per month at the 75% level.

Overhead Budget (75% capacity)		
Variable overhead costs		
Indirect materials	$22,500	
Indirect labor	90,000	
Power	22,500	
Repairs and maintenance	45,000	
Total variable overhead costs		$180,000
Fixed overhead costs		
Depreciation—Building	24,000	
Depreciation—Machinery	72,000	
Taxes and insurance	18,000	
Supervision	66,000	
Total fixed overhead costs		180,000
Total overhead costs		$360,000

The company incurred the following actual costs when it operated at 75% of capacity in December.

Direct materials (69,000 lbs. @ $6.10)		$ 420,900
Direct labor (22,800 hrs. @ $12.30)		280,440
Overhead costs		
Indirect materials	$21,600	
Indirect labor	82,260	
Power	23,100	
Repairs and maintenance	46,800	
Depreciation—Building	24,000	
Depreciation—Machinery	75,000	
Taxes and insurance	16,500	
Supervision	66,000	355,260
Total costs		$1,056,600

Required

1. Examine the monthly overhead budget to (a) determine the costs per unit for each variable overhead item and its total per unit costs, and (b) identify the total fixed costs per month.

2. Prepare flexible overhead budgets (as in Exhibit 24.12) for December showing the amounts of each variable and fixed cost at the 65%, 75%, and 85% capacity levels.

3. Compute the direct materials cost variance, including its price and quantity variances.

4. Compute the direct labor cost variance, including its rate and efficiency variances.

5. Compute the (a) variable overhead spending and efficiency variances, (b) fixed overhead spending and volume variances, and (c) total overhead controllable variance.

6. Prepare a detailed overhead variance report (as in Exhibit 24.19) that shows the variances for individual items of overhead.

Check (2) Budgeted total overhead at 17,000 units, $384,000

(3) Materials variances: Price, $6,900 U; Quantity, $9,000 U

(4) Labor variances: Rate, $6,840 U; Efficiency, $3,600 U

Problem 24-5B
Materials, labor, and overhead variances; and overhead variance report

C2 P2 P3

Guadelupe Company has set the following standard costs per unit for the product it manufactures.

Direct materials (10 lbs. @ $3.00 per lb.)	$30.00
Direct labor (4 hr. @ $6 per hr.)	24.00
Overhead (4 hr. @ $2.50 per hr.)	10.00
Total standard cost	$64.00

The predetermined overhead rate is based on a planned operating volume of 80% of the productive capacity of 10,000 units per month. The following flexible budget information is available.

	Operating Levels		
	70%	80%	90%
Production in units	7,000	8,000	9,000
Standard direct labor hours	28,000	32,000	36,000
Budgeted overhead			
Variable overhead costs			
Indirect materials	$ 8,750	$10,000	$11,250
Indirect labor	14,000	16,000	18,000
Power	3,500	4,000	4,500
Maintenance	1,750	2,000	2,250
Total variable costs	28,000	32,000	36,000
Fixed overhead costs			
Rent of factory building	12,000	12,000	12,000
Depreciation—Machinery	20,000	20,000	20,000
Taxes and insurance	2,400	2,400	2,400
Supervisory salaries	13,600	13,600	13,600
Total fixed costs	48,000	48,000	48,000
Total overhead costs	$76,000	$80,000	$84,000

During March, the company operated at 90% of capacity and produced 9,000 units, incurring the following actual costs.

Direct materials (92,000 lbs. @ $2.95 per lb.)		$ 271,400
Direct labor (37,600 hrs. @ $6.05 per hr.)		227,480
Overhead costs		
Indirect materials	$10,000	
Indirect labor	16,000	
Power	4,500	
Maintenance	3,000	
Rent of factory building	12,000	
Depreciation—Machinery	19,200	
Taxes and insurance	3,000	
Supervisory salaries	14,000	81,700
Total costs		$580,580

Required

1. Compute the direct materials cost variance, including its price and quantity variances.
2. Compute the direct labor variance, including its rate and efficiency variances.
3. Compute these variances: (a) variable overhead spending and efficiency, (b) fixed overhead spending and volume, and (c) total overhead controllable.
4. Prepare a detailed overhead variance report (as in Exhibit 24.19) that shows the variances for individual items of overhead.

Check (1) Materials variances: Price, $4,600 F; Quantity, $6,000 U.
 (2) Labor variances: Rate, $1,880 U; Efficiency, $9,600 U

Kenya Company's standard cost accounting system recorded this information from its June operations.

Problem 24-6B
Materials, labor, and overhead variances recorded and analyzed

C3   P4

Standard direct materials cost	$130,000
Direct materials quantity variance (favorable)	5,000
Direct materials price variance (favorable)	1,500
Actual direct labor cost	65,000
Direct labor efficiency variance (favorable)	3,000
Direct labor rate variance (unfavorable)	500
Actual overhead cost	250,000
Volume variance (unfavorable)	12,000
Controllable variance (unfavorable)	8,000

Required

Check (1) Dr. Goods in Process
Inventory (for overhead), $230,000

1. Prepare journal entries dated June 30 to record the company's costs and variances for the month.

Analysis Component

2. Identify the areas that would attract the attention of a manager who uses management by exception. Describe what action(s) the manager should consider.

PROBLEM SET C

 Problem Set C is available at the book's Website to further reinforce and assess your learning.

SERIAL PROBLEM

Success Systems

(This serial problem began in Chapter 1 and continues through most of the book. If previous chapter segments were not completed, the serial problem can begin at this point. It is helpful, but not necessary, for you to use the Working Papers that accompany the book.)

SP 24   Success Systems' second quarter 2009 fixed budget performance report for its computer furniture operations follows. The $174,150 budgeted expenses include $144,900 variable expenses and $29,250 fixed expenses. The actual expenses include $30,000 fixed expenses. Prepare a flexible budget performance report that shows any variances between budgeted results and actual results. List fixed and variable expenses separately.

	Fixed Budget	Actual Results	Variances
Desk sales (in units)	144	150	
Chair sales (in units)	72	80	
Desk sales (in dollars)	$162,000	$169,500	$7,500 F
Chair sales (in dollars)	$ 27,000	$ 30,000	$3,000 F
Total expenses	$174,150	$182,450	$8,300 U
Income from operations	$ 14,850	$ 17,050	$2,200 F

Check Variances: Fixed expenses,
$750 U

BEYOND THE NUMBERS

REPORTING IN ACTION

C1

BTN 24-1   Analysis of flexible budgets and standard costs emphasizes the importance of a similar unit of measure for meaningful comparisons and evaluations. When **Best Buy** compiles its financial reports in compliance with GAAP, it applies the same unit of measurement, U.S. dollars, for most measures of business operations. One issue for Best Buy is how best to adjust account values for its subsidiaries that compile financial reports in currencies other than the U.S. dollar.

Required

1. Read Best Buy's Note 1 in Appendix A and identify the financial statement where it reports foreign currency translation.

2. Record the annual amount of its foreign currency translation adjustment and its ending balance for the three fiscal years 2002 through 2005.

Fast Forward

3. Access Best Buy's financial statements for a fiscal year ending after February 26, 2005, from either its Website [BestBuy.com] or the SEC's EDGAR database [www.sec.gov]. (a) Identify its foreign currency translation adjustment. (b) Does this adjustment increase or decrease net income? Explain.

BTN 24-2   The usefulness of budgets, variances, and related analyses often depends on the accuracy of management's estimates of future sales activity.

Required

1. Identify and record the prior three years' sales (in dollars) for both **Best Buy** and **Circuit City** using their financial statements in Appendix A.

2. Using the data in part 1, predict both companies' sales activity for the next two to three years. (If possible, compare your predictions to actual sales figures for these years.)

**COMPARATIVE
ANALYSIS**

A2

BTN 24-3   Setting materials, labor, and overhead standards is challenging. If standards are set too low, companies might purchase inferior products and employees might not work to their full potential. If standards are set too high, companies could be unable to offer a quality product at a profitable rate and employees could be overworked. The ethical challenge is to set a high but reasonable standard. Assume that as a manager, you are asked to set the standard materials price and quantity for the new 1,000 CKB Mega-Max chip, a technically advanced product. To properly set the price and quantity standards, you assemble a team of specialists to provide input.

Required

Identify four types of specialists that you would assemble to provide information to help set the materials price and quantity standards. Briefly explain why you chose each individual.

**ETHICS
CHALLENGE**

C1

BTN 24-4   The reason we use the words *favorable* and *unfavorable* when evaluating variances is made clear when we look at the closing of accounts. To see this, consider that (1) all variance accounts are closed at the end of each period (temporary accounts), (2) a favorable variance is always a credit balance, and (3) an unfavorable variance is always a debit balance. Write a one-half page memorandum to your instructor with three parts that answer the three following requirements. (Assume that variance accounts are closed to Cost of Goods Sold.)

Required

1. Does Cost of Goods Sold increase or decrease when closing a favorable variance? Does gross margin increase or decrease when a favorable variance is closed to Cost of Goods Sold? Explain.

2. Does Cost of Goods Sold increase or decrease when closing an unfavorable variance? Does gross margin increase or decrease when an unfavorable variance is closed to Cost of Goods Sold? Explain.

3. Explain the meaning of a favorable variance and an unfavorable variance.

**COMMUNICATING
IN PRACTICE**

P4 C2

BTN 24-5   Access iSixSigma's Website (iSixSigma.com) to search for and read information about *benchmarking* to complete the following requirements.

Required

1. Write a one-paragraph explanation (in layperson's terms) of benchmarking.

2. How does standard costing relate to benchmarking?

**TAKING IT TO
THE NET**

C1

TEAMWORK IN ACTION

C2

BTN 24-6 Many service industries link labor rate and time (quantity) standards with their processes. One example is the standard time to board an aircraft. The reason time plays such an important role in the service industry is that it is viewed as a competitive advantage: best service in the shortest amount of time. Although the labor rate component is difficult to observe, the time component of a service delivery standard is often readily apparent, for example, "Lunch will be served in less than five minutes, or it is free."

Required

Break into teams and select two service industries for your analysis. Identify and describe all the time elements each industry uses to create a competitive advantage.

BusinessWeek **ACTIVITY**

C2

BTN 24-7 Read the article "The Shrinking Productivity Factor" from the December 28, 2005, issue of *BusinessWeek*. (The book's Website provides free access to the article.)

Required

1. The article predicts that worker productivity will increase in 2006. Which labor variance—the rate or efficiency variance—would this affect? How would it be affected?
2. The article predicts that labor costs will increase in 2006. Which labor variance—the rate or efficiency variance—would this affect? How would it be affected?
3. If productivity increases and labor costs increase, what is your prediction for a company's total labor costs? Explain.

ENTREPRENEURIAL DECISION

C1 C2

BTN 24-8 Entrepreneur Kevin Plank of **Under Armour** has implemented a costing system with standard costs for direct materials, direct labor, and overhead costs. Two comments frequently are mentioned in relation to standard costing and variance analysis: "Variances are not explanations" and "Management's goal is not to minimize variances."

Required

Write Kevin Plank a short memo interpreting these two comments.

HITTING THE ROAD

C1

BTN 24-9 Training employees to use standard amounts of materials in production is common. Typically, large companies invest in this training but small organizations do not. One can observe these different practices in a trip to two different pizza businesses. Visit both a local pizza business and a national pizza chain business and then complete the following.

Required

1. Observe and record the number of raw material items used to make a typical cheese pizza. Also observe how the person making the pizza applies each item when preparing the pizza.
2. Record any differences in how items are applied between the two businesses.
3. Estimate which business is more profitable from your observations. Explain.

GLOBAL DECISION

Dixons

BTN 24-10 Access the annual report of **Dixons** (at <u>Dixons-Group.com</u>) for the year ended May 1, 2004. The usefulness of its budgets, variances, and related analyses depends on the accuracy of management's estimates of future sales activity.

Required

1. Identify and record the prior two years' sales (in pounds) for Dixons from its income statement.
2. Using the data in part 1, predict sales activity for Dixons for the next two years. Explain your prediction process.

ANSWERS TO MULTIPLE CHOICE QUIZ

1. c; Fixed costs remain at $300,000; Variable costs = ($246,000/24,000 units) × 20,000 units = $205,000.

2. e; Budgeted direct materials + Unfavorable variance = Actual cost of direct materials used; or, 60,000 units × $10 per unit = $600,000 + $15,000 U = $615,000.

3. c; (AH × AR) − (AH × SR) = $1,599,040 − (84,160 hours × $20 per hour) = $84,160 F.

4. b; Actual variable overhead − Variable overhead applied to production = Variable overhead cost variance; or, $150,000 − (96,000 hours × $1.50 per hour) = $6,000 U.

5. a; Budgeted fixed overhead − Fixed overhead applied to production = Volume variance; or, $24,000 − (4,800 units × $4 per unit) = $4,800 U.

25

Capital Budgeting and Managerial Decisions

A Look Back

Chapter 24 discussed flexible budgets, variance analysis, and standard costs. It explained how management uses each to control and monitor business activities.

A Look at This Chapter

This chapter focuses on evaluating capital budgeting decisions. It also explains several tools and procedures used in making and evaluating short-term managerial decisions.

> *"If you're good at what you do and you are focused ... it will happen to you"*
> —Art Alaniz

Reaching for the Sky

EDINBURG, TX—Art Alaniz credits his Mexican-immigrant parents and their work ethic for much of his success. "I failed at my first two entrepreneurial attempts," explains Art. With his parents' help, says Art, "I picked myself up, dusted myself off, and went back in there." Art launched his current company, **Progressive Telecom** **(ProgressiveTelecom.com),** from a spare room in his mother's house. His mother, says Art, "always supported us and our dreams, [although she] speaks little English and has little formal education."

"I've always wanted to own my own business," recalls Art. "I started by advertising in the newspaper that I buy used Cell phones. Then I would refurbish them and sell them." Sales skyrocketed along with the proliferation of cell phones. The business quickly outgrew his mother's house. "We were doing good numbers," says Art. "Our company [went] from selling 20 to 50 phones to selling 20,000."

Soon, capital budgeting decisions became important for the financial health of his business as it built warehouses, juggled a large inventory, and determined the product mix it would carry. Art also implemented payback periods and return rates as a way to narrow business opportunities and to improve decision making.

Many new business questions also emerged, explains Art. Do we take this one-time deal? Do we scrap or rework certain inventory? Do we sell or further process particular items? What is the best product mix? These questions needed answers. Art learned to focus on relevant costs and incremental revenue concepts to arrive at a solution for these cases. "It was tough and is still," admits Art. "I know what I want to accomplish and I keep moving forward."

With an attention to managerial decisions and budgeting, this 34-year-old entrepreneur has guided the rapid growth of his company. In less than 10 years, Progressive Telecom's sales are nearing a remarkable $40 million.

Art still faces key business decisions every day, such as financing requirements, hurdle rates, payback periods, rates of return, net present values, and break-even time. But none of these faze him anymore. "What's the worst that could happen?" asks Art. "I have to start over again. That's not too difficult." We know he'll just pick himself up, dust himself off, and get right back in there.

[Sources: *Progressive Telecom Website,* May 2006; *The Monitor,* November 2004; *Entrepreneur,* November and October 2004; *PRNewswire,* October 2003; *TradeRoots.org Website,* March 2006; *Small Business Administration,* March 2006]

Making business decisions involves choosing between alternative courses of action. Many factors affect business decisions, yet analysis typically focuses on finding the alternative that offers the highest return on investment or the greatest reduction in costs. Some decisions are based on little more than an intuitive understanding of the situation because available information is too limited to allow a more systematic analysis. In other cases, intangible factors such as convenience, prestige, and environmental considerations are more important than strictly quantitative factors. In all situations, managers can reach a sounder decision if they identify the consequences of alternative choices in financial terms. This chapter explains several methods of analysis that can help managers make those business decisions.

Section 1—Capital Budgeting

C1 Explain the importance of capital budgeting.

The capital expenditures budget is management's plan for acquiring and selling plant assets. **Capital budgeting** is the process of analyzing alternative long-term investments and deciding which assets to acquire or sell. These decisions can involve developing a new product or process, buying a new machine or a new building, or acquiring an entire company. An objective for these decisions is to earn a satisfactory return on investment.

Capital budgeting decisions require careful analysis because they are usually the most difficult and risky decisions that managers make. These decisions are difficult because they require predicting events that will not occur until well into the future. Many of these predictions are tentative and potentially unreliable. Specifically, a capital budgeting decision is risky because (1) the outcome is uncertain, (2) large amounts of money are usually involved, (3) the investment involves a long-term commitment, and (4) the decision could be difficult or impossible to reverse, no matter how poor it turns out to be. Risk is especially high for investments in technology due to innovations and uncertainty.

Managers use several methods to evaluate capital budgeting decisions. Nearly all of these methods involve predicting cash inflows and cash outflows of proposed investments, assessing the risk of and returns on those flows, and then choosing the investments to make. Management often restates future cash flows in terms of their present value. This approach applies the time value of money: A dollar today is worth more than a dollar tomorrow. Similarly, a dollar tomorrow is worth less than a dollar today. The process of restating future cash flows in terms of their present value is called *discounting*. The time value of money is important when evaluating capital investments, but managers sometimes apply evaluation methods that ignore present value. This section describes four methods for comparing alternative investments.

Point: The nature of capital spending has changed with the business environment. Budgets for information technology have increased from about 25% of corporate capital spending 20 years ago to an estimated 35% today.

Methods Not Using Time Value of Money

All investments, whether they involve the purchase of a machine or another long-term asset, are expected to produce net cash flows. *Net cash flow* is cash inflows minus cash outflows. Sometimes managers perform simple analyses of the financial feasibility of an investment's net cash flow without using the time value of money. This section explains two of the most common methods in this category: (1) payback period and (2) accounting rate of return.

Payback Period

An investment's **payback period (PBP)** is the expected time period to recover the initial investment amount. Managers prefer investing in assets with shorter payback periods to reduce the risk of an unprofitable investment over the long run. Acquiring assets with short payback periods reduces a company's risk from potentially inaccurate long-term predictions of future cash flows.

P1 Compute payback period and describe its use.

Computing Payback Period with Even Cash Flows   To illustrate use of the payback period for an investment with even cash flows, we look at data from FasTrac, a manufacturer of exercise equipment and supplies. (*Even cash flows* are cash flows that are the same each and every year; *uneven cash flows* are cash flows that are not all equal in amount.) FasTrac is considering several different capital investments, one of which is to purchase a machine to use in manufacturing a new product. This machine costs $16,000 and is expected to have an eight-year life with no salvage value. Management predicts this machine will produce 1,000 units of product each year and that the new product will be sold for $30 per unit. Exhibit 25.1 shows the expected annual net cash flows for this asset over its life as well as the expected annual revenues and expenses (including depreciation and income taxes) from investing in the machine.

Decision Insight

Payback Phones   Profits of telecoms declined as too much capital investment chased too little revenue. Telecom success depends on new technology, and communications gear is evolving at a dizzying rate. Consequently, managers of telecoms often demand short payback periods and large expected net cash flows to compensate for the investment risk.

FASTRAC		
Cash Flow Analysis—Machinery Investment		
January 15, 2008		
	Expected Accrual Figures	Expected Net Cash Flows
Annual sales of new product	$30,000	$30,000
Deduct annual expenses		
Cost of materials, labor, and overhead (except depreciation)	15,500	15,500
Depreciation—Machinery	2,000	
Additional selling and administrative expenses	9,500	9,500
Annual pretax accrual income	3,000	
Income taxes (30%)	900	900
Annual net income	$ 2,100	
Annual net cash flow		$ 4,100

Exhibit 25.1

Cash Flow Analysis

The amount of net cash flow from the machinery is computed by subtracting expected cash outflows from expected cash inflows. The cash flows column of Exhibit 25.1 excludes all noncash revenues and expenses. Depreciation is FasTrac's only noncash item. Alternatively, managers can adjust the projected net income for revenue and expense items that do not affect

Point: Annual net cash flow in Exhibit 25.1 equals net income plus depreciation (a noncash expense).

cash flows. For FasTrac, this means taking the $2,100 net income and adding back the $2,000 depreciation.

The formula for computing the payback period of an investment that yields even net cash flows is in Exhibit 25.2.

Exhibit 25.2

Payback Period Formula with Even Cash Flows

$$\text{Payback period} = \frac{\text{Cost of investment}}{\text{Annual net cash flow}}$$

The payback period reflects the amount of time for the investment to generate enough net cash flow to return (or pay back) the cash initially invested to purchase it. FasTrac's payback period for this machine is just under four years:

$$\text{Payback period} = \frac{\$16,000}{\$4,100} = 3.9 \text{ years}$$

Example: If an alternative machine (with different technology) yields a payback period of 3.5 years, which one does a manager choose? Answer: The alternative (3.5 is less than 3.9).

The initial investment is fully recovered in 3.9 years, or just before reaching the halfway point of this machine's useful life of eight years.

Computing Payback Period with Uneven Cash Flows Computing the payback period in the prior section assumed even net cash flows. What happens if the net cash flows are uneven? In this case, the payback period is computed using the *cumulative total of net cash flows*. The word *cumulative* refers to the addition of each period's net cash flows as we progress through time. To illustrate, consider data for another investment that FasTrac is considering. This machine is predicted to generate uneven net cash flows over the next eight years. The relevant data and payback period computation are shown in Exhibit 25.3.

Exhibit 25.3

Payback Period Calculation with Uneven Cash Flows

Period*	Expected Net Cash Flows	Cumulative Net Cash Flows
Year 0	$(16,000)	$(16,000)
Year 1	3,000	(13,000)
Year 2	4,000	(9,000)
Year 3	4,000	(5,000)
Year 4	4,000	(1,000)
Year 5	5,000	4,000
Year 6	3,000	7,000
Year 7	2,000	9,000
Year 8	2,000	11,000
		Payback period = 4.2 years

* All cash inflows and outflows occur uniformly during the year.

Example: Find the payback period in Exhibit 25.3 if net cash flows for the first 4 years are:
Year 1 = $6,000; Year 2 = $5,000;
Year 3 = $4,000; Year 4 = $3,000.
Answer: 3.33 years

Year 0 refers to the period of initial investment in which the $16,000 cash outflow occurs at the end of year 0 to acquire the machinery. By the end of year 1, the cumulative net cash flow is reduced to $(13,000), computed as the $(16,000) initial cash outflow plus year 1's $3,000 cash inflow. This process continues throughout the asset's life. The cumulative net cash flow amount changes from negative to positive in year 5. Specifically, at the end of year 4, the cumulative net cash flow is $(1,000). As soon as FasTrac receives net cash inflow of $1,000 during the fifth year, it has fully recovered the investment. If we assume that cash flows are received uniformly *within* each year, receipt of the $1,000 occurs about one-fifth of the way through the year. This is computed as $1,000 divided by year 5's total net cash flow of $5,000, or 0.20. This yields a payback period of 4.2 years, computed as 4 years plus 0.20 of year 5.

Using the Payback Period Companies desire a short payback period to increase return and reduce risk. The more quickly a company receives cash, the sooner it is available for other uses and the less time it is at risk of loss. A shorter payback period also improves the company's ability to respond to unanticipated changes and lowers its risk of having to keep an unprofitable investment.

Payback period should never be the only consideration in evaluating investments. This is so because it ignores at least two important factors. First, it fails to reflect differences in the timing of net cash flows within the payback period. In Exhibit 25.3, FasTrac's net cash flows in the first five years were $3,000, $4,000, $4,000, $4,000, and $5,000. If another investment had predicted cash flows of $9,000, $3,000, $2,000, $1,800, and $1,000 in these five years, its payback period would also be 4.2 years, but this second alternative could be more desirable because it provides cash more quickly. The second important factor is that the payback period ignores *all* cash flows after the point where its costs are fully recovered. For example, one investment might pay back its cost in 3 years but stop producing cash after 4 years. A second investment might require 5 years to pay back its cost yet continue to produce net cash flows for another 15 years. A focus on only the payback period would mistakenly lead management to choose the first investment over the second.

"So what if I underestimated costs and overestimated revenues? It all averages out in the end."

Quick Check

Answers—p. 1020

1. Capital budgeting is (a) concerned with analyzing alternative sources of capital, including debt and equity, (b) an important activity for companies when considering what assets to acquire or sell, or (c) best done by intuitive assessments of the value of assets and their usefulness.

2. Why are capital budgeting decisions often difficult?

3. A company is considering purchasing equipment costing $75,000. Future annual net cash flows from this equipment are $30,000, $25,000, $15,000, $10,000, and $5,000. The payback period is (a) 4 years, (b) 3.5 years, or (c) 3 years.

4. If depreciation is an expense, why is it added back to an investment's net income to compute the net cash flow from that investment?

5. If two investments have the same payback period, are they equally desirable? Explain.

Accounting Rate of Return

The **accounting rate of return,** also called *return on average investment,* is computed by dividing a project's after-tax net income by the average amount invested in it. To illustrate, we return to FasTrac's $16,000 machinery investment described in Exhibit 25.1. We first compute (1) the after-tax net income and (2) the average amount invested. The $2,100 after-tax net income is already available from Exhibit 25.1. To compute the average amount invested, we assume that net cash flows are received evenly throughout each year. Thus, the average investment for each year is computed as the average of its beginning and ending book values. If FasTrac's $16,000 machine is depreciated $2,000 each year, the average amount invested in the machine for each year is computed as shown in Exhibit 25.4. The average for any year is the average of the beginning and ending book values.

P2 Compute accounting rate of return and explain its use.

	Beginning Book Value	Annual Depreciation	Ending Book Value	Average Book Value
Year 1	$16,000	$2,000	$14,000	$15,000
Year 2	14,000	2,000	12,000	13,000
Year 3	12,000	2,000	10,000	11,000
Year 4	10,000	2,000	8,000	9,000
Year 5	8,000	2,000	6,000	7,000
Year 6	6,000	2,000	4,000	5,000
Year 7	4,000	2,000	2,000	3,000
Year 8	2,000	2,000	0	1,000
All years				**$ 8,000**

Exhibit 25.4

Computing Average Amount Invested

Next we need the average book value for the asset's entire life. This amount is computed by taking the average of the individual yearly averages. This average equals $8,000, computed as $64,000 (the sum of the individual years' averages) divided by eight years (see last column of Exhibit 25.4).

Point: General formula for *annual average investment* is the sum of individual years' average book values divided by the number of years of the planned investment.

If a company uses straight-line depreciation, we can find the average amount invested by using the formula in Exhibit 25.5. Because FasTrac uses straight-line depreciation, its average amount invested for the eight years equals the sum of the book value at the beginning of the asset's investment period and the book value at the end of its investment period, divided by 2, as shown in Exhibit 25.5.

Exhibit 25.5

Computing Average Amount Invested under Straight-Line Depreciation

$$\text{Annual average investment} = \frac{\text{Beginning book value} + \text{Ending book value}}{2}$$

(straight-line case only)

$$= \frac{\$16,000 + \$0}{2} = \$8,000$$

If an investment has a salvage value, the average amount invested when using straight-line depreciation is computed as (Beginning book value + Salvage value)/2.

Once we determine the after-tax net income and the average amount invested, the accounting rate of return on the investment can be computed from the annual after-tax net income divided by the average amount invested, as shown in Exhibit 25.6.

Exhibit 25.6

Accounting Rate of Return Formula

$$\text{Accounting rate of return} = \frac{\text{Annual after-tax net income}}{\text{Annual average investment}}$$

This yields an accounting rate of return of 26.25% ($2,100/$8,000). FasTrac management must decide whether a 26.25% accounting rate of return is satisfactory. To make this decision, we must factor in the investment's risk. For instance, we cannot say an investment with a 26.25% return is preferred over one with a lower return unless we recognize any differences in risk. Thus, an investment's return is satisfactory or unsatisfactory only when it is related to returns from other investments with similar lives and risk.

When accounting rate of return is used to choose among capital investments, the one with the least risk, the shortest payback period, and the highest return for the longest time period is often identified as the best. However, use of accounting rate of return to evaluate investment opportunities is limited because it bases the amount invested on book values (not predicted market values) in future periods. Accounting rate of return is also limited when an asset's net incomes are expected to vary from year to year. This requires computing the rate using *average* annual net incomes, yet this accounting rate of return fails to distinguish between two investments with the same average annual net income but different amounts of income in early years versus later years or different levels of income variability.

Quick Check   Answers—p. 1020

6. The following data relate to a company's decision on whether to purchase a machine:

Cost	$180,000
Salvage value	15,000
Annual after-tax net income	40,000

The machine's accounting rate of return, assuming the even receipt of its net cash flows during the year and use of straight-line depreciation, is (a) 22%, (b) 41%, or (c) 21%.

7. Is a 15% accounting rate of return for a machine a good rate?

Methods Using Time Value of Money

This section describes two methods that help managers with capital budgeting decisions and that use the time value of money: (1) net present value and (2) internal rate of return. *(To apply these methods, you need a basic understanding of the concept of present value. An expanded*

explanation of present value concepts is in Appendix B near the end of the book. You can use the present value tables at the end of Appendix B to solve many of this chapter's assignments that use the time value of money.)

P3 Compute net present value and describe its use.

Net Present Value

Net present value analysis applies the time value of money to future cash inflows and cash outflows so management can evaluate a project's benefits and costs at one point in time. Specifically, **net present value (NPV)** is computed by discounting the future net cash flows from the investment at the project's required rate of return and then subtracting the initial amount invested.

Topic Tackler
PLUS
25-1

To illustrate, let's return to FasTrac's proposed machinery purchase described in Exhibit 25.1. Does this machine provide a satisfactory return while recovering the amount invested? Recall that the machine requires a $16,000 investment and is expected to provide $4,100 annual net cash inflows for the next eight years. If we assume that net cash flows from this machine are received at each year-end and that FasTrac requires a 12% annual return, net present value can be computed as in Exhibit 25.7.

Point: The assumption of end-of-year cash flows simplifies computations and is common in practice.

	Net Cash Flows*	Present Value of 1 at 12%†	Present Value of Net Cash Flows
Year 1	$ 4,100	0.8929	$ 3,661
Year 2	4,100	0.7972	3,269
Year 3	4,100	0.7118	2,918
Year 4	4,100	0.6355	2,606
Year 5	4,100	0.5674	2,326
Year 6	4,100	0.5066	2,077
Year 7	4,100	0.4523	1,854
Year 8	4,100	0.4039	1,656
Totals	$32,800		$20,367
Amount invested			(16,000)
Net present value			$ 4,367

* Cash flows occur at the end of each year.

† Present value of 1 factors are taken from Table B.1 in Appendix B.

Exhibit 25.7

Net Present Value Calculation with Equal Cash Flows

The first number column of Exhibit 25.7 shows the annual net cash flows. Present value of 1 factors, also called *discount factors,* are shown in the second column. Taken from Table B.1 in Appendix B, they assume that net cash flows are received at each year-end. *(To simplify present value computations and for assignment material at the end of this chapter, we assume that net cash flows are received at each year-end.)* Annual net cash flows from the first column of Exhibit 25.7 are multiplied by the discount factors in the second column to give present values shown in the third column. The last three lines of this exhibit show the final NPV computations. The asset's $16,000 initial cost is deducted from the $20,367 total present value of all future net cash flows to give this asset's NPV of $4,367. The machine is thus expected to (1) recover its cost, (2) provide a 12% compounded return, and (3) generate $4,367 above cost. We summarize this analysis by saying the present value of this machine's future net cash flows to FasTrac exceeds the $16,000 investment by $4,367.

Point: The amount invested includes all costs that must be incurred to get the asset in its proper location and ready for use.

Example: What is the net present value in Exhibit 25.7 if a 10% return is applied? *Answer:* $5,873

Net Present Value Decision Rule The decision rule in applying NPV is as follows: When an asset's expected cash flows are discounted at the required rate and yield a *positive* net present value, the asset should be acquired. This decision rule is reflected in the graphic at the right. When comparing several investment opportunities of about the same cost and same risk, we prefer the one with the highest positive net present value.

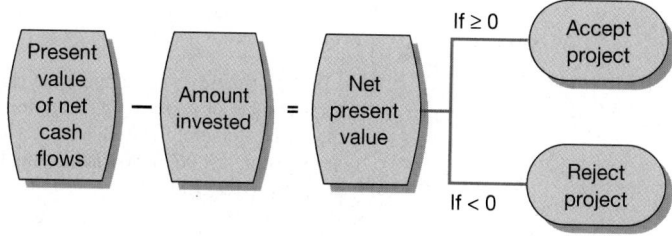

Example: Why does the net present value of an investment increase when a lower discount rate is used? *Answer:* Time value of money.

Simplifying Computations   The computations in Exhibit 25.7 use separate present value of 1 factors for each of the eight years. Each year's net cash flow is multiplied by its present value of 1 factor to determine its present value. The individual present values for each of the eight net cash flows are added to give the asset's total present value. This computation can be simplified in two ways if annual net cash flows are equal in amount. One way is to add the eight annual present value of 1 factors for a total of 4.9676 and multiply this amount by the annual $4,100 net cash flow to get the $20,367 total present value of net cash flows.[1] A second simplification is to use a calculator with compound interest functions or a spreadsheet program. Whatever procedure you use, it is important to understand the concepts behind these computations.

Decision Ethics

Answer—p. 1020

Systems Manager   Top management adopts a policy requiring purchases in excess of $5,000 to be submitted with cash flow projections to the cost analyst for capital budget approval. As systems manager, you want to upgrade your computers at a $25,000 cost. You consider submitting several orders all under $5,000 to avoid the approval process. You believe the computers will increase profits and wish to avoid a delay. What do you do?

Uneven Cash Flows   Net present value analysis can also be applied when net cash flows are uneven (unequal). To illustrate, assume that FasTrac can choose only one capital investment from among projects A, B, and C. Each project requires the same $12,000 initial investment. Future net cash flows for each project are shown in the first three number columns of Exhibit 25.8.

Exhibit 25.8

Net Present Value Calculation with Uneven Cash Flows

	Net Cash Flows			Present Value of 1 at 10%	Present Value of Net Cash Flows		
	A	**B**	**C**		**A**	**B**	**C**
Year 1	$ 5,000	$ 8,000	$ 1,000	0.9091	$ 4,546	$ 7,273	$ 909
Year 2	5,000	5,000	5,000	0.8264	4,132	4,132	4,132
Year 3	5,000	2,000	9,000	0.7513	3,757	1,503	6,762
Totals	$15,000	$15,000	$15,000		12,435	12,908	11,803
Amount invested					(12,000)	(12,000)	(12,000)
Net present value . . .					$ 435	$ 908	$ (197)

Example: If 12% is the required return in Exhibit 25.8, which project is preferred? *Answer:* Project B. Net present values are: A = $10; B = $553; C = $(715).

Example: Will the rankings of Projects A, B, and C change with the use of different discount rates, assuming the same rate is used for all projects? *Answer:* No; only the NPV amounts will change.

Point: Projects with higher cash flows in earlier years generally yield higher net present values.

The three projects in Exhibit 25.8 have the same expected total net cash flows of $15,000. Project A is expected to produce equal amounts of $5,000 each year. Project B is expected to produce a larger amount in the first year. Project C is expected to produce a larger amount in the third year. The fourth column of Exhibit 25.8 shows the present value of 1 factors from Table B.1 assuming 10% required return.

Computations in the right-most columns show that Project A has a $435 positive NPV. Project B has the largest NPV of $908 because it brings in cash more quickly. Project C has a $(197) *negative* NPV because its larger cash inflows are delayed. If FasTrac requires a 10% return, it should reject Project C because its NPV implies a return *under* 10%. If only one project can be accepted, project B appears best because it yields the highest NPV.

Salvage Value and Accelerated Depreciation   FasTrac predicted the $16,000 machine to have zero salvage value at the end of its useful life (recall Exhibit 25.1). In many

---

[1] We can simplify this computation using Table B.3, which gives the present value of 1 to be received periodically for a number of periods. To determine the present value of these eight annual receipts discounted at 12%, go down the 12% column of Table B.3 to the factor on the eighth line. This cumulative discount factor, also known as an *annuity* factor, is 4.9676. We then compute the $20,367 present value for these eight annual $4,100 receipts, computed as 4.9676 × $4,100.

cases, assets are expected to have salvage values. If so, this amount is an additional net cash inflow received at the end of the final year of the asset's life. All other computations remain the same.

Depreciation computations also affect net present value analysis. FasTrac computes depreciation using the straight-line method. Accelerated depreciation is also commonly used, especially for income tax reports. Accelerated depreciation produces larger depreciation deductions in the early years of an asset's life and smaller deductions in later years. This pattern results in smaller income tax payments in early years and larger payments in later years. Accelerated depreciation does not change the basics of a present value analysis, but it can change the result. Using accelerated depreciation for tax reporting affects the NPV of an asset's cash flows because it produces larger net cash inflows in the early years of the asset's life and smaller ones in later years. Being able to use accelerated depreciation for tax reporting always makes an investment more desirable because early cash flows are more valuable than later ones.

Use of Net Present Value In deciding whether to proceed with a capital investment project, we approve the proposal if the NPV is positive but reject it if the NPV is negative. When considering several projects of similar investment amounts and risk levels, we can compare the different projects' NPVs and rank them on the basis of their NPVs. However, if the amount invested differs substantially across projects, the NPV is of limited value for comparison purposes. To illustrate, suppose that Project X requires a $1 million investment and provides a $100,000 NPV. Project Y requires an investment of only $100,000 and returns a $75,000 NPV. Ranking on the basis of NPV puts Project X ahead of Y, yet X's NPV is only 10% of the initial investment whereas Y's NPV is 75% of its investment. We must also remember that when reviewing projects with different risks, we computed the NPV of individual projects using different discount rates. The higher the risk, the higher the discount rate.

Example: When is it appropriate to use different discount rates for different projects? *Answer:* When risk levels are different.

Internal Rate of Return

Another means to evaluate capital investments is to use the **internal rate of return,** which equals the rate that yields an NPV of zero for an investment. This means that if we compute the total present value of a project's net cash flows using the IRR as the discount rate and then subtract the initial investment from this total present value, we get a zero NPV.

To illustrate, we use the data for FasTrac's Project A from Exhibit 25.8 to compute its IRR. Exhibit 25.9 shows the two-step process in computing IRR.

P4 Compute internal rate of return and explain its use.

Step 1: Compute the present value factor for the investment project.

$$\text{Present value factor} = \frac{\text{Amount invested}}{\text{Net cash flows}} = \frac{\$12,000}{\$5,000} = 2.4000$$

Step 2: Identify the discount rate (IRR) yielding the present value factor

Search Table B.3 for a present value factor of 2.4000 in the three-year row (equaling the 3-year project duration). The 12% discount rate yields a present value factor of 2.4018. This implies that the IRR is approximately 12%.*

* Since the present value factor of 2.4000 is not exactly equal to the 12% factor of 2.4018, we can more precisely estimate the IRR as follows:

Discount rate	Present Value Factor from Table B.3
12%	2.4018
15%	2.2832
	0.1186 = difference

Then, $\text{IRR} = 12\% + \left[(15\% - 12\%) \times \dfrac{2.4018 - 2.4000}{0.1186} \right] = \underline{\underline{12.05\%}}$

Exhibit 25.9

Computing Internal Rate of Return (with even cash flows)

When cash flows are equal, as with Project A, we compute the present value factor (as shown in Exhibit 25.9) by dividing the initial investment by its annual net cash flows. We then use an annuity table to determine the discount rate equal to this present value factor. For FasTrac's Project A, we look across the three-period row of Table B.3 and find that the discount rate corresponding to the present value factor of 2.4000 roughly equals the 2.4018 value for the 12% rate. This row is reproduced here:

Present Value of an Annuity of 1 for Three Periods

Periods	Rate				
	1%	5%	10%	12%	15%
3	2.9410	2.7232	2.4869	2.4018	2.2832

The 12% rate is the Project's IRR. A more precise IRR estimate can be computed following the procedure shown in the note to Exhibit 25.9. Spreadsheet software and calculators can also compute this IRR.

Uneven Cash Flows If net cash flows are uneven, we must use trial and error to compute the IRR. We do this by selecting any reasonable discount rate and computing the NPV. If the amount is positive (negative), we recompute the NPV using a higher (lower) discount rate. We continue these steps until we reach a point where two consecutive computations result in NPVs having different signs (positive and negative). Because the NPV is zero using IRR, we know that the IRR lies between these two discount rates. We can then estimate its value. Spreadsheet programs and calculators can do these computations for us.

C2 Describe the selection of a hurdle rate for an investment.

Use of Internal Rate of Return When we use the IRR to evaluate a project, we compare it to a predetermined **hurdle rate,** which is a minimum acceptable rate of return and is applied as follows.

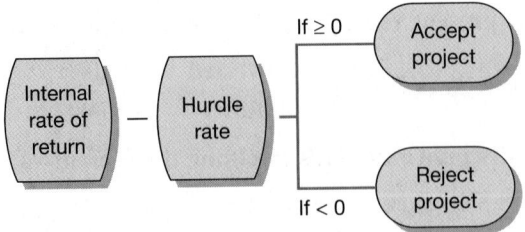

Example: How can management evaluate the risk of an investment? *Answer:* It must assess the uncertainty of future cash flows.

Top management selects the hurdle rate to use in evaluating capital investments. Financial formulas aid in this selection, but the choice of a minimum rate is subjective and left to management. For projects financed from borrowed funds, the hurdle rate must exceed the interest rate paid on these funds. The return on an investment must cover its interest and provide an additional profit to reward the company for its risk. For instance, if money is borrowed at 10%, an average risk investment often requires an after-tax return of 15% (or 5% above the borrowing rate). Remember that lower-risk investments require a lower rate of return compared with higher-risk investments.

If the project is internally financed, the hurdle rate is often based on actual returns from comparable projects. If the IRR is higher than the hurdle rate, the project is accepted. Multiple projects are often ranked by the extent to which their IRR exceeds the hurdle rate. The hurdle rate for individual projects is often different, depending on the risk involved. IRR is not subject to the limitations of NPV when comparing projects with different amounts invested because the IRR is expressed as a percent rather than as an absolute dollar value in NPV.

Comparison of Capital Budgeting Methods

We explained four methods that managers use to evaluate capital investment projects. How do these methods compare with each other? Exhibit 25.10 addresses that question. Neither the payback period nor the accounting rate of return considers the time value of money. On the other hand, both the net present value and the internal rate of return do.

Exhibit 25.10

Comparing Capital Budgeting Methods

	Payback Period	**Accounting Rate of Return**	**Net Present Value**	**Internal Rate of Return**
Measurement basis	■ Cash flows	■ Accrual income	■ Cash flows ■ Profitability	■ Cash flows ■ Profitability
Measurement unit	■ Years	■ Percent	■ Dollars	■ Percent
Strengths	■ Easy to understand ■ Allows comparison of projects	■ Easy to understand ■ Allows comparison of projects	■ Reflects time value of money ■ Reflects varying risks over project's life	■ Reflects time value of money ■ Allows comparisons of dissimilar projects
Limitations	■ Ignores time value of money ■ Ignores cash flows after payback period	■ Ignores time value of money ■ Ignores annual rates over life of project	■ Difficult to compare dissimilar projects	■ Ignores varying risks over life of project

The payback period is probably the simplest method. It gives managers an estimate of how soon they will recover their initial investment. Managers sometimes use this method when they have limited cash to invest and a number of projects to choose from. The accounting rate of return yields a percent measure computed using accrual income instead of cash flows. The accounting rate of return is an average rate for the entire investment period. Net present value considers all estimated net cash flows for the project's expected life. It can be applied to even and uneven cash flows and can reflect changes in the level of risk over a project's life. Since it yields a dollar measure, comparing projects of unequal sizes is more difficult. The internal rate of return considers all cash flows from a project. It is readily computed when the cash flows are even but requires some trial and error estimation when cash flows are uneven. Because the IRR is a percent measure, it is readily used to compare projects with different investment amounts. However, IRR does not reflect changes in risk over a project's life.

Decision Insight

And the Winner Is . . .
How do we choose among the methods for evaluating capital investments? Management surveys consistently show the internal rate of return (IRR) as the most popular method followed by the payback period and net present value (NPV). Few companies use the accounting rate of return (ARR), but nearly all use more than one method.

Company Usage for Capital Budgeting Methods

8. A company can invest in only one of two projects, A or B. Each project requires a $20,000 investment and is expected to generate end-of-period, annual cash flows as follows:

	Year 1	Year 2	Year 3	Total
Project A	$12,000	$8,500	$4,000	$24,500
Project B	4,500	8,500	13,000	26,000

Assuming a discount rate of 10%, which project has the higher net present value?

9. Two investment alternatives are expected to generate annual cash flows with the same net present value (assuming the same discount rate applied to each). Using this information, can you conclude that the two alternatives are equally desirable?

10. When two investment alternatives have the same total expected cash flows but differ in the timing of those flows, which method of evaluating those investments is superior, (*a*) accounting rate of return or (*b*) net present value?

Section 2—Managerial Decisions

This section focuses on methods that use accounting information to make several important managerial decisions. Most of these involve short-term decisions. This differs from methods used for longer-term managerial decisions that are described in the first section of this chapter and in several other chapters of this book.

Decisions and Information

This section explains how managers make decisions and the information relevant to those decisions.

Decision Making

Managerial decision making involves five steps: (1) define the decision task, (2) identify alternative courses of action, (3) collect relevant information and evaluate each alternative, (4) select the preferred course of action, and (5) analyze and assess decisions made. These five steps are illustrated in Exhibit 25.11.

Exhibit 25.11

Managerial Decision Making

| Define Task and Goal | Identify Alternative Actions | Collect Relevant Information | Select Course of Action | Analyze and Assess Decision |

Both managerial and financial accounting information play an important role in most management decisions. The accounting system is expected to provide primarily *financial* information such as performance reports and budget analyses for decision making. *Nonfinancial* information is also relevant, however; it includes information on environmental effects, political sensitivities, and social responsibility.

Relevant Costs

Most financial measures of revenues and costs from accounting systems are based on historical costs. Although historical costs are important and useful for many tasks such as product pricing and the control and monitoring of business activities, we sometimes find that an analysis of *relevant costs,* or *avoidable costs,* is especially useful. Three types of costs are pertinent to our discussion of relevant costs: sunk costs, out-of-pocket costs, and opportunity costs.

A *sunk cost* arises from a past decision and cannot be avoided or changed; it is irrelevant to future decisions. An example is the cost of computer equipment previously purchased by a company. Most of a company's allocated costs, including fixed overhead items such as depreciation and administrative expenses, are sunk costs.

An *out-of-pocket cost* requires a future outlay of cash and is relevant for current and future decision making. These costs are usually the direct result of management's decisions. For instance, future purchases of computer equipment involve out-of-pocket costs.

An *opportunity cost* is the potential benefit lost by taking a specific action when two or more alternative choices are available. An example is a student giving up wages from a job to attend summer school. Companies continually must choose from alternative courses of action. For instance, a company making standardized products might be approached by a customer to supply a special (nonstandard) product. A decision to accept or reject the special order must consider not only the profit to be made from the special order but also the profit given up by devoting time and resources to this order instead of pursuing an alternative project. The profit given up is an opportunity cost. Consideration of opportunity costs is important. The implications extend to internal resource allocation decisions. For instance, a computer manufacturer must decide between internally manufacturing a chip versus buying it externally. In another case, management of a multidivisional company must decide whether to continue operating or close a particular division.

Besides relevant costs, management must also consider the relevant benefits associated with a decision. **Relevant benefits** refer to the additional or *incremental* revenue generated by selecting a particular course of action over another. For instance, a student must decide the relevant benefits of taking one course over another. In sum, both relevant costs and relevant benefits are crucial to managerial decision making.

C3 Describe the importance of relevant costs for short-term decisions.

Example: Depreciation and amortization are allocations of the original cost of plant and intangible assets. Are they out-of-pocket costs? *Answer:* No; they are sunk costs.

Point: Opportunity costs are not entered in accounting records. This does not reduce their relevance for managerial decisions.

Managerial Decision Scenarios

Managers experience many different scenarios that require analyzing alternative actions and making a decision. We describe several different types of decision scenarios in this section. We set these tasks in the context of FasTrac, the exercise supplies and equipment manufacturer introduced earlier. *We treat each of these decision tasks as separate from each other.*

A1 Evaluate short-term managerial decisions using relevant costs.

Additional Business

FasTrac is operating at its normal level of 80% of full capacity. At this level, it produces and sells approximately 100,000 units of product annually. Its per unit and annual total costs are shown in Exhibit 25.12.

	Per Unit	Annual Total
Sales (100,000 units)	$10.00	$1,000,000
Direct materials	(3.50)	(350,000)
Direct labor	(2.20)	(220,000)
Overhead	(1.10)	(110,000)
Selling expenses	(1.40)	(140,000)
Administrative expenses	(0.80)	(80,000)
Total costs and expenses	(9.00)	(900,000)
Operating income	$ 1.00	$ 100,000

Exhibit 25.12

Selected Operating Income Data

A current buyer of FasTrac's products wants to purchase additional units of its product and export them to another country. This buyer offers to buy 10,000 units of the product at $8.50 per unit, or $1.50 less than the current price. The offer price is low, but FasTrac is considering the proposal because this sale would be several times larger than any single previous sale and it would use idle capacity. Also, the units will be exported, so this new business will not affect current sales.

To determine whether to accept or reject this order, management needs to know whether accepting the offer will increase net income. The analysis in Exhibit 25.13 shows that if management relies on per unit historical costs, it would reject the sale because it yields a loss. However, historical costs are *not* relevant to this decision. Instead, the relevant costs are the additional costs called **incremental costs.** These costs, also called *differential costs,* are the additional costs incurred if a company pursues a certain course of action. FasTrac's incremental costs are those related to the added volume that this new order would bring.

Exhibit 25.13

Analysis of Additional Business Using Historical Costs

	Per Unit	Total
Sales (10,000 additional units)	$ 8.50	$ 85,000
Direct materials	(3.50)	(35,000)
Direct labor	(2.20)	(22,000)
Overhead	(1.10)	(11,000)
Selling expenses	(1.40)	(14,000)
Administrative expenses	(0.80)	(8,000)
Total costs and expenses . . . . : . .	(9.00)	(90,000)
Operating loss	$(0.50)	$ (5,000)

To make its decision, FasTrac must analyze the costs of this new business in a different manner. The following information regarding the order is available:

- Manufacturing 10,000 additional units requires direct materials of $3.50 per unit and direct labor of $2.20 per unit (same as for all other units).
- Manufacturing 10,000 additional units adds $5,000 of incremental overhead costs for power, packaging, and indirect labor (all variable costs).
- Incremental commissions and selling expenses from this sale of 10,000 additional units would be $2,000 (all variable costs).
- Incremental administrative expenses of $1,000 for clerical efforts are needed (all fixed costs) with the sale of 10,000 additional units.

We use this information, as shown in Exhibit 25.14, to assess how accepting this new business will affect FasTrac's income.

Exhibit 25.14

Analysis of Additional Business Using Relevant Costs

	Current Business	Additional Business	Combined
Sales	$1,000,000	$ 85,000	$1,085,000
Direct materials	(350,000)	(35,000)	(385,000)
Direct labor	(220,000)	(22,000)	(242,000)
Overhead	(110,000)	(5,000)	(115,000)
Selling expenses	(140,000)	(2,000)	(142,000)
Administrative expense	(80,000)	(1,000)	(81,000)
Total costs and expenses	(900,000)	(65,000)	(965,000)
Operating income	$ 100,000	$ 20,000	$ 120,000

The analysis of relevant costs in Exhibit 25.14 suggests that the additional business be accepted. It would provide $85,000 of added revenue while incurring only $65,000 of added costs. This would yield $20,000 of additional pretax income, or a pretax profit margin of 23.5%. More generally, FasTrac would increase its income with any price that exceeded $6.50 per unit ($65,000 incremental cost/10,000 additional units).

An analysis of the incremental costs pertaining to the additional volume is always relevant for this type of decision. We must proceed cautiously, however, when the additional volume approaches or exceeds the factory's existing available capacity. If the additional volume requires the company to expand its capacity by obtaining more equipment, more space, or more personnel, the incremental costs could quickly exceed the incremental revenue. Another cautionary note is the effect on existing sales. All new units of the extra business will be sold outside FasTrac's normal domestic sales channels. If accepting additional business would cause existing sales to decline, this information must be included in our analysis. The contribution margin lost from a decline in sales is an opportunity cost. If future cash flows over several time periods are affected, their net present value also must be computed and used in this analysis.

The key point is that management must not blindly use historical costs, especially allocated overhead costs. Instead, the accounting system needs to provide information about the incremental costs to be incurred if the additional business is accepted.

Decision Maker	Answer—p. 1020

Partner You are a partner in a small accounting firm that specializes in keeping the books and preparing taxes for clients. A local restaurant is interested in obtaining these services from your firm. Identify factors that are relevant in deciding whether to accept the engagement.

Make or Buy

The managerial decision to make or buy a component for one of its current products is commonplace and depends on incremental costs. To illustrate, FasTrac has excess productive capacity it can use to manufacture Part 417, a component of the main product it sells. The part is currently purchased and delivered to the plant at a cost of $1.20 per unit. FasTrac estimates that making Part 417 would cost $0.45 for direct materials, $0.50 for direct labor, and an undetermined amount for overhead. The task is to determine how much overhead to add to these costs so we can decide whether to make or buy Part 417. If FasTrac's normal predetermined overhead application rate is 100% of direct labor cost, we might be tempted to conclude that overhead cost is $0.50 per unit, computed as 100% of the $0.50 direct labor cost. We would then mistakenly conclude that total cost is $1.45 ($0.45 of materials + $0.50 of labor + $0.50 of overhead). A wrong decision in this case would be to conclude that the company is better off buying the part at $1.20 each than making it for $1.45 each.

Topic Tackler

PLUS

25-2

Instead, as we explained earlier, only incremental overhead costs are relevant in this situation. Thus, we must compute an *incremental overhead rate*. Incremental overhead costs might include, for example, additional power for operating machines, extra supplies, added cleanup costs, materials handling, and quality control. We can prepare a per unit analysis in this case as shown in Exhibit 25.15.

We can see that if incremental overhead costs are less than $0.25 per unit, the total cost of making the component is less than the purchase price of $1.20 and FasTrac should make the part. FasTrac's decision rule in this case is that any amount of overhead less than $0.25 per unit yields a total cost for Part 417 that is less than the $1.20 purchase price. FasTrac must consider several nonfinancial

	Make	Buy
Direct materials	$0.45	—
Direct labor	0.50	—
Overhead costs	[?]	—
Purchase price	—	$1.20
Total incremental costs ..	$0.95 + [?]	$1.20

Exhibit 25.15

Make or Buy Analysis

factors in the make or buy decision, including product quality, timeliness of delivery (especially in a just-in-time setting), reactions of customers and suppliers, and other intangibles such as employee morale and workload. It must also consider whether making the part requires incremental fixed costs to expand plant capacity. When these added factors are considered, small cost differences may not matter.

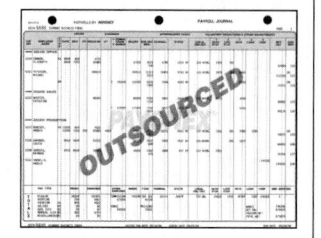

Scrap or Rework

Managers often must make a decision on whether to scrap or rework products in process. Remember that costs already incurred in manufacturing the units of a product that do not meet quality standards are sunk costs that have been incurred and cannot be changed. Sunk costs are irrelevant in any decision on whether to sell the substandard units as scrap or to rework them to meet quality standards.

To illustrate, assume that FasTrac has 10,000 defective units of a product that have already cost $1 per unit to manufacture. These units can be sold as is (as scrap) for $0.40 each, or they can be reworked for $0.80 per unit and then sold for their full price of $1.50 each. Should FasTrac sell the units as scrap or rework them?

To make this decision, management must recognize that the already incurred manufacturing costs of $1 per unit are sunk (unavoidable). These costs are *entirely irrelevant* to the decision. In addition, we must be certain that all costs of reworking defects, including interfering with normal operations, are accounted for in our analysis. For instance, reworking the defects means that FasTrac is unable to manufacture 10,000 *new* units with an incremental cost of $1 per unit and a selling price of $1.50 per unit, meaning it incurs an opportunity cost equal to the lost $5,000 net return from making and selling 10,000 new units. This opportunity cost is the difference between the $15,000 revenue (10,000 units × $1.50) from selling these new units and their $10,000 manufacturing costs (10,000 units × $1). Our analysis is reflected in Exhibit 25.16.

Exhibit 25.16

Scrap or Rework Analysis

	Scrap	Rework
Sale of scrapped/reworked units	$ 4,000	$ 15,000
Less costs to rework defects		(8,000)
Less opportunity cost of not making new units		**(5,000)**
Incremental net income	**$4,000**	**$ 2,000**

The analysis yields a $2,000 difference in favor of scrapping the defects, yielding a total incremental net income of $4,000. If we had failed to include the opportunity costs of $5,000, the rework option would have shown an income of $7,000 instead of $2,000, mistakenly making the reworking appear more favorable than scrapping.

Quick Check   Answers—p. 1020

11. A company receives a special order for 200 units that requires stamping the buyer's name on each unit, yielding an additional fixed cost of $400 to its normal costs. Without the order, the company is operating at 75% of capacity and produces 7,500 units of product at the following costs:

Direct materials	$37,500
Direct labor	60,000
Overhead (30% variable)	20,000
Selling expenses (60% variable)	25,000

The special order will not affect normal unit sales and will not increase fixed overhead and selling expenses. Variable selling expenses on the special order are reduced to one-half the normal amount. The price per unit necessary to earn $1,000 on this order is (*a*) $14.80, (*b*) $15.80, (*c*) $19.80, (*d*) $20.80, or (*e*) $21.80.

12. What are the incremental costs of accepting additional business?

Sell or Process

The managerial decision to sell partially completed products as is or to process them further for sale depends significantly on relevant costs. To illustrate, suppose that FasTrac has 40,000 units of partially finished Product Q. It has already spent $0.75 per unit to manufacture these 40,000 units at a $30,000 total cost. FasTrac can sell the 40,000 units to another manufacturer as raw material for $50,000. Alternatively, it can process them further and produce finished products X, Y, and Z at an incremental cost of $2 per unit. The added processing yields the products and revenues shown in Exhibit 25.17. FasTrac must decide whether the added revenues from selling finished products X, Y, and Z exceed the costs of finishing them.

Exhibit 25.18 shows the two-step analysis for this decision. First, FasTrac computes its incremental revenue from further processing Q into products X, Y, and Z. This amount is the difference between the $220,000 revenue from the further processed products and the $50,000 FasTrac will give up by not selling Q as is (a $50,000 opportunity cost). Second, FasTrac computes its incremental costs from further processing Q into X, Y, and Z. This amount is $80,000 (40,000 units × $2 incremental cost). The analysis shows that FasTrac can earn incremental net income of $90,000 from a decision to further process Q. (Notice that the earlier incurred $30,000 manufacturing cost for the 40,000 units of Product Q does not appear in Exhibit 25.18 because it is a sunk cost and as such is irrelevant to the decision.)

Product	Price	Units	Revenues
Product X	$4.00	10,000	$ 40,000
Product Y	6.00	22,000	132,000
Product Z	8.00	6,000	48,000
Spoilage	—	2,000	0
Totals		40,000	$220,000

Exhibit 25.17

Revenues from Processing Further

Revenue if processed	$220,000
Revenue if sold as is	(50,000)
Incremental revenue	170,000
Cost to process	(80,000)
Incremental net income	**$ 90,000**

Exhibit 25.18

Sell or Process Analysis

Example: Does the decision change if incremental costs in Exhibit 25.18 increase to $4 per unit and the opportunity cost increases to $95,000? *Answer:* Yes. There is now an incremental net loss of $35,000.

Quick Check   Answers—p. 1020

13. A company has already incurred a $1,000 cost in partially producing its four products. Their selling prices when partially and fully processed follow with additional costs necessary to finish these partially processed units:

Product	Unfinished Selling Price	Finished Selling Price	Further Processing Costs
Alpha	$300	$600	$150
Beta	450	900	300
Gamma	275	425	125
Delta	150	210	75

Which product(s) should *not* be processed further, (*a*) Alpha, (*b*) Beta, (*c*) Gamma, or (*d*) Delta?

14. Under what conditions is a sunk cost relevant to decision making?

Sales Mix Selection

When a company sells a mix of products, some are likely to be more profitable than others. Management is often wise to concentrate sales efforts on more profitable products. If production facilities or other factors are limited, an increase in the production and sale of one product usually requires reducing the production and sale of others. In this case, management must identify the most profitable combination, or *sales mix* of products. To identify the best sales mix, management must know the contribution

Decision Insight

Companies such as **Gap, Abercrombie & Fitch,** and **American Eagle** must continuously monitor and manage the sales mix of their product lists. Selling their products in hundreds of countries and territories further complicates their decision process. The contribution margin of each product is crucial to their product mix strategies.

margin of each product, the facilities required to produce each product, any constraints on these facilities, and its markets.

To illustrate, assume that FasTrac makes and sells two products, A and B. The same machines are used to produce both products. A and B have the following selling prices and variable costs per unit:

	Product A	Product B
Selling price per unit	$5.00	$7.50
Variable costs per unit	3.50	5.50
Contribution margin per unit	$1.50	$2.00

The variable costs are included in the analysis because they are the incremental costs of producing these products within the existing capacity of 100,000 machine hours per month. We consider three separate cases.

Case 1: Assume that (1) each product requires 1 machine hour per unit for production and (2) the markets for these products are unlimited. Under these conditions, FasTrac should produce as much of Product B as it can because of its larger contribution margin of $2 per unit. At full capacity, FasTrac would produce $200,000 of total contribution margin per month, computed as $2 per unit times 100,000 machine hours.

Case 2: Assume that (1) Product A requires 1 machine hour per unit, (2) Product B requires 2 machine hours per unit, and (3) the markets for these products are unlimited. Under these conditions, FasTrac should produce as much of Product A as it can because it has a contribution margin of $1.50 per machine hour compared with only $1 per machine hour for Product B. Exhibit 25.19 shows the relevant analysis.

Exhibit 25.19

Sales Mix Analysis

	Product A	Product B
Selling price per unit	$ 5.00	$ 7.50
Variable costs per unit	3.50	5.50
Contribution margin per unit	$ 1.50	$ 2.00
Machine hours per unit	1.0	2.0
Contribution margin per machine hour	$1.50	$1.00

Example: For Case 2, if Product B's variable costs per unit increase to $6, Product A's variable costs per unit decrease to $3, and the same machine hours per unit are used, which product should FasTrac produce? *Answer:* Product A. Its contribution margin of $2 per machine hour is higher than B's $.75 per machine hour.

At its full capacity of 100,000 machine hours, FasTrac would produce 100,000 units of Product A, yielding $150,000 of total contribution margin per month. In contrast, if it uses all 100,000 hours to produce Product B, only 50,000 units would be produced yielding a contribution margin of $100,000. These results suggest that when a company faces excess demand and limited capacity, only the most profitable product per input should be manufactured.

Case 3: The need for a mix of different products arises when market demand is not sufficient to allow a company to sell all that it produces. For instance, assume that (1) Product A requires 1 machine hour per unit, (2) Product B requires 2 machine hours per unit, and (3) the market for Product A is limited to 80,000 units. Under these conditions, FasTrac should produce no more than 80,000 units of Product A. This would leave another 20,000 machine hours of capacity for making Product B. FasTrac should use this spare capacity to produce 10,000 units of Product B. This sales mix would maximize FasTrac's total contribution margin per month at an amount of $140,000.

Point: A method called *linear programming* is useful for finding the optimal sales mix for several products subject to many market and production constraints. This method is described in advanced courses.

Segment Elimination

When a segment such as a department or division is performing poorly, management must consider eliminating it. Segment information on either net income (loss) or its contribution to overhead is not sufficient for this decision. Instead, we must look at the segment's avoidable expenses and unavoidable expenses. **Avoidable expenses,** also called *escapable expenses,* are amounts the company would not incur if it eliminated the segment. **Unavoidable**

expenses, also called *inescapable expenses,* are amounts that would continue even if the segment is eliminated.

To illustrate, FasTrac considers eliminating its treadmill division because its $48,300 total expenses are higher than its $47,800 sales. Classification of this division's operating expenses into avoidable or unavoidable expenses is shown in Exhibit 25.20.

	Total	Avoidable Expenses	Unavoidable Expenses
Cost of goods sold	$ 30,000	$ 30,000	—
Direct expenses			
Salaries expense	7,900	7,900	—
Depreciation expense—Equipment	200	—	$ 200
Indirect expenses			
Rent and utilities expense	3,150	—	3,150
Advertising expense	400	400	—
Insurance expense	400	300	100
Service department costs			
Share of office department expenses	3,060	2,200	860
Share of purchasing expenses	3,190	1,000	2,190
Total	$48,300	$41,800	$6,500

Exhibit 25.20

Classification of Segment Operating Expenses for Analysis

FasTrac's analysis shows that it can avoid $41,800 expenses if it eliminates the treadmill division. Because this division's sales are $47,800, eliminating it will cause FasTrac to lose $6,000 of income. *Our decision rule is that a segment is a candidate for elimination if its revenues are less than its avoidable expenses.* Avoidable expenses can be viewed as the costs to generate this segment's revenues.

When considering elimination of a segment, we must assess its impact on other segments. A segment could be unprofitable on its own, but it might still contribute to other segments' revenues and profits. It is possible then to continue a segment even when its revenues are less than its avoidable expenses. Similarly, a profitable segment might be discontinued if its space, assets, or staff can be more profitably used by expanding existing segments or by creating new ones. Our decision to keep or eliminate a segment requires a more complex analysis than simply looking at a segment's performance report. Such reports provide useful information, but they do not provide all the information necessary for this decision.

Example: How can insurance be classified as either avoidable or unavoidable? *Answer:* Depends on whether the assets insured can be removed and the premiums canceled.

Example: Give an example of a segment that a company might profitably use to attract customers even though it might incur a loss. *Answer:* Warranty and post-sales services.

Qualitative Decision Factors

Managers must consider qualitative factors in making managerial decisions. Consider a decision on whether to buy a component from an outside supplier or continue to make it. Several qualitative decision factors must be considered. For example, the quality, delivery, and reputation of the proposed supplier are important. The effects from deciding not to make the component can include potential layoffs and impaired worker morale. Consider another situation in which a company is considering a one-time sale to a new customer at a special low price. Qualitative factors to consider in this situation include the effects of a low price on the company's image and the threat that regular customers might demand a similar price. The company must also consider whether this customer is really a one-time customer. If not, can it continue to offer this low price in the long run? Clearly, management cannot rely solely on financial data to make such decisions.

Quick Check

Answers—p. 1020

15. What is the difference between avoidable and unavoidable expenses?

16. A segment is a candidate for elimination if (*a*) its revenues are less than its avoidable expenses, (*b*) it has a net loss, (*c*) its unavoidable expenses are higher than its revenues.

Decision Analysis | Break-Even Time

A2 Analyze a capital investment project using break-even time.

The first section of this chapter explained several methods to evaluate capital investments. Break-even time of an investment project is a variation of the payback period method that overcomes the limitation of not using the time value of money. **Break-even time (BET)** is a time-based measure used to evaluate a capital investment's acceptability. Its computation yields a measure of expected time, reflecting the time period until the *present value* of the net cash flows from an investment equals the initial cost of the investment. In basic terms, break-even time is computed by restating future cash flows in terms of present values and then determining the payback period using these present values.

To illustrate, we return to the FasTrac case described in Exhibit 25.1 involving a $16,000 investment in machinery. The annual net cash flows from this investment are projected at $4,100 for eight years. Exhibit 25.21 shows the computation of break-even time for this investment decision.

Exhibit 25.21

Break-Even Time Analysis*

Year	Cash Flows	Present Value of 1 at 10%	Present Value of Cash Flows	Cumulative Present Value of Cash Flows
0	$(16,000)	1.0000	$(16,000)	$(16,000)
1	4,100	0.9091	3,727	(12,273)
2	4,100	0.8264	3,388	(8,885)
3	4,100	0.7513	3,080	(5,805)
4	4,100	0.6830	2,800	(3,005)
5	4,100	0.6209	2,546	(459)
6	4,100	0.5645	2,314	1,855
7	4,100	0.5132	2,104	3,959
8	4,100	0.4665	1,913	5,872

* The time of analysis is the start of year 1 (same as end of year 0). All cash flows occur at the end of each year.

The right-most column of this exhibit shows that break-even time is between 5 and 6 years, or about 5.2 years. This is the time the project takes to break even after considering the time value of money (recall that the payback period computed without considering the time value of money was 3.9 years). We interpret this as cash flows earned after 5.2 years contribute to a positive net present value that, in this case, eventually amounts to $5,872.

Break-even time is a useful measure for managers because it identifies the point in time when they can expect the cash flows to begin to yield net positive returns. Managers expect a positive net present value from an investment if break-even time is less than the investment's estimated life. The method allows managers to compare and rank alternative investments, giving the project with the shortest break-even time the highest rank.

Decision Maker

Answer—p. 1020

Investment Manager Management asks you, the investment manager, to evaluate three alternative investments. Investment recovery time is crucial because cash is scarce. The time value of money is also important. Which capital budgeting method(s) do you use to assess the investments?

Demonstration Problem

Determine the appropriate action in each of the following managerial decision situations.

1. Packer Company is operating at 80% of its manufacturing capacity of 100,000 product units per year. A chain store has offered to buy an additional 10,000 units at $22 each and sell them to customers so as not to compete with Packer Company. The following data are available.

Costs at 80% Capacity	Per Unit	Total
Direct materials	$ 8.00	$ 640,000
Direct labor	7.00	560,000
Overhead (fixed and variable)	12.50	1,000,000
Totals	$27.50	$2,200,000

In producing 10,000 additional units, fixed overhead costs would remain at their current level but incremental variable overhead costs of $3 per unit would be incurred. Should the company accept or reject this order?

2. Green Company uses Part JR3 in manufacturing its products. It has always purchased this part from a supplier for $40 each. It recently upgraded its own manufacturing capabilities and has enough excess capacity (including trained workers) to begin manufacturing Part JR3 instead of buying it. The company prepares the following cost projections of making the part, assuming that overhead is allocated to the part at the normal predetermined rate of 200% of direct labor cost.

Direct materials	$11
Direct labor	15
Overhead (fixed and variable) (200% of direct labor)	30
Total	$56

The required volume of output to produce the part will not require any incremental fixed overhead. Incremental variable overhead cost will be $17 per unit. Should the company make or buy this part?

3. Gold Company's manufacturing process causes a relatively large number of defective parts to be produced. The defective parts can be (a) sold for scrap, (b) melted to recover the recycled metal for reuse, or (c) reworked to be good units. Reworking defective parts reduces the output of other good units because no excess capacity exists. Each unit reworked means that one new unit cannot be produced. The following information reflects 500 defective parts currently available.

Proceeds of selling as scrap	$2,500
Additional cost of melting down defective parts	400
Cost of purchases avoided by using recycled metal from defects	4,800
Cost to rework 500 defective parts	
Direct materials	0
Direct labor	1,500
Incremental overhead	1,750
Cost to produce 500 new parts	
Direct materials	6,000
Direct labor	5,000
Incremental overhead	3,200
Selling price per good unit	40

Should the company melt the parts, sell them as scrap, or rework them?

4. White Company can invest in one of two projects, TD1 or TD2. Each project requires an initial investment of $100,000 and produces the year-end cash inflows shown in the following table. Use net present values to determine which project, if any, should be chosen. Assume that the company requires a 10% return from its investments.

	Net Cash Flows	
	TD1	**TD2**
Year 1	$ 20,000	$ 40,000
Year 2	30,000	40,000
Year 3	70,000	40,000
Totals	$120,000	$120,000

Planning the Solution

- Determine whether Packer Company should accept the additional business by finding the incremental costs of materials, labor, and overhead that will be incurred if the order is accepted. Omit fixed costs that the order will not increase. If the incremental revenue exceeds the incremental cost, accept the order.

- Determine whether Green Company should make or buy the component by finding the incremental cost of making each unit. If the incremental cost exceeds the purchase price, the component should be purchased. If the incremental cost is less than the purchase price, make the component.

- Determine whether Gold Company should sell the defective parts, melt them down and recycle the metal, or rework them. To compare the three choices, examine all costs incurred and benefits received from the alternatives in working with the 500 defective units versus the production of 500 new units. For the scrapping alternative, include the costs of producing 500 new units and subtract the $2,500 proceeds from selling the old ones. For the melting alternative, include the costs of melting the defective units, add the net cost of new materials in excess over those obtained from recycling, and add the direct labor and overhead costs. For the reworking alternative, add the costs of direct labor and incremental overhead. Select the alternative that has the lowest cost. The cost assigned to the 500 defective units is sunk and not relevant in choosing among the three alternatives.

- Compute White Company's net present value of each investment using a 10% discount rate.

Solution to Demonstration Problem

1. This decision involves accepting additional business. Since current unit costs are $27.50, it appears initially as if the offer to sell for $22 should be rejected, but the $27.50 cost includes fixed costs. When the analysis includes only *incremental* costs, the per unit cost is as shown in the following table. The offer should be accepted because it will produce $4 of additional profit per unit (computed as $22 price less $18 incremental cost), which yields a total profit of $40,000 for the 10,000 additional units.

Direct materials	$ 8.00
Direct labor	7.00
Variable overhead (given)	3.00
Total incremental cost	$18.00

2. For this make or buy decision, the analysis must not include the $13 nonincremental overhead per unit ($30 − $17). When only the $17 incremental overhead is included, the relevant unit cost of manufacturing the part is shown in the following table. It would be better to continue buying the part for $40 instead of making it for $43.

Direct materials	$11.00
Direct labor	15.00
Variable overhead	17.00
Total incremental cost	$43.00

3. The goal of this scrap or rework decision is to identify the alternative that produces the greatest net benefit to the company. To compare the alternatives, we determine the net cost of obtaining 500 marketable units as follows:

Incremental Cost to Produce 500 Marketable Units	Sell as Is	Melt and Recycle	Rework Units
Direct materials			
New materials	$ 6,000	$6,000	
Recycled metal materials		(4,800)	
Net materials cost		1,200	
Melting costs		400	
Total direct materials cost	6,000	1,600	
Direct labor	5,000	5,000	$1,500
Incremental overhead	3,200	3,200	1,750
Cost to produce 500 marketable units	14,200	9,800	3,250
Less proceeds of selling defects as scrap	(2,500)		
Opportunity costs*			5,800
Net cost	$11,700	$9,800	$9,050

* The $5,800 opportunity cost is the lost contribution margin from not being able to produce and sell 500 units because of reworking, computed as ($40 − $14,200/500 units) × 500 units.

The incremental cost of 500 marketable parts is smallest if the defects are reworked.

4. TD1:

	Net Cash Flows	Present Value of 1 at 10%	Present Value of Net Cash Flows
Year 1	$ 20,000	0.9091	$ 18,182
Year 2	30,000	0.8264	24,792
Year 3	70,000	0.7513	52,591
Totals	$120,000		95,565
Amount invested			(100,000)
Net present value			$ (4,435)

TD2:

	Net Cash Flows	Present Value of 1 at 10%	Present Value of Net Cash Flows
Year 1	$ 40,000	0.9091	$ 36,364
Year 2	40,000	0.8264	33,056
Year 3	40,000	0.7513	30,052
Totals	$120,000		99,472
Amount invested			(100,000)
Net present value			$ (528)

White Company should not invest in either project. Both are expected to yield a negative net present value, and it should invest only in positive net present value projects.

Summary

C1 Explain the importance of capital budgeting. Capital budgeting is the process of analyzing alternative investments and deciding which assets to acquire or sell. It involves predicting the cash flows to be received from the alternatives, evaluating their merits, and then choosing which ones to pursue.

C2 Describe the selection of a hurdle rate for an investment. Top management should select the hurdle (discount) rate to use in evaluating capital investments. The required hurdle rate should be at least higher than the interest rate on money borrowed because the return on an investment must cover the interest and provide an additional profit to reward the company for risk.

C3 Describe the importance of relevant costs for short-term decisions. A company must rely on relevant costs pertaining to alternative courses of action rather than historical costs. Out-of-pocket expenses and opportunity costs are relevant because these are avoidable; sunk costs are irrelevant because they result from past decisions and are therefore unavoidable. Managers must also consider the relevant benefits associated with alternative decisions.

A1 Evaluate short-term managerial decisions using relevant costs. Relevant costs are useful in making decisions such as to accept additional business, make or buy, and sell as is or process further. For example, the relevant factors in deciding whether to produce and sell additional units of product are incremental costs and incremental revenues from the additional volume.

A2 Analyze a capital investment project using break-even time. Break-even time (BET) is a method for evaluating capital investments by restating future cash flows in terms of their present values (discounting the cash flows) and then calculating the payback period using these present values of cash flows.

P1 Compute payback period and describe its use. One way to compare potential investments is to compute and compare their payback periods. The payback period is an estimate of the expected time before the cumulative net cash inflow from the investment equals its initial cost. A payback period analysis fails to reflect risk of the cash flows, differences in the timing of cash flows within the payback period, and cash flows that occur after the payback period.

P2 Compute accounting rate of return and explain its use. A project's accounting rate of return is computed by dividing the expected annual after-tax net income by the average amount of investment in the project. When the net cash flows are received evenly throughout each period and straight-line depreciation is used, the average investment is computed as the average of the investment's initial book value and its salvage value.

P3 Compute net present value and describe its use. An investment's net present value is determined by predicting the future cash flows it is expected to generate, discounting them at a rate that represents an acceptable return, and then by subtracting the investment's initial cost from the sum of the present values. This technique can deal with any pattern of expected cash flows and applies a superior concept of return on investment.

P4 Compute internal rate of return and explain its use. The internal rate of return (IRR) is the discount rate that results in a zero net present value. When the cash flows are equal, we can compute the present value factor corresponding to the IRR by dividing the initial investment by the annual cash flows. We then use the annuity tables to determine the discount rate corresponding to this present value factor.

Guidance Answers to **Decision Maker** and **Decision Ethics**

Systems Manager   Your dilemma is whether to abide by rules designed to prevent abuse or to bend them to acquire an investment that you believe will benefit the firm. You should not pursue the latter action because breaking up the order into small components is dishonest and there are consequences of being caught at a later stage. Develop a proposal for the entire package and then do all you can to expedite its processing, particularly by pointing out its benefits. When faced with controls that are not working, there is rarely a reason to overcome its shortcomings by dishonesty. A direct assault on those limitations is more sensible and ethical.

Entrepreneur   The banker is probably concerned because new products are risky and should therefore be evaluated using a higher rate of return. You should conduct a thorough technical analysis and obtain detailed market data and information about any similar products available in the market. These factors might provide sufficient information to support the use of a lower return. You must convince yourself that the risk level is consistent with the discount rate used.

You should also be confident that your company has the capacity and the resources to handle the new product.

Partner   You should identify the differences between existing clients and this potential client. A key difference is that the restaurant business has additional inventory components (groceries, vegetables, meats, etc.) and is likely to have a higher proportion of depreciable assets. These differences imply that the partner must spend more hours auditing the records and understanding the business, regulations, and standards that pertain to the restaurant business. Such differences suggest that the partner must use a different "formula" for quoting a price to this potential client vis-à-vis current clients.

Investment Manager   You should probably focus on either the payback period or break-even time because both the time value of money and recovery time are important. Break-even time method is superior because it accounts for the time value of money, which is an important consideration in this decision.

Guidance Answers to **Quick Checks**

1. *b*

2. A capital budgeting decision is difficult because (1) the outcome is uncertain, (2) large amounts of money are usually involved, (3) a long-term commitment is required, and (4) the decision could be difficult or impossible to reverse.

3. *b*

4. Depreciation expense is subtracted from revenues in computing net income but does not use cash and should be added back to net income to compute net cash flows.

5. Not necessarily. One investment can continue to generate cash flows beyond the payback period for a longer time period than the other. The timing of their cash flows within the payback period also can differ.

6. *b*; Annual average investment = ($180,000 + $15,000)/2
                            = $97,500
   Accounting rate of return = $40,000/$97,500 = 41%

7. For this determination, we need to compare it to the returns expected from alternative investments with similar risk.

8. Project A has the higher net present value as follows:

Year	Present Value of 1 at 10%	Project A		Project B	
		Net Cash Flows	Present Value of Net Cash Flows	Net Cash Flows	Present Value of Net Cash Flows
1	0.9091	$12,000	$10,909	$ 4,500	$ 4,091
2	0.8264	8,500	7,024	8,500	7,024
3	0.7513	4,000	3,005	13,000	9,767
Totals		$24,500	$20,938	$26,000	$20,882
Amount invested			(20,000)		(20,000)
Net present value			**$ 938**		**$ 882**

9. No, the information is too limited to draw that conclusion. For example, one investment could be riskier than the other, or one could require a substantially larger initial investment.

10. *b*

11. *e*; Variable costs per unit for this order of 200 units follow:

Direct materials ($37,500/7,500)	$ 5.00
Direct labor ($60,000/7,500)	8.00
Variable overhead [(0.30 × $20,000)/7,500]	0.80
Variable selling expenses [(0.60 × $25,000 × 0.5)/7,500]	1.00
Total variable costs per unit	$14.80

   Cost to produce special order: (200 × $14.80) + $400
                          = $3,360.

   Price per unit to earn $1,000: ($3,360 + $1,000)/200 = 21.80.

12. They are the additional (new) costs of accepting new business.

13. *d*;

	Incremental benefits		Incremental costs
Alpha	$300 ($600 − $300)	>	$150 (given)
Beta	$450 ($900 − $450)	>	$300 (given)
Gamma	$150 ($425 − $275)	>	$125 (given)
Delta	$ 60 ($210 − $150)	<	$ 75 (given)

14. A sunk cost is *never* relevant because it results from a past decision and is already incurred.

15. Avoidable expenses are ones a company will not incur by eliminating a segment; unavoidable expenses will continue even after a segment is eliminated.

16. *a*

Key Terms   mhhe.com/wildFAP18e

Key Terms are available at the book's Website for learning and testing in an online Flashcard Format.

Accounting rate of return (p. 1001)   **Hurdle rate** (p. 1006)   **Payback period (PBP)** (p. 999)
Avoidable expense (p. 1014)   **Incremental cost** (p. 1010)   **Relevant benefits** (p. 1009)
Break-even time (BET) (p. 1016)   **Internal rate of return (IRR)** (p. 1005)   **Unavoidable expense** (p. 1014)
Capital budgeting (p. 998)   **Net present value (NPV)** (p. 1003)

Multiple Choice Quiz   Answers on p. 1036   mhhe.com/wildFAP18e

Multiple Choice Quizzes A and B are available at the book's Website.

1. A company inadvertently produced 3,000 defective MP3 players. The players cost $12 each to produce. A recycler offers to purchase the defective players as they are for $8 each. The production manager reports that the defects can be corrected for $10 each, enabling them to be sold at their regular market price of $19 each. The company should:
  a. Correct the defect and sell them at the regular price.
  b. Sell the players to the recycler for $8 each.
  c. Sell 2,000 to the recycler and repair the rest.
  d. Sell 1,000 to the recycler and repair the rest.
  e. Throw the players away.

2. A company's productive capacity is limited to 480,000 machine hours. Product X requires 10 machine hours to produce; and Product Y requires 2 machine hours to produce. Product X sells for $32 per unit and has variable costs of $12 per unit; Product Y sells for $24 per unit and has variable costs of $10 per unit. Assuming that the company can sell as many of either product as it produces, it should:
  a. Produce X and Y in the ratio of 57% and 43%.
  b. Produce X and Y in the ratio of 83% X and 17% Y.
  c. Produce equal amounts of Product X and Product Y.
  d. Produce only Product X.
  e. Produce only Product Y.

3. A company receives a special one-time order for 3,000 units of its product at $15 per unit. The company has excess capacity and it currently produces and sells the units at $20 each to its regular customers. Production costs are $13.50 per unit, which includes $9 of variable costs. To produce the special order, the company must incur additional fixed costs of $5,000. Should the company accept the special order?
  a. Yes, because incremental revenue exceeds incremental costs.
  b. No, because incremental costs exceed incremental revenue.
  c. No, because the units are being sold for $5 less than the regular price.
  d. Yes, because incremental costs exceed incremental revenue.
  e. No, because incremental cost exceeds $15 per unit when total costs are considered.

4. A company is considering the purchase of equipment for $270,000. Projected annual cash inflow from this equipment is $61,200 per year. The payback period is:
  a. 0.2 years
  b. 5.0 years
  c. 4.4 years
  d. 2.3 years
  e. 3.9 years

5. A company buys a machine for $180,000 that has an expected life of nine years and no salvage value. The company expects an annual net income (after taxes of 30%) of $8,550. What is the accounting rate of return?
  a. 4.75%
  b. 42.75%
  c. 2.85%
  d. 9.50%
  e. 6.65%

Discussion Questions

1. What is capital budgeting?

2. Identify four reasons that capital budgeting decisions by managers are risky.

3. Capital budgeting decisions require careful analysis because they are generally the _____ _____ and _____ decisions that management faces.

4. Identify two disadvantages of using the payback period for comparing investments.

5. Why is an investment more attractive to management if it has a shorter payback period?

6. What is the average amount invested in a machine during its predicted five-year life if it costs $200,000 and has a $20,000 salvage value? Assume that net income is received evenly throughout each year and straight-line depreciation is used.

7. If the present value of the expected net cash flows from a machine, discounted at 10%, exceeds the amount to be invested, what can you say about the investment's expected rate of return? What can you say about the expected rate of return if the present value of the net cash flows, discounted at 10%, is less than the investment amount?

8. Why is the present value of $100 that you expect to receive one year from today worth less than $100 received today? What is the present value of $100 that you expect to receive one year from today, discounted at 12%?

9. Why should managers set the required rate of return higher than the rate at which money can be borrowed when making a typical capital budgeting decision?

10. Why does the use of the accelerated depreciation method (instead of straight line) for income tax reporting increase an investment's value?

11. What is an out-of-pocket cost? What is an opportunity cost? Are opportunity costs recorded in the accounting records?

12. Why are sunk costs irrelevant in deciding whether to sell a product in its present condition or to make it into a new product through additional processing?

13. Identify the incremental costs incurred by Best Buy for shipping one additional iPod from a warehouse to a retail store along with the store's normal order of 75 iPods.

14. Circuit City is considering expanding a store. Identify three methods management can use to evaluate whether to expand.

15. Assume that Apple manufactures and sells 500,000 units of a product at $30 per unit in domestic markets. It costs $20 per unit to manufacture ($13 variable cost per unit, $7 fixed cost per unit). Can you describe a situation under which the company is willing to sell an additional 25,000 units of the product in an international market at $15 per unit?

 Red numbers denote Discussion Questions that involve decision-making.

QUICK STUDY

QS 25-1
Analyzing payback periods　P1

Park Company is considering two alternative investments. The payback period is 3.5 years for Investment A and 4 years for Investment B. (1) If management relies on the payback period, which investment is preferred? (2) Why might Park's analysis of these two alternatives lead to the selection of B over A?

QS 25-2
Payback period　P1

Freeman Company is considering an investment that requires immediate payment of $27,000 and provides expected cash inflows of $9,000 annually for four years. What is the investment's payback period?

QS 25-3
Computation of
net present value　P3

If Quail Company invests $50,000 today, it can expect to receive $10,000 at the end of each year for the next seven years plus an extra $6,000 at the end of the seventh year. What is the net present value of this investment assuming a required 10% return on investments?

QS 25-4
Computation of
accounting rate of return　P2

Peng Company is considering an investment expected to generate an average net income after taxes of $1,950 for three years. The investment costs $45,000 and has an estimated $6,000 salvage value. Compute the accounting rate of return for this investment.

QS 25-5
Selection of sales mix

C3　A1　

Excel Memory Company can sell all units of computer memory X and Y that it can produce, but it has limited production capacity. It can produce two units of X per hour *or* three units of Y per hour, and it has 4,000 production hours available. Contribution margin is $5 for Product X and $4 for Product Y. What is the most profitable sales mix for this company?

QS 25-6
Analysis of incremental costs

C3　A1　

Kando Company incurs a $9 per unit cost for Product A, which it currently manufactures and sells for $13.50 per unit. Instead of manufacturing and selling this product, Kando can purchase Product B for $5 per unit and sell it for $12 per unit. If it does so, unit sales would remain unchanged and $5 of the $9 per unit costs assigned to Product A would be eliminated. Should the company continue to manufacture Product A or purchase Product B for resale?

QS 25-7
Computation of break-even time

A2

Quick Feet, a shoe manufacturer, is evaluating the costs and benefits of new equipment that would custom fit each pair of athletic shoes. The customer would have his or her foot scanned by digital computer equipment; this information would be used to cut the raw materials to provide the customer a perfect fit. The new equipment costs $150,000 and is expected to generate an additional $52,500 in cash flows for five years. A bank will make a $150,000 loan to the company at a 10% interest rate for this equipment's purchase. Use the following table to determine the break-even time for this equipment.

Year	Cash Flows*	Present Value of 1 at 10%	Present Value of Cash Flows	Cumulative Present Value of Cash Flows
0	$(150,000)	1.0000		
1	52,500	0.9091		
2	52,500	0.8264		
3	52,500	0.7513		
4	52,500	0.6830		
5	52,500	0.6209		

* All cash flows occur at year-end.

EXERCISES

Compute the payback period for each of these two separate investments:

a. A new operating system for an existing machine is expected to cost $520,000 and have a useful life of six years. The system yields an incremental after-tax income of $150,000 each year after deducting its straight-line depreciation. The predicted salvage value of the system is $10,000.

b. A machine costs $380,000, has a $20,000 salvage value, is expected to last eight years, and will generate an after-tax income of $60,000 per year after straight-line depreciation.

Exercise 25-1
Payback period computation; even cash flows

P1

Beyer Company is considering the purchase of an asset for $180,000. It is expected to produce the following net cash flows. The cash flows occur evenly throughout each year. Compute the payback period for this investment.

	Year 1	Year 2	Year 3	Year 4	Year 5	Total
Net cash flows	$60,000	$40,000	$70,000	$120,000	$38,000	$328,000

Exercise 25-2
Payback period computation; uneven cash flows

P1

Check   3.083 years

A machine can be purchased for $150,000 and used for 5 years, yielding the following net incomes. In projecting net incomes, double-declining balance depreciation is applied, using a 5-year life and a zero salvage value. Compute the machine's payback period. Ignore taxes.

	Year 1	Year 2	Year 3	Year 4	Year 5
Net incomes	$10,000	$25,000	$50,000	$37,500	$100,000

Exercise 25-3
Payback period computation; declining-balance depreciation

P1

Check   2.265 years

A machine costs $700,000 and is expected to yield an after-tax net income of $52,000 each year. Management predicts this machine has a 10-year service life and a $100,000 salvage value, and it uses straight-line depreciation. Compute this machine's accounting rate of return.

Exercise 25-4
Accounting rate of return   P2

B2B Co. is considering the purchase of equipment that would allow the company to add a new product to its line. The equipment is expected to cost $360,000 with a 6-year life and no salvage value. It will be depreciated on a straight-line basis. The company expects to sell 144,000 units of the equipment's product each year. The expected annual income related to this equipment follows. Compute the (1) payback period and (2) accounting rate of return for this equipment.

Exercise 25-5
Payback period and accounting rate of return on investment

P1   P2

Sales	$225,000
Costs	
Materials, labor, and overhead (except depreciation)	120,000
Depreciation on new equipment	30,000
Selling and administrative expenses	22,500
Total costs and expenses	172,500
Pretax income	52,500
Income taxes (30%)	15,750
Net income	$ 36,750

Check   (1) 5.39 years (2) 20.42%

Exercise 25-6
Computing net present value   P3

After evaluating the risk of the investment described in Exercise 25-5, B2B Co. concludes that it must earn at least an 8% return on this investment. Compute the net present value of this investment.

Exercise 25-7
Computation and interpretation of net present value and internal rate of return

P3   P4

Phoenix Company can invest in each of three cheese-making projects: C1, C2, and C3. Each project requires an initial investment of $228,000 and would yield the following annual cash flows.

	C1	C2	C3
Year 1	$ 12,000	$ 96,000	$180,000
Year 2	108,000	96,000	60,000
Year 3	168,000	96,000	48,000
Totals	$288,000	$288,000	$288,000

(1) Assuming that the company requires a 12% return from its investments, use net present value to determine which projects, if any, should be acquired. (2) Using the answer from part 1, explain whether the internal rate of return is higher or lower than 12% for project C2. (3) Compute the internal rate of return for project C2.

Check   (3) IRR = 13%

Exercise 25-8
Decision to accept additional business or not

C3   A1

Farrow Co. expects to sell 150,000 units of its product in the next period with the following results.

Sales (150,000 units)	$2,250,000
Costs and expenses	
Direct materials	300,000
Direct labor	600,000
Overhead	150,000
Selling expenses	225,000
Administrative expenses	385,500
Total costs and expenses	1,660,500
Net income	$ 589,500

The company has an opportunity to sell 15,000 additional units at $12 per unit. The additional sales would not affect its current expected sales. Direct materials and labor costs would be the same for the additional units as they are for the regular units. However, the additional volume would create the following incremental costs: (1) total overhead would increase by 15% and (2) administrative expenses would increase by $64,500. Prepare an analysis to determine whether the company should accept or reject the offer to sell additional units at the reduced price of $12 per unit.

Check   Income increase, $3,000

Gilberto Company currently manufactures one of its crucial parts at a cost of $4.45 per unit. This cost is based on a normal production rate of 65,000 units per year. Variable costs are $1.95 per unit, fixed costs related to making this part are $65,000 per year, and allocated fixed costs are $58,500 per year. Allocated fixed costs are unavoidable whether the company makes or buys the part. Gilberto is considering buying the part from a supplier for a quoted price of $3.50 per unit guaranteed for a three-year period. Should the company continue to manufacture the part, or should it buy the part from the outside supplier? Support your answer with analyses.

Exercise 25-9

Make or buy decision

C3 A1

Check $35,750 increased costs to buy

Cobe Company has already manufactured 28,000 units of Product A at a cost of $28 per unit. The 28,000 units can be sold at this stage for $700,000. Alternatively, it can be further processed at a $420,000 total additional cost and be converted into 5,600 units of Product B and 11,200 units of Product C. Per unit selling price for Product B is $105 and for Product C is $70. Prepare an analysis that shows whether the 28,000 units of Product A should be processed further or not.

Exercise 25-10

Sell or process decision

C3 A1

Suresh Co. expects its five departments to yield the following income for next year.

Exercise 25-11

Analysis of income effects from eliminating departments

C3 A1

	Dept. M	Dept. N	Dept. O	Dept. P	Dept. T
Sales	$63,000	$ 35,000	$56,000	$42,000	$ 28,000
Expenses					
Avoidable	9,800	36,400	22,400	14,000	37,800
Unavoidable	51,800	12,600	4,200	29,400	9,800
Total expenses	61,600	49,000	26,600	43,400	47,600
Net income (loss)	$ 1,400	$(14,000)	$29,400	$ (1,400)	$(19,600)

Recompute and prepare the departmental income statements (including a combined total column) for the company under each of the following separate scenarios: Management (1) does not eliminate any department, (2) eliminates departments with expected net losses, and (3) eliminates departments with sales dollars that are less than avoidable expenses. Explain your answers to parts 2 and 3.

Check Total income (loss):
(2) $(21,000), (3) $7,000

Colt Company owns a machine that can produce two specialized products. Production time for Product TLX is two units per hour and for Product MTV is five units per hour. The machine's capacity is 2,750 hours per year. Both products are sold to a single customer who has agreed to buy all of the company's output up to a maximum of 4,700 units of Product TLX and 2,500 units of Product MTV. Selling prices and variable costs per unit to produce the products follow. Determine (1) the company's most profitable sales mix and (2) the contribution margin that results from that sales mix.

Exercise 25-12

Sales mix determination and analysis

C3 A1

	Product TLX	Product MTV
Selling price per unit	$15.00	$9.50
Variable costs per unit	4.80	5.50

Check (2) $55,940

This chapter explained two methods to evaluate investments using recovery time, the payback period and break-even time (BET). Refer to QS 25-7 and (1) compute the recovery time for both the payback period and break-even time, (2) discuss the advantage(s) of break-even time over the payback period, and (3) list two conditions under which payback period and break-even time are similar.

Exercise 25-13

Comparison of payback and BET

P1 A2

PROBLEM SET A

Problem 25-1A
Computation of payback period, accounting rate of return, and net present value

P1   P2   P3

mhhe.com/wildFAP18e

Factor Company is planning to add a new product to its line. To manufacture this product, the company needs to buy a new machine at a $480,000 cost with an expected four-year life and a $20,000 salvage value. All sales are for cash, and all costs are out of pocket except for depreciation on the new machine. Additional information includes the following.

Expected annual sales of new product	$1,840,000
Expected annual costs of new product	
Direct materials	480,000
Direct labor	672,000
Overhead excluding straight-line depreciation on new machine	336,000
Selling and administrative expenses	160,000
Income taxes	30%

Required

1. Compute straight-line depreciation for each year of this new machine's life.
2. Determine expected net income and net cash flow for each year of this machine's life.
3. Compute this machine's payback period, assuming that cash flows occur evenly throughout each year.
4. Compute this machine's accounting rate of return, assuming that income is earned evenly throughout each year.
5. Compute the net present value for this machine using a discount rate of 7% and assuming that cash flows occur at each year-end. (*Hint:* Salvage value is a cash inflow at the end of the asset's life.)

Check   (4) 21.56%

(5) $107,356

Problem 25-2A
Analysis and computation of payback period, accounting rate of return, and net present value

P1   P2   P3

Most Company has an opportunity to invest in one of two new projects. Project Y requires a $350,000 investment for new machinery with a four-year life and no salvage value. Project Z requires a $350,000 investment for new machinery with a three-year life and no salvage value. The two projects yield the following predicted annual results. The company uses straight-line depreciation, and cash flows occur evenly throughout each year.

	Project Y	Project Z
Sales	$350,000	$280,000
Expenses		
Direct materials	49,000	35,000
Direct labor	70,000	42,000
Overhead including depreciation	126,000	126,000
Selling and administrative expenses	25,000	25,000
Total expenses	270,000	228,000
Pretax income	80,000	52,000
Income taxes (30%)	24,000	15,600
Net income	$ 56,000	$ 36,400

Required

1. Compute each project's annual expected net cash flows.
2. Determine each project's payback period.
3. Compute each project's accounting rate of return.
4. Determine each project's net present value using 8% as the discount rate. For part 4 only, assume that cash flows occur at each year-end.

Check   For Project Y: (2) 2.44 years, (3) 32%, (4) $125,286

Analysis Component

5. Identify the project you would recommend to management and explain your choice.

Manning Corporation is considering a new project requiring a $90,000 investment in test equipment with no salvage value. The project would produce $66,000 of pretax income before depreciation at the end of each of the next six years. The company's income tax rate is 40%. In compiling its tax return and computing its income tax payments, the company can choose between the two alternative depreciation schedules shown in the table.

Problem 25-3A
Computation of cash flows and net present values with alternative depreciation methods

P3

	Straight-Line Depreciation	MACRS Depreciation*
Year 1	$ 9,000	$18,000
Year 2	18,000	28,800
Year 3	18,000	17,280
Year 4	18,000	10,368
Year 5	18,000	10,368
Year 6	9,000	5,184
Totals	$90,000	$90,000

* The modified accelerated cost recovery system (MACRS) for depreciation is discussed in Chapter 10.

Required

1. Prepare a five-column table that reports amounts (assuming use of straight-line depreciation) for each of the following for each of the six years: (a) pretax income before depreciation, (b) straight-line depreciation expense, (c) taxable income, (d) income taxes, and (e) net cash flow. Net cash flow equals the amount of income before depreciation minus the income taxes.

2. Prepare a five-column table that reports amounts (assuming use of MACRS depreciation) for each of the following for each of the six years: (a) pretax income before depreciation, (b) MACRS depreciation expense, (c) taxable income, (d) income taxes, and (e) net cash flow. Net cash flow equals the income amount before depreciation minus the income taxes.

3. Compute the net present value of the investment if straight-line depreciation is used. Use 10% as the discount rate.

4. Compute the net present value of the investment if MACRS depreciation is used. Use 10% as the discount rate.

Check Net present value:
(3) $108,518, (4) $110,303

Analysis Component

5. Explain why the MACRS depreciation method increases this project's net present value.

Jones Products manufactures and sells to wholesalers approximately 400,000 packages per year of underwater markers at $6 per package. Annual costs for the production and sale of this quantity are shown in the table.

Problem 25-4A
Analysis of income effects of additional business

C3 A1

mhhe.com/wildFAP18e

Direct materials	$ 576,000
Direct labor	144,000
Overhead	320,000
Selling expenses	150,000
Administrative expenses	100,000
Total costs and expenses	$1,290,000

A new wholesaler has offered to buy 50,000 packages for $5.20 each. These markers would be marketed under the wholesaler's name and would not affect Jones Products' sales through its normal channels. A study of the costs of this additional business reveals the following:

• Direct materials costs are 100% variable.

• Per unit direct labor costs for the additional units would be 50% higher than normal because their production would require overtime pay at one-and-one-half times the usual labor rate.

• 25% of the normal annual overhead costs are fixed at any production level from 350,000 to 500,000 units. The remaining 75% of the annual overhead cost is variable with volume.

- Accepting the new business would involve no additional selling expenses.
- Accepting the new business would increase administrative expenses by a $5,000 fixed amount.

Required

Prepare a three-column comparative income statement that shows the following:

1. Annual operating income without the special order (column 1).
2. Annual operating income received from the new business only (column 2).
3. Combined annual operating income from normal business and the new business (column 3).

Check Operating income:
(1) $1,110,000, (2) $126,000

Problem 25-5A
Analysis of sales mix strategies

C3   A1

Edgerron Company is able to produce two products, G and B, with the same machine in its factory. The following information is available.

	Product G	Product B
Selling price per unit	$120	$160
Variable costs per unit	40	90
Contribution margin per unit	$ 80	$ 70
Machine hours to produce 1 unit	0.4 hours	1.0 hours
Maximum unit sales per month	600 units	200 units

The company presently operates the machine for a single eight-hour shift for 22 working days each month. Management is thinking about operating the machine for two shifts, which will increase its productivity by another eight hours per day for 22 days per month. This change would require $15,000 additional fixed costs per month.

Required

1. Determine the contribution margin per machine hour that each product generates.
2. How many units of Product G and Product B should the company produce if it continues to operate with only one shift? How much total contribution margin does this mix produce each month?
3. If the company adds another shift, how many units of Product G and Product B should it produce? How much total contribution margin would this mix produce each month? Should the company add the new shift? Explain.
4. Suppose that the company determines that it can increase Product G's maximum sales to 700 units per month by spending $12,000 per month in marketing efforts. Should the company pursue this strategy and the double shift? Explain.

Check Units of Product G: (2) 440,
(3) 600, (4) 700

Problem 25-6A
Analysis of possible elimination
of a department

C3   A1

Elegant Decor Company's management is trying to decide whether to eliminate Department 200, which has produced losses or low profits for several years. The company's 2008 departmental income statement shows the following.

ELEGANT DECOR COMPANY **Departmental Income Statements** **For Year Ended December 31, 2008**	Dept. 100	Dept. 200	Combined
Sales	$436,000	$290,000	$726,000
Cost of goods sold	262,000	207,000	469,000
Gross profit	174,000	83,000	257,000
Operating expenses			
Direct expenses			
Advertising	17,000	12,000	29,000
Store supplies used	4,000	3,800	7,800
Depreciation—Store equipment	5,000	3,300	8,300
Total direct expenses	26,000	19,100	45,100

[continued on next page]

[continued from previous page]

Allocated expenses			
Sales salaries	65,000	39,000	104,000
Rent expense	9,440	4,720	14,160
Bad debts expense	9,900	8,100	18,000
Office salary	18,720	12,480	31,200
Insurance expense	2,000	1,100	3,100
Miscellaneous office expenses	2,400	1,600	4,000
Total allocated expenses	107,460	67,000	174,460
Total expenses	133,460	86,100	219,560
Net income (loss)	$ 40,540	$ (3,100)	$ 37,440

In analyzing whether to eliminate Department 200, management considers the following:

a. The company has one office worker who earns $600 per week, or $31,200 per year, and four sales-clerks who each earn $500 per week, or $26,000 per year.

b. The full salaries of two salesclerks are charged to Department 100. The full salary of one sales clerk is charged to Department 200. The salary of the fourth clerk, who works half-time in both departments, is divided evenly between the two departments.

c. Eliminating Department 200 would avoid the sales salaries and the office salary currently allocated to it. However, management prefers another plan. Two salesclerks have indicated that they will be quitting soon. Management believes that their work can be done by the other two clerks if the one office worker works in sales half-time. Eliminating Department 200 will allow this shift of duties. If this change is implemented, half the office worker's salary would be reported as sales salaries and half would be reported as office salary.

d. The store building is rented under a long-term lease that cannot be changed. Therefore, Department 100 will use the space and equipment currently used by Department 200.

e. Closing Department 200 will eliminate its expenses for advertising, bad debts, and store supplies; 70% of the insurance expense allocated to it to cover its merchandise inventory; and 25% of the miscellaneous office expenses presently allocated to it.

Required

1. Prepare a three-column report that lists items and amounts for (a) the company's total expenses (including cost of goods sold)—in column 1, (b) the expenses that would be eliminated by closing Department 200—in column 2, and (c) the expenses that will continue—in column 3.

2. Prepare a forecasted annual income statement for the company reflecting the elimination of Department 200 assuming that it will not affect Department 100's sales and gross profit. The statement should reflect the reassignment of the office worker to one-half time as a salesclerk.

Check (1) Total expenses: (a) $688,560, (b) $284,070

(2) Forecasted net income without Department 200, $31,510

Analysis Component

3. Reconcile the company's combined net income with the forecasted net income assuming that Department 200 is eliminated (list both items and amounts). Analyze the reconciliation and explain why you think the department should or should not be eliminated.

Cortino Company is planning to add a new product to its line. To manufacture this product, the company needs to buy a new machine at a $300,000 cost with an expected four-year life and a $20,000 salvage value. All sales are for cash and all costs are out of pocket, except for depreciation on the new machine. Additional information includes the following.

Expected annual sales of new product	$1,150,000
Expected annual costs of new product	
Direct materials	300,000
Direct labor	420,000
Overhead excluding straight-line depreciation on new machine	210,000
Selling and administrative expenses	100,000
Income taxes	30%

PROBLEM SET B

Problem 25-1B
Computation of payback period, accounting rate of return, and net present value

P1 P2 P3

Required

1. Compute straight-line depreciation for each year of this new machine's life.
2. Determine expected net income and net cash flow for each year of this machine's life.
3. Compute this machine's payback period, assuming that cash flows occur evenly throughout each year.
4. Compute this machine's accounting rate of return, assuming that income is earned evenly throughout each year.
5. Compute the net present value for this machine using a discount rate of 7% and assuming that cash flows occur at each year-end. (*Hint:* Salvage value is a cash inflow at the end of the asset's life.)

Check (4) 21.88%

(5) $70,915

Problem 25-2B

Analysis and computation of payback period, accounting rate of return, and net present value

P1 P2 P3

Aikman Company has an opportunity to invest in one of two projects. Project A requires a $240,000 investment for new machinery with a four-year life and no salvage value. Project B also requires a $240,000 investment for new machinery with a three-year life and no salvage value. The two projects yield the following predicted annual results. The company uses straight-line depreciation, and cash flows occur evenly throughout each year.

	Project A	Project B
Sales	$250,000	$200,000
Expenses		
Direct materials	35,000	25,000
Direct labor	50,000	30,000
Overhead including depreciation	90,000	90,000
Selling and administrative expenses	18,000	18,000
Total expenses	193,000	163,000
Pretax income	57,000	37,000
Income taxes (30%)	17,100	11,100
Net income	$ 39,900	$ 25,900

Required

1. Compute each project's annual expected net cash flows.
2. Determine each project's payback period.
3. Compute each project's accounting rate of return.
4. Determine each project's net present value using 8% as the discount rate. For part 4 only, assume that cash flows occur at each year-end.

Check For Project A: (2) 2.4 years, (3) 33.3%, (4) $90,879

Analysis Component

5. Identify the project you would recommend to management and explain your choice.

Problem 25-3B

Computation of cash flows and net present values with alternative depreciation methods

P3

Grossman Corporation is considering a new project requiring a $30,000 investment in an asset having no salvage value. The project would produce $12,000 of pretax income before depreciation at the end of each of the next six years. The company's income tax rate is 40%. In compiling its tax return and computing its income tax payments, the company can choose between two alternative depreciation schedules as shown in the table.

	Straight-Line Depreciation	MACRS Depreciation*
Year 1	$ 3,000	$ 6,000
Year 2	6,000	9,600
Year 3	6,000	5,760
Year 4	6,000	3,456
Year 5	6,000	3,456
Year 6	3,000	1,728
Totals	$30,000	$30,000

* The modified accelerated cost recovery system (MACRS) for depreciation is discussed in Chapter 10.

Required

1. Prepare a five-column table that reports amounts (assuming use of straight-line depreciation) for each of the following items for each of the six years: (a) pretax income before depreciation, (b) straight-line depreciation expense, (c) taxable income, (d) income taxes, and (e) net cash flow. Net cash flow equals the amount of income before depreciation minus the income taxes.

2. Prepare a five-column table that reports amounts (assuming use of MACRS depreciation) for each of the following items for each of the six years: (a) income before depreciation, (b) MACRS depreciation expense, (c) taxable income, (d) income taxes, and (e) net cash flow. Net cash flow equals the amount of income before depreciation minus the income taxes.

3. Compute the net present value of the investment if straight-line depreciation is used. Use 10% as the discount rate.

4. Compute the net present value of the investment if MACRS depreciation is used. Use 10% as the discount rate.

Check   Net present value:
(3) $10,041, (4) $10,635

Analysis Component

5. Explain why the MACRS depreciation method increases the net present value of this project.

Windmire Company manufactures and sells to local wholesalers approximately 300,000 units per month at a sales price of $4 per unit. Monthly costs for the production and sale of this quantity follow.

Problem 25-4B
Analysis of income effects of additional business

C3   A1

Direct materials	$ 384,000
Direct labor	96,000
Overhead	288,000
Selling expenses	120,000
Administrative expenses	80,000
Total costs and expenses	$ 968,000

A new out-of-state distributor has offered to buy 50,000 units next month for $3.44 each. These units would be marketed in other states and would not affect Windmire's sales through its normal channels. A study of the costs of this new business reveals the following:

• Direct materials costs are 100% variable.

• Per unit direct labor costs for the additional units would be 50% higher than normal because their production would require time-and-a-half overtime pay to meet the distributor's deadline.

• Twenty-five percent of the normal annual overhead costs are fixed at any production level from 250,000 to 400,000 units. The remaining 75% is variable with volume.

• Accepting the new business would involve no additional selling expenses.

• Accepting the new business would increase administrative expenses by a $4,000 fixed amount.

Required

Prepare a three-column comparative income statement that shows the following:

1. Monthly operating income without the special order (column 1).
2. Monthly operating income received from the new business only (column 2).
3. Combined monthly operating income from normal business and the new business (column 3).

Check   Operating income:
(1) $232,000, (2) $44,000

Sung Company is able to produce two products, R and T, with the same machine in its factory. The following information is available.

Problem 25-5B
Analysis of sales mix strategies

C3   A1

	Product R	Product T
Selling price per unit	$ 60	$ 80
Variable costs per unit	20	45
Contribution margin per unit	$ 40	$ 35
Machine hours to produce 1 unit	0.4 hours	1.0 hours
Maximum unit sales per month	550 units	175 units

The company presently operates the machine for a single eight-hour shift for 22 working days each month. Management is thinking about operating the machine for two shifts, which will increase its productivity by another eight hours per day for 22 days per month. This change would require $3,250 additional fixed costs per month.

Required

1. Determine the contribution margin per machine hour that each product generates.

2. How many units of Product R and Product T should the company produce if it continues to operate with only one shift? How much total contribution margin does this mix produce each month?

Check Units of Product R: (2) 440, (3) 550, (4) 675

3. If the company adds another shift, how many units of Product R and Product T should it produce? How much total contribution margin would this mix produce each month? Should the company add the new shift? Explain.

4. Suppose that the company determines that it can increase Product R's maximum sales to 675 units per month by spending $4,500 per month in marketing efforts. Should the company pursue this strategy and the double shift? Explain.

Problem 25-6B

Analysis of possible elimination of a department

C3 A1

Esme Company's management is trying to decide whether to eliminate Department Z, which has produced low profits or losses for several years. The company's 2008 departmental income statement shows the following.

ESME COMPANY **Departmental Income Statements** **For Year Ended December 31, 2008**			
	Dept. A	**Dept. Z**	**Combined**
Sales	$700,000	$175,000	$875,000
Cost of goods sold	461,300	125,100	586,400
Gross profit	238,700	49,900	288,600
Operating expenses			
Direct expenses			
Advertising	27,000	3,000	30,000
Store supplies used	5,600	1,400	7,000
Depreciation—Store equipment	14,000	7,000	21,000
Total direct expenses	46,600	11,400	58,000
Allocated expenses			
Sales salaries	70,200	23,400	93,600
Rent expense	22,080	5,520	27,600
Bad debts expense	21,000	4,000	25,000
Office salary	20,800	5,200	26,000
Insurance expense	4,200	1,400	5,600
Miscellaneous office expenses	1,700	2,500	4,200
Total allocated expenses	139,980	42,020	182,000
Total expenses	186,580	53,420	240,000
Net income (loss)	$ 52,120	$ (3,520)	$ 48,600

In analyzing whether to eliminate Department Z, management considers the following items:

a. The company has one office worker who earns $500 per week or $26,000 per year and four salesclerks who each earn $450 per week or $23,400 per year.

b. The full salaries of three salesclerks are charged to Department A. The full salary of one salesclerk is charged to Department Z.

c. Eliminating Department Z would avoid the sales salaries and the office salary currently allocated to it. However, management prefers another plan. Two salesclerks have indicated that they will be quitting soon. Management believes that their work can be done by the two remaining clerks if the one office worker works in sales half time. Eliminating Department Z will allow this shift of duties. If this change is implemented, half the office worker's salary would be reported as sales salaries and half would be reported as office salary.

d. The store building is rented under a long-term lease that cannot be changed. Therefore, Department A will use the space and equipment currently used by Department Z.

e. Closing Department Z will eliminate its expenses for advertising, bad debts, and store supplies; 65% of the insurance expense allocated to it to cover its merchandise inventory; and 30% of the miscellaneous office expenses presently allocated to it.

Required

1. Prepare a three-column report that lists items and amounts for (a) the company's total expenses (including cost of goods sold)—in column 1, (b) the expenses that would be eliminated by closing Department Z—in column 2, and (c) the expenses that will continue—in column 3.

2. Prepare a forecasted annual income statement for the company reflecting the elimination of Department Z assuming that it will not affect Department A's sales and gross profit. The statement should reflect the reassignment of the office worker to one-half time as a salesclerk.

Check (1) Total expenses: (a) $826,400, (b) $181,960

(2) Forecasted net income without Department Z, $55,560

Analysis Component

3. Reconcile the company's combined net income with the forecasted net income assuming that Department Z is eliminated (list both items and amounts). Analyze the reconciliation and explain why you think the department should or should not be eliminated.

 Problem Set C is available at the book's Website to further reinforce and assess your learning.

PROBLEM SET C

(This serial problem began in Chapter 1 and continues through most of the book. If previous chapter segments were not completed, the serial problem can begin at this point. It is helpful, but not necessary, that you use the Working Papers that accompany the book.)

SERIAL PROBLEM

Success Systems

SP 25 Adriana Lopez is considering the purchase of equipment for Success Systems that would allow the company to add a new product to its computer furniture line. The equipment is expected to cost $240,000 and to have a six-year life and no salvage value. It will be depreciated on a straight-line basis. Success Systems expects to sell 100 units of the equipment's product each year. The expected annual income related to this equipment follows.

Sales	$300,000
Costs	
Materials, labor, and overhead (except depreciation)	160,000
Depreciation on new equipment	40,000
Selling and administrative expenses	30,000
Total costs and expenses	230,000
Pretax income	70,000
Income taxes (30%)	21,000
Net income	$ 49,000

Required

Compute the (1) payback period and (2) accounting rate of return for this equipment.

BEYOND THE NUMBERS

BTN 25-1 In fiscal 2005, **Best Buy** invested $145 million in store-related projects that included store remodels, relocations, expansions, and various merchandising projects. Assume that these projects have a seven-year life, and that Best Buy requires a 15% internal rate of return on these projects.

REPORTING IN ACTION

C1 A1 P3

Required

1. What is the amount of annual cash flows that Best Buy must earn from these projects to have a 15% internal rate of return? (*Hint:* Identify the seven-period, 15% factor from the present value of an annuity table, and then divide $145 million by this factor to get the annual cash flows necessary.)

Fast Forward

2. Access Best Buy's financial statements for fiscal years ended after February 26, 2005, from its Website (BestBuy.com) or the SEC's Website (SEC.gov).

    a. Determine the amount that Best Buy invested in similar store-related projects for the most recent year.

    b. Assume a seven-year life and a 15% internal rate of return. What is the amount of cash flows that Best Buy must earn on these new projects?

COMPARATIVE ANALYSIS

C3

BTN 25-2 Best Buy and Circuit City sell several different products; most are profitable but some are not. Teams of employees in each company make advertising, investment, and product mix decisions. A certain portion of advertising for both companies is on a local basis to a target audience.

Required

1. Find one major advertisement of a product or group of products for each company in your local newspaper. Contact the newspaper and ask the approximate cost of this ad space (for example, cost of one page or one-half page of advertising).

2. Estimate how many products this advertisement must sell to justify its cost. Begin by taking the product's sales price advertised for each company and assume a 20% contribution margin.

3. Prepare a one-half page memorandum explaining the importance of effective advertising when making a product mix decision. Be prepared to present your ideas in class.

ETHICS CHALLENGE

P3

BTN 25-3 A consultant commented that "too often the numbers look good but feel bad." This comment often stems from estimation error common to capital budgeting proposals that relate to future cash flows. Three reasons for this error often exist. First, reliably predicting cash flows several years into the future is very difficult. Second, the present value of cash flows many years into the future (say, beyond 10 years) is often very small. Third, it is difficult for personal biases and expectations not to unduly influence present value computations.

Required

1. Compute the present value of $100 to be received in 10 years assuming a 12% discount rate.

2. Why is understanding the three reasons mentioned for estimation errors important when evaluating investment projects? Link this response to your answer for part 1.

COMMUNICATING IN PRACTICE

P1 P2 P3 P4

BTN 25-4 Payback period, accounting rate of return, net present value, and internal rate of return are common methods to evaluate capital investment opportunities. Assume that your manager asks you to identify the type of measurement basis and unit that each method offers and to list the advantages and disadvantages of each. Present your response in memorandum format of less than one page.

TAKING IT TO THE NET

BTN 25-5 Many companies must determine whether to internally produce their component parts or to outsource them. Further, some companies now outsource key components to international providers. Access the Website BizBrim.com and review the available information on outsourcing—especially as it relates to both the advantages and the negative effects of outsourcing.

Required

1. What does Bizbrim identify as the major advantages and the major disadvantages of outsourcing?

2. Does it seem that Bizbrim is generally in favor of or opposed to outsourcing? Explain.

TEAMWORK IN ACTION

P1 P3

BTN 25-6 Break into teams and identify four reasons that an international airline such as Southwest, Northwest, or American would invest in a project when its direct analysis using both payback period and net present value indicate it to be a poor investment. (*Hint:* Think about qualitative factors.) Provide an example of an investment project supporting your answer.

BTN 25-7   Read the article "Don't Be Afraid to Ask" by Liz Ryan in the December 27, 2005, issue of *BusinessWeek*. (The book's Website provides free access to the article.) This article deals with various business decision-making activities.

BusinessWeek
ACTIVITY

C1

Required

1. What role does asking the right question have in the management decision-making process?

2. How do the methods described in this chapter fit into the "don't be afraid to ask" framework?

BTN 25-8   Art Alaniz of **Progressive Telecom** buys used cell phones, refurbishes them, and resells them. He often must decide whether to scrap or rework his inventory. Assume that he purchases 1,000 cell phones from a recycler at a cost of $3,000. Art says the phones include 400 units of Model XR and 600 units of Model CT. Each of the Models can either be (1) refurbished and sold or (2) disassembled and the components sold to wholesalers. Details of each model's estimated refurbishing costs, value after refurbishing, cost to disassemble, and value if disassembled follow.

ENTREPRENEURIAL DECISION

A1

	Model XR	Model CT
Cost to refurbish phones for resale	$18,500	$20,000
Resale value of phones after refurbishing	20,000	27,000
Cost to disassemble for component resale	1,500	1,800
Resale value of disassembled components	4,000	6,000

Required

1. Compute the incremental revenue from each model if Alaniz decides to refurbush the cell phones for resale.

2. Compute the incremental revenue from each model if Alaniz disassembles the cell phones for component resale.

3. What business decision should Alaniz implement for each model? Explain.

BTN 25-9   Visit or call a local auto dealership and inquire about leasing a car. Ask about the down payment and the required monthly payments. You will likely find the salesperson does not discuss the cost to purchase this car but focuses on the affordability of the monthly payments. This chapter gives you the tools to compute the cost of this car using the lease payment schedule in present dollars and to estimate the profit from leasing for an auto dealership.

HITTING THE ROAD

C1   P3

Required

1. Compare the cost of leasing the car to buying it in present dollars using the information from the dealership you contact. (Assume you will make a final payment at the end of the lease and then own the car.)

2. Is it more costly to lease or buy the car? Support your answer with computations.

BTN 25-10   Access **Dixons'** 2004 annual report dated May 1, 2004, from its Website Dixons-Group.com. Identify its report on social responsibility.

GLOBAL DECISION

C1

Dixons

Required

1. Dixons reports that it recycled 2,611 tons of cardboard, paper, and plastic. Further, it reports a reduced amount of average emissions from its company cars. Efforts such as these can be costly to a company. Why would a company like Dixons pursue these costly efforts?

2. Dixons reports that it is working to recycle old appliances from its customers. This activity would be a costly undertaking for the company. Why would Dixons initiate such a program?

ANSWERS TO MULTIPLE CHOICE QUIZ

1. a; Reworking provides incremental revenue of $11 per unit ($19 − $8); and, it costs $10 to rework them. The company is better off by $1 per unit when it reworks these products and sells them at the regular price.

2. e; Product X has a $2 contribution margin per machine hour [($32 − $12)/10 MH]; Product Y has a $7 contribution margin per machine hour [($24 − $10)/2 MH]. It should produce as much of Product Y as possible.

3. a; Total revenue from the special order = 3,000 units × $15 per unit = $45,000; and, Total costs for the special order = (3,000 units × $9 per unit) + $5,000 = $32,000. Net income from the special order = $45,000 − $32,000 = $13,000. Thus, yes, it should accept the order.

4. c; Payback = $270,000/$61,200 per year = 4.4 years.

5. d; Accounting rate of return = $8,550/[($180,000 + $0)/2] = 9.5%.

Financial Statement Information

This appendix includes financial information for (1) **Best Buy**, (2) **Circuit City**, and (3) **Apple Computer**. This information is taken from their annual 10-K reports filed with the SEC. An **annual report** is a summary of a company's financial results for the year along with its current financial condition and future plans. This report is directed to external users of financial information, but it also affects the actions and decisions of internal users.

A company uses an annual report to showcase itself and its products. Many annual reports include attractive photos, diagrams, and illustrations related to the company. The primary objective of annual reports, however, is the *financial section,* which communicates much information about a company, with most data drawn from the accounting information system. The layout of an annual report's financial section is fairly established and typically includes the following:

- Letter to Shareholders
- Financial History and Highlights
- Management Discussion and Analysis
- Management's Report on Financial Statements and on Internal Controls
- Report of Independent Accountants (Auditor's Report) and on Internal Controls
- Financial Statements
- Notes to Financial Statements
- List of Directors and Officers

This appendix provides the financial statements for Best Buy (plus selected notes), Circuit City, and Apple Computer. The appendix is organized as follows:

- **Best Buy** **A-2** through **A-18**
- **Circuit City** **A-19** through **A-23**
- **Apple Computer** **A-24** through **A-28**

Many assignments at the end of each chapter refer to information in this appendix. We encourage readers to spend time with these assignments; they are especially useful in showing the relevance and diversity of financial accounting and reporting.

Special note: The SEC maintains the EDGAR (**E**lectronic **D**ata **G**athering, **A**nalysis, and **R**etrieval) database at www.SEC.gov. The **Form 10-K** is the annual report form for most companies. It provides electronically accessible information. The **Form 10-KSB** is the annual report form filed by "small businesses." It requires slightly less information than the Form 10-K. One of these forms must be filed within 90 days after the company's fiscal year-end. (Forms 10-K405, 10-KT, 10-KT405, and 10-KSB405 are slight variations of the usual form due to certain regulations or rules.)

Financial Report

Selected Financial Data

The following table presents our selected financial data. Certain prior-year amounts have been reclassified to conform to the current-year presentation. All fiscal years presented reflect the classification of Musicland's financial results as discontinued operations.

Five-Year Financial Highlights

$ in millions, except per share amounts

Fiscal Year	2005	2004	2003	2002	2001
Consolidated Statements of Earnings Data					
Revenue	$27,433	$24,548	$20,943	$17,711	$15,189
Operating income	1,442	1,304	1,010	908	611
Earnings from continuing operations	934	800	622	570	401
Loss from discontinued operations, net of tax	—	(29)	(441)	—	(5)
Gain (loss) on disposal of discontinued operations, net of tax	50	(66)	—	—	—
Cumulative effect of change in accounting principles, net of tax	—	—	(82)	—	—
Net earnings	984	705	99	570	396
Per Share Data					
Continuing operations	$2.79	$2.41	$1.90	$1.77	$1.26
Discontinued operations	—	(0.09)	(1.34)	—	(0.02)
Gain (loss) on disposal of discontinued operations	0.15	(0.20)	—	—	—
Cumulative effect of accounting changes	—	—	(0.25)	—	—
Net earnings	2.94	2.13	0.31	1.77	1.24
Cash dividends declared and paid	0.42	0.40	—	—	—
Common stock price:					
High	62.20	62.70	53.75	51.47	59.25
Low	43.87	25.55	16.99	22.42	14.00
Operating Statistics					
Comparable store sales change	4.3%	7.1%	2.4%	1.9%	4.9%
Gross profit rate	23.7%	23.9%	23.6%	20.0%	18.5%
Selling, general and administrative expense rate	18.4%	18.6%	18.8%	14.9%	14.5%
Operating income rate	5.3%	5.3%	4.8%	5.1%	4.0%
Year-End Data					
Current ratio	1.4	1.3	1.3	1.2	1.1
Total assets	$10,294	$8,652	$7,694	$7,367	$4,840
Long-term debt, including current portion	600	850	834	820	296
Total shareholders' equity	4,449	3,422	2,730	2,521	1,822
Number of stores					
U.S. Best Buy stores	668	608	548	481	419
Magnolia Audio Video stores	20	22	19	13	13
International stores	144	127	112	95	—
Total retail square footage (000s)					
U.S. Best Buy stores	28,260	26,421	24,243	21,599	19,010
Magnolia Audio Video stores	194	218	189	133	133
International stores	3,139	2,800	2,375	1,923	—

Fiscal 2001 included 53 weeks. All other periods presented included 52 weeks.

BEST BUY

Consolidated Balance Sheets

$ in millions, except per share amounts

Assets	February 26, 2005	February 28, 2004
Current Assets		
Cash and cash equivalents	$ 470	$ 245
Short-term investments	2,878	2,355
Receivables	375	343
Merchandise inventories	2,851	2,607
Other current assets	329	174
Total current assets	6,903	5,724
Property and Equipment		
Land and buildings	506	484
Leasehold improvements	1,139	861
Fixtures and equipment	2,458	2,151
Property under master and capital lease	89	78
	4,192	3,574
Less accumulated depreciation	1,728	1,330
Net property and equipment	2,464	2,244
Goodwill	513	477
Tradename	40	37
Long-Term Investments	148	—
Other Assets	226	170
Total Assets	$10,294	$8,652
Liabilities and Shareholders' Equity		
Current Liabilities		
Accounts payable	$ 2,824	$2,460
Unredeemed gift card liabilities	410	300
Accrued compensation and related expenses	234	269
Accrued liabilities	844	724
Accrued income taxes	575	380
Current portion of long-term debt	72	368
Total current liabilities	4,959	4,501
Long-Term Liabilities	358	247
Long-Term Debt	528	482
Shareholders' Equity		
Preferred stock, $1.00 par value: Authorized — 400,000 shares; Issued and outstanding — none	—	—
Common stock, $.10 par value: Authorized — 1 billion shares; Issued and outstanding — 328,342,000 and 324,648,000 shares, respectively	33	32
Additional paid-in capital	952	836
Retained earnings	3,315	2,468
Accumulated other comprehensive income	149	86
Total shareholders' equity	4,449	3,422
Total Liabilities and Shareholders' Equity	$10,294	$8,652

See Notes to Consolidated Financial Statements.

Consolidated Statements of Earnings

$ in millions, except per share amounts

For the Fiscal Years Ended	February 26, 2005	February 28, 2004	March 1, 2003
Revenue	$27,433	$24,548	$20,943
Cost of goods sold	20,938	18,677	15,998
Gross profit	6,495	5,871	4,945
Selling, general and administrative expenses	5,053	4,567	3,935
Operating income	1,442	1,304	1,010
Net interest income (expense)	1	(8)	4
Earnings from continuing operations before income tax expense	1,443	1,296	1,014
Income tax expense	509	496	392
Earnings from continuing operations	934	800	622
Loss from discontinued operations (Note 2), net of $17 and $119 tax	—	(29)	(441)
Gain (loss) on disposal of discontinued operations (Note 2)	50	(66)	—
Cumulative effect of change in accounting principle for goodwill (Note 1), net of $24 tax	—	—	(40)
Cumulative effect of change in accounting principle for vendor allowances (Note 1), net of $26 tax	—	—	(42)
Net earnings	$ 984	$ 705	$ 99
Basic earnings (loss) per share:			
Continuing operations	$ 2.87	$ 2.47	$ 1.93
Discontinued operations	—	(0.09)	(1.37)
Gain (loss) on disposal of discontinued operations	0.15	(0.20)	—
Cumulative effect of accounting changes	—	—	(0.25)
Basic earnings per share	$ 3.02	$ 2.18	$ 0.31
Diluted earnings (loss) per share:[1]			
Continuing operations	$ 2.79	$ 2.41	$ 1.90
Discontinued operations	—	(0.09)	(1.34)
Gain (loss) on disposal of discontinued operations	0.15	(0.20)	—
Cumulative effect of accounting changes	—	—	(0.25)
Diluted earnings per share	$ 2.94	$ 2.13	$ 0.31
Basic weighted average common shares outstanding (in millions)	325.9	323.3	321.1
Diluted weighted average common shares outstanding (in millions)[1]	336.6	333.9	330.7

[1]   The calculation of diluted earnings per share assumes the conversion of our convertible debentures due in 2022 into 5.8 million shares of common stock and adds back related after-tax interest expense of $6.5 for all periods presented.

See Notes to Consolidated Financial Statements.

Consolidated Statements of Changes in Shareholders' Equity

$ and shares in millions

	Common Shares	Common Stock	Additional Paid-In Capital	Retained Earnings	Accumulated Other Comprehensive Income (Loss)	Total
Balances at March 2, 2002	**319**	**$31**	**$ 702**	**$1,794**	**$ (6)**	**$2,521**
Net earnings	—	—	—	99	—	99
Other comprehensive income (loss), net of tax:						
Foreign currency translation adjustments	—	—	—	—	34	34
Other	—	—	—	—	(1)	(1)
Total comprehensive income						132
Stock options exercised	3	1	43	—	—	44
Tax benefit from stock options exercised	—	—	33	—	—	33
Balances at March 1, 2003	**322**	**32**	**778**	**1,893**	**27**	**2,730**
Net earnings	—	—	—	705	—	705
Foreign currency translation adjustments	—	—	—	—	59	59
Total comprehensive income						764
Stock options exercised	5	—	114	—	—	114
Tax benefit from stock options exercised	—	—	41	—	—	41
Vesting of restricted stock awards	—	—	3	—	—	3
Common stock dividends, $0.40 per share	—	—	—	(130)	—	(130)
Repurchase of common stock	(2)	—	(100)	—	—	(100)
Balances at February 28, 2004	**325**	**32**	**836**	**2,468**	**86**	**3,422**
Net earnings	—	—	—	984	—	984
Other comprehensive income, net of tax:						
Foreign currency translation adjustments	—	—	—	—	59	59
Other	—	—	—	—	4	4
Total comprehensive income						1,047
Stock options exercised	6	1	219	—	—	220
Tax benefit from stock options exercised and employee stock purchase plan	—	—	60	—	—	60
Issuance of common stock under employee stock purchase plan	1	—	36	—	—	36
Vesting of restricted stock awards	—	—	1	—	—	1
Common stock dividends, $0.42 per share	—	—	—	(137)	—	(137)
Repurchase of common stock	(4)	—	(200)	—	—	(200)
Balances at February 26, 2005	**328**	**$33**	**$ 952**	**$3,315**	**$149**	**$4,449**

See Notes to Consolidated Financial Statements.

Consolidated Statements of Cash Flows

$ in millions

For the Fiscal Years Ended	February 26, 2005	February 28, 2004	March 1, 2003
Operating Activities			
Net earnings	$ 984	$ 705	$ 99
(Gain) loss from and disposal of discontinued operations, net of tax	(50)	95	441
Cumulative effect of change in accounting principles, net of tax	—	—	82
Earnings from continuing operations	934	800	622
Adjustments to reconcile earnings from continuing operations to total cash provided by operating activities from continuing operations:			
Depreciation	459	385	310
Asset impairment charges	22	22	11
Deferred income taxes	(28)	(14)	(37)
Other	23	16	15
Changes in operating assets and liabilities, net of acquired assets and liabilities:			
Receivables	(30)	(27)	(89)
Merchandise inventories	(240)	(507)	(256)
Other assets	(190)	(25)	(21)
Accounts payable	347	272	(5)
Other liabilities	243	250	117
Accrued income taxes	301	197	111
Total cash provided by operating activities from continuing operations	1,841	1,369	778
Investing Activities			
Additions to property and equipment	(502)	(545)	(725)
Purchases of available-for-sale securities	(7,789)	(2,989)	(1,844)
Sales of available-for-sale securities	7,118	2,175	1,610
Other, net	7	1	49
Total cash used in investing activities from continuing operations	(1,166)	(1,358)	(910)
Financing Activities			
Long-term debt payments	(371)	(17)	(13)
Issuance of common stock under employee stock purchase plan and for the exercise of stock options	256	114	40
Repurchase of common stock	(200)	(100)	—
Dividends paid	(137)	(130)	—
Net proceeds from issuance of long-term debt	—	—	18
Other, net	(7)	46	(15)
Total cash (used in) provided by financing activities from continuing operations	(459)	(87)	30
Effect of Exchange Rate Changes on Cash	9	1	—
Net Cash Used in Discontinued Operations	—	(53)	(79)
Increase (Decrease) in Cash and Cash Equivalents	225	(128)	(181)
Cash and Cash Equivalents at Beginning of Year	245	373	554
Cash and Cash Equivalents at End of Year	$ 470	$ 245	$ 373
Supplemental Disclosure of Cash Flow Information			
Income tax paid	$ 241	$ 306	$ 283
Interest paid	35	22	24
Capital and financing lease obligations incurred	117	26	—

See Notes to Consolidated Financial Statements.

Best Buy

SELECTED Notes to Consolidated Financial Statements

$ in millions, except per share amounts

1.   Summary of Significant Accounting Policies
Description of Business

Best Buy Co., Inc. is a specialty retailer of consumer electronics, home-office products, entertainment software, appliances and related services.

We operate two reportable segments: Domestic and International. The Domestic segment is comprised of U.S. Best Buy and Magnolia Audio Video operations. At February 26, 2005, we operated 668 U.S. Best Buy stores in 48 states and the District of Columbia. At February 26, 2005, we operated 20 Magnolia Audio Video stores in California, Washington and Oregon. The International segment is comprised of Future Shop and Best Buy operations in Canada. At February 26, 2005, we operated 114 Future Shop stores throughout all Canadian provinces and 30 Canadian Best Buy stores in Ontario, Alberta, British Columbia, Manitoba and Saskatchewan. Future Shop and Canadian Best Buy stores offer products and services similar to those offered by U.S. Best Buy stores except that Canadian Best Buy stores do not sell appliances.

In support of our retail store operations, we also operate Geek Squad, a computer repair and service provider, and Web sites for each of our brands (BestBuy.com, BestBuyCanada.ca, FutureShop.ca, MagnoliaAV.com and GeekSquad.com).

Fiscal Year

Our fiscal year ends on the Saturday nearest the end of February. Fiscal 2005, 2004 and 2003 each included 52 weeks.

Cash and Cash Equivalents

Cash primarily consists of cash on hand and bank deposits. Cash equivalents primarily consist of money market accounts and other highly liquid investments with an original maturity of three months or less when purchased. We carry these investments at cost, which approximates market value. The amount of cash equivalents at February 26, 2005, and February 28, 2004, was $156 and $73, respectively, and the weighted average interest rates were 2.9% and 0.9%, respectively.

Outstanding checks in excess of funds on deposit totaled $393 and $351 at February 26, 2005, and February 28, 2004, respectively, and are reflected as current liabilities.

Merchandise Inventories

Merchandise inventories are recorded at the lower of average cost or market. In-bound freight-related costs from our vendors are included as part of the net cost of merchandise inventories. Also included in the cost of inventory are certain vendor allowances that are not a reimbursement of specific, incremental and identifiable costs to promote a vendor's products. Other costs associated with acquiring, storing and transporting merchandise inventories to our retail stores are expensed as incurred and included in cost of goods sold.

Our inventory loss reserve represents anticipated physical inventory losses (e.g., theft) that have occurred since the last physical inventory date. Independent physical inventory counts are taken on a regular basis to ensure that the inventory reported in our consolidated financial statements is accurately stated. During the interim period between physical inventory counts, we reserve for anticipated physical inventory losses on a location-by-location basis.

Property and Equipment

Property and equipment are recorded at cost. We compute depreciation using the straight-line method over the estimated useful lives of the assets. Leasehold improvements are depreciated over the shorter of their estimated useful lives or the period from the date the assets are placed in service to the end of the initial lease

$ in millions, except per share amounts

term. Accelerated depreciation methods are generally used for income tax purposes.

Repairs and maintenance costs are charged directly to expense as incurred. Major renewals or replacements that substantially extend the useful life of an asset are capitalized and depreciated.

Estimated useful lives by major asset category are as follows:

Asset	Life (in years)
Buildings	30-40
Leasehold improvements	10-25
Fixtures and equipment	3-15
Property under master and capital lease	3-35

Goodwill and Intangible Assets

Goodwill

Goodwill is the excess of the purchase price over the fair value of identifiable net assets acquired in business combinations accounted for under the purchase method. Effective March 3, 2002, we adopted SFAS No. 142, *Goodwill and Other Intangible Assets,* which eliminated the systematic amortization of goodwill. This Statement also requires that we review goodwill for impairment at adoption and at least annually thereafter.

During the fourth quarter of fiscal 2005, we completed our annual impairment testing of our goodwill and tradename, using the same valuation techniques as described above, and determined there was no impairment.

Tradename

We have an indefinite-lived intangible asset related to our Future Shop tradename that totaled $40 and $37 at February 26, 2005, and February 28, 2004, respectively, which is included in the International segment. The change in the indefinite-lived intangible asset balance from February 28, 2004, was the result of fluctuations in foreign currency exchange rates.

Lease Rights

Lease rights, representing costs incurred to acquire the lease of a specific commercial property, are recorded at cost and are amortized to rent expense over the remaining lease term, which ranges up to 16 years, beginning with the date we take possession of the property.

The gross cost and accumulated amortization of lease rights were $27 and $29; and $9 and $6, respectively, at February 26, 2005, and February 28, 2004, respectively. Lease rights amortization was $4, $4 and $2 for fiscal 2005, 2004 and 2003, respectively. Current lease rights amortization is expected to be approximately $3 for each of the next five fiscal years.

Income Taxes

We account for income taxes under the liability method. Under this method, deferred tax assets and liabilities are recognized for the estimated future tax consequences attributable to differences between the financial statement carrying amounts of existing assets and liabilities and their respective tax bases, and operating loss and tax credit carryforwards. Deferred tax assets and liabilities are measured using enacted income tax rates in effect for the year in which those temporary differences are expected to be recovered or settled. The effect on deferred tax assets and liabilities of a change in income tax rates is recognized in our statement of earnings in the period that includes the enactment date. A valuation allowance is recorded to reduce the carrying amounts of deferred tax assets if it is more likely than not that such assets will not be realized.

Long-Term Liabilities

The major components of long-term liabilities at February 26, 2005, and February 28, 2004, included deferred compensation plan liabilities, long-term rent-related liabilities, deferred income taxes and advances received under vendor alliance programs.

Foreign Currency

Foreign currency denominated assets and liabilities are translated into U.S. dollars using the exchange rates in effect at the balance sheet date. Results of operations and cash flows are translated using the average exchange rates throughout the period. The effect of exchange rate

$ in millions, except per share amounts

fluctuations on translation of assets and liabilities is included as a component of shareholders' equity in accumulated other comprehensive income. Gains and losses from foreign currency transactions, which are included in SG&A, have not been significant.

Revenue Recognition

We recognize revenue from the sale of merchandise at the time the customer takes possession of the merchandise. We recognize service revenue at the time the service is provided, the sales price is fixed or determinable, and collectibility is reasonably assured. Proceeds from the sale of gift cards are deferred until the customer uses the gift card to acquire merchandise or services. Amounts billed to customers for shipping and handling are included in revenue. An allowance has been established for estimated sales returns.

We sell extended service contracts on behalf of an unrelated third party. In jurisdictions where we are not deemed to be the obligor on the contract, commissions are recognized in revenue at the time of sale. In jurisdictions where we are deemed to be the obligor on the contract, commissions are recognized in revenue ratably over the term of the service contract.

Sales Incentives

We frequently offer sales incentives that entitle our customers to receive a reduction in the price of a product or service. Sales incentives include discounts, coupons and other offers that entitle a customer to receive a reduction in the price of a product or service by submitting a claim for a refund or rebate. For sales incentives in which we are the obligor, the reduction in revenue is recognized at the time the product is sold.

We have a customer loyalty program which allows members to earn points for each purchase completed at U.S. Best Buy stores. Points earned enable members to receive a certificate that may be redeemed on future purchases at U.S. Best Buy stores. The value of points earned by our loyalty program members is included in accrued liabilities and recorded as a reduction of revenue at the time the points are earned, based on the percentage of points that are projected to be redeemed.

Costs of Goods Sold and Selling, General and Administrative Expenses

The following table illustrates the primary costs classified in each major expense category.

Cost of Goods Sold	SG&A
<ul><li>Total cost of products sold including:<ul><li>— Freight expenses associated with moving merchandise inventories from our vendors to our distribution centers;</li><li>— Vendor allowances that are not a reimbursement of specific, incremental and identifiable costs to promote a vendor's products;</li></ul></li><li>Costs of services provided;</li><li>Physical inventory losses;</li><li>Markdowns;</li><li>Customer shipping and handling expenses;</li><li>Costs associated with operating our distribution network, including payroll and benefit costs, occupancy costs, and depreciation; and</li><li>Freight expenses associated with moving merchandise inventories from our distribution centers to our retail stores.</li></ul>	<ul><li>Payroll and benefit costs for retail and corporate employees;</li><li>Occupancy costs of retail, services and corporate facilities;</li><li>Depreciation related to retail, services and corporate assets;</li><li>Advertising;</li><li>Vendor allowances that are a reimbursement of specific, incremental and identifiable costs to promote a vendor's products;</li><li>Outside service fees;</li><li>Long-lived asset impairment charges; and</li><li>Other administrative costs, such as credit card service fees, supplies, and travel and lodging.</li></ul>

BEST BUY

$ in millions, except per share amounts

Advertising Costs

Advertising costs, which are included in SG&A, are expensed the first time the advertisement runs. Advertising costs consist primarily of print and television advertisements as well as promotional events. Gross advertising expenses, before expense reimbursement from vendor allowances, for fiscal 2005, 2004 and 2003 were $712, $675 and $567, respectively.

Stock-Based Compensation

We have a stock-based compensation plan that includes stock options and restricted stock. We also have an employee stock purchase plan. The table below illustrates the effect on net earnings and earnings per share as if we had applied the fair value recognition provisions of SFAS No. 123 to stock-based compensation for each of the last three fiscal years.

	2005	2004	2003
Net earnings, as reported	$ 984	$ 705	$ 99
Add: Stock-based compensation expense included in reported net earnings, net of tax[1]	(1)	5	1
Deduct: Stock-based compensation expense determined under fair value method for all awards, net of tax[2]	(60)	(101)	(85)
Net earnings, pro forma	$ 923	$ 609	$ 15
Earnings per share:			
Basic — as reported	$3.02	$2.18	$0.31
Basic — pro forma	$2.83	$1.88	$0.05
Diluted — as reported	$2.94	$2.13	$0.31
Diluted — pro forma	$2.80	$1.88	$0.05

[1]   Amounts represent the after-tax compensation costs for restricted stock awards.

[2]   In the fourth quarter of fiscal 2005, we increased our expected participant stock option forfeiture rate as a result of transferring to a third-party provider certain corporate employees, and the departure of certain senior executives. This higher level of expected stock option forfeitures reduced our fiscal 2005 pro forma stock-based compensation expense. Fiscal 2005 pro forma stock-based compensation expense may not be indicative of future stock-based compensation expense.

2.   Discontinued Operations

In fiscal 2004, we sold our interest in Musicland. The buyer assumed all of Musicland's liabilities, including approximately $500 in lease obligations, in exchange for all of the capital stock of Musicland and paid no cash consideration. The transaction also resulted in the transfer of all of Musicland's assets, other than a distribution center in Franklin, Indiana, and selected nonoperating assets. The loss from discontinued operations for fiscal 2004 included a loss on the disposal of discontinued operations (which was primarily noncash) of $66, net of tax, related to the sale of Musicland. In connection with the sale, Musicland purchased transition support services from us for approximately one year from the date of the sale.

In accordance with SFAS No. 144, Musicland's financial results are reported separately as discontinued operations for all periods presented.

During fiscal 2003, we recorded an after-tax, noncash impairment charge of $308 for the full write-off of goodwill related to our acquisition of Musicland. In addition, we recorded an after-tax, noncash charge of $8 for the change in our method of accounting for Musicland vendor allowances. The charges are classified as cumulative effects of changes in accounting principles in discontinued operations (see Note 1, *Summary of Significant Accounting Policies*).

Also during fiscal 2003, in accordance with SFAS No. 144, we recorded a pre-tax impairment charge of $166 related to a reassessment of the carrying value of

$ in millions, except per share amounts

Musicland's long-lived assets. The $166 charge was recorded in loss before income taxes, in the table below. We determined fair values utilizing widely accepted valuation techniques, including discounted cash flows. We based fair values on the then-current expectations for the business in light of the then-existing retail environment and the uncertainty associated with future trends in prerecorded music products.

The financial results of Musicland, included in discontinued operations, were as follows:

For the Fiscal Years Ended	Feb. 26, 2005	Feb. 28, 2004[1]	March 1, 2003
Revenue	$—	$354	$1,727
Loss before income taxes	—	(46)	(244)
Loss before the disposal and the cumulative effect of accounting changes, net of $17 and $119 tax, respectively	—	(29)	(125)
Gain (loss) on disposal of discontinued operations[2]	50	(66)	—
Cumulative effect of change in accounting principles, net of $5 tax	—	—	(316)
Gain (loss) from discontinued operations, net of tax	$50	$ (95)	$ (441)

[1] Fiscal 2004 includes operating results from March 2, 2003, through June 16, 2003, the date we sold our interest in Musicland.

[2] Fiscal 2005 gain on disposal of discontinued operations represents the reversal of valuation allowances on deferred tax assets as described below. Fiscal 2004 loss on disposal of discontinued operations is net of $25 tax benefit offset by a $25 valuation allowance.

3. Investments in Debt Securities

Our short-term and long-term investments are comprised of municipal and United States government debt securities. In accordance with SFAS No. 115, *Accounting for Certain Investments in Debt and Equity Securities,* and based on our ability to market and sell these instruments, we classify auction-rate debt securities and other investments in debt securities as available-for-sale and carry them at amortized cost. Auction-rate debt securities are long-term bonds that are similar to short-term instruments because their interest rates are reset periodically and investments in these securities can be sold for cash on the auction date. We classify auction-rate debt securities as short-term or long-term investments based on the reset dates.

In accordance with our investment policy, we place our investments in debt securities with issuers who have high-quality credit and limit the amount of investment exposure to any one issuer. We seek to preserve principal and minimize exposure to interest-rate fluctuations by limiting default risk, market risk and reinvestment risk.

On an annual basis, we review the key characteristics of our debt securities portfolio and their classification in accordance with GAAP. If a decline in the fair value of a security is deemed by management to be other than temporary, the cost basis of the investment is written down to fair value, and the amount of the write-down is included in the determination of income.

During our annual review in the fourth quarter of fiscal 2005, we reclassified our auction-rate debt securities from cash and cash equivalents to short-term investments or long-term investments, as appropriate, for all periods presented. The amortized cost of the securities reclassified for fiscal 2004 was $2,355. The unrealized gain on the securities in conjunction with this reclassification was not significant.

We also revised the presentation in the consolidated statements of cash flows for the years ended February 28, 2004, and March 1, 2003, to reflect the gross purchases and sales of these securities as investing activities rather than as a component of cash and cash equivalents, which is consistent with the presentation for the fiscal year ended February 26, 2005.

$ in millions, except per share amounts

The carrying amount of our investments in debt securities approximated fair value of February 26, 2005, and February 28, 2004, respectively, due to the rapid turnover of our portfolio and the highly liquid nature of these investments. Therefore, there were no significant unrealized holding gains or losses.

The following table presents the amortized principal amounts, related weighted average interest rates, maturities and major security types for our investments in debt securities:

	February 26, 2005		February 28, 2004	
	Amortized Principal Amount	Weighted Average Interest Rate	Amortized Principal Amount	Weighted Average Interest Rate
Short-term investments (less than one year)	$2,878	3.22%	$2,355	1.59%
Long-term investments (one to three years)	148	3.73%	—	—
Total	$3,026		$2,355	
Municipal debt securities	$3,019		$2,355	
Debt securities issued by U.S. Treasury and other U.S. government entities	7		—	
Total	$3,026		$2,355	

4. Debt

	Feb. 26, 2005	Feb. 28, 2004
Convertible subordinated debentures, unsecured, due 2022, initial interest rate 2.25%	$402	$ 402
Convertible debentures, unsecured, due 2021, interest rate 2.75%[1]	—	353
Master lease obligations, due 2006, interest rate 5.9%	55	58
Capital lease obligations, due 2005, interest rates ranging from 5.5% to 8.0%	13	16
Financing lease obligations, due 2008 to 2022, interest rates ranging from 5.6% to 6.0%[2]	107	—
Mortgage and other debt, interest rates ranging from 1.8% to 8.9%	23	21
Total debt	600	850
Less: current portion	(72)	(368)
Total long-term debt	$528	$ 482

[1]   In June 2004, we redeemed our convertible debentures due in 2021, for $355. No gain or loss was incurred.

[2]   In fiscal 2005, we recorded $107 of financing leases as a result of our review of our lease accounting practices. See Note 7, *Leases,* for further information.

The mortgage and other debt are secured by certain property and equipment with a net book value of $98 and $97 at February 26, 2005, and February 28, 2004, respectively.

Convertible Debentures

In January 2002, we sold convertible subordinated debentures having an aggregate principal amount of $402. The proceeds from the offering, net of $6 in offering expenses, were $396. The debentures mature in 2022 and are callable at par, at our option, for cash on or after January 15, 2007.

Holders may require us to purchase all or a portion of their debentures on January 15, 2007; January 15, 2012; and January 15, 2017, at a purchase price equal

$ in millions, except per share amounts

to 100% of the principal amount of the debentures plus accrued and unpaid interest up to but not including the date of purchase. We have the option to settle the purchase price in cash, stock, or a combination of cash and stock.

The debentures will be convertible into shares of our common stock at a conversion rate of 14.4927 shares per $0.001 principal amount of debentures, equivalent to an initial conversion price of $69.00 per share, if the closing price of our common stock exceeds a specified price for a specified period of time, if our credit rating falls below specified levels, if the debentures are called for redemption or if certain specified corporate transactions occur. At February 26, 2005, none of the criteria for conversion had been met. The debentures have an initial interest rate of 2.25% per annum. The interest rate may be reset, but not below 2.25% or above 3.25%, on July 15, 2006; July 15, 2011; and July 15, 2016. One of our subsidiaries has guaranteed the convertible debentures.

Credit Facilities

We have a $200 bank revolving credit facility which is guaranteed by certain of our subsidiaries. The facility expires on December 22, 2009. Borrowings under this facility are unsecured and bear interest at rates specified in the credit agreement. We also pay certain facility and agent fees. The agreement contains convenants that require us to maintain certain financial ratios.

Other

The fair value of long-term debt approximated $603 and $902 as of February 26, 2005, and February 28, 2004, respectively, based on the ask prices quoted from external sources, compared with carrying values of $600 and $850, respectively.

The future maturities of long-term debt, including master and capitalized leases, consist of the following:

Fiscal Year	
2006	$ 72
2007[1]	415
2008	14
2009	14
2010	20
Thereafter	65
	$600

[1] Holders of our debentures due in 2022 may require us to purchase all or a portion of their debentures on January 15, 2007. The table above assumes that all holders of our debentures exercise their redemption options.

5. Shareholders Equity Stock Compensation Plans

Outstanding options were granted at exercise prices equal to the fair market value of our common stock on the date of grant and have a 10-year term. Options issued to employees generally vest over a four-year period. Options issued to our directors vest immediately upon grant.

Earnings per Share

Basic earnings per share is computed based on the weighted average number of common shares outstanding. Diluted earnings per share is computed based on the weighted average number of common shares outstanding adjusted by the number of additional shares that would have been outstanding had the potentially dilutive common shares been issued. Potentially dilutive shares of common stock include stock options, unvested restricted stock awards, shares issuable under our ESPP as well as common shares that would have resulted from the assumed conversion of our convertible debentures (see Note 4, *Debt*). Since the potentially dilutive shares related to the convertible debentures are included in the calculation, the related interest, net of tax, is added back to income from continuing operations, as the interest would not have been paid if the convertible debentures were converted to common stock.

$ in millions, except per share amounts

The following table presents a reconciliation of the numerators and denominators of basic and diluted earnings per share from continuing operations for fiscal 2005, 2004 and 2003:

	2005	2004	2003
Numerator:			
Earnings from continuing operations, basic	$ 934	$ 800	$ 622
Adjustment for assumed dilution:			
Interest on convertible debentures due in 2022, net of tax	7	6	6
Earnings from continuing operations, diluted	$ 941	$ 806	$ 628
Denominator (in millions):			
Weighted average common shares outstanding	325.9	323.3	321.1
Effect of dilutive securities:			
Shares from assumed conversion of convertible debentures	5.8	5.8	5.8
Stock options and other	4.9	4.8	3.8
Weighted average common shares outstanding, assuming dilution	336.6	333.9	330.7
Basic earnings per share — continuing operations	$ 2.87	$ 2.47	$ 1.93
Diltuted earnings per share — continuing operations	$ 2.79	$ 2.41	$ 1.90

Repurchase of Common Stock

In June 2004, our Board authorized the purchase of up to $500 of our common stock from time to time through open market purchases. The $500 share repurchase program, which became effective on June 24, 2004, terminated and replaced the $400 share repurchase program authorized by our Board in fiscal 2000.

In April 2005, our Board authorized the purchase of up to $1.5 billion of our common stock from time to time through open market purchases. This share repurchase program has no stated expiration date. The $1.5 billion share repurchase program terminated and replaced the $500 share repurchase program authorized by our Board in June 2004.

During fiscal 2005, we purchased and retired 2.3 million shares at a cost of $118 under the $500 share repurchase program, and 1.6 million shares at a cost of $82 under the $400 share repurchase program.

Comprehensive Income

Comprehensive income is computed as net earnings plus certain other items that are recorded directly to shareholders' equity. The only significant other item included in comprehensive income is foreign currency translation adjustments. Foreign currency translation adjustments do not include a provision for income tax because earnings from foreign operations are considered to be indefinitely reinvested outside the U.S. Investment gains/losses were not significant.

BEST BUY

$ in millions, except per share amounts

6. Net Interest Income (Expense)

Net interest income (expense) for fiscal 2005, 2004 and 2003 was comprised of the following

	2005	2004	2003
Interest expense[1]	$(44)	$(32)	$(30)
Capitalized interest	—	1	5
Interest income	45	23	23
Net interest income (expense)	1	(8)	(2)
Interest expense allocated to discontinued operations[2]	—	—	(6)
Net interest income (expense) from continuing operations	$ 1	$ (8)	$ 4

[1] Fiscal 2005 interest expense includes $21 of expense related to our lease accounting corrections.

[2] We allocated interest expense to discontinued operations based upon debt that was attributable to Musicland's operation.

7. Leases

We lease portions of our corporate facilities and conduct the majority of our retail and distribution operations from leased locations. The leases require payment of real estate taxes, insurance and common area maintenance, in addition to rent. The terms of our lease agreements generally range up to 20 years. Most of the leases contain renewal options and escalation clauses, and certain store leases require contingent rents based on specified percentages of revenue. Other leases contain covenants related to the maintenance of financial ratios.

For leases that contain predetermined fixed escalations of the minimum rent, we recognize the related rent expense on a straight-line basis from the date we take possession of the property to the end of the initial lease term. We record any difference between the straight-line rent amounts and amounts payable under the leases as part of deferred rent, in accrued liabilities or long-term liabilities, as appropriate.

Cash or lease incentives (tenant allowances) received upon entering into certain store leases are recognized on a straight-line basis as a reduction to rent from the date we take possession of the property though the end of the initial lease term. We record the unamortized portion of tenant allowances as a part of deferred rent, in accrued liabilities or long-term liabilities, as appropriate.

At February 26, 2005, and February 28, 2004, deferred rent included in accrued liabilities was approximately $11 and $3, respectively, and deferred rent included in long-term liabilities was approximately $171 and $73, respectively.

We also lease certain equipment under noncancelable operating and capital leases. Assets acquired under capital leases are depreciated over the shorter of the useful life of the asset or the initial lease term.

Rental expense for all operating leases, during the past three fiscal years, including leases of property and equipment, was as follows:

	2005	2004	2003
Net rent expense for continuing operations	$501	$468	$440

$ in millions, except per share amounts

The future minimum lease payments under our capital, financing and operating leases by fiscal year (not including contingent rentals) as of February 26, 2005, are as follows:

Fiscal Year	Capital Leases	Financing Leases	Operating Leases
2006	$ 6	$ 16	$ 541
2007	2	15	541
2008	2	15	524
2009	2	14	511
2010	2	14	486
Thereafter	1	79	3,247
Subtotal	15	153	$5,850
Less: imputed interest	(2)	(46)	
Present value of lease obligations	$13	$107	

8. Benefit Plans

We sponsor retirement savings plans for employees meeting certain age and service requirements. The plans provide for company-matching contributions, which are subject to annual approval by our Board. The total matching contributions were $14, $13 and $13 in fiscal 2005, 2004 and 2003, respectively.

9. Income Taxes

Income tax expense was comprised of the following for the past three fiscal years:

	2005	2004	2003
Current:			
Federal	$502	$456	$375
State	36	49	51
Foreign	(1)	5	3
	537	510	429
Deferred:			
Federal	(4)	(9)	(22)
State	(20)	(1)	(3)
Foreign	(4)	(4)	(12)
	(28)	(14)	(37)
Income tax expense	$509	$496	$392

Deferred taxes are the result of differences between the bases of assets and liabilities for financial reporting and income tax purposes.

10. Segments

We operate two reportable segments: Domestic and International. The Domestic segment is comprised of U.S. Best Buy and Magnolia Audio Video operations. The International segment is comprised of Future Shop and Best Buy operations in Canada. Our segments are evaluated on an operating income basis, and a stand-alone tax provision is not calculated for each segment.

The following table presents our business segment information for continuing operations.

	2005
Revenue	
Domestic	$24,616
International	2,817
Total revenue	$27,433
Operating Income	
Domestic	$ 1,393
International	49
Total operating income	1,442
Net interest income (expense)	1
Earnings from continuing operations before income tax expense	$ 1,443
Assets	
Domestic	$ 8,372
International	1,922
Total assets	$10,294

$ in millions, except per share amounts

11. Contingencies and Commitments

Contingencies

We are involved in various other legal proceedings arising in the normal course of conducting business. We believe the amounts provided in our consolidated financial statements, as prescribed by GAAP, are adequate in light of the probable and estimable liabilities. The resolution of those proceedings is not expected to have a material impact on our results of operation or financial condition.

Commitments

In 2004, we engaged Accenture LLP to assist us with improving our operational capabilities and reducing our costs in the Human Resources and Information Systems areas. Our future contractual obligations to Accenture are expected to range from $124 to $235 per year through 2011, the end of the contract period. Prior to our engagement of Accenture, a significant portion of these costs were incurred as part of normal operations.

We had outstanding letters of credit for purchase obligations with a fair value of $92 as of February 26, 2005.

As of February 26, 2005, we had commitments for the purchase and construction of facilities valued at approximately $83. Also, as of February 26, 2005, we had entered into lease commitments for land and buildings for 73 future locations. These lease commitments with real estate developers provide for minimum rentals ranging from 10 to 20 years, which if consummated based on current cost estimates, will approximate $53 annually over the lease terms.

We assumed a liability for certain extended service contracts when we acquired Future Shop in fiscal 2002. We established an accrued liability for the acquired extended service contracts based on historical trends in product failure rates and the expected material and labor costs necessary to provide the services. The remaining terms of these acquired extended service contracts vary by product and extend through fiscal 2007. The estimated remaining liability for acquired extended service contracts at February 26, 2005, was $9. Subsequent to the acquisition, all new extended service contracts were sold on behalf of an unrelated third party, without recourse.

Financial Report

CONSOLIDATED BALANCE SHEETS

	At February 28 or 29	
(Amounts in thousands except share data)	2005	2004

ASSETS

CURRENT ASSETS:

	2005	2004
Cash and cash equivalents	$ 879,660	$ 783,471
Short-term investments	125,325	–
Accounts receivable, net of allowance for doubtful accounts of $120 and $547	172,995	170,568
Retained interests in securitized receivables	–	425,678
Merchandise inventory	1,459,520	1,517,256
Deferred income taxes	29,518	–
Prepaid expenses and other current assets	18,697	22,088
TOTAL CURRENT ASSETS	2,685,715	2,919,061
Property and equipment, net	738,802	677,107
Deferred income taxes	73,558	88,146
Goodwill	215,884	–
Other intangible assets	31,331	–
Other assets	44,092	46,212
TOTAL ASSETS	$3,789,382	$3,730,526

LIABILITIES AND STOCKHOLDERS' EQUITY

CURRENT LIABILITIES:

	2005	2004
Accounts payable	$ 961,718	$ 833,825
Accrued expenses and other current liabilities	228,966	149,605
Accrued income taxes	72,274	71,163
Deferred income taxes	–	79,422
Current installments of long-term debt	888	1,115
Liabilities of discontinued operations	–	3,068
TOTAL CURRENT LIABILITIES	1,263,846	1,138,198
Long-term debt, excluding current installments	11,522	22,691
Accrued straight-line rent and deferred rent credits	230,426	206,784
Accrued lease termination costs	104,234	75,722
Other liabilities	91,920	63,170
TOTAL LIABILITIES	1,701,948	1,506,565

STOCKHOLDERS' EQUITY:

	2005	2004
Common stock, $0.50 par value; 525,000,000 shares authorized; 188,150,383 shares issued and outstanding (203,899,395 in 2004)	94,075	101,950
Capital in excess of par value	721,038	922,600
Retained earnings	1,247,221	1,199,411
Accumulated other comprehensive income	25,100	–
TOTAL STOCKHOLDERS' EQUITY	2,087,434	2,223,961
Commitments and contingent liabilities [NOTES 12, 13 AND 16]		
TOTAL LIABILITIES AND STOCKHOLDERS' EQUITY	$3,789,382	$3,730,526

See accompanying notes to consolidated financial statements.

CIRCUIT CITY

CONSOLIDATED STATEMENTS OF OPERATIONS

(Amounts in thousands except per share data)	2005	%	2004	%	2003	%
NET SALES AND OPERATING REVENUES	$10,472,364	100.0	$9,857,057	100.0	$10,054,864	100.0
Cost of sales, buying and warehousing	7,903,641	75.5	7,573,049	76.8	7,647,992	76.1
GROSS PROFIT	2,568,723	24.5	2,284,008	23.2	2,406,872	23.9
Finance income	5,564	0.1	32,693	0.3	27,292	0.3
Selling, general and administrative expenses	2,457,032	23.5	2,277,479	23.1	2,385,310	23.7
Stock-based compensation expense	19,400	0.2	38,658	0.4	53,251	0.5
Interest expense	2,066	–	1,804	–	1,093	–
Earnings (loss) from continuing operations before income taxes	95,789	0.9	(1,240)	–	(5,490)	(0.1)
Income tax provision (benefit)	35,878	0.3	(453)	–	(181)	–
NET EARNINGS (LOSS) FROM CONTINUING OPERATIONS	59,911	0.6	(787)	–	(5,309)	(0.1)
NET EARNINGS (LOSS) FROM DISCONTINUED OPERATIONS	1,747	–	(88,482)	(0.9)	87,572	0.9
NET EARNINGS (LOSS)	$ 61,658	0.6	$ (89,269)	(0.9)	$ 82,263	0.8
Net earnings (loss) from discontinued operations attributed to:						
Circuit City common stock	$ 1,747		$ (88,482)		$ 65,264	
CarMax Group common stock	$ –		$ –		$ 22,308	
Weighted average common shares:						
Circuit City:						
Basic	193,466		205,865		207,217	
Diluted	196,227		205,865		207,217	
CarMax Group:						
Basic	–		–		37,023	
Diluted	–		–		38,646	
NET EARNINGS (LOSS) PER SHARE:						
Basic:						
Continuing operations	$ 0.31		$ –		$ (0.03)	
Discontinued operations attributed to Circuit City common stock	0.01		(0.43)		0.31	
	$ 0.32		$ (0.43)		$ 0.29	
Discontinued operations attributed to CarMax Group common stock	$ –		$ –		$ 0.60	
Diluted:						
Continuing operations	$ 0.31		$ –		$ (0.03)	
Discontinued operations attributed to Circuit City common stock	0.01		(0.43)		0.31	
	$ 0.31		$ (0.43)		$ 0.29	
Discontinued operations attributed to CarMax Group common stock	$ –		$ –		$ 0.58	

See accompanying notes to consolidated financial statements.

CIRCUIT CITY

CIRCUIT CITY

CONSOLIDATED STATEMENTS OF STOCKHOLDERS' EQUITY AND COMPREHENSIVE INCOME

(Amounts in thousands except per share data)	Shares Outstanding Circuit City	Shares Outstanding CarMax Group	Common Stock Circuit City	Common Stock CarMax Group	Capital In Excess of Par Value	Retained Earnings	Accumulated Other Comprehensive Income	Total
BALANCE AT FEBRUARY 28, 2002	208,823	36,851	$104,411	$ 18,426	$893,537	$1,744,129	$ —	$2,760,503
Net earnings and comprehensive income	—	—	—	—	—	82,263	—	82,263
Compensation for stock options	—	—	—	—	34,637	—	—	34,637
Exercise of common stock options	311	246	156	123	5,035	—	—	5,314
Shares issued under employee stock purchase plans	457	—	229	—	7,400	—	—	7,629
Shares issued under stock incentive plans	843	—	421	—	17,207	—	—	17,628
Tax effect from stock issued	—	—	—	—	5,986	—	—	5,986
Cancellation of restricted stock	(479)	(8)	(240)	(4)	(8,081)	—	—	(8,325)
Unearned compensation restricted stock	—	—	—	—	9,830	—	—	9,830
Cash dividends — common stock ($0.07 per share)	—	—	—	—	—	(14,687)	—	(14,687)
Distribution of CarMax, Inc. common stock to stockholders	—	(37,089)	—	(18,545)	—	(536,765)	—	(555,310)
Special dividend from CarMax	—	—	—	—	—	28,400	—	28,400
BALANCE AT FEBRUARY 28, 2003	209,955	—	104,977	—	965,551	1,303,340	—	2,373,868
Net loss and comprehensive loss	—	—	—	—	—	(89,269)	—	(89,269)
Repurchases of common stock	(9,266)	—	(4,633)	—	(79,720)	—	—	(84,353)
Compensation for stock options	—	—	—	—	24,184	—	—	24,184
Exercise of common stock options	1,369	—	685	—	11,843	—	—	12,528
Shares issued under stock incentive plans	2,546	—	1,273	—	19,312	—	—	20,585
Tax effect from stock issued	—	—	—	—	(10,595)	—	—	(10,595)
Cancellation of restricted stock	(705)	—	(352)	—	(10,074)	—	—	(10,426)
Unearned compensation restricted stock	—	—	—	—	2,099	—	—	2,099
Cash dividends — common stock ($0.07 per share)	—	—	—	—	—	(14,660)	—	(14,660)
BALANCE AT FEBRUARY 29, 2004	203,899	—	101,950	—	922,600	1,199,411	—	2,223,961
Comprehensive income:								
Net earnings	—	—	—	—	—	61,658	—	61,658
Other comprehensive income, net of taxes:								
Foreign currency translation adjustment (net of deferred taxes of $13,707)	—	—	—	—	—	—	25,100	25,100
Comprehensive income								86,758
Repurchases of common stock	(19,163)	—	(9,582)	—	(250,250)	—	—	(259,832)
Compensation for stock options	—	—	—	—	18,739	—	—	18,739
Exercise of common stock options	3,489	—	1,745	—	26,761	—	—	28,506
Shares issued under stock incentive plans	723	—	361	—	7,393	—	—	7,754
Tax effect from stock issued	—	—	—	—	(1,564)	—	—	(1,564)
Cancellation of restricted stock	(798)	—	(399)	—	(6,378)	—	—	(6,777)
Shares issued in acquisition of InterTAN, Inc.	—	—	—	—	6,498	—	—	6,498
Unearned compensation restricted stock	—	—	—	—	(2,761)	—	—	(2,761)
Cash dividends — common stock ($0.07 per share)	—	—	—	—	—	(13,848)	—	(13,848)
BALANCE AT FEBRUARY 28, 2005	188,150	—	$ 94,075	$ —	$721,038	$1,247,221	$25,100	$2,087,434

See accompanying notes to consolidated financial statements.

CONSOLIDATED STATEMENTS OF CASH FLOWS

(Amounts in thousands)	Years Ended February 28 or 29 2005	2004	2003
OPERATING ACTIVITIES:			
Net earnings (loss)	$ 61,658	$ (89,269)	$ 82,263
Adjustments to reconcile net earnings (loss) to net cash provided by (used in) operating activities of continuing operations:			
Net (earnings) loss from discontinued operations	(1,747)	88,482	(87,572)
Depreciation and amortization	154,788	197,607	159,800
Stock option expense	18,739	24,184	30,823
Amortization of restricted stock awards	(434)	13,395	20,828
(Gain) loss on dispositions of property and equipment	(206)	7,500	15,659
Provision for deferred income taxes	(116,455)	(35,618)	(18,664)
Changes in operating assets and liabilities:			
(Increase) decrease in accounts receivable, net	(65,112)	(30,183)	6,229
Decrease (increase) in retained interests in securitized receivables	32,867	(186,537)	(92,888)
Decrease (increase) in merchandise inventory	159,278	(107,520)	(175,493)
Decrease (increase) in prepaid expenses and other current assets	7,148	(3,923)	21,081
Decrease (increase) in other assets	3,925	12,553	(26,181)
Increase (decrease) in accounts payable	101,991	(85,727)	(58,041)
Increase (decrease) in accrued expenses and other current liabilities, and accrued income taxes	36,008	50,577	(48,069)
Increase in other long-term liabilities	63,549	18,966	7,116
NET CASH PROVIDED BY (USED IN) OPERATING ACTIVITIES OF CONTINUING OPERATIONS	455,879	(125,513)	(163,109)
INVESTING ACTIVITIES:			
Proceeds from the sale of the private-label operation	475,857	–	–
Acquisitions, net of cash acquired of $30,615	(268,774)	–	–
Purchases of property and equipment	(269,166)	(175,769)	(150,757)
Proceeds from sales of property and equipment	106,369	40,427	59,888
Purchases of investment securities	(125,325)	–	–
NET CASH USED IN INVESTING ACTIVITIES OF CONTINUING OPERATIONS	(81,039)	(135,342)	(90,869)
FINANCING ACTIVITIES:			
Payments on short-term debt	(1,853)	–	(397)
Principal payments on long-term debt	(28,008)	(1,458)	(24,865)
Repurchases of common stock	(259,832)	(84,353)	–
Issuances of Circuit City common stock, net	27,156	11,391	8,901
Issuances of CarMax Group common stock, net	–	–	298
Dividends paid	(13,848)	(14,660)	(14,687)
NET CASH USED IN FINANCING ACTIVITIES OF CONTINUING OPERATIONS	(276,385)	(89,080)	(30,750)
CASH (USED IN) PROVIDED BY DISCONTINUED OPERATIONS:			
BANKCARD OPERATION	(4,282)	248,736	(94,533)
CARMAX OPERATION	–	–	26,185
DIVX OPERATION	–	–	(10,500)
EFFECT OF EXCHANGE RATE CHANGES ON CASH	2,016	–	–
Increase (decrease) in cash and cash equivalents	96,189	(101,199)	(363,576)
Cash and cash equivalents at beginning of year	783,471	884,670	1,248,246
CASH AND CASH EQUIVALENTS AT END OF YEAR	$ 879,660	$ 783,471	$ 884,670

See accompanying notes to consolidated financial statements.

Apple Financial Report

CONSOLIDATED BALANCE SHEETS
(In millions, except share amounts)

	September 25, 2004	September 27, 2003
ASSETS:		
Current assets:		
Cash and cash equivalents	$2,969	$3,396
Short-term investments	2,495	1,170
Accounts receivable, less allowances of $47 and $49, respectively	774	766
Inventories	101	56
Deferred tax assets	231	190
Other current assets	485	309
Total current assets	7,055	5,887
Property, plant, and equipment, net	707	669
Goodwill	80	85
Acquired intangible assets	17	24
Other assets	191	150
Total assets	$8,050	$6,815
LIABILITIES AND SHAREHOLDERS' EQUITY:		
Current liabilities:		
Accounts payable	$1,451	$1,154
Accrued expenses	1,229	899
Current debt	—	304
Total current liabilities	2,680	2,357
Deferred tax liabilities and other non-current liabilities	294	235
Total liabilities	2,974	2,592
Shareholders' equity:		
Common stock, no par value; 900,000,000 shares authorized; 391,443,617 and 366,726,584 shares issued and outstanding, respectively	2,514	1,926
Deferred stock compensation	(93)	(62)
Retained earnings	2,670	2,394
Accumulated other comprehensive income (loss)	(15)	(35)
Total shareholders' equity	5,076	4,223
Total liabilities and shareholders' equity	$8,050	$6,815

See accompanying notes to consolidated financial statements.

APPLE COMPUTER

CONSOLIDATED STATEMENTS OF OPERATIONS

(In millions, except share and per share amounts)

Three fiscal years ended September 25, 2004	2004	2003	2002
Net sales	$ 8,279	$ 6,207	$ 5,742
Cost of sales	6,020	4,499	4,139
Gross margin	2,259	1,708	1,603
Operating expenses:			
Research and development	489	471	446
Selling, general, and administrative	1,421	1,212	1,109
Restructuring costs	23	26	30
Purchased in-process research and development	—	—	1
Total operating expenses	1,933	1,709	1,586
Operating income (loss)	326	(1)	17
Other income and expense:			
Gains (losses) on non-current investments, net	4	10	(42)
Interest and other income, net	53	83	112
Total other income and expense	57	93	70
Income before provision for income taxes	383	92	87
Provision for income taxes	107	24	22
Income before accounting changes	276	68	65
Cumulative effects of accounting changes, net of income taxes	—	1	—
Net income	$ 276	$ 69	$ 65
Earnings per common share before accounting changes:			
Basic	$ 0.74	$ 0.19	$ 0.18
Diluted	$ 0.71	$ 0.19	$ 0.18
Earnings per common share:			
Basic	$ 0.74	$ 0.19	$ 0.18
Diluted	$ 0.71	$ 0.19	$ 0.18
Shares used in computing earnings per share (in thousands):			
Basic	371,590	360,631	355,022
Diluted	387,311	363,466	361,785

See accompanying notes to consolidated financial statements.

APPLE COMPUTER

CONSOLIDATED STATEMENTS OF SHAREHOLDERS' EQUITY

(In millions, except share amounts which are in thousands)

	Common Stock		Deferred Stock Compensation	Retained Earnings	Accumulated Other Comprehensive Income (Loss)	Total Shareholders' Equity
	Shares	Amount				
Balances as of September 29, 2001	350,922	$1,693	$(11)	$2,260	$(22)	$3,920
Components of comprehensive income:						
Net income	—	—	—	65	—	65
Change in foreign currency translation	—	—	—	—	5	5
Change in unrealized gain on available-for-sale securities, net of tax	—	—	—	—	(17)	(17)
Change in unrealized gain on derivative investments, net of tax	—	—	—	—	(15)	(15)
Total comprehensive income						38
Amortization of deferred stock compensation	—	—	4	—	—	4
Common stock issued under stock plans	8,037	105	—	—	—	105
Tax benefit related to stock options	—	28	—	—	—	28
Balances as of September 28, 2002	358,959	$1,826	$ (7)	$2,325	$(49)	$4,095
Components of comprehensive income:						
Net income	—	—	—	69	—	69
Change in foreign currency translation	—	—	—	—	31	31
Change in unrealized gain on available-for-sale securities, net of tax	—	—	—	—	(12)	(12)
Change in unrealized gain on derivative investments, net of tax	—	—	—	—	(5)	(5)
Total comprehensive income						83
Amortization of deferred stock compensation	—	—	15	—	—	15
Write-off of deferred stock compensation	—	—	5	—	—	5
Common stock issued under stock plans	9,299	128	(75)	—	—	53
Settlement of forward purchase agreement	(1,531)	(35)	—	—	—	(35)
Tax benefit related to stock options	—	7	—	—	—	7
Balances as of September 27, 2003	366,727	$1,926	$(62)	$2,394	$(35)	$4,223
Components of comprehensive income:						
Net income	—	—	—	276	—	276
Change in foreign currency translation	—	—	—	—	13	13
Change in unrealized gain on available-for-sale securities, net of tax	—	—	—	—	(5)	(5)
Change in unrealized loss on derivative investments, net of tax	—	—	—	—	12	12
Total comprehensive income						296
Issuance of restricted stock units	—	64	(64)	—	—	—
Adjustment to common stock related to a prior year acquisition	(79)	(2)	—	—	—	(2)
Amortization of deferred stock compensation	—	—	33	—	—	33
Common stock issued under stock plans	24,796	427	—	—	—	427
Tax benefit related to stock options	—	99	—	—	—	99
Balances as of September 25, 2004	391,444	$2,514	$(93)	$2,670	$(15)	$5,076

See accompanying notes to consolidated financial statements.

APPLE COMPUTER

CONSOLIDATED STATEMENTS OF CASH FLOWS

(In millions)

Three fiscal years ended September 25, 2004	2004	2003	2002
Cash and cash equivalents, beginning of the year	$ 3,396	$ 2,252	$ 2,310
Operating Activities:			
Net income	276	69	65
Cumulative effects of accounting changes, net of taxes	—	(1)	—
Adjustments to reconcile net income to cash generated by operating activities:			
Depreciation, amortization and accretion	150	113	114
Stock-based compensation expense	33	16	5
Non-cash restructuring	5	12	8
Provision for (benefit from) deferred income taxes	20	(11)	(34)
Loss on disposition of property, plant, and equipment	7	2	7
Gains on sales of short-term investments, net	(1)	(21)	(7)
(Gains) losses on non-current investments, net	(4)	(10)	42
Gain on forward purchase agreement	—	(6)	—
Purchased in-process research and development	—	—	1
Changes in operating assets and liabilities:			
Accounts receivable	(8)	(201)	(99)
Inventories	(45)	(11)	(34)
Other current assets	(176)	(34)	(114)
Other assets	(39)	(30)	(11)
Accounts payable	297	243	110
Other liabilities	419	159	36
Cash generated by operating activities	934	289	89
Investing Activities:			
Purchases of short-term investments	(3,270)	(2,648)	(4,144)
Proceeds from maturities of short-term investments	1,141	2,446	2,846
Proceeds from sales of short-term investments	801	1,116	1,254
Proceeds from sales of non-current investments	5	45	25
Purchases of property, plant, and equipment	(176)	(164)	(174)
Cash used for business acquisitions	—	—	(52)
Other	11	33	(7)
Cash generated by (used for) investing activities	(1,488)	828	(252)
Financing Activities:			
Payment of long-term debt	(300)	—	—
Proceeds from issuance of common stock	427	53	105
Cash used for repurchase of common stock	—	(26)	—
Cash generated by financing activities	127	27	105
Increase (decrease) in cash and cash equivalents	(427)	1,144	(58)
Cash and cash equivalents, end of the year	$ 2,969	$ 3,396	$ 2,252
Supplemental cash flow disclosures:			
Cash paid during the year for interest	$ 10	$ 20	$ 20
Cash paid (received) for income taxes, net	$ (7)	$ 45	$ 11

See accompanying notes to consolidated financial statements.

B Time Value of Money

Learning Objectives

CAP

Conceptual

C1 Describe the earning of interest and the concepts of present and future values. *(p. B-2)*

Procedural

P1 Apply present value concepts to a single amount by using interest tables. *(p. B-3)*

P2 Apply future value concepts to a single amount by using interest tables. *(p. B-5)*

P3 Apply present value concepts to an annuity by using interest tables. *(p. B-6)*

P4 Apply future value concepts to an annuity by using interest tables. *(p. B-7)*

The concepts of present and future values are important to modern business activity. The purpose of this appendix is to explain, illustrate, and compute present and future values. This appendix applies these concepts with reference to both business and everyday activities.

Present and Future Value Concepts

C1 Describe the earning of interest and the concepts of present and future values.

The old saying "Time is money" reflects the notion that as time passes, the values of our assets and liabilities change. This change is due to *interest,* which is a borrower's payment to the owner of an asset for its use. The most common example of interest is a savings account asset. As we keep a balance of cash in the account, it earns interest that the financial institution pays us. An example of a liability is a car loan. As we carry the balance of the loan, we accumulate interest costs on it. We must ultimately repay this loan with interest.

Present and future value computations enable us to measure or estimate the interest component of holding assets or liabilities over time. The present value computation is important when we want to know the value of future-day assets *today.* The future value computation is important when we want to know the value of present-day assets *at a future date.* The first section focuses on the present value of a single amount. The second section focuses on the future value of a single amount. Then both the present and future values of a series of amounts (called an *annuity*) are defined and explained.

Present Value of a Single Amount

We graphically express the present value, called p, of a single future amount, called f, that is received or paid at a future date in Exhibit B.1.

Exhibit B.1

Present Value of a Single Amount Diagram

The formula to compute the present value of a single amount is shown in Exhibit B.2, where p = present value; f = future value; i = rate of interest per period; and n = number of periods. (Interest is also called the *discount,* and an interest rate is also called the *discount rate.*)

Exhibit B.2

Present Value of a Single Amount Formula

$$p = \frac{f}{(1 + i)^n}$$

To illustrate present value concepts, assume that we need $220 one period from today. We want to know how much we must invest now, for one period, at an interest rate of 10% to provide for this $220. For this illustration, the p, or present value, is the unknown amount—the specifics are shown graphically as follows:

$(i = 0.10)$ $f = \$220$

$p = ?$

Conceptually, we know p must be less than $220. This is obvious from the answer to this question: Would we rather have $220 today or $220 at some future date? If we had $220 today, we could invest it and see it grow to something more than $220 in the future. Therefore, we would prefer the $220 today. This means that if we were promised $220 in the future, we would take less than $220 today. But how much less? To answer that question, we compute an estimate of the present value of the $220 to be received one period from now using the formula in Exhibit B.2 as follows:

$$p = \frac{f}{(1 + i)^n} = \frac{\$220}{(1 + 0.10)^1} = \$200$$

We interpret this result to say that given an interest rate of 10%, we are indifferent between $200 today or $220 at the end of one period.

We can also use this formula to compute the present value for *any number of periods*. To illustrate, consider a payment of $242 at the end of two periods at 10% interest. The present value of this $242 to be received two periods from now is computed as follows:

$$p = \frac{f}{(1 + i)^n} = \frac{\$242}{(1 + 0.10)^2} = \$200$$

Together, these results tell us we are indifferent between $200 today, or $220 one period from today, or $242 two periods from today given a 10% interest rate per period.

The number of periods (n) in the present value formula does not have to be expressed in years. Any period of time such as a day, a month, a quarter, or a year can be used. Whatever period is used, the interest rate (i) must be compounded for the same period. This means that if a situation expresses n in months and i equals 12% per year, then i is transformed into interest earned per month (or 1%). In this case, interest is said to be *compounded monthly*.

A present value table helps us with present value computations. It gives us present values (factors) for a variety of both interest rates (i) and periods (n). Each present value in a present value table assumes that the future value (f) equals 1. When the future value (f) is different from 1, we simply multiply the present value (p) from the table by that future value to give us the estimate. The formula used to construct a table of present values for a single future amount of 1 is shown in Exhibit B.3.

> I will pay your allowance at the end of the month. Do you want to wait or receive its present value today?

$$p = \frac{1}{(1 + i)^n}$$

Exhibit B.3

Present Value of 1 Formula

This formula is identical to that in Exhibit B.2 except that f equals 1. Table B.1 at the end of this appendix is such a present value table. It is often called a **present value of 1 table**. A present value table involves three factors: p, i, and n. Knowing two of these three factors allows us to compute the third. (A fourth is f, but as already explained, we need only multiply the 1 used in the formula by f.) To illustrate the use of a present value table, consider three cases.

P1   Apply present value concepts to a single amount by using interest tables.

Case 1 (solve for *p* when knowing *i* and *n*). To show how we use a present value table, let's look again at how we estimate the present value of $220 (the *f* value) at the end of one period (*n* = 1) where the interest rate (*i*) is 10%. To solve this case, we go to the present value table (Table B.1) and look in the row for 1 period and in the column for 10% interest. Here we find a present value (*p*) of 0.9091 based on a future value of 1. This means, for instance, that $1 to be received one period from today at 10% interest is worth $0.9091 today. Since the future value in this case is not $1 but $220, we multiply the 0.9091 by $220 to get an answer of $200.

    Case 2 (solve for *n* when knowing *p* and *i*). To illustrate, assume a $100,000 future value (*f*) that is worth $13,000 today (*p*) using an interest rate of 12% (*i*) but where *n* is unknown. In particular, we want to know how many periods (*n*) there are between the present value and the future value. To put this in context, it would fit a situation in which we want to retire with $100,000 but currently have only $13,000 that is earning a 12% return. How long will it be before we can retire? To answer this, we go to Table B.1 and look in the 12% interest column. Here we find a column of present values (*p*) based on a future value of 1. To use the present value table for this solution, we must divide $13,000 (*p*) by $100,000 (*f*), which equals 0.1300. This is necessary because *a present value table defines* f *equal to 1, and* p *as a fraction of 1.* We look for a value nearest to 0.1300 (*p*), which we find in the row for 18 periods (*n*). This means that the present value of $100,000 at the end of 18 periods at 12% interest is $13,000 or, alternatively stated, we must work 18 more years.

    Case 3 (solve for *i* when knowing *p* and *n*). In this case, we have, say, a $120,000 future value (*f*) worth $60,000 today (*p*) when there are nine periods (*n*) between the present and future values, but the interest rate is unknown. As an example, suppose we want to retire with $120,000, but we have only $60,000 and hope to retire in nine years. What interest rate must we earn to retire with $120,000 in nine years? To answer this, we go to the present value table (Table B.1) and look in the row for nine periods. To use the present value table, we must divide $60,000 (*p*) by $120,000 (*f*), which equals 0.5000. Recall that this step is necessary because a present value table defines *f* equal to 1 and *p* as a fraction of 1. We look for a value in the row for nine periods that is nearest to 0.5000 (*p*), which we find in the column for 8% interest (*i*). This means that the present value of $120,000 at the end of nine periods at 8% interest is $60,000 or, in our example, we must earn 8% annual interest to retire in nine years.

Quick Check   Answer—p. B-8

  1. A company is considering an investment expected to yield $70,000 after six years. If this company demands an 8% return, how much is it willing to pay for this investment?

Future Value of a Single Amount

Exhibit B.4

Future Value of a Single Amount Formula

We must modify the formula for the present value of a single amount to obtain the formula for the future value of a single amount. In particular, we multiply both sides of the equation in Exhibit B.2 by $(1 + i)^n$ to get the result shown in Exhibit B.4.

$$f = p \times (1 + i)^n$$

    The future value (*f*) is defined in terms of *p*, *i*, and *n*. We can use this formula to determine that $200 (*p*) invested for 1 (*n*) period at an interest rate of 10% (*i*) yields a future value of

$220 as follows:

$$f = p \times (1 + i)^n$$
$$= \$200 \times (1 + 0.10)^1$$
$$= \$220$$

This formula can also be used to compute the future value of an amount for *any number of periods* into the future. To illustrate, assume that $200 is invested for three periods at 10%. The future value of this $200 is $266.20, computed as follows:

$$f = p \times (1 + i)^n$$
$$= \$200 \times (1 + 0.10)^3$$
$$= \$266.20$$

A future value table makes it easier for us to compute future values (f) for many different combinations of interest rates (i) and time periods (n). Each future value in a future value table assumes the present value (p) is 1. As with a present value table, if the future amount is something other than 1, we simply multiply our answer by that amount. The formula used to construct a table of future values (factors) for a single amount of 1 is in Exhibit B.5.

P2   Apply future value concepts to a single amount by using interest tables.

$$f = (1 + i)^n$$

Exhibit B.5

Future Value of 1 Formula

Table B.2 at the end of this appendix shows a table of future values for a current amount of 1. This type of table is called a **future value of 1 table**.

There are some important relations between Tables B.1 and B.2. In Table B.2, for the row where $n = 0$, the future value is 1 for each interest rate. This is so because no interest is earned when time does not pass. Also notice that Tables B.1 and B.2 report the same information but in a different manner. In particular, one table is simply the *inverse* of the other. To illustrate this inverse relation, let's say we invest $100 annually for a period of five years at 12% per year. How much do we expect to have after five years? We can answer this question using Table B.2 by finding the future value (f) of 1, for five periods from now, compounded at 12%. From that table we find $f = 1.7623$. If we start with $100, the amount it accumulates to after five years is $176.23 ($100 \times 1.7623$). We can alternatively use Table B.1. Here we find that the present value (p) of 1, discounted five periods at 12%, is 0.5674. Recall the inverse relation between present value and future value. This means that $p = 1/f$ (or equivalently, $f = 1/p$). We can compute the future value of $100 invested for five periods at 12% as follows: $f = \$100 \times (1/0.5674) = \$176.24$.

A future value table involves three factors: f, i, and n. Knowing two of these three factors allows us to compute the third. To illustrate, consider these three possible cases.

Case 1 (solve for f when knowing i and n). Our preceding example fits this case. We found that $100 invested for five periods at 12% interest accumulates to $176.24.

Case 2 (solve for n when knowing f and i). In this case, we have, say, $2,000 ($p$) and we want to know how many periods (n) it will take to accumulate to $3,000 ($f$) at 7% ($i$) interest. To answer this, we go to the future value table (Table B.2) and look in the 7% interest column. Here we find a column of future values (f) based on a present value of 1. To use a future value table, we must divide $3,000 ($f$) by $2,000 ($p$), which equals 1.500. This is necessary because *a future value table defines* p *equal to 1, and* f *as a multiple of 1*. We look for a value nearest to 1.50 (f), which we find in the row for six periods (n). This means that $2,000 invested for six periods at 7% interest accumulates to $3,000.

Case 3 (solve for i when knowing f and n). In this case, we have, say, $2,001 ($p$) and in nine years ($n$), we want to have $4,000 ($f$). What rate of interest must we earn to accomplish this? To answer that, we go to Table B.2 and search in the row for nine periods. To use a future value table, we must divide $4,000 ($f$) by $2,001 ($p$), which equals 1.9990. Recall that this is necessary because a future value table defines p equal to 1 and f as a multiple of 1. We look for a value nearest to 1.9990 (f), which we find in the column for 8% interest (i). This means that $2,001 invested for nine periods at 8% interest accumulates to $4,000.

Answer—p. B-8

Quick Check

2. Assume that you win a $150,000 cash sweepstakes. You decide to deposit this cash in an account earning 8% annual interest, and you plan to quit your job when the account equals $555,000. How many years will it be before you can quit working?

Present Value of an Annuity

An *annuity* is a series of equal payments occurring at equal intervals. One example is a series of three annual payments of $100 each. An *ordinary annuity* is defined as equal end-of-period payments at equal intervals. An ordinary annuity of $100 for 3 periods and its present value (p) are illustrated in Exhibit B.6.

Exhibit B.6

Present Value of an Ordinary Annuity Diagram

P3 Apply present value concepts to an annuity by using interest tables.

One way to compute the present value of an ordinary annuity is to find the present value of each payment using our present value formula from Exhibit B.3. We then add each of the three present values. To illustrate, let's look at three $100 payments at the end of each of the next three periods with an interest rate of 15%. Our present value computations are

$$p = \frac{\$100}{(1 + 0.15)^1} + \frac{\$100}{(1 + 0.15)^2} + \frac{\$100}{(1 + 0.15)^3} = \$228.32$$

This computation is identical to computing the present value of each payment (from Table B.1) and taking their sum or, alternatively, adding the values from Table B.1 for each of the three payments and multiplying their sum by the $100 annuity payment.

A more direct way is to use a present value of annuity table. Table B.3 at the end of this appendix is one such table. This table is called a **present value of an annuity of 1 table**. If we look at Table B.3 where $n = 3$ and $i = 15\%$, we see the present value is 2.2832. This means that the present value of an annuity of 1 for three periods, with a 15% interest rate, equals 2.2832.

Decision Insight

Aw-Shucks "I don't have good luck—I'm blessed," proclaimed Andrew "Jack" Whittaker, 55, a sewage treatment contractor, after winning the largest-ever, undivided jackpot in a U.S. lottery. Whittaker had to choose between $315 million in 30 annual installments or $170 million in one lump sum ($112 million after-tax). Says Whittaker, "My biggest problem is to keep my daughter and granddaughter from spending all their money in one week."

A present value of an annuity formula is used to construct Table B.3. It can also be constructed by adding the amounts in a present value of 1 table. To illustrate, we use Tables B.1 and B.3 to confirm this relation for the prior example:

From Table B.1		From Table B.3	
$i = 15\%, n = 1$	0.8696		
$i = 15\%, n = 2$	0.7561		
$i = 15\%, n = 3$	0.6575		
Total	2.2832	$i = 15\%, n = 3$	2.2832

We can also use business calculators or spreadsheet programs to find the present value of an annuity.

3. A company is considering an investment paying $10,000 every six months for three years. The first payment would be received in six months. If this company requires an 8% annual return, what is the maximum amount it is willing to pay for this investment?

Future Value of an Annuity

The future value of an *ordinary annuity* is the accumulated value of each annuity payment with interest as of the date of the final payment. To illustrate, let's consider the earlier annuity of three annual payments of $100. Exhibit B.7 shows the point in time for the future value (f). The first payment is made two periods prior to the point when future value is determined, and the final payment occurs on the future value date.

Exhibit B.7

Future Value of an Ordinary Annuity Diagram

One way to compute the future value of an annuity is to use the formula to find the future value of *each* payment and add them. If we assume an interest rate of 15%, our calculation is

$$f = \$100 \times (1 + 0.15)^2 + \$100 \times (1 + 0.15)^1 + \$100 \times (1 + 0.15)^0 = \$347.25$$

This is identical to using Table B.2 and summing the future values of each payment, or by adding the future values of the three payments of 1 and multiplying the sum by $100.

A more direct way is to use a table showing future values of annuities. Such a table is called a **future value of an annuity of 1 table**. Table B.4 at the end of this appendix is one such table. Note that in Table B.4 when $n = 1$, the future values equal 1 ($f = 1$) for all rates of interest. This is so because such an annuity consists of only one payment and the future value is determined on the date of that payment—no time passes between the payment and its future value. The future value of an annuity formula is used to construct Table B.4. We can also construct it by adding the amounts from a future value of 1 table. To illustrate, we use Tables B.2 and B.4 to confirm this relation for the prior example:

P4   Apply future value concepts to an annuity by using interest tables.

From Table B.2		From Table B.4	
$i = 15\%, n = 0$	1.0000		
$i = 15\%, n = 1$	1.1500		
$i = 15\%, n = 2$	1.3225		
Total	3.4725	$i = 15\%, n = 3$	3.4725

Note that the future value in Table B.2 is 1.0000 when $n = 0$, but the future value in Table B.4 is 1.0000 when $n = 1$. Is this a contradiction? No. When $n = 0$ in Table B.2, the future value is determined on the date when a single payment occurs. This means that no interest is earned because no time has passed, and the future value equals the payment. Table B.4 describes annuities with equal payments occurring at the end of each period. When $n = 1$, the annuity has one payment, and its future value equals 1 on the date of its final and only payment. Again, no time passes between the payment and its future value date.

Quick Check
Answer—p. B-8

4. A company invests $45,000 per year for five years at 12% annual interest. Compute the value of this annuity investment at the end of five years.

Summary

C1 **Describe the earning of interest and the concepts of present and future values.** Interest is payment by a borrower to the owner of an asset for its use. Present and future value computations are a way for us to estimate the interest component of holding assets or liabilities over a period of time.

P1 **Apply present value concepts to a single amount by using interest tables.** The present value of a single amount received at a future date is the amount that can be invested now at the specified interest rate to yield that future value.

P2 **Apply future value concepts to a single amount by using interest tables.** The future value of a single amount

invested at a specified rate of interest is the amount that would accumulate by the future date.

P3 **Apply present value concepts to an annuity by using interest tables.** The present value of an annuity is the amount that can be invested now at the specified interest rate to yield that series of equal periodic payments.

P4 **Apply future value concepts to an annuity by using interest tables.** The future value of an annuity invested at a specific rate of interest is the amount that would accumulate by the date of the final payment.

Guidance Answers to Quick Checks

1. $70,000 × 0.6302 = $44,114 (use Table B.1, $i = 8\%$, $n = 6$).

2. $555,000/$150,000 = 3.7000; Table B.2 shows this value is not achieved until after 17 years at 8% interest.

3. $10,000 × 5.2421 = $52,421 (use Table B.3, $i = 4\%$, $n = 6$).

4. $45,000 × 6.3528 = $285,876   (use   Table   B.4, $i = 12\%$, $n = 5$).

QUICK STUDY

QS B-1
Identifying interest
rates in tables
C1

Assume that you must make future value estimates using the *future value of 1 table* (Table B.2). Which interest rate column do you use when working with the following rates?

1. 8% compounded quarterly
2. 12% compounded annually
3. 6% compounded semiannually
4. 12% compounded monthly

QS B-2
Interest rate
on an investment   P1

Ken Francis is offered the possibility of investing $2,745 today and in return to receive $10,000 after 15 years. What is the annual rate of interest for this investment? (Use Table B.1.)

QS B-3
Number of periods
of an investment   P1

Megan Brink is offered the possibility of investing $6,651 today at 6% interest per year in a desire to accumulate $10,000. How many years must Brink wait to accumulate $10,000? (Use Table B.1.)

QS B-4
Present value
of an amount   P1

Flaherty is considering an investment that, if paid for immediately, is expected to return $140,000 five years from now. If Flaherty demands a 9% return, how much is she willing to pay for this investment?

CII, Inc., invests $630,000 in a project expected to earn a 12% annual rate of return. The earnings will be reinvested in the project each year until the entire investment is liquidated 10 years later. What will the cash proceeds be when the project is liquidated?

QS B-5
Future value
of an amount   P2

Beene Distributing is considering a project that will return $150,000 annually at the end of each year for six years. If Beene demands an annual return of 7% and pays for the project immediately, how much is it willing to pay for the project?

QS B-6
Present value
of an annuity   P3

Claire Fitch is planning to begin an individual retirement program in which she will invest $1,500 at the end of each year. Fitch plans to retire after making 30 annual investments in the program earning a return of 10%. What is the value of the program on the date of the last payment?

QS B-7
Future value
of an annuity   P4

Bill Thompson expects to invest $10,000 at 12% and, at the end of a certain period, receive $96,463. How many years will it be before Thompson receives the payment? (Use Table B.2.)

EXERCISES

Exercise B-1
Number of periods
of an investment   P2

Ed Summers expects to invest $10,000 for 25 years, after which he wants to receive $108,347. What rate of interest must Summers earn? (Use Table B.2.)

Exercise B-2
Interest rate on
an investment   P2

Jones expects an immediate investment of $57,466 to return $10,000 annually for eight years, with the first payment to be received one year from now. What rate of interest must Jones earn? (Use Table B.3.)

Exercise B-3
Interest rate on
an investment   P3

Keith Riggins expects an investment of $82,014 to return $10,000 annually for several years. If Riggins earns a return of 10%, how many annual payments will he receive? (Use Table B.3.)

Exercise B-4
Number of periods
of an investment   P3

Algoe expects to invest $1,000 annually for 40 years to yield an accumulated value of $154,762 on the date of the last investment. For this to occur, what rate of interest must Algoe earn? (Use Table B.4.)

Exercise B-5
Interest rate on
an investment   P4

Kate Beckwith expects to invest $10,000 annually that will earn 8%. How many annual investments must Beckwith make to accumulate $303,243 on the date of the last investment? (Use Table B.4.)

Exercise B-6
Number of periods
of an investment   P4

Sam Weber finances a new automobile by paying $6,500 cash and agreeing to make 40 monthly payments of $500 each, the first payment to be made one month after the purchase. The loan bears interest at an annual rate of 12%. What is the cost of the automobile?

Exercise B-7
Present value
of an annuity   P3

Spiller Corp. plans to issue 10%, 15-year, $500,000 par value bonds payable that pay interest semiannually on June 30 and December 31. The bonds are dated December 31, 2008, and are issued on that date. If the market rate of interest for the bonds is 8% on the date of issue, what will be the total cash proceeds from the bond issue?

Exercise B-8
Present value of bonds
P1   P3

McAdams Company expects to earn 10% per year on an investment that will pay $606,773 six years from now. Use Table B.1 to compute the present value of this investment.

Exercise B-9
Present value
of an amount   P1

Exercise B-10
Present value of
an amount and
of an annuity   P1   P3

Compute the amount that can be borrowed under each of the following circumstances:

1. A promise to repay $90,000 seven years from now at an interest rate of 6%.

2. An agreement made on February 1, 2008, to make three separate payments of $20,000 on February 1 of 2009, 2010, and 2011. The annual interest rate is 10%.

Exercise B-11
Present value
of an amount   P1

On January 1, 2008, a company agrees to pay $20,000 in three years. If the annual interest rate is 10%, determine how much cash the company can borrow with this agreement.

Exercise B-12
Present value
of an amount   P1

Find the amount of money that can be borrowed today with each of the following separate debt agreements *a* through *f*:

Case	Single Future Payment	Number of Periods	Interest Rate
a.	$40,000	3	4%
b.	75,000	7	8
c.	52,000	9	10
d.	18,000	2	4
e.	63,000	8	6
f.	89,000	5	2

Exercise B-13
Present values of annuities

P3

C&H Ski Club recently borrowed money and agrees to pay it back with a series of six annual payments of $5,000 each. C&H subsequently borrows more money and agrees to pay it back with a series of four annual payments of $7,500 each. The annual interest rate for both loans is 6%.

1. Use Table B.1 to find the present value of these two separate annuities. (Round amounts to the nearest dollar.)

2. Use Table B.3 to find the present value of these two separate annuities.

Exercise B-14
Present value with semiannual
compounding

C1   P3

Otto Co. borrows money on April 30, 2008, by promising to make four payments of $13,000 each on November 1, 2008; May 1, 2009; November 1, 2009; and May 1, 2010.

1. How much money is Otto able to borrow if the interest rate is 8%, compounded semiannually?

2. How much money is Otto able to borrow if the interest rate is 12%, compounded semiannually?

3. How much money is Otto able to borrow if the interest rate is 16%, compounded semiannually?

Exercise B-15
Future value
of an amount   P2

Mark Welsch deposits $7,200 in an account that earns interest at an annual rate of 8%, compounded quarterly. The $7,200 plus earned interest must remain in the account 10 years before it can be withdrawn. How much money will be in the account at the end of 10 years?

Exercise B-16
Future value
of an annuity   P4

Kelly Malone plans to have $50 withheld from her monthly paycheck and deposited in a savings account that earns 12% annually, compounded monthly. If Malone continues with her plan for two and one-half years, how much will be accumulated in the account on the date of the last deposit?

Exercise B-17
Future value of
an amount plus
an annuity   P2   P4

Starr Company decides to establish a fund that it will use 10 years from now to replace an aging production facility. The company will make a $100,000 initial contribution to the fund and plans to make quarterly contributions of $50,000 beginning in three months. The fund earns 12%, compounded quarterly. What will be the value of the fund 10 years from now?

Exercise B-18
Future value of
an amount   P2

Catten, Inc., invests $163,170 today earning 7% per year for nine years. Use Table B.2 to compute the future value of the investment nine years from now.

For each of the following situations, identify (1) the case as either (*a*) a present or a future value and (*b*) a single amount or an annuity, (2) the table you would use in your computations (but do not solve the problem), and (3) the interest rate and time periods you would use.

a. You need to accumulate $10,000 for a trip you wish to take in four years. You are able to earn 8% compounded semiannually on your savings. You plan to make only one deposit and let the money accumulate for four years. How would you determine the amount of the one-time deposit?

b. Assume the same facts as in part (*a*) except that you will make semiannual deposits to your savings account.

c. You want to retire after working 40 years with savings in excess of $1,000,000. You expect to save $4,000 a year for 40 years and earn an annual rate of interest of 8%. Will you be able to retire with more than $1,000,000 in 40 years? Explain.

d. A sweepstakes agency names you a grand prize winner. You can take $225,000 immediately or elect to receive annual installments of $30,000 for 20 years. You can earn 10% annually on any investments you make. Which prize do you choose to receive?

Exercise B-19
Using present and future value tables

C1 P1 P2 P3 P4

Table B.1

Present Value of 1

$$p = 1/(1 + i)^n$$

						Rate						
Periods	1%	2%	3%	4%	5%	6%	7%	8%	9%	10%	12%	15%
1	0.9901	0.9804	0.9709	0.9615	0.9524	0.9434	0.9346	0.9259	0.9174	0.9091	0.8929	0.8696
2	0.9803	0.9612	0.9426	0.9246	0.9070	0.8900	0.8734	0.8573	0.8417	0.8264	0.7972	0.7561
3	0.9706	0.9423	0.9151	0.8890	0.8638	0.8396	0.8163	0.7938	0.7722	0.7513	0.7118	0.6575
4	0.9610	0.9238	0.8885	0.8548	0.8227	0.7921	0.7629	0.7350	0.7084	0.6830	0.6355	0.5718
5	0.9515	0.9057	0.8626	0.8219	0.7835	0.7473	0.7130	0.6806	0.6499	0.6209	0.5674	0.4972
6	0.9420	0.8880	0.8375	0.7903	0.7462	0.7050	0.6663	0.6302	0.5963	0.5645	0.5066	0.4323
7	0.9327	0.8706	0.8131	0.7599	0.7107	0.6651	0.6227	0.5835	0.5470	0.5132	0.4523	0.3759
8	0.9235	0.8535	0.7894	0.7307	0.6768	0.6274	0.5820	0.5403	0.5019	0.4665	0.4039	0.3269
9	0.9143	0.8368	0.7664	0.7026	0.6446	0.5919	0.5439	0.5002	0.4604	0.4241	0.3606	0.2843
10	0.9053	0.8203	0.7441	0.6756	0.6139	0.5584	0.5083	0.4632	0.4224	0.3855	0.3220	0.2472
11	0.8963	0.8043	0.7224	0.6496	0.5847	0.5268	0.4751	0.4289	0.3875	0.3505	0.2875	0.2149
12	0.8874	0.7885	0.7014	0.6246	0.5568	0.4970	0.4440	0.3971	0.3555	0.3186	0.2567	0.1869
13	0.8787	0.7730	0.6810	0.6006	0.5303	0.4688	0.4150	0.3677	0.3262	0.2897	0.2292	0.1625
14	0.8700	0.7579	0.6611	0.5775	0.5051	0.4423	0.3878	0.3405	0.2992	0.2633	0.2046	0.1413
15	0.8613	0.7430	0.6419	0.5553	0.4810	0.4173	0.3624	0.3152	0.2745	0.2394	0.1827	0.1229
16	0.8528	0.7284	0.6232	0.5339	0.4581	0.3936	0.3387	0.2919	0.2519	0.2176	0.1631	0.1069
17	0.8444	0.7142	0.6050	0.5134	0.4363	0.3714	0.3166	0.2703	0.2311	0.1978	0.1456	0.0929
18	0.8360	0.7002	0.5874	0.4936	0.4155	0.3503	0.2959	0.2502	0.2120	0.1799	0.1300	0.0808
19	0.8277	0.6864	0.5703	0.4746	0.3957	0.3305	0.2765	0.2317	0.1945	0.1635	0.1161	0.0703
20	0.8195	0.6730	0.5537	0.4564	0.3769	0.3118	0.2584	0.2145	0.1784	0.1486	0.1037	0.0611
25	0.7798	0.6095	0.4776	0.3751	0.2953	0.2330	0.1842	0.1460	0.1160	0.0923	0.0588	0.0304
30	0.7419	0.5521	0.4120	0.3083	0.2314	0.1741	0.1314	0.0994	0.0754	0.0573	0.0334	0.0151
35	0.7059	0.5000	0.3554	0.2534	0.1813	0.1301	0.0937	0.0676	0.0490	0.0356	0.0189	0.0075
40	0.6717	0.4529	0.3066	0.2083	0.1420	0.0972	0.0668	0.0460	0.0318	0.0221	0.0107	0.0037

Table B.2

Future Value of 1

$$f = (1 + i)^n$$

						Rate						
Periods	1%	2%	3%	4%	5%	6%	7%	8%	9%	10%	12%	15%
0	1.0000	1.0000	1.0000	1.0000	1.0000	1.0000	1.0000	1.0000	1.0000	1.0000	1.0000	1.0000
1	1.0100	1.0200	1.0300	1.0400	1.0500	1.0600	1.0700	1.0800	1.0900	1.1000	1.1200	1.1500
2	1.0201	1.0404	1.0609	1.0816	1.1025	1.1236	1.1449	1.1664	1.1881	1.2100	1.2544	1.3225
3	1.0303	1.0612	1.0927	1.1249	1.1576	1.1910	1.2250	1.2597	1.2950	1.3310	1.4049	1.5209
4	1.0406	1.0824	1.1255	1.1699	1.2155	1.2625	1.3108	1.3605	1.4116	1.4641	1.5735	1.7490
5	1.0510	1.1041	1.1593	1.2167	1.2763	1.3382	1.4026	1.4693	1.5386	1.6105	1.7623	2.0114
6	1.0615	1.1262	1.1941	1.2653	1.3401	1.4185	1.5007	1.5869	1.6771	1.7716	1.9738	2.3131
7	1.0721	1.1487	1.2299	1.3159	1.4071	1.5036	1.6058	1.7138	1.8280	1.9487	2.2107	2.6600
8	1.0829	1.1717	1.2668	1.3686	1.4775	1.5938	1.7182	1.8509	1.9926	2.1436	2.4760	3.0590
9	1.0937	1.1951	1.3048	1.4233	1.5513	1.6895	1.8385	1.9990	2.1719	2.3579	2.7731	3.5179
10	1.1046	1.2190	1.3439	1.4802	1.6289	1.7908	1.9672	2.1589	2.3674	2.5937	3.1058	4.0456
11	1.1157	1.2434	1.3842	1.5395	1.7103	1.8983	2.1049	2.3316	2.5804	2.8531	3.4785	4.6524
12	1.1268	1.2682	1.4258	1.6010	1.7959	2.0122	2.2522	2.5182	2.8127	3.1384	3.8960	5.3503
13	1.1381	1.2936	1.4685	1.6651	1.8856	2.1329	2.4098	2.7196	3.0658	3.4523	4.3635	6.1528
14	1.1495	1.3195	1.5126	1.7317	1.9799	2.2609	2.5785	2.9372	3.3417	3.7975	4.8871	7.0757
15	1.1610	1.3459	1.5580	1.8009	2.0789	2.3966	2.7590	3.1722	3.6425	4.1772	5.4736	8.1371
16	1.1726	1.3728	1.6047	1.8730	2.1829	2.5404	2.9522	3.4259	3.9703	4.5950	6.1304	9.3576
17	1.1843	1.4002	1.6528	1.9479	2.2920	2.6928	3.1588	3.7000	4.3276	5.0545	6.8660	10.7613
18	1.1961	1.4282	1.7024	2.0258	2.4066	2.8543	3.3799	3.9960	4.7171	5.5599	7.6900	12.3755
19	1.2081	1.4568	1.7535	2.1068	2.5270	3.0256	3.6165	4.3157	5.1417	6.1159	8.6128	14.2318
20	1.2202	1.4859	1.8061	2.1911	2.6533	3.2071	3.8697	4.6610	5.6044	6.7275	9.6463	16.3665
25	1.2824	1.6406	2.0938	2.6658	3.3864	4.2919	5.4274	6.8485	8.6231	10.8347	17.0001	32.9190
30	1.3478	1.8114	2.4273	3.2434	4.3219	5.7435	7.6123	10.0627	13.2677	17.4494	29.9599	66.2118
35	1.4166	1.9999	2.8139	3.9461	5.5160	7.6861	10.6766	14.7853	20.4140	28.1024	52.7996	133.1755
40	1.4889	2.2080	3.2620	4.8010	7.0400	10.2857	14.9745	21.7245	31.4094	45.2593	93.0510	267.8635

$$p = \left[1 - \frac{1}{(1 + i)^n}\right]/i$$

Table B.3

Present Value of an Annuity of 1

						Rate						
Periods	**1%**	**2%**	**3%**	**4%**	**5%**	**6%**	**7%**	**8%**	**9%**	**10%**	**12%**	**15%**
1	0.9901	0.9804	0.9709	0.9615	0.9524	0.9434	0.9346	0.9259	0.9174	0.9091	0.8929	0.8696
2	1.9704	1.9416	1.9135	1.8861	1.8594	1.8334	1.8080	1.7833	1.7591	1.7355	1.6901	1.6257
3	2.9410	2.8839	2.8286	2.7751	2.7232	2.6730	2.6243	2.5771	2.5313	2.4869	2.4018	2.2832
4	3.9020	3.8077	3.7171	3.6299	3.5460	3.4651	3.3872	3.3121	3.2397	3.1699	3.0373	2.8550
5	4.8534	4.7135	4.5797	4.4518	4.3295	4.2124	4.1002	3.9927	3.8897	3.7908	3.6048	3.3522
6	5.7955	5.6014	5.4172	5.2421	5.0757	4.9173	4.7665	4.6229	4.4859	4.3553	4.1114	3.7845
7	6.7282	6.4720	6.2303	6.0021	5.7864	5.5824	5.3893	5.2064	5.0330	4.8684	4.5638	4.1604
8	7.6517	7.3255	7.0197	6.7327	6.4632	6.2098	5.9713	5.7466	5.5348	5.3349	4.9676	4.4873
9	8.5660	8.1622	7.7861	7.4353	7.1078	6.8017	6.5152	6.2469	5.9952	5.7590	5.3282	4.7716
10	9.4713	8.9826	8.5302	8.1109	7.7217	7.3601	7.0236	6.7101	6.4177	6.1446	5.6502	5.0188
11	10.3676	9.7868	9.2526	8.7605	8.3064	7.8869	7.4987	7.1390	6.8052	6.4951	5.9377	5.2337
12	11.2551	10.5753	9.9540	9.3851	8.8633	8.3838	7.9427	7.5361	7.1607	6.8137	6.1944	5.4206
13	12.1337	11.3484	10.6350	9.9856	9.3936	8.8527	8.3577	7.9038	7.4869	7.1034	6.4235	5.5831
14	13.0037	12.1062	11.2961	10.5631	9.8986	9.2950	8.7455	8.2442	7.7862	7.3667	6.6282	5.7245
15	13.8651	12.8493	11.9379	11.1184	10.3797	9.7122	9.1079	8.5595	8.0607	7.6061	6.8109	5.8474
16	14.7179	13.5777	12.5611	11.6523	10.8378	10.1059	9.4466	8.8514	8.3126	7.8237	6.9740	5.9542
17	15.5623	14.2919	13.1661	12.1657	11.2741	10.4773	9.7632	9.1216	8.5436	8.0216	7.1196	6.0472
18	16.3983	14.9920	13.7535	12.6593	11.6896	10.8276	10.0591	9.3719	8.7556	8.2014	7.2497	6.1280
19	17.2260	15.6785	14.3238	13.1339	12.0853	11.1581	10.3356	9.6036	8.9501	8.3649	7.3658	6.1982
20	18.0456	16.3514	14.8775	13.5903	12.4622	11.4699	10.5940	9.8181	9.1285	8.5136	7.4694	6.2593
25	22.0232	19.5235	17.4131	15.6221	14.0939	12.7834	11.6536	10.6748	9.8226	9.0770	7.8431	6.4641
30	25.8077	22.3965	19.6004	17.2920	15.3725	13.7648	12.4090	11.2578	10.2737	9.4269	8.0552	6.5660
35	29.4086	24.9986	21.4872	18.6646	16.3742	14.4982	12.9477	11.6546	10.5668	9.6442	8.1755	6.6166
40	32.8347	27.3555	23.1148	19.7928	17.1591	15.0463	13.3317	11.9246	10.7574	9.7791	8.2438	6.6418

$$f = [(1 + i)^n - 1]/i$$

Table B.4

Future Value of an Annuity of 1

						Rate						
Periods	**1%**	**2%**	**3%**	**4%**	**5%**	**6%**	**7%**	**8%**	**9%**	**10%**	**12%**	**15%**
1	1.0000	1.0000	1.0000	1.0000	1.0000	1.0000	1.0000	1.0000	1.0000	1.0000	1.0000	1.0000
2	2.0100	2.0200	2.0300	2.0400	2.0500	2.0600	2.0700	2.0800	2.0900	2.1000	2.1200	2.1500
3	3.0301	3.0604	3.0909	3.1216	3.1525	3.1836	3.2149	3.2464	3.2781	3.3100	3.3744	3.4725
4	4.0604	4.1216	4.1836	4.2465	4.3101	4.3746	4.4399	4.5061	4.5731	4.6410	4.7793	4.9934
5	5.1010	5.2040	5.3091	5.4163	5.5256	5.6371	5.7507	5.8666	5.9847	6.1051	6.3528	6.7424
6	6.1520	6.3081	6.4684	6.6330	6.8019	6.9753	7.1533	7.3359	7.5233	7.7156	8.1152	8.7537
7	7.2135	7.4343	7.6625	7.8983	8.1420	8.3938	8.6540	8.9228	9.2004	9.4872	10.0890	11.0668
8	8.2857	8.5830	8.8923	9.2142	9.5491	9.8975	10.2598	10.6366	11.0285	11.4359	12.2997	13.7268
9	9.3685	9.7546	10.1591	10.5828	11.0266	11.4913	11.9780	12.4876	13.0210	13.5795	14.7757	16.7858
10	10.4622	10.9497	11.4639	12.0061	12.5779	13.1808	13.8164	14.4866	15.1929	15.9374	17.5487	20.3037
11	11.5668	12.1687	12.8078	13.4864	14.2068	14.9716	15.7836	16.6455	17.5603	18.5312	20.6546	24.3493
12	12.6825	13.4121	14.1920	15.0258	15.9171	16.8699	17.8885	18.9771	20.1407	21.3843	24.1331	29.0017
13	13.8093	14.6803	15.6178	16.6268	17.7130	18.8821	20.1406	21.4953	22.9534	24.5227	28.0291	34.3519
14	14.9474	15.9739	17.0863	18.2919	19.5986	21.0151	22.5505	24.2149	26.0192	27.9750	32.3926	40.5047
15	16.0969	17.2934	18.5989	20.0236	21.5786	23.2760	25.1290	27.1521	29.3609	31.7725	37.2797	47.5804
16	17.2579	18.6393	20.1569	21.8245	23.6575	25.6725	27.8881	30.3243	33.0034	35.9497	42.7533	55.7175
17	18.4304	20.0121	21.7616	23.6975	25.8404	28.2129	30.8402	33.7502	36.9737	40.5447	48.8837	65.0751
18	19.6147	21.4123	23.4144	25.6454	28.1324	30.9057	33.9990	37.4502	41.3013	45.5992	55.7497	75.8364
19	20.8109	22.8406	25.1169	27.6712	30.5390	33.7600	37.3790	41.4463	46.0185	51.1591	63.4397	88.2118
20	22.0190	24.2974	26.8704	29.7781	33.0660	36.7856	40.9955	45.7620	51.1601	57.2750	72.0524	102.4436
25	28.2432	32.0303	36.4593	41.6459	47.7271	54.8645	63.2490	73.1059	84.7009	98.3471	133.3339	212.7930
30	34.7849	40.5681	47.5754	56.0849	66.4388	79.0582	94.4608	113.2832	136.3075	164.4940	241.3327	434.7451
35	41.6603	49.9945	60.4621	73.6522	90.3203	111.4348	138.2369	172.3168	215.7108	271.0244	431.6635	881.1702
40	48.8864	60.4020	75.4013	95.0255	120.7998	154.7620	199.6351	259.0565	337.8824	442.5926	767.0914	1,779.0903

Glossary

Absorption costing Costing method that assigns both variable and fixed costs to products.

Accelerated depreciation method Method that produces larger depreciation charges in the early years of an asset's life and smaller charges in its later years. *(p. 392)*

Account Record within an accounting system in which increases and decreases are entered and stored in a specific asset, liability, equity, revenue, or expense. *(p. 49)*

Account balance Difference between total debits and total credits (including the beginning balance) for an account. *(p. 53)*

Account form balance sheet Balance sheet that lists assets on the left side and liabilities and equity on the right. *(p. 18)*

Account payable Liability created by buying goods or services on credit; backed by the buyer's general credit standing. *(p. 50)*

Accounting Information and measurement system that identifies, records, and communicates relevant information about a company's business activities. *(p. 4)*

Accounting cycle Recurring steps performed each accounting period, starting with analyzing transactions and continuing through the post-closing trial balance (or reversing entries). *(p. 144)*

Accounting equation Equality involving a company's assets, liabilities, and equity; Assets = Liabilities + Equity; also called *balance sheet equation*. *(p. 12)*

Accounting information system People, records, and methods that collect and process data from transactions and events, organize them in useful forms, and communicate results to decision makers. *(p. 266)*

Accounting period Length of time covered by financial statements; also called *reporting period. (p. 92)*

Accounting rate of return Rate used to evaluate the acceptability of an investment; equals the after-tax periodic income from a project divided by the average investment in the asset; also called *rate of return on average investment. (p. 1001)*

Accounts payable ledger Subsidiary ledger listing individual creditor (supplier) accounts. *(p. 271)*

Accounts receivable Amounts due from customers for credit sales; backed by the customer's general credit standing. *(p. 354)*

Accounts receivable ledger Subsidiary ledger listing individual customer accounts. *(p. 271)*

Accounts receivable turnover Measure of both the quality and liquidity of accounts receivable; indicates how often receivables are received and collected during the period; computed by dividing net sales by average accounts receivable. *(p. 368)*

Accrual basis accounting Accounting system that recognizes revenues when earned and expenses when incurred; the basis for GAAP. *(p. 93)*

Accrued expenses Costs incurred in a period that are both unpaid and unrecorded; adjusting entries for recording accrued expenses involve increasing expenses and increasing liabilities. *(p. 99)*

Accrued revenues Revenues earned in a period that are both unrecorded and not yet received in cash (or other assets); adjusting entries for recording accrued revenues involve increasing assets and increasing revenues. *(p. 100)*

Accumulated depreciation Cumulative sum of all depreciation expense recorded for an asset. *(p. 97)*

Acid-test ratio Ratio used to assess a company's ability to settle its current debts with its most liquid assets; defined as quick assets (cash, short-term investments, and current receivables) divided by current liabilities. *(p. 193)*

Activity-based budgeting (ABB) Budget system based on expected activities. *(p. 929)*

Activity-based costing (ABC) Cost allocation method that focuses on activities performed; traces costs to activities and then assigns them to cost objects. *(p. 844)*

Activity cost driver Variable that causes an activity's cost to go up or down; a causal factor. *(p. 844)*

Activity cost pool Temporary account that accumulates costs a company incurs to support an activity. *(p. 845)*

Adjusted trial balance List of accounts and balances prepared after period-end adjustments are recorded and posted. *(p. 103)*

Adjusting entry Journal entry at the end of an accounting period to bring an asset or liability account to its proper amount and update the related expense or revenue account. *(p. 94)*

Aging of accounts receivable Process of classifying accounts receivable by how long they are past due for purposes of estimating uncollectible accounts. *(p. 362)*

Allowance for Doubtful Accounts Contra asset account with a balance approximating uncollectible accounts receivable; also called *Allowance for Uncollectible Accounts. (p. 359)*

Allowance method Procedure that (a) estimates and matches bad debts expense with its sales for the period and/or (b) reports accounts receivable at estimated realizable value. *(p. 359)*

Amortization Process of allocating the cost of an intangible asset to expense over its estimated useful life. *(p. 401)*

Annual financial statements Financial statements covering a one-year period; often based on a calendar year, but any consecutive 12-month (or 52-week) period is acceptable. *(p. 93)*

Annual report Summary of a company's financial results for the year with its current financial condition and future plans; directed to external users of financial information. *(p. A-1)*

Annuity Series of equal payments at equal intervals. *(p. 562)*

Appropriated retained earnings Retained earnings separately reported to inform stockholders of funding needs. *(p. 517)*

Assets Resources a business owns or controls that are expected to provide current and future benefits to the business. *(p. 12)*

Audit Analysis and report of an organization's accounting system, its records, and its reports using various tests. *(p. 11)*

Authorized stock Total amount of stock that a corporation's charter authorizes it to issue. *(p. 503)*

Available-for-sale (AFS) securities Investments in debt and equity securities that are not classified as trading securities or held-to-maturity securities. *(p. 590)*

Average cost See *weighted average. (p. 230)*

Avoidable expense Expense (or cost) that is relevant for decision making; expense that is not incurred if a department, product, or service is eliminated. *(p. 1014)*

Bad debts Accounts of customers who do not pay what they have promised to pay; an expense of selling on credit; also called *uncollectible accounts. (p. 358)*

Balance column account Account with debit and credit columns for recording entries and another column for showing the balance of the account after each entry. *(p. 56)*

Balance sheet Financial statement that lists types and dollar amounts of assets, liabilities, and equity at a specific date. *(p. 17)*

Balance sheet equation (See *accounting equation.*) *(p. 12)*

Bank reconciliation Report that explains the difference between the book (company) balance of cash and the cash balance reported on the bank statement. *(p. 326)*

Bank statement Bank report on the depositor's beginning and ending cash balances, and a listing of its changes, for a period. *(p. 325)*

Basic earnings per share Net income less any preferred dividends and then divided by weighted-average common shares outstanding. *(p. 518)*

Batch processing Accumulating source documents for a period of time and then processing them all at once such as once a day, week, or month. *(p. 281)*

Bearer bonds Bonds made payable to whoever holds them (the *bearer*); also called *unregistered bonds. (p. 557)*

Benchmarking Practice of comparing and analyzing company financial performance or position with other companies or standards.

Betterments Expenditures to make a plant asset more efficient or productive; also called *improvements. (p. 397)*

Bond Written promise to pay the bond's par (or face) value and interest at a stated contract rate; often issued in denominations of $1,000. *(p. 544)*

Bond certificate Document containing bond specifics such as issuer's name, bond par value, contract interest rate, and maturity date. *(p. 546)*

Bond indenture Contract between the bond issuer and the bondholders; identifies the parties' rights and obligations. *(p. 546)*

Book value Asset's acquisition costs less its accumulated depreciation (or depletion, or amortization); also sometimes used synonymously as the *carrying value* of an account. *(pp. 97 & 391)*

Book value per common share Recorded amount of equity applicable to common shares divided by the number of common shares outstanding. *(p. 520)*

Book value per preferred share Equity applicable to preferred shares (equals its call price [or par value if it is not callable] plus any cumulative dividends in arrears) divided by the number of preferred shares outstanding. *(p. 520)*

Bookkeeping (See *recordkeeping.*) *(p. 5)*

Break-even point Output level at which sales equals fixed plus variable costs; where income equals zero. *(p. 888)*

Break-even time (BET) Time-based measurement used to evaluate the acceptability of an investment; equals the time expected to pass before the present value of the net cash flows from an investment equals its initial cost. *(p. 1016)*

Budget Formal statement of future plans, usually expressed in monetary terms. *(p. 916)*

Budget report Report comparing actual results to planned objectives; sometimes used as a progress report. *(p. 954)*

Budgetary control Management use of budgets to monitor and control company operations. *(p. 954)*

Budgeted balance sheet Accounting report that presents predicted amounts of the company's assets, liabilities, and equity balances as of the end of the budget period. *(p. 928)*

Budgeted income statement Accounting report that presents predicted amounts of the company's revenues and expenses for the budget period. *(p. 928)*

Budgeting Process of planning future business actions and expressing them as formal plans. *(p. 916)*

Business An organization of one or more individuals selling products and/or services for profit. *(p. 10)*

Business entity principle Principle that requires a business to be accounted for separately from its owner(s) and from any other entity. *(p. 10)*

Business segment Part of a company that can be separately identified by the products or services that it provides or by the geographic markets that it serves; also called *segment. (p. 697)*

C corporation Corporation that does not qualify for nor elect to be treated as a proprietorship or partnership for income tax purposes and therefore is subject to income taxes; also called *C corp. (p. 474)*

Call price Amount that must be paid to call and retire a callable preferred stock or a callable bond. *(p. 513)*

Callable bonds Bonds that give the issuer the option to retire them at a stated amount prior to maturity. *(p. 557)*

Callable preferred stock Preferred stock that the issuing corporation, at its option, may retire by paying the call price plus any dividends in arrears. *(p. 513)*

Canceled checks Checks that the bank has paid and deducted from the depositor's account. *(p. 326)*

Capital budgeting Process of analyzing alternative investments and deciding which assets to acquire or sell. *(p. 998)*

Capital expenditures Additional costs of plant assets that provide material benefits extending beyond the current period; also called *balance sheet expenditures. (p. 396)*

Capital expenditures budget Plan that lists dollar amounts to be both received from disposal of plant assets and spent to purchase plant assets. *(p. 925)*

Capital leases Long-term leases in which the lessor transfers substantially all risk and rewards of ownership to the lessee. *(p. 568)*

Capital stock General term referring to a corporation's stock used in obtaining capital (owner financing). *(p. 503)*

Capitalize Record the cost as part of a permanent account and allocate it over later periods. *(p. 396)*

Carrying value of bonds Net amount at which bonds are reported on the balance sheet; equals the par value of the bonds less any unamortized discount or plus any unamortized premium; also called *carrying amount* or *book value. (p. 548)*

Cash Includes currency, coins, and amounts on deposit in bank checking or savings accounts. *(p. 317)*

Cash basis accounting Accounting system that recognizes revenues when cash is received and records expenses when cash is paid. *(p. 93)*

Cash budget Plan that shows expected cash inflows and outflows during the budget period, including receipts from loans needed to maintain a minimum cash balance and repayments of such loans. *(p. 926)*

Cash disbursements journal Special journal normally used to record all payments of cash; also called *cash payments journal. (p. 278)*

Cash discount Reduction in the price of merchandise granted by a seller to a buyer when payment is made within the discount period. *(p. 181)*

Cash equivalents Short-term, investment assets that are readily convertible to a known cash amount or sufficiently close to their maturity date (usually within 90 days) so that market value is not sensitive to interest rate changes. *(p. 317)*

Cash flow on total assets Ratio of operating cash flows to average total assets; not sensitive to income recognition and measurement; partly reflects earnings quality. *(p. 640)*

Cash Over and Short Income statement account used to record cash overages and cash shortages arising from errors in cash receipts or payments. *(p. 318)*

Cash receipts journal Special journal normally used to record all receipts of cash. *(p. 275)*

Change in an accounting estimate Change in an accounting estimate that results from new information, subsequent developments, or improved judgment that impacts current and future periods. *(pp. 395 & 517)*

Chart of accounts List of accounts used by a company; includes an identification number for each account. *(p. 52)*

Check Document signed by a depositor instructing the bank to pay a specified amount to a designated recipient. *(p. 323)*

Check register Another name for a cash disbursements journal when the journal has a column for check numbers. *(pp. 279 & 334)*

Classified balance sheet Balance sheet that presents assets and liabilities in relevant subgroups, including current and noncurrent classifications. *(p. 145)*

Clock card Source document used to record the number of hours an employee works and to determine the total labor cost for each pay period. *(p. 767)*

Closing entries Entries recorded at the end of each accounting period to transfer end-of-period balances in revenue, gain, expense, loss, and withdrawal (dividend for a corporation) accounts to the capital account (to retained earnings for a corporation). *(p. 141)*

Closing process Necessary end-of-period steps to prepare the accounts for recording the transactions of the next period. *(p. 140)*

Columnar journal Journal with more than one column. *(p. 272)*

Common stock Corporation's basic ownership share; also generically called *capital stock. (pp. 11 & 502)*

Common-size financial statement Statement that expresses each amount as a percent of a base amount. In the balance sheet, total assets is usually the base and is expressed as 100%. In the income statement, net sales is usually the base. *(p. 681)*

Comparative financial statement Statement with data for two or more successive periods placed in side-by-side columns, often with changes shown in dollar amounts and percents. *(p. 676)*

Compatibility principle Information system principle that prescribes an accounting system to conform with a company's activities, personnel, and structure. *(p. 267)*

Complex capital structure Capital structure that includes outstanding rights or options to purchase common stock, or securities that are convertible into common stock. *(p. 519)*

Components of accounting systems Five basic components of accounting systems are source documents, input devices, information processors, information storage, and output devices. *(p. 267)*

Composite unit Generic unit consisting of a specific number of units of each product; unit comprised in proportion to the expected sales mix of its products. *(p. 895)*

Compound journal entry Journal entry that affects at least three accounts. *(p. 59)*

Comprehensive income Net change in equity for a period, excluding owner investments and distributions. *(p. 593)*

Computer hardware Physical equipment in a computerized accounting information system. *(p. 268)*

Computer network Linkage giving different users and different computers access to common databases and programs. *(p. 281)*

Computer software Programs that direct operations of computer hardware. *(p. 268)*

Conservatism principle Principle that prescribes the less optimistic estimate when two estimates are about equally likely. *(p. 234)*

Consignee Receiver of goods owned by another who holds them for purposes of selling them for the owner. *(p. 224)*

Consignor Owner of goods who ships them to another party who will sell them for the owner. *(p. 224)*

Consistency principle Principle that prescribes use of the same accounting method(s) over time so that financial statements are comparable across periods. *(p. 232)*

Consolidated financial statements Financial statements that show all (combined) activities under the parent's control, including those of any subsidiaries. *(p. 593)*

Contingent liability Obligation to make a future payment if, and only if, an uncertain future event occurs. *(p. 439)*

Continuous budgeting Practice of preparing budgets for a selected number of future periods and revising those budgets as each period is completed. *(p. 918)*

Continuous improvement Concept requiring every manager and employee continually to look to improve operations. *(p. 724)*

Contra account Account linked with another account and having an opposite normal balance; reported as a subtraction from the other account's balance. *(p. 97)*

Contract rate Interest rate specified in a bond indenture (or note); multiplied by the par value to determine the interest paid each period; also called *coupon rate, stated rate,* or *nominal rate. (p. 547)*

Contributed capital Total amount of cash and other assets received from stockholders in exchange for stock; also called *paid-in capital.*

Contributed capital in excess of par value Difference between the par value of stock and its issue price when issued at a price above par.

Contribution margin Sales revenue less total variable costs.

Contribution margin income statement Income statement that separates variable and fixed costs; highlights the contribution margin, which is sales less variable expenses.

Contribution margin per unit Amount that the sale of one unit contributes toward recovering fixed costs and earning profit; defined as sales price per unit minus variable expense per unit. *(p. 888)*

Contribution margin ratio Product's contribution margin divided by its sale price. *(p. 888)*

Control Process of monitoring planning decisions and evaluating the organization's activities and employees. *(p. 721)*

Control principle Information system principle that prescribes an accounting system to aid managers in controlling and monitoring business activities. *(p. 266)*

Controllable costs Costs that a manager has the power to control or at least strongly influence. *(pp. 726 & 855)*

Controllable variance Combination of both overhead spending variances (variable and fixed) and the variable overhead efficiency variance. *(p. 967)*

Controlling account General ledger account, the balance of which (after posting) equals the sum of the balances in its related subsidiary ledger. *(p. 271)*

Conversion costs Expenditures incurred in converting raw materials to finished goods; includes direct labor costs and overhead costs. *(p. 731)*

Convertible bonds Bonds that bondholders can exchange for a set number of the issuer's shares. *(p. 557)*

Convertible preferred stock Preferred stock with an option to exchange it for common stock at a specified rate. *(p. 513)*

Copyright Right giving the owner the exclusive privilege to publish and sell musical, literary, or artistic work during the creator's life plus 70 years. *(p. 402)*

Corporation Business that is a separate legal entity under state or federal laws with owners called *shareholders* or *stockholders. (pp. 11 & 500)*

Cost All normal and reasonable expenditures necessary to get an asset in place and ready for its intended use. *(p. 387)*

Cost accounting system Accounting system for manufacturing activities based on the perpetual inventory system. *(p. 762)*

Cost-benefit principle Information system principle that prescribes the benefits from an activity in an accounting system to outweigh the costs of that activity. *(p. 267)*

Cost center Department that incurs costs but generates no revenues; common example is the accounting or legal department. *(p. 848)*

Cost object Product, process, department, or customer to which costs are assigned. *(p. 725)*

Cost of goods available for sale Consists of beginning inventory plus net purchases of a period. *(p. 200)*

Cost of goods manufactured Total manufacturing costs (direct materials, direct labor, and factory overhead) for the period plus beginning goods in process less ending goods in process; also called *net cost of goods manufactured* and *cost of goods completed. (p. 811)*

Cost of goods sold Cost of inventory sold to customers during a period; also called *cost of sales. (p. 179)*

Cost principle Accounting principle that prescribes financial statement information to be based on actual costs incurred in business transactions. *(p. 9)*

Cost variance Difference between the actual incurred cost and the standard cost. *(p. 961)*

Cost-volume-profit (CVP) analysis Planning method that includes predicting the volume of activity, the costs incurred, sales earned, and profits received. *(p. 882)*

Coupon bonds Bonds with interest coupons attached to their certificates; bondholders detach coupons when they mature and present them to a bank or broker for collection. *(p. 557)*

Credit Recorded on the right side; an entry that decreases asset and expense accounts, and increases liability, revenue, and most equity accounts; abbreviated Cr. *(p. 53)*

Credit memorandum Notification that the sender has credited the recipient's account in the sender's records. *(p. 187)*

Credit period Time period that can pass before a customer's payment is due. *(p. 181)*

Credit terms Description of the amounts and timing of payments that a buyer (debtor) agrees to make in the future. *(p. 181)*

Creditors Individuals or organizations entitled to receive payments. *(p. 50)*

Cumulative preferred stock Preferred stock on which undeclared dividends accumulate until paid; common stockholders cannot receive dividends until cumulative dividends are paid. *(p. 511)*

Current assets Cash and other assets expected to be sold, collected, or used within one year or the company's operating cycle, whichever is longer. *(p. 146)*

Current liabilities Obligations due to be paid or settled within one year or the company's operating cycle, whichever is longer. *(pp. 147 & 429)*

Current portion of long-term debt Portion of long-term debt due within one year or the operating cycle, whichever is longer; reported under current liabilities. *(p. 437)*

Current ratio Ratio used to evaluate a company's ability to pay its short-term obligations, calculated by dividing current assets by current liabilities. *(p. 148)*

Curvilinear cost Cost that changes with volume but not at a constant rate. *(p. 884)*

Customer orientation Company position that its managers and employees be in tune with the changing wants and needs of consumers. *(p. 723)*

CVP chart Graphic representation of cost-volume-profit relations. *(p. 890)*

Cycle efficiency (CE) A measure of production efficiency, which is defined as value-added (process) time divided by total cycle time. *(p. 735)*

Cycle time (CT) A measure of the time to produce a product or service, which is the sum of process time, inspection time, move time, and wait time; also called *throughput time. (p. 735)*

Date of declaration Date the directors vote to pay a dividend. *(p. 507)*

Date of payment Date the corporation makes the dividend payment. *(p. 507)*

Date of record Date directors specify for identifying stockholders to receive dividends. *(p. 507)*

Days' sales in inventory Estimate of number of days needed to convert inventory into receivables or cash; equals ending inventory divided by cost of goods sold and then multiplied by 365; also called *days' stock on hand.* *(p. 236)*

Days' sales uncollected Measure of the liquidity of receivables computed by dividing the current balance of receivables by the annual credit (or net) sales and then multiplying by 365; also called *days' sales in receivables.* *(p. 329)*

Debit Recorded on the left side; an entry that increases asset and expense accounts, and decreases liability, revenue, and most equity accounts; abbreviated Dr. *(p. 53)*

Debit memorandum Notification that the sender has debited the recipient's account in the sender's records. *(p. 182)*

Debt ratio Ratio of total liabilities to total assets; used to reflect risk associated with a company's debts. *(p. 67)*

Debt-to-equity ratio Defined as total liabilities divided by total equity; shows the proportion of a company financed by non-owners (creditors) in comparison with that financed by owners. *(p. 558)*

Debtors Individuals or organizations that owe money. *(p. 49)*

Declining-balance method Method that determines depreciation charge for the period by multiplying a depreciation rate (often twice the straight-line rate) by the asset's beginning-period book value. *(p. 392)*

Deferred income tax liability Corporation income taxes that are deferred until future years because of temporary differences between GAAP and tax rules. *(p. 451)*

Degree of operating leverage (DOL) Ratio of contribution margin divided by pretax income; used to assess the effect on income of changes in sales. *(p. 896)*

Departmental accounting system Accounting system that provides information useful in evaluating the profitability or cost effectiveness of a department. *(p. 847)*

Departmental contribution to overhead Amount by which a department's revenues exceed its direct expenses. *(p. 854)*

Depletion Process of allocating the cost of natural resources to periods when they are consumed and sold. *(p. 400)*

Deposit ticket Lists items such as currency, coins, and checks deposited and their corresponding dollar amounts. *(p. 323)*

Deposits in transit Deposits recorded by the company but not yet recorded by its bank. *(p. 326)*

Depreciable cost Cost of a plant asset less its salvage value. *(p. 390)*

Depreciation Expense created by allocating the cost of plant and equipment to periods in which they are used; represents the expense of using the asset. *(pp. 97 & 389)*

Diluted earnings per share Earnings per share calculation that requires dilutive securities be added to the denominator of the basic EPS calculation. *(p. 519)*

Dilutive securities Securities having the potential to increase common shares outstanding; examples are options, rights, convertible bonds, and convertible preferred stock. *(p. 519)*

Direct costs Costs incurred for the benefit of one specific cost object. *(p. 725)*

Direct expenses Expenses traced to a specific department (object) that are incurred for the sole benefit of that department. *(p. 849)*

Direct labor Efforts of employees who physically convert materials to finished product. *(p. 731)*

Direct labor costs Wages and salaries for direct labor that are separately and readily traced through the production process to finished goods. *(p. 731)*

Direct material Raw material that physically becomes part of the product and is clearly identified with specific products or batches of product. *(p. 730)*

Direct material costs Expenditures for direct material that are separately and readily traced through the production process to finished goods. *(p. 730)*

Direct method Presentation of net cash from operating activities for the statement of cash flows that lists major operating cash receipts less major operating cash payments. *(p. 628)*

Direct write-off method Method that records the loss from an uncollectible account receivable at the time it is determined to be uncollectible; no attempt is made to estimate bad debts. *(p. 358)*

Discount on bonds payable Difference between a bond's par value and its lower issue price or carrying value; occurs when the contract rate is less than the market rate. *(p. 547)*

Discount on note payable Difference between the face value of a note payable and the (lesser) amount borrowed; reflects the added interest to be paid on the note over its life.

Discount on stock Difference between the par value of stock and its issue price when issued at a price below par value. *(p. 505)*

Discount period Time period in which a cash discount is available and the buyer can make a reduced payment. *(p. 181)*

Discount rate Expected rate of return on investments; also called *cost of capital, hurdle rate,* or *required rate of return. (p. B-2)*

Discounts lost Expenses resulting from not taking advantage of cash discounts on purchases. *(p. 335)*

Dividend in arrears Unpaid dividend on cumulative preferred stock; must be paid before any regular dividends on preferred stock and before any dividends on common stock. *(p. 511)*

Dividend yield Ratio of the annual amount of cash dividends distributed to common shareholders relative to the common stock's market value (price). *(p. 519)*

Dividends Corporation's distributions of assets to its owners.

Double-declining-balance (DDB) depreciation Depreciation equals beginning book value multiplied by 2 times the straight-line rate. *(p. 392)*

Double-entry accounting Accounting system in which each transaction affects at least two accounts and has at least one debit and one credit. *(p. 53)*

Double taxation Corporate income is taxed and then its later distribution through dividends is normally taxed again for shareholders. *(p. 11)*

Earnings (See *net income.*) *(p. 13)*

Earnings per share (EPS) Amount of income earned by each share of a company's outstanding common stock; also called *net income per share. (p. 518)*

Effective interest method Allocates interest expense over the bond life to yield a constant rate of interest; interest expense for a period is found by multiplying the balance of the liability at the beginning of the period by the bond market rate at issuance; also called *interest method. (p. 563)*

Efficiency Company's productivity in using its assets; usually measured relative to how much revenue a certain level of assets generates. *(p. 675)*

Efficiency variance Difference between the actual quantity of an input and the standard quantity of that input. *(p. 966)*

Electronic funds transfer (EFT) Use of electronic communication to transfer cash from one party to another. *(p. 324)*

Employee benefits Additional compensation paid to or on behalf of employees, such as premiums for medical, dental, life, and disability insurance, and contributions to pension plans. *(p. 437)*

Employee earnings report Record of an employee's net pay, gross pay, deductions, and year-to-date payroll information. *(p. 448)*

Enterprise resource planning (ERP) software Programs that manage a company's vital operations, which range from order taking to production to accounting. *(p. 281)*

Entity Organization that, for accounting purposes, is separate from other organizations and individuals. *(p. 10)*

EOM Abbreviation for *end of month;* used to describe credit terms for credit transactions. *(p. 181)*

Equity Owner's claim on the assets of a business; equals the residual interest in an entity's assets after deducting liabilities; also called *net assets. (p. 12)*

Equity method Accounting method used for long-term investments when the investor has "significant influence" over the investee. *(p. 592)*

Equity ratio Portion of total assets provided by equity, computed as total equity divided by total assets. *(p. 689)*

Equity securities with controlling influence Long-term investment when the investor is able to exert controlling influence over the investee; investors owning 50% or more of voting stock are presumed to exert controlling influence. *(p. 593)*

Equity securities with significant influence Long-term investment when the investor is able to exert significant influence over the investee; investors owning 20 percent or more (but less than 50 percent) of voting stock are presumed to exert significant influence. *(p. 591)*

Equivalent units of production (EUP) Number of units that would be completed if all effort during a period had been applied to units that were started and finished. *(p. 805)*

Estimated liability Obligation of an uncertain amount that can be reasonably estimated. *(p. 437)*

Estimated line of cost behavior Line drawn on a graph to visually fit the relation between cost and sales. *(p. 885)*

Ethics Codes of conduct by which actions are judged as right or wrong, fair or unfair, honest or dishonest. *(p. 8)*

Events Happenings that both affect an organization's financial position and can be reliably measured. *(p. 13)*

Expanded accounting equation Assets = Liabilities + Equity; Equity equals [Owner capital − Owner withdrawals + Revenues − Expenses] for a noncorporation; Equity equals [Contributed capital + Retained earnings + Revenues − Expenses] for a corporation where dividends are subtracted from retained earnings. *(p. 13)*

Expenses Outflows or using up of assets as part of operations of a business to generate sales. *(p. 13)*

External transactions Exchanges of economic value between one entity and another entity. *(p. 13)*

External users Persons using accounting information who are not directly involved in running the organization. *(p. 5)*

Extraordinary gains or losses Gains or losses reported separately from continuing operations because they are both unusual and infrequent. *(p. 697)*

Extraordinary repairs Major repairs that extend the useful life of a plant asset beyond prior expectations; treated as a capital expenditure. *(p. 397)*

Factory overhead Factory activities supporting the production process that are not direct material or direct labor; also called *overhead* and *manufacturing overhead. (p. 731)*

Factory overhead costs Expenditures for factory overhead that cannot be separately or readily traced to finished goods; also called *overhead costs.* (p. 73)

Favorable variance Difference in actual revenues or expenses from the budgeted amount that contributes to a higher income. (p. 956)

Federal depository bank Bank authorized to accept deposits of amounts payable to the federal government. (p. 446)

Federal Insurance Contributions Act (FICA) Taxes Taxes assessed on both employers and employees; for Social Security and Medicare programs. (p. 434)

Federal Unemployment Taxes (FUTA) Payroll taxes on employers assessed by the federal government to support its unemployment insurance program. (p. 436)

FIFO method (See *first-in, first-out.*) (p. 816)

Financial accounting Area of accounting mainly aimed at serving external users. (p. 5)

Financial Accounting Standards Board (FASB) Independent group of full-time members responsible for setting accounting rules. (p. 9)

Financial leverage Earning a higher return on equity by paying dividends on preferred stock or interest on debt at a rate lower than the return earned with the assets from issuing preferred stock or debt; also called *trading on the equity.* (p. 513)

Financial reporting Process of communicating information relevant to investors, creditors, and others in making investment, credit, and business decisions. (p. 675)

Financial statement analysis Application of analytical tools to general-purpose financial statements and related data for making business decisions. (p. 674)

Financial statements Includes the balance sheet, income statement, statement of owner's (or stockholders') equity, and statement of cash flows. (p. 17)

Financing activities Transactions with owners and creditors that include obtaining cash from issuing debt, repaying amounts borrowed, and obtaining cash from or distributing cash to owners. (p. 624)

Finished goods inventory Account that controls the finished goods files, which acts as a subsidiary ledger (of the Inventory account) in which the costs of finished goods that are ready for sale are recorded. (pp. 729 & 764)

First-in, first-out (FIFO) Method to assign cost to inventory that assumes items are sold in the order acquired; earliest items purchased are the first sold. (p. 229)

Fiscal year Consecutive 12-month (or 52-week) period chosen as the organization's annual accounting period. (p. 93)

Fixed budget Planning budget based on a single predicted amount of volume; unsuitable for evaluations if the actual volume differs from predicted volume. (p. 955)

Fixed budget performance report Report that compares actual revenues and costs with fixed budgeted amounts and identifies the differences as favorable or unfavorable variances. (p. 955)

Fixed cost Cost that does not change with changes in the volume of activity. (p. 725)

Flexibility principle Information system principle that prescribes an accounting system be able to adapt to changes in the company, its operations, and needs of decision makers. (p. 267)

Flexible budget Budget prepared (using actual volume) once a period is complete that helps managers evaluate past performance; uses fixed and variable costs in determining total costs. (p. 956)

Flexible budget performance report Report that compares actual revenues and costs with their variable budgeted amounts based on actual sales volume (or other level of activity) and identifies the differences as variances. (p. 958)

FOB Abbreviation for *free on board;* the point when ownership of goods passes to the buyer; *FOB shipping point* (or *factory*) means the buyer pays shipping costs and accepts ownership of goods when the seller transfers goods to carrier; *FOB destination* means the seller pays shipping costs and buyer accepts ownership of goods at the buyer's place of business. (p. 183)

Foreign exchange rate Price of one currency stated in terms of another currency. (p. 599)

Form 940 IRS form used to report an employer's federal unemployment taxes (FUTA) on an annual filing basis. (p. 446)

Form 941 IRS form filed to report FICA taxes owed and remitted. (p. 444)

Form 10-K (or 10-KSB) Annual report form filed with SEC by businesses (small businesses) with publicly-traded securities. (p. A-1)

Form W-2 Annual report by an employer to each employee showing the employee's wages subject to FICA and federal income taxes along with amounts withheld. (p. 446)

Form W-4 Withholding allowance certificate, filed with the employer, identifying the number of withholding allowances claimed. (p. 448)

Franchises Privileges granted by a company or government to sell a product or service under specified conditions. (p. 403)

Full-disclosure principle Principle that prescribes financial statements (including notes) to report all relevant information about an entity's operations and financial condition. (p. 366)

GAAP (See *generally accepted accounting principles.*) (p. 9)

General accounting system Accounting system for manufacturing activities based on the *periodic* inventory system. (p. 762)

General and administrative expenses Expenses that support the operating activities of a business. (p. 191)

General and administrative expense budget Plan that shows predicted operating expenses not included in the selling expenses budget. (p. 924)

General journal All-purpose journal for recording the debits and credits of transactions and events. (pp. 54 & 270)

General ledger (See *ledger.*) (p. 49)

General partner Partner who assumes unlimited liability for the debts of the partnership; responsible for partnership management. (p. 473)

General partnership Partnership in which all partners have mutual agency and unlimited liability for partnership debts. (p. 473)

Generally accepted accounting principles (GAAP) Rules that specify acceptable accounting practices. (p. 9)

Generally accepted auditing standards (GAAS) Rules that specify acceptable auditing practices.

General-purpose financial statements Statements published periodically for use by a variety of interested parties; includes the income statement, balance sheet, statement of owner's equity (or statement of retained earnings for a corporation), statement of cash flows, and notes to these statements. *(p. 675)*

Going-concern principle Principle that prescribes financial statements to reflect the assumption that the business will continue operating. *(p. 10)*

Goods in process inventory Account in which costs are accumulated for products that are in the process of being produced but are not yet complete; also called *work in process inventory*. *(pp. 729 & 764)*

Goodwill Amount by which a company's (or a segment's) value exceeds the value of its individual assets less its liabilities. *(p. 403)*

Gross margin (See *gross profit*.) *(p. 179)*

Gross margin ratio Gross margin (net sales minus cost of goods sold) divided by net sales; also called *gross profit ratio*. *(p. 193)*

Gross method Method of recording purchases at the full invoice price without deducting any cash discounts. *(p. 335)*

Gross pay Total compensation earned by an employee. *(p. 433)*

Gross profit Net sales minus cost of goods sold; also called *gross margin*. *(p. 179)*

Gross profit method Procedure to estimate inventory when the past gross profit rate is used to estimate cost of goods sold, which is then subtracted from the cost of goods available for sale. *(p. 246)*

Held-to-maturity (HTM) securities Debt securities that a company has the intent and ability to hold until they mature. *(p. 590)*

High-low method Procedure that yields an estimated line of cost behavior by graphically connecting costs associated with the highest and lowest sales volume. *(p. 886)*

Horizontal analysis Comparison of a company's financial condition and performance across time. *(p. 676)*

Hurdle rate Minimum acceptable rate of return (set by management) for an investment. *(p. 1006)*

Impairment Diminishment of an asset value. *(p. 401)*

Imprest system Method to account for petty cash; maintains a constant balance in the fund, which equals cash plus petty cash receipts. *(p. 321)*

Inadequacy Condition in which the capacity of plant assets is too small to meet the company's production demands. *(p. 389)*

Income (See *net income*.) *(p. 13)*

Income statement Financial statement that subtracts expenses from revenues to yield a net income or loss over a specified period of time; also includes any gains or losses. *(p. 17)*

Income Summary Temporary account used only in the closing process to which the balances of revenue and expense accounts (including any gains or losses) are transferred; its balance is transferred to the capital account (or retained earnings for a corporation). *(p. 141)*

Incremental cost Additional cost incurred only if a company pursues a specific course of action. *(p. 1010)*

Indefinite useful life Asset life that is not limited by legal, regulatory, contractual, competitive, economic, or other factors. *(p. 401)*

Indirect costs Costs incurred for the benefit of more than one cost object. *(p. 725)*

Indirect expenses Expenses incurred for the joint benefit of more than one department (or cost object). *(p. 849)*

Indirect labor Efforts of production employees who do not work specifically on converting direct materials into finished products and who are not clearly identified with specific units or batches of product. *(p. 731)*

Indirect labor costs Labor costs that cannot be physically traced to production of a product or service; included as part of overhead. *(p. 731)*

Indirect material Material used to support the production process but not clearly identified with products or batches of product. *(p. 728)*

Indirect method Presentation that reports net income and then adjusts it by adding and subtracting items to yield net cash from operating activities on the statement of cash flows. *(p. 628)*

Information processor Component of an accounting system that interprets, transforms, and summarizes information for use in analysis and reporting. *(p. 268)*

Information storage Component of an accounting system that keeps data in a form accessible to information processors. *(p. 268)*

Infrequent gain or loss Gain or loss not expected to recur given the operating environment of the business. *(p. 697)*

Input device Means of capturing information from source documents that enables its transfer to information processors. *(p. 268)*

Installment note Liability requiring a series of periodic payments to the lender. *(p. 554)*

Intangible assets Long-term assets (resources) used to produce or sell products or services; usually lack physical form and have uncertain benefits. *(pp. 147 & 401)*

Interest Charge for using money (or other assets) loaned from one entity to another. *(p. 364)*

Interim financial statements Financial statements covering periods of less than one year; usually based on one-, three-, or six-month periods. *(pp. 93 & 245)*

Internal controls or **Internal control system** All policies and procedures used to protect assets, ensure reliable accounting, promote efficient operations, and urge adherence to company policies. *(pp. 266 & 312)*

Internal rate of return (IRR) Rate used to evaluate the acceptability of an investment; equals the rate that yields a net present value of zero for an investment. *(p. 1005)*

Internal transactions Activities within an organization that can affect the accounting equation. *(p. 13)*

Internal users Persons using accounting information who are directly involved in managing the organization. *(p. 6)*

International Accounting Standards Board (IASB) Group that identifies preferred accounting practices and encourages global acceptance; issues International Financial Reporting Standards (IFRS). *(p. 9)*

Inventory Goods a company owns and expects to sell in its normal operations. *(p. 179)*

Inventory turnover Number of times a company's average inventory is sold during a period; computed by dividing cost of goods sold by average inventory; also called *merchandise turnover. (p. 236)*

Investing activities Transactions that involve purchasing and selling of long-term assets, includes making and collecting notes receivable and investments in other than cash equivalents. *(p. 624)*

Investment center Center of which a manager is responsible for revenues, costs, and asset investments. *(p. 858)*

Investment center return on total assets Center net income divided by average total assets for the center. *(p. 858)*

Invoice Itemized record of goods prepared by the vendor that lists the customer's name, items sold, sales prices, and terms of sale. *(p. 332)*

Invoice approval Document containing a checklist of steps necessary for approving the recording and payment of an invoice; also called *check authorization. (p. 333)*

Job Production of a customized product or service. *(p. 762)*

Job cost sheet Separate record maintained for each job. *(p. 764)*

Job lot Production of more than one unit of a customized product or service. *(p. 763)*

Job order cost accounting system Cost accounting system to determine the cost of producing each job or job lot. *(pp. 764 & 801)*

Job order production Production of special-order products; also called *customized production. (p. 762)*

Joint cost Cost incurred to produce or purchase two or more products at the same time. *(p. 861)*

Journal Record in which transactions are entered before they are posted to ledger accounts; also called *book of original entry. (p. 54)*

Journalizing Process of recording transactions in a journal. *(p. 54)*

Just-in-time (JIT) manufacturing Process of acquiring or producing inventory only when needed. *(p. 724)*

Known liabilities Obligations of a company with little uncertainty; set by agreements, contracts, or laws; also called *definitely determinable liabilities. (p. 430)*

Land improvements Assets that increase the benefits of land, have a limited useful life, and are depreciated. *(p. 388)*

Large stock dividend Stock dividend that is more than 25% of the previously outstanding shares. *(p. 508)*

Last-in, first-out (LIFO) Method to assign cost to inventory that assumes costs for the most recent items purchased are sold first and charged to cost of goods sold. *(p. 229)*

Lean business model Practice of eliminating waste while meeting customer needs and yielding positive company returns. *(p. 724)*

Lease Contract specifying the rental of property. *(pp. 402 & 567)*

Leasehold Rights the lessor grants to the lessee under the terms of a lease. *(p. 402)*

Leasehold improvements Alterations or improvements to leased property such as partitions and storefronts. *(p. 403)*

Least-squares regression Statistical method for deriving an estimated line of cost behavior that is more precise than the high-low method and the scatter diagram. *(p. 887)*

Ledger Record containing all accounts (with amounts) for a business; also called *general ledger. (p. 49)*

Lessee Party to a lease who secures the right to possess and use the property from another party (the lessor). *(p. 402)*

Lessor Party to a lease who grants another party (the lessee) the right to possess and use its property. *(p. 402)*

Liabilities Creditors' claims on an organization's assets; involves a probable future payment of assets, products, or services that a company is obligated to make due to past transactions or events. *(p. 12)*

Licenses (See *franchises.) (p. 403)*

Limited liability Owner can lose no more than the amount invested. *(p. 11)*

Limited liability company Organization form that combines select features of a corporation and a limited partnership; provides limited liability to its members (owners), is free of business tax, and allows members to actively participate in management. *(p. 474)*

Limited liability partnership Partnership in which a partner is not personally liable for malpractice or negligence unless that partner is responsible for providing the service that resulted in the claim. *(p. 473)*

Limited partners Partners who have no personal liability for partnership debts beyond the amounts they invested in the partnership. *(p. 473)*

Limited partnership Partnership that has two classes of partners, limited partners and general partners. *(p. 473)*

Liquid assets Resources such as cash that are easily converted into other assets or used to pay for goods, services, or liabilities. *(p. 317)*

Liquidating cash dividend Distribution of assets that returns part of the original investment to stockholders; deducted from contributed capital accounts. *(p. 508)*

Liquidation Process of going out of business; involves selling assets, paying liabilities, and distributing remainder to owners.

Liquidity Availability of resources to meet short-term cash requirements. *(pp. 317 & 675)*

List price Catalog (full) price of an item before any trade discount is deducted. *(p. 180)*

Long-term investments Long-term assets not used in operating activities such as notes receivable and investments in stocks and bonds. *(pp. 147 & 586)*

Long-term liabilities Obligations not due to be paid within one year or the operating cycle, whichever is longer. *(pp. 147 & 429)*

Lower of cost or market (LCM) Required method to report inventory at market replacement cost when that market cost is lower than recorded cost. *(p. 233)*

Maker of the note Entity who signs a note and promises to pay it at maturity. *(p. 364)*

Management by exception Management process to focus on significant variances and give less attention to areas where performance is close to the standard. *(p. 970)*

Managerial accounting Area of accounting mainly aimed at serving the decision-making needs of internal users; also called *management accounting*. *(pp. 6 & 720)*

Manufacturer Company that uses labor and operating assets to convert raw materials to finished goods. *(p. 13)*

Manufacturing budget Plan that shows the predicted costs for direct materials, direct labor, and overhead to be incurred in manufacturing units in the production budget. *(p. 935)*

Manufacturing statement Report that summarizes the types and amounts of costs incurred in a company's production process for a period; also called *cost of goods manufacturing statement*. *(p. 733)*

Margin of safety Excess of expected sales over the level of break-even sales. *(p. 893)*

Market prospects Expectations (both good and bad) about a company's future performance as assessed by users and other interested parties. *(p. 675)*

Market rate Interest rate that borrowers are willing to pay and lenders are willing to accept for a specific lending agreement given the borrowers' risk level. *(p. 547)*

Market value per share Price at which stock is bought or sold. *(p. 503)*

Master budget Comprehensive business plan that includes specific plans for expected sales, product units to be produced, merchandise (or materials) to be purchased, expenses to be incurred, plant assets to be purchased, and amounts of cash to be borrowed or loans to be repaid, as well as a budgeted income statement and balance sheet. *(p. 920)*

Matching principle Prescribes expenses to be reported in the same period as the revenues that were earned as a result of the expenses. *(pp. 94 & 358)*

Materiality principal Prescribes that accounting for items that significantly impact financial statement and any inferences from them adhere strictly to GAAP. *(p. 358)*

Materials consumption report Document that summarizes the materials a department uses during a reporting period; replaces materials requisitions. *(p. 802)*

Materials ledger card Perpetual record updated each time units are purchased or issued for production use. *(p. 765)*

Materials requisition Source document production managers use to request materials for production; used to assign materials costs to specific jobs or overhead. *(p. 767)*

Maturity date of a note Date when a note's principal and interest are due. *(p. 364)*

Merchandise (See *merchandise inventory*.) *(p. 178)*

Merchandise inventory Goods that a company owns and expects to sell to customers; also called *merchandise* or *inventory*. *(p. 179)*

Merchandise purchases budget Plan that shows the units or costs of merchandise to be purchased by a merchandising company during the budget period. *(p. 923)*

Merchandiser Entity that earns net income by buying and selling merchandise. *(p. 178)*

Merit rating Rating assigned to an employer by a state based on the employer's record of employment. *(p. 436)*

Minimum legal capital Amount of assets defined by law that stockholders must (potentially) invest in a corporation; usually defined as par value of the stock; intended to protect creditors. *(p. 503)*

Mixed cost Cost that behaves like a combination of fixed and variable costs. *(p. 883)*

Modified Accelerated Cost Recovery System (MACRS) Depreciation system required by federal income tax law. *(p. 394)*

Monetary unit principle Principle that assumes transactions and events can be expressed in money units. *(p. 10)*

Mortgage Legal loan agreement that protects a lender by giving the lender the right to be paid from the cash proceeds from the sale of a borrower's assets identified in the mortgage. *(p. 556)*

Multinational Company that operates in several countries. *(p. 599)*

Multiple-step income statement Income statement format that shows subtotals between sales and net income, categorizes expenses, and often reports the details of net sales and expenses. *(p. 191)*

Mutual agency Legal relationship among partners whereby each partner is an agent of the partnership and is able to bind the partnership to contracts within the scope of the partnership's business. *(p. 473)*

Natural business year Twelve-month period that ends when a company's sales activities are at their lowest point. *(p. 93)*

Natural resources Assets physically consumed when used; examples are timber, mineral deposits, and oil and gas fields; also called *wasting assets*. *(p. 400)*

Net assets (See *equity*.) *(p. 12)*

Net income Amount earned after subtracting all expenses necessary for and matched with sales for a period; also called *income, profit,* or *earnings*. *(p. 13)*

Net loss Excess of expenses over revenues for a period. *(p. 18)*

Net method Method of recording purchases at the full invoice price less any cash discounts. *(p. 335)*

Net pay Gross pay less all deductions; also called *take-home pay*. *(p. 433)*

Net present value (NPV) Dollar estimate of an asset's value that is used to evaluate the acceptability of an investment; computed by discounting future cash flows from the investment at a satisfactory rate and then subtracting the initial cost of the investment. *(p. 1003)*

Net realizable value Expected selling price (value) of an item minus the cost of making the sale. *(p. 224)*

Noncontrollable costs Costs that a manager does not have the power to control or strongly influence. *(p. 726)*

Noncumulative preferred stock Preferred stock on which the right to receive dividends is lost for any period when dividends are not declared. *(p. 511)*

Noninterest-bearing note Note with no stated (contract) rate of interest; interest is implicitly included in the note's face value.

Nonparticipating preferred stock Preferred stock on which dividends are limited to a maximum amount each year. *(p. 512)*

No-par value stock Stock class that has not been assigned a par (or stated) value by the corporate charter. *(p. 503)*

Nonsufficient funds (NSF) check Maker's bank account has insufficient money to pay the check; also called *hot check*. *(p. 326)*

Non-value-added time The portion of cycle time that is not directed at producing a product or service; equals the sum of inspection time, move time, and wait time. *(p. 735)*

Note (See promissory note.) *(p. 364)*

Note payable Liability expressed by a written promise to pay a definite sum of money on demand or on a specific future date(s). *(p. 364)*

Note receivable Asset consisting of a written promise to receive a definite sum of money on demand or on a specific future date(s). *(p. 49)*

Objectivity principle Principle that prescribes independent, unbiased evidence to support financial statement information. *(p. 9)*

Obsolescence Condition in which, because of new inventions and improvements, a plant asset can no longer be used to produce goods or services with a competitive advantage. *(p. 389)*

Off-balance-sheet financing Acquisition of assets by agreeing to liabilities not reported on the balance sheet. *(p. 568)*

Online processing Approach to inputting data from source documents as soon as the information is available. *(p. 281)*

Operating activities Activities that involve the production or purchase of merchandise and the sale of goods or services to customers, including expenditures related to administering the business. *(p. 623)*

Operating cycle Normal time between paying cash for merchandise or employee services and receiving cash from customers. *(p. 145)*

Operating leases Short-term (or cancelable) leases in which the lessor retains risks and rewards of ownership. *(p. 567)*

Operating leverage Extent, or relative size, of fixed costs in the total cost structure. *(p. 896)*

Opportunity cost Potential benefit lost by choosing a specific action from two or more alternatives. *(p. 726)*

Ordinary repairs Repairs to keep a plant asset in normal, good operating condition; treated as a revenue expenditure and immediately expensed. *(p. 397)*

Organization expenses (costs) Costs such as legal fees and promoter fees to bring an entity into existence. *(pp. 501 & 506)*

Out-of-pocket cost Cost incurred or avoided as a result of management's decisions. *(p. 726)*

Output devices Means by which information is taken out of the accounting system and made available for use. *(p. 269)*

Outsourcing Manager decision to buy a product or service from another entity; part of a *make-or-buy* decision; also called *make or buy*. *(p. 997)*

Outstanding checks Checks written and recorded by the depositor but not yet paid by the bank at the bank statement date. *(p. 326)*

Outstanding stock Corporation's stock held by its shareholders.

Overapplied overhead Amount by which the overhead applied to production in a period using the predetermined overhead rate exceeds the actual overhead incurred in a period. *(p. 774)*

Overhead cost variance Difference between the total overhead cost applied to products and the total overhead cost actually incurred. *(p. 966)*

Owner, capital Account showing the owner's claim on company assets; equals owner investments plus net income (or less net losses) minus owner withdrawals since the company's inception; also referred to as *equity*. *(p. 13)*

Owner investment Assets put into the business by the owner. *(p. 12)*

Owner's equity (See *equity*.) *(p. 12)*

Owner withdrawals (See *withdrawals*.) *(p. 13)*

Paid-in capital (See *contributed capital*.) *(p. 504)*

Paid-in capital in excess of par value Amount received from issuance of stock that is in excess of the stock's par value. *(p. 505)*

Par value Value assigned a share of stock by the corporate charter when the stock is authorized. *(p. 503)*

Par value of a bond Amount the bond issuer agrees to pay at maturity and the amount on which cash interest payments are based; also called *face amount* or *face value* of a bond. *(p. 544)*

Par value stock Class of stock assigned a par value by the corporate charter. *(p. 503)*

Parent Company that owns a controlling interest in a corporation (requires more than 50% of voting stock). *(p. 593)*

Participating preferred stock Preferred stock that shares with common stockholders any dividends paid in excess of the percent stated on preferred stock. *(p. 512)*

Partner return on equity Partner net income divided by average partner equity for the period. *(p. 484)*

Partnership Unincorporated association of two or more persons to pursue a business for profit as co-owners. *(pp. 10 & 472)*

Partnership contract Agreement among partners that sets terms under which the affairs of the partnership are conducted; also called *articles of partnership*. *(p. 472)*

Partnership liquidation Dissolution of a partnership by (1) selling noncash assets and allocating any gain or loss according to partners' income-and-loss ratio, (2) paying liabilities, and (3) distributing any remaining cash according to partners' capital balances. *(p. 482)*

Patent Exclusive right granted to its owner to produce and sell an item or to use a process for 17 years. *(p. 402)*

Payback period (PBP) Time-based measurement used to evaluate the acceptability of an investment; equals the time expected to pass before an investment's net cash flows equal its initial cost. *(p. 999)*

Payee of the note Entity to whom a note is made payable. *(p. 364)*

Payroll bank account Bank account used solely for paying employees; each pay period an amount equal to the total employees' net pay is deposited in it and the payroll checks are drawn on it. *(p. 448)*

Payroll deductions Amounts withheld from an employee's gross pay; also called *withholdings. (p. 434)*

Payroll register Record for a pay period that shows the pay period dates, regular and overtime hours worked, gross pay, net pay, and deductions. *(p. 446)*

Pension plan Contractual agreement between an employer and its employees for the employer to provide benefits to employees after they retire; expensed when incurred. *(p. 569)*

Period costs Expenditures identified more with a time period than with finished products costs; includes selling and general administrative expenses. *(p. 726)*

Periodic inventory system Method that records the cost of inventory purchased but does not continuously track the quantity available or sold to customers; records are updated at the end of each period to reflect the physical count and costs of goods available. *(p. 180)*

Permanent accounts Accounts that reflect activities related to one or more future periods; balance sheet accounts whose balances are not closed; also called *real accounts. (p. 140)*

Perpetual inventory system Method that maintains continuous records of the cost of inventory available and the cost of goods sold. *(p. 179)*

Petty cash Small amount of cash in a fund to pay minor expenses; accounted for using an imprest system. *(p. 321)*

Planning Process of setting goals and preparing to achieve them. *(p. 721)*

Plant assets Tangible long-lived assets used to produce or sell products and services; also called *property, plant and equipment (PP&E)* or *fixed assets.* *(pp. 96 & 386)*

Pledged assets to secured liabilities Ratio of the book value of a company's pledged assets to the book value of its secured liabilities.

Post-closing trial balance List of permanent accounts and their balances from the ledger after all closing entries are journalized and posted. *(p. 144)*

Posting Process of transferring journal entry information to the ledger; computerized systems automate this process. *(p. 54)*

Posting reference (PR) column A column in journals in which individual ledger account numbers are entered when entries are posted to those ledger accounts. *(p. 55)*

Predetermined overhead rate Rate established prior to the beginning of a period that relates estimated overhead to another variable, such as estimated direct labor, and is used to assign overhead cost to production. *(p. 770)*

Preemptive right Stockholders' right to maintain their proportionate interest in a corporation with any additional shares issued. *(p. 502)*

Preferred stock Stock with a priority status over common stockholders in one or more ways, such as paying dividends or distributing assets. *(p. 510)*

Premium on bonds Difference between a bond's par value and its higher carrying value; occurs when the contract rate is higher than the market rate; also called *bond premium. (p. 550)*

Premium on stock (See *contributed capital in excess of par value.) (p. 505)*

Prepaid expenses Items paid for in advance of receiving their benefits; classified as assets. *(p. 95)*

Price-earnings (PE) ratio Ratio of a company's current market value per share to its earnings per share; also called *price-to-earnings. (p. 519)*

Price variance Difference between actual and budgeted revenue or cost caused by the difference between the actual price per unit and the budgeted price per unit. *(p. 958)*

Prime costs Expenditures directly identified with the production of finished goods; include direct materials costs and direct labor costs. *(p. 731)*

Principal of a note Amount that the signer of a note agrees to pay back when it matures, not including interest. *(p. 364)*

Principles of internal control Principles prescribing management to establish responsibility, maintain records, insure assets, separate recordkeeping from custody of assets, divide responsibility for related transactions, apply technological controls, and perform reviews. *(p. 313)*

Prior period adjustment Correction of an error in a prior year that is reported in the statement of retained earnings (or statement of stockholders' equity) net of any income tax effects. *(p. 517)*

Pro forma financial statements Statements that show the effects of proposed transactions and events as if they had occurred. *(p. 140)*

Process cost accounting system System of assigning direct materials, direct labor, and overhead to specific processes; total costs associated with each process are then divided by the number of units passing through that process to determine the cost per equivalent unit. *(p. 801)*

Process cost summary Report of costs charged to a department, its equivalent units of production achieved, and the costs assigned to its output. *(p. 809)*

Process operations Processing of products in a continuous (sequential) flow of steps; also called *process manufacturing* or *process production. (p. 798)*

Product costs Costs that are capitalized as inventory because they produce benefits expected to have future value; include direct materials, direct labor, and overhead. *(p. 726)*

Production budget Plan that shows the units to be produced each period. *(p. 935)*

Profit (See *net income.) (p. 13)*

Profit center Business unit that incurs costs and generates revenues. *(p. 848)*

Profit margin Ratio of a company's net income to its net sales; the percent of income in each dollar of revenue; also called *net profit margin. (p. 105)*

Profitability Company's ability to generate an adequate return on invested capital. *(p. 675)*

Promissory note (or **note**) Written promise to pay a specified amount either on demand or at a definite future date; is a *note receivable* for the lender but a *note payable* for the lendee. *(p. 364)*

Proprietorship (See *sole proprietorship.) (p. 10)*

Proxy Legal document giving a stockholder's agent the power to exercise the stockholder's voting rights. *(p. 502)*

Purchase discount Term used by a purchaser to describe a cash discount granted to the purchaser for paying within the discount period. *(p. 181)*

Purchase order Document used by the purchasing department to place an order with a seller (vendor). *(p. 332)*

Purchase requisition Document listing merchandise needed by a department and requesting it be purchased. *(p. 332)*

Purchases journal Journal normally used to record all purchases on credit. *(p. 277)*

Quantity variance Difference between actual and budgeted revenue or cost caused by the difference between the actual number of units and the budgeted number of units. *(p. 958)*

Ratio analysis Determination of key relations between financial statement items as reflected in numerical measures. *(p. 676)*

Raw materials inventory Goods a company acquires to use in making products. *(p. 728)*

Realizable value Expected proceeds from converting an asset into cash. *(p. 359)*

Receiving report Form used to report that ordered goods are received and to describe their quantity and condition. *(p. 333)*

Recordkeeping Part of accounting that involves recording transactions and events, either manually or electronically; also called *bookkeeping*. *(p. 5)*

Registered bonds Bonds owned by investors whose names and addresses are recorded by the issuer; interest payments are made to the registered owners. *(p. 557)*

Relevance principle Information system principle prescribing that its reports be useful, understandable, timely, and pertinent for decision making. *(p. 266)*

Relevant benefits Additional or incremental revenue generated by selecting a particular course of action over another. *(p. 1009)*

Relevant range of operations Company's normal operating range; excludes extremely high and low volumes not likely to occur. *(p. 891)*

Report form balance sheet Balance sheet that lists accounts vertically in the order of assets, liabilities, and equity. *(p. 18)*

Responsibility accounting budget Report of expected costs and expenses under a manager's control. *(p. 856)*

Responsibility accounting performance report Responsibility report that compares actual costs and expenses for a department with budgeted amounts. *(p. 856)*

Responsibility accounting system System that provides information that management can use to evaluate the performance of a department's manager. *(p. 848)*

Restricted retained earnings Retained earnings not available for dividends because of legal or contractual limitations. *(p. 516)*

Retail inventory method Method to estimate ending inventory based on the ratio of the amount of goods for sale at cost to the amount of goods for sale at retail. *(p. 245)*

Retailer Intermediary that buys products from manufacturers or wholesalers and sells them to consumers. *(p. 178)*

Retained earnings Cumulative income less cumulative losses and dividends. *(p. 504)*

Retained earnings deficit Debit (abnormal) balance in Retained Earnings; occurs when cumulative losses and dividends exceed cumulative income; also called *accumulated deficit*. *(p. 507)*

Return Monies received from an investment; often in percent form. *(p. 23)*

Return on assets (See *return on total assets*) *(p. 20)*

Return on total assets Ratio reflecting operating efficiency; defined as net income divided by average total assets for the period; also called *return on assets* or *return on investment*. *(p. 594)*

Return on equity Ratio of net income to average equity for the period.

Revenue expenditures Expenditures reported on the current income statement as an expense because they do not provide benefits in future periods. *(p. 396)*

Revenue recognition principle The principle prescribing that revenue is recognized when earned. *(p. 10)*

Revenues Gross increase in equity from a company's business activities that earn income; also called *sales*. *(p. 13)*

Reverse stock split Occurs when a corporation calls in its stock and replaces each share with less than one new share; increases both market value per share and any par or stated value per share. *(p. 510)*

Reversing entries Optional entries recorded at the beginning of a period that prepare the accounts for the usual journal entries as if adjusting entries had not occurred in the prior period. *(p. 151)*

Risk Uncertainty about an expected return. *(p. 24)*

Rolling budget New set of budgets a firm adds for the next period (with revisions) to replace the ones that have lapsed. *(p. 918)*

S corporation Corporation that meets special tax qualifications so as to be treated like a partnership for income tax purposes. *(p. 474)*

Safety stock Quantity of inventory or materials over the minimum needed to satisfy budgeted demand. *(p. 923)*

Sales (See *revenues*.) *(p. 13)*

Sales budget Plan showing the units of goods to be sold or services to be provided; the starting point in the budgeting process for most departments. *(p. 922)*

Sales discount Term used by a seller to describe a cash discount granted to buyers who pay within the discount period. *(p. 181)*

Sales journal Journal normally used to record sales of goods on credit. *(p. 271)*

Sales mix Ratio of sales volumes for the various products sold by a company. *(p. 895)*

Salvage value Estimate of amount to be recovered at the end of an asset's useful life; also called *residual value* or *scrap value*. *(p. 389)*

Sarbanes-Oxley Act Created the Public *Company Accounting Oversight Board*, regulates analyst conflicts, imposes corporate governance requirements, enhances accounting and control disclosures, impacts insider transactions and executive loans, establishes new types of criminal conduct, and expands penalties for violations of federal securities laws. *(p. 11)*

Scatter diagram Graph used to display data about past cost behavior and sales as points on a diagram. *(p. 885)*

Schedule of accounts payable List of the balances of all accounts in the accounts payable ledger and their total. *(p. 278)*

Schedule of accounts receivable List of the balances for all accounts in the accounts receivable ledger and their total. *(p. 273)*

Secured bonds Bonds that have specific assets of the issuer pledged as collateral. *(p. 557)*

Securities and Exchange Commission (SEC) Federal agency Congress has charged to set reporting rules for organizations that sell ownership shares to the public. *(p. 9)*

Segment return on assets Segment operating income divided by segment average (identifiable) assets for the period. *(p. 282)*

Selling expense budget Plan that lists the types and amounts of selling expenses expected in the budget period. *(p. 924)*

Selling expenses Expenses of promoting sales, such as displaying and advertising merchandise, making sales, and delivering goods to customers. *(p. 191)*

Serial bonds Bonds consisting of separate amounts that mature at different dates. *(p. 557)*

Service company Organization that provides services instead of tangible products. *(p. 178)*

Shareholders Owners of a corporation; also called *stockholders. (p. 11)*

Shares Equity of a corporation divided into ownership units; also called *stock. (p. 11)*

Short-term investments Debt and equity securities that management expects to convert to cash within the next 3 to 12 months (or the operating cycle if longer); also called *temporary investments* or *marketable securities. (p. 586)*

Short-term note payable Current obligation in the form of a written promissory note. *(p. 431)*

Shrinkage Inventory losses that occur as a result of theft or deterioration. *(p. 188)*

Signature card Includes the signatures of each person authorized to sign checks on the bank account. *(p. 323)*

Simple capital structure Capital structure that consists of only common stock and nonconvertible preferred stock; consists of no dilutive securities. *(p. 519)*

Single-step income statement Income statement format that includes cost of goods sold as an expense and shows only one subtotal for total expenses. *(p. 192)*

Sinking fund bonds Bonds that require the issuer to make deposits to a separate account; bondholders are repaid at maturity from that account. *(p. 557)*

Small stock dividend Stock dividend that is 25% or less of a corporation's previously outstanding shares. *(p. 508)*

Social responsibility Being accountable for the impact that one's actions might have on society. *(p. 8)*

Sole proprietorship Business owned by one person that is not organized as a corporation; also called *proprietorship. (p. 10)*

Solvency Company's long-run financial viability and its ability to cover long-term obligations. *(p. 675)*

Source documents Source of information for accounting entries that can be in either paper or electronic form; also called *business papers. (p. 49)*

Special journal Any journal used for recording and posting transactions of a similar type. *(p. 270)*

Specific identification Method to assign cost to inventory when the purchase cost of each item in inventory is identified and used to compute cost of inventory. *(p. 227)*

Spending variance Difference between the actual price of an item and its standard price. *(p. 966)*

Spreadsheet Computer program that organizes data by means of formulas and format; also called *electronic work sheet. (p. 136)*

Standard costs Costs that should be incurred under normal conditions to produce a product or component or to perform a service. *(p. 959)*

State Unemployment Taxes (SUTA) State payroll taxes on employers to support its unemployment programs. *(p. 436)*

Stated value stock No-par stock assigned a stated value per share; this amount is recorded in the stock account when the stock is issued. *(p. 504)*

Statement of cash flows A financial statement that lists cash inflows (receipts) and cash outflows (payments) during a period; arranged by operating, investing, and financing. *(pp. 17 & 622)*

Statement of owner's equity Report of changes in equity over a period; adjusted for increases (owner investment and net income) and for decreases (withdrawals and net loss). *(p. 17)*

Statement of partners' equity Financial statement that shows total capital balances at the beginning of the period, any additional investment by partners, the income or loss of the period, the partners' withdrawals, and the partners' ending capital balances; also called *statement of partners' capital. (p. 477)*

Statement of retained earnings Report of changes in retained earnings over a period; adjusted for increases (net income), for decreases (dividends and net loss), and for any prior period adjustment.

Statement of stockholders' equity Financial statement that lists the beginning and ending balances of each major equity account and describes all changes in those accounts. *(p. 517)*

Statements of Financial Accounting Standards (SFAS) FASB publications that establish U.S. GAAP. *(p. 9)*

Step-wise cost Cost that remains fixed over limited ranges of volumes but changes by a lump sum when volume changes occur outside these limited ranges. *(p. 884).*

Stock (See *shares.) (p. 11)*

Stock dividend Corporation's distribution of its own stock to its stockholders without the receipt of any payment. *(p. 508)*

Stock options Rights to purchase common stock at a fixed price over a specified period of time. *(p. 517)*

Stock split Occurs when a corporation calls in its stock and replaces each share with more than one new share; decreases both the market value per share and any par or stated value per share. *(p. 510)*

Stock subscription Investor's contractual commitment to purchase unissued shares at future dates and prices.

Stockholders (See *shareholders*.) *(p. 11)*

Stockholders' equity A corporation's equity; also called *shareholders' equity* or *corporate capital*. *(p. 504)*

Straight-line depreciation Method that allocates an equal portion of the depreciable cost of plant asset (cost minus salvage) to each accounting period in its useful life. *(pp. 97 & 390)*

Straight-line bond amortization Method allocating an equal amount of bond interest expense to each period of the bond life. *(p. 548)*

Subsidiary Entity controlled by another entity (parent) in which the parent owns more than 50% of the subsidiary's voting stock. *(p. 593)*

Subsidiary ledger List of individual sub-accounts and amounts with a common characteristic; linked to a controlling account in the general ledger. *(p. 270)*

Sunk cost Cost already incurred and cannot be avoided or changed. *(p. 726)*

Supplementary records Information outside the usual accounting records; also called *supplemental records*. *(p. 184)*

Supply chain Linkages of services or goods extending from suppliers, to the company itself, and on to customers.

T-account Tool used to show the effects of transactions and events on individual accounts. *(p. 53)*

Target cost Maximum allowable cost for a product or service; defined as expected selling price less the desired profit. *(p. 763)*

Temporary accounts Accounts used to record revenues, expenses, and withdrawals (dividends for a corporation); they are closed at the end of each period; also called *nominal accounts*. *(p. 140)*

Term bonds Bonds scheduled for payment (maturity) at a single specified date. *(p. 557)*

Throughput time (See *cycle time*.)

Time period principle Assumption that an organization's activities can be divided into specific time periods such as months, quarters, or years. *(p. 92)*

Time ticket Source document used to report the time an employee spent working on a job or on overhead activities and then to determine the amount of direct labor to charge to the job or the amount of indirect labor to charge to overhead. *(p. 768)*

Times interest earned Ratio of income before interest expense (and any income taxes) divided by interest expense; reflects risk of covering interest commitments when income varies. *(p. 441)*

Total asset turnover Measure of a company's ability to use its assets to generate sales; computed by dividing net sales by average total assets. *(p. 404)*

Total quality management (TQM) Concept calling for all managers and employees at all stages of operations to strive toward higher standards and reduce number of defects. *(p. 724)*

Trade discount Reduction from a list or catalog price that can vary for wholesalers, retailers, and consumers. *(p. 180)*

Trademark or **Trade (Brand) name** Symbol, name, phrase, or jingle identified with a company, product, or service. *(p. 403)*

Trading on the equity (See *financial leverage*.)

Trading securities Investments in debt and equity securities that the company intends to actively trade for profit. *(p. 589)*

Transaction Exchange of economic consideration affecting an entity's financial position that can be reliably measured. *(p. 13)*

Treasury stock Corporation's own stock that it reacquired and still holds. *(p. 514)*

Trial balance List of accounts and their balances at a point in time; total debit balances equal total credit balances. *(p. 63)*

Unadjusted trial balance List of accounts and balances prepared before accounting adjustments are recorded and posted. *(p. 103)*

Unavoidable expense Expense (or cost) that is not relevant for business decisions; an expense that would continue even if a department, product, or service is eliminated. *(p. 1014)*

Unclassified balance sheet Balance sheet that broadly groups assets, liabilities, and equity accounts. *(p. 145)*

Uncontrollable costs Costs that a manager does not have the power to determine or strongly influence. *(p. 856)*

Underapplied overhead Amount by which overhead incurred in a period exceeds the overhead applied to that period's production using the predetermined overhead rate. *(p. 773)*

Unearned revenue Liability created when customers pay in advance for products or services; earned when the products or services are later delivered. *(pp. 51 & 98)*

Unfavorable variance Difference in revenues or costs, when the actual amount is compared to the budgeted amount, that contributes to a lower income. *(p. 956)*

Unit contribution margin Amount a product's unit selling price exceeds its total unit variable cost.

Units-of-production depreciation Method that charges a varying amount to depreciation expense for each period of an asset's useful life depending on its usage. *(p. 391)*

Unlimited liability Legal relationship among general partners that makes each of them responsible for partnership debts if the other partners are unable to pay their shares. *(p. 473)*

Unrealized gain (loss) Gain (loss) not yet realized by an actual transaction or event such as a sale. *(p. 589)*

Unsecured bonds Bonds backed only by the issuer's credit standing; almost always riskier than secured bonds; also called *debentures*. *(p. 557)*

Unusual gain or loss Gain or loss that is abnormal or unrelated to the company's ordinary activities and environment. *(p. 697)*

Useful life Length of time an asset will be productively used in the operations of a business; also called *service life*. *(p. 389)*

Value-added time The portion of cycle time that is directed at producing a product or service; equals process time. *(p. 735)*

Value chain Sequential activities that add value to an entity's products or services; includes design, production, marketing, distribution, and service. *(p. 732)*

Variable cost Cost that changes in proportion to changes in the activity output volume. *(p. 725)*

Variance analysis Process of examining differences between actual and budgeted revenues or costs and describing them in terms of price and quantity differences. *(p. 958)*

Vendee Buyer of goods or services. *(p. 332)*

Vendor Seller of goods or services. *(p. 332)*

Vertical analysis Evaluation of each financial statement item or group of items in terms of a specific base amount. *(p. 676)*

Volume variance Difference between two dollar amounts of fixed overhead cost; one amount is the total budgeted overhead cost, and the other is the overhead cost allocated to products using the predetermined fixed overhead rate. *(p. 967)*

Voucher Internal file used to store documents and information to control cash disbursements and to ensure that a transaction is properly authorized and recorded. *(p. 320)*

Voucher register Journal (referred to as *book of original entry*) in which all vouchers are recorded after they have been approved. *(p. 334)*

Voucher system Procedures and approvals designed to control cash disbursements and acceptance of obligations. *(p. 319)*

Wage bracket withholding table Table of the amounts of income tax withheld from employees' wages. *(p. 448)*

Warranty Agreement that obligates the seller to correct or replace a product or service when it fails to perform properly within a specified period. *(p. 438)*

Weighted average Method to assign inventory cost to sales; the cost of available-for-sale units is divided by the number of units available to determine per unit cost prior to each sale that is then multiplied by the units sold to yield the cost of that sale. *(p. 230)*

Weighted-average method (See *weighted average.*) *(p. 808)*

Wholesaler Intermediary that buys products from manufacturers or other wholesalers and sells them to retailers or other wholesalers. *(p. 178)*

Withdrawals Payment of cash or other assets from a proprietorship or partnership to its owner or owners. *(p. 13)*

Work sheet Spreadsheet used to draft an unadjusted trial balance, adjusting entries, adjusted trial balance, and financial statements. *(p. 136)*

Working capital Current assets minus current liabilities at a point in time. *(p. 685)*

Working papers Analyses and other informal reports prepared by accountants and managers when organizing information for formal reports and financial statements. *(p. 136)*

Credits

Index

Chart of Accounts

Following is a typical chart of accounts. Each company has its own unique accounts and numbering system.

Assets

Current Assets

101 Cash
102 Petty cash
103 Cash equivalents
104 Short-term investments
105 Market adjustment, _____ securities (S-T)
106 Accounts receivable
107 Allowance for doubtful accounts
108 Legal fees receivable
109 Interest receivable
110 Rent receivable
111 Notes receivable
119 Merchandise inventory
120 _____ inventory
121 _____ inventory
124 Office supplies
125 Store supplies
126 _____ supplies
128 Prepaid insurance
129 Prepaid interest
131 Prepaid rent
132 Raw materials inventory
133 Goods in process inventory, _____
134 Goods in process inventory, _____
135 Finished goods inventory

Long-Term Investments

141 Long-term investments
142 Market adjustment, _____ securities (L-T)
144 Investment in _____
145 Bond sinking fund

Plant Assets

151 Automobiles
152 Accumulated depreciation—Automobiles
153 Trucks
154 Accumulated depreciation—Trucks
155 Boats
156 Accumulated depreciation—Boats
157 Professional library
158 Accumulated depreciation—Professional library
159 Law library
160 Accumulated depreciation—Law library
161 Furniture
162 Accumulated depreciation—Furniture
163 Office equipment
164 Accumulated depreciation—Office equipment
165 Store equipment
166 Accumulated depreciation—Store equipment
167 _____ equipment
168 Accumulated depreciation—_____ equipment
169 Machinery
170 Accumulated depreciation—Machinery
173 Building _____
174 Accumulated depreciation—Building _____
175 Building _____
176 Accumulated depreciation—Building _____
179 Land improvements _____
180 Accumulated depreciation—Land improvements _____
181 Land improvements _____
182 Accumulated depreciation—Land improvements _____
183 Land

Natural Resources

185 Mineral deposit
186 Accumulated depletion—Mineral deposit

Intangible Assets

191 Patents
192 Leasehold
193 Franchise
194 Copyrights
195 Leasehold improvements
196 Licenses
197 Accumulated amortization—_____

Liabilities

Current Liabilities

201 Accounts payable
202 Insurance payable
203 Interest payable
204 Legal fees payable
207 Office salaries payable
208 Rent payable
209 Salaries payable
210 Wages payable
211 Accrued payroll payable
214 Estimated warranty liability
215 Income taxes payable
216 Common dividend payable
217 Preferred dividend payable
218 State unemployment taxes payable
219 Employee federal income taxes payable
221 Employee medical insurance payable
222 Employee retirement program payable
223 Employee union dues payable
224 Federal unemployment taxes payable
225 FICA taxes payable
226 Estimated vacation pay liability

Unearned Revenues

230 Unearned consulting fees
231 Unearned legal fees
232 Unearned property management fees
233 Unearned _____ fees
234 Unearned _____ fees
235 Unearned janitorial revenue
236 Unearned _____ revenue
238 Unearned rent

Notes Payable

240 Short-term notes payable
241 Discount on short-term notes payable
245 Notes payable
251 Long-term notes payable
252 Discount on long-term notes payable

Long-Term Liabilities

253 Long-term lease liability
255 Bonds payable
256 Discount on bonds payable
257 Premium on bonds payable
258 Deferred income tax liability

Equity

Owner's Equity

301 _____, Capital
302 _____, Withdrawals
303 _____, Capital
304 _____, Withdrawals
305 _____, Capital
306 _____, Withdrawals

Paid-In Capital

307 Common stock, $_____ par value
308 Common stock, no-par value
309 Common stock, $_____ stated value
310 Common stock dividend distributable
311 Paid-in capital in excess of par value, Common stock
312 Paid-in capital in excess of stated value, No-par common stock
313 Paid-in capital from retirement of common stock
314 Paid-in capital, Treasury stock
315 Preferred stock
316 Paid-in capital in excess of par value, Preferred stock

Retained Earnings

318 Retained earnings
319 Cash dividends (or Dividends)
320 Stock dividends

Other Equity Accounts

321 Treasury stock, Common
322 Unrealized gain—Equity
323 Unrealized loss—Equity

Revenues

401 _____ fees earned
402 _____ fees earned
403 _____ services revenue
404 _____ services revenue
405 Commissions earned
406 Rent revenue (or Rent earned)
407 Dividends revenue (or Dividend earned)
408 Earnings from investment in _____
409 Interest revenue (or Interest earned)
410 Sinking fund earnings
413 Sales
414 Sales returns and allowances
415 Sales discounts

Cost of Sales

Cost of Goods Sold

502 Cost of goods sold
505 Purchases
506 Purchases returns and allowances
507 Purchases discounts
508 Transportation-in

Manufacturing

520 Raw materials purchases
521 Freight-in on raw materials
530 Factory payroll
531 Direct labor
540 Factory overhead
541 Indirect materials
542 Indirect labor
543 Factory insurance expired
544 Factory supervision
545 Factory supplies used
546 Factory utilities
547 Miscellaneous production costs
548 Property taxes on factory building
549 Property taxes on factory equipment
550 Rent on factory building
551 Repairs, factory equipment
552 Small tools written off
560 Depreciation of factory equipment
561 Depreciation of factory building

Standard Cost Variance

580 Direct material quantity variance
581 Direct material price variance
582 Direct labor quantity variance
583 Direct labor price variance
584 Factory overhead volume variance
585 Factory overhead controllable variance

Expenses

Amortization, Depletion, and Depreciation

601 Amortization expense—_____
602 Amortization expense—_____
603 Depletion expense—_____
604 Depreciation expense—Boats
605 Depreciation expense—Automobiles
606 Depreciation expense—Building _____
607 Depreciation expense—Building _____
608 Depreciation expense—Land
   improvements _____
609 Depreciation expense—Land
   improvements _____
610 Depreciation expense—Law library
611 Depreciation expense—Trucks
612 Depreciation expense—_____ equipment
613 Depreciation expense—_____ equipment
614 Depreciation expense—_____
615 Depreciation expense—_____

Employee-Related Expenses

620 Office salaries expense
621 Sales salaries expense
622 Salaries expense
623 _____ wages expense
624 Employees' benefits expense
625 Payroll taxes expense

Financial Expenses

630 Cash over and short
631 Discounts lost
632 Factoring fee expense
633 Interest expense

Insurance Expenses

635 Insurance expense—Delivery equipment
636 Insurance expense—Office equipment
637 Insurance expense—_____

Rental Expenses

640 Rent expense
641 Rent expense—Office space
642 Rent expense—Selling space
643 Press rental expense
644 Truck rental expense
645 _____ rental expense

Supplies Expenses

650 Office supplies expense
651 Store supplies expense
652 _____ supplies expense
653 _____ supplies expense

Miscellaneous Expenses

655 Advertising expense
656 Bad debts expense
657 Blueprinting expense
658 Boat expense
659 Collection expense
661 Concessions expense
662 Credit card expense
663 Delivery expense
664 Dumping expense
667 Equipment expense
668 Food and drinks expense
671 Gas and oil expense
672 General and administrative expense
673 Janitorial expense
674 Legal fees expense
676 Mileage expense
677 Miscellaneous expenses
678 Mower and tools expense
679 Operating expense
680 Organization expense
681 Permits expense
682 Postage expense
683 Property taxes expense
684 Repairs expense—_____
685 Repairs expense—_____
687 Selling expense
688 Telephone expense
689 Travel and entertainment expense
690 Utilities expense
691 Warranty expense
695 Income taxes expense

Gains and Losses

701 Gain on retirement of bonds
702 Gain on sale of machinery
703 Gain on sale of investments
704 Gain on sale of trucks
705 Gain on _____
706 Foreign exchange gain or loss
801 Loss on disposal of machinery
802 Loss on exchange of equipment
803 Loss on exchange of _____
804 Loss on sale of notes
805 Loss on retirement of bonds
806 Loss on sale of investments
807 Loss on sale of machinery
808 Loss on _____
809 Unrealized gain—Income
810 Unrealized loss—Income

Clearing Accounts

901 Income summary
902 Manufacturing summary

A Rose by Any Other Name

The same financial statement sometimes receives different titles. Below are some of the more common aliases.*

Balance Sheet	Statement of Financial Position Statement of Financial Condition
Income Statement	Statement of Income Operating Statement Statement of Operations Statement of Operating Activity Earnings Statement Statement of Earnings Profit and Loss (P&L) Statement
Statement of Cash Flows	Statement of Cash Flow Cash Flows Statement Statement of Changes in Cash Position Statement of Changes in Financial Position
Statement of Owner's Equity	Statement of Changes in Owner's Equity Statement of Changes in Owner's Capital Statement of Shareholders' Equity[†] Statement of Changes in Shareholders' Equity[†] Statement of Stockholders' Equity and Comprehensive Income[†] Statement of Changes in Capital Accounts[†]

*The term **Consolidated** often precedes or follows these statement titles to reflect the combination of different entities, such as a parent company and its subsidiaries.
[†]Corporation only.

We thank Dr. Louella Moore from Arkansas State University for suggesting this listing.